Alberto Sanfeliu
Manuel Lazo Cortés (Eds.)

Progress in Pattern Recognition, Image Analysis and Applications

10th Iberoamerican Congress on Pattern Recognition, CIARP 2005
Havana, Cuba, November 15-18, 2005
Proceedings

Springer

Volume Editors

Alberto Sanfeliu
Universitat Politènica de Catalunya
Institut de Robòtica i Informàtica Industrial
Llorens Artigas 4-6, 08028 Barcelona, Spain
E-mail: sanfeliu@iri.upc.es

Manuel Lazo Cortés
Instituto de Cibernética, Matemática y Fisica
15 No. 551 C y D. Vedado Havanna 10400, Cuba
E-mail:mlazo@icmf.cu

Library of Congress Control Number: 200593483

CR Subject Classification (1998): I.5, I.4, I.2.10, I.2.7, F.2.2

ISSN 0302-9743
ISBN-10 3-540-29850-9 Springer Berlin Heidelberg New York
ISBN-13 978-3-540-29850-2 Springer Berlin Heidelberg New York

Springer is a part of Springer Science+Business Media

springeronline.com

Printed in Germany

Typesetting: Camera-ready by author, data conversion by Scientific Publishing Services, Chennai, India
Printed on acid-free paper SPIN: 11578079 06/3142 5 4 3 2 1 0

Lecture Notes in Computer Science 3773

Preface

CIARP 2005 (10th Iberoamerican Congress on Pattern Recognition, X CIARP) is the 10th event in the series of pioneer congresses on pattern recognition in the Iberoamerican community, which takes place in La Habana, Cuba. As in previous years, X CIARP brought together international scientists to promote and disseminate ongoing research and mathematical methods for pattern recognition, image analysis, and applications in such diverse areas as computer vision, robotics, industry, health, entertainment, space exploration, telecommunications, data mining, document analysis, and natural language processing and recognition, to name a few. Moreover, X CIARP was a forum for scientific research, experience exchange, share of new knowledge and increase in cooperation between research groups in pattern recognition, computer vision and related areas.

The 10th Iberoamerican Congress on Pattern Recognition was organized by the Cuban Association for Pattern Recognition (ACRP) and sponsored by the Institute of Cybernetics, Mathematics and Physics (ICIMAF), the Advanced Technologies Application Center (CENATAV), the University of Oriente (UO), the Polytechnic Institute "José A Echevarria" (ISPJAE), the Central University of Las Villas (UCLV), the Ciego de Avila University (UNICA), as well as the Center of Technologies Research on Information and Systems (CITIS-UAEH) in Mexico.

The conference was also co-sponsored by the Portuguese Association for Pattern Recognition (APRP), the Spanish Association for Pattern Recognition and Image Analysis (AERFAI), the Special Interest Group of the Brazilian Computer Society (SIGPR-SBC), and the Mexican Association for Computer Vision, Neurocomputing and Robotics (MACVNR). X CIARP was endorsed by the International Association for Pattern Recognition (IAPR).

The number of papers and interest in the congress grow every year, and on this occasion we received more than 200 papers from 29 countries. Of these, 107 were accepted for publication in these proceedings and for presentation at the conference. The review process was carried out by the Scientific Committee, on all contributions, double blind, and assessed by at least two reviewers who prepared an excellent selection dealing with outgoing research. We are especially indebted to them for their efforts and the quality of the reviews.

The conference was organized in four tutorials, three keynote addresses, and oral and poster presentations, that took place on November 15–18, 2005. The keynote addresses dealt with topics on computer vision, image annotation and computational geometry, with distinguished lectures by Dr. Josef Kittler, professor at the School of Electronics and Physical Sciences, University of Surrey, United Kingdom, Dr. Alberto Del Bimbo University of Florence, Italy, and Dr. Eduardo Bayro Corrochano, Computer Science Department, Center of Research and Advanced Studies, Guadalajara, Mexico.

We would like to thank the members of the Organizing Committee for their enormous effort that allowed for an excellent conference and proceedings. We hope that this congress was a fruitful precedent for future CIARP events.

November 2005

Manuel Lazo
Alberto Sanfeliu

Organization

Volume Editors

Alberto Sanfeliu Cortés
Institut de Robòtica i Informàtica Industrial
Universitat Politècnica de Catalunya
Llorens Artigas 4-6, 08028 Barcelona, España

Manuel Lazo Cortés
Instituto de Cibernética, Matemática y Física
15 No. 551 C y D. Vedado, Havana 10400, Cuba

General Co-chairs

Alberto Sanfeliu Cortés
Institut de Robòtica i Informàtica Industrial, Universitat Politècnica de Catalunya, Spain
Manuel Lazo Cortés
Instituto de Cibernética, Matemática y Física, Cuba
Sergio Cano Ortiz
Universidad de Oriente, Cuba

Steering Committee

José Ruiz Shulcloper (ACRP, Cuba)
Eduardo Bayro Corrochano (MACVNR, Mexico)
Dibio Leandro Borges (SIGPR-SBC, Brazil)
Alberto Sanfeliu Cortés (AERFAI, Spain)
Aurélio J. C. Campilho (APRP, Portugal)

Local Committee

Victoria de la Rosa
Margarita Pie
Esther Ponte Cachafeiro
Grisel Reyes León
Maite Romero Duran
Marlenis Salgado
Carmen Seara
Isneri Talavera Bustamante

Scientific Committee

Aguilar, J.	Univ. Los Andes, Venezuela
Alquezar Mancho, R.	Universitat Politecnica de Catalunya, Spain
Araujo, H.	University of Coimbra, Portugal
Bayro, E.	CINVESTAV-Guadalajara, Mexico
Benedi, J. M.	Polytechnic University of Valencia, Spain
Bioucas-Dias, J.	Instituto Superior Técnico, Portugal
Bloch, I.	École Nationale Supérieure des Télécommunications, France
Borges, D. L.	Pontifical Catholic University of Parana, Brazil
Bourlard, H.	Swiss Federal Institute of Technology, Switzerland
Bunke, H.	University of Bern, Switzerland
Caldas Pinto, J. R.	Instituto Superior Técnico, Portugal
Cano-Ortiz, S. D.	Universidad de Oriente, Cuba
Cardenas-Barrera, J.	Universidad Central de Las Villas, Cuba
Carrasco, J. A.	INAOE-Mexico
Colmenares, G. A.	Universidad de los Andes, Venezuela
d'Ávila-Mascarenhas, N. D.	Universidade Federal de São Carlos, Brazil
Del Bimbo, A.	Università di Firenze, Italy
Desachy, J.	Université des Antilles et de la Guyane, France
Escalante-Ramírez, B.	UNAM, México
Facon, J.	Pontifical Catholic University of Parana , Brazil
Fuertes Garcia, J. M.	Universidad de Jaèn, Spain
Gelbukh, A.	CIC-IPN, Mexico
Gibert, K.	Universitat Politècnica de Catalunya, Spain
Goldfarb, L.	University of New Brunswick, Canada
Gomez Gil, M. P.	UDLA, Mexico
Gomez-Ramirez, E.	Universidad de La Salle, Mexico
Gordillo, J. L.	ITESM, Mexico
Graña, M.	University of the Basque Country, Spain
Grau, A.	Universitat Politècnica de Catalunya, Spain
Guevara, M. A.	Universidad de Ciego de Ávila, Cuba
Hancock, E. R.	University of York, UK
Hernandez- Diaz, M. E.	Universidad Central de Las Villas
Hernando, J.	Universitat Politècnica de Catalunya, Spain
Kasturi, R.	The Pennsylvania State University, USA
Katsaggelos, A.	Northwestern University, USA
Kittler, J.	University of Surrey, UK
Lira-Chavez, J.	UNAM, Mexico
Lopez de Ipiña, K.	University of the Basque Country, Spain
Lorenzo-Ginori, J. V.	Universidad Central de Las Villas, Cuba
Lovell, B.	University of Queensland, Australia
Martínez, J. F.	INAOE-Mexico

Medioni, G.	University of Southern California, USA
Mejail, M.	Universidad de Buenos Aires, Argentina
Moctezuma, M.	UNAM, Mexico
Nascimento, J.	Instituto Superior Técnico, Portugal
Ney, H.	University of Aachen, Germany
Novovicova, J.	Academy of Sciences, Czech Republic
Ochoa, A.	ICIMAF, Cuba
Pardo, A.	Universidad de la República, Uruguay
Perez de la Blanca, N.	Universidad de Granada, Spain
Petrou, M.	University of Surrey, UK
Pina, P.	Instituto Superior Técnico, Portugal
Pinho, A.	University of Aveiro, Portugal
Pla, F.	Universitat Jaume I, Spain
Pons-Porrata, A.	Universidad de Oriente, Cuba
Randall, G.	Universidad de la República, Uruguay
Rodríguez Hourcadette, M.	University of Los Andes, Venezuela
Rodríguez, R.	ICIMAF, Cuba
Ruiz-Shulcloper, J.	CENATAV, Cuba
Sanches, J.	Instituto Superior Técnico, Portugal
Sanniti di Baja, G.	Istituto di Cibernetica, CNR, Italy
Sansone, C.	Università di Napoli, Italy
Silva, A.	Universidade de Aveiro, Portugal
Serra, J.	École des Mines de Paris, France
Sossa Azuela, J. H.	CIC-IPN, Mexico
Soto, M. R.	ICIMAF, Cuba
Sousa Santos, B.	Universidade de Aveiro, Portugal
Taboada Crispi, A.	Universidad Central de Las Villas, Cuba
Tombre, K.	Institut National Polytechnique de Lorraine, France
Torres, M. I.	University of the Basque Country, Spain
Trucco, E.	Heriot-Watt University, UK
Verri, A.	University of Genova, Italy
Villanueva, J. J.	Universitat Autònoma de Barcelona, Spain

Additional Referees

Anaya Sanchez, H.
Berreti, S.
Bungeroth, J.
Deselaers, T.
Dreuw, P.
Gil, R.
Grim, J.
Haindl, M.
Hasan, S.

Hoffmeister, B.
Jacobo-Berlles, J.
Jose Erthal, G.
Luan Ling, L.
Neves, A. J. R.
Percannella, G.
Risk, M.
Ruedin, A.
Vilar, D.

Table of Contents

Regular Papers

Keynote Lectures

CT and PET Registration Using Deformations Incorporating Tumor-Based Constraints

Antonio Moreno[1,2], Gaspar Delso[3], Oscar Camara[4], and Isabelle Bloch[1]

[1] Ecole Nationale Supérieure des Télécommunications, TSI Department, CNRS UMR 5141, 46 rue Barrault, 75634, Paris Cedex 13, France
Antonio.Moreno@enst.fr
[2] Segami, 22 avenue de la Sibelle, F-75014 Paris, France
[3] Philips Medical Systems, Suresnes, France
[4] Center for Medical Image Computing, Department of Medical Physics, University College London, London WC1E 6BT, UK

Abstract. Registration of CT and PET thoracic images has to cope with deformations of the lungs during breathing. Possible tumors in the lungs usually do not follow the same deformations, and this should be taken into account in the registration procedure. We show in this paper how to introduce tumor-based constraints into a non-linear registration of thoracic CT and PET images. Tumors are segmented by means of a semi-automatic procedure and they are used to guarantee relevant deformations near the pathology. Results on synthetic and real data demonstrate a significant improvement of the combination of anatomical and functional images for diagnosis and for oncology applications.

1 Introduction

Computed Tomography (CT) and Positron Emission Tomography (PET), particularly dealing with thoracic and abdominal regions, furnish complementary information about the anatomy and the metabolism of human body. Their combination has a significant impact on improving medical decisions for diagnosis and therapy [3] even with the combined PET/CT devices where registration remains necessary to compensate patient respiration and heart beating. In particular, accuracy is fundamental when there is pathology.

Registration of these two modalities is a challenging application due to the poor quality of the PET image and the large deformations involved in these regions.

Most of the existing methods have as a limitation that regions placed inside or near the main structures will be deformed more or less according to the registration computed for the latter, depending on how local is the deformation. A critical example of this situation occurs when a tumor is located inside the lungs and there is a large volume difference between CT and PET images (due to the breathing). In this case, the tumor can be registered according to the transformation computed for the lungs, taking absurd shapes, such as shown in Figure 1. Therefore, the aim of this paper is to avoid this undesired tumor

M. Lazo and A. Sanfeliu (Eds.): CIARP 2005, LNCS 3773, pp. 1–12, 2005.

misregistrations in order to preserve tumor geometry and, in particular, intensity since it is critical for clinical studies, for instance based on SUV (Standardized Uptake Value).

In Section 2, we summarize existing work related to this subject and we provide an overview of the proposed approach. In Section 3, we describe the segmentation of the targeted structures, i.e., the body, the lungs and the tumors. The introduction of tumor-based constraints into the registration algorithm is detailed in Section 4. Section 5 presents some results obtained on synthetic and real data. Finally, conclusions and future works are discussed in Section 6.

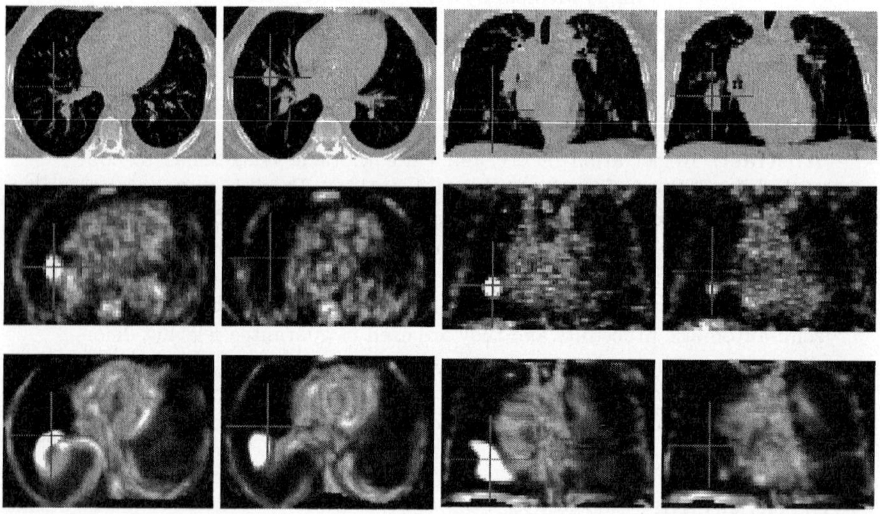

Fig. 1. Axial and coronal slices in CT (first row) and in PET (second row). Result of the non-linear registration without tumor-based constraints (third row). The absence of these constraints leads to undesired and irrelevant deformations of the pathology. On the images of the first and third columns, the cursor is positioned on the tumor localization in PET data, while in the second and fourth columns, it is positioned on the tumor localization in CT data. This example shows an erroneous positioning of the tumor and illustrates the importance of tumor segmentation and the use of tumor-specific constraints.

2 Related Work and Overview of the Proposed Approach

Some approaches have already been developed for registration of multimodality images in pathological cases (pulmonary nodules, cancer), such as in [5]. However these approaches compute a rigid (or affine) registration for all the structures and they do not take into account the local nature of the deformations.

Rohlfing and Maurer [9] have developed a method of non-rigid registration based on B-spline Free-Form Deformations as in [1], but they have added some incompressibility constraints (using the properties of the Jacobian) which only guarantee the preservation of the volume of the structures but not their shape. Loeckx et al. [10] have added a local rigidity constraint and they have obtained very promising results.

A different approach, that we consider closer to physical reality of human body, is based on the combination of rigid and non-rigid deformations, as suggested by Little et al. [7] and Huesman et al. [6]. These methods are based on the use of point interpolation techniques, together with a weighting of the deformation according to a distance function. Castellanos et al. [8] developed a slightly different methodology, in which local non-rigid warpings are used to guarantee the continuity of the transformation.

The advantage of the approach by Little is that it takes into account rigid structures and the deformations applied to the image are continuous and smooth. The method we propose is inspired by this one and adapted to develop a registration algorithm for the thoracic region in the presence of pathologies.

The data consist of 3D CT and PET images of pathological cases, exhibiting tumors in the lungs. We assume that the tumor is rigid and thus a linear transformation is sufficient to cope with its movements between CT and PET images. This hypothesis is relevant and in accordance with the clinicians' point of view, since tumors are often a compact mass of pathological tissue. In order to guarantee a good registration of both normal and pathological structures, the first step consists of a segmentation of all structures which are visible in both modalities. Then we define two groups of landmarks in both images, which correspond to homologous points, and will guide the deformation of the PET image towards the CT image. The positions of the landmarks are therefore adapted to anatomical shapes. This is an important feature and one of the originalities of our method. The deformation at each point is computed using an interpolation procedure based on the landmarks, on the specific type of deformation of each landmark depending on the structure it belongs to, and weighted by a distance function, which guarantees that the transformation will be continuous.

The proposed approach has two main advantages:

1. As the transformation near the tumor is reduced by using the distance weight, even if we have some small errors in the tumor segmentation (often quite challenging, mainly in CT), we will obtain a consistent and robust transformation.
2. In the considered application, one important fact is that the objects to register are not the same in the two images. For instance, the volume of the "anatomical" tumor in CT is not necessarily the same as the volume of the "functional" tumor in PET because the two modalities highlight different characteristics of the objects. The registration of these two views of the tumor must preserve these local differences, which can be very useful because we could discover a part of the anatomy that is touched by the pathology and could not be seen in the CT image. This also advocates in favor of a rigid local registration.

3 Segmentation

The first stage of our method consists in segmenting the most relevant structures that can be observed in both modalities. In this paper, we have segmented the body contours and the lungs. The body is segmented using automatic thresholding and mathematical morphology operators. Lung segmentation is achieved using the procedure introduced in [2] based on a hierarchical method that uses mathematical morphology guided by the previously segmented structures. These structures will be the base for our algorithm as landmarks will lean on them.

Nevertheless, the most important objects to segment are the tumors. In a first approach, tumors have been segmented by a semi-interactive segmentation algorithm, using the coordinates furnished by a "click" of an expert inside the pathology. More precisely, the interaction consists for the physician in defining a seed-point in the tumor of interest (in both CT and PET images). Next, both selected points are used as the input to a relaxation region growing algorithm [4]. This semi-interactive approach has been chosen due to the complexity of a fully automatic tumor segmentation method, mainly in CT images. In addition, this very reduced interaction is well accepted by the users, and even required because it is faster than any non-supervised method and it assures consistent results.

The segmented tumors in CT and PET images are used in the following in order to:

1. calculate the rigid transformation (translation) of the tumor from PET image (source image) to CT image (target image);
2. calculate the distance map to the tumor in PET that will constrain the deformation to be rigid inside the tumor and increasingly non-rigid away from it.

Figure 2 shows some results of the body contour, lungs and tumor segmentations.

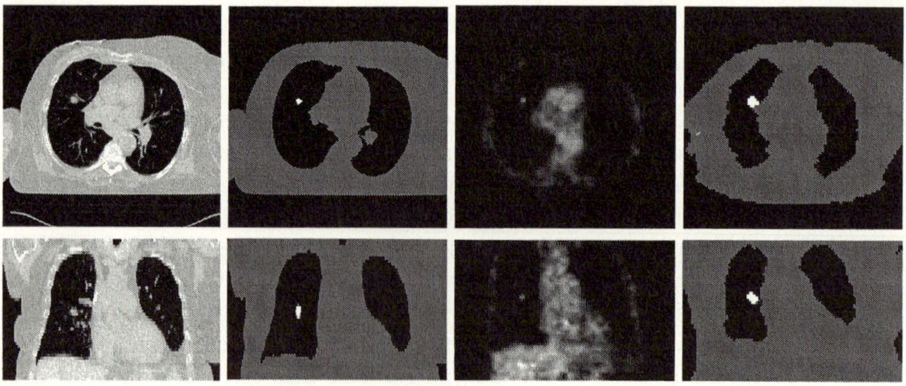

Fig. 2. Segmentation results. First and third columns: original CT and PET images (axial and coronal views). Second and fourth columns: results of the segmentation of the body contour, the lungs and the tumor in both modalities.

4 Combining Rigid and Non-linear Deformations Using a Continuous Distance Function

Based on pairs of corresponding landmarks in both images, the transformation is interpolated through the whole image using the approach in [7]. We introduce the rigid structure constraint so that the non-rigid transformation is gradually weighted down in the proximity of predefined rigid objects.

In this paper, we apply this theoretical framework to a particular 3D case dealing with just one rigid structure (only one tumor is present in each image).

4.1 Point-Based Displacement Interpolation

The first step in a point-based interpolation algorithm concerns the selection of the landmarks guiding the transformation. Thus, homologous structures in both images are registered based on landmarks points defined on their surface. The resulting deformation will be exact at these landmarks and smooth elsewhere, which is achieved by interpolation.

Let us denote by $\boldsymbol{t}_i$ the n landmarks on the source image that we want to transform to new sites $\boldsymbol{u}_i$ (the homologous landmarks) in the target image.

The deformation at each point $\boldsymbol{t}$ in the image is defined as:

$$\boldsymbol{f}(\boldsymbol{t}) = \mathcal{L}(\boldsymbol{t}) + \sum_{j=1}^{n} B_j^T \sigma(\boldsymbol{t}, \boldsymbol{t}_j) \tag{1}$$

under the constraints

$$\forall i, \quad \boldsymbol{u}_i = \boldsymbol{f}(\boldsymbol{t}_i). \tag{2}$$

The first term, $\mathcal{L}(\boldsymbol{t})$, represents the linear transformation of every point $\boldsymbol{t}$ in the source image. The second term represents the non-linear transformation which is, for a point $\boldsymbol{t}$, the sum of n terms, one for each landmark. Each term is the product of the coefficients of a matrix B (that will be computed in order to satisfy the constraints on the landmarks) with a function $\sigma(\boldsymbol{t}, \boldsymbol{t}_j)$, depending on the distance between $\boldsymbol{t}$ and $\boldsymbol{t}_j$:

$$\sigma(\boldsymbol{t}, \boldsymbol{t}_j) = |\boldsymbol{t} - \boldsymbol{t}_j|. \tag{3}$$

This form has favorable properties for image registration [11]. However, different functions can be used as the one described in [7].

With the constraints given by Equation 2, we can calculate the coefficients B of the non-linear term by expressing Equation 1 for $\boldsymbol{t} = \boldsymbol{t}_i$. The transformation can then be defined in a matricial way:

$$\Sigma B + L = U \tag{4}$$

where U is the matrix of the landmarks $\boldsymbol{u}_i$ in the target image (the constraints), $\Sigma_{ij} = \sigma(\boldsymbol{t}_i, \boldsymbol{t}_j)$ (given by Equation 3), B is the matrix of the coefficients of the non-linear term and L represents the application of the linear transformation to the landmarks in the source image, $\boldsymbol{t}_i$. In our specific case, this linear transformation L is the translation of the tumor (between PET and CT images) found in the preprocessing.

From Equation 4, the matrix B is obtained as:

$$B = \Sigma^{-1}(U - L). \tag{5}$$

Once the coefficients of B are found, we can calculate the general interpolation solution for every point in $\mathbb{R}^3$ as shown in Equation 1.

4.2 Introducing Rigid Structures

In this section, we show how to introduce the constraint imposed by the rigid structures in the images. As mentioned in Section 2, the tumor has not exactly the same size nor the same shape in PET and CT images. However, we know that they correspond to the same structure and we register them in a linear way (translation defined by the difference of their centers of mass).

To add the influence of the rigid structure O, we have redefined the function $\sigma(\boldsymbol{t}, \boldsymbol{t}_j)$ as $\sigma'(\boldsymbol{t}, \boldsymbol{t}_j)$ in the following way:

$$\sigma'(\boldsymbol{t}, \boldsymbol{t}_j) = d(\boldsymbol{t}, O)d(\boldsymbol{t}_i, O)\sigma(\boldsymbol{t}, \boldsymbol{t}_j) \tag{6}$$

where $d(\boldsymbol{t}, O)$ is a distance function from point $\boldsymbol{t}$ to object O. It is equal to zero for $\boldsymbol{t} \in O$ (inside the rigid structure) and takes small values when $\boldsymbol{t}$ is near the structure. This distance function is continuous over $\mathbb{R}^3$ and it weights the function $\sigma(\boldsymbol{t}, \boldsymbol{t}_j)$ (see Equation 3). So the importance of the non-linear deformation will be controlled by the distance to the rigid object in the following manner:

- $d(\boldsymbol{t}, O)$ makes $\sigma'(\boldsymbol{t}, \boldsymbol{t}_j)$ tend towards zero when the point for which we are calculating the transformation is close to the rigid object;
- $d(\boldsymbol{t}_i, O)$ makes $\sigma'(\boldsymbol{t}, \boldsymbol{t}_j)$ tend towards zero when the landmark $\boldsymbol{t}_j$ is near the rigid object. This means that the landmarks close to the rigid structure will hardly contribute to the non-linear transformation computation.

Equation 4 is then rewritten by replacing Σ by Σ', leading to a new matrix B'. Finally, we can calculate the general interpolation solution for every point in $\mathbb{R}^3$ as in Equation 1.

5 Results

We present in this section some results that we have obtained on synthetic images, on segmented images and, finally, on real images.

5.1 Synthetic Images

This first experiment on synthetic images aims at checking that the rigid structures are transformed rigidly, that the landmarks are correctly translated too and, finally, that the transformation elsewhere is consistent and smooth.

This simulation was designed to be similar to the effect we can find with real images. The rigid structure is the "tumor" and it is just translated. The frame of our synthetic images simulate the contour of the body and the internal black square replace the lungs. As we are taking the PET image as the one to be deformed (source image), we simulate an expansive transformation because the lungs in PET are usually smaller than in CT images. This is due to the fact that the CT image is often acquired in maximal inspiration of the patient. The result in this case is shown in the second row of Figure 3.

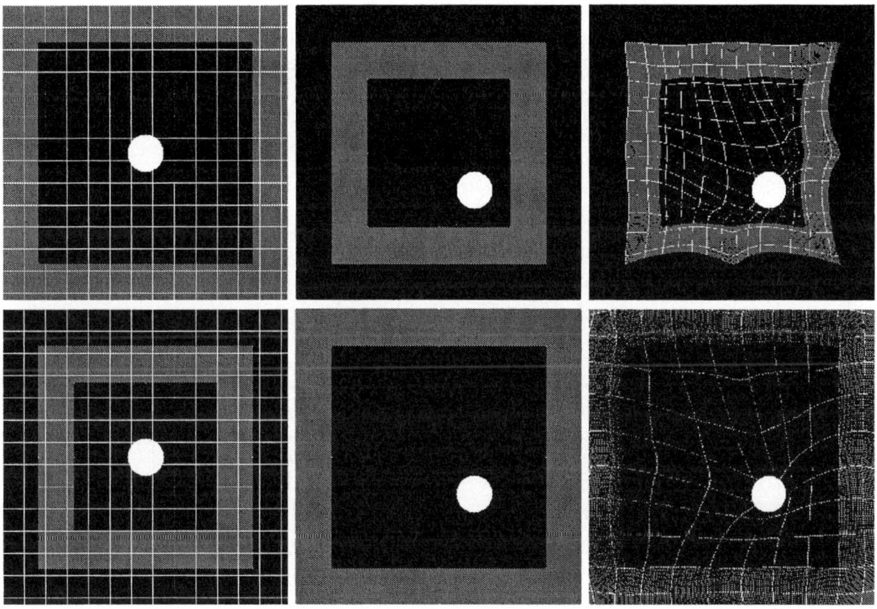

Fig. 3. Results on synthetic images. First row: effects of shrinking a frame (in grey in the figure) and translating the "tumor" (in white in the figure). Second row: effects of expanding a frame and translating the "tumor". Source images (with a grid) are shown on the left, target images are in the middle and the results of the transformation on the right. The landmarks are located on the internal and external edges of the frame in grey (on the corners and in the middle of the sides). The total number of landmarks is 16 in both examples.

In order to observe the transformation all over the image, we have plotted a grid on it. To illustrate the effect of the transformation we have simulated a compression and an expansion of a frame and a simple translation of the "tumor". It can be seen in Figure 3 that the results with our synthetic images are satisfactory as the shape of the rigid structure (the "tumor") is conserved and the landmarks are translated correctly. The frame, on which the landmarks are put, is deformed in a continuous and smooth way. If we do not apply the constraints on the rigid structure we obtain an undesired transformation as illustrated in Figure 4 (the tumor is expanded).

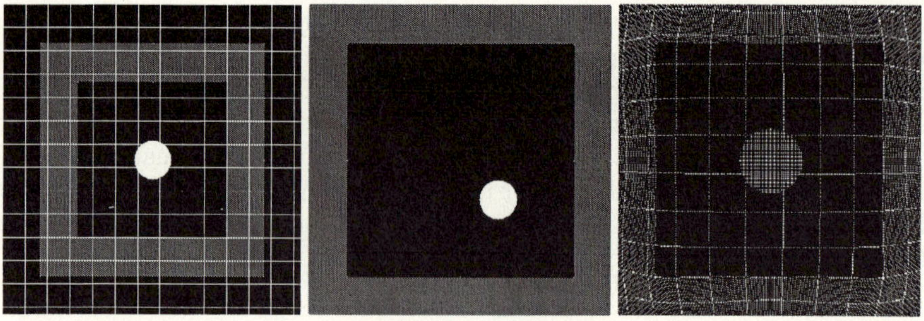

Fig. 4. Result on a synthetic image without constraints on the rigid structure when we apply an expansion to the frame using 16 landmarks. Source image (with a grid) is shown on the left, target image is in the middle and the result of the transformation on the right.

However, it must be noticed that the edges of the frame are not totally straight after the transformation. In general, the more landmarks we have, the better the result will be. The positions of the landmarks are important too. Here we have chosen to spread them uniformly over the internal and external edges of the frame.

The algorithm has also been tested on 3D synthetic images with similar results. We only show here the results on bi-dimensional images for the sake of simplicity.

5.2 Segmented Images

In order to appreciate more clearly the effect of the transformation, we have first used the results of the segmentation to create the simplified real images. They are not only useful to analyze the deformation but it is also easier to define the landmarks on them.

Landmarks have to correspond to the same anatomical reality in both images. Thus we have decided to place them (uniformly distributed) on the surfaces of the lungs.

Figure 5 shows some results on the simplified images. A grid is superimposed on the segmented PET image for better visualization. In these cases, we have fixed the corners of the images to avoid undesired deformations. In Figure 6, we can see the undesired effect produced if there is no landmark to retain the borders of the image.

For any number of landmarks, the tumor is registered correctly with a rigid transformation. Nevertheless, the quality of the result depends on the quantity of landmarks and their positions. If the number of landmarks is too low, the algorithm does not have enough constraints to find the desired transformation.

Here the results are obtained by applying the direct transformation in order to better appreciate the influence of the deformation in every region of the image. However it is clear that the final result should be based on the computation of

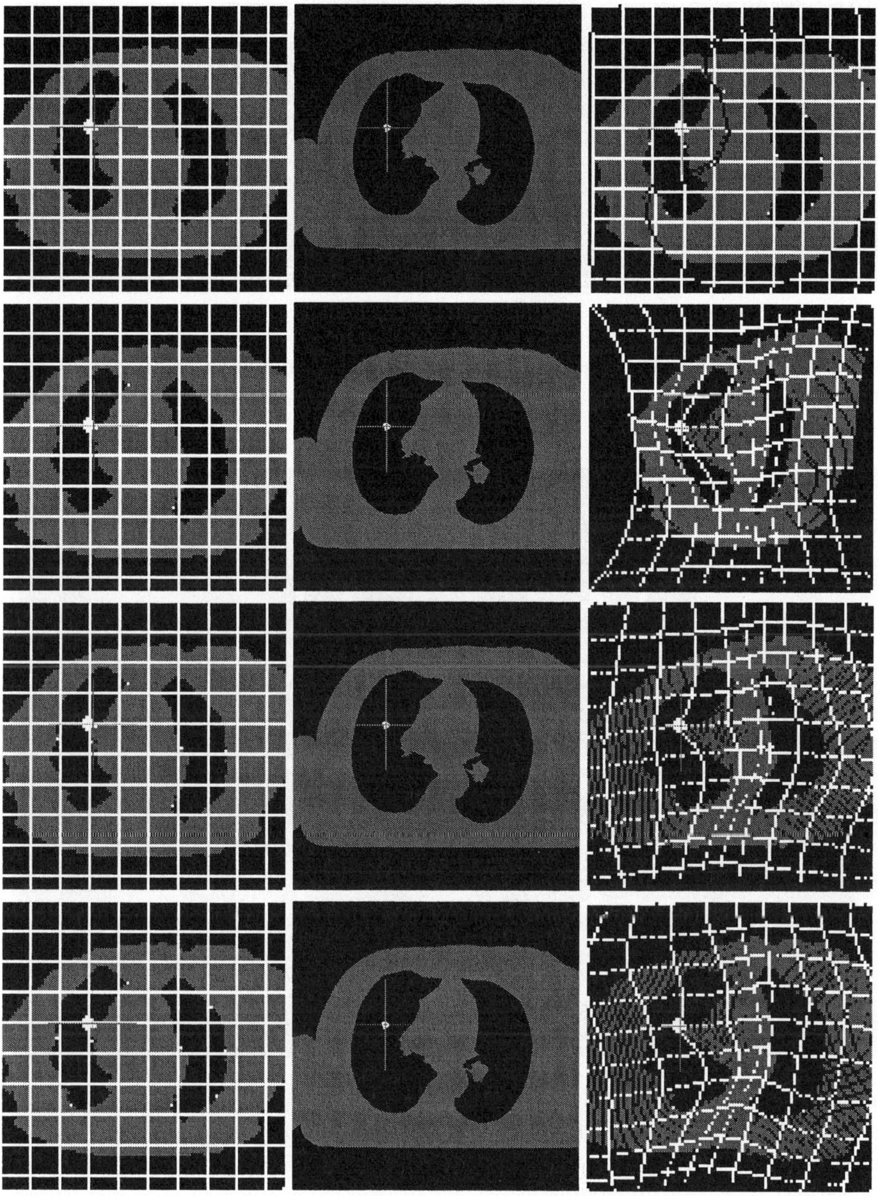

Fig. 5. Results on simplified images. First column: segmented PET images with a grid for visualization purpose (landmarks are also marked in white). Second column: segmented CT images with the corresponding landmarks. Third column: results of the registration of the simplified PET and CT images. In the first row 4 landmarks have been used (fixed on the corners of the image). Then additional landmarks are chosen on the walls of the lungs (uniformly distributed): 4 in the second line, 8 in the third one and 12 in the last one. In all the images the cursor is centered on the tumor in the CT image.

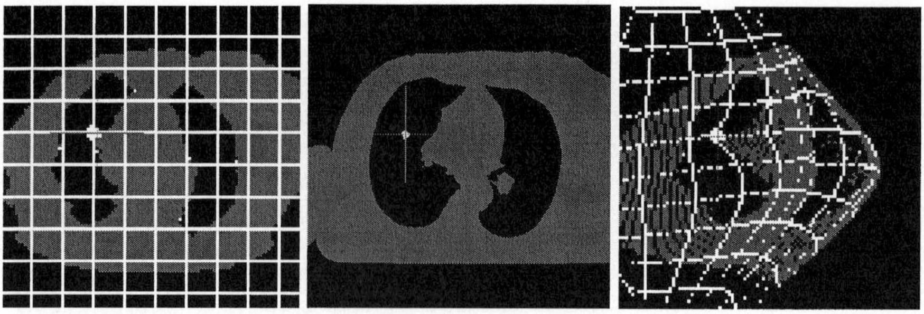

Fig. 6. Result on the simplified images. This is the kind of result we obtain if we do not fix the corners of the image. Here we have only 8 landmarks on the walls of the lungs.

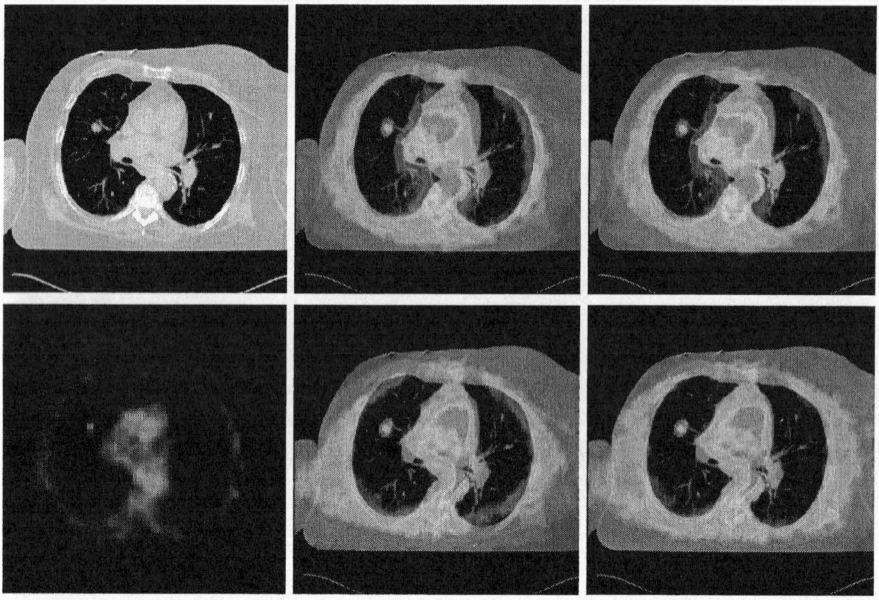

Fig. 7. Results on real images. The CT image and the original PET image are shown in the first column. Second and third columns, from left to right and from top to bottom: superimposition of the CT image with the deformed PET image with 0 (only global translation), 4, 12 and 16 landmarks.

the inverse transformation at each point of the result image in order to avoid unassigned points.

5.3 Real Images

Figure 7 shows the results on real images. As happened with the simplified images, we have to fix the corners of the images to avoid misregistrations.

As previously, the tumor is registered correctly with a rigid transformation in all the cases. However, the accuracy of the registration depends on the number and the distribution of the landmarks. If the number of landmarks is not sufficient there are errors. It can be seen that with an appropriate number of landmarks the registration is very satisfactory. Figure 7 shows that with only 16 landmarks in CT and in PET, the results are good and the walls of the lungs are perfectly superimposed. The results are considerably improved, compared to those obtained with 4 or 12 landmarks.

This shows that the minimal number of landmarks does not need to be very large if the landmarks are correctly distributed, i.e., if they are located on the points that suffer the most important deformations.

6 Conclusion and Future Work

We have developed a CT/PET registration method adapted to pathological cases. It consists in computing a deformation of the PET image guided by a group of landmarks and with tumor-based constraints. Our algorithm avoids undesired tumor misregistrations and it preserves tumor geometry and intensity.

One of the originalities of our method is that the positions of the landmarks are adapted to anatomical shapes. In addition to this, as the transformation near the tumor is reduced by the distance weight, even if the tumor segmentation is not perfect, the registration remains consistent and robust. Moreover, the tumor in CT and PET has not necessarily the same size and shape, therefore the registration of these two modalities is very useful because all the information of the PET image is preserved. This is very important in order to know the true extension of the pathology for diagnosis and for the treatment of the tumor with radiotherapy, for example.

Future work will focus on the automatic selection of the landmarks in order to furnish a consistent distribution on the surfaces of the structures and to guarantee a satisfactory registration.

A comparison with other methods (as Loeckx's one) will provide some conclusions on the limits of each method and their application fields.

Although validation is a common difficulty in registration [12], we plan an evaluation phase in collaboration with clinicians.

Acknowledgments

The authors would like to thank Liège, Lille, Louisville and Val de Grâce Hospitals for the images and helpful discussions and the members of Segami Corporation for their contribution to this project. This work was partially supported by the French Ministry for Research.

References

1. O. Camara-Rey: "Non-Linear Registration of Thoracic and Abdominal CT and PET Images: Methodology Study and Application in Clinical Routine", PhD dissertation, ENST (ENST 2003 E 043), Paris, France, December 2003
2. G. Delso: "Registro Elástico de Imágenes Médicas Multimodales. Aplicación en Oncología", PhD dissertation, Centre de Recerca en Enginyeria Biomèdica, Universitat Politècnica de Catalunya, Barcelona, Spain, October 2003
3. H.N. Wagner, Jr., MD: "Creating Lifetime Images of Health and Disease", 2004 SNM Highlights Lecture, pp. 11N-41N and "PET and PET/CT: Progress, Rewards, and Challenges", The Journal of Nuclear Medicine, Vol. 44, No. 7, pp. 10N-14N, July 2003
4. R. Adams, and L. Bischof: "Seeded region growing", IEEE Transactions on Pattern Analysis and Machine Intelligence, 16, pp. 641-647, 1994
5. T. Blaffert, and R. Wiemker: "Comparison of different follow-up lung registration methods with and without segmentation", Medical Imaging 2004, Proceedings of SPIE Vol. 5370, pp. 1701-1708
6. R.H. Huesman, G.J. Klein, J.A. Kimdon, C. Kuo, and S. Majumdar: "Deformable Registration of Multimodal Data Including Rigid Structures", IEEE Transactions on Nuclear Science, Vol. 50, No. 3, June 2003
7. J.A. Little, D.L.G. Hill, and D.J. Hawkes: "Deformations Incorporating Rigid Structures", Computer Vision and Image Understanding, Vol. 66, No. 2, pp. 223-232, May 1997
8. N.P. Castellanos, P.L.D. Angel, and V. Medina: "Nonrigid medical image registration technique as a composition of local warpings", Pattern Recognition 37, pp. 2141-2154, 2004
9. T. Rohlfing, and C.R. Maurer: "Intensity-Based Non-rigid Registration Using Adaptive Multilevel Free-Form Deformation with an Incompressibility Constraint", Proceedings of MICCAI 2001, LNCS 2208, pp. 111-119, 2001
10. D. Loeckx, F. Maes, D. Vandermeulen, and P. Suetens: "Nonrigid Image Registration Using Free-Form Deformations with Local Rigidity Constraint", Proceedings of MICCAI 2004, LNCS 3216, pp. 639-646, 2004
11. R. Wiemker, K. Rohr, L. Binder, R. Sprengel, and H.S. Stiehl: "Application of elastic registration to imagery from airbone scanners", Congress of the International Society for Photogrammetry and Remote Sensing (ISPRS'96), pp. 949-954, 1996
12. J.A. Schnabel, C. Tanner, A.D. Castellano-Smith, A. Degenhard, M.O. Leach, D.R. Hose, D.L.G. Hill, and D.J. Hawkes: "Validation of Nonrigid Image Registration Using Finite-Element Methods: Application to Breast MR Images", IEEE Transactions on Medical Imaging, Vol. 22, No. 2, February 2003

Surface Grading Using Soft Colour-Texture Descriptors

Fernando López, José-Miguel Valiente, and José-Manuel Prats

Universidad Politécnica de Valencia, Camino de Vera s/n, 46022 Valencia, Spain
flopez@disca.upv.es

Abstract. This paper presents a new approach to the question of surface grading based on *soft colour texture descriptors* and well known classifiers. These descriptors come from global image statistics computed in perceptually uniform colour spaces (CIE Lab or CIE Luv). The method has been extracted and validated using a statistical procedure based on *experimental design* and *logistic regression*. The method is not a new theoretical contribution, but we have found and demonstrate that a simple set of global statistics softly describing colour and texture properties, together with well-known classifiers, are powerful enough to meet stringent factory requirements for real-time and performance. These requirements are on-line inspection capability and 95% surface grading accuracy. The approach is also compared with two other methods in the surface grading literature; colour histograms [1] and centile-LBP [8]. This paper is an extension and in-depth development of ideas reported in a previous work [11].

1 Introduction

There are many industries manufacturing flat surface materials that need to split their production into homogeneous series grouped by the global appearance of the final product. These kinds of products are used as wall and floor coverings. Some of them are natural products such as marble, granite or wooden boards, and others are artificial, such as ceramic tiles. At present, the industries rely on human operators to carry out the task of surface grading. Human grading is subjective and often inconsistent between different graders [7]. Thus, automatic and reliable systems are needed. Capacity to inspect overall production at on-line rates is also an important consideration.

In recent years many approaches to surface grading have been developed (see Table 1). Boukouvalas et al [1][2][3] proposed colour histograms and dissimilarity measures of these distributions to grade ceramic tiles.

Other works consider specific types of ceramic tiles; *polished porcelain* tiles, which imitate granite. These works include texture features. Baldrich et al [4] proposed a perceptual approximation based on the use of discriminant features defined by human classifiers at factory. These features mainly concerned grain distribution and size. The method included grain segmentation and features

M. Lazo and A. Sanfeliu (Eds.): CIARP 2005, LNCS 3773, pp. 13–23, 2005.

measurement. Lumbreras et al [5] joined colour and texture through multiresolution decompositions on several colour spaces. They tested combinations of multiresolution decomposition schemes (Mallat's, *àtrous* and wavelet packets), decomposition levels and colour spaces (Grey, RGB, Otha and Karhunen-Loève transform). Peñaranda et al [6] used the first and second histogram moments of each RGB space channel.

Kauppinnen [7] developed a method for grading wood based on the Percentile (or centile) features of histograms calculated for RGB channels. Kyllönen et al´s [8] approach used colour and texture features. They chose centiles for colour, and LBP (Local Binary Pattern) histograms for texture description.

Lebrun and Macaire [9] described the surfaces of the Portuguese "Rosa Aurora" marble using the mean colour of the background and mean colour, absolute density and contrast of marble veins. They achieved good results but their approach is very dependent on the properties of this marble. Finally, Kukkonen et al [10] presented a system for grading ceramic tiles using spectral images. Spectral images have the drawback of producing great amounts of data.

Table 1. Summary of surface grading literature

	ground truth	features	time study	accuracy %
Boukouvalas	ceramic tiles	colour	no	-
Baldrich	polished tiles	colour/texture	no	92.0
Lumbreras	polished tiles	colour/texture	no	93.3
Peñaranda	polished tiles	colour/texture	yes	-
Kauppinen	wood	colour	yes	80.0
Kyllönen	wood	colour/texture	no	-
Lebrun	marble	colour/texture	no	98.0
Kukkonen	ceramic tiles	colour	no	80.0

Many of these approaches specialized in a specific type of surface, others were not accurate enough, and others did not take into account time restrictions in a real inspection at factory. Thus, we think surface grading is still an open research field and in this paper present a generic method suitable for use in a wide range of random surfaces. The approach uses what we call *soft colour-texture descriptors*, which are simple and fast [to compute] global colour and texture statistics. The method achieves good results with a representative data set of ceramic tiles. Furthermore, the approach is appropriate for use in systems with real-time requirements.

The final approach based on soft colour-texture descriptors (the proposed method) was extracted from a statistical procedure used to determine the best combination of quantitative/categorical factors in terms of a set of experiments that maximize or minimize one response variable also involved in the experiments. We used the accuracy rate of classifications as response variable. The statistical procedure is a combination of experimental design [13] and logistic regression [14] methods which have also been used for the literature approaches.

2 Literature Methods

For comparison purposes we selected two methods from the literature: colour histograms [1] and centile-LBP [8]. They are similar to ours, both are generic solutions with low computational costs. Colour histograms are 3D histograms (one axis per space channel) which are compared using dissimilarity measures. In [1] the authors used the *chi square test* and the *linear correlation coefficient*.

$$\chi^2 = \sum_i \frac{(R_i - S_i)^2}{R_i + S_i} \qquad r = \frac{\sum_i (x_i - \bar{x})(y_i - \bar{y})}{\sqrt{\sum_i (x_i - \bar{x})}\sqrt{\sum_i (y_i - \bar{y})}}$$

When comparing two binned data sets with the same number of data points the *chi square* statistic (χ^2) is defined as above, where R_i is the number of events in bin i for the first data set, and S_i is the number of events in the same bin for the second data set. The *linear correlation coefficient* (r) measures the association between random variables for pairs of quantities (x_i, y_i), $i = 1,...,N$. The mean of the x_i values is $\bar{x}$ and $\bar{y}$ is the mean of the y_i values.

The Centiles, are calculated from a cumulative histogram $C_k(x)$, which is defined as a sum of all the values smaller than x or equal to x in the normalized histogram $P_k(x)$, corresponding to the colour channel k. The percentile value gives x when $C_k(x)$ is known, so an inverse function of $C_k(x)$ is required. Let $F_k(y)$ be the percentile feature, then $F_k(y) = C_k^{-1}(y) = x$, where y is a value of the cumulative histogram in the range [0%,100%].

The Local Binary Pattern (LBP) is a texture operator where the original 3x3 neighbourhood is thresholded by the value of the centre pixel (Figure 1b). Pixel values in the thresholded neighbourhood are multiplied by the weights given to the corresponding pixels (Figure 1c). Finally, the values of the eight pixels are summed to obtain the number of this texture unit. Using LBP there are 2^8 possible combinations of texture numbers, then a histogram collects the LBP texture description of an image.

6	5	3
7	5	2
9	3	7

(a)

1	1	0
1		0
1	0	1

(b)

1	2	4
8		16
32	64	128

(c)

1	2	0
8		0
32	0	128

(d)

LBP=1+2+8+32+128=171

Fig. 1. Computation of local binary pattern (LBP)

In [8] centile and LBP features were combined in one measure of distance and then used the k-NN classifier. The Euclidean distance in the feature space was used for centile features. For LBP they used a log-likelihood measure: $L(S, R) = -\sum_{n=0}^{N-1} S_n ln R_n$, where N is the number of bins. S_n and R_n are the sample and reference probabilities of bin n. The distances were joined by simply adding them. Previously both distances were normalized using the min and max values of all the distances found in the training set.

3 Soft Colour-Texture Descriptors

The presented method is simple, a set of statistical features describing colour and texture properties are collected [15]. The features are computed in a perceptually uniform colour space (CIE Lab or CIE Luv). These statistics form a feature vector used in the classification stage where the well known k-NN and leaving-one-out methods [16] were chosen as classifiers.

CIE Lab and CIE Luv were designed to be perceptually uniform. The term 'perceptual' refers to the way that humans perceive colours, and 'uniform' implies that the perceptual difference between two coordinates (two colours) will be related to a measure of distance, which commonly is the Euclidean distance. Thus, colour differences can be measured in a way close to the human perception of colours. These spaces were chosen to provide accuracy and perceptual approach to colour difference computation. As the data set images were acquired originally in RGB, conversion to CIE Lab or CIE Luv coordinates was needed. This conversion is performed using the standard RGB to CIE Lab and RGB to CIE Luv transformations [17] as follows.

RGB to XYZ:

$$\begin{bmatrix} X \\ Y \\ Z \end{bmatrix} = \begin{bmatrix} 0.412453 & 0.357580 & 0.180423 \\ 0.212671 & 0.715160 & 0.072169 \\ 0.019334 & 0.119193 & 0.950227 \end{bmatrix} \begin{bmatrix} R \\ G \\ B \end{bmatrix}$$

XYZ to CIE Lab:

$$L = 116(Y/Y_n)^{1/3} - 16$$
$$a = 500((X/X_n)^{1/3} - (Y/Y_n)^{1/3})$$
$$b = 200((Y/Y_n)^{1/3} - (Z/Z_n)^{1/3})$$

XYZ to CIE Luv:

$$L = 116(Y/Y_n)^{1/3} - 16$$
$$u = 13L(u' - u'_n)$$
$$v = 13L(v' - v'_n)$$

where

$$u' = 4X/X + 15Y + 3Z \qquad v' = 9X/X + 15Y + 3Z$$
$$u'_n = 4X_n/X_n + 15Y_n + 3Z_n \qquad v'_n = 9X_n/X_n + 15Y_n + 3Z_n$$

X_n, Y_n, and Z_n are the values of X, Y and Z for the illuminant (reference white point). We followed the ITU-R Recommendation BT.709, and used the illuminant D_{65}, where $[X_n\, Y_n\, Z_n] = [0.95045\ \ 1\ \ 1.088754]$.

We proposed several statistical features for describing surface appearance. For each channel we chose the mean and the standard deviation. Also, by computing the histogram of each channel, we were able to calculate histogram moments. The nth moment of z about the mean is defined as

$$\mu_n(z) = \sum_{i=1}^{L} (z_i - m)^n p(z_i)$$

where z is the random variable, $p(z_i)$, $i = 1, 2, \ldots, L$ the histogram, L the number of different variable values and m the mean value of z.

Colour histograms can easily collect 80,000 bins (different colours) which are all used to compute histogram dissimilarities. Centile-LBP approach uses 171 centile measures to compile colour property, and LBP histograms of 256 components to collect texture property. We can consider that these approaches use 'hard' colour and texture descriptors in comparison to our method which only uses the mean, standard deviation and histogram moments from 2nd to 5th to compile colour and texture properties (a maximum feature vector of 18 components). By comparison we named the proposed method *soft colour-texture descriptors*. This assertion is even more acceptable if we revise classical approaches to texture description in the literature.

4 Experiments and Results

All the experiments were carried out using the same data set. The ground truth was formed by the digital RGB images of 960 tiles acquired from 14 different models, each one with three different surface classes given by specialized graders at factory (see Table 2 and Figure 2). For each model two classes were close and one was far away. Models were chosen representing the extensive variety that factories can produce, a catalogue of 700 models is common. But, in spite of this great number of models, almost all of them imitate one of the following mineral textures; marble, granite or stone.

Table 2. Ground truth formed by 14 models of ceramic tiles

	classes	tiles/class	size (cm)	aspect
Agata	13, 37, 38	16	33x33	marble
Antique	4, 5, 8	14	23x33	stone
Berlin	2, 3, 11	24	16x16	granite
Campinya	8, 9, 25	30	20x20	stone
Firenze	9, 14, 16	20	20x25	stone
Lima	1, 4, 17	24	16x16	granite
Marfil	27, 32, 33	14	23x33	marble
Mediterranea	1, 2, 7	30	20x20	stone
Oslo	2, 3, 7	24	16x16	granite
Petra	7, 9, 10	28	16x16	stone
Santiago	22, 24, 25	28	19x19	stone
Somport	34, 35, 38	28	19x19	stone
Vega	30, 31, 37	20	20x25	marble
Venice	12, 17, 18	20	20x25	marble

Digital images of tiles were acquired using a spatially and temporally uniform illumination system. Spatial and temporal uniformity is important in surface grading [1,4,6] because variations in illumination can produce different shades for the same surface and then misclassifications. The illumination system was formed by two special high frequency fluorescent lamps with uniform illuminance

Fig. 2. Samples from the ground truth. From up to down; three samples of petra and marfil models, each one corresponding to a different surface grade.

along their length. To overcome variations along time, the power supply was automatically regulated by a photoresistor located near the fluorescents.

In order to study the feasibility of the soft colour-texture descriptors on perceptually uniform colour spaces we carried out a statistical experiment design. Our aim was to test several factors to determine which combination gave the best accuracy results. These factors related to colour spaces, classifiers, and sets of soft colour-texture descriptors. Colour space: CIE Lab, CIE Luv, RGB and Grey scale. Classifier: k-NN (k=1,3,5,7) and leaving-one-out (k=1,3,5,7). Soft colour-texture descriptors: mean, standard deviation and 2nd to 5th histogram moments.

The factors and their possible values defined 4096 different classification experiments for each tile model. As the ground truth was formed by 14 tile models, 57,344 experiments had to be carried out. We decided to use a statistical tool, the *experiment design* [13], in order to manage the large quantity of experiments and results. This tool, in combination with the *logistic-regression* [14] method, provides a methodology for finding the best combination of factors in a set of experiments that maximize or minimize one response variable. In our case, we were looking to maximize classification accuracy rates. This methodology follows the plan presented in Figure 3.

When we want to perform a complex experiment or set of experiments efficiently we need a scientific approach to planning the experiment. Experimental design is a statistical tool which refers to the process of planning experiments so that appropriate data can be collected for analysis with statistical methods. This would lead to objective and valid conclusions. We chose to use a complete factorial approach in the design of our experiment. This is the most advisable approach for dealing with several factors [13]. Complete factorial design means

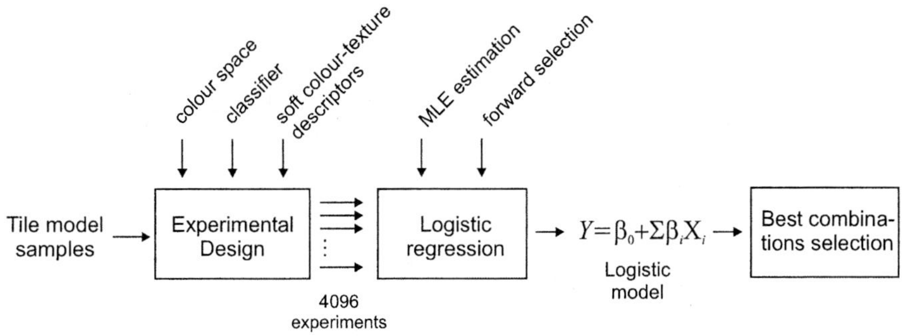

Fig. 3. Block diagram representing the statistical procedure for extracting the best combinations of factor values in a set of experiments or experimental design

that we select a fixed number of possible values for each factor and then carry out experiments with all the possible combinations of them. In our case, each combination of factors is a single experiment with a classification of surface grades. By varying the factor values in a nested way independence between factors, iterations and experiments is achieved, guaranteeing that simple and interaction effects are orthogonal.

From the set of performed experiments we computed the logistic model using a logistic regression [14]. The achieved mean accuracy of all models is used as the output variable (response variable). Thus, we summarize the 14 groups of 4096 experiments for tile models in a single set of 4096 experiments. We used a logistic (logarithmic) approach rather than a linear one because the output variable is probabilistic and the logarithmic method fits the extracted model better. Using the extracted logistic model, $y = \beta_0 + \sum \beta_i X_i$, we compute the predicted accuracy rate for each combination of factors using $p = \frac{e^y}{1+e^y}$. Then we can sort the combinations by their predicted accuracies. The one with the best accuracy will reveal the best combination of factors.

The best predicted accuracy rate in the experimental design carried out for soft colour-texture descriptors was 97.36% with a confidence interval at 95% [96.25%, 98.36%]. This result was achieved using CIE Lab colour space, 1 leaving-one-out classifier and all the proposed soft colour-texture descriptors (mean, standard deviation and 2nd to 5th histogram moments). The measured accuracy with this combination was 96.7%.

Figure 4 shows that CIE Lab and CIE Luv spaces featured strongly in the best sets of factor combinations. RGB space achieved almost null presence in the 1000 best combinations rising to 11.9% and 16.3% in 1500 and 2000 combinations. The Grey scale (with no colour information) was not among the best combinations. Thus, perceptually uniform colour spaces show clearly better performance than RGB with the soft colour-texture descriptors method. Also, this figure suggests that best classifiers are derived from the leaving-one-out method.

A similar experimental design was performed for the literature methods. In this case, we used the following factors and possible values. Colour space: CIE

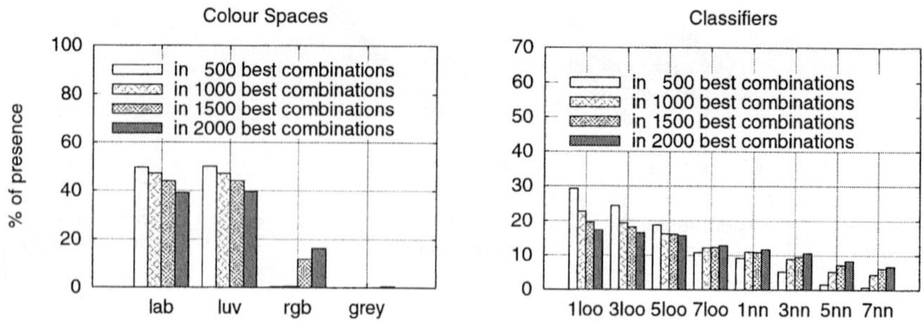

Fig. 4. Presence percentage of colour spaces and classifiers in the best combinations sets ordered by the predicted accuracy rate in the experimental design performed for soft colour-texture descriptors

Lab, CIE Luv, RGB and Grey scale. Classifier: k-NN (k=1,3,5,7) and leaving-one-out (k=1,3,5,7). Distance measure: chi square test, linear correlation coefficient, log-likelihood measure. Distance measures are used in these methods to determine colour histograms and LBP histograms dissimilarities. In a study similar to the one in Figure 4 it was concluded that RGB was the best space for the colour histograms approach closely followed by CIE Lab. Nevertheless, in centile-LBP, CIE Lab was the best followed by RGB. Chi square test was the best distance in colour histograms, and linear correlation performed better in centile-LBP. In both methods the leaving-one-out classifiers again showed the best performance. Table 3 shows the best results achieved in each surface grading method and its corresponding combination of factors.

In all methods the achieved performance is very good and quite similar. For all of them predicted accuracy and confidence interval exceed factory demands of 95%. Differences between the methods arose in terms of timing costs.

Figure 5 presents a comparison of the methods by timing costs (measured on a common PC) for nine of the fourteen tile models. The soft colour-texture

Table 3. Best result of each surface grading approach

	factors	predicted accuracy	c.i. 95%	measured accuracy
Soft colour-texture descriptors	CIE Lab, 1-loo, all descriptors	97.36%	[96.25%, 98.36%]	96.7%
Colour histograms	RGB, 1-loo chi square	97.82%	[96.50%, 98.54%]	98.67%
Centile-LBP	CIE Lab, 1-loo, linear correlation	98.26%	[97.27%, 99.03%]	98.25%

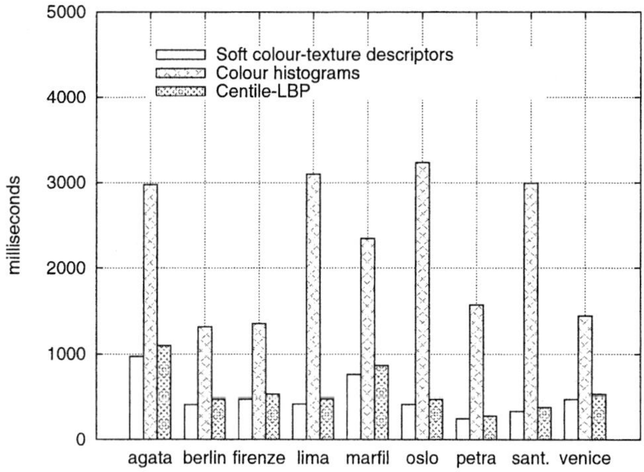

Fig. 5. Timing comparison of surface grading approaches using the corresponding best combination of factors in each method

descriptors method provides the best performance, closely followed by centile-LBP. The colour histograms approach compile by far the worst timing despite the fact that this method does not need to translate the image data, originally in RGB, into CIE Lab or CIE Luv spaces. Also, this method presents irregular timing for the same data size. The berlin, lima and oslo models share data size (tile and image size) but the method achieves significant timing differences among them. This effect is due to the use of binary trees to store the colour histograms of images. Images with larger numbers of different colours need larger trees and more time to compute the differences between histograms. This timing dependence related to data values does not appear in the other two methods whose computational costs only depend on image size and the algorithm; $\Theta(n)+C$ where n is the image size and C is a constant related to the algorithm used for implementing the approach.

5 Conclusions

In this paper we present a new approach for the purpose of surface grading. This approach is based on the use of soft colour-texture descriptors and perceptually uniform colour spaces. Two statistics tools, experimental design and logistic regression, has been used to study and determine the best combination of factors providing the best accuracy rates using a ground truth composed of 14 ceramic tile models. The best combination was: CIE Lab colour space, 1 leaving-one-out classifier and all the soft colour-texture descriptors.

For comparison purposes, a similar study was performed for two literature methods; colour histograms and centile-LBP. In this study we used the factor of inter-histograms distance measures instead of soft colour-texture descriptors.

Best combinations of factors were RGB colour space, 1 leaving-one-out classifier and chi square distance for the colour histograms method, and CIE Lab, 1 leaving-one-out classifier and linear correlation for centile-LBP.

All the approaches achieved factory compliance exceeding the 95% of minimum accuracy. The achieved percentages of all methods vary in less than 1%, thus the accuracy results are quite similar. The differences among the methods arose more clearly when we studied the timing costs. The best in timing was the method based on soft colour-texture descriptors closely followed by centile-LBP. Colour histograms performed worse and irregularly due to binary trees which are used to efficiently store the histograms.

In a work recently reported [12] we studied and demonstrate the on-line inspection capability of soft colour-texture descriptors carrying out a study of real-time comliance and parallelization based on MPI-cluster technology.

Acknowledgements

This work was partially founded by FEDER-CICYT (DPI2003-09173-C02-01). We also want to thank the collaboration of Keraben S.A. for providing the ceramic tile samples.

References

[1] C. Boukouvalas, J. Kittler, R. Marik and M. Petrou. Color grading of randomly textured ceramic tiles using color histograms. IEEE Trans. Industrial Electronics, 46(1):219–226, 1999.

[2] C. Boukouvalas and M. Petrou. Perceptual correction for colour grading using sensor transformations and metameric Data. Machine Vision and Applications, 11:96-104, 1998.

[3] C. Boukouvalas and M. Petrou. Perceptual correction for colour grading of random textures. Machine Vision and Appl., 12:129-136, 2000.

[4] R. Baldrich, M. Vanrell and J.J. Villanueva. Texture-color features for tile classification. EUROPTO/SPIE Conf. on Color and Polarisation Techniques in Indust. Inspection, Germany, 1999.

[5] F. Lumbreras, J. Serrat, R. Baldrich, M. Vanrell and J.J. Villanueva. Color texture recognition through multiresolution features. Int. Conf. on Quality Control by Artificial Vision. 1:114–121, France, 2001.

[6] J. A. Peñaranda, L. Briones and J. Florez. Color machine vision system for process control in ceramics industry. SPIE. 3101:182–192, 1997.

[7] H. Kauppinen. Development of a color machine vision method for wood surface inspection. Phd Thesis, Oulu University, 1999.

[8] J. Kyllönen and M. Pietikäinen Visual inspection of parquet slabs by combining color and texture. Proc. IAPR Workshop on Machine Vision Appl., Japan, 2000.

[9] V. Lebrun and L. Macaire. Aspect inspection of marble tiles by color line-scan camera. Int. Conf. on Quality Control by Artificial Vision, France, 2001.

[10] S. Kukkonen, H. Kvinen and J. Parkkinen. Color Features for Quality Control in Ceramic Tile Industry. Optical Engineering. 40(2):170–177, 2001.

[11] F. López, J.M. Valiente, R. Baldrich and M. Vanrell. Fast surface grading using color statistics in the CIE Lab space. 2nd Iberian Conference on Pattern Recognition and Image Analysis (IbPRIA2005). Lecture Notes in Computer Science. 3523:666-673, 2005.
[12] F. López, J.M. Valiente and G. Andreu. A study of real-time compliance and parallelization for the purpose of surface grading. XVI Jornadas de Paralelismo, I Congreso Español de Informática, 2005.
[13] D.C. Montgomery. Design and analysis of experiments. (4th Edition), John Wiley and Sons, Inc. New York, 1997.
[14] R. Christensen. Log-linear models and logistic regression. (2nd Edition), Springer-Verlag, New York, 1997.
[15] R.C. Gonzalez and P. Wintz. Digital image processing. Addison-Wesley, 2nd Edition, 1987.
[16] R.O. Duda and P.E. Hart. Pattern classification and scene analysis. John Wiley and Sons, New York, 1973.
[17] G. Wyszecki and W.S. Stiles. Color sciencie: concepts and methods, quantitative data and formulae. Wiley, 2nd Edition, New York, 1982.

Support Vector Machines with Huffman Tree Architecture for Multiclass Classification*

Gexiang Zhang**

School of Electrical Engineering, Southwest Jiaotong University,
Chengdu 610031 Sichuan, China
gxzhang@ieee.org

Abstract. This paper proposes a novel multiclass support vector machine with Huffman tree architecture to quicken decision-making speed in pattern recognition. Huffman tree is an optimal binary tree, so the introduced architecture can minimize the number of support vector machines for binary decisions. Performances of the introduced approach are compared with those of the existing 6 multiclass classification methods using U.S. Postal Service Database and an application example of radar emitter signal recognition. The 6 methods includes one-against-one, one-against-all, bottom-up binary tree, two types of binary trees and directed acyclic graph. Experimental results show that the proposed approach is superior to the 6 methods in recognition speed greatly instead of decreasing classification performance.

1 Introduction

Support vector machine (SVM), developed principally by Vapnik [1], provides a novel means of classification using the principles of structure risk minimization. The subject of SVM covers emerging techniques that have been proven to be successful in many traditional neural network-dominated applications [2]. SVM is primarily designed for binary classification problems. In real world, there are many multiclass classification problems. So how to extend effectively it to multiclass classification is still an ongoing research issue [3]. The popular methods are that multiclass classification problems are decomposed into many binary-class problems and these binary-class SVMs are incorporated in a certain way [4]. Some experimental results [3-9] verify that the combination of several binary SVMs is a valid and practical way for solving muticlass classification problems. Currently, there are mainly 6 methods for combining binary-class SVMs. They are respectively one-against-all (OAA) [3,5], one-against-one (OAO) [3,6], directed acyclic graph (DAG) [3,7], bottom-up binary tree (BUBT) [8,9], two types of binary trees labeled as BT1 and BT2 [10]. For an N-class classification problem, these methods need test at least $\log_2 N$ binary SVMs for classification

* This work was supported by the National EW Laboratory Foundation (NEWL51435QT220401)

** Student Member, IEEE

M. Lazo and A. Sanfeliu (Eds.): CIARP 2005, LNCS 3773, pp. 24–33, 2005.

decision. To decrease the number of binary SVMs needed in testing procedure, a novel multiclass SVM with Huffman tree architecture (HTA) is proposed in this paper. The outstanding characteristic of the introduced method lies in faster recognition speed than OAA, OAO, DAG, BUBT, BT1 and BT2 instead of lowering classification capability.

2 Support Vector Machines

For many practical problems, including pattern matching and classification, function approximation, optimization, data clustering and forecasting, SVMs have drawn much attention and been applied successfully in recent years [1-9]. An interesting property of SVM is that it is an approximate implementation of the structure risk minimization induction principle that aims at minimizing a bound on the generation error of a model, rather than minimizing the mean square error over the data set [2]. SVM is considered as a good learning method that can overcome the internal drawbacks of neural network [1].

The main idea of SVM classification is to construct a hyperplane to separate the two classes (labelled $y \in \{-1, +1\}$) [1]. Let the decision function be

$$f(x) = sign(\mathbf{w} \cdot \mathbf{x} + b) \tag{1}$$

where $\mathbf{w}$ is weighting vector, and b is bias and $\mathbf{x}$ is sample vector. The following optimization problem is given to maximize the margin [1], i.e. to minimize the following function

$$\phi(\mathbf{w}, \xi) = \frac{1}{2}||\mathbf{w}||^2 + C\sum_{i=1}^{l} \xi_i \tag{2}$$

Subject to

$$\begin{array}{ll} y_i((\mathbf{w} \cdot \mathbf{x}_i) + b) \geq 1 - \xi_i & \\ \xi_i \geq 0 & i = 1, 2, \cdots, l \end{array} \tag{3}$$

In (4) and (5), y_i is the label of the ith sample vector $\mathbf{x}_i$; ξ_i and l are the ith relax variable of the ith sample vector and the dimension of sample vector, respectively [1].

The dual optimization problem of the above optimization problem is represented as

$$W(\alpha) = \sum_{i=1}^{l} \alpha_i - \frac{1}{2} \sum_{i,j=1}^{l} y_i y_j \alpha_i \alpha_j \mathbf{K}(\mathbf{x}_i, \mathbf{x}_j) \tag{4}$$

Subject to

$$0 \leq \alpha_i \leq C, \quad \sum_{i=1}^{l} \alpha_i y_i, \quad i = 1, 2, \cdots, l \tag{5}$$

where $\mathbf{K}(\mathbf{x}_i, \mathbf{x}_j)$ is a kernel function. $\mathbf{x}_i$ and $\mathbf{x}_j$ are the ith sample vector and the jth sample vector, respectively. α is a coefficient vector,$\alpha = [\alpha_1, \alpha_2, \cdots, \alpha_l]$ [1]. The decision function of the dual optimization problem becomes the form:

$$f(x) = sign[(\sum_{i=1}^{l} \alpha_i y_i \mathbf{K}(\mathbf{x}_i, \mathbf{x}_j) + b)] \qquad (6)$$

3 SVM with HTA

On the basis of fast-speed and powerful-function computers, various methods for signal recognition, character recognition and image recognition were presented [11]. However, comparing with human brain, the methods are obviously too slow. One of the most important reasons is that man identifies objects or patterns in an unequal probability way and most of the existing pattern recognition methods are based on a consideration: all patterns appear in an equal probability. However, in some applications such as radar emitter signal recognition, handwritten digit recognition in postal service and letter recognition in natural text, some patterns may come up frequently, while the others emerge rarely. If all patterns are recognized equiprobably, the efficiency may be very low. On the contrary, if the patterns with high probability are classified preferentially, the speed of recognizing all patterns can be quickened greatly. According to this idea, Huffman tree architecture is introduced to combine multiple binary-SVMs for multiclass classification problems.

An example of HTA with 8 nodes is given in Fig.1. HTA solves an N-class pattern recognition problem with a hierarchical binary tree, of which each node makes binary decision with an SVM. Using different probabilities of occurrence of different patterns, Huffman tree can be constructed using the following algorithm [12,13].

Step 1. According to N probability values $\{p_1, p_2, \cdots, p_N\}$ given, a set $F = \{T_1, T_2, \cdots, T_N\}$ of N binary trees is constructed. For every binary tree T_i $(i = 1, 2, \cdots, N)$, there is only one root node with probability value p_i and its both left-child tree and right-child tree are empty.

Step 2. Two trees in which root nodes have the minimal probability values in F are chosen as left and right child trees to construct a new binary tree. The probability value of root node in the new tree is summation of the probability values of root nodes of its left and right child trees.

Step 3. In step 2, the two trees chosen in F are deleted and the new binary tree constructed is added to the set F.

Step 4. Step 2 and step 3 are repeated till only one tree left in F. The final tree is Huffman tree.

Huffman tree is an optimal binary tree [13], which can minimize the number of SVMs for binary decisions. Once the probabilities of all nodes are given, the structure of HTA is determinate and unique. The SVM-HTA classifier takes advantage of both the efficient computation of HTA and the high classification accuracy of SVMs.

To bring into comparison, the performances of the 7 methods including OAA, OAO, DAG, BUBT, BT1, BT2 and HTA are analyzed in the following description.

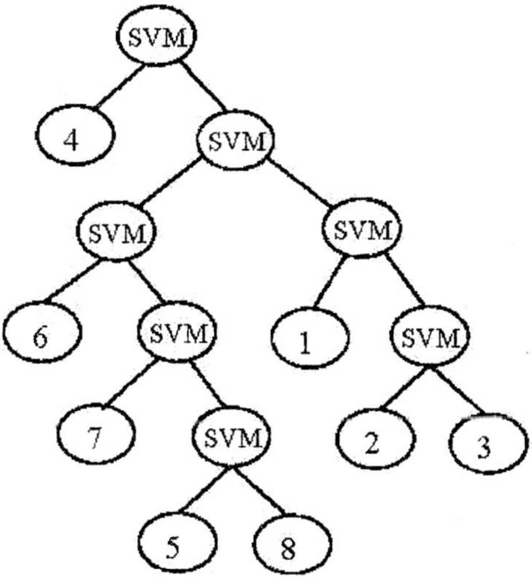

Fig. 1. Huffman tree architecture with 8 nodes

OAA is perhaps the simplest scheme for combining binary SVMs to solve multiclass problems. In OAA, every class need train to distinguish the rest classes, so there are N binary SVMs to be trained for an N-class classification problem, while in testing procedure, *Max Wins* strategy is usually used to classify a new example and consequently N binary decision functions are required to solve. The *Max Wins* strategy is

$$f(x) = arg \max_{i}(\mathbf{w}_i \cdot \mathbf{x} + b_i) \tag{7}$$

Another scheme called pairwise is used in OAO, DAG and BUBT. In this approach, each binary SVM separates a pair of classes and $N(N-1)/2$ binary SVMs in total are trained when there are N classes. In decision phase, there is much difference among the three methods. OAO uses traditional *Max Wins* strategy and need test $N(N-1)/2$ SVMs. DAG employs directed acyclic graph in which every class is eliminated step by step from the list composed of all classes. Thus, for a problem with N classes, $N-1$ binary SVMs will be tested in order to drive an answer. In BUBT, a bottom-up binary tree architecture is introduced to incorporate $N(N-1)/2$ binary SVMs trained and a tournament strategy is used to classify a new example. Similar to DAG, BUBT also need test $(N-1)$ binary SVMs for the classification decision. BT1 and BT2 use a hierarchical scheme that a multiclass classification problem is decomposed into a series of binary classification sub-problems. The difference between BT1 and BT2 lies in different decomposition method. BT1 separates one class from the rest classes with an SVM. In every step of decomposition, there is at least one terminal node between two siblings. Thus, for an N-class problem, BT1 need train $(N-1)$ binary SVMs and $(N^2+N-2)/(2N)$ binary decision functions are required to solve in testing procedure. While BT2 usually decomposes an N-class problem in a peer-to-peer way into $(N-1)$ binary classification subproblems. So there are $(N-1)$ binary SVMs to train in training procedure and only $\log_2 N$ binary SVMs need test in decision phase.

According to the above analysis, OAA, OAO, DAG, BUBT, BT1 and BT2 need train at least $(N-1)$ SVMs and require to test at least $\log_2 N$ SVMs for an N-class classification problem. While in HTA illustrated in Fig.1, only $(N-1)$ binary SVMs need be trained for N-class problem. Because Huffman tree is the optimal binary tree that has the minimal average depth, HTA need test much smaller than $\log_2 N$ SVMs for the classification decision. For example, in Fig.1, if the probability values of node 1 to node 8 are 0.135, 0.048, 0.058, 0.39, 0.039, 0.23, 0.067 and 0.033, respectively, HTA need test 2537 SVMs and BT2 need test 3000 SVMs when the number of testing samples is 1000. So among the 7 multiclass SVM classifiers, HTA need the minimal SVMs both in training and in testing procedures.

4 Simulations

4.1 Performance Test

HTA is evaluated on the normalized handwritten digit data set, automatically scanned from envelops by U.S. Postal Service (USPS) [7,14,15]. The USPS database contains zipcode samples from actual mails. This database is composed of separate training and testing sets. The USPS digit data consists of 10 classes (the integer 0 through 9), whose inputs are pixels of a scaled image. The numbers 0 through 9 have 1194, 1005, 731, 658, 652, 556, 664, 645, 542, 644 training samples respectively and have 359, 264, 198, 166, 200, 160, 170, 147, 166, 177 testing samples respectively. Thus, there are totally 7291 samples in training set and 2007 samples in the testing set. Every sample is made up of 256 features. The difference of the number of the 10 integers extracted from actual mails verifies that the 10 integers occur in an unequal probability. To be convenient for testing, the occurring probabilities of the 10 classes 0 through 9 in testing set are used to construct a Huffman tree. The probabilities of 0 through 9 are respectively 0.1789, 0.1315, 0.0987, 0.0827, 0.0997, 0.0797, 0.0847, 0.0732, 0.0827 and 0.0882. The constructed Huffman tree architecture is illustrated in Fig.2.

Seven approaches OAA, OAO, DAG, BUBT, BT1, BT2 and HTA are used to make comparison experiments. The computational experiments are done on a Pentium IV-2.0 with 512 MB RAM using MATLAB implementation by Steve Gunn. Gaussian kernel function $\mathbf{K}(\mathbf{x}_i, \mathbf{x}_j)$

$$\mathbf{K}(\mathbf{x}_i, \mathbf{x}_j) = e^{\frac{|\mathbf{x}_i - \mathbf{x}_j|^2}{2\sigma}} \quad (8)$$

and the same parameter C and σ are used in 7 SVM classifiers. We use similar stop-ping criteria that the KKT violation is less than 10^{-3}. For each class, 504

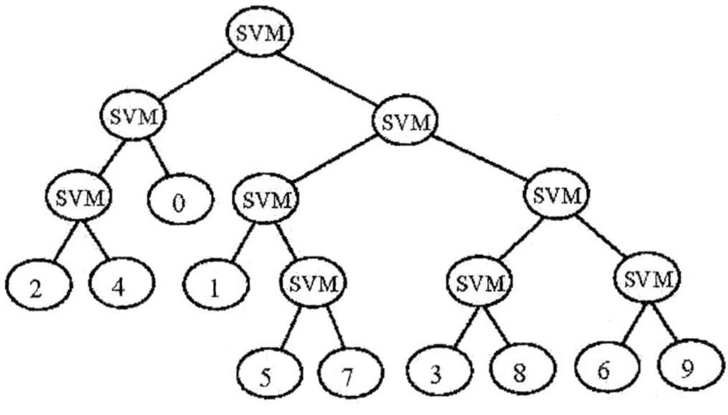

Fig. 2. Huffman tree architecture for digit recognition

samples selected randomly from its training set are used to train the SVM classifiers. The criterions for evaluating the performances of the 7 classifiers are their error rate and recognition efficiency including training time and testing time. All samples in the testing set are used to test the performances of the 7 classifiers. Statistical results of many experiments using the 7 classifiers respectively are given in Table 1.

Table 1 shows the results of experiments. HTA, BT1, BT2 and OAA consume much shorter training time than OAO, DAG and BUBT. Because HTA, BT1 and BT2 need train the same number of binary SVMs, the training time of the three methods has small difference. Similarly, the three methods including OAA, BUBT and DAG consume nearly same training time because they train the same number of SVMs. In the 7 methods, the testing time of HTA is the shortest. In Table 1, HTA consumes 445.44 seconds of testing time, which is a litter shorter than that of BT1 and BT2 and much shorter than that of OAA, OAO, DAG and BUBT. From the recognition error rate, HTA is much superior to OAA and OAO; HTA is a little superior to BUBT and BT1; HTA is not

Table 1. Experimental results of digit recognition

Methods	Training Time (sec.)	Testing time (sec.)	Error rate (%)
HTA	8499.21	445.44	3.42
OAA	9470.81	1391.57	95.59
OAO	44249.48	6068.75	89.57
DAG	43153.70	1217.69	2.32
BUBT	44938.34	1255.61	3.52
BT1	8397.35	641.14	4.83
BT2	8125.30	463.57	3.40

inferior to DAG and BT2. In a word, experimental results indicate that HTA has high recognition efficiency and good classification capability.

4.2 Application

In this subsection, an application example of radar emitter signal recognition is applied to make the comparison experiments of OAA, OAO, DAG, BUBT, BT1, BT2 and HTA. In the example, there are 8 modulation radar emitter signals (labeled as RES1, RES2, RES3, RES4, RES5, RES6, RES7, RES8, respectively). Some features of these radar emitter signals have been extracted in our prior work [21,22]. Two features obtained by the feature selection method [23] are used to recognize the 8 modulation radar emitter signals. In experiments, every radar emitter signal uses 360 training samples and thereby there are 2880 training samples in total. The training samples are employed to draw a feature distribution graph shown in Fig.3 to illustrate distribution of radar emitter signal features in feature space.

According to experts' experiences, the occurrence probabilities of the 8 modulation signals can be approximately considered as 0.135, 0.048, 0.058, 0.39, 0.039, 0.23, 0.067 and 0.033, respectively. Thus, the Huffman tree architecture constructed using 8 radar emitter signals is shown in Fig.1. In testing phase, there are 8000 testing samples in total and the number of testing samples of 8 radar emitter signals is computed in the proportion of 13.5%, 4.8%, 5.8%, 39%, 3.9%, 23%, 6.7% and 3.3%, respectively. Both training samples and testing sam-

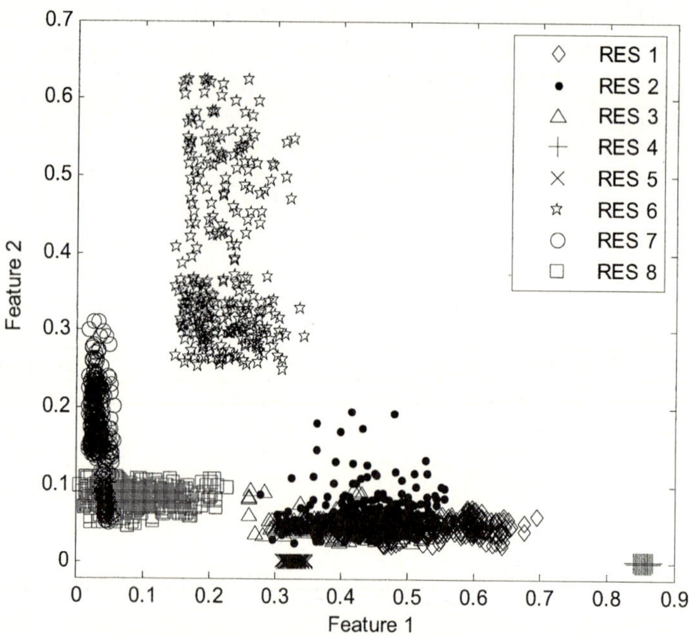

Fig. 3. Feature distribution graph

Table 2. Experimental results of RES recognition

Methods	Training Time (sec.)	Testing time (sec.)	Error rate (%)
HTA	1917.70	85.55	12.28
OAA	2154.95	255.08	45.64
OAO	8007.84	815.58	84.83
DAG	8151.94	199.75	13.40
BUBT	7737.49	238.01	12.25
BT1	1951.73	134.31	26.85
BT2	1910.94	112.59	22.00

ples are extracted from radar emitter signals when signal-to-noise (SNR) varies from 5 dB to 20 dB. Experimental results of OAA, OAO, DAG, BUBT, BT1, BT2 and HTA are given in Table 2.

Figure 3 shows that there are some overlaps between RES 7 and RES 8 and there is much confusion among RES 1, RES 2 and RES 3. This brings many difficulties to correct recognition. Also, the features of 8 radar emitter signals have good clustering. Table 2 presents the results of comparing 7 multiclass SVM classifiers. Although HTA is appreciably inferior to BUBT in recognition error rate and it needs a little more training time than BT2, HTA has higher recognition efficiency than OAA, OAO, BUBT, DAG and BT1. Especially, HTA is the best among the 7 methods for the testing time and it achieves lower recognition error rate than OAA, OAO, DAG, BT1 and BT2.

The experimental results of digit recognition and radar emitter signal recognition are consistent with theoretical analysis in Section 3. In pattern recognition including radar emitter signal recognition and USPS digit recognition, training is off-line operation, while testing is usually on-line operation. So the testing speed of classifiers is more important, especially in radar emitter signal recognition. Experimental results verify that HTA is the fastest among the 7 multiclass SVM classifiers instead of decreasing classification performance. This benefit is especially useful when the number of classes is very large.

5 Concluding Remarks

In the methods for combining multiple binary SVMs to solve multiclass classification problems, binary tree architecture is a good one because it needs small binary SVMs both in training phase and in testing phase. However, how to choose the root nodes in each layer is a very important issue in engineering applications when binary tree architecture is used to combine multiple binary-support-vector-machines. From the view of intelligent aspects of human brain in pattern recognition, this paper introduces Huffman tree architecture to design a multiclass classifier. For a real problem, the Huffman tree architecture is unique. The outstanding characteristic of the introduced architecture lies in faster recognition speed than the existing 6 methods. Though, this paper discusses the technique for quickening recognition speed only from the architecture for combining support vector machines. In fact, the recognition speed has also relation to the number of support vectors obtained in training phase of support vector machines. This problem will be further discussed in later paper.

References

1. Vapnik, V.N.: Statistical Learning Theory. New York, Wiley, (1998)
2. Dibike, Y.B., Velickov, S., and Solomatine, D.: Support Vector Machines: Review and Applications in Civil Engineering. Proceedings of the 2nd Joint Workshop on Application of AI in Civil Engineering, (2000) 215-218
3. Hsu, C.W., Lin, C. J.: A Comparison of Methods for Multiclass Support Vector Machines. IEEE Transactions on Neural Networks. Vol.13, No.2. (2002) 415-425
4. Cheong, S.M., Oh,S.H., and Lee, S.Y.: Support Vector Machines with Binary Tree Architecture for MultiClass Classification. Neural Information Processing: Letters and Reviews. Vol.2, No.3. (2004) 47-51
5. Rifkin, R., Klautau, A.: In Defence of One-Vs-All Classification. Journal of Machine Learning Research. Vol.5, No.1. (2004) 101-141
6. Furnkranz, J.: Round Robin Classification. Vol.2, No.2. (2002) 721-747
7. Platt, J.C., Cristianini, N., and Shawe-Taylor, J.: Large Margin DAG's for Multiclass Classification. Advances in Neural Information Processing Systems. Cambridge, MA: MIT Press, Vol.12. (2000) 547-553
8. Guo, G.D., Li, S.Z.: Content-based Audio Classification and Retrieval by Support Vector Machines. IEEE Transactions on Neural Networks. Vol.14, No.1. (2003) 209-215
9. Guo, G.D., Li, S.Z., and Chan, K.L.: Support Vector Machines for Face Recognition. Image and Vision Computing, Vol.19, No.9. (2001) 631-638
10. Huo, X.M., Chen, J.H., and Wang, S.C., et al: Support Vector Trees: Simultaneously Realizing the Principles of Maximal Margin and Maximal Purity. Technical report. (2002) 1-19 (Available: www.isye.gatech.edu /research /files/tsui-2002-01.pdf)
11. Jain, A.K., Duin, R.P.W., and Mao, J.C.: Statistical Pattern Recognition: a Review. IEEE Transactions on Pattern Analysis and Machine Intelligence. Vol.22, No.1. (2000) 4-37
12. Huang, J.H., Lai, Y.C.: Reverse Huffman Tree for Nonuniform Traffic Pattern. Electronics Letters. Vol.27, No.20. (1991) 1884-1886
13. Weiss, M.A.: Data Structures and Algorithm Analysis in C (2nd Edition). Addison Wesley, New York (1996)
14. Bredensteiner, E.J., Bennett, K.P.: Multicategory Classification by Support Vector Machines. Computational Optimization and Applications, Vol.12, No.1-3. (1999) 53-79
15. www-stat.Stanford.edu/ tibs/ElemStaLearn/datasets/zip.digits
16. Frey, P.W., Slate, D.J.: Letter Recognition Using Holland-Style Adaptive Classifiers. Machine Learning, Vol.6, No.2. (1991) 161-182
17. Murphy, P., Aha, D.W.: UCI Repository of Machine Learning Databases and Domain Theories. Available from [http: //www.ics.uci.edu / mlearn /MLRepository.html] (1995)
18. Gao, D.Q., Li, R.L., and Nie, G.P., et al.: Adaptive Task Decomposition and Modular Multilayer Perceptions for Letter Recognition. Proceedings of IEEE International Joint Conference on Neural Networks, Vol.4. (2004) 2937-2942

19. Vlad, A., Mitrea, A., and Mitrea, M., et al.: Statistical Methods for Verifying the Natural Language Stationarity Based on the First Approximation. Case Study: Printed Romanian. Proceedings of the International Conference Venezia per il trattamento automatico dellalingue, (1999) 127-132
20. Vlad, A., Mitrea, A., and Mitrea, M.: Two Frequency-Rank Laws For Letters In Printed Romanian. Procesamiento on Natural Language, No.24. (2000) 153-160
21. Zhang, G.X., Hu, L.Z., and Jin, W.D.: Intra-pulse Feature Analysis of Radar Emitter Sig-nals. Journal of Infrared and Millimeter Waves, Vol.23, No.6. (2004) 477-480
22. Zhang, G.X., Hu, L.Z., and Jin, W.D.: Resemblance Coefficient Based Intrapulse Feature Extraction Approach for Radar Emitter Signals. Chinese Journal of Electronics, Vol.14, No.2. (2005) 337-341
23. Zhang, G.X., Jin, W.D., Hu, L.Z.: A novel feature selection approach and its application. Lecture Notes in Computer Science. Vol.3314. (2004) 665-671.

Automatic Removal of Impulse Noise from Highly Corrupted Images

Vitaly Kober[1], Mikhail Mozerov[2], and Josué Álvarez-Borrego[3]

[1]Department of Computer Science, Division of Applied Physics,
CICESE, Ensenada, B.C. 22860, Mexico
vkober@cicese.mx
[2]Laboratory of Digital Optics, Institute for Information Transmission Problems,
Bolshoi Karetnii 19, 101447 Moscow, Russia
mozer@iitp.ru
[3]Dirección de Telemática,
CICESE, Ensenada, B.C. 22860, Mexico
josue@cicese.mx

Abstract. An effective algorithm for automatic removal impulse noise from highly corrupted monochromatic images is proposed. The method consists of two steps. Outliers are first detected using local spatial relationships between image pixels. Then the detected noise pixels are replaced with the output of a rank-order filter over a local spatially connected area excluding the outliers, while noise-free pixels are left unaltered. Simulation results in test images show a superior performance of the proposed filtering algorithm comparing with conventional filters. The comparisons are made using mean square error, mean absolute error, and subjective human visual error criterion.

1 Introduction

Digital images are often corrupted by impulse noise due to a noise sensor or channel transmission errors. The major objective of impulse noise removal is to suppress the noise while preserving the image details. Various algorithms have been proposed for impulse noise removal [1-5]. Basically the most of these algorithms are based on the calculation of rank-order statistics [6]. If filters are implemented uniformly across an image then they tend to modify pixels that are undisturbed by noise. Moreover, they are prone to edge jitter when the percentage of impulse noise is large. Consequently, suppression of impulses is often at expense of blurred and distorted features. Effective techniques usually consist of two steps. First a filter detects corrupted pixels and then a noise cancellation scheme is applied only to detected noisy pixels. Recently nonlinear filters for monochrome images with a signal-dependent shape of the moving window have been proposed [7]. In this paper, we extend this approach to automatic suppressing the impulse noise in highly corrupted images. First outliers are detected using local spatial relationships between image pixels. Then the detected noise pixels are replaced with the output of an appropriate rank-order filter computed over a local spatially connected area excluding the outliers from the area. In the case of

M. Lazo and A. Sanfeliu (Eds.): CIARP 2005, LNCS 3773, pp. 34–41, 2005.

independent impulse noise, the proposed detector greatly reduces the miss probability of impulse noise. The performance of the proposed filter is compared with that of conventional algorithms.

The presentation is organized as follows. In Section 2, we present a new efficient algorithm for automatic detection of noise impulses. A modified filtering algorithm using the proposed detector is also described. In Section 3, with the help of computer simulation we test the performance of the conventional and proposed filters. Section 4 summarizes our conclusions.

2 Automatic Detection and Removal Impulse Noise

In impulse noise models, corrupted pixels are often replaced with values near to the maximum and minimum of the dynamic range of a signal. In our experiments, we consider a similar model in which a noisy pixel can take a random value either from sub-ranges of the maximum or the minimum values with a given probability. The distribution of impulse noise in the sub-ranges can be arbitrary. To detect impulse noise in an image, we use the concept of a spatially connected neighborhood (*SCN*). An underlying assumption is as follows: image pixels geometrically close to each other belong to the same structure or detail. The spatially connected neighborhood is defined as a subset of pixels $\{v_{n,m}\}$ of a moving window, which are spatially connected with the central pixel of the window, and whose values deviate from the value of the central pixel $v_{k,l}$ at most predetermined quantities $-\varepsilon_v$ and $+\varepsilon_v$ [7]:

$$SCN\left(v_{k,l}\right) = CON\ \left(\left\{v_{n,m} : v_{k,l} - \varepsilon_v \le v_{n,m} \le v_{k,l} + \varepsilon_v\right\}\right), \tag{1}$$

where *CON(X)* denotes four- or eight-connected region including the central pixel of the moving window. The size and shape of a spatially connected neighborhood are dependent on characteristics of image data and on parameters, which define measures of homogeneity of pixel sets. So the spatially connected neighborhood is a spatially connected region constructed for each pixel, and it consists of all the spatially connected pixels, which satisfy a property of similarity with the central pixel.

We assume that the size of the *SCN* of a noise cluster is relatively small comparing to that of details of image to be processed. Therefore impulsive noise can be detected by checking the size of the cluster; that is, if $S \le \mathrm{M}$ then the impulse is detected. Here *S*=SIZE(*SCN*) is the number of pixels included in the *SCN* constructed around the central pixel of the moving window with the parameter ε_v for adjacent pixels, *M* is a given threshold value for detection of noise clusters. Actually the detection depends on two integer parameters; that is, ε_v and *M*. Extensive computer simulations have shown that the best value of *M*, which yields minimum detection errors of noise clusters for various noise distributions, can be expressed as a function of a given noise distribution and a chosen value of ε_v. Let us consider model of impulsive noise. A test gray scale image has *Q*=256 quantization levels and *N* pixels. The probability of independent corruption of image pixels by impulse noise at the level *q* is equal to *P(q)* ($0 \le q \le Q-1$). The probability of noise impulse occurring can be calculated as

$$p = \sum_{q=0}^{Q-1} P(q)\,, \tag{2}$$

and the expected number of impulses in the image is given by

$$N_{imp} = pN . \tag{3}$$

For the considering detector, if the absolute difference between the noise impulse and pixels of neighborhood is less or equal to a chosen value of ε_v then the impulse is invisible for the detector. Therefore the total number of detectable impulses is less than N_{imp} in Eq. (3). In this case the expected number of outliers is given by

$$\tilde{N}_{imp} = N\sum_{q=0}^{Q-1}\tilde{P}(q), \tag{4}$$

where $\tilde{P}(q)$ is the probability of detection of an impulse at the level q. If the distribution of the image signal is spatially homogeneous then the probability of noise impulse detection can be approximately estimated with the help of the histogram of uncorrupted test image,

$$\tilde{P}(q) \approx P(q)\left(1-\sum_{l=0}^{Q-1}h_l\left[|l-q|\le\varepsilon_v\right]\Big/N\right), \tag{5}$$

where $\{h_q\}$ is the histogram of uncorrupted image, [.] denotes the following function: 1, if the statement in brackets is true and 0, otherwise.

Since the histogram of the uncorrupted image is usually inaccessible then the estimation of this histogram can be written as

$$h_q = \frac{\tilde{h}_q - NP(q)}{1-p}, \tag{6}$$

where $\left\{\tilde{h}_q\right\}$ is the available histogram of the observed noisy image.

The proposed detector of impulse noise takes into account the size of the *SCN*. Now we know how many impulses can be detected by the detector. Obviously, such detector omits impulses with the size greater than *M*. The probability *Pr*(M) of occurrence of four-connected noise clusters of the size *M* can be computed using the formulas given in the papers [8, 9]. In this way the expected number and the probability of occurrence of all clusters of the size greater than *M* can be obtained. We can state that if the expected number of clusters of the size greater than *M* (for a given image and a noise distribution) is less than unity then the value of the threshold *M* is optimal. Formally the statement can be written as

$$M = S \text{ if } N_{imp>S} = N_{imp} - N\sum_{m=1}^{S}Pr(m) < 1 \le N_{imp} - N\sum_{m=1}^{S-1}Pr(m) \tag{7}$$

where $N_{imp>S}$ is the expected number of clusters of the size greater than *S* pixels.

The probability of occurrence of a four-connected noise cluster of the size *M* in a moving window can be computed using the addition formula of probabilities. The noise cluster occurs simultaneously with one of the mutually exclusive events $H_1,\ldots, H_N$. Here H_k is the event denoting that there is a noise cluster of the size exactly *M* noise impulses surrounded by uncorrupted image pixels. The probability of occurrence of a noise cluster of the size M at a given image pixel is given as [8, 9]

$$Pr(M) = \sum_{k=1}^{N} Pr(H_k), \tag{8}$$

where the probability of the event H_k is $Pr(H_k) = P^M (1-P)^{E_k(M)}$, $E_k(M)$ is the number of surrounded uncorrupted image pixels. Taking into account that some of the probabilities $Pr(H_k)$ are equal, the Eq.(8) is computationally simplified to

$$Pr(M) = p^M \sum_{k=1}^{K(M)} C_k(M)(1-p)^{E_k(M)}, \tag{9}$$

where $K(M)$ is the number of groups, each of them contains $C_k(M)$ events H_k with the equal probabilities $Pr(H_k)$, k=1,...$K(M)$. $C_k(M)$, $E_k(M)$ are coefficients determined from the geometry (binary region of support) of the cluster of noise. For example, the number of groups with M=2 is $K(2)$=1, and the number of surrounding four-connected uncorrupted pixels is $E_1(M)$=6. The number of the events is $C_1(M)$=4 (four possible variants of the noise cluster on the grid including the given pixel). These coefficients are provided in Table 1.

Table 1. Coefficients for calculating the probability of impulsive clusters

Size of cluster M	$K(M)$	k	$C_k(M)$	$E_k(M)$
1	1	1	1	4
2	1	1	4	6
3	2	1	12	7
		2	6	8
4	3	1	36	8
		2	32	9
		3	8	10
5	5	1	5	8
		2	100	9
		3	140	10
		4	60	11
		5	10	12

With the help of Table 1 and Eq. (9), the probability of occurrence of a four-connected impulse noise cluster of the size M can be easily calculated. Table 2 presents the probability of occurrence of impulse cluster of size M versus the probability of impulse noise on a rectangular grid. We see that when the probability of impulse noise is high, the occurrence of impulse cluster is very likely.

Table 2. The probability of occurrence of impulse clusters of the size M versus the probability p of impulse noise

M	Probability of impulse noise		
	p=0.01	p=0.1	p=0.2
0	0.99	0.9	0.8
1	$5.6\text{x}10^{-3}$	$6.5\text{x}10^{-2}$	$8.2\text{x}10^{-2}$
2	$3.7\text{x}10^{-4}$	$2.1\text{x}10^{-2}$	$4.2\text{x}10^{-2}$
3	$1.7\text{x}10^{-5}$	$8.3\text{x}10^{-3}$	$2.8\text{x}10^{-2}$
4	$7\text{x}10^{-7}$	$3\text{x}10^{-3}$	$1.8\text{x}10^{-2}$
5	$2.8\text{x}10^{-8}$	$1.1\text{x}10^{-3}$	$1.1\text{x}10^{-2}$

Finally the proposed algorithm of impulse noise detection consists of the following steps.

- Choose two initial values for $\varepsilon_v \in [1,(Q-1)]$, say $\varepsilon_{v\ max}$ and $\varepsilon_{v\ min}$, and then calculate $\varepsilon_v=(\varepsilon_{v\ max}+\varepsilon_{v\ min})/2$.
- Compute $\tilde{N}_{imp}$ and M using Eqs. (4)-(7), noise distribution and threshold ε_v.
- Form the *SCN* with ε_v and calculate the number of detected impulses, say D.
- Compare D with $\tilde{N}_{imp}$, and if ($D=\tilde{N}_{imp}$ or $\varepsilon_v=\varepsilon_{v\ max}$ or $\varepsilon_v=\varepsilon_{v\ min}$) then the optimal pair of ε_v and M is found, else go to the next step.
- If $D>\tilde{N}_{imp}$ then set $\varepsilon_{v\ min}=\varepsilon_v$, else set $\varepsilon_{v\ max}=\varepsilon_v$. Calculate $\varepsilon_v=(\varepsilon_{v\ max}+\varepsilon_{v\ min})/2$ and go to the second step.

Computer experiments with test images corrupted by various kinds of impulse noise have showed that the integer function $D(\varepsilon_v)$ is monotonically decreasing. Thus the solution of the proposed iterative algorithm with respect to ε_v is unique. Since $\varepsilon_{v\ max}$, ε_{vmin}, and ε_v are integer then the number of iterations for Q=256 is limited by 7.

When the map of detected impulses with the calculated parameters is obtained, the noisy pixels are replaced with the output of any appropriate filter. In our case the median value of at least 3 uncorrupted neighboring pixels is used.

3 Computer Experiments

Signal processing of an image degraded due to impulse noise is of interest in a variety of tasks. Computer experiments are carried out to illustrate and compare the performance of conventional and proposed algorithms. In this paper, we will base our comparisons on the mean square error (MSE), the mean absolute error (MAE), and a subjective visual criterion. The empirical normalized mean square error is given by

$$MSE = \frac{\sum_{n=1}^{N_x}\sum_{m=1}^{M_y}\left|v_{n,m}-\hat{v}_{n,m}\right|^2}{\sum_{n=1}^{N_x}\sum_{m=1}^{M_y}v_{n,m}^{\ 2}}, \qquad (10)$$

where $\{v_{n,m}\}$ and $\{\hat{v}_{n,m}\}$ are the original image and its estimate (filtered image), respectively. In our simulations, N_x=256, M_y=256 (256x256 image resolution), and each pixel has 256 levels of quantization. The empirical normalized mean absolute error is defined as

$$MAE = \frac{\sum_{n=1}^{N_x}\sum_{m=1}^{M_y}\left|v_{n,m,k} - \hat{v}_{n,m,k}\right|}{\sum_{n=1}^{N_x}\sum_{m=1}^{M_y}\left|v_{n,m,k}\right|}. \quad (11)$$

The use of these error measures allows us to compare the performance of each filter. Fig. 1 shows a test image. The test image degraded due to impulsive noise is shown in Fig. 2.

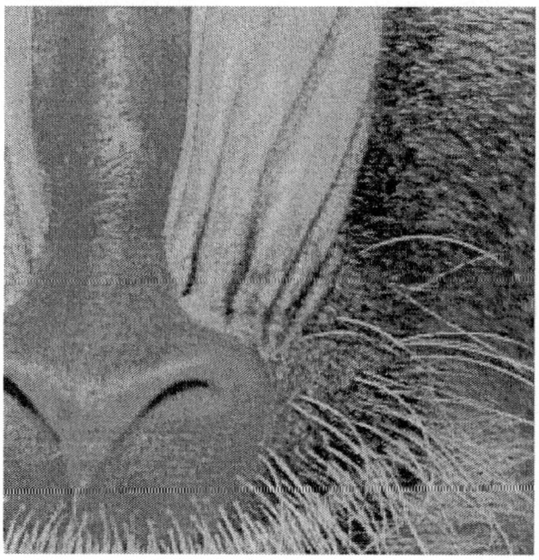

Fig. 1. Original image

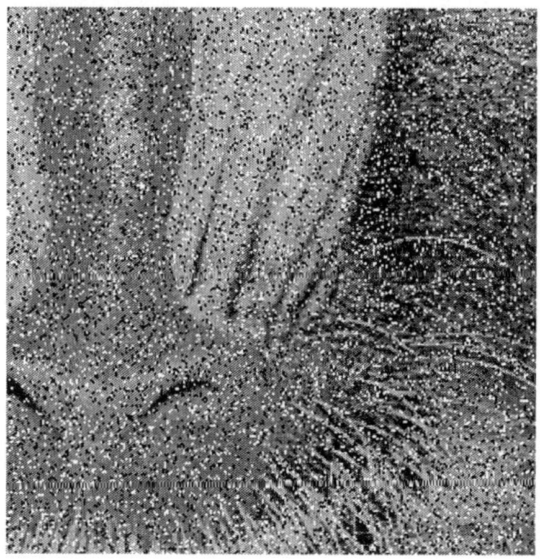

Fig. 2. Noisy image

The probability of independent noise impulse occurrence is 0.2. In computer simulation, the values of impulses were set to 0-15 or 240-255 with equal probability. Table 3 shows the errors under the MSE and MAE criteria for the median filter (MED) of 3x3 pixels, fuzzy technique (FF) [5], and the proposed filter.

Table 3. Impulse noise suppression with different filters

Type of Filters	Measured Errors	
	MSE	MAE
Noisy image	0.17	0.162
MED 3x3	0.065	0.012
FF algorithm	0.023	0.009
Proposed algorithm	0.019	0.005

The parameters M and ε_v are automatically calculated with the proposed algorithm described in Section 2. We see that in this case the proposed filter has the best performance with respect to the MSE and MAE. Now we carry out visual comparison of the filtering results with the median and the proposed filters. Figures 3 and 4 show the filtered images obtained from the noisy image with the median filter and the proposed filter, respectively. The proposed filter using the spatial pixel connectivity has a strong ability in impulse noise suppression and a very good preservation of fine structures and details. The visual comparison shows that the filtered image with the median filter is much smoother than the output image after filtering with proposed method.

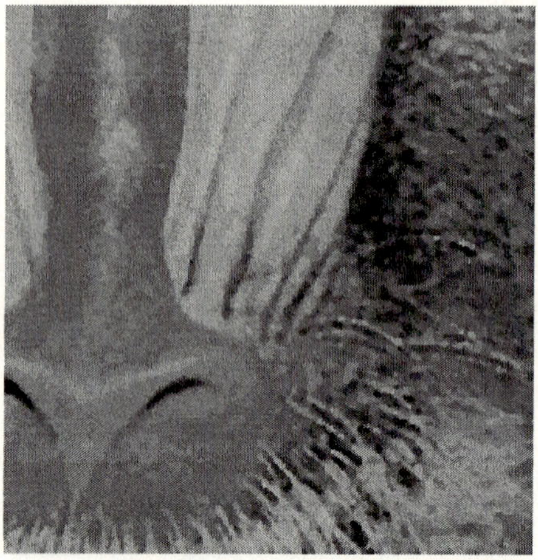

Fig. 3. Filtered image by MED filter

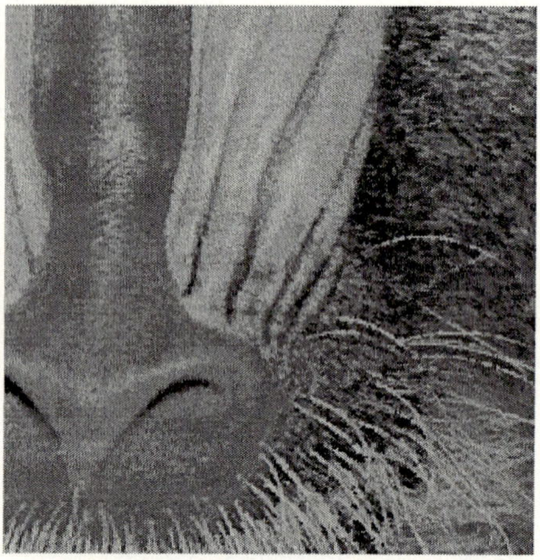

Fig. 4. Filtered image by the proposed method

4 Conclusion

In this paper, we have presented a new algorithm for automatic detection and suppression of impulse noise in highly corrupted images. The filter utilizes an explicit use of spatial relations between image elements. When the input image is degraded due impulse noise, extensive testing has shown that the proposed spatially adaptive filter outperforms conventional filters in terms of the mean square error, the mean absolute error, and the subjective visual criterion.

References

1. Pitas I. and Venetsanopoulos A.N., Nonlinear digital filters. Principles and applications, Kluwer Academic Publishers, Boston (1990).
2. Tsekeridou S., Kotropoulos C., Pitas I., Adaptive order statistic filters for the removal of noise from corrupted images, Optical Engineering, Vol. 37, (1998), 2798-2815.
3. Abreu E., Linghtstone M., Mitra S.K., and Arakawa K., A new efficient approach for the removal of impulse noise from highly corrupted images, IEEE Trans. on Image Processing, Vol. 2, No. 6, (1993), 1012-1025.

4. Lehmann T., Oberschelp W., Pelikan E., Repges R., Image processing for medical images, Springer-Verlag, Berlin, Heidelberg, New York (1997).
5. Zhang D. and Wang Z., Impulse noise detection and removal using fuzzy techniques, Electronics Letter, Vol. 33, No. 5, (1997), 378-379.
6. David H.A., Order statistics, Wiley, New York (1970).
7. Kober V., Mozerov M., Alvarez-Borrego J., Nonlinear filters with spatially connected neighborhoods, Optical Engineering, Vol. 40, No. 6, (2001), 971-983.
8. Mozerov M., Kober V., Choi T., Noise Removal from highly corrupted color images with adaptive neighborhoods, IEICE Trans. on Fund., Vol. E86-A, No. 10, 2003, 2713-2717.
9. Kober V., Mozerov M., Alvarez-Borrego J., Spatially adaptive algorithms for impulse noise removal from color images, Lecture Notes in Computer Science, Vol. 2905, (2003), 113-120.

Smoothing of Polygonal Chains for 2D Shape Representation Using a G^2-Continuous Cubic A-Spline*

Sofía Behar[1], Jorge Estrada[2], Victoria Hernández[2], and Dionne León[2]

[1] Faculty of Mathematics and Computer Sciences, Havana University, Cuba
[2] Institute of Mathematics and Theoretical Physics, CITMA, Cuba

Abstract. We have developed a G^2-continuous cubic A-spline, suitable for smoothing polygonal chains used in 2D shape representation. The proposed A-spline scheme interpolates an ordered set of data points in the plane, as well as the direction and sense of tangent vectors associated to these points. We explicitly characterize curve families which are used to construct the A-spline sections, whose members have the required interpolating properties and possess a minimal number of inflection points. The A-spline considered here has many attractive features: it is very easy to construct, it provides us with convenient geometric control handles to locally modify the shape of the curve and the error of approximation is controllable. Furthermore, it can be rapidly displayed, even though its sections are implicitly defined algebraic curves.

Keywords: Algebraic cubic splines, polygonal chain, data interpolation and fitting, 2D shape representation.

Mathematics Subject Classification: 65D07(splines), 65D05 (interpolation), 65D17 (Computer Aided Design).

1 Introduction

Several geometry processing tasks use polygonal chains for 2D shape representation. Digital image contouring, snakes, fitting from "noisy" data, interactive shape or font design and level set methods (see for instance [5], [7], [10], [11]) are some illustrating examples. Suppose a curve is sampled within some error band of width $2\,\varepsilon$ around the curve. Since the sampled point sequence $\mathcal{S}$ could be dense, a simplification step is often used to obtain coarser or multiresolution representations. A polygonal chain $\mathcal{C}$ approximating the points of $\mathcal{S}$ is constructed, with the property that all points in $\mathcal{S}$ are within an ε-neighborhood of the simplified polygonal chain $\mathcal{C}$.

Prior work on using algebraic curve spline in data interpolation and fitting focus on using bivariate barycentric BB-form polynomials defined on plane triangles ([1], [5],[8],[9]) Some other authors use tensor product A-splines ([2]).

* The results presented in this work were obtained with the support of a FONCI/2003 grant.

M. Lazo and A. Sanfeliu (Eds.): CIARP 2005, LNCS 3773, pp. 42–50, 2005.

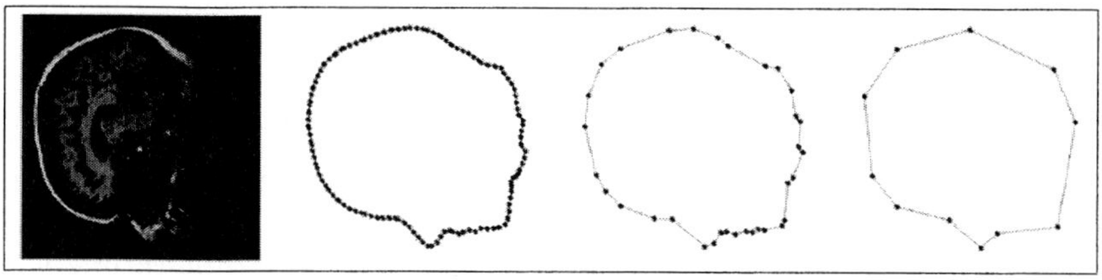

Fig. 1. Sequence of polygonal chains

These A-spline functions are easy to construct. The coefficients of the bivariate polynomial that define the curve are explicitly given. There exist convenient geometric control handles to locally modify the shape of the curve, essential for interactive curve design. Each curve section of the A-spline curve has either no inflection points if the corresponding edge is convex, or one inflection point otherwise, therefore the A-spline sections have a minimal number of inflection points. Since their degree is low, the A-spline sections can be evaluated and displayed very fast. Moreover, some of them are also ε-error controllable.

All that features make these error-bounded A-spline curves promising in the above mentioned applications, which happen to be equivalent to the interpolation and/or approximation a polygonal chain of line segments with error bounds.

Given an input polygonal chain $\mathcal{C}$, we use a cubic A-spline curve $\mathcal{A}$ to smoothly approximate the polygon by interpolating the vertices as well as the direction and sense of the given tangent vectors at the vertices. We also interpolate curvatures at the polygon vertices to achieve G^2-continuity.

The present work is a natural generalization of [5], where once the contour of digital image data has been extracted, the algorithm computes the breakpoints of the A-spline, i.e the junction points for the sections that make up the A-spline curve. Inflection points are also added to the set of junction points of the A-spline. Tangent lines at the junction points are computed using a weighted least square linear fit (fitting line), instead of the classical techniques. This G^1-continuous A-spline scheme interpolates the junction points along with the tangent directions and least-squares approximates the given data between junction points.

2 Some Notations and Preliminaries

The A-spline curve $\mathcal{A}$ discussed in this paper consists of a chain of curve sections $\mathcal{A}_i$. Each section is defined as the zero contour of a bivariate BB-polynomial of degree 3. We show that these curve sections are convex, connected and nonsingular in the interior of the regions of interest.

2.1 Derivative Data

On each vertex Q_i of the polygonal chain $\mathcal{C}$, we assume that the slope of the tangent line t_i as well as the curvature κ_i of $\mathcal{A}$ at Q_i are given. The values t_i can be estimated from the given dense sample data $\mathcal{S}$ by means of a weighted least square linear fit (fitting line) technique, such as proposed in [5], which has a better performance as the ones usually recommended in the literature (see for instance [1] or [2]). Figure 2 illustrates the performance of different methods. The direction of vector $\overrightarrow{v_i}$ may be determined by the estimated value t_i.

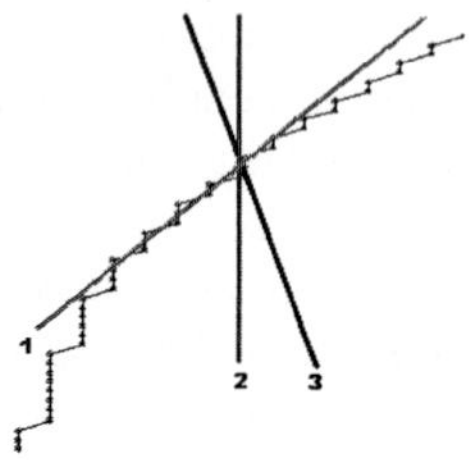

Fig. 2. Selecting the tangent vector using: 1. Fitting line, 2. Interpolation parabola, 3. Fourth degree interpolation polynomial

To compute the curvature values κ_i, we propose the following procedure. Among all (implicitly defined) plane quadratic curves $f(x,y) = 0$ passing through Q_i, such that the tangent line of f at Q_i has slope t_i, compute the quadratic curve with implicit equation $f^*(x,y) = 0$ minimizing the weighted sum

$$W_i := \sum_k \left(\frac{f(P_i^k)}{d_i^k} \right)^2$$

where P_i^k are points in $\mathcal{S}$ which are in a neighborhood of Q_i, $P_i^k \neq Q_i$, and $d_i^k := \|Q_i - P_i^k\|$. Then, set κ_i equal to the curvature of $f^*(x,y) = 0$ at Q_i. The computation of $f^*(x,y) = 0$ reduces to a linear least squares problem, hence it is not expensive.

2.2 Convexity of an Edge

Definition 1. *Given two consecutive vertices of $\mathcal{C}$, we call the edge passing through them* ***convex*** *if the associated tangent vectors point to opposite sides of the edge. Otherwise, we call the edge* ***non convex*** *(see Fig. 3).*

In the non convex case, in an analogous way as explained in [5], we insert to $\mathcal{C}$ a new intermediate vertex for the position of the inflection point and the

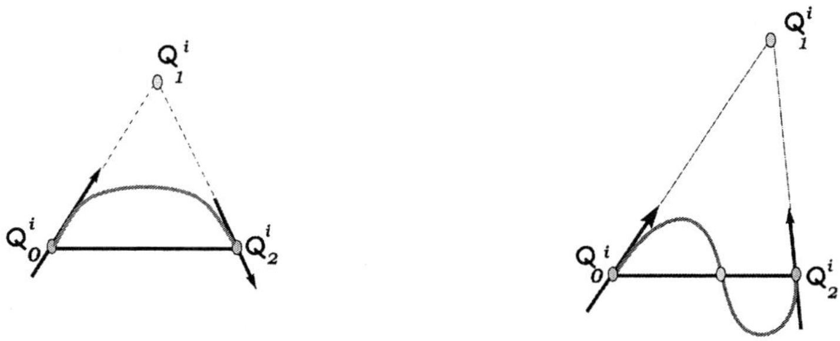

Fig. 3. Examples of convex and non convex cases

tangent line at this new vertex is computed using a weighted least square linear fit. Further, the corresponding curvature value is set equal to 0, since it happens to be an inflection point. In this way we reduce a non convex edge of $\mathcal{C}$ to the union of two consecutive convex edges.

2.3 ε-Error Controllability

Definition 2. *Given a magnitude $\varepsilon > 0$, we call an A-spline* ε-**controllable** *if the points of each section $\mathcal{A}_i$ are at most at distance ε to the corresponding edge $\mathcal{A}$.*

We show that the proposed A-spline scheme is ε-**controllable**. Note that if we use barycentric coordinates (u, v) with respect to a triangle, such that the edge E_i corresponds to the line $v = 0$, then $\mathcal{A}_i$ is ε-**controllable** iff $|v| \leq \varepsilon_i$, for some $0 \leq \varepsilon_i$ depending on ε and of the geometry of the triangle.

3 Polygonal Chain Approximation by Cubic A-Spline Curves

Given an ordered set of n points in the plane $\mathcal{C}$ and prescribed tangent vectors at these points, we want to construct a cubic G^2-continuous A-spline curve $\mathcal{A}$, interpolating these points, as well as the direction and sense of their prescribed tangent vectors.

3.1 Triangle Chain

Abusing of notation, let us introduce a new sequence of points Q^i_j. First, set $Q^i_0 := Q_i$ and $Q^i_2 := Q_{i+1}$. Each pair of consecutive points $Q^i_0, Q^i_2 \in \mathcal{C}$ with their tangent directions define a triangle T_i, with vertices Q^i_0, Q^i_1, Q^i_2, where Q^i_1

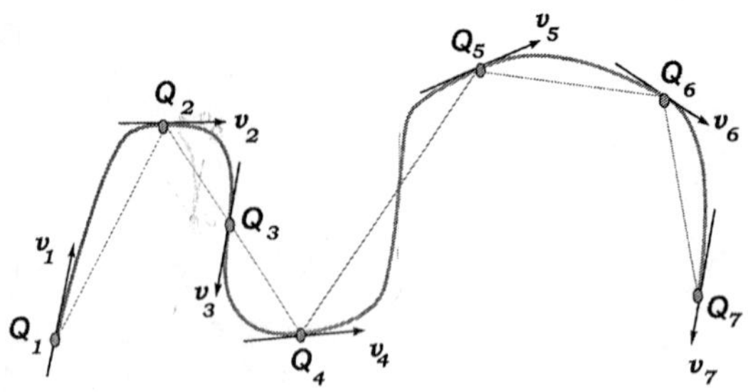

Fig. 4. Interpolating points Q_i with their prescribed tangent vectors $\overrightarrow{v_i}$

is the point of intersection of the tangent directions at Q_0^i and Q_2^i. In order to obtain a continuous curve $\mathcal{A}$, we must require that $Q_2^i = Q_0^{i+1}$ for $i = 1, ...n-1$. Additionally, to construct a closed curve, it is necessary that $Q_2^n = Q_0^1$.

3.2 G^1-Continuity

$\mathcal{A}_i$ may be written in barycentric coordinates (u, v, w), $w = 1 - u - v$ with respect to the vertices of T_i as,

$$\mathcal{A}_i : f_i(u, v) = \sum_{j=0}^{3} \sum_{k=0}^{3-j} a_{kj}^i u^k v^j w^{3-k-j} = 0 \tag{1}$$

Note that after introducing barycentric coordinates the vertex Q_0^i is transformed in the point $(1, 0)$, while the vertex Q_2^i is transformed in the point $(0, 0)$.

It is well known that $\mathcal{A}_i$ interpolates Q_0^i and Q_2^i if the coefficients $a_{0,0}^i$ and $a_{3,0}^i$ in (1) vanish. Furthermore, the tangent lines to $\mathcal{A}_i$ at Q_0^i and Q_2^i are the corresponding sides of the triangle T_i iff $a_{0,1}^i$ and $a_{2,1}^i$ vanish. Assuming that the previous restrictions on the coefficients of are satisfied, then $\mathcal{A}$ is G^1–continuous.

3.3 Explicit Expressions for $\mathcal{A}_i$

Since the section $\mathcal{A}_i$ is traced out from the initial point Q_0^i to the point Q_2^i then, according to the sense of vector $\overrightarrow{v_i}$ associated to Q_0^i we must consider two cases (see Fig. 5):

- **Inner case:** $\overrightarrow{v_i}$ points out to the halfplane containing Q_0^i.
- **Outer case:** $\overrightarrow{v_i}$ does not point out to the halfplane containing Q_0^i.

In the **inner case**, section $\mathcal{A}_i$ is the zero contour of the cubic curve with equation

$$\begin{aligned} I^i(u, v) : \quad & -v^3 + \frac{(1-2u_i)^3}{2u_i^3} uw^2 + \frac{(1-2u_i)^3}{2u_i^3} u^2 w - k_2^i \frac{(1-2u_i)^3}{2u_i^3} v^2 w \\ & - k_0^i \frac{(1-2u_i)^3}{2u_i^3} uv^2 + (k_2^i + k_0^i) \frac{(1-2u_i)^4}{2u_i^4} uvw = 0 \end{aligned}$$

Fig. 5. Interpolating the sense of tangent vectors. (a) **Inner case** (b) **Outer case**.

In the **outer case**, section $\mathcal{A}_i$ is the zero contour of the cubic curve with equation

$$O^i(u,v): \quad -v^3 - \frac{(1-2u_i)^3}{2u_i^3}uw^2 - \frac{(1-2u_i)^3}{2u_i^3}u^2w + k_2^i\frac{(1-2u_i)^3}{2u_i^3}v^2w + k_0^i\frac{(1-2u_i)^3}{2u_i^3}uv^2 + (k_2^i + k_0^i)\frac{(1-2u_i)^4}{2u_i^4}uvw = 0$$

In the next theorem we show that $\mathcal{A}_i$ is contained in the plane region Ω_i. In the **inner case**, Ω_i is the interior of the triangle $\mathcal{T}$ with vertices $(0,0),(1,0),(0,1)$ otherwise, Ω_i is equal to $\mathcal{R} = \{(u,v): -0.5 < v < 0, \quad 0 < u < 1-u-v\}$.

Theorem 1. *The plane cubic curves $I^i(u,v), O^i(u,v)$, satisfy the following properties:*

1. *They interpolate the points Q_0^i, Q_2^i. Their tangent lines at Q_0^i and Q_2^i are the corresponding sides of T_i.*
2. *At Q_0^i they have curvature $\kappa_2^i = \frac{k_2^i\Delta_i}{(g_2^i)^3}$ and at Q_2^i have curvature $\kappa_0^i = \frac{k_0^i\Delta_i}{(g_0^i)^3}$. Here $g_j^i = \|Q_j^i - Q_1^i\|$ and Δ_i denotes the area of T_i.*
3. *Geometric handles: The curves I^i interpolate the point with barycentric coordinates $(u_i, 1-2u_i)$ while the curves O^i interpolate the point with barycentric coordinates $(\frac{u_i}{4u_i-1}, \frac{2u_i-1}{4u_i-1})$. Recall that these interpolation points lay on the line $1-2u-v=0$.*
4. *In Ω_i, I^i and O^i are non singular, connected and convex.*
5. *If $\varepsilon_i \geq 1$ then, curves I^i and O^i are ε_i-controllable. Otherwise, for $0 \leq u_i \leq \frac{1-\varepsilon_i}{2-\varepsilon_i}$, I^i are ε_i-controllable and for $0 \leq u_i \leq \frac{\varepsilon_i-1}{3\varepsilon_i-2}$, O^i are ε_i-controllable.*

The proof of this theorem is somewhat long and due page limitation could not be completely included. We will present some arguments:

1. See the section G^1-**continuity**.
2. See [6].

3. It is a straightforward computation.

4. For the **inner case**, see [1], [6] and [8]. For the **outer case**, the techniques used in the **inner case** do not apply, furthermore, the curves O^i have not been studied before. Considering the pencil $\mathcal{L}$ of lines passing through Q_1^i, the value of the v-coordinate of the intersection of each line $l \in \mathcal{L}$ with any of the curves O^i satisfies a cubic equation, that rewritten in BB-form permits, using range analysis such as in [4], to ensure that inside of $\mathcal{R}$, l and each curve have only one intersection point, counting multiplicity. Hence these new curves are connected and non singular inside $\mathcal{R}$. Assuming the existence of an inflection point in $\mathcal{R}$, since the curves O^i are connected and additionally they are convex in a neighborhood of Q_0^i as well as of Q_2^i, then there are at least two inflection points in $\mathcal{R}$. Thus considering the line passing through two consecutive inflexion points in $\mathcal{R}$, it is straightforward to show that this line cuts the curve at least in 4 points, but the curves are cubic, a contradiction to Bezout Theorem.

5. For each of the curves I^i, O^i, let us denote them as $f^i(u,v) = 0$, it was computed their partial derivatives with respect to the variable u, $f_u^i(u,v) = 0$ and using elimination theory, we eliminated the variable u from the system of equations $\{f^i(u,v) = 0,\ f_u^i(u,v) = 0\}$, obtaining a polynomial $p^i(v, u_i, k_0^i, k_2^i)$, such that for fixed values of the parameters (u_i, k_0^i, k_2^i), the roots v of $p^i(v, u_i, k_0^i, k_2^i) = 0$ correspond to the v-coordinate of the relative extremes of $v = v(u)$ on the graph of curve $f^i(u,v) = 0$. Considering the limit cases ($k_j^i = 0$ and $k_j^i \to \infty$, $j = 0, 2$), we obtained the above mentioned intervals for the parameter u_i in order to ensure $|v| \leq \varepsilon_i$.

3.4 G^2-Continuity

We already have shown that $\mathcal{A}$ is G^1-continuous. The above proposed cubic sections $\mathcal{A}_i$ have, by construction, free parameters $k_j^i, j = 0, 2$ that permit us to set the curvature value of $\mathcal{A}_i$ at Q_i equal to the curvature values κ_i estimated at each vertex $Q_i \in \mathcal{C}$ in the above section **Derivative data**. Hence, $\mathcal{A}$ is G^2-continuous.

3.5 Shape Control Handles

Given a polygonal chain $\mathcal{C}$, for each section $\mathcal{A}_i$ we have a free parameter, which plays the role of a shape control handle: the selection of an additional point in the interior of the region of interest Ω_i to be interpolated. If one wishes to choose this point (with barycentric coordinates (u_i, v_i)) in a non supervised way, we propose the following procedure: compute the barycentric coordinates (u_i^c, v_i^c) of the center of mass of all points in Ω_i, and set $u_i := \frac{2+u_i^c-2v_i^c}{5}$, hence the interpolating point is the point on the line $1 - 2u - v = 0$ with minimal distance to the points in Ω_i.

3.6 Curve Evaluation and Display

For intensive evaluation of the curve, a quadtree subdivision process on the triangle T_i could be used . On each sub-triangle, by means of blossom principle for triangular BB-functions, the BB-net corresponding to the sub-triangle is computed and we discard those sub-triangles on which the BB-polynomials have only positive or negative coefficients. After few recursion steps, we obtain a set of sub-triangles providing us a set of pixels, whose centers are approximately on the curve. See [4] for more details.

3.7 Numerical Examples

The algorithm proposed in this paper was successfully applied to the approximation of the contours of magnetic resonance images (MRI) of a human head (from Rendering test data set, North Carolina University, ftp.cs.unc.edu). In the same plot, the figure shows the A-splines which approximate 25 contours. Each contour was obtained from a previous processing of a digital image that corresponds to a cross section of the human head. The results were obtained from a MATLAB program that constructs and displays the A-spline curve approximating the contour data.

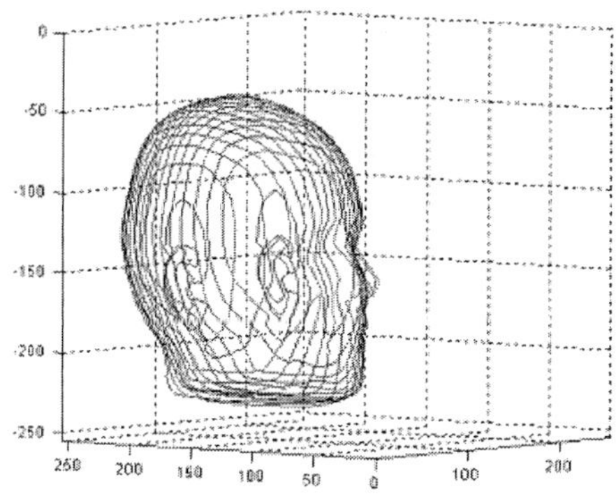

Fig. 6. Approximation of the contours of MRI of a human head

3.8 Conclusions

In comparison to [2], the A-spline proposed in the present work achieves G^2-continuity with the minimal degree (3) and we do not impose restrictions for the interpolation of tangent vectors. On the other hand, we interpolate not only the directions of the tangent vectors but also their sense, which is a completely new feature in this context. Moreover, the high flexibility of our A-spline scheme facilitates, with few adaptations, to solve efficiently another related problems such as free design of generatrix curves as well as the computation of the structural parameters of the corresponding revolution surfaces (see [3] and [6]) and smoothing and fitting of stream lines from a finite sample of flow data.

References

[1] Bajaj C., Xu G. A-Splines (1999), Local Interpolation and Approximation using G^k-Continuous Piecewise Real Algebraic Curves, Computer Aided Geometric Desing, 16: 557-578.
[2] Bajaj C., Xu G. (2001), Regular algebraic curve sections (III) - Applications in interactive design and data fitting. Computer Aided Geometric Desing, 18: 149-173.
[3] Behar S., Hernández V., Alvarez L., Estrada J., Computing a revolution shell using a G^2-continuous A-spline and a semidiscrete method for the EDPs, Proceedings IV, ITLA, 2001, 241-250, ISBN: 959-7056-13-5.
[4] Estrada, J. , Martínez D., León, D., Theisel, H. , Solving Geometric Problems using Subdivision Methods and Range Analysis, in: Mathematical Methods for Curves and Surfaces: Tromso 2004, M. Daehlen, K. Morken and L.L. Shumaker (eds.), 2005, 101-114, Nashboro Press, Brentwood, TN.
[5] Hernández, V., Martínez D., Estrada J. (2002), Fitting a conic A-spline to contour image data, Revista Investigación Operacional, Vol. 29, 55-64.
[6] Hernández, V., Behar, S., Estrada J., Geometric design by means of a G^2 continuous A-spline, Approximation, Optimization and Mathematical Economics, Physica-Verlag, Heidelberg, 2001, 133-145.
[7] Kass,M., Witkin, A., Terzopoulos, D. (1988), Snakes: active contour models, International. J. Comput. Vision, 321-331.
[8] Paluszny M, Patterson R., G^2-continuous cubic algebraic splines and their efficient display , Curves and Surfaces II , P.J. Laurent , A. Le Méhauté , and L.L. Schumacker (eds.), 1994, 353-359.
[9] Paluszny M, Patterson R. (1998), Geometric control of G^2-cubic A-splines, Computer Aided Geometric Design 15: 261-287.
[10] Ray B., Ray K. (1994), A non-parametric sequential method for polygonal approximation of digital curves, Pattern Recognition Letters 15: 161-167.
[11] Sethian, J., A., Level Set Methods, Cambridge Univ. Press., Cambridge, 1996.

A Robust Statistical Method for Brain Magnetic Resonance Image Segmentation

Bo Qin[1], JingHua Wen[2], and Ming Chen[1]

[1] Department of Automatic Control of Northwestern Polytechnical University, Xi'an, 710072, P.R. China
qinbo_2000@163.com

[2] School of Medicine of Xi'an JiaoTong University, Xi'an, 710049, P.R. China

Abstract. In this paper, a robust statistical model-based brain MRI image segmentation method is presented. The MRI images are modeled by Gaussian mixture model. This method, based on the statistical model, approximately finds the maximum a posteriori estimation of the segmentation and estimates the model parameters from the image data. The proposed strategy for segmentation is based on the EM and FCM algorithm. The prior model parameters are estimated via EM algorithm. Then, in order to obtain a good segmentation and speed up the convergence rate, initial estimates of the parameters were done by FCM algorithm. The proposed image segmentation methods have been tested using phantom simulated MRI data. The experimental results show the proposed method is effective and robust.

1 Introduction

Automatic and robust brain tissue classification from magnetic resonance images (MRI) is of great importance for anatomical imaging in brain research. Segmentation brain images can be used in the three-dimensional visualization and quantitative analysis of brain morphometry and functional cortical structures. Segmentation of the brain MRI image into different tissues, such as the gray matter (GM), the white matter (WM), the cerebrospinal fluid (CSF).Now, brain segmentation methods can be categorized as manual methods and semi automated and automated methods. In the study of brain disorders, a large amount of data is necessary but in most clinical applications, the manual slice segmentation is the only method of choice and is time consuming. Even if experts do it, these types of segmentation stays subjective and show some intra and inter variability. Fully automatic, robust tissue classification is required for batch processing the data from large-scale, multi-site clinical trials or research projects.

The automatic segmentation of brain MR images, however, remains a persistent difficult problem. The main artifacts affecting brain MRI scans such as Intensity non-uniformity, and image Noise and Partial volume effect. Currently available methods for MR image segmentation can be categorized into Region-based and clustering-based techniques[1]. Region-based techniques include the use of standard image

M. Lazo and A. Sanfeliu (Eds.): CIARP 2005, LNCS 3773, pp. 51 – 58, 2005.

processing techniques such as threshold-based, and mathematical morphology-based, and probability-based, and clustering-based, and prior knowledge-based and neural network-based techniques [2-8].

This paper aims to develop an algorithm for the automatic estimation of the statistics of the main tissues of the brain [the gray matter (GM), the white matter (WM), the cerebrospinal fluid (CSF)] from MRI images. These statistics can be used for segmenting the brain from its surrounding tissues for 3-D visualization or for a quantitative analysis of the different tissues. Segmentation of MR brain images was carried out on original images using the Gaussian mixture model models (GMMS)[9-10] and fuzzy c-means [2] techniques. The segmentation method presented in this work models the intensity distributions of MRI images as a mixture of Gaussians. The prior model parameters are estimated via EM algorithm [8]. Then, in order to obtain a good segmentation and speed up the convergence rate, initial estimates of the parameters were done by FCM algorithm. The performance of the algorithm is evaluated using phantom images. The experiments on simulated MR images prove that our algorithm is insensitive to noise and can more precisely segment brain MRI images into different tissues: the gray matter, the white matter and the cerebrospinal fluid.

2 Image Model

In this section, we derive a model for the tissues of the brain. For this purpose, we consider a normal human brain consists of three types of tissues: the white matter (WM), the gray matter (GM) and the cerebrospinal fluid (CSF). It is simplified in the case where only T1 weight images are considered. The image is defined by $y = (y_i, i \in I)$ where y_i denotes the image intensity as the voxel indexed by i. We assume only one class of tissue occupies the spatial volume of each voxel. Let the total number of tissue classes in the image be K and each of them be represented by a label from $\Lambda = \{1,2,\cdots K\}$ and x_i represents the tissue class of voxel at the image site $i, x_i = k$ denote an assignment of the kth tissue class to the site i. A segmentation of the image is given by $x_i = (x_i; i \in I)$. The process of segmentation is to find x, which represents the correct tissue class at each voxel of image y., our attempt was to find $x = x^*$ which represents optimal segmentation is given by:

$$x^* = \arg\max_x p(x \mid y) \tag{1}$$

From Baye's theorem, the posterior probability of segmentation $p(x \mid y)$ can be written as:

$$p(x \mid y) \propto p(x, y) = p(y \mid x) p(x) \tag{2}$$

where $p(y \mid x)$ is the conditional probability of the image y given the segmentation x and $p(x)$ is the prior density of x .our attempt is to find the maximum a posteriori(MAP)estimate by modeling $p(y \mid x)$ the measurement model. Each tissue class has a signature, or mean intensity and variance at a particular site. For each tissue class, a gaussian distribution is assumed and the entire image can be assumed as a Gaussian mixture density. A tissue can be modeled by a multivatiate Gaussian density with mean vector μ and covariance matrix Σ, i.e.;

$$p(x|\theta)=(2\pi)^{-M/2}\Sigma_k^{-1/2}\cdot\exp(-\frac{1}{2}(x_i-\mu_k)^t\Sigma_k^{-1}(x_i-\mu_i)) \tag{3}$$

Where $\theta=(\mu_k,\Sigma_k)$ is the vector of parameters associated with each type of tissue k, $\mu_k=(\mu_{k1},\mu_{k2},\cdots,\mu_{kM})^t$ is the mean vector, and $\Sigma_k=E[(x_i-\mu_k)(x_i-\mu_k)']$ is the covariance matrix associated with class $k, 1\le k\le c$ where c is the number of classes. In our case, since the input is intensity at a given point i, the dimension is one, and the number of classes $K=3$ corresponding to the gray matter(GM),the white matter(WM) and the cerebrospibal fluid.(CSF).

3 MR Image Segmentation Framework

3.1 Initial Parameter Estimation

The choice of initial parameter is very important. The initial classification can be obtained either directly through the thresholding or through ML estimation with those known parameters .In this work; we use a modified FCM algorithm [11] for initial classification. The modified fuzzy c-means (FCM) algorithm is the best known and the most widely used fuzzy clustering technique. This algorithm iteratively minimizes the following objective function:

$$J=\sum_{i=1}^{C}\sum_{j=1}^{N}(u_{ij})^m d^2(x_j,c_i)-a\sum_{i=1}^{C}p_i\log(p_i) \tag{4}$$

Where u_{ij} is the membership value at pixel j in the class i such that $\sum_{i=1}^{C}u_{ij}=1$, $\forall j\in[0,N].p_i=\frac{1}{N}\sum_{j=1}^{N}u_{ij}$ is interpreted as "probability" of all the pixels. $d^2(x_j,c_i)$ is the standard Euclidian distance and the fuzziness index m is a weighting coefficient on each fuzzy membership.

3.2 Parameters Estimation

Now that we have defined a model for our data, the problem is to estimate the different parameters of the mixture. The aim of estimation is find the parameters that maximize the likelihood of the GMM, given the image $Y=\{y_1,y_2,\cdots,y_T\}$ the GMM likelihood can be written as

$$p(Y|\theta)=\prod_{i=1}^{T}p(y_i|\theta) \tag{5}$$

if $p(Y \mid \theta)$ is a well behaved, differentiable of θ, then θ can be found by the standard methods of differential calculus. This expression is a nonlinear function of the parameters θ and direct maximization is not possible. However, ML parameter estimates can be obtained iteratively using a special case of the expectation-maximization (EM) algorithm.

The EM algorithm estimates the maximum likelihood parameter θ ,we seek:

$$\hat{\theta} = \arg\max_{\theta} \log p(y \mid \theta) \tag{6}$$

The EM algorithm is an iterative procedure for finding the ML estimate of the parameters. Each iteration consists of two steps:

$$\text{E-Step: Find } \quad Q(\theta \mid \theta^{(t)}) = E[\log f(x,\theta) \mid y, \theta^{(t)}] \tag{7}$$

$$\text{M-Step:Find } \theta^{(t+1)} = \arg\max_{\theta}\{Q(\theta, \theta^{(t)})\} \tag{8}$$

The EM algorithm begins with an initial model θ, and estimates a new model $\hat{\theta}$, such that $p(Y \mid \hat{\theta}) \geq p(Y \mid \theta)$. The new model then becomes the initial model for the next iteration and the process is repeated until some convergence threshold is reached .In the case of the univariate normal mixture, the maximum likelihood estimates $\hat{w}_i$ of the mixture coefficients, $\hat{\mu}_i$ of the mean and Σ_i of the variance are expressed as fllows:

$$\hat{w}_{ij} = \frac{a_i p(y_i \mid \mu_i, \Sigma_i)}{\sum_{l=1}^{K} a_l p(y_j \mid \mu_l, \Sigma_l)} \tag{9}$$

$$\hat{a}_i = \frac{1}{N} \sum_{i=1}^{N} w_{ij}, \quad i = 1,2,\ldots, K \tag{10}$$

$$\hat{\mu}_i = \frac{\sum_{j=1}^{N} w_{ij} y_j}{\sum_{j=1}^{N} w_{ij}}, \quad i = 1,2,\ldots, K \tag{11}$$

$$\Sigma_i = \frac{\sum_{j=1}^{N} w_{ij} (y_j - \mu_i)(y_j - \mu_i)'}{\sum_{j=1}^{N} w_{ij}}, \quad i = 1,2,\ldots, K \tag{12}$$

In our work, as mentioned earlier a three-tissue gaussian model was assumed to characterize the gray matter, the white matter and the cerebrospinal fluid. The EM algorithm was used to estimate the parameters of the gaussian mixture. Improved segmentation resulted when images were used. The convergence of EM algorithm was faster when initial estimates of the parameters were done by Fuzzy c- means.

4 Experimental Results

In this section we describe the performance of our method to the segmentation of the brain into white matter and gray matter and CSF. To validate the performance of our method, we use the Brainweb MRI simulator(http://www.bic.mni.mcgill.ca/brainweb),which consists of 3-dimensional MR data simulated using TI weight image, each data set is composed of voxels of 181X217X181, the slice thickness is 1mm.The 2-D images are slice from the 3-D data sets.2-D segmentation is the clustering of the slice images,3-D segmentation is the clustering of the whole 3-D data sets. We use several simulated MRI acquisitions of this phantom including RF non-uniformities and noise levels. Segment has been done on MR images containing 3, 5 and 9% noise and of 20% RF non-uniformity. The brain data were classified into three clusters: gray matter, white matter and cerebrospinal fluid. Fig.1-

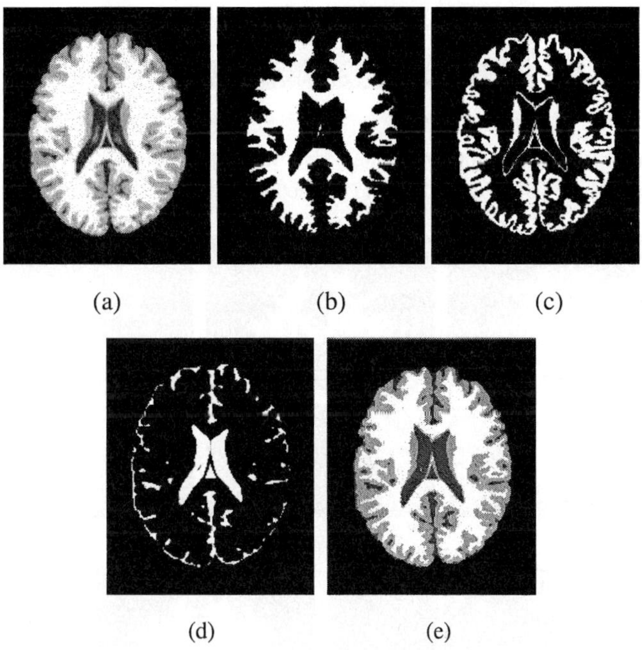

Fig. 1. Segmentation Result under 3% noise (a) T1 weight image (b)-(d) GM, WM and CSF posterior functions computed by our method respectively (e) segmentation result

Fig.3 show the segmentation results on the simulated MRI images with different noise level. Although the images with 9%, 5% noise look much worse than the images with 3% noise, there is noticeable difference on the segmentation images by the proposed method as shown in Fig.2-Fig.3.Fig.4 shows the final 3D rendering of the gray matter and white matter volume using the proposed segmentation method.

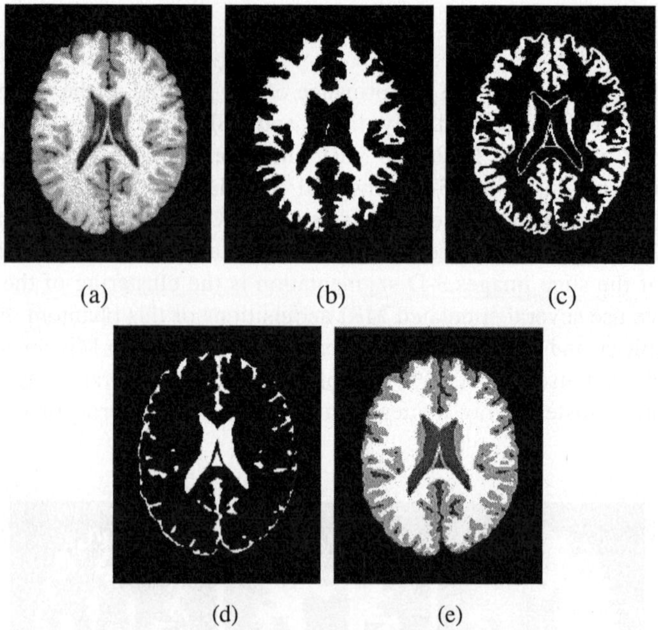

Fig. 2. Segmentation Result under 5% noise: (a) T1 weight image (b)-(d) GM, WM and CSF posterior functions computed by our method respectively (e) segmentation result

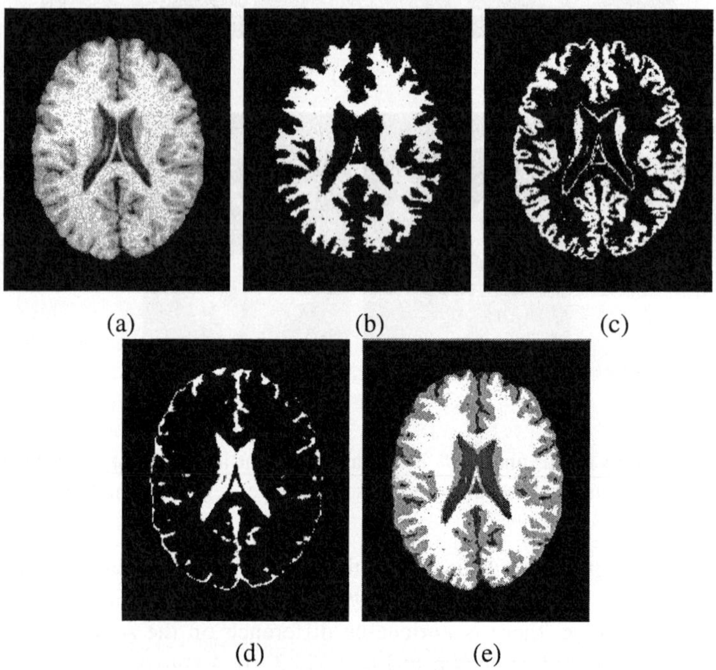

Fig. 3. Segmentation Result under 9% noise: (a) T1 weight image (b)-(d) GM, WM and CSF posterior functions computed by our method respectively (e) segmentation result

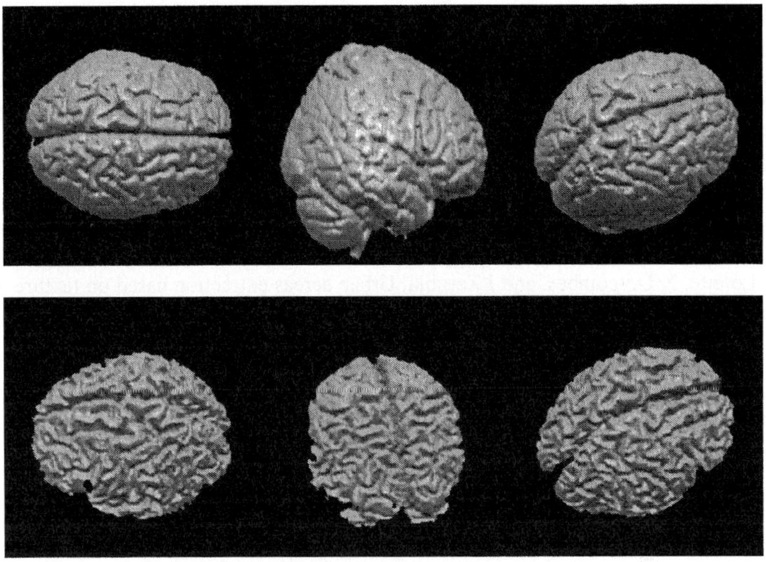

Fig. 4. 3D rendering of the gray matter and white matter

5 Conclusions

We have presented an approach combining Gaussian mixture model finite mixture model and FCM clustering algorithm. The parameters initialization using Fuzzy c-means algorithms. The proposed image segmentation methods have been tested using phantom simulated MRI data and real MRI brain data. The experiments on simulated MR T1-Weight brain images prove that our algorithm is insensitive to noise and can more precisely segment brain MRI images into different tissues: gray matter, white matter and cerebrospinal fluid.

References

[1] Pham, D.L., Xu, C., Prince, J.L.: Current methods in medical image segmentation.Annual Review of Biomedical Engineering,Vol. 2, pp.315-337,2000.

[2] M.C.Clark,L.O.Hall, and D.B,Goldgof, MRI segmentation using fuzzy clustering techniques: integrating knowledge, IEEE Eng Med Biol;Vol.13(5),pp.730-742, 1994.

[3] M.Ozkan, and B. M. Dawant, Neural-Network Based Segmentation of Multi-Modal Medical Images, IEEE Transaction on Medical Imaging, Vol.12, pp.534–544, 1993.

[4] Kapur, T., Grimson, W.E., Wells, W.M., Kikinis, R., Segmentation of brain tissue from magnetic resonance images. Med Image Anal. Vol. 1 pp.109-127, 1996.

[5] Y.Wang,and T.Adali, Quantification and segmentation of brain tissues from MR images: A probabilistic neural network approach, IEEE Trans. on Image Processing, Vol.7, pp.1165–1180, 1998.

[6] C.Tsai, BS.Manjunath, and R.Jagadeesan, Automated segmentation of brain MR images", Pattern Recogn, Vol.28, pp.1825-1862, 1995.

[7] W. M. Wells, and W. E. L. Grimson, Adaptive Segmentation of MRI data, IEEE Transaction on Medical Imaging, Vol.15, pp.429–442, 1996.
[8] Leemput, K.V., Maes, F., Vandermeulen, D., Suetens, P, Automated model-based tissue classi¯cation of MR images of the brain. IEEE trans. on medical imaging,Vol.18, pp.897-908, 1999.
[9] G. J. McLachlan, and T. Krishnan. The EM algorithm and extensions. John Wiley and Sons, New York, 1996.
[10] G. M. McLachlan and D. Peel, Finite Mixture Models. New York: John Wiley & Sons, Inc., 2001.
[11] A.Lorette, X.Descombes, and J.Zerubia, Urban aereas extraction based on texture analysis through a markovian modeling, International journal of computer vision Vol.36, pp,219-234,2000.

Inference Improvement by Enlarging the Training Set While Learning DFAs*

Pedro García[1], José Ruiz[1], Antonio Cano[1], and Gloria Alvarez[2]

[1] Universidad Politécnica de Valencia,
Departamento de Sistemas Informáticos y Computación,
Camino de Vera s/n, 46022 Valencia, Spain
{pgarcia, jruiz, acano}@dsic.upv.es
http://www.dsic.upv.es/users/tlcc/tlcc.html

[2] Pontificia Universidad Javeriana - Seccional Cali,
Grupo de Investigación DESTINO, Calle 18 118-250,
Cali, Colombia
galvarez@dsic.upv.es

Abstract. A new version of the *RPNI* algorithm, called *RPNI2*, is presented. The main difference between them is the capability of the new one to extend the training set during the inference process. The effect of this new feature is specially notorious in the inference of languages generated from regular expressions and Non-deterministic Finite Automata (NFA). A first experimental comparison is done between *RPNI2* and *DeLeTe2*, other algorithm that behaves well with the same sort of training data. [1]

1 Introduction

One of the best known algorithms for regular language identification, *RPNI* (Regular Positive and Negative Inference) [9], converges to the minimal Deterministic Finite Automaton (DFA) of the target language. It finds equivalence relations in the data from the prefix tree acceptor of the sample.

Recently an algorithm called *DeLeTe2* [3] that outputs Non-deterministic Finite Automata (NFA) instead of DFAs has been proposed. *DeLeTe2* looks for a special type of NFA called RFSA (Residual Finite State Automata), whose states represent residuals of the target language. Every regular language is recognized by a unique minimal RFSA, called the canonical RFSA. Canonical RFSA consists only of prime residual states (i.e. states that can not be obtained as union of other residuals).

The basis of *DeLeTe2* algorithm is to obtain RFSAs by looking for inclusion relations in the residuals of the target language using the prefix tree acceptor of the data. Its authors have shown that when the target automaton is a randomly generated DFA [8], the probability of occurrence of inclusion relation between

* Work partially supported by Spanish CICYT under TIC2003-09319-C03-02

[1] A two pages abstract presented in the Tenth International Conference on Implementation and Application of Automata [5] gives a shallow description of this work.

M. Lazo and A. Sanfeliu (Eds.): CIARP 2005, LNCS 3773, pp. 59–70, 2005.

states is very small and then, the size of the canonical RFSA and the minimal DFA of a language are the same. Hence, in this case, *DeLeTe2* behaves worse than *RPNI*. On the other hand, when the target languages are generated using random regular expressions or NFAs, the experiments in [3] show that *DeLeTe2* performs better than *RPNI*.

In this work we propose a modification of *RPNI* algorithm, called *RPNI2*. It extends *RPNI* by finding inclusion relations among residuals aiming to predict whether the prefixes of the data belong to the target language or to its complement.

RPNI2 outputs a DFA and converges to the minimal DFA of the target language. When the source of the learning data is a non-deterministic model, its performance is very similar to *DeLeTe2* performance. However, the average descriptive complexity of the hypothesis that *RPNI2* obtains is substantially smaller than the one obtained by *DeLeTe2*.

Next sections have the following structure: section 2 reminds useful definitions, notation and algorithms. Section 3 presents the *RPNI2* algorithm, a brief example is shown in section 4. The experimental results are in section 5 and finally, section 6 contains the conclusions.

2 Definitions and Notation

Definitions not contained in this section can be found in [7,10]. Definitions and previous works concerning RFSAs can be found in [1,2,3].

Let A be a finite alphabet and let A^* be the free monoid generated by A with concatenation as the internal operation and ε as neutral element. A *language* L over A is a subset of A^*. The elements of L are called *words*. The length of a word $w \in A^*$ is noted $|w|$. Given $x \in A^*$, if $x = uv$ with $u, v \in A^*$, then u (resp. v) is called *prefix* (resp. *suffix*) of x. $\mathrm{Pr}(L)$ (resp. $\mathrm{Suf}(L)$) denotes the set of prefixes (resp. suffixes) of L. The product of two languages $L_1, L_2 \subseteq A^*$ is defined as: $L_1 \cdot L_2 = \{u_1u_2 | u_1 \in L_1 \wedge u_2 \in L_2\}$. Sometimes $L_1 \cdot L_2$ will be notated simply as L_1L_2. Throughout the paper, the *lexicographical order* in A^* will be denoted as $\ll$. Assuming that A is totally ordered by $<$ and given $u, v \in A^*$ with $u = u_1 \dots u_m$ and $v = v_1 \dots v_n$, $u \ll v$ if and only if ($|u| < |v|$) or ($|u| = |v|$ and $\exists j$, $1 \leq j \leq n, m$ such that $u_1 \dots u_j = v_1 \dots v_j$ and $u_{j+1} < v_{j+1}$).

A *Non-deterministic Finite Automaton* (NFA) is a 5-tuple $\mathcal{A} = (Q, A, \delta, Q_0, F)$ where Q is the (finite) set of states, A is a finite alphabet, $Q_0 \subseteq Q$ is the set of initial states, $F \subseteq Q$ is the set of final states and δ is a partial function that maps $Q \times A$ in 2^Q. The extension of this function to words is also denoted δ. A word x is accepted by $\mathcal{A}$ if $\delta(Q_0, x) \cap F \neq \emptyset$. The set of words accepted by $\mathcal{A}$ is denoted by $L(\mathcal{A})$.

Given a finite set of words D_+, the *prefix tree acceptor of* D_+ is defined as the automaton $\mathcal{A} = (Q, A, \delta, q_0, F)$ where $Q = Pr(D_+)$, $q_0 = \varepsilon$, $F = D_+$ and $\delta(u, a) = ua$, $\forall u, ua \in Q$.

A Moore machine is a 6-tuple $M = (Q, A, B, \delta, q_0, \Phi)$, where A (resp. B) is the input (resp. output) alphabet, δ is a partial function that maps $Q \times A$ in

Q and Φ is a function that maps Q in B called *output function*. Throughout this paper $B = \{0, 1, ?\}$. A nondeterministic Moore machine is defined in a similar way except for the fact that δ maps $Q \times A$ in 2^Q and the set of initial states is I. The automaton related to a Moore machine $M = (Q, A, B, \delta, I, \Phi)$ is $\mathcal{A} = (Q, A, \delta, I, F)$ where $F = \{q \in Q : \Phi(q) = 1\}$. The *restriction* of M to $P \subseteq Q$ is the machine M_P defined as in the case of automata.

The behavior of M is given by the partial function $t_M : A^* \to B$ defined as $t_M(x) = \Phi(\delta(q_0, x))$, for every $x \in A^*$ such that $\delta(q_0, x)$ is defined.

Given two disjoint finite sets of words D_+ and D_-, we define the (D_+, D_-)-*Prefix Tree Moore Machine* ($PTMM(D_+, D_-)$) as the Moore machine having $B = \{0, 1, ?\}$, $Q = \Pr(D_+ \cup D_-)$, $q_0 = \varepsilon$ and $\delta(u, a) = ua$ if $u, ua \in Q$ and $a \in A$. For every state u, the value of the output function associated to u is 1, 0 or ? (undefined) depending whether u belongs to D_+, to D_- or to $Q - (D_+ \cup D_-)$ respectively. The size of the sample (D_+, D_-) is $\sum_{w \in D_+ \cup D_-} |w|$.

A Moore machine $M = (Q, A, \{0, 1, ?\}, \delta, q_0, \Phi)$ is *consistent* with (D_+, D_-) if $\forall x \in D_+$ we have $\Phi(x) = 1$ and $\forall x \in D_-$ we have $\Phi(x) = 0$.

2.1 Residual Finite State Automata (RFSA)

The *derivative* of a language L by a word u, also called *residual language* of L associated to u is $u^{-1}L = \{v \in A^* : uv \in L\}$. A residual language $u^{-1}L$ is *composite* if $u^{-1}L = \cup_{v^{-1}L \subsetneq u^{-1}L} v^{-1}L$. A residual language is *prime* if it is not composite.

If $\mathcal{A} = (Q, A, \delta, I, F)$ is an NFA and $q \in Q$, we define the language accepted in automaton $\mathcal{A}$ from state q as $L(\mathcal{A}, q) = \{v \in A^* : \delta(q, v) \cap F \neq \emptyset\}$.

A Residual Finite State Automata RFSA [2] is an automaton $\mathcal{A} = \langle Q, A, \delta, I, F\rangle$ such that, for each $q \in Q$, $L(\mathcal{A}, q)$ is a residual language of the language L recognized by $\mathcal{A}$. So $\forall q \in Q, \exists u \in A^*$ such that $L(\mathcal{A}, q) = u^{-1}L$. In other words, a *Residual Finite State Automaton* (RFSA) $\mathcal{A}$ is an NFA such that every state defines a residual language of $L(\mathcal{A})$.

Two operators are defined [2] on RFSAs that preserve equivalence. The saturation and reduction operators. Given $\mathcal{A} = (Q, A, \delta, I, F)$ the *saturated automaton* of $\mathcal{A}$ is the automaton $\mathcal{A}^s = (Q, A, \delta^s, I^s, F)$, where $I^s = \{q \in Q : L(\mathcal{A}, q) \subseteq L(\mathcal{A})\}$ and $\forall q \in Q$, $\forall a \in A$, $\delta^s(q, a) = \{q' \in Q : L(\mathcal{A}, q') \subseteq a^{-1}L(\mathcal{A}, q)\}$. If in automaton $\mathcal{A}$ all the residual languages (not only the prime ones) are considered as states, the new automata is known as saturated RFSA of the minimal DFA for L. The *reduction* operator allows to eliminate from an automaton $\mathcal{A}^s$ the composite states and the transitions related to them. Both operations are useful to get the *canonical RFSA* associated with $\mathcal{A}$: first the saturation operator is applied to $\mathcal{A}$, later the reduction operator is applied to the result. It is known [2] that every regular language L is recognized by a unique reduced saturated RFSA, the *canonical RFSA* of L.

Formally, given a language $L \subseteq A^*$ the *canonical RFSA* of L is the automaton $\mathcal{A} = (Q, A, \delta, I, F)$ where:

- $Q = \{u^{-1}L : u^{-1}L \text{ is prime}, u \in A^*\}$
- A is the alphabet of L
- $\delta(u^{-1}L, a) = \{v^{-1}L \in Q : v^{-1}L \subseteq (ua)^{-1}L\}$
- $I = \{u^{-1}L \in Q : u^{-1}L \subseteq L\}$
- $F = \{u^{-1}L \in Q : \varepsilon \in u^{-1}L\}$

Two relations defined in the set of states of an automaton link RFSAs with grammatical inference. Let $D = (D_+, D_-)$ be a sample, let $u, v \in Pr(D_+)$. We say that $u \prec v$ if no word w exists such that $uw \in D_+$ and $vw \in D_-$. We say that $u \simeq v$ [2] if $u \prec v$ and $v \prec u$.

Example of RFSAs. The following example has been taken from [2]. Let $A = \{0, 1\}$ and let $L = A^*0A$. L can be recognized by the three automata of Figure 1. States that output 1 (resp. 0) are drawn using thick (resp. thin) lines.

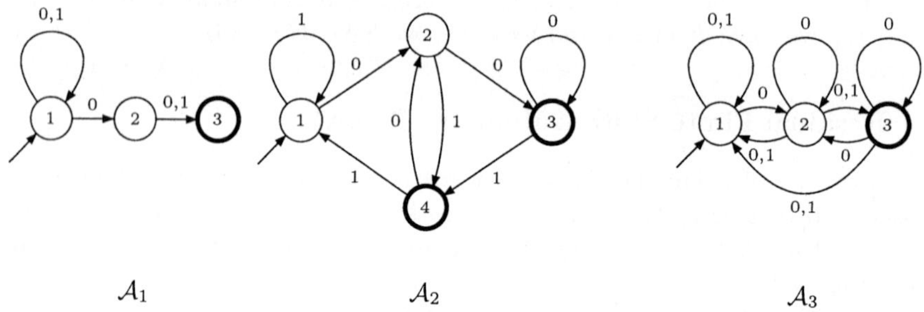

Fig. 1. $\mathcal{A}_1$ is an automaton recognizing $L = A^*0A$ which is neither a NFA nor a RFSA. $\mathcal{A}_2$ is a DFA recognizing L which is also RFSA. $\mathcal{A}_3$ is the canonical RFSA for L.

- The first one $\mathcal{A}_1$ is neither DFA nor RFSA. The languages associated with states are: $L(\mathcal{A}_1, 1) = A^*0A$, $L(\mathcal{A}_1, 2) = A$ and $L(\mathcal{A}_1, 3) = \varepsilon$. One can see that $L(\mathcal{A}_1, 3) = \varepsilon$ and $\nexists u \in A^*$ such that $L(\mathcal{A}_1, 3) = u^{-1}L$.
- Automaton $\mathcal{A}_2$ is a minimal automaton recognizing L and thus, is a RFSA, in this case $L(\mathcal{A}_2, 1) = A^*0A$, $L(\mathcal{A}_2, 2) = A^*0A + A$, $L(\mathcal{A}_2, 3) = A^*0A + A + \varepsilon$, $L(\mathcal{A}_2, 4) = A^*0A + \varepsilon$.
- Automaton $\mathcal{A}_3$ is the L's canonical RFSA, which is not a DFA. The languages associated with states are: $L(\mathcal{A}_3, 1) = \varepsilon^{-1}L$, $L(\mathcal{A}_3, 2) = 0^{-1}L$ and $L(\mathcal{A}_3, 3) = 01^{-1}L$.

2.2 The *RPNI* Algorithm

The aim of grammatical inference is to obtain a description of a language L by means of a sample (a set of words labelled as belonging to L or to its complement). Throughout this work we will assume that the target language L is regular; then, the description we will look for is an automaton.

[2] This relation is known in the terminology set up by Gold as *not obviously different states.* Other authors call it *compatible states.*

We will use the convergence criterion called *identification in the limit*, introduced by Gold [6].

The *RPNI* algorithm [9] is used for inference of regular languages. It receives as input a sample of the target language and outputs, in polynomial time, a DFA consistent with the input. *RPNI* converges to the minimal automaton of the target language in the limit.

Algorithm *RPNI* (D_+, D_-) starts from the $PTMM(D_+, D_-)$, and recursively merges every state with the previous ones to keep a deterministic automaton under the condition that it does not accept a negative sample. State merging is done by the function $\texttt{detmerge}(M, p, q)$ shown in Algorithm 1, which merges states p and q in M if they are compatible. If one of the merging states is undefined and the other is not, the merged state takes the value of the latter state.

Algorithm 1 Function detmerge

```
detmerge(M, p, q) //p ≪ q in lexicographical order//
    M' := M
    list := {(p, q)}
    while list' ≠ ∅
        (r, s) := first(list)
        M1 := merge(M', r, s)
        if M1 = M'
            Return M
        else
            M' := M1
            for a ∈ A
                if δ(p, a) and δ(q, a) are defined
                    list := append(list, (δ(p, a), δ(q, a)))
                endif
            endfor
        endif
    endwhile
    Return M'
```

The merging process is recursively repeated with the successors of the merged states until either the nondeterminism disappears or the algorithm tries to merge incompatible states. In the former case, the output of the algorithm is the deterministic automaton resulting of merging states, whereas in the latter the output of $\texttt{detmerge}(M, p, q)$ is M.

2.3 *DeLeTe2* Algorithm

The *DeLeTe* and *DeLeTe2* algorithms output residual nondeterministic finite automata (RFSA). The algorithms look for inclusion relations between the residual languages and reflect those situations in the automaton using the saturation operator. As it can be expected, the method becomes more interesting when the target automaton contains many composite residual languages, because then may exist many inclusion relations between states that make the size of the hypothesis to decrease. Otherwise, if most of the residual languages of the target automaton are prime the output automaton would have a size similar to the size of the minimal DFA [3].

It is known [3] that *DeLeTe2* is an improvement to *DeLeTe* algorithm (algorithm 2) it solves the eventual lack of consistency with the sample of *DeLeTe*, unfortunately the details of this improvement have not been published yet.

Algorithm 2 Algorithm *DeLeTe*

```
DeLeTe(D+, D-)
    let Pref be the set of prefixes of D+ in lexicographical order
    Q := ∅; I := ∅; F := ∅; δ := ∅; u := ε
    stop := false
    while not stop
        if ∃u'|u ≃ u'
            delete uA* from Pref
        else
            Q := Q ∪ {u}
            if u ≺ u'
                I := I ∪ {u}
            endif
            if u ∈ D+
                F := F ∪ {u}
            endif
            δ := δ ∪ {(u', x, u)|u' ∈ Q, u'x ∈ Pref, u ≺ u'x}∪
                      {(u, x, u')|u' ∈ Q, ux ∈ Pref, u' ≺ ux}
        endif
        if u is the last word of Pref or
        A = ⟨Q, A, I, F, δ⟩ is consistent with D+, D-
            stop := true
        else
            u := next word in Pref
        endif
    endwhile
    Return A = ⟨Q, A, I, F, δ⟩
```

3 The *RPNI2* Algorithm

The idea behind *RPNI2* is to try to establish the possible inclusion relation between states that can not be merged. Sometimes this will allow us to define the output associated to states that were previously undefined.

The following definitions are useful to understand functions `tryInclusion` and `defineStates` shown in Algorithms 4 and 5 respectively. These functions are used in *RPNI2* to represent the new ideas stated above. Algorithm *RPNI2* is shown in Algorithm 3.

Algorithm 3 Algorithm *RPNI2*

```
RPNI2(D+, D-)
    M := PTMM(D+, D-)
    list := {u0, u1, ..., ur} //states of M in lexicographical order, u0 = λ//
    list' := {u1, ..., ur}
    q := u1
    while list' ≠ ∅
        for p ∈ list and p ≪ q (in lexicographical order)
            if detmerge(M, p, q) = M
                defineStates(M,p,q)
            else
                M := detmerge(M, p, q)
                exit for
            endif
        endfor
        list := Delete from list the states which are not in M
        list' := Delete from list' the states which are not in M
        q := first(list')
    endwhile
    Return M
```

Definition 1. *States p and q are non-comparable (for inclusion relations) in a Moore machine if there exist $u, v \in A^*$ such that $\Phi(\delta(p,u)) = 1 \wedge \Phi(\delta(q,u)) = 0$ and $\Phi(\delta(p,v)) = 0 \wedge \Phi(\delta(q,v)) = 1$.*

Definition 2. *Given $p, q \in Q$, we say that state p is potentially lesser than state q if they are not non-comparable and there does not exist $u \in A^*$ such that $\Phi(\delta(p,u)) = 1 \wedge \Phi(\delta(q,u)) = 0$.*

When states p and q can not be merged while running *RPNI*, that is, when $\texttt{detmerge}(M,p,q) = M$, the new algorithm tries to define the output for the undefined states using the function `defineStates` shown in Algorithm 5.

To explain the behavior of the function `defineStates` we will use the Moore machine M in Fig. 2; in this figure and the next ones the output value of each state q will be represented as a thin circle if $\Phi(q) = 0$, a thick one if $\Phi(q) = 1$ and a dashed one if $\Phi(q) =?$. Following the algorithm it is possible to see that $\texttt{defineStates}(M,1,2) = M$, since otherwise the negative sample 1000010 should be accepted.

Algorithm 4 Function tryInclusion

```
tryInclusion(M,p,q)
    M' := M
    while p and q are not non-comparable
        for any u common successor of p and q
            if φ(δ(p,u)) = 1 ∧ φ(δ(q,u)) =?
                φ(δ(q,u)) = 1; Update M'
            endif
            if φ(δ(p,u)) =? ∧ φ(δ(q,u)) = 0
                φ(δ(p,u)) = 0; Update M'
            endif
        endfor
    endwhile
    if p and q are non-comparable
        Return M
    else
        Return M'
```

Algorithm 5 Function defineStates

```
defineStates(M,p,q)
    if p and q are non-comparable
        Return M
    else
        if p is potentially lesser than q
            tryInclusion(M,p,q)
        endif
        if q is potentially lesser than p
            tryInclusion(M,q,p)
        endif
    endif
```

In the tree in Fig. 3, the signs preceding the state name represent its output value; for example: $(+2, 11)$ means $\Phi(2) = 1$ and $\Phi(11) =?$. Since the states of the same node do not have different labels named "+" and "-", states 1 and 2 are not non-comparable with respect to inclusion.

Executing `tryInclusion`$(M, 1, 2)$ returns M; otherwise the node $(4, -13)$ would imply $\Phi(4) = 0$ and at the same time the node $(+1, 4)$ would imply $\Phi(4) = 1$. However, executing `tryInclusion`$(M, 2, 1)$ changes the output of states 4 and 8 and then the function `defineStates`$(M, 1, 2)$ changes M to $\Phi(4) = 1$ and $\Phi(8) = 1$. Notice that the change of the output value of a state from ? (indefinite)

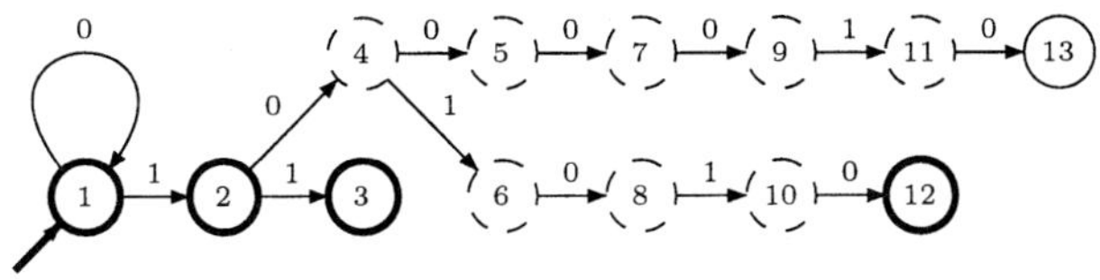

Fig. 2. Initial Moore machine used to describe the behavior of function `defineStates`

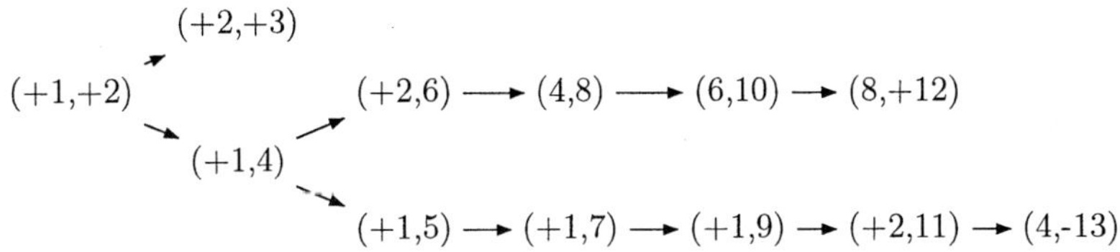

Fig. 3. Scheme used to compare states in function `defineStates`

to 0 or 1 is equivalent to suppose that a new word is present in the input sample. Hence, this process can be seen as an enlargement of the training set.

4 Example

We are going to describe the behavior of algorithm *RPNI2* using the sample $D_+ = \{0, 001, 000011, 0101010\}$ and $D_- = \{01000010\}$ that gives different outputs for the three algorithms. We also show the automata that *RPNI* and *DeLeTe2* output. The Prefix Tree Moore machine is depicted in Fig. 4.

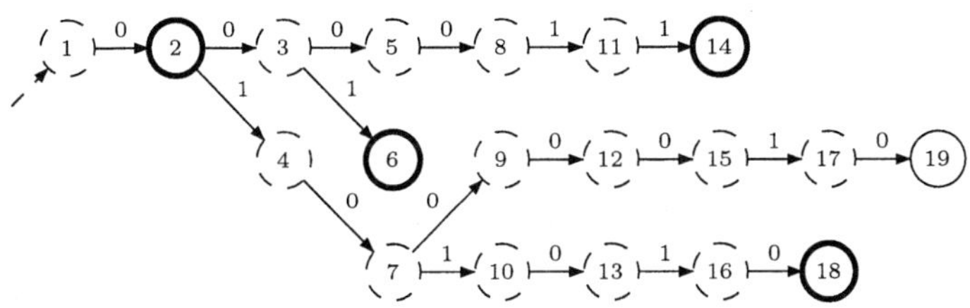

Fig. 4. Prefix Tree Moore machine of the sample

With this sample as input, *RPNI2* first merges states 1 and 2, then tries to merge 1 and 4. These states can not be merged, but the function `defineStates` changes the value of states 7 and 13 to positive. The same happens with states 4 and 7. The function `defineStates` changes now the value of states 9, 10, 12 and 15 to positive. Finally, the algorithm merges states 4 and 9 and then it merges states 1 and 10.

Fig. 5 depicts the outputs given by algorithms *RPNI*, *DeLeTe2* and *RPNI2* when using the above sample input. It should be noted that during the execution of *RPNI2*, states 7, 9, 10, 12, 13 and 15 are labelled as positive.

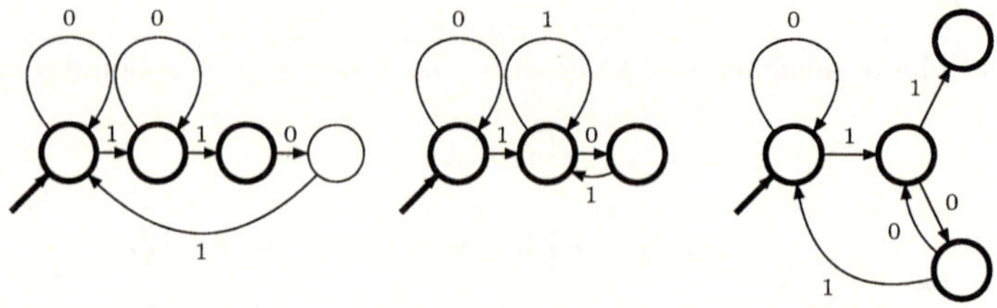

RPNI ***DeLeTe2*** ***RPNI2***

Fig. 5. Output automata given by the three algorithms compared in this work on input $D_+ = \{0, 001, 000011, 0101010\}$ and $D_- = \{01000010\}$

5 Results

The aim of the experiments is to analyze the behaviour of *RPNI2* and to compare it with the *DeLeTe2* algorithm. Both the training/test samples and the *DeLeTe2* program used in this experimentation are provided by their authors and are available in Aurélien Lemay's web page `http://www.grappa.univ-lille3.fr/~lemay/`. The samples have the following features [3]:

- The target language are regular expressions or NFAs.
- The probability distribution of the sample generation methods are different in each case: NFAs or regular expressions.
- The NFAs sample generation method chooses randomly the states number n, the alphabet size $|\Sigma|$, the transitions number per state n_δ and the initial and final state probabilities (p_I and p_F respectively) for each state. Each state has exactly n_δ successors. The symbol and destination state of each transition are chosen randomly. Once the automaton is trimmed some states will have fewer than n_δ transitions. The parameter values used in these experiments were: $n = 10$, $|\Sigma| = 2$, $n_\delta = 2$, $p_I = p_F = 0.5$.
- The regular expressions generation method consider a set of operators $Op = \{\emptyset, 0, 1, *, \cdot, +\}$. An upper bound n_{op} for the number of operators used is chosen and a probability distribution p on Op is defined. The root operator is chosen by means of the distribution p. If the operator is 0-ary the expression ends, if it is 1-ary the procedure is called recursively with parameter $n_{op} - 1$ and if it is binary, it is called twice with parameters $\lceil n_{op}/2 \rceil$ and $\lfloor (n_{op}-1)/2 \rfloor$. The parameter values used in these experiments are: $n_{op} = 100$, $p_\varepsilon = 0.02$, $p_0 = p_1 = 0.05$, $p_* = 0.13$, $p_\cdot = 0.5$ and $p_+ = 0.25$.

Two kinds of experiments are reported in table 1, depending on the source of the training and test samples: er_* if they come from regular expressions and nfa_* from NFAs. The number in the identifier of the experiment represents the number of training samples. Each experiment consist of 30 different languages to be learned. Each experiment has 1000 test samples. Table 1 reports the recognition rate and the average size of the inferred hypothesis. These results are calculated as follows: each test sample is presented to the inference program, the program tags the sample as belonging to the target language or not, if this classification agrees with the real sample tag, the sample is considered correct and increases a counter; at the end, the number of correct samples is divided by 1000 (the total of test samples) and this value is reported as recognition rate. The average size is computed adding up the number of states of the 30 hypothesis generated in each experiment and dividing by 30. As it can be seen in Table 1, the error rate of the new algorithm *RPNI2* is better than the previous *RPNI* but slightly worse than *DeLeTe2*. The opposite happens with the description complexity (i.e. states number) of the output hypothesis: the results obtained by *RPNI2* are then better than those of *DeLeTe2*.

It should be noted that the results obtained with our implementation of *RPNI* slightly differ from those obtained in [3] with the same data, maybe because of different implementations of the algorithm. To be more specific about the cause of these differences would be required to know the code used by the authors. The results corresponding to *DeLeTe2* execution, are slightly different too, although they were generated with their own program.

Table 1. Inference results with *RPNI*, *RPNI2* and *DeLeTe2* algorithms

	RPNI		*RPNI2*		*DeLeTe2*	
Iden.	Recogn. rate	Avg. size	Recogn. rate	Avg. size	Recogn. rate	Avg. size
er_50	76.36%	9.63	80.03%	16.32	81.68%	32.43
er_100	80.61%	14.16	88.68%	19.24	91.72%	30.73
er_150	84.46%	15.43	90.61%	26.16	92.29%	60.96
er_200	91.06%	13.3	93.38%	27.37	95.71%	47.73
nfa_50	64.8%	14.3	66.43%	30.64	69.80%	71.26
nfa_100	68.25%	21.83	72.79%	53.14	74.82%	149.13
nfa_150	71.21%	28.13	75.69%	71.87	77.14%	218.26
nfa_200	71.74%	33.43	77.25%	88.95	79.42%	271.3

6 Conclusions

The *RPNI2* strategy behaves better than the original *RPNI* when the language to learn comes from a regular expression or a NFA. In this case, because of the inclusion relation between residual automata, the output values assigned to some states, provide significant information to the inference process thus improving the recognition rate with the test samples.

The experiments presented in [3], which we have also reproduced with *RPNI2*, do not seem to obtain decisive conclusions about the usefulness of inferring RFSAs, because the main reason for its use (the smaller size of the hypothesis)

does not hold. Although the experiments are still preliminary, it seems that the slightly better results obtained by *DeLeTe2* with respect to *RPNI2* do not compensate the fact that the size of the representations obtained by *RPNI2* are clearly smaller.

References

1. Denis, F. Lemay, A. and Terlutte, A. *Learning regular languages using nondeterministic finite automata.*A.L. Oliveira (Ed.), ICGI 2000, LNAI 1891, pp 39-50 (2000).
2. Denis, F. Lemay, A. and Terlutte, A. *Residual finite state automata.*In STACS 2001, LNAI 2010, pp 144-157 (2001).
3. Denis, F., Lemay, A., Terlutte, A. Learning regular languages using RFSAs. Theoretical Computer Science 313(2), pp 267-294 (2004).
4. García, P., Cano, A., Ruiz, J. A comparative study of two algorithms for Automata Identification. A.L. Oliveira(Ed.), LNAI 1891, pp 115-126 (2000).
5. García, P., Ruiz, J., Cano, A., Alvarez G. Is learning RFSAs better than learning DFAs. Proceedings of Tenth International Conference on Implementation and Application of Automata. 2005. To be published.
6. Gold, E.M. Language identification in the limit. Information and Control 10, pp 447-474 (1967).
7. Hopcroft, J. and Ullman, J. *Introduction to Automata Theory, Languages and Computation.* Addison-Wesley (1979).
8. Nicaud, C. Etude du comportment des automates finis et des langages rationnels. Ph.D. Thesis, Université de Marne la Vallée. 2001.
9. Oncina, J., García, P. Inferring Regular Languages in Polynomial Updated Time. In Pattern Recognition and Image Analysis. Pérez de la Blanca, Sanfeliú and Vidal (Eds.) World Scientific (1992).
10. Trakhtenbrot B., Barzdin Y. Finite Automata: Behavior and Synthesis. North Holland Publishing Company (1973).

A Computational Approach to Illusory Contour Perception Based on the Tensor Voting Technique

Marcus Hund and Bärbel Mertsching *

University of Paderborn, Dept. of Electrical Engineering, GET-Lab,
Pohlweg 47-49, D-33098 Paderborn, Germany
{hund, mertsching}@get.upb.de

Abstract. A computational approach to the perception of illusory contours is introduced. The approach is based on the *tensor voting* technique and applied to several real and synthetic images. Special interest is given to the design of the communication pattern for spatial contour integration, called voting field.

1 Introduction

Illusory contours, also called virtual contours, are perceived contours that have no counterpart in the retinal image of the human vision system. Neurophysical studies have shown that the perception of illusory contours can be found in mammals, birds and insects [20]. The importance of illusory contours becomes obvious regarding the fact that the brains of these animals have developed independently throughout evolution. We can therefore assume that illusory contour perception is not just a malfunction of these visual processing systems, but instead is necessary for object border completion. Also for technical vision systems, the completion of object boundaries that are interrupted due to occlusions or low luminance contrast is an important issue.

For the human vision system, illusory contours have been studied by Gestalt psychologists from the early 20th century on [10, 2, 25]. Schuhmann was one of the first to mention this phenomenon in 1900 [24]. He described illusory contours as contours that are not "objectively present". In the following years the contributions to the field of illusory contour perception comprised the description of optical illusions based on contour perception rather than explaining these illusions. The most famous examples for optical illusions caused by illusory contour perception are the Kanizsa figures shown in Fig. 1 (see also [8]).

In the following we present a computational approach to illusory contour perception in natural scenes. The model uses the position and orientation of detected corners. We therefore developed an algorithm for threshold-free edge detection and a subsequent corner detection, which leads to the question of the

* We gratefully acknowledge partial funding of this work by the Deutsche Forschungsgemeinschaft under grant Me1289/7-1 "KomForm".

M. Lazo and A. Sanfeliu (Eds.): CIARP 2005, LNCS 3773, pp. 71–80, 2005.

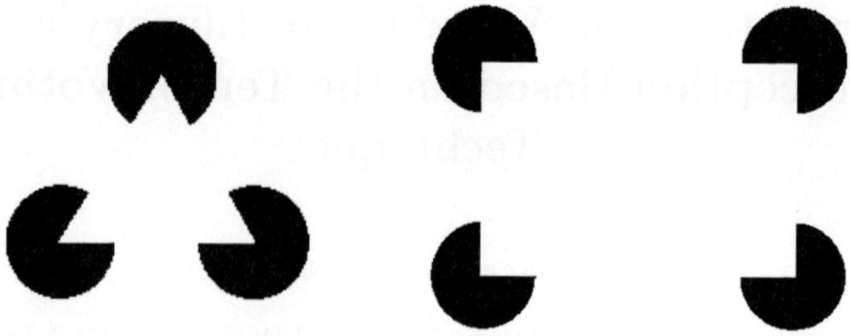

(a) Kanizsa Triangle (b) Kanizsa Rectangle

Fig. 1. Kanizsa figures: The black "pacmen" induce the perception of a triangle in (a) and a rectangle in (b)

dependency of the presented results on the preceding low level image processes. On the one hand it can be argued that results on real images suffer from the systematic errors in preceding steps, on the other hand a real image offers a much more complex and realistic test bed. Furthermore few attempts have been made so far to apply illusory contour perception to real images.

2 Related Work

The majority of approaches or models dealing with the problem of spatial contour integration use some kind of bipole connection scheme [6,21], as introduced by Grossberg and Mingolla [23]. This perceptual grouping kernel usually consists of two symmetric lobes encoding the connection strength and orientation. In [26], Williams and Thornber address the comparison of different methods of aggregating the contributions of neighboring sites of the grouping kernel. For a detailed overview of contour integration approaches, see [5] or [19]. In [19], emphasis is placed on models including illusory contour perception, namely the model of Heitger et al. [7,22] as a neurophysical inspired computational model and the approach of Zweck and Williams [28] which models the Brownian motion of a particle from source to sink.

The method proposed in this paper uses the tensor voting technique introduced by Medioni et al. [4]. Tensor voting was applied successfully to contour inference problems on synthetic and binary input images in [17]. In [13] and [12], this approach was extended to greyscale images as input, using gabor filtering as a preceding image processing step. In the tensor voting framework the grouping kernel, called stick voting field, is orientational, i.e. with angles from 0° to 180°, and designed for contour inference. Considering illusory contour perception, the use of this stick voting field could make sense in the context of a unified treatment of all contour elements, but would lead to interference of contour elements, especially in the case of amodal completions behind a textured foreground. What is needed for illusory contours including amodal completions is a directional communication pattern (with angles from 0° to 360°), e.g. one lobe, which was already used in [15] and [16], but addressed to spontaneously splitting figures and binary input images.

3 Edge and Corner Detection

As a preprocessing step we have developed a method for threshold-free edge detection and a subsequent corner detection. This is achieved by applying a recursive search to edge candidates. The edge candidates are local extrema and zero-crossings of the responses of several Gaussian-based filter banks. For an overview of edge detection algorithms, see [3] and [27].

The kernels of our filter functions are shown in Fig. 2. In the case of the edge-filter, Fig. 2(a), the behaviour of the filter is similar to that of the first derivative of a Gaussian. For example, edges produce local extrema in the filter responses with corresponding orientation. Like the edge filters, the corner filters in Fig. 2(b) are defined for different orientation angles. The center-surround filter shown in Fig. 2(c) behaves like the Mexican Hat Operator [11]. Edges produce zero crossings, while lines result in local extrema of the filter responses.

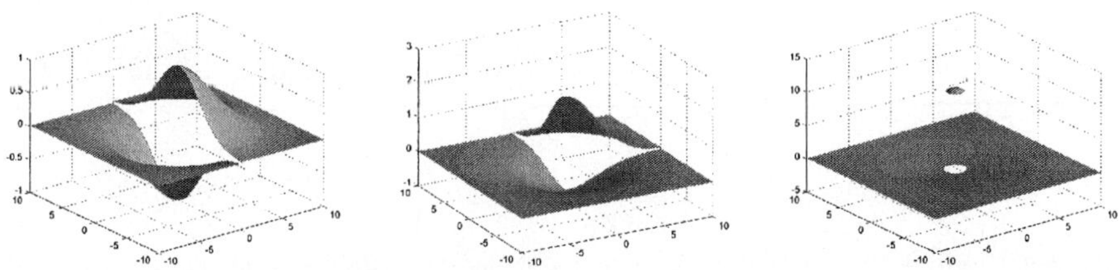

(a) (b) (c)

Fig. 2. Filter Masks: (a) Edge filter (b) Corner filter (c) Center-surround filter

In general, edge detection is performed by convolving one filter mask with the image data and in many cases, the filter mask is rotated to gain orientation-sensitive filter responses. Like all differential edge detection schemes these methods suffer from the necessity of defining a threshold. This makes the results of an edge detector highly dependent on the image and on its brightness. Furthermore, to avoid the influence of noise, the size of the convolution mask has to be sufficiently large. This often leads to rounded corners and poor localization. To avoid these disadvantages we use several convolution masks with different shapes and compare their filter responses with each other to decide whether a given point belongs to an edge.

Taken on their own, these convolution masks have several problems in detecting edges or corners, but in spite of these problems, some image positions can be labled as edges with a high probability. If an image position belongs to a zero crossing of the center-surround filter and to a local maximum of the edge filter and furthermore, if this maximum is higher than the corresponding corner

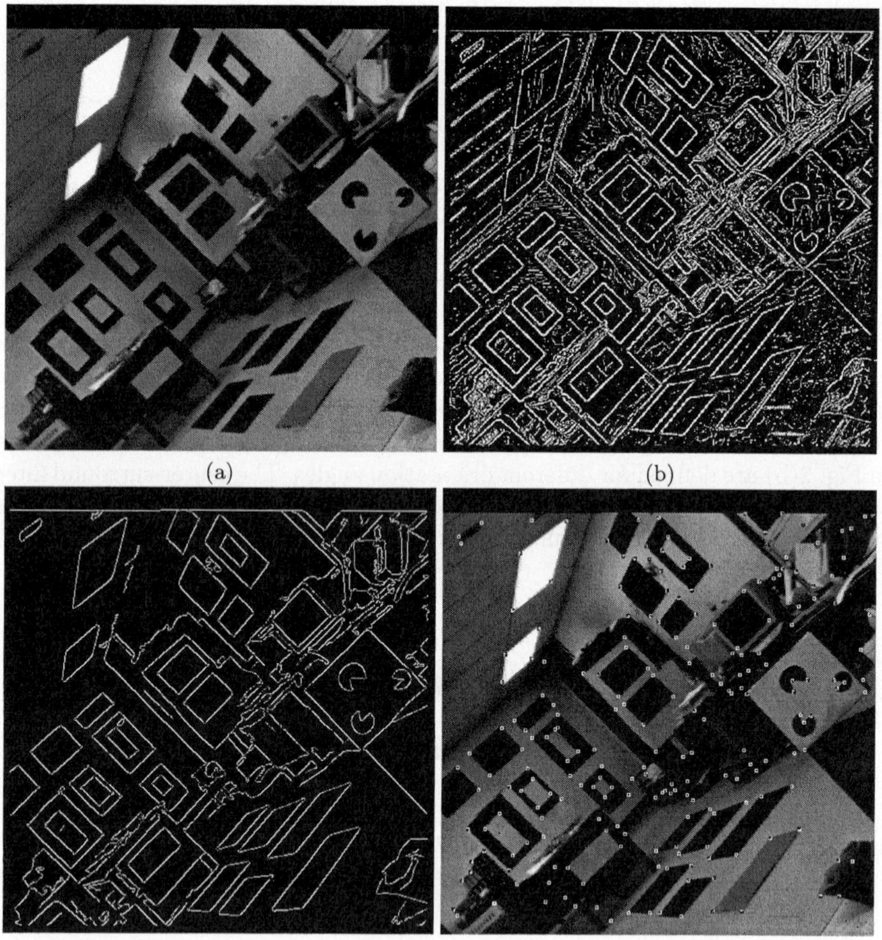

(a) (b) (c) (d)

Fig. 3. Lab scene: (a) Input image (b) Edge Candidates (c) Detected edges (d) Detected corners

filter response, the position is very likely to belong to an edge. Starting from these "ideal" edges, we now recursively try to find a good continuation of the edge, using a ranking list that defines e.g. that a zero crossing combined with an edge filter maximum is preferred to a simple zero crossing.

With a search for local minima on the absolute center-surround filter responses, most of the corners are found correctly, except for those that lie on "ideal" edges. Here we have to use the classic approach and compute the orientation differences between neighboring edgels.

The result of the recursive search is shown in Fig. 3(c), detected corners are shown superposed to the input image in Fig. 3(d). A comparison to other corner detectors is given in [18]. Note that the used method for corner and edge detection is not an integral part of the proposed computational approach to illusory contour perception and can therefore be replaced by any other corner detector providing not only the corner positions but also the associated orientation angles.

4 Tensor Voting

In [17], Medioni, Lee and Tang describe a framework for feature inference from sparse and noisy data called tensor voting. The most important issue is the representation of edge elements as tensors. In the 2D-case, a tensor over $\mathbb{R}^2$ can be denoted by a symmetric 2×2 matrix T with two perpendicular eigenvectors $\boldsymbol{e}_1, \boldsymbol{e}_2$ and two corresponding real eigenvalues $\lambda_1 > \lambda_2$. A tensor can be visualized as an ellipse in 2-D with the major axis representing the estimated tangent direction $\boldsymbol{e}_1$ and its length λ_1 reflecting the saliency of this estimation. The length λ_2 assigned to the perpendicular eigenvector $\boldsymbol{e}_2$ encodes the orientation uncertainty. The definition of saliency measures is deducted from the following decomposition of a tensor into $T = \lambda_1 \boldsymbol{e}_1 \boldsymbol{e}_1^\top + \lambda_2 \boldsymbol{e}_2 \boldsymbol{e}_2^\top$ or equivalently $T = (\lambda_1 - \lambda_2) \boldsymbol{e}_1 \boldsymbol{e}_1^\top + \lambda_2 (\boldsymbol{e}_1 \boldsymbol{e}_1^\top + \boldsymbol{e}_2 \boldsymbol{e}_2^\top)$. Then, the weighting factor $(\lambda_1 - \lambda_2)$ represents an orientation in the direction of the eigenvector $\boldsymbol{e}_1$ and thus will be called *curve-* or *stick-saliency*. The second weight λ_2 is applied to a circle, hence it is called *junction-* or *ball-saliency* as its information about multiple orientations measures the confidence in the presence of a junction.

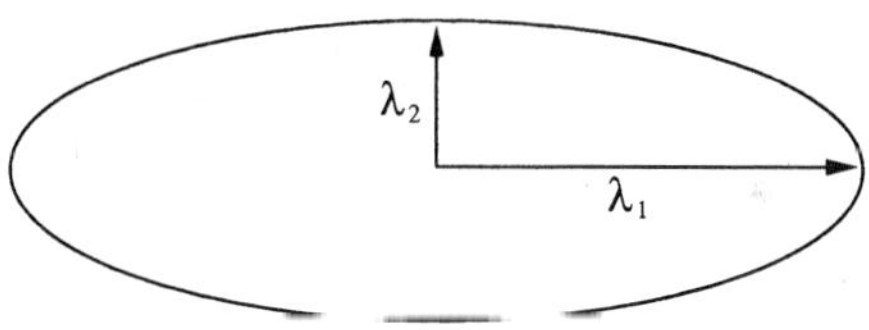

Fig. 4. Visualization of a tensor as an ellipse

Grouping can now be formulated as the combination of elements according to their stick-saliency or ball-saliency. In stick-voting, for each oriented input token the grouping kernel called stick-voting-field (see next section) is aligned to the eigenvector $\boldsymbol{e}_1$. In the following the input tokens consist of detected corners and their associated directions. All fields are combined by tensor addition, i.e. addition of the matrices and spectral decomposition of the sum into eigenvectors and -values. The field is designed to create groupings with neighboring tokens which fulfill the minimal curvature constraint. Hence the orientation of each token of the voting field is defined to lie on a cocircular path.

Note that for junctions or corners neither the tensor representation suffices to encode the at least two different orientations nor is the ball saliency a trustable measure for junctions, since it is highly dependent on the orientations of incoming edges [14].

5 Voting Fields

Given a point P with an associated tangent direction and a point Q with the orientation difference θ between the tangent direction and the direct connection of P and Q. Let ℓ be the distance between P and Q. Then, with

$$r = \frac{\ell}{2sin\theta} \quad \text{and} \quad s = \frac{\ell \cdot \theta}{sin\theta} \quad ,$$

r is the radius of the tangent circle to P going through Q and s is the arc length distance along the circular path (radian).

Most approaches to spatial contour integration define the connection strength V for P and Q and therefore the shape of the bipole connection scheme via $V = V_d \cdot V_c$ with a distance term V_d and a curvature term V_c. In [7], Heitger et al. use

$$V_{d1} = e^{-\frac{\ell^2}{2\sigma^2}} \quad \text{and} \quad V_{c1} = \begin{cases} \cos^k(\frac{\pi/2}{\alpha} \cdot \theta) & \text{if } |\theta| < \alpha \\ 0 & \text{otherwise} \end{cases}$$

with $k = 2n$, $n \in \mathbb{N}$ and an opening angle $2\alpha = \pi$. Hansen and Neumann also use V_{d1} and V_{c1}, but with $k = 1$ and $\alpha = 10°$ [6]. In [17], Medioni et al. define the proximity term V_{d2} and the curvature term V_{c2} as follows:

$$V_{d2} = e^{-\frac{s^2}{2\sigma^2}} \quad \text{and} \quad V_{c2} = e^{-\frac{c \cdot \rho^2}{\sigma^2}} \quad \text{with} \quad \rho = \frac{2sin\theta}{\ell}$$

c is a positive constant and ρ is nothing else than the inverse radius of the osculating circle. This results in a curvature measure that is highly dependent on scale.

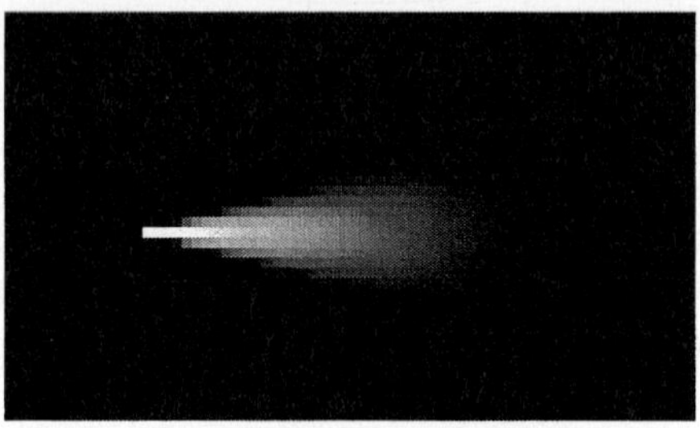

Fig. 5. Stick saliency for the half lobe stick voting field with $V = V_{d2} \cdot V_{c1}$, $k = 1$ and $\alpha = 15°$

To achieve a clear separation of distance along the circular path and its curvature, we choose V_{d2} and V_{c1}. The results presented in the next chapter are computed with a directional one-lobe voting field and $V = V_{d2} \cdot V_{c1}$, $k = 1$ and $\alpha = 15°$, i.e. an opening angle of 30°.

6 Results

Fig. 6(a), (d) and (g) show detected edges and corners and their associated orientations, (b), (e) and (f) show stick saliencies after tensor voting and (c), (f) and (i) show extracted illusory contours superposed to the previously detected contours. It is remarkable, that in Fig. 6(f) the amodal completions of the circles are found while this is not the case in Fig. 6(c) and (i). This is due to the acute connection angles in the latter two cases as can be seen in the images showing the stick saliencies.

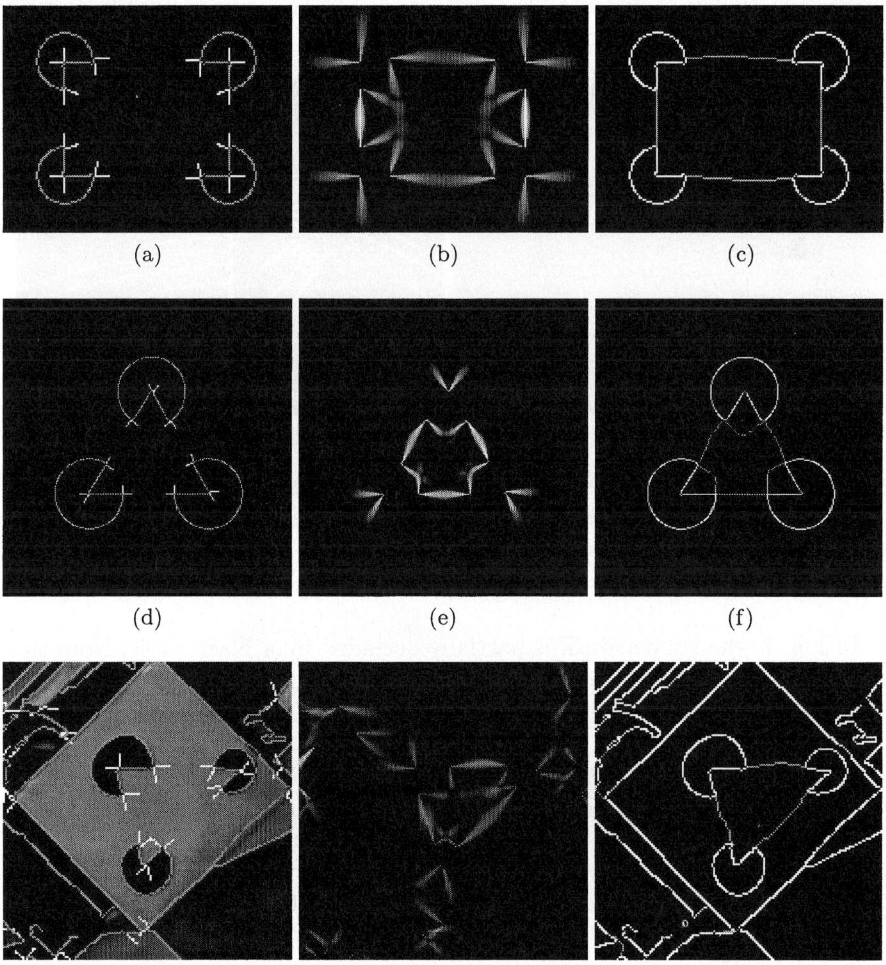

(a) (b) (c)

(d) (e) (f)

(g) (h) (i)

Fig. 6. Top row: Results for Fig. 1(b), middle row: results for Fig. 1(a), bottom row: results for the Kanizsa triangle in Fig. 3. For further description see text.

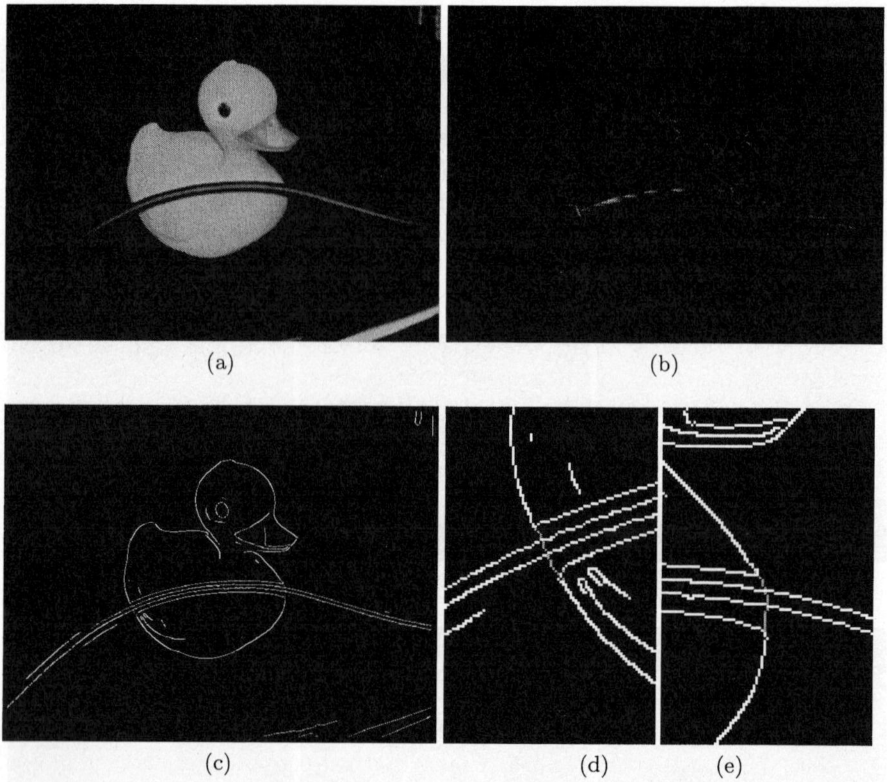

Fig. 7. Rubber duck image: (a) input image, (b) stick saliencies induced by corners and associated orientations, (c) illusory contours superposed to detected edges, (d) and (e) magnification of regions containing illusory contours

In Fig. 7, the rubber duck is partially occluded by a black cable. Note that there are some false assigned corners due to light reflections on the cable. The voting fields cast by these corners interfere with the fields generated at the duck's object boundary and hence compromise the correct detection of amodal completions (Fig. 7(b)). This illustrates that a unified treatment of edge segments and corners would disturb the perception of amodal completions, at least for this low level image processing step. Anyhow just the two desired amodal completions of the duck's object boundary are marked as illusory contours, see Fig. 7(d) and (e), so the correct virtual contours are found.

7 Conclusion

An approach to illusory contour perception has been introduced and successfully applied to synthetic and real images. There are some natural limitations to a low level image processing model for illusory contour perception. For a certain stage of grouping a knowledge base is required which leaves the field of low level image processing. Furthermore, the human vision system derives its enormous capabilities not only from the "hardware implementation" as a parallel network but also from the fact that several cues like depth and motion are considered when detecting object boundaries.

With our approach we have shown that good results for illusory contour perception can be achieved even in a low level image processing step.

8 Future Work

Currently, our model does not distinguish between modal and amodal completions and the contours are not assigned to certain object boundaries. Consequently, unit formation will be substantial for future research. For further discussion about unit formation, see [9] and [1].

References

1. B. L. Anderson, M Singh, and R. W. Fleming. The interpolation of object and surface structure. *Cognitive Psychology*, 44:148–190, 2002.
2. Walter H. Ehrenstein, Lothar Spillmann, and Viktor Sarris. Gestalt issues in modern neuroscience. *Axiomathes*, 13(3):433–458, 2003.
3. Rafael C. Gonzalez and Richard E. Woods. *Digital Image Processing.* Prentice Hall, 2002.
4. Gideon Guy and Gerard Medioni. Inferring global perceptual contours from local features. *International Journal of Computer Vision*, 20(1-2):113–133, 1996.
5. Thorsten Hansen. *A neural model of early vision: Contrast, contours, corners and surfaces.* PhD thesis, Universität Ulm, 2003.
6. Thorsten Hansen and Heiko Neumann. Neural mechanisms for representing surface and contour features. In *Emergent Neural Computational Architectures Based on Neuroscience - Towards Neuroscience-Inspired Computing*, pages 139–153. Springer-Verlag, 2001.
7. F. Heitger and R. von der Heydt. A computational model of neural contour processing: Figure-ground segregation and illusory contours. In *International Conference on Computer Vision*, pages 32–40, 1993.
8. G. Kanizsa, editor. *Organization in Vision.* Praeger, 1979.
9. P.J. Kellman, S. E. Guttman, and T. D. Wickens. Geometric and neural models of object perception. In *From fragments to objects: Segmentation and grouping in vision.* T. F. Shipley, Ed, and P.J. Kellman, Ed. . Oxford, UK: Elsevier Science, 2001.
10. K. Koffka. *Principles of Gestalt psychology.* Harcourt Brace, New York, 1935.
11. D. Marr. *Vision: a computational investigation into the human representation and processing of visual information.* W. H. Freeman, San Francisco, 1982.
12. A. Massad, M. Babos, and B. Mertsching. Application of the tensor voting technique for perceptual grouping to grey-level images. In L. van Gool, editor, *Pattern Recognition, 24th DAGM Symposium (DAGM2002)*, pages 306–313, 2002.
13. A. Massad, M. Babos, and B. Mertsching. Perceptual grouping in grey level images by combination of gabor filtering and tensor voting. In R. Kasturi, D. Laurendeau, and C. Suen, editors, *ICPR*, volume 2, pages 677–680, 2002.

14. A. Massad, M.Babos, and B. Mertsching. Application of the tensor voting technique for perceptual grouping to grey-level images: Quantitative evaluation. 2003. Intl. Symposium on Image and Signal Processing and Analysis.
15. A. Massad and G. Medioni. 2-D Shape Decomposition into Overlapping Parts. In C. Arcelli, L. Cordella, and G. Sanniti di Baja, editors, *Visual Form 2001, 4th International Workshop on Visual Form (IWVF 4)*, pages 398 – 409, Capri, Italy, January 2001.
16. A. Massad and B. Mertsching. Segmentation of Spontaneously Splitting Figures into Overlapping Parts. In B. Radig and S. Florcyk, editors, *Pattern Recognition, 23rd DAGM Symposium*, pages 25 – 31, January 2001.
17. G. Medioni, M.-S. Lee, and C.-K. Tang. *A Computational Framework for Segmentation and Grouping*. Elsevier Science, 2000.
18. Farzin Mokhtarian and Riku Suomela. Robust image corner detection through curvature scale space. *IEEE Trans. Pattern Anal. Mach. Intell.*, 20(12):1376–1381, 1998.
19. H. Neumann and E. Mingolla. Computational neural models of spatial integration in perceptual grouping. In T. Shipley and P. Kellman, editors, *From fragments to units: Segmentation and grouping in vision*, pages 353–400. Elsevier Science, Oxford, UK, 2001.
20. Andreas Nieder. Seeing more than meets the eye: processing of illusory contours in animals. *Journal of Comparative Physiology A: Sensory, Neural, and Behavioral Physiology*, 188(4):249–260, 2002.
21. Pierre Parent and Steven Zucker. Trace inference, curvature consistency, and curve detection. *IEEE Trans. Pattern Anal. Mach. Intell.*, 11(8):823–839, 1989.
22. Esther Peterhans and Friedrich Heitger. Simulation of neuronal responses defining depth order and contrast polarity at illusory contours in monkey area v2. *Journal of Computational Neuroscience*, 10(2):195–211, 2001.
23. W. D. Ross, S. Grossberg, and E. Mingolla. Visual cortical mechanisms of perceptual grouping: interacting layers, networks, columns, and maps. *Neural Netw.*, 13(6):571–588, 2000.
24. F. Schumann. Beiträge zur Analyse der Gesichtswahrnehmungen. Erste Abhandlung. Einige Beobachtungen über die Zusammenfassung von Gesichtseindrücken zu Einheiten. *Zeitschrift für Psychologie und Physiologie der Sinnesorgane*, 23:1–32, 1900. English translation by A. Hogg (1987) in The perception of Illusory Contours Eds S Petry, G.E. Meyer (New Yourk: Springer) pp 40-49.
25. Max Wertheimer. Untersuchungen zur Lehre von der Gestalt II. *Psychologische Forschung*, 4:301–350, 1923.
26. Lance R. Williams and Karvel K. Thornber. A comparison of measures for detecting natural shapes in cluttered backgrounds. *International Journal of Computer Vision*, 34(2/3):81–96, 2000.
27. D. Ziou and S. Tabbone. Edge detection techniques: an overview. *International Journal on Pattern Recognition and Image Analysis*, 8(4):537–559, 1998.
28. John W. Zweck and Lance R. Williams. Euclidean group invariant computation of stochastic completion fields using shiftable-twistable functions. In *ECCV (2)*, pages 100–116, 2000.

A Novel Clustering Technique Based on Improved Noising Method

Yongguo Liu[1,2,4], Wei Zhang[3], Dong Zheng[4], and Kefei Chen[4]

[1] College of Computer Science and Engineering,
University of Electronic Science and Technology of China,
Chengdu 610054, P. R. China
[2] State Key Laboratory for Novel Software Technology,
Nanjing University, Nanjing 210093, P. R. China
[3] Department of Computer and Modern Education Technology,
Chongqing Education College, Chongqing 400067, P. R. China
[4] Department of Computer Science and Engineering,
Shanghai Jiaotong University, Shanghai 200030, P. R. China

Abstract. In this article, the clustering problem under the criterion of minimum sum of squares clustering is considered. It is known that this problem is a nonconvex program which possesses many locally optimal values, resulting that its solution often falls into these traps. To explore the proper result, a novel clustering technique based on improved noising method called INMC is developed, in which one-step DHB algorithm as the local improvement operation is integrated into the algorithm framework to fine-tune the clustering solution obtained in the process of iterations. Moreover, a new method for creating the neighboring solution of the noising method called mergence and partition operation is designed and analyzed in detail. Compared with two noising method based clustering algorithms recently reported, the proposed algorithm greatly improves the performance without the increase of the time complexity, which is extensively demonstrated for experimental data sets.

1 Introduction

The clustering problem is a fundamental problem that frequently arises in a great variety of application fields such as pattern recognition, machine learning, and statistics. In this article, we focus on the minimum sum of squares clustering problem stated as follows: Given N objects in R^m, allocate each object to one of K clusters such that the sum of squared Euclidean distances between each object and the center of its belonging cluster for every such allocated object is minimized. This problem can be mathematically described as follows:

$$\min_{W,C} J(W,C) = \sum_{i=1}^{N}\sum_{j=1}^{K} w_{ij}\|\mathbf{x}_i - \mathbf{c}_j\|^2 \tag{1}$$

where $\sum_{j=1}^{K} w_{ij} = 1$, $i = 1, \ldots, N$. If object $\mathbf{x}_i$ is allocated to cluster C_j, then w_{ij} is equal to 1; otherwise w_{ij} is equal to 0. Here, N denotes the number of objects,

M. Lazo and A. Sanfeliu (Eds.): CIARP 2005, LNCS 3773, pp. 81–92, 2005.

m denotes the number of object attributes, K denotes the number of clusters, $X = \{\mathbf{x}_1, \ldots, \mathbf{x}_N\}$ denotes the set of N objects, $C = \{C_1, \ldots, C_K\}$ denotes the set of K clusters, and $W = [w_{ij}]$ denotes the $N \times K$ $0-1$ matrix. Cluster center $\mathbf{c}_j$ is calculated as follows:

$$\mathbf{c}_j = \frac{1}{n_j} \sum_{\mathbf{x}_i \in C_j} \mathbf{x}_i \tag{2}$$

where n_j denotes the number of objects belonging to cluster C_j. This clustering problem is a nonconvex program which possesses many locally optimal values, resulting that its solution often falls into these traps. It is known that this problem is NP-hard [1]. If exhaustive enumeration is used to solve this problem, then one requires to evaluate

$$\frac{1}{K!} \sum_{j=1}^{K} (-1)^{K-j} \binom{K}{j} j^N \tag{3}$$

partitions. It is seen that exhaustive enumeration cannot lead to the required solution for most problems in reasonable computation time [2].

Many methods have been reported to deal with this problem [2,3]. Among them, K-means algorithm is a very popular one but it converges to local minima in many cases [4]. Moreover, many researchers attempt to solve this problem by stochastic optimization methods including evolutionary computation [5,6,7], tabu search [8], and simulated annealing [9]. By adopting these techniques, researchers obtain better performance than by using local iteration methods such as K-means algorithm. In [10], the noising method, a recent metaheuristic technique firstly reported in [11], is introduced to deal with the clustering problem under consideration. In the field of metaheuristic algorithms, to efficiently use them in various kinds of applications, researchers often combine them with local descent approaches [12,13]. To efficiently use the noising method in the clustering problem, in [10], the authors introduced K-means algorithm as the local improvement operation to improve the performance of the clustering algorithm. As a result, two methods called NMC and KNMC, respectively, are developed. NMC does not own K-means operation but KNMC does. The choice of the algorithm parameters is extensively discussed, and performance comparisons between these two methods and K-means algorithm, GAC [5], TSC [8], and SAC [9] are conducted on experimental data sets. It is concluded that, with much less computational cost than GAC, TSC, and SAC, KNMC can get much better clustering results sooner than NMC, GAC, and TSC, and obtain results close to those of SAC. Meanwhile, it is found that the results of KNMC are still inferior to those of SAC in most cases.

The motivation of this article is how to design a new noising method based clustering algorithm. On one hand, the low complexity should be kept, and on the other hand, the quality of outputs should be further improved. Here, we find there are still some problems in KNMC. Firstly, methods better than K-means algorithm are not considered, and secondly, the probability threshold employed in [10] need be determined in advance. But it is very difficult for the designer to choose the proper value in different cases. In this paper, two novel operations are introduced, DHB operation and mergence and partition operation. The role of DHB operation is similar to that of K-means operation in [10], but the former can further improve the current solution. Mergence and partition operation similar to the probability threshold is used to establish the neighboring solution, but it does not need any parameter and can attain much better results than the latter. By introducing these two modules, we develop a new clustering technique based on improved noising method called INMC. By extensive computer simulations, its superiority over NMC, KNMC, and even SAC is demonstrated.

The remaining part of this paper is organized as follows: In Section 2, INMC algorithm and its components are described in detail. In Section 3, how to determine proper modules is extensively discussed. Performance comparisons between the proposed algorithm and other techniques are conducted on experimental data sets. Finally, some conclusions are drawn in Section 4.

2 INMC Algorithm

As stated in [10,14], instead of taking the genuine data into account directly, the noising method considers the optimal result as the outcome of a series of fluctuating data converging towards the genuine ones. Figure 1 gives the general description of INMC. The architecture of INMC is similar to that of KMNC and their most procedures observe the main architecture of the noising method. The difference between KNMC and INMC lies that two new operations are introduced in INMC. The detail discussion about KNMC and the noising method can be found in [10] and [14], respectively. Here, DHB operation consisting of one-step DHB algorithm is used to fine-tune solution X_c and accelerate the convergence speed of the clustering algorithm. Moreover, mergence and partition operation is designed to establish the neighboring solution.

```
Begin
  set parameters and the current solution X_c at random
  while N_i ≤ N_t do
    N_i ← N_i + 1
    perform DHB operation to fine-tune solution X_c
    perform mergence and partition operation to create the neighbor X'
    if f(X') − f(X_c) + noise < 0, then X_c ← X'
    if f(X_c) < f(X_b), then update the best solution X_b ← X_c
    if N_i = 0(mod N_f), then decrease the noise rate r_n
  end do
  output solution X_b
end
```

Fig. 1. General description of INMC

2.1 DHB Operation

In [15], an iterative method called DHB algorithm, a breadth-first search technique, for the clustering problem is reported. According to this algorithm, another alternative approach called DHF algorithm, a depth-first search technique, is described in [16]. In [17], two algorithms called AFB algorithm and ABF algorithm, respectively, based on hybrid alternating searching strategies, are presented to overcome the drawbacks of either a breadth-first search or a depth-first search in the clustering problem. In [18], five iteration methods (DHB, DHF, ABF, AFB, and K-means) are compared. First four methods have the similar performance and own stronger convergence states than K-means algorithm. Their time complexities are the same as that of K-means algorithm. In [18], the conclusion is drawn that first four algorithms can get much better clustering results sooner than K-means algorithm and DHB algorithm is recommended to perform the clustering task. The detail descriptions of five methods can be found in the corresponding references. In this paper, we choose DHB algorithm as the local improvement operation to fine-tune solution X_c. Firstly, we define several variables so as to describe DHB operation. For cluster C_j, its objective function value is defined as:

$$J_j = \sum_{\mathbf{x}_i \in C_j} \|\mathbf{x}_i - \mathbf{c}_j\|^2 \tag{4}$$

If object $\mathbf{x}_i$ belonging to cluster C_j is reassigned to C_k, then cluster centers are moved accordingly, J_j decreases by ΔJ_{ij}, J_k increases by ΔJ_{ik}, and the objective function value J is updated as follows:

$$\begin{cases} \Delta J_{ij} = n_j \|\mathbf{x}_i - \mathbf{c}_j\|^2/(n_j - 1) \\ \Delta J_{ik} = n_k \|\mathbf{x}_i - \mathbf{c}_k\|^2/(n_k + 1) \\ J' = J - \Delta J_{ij} + \Delta J_{ik} \end{cases} \tag{5}$$

and C_j and C_k are modulated as follows:

$$\begin{cases} \mathbf{c}'_j = (n_j \mathbf{c}_j - \mathbf{x}_i)/(n_j - 1) \\ \mathbf{c}'_k = (n_k \mathbf{c}_k + \mathbf{x}_i)/(n_k + 1) \end{cases} \tag{6}$$

Then, DHB operation is described as follows: Object $\mathbf{x}_i$ belonging to cluster C_j is reassigned to cluster C_k, iff

$$\min(\Delta J_{ik}) < \Delta J_{ij} \tag{7}$$

where $i = 1, \ldots, N$, $j, k = 1, \ldots, K$, and $j \neq k$. According to Equations 5 and 6, the corresponding parameters are updated. After all objects are considered, the modified solution is obtained.

2.2 Mergence and Partition Operation

In [10], the probability threshold popularly used to create the neighborhood of tabu search is adopted to establish the neighboring solution of the current solution X_c. But the designer has to determine the value of this parameter in advance by computer simulations. In this paper, mergence and partition operation is designed to create the neighboring solution and no parameter is needed any longer. In [19], three clustering concepts, under-partitioned state, optimal-partitioned state, and over-partitioned state, are given to describe the variation of two partition functions so as to establish the cluster validity index. In this article, we introduce these concepts to explain why and how we establish the neighboring solution by mergence and partition operation. In general, for a cluster, there are only three partition states, under-partitioned state, optimal-partitioned state, and over-partitioned state. In over-partitioned case, an original cluster is improperly divided into several parts. In under-partitioned case, more than two original clusters or parts of them are improperly grouped together. Only in optimal-partitioned one, all original clusters are correctly partitioned. For a suboptimal clustering solution, there must be the under-partitioned cluster and the over-partitioned cluster. Therefore, it is seen that further partitioning the under-partitioned cluster and merging the over-partitioned cluster are natural and suitable for establishing the neighboring solution and exploring the correct clustering result. By improving all improperly partitioned clusters, we can expect to achieve the proper result at last. Here, we randomly perform one partition and one mergence on solution X_c, keep the number of clusters constant, and form the neighbor. As the increase of the number of iterations, this operation are repeatedly performed on suboptimal solutions and the proper solution will be finally achieved. Mergence and partition operation includes four sub-operations: mergence cluster selection, partition cluster selection, cluster mergence, and cluster partition. Here, the cluster to be merged C_m and the cluster to be partitioned C_p are randomly determined. For cluster C_m, its belonging objects will be reassigned to their respective nearest clusters. That is, object $\mathbf{x}_i \in C_m$ is reassigned to cluster C_j, iff

$$\|\mathbf{x}_i - \mathbf{c}_j\|^2 < \|\mathbf{x}_i - \mathbf{c}_k\|^2 \tag{8}$$

where $k, j = 1, \ldots, K$, $C_j, C_k \neq C_m$, and $C_j \neq C_k$. After this sub-operation, cluster C_m disappears and the number of clusters decreases by one. Meanwhile, For cluster C_p, we view objects belonging to cluster C_p as a new data set, and adopt iteration methods such as K-means algorithm to divide its belonging objects into two new clusters. Here, K-means algorithm is chosen to perform this task by computer simulations. After this sub-operation, cluster C_p is divided into two new clusters and the number of clusters increases by one. Above four steps are performed on solution X_c and the neighboring solution X' is established.

3 Experimental Results

In order to analyze the performance of the proposed algorithm, we firstly evaluate the individual contributions made by different operations. Then the proposed algorithm is applied to seven data sets and compared with SAC, NMC, and KNMC. These experimental data sets are chosen because they represent different situations and provide the extensive tests of the adaptability of the proposed algorithm. Simulation experiments are conducted in Matlab on an Intel Pentium III processor running at 800MHz with 128MB real memory. Each experiment includes 20 independent trials.

3.1 Performance Evaluation

In this section, the experiments are performed to compare performance of different modules. Due to space limitations, here, the well-known data set, German Towns with eight clusters, is chosen to show the comparison results. For other experimental data sets, the similar results are obtained.

Three local improvement operations (No operation, K-means operation, and DHB operation) adopted by NMC, KNMC, and INMC, respectively, are compared. In NMC, there is no local improvement operation. Here, the probability threshold is used to create the neighboring solution. The best results obtained by the methods equipped with different operations in the process of iterations are compared as shown in Figure 2. It is seen that No operation is the worst. For other two operations, it seems that their results are almost equal to each other. But after No operation is removed, the real results are shown as Figure 3. It is clear that K-means operation is obviously inferior to DHB operation. As a result, the algorithm equipped with DHB operation can attain the best results more quickly and stably than ones with other two operations.

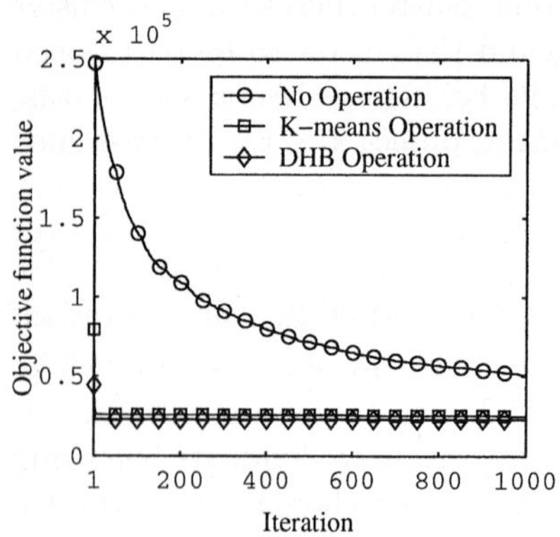

Fig. 2. Comparison of three operations for improving solution X_c

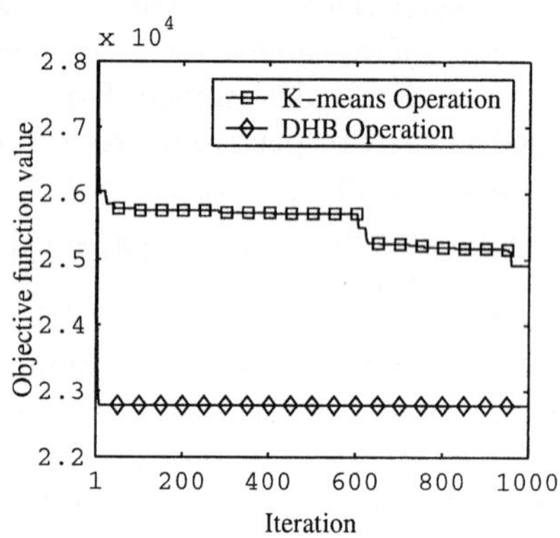

Fig. 3. Comparison of K-means operation and DHB operation

We now discuss the issue of creating the neighboring solution. Here, to compare performance of the probability threshold and mergence and partition operation, we do not adopt the local improvement operation to improve the current solution. Figure 4 shows that mergence and partition operation is far superior to the probability threshold and greatly improve the performance of the clustering algorithm. Without the cooperation of the local improvement operation, the neighboring solution provided by mergence and partition operation still accelerates the clustering algorithm to attain the best result stably and quickly. Therefore, it can be expected the combination of DHB operation and mergence and partition operation can further improve the performance of the clustering method.

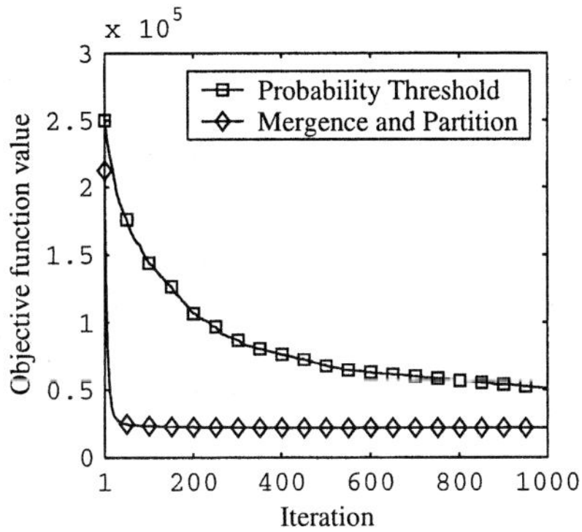

Fig. 4. Comparison of two modes for creating the neighboring solution

3.2 Performance Comparison

In this paper, seven data sets are chosen to perform computer simulations besides the ones adopted in [10]. Two well-known data sets are added: German Towns [2] and British Towns [20]. Here, we consider two cases: one is that the number of clusters is variable; the other is that this parameter is fixed. Among data sets, the number of clusters in German Towns varies in the range [4, 10]. We label them as GT4C, GT5C, GT6C, GT7C, GT8C, GT9C, and GT10C, respectively. This data set consists of Cartesian coordinates of 59 towns in Germany. The case of British Towns is the same as that of German Towns. This data set is composed of 50 samples each of four variables corresponding to the first four principal components of the original data. In other data sets, the number of clusters is fixed. The detail descriptions of these five data sets (Data52, Data62, Iris, Crude Oil, and Vowel) can be found in [10].

In this paper, our aim is to improve the noising method for the clustering problem under consideration and to further explore better results than those of KNMC and even SAC. In [10], it is shown that KNMC is better than K-means algorithm, GAC, and TSC. Therefore, we here focus on SAC, NMC, KNMC, and INMC. For SAC, according to the recommendation of the reference, the number of iterations at a temperature is set to be 20, the initial annealing temperature is set to be 100, α is set to be 0.05, and the terminal annealing temperature is set to be 0.01. In [10], The choice of the algorithm parameters is determined by computer simulations as follows: the noise range is equal to 10, the terminal noise rate is equal to 0, the original noise rate is equal to 10, the number of iterations at the fixed noise rate is equal to 20, and the total number of iterations is equal to 1000. For INMC, its parameter settings are the same as those of NMC and KNMC.

Before conducting comparison experiments, we analyze the time complexities of methods adopted in this article. The time complexities of SAC, NMC, and KNMC are $O(GN_sKmN)$, $O(N_tmN)$, and $O(N_tKmN)$, respectively, where G denotes the number of iterations during the process that the annealing temperature drops, N_s denotes the number of iterations at the fixed temperature, and N_t denotes the total number of iterations in the noising method. It is known that the cost of NMC is lower than that of KNMC, but the performance of NMC is far inferior to that of KNMC. For INMC, the complexity of DHB operation is $O(KmN)$. The complexity of mergence and partition operation is $O(KmN)$. Therefore, the time complexity of INMC is $O(N_tKmN)$ that is equal to that of KNMC. Under this condition, the complexity of SAC is over thrice as much as those of INMC and KNMC.

Table 1. Comparison of the clustering results of four methods for German Towns

		SAC	NMC	KNMC	INMC
GT4C	Avg	49600.59	75063.93	51610.14	49600.59
	SD	0.00	7917.87	6652.60	0.00
	Min	49600.59	63245.97	49600.59	49600.59
GT5C	Avg	39496.39	67157.79	40075.44	39091.02
	SD	783.34	6897.88	1094.02	376.04
	Min	38716.02	58374.91	38716.02	38716.02
GT6C	Avg	32220.44	62077.15	33837.61	31502.50
	SD	1548.73	7178.90	1369.15	975.98
	Min	30535.39	49445.41	30535.39	30535.39
GT7C	Avg	26964.11	54509.46	29009.23	24511.56
	SD	1707.07	6077.62	2146.84	136.82
	Min	24432.57	40164.41	25743.20	24432.57
GT8C	Avg	22603.12	52753.38	24496.94	21573.29
	SD	1458.92	5527.67	1591.55	153.88
	Min	21499.99	45283.29	22114.03	21483.02
GT9C	Avg	19790.99	47585.86	21746.58	18791.13
	SD	420.20	4602.09	1925.25	175.83
	Min	19130.63	35490.28	19521.02	18550.44
GT10C	Avg	18028.90	42796.75	20451.51	16515.07
	SD	633.67	4078.29	1643.82	125.47
	Min	16864.78	35015.27	18462.07	16307.96

The average (Avg), standard deviation (SD), and minimum (Min) values of the clustering results of four methods for German Towns are compared as shown in Table 1. In face of German Towns in which the number of clusters is variable, NMC is the worst and fails to attain the best values even once within specified iterations and its best values obtained are far worse than the best ones. KNMC equipped with K-means operation can attain much better results than NMC. KNMC can attain the optimal results of German Towns when the number of clusters is small. But when this number is greater than and equal to seven, KNMC cannot obtain the ideal results any longer. SAC spending much more computational resource than KNMC obtains better performance than KNMC as stated in [10]. SAC can attain the optimal results of German Towns when the number of clusters is up to seven. As the increase of this number, it does not attain the best results but its results are still superior to those of KNMC.

With the cooperation of DHB operation and mergence and partition operation, INMC can achieve the best value in each case. Its stability and solution quality are far superior to those of NMC, KNMC, and even SAC. Meanwhile, its time complexity the same as that of KNMC does not increase.

The average (Avg), standard deviation (SD), and minimum (Min) values of the clustering results of four methods for British Towns are compared as shown in Table 2. In face of British Towns, NMC is still the worst and fails to attain the best value in each case. At this time, KNMC can attain the optimal results of British Towns when the number of clusters is up to five. As the increase of the number of clusters, KNMC cannot obtain the best results any longer. In face of British Towns, the performance of SAC also becomes bad. It only attains the best values of British Towns with four and six clusters. But SAC still obtains better performance than KNMC in most case. In face of British Towns with different clusters, INMC can still attain the best value in each case. It is shown that the stability and solution quality of INMC are far superior to those of NMC, KNMC, and SAC.

Table 2. Comparison of the clustering results of four methods for British Towns

		SAC	NMC	KNMC	INMC
BT4C	Avg	180.91	213.74	182.05	180.91
	SD	0.00	13.05	1.96	0.00
	Min	180.91	186.25	180.91	180.91
BT5C	Avg	160.56	189.45	162.76	160.23
	SD	0.00	9.82	3.12	0.00
	Min	160.56	172.64	160.23	160.23
BT6C	Avg	145.37	178.18	147.29	141.46
	SD	3.30	10.17	2.97	0.00
	Min	141.46	167.61	142.30	141.46
BT7C	Avg	130.26	175.20	132.69	126.60
	SD	2.45	12.01	3.86	0.29
	Min	128.68	156.40	128.28	126.28
BT8C	Avg	120.07	163.48	121.18	113.82
	SD	3.01	8.93	3.96	0.57
	Min	114.07	141.67	116.65	113.50
BT9C	Avg	111.18	155.78	111.30	103.24
	SD	2.47	9.83	3.25	0.22
	Min	103.75	142.75	104.31	102.74
BT10C	Avg	100.71	148.21	103.14	92.81
	SD	3.36	10.69	4.14	0.17
	Min	93.19	131.07	98.47	92.68

After considering the case in which the number of clusters is variable, we focus on the other case. The average (Avg), standard deviation (SD), and minimum (Min) values of the clustering results of four methods for other five data sets are compared as shown in Table 3. In these experiments, the number of clusters is constant. As stated in [10], NMC is the worst, KNMC is the second, and SAC is the best. SAC can attain the best values of Data52, Iris, and Crude Oil in all trials. But after INMC is considered, more promising results are expected. INMC can stably obtain the best values of Data52, Data62, Iris, and Crude Oil in all trials. For Vowel, its solution quality and stability are much better than other three methods.

Table 3. Comparison of the clustering results of four methods for Data52, Data62, Iris, Crude Oil, and Vowel

		SAC	NMC	KNMC	INMC
Data52	Avg	488.02	2654.52	488.69	488.02
	SD	0.00	55.52	0.58	0.00
	Min	488.02	2557.31	488.09	488.02
Data62	Avg	1103.11	19303.58	1230.02	543.17
	SD	366.63	422.77	1382.50	0.00
	Min	543.17	18005.98	543.17	543.17
Iris	Avg	78.94	302.99	85.37	78.94
	SD	0.00	37.43	19.26	0.00
	Min	78.94	242.15	78.94	78.94
Crude Oil	Avg	1647.19	1995.44	1647.27	1647.19
	SD	0.00	124.27	0.12	0.00
	Min	1647.19	1787.43	1647.19	1647.19
Vowel	Avg	31941263.99	250796549.46	31554139.24	31389900.02
	SD	1205116.61	2866658.66	1209301.09	412724.00
	Min	30720909.84	245737316.31	30718120.60	30690583.33

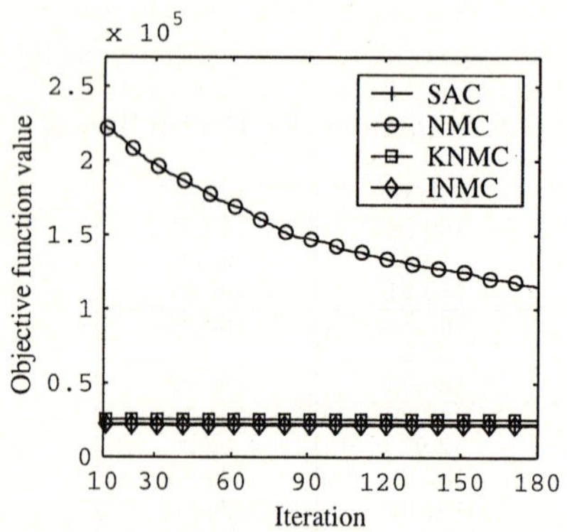

Fig. 5. Comparison of four methods for German Towns

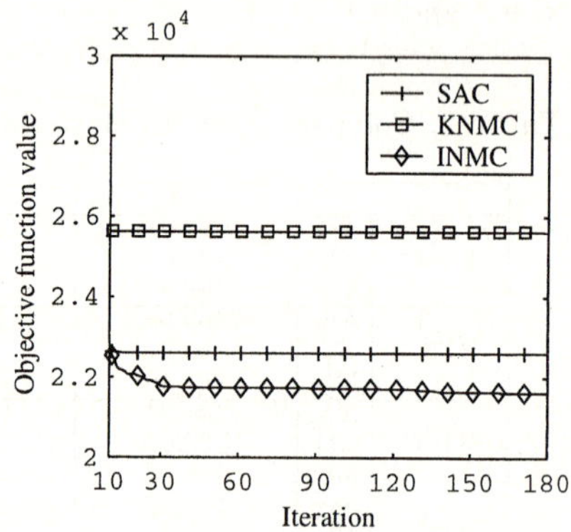

Fig. 6. Comparison of SAC, KNMC, and INMC for German Towns

In order to understand the performance of four methods better, we use German Towns with eight clusters to show the iteration process. In Figure 5, it is seen that NMC is obviously much inferior to other three methods. For other three algorithms, it seems that their results are almost equal to each other. But after NMC is removed, the real results are shown as Figure 6. It is seen that INMC is superior to SAC and KNMC, which shows that without the increase of the time complexity, the performance of the noising method based clustering algorithm can be greatly improved by introducing proper components into the algorithm framework.

4 Conclusions

In this article, in order to further improve the performance of the noising method based clustering algorithm, a novel algorithm called INMC is proposed. Two new operations are described in detail, DHB operation and mergence and partition operation. In the algorithm framework, DHB operation is used to modulate the current solution obtained in the process of iterations and to accelerate the convergence speed of INMC, and mergence and partition operation is developed to establish the neighboring solution. With the same time complexity as KNMC, INMC can get much better results more quickly and stably than NMC and KNMC. Moreover, compared with SAC, INMC spends much less resource and obtains much better results, which is not solved in [10]. In future, the estimation of the number of clusters should be considered. Meanwhile, improving the stability of the proposed algorithm to the best results in complicate cases will be the subject of future publications.

Acknowledgements

This research was supported in part by the National Natural Science Foundation of China (Grants 60473020, 60273049, 90104005) and State Key Laboratory for Novel Software Technology at Nanjing University.

References

1. Brucker, P.: On the complexity of clustering problems. Lecture Notes in Economics and Mathematical Systems. **157** (1978) 45–54
2. Spath, H.: Cluster analysis algorithms. Wiley, Chichester (1980)
3. Jain, A.K., Dubes, R.: Algorithms for clustering data. Prentice-Hall, New Jersey (1988)
4. Selim, S.Z., Ismail, M.A.: K-Means-type algorithm: generalized convergence theorem and characterization of local optimality. IEEE Trans Pattern Anal Mach Intell. **6**(1984) 81–87
5. Murthy, C.A., Chowdhury, N.: In search of optimal clusters using genetic algorithms. Pattern Recognit Lett. **17** (1996) 825–832
6. Babu, G.P., Murthy, M.N.: Clustering with evolutionary strategies. Pattern Recognit. **27** (1994) 321–329
7. Babu, G.P.: Connectionist and evolutionary approaches for pattern clustering. PhD dissertation. Indian Institute of Science, India (1994)
8. Al-sultan, K.S.: A tabu search approach to the clustering problem. Pattern Recognit. **28** (1995) 1443–1451
9. Bandyopadhyay, S., Maulik, U., Pakhira, M.K.: Clustering using simulated annealing with probabilisitc redistribution. Int J Pattern Recognit Artif Intell. **15** (2001) 269–285
10. Liu, Y.G., Liu, Y., Chen, K.F.: Clustering with noising method. Lecture Notes in Artificial Intelligence. **3584** (2005) 209–216
11. Charon, I., Hudry, O.: The noising method: a new method for combinatorial optimization. Oper Res Lett. **14** (1993) 133–137
12. Chelouah, R., Siarry, P.: Genetic and Nelder-Mead algorithms hybridized for a more accurate global optimization of continuous multiminima functions. Eur J Oper Res. **148** (2003) 335–348

13. Chelouah, R., Siarry, P.: A hybrid method combining continuous tabu search and Nelder-Mead simplex algorithms for the global optimization of multiminima functions. Eur J Oper Res. **161** (2005) 636–654
14. Charon, I., Hudry, O.: The noising method: a generalization of some metaheuristics. Eur J Oper Res. **135** (2001) 86–101
15. Duda, R.O., Hart, P.E.: Pattern classification and scene analysis. Wiley, New York (1972)
16. Ismail, M.A., Selim, S.Z., Arora, S.K.: Efficient clustering of multidimensional data. In: Proceedings of 1984 IEEE International Confference on System, Man, and Cybernetics. Halifax. (1984) 120–123
17. Ismail, M.A., Kamel, M.S.: Multidimensional data clustering utilizing hybrid search strategies. Pattern Recognit. **22** (1989) 75–89
18. Zhang, Q.W., Boyle, R.D.: A new clustering algorithm with multiple runs of iterative procedures. Pattern Recognit. **24** (1991) 835–848
19. Kim, D.J., Park, Y.W., Park, D.J.: A novel validity index for determination of the optimal number of clusters. IEICE Trans Inf Syst. **E84-D** (2001) 281–285
20. Chien, Y.T.: Interactive Pattern Recognition. Marcel-Dekker, New York (1978)

Object Recognition in Indoor Video Sequences by Classifying Image Segmentation Regions Using Neural Networks

Nicolás Amezquita Gómez and René Alquézar

Dept. Llenguatges i Sistemes Informàtics, Universitat Politècnica de Catalunya,
Campus Nord, Edifici Omega, 08034 Barcelona, Spain
{amezquita, alquezar}@lsi.upc.edu
http://www.lsi.upc.edu/~alquezar/

Abstract. This paper presents the results obtained in a real experiment for object recognition in a sequence of images captured by a mobile robot in an indoor environment. The purpose is that the robot learns to identify and locate objects of interest in its environment from samples of different views of the objects taken from video sequences. In this work, objects are simply represented as an unstructured set of spots (image regions) for each frame, which are obtained from the result of an image segmentation algorithm applied on the whole sequence. Each spot is semi-automatically assigned to a class (one of the objects or the background) and different features (color, size and invariant moments) are computed for it. These labeled data are given to a feed-forward neural network which is trained to classify the spots. The results obtained with all the features, several feature subsets and a backward selection method show the feasibility of the approach and point to color as the fundamental feature for discriminative ability.

1 Introduction

One of the most general and challenging problems a mobile robot has to confront is to identify and locate objects that are common in its environment. Suppose an indoor environment composed by halls, corridors, offices, meeting rooms, etc., where a robot navigates and is expected to perform some helping tasks (in response to orders such as "bring me a coke from the machine in the corridor" or "throw these papers to the nearest waste paper basket"). To accomplish these tasks, the robot must be able to locate and identify different objects such as a beverage machine or a waste paper basket. Of course, a possible approach is to program the robot with recognition procedures specific for each object of interest; in this way, the knowledge about the object and its characteristics is directly injected by the programmer in the recognition code. However, this approach is somewhat tedious and costly, and a preferable one would be to show to the robot in an easy way what the object is from images taken in different views and to rely on the general learning abilities of the robot, which could be based on neural networks or other machine learning paradigms, to obtain a certain model of the object and an associated recognition procedure.

M. Lazo and A. Sanfeliu (Eds.): CIARP 2005, LNCS 3773, pp. 93 – 102, 2005.

A very important issue is to determine the type of object model to learn. In this respect, a wide range of object representation schemes has been proposed in the literature [1]. In our point of view, a useful model should be relatively simple and easy to acquire from the result of image processing steps. For instance, the result of a color image segmentation process, consisting of a set of regions (spots, from now on) characterized by different features (related to size, color and shape), may be a good starting point to learn the model. Although structured models like adjacency attributed graphs or random graphs can be synthesized for each object from several segmented images [2], we have decided to investigate first a much simpler approach in which the object is just represented as an unstructured set of spots and the spots are classified directly as belonging to one of a finite set of objects or the background (defined as everything else) using a feed-forward neural network.

The classification of segmented image regions for object recognition has been addressed in several works. In [3], *eigenregions*, which are geometrical features that encompass several properties of an image region, are introduced to improve the identification of semantic image classes. Neural networks are used in [4] not only to classify known objects but to detect new image objects as well in video sequences. In [5], objects of interest are first localized, then features are extracted from the regions of interest and finally a neural network is applied to classify the objects. Support vector machines are used in [6] to classify a segmented image region in two categories, either a single object region or a mixture of background and foreground (multiple object region), in order to derive a top-down segmentation method.

The rest of the paper is organized as follows. In Section 2, image acquisition, preprocessing and segmentation steps are described as well as the semiautomatic method to assign class labels to spots. In Section 3, the features computed for each spot are defined. Neural network training and test together with the experimental methodology followed are commented in Section 4. The experimental results are presented in Section 5, and finally, in Section 6, some conclusions are drawn and future work discussed.

2 Image Acquisition, Pre-processing and Segmentation

A digital video sequence of 88 images was captured by an RGB camera installed on the MARCO mobile robot at the *Institute of Robotics and Industrial Informatics* (IRI, UPC-CSIC) in Barcelona. The sequence shows an indoor scene with some slight perspective and scale changes caused by the movement of the robot while navigating through a room. The objects of interest in the scene were a box, a chair and a pair of identical wastebaskets put together side by side (see Figure 1), and the objective was to discriminate them from the rest of the scene (background) and locate them in the images.

Before segmentation, the images in the sequence were preprocessed by applying a median filter on the RGB planes to smooth the image and reduce some illumination reflectance effects and noise. Then, the image segmentation module was applied to the whole sequence, trying to divide the images in homogeneous regions, which should correspond to the different objects in the image or parts of them. We used an implementation of the Felzenszwalb – Huttenlocher algorithm [7], which is a pixel merge method based on sorted edge weights and minimum spanning tree, to segment each image separately. Note that this is a method working on static images that does not exploit the dynamic continuity of image changes through the sequence.

The output of the segmentation process for each image consists of a list of regions (spots) that partition the image in homogeneous pieces, where each region is defined by the set of coordinates of the pixels it contains. For each spot, the mass center was calculated, and for all the spots whose mass center lied in some *region-of-interest* (ROI) rectangular windows, several features listed in Section 3 were computed as well. These windows were manually marked on the images with a graphics device to encompass the three objects of interest and a large region on the floor. Figure 1 shows one of the images and its segmentation together with the ROI windows on them.

The remaining set of spots, those with the mass center inside the ROI windows, was further filtered by removing all the spots with a size lower than 100 pixels, with the purpose of eliminating small noisy regions caused by segmentation defects. Hence, from the 88 images, a total number of 7853 spots were finally obtained.

In order to assign a class label to each spot, to be used as target for the spot pattern in the neural network training and test processes, a simple decision was made: each one of the four ROI windows constituted a class and all the spots in a window were assigned the same class label. Note that this is a rough decision, since several background spots are included in the ROI windows of the box, the chair and the wastebaskets, and therefore are not correctly labeled really. This is a clear source of error (incorrectly labeled patterns) that puts some bounds on the level of classification accuracy that the learning system, in this case the neural network, may reach. However, we preferred to carry out this simple but more practical approach instead of manually labeling each spot, which is obviously a very tedious task, although it would probably have raised the classification performance of the trained networks.

For illustrative purposes, the spots of Figure 1 that were assigned to each of the four classes are displayed in Figure 2; for the three objects (Figure 2 (a)-(c)), the union of selected spots is shown in the left and isolated spots that belong to the class are shown in the right. In addition, Figure 3 displays some of the ROI windows in other images of the sequence.

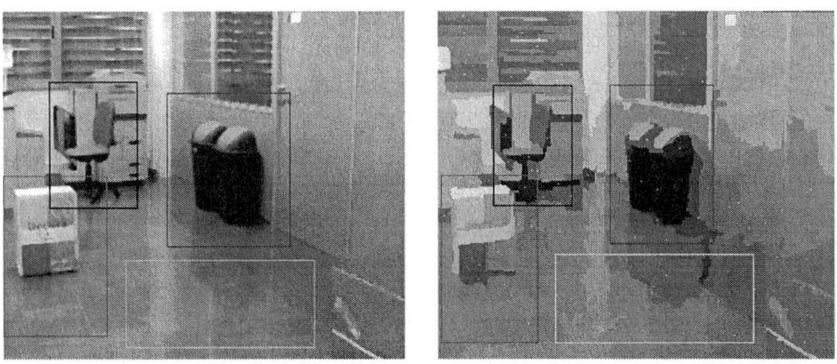

Fig. 1. One of the original images *(left)* and the corresponding segmented image *(right)*, with the four ROI windows marked on them. Spot mass centers are also displayed in the right image.

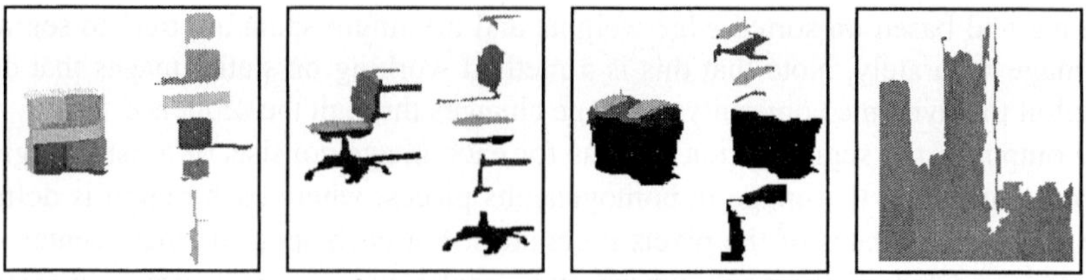

(a) Class 1 (b) Class 2 (c) Class 3 (d) Class 4

Fig. 2. Labeling of the spots selected from the segmented image in Figure 1

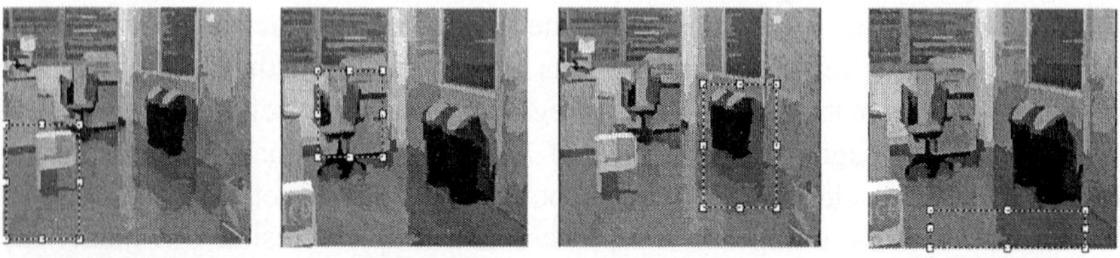

Window of the class 1 Window of the class 2 Window of the class 3 Window of the class 4

Fig. 3. Selection of ROI windows for two other images in the video sequence

3 Features Computed for the Image Regions

In order to be processed as a pattern by a neural network, a spot must be described by a feature vector. Table 1 displays the 14 variables that were initially considered to form the feature vector for training and testing the networks. In Section 5 we will also present results obtained from several different subsets of these 14 variables.

Two types of information were used in the computation of the spot features: color and geometry. With regards to color, average and variance values for each one of the three RGB bands were calculated for each spot on the basis of the corresponding intensity values of the spot pixels in the original image (not in the segmented image, for which spot color variance would be zero). This is, the result of the segmentation algorithm served to identify the pixels of every spot, but the color characteristics of these pixels were taken from the original RGB image.

The geometrical information may include features related to position, orientation, size and shape. Because of the robot movement, we were mainly interested in shape descriptors that were invariant to translation and scale, and to this end, we decided to use the seven invariant geometric moments defined by Hu [8]. In addition and since the range of variation of the objects' size was rather limited in the video sequence, we also calculated and used the size of each spot, i.e. its area measured in number of pixels.

For the calculation of the moments corresponding to a spot, all the pixels that form the spot are involved (not only its boundary pixels). More precisely, the seven invariant moments, independent of position and size of the region, that we used in this work are defined by the following equations:

$$I_1=N(2,0)+N(0,2) \tag{1}$$

$$I_2=(N(2,0)-N(0,2))^2+4(N(1,1))^2 \tag{2}$$

$$I_3=(N(3,0)-3N(1,2))^2 +(3N(2,1)-N(0,3))^2 \tag{3}$$

$$I_4=(N(3,0)+N(1,2))^2+(N(2,1)+N(0,3))2 \tag{4}$$

$$I_5=(N(3,0)-3N(1,2))(N(3,0)+N(1,2))[(N(3,0)+N(1,2))^2 -3(N(2,1)+N(0,3))^2] +(3N(2,1) -N(0,3))(N(2,1)+N(0,3))[3(N(3,0)+N(1,2))^2-(N(2,1)+N(0,3))^2] \tag{5}$$

$$I_6=(N(2,0) - N(0,2)) [(N(0,3)+N(1,2))^2-(N(2,1)+N(0,3))^2] +4N(1,1)(N(3,0)+N(1,2))(N(2,1)+N(0,3)) \tag{6}$$

$$I_7=(3N(2,1)-N(0,3)) (N(3,0)+N(1,2))[(N(3,0)+N(1,2))^2-3(N(2,1)+N(0,3))^2] +(3N(1,2)-N(3,0))(N(2,1)+N(0,3))[3(N(3,0)+N(1,2)^2)-(N(2,1)+N(0,3))^2] \tag{7}$$

where N (p, q) are the normalized central moments of order two, which are given by:

$$N (p, q) - MC (p, q) / MC^{\beta} (0, 0) \ ; \beta = ((p + q) / 2) + 1 \tag{8}$$

$$MC(p,q) = \Sigma\Sigma (x-X)^{p} (y-Y)^{q} f(x, y) \tag{9}$$

Table 1. Initial set of 14 variables that formed the feature vector for every spot and were used as input to the neural network for training and test

Set of variables	
Number of variable	**Feature**
1	Size of spot
2	Average red plane
3	Average green plane
4	Average blue plane
5	I1RGB invariant moment
6	I2RGB invariant moment
7	I3RGB invariant moment
8	I4RGB invariant moment
9	I5RGB invariant moment
10	I6RGB invariant moment
11	I7RGB invariant moment
12	Variance red plane
13	Variance green plane
14	Variance blue plane

$$MC(0,0)= \sum\sum f(x,y) \tag{10}$$

where f (x, y) is the intensity value of the pixel (x,y) in the segmented image, as given by the average of the three planes RGB, and (X,Y) are the mean coordinates of the spot. It must be noted that, in this case, all pixels in the same spot share the same value f(x,y), which depends on the color assigned to the spot as result of the segmentation process.

4 Neural Networks and Experimental Methodology

Neural networks (NNs) are used for a wide variety of object classification tasks [9]. An object is represented by a number of features that form a *d*-dimensional feature vector **x** within an input space $X \subseteq R^d$. A classifier therefore realizes a mapping from input space X to a finite set of classes $C = \{1,...,l\}$. A neural network is trained to perform a classification task from a set of training examples $S = \{(\mathbf{x}^\mu, t^\mu), \mu = 1,...,M\}$ using a supervised learning algorithm. The training set S consists of M feature vectors $\mathbf{x}^\mu \in R^d$ each labeled with a class membership $t^\mu \in C$. The network typically has as many outputs as classes and the target labels are translated into *l*-dimensional target vectors following a local unary representation. During the training phase the network parameters are adapted to approximate this mapping as accurately as possible (unless some technique, such as early stopping, is applied to avoid over-fitting). In the classification phase an unlabeled feature vector $\mathbf{x} \in R^d$ is presented to the trained network and the network outputs provide an estimation of the *a-posteriori* class probabilities for the input **x**, from which a classification decision is made, usually an assignment to the class with maximum *a-posteriori* probability [10].

In this work, we used a feed-forward 2-layer perceptron architecture (i.e. one hidden layer of neurons and an output layer) using standard backpropagation as training algorithm. For processing the full feature vectors, the networks consisted of 14 inputs, *n* hidden units and 4 output units, where *n* took different values from 10 to 200 (see Table 2). Hyperbolic tangent and sine functions were used as activation functions in the hidden layer and the output layer, respectively. A modified version of the PDP simulator of Rumelhart and McClelland [11] was employed for the experiments, setting a learning rate of 0.003 and a momentum parameter of zero for backpropagation, and a maximum number of 2,000 training epochs for each run.

As mentioned before, a dataset containing 7853 labeled patterns (spots) was available after the image segmentation and feature calculation processes described in previous sections. For each network tested, a kind of cross-validation procedure was carried out by generating 10 different random partitions of this dataset, each including 60% of the patterns for the training set, 15% for the validation set and 25% for the test set. The validation sets were used for early stopping the training phase. Actually, the network chosen at the end of the training phase was the one that yielded the best classification result on the validation set among the networks obtained after each training epoch. Then, this network was evaluated on the corresponding test set.

After the experiments with the whole set of features, we performed similar cross-validation experiments with different subsets of features (as indicated in Table 3), using the same experimental parameters aforementioned, except that the number of hidden units was fixed to 160 (since this provided the best test result with all features) and that the number of inputs was obviously set to the dimension of the feature subset.

Finally, starting from the architecture selected for the full set of features, a sequential backward selection method [12] was applied trying to determine a good subset of input features by eliminating variables one by one and retraining the network each time a variable is temporarily removed. In this case, each partition of the cross-validation procedure divided the dataset in 60% of patterns for training and 40% for test (no validation set) and the training stop criterion was to obtain the best result in the training set for a maximum of 2,000 epochs.

5 Experimental Results

The results obtained for the full set of features with the different networks tested are displayed in Table 2. For each one of the three sets (training, validation and test set), the classification performance is measured as the average percentage of correctly classified patterns in the ten cross-validation partitions, evaluated in the networks selected after training (the ones that maximize the performance on the validation set). Although the classification performance is shown for the three sets, the main result for assessing the network classification and generalization ability is naturally the classification performance in the test set. Hence, a best correct classification rate of 75.94 % was obtained for the architecture with 160 hidden units, even though the generalization performance was rather similar in the range from 60 to 200 hidden units. It appears to be an upper bound for both the training and test sets that might be caused in part by the incorrectly labeled patterns mentioned in Section 2.

Table 2. Classification performance obtained for different network configurations (hidden layer sizes) for the full set of 14 features using 10-partition cross-validation and early stopping

Classification performance (all features)			
Hidden units	**Training**	**Validation**	**Test**
200	80.27 %	77,00 %	75.63 %
180	80.04 %	77.47 %	75.81 %
160	80.33 %	77.38 %	**75.94** %
140	80.24 %	77.46 %	75.74 %
120	80.03 %	77.06 %	75.23 %
100	79.74 %	76.94 %	75.74 %
80	79,43 %	77,12 %	75,54 %
60	79,22 %	77,30 %	75,77 %
40	77,86 %	76,08 %	74,33 %
20	74,92 %	74,84 %	73,46 %
10	72.11 %	71.60 %	70.18 %

Table 3. It presents the classification results for several groups of selected variables to assess the relative importance of the different types of features (size, color averages, color variances and shape invariant moments)

Classification performance (with feature subsets)			
Feature Subsets	**Training**	**Validation**	**Test**
spot size, average and variance r,g,b	79.69	78.02	**76.17**
all variables	80.33	77.38	75.94
spot size and average r,g,b	77.77	77.49	75.92
spot size, average r,g,b and three first invariant moments	79.32	77.68	75.90
average r,g,b and seven invariants	77.51	77.23	75.38
average r,g,b and three first invariants	76.90	76.91	74.83
spot size and variance r,g,b	45.12	45.82	45.61
spot size, variance r,g,b and three first invariant moments	45.10	45.59	45.08
Seven invariant moments, variance r,g,b	40.95	41.12	40.79
Seven invariant moments	30.30	30.34	29.96

Table 4. It presents top-down the order of the variables eliminated in the sequential backward selection process and the associated performance in the training and test sets after each step

Backward selection process – Classification performance			
Num. var.	**Feature eliminated**	**Training**	**Test**
BASELINE	No variable removed	79.88	75.64
5	I1RGB invariant moment	80.14	76.40
13	variance of green plane	80.16	76.22
14	Variance of blue plane	79.77	76.55
11	I7RGB moment invariant	80.04	76.26
12	variance of red plane	78.90	**77.13**
9	I5RGB moment invariant	78.60	76.24
8	I4RGB moment invariant	78.07	75.99
7	I3RGB moment invariant	78.14	75.73
6	I2RGB moment invariant	77.81	75.89
10	I6RGB moment invariant	77.04	74.18
1	spot size	73.35	72.49
3	average of green plane	65.89	63.96
4	Average of blue plane	40.36	39.86
2	Average of red plane	30.48	30.83

The results obtained for different subsets of features are displayed in Table 3, ordered decreasingly by test classification performance. It can be noted that similar results are obtained if the average color features are taken into account, but the performance falls down dramatically when they are not used. The best result here was

76.17% test classification performance for a subset comprising color features (both RGB averages and variances) and spot size (and with the shape invariant moments removed). Using only the seven invariant moments, the performance is almost as poor as that of a random classification decision rule.

The results of the sequential backward feature selection, shown in Table 4, clearly confirmed that RGB color variances and invariant moments were practically useless (they were the first features removed without a significant performance degradation, indeed the test classification rate grew up to a 77.13% after the elimination of six of these variables) and that RGB color averages provided almost all the relevant information to classify the spots.

6 Conclusions and Future Work

A simple approach to object recognition in video sequences has been tested in which a feed-forward neural network is trained to classify image segmentation regions (spots) as belonging to one of the objects of interest or to the background. Hence, objects are implicitly represented as an unstructured set of spots; no adjacency graph or description of the structure of the object is used.

In order to provide labeled examples for the supervised training of the network, a semiautomatic procedure for assigning object labels (classes) to spots has been carried out based on the manual definition of graphical region-of-interest windows. However, this procedure produces some incorrectly labeled examples that affect negatively the learning of the objects and the posterior classification performance.

Spot RGB color averages and, to a less extent, spot size have been determined empirically in this work as adequate features to discriminate objects based on segmentation regions, whereas spot shape invariant moments and spot RGB color variances have been shown to be of very little help. The obtained classification results are rather good taking into account the simplicity of the approach (for instance, two very similar spots could perfectly belong to different objects) and the presence of incorrectly labeled patterns in the training and test sets caused by the semiautomatic labeling procedure.

In order to increase the classification performance, there are several actions that can be attempted. First, the labeling procedure may be improved to reduce (or even eliminate) the presence of incorrectly labeled spots. Second, some model of the structure of the object can be used in the learning and test phases; for instance, attributed graphs and random graphs with spots as nodes may be tried [2]. Third, a better image segmentation algorithm may be used, for instance, one based on the dynamic sequence of images (instead of using only single images separately) may be more robust.

In the long-term, our purpose is to design a dynamic object recognition method for video sequences by exploiting the intrinsic continuity in the object views represented by the successive images the mobile robot capture while navigating in an indoor environment.

Acknowledgements

We would like to thank the people of the Learning and Vision Mobile Robotics group led by Dr. Alberto Sanfeliu at the *Institute of Robotics and Industrial Informatics* (IRI) in Barcelona for providing us with the video sequence data and for their constant support, especially to Juan Andrade Cetto and Joan Purcallà. This work was partially funded by the Spanish CICYT project DPI 2004-05414.

References

1. Pope A. R. "Model-Based Object Recognition. A survey of recent research", University of British Columbia, Vancouver, Canada, Technical Report 94-04, January 1994.
2. Sanfeliu A., Serratosa F., Alquézar R., "Second-order random graphs for modeling sets of attributed graphs and their application to object learning and recognition", Int. Journal of Pattern Recognition and Artificial Intelligence, Vol. 18 (3), 375-396, 2004.
3. Fredembach C., Schröder M. and Süsstrunk S., "Eigenregions for image classification", IEEE Transactions on Pattern Analysis and Machine Intelligence (PAMI), Vol. 26 (12), pp. 1645-1649, 2004.
4. Singh S., Markou M., Haddon J., "Detection of new image objects in video sequences using neural networks", Proc. SPIE Vol. 3962, p. 204-213, Applications of Artificial Neural Networks in Image Processing V, Nasser M. Nasrabadi; Aggelos K. Katsaggelos; Eds., 2000.
5. Fay R., Kaufmann U., Schwenker F., Palm G., "Learning object recognition in a neurobotic system". In: Horst-Michael Groß, Klaus Debes, Hans-Joachim Böhme (Eds.) *3rd Workshop on SelfOrganization of AdaptiVE Behavior (SOAVE 2004).* Fortschritt -Berichte VDI, Reihe 10 Informatik / Kommunikation, Nr. 743, pp. 198-209, VDI Verlag, Düsseldorf, 2004.
6. Wang W., Zhang A. and Song Y., "Identification of objects from image regions", IEEE International Conference on Multimedia and Expo (ICME 2003), Baltimore, July 6-9, 2003.
7. Felzenszwalb P. and Huttenlocher D., "Efficiently computing a good segmentation". In IEEE Conference on Computer Vision and Pattern Recognition, 98-104, 1998.
8. Hu M-K., "Visual pattern recognition by moment invariants", IRE Trans. on Information Theory, Vol. 8 (2), pp. 179-187, 1962.
9. Fiesler E. and Beale R. (eds.), *Handbook of Neural Computation*, IOP Publishing Ltd and Oxford University Press, 1997.
10. Bishop C.M., *Neural Networks for Pattern Recognition*, Oxford University Press, 1995.
11. Rumelhart D.E., McClelland J.L. and the PDP Research Group (eds.), *Parallel Distributed Processing: Explorations in the Microstructure of Cognition*, MIT Press, 1986.
12. Romero E., Sopena J.M., Navarrete G., Alquézar R., "Feature selection forcing overtraining may help to improve performance", Proc. Int. Joint Conference on Neural Networks, IJCNN-2003, Portland, Oregon, Vol.3, pp.2181-2186, 2003.

Analysis of Directional Reflectance and Surface Orientation Using Fresnel Theory

Gary A. Atkinson and Edwin R. Hancock

Department of Computer Science,
University of York, York, YO10 5DD, UK
{atkinson, erh}@cs.york.ac.uk

Abstract. Polarization of light caused by reflection from dielectric surfaces has been widely studied in computer vision. This paper presents an analysis of the accuracy of a technique that has been developed to acquire surface orientation from the polarization state of diffusely reflected light. This method employs a digital camera and a rotating linear polarizer. The paper also explores the possibility of linking polarization vision with shading information by means of a computationally efficient BRDF estimation algorithm.

1 Introduction

Many attempts have been made by the computer vision community to exploit the phenomenon of the partial polarization of light caused by reflection from smooth surfaces. Existing work has demonstrated the usefulness of polarization in surface height recovery [7,6,8,1]; overcoming the surface orientation ambiguity associated with photometric stereo [3,4]; image segmentation [11]; recognition and separation of reflection components [10,11]; and distinguishing true laser stripes from inter-reflections for triangulation based laser scanning [2]. Polarization vision has been studied for both metallic and dielectric surfaces and both specular and diffuse reflection. However, little work has been carried out that assesses the accuracy of these techniques or to couple these methods with shape from shading or other intensity-based methods.

This paper is concerned with what is probably the most studied of the above applications: shape recovery. In particular, we focus on shape recovery from *diffuse* reflection from *dielectric* surfaces since this is the most commonly occurring situation. The paper uses a technique to recover surface normals from polarization that involves a linear polarizer being mounted on a digital camera and images taken as the transmission axis of the polarizer is rotated. We apply this method to objects made from a variety of materials of known shape. The surface orientation prediction based on polarization is then compared to the exact values calculated from the known geometry. The analysis reveals several unstudied features of surface polarization that help to demonstrate where current techniques of polarization vision are adequate and where its use is inappropriate or where more detailed models are required.

M. Lazo and A. Sanfeliu (Eds.): CIARP 2005, LNCS 3773, pp. 103–111, 2005.

We also use polarization to estimate the "slice" of the *bidirectional reflectance distribution function* (BRDF) corresponding to the case where the camera and light source are coincident. We do this for objects of unknown shape and compare the results to objects of the same material but known shape. This is of interest for three reasons. Firstly, it complements the accuracy analysis since, again, exact values can be deduced from the known shapes. Secondly, BRDF data may be useful for the shape recovery of surface regions that cause difficulty for polarization vision such as inter-reflections [1]. Finally, BRDF data can be used for realistic image rendering.

2 Polarization and Reflection

The Fresnel equations give the ratios of the reflected wave amplitude to the incident wave amplitude for incident light that is linearly polarized perpendicular to, or parallel to, the plane of specular incidence. These ratios depend upon the angle of incidence and the refractive index, n, of the reflecting medium. Since the incident light can always be resolved into two perpendicular components, the Fresnel equations are applicable to all incident polarization states. Indeed, throughout this work, we assume that the incident light is unpolarized.

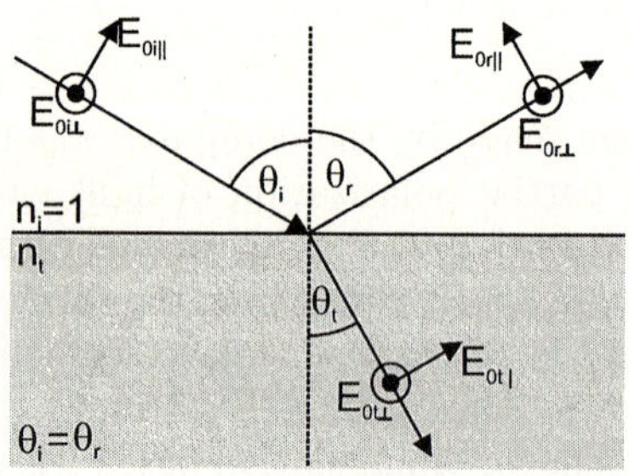

Fig. 1. Definitions. Directions of electric fields are indicated.

For the geometry of Fig. 1, the Fresnel reflection coefficients are [5]

$$r_{\perp}\left(n_i, n_t, \theta_i\right) \equiv \frac{E_{0r\perp}}{E_{0i\perp}} = \frac{n_i \cos\theta_i - n_t \cos\theta_t}{n_i \cos\theta_i + n_t \cos\theta_t} \tag{1}$$

$$r_{\parallel}\left(n_i, n_t, \theta_i\right) \equiv \frac{E_{0r\parallel}}{E_{0i\parallel}} = \frac{n_t \cos\theta_i - n_i \cos\theta_t}{n_t \cos\theta_i + n_i \cos\theta_t} \tag{2}$$

where (1) gives the reflection ratio for light polarized perpendicular to the plane of incidence and (2) is for light polarized parallel to the plane of incidence. The angle θ_t can be obtained from the well-known Snell's Law: $n_i \sin\theta_i = n_t \sin\theta_t$. Cameras do not measure the amplitude of a wave but the square of the amplitude, or *intensity*. With this in mind, it is possible to show that the *intensity coefficients*, which relate the reflected power to the incident power, are $R_\perp = r_\perp^2$ and $R_\parallel = r_\parallel^2$ [5].

Figure 2 shows the Fresnel intensity coefficients for a typical dielectric as a function of the angle of the incident light. Both reflection and transmission coefficients are shown, where the latter refers to the ratio of transmitted to incident power (the transmission coefficients are simply $T_\perp = 1 - R_\perp$ and $T_\parallel = 1 - R_\parallel$).

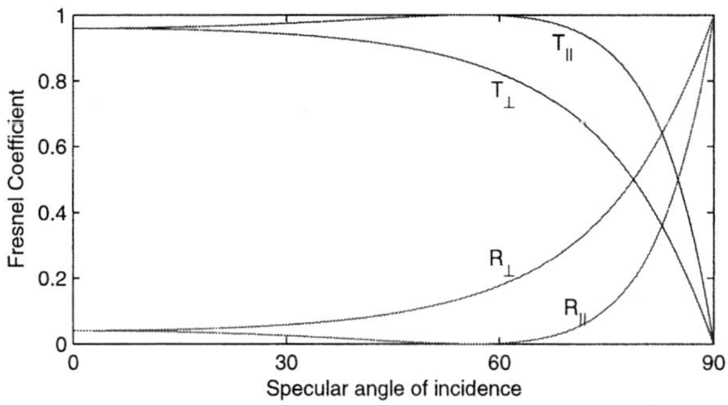

Fig. 2. Reflection and transmission coefficients for a dielectric ($n = 1.5$)

The work reported here relies on taking a succession of images of objects with a polarizer mounted on the camera at different angles. As the polarizer is rotated, the measured pixel brightness at a given point varies sinusoidally. Let $I_{\max}$ and $I_{\min}$ be the maximum and minimum intensities in this sinusoid respectively. The *degree of polarization* is defined to be

$$\rho = \frac{I_{\max} - I_{\min}}{I_{\max} + I_{\min}} \tag{3}$$

Careful consideration of Fig. 2 and the Fresnel equations leads to an expression for the degree of polarization in terms of the refractive index and the zenith angle, that is, the angle between the surface normal and the viewing direction. Unfortunately, this equation is only applicable to specular reflection since the process that causes diffuse polarization, the sole concern of this paper, is different, as explained below.

Diffuse polarization is a result of the following process [11]: A portion of the incident light penetrates the surface and is scattered internally. Due to the random nature of internal scattering, the light becomes depolarized. Some of the light is then refracted back into the air, being partially polarized in the process. Snell's Law and the Fresnel equations can be used to predict the degree of polarization of light emerging from the surface at a given angle. Figure 3 shows the Fresnel coefficients for light being refracted back into air.

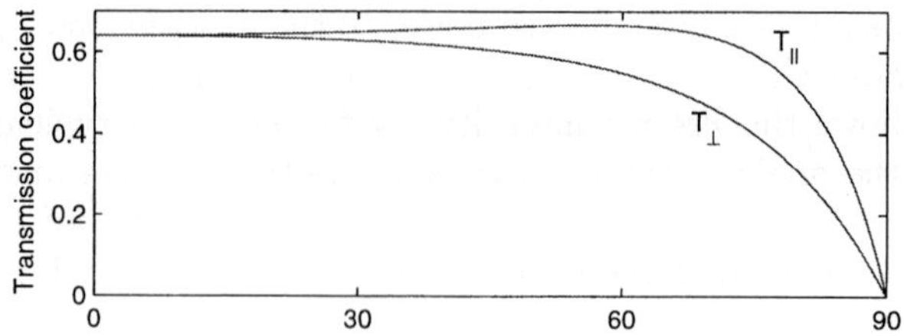

Fig. 3. Fresnel coefficients for light leaving a medium ($n = 1.5$)

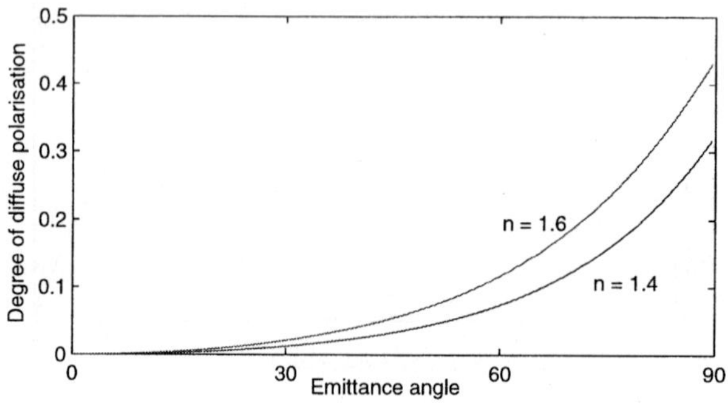

Fig. 4. Degree of polarization for diffuse reflection for two different refractive indices

Using a similar method to that used for specular polarization, an equation for the degree of polarization in terms of the zenith angle and refractive index can be derived:

$$\rho = \frac{(n - 1/n)^2 \sin^2 \theta}{2 - 2n^2 - (n + 1/n)^2 \sin^2 \theta + 4 \cos \theta \sqrt{n^2 - \sin^2 \theta}} \quad (4)$$

The dependence of the diffuse polarization ρ on the zenith angle θ is shown in Fig. 4.

The azimuth angle of the surface normal, i.e. the angle of the projection of the surface normal onto the image plane, is also intimately related to the Fresnel equations. As Fig. 3 shows, diffusely reflected light is reflected most efficiently when polarized parallel to the plane containing the surface normal and the ray reflected towards the camera. The azimuth angle therefore exactly matches the angle of the polarizer that permits greatest transmission.

3 Polarization Analysis

Equations (3) and (4) are central to the technique of recovering surface orientation from diffuse polarization. For the experiments described below, the surface normal azimuth and zenith angles were recovered using the following method: For each object, 36 images were taken with a Nikon D70 digital SLR camera, with a linear polarizer mounted on the lens, which was rotated by 5° between successive images. There was just one light source, a small but intense collimated tungsten lamp. The walls, floor and ceiling of the laboratory, as well as the table on which the objects lay, were matte black to avoid inter-reflections from the environment.

As mentioned earlier, pixel brightness varies sinusoidally with polarizer angle. A sinusoid was therefore fitted to the pixel brightnesses for each point on the images. With I_{max} and I_{min} taken from this fit, (3) and (4) were used to estimate the zenith angles. The azimuth angle of the surface was taken to match the polarizer angle that allowed greatest transmission.

To assess the accuracy of the method, a set of vertically oriented cylinders of various materials were used. The geometry of a cylinder is convenient for three reasons. First, the analysis can easily be performed for all possible zenith angles. Second, noise can be reduced by taking the average image intensity for each column of pixels. Finally, the structure is simple enough for shape recovery to be performed exactly from a single image. This is simply done by isolating the cylinder from the background and placing semicircles that arch from one side of the object to the other.

Using the method described above, we obtained a set of graphs showing the measured and theoretical zenith angles against position across the cylinder for different materials. Since the azimuth angle of the cylinder is constant, we can also see how the accuracy of azimuth angle estimates vary with zenith angle, if at all. A sample of these results for porcelain, blank photographic paper, photographic paper coated with cling film and normal paper are shown in Fig. 5. The photographic paper is much smoother than normal paper due to its coating. Several other material samples were also analysed, including different paper types, plastics, wax, terracotta and papers coated with inks. The graphs of Fig. 5 provide a good overall representation.

The first point to note about the figures is that, even for normal paper which at the fine scale is very rough, the azimuth angles have been accurately recovered. However, more noise is associated with the rougher surfaces.

There was greater variation in the accuracy of the zenith angle estimates. For Fig. 5, the refractive index used was simply the value that produced greatest similarity between theory and experiment for the material in question. The shiny white porcelain object produced excellent agreement with theory down to very small zenith angles.

The remaining graphs in Fig. 5 demonstrate the complications that can cause the measured zenith angles to deviate from the expected values. The result for blank white photographic paper, for example, is very accurate for large zenith angles but an increasing discrepancy is present as the zenith angle approaches zero. When the paper is coated in cling film, the discrepancy is less marked. Clearly, this suggests that there is a process occurring that is not accounted for by the theory. It is not considered useful to investigate this phenomenon further because the intensity may vary by just a few grey levels in such regions. Therefore, intensity quantization errors prevent extraction of useful data. The

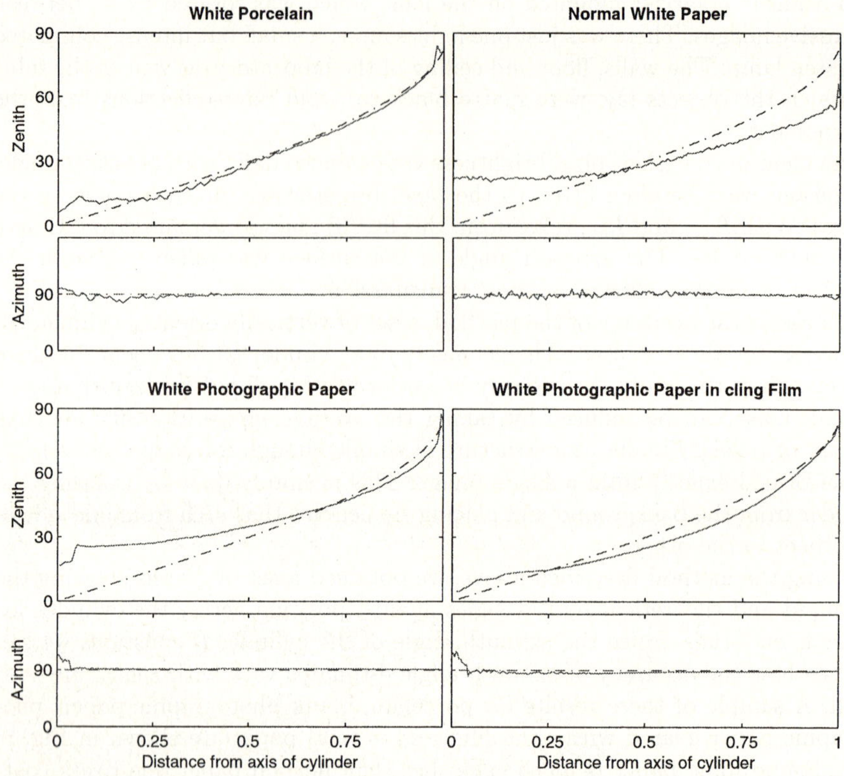

Fig. 5. Plots of measured zenith and azimuth angles (solid lines) across the surfaces of cylinders of different materials. The exact values are indicated by the broken curves.

results for paper, which of course, is a rough matte surface, also show the phenomenon of finite polarization at low zenith angles, as well as depolarizing effects of roughness nearer to the limbs.

4 Shading Analysis and BRDF Estimation

We now turn our attention to information contained within the *shading* of the images. For this analysis normal digital photographs were used (i.e. the polarizer was removed from the camera) although taking the sum of two images with the polarizer angle 90° different gives the same result (except for an overall intensity reduction due to non-ideal filters). This analysis demonstrates the relative strengths of polarization and shading analysis.

It is not our intention here to present a detailed survey of reflectance models [12] but we are interested in where shading information should be used in place of polarization. First consider the simplest reflectance model: the Lambertian

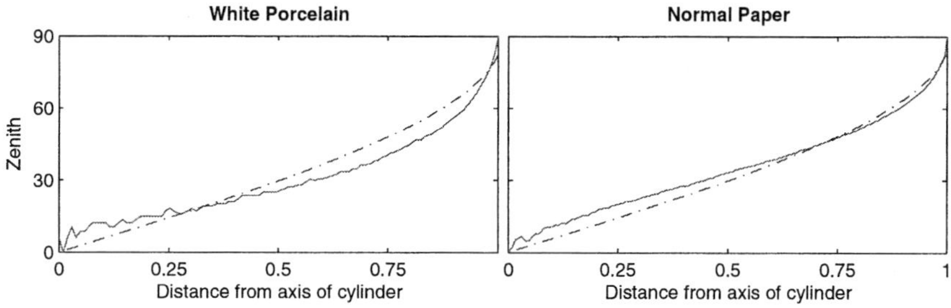

Fig. 6. Estimation of zenith angles using the Lambertian reflectance model (solid lines) compared to ground truth for two materials

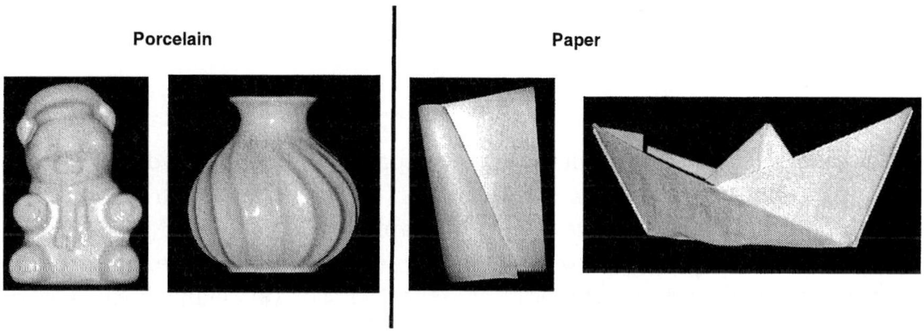

Fig. 7. Some of the objects used in BRDF estimation

approximation. Figure 6 shows the zenith angle prediction using this model for the porcelain and paper samples from Fig. 5. Polarization clearly gave much better results for porcelain, but for paper (a genuinely Lambertian surface), polarization was weaker due to roughness. Note however that the Lambertian model tells us little about the surface azimuth angle, whereas even for paper, this was accurately recovered from polarization up to a 180° ambiguity caused by the equivalence of phase angles separated by this angle.

For the final contribution of this paper, we consider the BRDF of these two very different materials. In full, the BRDF is the ratio of reflected light to incident light for all possible viewing and illumination directions. Here, we are concerned with estimating the "slice" of the BRDF where the light source and camera are coincident using a single polarization image. The method is very simple and computationally efficient and we compare the results to ground truth and to an intensity based method.

The polarization-based method simply bins the zenith angles recovered from a polarization image (here bin sizes were taken to be 1° wide) and plots intensity against zenith angle. The intensity based method uses the cumulative distribution of intensity gradients to estimate the zenith angles which then approximates the BRDF in the form of a polar function on a Gauss sphere. Details of this method can be found in [9].

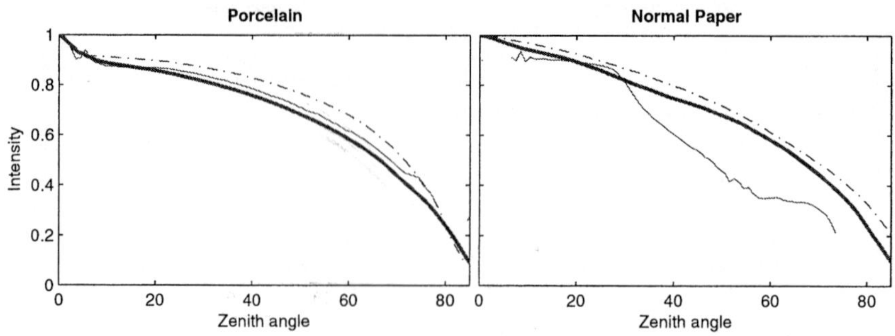

Fig. 8. Estimation of BRDF for porcelain and paper using polarization (thin solid line) and intensity (thick line) compared to the exact curve (broken line). Note the near-perfect overlap between the exact and polarization measurements for large zenith angles for porcelain.

These BRDF estimation methods were applied to objects made of porcelain and paper, some of which are shown in Fig. 7. A BRDF graph was obtained for each object. Figure 8 shows the mean graph for each material. Zenith angles above 85° are not shown due to the difficulty in obtaining reliable intensity data for these areas. Results are broadly as expected. For porcelain, both methods gave good results with polarization being more accurate. In particular, the polarization method gives almost exact results above about 70°. The random-looking curve for paper shows that BRDF estimation is highly sensitive to surface geometry for that material so intensity-based methods should clearly be used here. The BRDF can be estimated in full by repeating the experiment under many different lighting conditions and interpolating between the positions used to estimate the BRDF under arbitrary illumination conditions.

5 Conclusion

This work has presented a sensitivity study of shape from diffuse polarization for various materials. The difference in the accuracy of the method between regions of high and low zenith angles is clearly illustrated by Fig. 5, which also provides a detailed picture of the effects of roughness. Importantly, we see that the surface normal *azimuth* angles can be *accurately* determined even for moderately rough surfaces. The BRDF experiments have demonstrated very efficient methods for BRDF estimation from polarization and intensity and has applications in image rendering and combining shape from shading with polarization. The paper clearly identifies strengths and weaknesses of shape from polarization over shape from shading.

References

1. G. A. Atkinson and E. R. Hancock. Recovery of Surface Orientation from Diffuse Polarization. To appear: *Trans. Image Proc.*
2. J. Clark, E. Trucco, and L.B. Wolff. Using light polarization in laser scanning. *Image and Vision Computing*, 15:107–117, 1997.
3. O. Drbohlav and R. Šára. Unambiguous determination of shape from photometric stereo with unknown light sources. In *Proc. of ICCV*, pages 581–586, 2001.
4. O. Drbohlav and R. Šára. Specularities reduce ambiguity of uncalibrated photometric stereo. In *Proc. of ECCV*, volume 2, pages 46–62, 2002.
5. E. Hecht. *Optics*. Addison Wesley Longman, third edition, 1998.
6. D. Miyazaki, M. Kagesawa, and K. Ikeuchi. Transparent surface modelling from a pair of polarization images. *IEEE Trans. Patt. Anal. Mach. Intell.*, 26:73–82, 2004.
7. D. Miyazaki, M. Saito, Y. Sato, and K. Ikeuchi. Determining surface orientations of transparent objects based on polarization degrees in visible and infrared wavelengths. *J. Opt. Soc. Am. A*, 19:687–694, 2002.
8. S. Rahmann and N. Canterakis. Reconstruction of specular surfaces using polarization imaging. In *Proc. CVPR*, pages 149–155, 2001.
9. A. Robles-Kelly and E. R. Hancock. Estimating the surface radiance function from single images. To appear: *Graphical Models.*
10. S. Umeyama. Separation of diffuse and specular components of surface reflection by use of polarization and statistical analysis of images. *IEEE Trans. Patt. Anal. Mach. Intell*, 26:639–647, 2004.
11. L. B. Wolff and T. E. Boult. Constraining object features using a polarization reflectance model. *IEEE Trans. Pattern Anal. Mach. Intell*, 13:635–657, 1991.
12. L. B. Wolff, S. K. Nayar, and M. Oren. Improved diffuse reflection models for computer vision. *Intl. J. Computer Vision*, 30:55–71, 1998.

Lacunarity as a Texture Measure for Address Block Segmentation

Jacques Facon[1], David Menoti[1,2], and Arnaldo de Albuquerque Araújo[2]

[1] PUCPR - Pontifícia Universidade Católica do Paraná,
Grupo de Imagem e Visão - Programa de Pós-Graduação em Informática Aplicada,
Rua Imaculada Conceição, 1155, Prado Velho - 80.215-901, Curitiba-PR, Brazil
{facon, menoti}@ppgia.pucpr.br

[2] UFMG - Universidade Federal de Minas Gerais,
Grupo de Processamento Digital de Imagens - Departamento de Ciência da Computação,
Av. Antônio Carlos, 6627, Pampulha - 31.270-010, Belo Horizonte-MG, Brazil
{menoti, arnaldo}@dcc.ufmg.br

Abstract. In this paper, an approach based on lacunarity to locate address blocks in postal envelopes is proposed. After computing the lacunarity of a postal envelope image, a non-linear transformation is applied on it. A thresholding technique is then used to generate evidences. Finally, a region growing is applied to reconstruct semantic objects like stamps, postmarks, and address blocks. Very little *a priori* knowledge of the envelope images is required. By using the lacunarity for several ranges of neighbor window sizes r onto 200 postal envelope images, the proposed approach reached a success rate over than 97% on average.

1 Introduction

Postal Service processes postal envelopes through manual and automated operations. The former require an employee to read the address before sorting the mail. The latter requires that an employee simply feed mail into and remove mail from a machine that both "reads" and sorts. Due to wide variety of postal envelope attributes like layouts, colors, texture, and handwritten address block mixed up with postmarks or stamps, many mails have to be processed manually. Mail-handling is a very labor intensive process and the knowledge level required for the sorting process is quite considerable. The use of automation is the logical choice for improving productivity and reducing expenses. Mail sorting and postal automation represent an important area of application for Image Processing and Pattern Recognition techniques. The main function required in postal automation, involving Computer Vision, is definitely address reading and interpretation.

Here, we have focused our attention on segmentation of a postal envelope image into stamps, postmarks and address blocks. Other works in the literature have tackled different aspects of that problem. An address block location method is proposed in [1] for working with both machine and hand printed addresses. The method is based on dividing the input image into blocks where the homogeneity of each block gradient magnitude is measured. Heuristically given thresholds are used to decide upon the gradient magnitude of a typical address block candidate. In their tests 1600 machine

M. Lazo and A. Sanfeliu (Eds.): CIARP 2005, LNCS 3773, pp. 112–119, 2005.

printed addresses and 400 hand printed ones were used, reporting over 91% successful location. The solution appears to work fast for well-constrained envelopes, whereby a large separation exists between the image regions since they mentioned a large drawback in the figures if the envelopes have more than one stamp for example. Eiterer et al [2] present a segmentation method based on calculation of fractal dimension from 2D variation procedure and k-means clustering. The authors have also computed the influence of box size r used in each image pixel. Best values, on a 200 postal envelope database, were obtained for range $r = \{3, 9\}$, where the segmentation recovered address blocks ($97.24\% \pm 13.64\%$) with quite noise ($6.43\% \pm 6.52\%$).

The purpose of this study is to investigate the potential usefulness of lacunarity in quantifying the texture of postal envelope images to locate handwritten address blocks, postmarks and stamps, with little *a priori* knowledge of the envelope images.

The rest of this paper is organized as follows: Section 2 describes the segmentation task for postal automation and the proposed approach. Section 3 presents some experimental results, the evaluation process used and briefly a discussion. Finally, some conclusions are drawn in Section 4.

2 The Proposed Segmentation Approach for Postal Automation

The segmentation task to be performed for postal automation consists in separating the background, and locating the address block, stamps, and postmarks. Our postal envelope segmentation approach is based on evidence generation by lacunarity associated with a region-growing algorithm. The 4 main steps are (Figure 1):

- Feature Extraction: it is performed on an input image I_{in} by means of Lacunarity generating a feature image I_{FE};
- Feature Normalization: New features I_{FN} are devised by non-linear normalization from I_{FE}, in order to enhance singularities (discontinuities) between background and objects and enhance extracted features;
- Saliency Identification: it is performed from I_{FN} by a thresholding algorithm generating I_{SI}, which contains enough evidence for segmentation objects;
- Region-growing: it is applied on the evidences in I_{SI} in order to recover all remaining pixels belonging to segmentation objects of interest, yelding the final segmentation I_{out}.

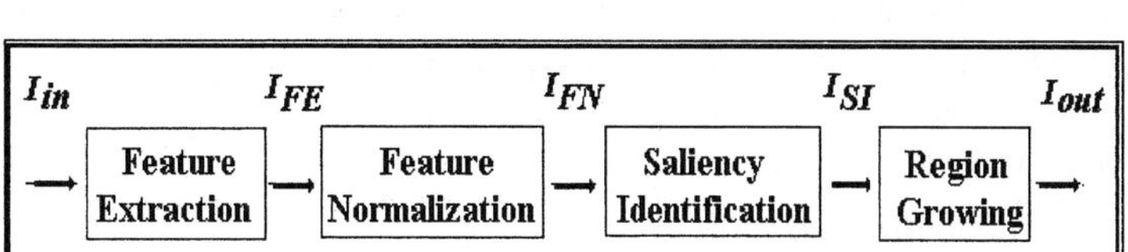

Fig. 1. Flowchart of the segmentation approach proposed

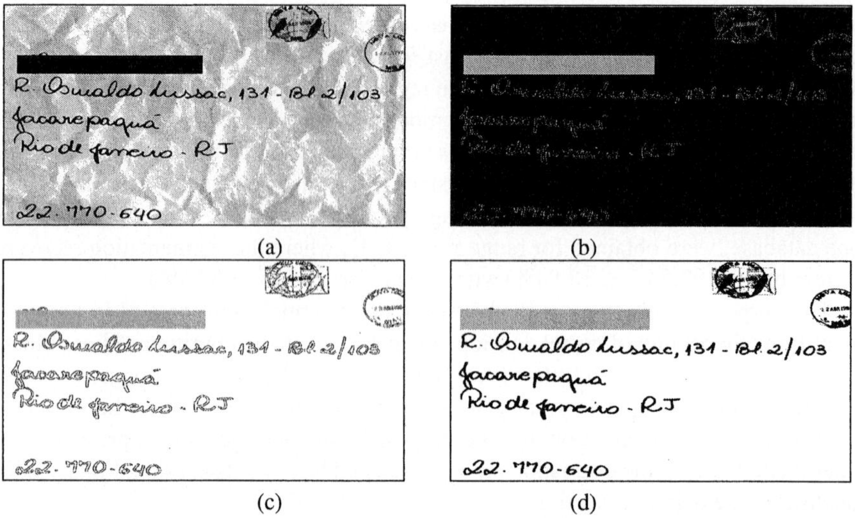

Fig. 2. Input image and outputs of the last three steps: (a) Envelope image, (b) Feature Normalization, (c) Saliency Identification, (d) Region Growing

2.1 Feature Extraction

Lacunarity is a multi-scale measure describing the distribution of gaps within a texture: the greater the range in gap size distribution, the more lacunar the data [3]. Higher lacunarity values represent a wider range of sizes of structures within an image. Lacunarity is sensitive to both the image density and its spatial configuration [4].

A number of algorithms have been proposed for measuring this property [5], [6]. The Allain 's and Cloitre 's [7] algorithm for lacunarity estimation gliding box method has been adopted. The gliding-box samples an image using overlapping square windows of length r. Lacunarity is defined in terms of the local first and second moments, measured for each neighborhood size, about every pixel in the image [4]:

$$L(r) = 1 + \frac{var(r)}{mean^2(r)} \tag{1}$$

where $mean(r)$ and $var(r)$ are the mean and variance of the pixel values, respectively, for a neighborhood size r.

Thus, lacunarity is used as evidence to distinguish between background and objects. Feature extraction (I_{FE}) is performed by using Equation 1, where $mean(r)$ and $var(r)$ will be computed for different neighborhood sizes r.

2.2 Feature Normalization

The distribution in I_{FE} is very sparse and non-uniform. How to detect the lacunarity values that can capture texture characteristic for homogeneous areas or for transition areas is the main challenge for this feature-developing task. The variations of handwritten object sizes and background illumination in image directly affect lacunarity distribution. To take into account the variation of lacunarity distributions, a non-linear normalization was used:

$$I_{FN} = \arctan\left(\frac{I_{FE}}{(k * std(I_{FE})}\right) \quad (2)$$

where $\arctan(\bullet)$ is a trigonometric and well-known non-linear function, $std(I_{FE})$ is standard deviation of I_{FE} and k is a multiplicative factor. Figure 2-(b) depicts an example where it is easy to observe the enhancement of evidences.

2.3 Saliency Identification

To separate evidences into objects and background, the Otsu 's thresholding algorithm [8] was used, producing the output I_{SI} (Figure 2-(c)).

Once features devised in the first two steps are thresholded, saliencies for segmentation objects are detected. Thus, they are working as evidences for next step to reconstruct desired objects. Figure 2-(d) depicts this step.

2.4 Region Growing

At this stage, the image I_{SI} contains the selected evidences likely to belong to either address block, stamps or postmarks. However, these evidences have to be properly used in order to select the coherent pixels for I_{SI}.

Thus, each point in I_{SI} will be selected if the gray value, i_v, of respective pixel falls inside $\lambda\%$ of image distribution (Gaussian):

$$i_v \leq I_\mu - Z_{50\%-\lambda} \times I_\sigma \quad (3)$$

where, I_μ and I_σ are the global mean and global standard deviation of image, respectively, $Z_{50\%-\lambda}$ is the normalized point for probability of $50\% - \lambda$. In fact, we suppose that objects to be recovered are the $\lambda\%$ (in Gaussian distribution) darker ones.

After verifying all points i_v indicated through I_{SI}, only ones that hold the global constrains (Equation 3) will be stored:

$$i_v \leq i_g \quad (4)$$

where, i_g is the greatest gray value of each initial saliency so far.

If a dequeued point holds Equation 4, its neighbor points will be enqueued if they hold Equation 3. The region-growing process will stop when there is no more points in queue. Figure 2-(d) shows an example of this process.

3 Experiments, Numerical Results and Discussion

A database composed of 200 complex postal envelope images, with no fixed position for the handwritten address blocks, postmarks and stamps was used. Each grayscale image, approximately 1500×2200 pixels, was digitized at 200 dpi. We could verify that the address blocks, stamps and postmarks represent only 1.5%, 4.0% and 1.0% on

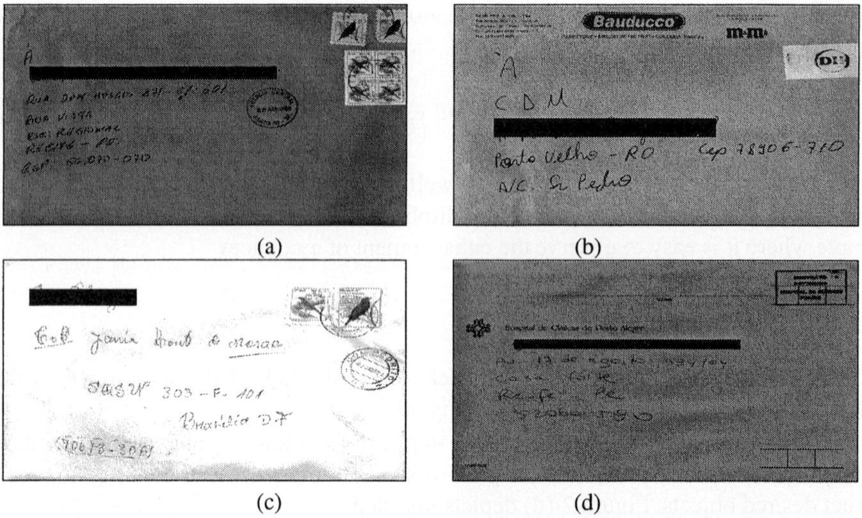

Fig. 3. Four (4) different images of postal envelopes used, as I_{in}, in the experiments

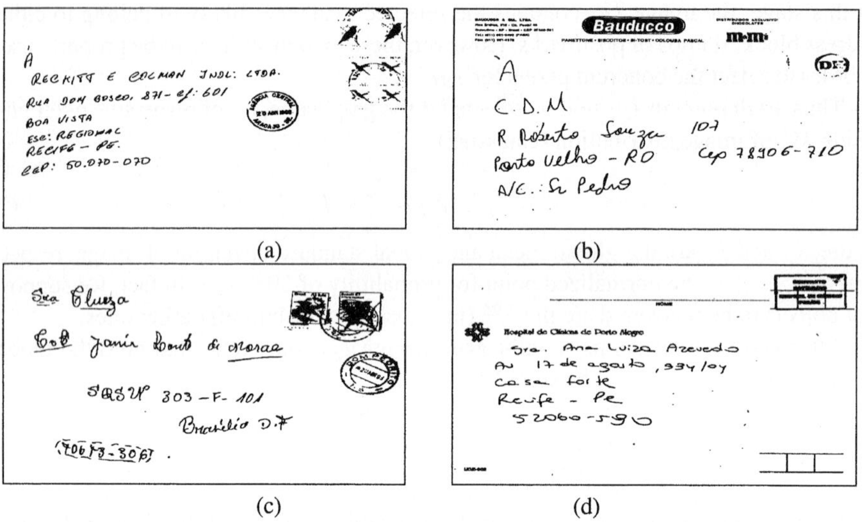

Fig. 4. Final results I_{out} obtained by our proposed approach with recovered address block, stamps and postmarks without background, for 4 different envelopes

average of the envelope area, respectively and that the great majority of pixels of these images belong to the envelope background (approximately 93.5%). Figure 3 depicts 4 envelopes issued from this database.

A ground-truth strategy was employed to evaluate the accuracy of the proposed approach. The ideal result (ground-truth segmentation) regarding each class (handwritten address block, postmarks and stamps) has been generated for each envelope image. By comparing identical pixels at the same location in the ground-truth images and segmented ones, a score of segmentation was computed.

The accuracy evaluation of the proposed method was carried out focusing the attention to address block. The tradeoff between high address block accuracy and low noise rates has been taken into account. Table 1 depicts the best results, where the lacunarity box size $r = 3$, $k = 2$, and $\lambda = 10\%$ (and $Z_{50\%-\lambda} = 1.28$).

Table 1. Best results. Average results with identification of regions (pixel by pixel accuracy) for the images tested.

Objects	Accuracy pixel by pixel ($\mu \pm \sigma$)
Address Block	$97.52\% \pm 5.72\%$
Stamp	$31.94\% \pm 15.10\%$
Postmarks	$88.07\% \pm 16.79\%$
Noise	$0.51\% \pm 0.75\%$

Independently of the layout and background in the input images (Figure 3), one can observe that the segmentation has succeeded in recovering address blocks, postmarks and stamps, and eliminating the background (Figure 4).

In order to quantify their influence in accuracy, experiments to test each step of the proposed approach have been run. Thus, we have focused our attention on automation purposes, and only address block accuracy and noise have been reported. Table 2 depicts variations in results when the box size r changes. By increasing r, the address block accuracy decreases and the noise increases. In addition, by increasing r, the approach time complexity increases, since it is $O(r^2n)$ in lacunarity feature extraction. From these experiments, one can conclude that $r = 3$ is the best box size.

Table 2. Testing Lacunarity varying box size r

	Accuracy pixel by pixel ($\mu \pm \sigma$)	
Lac	Address Block	Noise
3	$97.52\% \pm 5.72\%$	$0.51\% \pm 0.75\%$
5	$97.37\% \pm 5.95\%$	$0.52\% \pm 0.76\%$
7	$97.14\% \pm 6.42\%$	$0.52\% \pm 0.77\%$
9	$96.80\% \pm 7.10\%$	$0.53\% \pm 0.76\%$

The influence of multiplicative factor of non-linear normalization has also been tested (Table 3). No meaningful modification in accuracy has occurred. We can conclude that feature extraction and proposed non-linear normalization based on standard deviation are robust.

The influence of parameter λ has also been analyzed (Table 4). By observing the results regarding accuracy for address block and noise, one can clearly observe how λ

Table 3. Testing non-linearity factor normalization k

	Accuracy pixel by pixel ($\mu \pm \sigma$)	
factor	Address Block	Noise
0.25	$97.80\% \pm 5.35\%$	$0.80\% \pm 1.04\%$
0.5	$97.77\% \pm 5.37\%$	$0.66\% \pm 0.88\%$
1	$97.71\% \pm 5.46\%$	$0.59\% \pm 0.82\%$
2	$97.52\% \pm 5.72\%$	$0.51\% \pm 0.75\%$
3	$97.33\% \pm 5.97\%$	$0.48\% \pm 0.72\%$
4	$97.13\% \pm 6.28\%$	$0.45\% \pm 0.72\%$

parameter can affect the accuracy. Increasing (decreasing) λ increases (decreases) both address block and noise accuracies. By considering 0.51% a good noise rate on average, $\lambda = 10\%$ has been chosen.

Table 4. Testing objects image distribution, the λ parameter

	Accuracy pixel by pixel ($\mu \pm \sigma$)	
λ	Address Block	Noise
17%	$98.56\% \pm 3.71\%$	$0.87\% \pm 1.21\%$
15%	$98.34\% \pm 4.10\%$	$0.77\% \pm 1.11\%$
10%	$97.52\% \pm 5.72\%$	$0.51\% \pm 0.75\%$
5%	$94.77\% \pm 9.32\%$	$0.28\% \pm 0.45\%$
2.5%	$91.98\% \pm 12.97\%$	$0.17\% \pm 0.29\%$

These experiments have shown that the accuracy is biased only for λ parameter, which is used to apply the knowledge about database images. One can say that the Gaussian supposition works well (global constrain - Equation 3). On other hand, the value choice of the other parameters was not critical in our proposed segmentation method.

4 Conclusions

A new postal envelope segmentation method based on saliency identification from lacunarity feature was proposed. The obtained results have shown this approach very promising. The lacunarity algorithm is simple to implement, depending only on local means and variances calculated for window sizes throughout the image. There is no need to correct for noise in the image. Hence, lacunarity by itself may be sufficient to characterize postal envelope texture, address block, postmarks and stamps, resulting in a major advantage over other approaches. The time complexity ($O(n)$) of the region-growing algorithm is the same as in other approaches. But, simplicity of this approach gives a time performance gain (6 times faster), compared with [2], which performs an iterative process (k-means algorithm) and uses large box sizes for computing the fractal dimension.

Acknowledgments

We would like to acknowledge support for this research from UFMG, PUCPR, CNPq/MCT, CAPES/MEC and the Brazilian Post Office Agency (Correios Brasileiros).

References

1. Wolf, M., Niemann, H., Schmidt, W.: Fast address block location on handwritten and machine printed mail–piece images. In: ICDAR'97 IEEE International Conference on Document Analysis and Recognition, Ulm, Germany (1997) 753–757
2. Eiterer, L., Facon, J., Menoti, D.: Postal envelope address block location by fractal-based approach. SIBGRAPI/SIACG 2004, XVII Brazilian Symposium on Computer Graphics and Image Processing **1** (2004) 90–97
3. Mandelbrot, B.: The Fractal Geometry of Nature. W. H. Freeman And Company, New york (1983)
4. Henebry, G., Kux, H.: Lacunarity as a texture measure for sar imagery. International Journal of Remote Sensing **16** (1995) 565–571
5. Lin, B., Yang, Z.R.: A suggested lacunarity expression for sierpinski carpets. Journal of Physics A: Mathematical and General **19** (1986) 49–52
6. Gefen, Y., Meir, Y., Mandelbrot, B.B., Aharony, A.: Geometric implementation of hypercubic lattices with noninteger dimensionality by use of low lacunarity fractal lattices. Physical Review Letters **50** (1983) 145–148
7. Allain, C., Cloitre, M.: Characterizing the lacunarity of random and deterministic fractal sets. Physical Review A **44** (1991) 3552–3558
8. Otsu, N.: A threshold selection method from gray-level histograms. IEEE Transactions on Systems, Man and Cybernetics **9** (62-66) 1979

Measuring the Quality Evaluation for Image Segmentation

Rodrigo Janasievicz Gomes Pinheiro and Jacques Facon

PUCPR-Pontifícia Universidade Católica do Paraná,
Rua Imaculada Conceição, 1155, Prado Velho,
80215-901 Curitiba-PR, Brazil
{pinheiro, facon}@ppgia.pucpr.br

Abstract. This paper proposes a measure of quality for evaluating the performance of region-based segmentation methods. Degradation mechanisms are used to compare segmentation evaluation methods onto deteriorated ground-truth segmentation images. Experiments showed the significance of using degradation mechanisms to compare segmentation evaluation methods. Encouraging results were obtained for a selection of degradation effects.

1 Introduction

Image Segmentation is a field that deals with the analysis of the spatial content of an image. It is used to separate semantic sets (regions, textures edges) and is an important step for image understanding. The region-based segmentation consists in estimating which class each pixel of the image belongs to. Due to the fact that none of the segmentation approaches are applicable to all images, several region-based segmentation approaches have been proposed. None of the algorithms are equally suitable for a particular application. It is the reason why establish certain criteria, other than human subjective ones, to evaluate the performance evaluation of segmentation algorithms is needed. Performance evaluation is a critical step for increasing the understanding rates in image processing. This work will focus on discrepancy evaluation methods of region-based segmentation, that consist in comparing the results obtained by applying a segmentation algorithm with a reference (ground-truth) and measuring the differences (or discrepancy). Zhang [1] has proposed a discrepancy evaluation method based on mis-classified pixels. Suppose an image segmented into N pixel classes, a confusion matrix C of dimension $N \times N$ can be constructed, where each entry C_{ij} represents the pixel number of class j classified as class i by the segmentation algorithms. A first error type named "multi-class Type I error" was defined as:

$$M_I^{(k)} = 100 \times \left[\left(\sum_{i=1}^{N} C_{ik} \right) - C_{kk} \right] / \left[\sum_{i=1}^{N} C_{ik} \right] \quad (1)$$

where the numerator represents the pixel number of class k not classified as k and the denominator is the total pixel number of class k. A second error type named "multi-class Type II error" was defined as:

M. Lazo and A. Sanfeliu (Eds.): CIARP 2005, LNCS 3773, pp. 120–127, 2005.

$$M_{II}^{(k)} = 100 \times \left[\left(\sum_{i=1}^{N} C_{ki} \right) - C_{kk} \right] / \left[\left(\sum_{i=1}^{N} \sum_{j=1}^{N} C_{ij} \right) \right] \tag{2}$$

where the numerator represents the pixel number of other classes called class k. The denominator is the total pixel number of other classes.

Yasnoff et al [2] have shown that measuring the discrepancy only on the number of mis-classified pixels does not consider the pixel position error. Possible solution is to use the distance between the mis-segmented pixel and the nearest pixel that actually belongs to the mis-segmented class. Let S be the number of mis-segmented pixels for the whole image and $d(i)$ be a metric to measure the distance between the ith mis-segmented pixel and the nearest pixel that actually is of the mis-classified class. Yasnoff et al [2] have defined a discrepancy measure D based on this distance:

$$D = \sum_{i=1}^{S} d^2(i) \tag{3}$$

To exempt the influence of image size, the discrepancy measure D is normalized ND:

$$ND = 100 \times \sqrt{D} \Big/ T \tag{4}$$

where T is the total pixel number in the image.

This work will focus on proposing a new discrepancy evaluation and a strategy for measuring its performance. This paper is organized as follows: A new discrepancy evaluation method taking into account the different "scenarios" occurred in a segmentation process is detailed in Section 2. Section 3 presents some experimental results and discussions. Section 4 shows the quality evaluation of two specific address block segmentation methods. Finally, some conclusions are drawn in Section 5.

2 New Discrepancy Evaluation Method

A discrepancy evaluation method taking into account the different "scenarios" occurred in a segmentation process is proposed. Let A be a segmentation algorithm to be evaluated. Let G_i (where i = 1 to G) be the ground-truth regions of a image and S_j (where j = 1 to S) be the segmented regions obtained from algorithm A. Let n_{Gi} be the pixel number of the ground-truth region G_i, and n_{Sj} be the pixel number of the segmented region S_j. Let also $w_{ij} = n_{Gi} \cap n_{Sj}$ be the number of well-classified pixels between regions G_i e S_j. A discrepancy measure D_i is defined for each ground-truth region. G_i. To characterize the discrepancy between G_i and S_j, four classifications of region segmentation are considered:

- Correct segmentation: The ground-truth region G_i has been segmented in an unique region S_j: the discrepancy measure is $D_i = w_{ij}$. In case of total overlap, $D_i = w_{ij} = n_{Gi} = n_{Sj}$.
- Over-segmentation: The segmentation process has fragmented the ground-truth region G_i in a set of s regions S_j: the discrepancy measure is $D_i = w_{ij}/s$;

- Under-segmentation: The segmentation process has merged a set of g ground-truth region G_i in an unique region S_j: the discrepancy measure is $D_i = w_{ij}/g$;
- mis-segmentation: The ground-truth region G_i has not been segmented. The discrepancy measure in this case represents a penalty: $D_i = -n_{Gi}$;

A general metric $\Upsilon(A)$, taking into account these four "scenarios", can qualify the segmentation method A, as follows:

$$\Upsilon(A) = \frac{\sum_{i=1}^{G} D_i}{\sum_{i=1}^{G} n_{Gi}} \tag{5}$$

This metric $\Upsilon(A)$ presents some properties:

- $\Upsilon(A) = -1$ when segmentation totally failed (the A algorithm has ignored all ground-truth regions);
- $\Upsilon(A) = 0$ when the number of correct, over or under-segmented pixels matches the number of "forgotten" pixels;
- $\Upsilon(A) = 1$ when segmentation has completely succeeded;
- Metric $\Upsilon(A)$ verifies $-1 \leq \Upsilon(A) \leq 1$.

3 Comparison Strategy and Results

In order to compare different segmentation methods, two strategies can be used: the first one consists in applying the evaluation methods to segmented images obtained from different segmentation approaches. The second one consists in simulating results of segmentation processes. The latter has been adopted and a set of test images synthetically deteriorated was used. A binary image (640 × 480 pixels) that represents the ground-truth segmentation has suffered deteriorations. By this way, the aim is evaluating the resistance of segmentation methods to noise, shrinking and stretching. The degradation processes are a combination of salt noise, pepper noise and salt-pepper noise ($\{1, 5, 10, 15, 20, 25, 30, 35, 40, 45, 50\%\}$), i ($\in [1, 5]$) erosions and dilations (both with cross and square structuring elements EE. Fig 1 depicts some of these test images used during the evaluation process.

Five discrepancy criteria have been applied to a database of 90 deteriorated images (Fig 1) where image 1-(a) represents the ground-truth image: The Zhang [1] multi-class Types I and II error criteria (equations 1 and 2) , the Yasnoff et al [2] discrepancy measure ND (equation 4), the new proposed evaluation metric (equation 5), respectively named $DBMCP-Type\ I$, $DBMCP-Type\ II$, $DBSMSP$ and $\Upsilon(.)$. By modifying the ND measure, a fifth discrepancy measure , named $DBSMSP-II$, has been used, where $d(i)$ measures the distance between the ith mis-segmented pixel and the gravity center of the nearest ground-truth class.

For the aim of comparison, results are depicted in Figures 2, 3, 4. $DBMCP-Type\ I$, $DBMCP-Type\ II$, $DBSMSP$, $DBSMSP-II$ measures have been inverted and $\Upsilon(.)$ metric normalized between 0 and 1.

Fig. 1. Test images: (a) Ground-truth image, (b) Salt Pepper (50%), (c) Dilation (cross EE 1 iteration), (d) Erosion (square EE 5 iterations)

It may be observed that:

- The $DBMCP - Type\ I$, $DBSMSP$ and $DBSMSP - II$ measures are totally insensitive with respect to "holed" segmentation simulated from salt noise (Figure 2-(a). The $DBMCP - Type\ II$ measure is few sensitive. In the opposite, the new $\Upsilon(.)$ criterion is very sensitive to the "salt" effect;
- No measure is really sensitive with respect to noisy segmentation simulated from pepper noise (Figure 2-(b);
- With respect to black set expansion simulated from dilation, $DBMCP - Type\ II$ and $\Upsilon(.)$ criteria is very sensitive (Figure 3-(b));
- With respect to black set shrinking simulated from erosion, no measure (Figure 3-(a)) shows high sensibility. The $DBMCP - Type\ I$ measure is the more sensitive;
- With respect to black set expansion and salt-pepper noise, all measures (Figure 4-(a)) show low sensibility. The proposed metric $\Upsilon(.)$ is less sensitive than other ones when erosion is combined with few salt-pepper. On the other hand, with increasing salt-pepper percent, the metric $\Upsilon(.)$ decreases faster than other ones;
- With respect to bad segmentation simulated from dilation and salt-pepper noise, $DBSMSP - II$, $DBMCP - Type\ I$ and $DBSMSP$ measures are not very sensitive (Figure 4-(b)). In case of serious degradation (one EE_{cross} dilation and 50% of salt-pepper noise), these criteria do not decrease below 77%. $DBMCP - Type\ II$ criterion is a little bit more sensitive and does not decrease below 80%. The new $\Upsilon(.)$ criterion is much more robust and reliable in evaluating this kind of bad segmentation.

Salt	DBMCP Type I	DBMCP Type II	DBSMSP	DBSMSP II	Υ(.)
1%	1,00	1,00	1,00	1,00	0,98
5%	1,00	0,98	1,00	1,00	0,91
10%	1,00	0,95	1,00	1,00	0,83
15%	1,00	0,93	1,00	1,00	0,75
20%	1,00	0,91	1,00	1,00	0,67
25%	1,00	0,89	1,00	1,00	0,57
30%	1,00	0,87	1,00	1,00	0,50
35%	1,00	0,85	1,00	1,00	0,43
40%	1,00	0,84	1,00	1,00	0,28
45%	1,00	0,82	1,00	1,00	0,11
50%	1,00	0,80	1,00	1,00	0,00

(a)

Pepper	DBMCP Type I	DBMCP Type II	DBSMSP	DBSMSP II	Υ(.)
1%	1,00	1,00	0,99	0,90	1,00
5%	0,98	1,00	0,97	0,90	1,00
10%	0,95	1,00	0,96	0,89	1,00
15%	0,93	1,00	0,96	0,89	1,00
20%	0,91	1,00	0,95	0,89	1,00
25%	0,89	1,00	0,95	0,88	0,99
30%	0,87	1,00	0,94	0,88	0,99
35%	0,85	1,00	0,94	0,88	0,99
40%	0,84	1,00	0,93	0,88	0,99
45%	0,82	1,00	0,93	0,88	0,97
50%	0,80	1,00	0,93	0,88	0,95

(b)

Fig. 2. Normalised measure values for:(a) Salt noise, (b) Pepper noise

Erosion	DBMCP Type I	DBMCP Type II	DBSMSP	DBSMSP II	Υ(.)
1	0,94	1,00	0,96	0,89	1,00
2	0,88	1,00	0,94	0,89	0,95
3	0,83	1,00	0,93	0,88	0,86
4	0,78	1,00	0,92	0,88	0,84
5	0,72	1,00	0,91	0,88	0,84

(a)

Dilation	DBMCP Type I	DBMCP Type II	DBSMSP	DBSMSP II	Υ(.)
1	1,00	0,73	1,00	1,00	0,80
2	1,00	0,47	1,00	1,00	0,60
3	1,00	0,23	1,00	1,00	0,38
4	1,00	0,05	1,00	1,00	0,19
5	1,00	0,01	1,00	1,00	0,00

(b)

Fig. 3. Normalized measure values for:(a) Erosion, (b) Dilation

Salt Pepper	DBMCP Type I	DBMCP Type II	DBSMSP	DBSMSP II	Υ(.)
1%	0,94	1,00	0,96	0,89	1,00
5%	0,92	0,98	0,95	0,90	0,98
10%	0,90	0,95	0,95	0,89	0,95
15%	0,88	0,93	0,94	0,89	0,93
20%	0,86	0,91	0,94	0,89	0,90
25%	0,85	0,89	0,94	0,88	0,88
30%	0,83	0,87	0,93	0,88	0,85
35%	0,81	0,85	0,93	0,88	0,82
40%	0,80	0,84	0,93	0,88	0,81
45%	0,78	0,82	0,92	0,88	0,78
50%	0,77	0,80	0,92	0,88	0,76

Salt Pepper	DBMCP Type I	DBMCP Type II	DBSMSP	DBSMSP II	Υ(.)
1%	1,00	0,72	0,99	0,90	0,73
5%	0,98	0,72	0,97	0,90	0,68
10%	0,95	0,70	0,96	0,89	0,65
15%	0,93	0,70	0,96	0,89	0,63
20%	0,91	0,79	0,95	0,89	0,60
25%	0,89	0,68	0,95	0,88	0,53
30%	0,87	0,67	0,94	0,88	0,50
35%	0,85	0,66	0,94	0,88	0,50
40%	0,84	0,65	0,93	0,88	0,44
45%	0,82	0,65	0,93	0,88	0,43
50%	0,80	0,64	0,93	0,88	0,37

Fig. 4. Normalized measure values with salt-pepper noise for: (a) Erosion, (b) Dilation

4 Real Application and Discussion

In order to test the accuracy of quality evaluation in real segmentation, the five discrepancy criteria were applied on two published approaches for postal envelopes; the first one based on feature selection in wavelet space [3] and the second one based on fractal dimension [4]. In both approaches, the same database composed of 200 complex postal envelope images, with no fixed position for the handwritten address blocks, postmarks and stamps was used. The authors have also employed a ground-truth strategy where the accuracy was computed by only taking in account the identical pixels at the same location.

According to [3], the wavelet-based segmentation rates are 97.36% for address block, 26.96% for stamps and 75.88% for postmarks. According to [4], the fractal-based approach rates are 97.24% for address block, 66.34% for stamps and 91.89% for postmarks.

By applying the five discrepancy criteria to [3] 's and [4] 's segmentation results, without separating the address block, stamp and postmark classes, we obtained the quality evaluation rates grouped in Table 1. This Table depicts that $DBMCP - Type\ I$ and $DBSMSP$ and $DBSMSP - II$ measures have the same sensibility than [3] 's and [4] 's address block evaluation. This fact means that these 3 measures were not able to accurately evaluate the results of real segmentation. The 3 measures have not evaluated that the stamp and postmark segmentation was worse than the address block one.

Table 1. Quality evaluation comparison for the database

Method	DBNMSP Type I	DBNMSP Type II	DBSMSP	DBSMSP II	$\Upsilon(.)$
Wavelet	0,993	0,645	0,996	0,983	0,404
Fractal	0,917	0,872	0,982	0,967	0,378

Table 2. Quality evaluation comparison for only images No 1 and No 2

Image	DBNMSP Type I	DBNMSP Type II	DBSMSP	DBSMSP II	$\Upsilon(.)$
No 1	0,999	0,303	0,999	0,983	0,192
No 2	0,995	0,999	0,997	0,993	0,975

$DBMCP{-}Type\ II$ measure has shown be more sensitive than the three first ones. The new $\Upsilon(.)$ criterion has shown be much more severe than other ones. This is due to the fact that $\Upsilon(.)$ criterion took in account all the classes. And one can observe that the rates are low because the stamp segmentation was inefficient. The defects occurred in stamp segmentation are similar to bad segmentation simulated from dilation or dilation and salt-pepper noise described in section 3. Figure 5 depicts the segmentation of two postal envelopes, the first one (Figure 5-(a), (b) and (c)) with stamps and the second

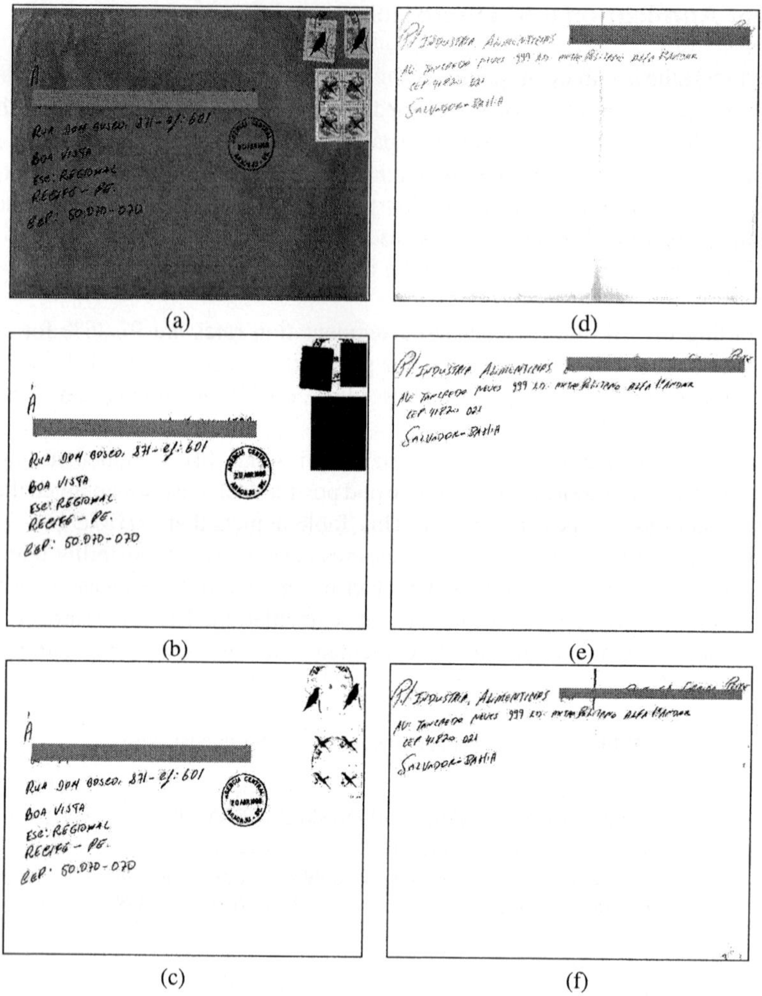

Fig. 5. Examples of address block segmentation: (a) Original image No 1, (b) Ground-truth image, (c) Segmentation Result, (d) Original image No 2, (e) Ground-truth image, (f) Segmentation Result

one (Figure 5-(d), (e) and (f)) without stamp neither postmark. Table 2 shows the five discrepancy criteria segmentation rates for the two above images. One can observe that, for Figure 5-(a) where the stamp segmentation was inefficient, whereas $DBMCP - Type\ I$ and $DBSMSP$ and $DBSMSP - II$ rates are high, $DBMCP - Type\ II$ and $\Upsilon(.)$ rates are low. For Figure 5-(d) without stamp neither postmark, the address block segmentation was efficient and $DBMCP - Type\ II$ and $\Upsilon(.)$ rates are very high. Due to noise occurred in address block segmentation, $\Upsilon(.)$ rate is lower than $DBMCP - Type\ II$ one. This point shows that the $\Upsilon(.)$ measure is more able to take in account different segmentation scenarios than other criteria.

5 Conclusions

A new discrepancy evaluation criterion considering different "scenarios" occurred in a segmentation process have been proposed. The new measure has been compared to traditional discrepancy evaluation criteria. A strategy for evaluating the new measure and other ones in the context of region-based segmentation was used. By applying the discrepancy criteria onto a test database of degradated images, the new discrepancy evaluation criterion has shown to be more sensitive than other ones.

By applying the discrepancy criteria in real segmentation onto wavelet based-segmentation and fractal based-segmentation methods for postal envelope segmentation, experiments have shown that the new measure is more severe than other ones and is able to take in account different segmentation scenarios.

As explained before, evaluation is a critical step. And this study has shown that it is possible to evaluate different segmentation "scenarios". In spite of its simplicity, the new measure was shown to be appropriated in the segmentation evaluation challenge. Another advantage is that, in opposite to the study of [5], that excludes bad segmentation, there is no restriction in applying our evaluation approach.

References

1. Zhang, Y.: A survey on evaluation methods for image segmentation. Pattern Recognition **29** (1996) 1335–1346
2. Yasnoff, W., Mui, J.K., Bacus, J.W.: Error measures for scene segmentation. Pattern Recognition **9** (1977) 217–231
3. Menoti, D., Facon, J., Borges, D.L., A.Souza: Segmentation of postal envelopes for address block location: an approach based on feature selection in wavelet space. ICDAR 2003 - 7th InternationalConference on Document Analysis and Recognition **2** (2003) 699–703
4. Eiterer, L.F., Facon, J., Menoti, D.: Fractal-based approach for segmentation of address block in postal envelopes. 9TH Iberoamerican Congress on Pattern Recognition LNCS Lecture Notes in Computer Science **1** (2004) 454–461
5. Roldán, R.R., Lopera, J.F.G., Allah, C.A., Aroza, J.M., Escamilla, P.L.L.: A measure of quality for evaluating methods of segmentation and edge detection. Pattern Recognition **34** (2001) 969–980

Frame Deformation Energy Matching of On-Line Handwritten Characters

Jakob Sternby

Centre for Mathematical Sciences,
Sölvegatan 18, Box 118,
S-221 00, Lund, Sweden
jakob@maths.lth.se

Abstract. The coarse to fine search methodology is frequently applied to a wide variety of problems in computer vision. In this paper it is shown that this strategy can be used to enhance the recognition of on-line handwritten characters. Some explicit knowledge about the structure of a handwritten character can be obtained through a structural parameterization. The Frame Deformation Energy matching (FDE) method is a method optimized to include such knowledge in the discrimination process. This paper presents a novel parameterization strategy, the Djikstra Curve Maximization (DCM) method, for the segments of the structural frame. Since this method distributes points unevenly on each segment, point-to-point matching strategies are not suitable. A new distance measure for these segment-to-segment comparisons have been developed. Experiments have been conducted with various settings for the new FDE on a large data set both with a single model matching scheme and with a kNN type template matching scheme. The results reveal that the FDE even in an ad hoc implementation is a robust matching method with recognition results well comparing to the existing state-of-the-art methods.

1 Introduction

Explicit usage of the structural information inherent to handwritten characters is highly uncommon in state-of-the-art recognition methods today. The tantalizing idea of automatic optimization of all kinds of features by means of statistical methods such as Neural Networks (NN) and/or Hidden Markov Models (HMM) seems to have caused researchers to abandon the more straightforward discrimination methods based on template matching [10]. The most successful of the template matching methods, which still seems to have some followers [13], is the Dynamic Time Warping (DTW) method which improves on static matching by enabling a dynamic match between different dimensions. Under equal training circumstances Hidden Markov Models seems to provide a higher hitrate than DTW [3]. It is probable that HMM can be somewhat less sensitive to the non-linearity of the variations of handwritten data since it models smaller segments of each character with hidden states based on features [6]. However, the Markov characteristic of such systems may also make it difficult to construct features that

M. Lazo and A. Sanfeliu (Eds.): CIARP 2005, LNCS 3773, pp. 128–137, 2005.

can discriminate between some models that have similar sets of hidden states but of varying durations [1]. Recently Bahlmann et al. [2] have shown how DTW and HMM relate to each other.

This paper presents considerable enhancements to the new template matching method called Frame Deformation Energy (FDE) matching. The method is based on a structural parameterization obtained by extracting a structurally defined subset of points called *core points* in two stages. A outer *core point frame* is obtained as the set of local extreme points in the direction orthogonal to the writing direction and then a fixed number of points is added to each such segment. This paper introduces a new method, here called the Djikstra Curve Maximization (DCM) method to extract the fixed number of points on each segment of the core point frame. Previously the extraction of such sets of *interesting* points have been performed mainly for segmentation of cursive script [9, 11]. It has previously been shown that a structural parameterization enhances the recognition performance for Euclidean matching. In this paper, implementation of a new curve segment matching strategy developed for the DCM parameterization method produces the highest recognition results obtained for the FDE strategy so far. In particular the method seems robust and delivers very reliable results for top two candidates.

2 Structural Reparameterization with Core Points

In the field of handwriting recognition (HWR) most of the techniques for extracting the most *interesting* points on a curve have been developed for segmentation of cursive script [8]. It has previously been shown that this strategy can be used also to decompose isolated characters into smaller segments of simple curves. The achievement of such a decomposition is that it enables a description of the non-linear variations of handwritten data into smaller less non-linear parts. In this paper a very simple yet effective method of dividing samples into segments has been studied. The extreme points in the direction orthogonal to the writing direction (normally y) define a subset here called the **core point frame**. Once such a method for fixing this greater structure of segments has been chosen, the problem of fixing a parameterization for the intermittent points can be addressed. Independently of the method chosen for accomplishing this the new parameterization of a core point frame with intermittent points, will be called the *core points* $C(X)$ of a sample X.

2.1 Choosing a Fixed Number of Intermittent Points

The most basic approach for picking middle points is to sample each segment in the core point frame by arclength. The weakness of this method is that segments may require a varied number of points in order to be described correctly. Of course one can choose to pick many points but this also effects the time complexity. This rudimentary method is here referred to as the *Segment Arclength* (SA) method. Aiming at enabling an upper bound for the required number of points on each segment, methods that try to approximate the segment by a few number of points have also been investigated below. For handwritten characters a study of the various allographs of the script reveals that there is a maximum of significant points on the segments. For the Latin-1 character set it has been empirically observed that this number is three on any individual segment. For this reason a fixed number of three points have been placed on each segment for both methods of choosing points described below.

Since each segment of the core point frame should be described as well as possible a method that chooses the most *interesting* points on this curve segment is needed. As stated previously such methods have been used in the past for cursive script segmentation [8]. A method inspired by these ideas have been tried and will be referred to as the *Curvature* (C) method. Instead of just spacing the points evenly on the segment as one would if one were to use conventional arclength parameterization, a search for points that have a significant curvature is performed first. This search is done recursively by picking any point with a diversion from the line between the start and end point that exceeds a threshold. If the number of curvature points chosen in this manner is less than the fixed number of points per segment, points are added in a manner that spaces them as evenly as possible.

Choosing the n points on a piece of a curve that *best* approximates it is a problem that has been thoroughly studied in the field of discrete geometry [5]. There it is common to refer to the best approximation the so called min-ϵ solution in terms of the uniform metric i.e. the n points on the (discrete) curve $X = \{x_i\}_{i=0}^{m}$ resulting in the smallest maximum distance between the removed points and the resulting piecewise linear curve.

Below we present a fundamentally different approach for finding an approximation of an m-polygon with n points. With a Euclidean metric the subset that maximizes the linear segment function is:

$$(x_{p_1}, \ldots, x_{p_n}) = \underset{(p_1,\ldots,p_n)\subset(1,\ldots,m)}{\operatorname{argmax}} \sum_{i=1}^{n} \|x_{p_j} - x_{p_{j-1}}\|. \quad (1)$$

We call the method of finding $(x_{p_1}, \ldots, x_{p_n})$ on a m-polygon according to (1), the *Djikstra Curve Maximization* (DCM) method since the set can be found by means of a modified version of the Djikstras algorithm. This is a clear strategy with the appealing characteristic that it is independent of threshold values and other tuning parameters indispensable for the C-method described above.

One can easily show that the DCM and the min-ϵ curve approximations are similar under some circumstances. One equally easily realizes that there are many cases when they differ. One interesting example are the respective solutions of the min-ϵ approach and the DCM to picking one point on a sinus curve on the interval $[0, 2\pi]$. Here the DCM has two optimal solutions lying close to the respective extreme points, whereas the min-ϵ approach will choose the middle point. In particular one easily observes that their behavior differ greatly when the number n is less than the number of local extreme points on the curve. The DCM gets many solutions in this case, all aiming at choosing one of the prominent features of the curve whereas the min-ϵ solution gives the mean path.

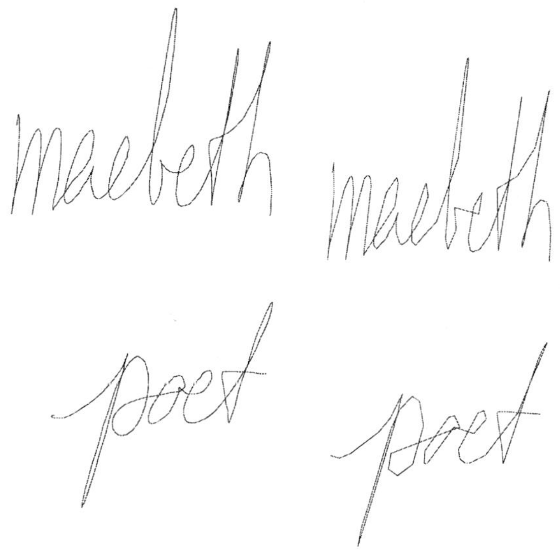

Fig. 1. Two cursive words with the original sampling to the left and the core point reparameterized words to the right. Here the DCM technique of Section 2.1 is used to find the intermittent points in the core point frame.

Examples of the extracting core points with DCM on some connected character sequences are shown in Figure 1. Apparently the DCM provides a nice and smooth curve.

3 The Frame Deformation Energy Model

One of the limitations of template matching techniques such as DTW lies in the fact that the normalization is global. Even though DTW is successful at enabling matching between samples of varying dimension it is still dependent on normalization and thereby also sensitive to non-linear variations. In other words a handwritten sample X is in general not only the result of global transformation of the reference template but also of individual transformations of each segment of the core point frame.

These facts motivate the search for a method that tries to find both the local segment transformations as well as calculate the resulting distance to the transformed segments. In short the matching process of a sample $X = \{x_i\}$ to a template (prototype) $P = \{p_i\}$ can be divided into three stages:

1. Find the best global linear transformation $\mathrm{A}_P = \mathrm{argmin}_{\mathrm{L}} \|P - \mathrm{L}X\|$
2. Find the frame bending transformation $\mathrm{B}_P, p_i = \mathrm{B}_P(x_i)$, $\forall x_i, pi$ in their respective core point frames
3. Calculate a distance value dependent on the transformations A_P, B_P and the remaining difference $P - \mathrm{B}_P(\mathrm{A}_P(X))$

Analysis of samples of on-line handwritten characters clearly show that in-class global transformations of handwritten characters are constrained linear transformations. There are no reflections and only limited rotation and skew. The frame bending transformations are defined as the transformations identifying the corresponding core point frames.

3.1 Distance Calculation

A popular method to achieve exact transformations between templates in pattern recognition is thin-plate splines. Although there have been successful applications of thin-plate splines to the character recognition problem in the past [4] it has obvious shortcomings. The main problem is that common variations in handwritten patterns involves points on the extension of a line being distributed on either side of the line causing folding of the thin-plate spline. To counter this problem a much simpler energy model for the frame is introduced. Let each segment be modelled by a robust spring that is equally sensitive to compression and prolongation and let the connection between each segment be a coiled spring that is equally sensitive to torque in both directions. The most simple distance measure for the bending energy of the frame between a sample X and a template P of m core points, with frames $F_X = (f_X(1), \ldots, f_X(n))$ to $F_P = (f_P(1), \ldots, f_P(n))$ is then given by

$$E_{\mathrm{B}}(X, P) = \sum_{i=2}^{n-1} k_x\left(\frac{\|f_X(i+1) - f_X(i)\|}{\|f_X(i) - f_X(i-1)\|} - \frac{\|f_P(i+1) - f_P(i)\|}{\|f_P(i) - f_P(i-1)\|}\right)^2 + \sum_{i=2}^{n-1} k_a\left(\frac{\theta_i^{F_X} - \theta_i^{F_P}}{\pi}\right)^2, \quad (2)$$

where k_x, k_a are the spring constants for the segment springs and the inter-segment springs respectively. The intermittent frame segment angles $\theta_i^{F_X}$ are defined as $\theta_i^{F_X} = \arg(f_X(i+1) - f_X(i), f_X(i) - f_X(i-1))$. For notational convenience a modula π for the angle retrieved with the arg operator is implied. As described in the previous section the result of the bent frame $\mathrm{B}_{F_P}(F_X)$ is that $\|\mathrm{B}_{F_P}(F_X) - F_P\| = 0$, however, the intermittent points are just Bookstein coordinates in their respective surrounding segment and will generally not be identical. To model their distance, the different models for selecting the intermittent points presented in Section 2.1, have been evaluated with various distance measures.

Distance Measures for Intermittent Core Points. From an implementation point of view the most simple way to model the energy of transforming points from one curve to the other is to to find a model that corresponds to the Euclidean measure. This is achieved by imagining that each of the intermittent points are attached to the corresponding point in the sample being matched by elastic strings. This induces an energy measure for the intermittent points after matching the frame

$$E_M^{\mathrm{Euc}}(\mathrm{B}_P(\mathrm{A}_P(X)), P) = \sum_{j=1}^{m} k_j \|\mathrm{B}_P(\mathrm{A}_P(x_j)) - p_j\|^2, \quad (3)$$

where k_j is the spring constant for the string attached to core point j in P. Evidently setting $k_j = 1, j = 1, \ldots, m$ gives the square Euclidean distance of the bent frame transformed sample $\|\mathrm{B}_P(\mathrm{A}_P(X)) - P\|^2$. This should only be suitable when there is a strong correspondence between points on the segments so it should not be used with selection methods that distributes points unevenly such as the DCM. Even though most of the parameterizational differences should have been depleted by the core point reparameterization one could also try a DTW measure on the intermittent points. However this has not been tested in this paper.

The DCM method presented in Section 2.1 is not suitable to use with either of these measures since points may be distributed anywhere on the curve segment. Instead some kind of curve comparison measure that is independent of the parameterization is needed. To accomplish a new distance function the *Djikstra Curve* distance E_M^{DC}, consisting of two individual components is proposed. The first component is a Point-to-curve distance function $d_{PC}(X, P)$, used for matching the intermittent core points of one curve to some line segment in the other curve. It is a DTW method with transitions $(1,0), (1,1)$ solving the problem of finding the correspondence function $\Phi(k) = (\phi_x(k), \phi_{\boldsymbol{p}}(k)), k = 1, \ldots, m$ that optimizes

$$d_{PC}(X, P) = \min_{\Phi} \sum_{i=1}^{m} \mathfrak{g}_{PL}(x_{\phi_x(i)}, \boldsymbol{p}_{\phi_{\boldsymbol{p}}(i)}), \tag{4}$$

where $\Phi(1) = (1, k_1), \Phi(m) = (m, k_m), k_i \leq k_{i+1}, \forall i \in (1, \ldots, m)$. Here $\mathfrak{g}_{PL}(x_k, \boldsymbol{p}_j)$ denotes the distance between point x_k and the line segment $\boldsymbol{p}_j = (p_{j-1}, p_j)$. Let l_j be the line passing through line segment $\boldsymbol{p}_j$ and let $x_{l_j}^{\perp}$ be the orthogonal projection of point x onto l_j, then

$$\mathfrak{g}_{PL}(x_k, \boldsymbol{p}_j) = \begin{cases} \min(\|x_k - p_{j-1}\|, \|x_k - p_j\|), & \text{if } x_{(l_j,k)}^{\perp} \notin \boldsymbol{p}_j, \\ \|x_k - x_{(l_j,k)}^{\perp}\|, & \text{otherwise}. \end{cases} \tag{5}$$

The d_{PC} distance function from (4) is found through the following recursive algorithm

Algorithm 1.
$D_j(1) := \mathfrak{g}_{PL}(1, j), j = 1, \ldots, m+1$
for $j = 1, \ldots, m+1$ ***do***
    for $k = 2, \ldots, m$ ***do***
        $D_j(k) := \mathfrak{g}_{PL}(k, j) + \min(D_{j-1}(k-1), D_j(k-1))$
    end for
end for
$d_{PC} := \mathrm{argmin}_j\, D_j(m)$

The second is a fuzzy DTW distance function computing a distance between the angles of consecutive core points. Denote the normalized angles of consecutive points in X and P by $\{\theta_i^X\}_{i=1}^m$ and $\{\theta_i^P\}_{i=1}^m$ respectively then the angular distance function corresponding to (5) is defined as

$$\mathfrak{g}_A(x_i, p_j) = (\kappa_\theta(\theta_i^X - \theta_j^P)/\pi)^2 + (\kappa_\lambda(\lambda_i^X - \lambda_j^P))^2, \tag{6}$$

where $\lambda_i^X = \frac{(x_i - x_1)^T (x_m - x_1)}{\|x_m - x_1\|}$ is the location of each angle in terms of the baseline. It has been found that results are improved if a certain fuzziness is added to the angular distance function. To enable this the definition of $\mathfrak{g}_A$ in (6) is extended to treat matching the angle on one curve segment to a flat segment on the other defined as a parameter $t \in [0, 1]$ between two points as

$$\mathfrak{g}_A(x_i, p_j + t) = (\kappa_\theta(\theta_i^X - \pi)/\pi)^2 + (\kappa_\lambda(\lambda_i^X - ((1-t)\lambda_j^P - t\lambda_{j+1}^P))^2. \quad (7)$$

The recursive update rule for the algorithm finding the best DTW distance corresponding to the inner statement of Algorithm 1 in this case becomes

$$D_j^A(k) = \min \begin{cases} \mathfrak{g}_A(x_j, p_k) + D_{j-1}^A(k) \\ 2\mathfrak{g}_A(x_j, p_k) + D_{j-1}^A(k-1) \\ \mathfrak{g}_A(x_j, p_k) + D_j^A(k-1) \\ 2\mathfrak{g}_A(x_j, p_k) + \min_{r \in (1,\ldots,j-1)} D_{j-r}^A(k-1) + \\ \qquad \sum_{i=1}^r \mathfrak{g}_A(x_{j-r+i}, p_{k-1} + i/(r+1)) \\ 2\mathfrak{g}_A(x_j, p_k) + \min_{r \in (1,\ldots,j-1)} D_{j-1}^A(k-r) + \\ \qquad \sum_{i=1}^r \mathfrak{g}_A(x_{j-1} + i/(r+1), p_{k-r+i}) \end{cases} \quad (8)$$

According to (8) the total angular distance will be $d_A(X, P) = D_m^A(m)$. Now the *Djikstra Curve* distance E_M^{DC} can be written as

$$E_M^{DC} = d_{PC}(X, P) + d_{PC}(P, X) + d_A(X, P). \quad (9)$$

The Frame Deformation Energy Distance (FDE). Above we have described methods to account for the two steps of frame bending and curve segment comparison. It is not entirely obvious how to fit a suitable penalization of global transformations into this. On one hand global transformations are natural variations of isolated handwritten character data and on the other some kind of penalization is necessary since the energy $E_{\mathrm{B}}(X, P)$ of (2) is invariant to global rotation. One could try global transformations of rotation and of the triple scale, rotation and skew. For these parameters of scale (λ_x, λ_y), rotation θ and skew η one can define a distance function similar to that of the bending energy by setting

$$E_{RSS}(X, P) = k_\lambda((\frac{\lambda_x}{\lambda_y})^{t_\lambda} - 1)^2 + k_\theta(\frac{\bmod(\theta, \pi)}{\pi})^2 + k_\eta(\frac{\bmod(\eta, \pi)}{\pi})^2, \quad (10)$$

where t_λ is 1 $\lambda_x < \lambda_y$ and -1 otherwise. However in the experiments of this paper only the rotational component in (10) denoted by $E_R(X, P)$ has been used.

Combining the distance components for global transformation, bending energy and curve segment into a weighted sum produces the following distance functions:

$$D_R^{method}(X, P) = w_{\mathrm{A}} E_R(X, P) + w_{BE} E_{\mathrm{B}}(\mathrm{A}(X), P) + w_M E_M^{method}(\mathrm{A}(\mathrm{B}(X)), P) \quad (11)$$

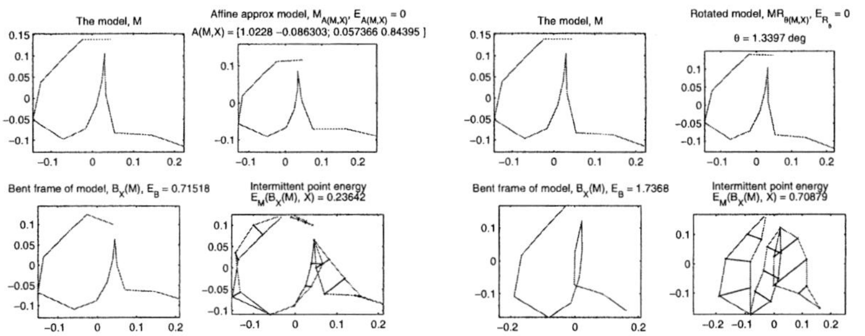

Fig. 2. One in-class and one inter-class example of a mean model matched to a sample according to the scheme of Section 3

Matching with the distance function in (11) will be referred to as Frame Deformation Energy Matching (FDE). The optimization problem of finding the optimal set of parameters $\{w\}, \{k\}$ could probably be solved by some Support Vector Machine inspired method but it is interesting enough to receive full attention in a separate paper.

4 Experiments

The recognition experiments in this paper have been conducted on the MIT single character database [7]. The set of 37161 samples from the w section (single characters from words) was selected as test set while the 2825 samples from the l section was selected as the training set.

For single models the new version of the template matching method FDE was compared to DTW as well as a Gaussian Active Shape Model (AS) such as it is described in thesis [12]. For the FDE and DTW methods a single model was constructed for each allograph as the mean of the samples belonging to that allograph class. For AS one model was built for each allograph class. The FDE was implemented with the D_R^{DC} measure in the most simple way by manually setting all the spring constants in (2), (3) as well as all of the weights in (11) to suitable values. Even with this simple ad hoc setting the results of template matching

Table 1. Results of k-NN matching on the MIT database. The different methods for selecting intermittent points are shown as CP-C (Curvature) and CP-DCM (Djikstra Curve Maximization). Where available the recognition result for best-two candidates is also displayed to the right.

k-Distance Measure	Arclength	CP-C	CP-DCM
1-Euclidean	86.3%	89.6 / 91.0 %	-
1-DTW	91,3%	89,5 %	-
1-D_{AFE}^{DC}	-	-	88.2 / **94.7 %**

Table 2. Results of single model matching on the MIT database

Method	Original data	CP-DCM
AS	77.2 %	82.4 %
DTW-mean	**89.6 / 90.7 %**	-
D_R^{DC}-mean	-	82.4 / 90.3 %

with single models performs as well as DTW on the original parameterization for top-two candidates Table 2 making it a promising method well worth further research. Especially since the results of the top two candidates when running the same FDE method on multiple models for each class as seen in Table 1. Although only two methods have been tried for second candidates in the 1-NN matching the significant increase in recognition accuracy for the FDE method is indicates a strong potential for improvement even at the single-model stage.

5 Discussion and Conclusions

This paper presents a new parameterization an distance measure for use with the novel Frame Deformation Energy (FDE) matching method. The main objective of the new method is to try to address the weak points of a global matching schemes by dividing the matching process of a handwritten character into natural segments called a core point frame. It has been shown that the new strategy provides a robust matching method with results comparable to state-of-the-art template matching methods such as DTW for top two candidates even in an ad hoc implementation of manually setting the spring constants of the energy model.

Further research will include automatic methods for optimizing spring constants for different allographs as well as hybrid methods for a final optimal recognition rate. It might be even more efficient to view the problem in a probabilistic way by determining the class C with a model M_C that has the highest probability $P(C|\mathrm{A}_X, \mathrm{B}_X, \mathrm{B}_X(\mathrm{A}_X(M_C)) - X)$. Since the novel FDE technique already at this early stage has shown a promising capacity for computationally efficient single models it will be especially useful in on-line cursive script systems based on segmentation graphs.

References

1. J. Andersson. Hidden markov model based handwriting recognition. Master's thesis, Dept. of Mathematics, Lund Institute of Technology, Sweden, 2002.
2. C. Bahlmann and H. Burkhardt. The writer independent online handwriting recognition system *frog on hand* and cluster generative statistical dynamic time warping. *IEEE Trans. Pattern Analysis and Machine Intelligence*, 26(3):299–310, March 2004.
3. E. J. Bellegarda, J. R. Bellegarda, D. Nahamoo, and K. Nathan. A fast statistical mixture algorithm for on-line handwriting recognition. *IEEE Trans. Pattern Analysis and Machine Intelligence*, 16(12):1227–1233, 1994.

4. S. Belongie, J. Malik, and J. Puzicha. Shape matching and object recognition using shape contexts. *IEEE Trans. Pattern Analysis and Machine Intelligence*, 24(24):509–522, 2002.
5. M. T. Goodrich. Efficient piecewise-linear function approximation using the uniform metric: (preliminary version). In *SCG '94: Proceedings of the tenth annual symposium on Computational geometry*, pages 322–331, New York, NY, USA, 1994. ACM Press.
6. J. Hu, S.G. Lim, and M. K. Brown. Writer independent on-line handwriting recognition using an hmm approach. *Pattern Recognition*, (33):133–147, 2000.
7. R. Kassel. The MIT on-line character database. ftp://lightning.lcs.mit.edu/pub/handwriting/mit.tar.Z.
8. X. Li, M. Parizeau, and R. Plamondon. Segmentation and reconstruction of on-line handwritten scripts. *Pattern Recognition*, 31(6):675–684, 1998.
9. M. Parizeau and R. Plamondon. A handwriting model for syntactic recognition of cursive script. In *Proc. 11th International Conference on Pattern Recognition*, volume II, pages 308–312, August 31 to September 3 1992.
10. R. Plamondon and S. Srihari. On-line and off-line handwriting recognition: A comprehensive survey. *IEEE Trans. Pattern Analysis and Machine Intelligence*, 22(1):63–84, January 2000.
11. C. De Stefano, M. Garutto, and A. Marcelli. A saliency-based multiscale method for on-line cursive handwriting shape description. In *Proceedings of the Ninth International Workshop on Frontiers in Handwriting Recognition*, pages 124–129, 2004.
12. J. Sternby. Core points - variable and reduced parameterization for symbol recognition. Technical report, 2005. Licentiate Thesis in Mathematical Sciences 2005:7.
13. V. Vuori. Adaptation in on-line recognition of handwriting. Master's thesis, Helsinki University of Technology, 1999.

Nonlinear Civil Structures Identification Using a Polynomial Artificial Neural Network

Francisco J. Rivero-Angeles[1,*], Eduardo Gomez-Ramirez[2], and Ruben Garrido[1]

[1] Centro de Investigacion y de Estudios Avanzados del IPN, CINVESTAV - Departamento de Control Automatico, Av. Instituto Politecnico Nacional #2508, Col. Zacatenco, A.P. 14-740, Mexico, D.F. 07360, Mexico

[2] Universidad La Salle - Laboratorio de Investigacion y Desarrollo, de Tecnologia Avanzada. Benjamin Franklin #47, Col. Condesa, Mexico, D.F. 06140, Mexico

frivero@candeingenieros.com

Abstract. Civil structures could undergo hysteresis cycles due to cracking or yielding when subjected to severe earthquake motions or even high wind. System identification techniques have been used in the past years to assess civil structures under lateral loads. The present research makes use of a polynomial artificial neural network to identify and predict, online, the behavior of such nonlinear structures. Simulations are carried out using the Loma Prieta and the Mexico City seismic records on two hysteretic models. Afterwards, two real seismic records acquired on a 24-story concrete building in Mexico City are used to test the proposed algorithm. Encouraging results are obtained: fast identification of the weights and fair prediction of the output acceleration.

1 Introduction

Health monitoring of structures has been a focus of interest for researchers in structural and control engineering for the past two decades. Civil structures, such as buildings and bridges, are instrumented to acquire output acceleration, velocity and displacement data due to lateral loads, which could be severe wind or strong earthquake motions. The data is later analyzed to assess the lateral resistant capacity of the structure and to check output maximums against those allowed by construction codes. In some instances, wind or earthquake forces may induce lateral loads to civil structures such that energy may dissipate through hysteretic phenomena, a nonlinear time-variante behavior which reduces their resistant capacity [5]. Many buildings have been instrumented around the world in order to monitor their structural health. The identification of such nonlinear systems is therefore an important task for engineers who work in areas affected by these natural hazards, and thus, the subject of the present paper.

Forecasting time series has been solved with a broad range of algorithms such as ARMAX [1], NARMAX [2], Fuzzy Logic [14], Neural Networks [3], etc. Some

* Corresponding author.

M. Lazo and A. Sanfeliu (Eds.): CIARP 2005, LNCS 3773, pp. 138–145, 2005.

researchers have succesfully identified nonlinear structures with a wide variety of proposed algorithms [4]. Some examples include: ERA-OKID, Subspace and Least Squares algorithms to estimate linear parameters of structures [9]. An Orthogonal NARMAX model is proposed in [6]. Sequential regression analysis, Gauss Newton optimization and Least Squares with extended Kalman filter is reviewed in [8]. Least Squares methods have also been used by [10], [13], and [16].

Although artificial neural networks have not been widely used in civil and structural engineering, some researchers have succesfully applied them ([11], [12], and [7]). Nonetheless, the models and architectures of those networks seem quite complex and computer time consuming.

The present research proposes the use of a polynomial artificial neural network [3] to identify a nonlinear structural system with a fairly small amount of samples for on-line training. One important issue to consider is the use of on-line algorithms for closed-loop control applications or simulation and fault detection analysis, that is the reason an on-line algorithm is proposed.

In the present research, the Loma Prieta (California, USA, 1989) and SCT (Mexico City, Mexico, 1985) seismic records are used to test the proposed algorithm on a hysteretic simulated shear building structure. A Bouc-Wen model [15] is used to simulate a hysteretic nonlinear single degree of freedom structure (SDOF). Simulation results show that the proposed network is able to identify the nonlinear system and predict with good accuracy the acceleration output with a fairly simple model. Later on, one actual seismic record, acquired on a real 24-story concrete structure in Mexico City in 2002, is used to identify the behavior of the building. The identified model is then used to predict the acceleration motion of the same real building, subjected to another actual record acquired ten months later, in 2003, and the results show that this simple model predicts with very good accuracy the behavior of the system.

The proposed network model has two interesting features: (1) the driving external forces are considered unknown and not needed, which for the case of wind loading this model is applicable; and (2) this model does not need physical structural parameters, which in turn is a nice advantage when an instrumentation is set up in an unknown structural system. A long term aim of the present research is to develop a technique that could be used in conjunction with fault detection analysis, structural health monitoring, and structural control.

2 Polynomial Artificial Neural Network

The model of a polynomial artificial neural network (PANN) is shown in (1).

$$\begin{aligned}\hat{y}_k = [\phi(&x_{1,k}, x_{2,k}, \ldots, x_{n_i,k}, x_{1,k-1}, x_{2,k-1}, \ldots,\\ &x_{n_i,k-n_1}, \ldots, y_{k-1}, y_{k-2}, \ldots, y_{k-n_2})]_{\phi_{min}}^{\phi_{max}};\end{aligned} \tag{1}$$

where $\hat{y}_k \in \Re$ is the estimated time series, $\phi(x, y) \in \Re$ is a nonlinear function, $x_i \in X$ are the inputs for $i = 1, \ldots, n_i$; and n_i is the number of inputs. $y_{k-j} \in Y$ are the previous values of the output, for $j = 1, \ldots, n_2$; n_1 is the number of delays of the input, n_2 is the number of delays on the output, X and Y are compact subsets of $\Re$. Simplifying the notation, it results into (2).

$$z = (x_{1,k}, x_{2,k}, \ldots, x_{n_1,k}, \ldots, y_{k-1}, y_{k-2}, \ldots, y_{k-n_2});$$
$$z = (z_1, z_2, z_3, \ldots, z_{n_v}); \tag{2}$$

where n_v is the total number of elements in description z, and $n_v = n_i + n_1 n_i + n_2$. The nonlinear function $\phi(z) \in \Phi_p$ belongs to a family Φ_p of polynomials that can be represented as (3)

$$\Phi_p(z_1, z_2, \ldots, z_{n_v}) = (\phi(z) : \phi(z) = a_0(z_1, z_2, \ldots, z_{n_v}) + a_1(z_1, z_2, \ldots, z_{n_v}), \\ +a_2(z_1, z_2, \ldots, z_{n_v}) + \ldots + a_p(z_1, z_2, \ldots, z_{n_v})). \tag{3}$$

The subindex p is the maximum power of the polynomials expression and $a_i(z_1, z_2, \ldots, z_{n_v})$ are homogeneous polynomials of total degree i, for $i = 0, \ldots, p$. Every homogeneous polynomial could be written as shown in (4)

$$\begin{aligned} a_0(z_1, z_2, \ldots, z_{n_v}) &= w_0 \\ a_1(z_1, z_2, \ldots, z_{n_v}) &= w_{1,1} z_1 + w_{1,2} z_2 + \ldots + w_{1,n_v} z_{n_v} \\ a_2(z_1, z_2, \ldots, z_{n_v}) &= w_{2,1} z_1^2 + w_{2,2} z_1 z_2 + \ldots + w_{2,N_2} z_{n_v}^2 \\ &\vdots \\ a_p(z_1, z_2, \ldots, z_{n_v}) &= w_{p,1} z_1^p + w_{p,2} z_1^{p-1} z_2 + \ldots + w_{p,N_p} z_{n_v}^p; \end{aligned} \tag{4}$$

where $w_{i,j}$ is the associated weight of the network. The term w_0 corresponds to the input bias of the network. The homogeneous polynomial $a_1(z)$ is equivalent to weight the inputs. The polynomials $a_2(z)$ to $a_p(z)$ represent the modulation between the inputs and the power of each polynomial. N_i is the number of terms of every polynomial with:

$$N_0 = 1; N_1 = n_v; N_2 = \sum_{i=1}^{n_v} i; N_3 = \sum_{s_1=0}^{n_v-1} \sum_{i=1}^{n_v-s_1} i; \ldots \\ \ldots; N_p = \underbrace{\sum_{s_{p-2}=0}^{n_v-1} \cdots \sum_{s_2=0}^{n_v-s_3} \sum_{s_1=0}^{n_v-s_2} \sum_{i=1}^{n_v-s_1}}_{p-1} i. \tag{5}$$

The dimension of N_Φ of each family Φ_p could be computed by $N_\Phi = \sum_{i=0}^{p} N_i$. The activation function is given by (6)

$$[\phi(z)]_{\phi_{min}}^{\phi_{max}} = \begin{cases} \phi_{max} & \phi(z) \geq \phi_{max} \\ \phi(z) & \phi_{min} < \phi(z) < \phi_{max} \\ \phi_{min} & \phi(z) \leq \phi_{min} \end{cases}. \tag{6}$$

The weights of the PANN could be found with a recursive Least Squares algorithm during training. It is worth noting that in [3] the PANN is shown to lead to better and faster results compared to a normal ANN. The architecture of the PANN model is shown in fig. 1.

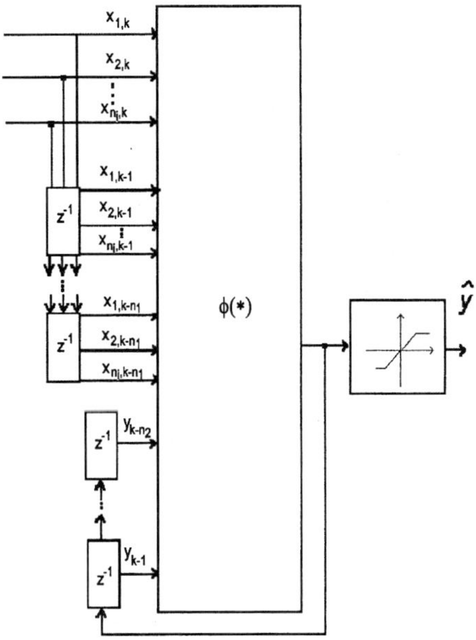

Fig. 1. PANN architecture

3 Simulations of Theoretical Models

The output acceleration, velocity and displacements of a one-story shear building (SDOF) are only lateral motion of the mass. In the simulations, two theoretical SDOF were introduced: (a) structure subjected to the Loma Prieta earthquake with mass m =1 kg, damping c =1.2566 $kgf \cdot s/cm$, and stiffness k =157.9137 kgf/cm; and (b) structure subjected to the Mexico City earthquake with mass m =1 kg, damping c =0.3142 $kgf \cdot s/cm$, and stiffness k =9.8696 kgf/cm. In both cases the theoretical acceleration output, sampled at 0.02 sec., was contaminated with 2% random noise, and the structure was subjected to smooth and compact hysteresis for stability purposes. In this sense, for SDOF (b) the seismic record had to be scaled to 30% amplitude.

A PANN with $p = 2$, $n_i = n_1 = 0$, and $n_2 = 4$ is used for training. Training neural networks is usually based on two criteria: (1) minimizing the error, or (2) by reaching a fixed number of iterations (epochs). Real-time techniques need a different approach due to the fact that the learning process has to be done on-line; thus, training criteria was done with the weight variance herein. One conclusion drawn from the results is that at least two cycles of motion are needed for training because the weight variance tends to zero after that time.

In our simulations, 100 samples (2 seconds) are required for training SDOF (a), and 200 (4 seconds) for SDOF (b). Fig. 2 shows the training and prediction of the hysteretic SDOF (a) in a three-second window.

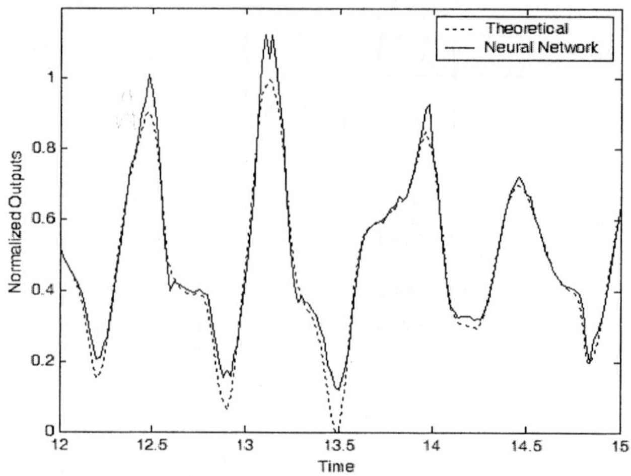

Fig. 2. Prediction of the intense part, Loma Prieta input

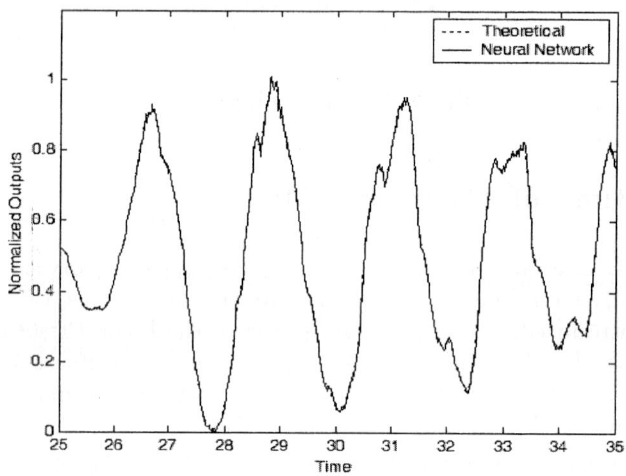

Fig. 3. Prediction of the intense part, Mexico City input

Training could identify a nonlinear model with very small hysteresis, and when the hysteresis cycles become wider at the intense part of the excitation, around 12 seconds of motion, the prediction looses some accuracy. Nonetheless, the proposed PANN is able to predict fairly well the acceleration output. Increasing training time could increase accuracy because hysteretic cycles become wider.

On the other hand, fig. 3 shows the prediction of the hysteretic SDOF (b) in a ten-second window. It is worth noting that the PANN is able to identify very well the nonlinear model, since a bit wider hysteresis occurs from the beginning, and when the intense part takes place the prediction is still very good.

4 Identification Using Real Data

In this section, the PANN is used to identify a model of a real instrumented building. This structure is a 24-story concrete building located in Mexico City. It is instrumented with accelerometer sensors located throughout the building, and several earthquakes have been acquired since its activation. The building has a period of around 3 seconds, thus, training was done with 6 seconds of the output acceleration motion at the centroid of the roof. The seismic event of April 18, 2002, was used for training and prediction.

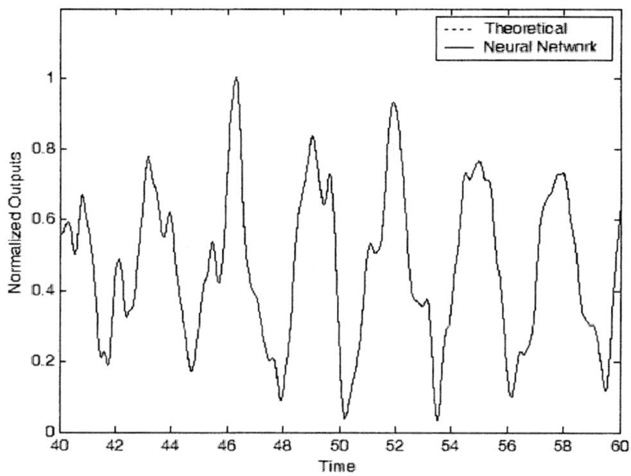

Fig. 4. Prediction of the intense part, April 18 2002 record

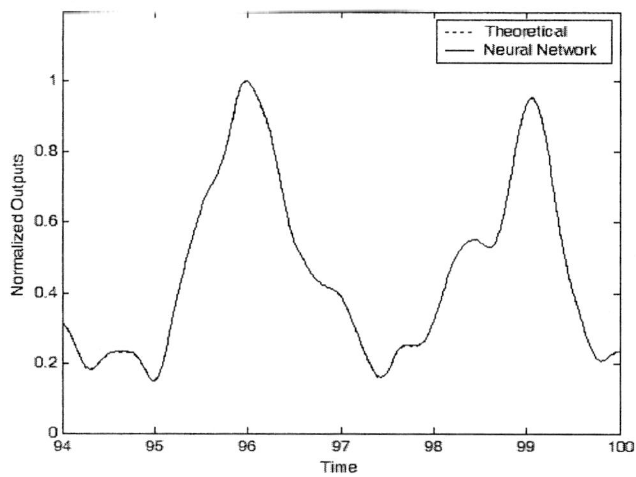

Fig. 5. Prediction of the intese part, January 21 2003 record

Fig. 4 shows the prediction of the motion of the building. It is worth noting that both lines seem overlapped due to the fact that the PANN is a very fine tool to identify this structure. The proposed approach is so efficient that no distinction between both lines could be observed.

After training, the weights of the network are kept unchanged to predict the acceleration output for the seismic event of January 21, 2003. Fig. 5 shows the prediction of the motion. Note again that both lines seem overlapped beause the prediction error is very small. In this case, this coud mean that the building has not suffered a noticeable change on its structural properties, since the model still predicts accurately the motion, even after ten months between both seismic events. Therefore, this technique could be used later as a tool for fault detection analysis.

5 Conclusions

In the last two decades, several buildings have been instrumented in order to monitor their structural health through the analysis of measured acceleration, velocity and displacement records. The present research proposes the use of a polynomial artificial neural network (PANN) to identify the nonlinear behavior of a building structure, and to forecast the acceleration output. The PANN is trained on-line with only the first two cycles of motion.

To test the effectiveness of the proposed algorithm, two theoretical simulations were introduced. The hysteretic structures were subjected to the seismic records of Loma Prieta (USA, 1989) and Mexico City (Mexico, 1985). The results show fast convergence speed of the weights, and good accuracy to forecast the nonlinear output.

Later on, a model of a real instrumented building was identified with the PANN. The real acquired seismic event of April 18, 2002, was used to train and forecast the motion of the roof.

Finally, the real acquired seismic event of January 21, 2003, was used to predict the motion of the roof using the model identified earlier. Very encouraging results are derived from the analysis. In the long run, the present research is aimed to develop a technique that could be used in conjunction with fault detection analysis, structural health monitoring, and structural control.

References

1. Box, G. E. P., & Jenkin, G. M., *Time Series Analysis: Forecasting and Control*, San Francisco, CA, Holden-Day (1970)
2. Chen, S., & Billings, A., "Representations of Nonlinear Systems: the NARMAX model", *Int. J. of Control*, Vol. 49, No. 3 (1989)
3. Gomez-Ramirez, E., Poznyak, A., Gonzalez-Yunes, A., & Avila-Alvarez, M., "Adaptive Architecture of Polynomial Artificial Neural Network to Forecast Nonlinear Time Series", *Congress on Evolutionary Computation, CEC '99*, Mayflower, Washington, D.C., USA, July 6 - 9 (1999)

4. Housner, G. W., Bergman, L. A., Caughey, T. K., Chassiakos, A. G., Claus, R. O., Masri, S. F., Skelton, R. E., Soong, T. T., Spencer, B. F., & Yao, J. T. P., "Structural Control: Past, Present and Future", *Journal of Engineering Mechanics*, Vol. 123, No. 9, Sep. (1997)
5. Humar, J. L., *Dynamics of Structures*, A. A. Balkema Publishers, 2nd Edition (2001)
6. Korenberg, M., Billings, S. A., Liu, Y. P., & McIlroy, P. J., "Orthogonal Parameter Estimation Algorithm for Non-Linear Stochastic Systems", *International Journal of Control*, Vol. 48, No. 1 (1988)
7. Kosmatopoulos, E. B., Smyth, A. W., Masri, S. F., & Chassiakos, A. G., "Robust Adaptive Neural Estimation of Restoring Forces in Nonlinear Structures", *Transactions of the ASME, Journal of Applied Mechanics*, Vol. 68, November (2001)
8. Loh, C. H., & Chung, S. T., "A Three-Stage Identification Approach for Hysteretic Systems", *Earthquake Engineering and Structural Dynamics*, Vol. 22, (1993) 129-150
9. Martinez-Garcia, J. C., Gomez-Gonzalez, B., Martinez-Guerra, R., & Rivero-Angeles, F. J., "Parameter Identification of Civil Structures Using Partial Seismic Instrumentation", *in 5th Asian Control Conference, ASCC*, Melbourne, Australia, July 20-23 (2004)
10. Masri, S. F., Miller, R. K., Saud, A. F., & Caughey, T. K., "Identification of Nonlinear Vibrating Structures: Part I - Formulation", *Transactions of the ASME, J. of Applied Mechanics*, Vol. 57, Dec. (1987)
11. Masri, S. F., Chassiakos, A. G., & Caughey, T. K., "Structure-unknown non-linear dynamic systems: identification through neural networks", *Smart Mater. Struct.*, 1, (1992) 45-56
12. Masri, S. F., Chassiakos, A. G., & Caughey, T. K., "Identification of nonlinear dynamic systems using neural networks", *J. of Applied Mechanics*, 60, (1993) 123-33
13. Mohammad, K. S., Worden, K., & Tomlinson, G. R., "Direct Parameter Estimation for Linear and Non-linear Structures", *Journal of Sound and Vibration*, 152 (3) (1992)
14. Sugeno, M., *Industrial Applications of Fuzzy Control*, Elsevier Science Pub. Co. (1985)
15. Wen, Y. K., "Method for Random Vibration of Hysteretic Systems", *Journal of Engineering Mechanics, ASCE*, 102(2), (1976) 249-263
16. Yar, M., & Hammond, J. K., "Parameter Estimation for Hysteretic Systems", *J. of Sound and Vibration*, 117 (1) (1987)

A Method of Automatic Speaker Recognition Using Cepstral Features and Vectorial Quantization

José Ramón Calvo de Lara

Advanced Technologies Application Center, CENATAV, Cuba
jcalvo@cenatav.co.cu

Abstract. *Automatic Speaker Recognition* techniques are increasing the use of the speaker's voice to control access to personalized telephonic services. This paper describes the use of vector quantization as a feature matching method, in an automatic speaker recognition system, evaluated with speech samples from a SALA Spanish Venezuelan database for fixed telephone network. Results obtained reflect a good performance of the method in a text independent job in the context of sequences of digits.

1 Introduction

Automatic Speaker Recognition techniques make it possible to use the speaker's voice to verify their identity and control access to services such as voice dialling, banking by telephone, telephone shopping, database access services, information services, voice mail, security control for confidential information areas, and remote access to computers [1].

These techniques can be classified into identification and verification. *Speaker identification* is the process of determining which registered speaker provides a given utterance. *Speaker verification* is the process of accepting or rejecting the identity claim of a speaker.

Speaker Recognition methods can be divided into *text-independent* and *text dependent*. In a *text-independent* method, speaker models capture characteristics of speaker's speech *irrespective of what one is saying*. In a *text-dependent* method the recognition of the speaker's identity is based on his/her *speaking specific phrases*, like passwords, card numbers, PIN codes, etc.

Speaker Recognition systems contain two main processes: *feature extraction* and *feature matching*. *Feature extraction* extracts a small amount of data from the voice signal that can be used later to represent each speaker. *Feature matching* involves the procedure to identify the unknown speaker by comparing extracted features from his/her voice input with the ones from a set of known speakers.

An Automatic Speaker Recognizer has to serve two pattern recognition phases. The first one is the *training phase* while the second one is the *testing phase*. In the *training phase*, each registered speaker provides samples of their speech so that the system can train a reference model for that speaker. In case of speaker verification

M. Lazo and A. Sanfeliu (Eds.): CIARP 2005, LNCS 3773, pp. 146 – 153, 2005.

systems, in addition, a speaker-specific threshold is also computed from the training samples. During the *testing phase*, the input speech is matched with stored reference model(s) and recognition decision is made.

This paper refers the author's experience in the design and test of a text independent speaker recognition method, with a vector quantization algorithm of feature matching, evaluated with speech samples obtained from SALA database for fixed telephone network.

2 Feature Extraction from Speech Samples

The feature extraction from the speech samples consists of a filtering process with pre-emphasis and an extraction process of spectral features using a short term analysis [2]. The 8bit μ-law samples of corpus recorded at a sampling rate of 8 kHz were converted to linear 16 bit PCM samples.

2.1 Filtering Process with Pre-emphasis

Pre-emphasis refers to filtering that emphasizes the higher frequencies of speech; its purpose is to balance the spectrum of voiced sounds that have a steep roll-off in the high frequency region. The pre-emphasis makes the upper harmonics of the fundamental frequency more distinct, and the distribution of energy across the frequency range more balanced.

2.2 Extraction of Spectral Features

The extraction process of spectral features using a short term analysis consists in:

- A frame blocking, where the continuous speech signal is blocked into frames of 256 samples, with adjacent frames separated by 100 samples.
- A frame windowing, a Hamming window is applied to each individual frame in order to minimize the signal discontinuities, and consequently the spectral distortion, at the beginning and end of each frame.
- A Discrete Fourier Transform process using a FFT algorithm, which converts each frame of 256 samples from the time domain into the frequency domain, the result obtained is the *signal's periodogram.*

A wide range of possibilities exist for representing the speech signal in Automatic Speech and Speaker Recognition with spectral features as Linear Prediction Coefficients (LPC), Linear Prediction Cepstrals Coefficients (LPCC) and Mel-Frequency Cepstrals Coefficients (MFCC) and others [3].

MFCC are perhaps the best known and most popular spectral features for representing the speech signal, widely used in many speech and speaker recognizers [4], these are used in this speaker recognizer. Dynamic spectral features known as *delta* and *delta-delta* features are calculated too, and appended to MFCC.

2.2.1 MFCC Features

Psychophysical studies have shown that human perception of the frequency contents of sounds for speech signals does not follow a linear scale. MFCC features are based on the known variation of the human ear's critical bandwidths with frequency; filters spaced linearly at low frequencies and logarithmically at high frequencies have been used to capture the phonetically important characteristics of speech.

Thus for each tone with an actual frequency, *f*, measured in Hz, a subjective pitch is measured on a scale called the *'mel'* scale. The *mel-frequency* scale is linear frequency spacing below 1000 Hz and a logarithmic spacing above 1000 Hz. As a reference point, the pitch of a 1 kHz tone, 40 dB above the perceptual hearing threshold, is defined as 1000 *mels*.

In order to simulate the frequency warping process, we use a filter bank, one filter for each desired *mel-frequency* component. That filter bank has a triangular band-pass frequency response, and the spacing as well as the bandwidth is determined by a constant *mel-frequency* interval. A *mel-spaced* filter bank with 12 filters is given in figure 1.

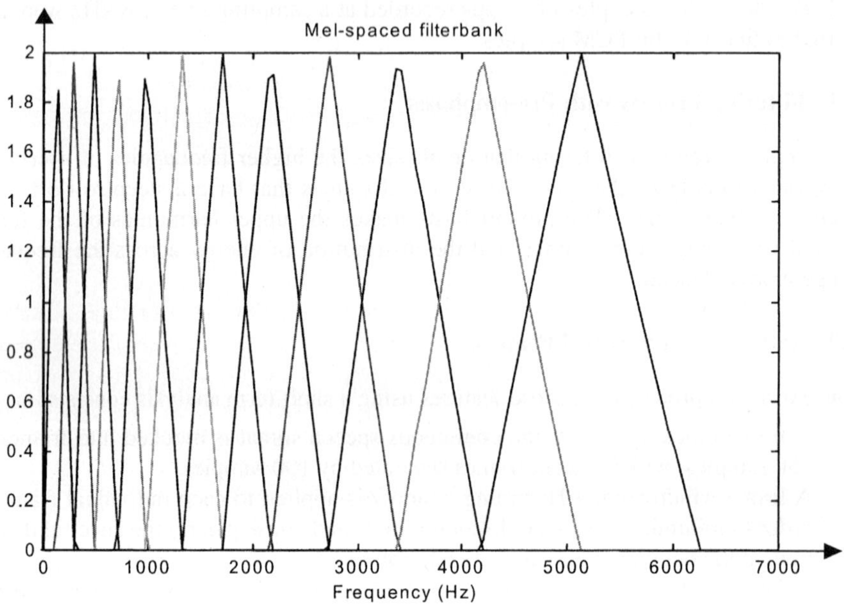

Fig. 1. Mel-spaced filter bank with 12 filters [1]

The modified or mel power spectrum consists of the output power of these filters applied to the periodogram. The number of mel-spaced filters and mel power spectrum coefficients is typically chosen as 20.

At last, we convert the log mel spectrum back to time, to obtain the mel-frequency Cepstrum Coefficients (MFCC). Because the mel spectrum coefficients (and so their logarithm) are real numbers, we can convert them to the time domain using the Discrete Cosine Transform (DCT).

The first component k= 0 is excluded from the DCT since it represents the mean value of the input signal which carried little speaker specific information. Twelve cepstral coefficients of the speech spectrum provides a good representation of the local spectral properties of the signal for the given frame analysis.

By applying the procedure described above for each speech frame, an acoustic vector of 12 mel-frequency cepstrum coefficients is computed. These are result of a cosine transform of the logarithm of the short-term power spectrum expressed on a mel-frequency scale. Therefore each input utterance is transformed into a temporal sequence of acoustic vectors. A block diagram of the MFCC extraction process is given in figure 2.

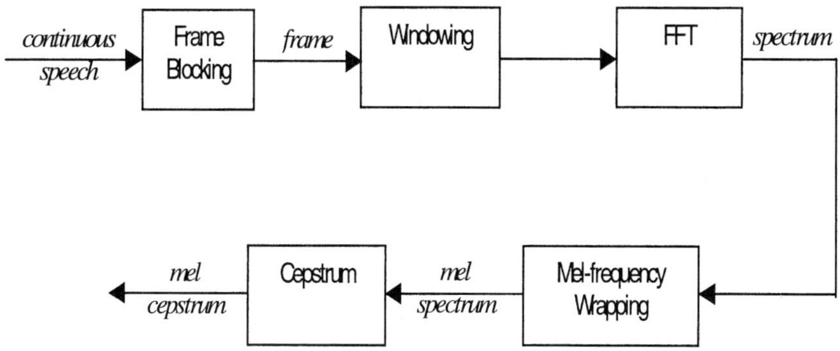

Fig. 2. Mel-Frequency Cepstrum Coefficients extraction process [1]

2.2.2 Extracting Delta and Delta-Delta Features

A widely method to encode some of the dynamic information over time of spectral features is known as *delta features* "Δ" [3, 5]. The time derivatives of each cepstral coefficient are obtained by differentiation and zero padding at begin and end of the utterance, then, the estimate of the derivative is appended to the acoustic vector, yielding a higher-dimensional feature vector. The time derivatives of the delta features are estimated also, using the same method, yielding *delta-delta features* "ΔΔ". These are again appended to the dimensional feature space. In our case we obtained a 36-dimmension acoustic vector: 12 MFCC + 12Δ + 12 ΔΔ.

3 Feature Matching

The problem of automatic speaker recognition is a pattern recognition problem. The goal of pattern recognition is to classify objects into one of a number of classes. In our case, the objects or patterns are sequences of acoustic vectors that are extracted from an input speech using the techniques described in the previous section. The classes refer to individual speakers. Since the classification procedure in our case is applied on extracted features, it can be referred to as feature matching.

Furthermore, if there are a set of patterns which classes are known, then it is a problem of supervised pattern recognition. During the training phase, we label the sequence of acoustic vectors of each input speech with the ID of the known speakers; these patterns comprise the training set and are used to derive a classification algorithm. The remaining sequences of acoustic vectors are then used to test the classification algorithm; these patterns are referred to as the test set. If the correct classes of the individual pattern in the test set are also known, then one can evaluate the performance of the algorithm.

3.1 Vector Quantization Method of Feature Matching

The state-of-the-art in feature matching techniques used in speaker recognition includes Dynamic Time Warping (DTW), Hidden Markov Modelling (HMM), and Vector Quantization (VQ). In this system, the VQ approach is used, due to ease of implementation and high accuracy.

VQ is a process of mapping vectors from a large vector space to a finite number of regions in that space. Each region is called a *cluster* and can be represented by its center called a *codeword.* The collection of all codeword is called a *codebook.* Figure 3 shows a diagram to illustrate this process.

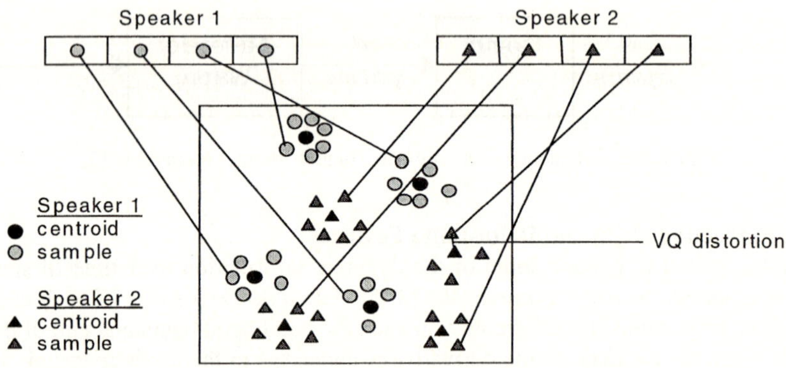

Fig. 3. Conceptual diagram illustrating vector quantization codebook formation [6]

In the figure, only two speakers and two dimensions of the acoustic vectors space are shown. The circles refer to the acoustic vectors from speaker 1 while the triangles are from speaker 2. In the *training phase*, a speaker-specific VQ codebook is generated for each known speaker by clustering his/her training acoustic vectors.

The result codewords (centroids) are shown by black circles and black triangles for speaker 1 and 2, respectively. The distance from any acoustic vector to the closest codeword of a codebook is called a VQ-distortion. In the *testing phase*, an input utterance of an unknown voice is *"vector-quantized"* using each trained codebook and the total VQ distortion is computed. The speaker corresponding to the VQ codebook with smallest total VQ-distortion is identified.

3.1.1 LBG Algorithm

In the training phase, a speaker-specific VQ codebook is generated for each known speaker by clustering his/her training acoustic vectors using a well-know algorithm namely LBG [7], this recursive algorithm cluster a set $X = \{x_1,\ldots\ldots, x_T\}$ of acoustic vectors into a codebook $C = \{c_1,\ldots\ldots c_M\}$ of M codewords (M power of 2) . The algorithm is formally implemented by the following recursive procedure [1]:

1. Design a 1-vector codebook, this is the centroid of the set of training vectors
2. Double the size of the codebook by splitting each current codebook $\mathbf{y}_n$ according to the rule:

$$\mathbf{y}_n^+ = \mathbf{y}_n(1+\varepsilon) \tag{1}$$

$$\mathbf{y}_n^- = \mathbf{y}_n(1-\varepsilon) \tag{2}$$

   Where n varies from 1 to the current size of the codebook, and ε is a splitting parameter (ε =0.01).
3. Nearest-Neighbor Search: for each training acoustic vector, find the codeword in the current codebook that is closest in terms of VQ-distortion, and assign that vector to the corresponding cluster associated with the closest codeword.
4. Centroid Update: update the codeword in each cluster using the centroid of the training acoustic vectors assigned to that cluster.
5. Repeat steps 3 and 4 until the VQ distortion falls below a preset threshold.
6. Repeat steps 2, 3 and 4 until a codebook size of M is designed.

The generated codebook C contains the codewords that better represents the training set of acoustics vectors X in terms of VQ-distortion.

3.1.2 Measure of VQ-Distortion

Consider an acoustic vector x_i generated by any speaker, and a codebook C, the VQ-distortion d_q of the acoustic vector x_i with respect to C is given by:

$$d_q(x_i, C) = \min d(x_i, c_j) \tag{3}$$

Where d (. , .) is a distance measure defined for the acoustic vectors. The codeword cj for which d (x_i , c_j) is minimum, is the nearest neighbor of x_i in the codebook C.

Euclidean distance is a distance measure used due the straightforward implementation and intuitive notion (Euclidean distance between two cepstral features, measures the squared distance between the corresponding short term log spectra) [3].

In the testing phase, all the sequences of acoustic vectors from an unknown speaker is "vector-quantized" computing the average quantization distortion D_Q with each trained codebook C, the known speaker corresponding to the codebook C with smallest D_Q is assigned to unknown speaker. The average quantization distortion D_Q is defined as the average of the individual distortions:

$$D_Q(X, C) = \frac{1}{T}\sum_{i=1}^{T} d_q(x_i, C) \tag{4}$$

4 Experimental Results

The proposed speaker recognizer was evaluated with sequences of digits obtained from 347 speakers of SALA database. A sequence of about 15 sec of duration was used for training and other sequence of similar duration was used for testing. Until now SALA Database had been used only in speech recognition studies[8].

4.1 SALA Database

The SALA Spanish Venezuelan Database for fixed telephone network was recorded within the scope of the SpeechDat Across Latin America project. [9] The design of the corpus and the collection was performed at the Universidad de los Andes, Mérida Venezuela, transcription and formatting was performed at the Universidad Politécnica de Cataluña, Spain.

This database comprises telephone recording from 1000 speakers recorded directly over the PSTN using two analogue lines, signals were sampled at 8 kHz and μ-law encoded without automatic gain control. Every speaker pronounces 44 different utterances.

The database has the following speaker demographic structure:

- Five dialectal regions: Central, Zuliana, Llanos, Sud-Oriental and Andes
- Five age groups: under 16, 16 to 30, 31 to 45, 46 to 60 and over 60

13 speakers called more than once using the same prompt sheet.

4.2 Evaluation Results

The following table shows the 30 distribution groups of the 347 speakers:

Table 1. Distribution of groups of speakers for the evaluation

Age	16-30		31-45		46-60	
Regions	**F**	**M**	**F**	**M**	**F**	**M**
Central	12	12	12	12	8	12
Zuliana	12	11	12	12	12	11
Llanos	12	12	12	12	12	12
Sud-Oriental	12	12	12	12	5	12
Andes	12	12	12	12	12	12

The speaker recognizer was evaluated within every one of the 30 groups, obtaining the following results:

Table 2. Results of the evaluation

	speakers	identified	%
F	169	168	**99.4**
M	178	175	**98.3**
	347	343	**98.8**

An additional evaluation, using the 13 speakers that called more than once, taking a sequence of digits of the first call for training and other sequence of digits of the second call for testing, shows a 92.3 % of identification rate.

5 Conclusion and Future Work

This paper describes the result of the application of a vector quantization speaker recognition method, used in a text independent job in the context of sequences of continuos digits and evaluated with a database for fixed telephone network. This kind of job and environment isn't usual for vector quantization methods [3,4].

Many as 98.8% of speakers in a group of 347 speakers of SALA Database were identified correctly. Such a result may be regarded as a promising way to a high-performance speaker identification system. However, it has to be taken into account that the speech data used in the experiments were recorded during one session. More exhaustive test must be performed in order to probe the method when there is a time interval between the recording of training and testing sentences.

References

1. Minh N. Do, "An Automatic Speaker Recognition System", Audio Visual Communications Laboratory, Swiss Federal Institute of Technology, Lausanne, Switzerland, 2001. http://lcavwww.epfl.ch/~minhdo/asr_project/asr_project.doc
2. Douglas A. Reynolds, "An Overview of Automatic Speaker Recognition Technology", MIT Lincoln Laboratory, Lexington, MA, USA, This paper appears in ICASSP 2002, pp 4072-4075.
3. Tomi Kinnunen, "Spectral Features for Automatic Text-Independent Speaker Recognition", University of Joensuu, Department of Computer Science, Joensuu, Finland, December 21, 2003. ftp://cs.joensuu.fi/pub/PhLic/2004_PhLic_Kinnunen_Tomi.pdf
4. Joseph P. Campbell, Jr, "Speaker Recognition: A tutorial", DoD. Proceedings of the IEEE, Vol 85, No. 9 September 1997, pp. 1437-1462.
5. Mason, J., and Zhang, X. "Velocity and acceleration features in speaker recognition", Department of Electrical & Electronic Engineering, Univ. Coll., Swansea. This paper appears in ICASSP 1991, pp. 3673–3676.
6. F.K. Song, A.E. Rosenberg and B.H. Juang, "A vector quantisation approach to speaker recognition", AT&T Technical Journal, Vol. 66-2, pp. 14-26, March 1987.
7. Y. Linde, A. Buzo & R. Gray, "An algorithm for vector quantizer design", *IEEE Transactions on Communications*, Vol. 28, pp.84-95, 1980.
8. L. Maldonado, E. Mora; Universidad de los Andes, Mérida, Venezuela: Personal communications with the author, 2004.
9. A. Moreno, R. Comeyne, K. Haslam, H. van den Heuvel, H. Höge, S. Horbach, G. Micca : "SALA: SpeechDat Across Latin America: .Results Of The First Phase",, LREC2000: 2nd International Conference on Language Resources & Evaluation, Athens, Greece 2000.

Classification of Boar Spermatozoid Head Images Using a Model Intracellular Density Distribution

Lidia Sánchez[1], Nicolai Petkov[2], and Enrique Alegre[1]

[1]Department of Electrical and Electronics Engineering,
University of León, Campus de Vegazana s/n, 24071 León, Spain
[2]Institute of Mathematics and Computing Science,
University of Groningen, P.O. Box 800, 9700 AV Groningen, The Netherlands
{lidia, enrique.alegre}@unileon.es, petkov@cs.rug.nl

Abstract. We propose a novel classification method to identify boar spermatozoid heads which present an intracellular intensity distribution similar to a model. From semen sample images, head images are isolated and normalized. We define a model intensity distribution averaging a set of head images assumed as normal by veterinary experts. Two training sets are also formed: one with images that are similar to the model and another with non-normal head images according to experts. Deviations from the model are computed for each set, obtaining low values for normal heads and higher values for assumed as non-normal heads. There is also an overlapped area. The decision criterion is determined to minimize the sum of the obtained false rejected and false acceptance errors. Experiments with a test set of normal and non-normal head images give a global error of 20.40%. The false rejection and the false acceptance rates are 13.68% and 6.72% respectively.

1 Introduction

Semen quality assessment is an important subject in fertility studies: semen analysis is a keystone in the clinical workup of infertile male patients and semen assessment is a critical stage in artificial insemination processes carried out in veterinary medicine. Pig and cattle farmers regularly acquire semen for artificial insemination from national and international breeding companies whose main objective is to generate and supply semen from boars and bulls of high genetic value. These companies are aware that they must maintain high standards of product, and therefore subject the semen to rigorous quality control procedures. Some of them use computerised methods for sperm evaluation, thus obtaining information about the quality of overall motility and morphology, and others couple this with tests to evaluate sperm plasma membrane and acrosomal integrity. A precise prediction of fertility cannot be provided, although problematic samples can usually be distinguished.

Whereas the majority of currently applied methods for inspection of animal gametes were developed for the analysis of human semen morphology and subsequently adapted for semen of other species, there is a continuing development of new methodologies [1,2]. Such improvements have increased the sensitivity of automated analysis, allowing the recognition of minuscule differences between sperm cells. However, experts do not know a lot about the influence of these morphological alterations in male

M. Lazo and A. Sanfeliu (Eds.): CIARP 2005, LNCS 3773, pp. 154–160, 2005.

fertility [3,4]. Several authors have proposed different approaches to classify subpopulations or to describe shape abnormalities using image processing techniques. Most of them use CASA (Computer Aided Sperm Analysis) systems [5,6] or propose new description and classification methods [7,8,9,10,11].

Although acrosome integrity and plasma membrane integrity determine the sperm viability because their enzymes take part in the oocyte penetration process, some possible features obtained of density distribution or intracellular texture are not considered. It is a visually observable fact that spermatozoid heads present a variety of cellular textures and the experts know that they are determined by their corresponding cytoplasmic densities. Our research is focused on finding a correlation between certain patterns of intracellular density distribution and semen fertility.

In this approach, veterinary experts first assume that a certain intracellular density distribution is characteristic of healthy cells. Then a distribution model for normal heads is obtained. Traditional techniques such as vital and fluorescent stains are used to assess the sperm capacitation of a sample, and experts try to find a correlation between the above mentioned classification and semen fertility. The aim of this research is to define a pattern of intracellular density distribution that corresponds to semen fertility, as determined by traditional techniques. This approach can lead to the use of digital image processing for sperm fertility estimation instead of expensive staining techniques.

In the current work, we analyse grey-level images of boar spermatozoid heads comprised in boar semen samples, Fig. 1a. To acquire the semen samples, veterinary experts used a phase-contrast microscope and fixed the spermatozoa in glutaraldehyde. We define a model intracellular density distribution of the spermatozoid heads, according to the hypothesis of experts. Hence, the typical deviations from the model for normal distributions and non-normal distributions give a classification criterion. The goal is to automatically classify spermatozoid head images as normal or not-normal by means of their deviation from the model intracellular density distribution.

In Section 2, we present the methods we have used and the obtained results. Discussion and conclusions are given in Section 3.

2 Methods and Results

2.1 Pre-processing and Segmentation

Boar sample images were captured by means of an optical phase-contrast microscope connected to a digital camera. The magnification used was $\times 40$ and the dimensions of each sample were 1600×1200 pixels. A boar sample image comprises a number of heads which can vary widely from one sample to the next (Fig. 1a). Spermatozoid heads also present different orientations and tilts. After morphological processing to smooth the contours of the cells, they are isolated using segmentation by threshold applying Otsu's method. Finally, those regions that are smaller than an experimental obtained value of 45% of the average of the head area are removed as well as the heads next to the image boundaries (Fig. 1b).

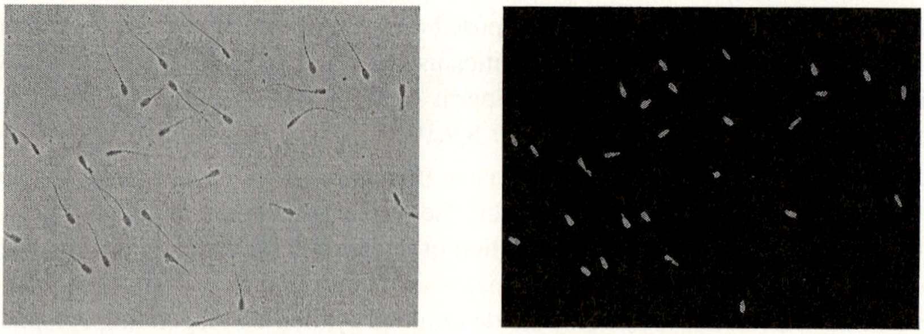

(a) (b)

Fig. 1. (a) Boar semen sample image acquired using a phase-contrast microscope. (b) Image obtained after pre-processing and segmentation. Spermatozoid heads are grey-level distributions in oval shapes on a black background.

2.2 Head Normalization

A spermatozoid head presents an oval shape with an eccentricity between 1.75 and 2. As heads in a sample have different orientations, we find the main axes of the ellipse that a head forms (Fig. 2a) to be able to rotate all the head images to the same horizontal orientation (Fig. 2b). Empirical measurements in head morphological analysis give a width from 4 to $5\mu m$ and a length from 7 to $10\mu m$. We re-scale all the head images to 19×35 pixels and consider a 2D function $f(x, y)$ defined by the grey levels of the image in the set of points which belongs to an ellipse whose major and minor axis are 35 and 19 respectively (Fig. 2c).

(a) (b) (c)

Fig. 2. (a) Spermatozoid head and main axes of the ellipse that it defines. (b) Rotated head. (c) After re-scaling and brightness and contrast normalization, 2D grey-level function obtained for the points of an ellipse with major and minor axis of 35 and 19 pixels, respectively.

Sample images differ in their brightness and contrast grey level. To normalise that, we develop a linear transformation of the 2D function to keep a determined mean and standard deviation (Fig. 2c). So, we define a new 2D function $g(x, y)$ as follows:

$$g(x, y) = af(x, y) + b, \tag{1}$$

Fig. 3. Model of an intracellular distribution image considered as normal by veterinary experts, obtained from the average of a set of head images assumed as normal

where the coefficients a and b are computed as:

$$a = \frac{\sigma_g}{\sigma_f}, \quad b = \mu_g - a\mu_f \; . \tag{2}$$

The spermatozoid head images which experts consider as potentially normal take values for the mean and the standard deviation around 8 and 10 respectively. For this reason, we set $\sigma_g = 8$ and $\mu_g = 100$. The values μ_f and σ_f correspond with the mean and the standard deviation of the function f, respectively.

2.3 Model of a Normal Intracellular Distribution

We describe a model density distribution as the average of a set of 34 heads assumed as normal by veterinary experts. Such heads have a grey-level intensity variation from left to right according to the dark post nucleus cap, the intermediate light area and a slightly darker part called acrosome that covers part of the cell nucleus. After the previous steps of pre-processing, segmentation and normalization, we compute a model 2D function as (Fig. 3):

$$m(x,y) = \frac{1}{n}\sum_{i=1}^{n} g_i(x,y) \; . \tag{3}$$

We also consider the standard deviation to assess the variability of the grey-levels for each point:

$$\sigma(x,y) = \sqrt{\sum_{i=1}^{n} \frac{(g_i(x,y) - m_i(x,y))^2}{n}} \; . \tag{4}$$

2.4 Classification of Spermatozoid Head Images

Apart from the set of images used to build the model, we employ two training sets of 44 head images labelled as "normal" (Fig. 4a) and 82 head images labelled as "non-normal" (Fig. 4b) by veterinary experts according to the similarity to the intracellular distribution considered as potentially normal. For each image of those training sets, we apply the above mentioned stages and then compute a deviation from the model function using the L_∞ norm:

$$d = \max\left(\frac{|g(x,y) - m(x,y)|}{\sigma_{xy}}\right) \; . \tag{5}$$

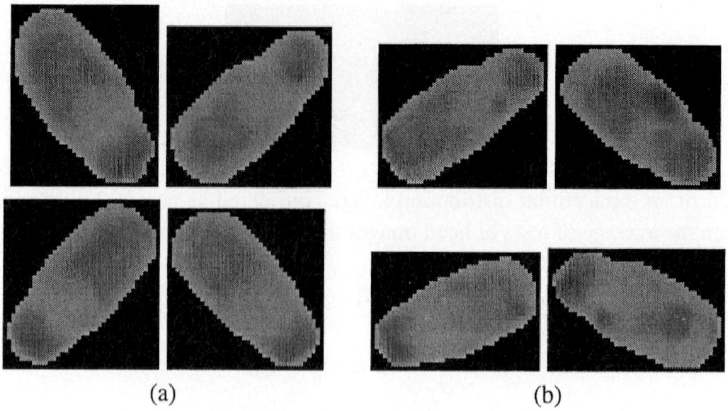

Fig. 4. Examples of heads that were classified by an expert as having an intracellular distribution that is (a) similar and (b) not similar to the assumed normal density distribution

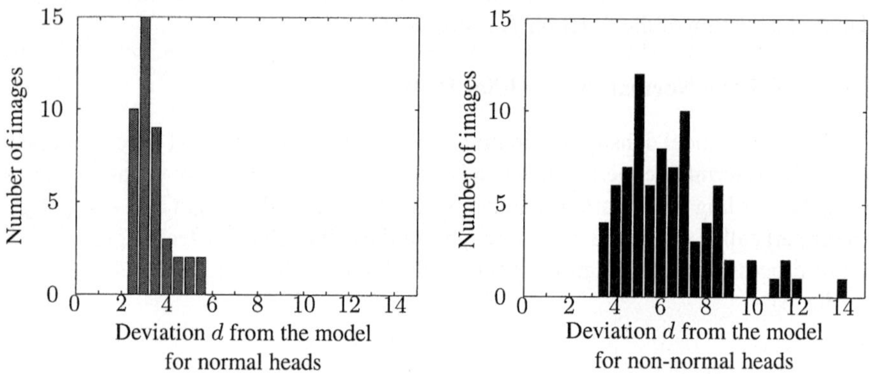

Fig. 5. Histograms of deviation from the model for (a) the set of head images considered as normal by the experts and (b) the set of spermatozoid head images that present intensity distributions not similar to the model

The obtained deviations for the 2D functions of the set of normal and non-normal head images yield two histograms, Fig. 5. In general, the deviation values obtained for normal heads are smaller than the ones obtained for non-normal ones. We can now classify heads by taking a certain value of the deviation as a decision criterion. If the deviation value obtained for a given head is below the decision criterion, that head is classified as normal, otherwise as non-normal. The two histograms overlap for values of the deviation between 3.5 and 5.5 and this means that it is not possible to achieve errorless classification by taking any value of the deviation as a decision criterion. If a high value of the decision criterion is taken (above 5.5), all normal heads will be classified as normal but a number of non-normal cells that have deviation values below 5.5 will be erroneously accepted as normal too. If a low decision criterion value (e.g. 3) is taken, all non-normal heads will be correctly rejected but a number of normal heads (with deviation values above 3) will be rejected as well. Fig. 6 shows the false acceptance and false rejection error as well as their sum as function of the value of the

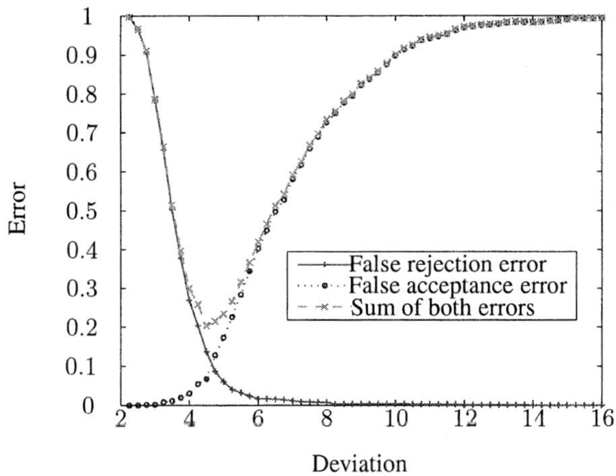

Fig. 6. Error rates in head classification obtained for the different values of the decision criterion. The red line shows the percentage of normal heads that are classified as non-normal (false rejection error); the blue line represents the fraction of non-normal heads misclassified (false acceptance error). The green line is the sum of both errors and it has a minimum for a decision criterion value of 4.25.

decision criterion. The sum of the two errors has a minimum for the value 4.25 of the decision criterion and in the following we use this value for classification. We also used a Bayer classifier but it yielded error rates higher than the method explained previously.

2.5 Experimental Results

We use a test set of 1400 images of spermatozoid heads: 775 images of heads with a normal density distribution pattern according to veterinary experts and 625 images of heads which are not perceived as normal by the experts. We calculate the deviation of each such image from the model and classify it as normal if that deviation is less than 4.25. Otherwise the image is considered as non-normal. The false rejection error of normal heads is 13.68%, and the false acceptance rate of non-normal heads is 6.72%. The overall classification error is 20.40%.

3 Discussion and Conclusions

We proposed a method to classify images of boar spermatozoid heads by means of their intracellular density distribution. A model of normal intensity distribution was defined using a set of head images that were assumed as potentially normal by veterinary experts. We used two training sets of images, one of normal and the other of non-normal heads, and computed the deviation of the grey-level intensity distribution of each such head image from the model distribution. That yields a histogram with the values of deviations of normal head distributions from the model and another histogram with the deviations of non-normal distributions from the model. These histograms were used to compute the value of a decision criterion in a two-class classification problem. Using this value of the decision criterion with a new test set of normal and non-normal head images, we obtained a global error of 20.40% with a false rejection error of normal heads of 13.68% and a false acceptance rate of non-normal heads of 6.72%.

This result can not be compared with another works since there are no approaches which solve this problem considering the intracellular density distribution. Hence, in future works we will try to reduce this error using a more robust classification method. The obtained results will be tested in veterinary praxis using staining techniques to correlate it with sperm fertility.

References

1. Gravance, C., Garner, D., Pitt, C., Vishwanath, R., Sax-Gravance, S., Casey, P.: Replicate and technician variation associated with computer aided bull sperm head morphometry analysis (ASMA). International Journal of Andrology **22** (1999) 77–82
2. Hirai, M., Boersma, A., Hoeflich, A., Wolf, E., Foll, J., Aumuller, T., Braun, J.: Objectively measured sperm motility and sperm head morphometry in boars (Sus scrofa): relation to fertility and seminal plasma growth factors. J. Androl **22** (2001) 104–110
3. Wijchman, J., Wolf, B.D., Graafe, R., Arts, E.: Variation in semen parameters derived from computer-aided semen analysis, within donors and between donors. J. Androl. **22** (2001) 773–780
4. Suzuki, T., Shibahara, H., Tsunoda, H., Hirano, Y., Taneichi, A., Obara, H., Takamizawa, S., Sato, I.: Comparison of the sperm quality analyzer IIC variables with the computer-aided sperm analysis estimates. International Journal of Andrology **25** (2002) 49–54
5. Rijsselaere, T., Soom, A.V., Hoflack, G., Maes, D., de Kruif, A.: Automated sperm morphometry and morphology analysis of canine semen by the Hamilton-Thorne analyser. Theriogenology **62** (2004) 1292–1306
6. Verstegen, J., Iguer-Ouada, M., Onclin, K.: Computer assisted semen analyzers in andrology research and veterinary practice. Theriogenology **57** (2002) 149–179
7. Linneberg, C., Salamon, P., Svarer, C., Hansen, L.: Towards semen quality assessment using neural networks. In: Proc. IEEE Neural Networks for Signal Processing IV. (1994) 509–517
8. Garrett, C., Baker, H.: A new fully automated system for the morphometric analysis of human sperm heads. Fertil. Steril. **63** (1995) 1306–1317
9. Ostermeier, G., Sargeant, G., Yandell, T., Parrish, J.: Measurement of bovine sperm nuclear shape using Fourier harmonic amplitudes. J. Androl. **22** (2001) 584–594
10. Alegre, E., Sánchez, L., Aláiz, R., Dominguez-Fernández, J.: Utilización de momentos estadísticos y redes neuronales en la clasificación de cabezas de espermatozoides de verraco. In: XXV Jornadas de Automática. (2004)
11. Beletti, M., Costa, L., Viana, M.: A comparison of morphometric characteristics of sperm from fertile Bos taurus and Bos indicus bulls in Brazil. Animal Reproduction Science **85** (2005) 105–116

Speech Recognition Using Energy Parameters to Classify Syllables in the Spanish Language

Sergio Suárez Guerra, José Luis Oropeza Rodríguez, Edgardo M. Felipe Riveron, and Jesús Figueroa Nazuno

Computing Research Center, National Polytechnic Institute,
Juan de Dios Batiz s/n, P.O. 07038, Mexico
{ssuarez, edgardo, jfn}@cic.ipn.mx, j_orope@yahoo.com.mx

Abstract. This paper presents an approach for the automatic speech recognition using syllabic units. Its segmentation is based on using the Short-Term Total Energy Function (STTEF) and the Energy Function of the High Frequency (ERO parameter) higher than 3,5 KHz of the speech signal. Training for the classification of the syllables is based on ten related Spanish language rules for syllable splitting. Recognition is based on a Continuous Density Hidden Markov Models and the bigram model language. The approach was tested using two voice corpus of natural speech, one constructed for researching in our laboratory (experimental) and the other one, the corpus Latino40 commonly used in speech researches. The use of ERO parameter increases speech recognition by 5% when compared with recognition using STTEF in discontinuous speech and improved more than 1.5% in continuous speech with three states. When the number of states is incremented to five, the recognition rate is improved proportionally to 97.5% for the discontinuous speech and to 80.5% for the continuous one.

1 Introduction

Using the syllable as the information unit for automatic segmentation applied to Portuguese improved the error rate in word recognition, as reported by [1]. It provides the framework for incorporating the syllable in Spanish language recognition because both languages, Spanish and Portuguese, have as a common characteristic well structured syllable content [2].

The dynamic nature of the speech signal is generally analyzed by means of characteristic models. Segmentation-based systems offer the potential for integrating the dynamics of speech at the phoneme boundaries. This capability of the phonemes is reflected in the syllables, like it has been demonstrated in [3].

As in many other languages, the syllabic units in Spanish are defined by rules (10 in total), which establish 17 distinct syllabic structures. In this paper the following acronyms are used: Consonant – C, Vocal – V; thus, the syllabic structures are formed as CV, VV, CCVCC, etc.

The use of syllabic units is motivated by:

M. Lazo and A. Sanfeliu (Eds.): CIARP 2005, LNCS 3773, pp. 161 – 170, 2005.

- A more perceptual model and better meaning of the speech signal.
- A better framework when dynamic modeling techniques are incorporated into a speech recognition system [4].
- Advantages of using sub words (i.e. phonemes, syllables, triphones, etc) into speech recognition tasks [5]. Phonemes are linguistically well defined; the number of them is little (27 in the Spanish language) [6]. However, syllables serve as naturally motivated minimal units of prosodic organization and for the manipulation of utterances [7]. Furthermore, the syllable has been defined as "a sequence of speech sounds having a maximum or peak of inherent sonority (that is apart from factors such as stress and voice pitched) between two minima of sonority" [8]. The triphones treat the co-articulation problem to segment words structure as a more useful method not only in Spanish language. The triphones, like the syllables, are going to be nowadays as a good alternative for the speech recognition [5].

The use of syllables has several potential benefits. First, syllabic boundaries are more precisely defined than phonetic segment boundaries in both speech waveforms and in spectrographic displays. Second, the syllable may serve as a natural organizational unit useful for reducing redundant computation and storage [4].

There are not antecedents of speech recognition systems using the syllables rules in the training system for the Spanish language. Table 1 lists the frequencies of occurrence of ten monosyllables used in corpus Latino40 and its percentage in the vocabulary. Table 2 shows the percentage of several syllabic structures in corpus Latino40. Both tables show the behavior of the syllables units for this corpus.

Table 1. Frequency of occurrence of ten monosyllables used in corpus Latino40

Word	Syllable configuration	Number of times	% in the vocabulary
De	Deaf Occlusive + Vocal	1760	11.15
La	Liquid + Vocal	1481	9.38
El	Vocal + Liquid	1396	8.85
En	Vocal + Nasal	1061	6.72
No	Nasal + Vocal	1000	6.33
Se	Fricative + Vocal	915	5.80
Que	Deaf Occlusive + Vocal	891	5.64
A	Vocal	784	4.97
Los	Liquid + Vocal + Fricative	580	3.67
Es	Vocal + Fricative	498	3.15

Table 2. Percentage of several syllabic structures in corpus Latino40

Syllable structure	Vocabulary Rate (%)	Accumulated in the vocabulary (%)
CV	50.72	50.72
CVC	23.67	74.39
V	5.81	80.2
CCV	5.13	85.33
VC	4.81	90.14
CVV	4.57	94.71
CVVC	1.09	95.8

2 Continuous Speech Recognition Using Syllables

In automatic speech recognition research (ASR) the characteristics of each basic phonetic unit in a large extent are modified by co-articulation. As a result, the phonetic features found in articulated continuous speech, and the phonetic features found in isolated speech, have different characteristics. Using the syllables the problem is the same, but in our approach the syllables were directly extracted from the speech waveform, whose grammatical solution were found later using a dedicated expert system. Figure 1 shows the result of the segmentation using STTEF [3].

It can be noted that the energy is more significant when the syllable is present and it is a minimum when it is not. The resulting relative minimum and maximum energy are used as the potential syllabic boundaries. The term syllabic unit is introduced to differentiate between the syllables defined generally on the phonological level and the syllabic segments.

Thus, each syllable can be independently stored in a file. Our database uses 10 phrases with 51 different syllables. For each phrase 20 utterances were used, 50% for training and the remainder for recognition, and there were produced by a single female speaker at a moderate speaking rate.

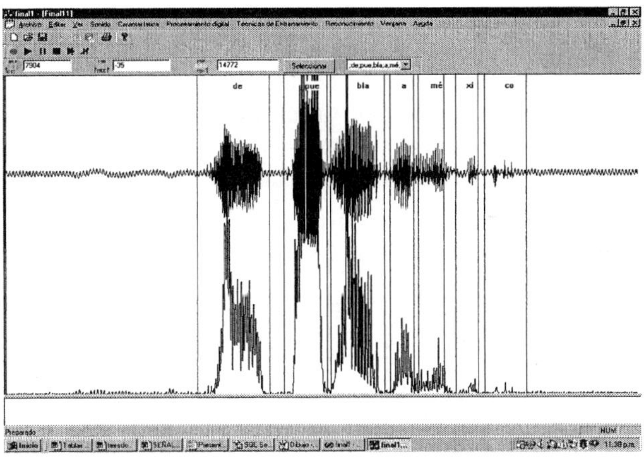

Fig. 1. Syllables speech segmentation labeling

3 Training Speech Model Using Data Segments

The Energy Function of the High Frequency (ERO parameter) is the energy level of the speech signal at high frequencies. The fricative letter, s, is the most significant example. When we use a high-pass filter, we obtain the speech signal above a given cut-off frequency f_c, the RO signal. In our approach, a cut-off frequency $f_c = 3500$ Hz is used as the threshold frequency for obtaining the RO signal. The speech signal at a lower frequency is attenuated. Afterwards, the energy is calculated from the Equation

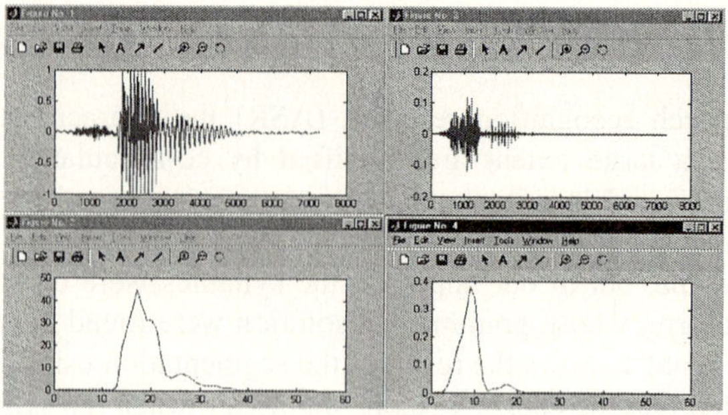

Fig. 2. STTEF (*left*) and ERO (*right*) parameters in the Spanish word 'cero'

(1) for the ERO parameter in each segment of the resultant RO signal. Figure 2 shows graphically the results of this procedure for Short-Term Total Energy Function (STTEF) and ERO parameter in the case of the word 'cero'.

$$ERO = \sum_{i=0}^{N-1} ROi^2 \tag{1}$$

Figure 3 shows the energy distribution for ten different words 'cero' spoken by the same speaker. We found an additional area between the two syllables (ce-ro) using our analysis. In the figure, the dark gray rectangle represents the energy before using the filter, ERO; a medium gray rectangle the energy of the signal after using the filter, STTEF; and a light gray rectangle represents the transition region between both parameters. We call this region the Transition Energy Region -RO.

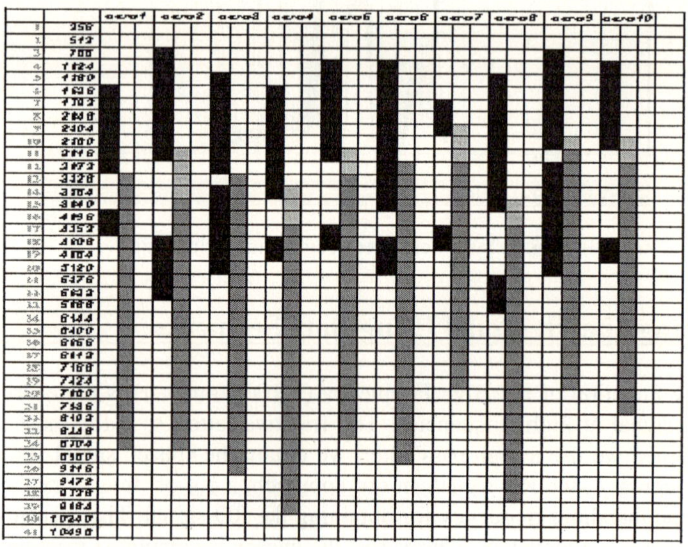

Fig. 3. Energy distribution for ten different words 'cero'

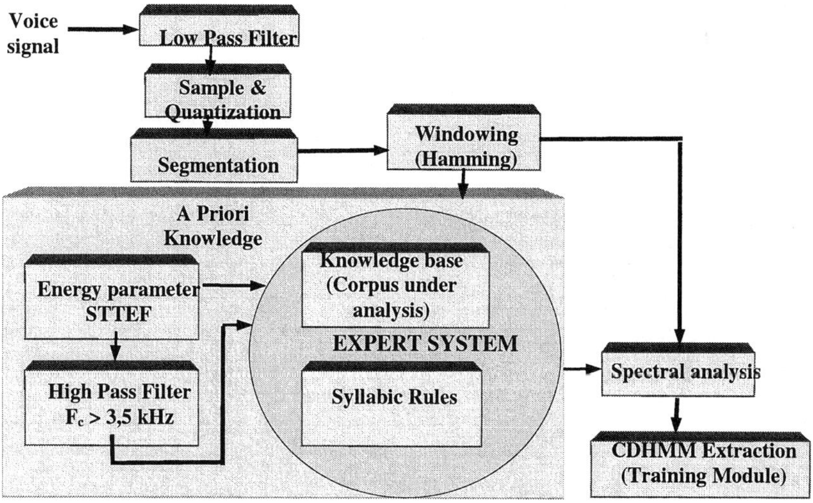

Fig. 4. Functional block diagram for syllable splitting

Figure 4 shows the functional block diagram representing the algorithm used in our approach to extract the signal characteristics.

In the training phase an expert system uses the ten rules for syllable splitting in Spanish. It receives the energy components STTEF and the ERO parameter extracted from the speech signal. Table 3 shows the basic sets in Spanish used by the expert system for the syllable splitting. Table 4 shows the inference rules created in the expert system, associated with the rules for splitting words in syllables.

The rules mentioned above are the postulates used by the recognition system. Syllable splitting is carried out taking into account the spectrogram shape, parameters and the statistics from the expert system. Figure 5 shows graphically the decision trees of the inference rules of the expert system.

After the execution by the expert system and for the voice corpus in process of the entire syllable splitting inference rules, the results are sent to the Training Module as the initial parameters. Then, the necessary models are created for each syllable during the process of recognition.

Table 3. Basic sets in Spanish used during the syllable splitting

CI = {br,bl,cr,cl,dr,fr,fl,gr,gl,kr,ll,pr,pl,tr,rr,ch,tl}	Non-separable Consonant
VD={ai,au,ei,eu,io,ou,ia,ua,ie,ue,oi,uo,ui,iu,ay,ey,oy}	Vocal Diphthong and hiatus
VA={a}	Open Vocal
VS={e,o}	Half-open Vocal
VC={i,u}	Close Vocal
CC={ll.rr,ch}	Compound Consonant
CS={b,c,d,f,g,h,j,k,l,m,n,ñ,p,q,r,s,t,v,w,x,y,z}	Simple Consonant
VT={iai, iei, uai, uei, uau, iau, uay, uey}	Vocal Triphthong and hiatus

Table 4. Inference rules of the expert system

Inference rules		
If CC ^ CC ∈ CI	→	/CC/
If VCV	→	/V/ /CV/
If VCCV	→	/VC/ /CV/
If VCCCV	→	/VCC/ /CV/
If C1C2 ^ C1='h' or C2='h'	→	/C1/ /C2/
If VV ∉ VA, VS	→	/VV/
If VV ∈ VA, VS	→	/V/ /V/
If VCV with C='h'	→	/VCV/
If V1V2 any with accent	→	/V1/ /V2/
If VVV ∈ VT	→	/VVV/

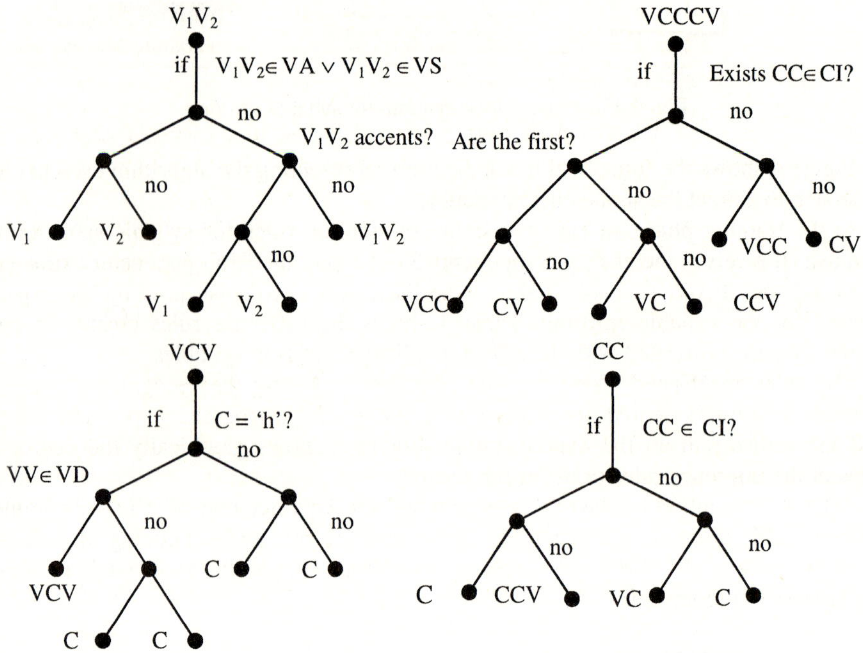

Fig. 5. Decision trees for the inference rules created in the expert system

During the recognition phase, the Recognition Module receives the Cepstral Linear Prediction Coefficients from the signal in processes. They are used to calculate the probabilities of each element in the corpus. The recognized element is that with a higher probability. The final result of this process is the entire speech recognition.

4 Model for Continuous Speech Recognition

In our approach, speech recognition is based on a Hidden Markov Model (HMM) with Continuous Density and the bigram [5] like a language model described by Equation (2).

$$P(W) = P(w_1)\prod_{i=2}^{N} P(w_i|w_{i-1}) \tag{2}$$

Where W represents the words in the phrase under analysis w_1 on the corpus; w_i represents a word in the corpus; P (W) is the probability of the language model; $P(w_i)$ is the probability of a given word in the corpus. In automatic speech recognition it is common to use expression (3) to achieve better performance:

$$\overset{*}{W} = \arg\max\left[P(O|W)P(W)\right] \tag{3}$$

Here, $\overset{*}{W}$ represents the word string, based on the acoustic observation sequence, so that the decoded string has the maximum a posteriori probability $P\,(O|W)$, called the acoustic model.

Language models require the estimation of a priori probability *P(W)* of the word sequence $w = w_1 + w_2 + \cdots + w_N$. *P(W)* can be factorized as the following conditional probability:

$$P(W) = P(w_1 \mid w_2 \mid \cdots + w_N) = P(w_1)\sum_{i=1}^{N} P(w_i \mid w_{i-1}) \tag{4}$$

The estimation of such a large set of probabilities from a finite set of training data is not feasible.

The bigram model is based on the approximation based on the fact that a word only depends statistically on the temporally previous word. In the bigram model shown by the equation (2), the probability of the word $w^{(m)}$ at the generic time index *i* when the previous word is $w^{(m^1)}$ is given by:

$$\hat{P}(w_i = w^{(m)} \mid w_{i-1} = w^{m^1}) = \frac{N(w_i = w^{(m)} \mid w_{i-1} = w^{(m^1)})}{N(w^{m^1})} \tag{5}$$

where the numerator is the number of occurrences of the sequence $\left\langle w_i = w^{(m)}, w_{i-1} = w^{(m^1)} \right\rangle$ in the training set.

5 Experiments and Results

Taking into account the small redundancy of syllables in the corpus Latino40, we have designed a new experimental corpus with more redundant syllables units, prepared by two women and three men, repeating ten phrases twenty times each to give one thousand phrases in total.

Table 5 shows the syllables and the number of times each one appear in phrases of our experimental corpus.

Table 5. Syllables and the number of each type into our experimental corpus

Syllable	#Items	Syllable	#Items	Syllable	#Items
de	2	es	3	zo	1
Pue	1	pa	2	rios	1
bla	1	cio	1	bio	1
a	5	e	2	lo	1
Me	1	o	1	gi	1
xi	1	ahu	1	cos	1
co	1	ma	2	el	1
cuauh	1	do	1	true	1
te	1	cro	1	que	1
moc	1	cia	1	ri	2
y	1	ta	1	ti	1
cuau	2	en	1	lla	1
tla	2	eu	1	se	2
mo	2	ro	1	ria	1
re	2	pro	1	po	1
los	1	to	1	si	1
ble	1	sis	1	tir	1

Table 6. Percentage of discontinuous recognition

Segmentation	Hidden Markov (%) with 3 states	Models states (%) with 5 states
STTEF	89.5	95.5
STTEF + ERO	95.0	97.5

Table 7. Percentage of continuous recognition

Segmentation	Hidden Markov(%) with 3 states	Models states (%) with 5 states
STTEF	77.5	78.5
STTEF + ERO	79.0	80.5

Three Gaussian mixtures were used for each state in the HMM with three and five states, using twelve Cepstral Linear Prediction Coefficients (CLPCs). Tables 6 and 7 show the results of recognition for the discontinuous and continuous cases, respectively, referred to the experimental corpus. The accentuation of Spanish words was not considered in the analysis.

6 Conclusion

The results shown in this paper demonstrate that we can use the syllables as an alternative to the phonemes in an automatic speech recognition system (ASRS) for the Spanish language. The use of syllables for speech recognition avoids the contextual dependency found when phonemes are used.

In our approach we used a new parameter: the Energy Function of the Cepstral High Frequency parameter, ERO. The incorporation of a training module as an expert system using the STTEF and the ERO parameter, taking into account the ten rules for syllable splitting in Spanish, improved considerably the percent of success in speech recognition. The use of the ERO parameter increased by 5% the speech recognition with respect to the use of STTEF in discontinuous speech and by more than 1.5% in continuous speech with three states. When the number of states was incremented to five, the improvement in the recognition was increased to 97.5% for discontinuous speech and to 80.5% for continuous speech.

CLPCs and CDHMMs were used for training and recognition, respectively.

It was also demonstrated that comparing our results with [9], for English, we obtained a better percent in the number of syllables recognized when our new alternative for modeling the ASRS was used for the Spanish language.

The improvement of the results shows that the use of expert systems or conceptual dependency [10] is relevant in speech recognition of the Spanish language when syllables are used as the basic features for recognition.

References

1. Meneido H., Neto J. Combination of Acoustic Models in Continuous Speech Recognition Hybrid Systems, INESC, Rua Alves Redol, 9, 1000- 029 Lisbon, Portugal. 2000.
2. Meneido, H. Joâo P. Neto, J., and Luis B. Almeida, L., INESC-IST. Syllable Onset Detection Applied to the Portuguese Language. 6th European Conference on Speech Communication and Technology (EUROSPEECH'99) Budapest, Hungary, September 5-9. 1999.
3. Suárez, S., Oropeza, J.L., Suso, K., del Villar, M., Pruebas y validación de un sistema de reconocimiento del habla basado en sílabas con un vocabulario pequeño. Congreso Internacional de Computación CIC2003. México, D.F. 2003.
4. Su-Lin Wu, Michael L. Shire, Steven Greenberg, Nelson Morgan., Integrating Syllable Boundary Information into Speech Recognition. Proc. ICASSP, 1998.
5. Rabiner, L. and Juang, B-H., Fundamentals of Speech Recognition, Prentice Hall
6. Serridge, B., 1998. Análisis del Español Mexicano, para la construcción de un sistema de reconocimiento de dicho lenguaje. Grupo TLATOA, UDLA, Puebla, México. 1993.

7. Fujimura, O., UCI Working Papers in Linguistics, Volume 2, Proceedings of the South Western Optimality Theory Workshop (SWOT II), Syllable Structure Constraints, a C/D Model Perspective. 1996.
8. Wu, S., Incorporating information from syllable-length time scales into automatic speech recognition. PhD Thesis, Berkeley University, California. 1998.
9. Bilmes, J.A. A Gentle Tutorial of the EM Algorithm and its Application to Parameter Estimation for Gaussian Mixture and Hidden Markov Models, International Computer Science Institute, Berkeley, CA. 1998.
10. Savage Carmona Jesus, A Hybrid System with Symbolic AI and Statistical Methods for Speech Recognition, Doctoral Thesis, University of Washington. 1995.

A Strategy for Atherosclerotic Lesions Segmentation

Roberto Rodríguez and Oriana Pacheco

Digital Signal Processing Group,
Institute of Cybernetics, Mathematics & Physics (ICIMAF)
rrm@.icmf.inf.cu

Abstract. The watersheds method is a powerful segmentation tool developed in mathematical morphology, which has the drawback of producing over-segmentation. In this paper, in order to prevent its over-segmentation, we present a strategy to obtain robust markers for atherosclerotic lesions segmentation of the thoracic aorta. In such sense, we introduced an algorithm, which was very useful in order to obtain the markers of atherosclerotic lesions. The obtained results by using our strategy were validated calculating the false negatives (FN) and false positives (FP) according to criterion of pathologists, where 0% for FN and less than 11% for FP were obtained. Extensive experimentation showed that, using real image data, the proposed strategy was very suitable for our application.

1 Introduction

Segmentation and contour extraction are important steps towards image analysis. Segmented images are now used routinely in a multitude of different applications, such as, diagnosis, treatment planning, localization of pathology, study of anatomical structure, computer-integrated surgery, among others. However, image segmentation remains a difficult task due to both the variability of object shapes and the variation in image quality. Particularly, medical images are often corrupted by noise and sampling artifacts, which can cause considerable difficulties when applying rigid methods.

The pathological anatomy is a speciality where the use of different techniques of digital image processing (DIP) allows to improve the accuracy of diagnosis of many diseases. One of the most important diseases to study is the atherosclerosis and its organic-consequences, which is one of the principal causes of death in the world [1]. The atherosclerosis produces as final consequence the loss of elasticity and increase of the wall of arteries. For example, heart attack, cerebral attack and ischemia are some of its principal consequences [2].

Many segmentation methods have been proposed for medical-image data [3-6]. Unfortunately, segmentation using traditional low-level image processing techniques, such as thresholding, histogram, and other classical operations, requires a considerable amount of interactive guidance in order to get satisfactory results. Automating these model-free approaches is difficult because of shape complexity, shadows, and variability within and across individual objects. Furthermore, noise and other image artifacts can cause incorrect regions or boundary discontinuities in objects recovered from these methods.

M. Lazo and A. Sanfeliu (Eds.): CIARP 2005, LNCS 3773, pp. 171 – 180, 2005.

In mathematical morphology (MM) important methods have been developed for image segmentation [7, 8]. One of the most powerful tools developed in MM is the watersheds transformation, which is classic in the field of topography and it has been used in many problems of image segmentation. However, the watersheds transformation has the disadvantage of producing over-segmentation. For that reason, the correct way to use watersheds for grayscale image segmentation is to mark the regions we want to segment, that is, the objects, but also the background.

The goal of this paper is to present a strategy to obtain robust markers for atherosclerotic lesions segmentation of the thoracic aorta. In such sense, we introduced an algorithm to obtain markers, which identifies correctly the atherosclerotic lesions and eliminates considerably all spurious information. The validity of our strategy was tested by using watersheds segmentation, where the atherosclerotic lesions were correctly delineated according to the criteria of pathologists.

This paper is organized as follows: Section 2 outlines the theoretical aspects and the method of evaluation. In section 3, we present the features of the studied images. In section 4, we introduce an algorithm to obtain the markers. In section 5, we show the validity of our strategy and we carry out a test of the obtained results. Finally, we describe our conclusions in Section 6.

2 Theoretical Aspects

This section presents the most important theoretical aspects.

2.1 Pre-processing

With the goal of diminishing the noise in the original images we used the Gauss filter. We carried out several researches with many images, arriving to the final conclusion that the best performance are obtained, according to our application, with $\sigma = 3$ and a 3x3 window size. We verified that with these parameters the noise was considerably smoothed and the edges of the interest objects (lesions) were not affected.

2.2 Contrast Enhancement

Contrast enhancement is a very used technique as previous step to segmentation. There are many methods in the literature that can be seen [9, 10]. In this work, we improve the contrast via histogram modification.

2.3 Morphological Grayscale Reconstruction

Let J and I be two grayscale images defined on the same domain D_I, taking their values in the discrete set $\{0, 1, ..., L-1\}$ and such that $J \leq I$ (i.e., for each pixel $p \in D_I$, $J(p) \leq I(p)$). L being an arbitrary positive integer. In this way, it is useful to introduce the geodesic dilations according to the following definition [7]:

Definition 2.3.1 (Geodesic dilation). The elementary geodesic dilation of $\delta_I^{(1)}(J)$ of grayscale image $J \leq I$ "under" I (J is called the *marker* image and I is the *mask*) is defined as,

$$\delta_I^{(1)}(J) = (J \oplus B) \wedge I \tag{1}$$

where the symbol $\wedge$ stands for the pointwise minimum and $J \oplus B$ is the dilation of J by flat structuring element B. The grayscale geodesic dilation of size $n \geq 0$ is obtained by,

$$\delta_I^{(n)}(J) = \delta_I^{(1)} \circ \delta_I^{(1)} \circ \cdots\cdots \circ \delta_I^{(1)}(J),\ n \text{ times} \tag{2}$$

This leads to the following definition of grayscale reconstruction,

Definition 2.3.2 (Grayscale reconstruction). The grayscale reconstruction $\rho_I(J)$ of I from J is obtained by iterating grayscale dilations of J "under" I until stability is reached, that is,

$$\rho_I(J) = \bigcup_{n \geq 1} \delta_I^{(n)}(J) \tag{3}$$

Definition 2.3.3 (Geodesic erosion). Similarly, the elementary geodesic erosion $\varepsilon_I^{(1)}(J)$ of grayscale image $J \geq I$ "above" I is given by,

$$\varepsilon_I^{(1)}(J) = (J\, \theta\, B) \vee I \tag{4}$$

where $\vee$ stands for the pointwise maximum and $J\, \theta\, B$ is the erosion of J by flat structuring element B. The grayscale geodesic erosion of size $n \geq 0$ is then given by,

$$\varepsilon_I^{(n)}(J) = \varepsilon_I^{(1)} \circ \varepsilon_I^{(1)} \circ \cdots\cdots\cdots \circ \varepsilon_I^{(1)}(J),\ n \text{ times} \tag{5}$$

Reconstruction turns out to provide a very efficient method to extract regional maxima and minima from grayscale images. Furthermore, the technique extends to the determination of maximal structures, which will be call *h-domes* and *h-basins*. The only parameter *(h)* is related to the height of these structures. The mathematical background and other definitions can be found in [7].

2.4 Watersheds Segmentation

In what follows, we consider grayscale images as numerical functions or as topographic relief.

Definition 2.4.1 (Catchment Basin). The catchment basin *C(M)* associated with a minimum *M* is the set of pixels *p* of D_I such that a water drop falling at *p* flows down along the relief, following a certain descending path called the downstream of *p*, and eventually reaches *M*.

Using the former definitions, it is possible to present the watershed definition. The notion of watershed will now serve as a guideline for the segmentation of grayscale images.

Definition 2.4.2 (Watersheds by Immersion). Suppose that we have pierced holes in each regional minimum of *I*, this picture being regarded as a topographic surface. We then slowly immerse this surface into a lake. Starting from the minimum of lowest altitude, the water will progressively fill up the different catchment basins of *I*. Now, at each pixel where the water coming from two different minima would merge, we build a dam (see Fig. 1). At the end of this immersion procedure, each minimum is completely surrounded by dams, which delimit its associated catchment basin. The whole set of dams which has been built thus provides a tessellation of I in its different catchment basins. These dams correspond to the watershed of I, that is, these represent the edges of objects.

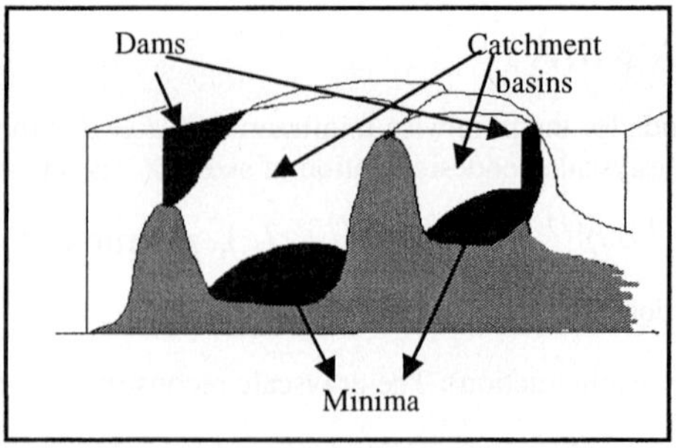

Fig. 1. Building dams at the places where the water coming from two different minima would merge

In many practical cases, one of the principal problems is the obtaining the regional minimum, due to the fact that, in general, images are corrupted by noise. Therefore, the correct way to use watersheds for grayscale image segmentation consists in first detecting markers of the objects to be extracted. When one works in the other way, then the watersheds transformation produces over-segmentation. The over-segmentation mainly comes from the fact that the markers are not perfectly appropriate to the objects to be contoured. In short, the quality of the segmentation is directly linked to the marking function. In this work, the proposed strategy permits to obtain good markers, which were useful for the segmentation process.

2.5 The Method of Evaluation

In order to evaluate the performance of the proposed strategy, we calculate the percent of false negatives (*FN,* atherosclerotic lesions, which are not classified by the strategy) and the false positives (*FP*, noise, which is classified as atherosclerotic lesion). These are defined according to the following expressions,

$$FP = \frac{f_p}{V_p + f_p} * 100$$

$$FN = \frac{f_n}{V_p + f_n} * 100 \tag{7}$$

where V_p is the real quantity of atherosclerotic lesions identified by the physician, f_n is the quantity of atherosclerotic lesions, which were not marked by the strategy and f_p is the number of spurious regions, which were marked as atherosclerotic lesions.

3 Features of the Studied Images

Studied images are of arteries, which have atherosclerotic lesions and these were obtained from different parts of the human body from more of 80 autopsies. These arteries were contrasted with a special tint in order to accentuate the different lesions in arteries. Later, the lesions are manually classified by the pathologists according to World Health Organization. They classified the lesions in type I, II, III and IV. For example, the lesions I and II, these are the fatty streaks and fibrous plaques respectively, while the lesions III and IV are respectively the complicated and calcified plaques. The arteries were digitalized directly from the working desk. It is possible to observe from the images that the different arterial structures are well defined. Other works have used the photograph of the arteries to digitalize the image [11, 12]. This constitutes an additional step, increases the cost of the research, and leads to a loss of information in the original image. The segmentation process is then more difficult too. These images were captured via the MADIP system with a resolution of 512x512x8 bit/pixels [13].

There are several remarkable characteristics of these images, which are common to typical images that we encounter in the atherosclerotic lesions:

1. High local variation of intensity is observed both, within the atherosclerotic lesions and the background. However, the local variation of intensities is higher within the lesions than in background regions.
2. The histograms showed that there is a low contrast in the images.
3. The lesions III and IV have better contrast than the lesions I and II
4. It is common of these images the diversity in shape and size of the atherosclerotic lesions.

4 Experimental Results. Discussion

It is very important to point out that the proposed strategy was obtained according to experimentation, that is, we carried out firstly a morphological reconstruction by erosion for each of the lesions, and secondly, we carried out a morphological reconstruction by dilation for each of the lesions. We verified that in all cases the best results for the lesions I and II using a reconstruction by dilation were obtained, while for the lesions III and IV the obtained results were much better for a reconstruction by erosion.

With the goal of extracting the approximate regions of interest, after the histogram modification, we carried out a morphological reconstruction. We verified that the reconstruction by erosion (for the lesions III and IV) led to an image where the dark zones correspond to these lesions. For example, in Fig. 2 is shown the obtained result for a lesions IV.

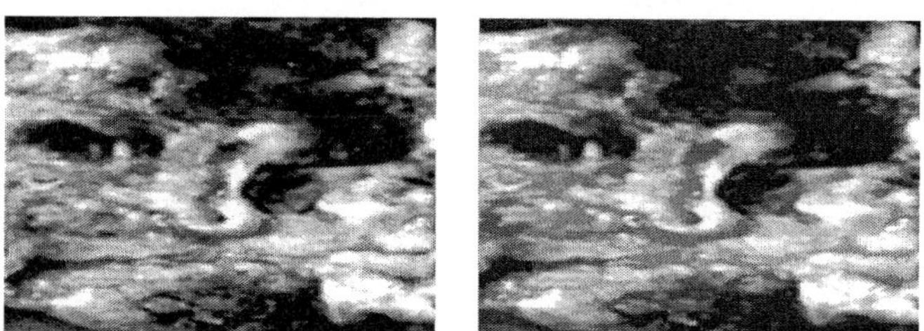

(a) (b)

Fig. 2. (a) Resulting image of the histogram modification. (b) Image obtained by a reconstruction by erosion. The dark parts correspond to the lesion IV.

The result in Fig. 2(b) was obtained by using a rhomb as structuring element of 5x5 pixels and a height equal to 60. The selection of this structuring element and its size was obtained via experimentation. These values were used for the lesion III too.

We carried out several experiments with different structuring element and with different size, which we did not put here for problem space. With respect to the height, we verified that for each of our images the optimal value was in the range from 40 to 60.

After obtaining both, the size of structuring element and the optimal height, the next stage of our strategy was to segment the approximate region of interest, that is, a region that contains the atherosclerotic lesions and its neighbouring background. This step was carried out by applying a simple threshold through Otsu method. The thresholding value does not have much influence on the performance, because the exact shape and size of this region are not important, and hence the region is referred to as an approximate region. In Fig. 3(b) one can see the region of interest.

After this result, we introduce the following algorithm to obtain markers for the atherosclerotic lesions.

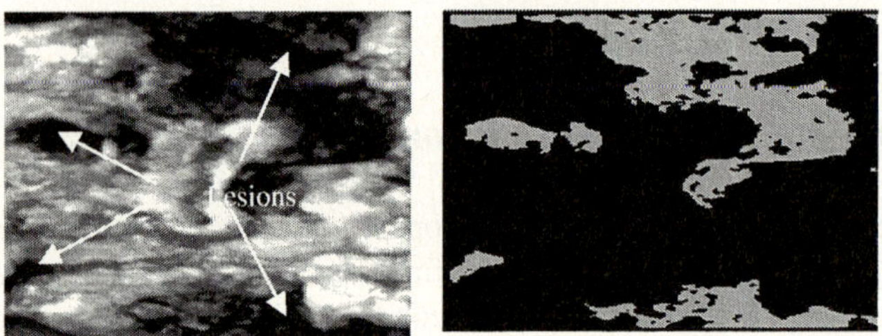

(a) (b)

Fig. 3. (a) Image of the reconstruction, where the arrows indicate the lesions. (b) Regions of interest.

4.1 Algorithm to Obtain Markers

The steps of the algorithm are described below:

1. Obtain the regions of interest. Let IREZI be the resulting image.
2. Label the resulting image of the step 1. Create an auxiliary image; let IA1 be this image. All pixels of this image are put in zero. Scan IREZI at iterative way and all the background in IA1 is labeled with a value equal to 1.
3. Scan IREZI again from the top to the bottom and from the left to the right. If there is a pixel, which belongs to a connected component and in the image IAl this pixel has zero value, then other iterative method begins to work. This new iterative method marks with a determined value within the image IA1 all pixels belonging to a connected component. In addition, pixels within the image IREZI are also marked with a value, which identifies the connected component to which they belong. As this step is finished, in the image IREZI all the connected components were filled and in the image IA1 all the connected components were labeled.
4. Create other auxiliary image (let IA2 be this image) with the same values of the image IA1. Create also an array, which controls if a connected component was reduced. In the image IA2 is where in each step the reduction of the connected components are obtained, the final result is represented in the image IA1.

5. Scan the labeled image (IA1). When in this image a pixel is found, which belongs to a connected component, through other iterative method, this component is reduced and in the image IA2 all the frontiers of the connected component are marked. If still there is some pixel within the connected component, which is no frontier, in the images IA2 and IA1, the mentioned pixel is eliminated and this function begins again until that all points are frontiers. In this case, the obtained result (reduction) is taken as the mark.
6. Finish when the image IREZI is completely scanned. When this step is concluded, in the image IA1 all marks of BV are. These marks are collocated in the image IREZI. Here, after the step two, the connected components (in IREZI) were filled. The image IREZI is the resulting image.

The result of applying this algorithm to the image of Fig. 3(b) is shown in Fig. 4. In Fig. 4(b) one can see that the mark is unique for each of the atherosclerotic lesions, which is always within these. This procedure was carried out for the lesions III and IV.

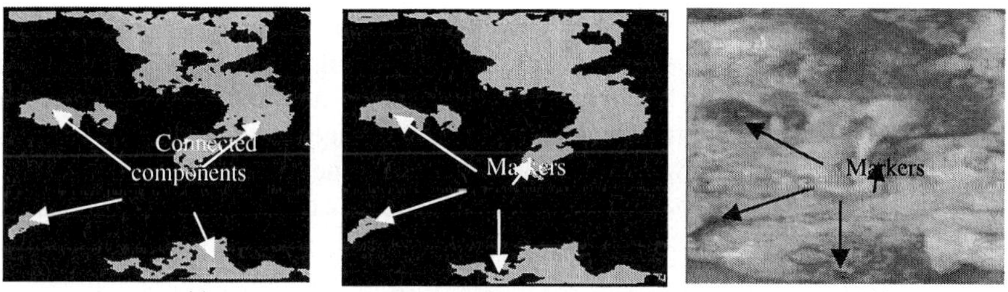

(a) (b) (c)

Fig. 4. (a) Image with regions of interest. (b) Marking image. (c) Marks superimposed on the original image.

Now, we will explain the steps that we carried out to obtain the marks for the lesions I and II. We carried out a reconstruction by dilation. This reconstruction improved more these lesions. Fig.5 shows the obtained result of the reconstruction.

Later, we obtained the approximate region of interest and the markers similarly as in the lesions III and IV. In Fig. 6 is shown the obtained result.

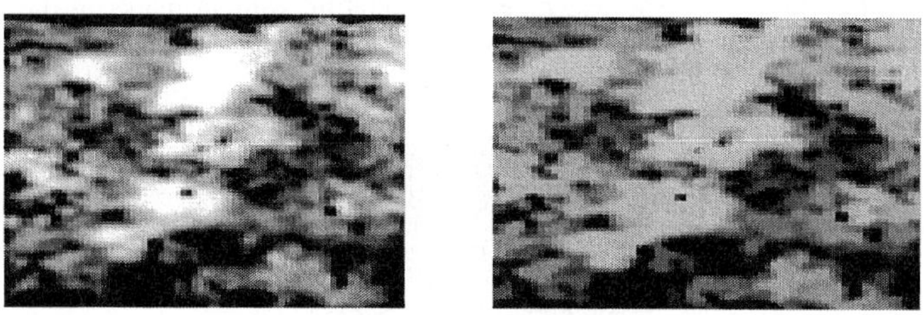

(a) (b)

Fig. 5. (a) Initial image. (b) Reconstruction by dilation (lesion II and II).

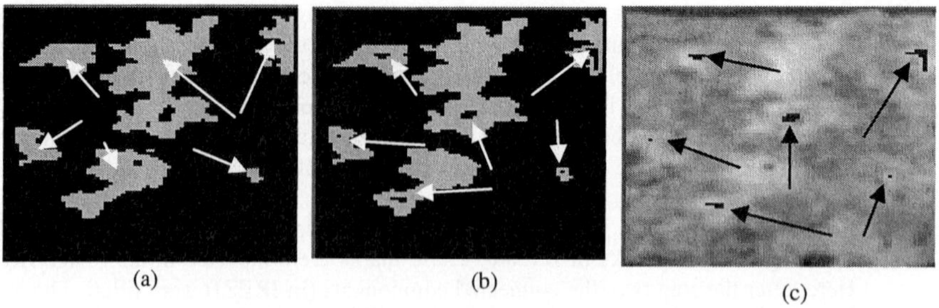

Fig. 6. (a) Regions of interest. The arrows indicate the connected components. (b) Image with marks. (c) The marks superimposed on the original image.

5 Application of the Proposed Strategy for Atherosclerosis Image Segmentation by Using the Watershed Method

As we have pointed out the watershed transformation has the drawback of producing an over-segmentation as it is applied directly to the original image or the gradient image. In fact, Fig. 7(b) shows the obtained result as we applied directly the watershed transformation to an atherosclerosis image without good markers. However, in Fig. 7(c) is shown the excellent result obtained according to our strategy and the introduced algorithm in this work. The contours of the atherosclerotic lesions were well defined.

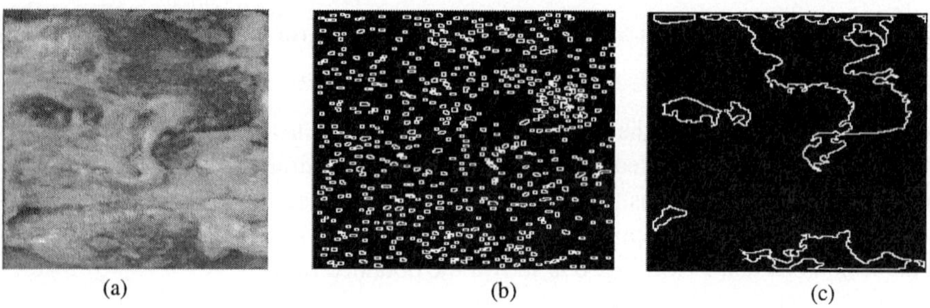

Fig. 7. (a) Original image. (b) The watershed segmentation without marks in the lesions. (c) The watershed segmentation according to our strategy.

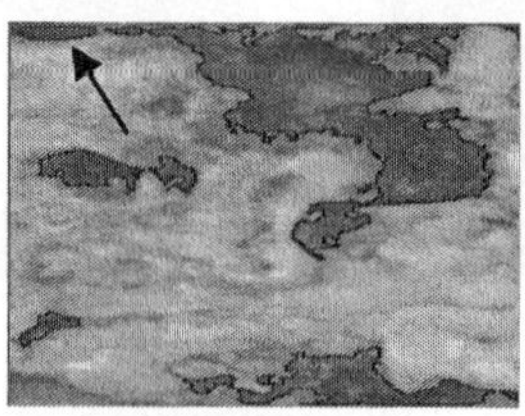

Fig. 8. The contours superimposed on the original image. The arrow indicates an object, which does not correspond to an atherosclerotic lesion.

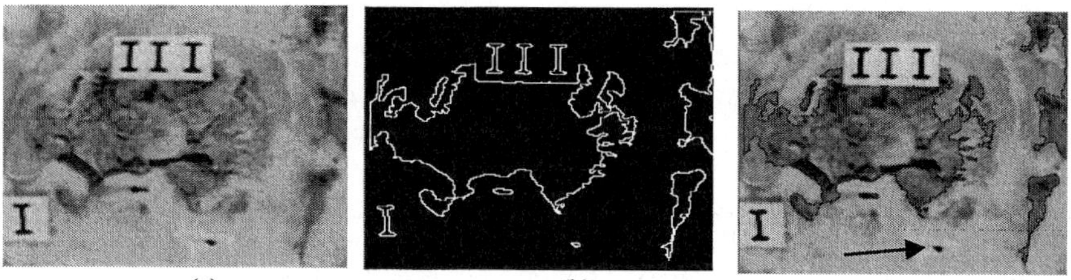

Fig. 9. (a) Original image. (b) Watershed transformation. (c) Contours superimposed on the original image. The arrow in Figure 9 (c) indicates an object, which does not belong to the lesion.

In Fig. 8, we show the contours superimposed on the original image in order to see the exact coincidence of the obtained contours. This result is evident

In Fig. 9, another example, with real image, of the application of our strategy is shown. The authors have several examples, which we did not present for problem space

6 Conclusions

In this work, we proposed a strategy to obtain robust markers for atherosclerotic lesions. In such sense, we introduced an algorithm, which identifies correctly the atherosclerotic lesions and all undesirable information is considerably eliminated. With our strategy the application of the watersheds transformation provided excellent results, and we obtained the exact contours of the atherosclerotic lesions. We showed by extensive experimentation by using real image data, that the proposed strategy was robust for the type of images considered. This strategy was tested, according to the criteria of pathologists, obtaining the false negatives (FN) and false positives (FP), where the percent for FN was equal to 0% and for FP minor than 11%. The results were obtained for more of 80 images.

References

1. Fernández-Britto, J. E., Carlevaro, P. V., Bacallao, J., Koch, A.S., Guski,H., Campos, R.: "*Coronary Atherosclerotic lesion: Its study applying an atherometric system using discriminant analysis*". Zentralbl.allg. Pathol. 134: 243-249, 1988.
2. Cotran, Robbins: Patología Estructural y Funcional, *Mc. Grow Hill, México, ISBN: 970-10-2787-6, 2002.*
3. W. Kenong, D. Gauthier and M. D. Levine, "*Live Cell Image Segmentation*", IEEE Transactions on Biomedical Engineering, vol.42, no. 1, enero 1995.
4. J. Sijbers, P. Scheunders, M. Verhoye, A. Van der Linden, D. Van Dyck, E. Raman, "*Watershed-based segmentation of 3D MR data for volume quatization*", Magnetic Resonance Imaging, vol. 15, no. 6, pp 679-688, 1997.
5. C. Chin-Hsing, J. Lee, J. Wang and C. W. Mao, "*Color image segmentation for bladder cancer diagnosis*", Mathl. Comput. Modeling, vol. 27, no. 2, pp. 103-120, 1998.

6. P. Schmid, "*Segmentation of digitized dermatoscopic images by two-dimensional color clustering*", IEEE Trans. Med. Imag., vol. 18, no. 2, Feb, 1999.
7. Vincent, L.: "*Morphological grayscale reconstruction in Image Analysis: Applications and Efficient Algorithms"*. IEEE Transactions on Image Processing, vol.2, pp. 176-201, April, 1993.
8. Vicent, L and Soille, P.*: "Watersheds in digital spaces: An efficient algorithm based on immersion simulations"*, IEEE Transact. Pattern Anal. Machine Intell., 13:583-593; 1991.
9. Fuh C-S, Maragos P., Vincent L.: *Region based approaches to visual motion correspondence*. Technical Report HRL, Harvard University, Cambridge, MA, 1991.
10. Roberto R. M.: " *The interaction and heuristic knowledge in digital image restoration and enhancement. An intelligent system (SIPDI)",* Ph.D Thesis, Institute of Technology, Havana, 1995.
11. Svindland, A. and Walloe, L.: *"Distribution pattern of sudanophilic plaques in the descending thoracic and proximal abdominal human aorta*". Atherosclerosis, 57: 219-224, 1985.
12. Cornill, J. F., Barrett, W. A., Herderick, E. E., Mahley, R. W. and Fry, D. L.: "*Topographic study of sudanophilic lesions in cholesterol-fed minipigs by image analysis*". Arteriosclerosis, 5: 415-426, 1985.
13. Rodríguez, R., Alarcón, T. and Sánchez, L.: "*MADIP: Morphometrical Analysis by Digital Image Processing*", Proceedings of the IX Spanish Symposium on Pattern Recognition and Image Analysis, Vol. I, pp. 291-298, ISBN 84-8021-349-3, 2001, Spain.

Image Scale-Space from the Heat Kernel

Fan Zhang and Edwin R. Hancock

Department of Computer Science,
University of York, York, YO10 5DD, UK

Abstract. In this paper, we show how the heat-kernel can be used to construct a scale-space for image smoothing and edge detection. We commence from an affinity weight matrix computed by exponentiating the difference in pixel grey-scale and distance. From the weight matrix, we compute the graph Laplacian. Information flow across this weighted graph-structure with time is captured by the heat-equation, and the solution, i.e. the heat kernel, is found by exponentiating the Laplacian eigen-system with time. Our scale-space is constructed by varying the time parameter of the heat-kernel. The larger the time the greater the the amount of information flow across the graph. The method has the effect of smoothing within regions, but does not blur region boundaries. Moreover, the boundaries do not move with time and this overcomes one of the problems with Gaussian scale-space. We illustrate the effectiveness of the method for image smoothing and edge detection.

1 Introduction

Witkin was one of the first to formalise the multi-scale descriptions of images and signals in terms of scale-space filtering [13]. The technique plays an important role in low-level computer vision. The basic idea is to use convolutions with the Gaussian kernel to generate fine to coarse resolution image descriptions. Babaud [7], Yuille [17] and Hummel [6] have analysed and further developed the method. Broadly speaking this work has shown that there is considerable information to be gained from the analysis of changes in image structure over different scales. Moreover, the study of multi-scale and multi-resolution image processing has lead the development of a diverse family of algorithms. For instance, Gidas [4] has extended Geman and Geman's [3] stochastic image restoration method to the multi-scale case using the renormalisation group to relate the processing at different scales. Spann and Wilson [16] combined the spatial and frequency domain locality to segment images using multiresolution techniques.

The formal description of Witkin's idea is as follows. From the image $\mathcal{I}_0(x,y)$ a series of coarser scale images $\mathcal{I}(x,y,\sigma)$ are generated through convolution with a Gaussian kernel $G(x,y;\sigma)$ of scale σ. The convolution is

$$\mathcal{I}(x,y,\sigma) = \mathcal{I}_0(x,y) * G(x,y;\sigma) = \int_{-\infty}^{+\infty}\int_{-\infty}^{+\infty} \mathcal{I}_0(x-u,y-v)\frac{1}{2\pi\sigma^2}e^{-\frac{u^2+v^2}{2\sigma^2}}dudv \tag{1}$$

M. Lazo and A. Sanfeliu (Eds.): CIARP 2005, LNCS 3773, pp. 181–192, 2005.

As the scale σ is increased, the resolution becomes coarser. Since the Gaussian smoothing process is linear and isotropic, it has an equal blurring effect at all image locations. Hence, while the region interiors are smoothed their boundaries are blurred. Another problem with linear scale-space is that the boundary locations move and sometimes coalesce at coarse scales. As illustrated by Perona and Malik [12], in 2-D images there is additional problem that edge junctions, which contain much of the spatial information of edge maps, are destroyed.

Hummel [6] and Koenderink [8] pointed out that the family of images derived from the Gaussian convolution operation are solutions of the heat equation

$$\frac{\partial \mathcal{I}}{\partial t} = \Delta \mathcal{I} = \frac{\partial^2 \mathcal{I}}{\partial x^2} + \frac{\partial^2 \mathcal{I}}{\partial y^2} \tag{2}$$

with the initial condition $\mathcal{I}(x, y, 0) = \mathcal{I}_0(x, y)$. Based on this observation, Koenderink [8] stated two criteria for features to generate multi-scale descriptions. The first of these is causality, whereby any feature at a coarse level of resolution is required to possess a "cause" at a finer level of resolution, although the reverse need not be true. The second criterion is that of homogeneity and isotropy. According to this requirement the scale-space blurring is required to be spatially invariant. In [12], Perona and Malik suggested another definition of scale-space which breaks the isotropy criterion and works better than Gaussian blurring. Since Gaussian blurring is governed by the heat equation, the thermal conductivity in all directions is constant. As a result boundaries will be blurred. Perona and Malik's idea is to halt the heat-flow process at object boundaries. To do this they control the thermal conductivity $c(x, y, t)$ using the magnitude of the image gradient. When the gradient is large, which indicates the existence of a likely edge, the value c is small. When the gradient is small, on the other hand, the value of c is large. They generate a family of coarse resolution images which are the solutions of the anisotropic diffusion equation

$$\frac{\partial \mathcal{I}}{\partial t} = div((c(x, y, t)(\frac{\partial \mathcal{I}}{\partial x} + \frac{\partial \mathcal{I}}{\partial y}))) \tag{3}$$

where *div* is the divergence operator. The method is demonstrated to outperform Gaussian blurring, preserving boundary sharpness and location.

Recently, there has been considerable interest in the use of graph-spectral methods for image segmentation. The pioneering work here was done by Shi and Malik [15]. The idea is to characterise the similarity of image pixels using a weight matrix which is computed by exponentiating the difference in pixel brightness. From the weight matrix the Laplacian matrix (the degree matrix minus the weight matrix) of the associated weighted graph is computed. The bi-partition of the graph that minimises the normalised cut is located using the Fiedler eigen-vector of the Laplacian.

This paper aims to exploit the close relationship between the heat-kernel and the Laplacian eigensystem to develop a graph-spectral method for scale-space image representation. Our method is motivated by the heat kernel on graphs [9] which is based on the heat equation for discrete structures, recently proposed in the machine learning domain. According to the heat-equation, the Laplacian determines the rate of heat-flow across the weighted graph with time. The solution to the heat equation, i.e. the heat-kernel, is found by exponentiating the Laplacian eigensystem with time. We exploit this property to develop a scale-space representation from the affinity weight matrix. According to our representation, time plays the role of scale. By varying time we control the amount of blurring resulting from heat-flow.

2 Heat Kernels on Graphs

To commence, suppose that the graph under study is denoted by $G = (V, E, W)$ where V is the set of nodes, $E \subseteq V \times V$ is the set of edges and $W : E \rightarrow [0, 1]$ is the weight function. Since we wish to adopt a graph-spectral approach we introduce the adjacency matrix A for the graph where the elements are

$$A(u,v) = \begin{cases} W(u,v) & \text{if } (u,v) \in E \\ 0 & \text{otherwise} \end{cases} \quad (4)$$

We also construct the diagonal degree matrix D, whose elements are given by $D(u,u) = deg(u) = \sum_{v \in V} A(u,v)$. ¿From the degree matrix and the adjacency matrix we construct the Laplacian matrix $L = D - A$, i.e. the degree matrix minus the adjacency matrix. The spectral decomposition of the Laplacian matrix is $L = \Phi \Lambda \Phi^T$ where $\Lambda = diag(\lambda_1, \lambda_2, ..., \lambda_{|V|})$ is the diagonal matrix with the decreasingly ordered eigenvalues $(0 = \lambda_1 < \lambda_2 \leq \lambda_3 ...)$ as elements and $\Phi = (\phi_1 | \phi_2 | .... | \phi_{|V|})$ is the matrix with the correspondingly ordered eigenvectors as columns. Since L is symmetric and positive semi-definite, the eigenvalues of the Laplacian are all positive. The eigenvector ϕ_2 associated with the smallest non-zero eigenvalue λ_2 is referred to as the Fiedler-vector. We are interested in the heat equation associated with the Laplacian and with the accompanying initial conditions $h_0 = \mathcal{I}$ where $\mathcal{I}$ is the identity matrix, i.e.

$$\frac{\partial h_t}{\partial t} = -L h_t \quad (5)$$

where h_t is the heat kernel and t is time. The heat kernel can hence be viewed as describing the flow of heat across the edges of the graph with time. The rate of flow is determined by the Laplacian of the graph. The solution to the heat equation is found by exponentiating the Laplacian eigen-spectrum, i.e.

$$h_t = \exp[-tL] = \Phi \exp[-t\Lambda] \Phi^T . \quad (6)$$

The heat kernel is a $|V| \times |V|$ matrix, and for the nodes u and v of the graph G the resulting element is

$$h_t(u,v) = \sum_{i=1}^{|V|} \exp[-\lambda_i t] \phi_i(u) \phi_i(v) \quad (7)$$

When t tends to zero, then $h_t \simeq I - Lt$, i.e. the kernel depends on the local connectivity structure or topology of the graph. If, on the other hand, t is large, then $h_t \simeq \exp[-\lambda_2]\phi_2\phi_2^T$, where λ_2 is the smallest non-zero eigenvalue and ϕ_2 is the associated eigenvector, i.e. the Fiedler vector. Hence, the large time behavior is governed by the global structure of the graph.

3 Graph Scale-Space

The heat kernel matrix h_t is real valued and from the well-known 'kernel trick' [14] can be interpreted as a inner-product or Gram matrix. As a result the nodes of the graph can be viewed as residing in a possibly infinite dimensional Hilbert space. In other words, $h_t(u,v)$ efficiently characterizes the similarity between the nodes u and v. The Laplacian L encodes the local structure of a graph and dominates the heat-kernel at small time, but as time t increases then the global structure emerges in h_t.

From the standpoint of heat diffusion, the heat kernel h_t is the solution of the heat equation (5). As pointed out in [10], for an equally weighted graph the heat kernel h_t is the counterpart of the Gaussian kernel for discrete spaces $R^{|V|}$ with variance $\sigma^2 = 2t$. The value of $h_t(u,v)$ decays exponentially with the distance or weight of edge $W(u,v)$. It is useful to consider the following picture of the heat diffusion process on graphs. Suppose we inject a unit amount of heat at the vertex k of a graph, and allow the heat diffuse through the edges of the graph. The rate of diffusion over the edge $E(u,v)$ is determined by the edge weight $W(u,v)$. At time t, the heat kernel value of $h_t(k,v)$ is the amount of heat accumulated at vertex v.

Following recent work on graph-spectral methods for image segmentation [15] [11] we abstract images using the graph $G = (V, E, W)$ where the vertices of G are the pixels of the image, and an edge is formed between each pair of vertices. We denote the pixel intensities of the image as a column vector $\mathcal{I}_0$. The weight of each edge, $W(u,v)$, is a function characterizing the relationship between the pixels u and v. We would like to generate a family of coarser resolution images from $\mathcal{I}_0$ using heat flow on the graph G. To do this we inject at each vertex an amount of heat energy equal to the intensity of the associated pixel. The heat at each vertex diffuses through the graph edges as time t progresses. The edge weight plays the role of thermal conductivity. If two pixels belong to the same region, then the associated edge weight is large. As a result heat can flow easily between them. On the other hand, if two pixels belong to different regions, then the associated edge weight is very small, and hence it is difficult for heat to flow from one region to another. We wish to minimize the influence of one region on another. This behaviour is of course captured by the standard weight matrix

$$W(u,v) = \begin{cases} e^{-\frac{|\mathcal{I}_0(u)-\mathcal{I}_0(v)|^2}{\sigma^2}} & \text{if } \|X(u)-X(v)\| \leq r \\ 0 & \text{otherwise} \end{cases} \tag{8}$$

where $\mathcal{I}_0(u)$ and $X(u)$ are the intensity and location of the pixel u respectively. This heat evolution model is similar to the graph heat kernel described in

Section 2, except that the initial heat residing at each vertex is determined by the pixel intensities. Since we wish to find the heat at each node of the graph at time t, the heat diffusion here is still controlled by the graph Laplacian. So the evolution of the image intensity $\mathcal{I}_0$ follows the equation

$$\frac{\partial \mathcal{I}_t}{\partial t} = -L\mathcal{I}_0. \tag{9}$$

The solution of the above equation is $\mathcal{I}_t = e^{-tL}\mathcal{I}_0 = h_t\mathcal{I}_0$. So the intensity of pixel v at time t is

$$\mathcal{I}_t(v) = \sum_{u=1}^{|V|} \mathcal{I}_0(u) \times h_t(u,v) \tag{10}$$

Since each row u of the heat kernel h_t satisfies the conditions $0 \leq h_t(u,v) \leq 1 \forall v$ and $\sum_{v=1}^{|V|} h_t(u,v) = 1$, the total intensity of the image at all scales (times) is preserved.

3.1 Lazy Random Walk View of Graph Scale-Space

Our proposed graph scale-space also has an explanation from the viewpoint of the continuous time lazy random walk. Consider a lazy random walk with transition matrix $T = (1-\alpha)I + \alpha D^{-1}A$ which migrates between different nodes with probability α and remains static at a node with probability $1-\alpha$. In the continuous time limit, i.e. $N \to \infty$, let $t = \alpha N$, then

$$\lim_{N\to\infty} T^N = \lim_{N\to\infty} ((1-\alpha)I + \alpha D^{-1}A)^N \tag{11}$$

$$= e^{-tD^{-1}L} \tag{12}$$

Let p_t be the vector whose element $p_t(i)$ is the probability of visiting node i of the graph under the random walk. The probability vector evolves under the equation $\frac{\partial p_t}{\partial t} = -Lp_t$, which has the solution $p_t = e^{-tL}p_0$. As a result

$$p_t = h_t p_0 \tag{13}$$

As a result, the heat kernel is the continuous time limit of the lazy random walk. If we normalize the image intensity vector $\mathcal{I}_0$ and consider it as the initial probability distribution of the associated graph, then the intensity or probability of each node at time t is given by (13).

3.2 Approximate Schemes to Estimate the Heat Kernel

Since in practice the number of image pixels is large, it is time consuming and demanding on memory space to calculate the heat kernel through finding all the eigenvalues and eigenvectors of the graph Laplacian matrix. However, we can perform a McLaurin expansion [2] on the heat-kernel to re-express it as a polynomial in t with the result

$$h_t = e^{-tL} = I - tL + \frac{t^2}{2!}L^2 - \frac{t^3}{3!}L^3 + \cdots \tag{14}$$

Hence, we can approximate h_t using the leading terms. However, in practice the graph Laplacian matrix L of an image is too large and this still proves computationally restrictive. To overcome this problem, we explore the following two simplification schemes:

Scheme 1: Since the graph Laplacian L is positive semi-definite, its eigenvalues are all positive (with the exception of one that is zero for a connected graph). Further, since $h_t = \Phi \exp[-t\Lambda]\Phi^T$, then only the largest few eigenvalues and corresponding eigenvectors of L make a significant contribution to h_t. As a result, since the graphs we use here are only locally connected and as result L is very sparse, then we can use the Lanczos algorithm [5] to find the leading few eigenvalues and eigenvectors. If we select the largest d eigenvalues, then

$$h_t \approx \Phi_d \exp[-t\Lambda_d]\Phi_d^T \tag{15}$$

where Φ_d is a $n \times d$ matrix with the first d columns of Φ and Λ_d is a $d \times d$ diagonal matrix containing the first d eigenvalues.

Scheme 2: An alternative is to restrict our attention to pixels that are close to one-another. We can then use a smaller $n_1 \times n_2$ window of each pixel to construct a smaller graph. As a result we can use the heat kernel of this smaller graph to calculate the intensity of the pixel at time t. This method has a high degree of potential parallelism and so could be implemented on a multi-processor machine.

We have used both of the above schemes in our experiments, and both give good performance. Moreover, unlike Perona and Malik, our method does not need iteration to compute the brightness of the image at different scales.

3.3 Properties of Graph Scale-Space

Anisotropic diffusion is based on the heat conduction equation for a two dimensional continuous function, and locates the solution using an iterative numerical scheme for discrete images. Our scale-space construction commences with the discrete image data and is derived from the diffusions (or lazy random walks) on the discrete image structures. Exact solutions are found using the graph spectrum. In our method the total pixel weight is invariant to the diffusion time t, while the weight or gradient in the numerical scheme for anisotropic diffusion needs to be updated at each step.

Our graph-based scale-space representation overcomes the drawbacks of the Gaussian scale-space outlined in Section 1 since it is anisotropic due to the difference in edge weights. Moreover, it has the following characteristics which are similar to the method of Perona and Malik:

1. Causality: The graph scale-space representation has no spurious details generated through the fine to coarse scale sampling. Witkin [13] and Koenderink [8] pointed out that any candidate multi-scale description must satisfy this criteria.
2. Object boundaries maintain sharpness at coarse scales and the locations of the boundaries do not shift through the scale-space.
3. Region smoothing is preferred over boundary smoothing.

4. The total intensity of the image does not change, and the contrast of different regions is maintained at different scales
5. The new scale-space can be efficiently calculated without iteration using approximation schemes.

4 Experiments

In this section we present the results of applying our method to synthetic and real world data, and provide some experimental evaluation. We have also compared our method with Gaussian smoothing and Perona and Malik's algorithm (Anisotropic diffusion). In the following, Figures 1 and 4 used simplification scheme 1 and the remaining results used scheme 2. In all our experiments we set $r = 1$.

We first constructed a synthetic image and generated a sequence of blurred images with different amounts of added noise. Then, both anisotropic diffusion and the heat kernel filter were applied to the sequence. The scale spaces of a sample image from the sequence are shown in Figure 1. To compare the two methods, we counted the number of error pixels of each image of the sequence at different scales or time. The image statistics are plotted in Figure 2. When the amount of noise is small, anisotropic diffusion works a little better than the heat kernel method. However, when the amount of added noise becomes larger, then the heat kernel method clearly outperforms anisotropic diffusion.

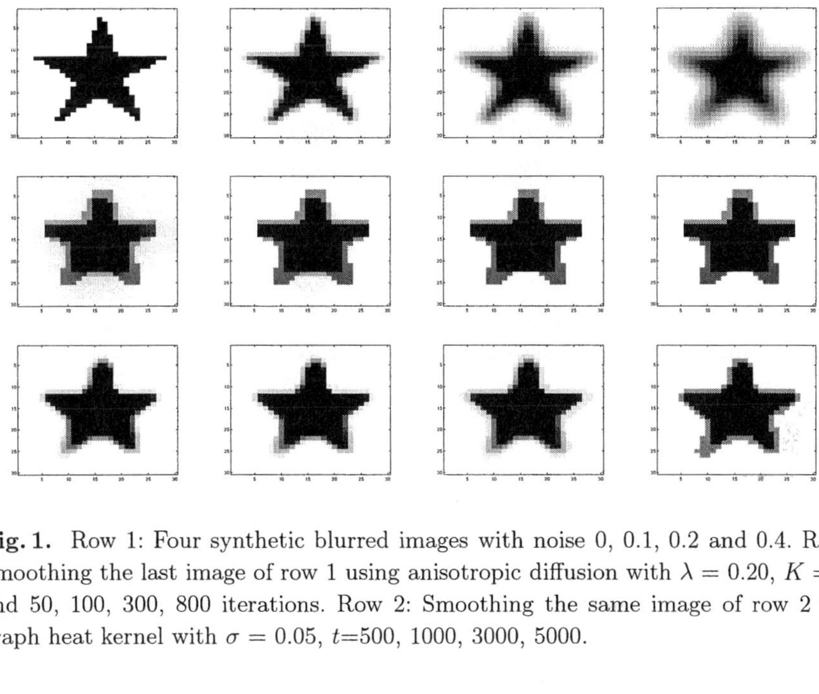

Fig. 1. Row 1: Four synthetic blurred images with noise 0, 0.1, 0.2 and 0.4. Row 2: Smoothing the last image of row 1 using anisotropic diffusion with $\lambda = 0.20$, $K = 0.1$, and 50, 100, 300, 800 iterations. Row 2: Smoothing the same image of row 2 using graph heat kernel with $\sigma = 0.05$, t=500, 1000, 3000, 5000.

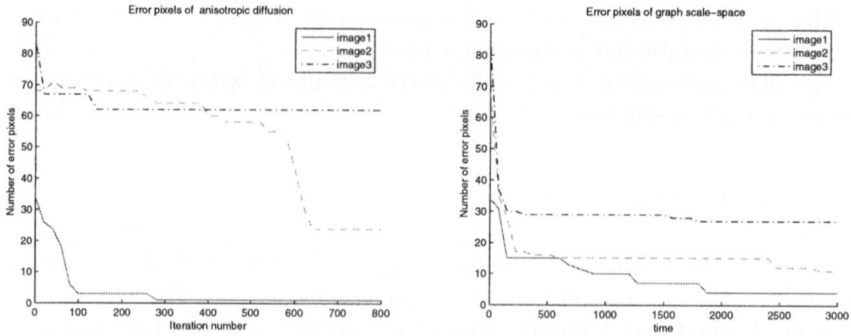

Fig. 2. Error pixels comparison of the the anisotropic diffusion (left) and graph scale space (left)

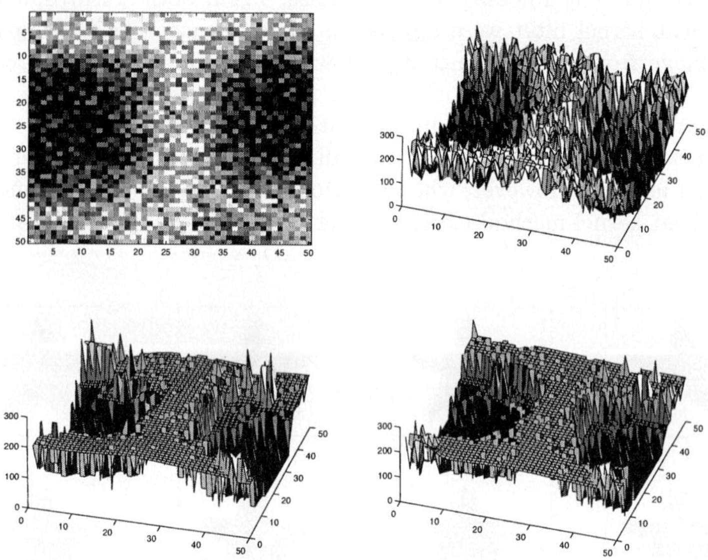

Fig. 3. (a) Synthetic heavily noisy image. (b) 3D brightness of original image. (c) 3D brightness using anisotropic diffusion after 350 iterations. (d) 3D brightness after using Graph heat kernel, window size: 13 × 13; $\sigma = 0.1$; $t = 25$.

In Figure 3 we illustrate the effect of the heat kernel method on another synthetic image. Panel (a) shows the original image, which is subject to considerable noise. Panel (b) displays the grey-scale values as an elevation plot. The second row shows the smoothed images after applying anisotropic diffusion and graph heat kernel filter. Here both methods recovered the main image structure, and the boundaries are well preserved. Comparing the two elevation plots it is clear that the heat kernel filter preserves the original structure a little better.

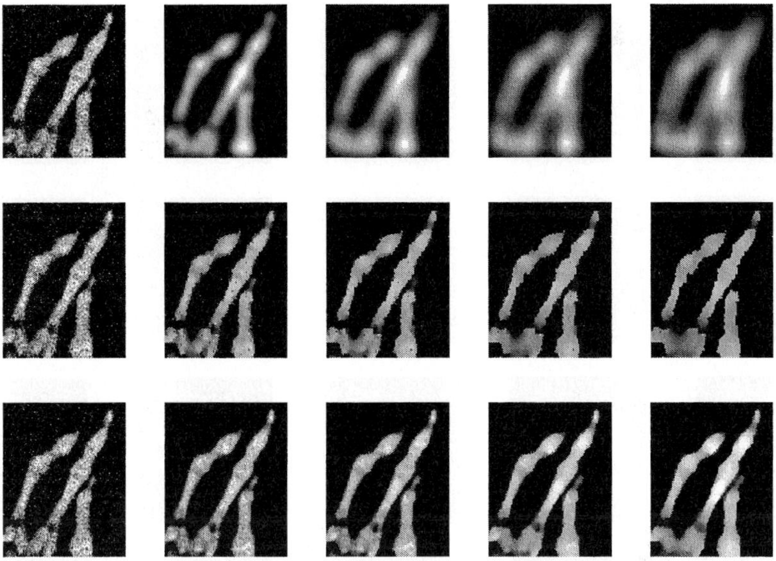

Fig. 4. CT hand with noise (image size: 94 × 110). Row 1: Linear Gaussian scale-space, $\sigma = 0, 2, 4, 8, 16$. Row 2: Anisotropic scale-space, 0, 10, 20, 30, 50 iterations. Row 3: Graph scale-space, $\sigma = 0.1$; $t = 0, 0.1, 1, 5, 15$. All scale parameters increase from left to right.

In Figure 4 we show the result of applying the method to a CT scan of a hand. The top row shows the result of Gaussian filtering. Here the different images are for different widths of the Gaussian filter. The middle row shows the result of anisotropic diffusion and the bottom row shows the result of heat kernel smoothing. Here the different images are for different values of scale or t. In the case of the Gaussian scale-space, the main effect of increased filter width is increased blurring. When the heat-kernel method is used, then the effect is to smooth noise while preserving fine image and boundary detail.

Another synthetic example is shown in Figure 5. Here the test image is a picture of a house, with 10% Gaussian noise added. The top two rows show the smoothed image obtained using a Gaussian filter and the resulting edge map detected using Canny's method [1]. The middle two rows and bottom two rows are the results of applying the anisotropic diffusion and heat-kernel filter respectively. In the first column, we show the original image and its edge-map. The remaining columns show the results obtained with increasing values of scale or time t. From the top two rows, although the results obtained with the Gaussian filter control the effects of noise, the edge-structures are badly eroded. For comparison, the effect of anisotropic diffusion and the heat kernel filter are to smooth away the noise present in the original image and edge-map, while preserving edge-structure. Comparing the edges detected, the heat kernel filter preserves the edges and junctions best.

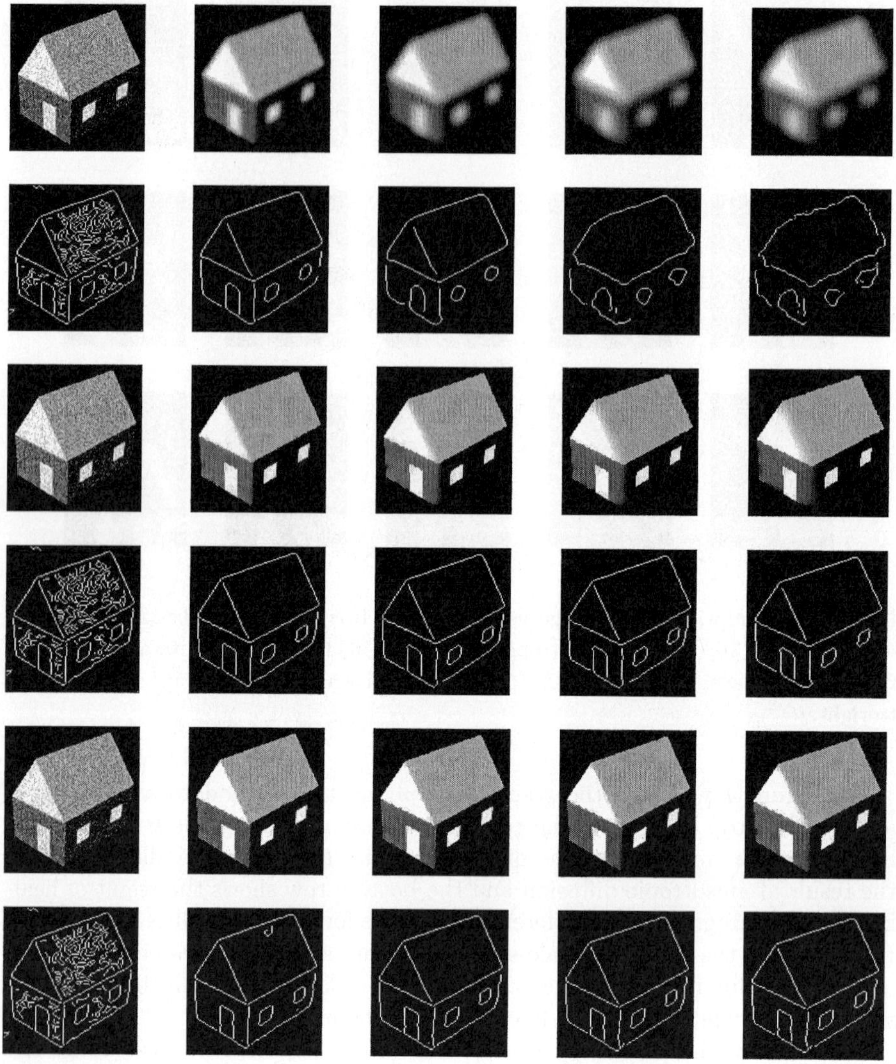

Fig. 5. Synthetic house with 10% noise (image size: 120 × 141). Row 1: Gaussian scale-space, σ = 0, 2, 4, 8, 16. Row 2: Edges detected using Canny detector [1] with Gaussian kernel variance as row 1. Edges are distorted and the junctions disappear. Row 3: Anisotropic scale-space, 0, 10, 20, 30, 40 iterations. Row 4: Edges using the same parameters of row 3. Row 5: Graph scale-space, window size: 11 × 11; $\sigma = 0.08$; t = 0, 2, 5, 10, 15. Row 6: Edges using the same parameters of row 5. The object shapes, boundaries and edge junctions are all preserved. All scale parameters increase from left to right.

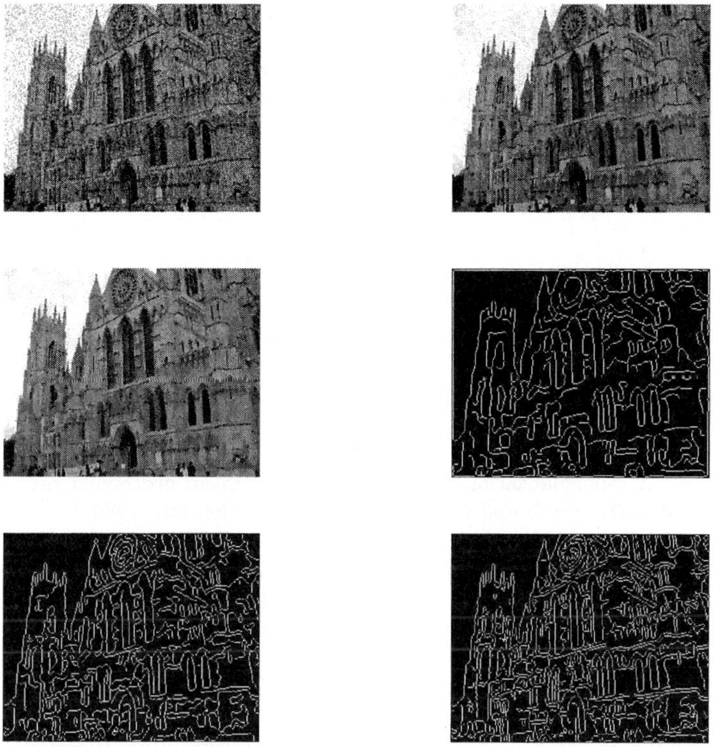

Fig. 6. York Minster with 15% noise (image size: 350 × 262). (a) original picture. (b) and (c) the results after using graph kernel with window size: 15 × 15; σ = 0.06; t = 2, 5. (d) edges detected using Gaussian kernel. (e) edges detected using anisotropic diffusion. (f) edges detected using graph heat kernel.

A complex real-world example is shown in Figure 6. Subfigure (a) shows the original image, and (b) and (c) show the results of applying the heat-kernel to the original image. Subfigure (f) shows the result of applying edge detection to the smoothed image in (b). For comparison subfigures (d) and (e) show the results of applying edge detection to the output of Gaussian filtering and anisotropic diffusion respectively. The main feature to note here is that the heat kernel best preserves the fine detail of the image.

5 Conclusions and Future Work

In this paper we have shown how the heat kernel can be used to smooth images without loss of fine boundary detail. Our approach is a graph-spectral one. We commence from an affinity matrix which measures the similarity of pixel grey-scale values. From the affinity matrix we compute the Laplacian, and the spectrum of the Laplacian matrix is used to estimate the elements of the heat-kernel. Experiments show that the boundaries and regions extracted from the smoothed images preserve fine detail.

Our future plans are to extend the method to the processing of vector fields. In particular we are interested in how the method can be used to segment structures from tensor MRI imagery.

References

1. J. Canny. A computational approach to edge detection. *IEEE Trans. Pattern Anal. and Machine Intell.*, 8(6):679 – 698, 1986.
2. F.R.K. Chung and S.-T. Yau. Discrete green's functions. In *J. Combin. Theory Ser.*, pages 191–214, 2000.
3. S. Geman and D. Geman. Stochastic relaxation, gibbs distributions, and the bayesian restoration of images. *IEEE Trans. Pattern Anal. and Machine Intell.*, 6(6):721–741, 1984.
4. Basilis Gidas. A renormalization group approach to image processing problems. *IEEE Trans. Pattern Anal. and Machine Intell.*, 11(2):164–180, 1989.
5. G.H. Golub and C.F. Van Loan. *Matrix Computations.* John Hopkins Press, 1989.
6. R. Hummel. The scale-space formulation of pyramid data structures. *Parallel Computer Vision, Ed. by L. Uhr, Academic Press*, 1987.
7. J. Babaud, A. Witkin, M. Baudin, and R. Duda. Uniqueness of the gaussian kernel for scale-space filtering. *IEEE Trans. Pattern Anal. and Machine Intell.*, 8(1):26–33, 1986.
8. J. Koenderink. The structure of images. *Biological Cybernetics*, 50:363–370, 1984.
9. R. Kondor and J. Lafferty. Diffusion kernels on graphs and other discrete structures. *19th Intl. Conf. on Machine Learning (ICML) [ICM02].*, 2002.
10. M. Lozano and F. Escolano. A significant improvement of softassign with diffusion kernels. In *SSPR and SPR 2004, LNCS 3138*, pages 76–84, 2004.
11. M.Meila and J.Shi. A random walks view of spectral segmentation. *In proceedings of AI and STATISTICS (AISTATS)*, 2001.
12. P. Perona and J. Malik. Scale-space and edge dectection using anisotropic diffusion. *IEEE Trans. Pattern Anal. and Machine Intell.*, 12(7):629–639, 1990.
13. Andrew P.Witkin. Scale-space filtering. In *8th Int. Joint Conf. on Artificial Intelligence, Karlsruhe, Germany*, pages 1019–1021, 1983.
14. M. Scholkopf and A. Smola. *Learning with kernels.* MIT Press, 2001.
15. J. Shi and J. Malik. Normalized cuts and image segmentation. *IEEE Transactions on Pattern Analysis and Machine Intelligence*, 22(8):888–905, 2000.
16. R. Wilson and M. Spann. Finite prolate spheroidal sequences and their application ii: Image feature description and segmentation. *IEEE Trans. Pattern Anal. and Machine Intell.*, 10(2):193–203, 1988.
17. A. Yuille and T. Poggio. Scaling theorems for zero crossings. *IEEE Trans. Pattern Anal. and Machine Intell.*, 8(1):15–25, 1986.

A Naive Solution to the One-Class Problem and Its Extension to Kernel Methods

Alberto Muñoz[1] and Javier M. Moguerza[2]

[1] University Carlos III, c/ Madrid 126, 28903 Getafe, Spain
alberto.munoz@uc3m.es
[2] University Rey Juan Carlos, c/ Tulipán s/n, 28933 Móstoles, Spain
javier.moguerza@urjc.es

Abstract. In this work, the problem of estimating high density regions from univariate or multivariate data samples is studied. To be more precise, we estimate minimum volume sets whose probability is specified in advance. This problem arises in outlier detection and cluster analysis, and is strongly related to One-Class Support Vector Machines (SVM). In this paper we propose a new simpler method to solve this problem. We show its properties and introduce a new class of kernels, relating the proposed method to One-Class SVMs.

1 Introduction

The task of estimating high density regions from data samples arises explicitly in a number of works involving interesting problems such as outlier detection or cluster analysis (see for instance [5,7] and references herein). One-Class Support Vector Machines (SVM) [10,12] are designed to solve this problem with tractable computational complexity. We refer to [10] and references therein for a complete description of the problem and its ramifications.

In the recent years papers showing failures in the estimations found by One-Class SVM have appeared [4,6]. In this work, a new algorithm to estimate high density regions from data samples is presented. The algorithm relaxes the density estimation problem in the following sense: instead of trying to estimate the density function at each data point, an easier to calculate data-based measure is introduced in order to establish a density ranking among the sample points.

The concrete problem to solve is the estimation of minimum volume sets of the form $S_\alpha(f) = \{x|f(x) \geq \alpha\}$, such that $P(S_\alpha(f)) = \nu$, where f is the density function and $0 < \nu < 1$. Throughout the paper, sufficient regularity conditions on f are assumed.

The rest of the paper is organized as follows. Section 2 introduces the method and its properties. In Section 3, a kernel formulation of the proposed algorithm is shown. Section 4 shows the numerical advantages of the new method over One-Class SVM. Section 5 concludes.

M. Lazo and A. Sanfeliu (Eds.): CIARP 2005, LNCS 3773, pp. 193–204, 2005.

2 The Naive One-Class Algorithm

There are data analysis problems where the knowledge of an accurate estimator of the density function $f(x)$ is sufficient to solve them, for instance, mode estimation [2], or the present task of estimating $S_\alpha(f)$. However, density estimation is far from trivial [11,10]. The next definition is introduced to relax the density estimation problem: the task of estimating the density function at each data point is replaced by a simpler measure that asymptotically preserves the order induced by f.

Definition 1. Neighbourhood Measures. *Consider a random variable X with density function $f(x)$ defined on $\mathbb{R}^d$. Let S_n denote the set of random independent identically distributed (iid) samples of size n (drawn from f). The elements of S_n take the form $s_n = (x_1, \cdots, x_n)$, where $x_i \in \mathbb{R}^d$. Let $M : \mathbb{R}^d \times S_n \longrightarrow \mathbb{R}$ be a real-valued function defined for all $n \in \mathbb{N}$. (a) If $f(x) < f(y)$ implies $\lim_{n\to\infty} P(M(x, s_n) > M(y, s_n)) = 1$, then M is a* ***sparsity measure****. (b) If $f(x) < f(y)$ implies $\lim_{n\to\infty} P(M(x, s_n) < M(y, s_n)) = 1$, then M is a* ***concentration measure****.*

Example 1. $M(x, s_n) \propto 1/\hat{f}(x, s_n)$, where $\hat{f}$ can be any consistent non-parametric density estimator, is a sparsity measure; while $M(x, s_n) \propto \hat{f}(x, s_n)$ is a concentration measure. A commonly used estimator is the kernel density one $\hat{f}(x, s_n) = \frac{1}{nh^d}\sum_{i=1}^{n} K(\frac{\|x-x_i\|}{h})$.

Example 2. Consider the distance from a point x to its kth-nearest neighbour in s_n, $x^{(k)}$: $M(x, s_n) = d_k(x, s_n) = d(x, x^{(k)})$: it is a sparsity measure. Note that d_k is neither a density estimator nor is it one-to-one related to a density estimator. Thus, the definition of 'sparsity measure' is not trivial. Another valid choice is given by the average distance over all the k nearest neighbours: $M(x, s_n) = \bar{d}_k = \frac{1}{k}\sum_{j=1}^{k} d_j = \frac{1}{k}\sum_{j=1}^{k} d(x, x^{(j)})$. Extensions to other centrality measures, such as trimmed-means are straightforward.

Our goal is to obtain some decision function $h(x)$ which solves the problem stated in the introduction, that is, $h(x) = +1$ if $x \in S_\alpha(f)$ and $h(x) = -1$ otherwise. We will show how to use sparsity measures to build $h(x)$.

Consider a sample $s_n = \{x_1, \ldots, x_n\}$. Consider the function $g(x) = M(x_i, s_n)$, where M is a sparsity measure. For the sake of simplicity we assume $g(x_i) \neq g(x_j)$ if $i \neq j$ (the complementary event has zero probability).

To solve the One-Class problem, thc following algorithm is introduced:

Naive One-Class Algorithm
(1) Choose a constant $\nu \in [0, 1]$.
(2) Consider the order induced in s_n by the sparsity measure $g(x)$, that is, $g(x_{\{1\}}) \leq g(x_{\{2\}}) \leq \ldots \leq g(x_{\{n\}})$, where $x_{\{i\}}$ denotes the ith-sample.
(3) Consider the value $\rho^* = g(x_{\{\nu n\}})$ if $\nu n \in \mathbb{N}$, $\rho^* = g(x_{\{[\nu n]+1\}})$ otherwise, where $[x]$ stands for the largest integer not greater than x.
(4) Define $h(x) = sign(\rho^* - g(x))$

Note that the choice of the function $g(x)$ is not involved in the algorithm; it has to be determined in advance. The role of ρ^* and ν will become clear with the next proposition, which shows that the decision function $h(x) = sign(\rho^* - g(x))$ will be non-negative for at least a proportion equal to ν of the training s_n sample. Following [10], this result is called ν-property.

Proposition 1. ν-property. *The following two statements hold for the value ρ^*:*

1. $\frac{1}{n}\sum_{i=1}^{n} I(g(x_i) < \rho) \leq \nu \leq \frac{1}{n}\sum_{i=1}^{n} I(g(x_i) \leq \rho)$, *where I stands for the indicator function and $x_i \in s_n$.*
2. *With probability 1, asymptotically, the preceding inequalities become equalities.*

Proof. 1. Regarding the right-hand side of the inequality, $\frac{1}{n}\sum_{i=1}^{n} I(g(x_i) \leq \rho) = \frac{\nu n}{n} = \nu$ if $\nu n \in \mathbb{N}$ and equals $\frac{[\nu n]+1}{n} > \nu$ if $\nu n \notin \mathbb{N}$. For the left-hand side a similar argument applies. 2. Regarding the right-hand side inequality, if $\nu n \in \mathbb{N}$ the result is immediate from the preceding argument. If $\nu n \notin \mathbb{N}$, $\frac{[\nu n]+1}{n} \to \nu$ as $n \to \infty$. Again, for the left-hand side a similar argument applies. □

Remark 1. If $g(x)$ is chosen to be a concentration measure, then the decision function has to be defined as $h(x) = sign(g(x) - \rho^*)$.

Notice that in the naive algorithm ν represents the fraction of points inside the support of the distribution if $g(x)$ is a sparsity measure. If a concentration measure is used, ν represents the fraction of outlying points. The role of ρ^* becomes now clear: it represents the decision value which, induced by the sparsity measure, determines if a given point belongs to the support of the distribution. As the next theorem states an asymptotical result, we will denote every quantity depending on the sample s_n with the subscript n. Also we will suppose $\nu n \in \mathbb{N}$. The theorem goes one step further from the ν-property, showing that, asymptotically, the naive One-Class algorithm finds the desired α-level sets. In order to formulate the theorem, we need a measure to estimate the difference between two sets. We will use the d_μ-distance. Given two sets A and B

$$d_\mu(A, B) = \mu(A \Delta B),$$

where μ is a measure on $\mathbb{R}^d$, Δ is the symmetric difference $A\Delta B = (A \cap B^c) \cup (B \cap A^c)$, and A^c denotes the complementary set of A.

Theorem 1. *Consider a measure μ absolutely continuous with respect to the Lebesgue measure. The set $R_n = \{x : h_n(x) = sign(\rho_n^* - g_n(x)) \geq 0\}$ d_μ-converges to a region of the form $S_\alpha(f) = \{x | f(x) \geq \alpha\}$, such that $P(S_\alpha(f)) = \nu$. Therefore, the naive One-Class method estimates a density contour cluster $S_\alpha(f)$ (which, in probability, includes the mode).*

Proof. For space reasons, we omit some mechanical steps. Consider the set $C_\nu = \{x_\nu \in \mathbb{R}^d : f(x_\nu) = \alpha\}$, where $\nu = P(S_\alpha(f))$. By Proposition 1, point 2, $\lim_{n\to\infty} P(g_n(x) < g_n(x_{\{\nu n\}})) = \nu$ (fact 1). Besides, it is easy to prove that given $C \subset S_{f(y)}(f)$ with $\mu(C) < \infty$, then $\mu(x \in C : g_n(x) < g_n(y))$ tends to $\mu(C)$. Thus $\lim_{n\to\infty} P(g_n(x) < g_n(x_\nu)) = \nu$, $\forall x_\nu \in C_\nu$ (fact 2). From facts 1 and 2, and using standard arguments from probability theory, it follows that $\forall \varepsilon > 0$, $\lim_{n\to\infty} P(\left|f(x_{\{\nu n\}}) - f(x_\nu)\right| > \varepsilon) = 0$, that is, $\lim_{n\to\infty} f(x_{\{\nu n\}}) = f(x_\nu)$ in probability.

Now consider $x \in S_\alpha(f)) \cap R_n^c$. From $f(x) > f(x_\nu)$ and Definition 1, it holds that $\lim_{n\to\infty} P(g_n(x) < g_n(x_\nu)) = 1$. Given that $\lim_{n\to\infty} f(x_{\{\nu n\}}) = f(x_\nu)$ in probability, it follows that $\lim_{n\to\infty} P(g_n(x) < g_n(x_{\{\nu n\}})) = 1$, that is, $P(h_n(x) < 0) \to 1$. Therefore, $\mu\left(S_\alpha(f)) \cap R_n^c\right) \to 0$.

Let now $x \in R_n \cap S_\alpha(f)^c$. From $f(x) < f(x_\nu)$, Definition 1 and $\lim_{n\to\infty} f(x_{\{\nu n\}}) = f(x_\nu)$ in probability, it holds that $P(g_n(x) \geq g_n(x_{\{\nu n\}})) \to 1$, that is, $P(h_n(x) > 0) \to 1$. Thus $\mu\left(R_n \cap S_\alpha(f)^c\right) \to 0$, which concludes the proof. □

We provide an estimate of a region $S_\alpha(f)$ with the property $P(S_\alpha(f)) = \nu$. Among regions S with the property $P(S) = \nu$, the region $S_\alpha(f)$ will have minimum volume as it has the form $S_\alpha(f) = \{x|f(x) \geq \alpha\}$. Therefore we provide an estimate that asymptotically, in probability, has minimum volume.

Finally, it is important to remark that the quality of the estimation procedure heavily depends on using a sparsity or a concentration measure (the particular choice is not – asymptotically – relevant). If the measure used is neither a concentration nor a sparsity measure, there is no reason why the method should work.

3 Kernel Formulation of the Naive Algorithm

In this section we will show the relation between the naive algorithm and One-Class SVM. In order to do so we have to define a class of neighbourhood measures.

Definition 2. Positive and Negative Neighbourhood Measures. $MP(x, s_n)$ *is said to be a* ***positive sparsity (concentration) measure*** *if* $MP(x, s_n)$ *is a sparsity (concentration) measure and* $MP(x, s_n) \geq 0$. $MN(x, s_n)$ *is said to be a* ***negative sparsity (concentration) measure*** *if* $-MN(x, s_n)$ *is a positive concentration (sparsity) measure.*

Given that negative neighbourhood measures are in one-to-one correspondence to positive neighbourhood measures, only positive neighbourhood measures need to be considered. The following classes of kernels can be defined using positive neighbourhood measures.

Definition 3. Neighbourhood Kernels. *Consider the mapping* $\phi : \mathbb{R}^d \to \mathbb{R}^+$ *defined by* $\phi(x) = MP(x, s_n)$, *where* $MP(x, s_n)$ *is a positive neighbourhood measure. The function* $K(x, y) = \phi(x)\phi(y)$ *is called a* ***neighbourhood kernel***. *If* $MP(x, s_n)$ *is a positive sparsity (concentration) measure,* $K(x, y)$ *is a* ***sparsity (concentration) kernel***.

Note that the set $\{\phi(x_i)\}$ is trivially separable from the origin in the sense of [10], since each $\phi(x_i) \in \mathbb{R}^+$. Separability is guaranteed by Definition 2.

The strategy of One-Class support vector methods is to map the data points into a feature space determined by a kernel function, and to separate them from the origin with maximum margin (see [10] for details). In order to build a separating hyperplane between the origin and the points $\{\phi(x_i)\}$, the quadratic One-Class SVM method solves the following problem:

$$\begin{aligned} \min_{w,\rho,\xi} \ & \frac{1}{2}\|w\|^2 - \nu n \rho + \sum_{i=1}^{n} \xi_i \\ \text{s.t.} \ & \langle w, \phi(x_i) \rangle \geq \rho - \xi_i \,, \\ & \xi_i \geq 0, \qquad\qquad i = 1, \ldots, n \,, \end{aligned} \tag{1}$$

where ϕ is the mapping defining the kernel function, ξ_i are slack variables, $\nu \in [0,1]$ is an a priori fixed constant, and ρ is a decision variable which determines if a given point belongs to the estimated high density region.

The next theorem illustrates the relation between our naive algorithm and One-Class SVMs when neighbourhood kernels are used.

Theorem 2. *Define the mapping $\phi(x) = MP(x, s_n)$. The decision function $h_V(x) = sign(\rho_V^* - w^*\phi(x))$ obtained from the solution ρ_V^* and w^* to the One-Class SVM problem (1) using the sparsity kernel $K(x,y) = \phi(x)\phi(y)$ coincides with the decision function $h(x)$ obtained by the naive algorithm.*

Proof. Consider the dual problem of (1):

$$\begin{aligned} \max_{\alpha} \ & \frac{1}{2}\sum_{i=1}^{n}\sum_{j=1}^{n} \alpha_i \alpha_j K(x_i, x_j) \\ \text{s.t.} \ & \sum_{i=1}^{n} \alpha_i = \nu n \,, \\ & 0 \leq \alpha_i \leq 1 \,, \qquad\qquad i = 1, \ldots, n \,, \end{aligned} \tag{2}$$

where $x_i \in s_n$. For the sake of simplicity we assume $\phi(x_i) \neq \phi(x_j)$ if $i \neq j$ (the complementary event has zero probability) and that $\nu n \in \mathbb{N}$ (the proof for $\nu n \notin \mathbb{N}$ can be derived with similar arguments to those in the proof of Proposition 1). Consider the order induced in s_n by the mapping $\phi(x)$ and denote $x_{\{i\}}$ the ith-sample and $\alpha_{\{i\}}$ the corresponding dual variable. Therefore $\phi(x_{\{1\}}) \leq \phi(x_{\{2\}}) \leq \ldots \leq \phi(x_{\{n\}})$. Since $K(x_i, x_j) = \phi(x_i)\phi(x_j)$ and, by Definition 2, $\phi(x_i) \in \mathbb{R}^+$, the maximum of the objective function of problem (2) will be attained for $\alpha_{\{i\}} = 1$, $i \in \{1, \ldots, \nu n\}$ and $\alpha_j = 0$ otherwise. At the solution, the objective function takes the value $-\frac{1}{2}\sum_{i=1}^{\nu n}\sum_{j=1}^{\nu n} K(x_{\{i\}}, x_{\{j\}})$. By the weak theorem of duality, the value of the objective function of problem (1) has to be equal or greater than the value of the objective function of problem (2) at the solution. Consider the solution $w^* = \sum_{i=1}^{\nu n} \phi(x_{\{i\}})$, $\rho_V^* = w^*\phi(x_{\{\nu n\}})$, $\xi_{\{i\}} = w^*\left[\phi(x_{\{\nu n\}}) - \phi(x_{\{i\}})\right]$ for $i \in \{1, \ldots, [\nu n]\}$. For the remaining indexes $\xi_j = 0$.

At this point the solution to problem (1) coincides with the solution to problem (2), that is, the duality gap is zero. The decision function takes the form $h_V(x) = sign(w^* \left[\phi(x_{\{\nu n\}}) - \phi(x)\right])$ which coincides with the decision function of the naive algorithm (the scalar $w^* > 0$ does not affect the sign). So the theorem holds. □

It remains open to show if the decision function obtained from One-Class SVM algorithms within the framework in [10,8] can be stated in terms of positive sparsity or concentration measures. The next remark provides the answer.

Remark 2. The exponential kernel $K_c(x, y) = e^{-\|x-y\|^2/c}$ is neither a sparsity kernel nor a concentration kernel. For instance, consider a univariate bimodal density f with finite modes m_1 and m_2 such that $f(m_1) = f(m_2)$. Consider any positive sparsity measure $MP(x, s_n)$ and the induced mapping $\phi(x) = MP(x, s_n)$. As $n \to \infty$, the sparsity kernel $K(x, y) = \phi(x)\phi(y)$ would attain its minimum at (m_1, m_2) (or at two points in the sample s_n near to the modes). On the other hand, as the exponential kernel $K_c(x, y)$ depends exclusively on the distance between x and y, any pair of points (a, b) whose distance is larger than $\|m_1 - m_2\|$ will provide a value $K_c(a, b) < K_c(m_1, m_2)$, which asymptotically can not happen for kernels induced by positive sparsity measures. In this case, the neighbourhood kernel has four minima while the exponential kernel has the whole diagonal as minima. The reasoning for concentration kernels is analogous. A similar argument applies for polinomial kernels with even degrees (odd degrees induce mapped data sets that are non separable from the origin, which discards them).

Note that, while the naive algorithm works with every neighbourhood measure, the separability condition of the mapped data is necessary when One-Class SVM are being used, restricting the use of neighbourhood measures to positive or negative ones. This restriction and the fact that our method provides a simpler approach make the use of the naive algorithm advisable when neighbourhood measures are being used.

4 Experiments

In this section we compare the performance of One-Class SVM and the naive algorithm for a variety of artificial and real data sets. Systematic comparisons of the two methods as data dimension increases are carried out. First of all we describe the implementation details concerning both algorithms.

With regards to One-Class SVM we adopt the proposal in [10], that is, the exponential kernel $K_c(x, y) = e^{-\|x-y\|^2/c}$ is used. This is the only kernel used for experimentation in [10], and it is also the only (non neighbourhood) kernel for which a clear relation to density estimation has been demonstrated (see [6]). To perform the experiments, a range of values for c has been chosen, following the widely used rule $c = hd$ (see [9,10]), where d is the data dimension and $h \in \{0.1, 0.2, 0.5, 0.8, 1.0\}$.

Concerning the naive algorithm, three different sparsity measures have been considered:

- $M_1(x, s_n) = d_k = d(x, x^{(k)})$, the distance from a point x to its kth-nearest neighbour $x^{(k)}$ in the sample s_n. The only parameter in M_1 is k, which takes a finite number of values (in the set $\{1, \cdots, n\}$). We have chosen k to cover a representative range of values, namely, k will equal the 10%, 20%, 30%, 40% and 50% sample proportions. Therefore we choose k as the closest integer to hn, where n is the sample size and $h \in \{0.1, 0.2, 0.3, 0.4, 0.5\}$.
- $M_2(x, s_n) = \dfrac{1}{\sum_{i=1}^{n} \exp\left(-\frac{\|x-x_i\|^2}{2\sigma}\right)}$, where $\sigma \in \mathbb{R}^+$. The only parameter in M_2 is σ. We want σ to be related to the sample variability and, at the same time, to scale well with respect to the data sample distances. We choose $\sigma = hs$, where $s = \max d_{ij}^2/\varepsilon$, $h \in \{0.1, 0.2, 0.5, 0.8, 1.0\}$, $d_{ij}^2 = \|x_i - x_j\|^2$ and ε is a small value which preserves scalability in M_2. For all the experiments we have chosen $\varepsilon = 10^{-8}$.
- $M_3(x, s_n) = \log\left(\dfrac{1}{\sum_{i=1}^{n} \frac{1}{\|x-x_i\|^p}}\right)$, where $p \in \mathbb{R}^+$. Parameter p in M_3 is related to data dimension [3]. We choose $p = hd$, where d is the data dimension and $h \in \{0.01, 0.02, 0.05, 0.08, 0.1\}$. In this case the values of h are smaller for smoothing reasons (see [3] for details).

Measure M_1 has been described in Example 2 in Section 2. Measures M_2 and M_3 are of the type described in Examples 1 and 4 in the same section. M_2 uses as density estimator the Parzen window [11], while M_3 is based on the Hilbert kernel density estimator [3] and could take negative values. Note that Theorem 1 guarantees that asymptotically every sparsity measure (and in particular the three chosen here) will lead to sets containing the true mode.

4.1 Artificial Data Sets

An Asymmetric Distribution. In the first experiment we have generated 2000 points from a gamma $\Gamma(\alpha, \beta)$ distribution, with $\alpha = 1.5$ and $\beta = 3$. Figure 1 shows the histogram, the gamma density curve, the true mode $(\alpha - 1)/\beta$ as a bold vertical line, the naive algorithm estimations with sparsity measure M_1 (five upper lines) and the One-Class SVM (five lower lines) estimations of the 50% highest density region. The parameters have been chosen as described at the beginning of Section 4, and lines are drawn for each method in increasing order in the h parameter, starting from the bottom. Being our goal to detect the shortest region of the form $S_\alpha(f) = \{x : f(x) > \alpha\}$ (that must contain the mode), it is apparent that the naive regions improve upon the One-Class SVM regions. All the naive regions regions contain the true mode and are connected. All the One-Class SVM regions are wider and show a strong bias towards less dense zones. Furthermore, only in two cases the true mode is included in the estimated SVM regions, but in these cases the intervals obtained are not simply connected. The naive algorithm using measures M_2 and M_3 provide similar intervals to those obtained using measure M_1, and are not shown for space reasons.

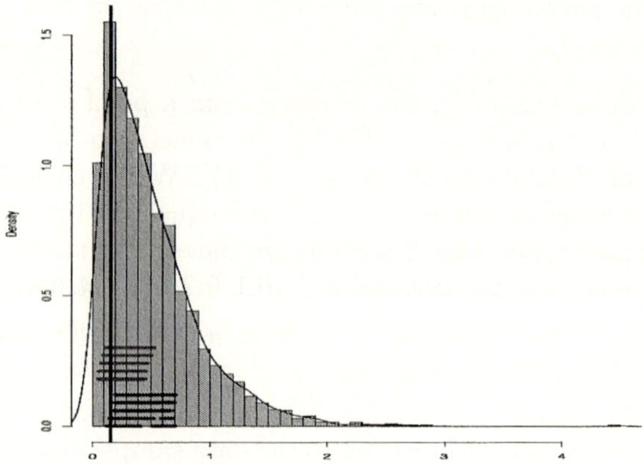

Fig. 1. Gamma sample with 2000 points. The figure shows the histogram, the density curve, a vertical line at the true mode, the naive estimations with sparsity measure M_1 (five upper lines) and One-Class SVM (five lower lines) estimations of the 50% highest density region.

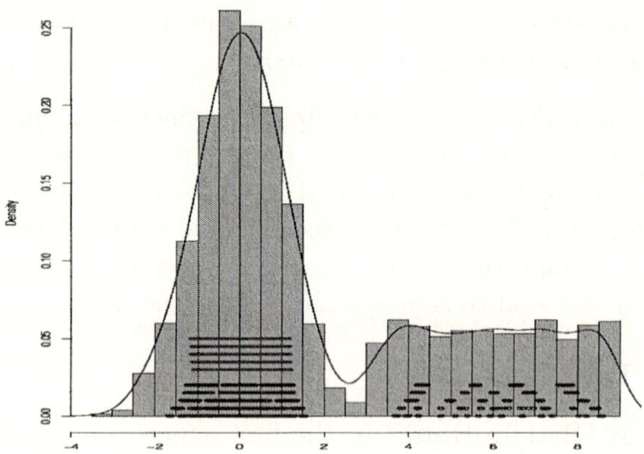

Fig. 2. Mixture sample with 3000 points. The figure shows the histogram, the estimated density curve, the naive estimations with sparsity measure M_1 (five upper lines) and One-Class SVM (five lower lines) estimations of the 50% highest density region.

A Mixture of Distributions. This second experiment considers a mixture of a normal $N(0,1)$ and a uniform $U(6,9)$ distribution. Figure 2 shows the histogram, the estimated density curve, the naive estimations with sparsity measure M_1 (five upper lines) and the One-Class SVM (five lower lines) estimations of the 50% highest density region. Again, the parameters have been chosen as described at the beginning of Section 4, and lines are drawn for each method in increasing order in the h parameter, starting from the bottom. Once more, the naive method using measures M_2 and M_3 provide similar intervals to those obtained using measure M_1, and are not shown for space reasons. Regarding the quality of the results, note that the 50% densest region corresponds to points from the normal distribution. All the naive estimations (upper lines) match the correct region, while the One-Class SVM (lower lines) spreads part of the points in the uniform zone. However, all points in the uniform zone have lower density than those found by the naive procedure.

Increasing the Data Dimension. In this experiment we want to evaluate whether the performance of the Naive method and One-Class SVM algorithms degrades as the data dimension increases. To this end, we have generated 20 data sets with increasing dimension from 2 to 200. Each data set contains 2000 points from a multivariate normal distribution $N(0, I_d)$, where I_d is the identity matrix in $\mathbb{R}^d$. Detailed results are not shown for space reasons. We will only show the conclusions. Since the data distribution is known, we can retrieve the true outliers, that is, the true points outside the support corresponding to any percentage specified in advance. For each dimension and each method, we have determined, from the points retrieved as outliers, the proportion of true ones.

As the data dimension increases, the performance of One-Class SVM degrades: it tends to retrieve as outliers an increasing number of points. The best results for One-Class SVM are obtained for the largest magnitudes of the parameter c (only when convergence for the optimization problem within was achieved).

Regarding the naive method, robustness with regard to the parameter choice is observed. Dimension barely affects the performance of our method, and results are consistently better than those obtained with One-Class SVM. For instance, for a percentage of outliers equal to 1%, the best result for One-Class SVM is 15%, against 100% using our method (for all the sparsity measures considered). For a percentage of outliers equal to 5%, the best result for One-Class SVM is 68%, against 99% using the naive method.

4.2 A Practical Example: Outlier Detection in Handwritten Digit Recognition

The database used next contains nearly 4000 instances of handwritten digits from Alpaydin and Kaynak [1]. Each digit is represented by a vector in $\mathbb{R}^{64}$ constructed from a 32×32 bitmap image. The calligraphy of the digits in the database seems to be easily perceivable, which is supported by the high success rate of various classifiers. In particular, for each digit, nearest neighbour classifiers accuracy is always over 97% [1].

In the present case there is a nice interpretation for points outside the sets $S_\alpha(f)$ (the support of the data set, see Section 1). The outlying points should correspond to 'badly'-written characters. In order to check out this behaviour, 10 apparent outliers (shown in Figure 3) have been added to the database. We will consider the whole database as a sample from a multivariate distribution, and we will verify if the proposed algorithm is able to detect this outlying instances. Note that there is an added difficulty in this case, namely, the underlying distribution is multimodal in a high dimensional environment.

Figure 4 shows the outliers obtained by the naive algorithm when the support for the 99.5% percentile is calculated. Using this support percentage exactly 20

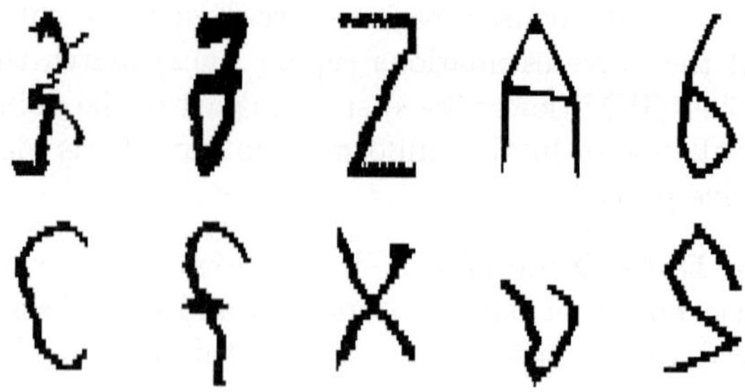

Fig. 3. Ten (apparent) outliers added to the original Alpaydin & Kaynak handwritten digits database

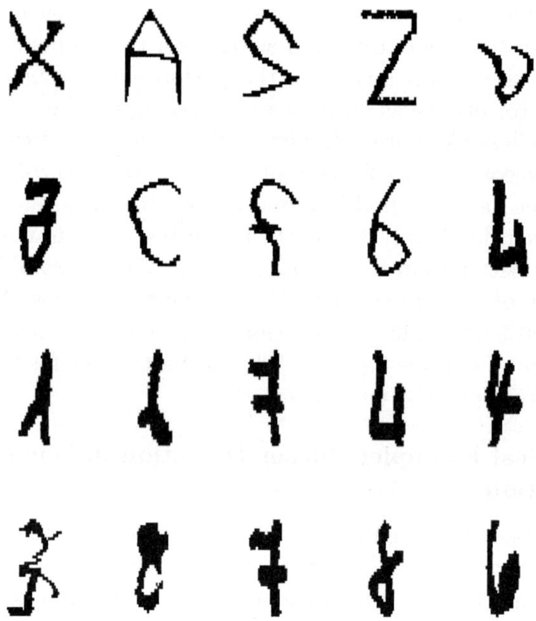

Fig. 4. The outlying digits found by the naive algorithm, ordered left–right and up–down using the sparsity measure $M(x, s_n) = d(x, x^{(k)})$

outliers are to be retrieved. We expect to detect the 10 outliers we have included, and we are curious about the aspect of the 10 other most outlying digits in the database. In Figure 4, the digits retrieved as outliers by the naive method using the sparsity measure M_1 are shown in decreasing order (left-right and up-down). Here $k = 1$, using $k = n^{4/(d+4)}$, where d is the space dimension. This value is known to be proportional to the (asymptotically) optimal value [11] for density estimation tasks. Nine of the ten added outliers are detected as the most outlying points. The remaining eleven outliers include the other added instance (similar to a '3'), and ten more figures whose calligraphy seems to be different from representative digits within each class. Similar results are obtained for sparsity measures M_2 and M_3.

Using a One-Class SVM with exponential kernel (trying a wide range of values for the c parameter, including those proposed in [9,10]) none of the ten added outliers was detected.

5 Conclusions

In this paper a new method to estimate minimum volume sets of the form $S_\alpha(f) = \{x|f(x) \geq \alpha\}$, has been proposed. Our proposal introduces the use of neighbourhood measures. These measures asymptotically preserve the order induced by the density function f. In this way we avoid the complexity of solving a pure density estimation problem. Regarding computational results, the naive method performs consistently better than One-Class SVM in all the tested problems (the ones shown here and many others omitted for space reasons). The advantage that the naive method has over the One-Class SVM is due to Theorem 1 which guarantees that it asymptotically finds the desired α-level sets. The suboptimal performance of One-Class SVM arises from the fact that its decision function is not based on sparsity or concentration measures and that there are no results of the nature of Theorem 1 for One-Class SVM. In particular, we have shown that the neither the exponential kernel nor polynomial kernels come from neighbourhood measures (and therefore Theorem 1 does not hold for these kernels).

Acknowledgments. This work was partially supported by spanish grants SEJ2004-03303, 06/HSE/0181/2004, TIC2003-05982-C05-05 (MCyT) and PPR-2004-05 (URJC).

References

1. E. Alpaydin and C. Kaynak. *Cascading Classifiers.* Kybernetika, 34(4):369-374, 1998.
2. L. Devroye. *Recursive estimation of the mode of a multivariate density.* The Canadian Journal of Statistics, 7(2):159-167, 1979.
3. L. Devroye and A. Krzyzak. *On the Hilbert kernel density estimate.* Statistics and Probability Letters, 44:299-308, 1999.
4. J.M. Moguerza and A. Muñoz. *Solving the One-Class Problem using Neighbourhood Measures.* LNCS 3138:680-688, Springer, 2004.
5. J.M. Moguerza, A. Muñoz and M. Martin-Merino. *Detecting the Number of Clusters Using a Support Vector Machine Approach.* LNCS 2415:763-768, Springer, 2002.
6. A. Muñoz and J.M. Moguerza. *One-Class Support Vector Machines and density estimation: the precise relation.* LNCS 3287:216-223, Springer, 2004.
7. A. Muñoz and J. Muruzabal. *Self-Organizing Maps for Outlier Detection.* Neurocomputing, 18:33-60, 1998.

8. G. Rätsch, S. Mika, B. Schölkopf and K.R. Müller. *Constructing Boosting Algorithms from SVMs: an Application to One-Class Classification.* IEEE Trans. on Pattern Analysis and Machine Intelligence, 24(9):1184-1199, 2002.
9. B. Schölkopf, C. Burges and V. Vapnik. *Extracting Support Data for a given Task.* Proc. of the First International Conference on Knowledge Discovery and Data Mining, AAAI Press, 1995.
10. B. Schölkopf, J.C. Platt, J. Shawe-Taylor, A.J. Smola and R.C. Williamson. *Estimating the Support of a High Dimensional Distribution.* Neural Computation, 13(7):1443-1471, 2001.
11. B.W. Silverman. *Density Estimation for Statistics and Data Analysis.* Chapman and Hall, 1990.
12. D.M.J. Tax and R.P.W. Duin. *Support Vector Domain Description.* Pattern Recognition Letters, 20:1991-1999, 1999.

Nonlinear Modeling of Dynamic Cerebral Autoregulation Using Recurrent Neural Networks*

Max Chacón[1], Cristopher Blanco[1], Ronney Panerai[2], and David Evans[2]

[1] Informatic Engineering Department, University of Santiago de Chile, Av. Ecuador 3659, PO Box 10233, Santiago, Chile
mchacon@diinf.usach.cl, christopher.blanco@usach.cl
[2] Medical Physics Group, Department of Cardiovascular Sciences, University of Leicester, Leicester Royal Infirmary, Leicester LE1 5WW, UK
{rp9, dhe}@le.ac.uk

Abstract. The function of the Cerebral Blood Flow Autoregulation (CBFA) system is to maintain a relatively constant flow of blood to the brain, in spite of changes in arterial blood pressure. A model that characterizes this system is of great use in understanding cerebral hemodynamics and would provide a pattern for evaluating different cerebrovascular diseases and complications. This work posits a non-linear model of the CBFA system through the evaluation of various types of neural networks that have been used in the field of systems identification. Four different architectures, combined with four learning methods were evaluated. The results were compared with the linear model that has often been used as a standard reference. The results show that the best results are obtained with the FeedForward Time Delay neural network, using the Levenberg-Marquardt learning algorithm, with an improvement of 24% over the linear model ($p<0.05$).

1 Introduction

The determination of a model for the Cerebral Blood Flow Autoregulation (CBFA) system, is an important physiological modeling problem, not only because of the importance of maintaining Cerebral Blood Flow (CBF) within narrow limits, but also because this flow self regulation system is present in a number of other organs [1].

The CBFA system has been the object of intense study recently, due to the development of transcranial Doppler as a tool for measuring CBF Velocity (CBFV), which can be assumed to be the equivalent to CBF [1,2]. A key element in the modeling of CBFA is the determination of the dynamic relationship that exists between Arterial Blood Pressure (ABP) and CBFV. The cerebral autoregulation literature includes a wide variety of studies that seek to characterize this relationship. In general these studies try to induce abrupt changes in patient ABP and then measure the effect of these changes on CBFV [1,3-4]. A non-invasive alternative, of great clinical importance in the modeling of CBFA is to analyze the relationship between ABP and CBFV by observing natural oscillations or spontaneous fluctuations in ABP

* This study has been supported by FONDECYT (Chile) project N° 1050082.

M. Lazo and A. Sanfeliu (Eds.): CIARP 2005, LNCS 3773, pp. 205 – 213, 2005.

and its effect on CBFV. The validity of this type of analysis was demonstrated previosuly [1,4-6]. This technique can be applied both to healthy and sick patients including premature neonates. Thus, the greatest possibilities of generating clinical tools lie in the use of models based on spontaneous fluctuations.

In order to characterize the ABP-CBFV relationship by measuring spontaneous fluctuations of ABP, a series of signal processing techniques have been used. Among these are transfer functions models, frequency analysis and impulse and step responses [4, 6-9]. Studies in the time domain have also been carried out using moving average filters such as the Wiener-Laguerre [4,6] and differential equations as proposed by Aaslid-Tiecks [6-10]. These models assume a linear relation between ABP and CBFV, which severely limits the results obtained, due to the existence of a number of non-linearities in the system [6] which are not considered in linear models. Up to now, there have been few attempts to model the system with non-linear methods. To our knowledge, there are only three studies that used neural networks [11-13]. Mitsis et al [11] used spontaneous fluctuations, but proposed a model based on a particular type of neural network. They have studied only five subjects and did not compare their findings with other models, such as the commonly used Aaslid-Tiecks linear model [6-10]. Thus, there is a dearth in the development of non-linear models of CBFA, especially with signals that facilitate the construction of diagnostic methods.

The present work proposes the modeling of the ABP-CBFV relationship through the use of non-linear system identification techniques, which hitherto have not been applied to autoregulation modeling. The different network architectures analyzed in the present work were: FeedForward Time Delay, Neural Net Output Error, Elman Net and Time Lagged FeedForward. These architectures were combined with the following learning methods: Backpropagation with momentum, Delta Bar Delta, Levenberg-Marquardt and One Step Secant [14-17]. Moreover, the results obtained with neural networks were compared with results obtained with the Aaslid-Tiecks model [1,3,6,10], the most often used linear model in the field of cerebral hemodynamics for evaluating autoregulation.

2 Methods

2.1 Data Collection and Pre-processing

The study included 16 volunteer subjects with no history of cardio-vascular or neurologic disease. The average ± standard deviation (SD) age was 30 ± 7 years, with a range of 23 to 47 years. Measurements were carried out at Leicester Royal Infirmary in a room with a temperature of approximately 23° C. The study was approved by the Leicestershire ethics committee and written consent was obtained from each subject.

CBFV was monitored in the medial cerebral artery using a Scimed QVL-120 Transcranial Doppler with a 2 MHz transducer. APB was measured with a non-invasive Finapres 2300 Ohmeda monitor.

Pressure and CBFV data were collected and stored on digital audio tape with a Sony PC108M 8-track recorder for posterior processing.

The data on the tape were transferred to a microcomputer in real time. FFT was used to extract the maximum velocity with a time window of 5 ms. The ABP signal was sampled at 200 samples/sec. Both signals were filtered with a Butterworth 8th order low pass filter with a cut off frequency of 20 Hz. The beginning of each cardiac cycle was detected from the end-diastolic value of the ABP wave, and mean values for ABP and CBFV were calculated for each cardiac cycle.

The data obtained from the samples were conditioned for further analysis with the models. The measures of ABP and CBFV for each patient consisted of a file with approximately 1500 samples taken every 0.2 seconds. Given that the Nyquist frequency for these signals is approximately 1 sec. it is possible to determine the mean of three samples, thus obtaining a sampling period of 0.6 seconds. In this way, the number of samples was reduced to 500 per patient.

2.2 Neural Network Models

Neural networks require short term memories in order to represent dynamic systems. Networks that include such memories are known as *recurrent neural networks*. These networks can be divided into two large groups, static neuronal networks with external recurrence, and networks with internal memory.

Networks with external recurrence are basically multilayer perceptrons which retard some of their inputs, and re-input their output with some delay. In this particular project we used FeedForward Time Delay and Neural Net Output Error networks which are representative of this type of model (also called NARX networks [18]).

Networks with internal memory attempt to extend the duration of short term memory provided by networks with external recurrence. In order to achieve this extension, so-called context memories are introduced. In this work two types of networks with internal memory were used: Elman Net and Time Lagged FeedForward.

The general structure for *FeedForward Time Delay (FFTD)* networks used for the CBFA model, is presented in Figure. 1.

An important characteristic of these networks, is the manner in which training is carried out. In contrast to the training of a static network, these networks follow a strict sequence for the order in which signal samples are presented.

The structure of a *Neural Net Output Error (NNOE)* [19-20] is essentially a FFTD network to which an error term is added that is represented by a white noise signal, the purpose of which is to represent a non-explained portion of the variance of the output variable, (in this case the CBFV). The inclusion of a signal that complements the chosen variables for this model allows a better fit between said model and the data being considered.

The *Elman Net (Elman)* [14-17] has a classic recurrent neural network topology, and has all the elements that are typical of a multilayer perceptron, which turn it into a universal function approximator. Moreover, it has context units which represent a recurrent link with the hidden layer. This property allows the network to address an important limitation of static neural networks with external recurrences which is the definition of a fixed time window that does not allow the gathering of information about samples that occurred at time prior to $D=max\{N,M\}$.

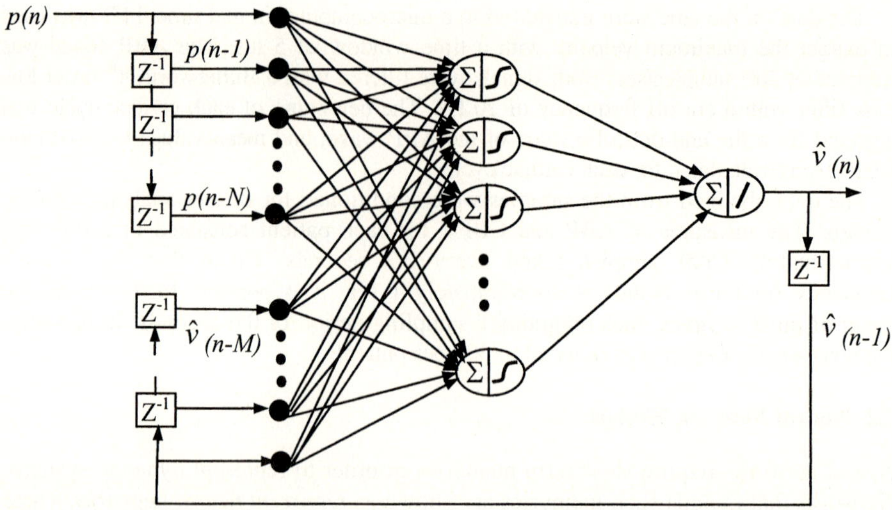

Fig. 1. Architecture of the FeedForward Time Delay (FFTD) neural network

Context memories can not only store information from the last D samples, but can also incorporate information from all the samples that the network has seen This is due to the fact that their output is generated as a function of the weighting of all the samples that have been seen during the network's training. The basic structure for context memories is shown in Figure 2.

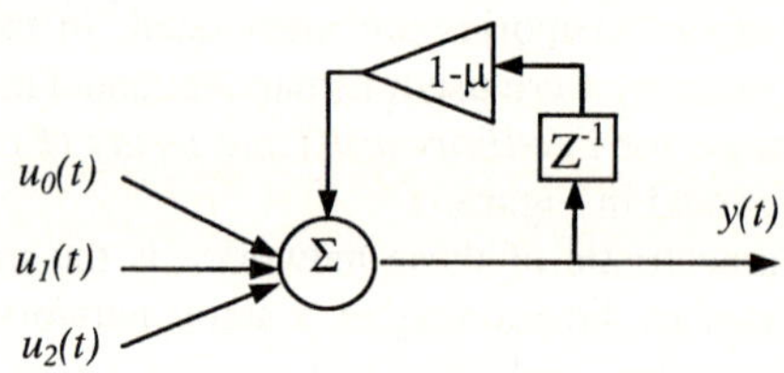

Fig. 2. Context memory for the Elman network

The principal shortcoming of these memories is that they do not deliver the exact value of the last D samples, these values are only approximated. In exchange, however, they are able to store approximate information about samples that have been seen outside the window of D samples. The memory parameter μ must be adjusted, making a compromise between the detail with which the memory recalls certain samples, and the number of samples in the past that it is able to recall.

An important property of the Elman network is that, because it has a fixed recurrent link, it can be easily trained using a variation of the Backpropagation algorithm [14-15]. This model does not require that the delay number be explicitly indicated either for the input or for the output; determining the number of neurons in the hidden layer is sufficient.

Time Lagged FeedForward (TLFF) networks use a topology that is similar to that of FFTD, but they include context units known as *Gamma* and *Laguerre memories* [14], considered to be more powerful than those used in Elman networks.

Figure 3a and 3b show Gamma and Laguerre memories. These memories are essentially a cascade of low-pass filters in the case of the Gamma memory, and band pass filters for the Laguerre memory (except for the first), all of which have a common parameter μ. When only one memory is used, this is the same as used in the Elman network. When μ is 1, the memory becomes a line of simple delays such as used in FFTD networks. Both memories have the same representational capacity. The difference lies in the response to impulse of the Laguerre memory which becomes more oscillatory than the Gamma memory. Nonetheless, the Laguerre memory has the advantage that it stabilizes in less time than the Gamma memory.

The different learning methods or algorithms evaluated, correspond to variations and improvements on the backpropagation algorithm. A momentum term is added to this classic algorithm to improve convergence. The second improvement consists of adopting variable linear learning rates for individual weights. In this case the Delta Bar Delta algorithm linearly increases the rate of learning when the sign of the slope does not vary, and reduces the rate exponentially when it does.

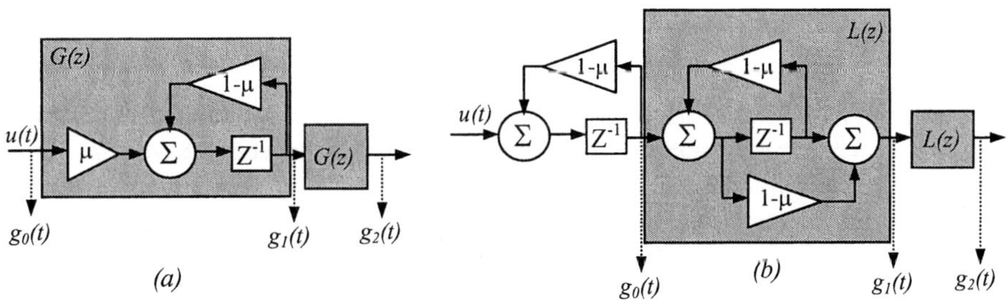

Fig. 3. a) Gamma Memory, b) Laguerre Memory, for the TLFF network

The other two algorithms correspond to quasi-Newton methods that avoid having to calculate the Hessian matrix. The Levenberg-Marquardt algorithm uses a combination of Jacobian matrices, which can be calculated with the Standard Backpropagation algorithm. The One Step Secant method uses an approximation of the combined Hessian matrix by calculating the direction of search of the slope which uses the directions of the previous slopes.

2.3 Selection of Parameters and Statistical Analysis

The different topologies were evaluated using a hidden layer [21], in which the number of neurons used varied from 2 to 20. The number of input and output signal delays varied from zero to 20 delays for each architecture, with the exception of the Elman network. Furthermore, to estimate the order of the system, the method proposed by He and Asada [20] was used, and an empirical verification was carried out to coincide with the combination that yields the best performance. The methods evaluated for stopping training were Early Stopping and Regularization [14-15].

The signals for each patient were divided into two groups of 2.5 minutes each. Thus, a crossed validation strategy was developed [14, 16, 22] in which a model was generated for the patient with the first part of the signal, evaluated by the second part, and vice-versa. In total, 32 models were generated for each topology used.

In order to measure the performance of the models, the correlation coefficient (*r*) was used as well as the normalized mean-square error (NMSE). The latter is defined as the sum of the squares of the error between the model's output ($\hat{v}$) and the real output value (v) divided by the square of the real value of the output [11,13].

In order to compare different model results in terms of error and correlation, Wilcoxon's non-parametric sign test was used, and two results were considered significantly different when $p<0.05$.

Further to comparing the results obtained with the different alternatives of non-linear networks, the data were evaluated with Aaslid-Tiecks [10] linear model, which estimated CBFV using a second degree linear differential equation made up of two state variables. The relevance of this lies in the consideration of physiological elements in the estimation of autoregulation of the subjects. Additionally, this model provides an index of dynamic autoregulation which allows the individual performance of CBFA to be assessed on a scale of 1 to 10.

3 Results

The different models were tested on 16 subjects, and the architecture that generated the best average result for all subjects was selected. For each architecture, (except the Elman network, which only determines the number of neurons in the hidden layer), the fundamental parameters that were adjusted were: the number of delays applied to the ABP (PD) signal, the number of delays applied to the CBFV (VD) signal, and the number of neurons in the hidden layer (HL). Table 1 shows the best average results for each model, including the Aaslid-Tiecks linear model [6-10]. Upon analyzing the results presented in Table 1, it is evident that the best model depends on the evaluation parameter being considered. We believe that due to the large variability present in the spontaneous fluctuation signals, the best parameter for evaluation is the correlation coefficient obtained with the test set, and that NMSE should be used only as a means of comparison with other works.

Table 1. Mean results for the different models, best architecture, best learning method, NMSE, and correlation coefficient (*r*) for training and testing

Model	Architecture	Learning	Training		Testing	
	PD-VD-HL	Method	NMSE ± SD	r ± SD	NMSE ± SD	r ± SD
Linear	2-2	-	62.3% ± 30.2 %	0.55 ± 0.15	66.5% ± 33.1 %	0.51 ± 0.20
FFTD	8-2-6	LM	51.5% ± 30.5 %	0.65 ± 0.14	57.3% ± 25.3 %	*0.63 ±0.13*
NNOE	6-2-10	LM	36.8% ± 12.9 %	*0.73 ±0.09*	78.8% ± 64.4 %	0.58 ± 0.09
Elman	20	Elman	51.5% ± 16.5 %	0.60 ± 0.13	63.2% ± 23.0 %	0.52 ± 0.16
TLFF	8-6-12	DBD	48.1% ± 8.4 %	0.56 ± 0.18	48.3% ± 8.9 %	0.53 ± 0.20

Figure 4 shows a typical CBFV prediction for a patient using the FFTD model (with the LM algorithm), who shows the highest mean correlation value in testing.

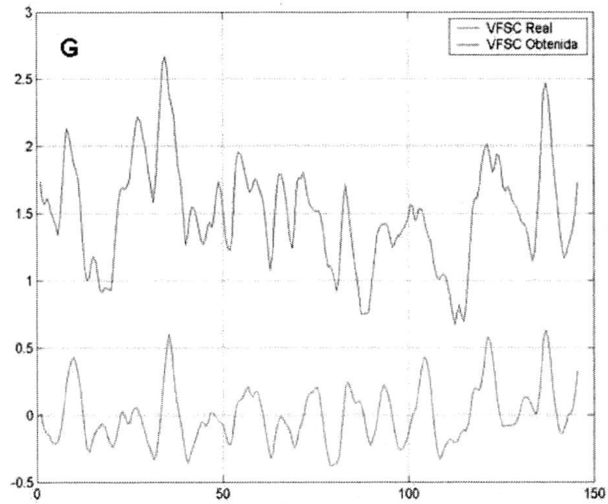

Fig. 4. Prediction for a CBFV segment with the FFTD model, and the LM learning algorithm, real signal v (above) and prediction $\hat{v}$ (below)

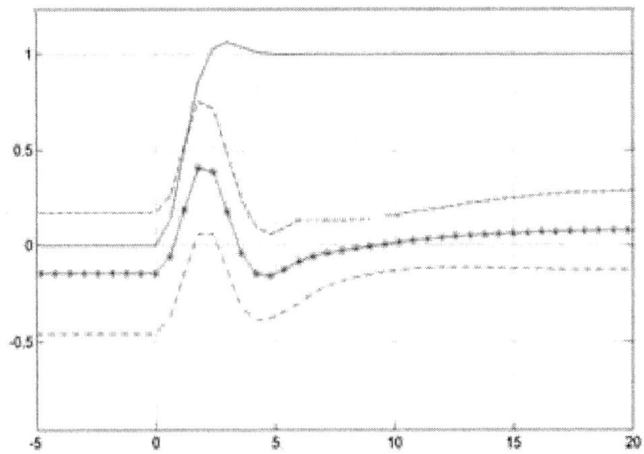

Fig. 5. Mean response of CBFV to the ABP step for 16 subjects. ABP step (solid line), mean CBFV response (asterisks), ± CBFV standard deviation (dotted line).

An important characteristic for evaluating a CBFA model is determining whether the model is able to capture the physiological dynamics of the CBFA system, or if the model has only managed a numerical fit for the data. One way of determining whether this is the case, or not, is to input an ABP step signal that simulates a thigh cuff technique, to an already trained model, and examine the CBFV response signal. Figure 5 shows the ABP step signal and the mean CBFV response for the various models for 16 subjects.

4 Discussion and Conclusions

Upon examining the correlations coefficients for the test set in Table 1, it is evident that the two models that noticeably surpass the correlation achieved by the linear model are the FFTD model (0.12 higher) and the NNOE model (0.07 higher).

Sign test results for the FFTD network with LM were significantly superior to the linear model. The next model that shows large differences with the linear model is the NNOE model, but its hypothesis test showed that the difference was not significant (p=0.010). The better performance of the non-linear models can also be seen when comparing them against the two linear models used by Panerai [6,8-9]. This shows that CBFA is a non-linear phenomenon.

In order to compare these results with non-linear models, we can refer to the work done by Mitsis et al [11], which is the only work that uses the same type of signal. Their study achieved an NMSE of 27.6% ± 9.5%, for its non-linear solution, which is inferior to our results. However, there are two important differences to consider which can narrow the difference between these results. Mitsis et al. analysed only 5 subjects, and they calculated the NMSE over the entire signal, whereas our errors correspond exclusively to the test set.

The mean response of CBFV to the models shown in Figure 5 represent an adequate physiological response to the ABP step signal, indicating that the non-linear model not only achieves a numerical fit, but also represents the normal physiological function of the CBFA system in healthy subjects.

The high correlation values of the NNOE model over the training set should be highlighted. The principal difference between this model and the others, is that it considers a white noise signal for modeling, which represents those elements that can affect CBFV and which cannot be completely represented by the ABP signal. Future work should consider the possibility of including other variables such as the partial pressure of carbon dioxide (pCO_2) and critical closing pressure [23].

The importance of the present work resides in that it proves, generally speaking, the superiority of neural network models in the modeling of CBFA. However, it leaves unaddressed a great deal of challenges, such as the evaluation with other signal types (thigh cuff technique and valsalva maneuver), the generation of multivariate models, and the development of classification systems to allow clinical assessment of CBFA in patients.

References

1. Panerai R. Assessment of cerebral pressure autoregulation in humans - a review of measurement methods. Physiological Measurement **19** (1998) 305-38.
2. Newell D, Aaslid R, Lam A, Mayberg T, Winn R. Comparison of flow and velocity during autoregulation testing in humans. Stroke **25** (1994) 793-7.
3. Panerai R, Evans D, Mahony P, Deverson S, Hayes P. Assessment of thigh cuff technique for measurement of dynamic cerebral autoregulation. Stroke **31** (2000)476-80.
4. Panerai RB, Dawson SL, Eames PJ and Potter JF. Cerebral blood flow velocity response to induced and spontaneous sudden changes in arterial blood pressure. Am J Physiol **280** (2001) H2162-H2174.

5. Panerai R, Kelsall A, Rennie J, and Evans D. Cerebral autoregulation dynamics in premature newborns. Stroke **26** (1995) 74-80.
6. Panerai R, Dawson S, Potter J. Linear and nonlinear analysis of human dynamic cerebral autoregulation. Am J Physiol **227** (1999) H1089-H1099.
7. Panerai R, White R, Markus H, Evans D. Grading of cerebral dynamic autoregulation from spontaneous fluctuations in arterial blood pressure. Stroke **29** (1998) 2341-6.
8. Panerai R, Rennie J, Kelsall A, Evans D. Frequency-domain analysis of cerebral autoregulation from spontaneous fluctuations in arterial blood pressure. Med. Biol. Eng. Comput **36** (1998) 315-22.
9. Simpson D, Panerai R, Evans D, Naylor R. A Parametric Approach to Measuring Cerebral Blood Flow Autoregulation from Spontaneous Variations in Blood Pressure. Annals of Biomedical Engineering **29** (2001)18-25.
10. Tiecks F, Lam A, Aaslid R, Newell D. Comparison of static and dynamic cerebral autoregulation measurements. Stroke **26** (1995) 1014-9.
11. Mitsis G, Zhang G, Levine BD, Marmarelis VZ. Modeling of Nonlinear Physiological Systems with fast and Slow Dynamics. II. Application to cerebral Autoregulation. Ann. Biomedical Engineering **30** (2002) 555-65.
12. Panerai R, Chacón M, Pereira R and Evans D. Neural Network Modeling of Dynamic Cerebral Autoregulation: Assessment and Comparison with Established Methods. Med Eng & Phys **26** (2004) 43-52.
13. Mitsis G, ZPoulin M Robbins A Marmarelis VZ. Nonlinear Modeling of the Dynamic Effects of Arterial Pressure and CO2 Variations on Cerebral Blood Flow in Healthy Humans. IEEE Trans. Bio. Eng **51** (2004) 1932-43.
14. Principe J, Euliano N, Lefebvre C. Neural and Adaptive Systems: Fundamentals Through Simulations. New York: John Wiley & Sons (2000).
15. Hilera J, Martínez V. Redes Neuronales Artificiales. Fundamentos, modelos y aplicaciones. Madrid: RA-MA (1995).
16. Bishop C. Neural Networks for Pattern Recognition. Oxford: Oxford University Press (1995).
17. Elman J. Finding Structure in Time. Cog. Sci **4** (1990) 141-66.
18. Lin T, Horne B, Tiňo P, Giles C. Learning Long-Term Dependencies in NARX Recurrent Neural Networks, IEEE Trans. on Neu. Net. **7** (1996) 1329-38.
19. Ljung L. System Identification – Theory for the User. New Yersey: Prentice Hall (1987).
20. He X, Asada H. A New Method for Identifying Orders of Input-Output Models for Nonlinear Dynamics Systems. Proc. of the American Control Conf, S F California (1993).
21. Hornick K, Stinchcombe M, White H. Multilayer feedforward networks are universal approximators. Neural Networks **2** (1997) 359-66.
22. Mitchell T. Machine Learning. New York: WCB/McGraw-Hill (1997).
23. Panerai R.B. The critical closing pressure of the cerebral circulation. Med. Eng. & Phy. **25** (2003) 621–32.

Neural Network Approach to Locate Motifs in Biosequences*

Marcelino Campos and Damián López

Departamento de Sistemas Informáticos y Computación,
Universidad Politécnica de Valencia,
Camino de Vera s/n, 46022 Valencia, Spain
{mcampos, dlopez}@dsic.upv.es

Abstract. In this work we tackle the task of detecting biological motifs, i.e. subsequences with an associated function. This task is important in bioinformatics because it is related to the prediction of the behaviour of the whole protein. Artificial neural networks are used to, somewhat, translate the sequence of amino acids of the protein into a code that shows the subsequences where the presence of the studied motif is expected. The experimentation performed prove the good performance of our approach.

1 Introduction

The quantity of biological data is increasing each day. Processing of this data implies sometimes to detect certain subsequences (domains or motifs) with some functional features.

Coiled coil motif is involved in protein interaction. It is known the role of this motif in some biological processes such as protein transport and membrane fusions and the infection of cells by parasites [12][2].

Briefly, the coiled coil is an ubiquitous protein folding and assembly motif made of α-helices wrapping around each other forming a super-coil. Coiled coil motifs are usually made of seven-residue repeats $(abcdefg)_n$, called heptads, in which hydrophobic core occurs mostly at positions a and d. The interaction between two α-helices in a coiled coil involves these hydrophobic residues. Its simplicity and regularity results in a highly versatile protein interaction mechanism (see Figure 1). Furthermore, this is the most extensively studied protein motif.

Several programs for predicting coiled coil domains have been described. The most relevant to large-scale annotations are *coils* [7] (probably the most widely used), *paircoil* [1] and *multicoil* [13]. All these programs are based on the probability of appearance of every amino acid in each position of the characteristic heptad. This information is extracted from known coiled coil motifs and stored in a matrix. This approach is known as a PSSM approach (Position Specific Scoring Matrix). Multicoil is the most specialized one, and aims to detect double or triple coiled coil domains.

* Work supported by the Spanish CICYT under contract TIC2003-09319-C03-02.

M. Lazo and A. Sanfeliu (Eds.): CIARP 2005, LNCS 3773, pp. 214–221, 2005.

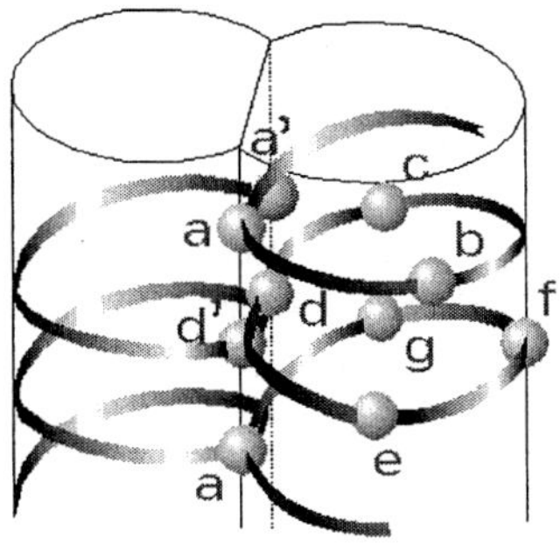

Fig. 1. We show a schematic representation of the coiled coil structure. Note that two α-helix are involved. Hydrophobic residues at the a and d positions are spatially close one each other because the helix structure. Their interaction result in a simple protein to protein fusion mechanism.

Lupas et al. [7] take into account that even very short proteins have stable coiled coils containing four or five heptads. The general scheme performs the analysis of the protein sequence using a sliding window of 21-35 amino acids. In that way, a score for each amino acid in the sequence of the protein is obtained using the probabilities stored in the PSSM. Berger's approach is the same but it considers correlation between amino acids where Lupas' consider probabilities of appearance. Berger et al. claim that the approach is useful to discard false positives detected by the Lupas' approach.

Hidden Markov Models and grammatical inference approaches has also been used in order to detect the presence of this motif [3,6,5]. Nevertheless, the problem of locating general coiled coil motifs is far of being solved. Several authors have noted several important coiled-proteins that are not detected when the previous approaches are used (among others, fusion-membrane proteins of the human and simian immunodeficiency virus or Ebola virus [10]). Thus, several other works propose solutions for more specific instances of the problem [11][10].

In our work, we use artificial neural networks to detect the subsequences which probably correspond to coiled coil. The experimentation carried out show that the performance of our approach is suitable for the task. This work is structured as follows: on section 2 we explain our neural net based approach and the process to select the parameters and topology of the net. Section 3 presents the experimentation that proves the validity of our approach. The conclusions of the work and some lines of future work end this paper.

2 Neural-Based Pattern Recognition

In our work we use Multilayer Perceptrons (MLPs). These neural nets are widely applied in pattern recognition tasks. For this purpose, the number of cells in the output layer is determined by the number of classes (C) involved in the task. In the same way, the input layer must hold the input patterns, and therefore the size of this layer depends on the data representation. Classification is based on the creation of boundaries between classes. These boundaries can be approximated by hyperplanes. Each unit in the hidden layer(s) of MLPs forms a hyperplane in the pattern space. If a sigmoid activation function [9] is used, MLPs can form smooth decision boundaries which are suitable to perform classification tasks. The activation level of an output unit can be interpreted as an approximation of the a posteriori probability that the input pattern belongs to the corresponding class. Therefore, an input pattern can be classified in the class $i^\star$ with maximum a posteriori probability:

$$i^\star = \operatorname*{argmax}_{i \in C} \Pr(i|x) \approx \operatorname*{argmax}_{i \in C} g_i(x, \omega) ,$$

where $g_i(x, \omega)$ is the i-th output of the MLP given the input pattern, x, and the set of parameters of the MLP, ω.

2.1 Input Data

In order to test our approach we used the *SwissProt Database* (release 40, April 2003). Each entry in the database contains the protein sequence and annotations for its known motifs (domains). Some of these motifs are annotated as *potential*, which means that have not yet been confirmed. We extracted from the database those entries corresponding non-potential coiled coil proteins, resulting in a set of 350 sequences (containing 720 coiled coil motifs).

Proteins are composed by a sequence of amino acids. When the amino acids are codified with one symbol, then protein sequences can be considered strings over an alphabet of 23 symbols: 20 amino acids, the glutamic and aspartic acids, plus a wildcard symbol. The wildcard symbol appear in the sequences whenever the true amino acid is not yet confirmed.

In order to standardize the input (the length of the proteins is not constant), the database was used to extract the set of segments of a given length (k). This parameter will closely determine the size of the input layer of the MLP. For each of these segments three output classes (three neurons in the output layer) were established in the following way:

- Class -1 whenever the segment does not overlap with a coiled coil motif
- Class 1 whenever the segment overlap but is not wholly contained in a coiled coil motif
- Class 2 whenever the segment is wholly contained in a coiled coil motif.

Three different numerical representations of the input data were tested. The first one considered the ordinal of each symbol, resulting in an input layer of k nodes. The second codification considered the symbols as a vector of 23 bits, obtaining an input layer of $23k$ nodes. The third codification is divided into two steps: first we used the Dayhoff codification (see Figure 1) to reduce the size of the input alphabet. Then we used the vector-based representation of the second representation. This option reduced the size of the input layer to $8k$.

Table 1. Dayhoff Amino acid codifications. This codification uses physic-chemical properties of the amino acids to group them into seven classes. Therefore, it is biologically justified.

amino acid	Dayhoff
C	a
A, P, G, S, T	b
N, Q, D, E	c
R, H, K,	d
L, V, M, I	e
F, W, Y	f
B, Z	g
X	x

2.2 Neural Network Topologies

The training of the MLPs was carried out with the software package *SNNS Stuttgart Neural Network Simulator* [14]. In order to properly use MLPs as classifiers we need to take some considerations. The more suitable input codification, the size of the input layer and the learning algorithm were studied in this order. To select the more suitable parameters, we randomly extracted 287 out of 350 sequences in the database to train different MLPs. The remaining 63 sequences were used to validate the resulting neural nets. The best results were obtained using the $23k$ codification, length of the segments $k = 28$ and backpropagation learning algorithm with learning rate of 0.1. Increasing number of nodes in the hidden layer of the MLPs (20, 40, 60, 80, 100, 200, 300 and 500 nodes), as well as MLPs with two hidden layers of 40 and 20 nodes respectively were also considered. Best results were obtained with one single hidden layer of 500 nodes.

3 Experimentation

For each test segment, it was expected that the MLP outputs 2 whenever the segment belonged with high probability to a coiled coil motif, -1 if the segment did not belong to a coiled coil motif and 1 otherwise. When a protein was analyzed, the different segments were processed sequentially. The output shows the appearance probability of a coiled coil motif (see Figure 2). In order to obtain statistically significant results, five balanced random partitions of the data were done (80% to train and 20% to test). Therefore, our final experiment entailed five runs obtaining a global 12.25% classification error rate. Confusion matrix is shown in Table 2.

3.1 Postprocessing

It is important to note that the result of any motif forecasting method ought to be confirmed in the laboratory. Thus, on the one hand it is important to reduce

Table 2. Confusion matrix for the final experiment

Classes	-1	1	2
-1	54.824 (89,36%)	3.752 (6,12%)	2.779 (4,53%)
1	4.045 (12,48%)	26.621 (82,13%)	1.747 (5,39%)
2	2.635 (5,61%)	2.312 (4,92%)	42.034 (89,47%)

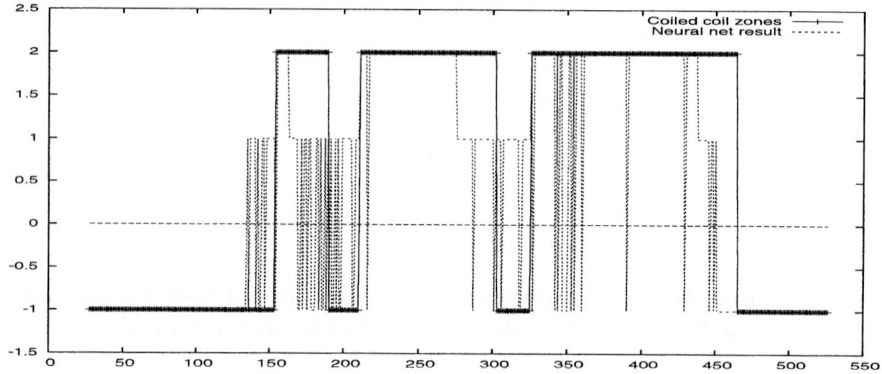

Fig. 2. Processing of a protein sequence. Note that the output fairly approximates the coiled coil database annotations.

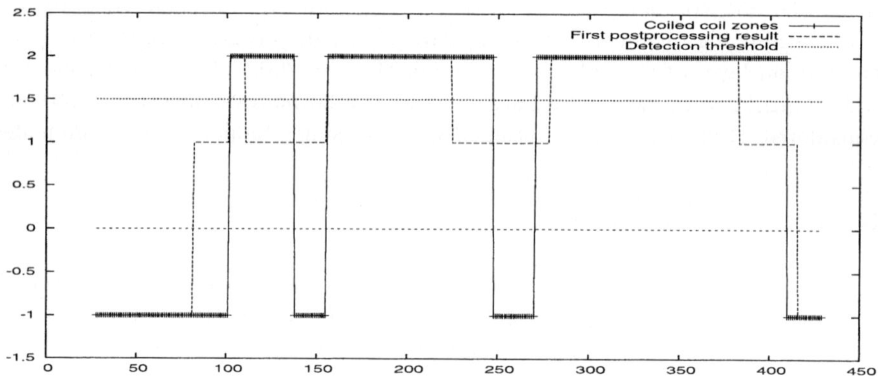

Fig. 3. Result of the first postprocessing method is shown. Note that in order a change to be considered, more than 7 consecutive amino acids with the same output are needed. The noise level of the postprocessed output is also highly reduced.

the rate of *false positive* detection. On the other hand, it is more important to roughly detect the more motifs the best rather than to accurately detect only some of them.

Before to analyze our approach in this way, we post-processed the output of our method. To do this, two procedures were tested.

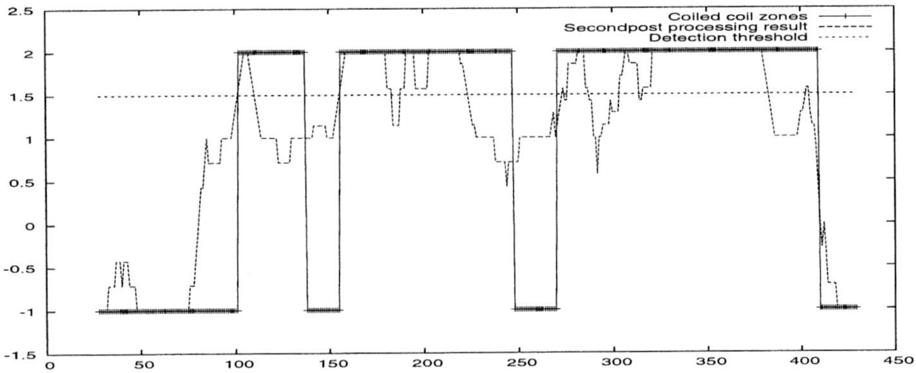

Fig. 4. Result of the second postprocessing method is shown. Note that there is no trouble with several predictions for a single coiled coil annotation.

The first one take into account that certain number of heptad repeats are needed to give stability to a coiled coil motif. Thus, the postprocessing did not considered those changes of length lower or equal to one heptad. Besides, this postprocess of the output reduced the noise level, because most of them was produced by very short predictions. Figure 3 shows the postprocessing of the output shown in Figure 2.

The second post-processing procedure is based on a smoothing of the output signal. To do this a one-heptad-length sliding window was considered to average the value of each output value. Figure 4 shows the postprocessing of the output shown in Figure 2.

In order to analyze the motif detection error, three categories were established:

- Error: Annotated coiled coil motif that has not been detected. The error detection rate is defined as the number of errors among the total number of coiled coil motifs in the database.
- False positive: prediction that overlap with no coiled coil annotation. Therefore, false positive detection rate is considered as the number of false predictions among the total number of coiled coil annotations in the database.
- Correct detection: Annotated coiled coil motifs that overlap with some coiled coil predictions.

Finally, we considered as a coiled coil prediction those regions with output over a value of 1.5, that is, the average between the probable and high probable coiled coil output. The results obtained are shown in Table 3. In order to compare our results with the most known prediction algorithms [7][1], we run available versions of the algorithms ([8][4] respectively) using the default parameter values. The results are also shown in Table 3.

The results obtained differ from each other considering the postprocessing procedure. On the one hand the first postprocessing procedure produces very

Table 3. Comparative experimental results. The error rate and the false positives detection rate is shown for each method tested.

	error rate	FP
MLP (1st postprocessing)	22,50%	1,80%
MLP (2nd postprocessing)	7,50%	14,44%
coils	19,30%	15,83%
paircoil	21,38%	10,27%

low rate of false positive detection. This reduction does not produce significant increase of the error rate (it is quite similar to the Lupas' and Berger's methods error rate). The second postprocessing procedure obtains better error rate than any other approach (the false positive rate is also similar to the Lupas' and Berger's methods rate).

4 Conclusions

We propose a neural net based method to detect coiled coil motifs from biosequences. This motif is related to protein interaction. Motif location is important in bioinformatics because it is related to the prediction of the behaviour of the whole protein.

MLPs are used to, somewhat, translate the sequence of amino acids of the protein into a code that shows the subsequences where the presence of the studied domain is expected. The output of the neural net is then postprocessed to obtain a motif location forecast. Two postprocessing procedures were tested. The behaviour of these procedure were different one each other.

In any case the results are improved respect previous prediction methods. This is proved by the experimentation carried out. We can select the postprocessing to obtain very low rate of false positive detection or low rate of error detection. The reduction of false positive rate is highly biologically demanded because it reduces the experimental effort. Comparison with two well-known coiled coil prediction algorithms [7][1] is shown.

It is very important to note that the database contains annotations only for those proteins that contain a coiled coil region. Furthermore, it is not assured that the coiled coil motifs are accurately annotated. Furthermore, there not exist any negative annotation, that is, information concerning non-coiled coil subsequences. This have to be considered as an important drawback. Of course, the availability of non-coiled protein sequences should improve our results. This sequences could be obtained by considering protein structural information.

Coiled coil is a well characterized motif. Its structure is the key stone of the most used prediction algorithms. MLPs could also be used to predict the location of other motifs whose structure is poorly known.

References

1. B. Berger, D.B. Wilson, E. Wolf, T. Tonchev, M. Milla, and P. S. Kim. Predicting coiled coils by use of pairwise residue correlation. Proc. Natl. Acac. Sci., 92:8259 8263, 1995.
2. D.C. Chan and P.S. Kim. Hiv entry and its inhibition. Cell, 93:681684, 1998.
3. M. Delorenzi and T. Speed. An hmm model for coiled-coil domains and a comparison with pssm-based predictions. Bioinformatics, 18(4):617625, 2002.
4. PAIRCOIL implementation by the authors, 1995. http://theory.lcs.mit.edu/bab/computing.
5. D. Lopez, A. Cano, M. Vazquez de Parga, B. Calles, J.M. Sempere, T. Perez, M. Campos, Jose Ruiz, and Pedro Garcia. Motifs discovery by k-tss grammatical inference. 2005. Submitted and accepte at the 19th IJCAI'05.
6. Damian Lopez, Antonio Cano, Manuel Vazquez de Parga, Belen Calles, Jose M. Sempere, Tomas Perez, Jose Ruiz, and Pedro Garcia. Detection of functional motifs in biosequences: A grammatical inference approach. In X. Messeguer and G. Valiente, editors, Proceedings of the 5th Annual Spanish Bioinformatics Conference, pages 7275. Univ. Politécnica de Catalunya. ISBN: 84-7653-863-4, 2004.
7. A. Lupas, M. Van Dyke, and J. Stock. Predicting coiled coild from protein sequences. Science, 252:11621164, 1991.
8. Source Code NCOILS, 1999. http://www.russell.embl.de/cgi-bin/coils-svr.pl.
9. D. E. Rumelhart, P. Smolensky, J. L. McClelland, and G. E. Hinton. Schemata and sequential thought processes in pdp models. In J. L. McClelland, D. E. Rumelhart, others, and eder, editors, Parallel Distributed Processing: Volume 2: Psychological and Biological Models, pages 757. MIT Press, Cambridge, MA, 1986.
10. M. Singh, B. Berger, and P.S. Kim. Learncoil-vmf: Computational evidence for coiled-coil-like motifs in many viral membrane fusion proteins. J. Mol. Biol., 290:10311041, 1999.
11. M. Singh, B. Berger, P.S. Kim, J.M. Berger, and A.G. Cochran. Computational learning reveals coiled coil-like motifs in histidine kinase linker domains. Proc. Natl. Acac. Sci., 95:27382743, 1998.
12. J.J. Skehel and D.C. Wiley. Coiled coils in both intracellular vesicle and viral membrane fusion. Cell, 95:871874, 1998.
13. E. Wolf, P.S. Kim, and B. Berger. Multicoil: a program for predicting two- and three-stranded coiled coils. Protein Science, 6:11791189, 1997.
14. Andreas Zell, Niels Mache, Ralf Huebner, Michael Schmalzl, Tilman Sommer, and Thomas Korb. SNNS: Stuttgart neural network simulator. Technical report, Stuttgart, 1992.

Free-Shaped Object Recognition Method from Partial Views Using Weighted Cone Curvatures

Santiago Salamanca[1], Carlos Cerrada[2], Antonio Adán[3], Jose A. Cerrada[2], and Miguel Adán[4]

[1] Escuela de Ingenierías Industriales, Universidad de Extremadura, Av. Elvas s/n, 06071 Badajoz, Spain
ssalaman@unex.es
[2] Escuela Técnica Superior de Ingeniería Informática, UNED juan del rosal 16, 28040 Madrid, Spain
{ccerrada, jcerrada}@issi.uned.es
[3] Escuela Superior de Informática, Universidad de Castilla La Mancha, Paseo de la Universidad 4, 13071 Ciudad Real, Spain
antonio.adan@uclm.es
[4] Escuela de Ingeniería Técnica Agrícola, Universidad de Castilla la Mancha, Ronda de Calatrava nº 7, 13071 Ciudad Real, Spain
miguel.adan@uclm.es

Abstract. This work presents a method for free-shaped object recognition from its partial views. Consecutive database reductions are achieved in three stages by using effective discriminant features. These features are extracted from the spherical mesh representation used to modeling the partial view and from the view range data itself. The used characteristics are global, which means that they can not represent the views univocally. However, their staged application allows the initial object database to be reduced to selecting just one candidate in the final stage with a high success rate. Yet, the most powerful search reduction is achieved in the first stage where the new Weighted Cone Curvature (WCC) parameter is processed. The work is devoted to describe the overall method making especial emphasis in the WCC feature and its application to partial views recognition. Results with real objects range data are also presented in the paper.

1 Introduction

The *recognition* problem tries to identify an object, called unknown or scene object, from a set of objects in an object database, generally called *models*. The problem of *positioning* or *alignment* solves the localization of an object in a scene with respect to a reference system linked to the model of this object. One of the most common ways of solving this problem is *matching* the unknown object on the corresponding object in the object database.

Although conceptually recognition and positioning are two different problems, in practice they are closely related. If we can align the unknown object precisely on one of the different objects in the database, we will have solved not only positioning but also recognition.

M. Lazo and A. Sanfeliu (Eds.): CIARP 2005, LNCS 3773, pp. 222 – 232, 2005.

The case that we present in this work is recognition of the range data of a partial view by matching the view on the range data of the complete objects stored in the object database. The resolution of the problem is of real practical interest since it can be used in tasks with industrial robots, mobile robot navigation, visual inspection, etc.

In order to tackle the problem posed it is necessary to generate a model that allows us to extract information from the source data and represent them. Regarding these representations there are two fundamental categories: object-based representation and view-centered representation.

The first creates models based on representative characteristics of the objects [8, 5, 3], while the second tries to generate the model according to the appearance of the object from different points of view [4, 7].

Some other methods [6, 9] are halfway between these two categories since they do not capture the appearance of the object from each point of view, but provide just a characteristic measurement of the object. This is our case since our basis will be different measurements on the meshes or on the range data of the objects, calculated from different points of view. In this particular direction is addressed the problem in [1] where a shape similarity measure is introduced and applied. Nevertheless, this solution does not solve satisfactorily the object recognition problem from real partial views, which is the main purpose of our method.

The structure of the work will be as follows: in section 2 we will do a general description of the three stages of method proposed. In section 3 we will study first stage and the WCC feature which is the key of our method. Some explanations of the two others stages are stated in section 4. Then, in section 5 we will give the experimental results of the method, making special emphasis in the high reduction rates achieved in the first stage, and in section 6 the conclusions of this work.

2 Overall Method: Functioning Principle

The method presented in this work obtains effective database reduction by applying sequentially different global characteristics calculated on the spherical meshes and the range data of partial views (Fig. 1).

In the first stage we use a new invariant that we call *Weihgted Cone-Curvature (WCC)* to determine a first approximation to the possible axes of vision from which this partial view has been acquired. Discretization of the vision space is obtained by circumscribing a spherical mesh around the model of the complete object. Each node in this mesh, together with the origin of coordinates, defines the initial axes of vision around this model. Therefore, determining the possible axes of vision from which the partial view has been acquired is equivalent to selecting a set of nodes on the mesh and rejecting the others. It is important to bear in mind that with this reduction what we are doing implicitly is a reduction of the possible rotations that could be applied on the partial view to match it on the model of the complete object.

We will call the nodes obtained after this first step $\mathbf{N}_i^{cc} \subset \mathbf{N}_i$, where $\mathbf{N}_i$ are the initial nodes of the spherical mesh circumscribed in the *i*-th object of the database. As is deduced from the explanation, in this stage the number of models in the object database is not reduced.

Another invariant based on the principal components (eigen values + eigen vectors) of the partial view and complete object range data will be applied in a second stage on the selected nodes. After this features comparison a list for each of the objects in the database will be created with the nodes $\mathbf{N}_i^{cc}$ ordered according to the error existing in the eigen values comparison. This ordering in turn means that it is possible to identify which object has the greatest probability of matching the partial view. At the end of this second stage a reduction of the models in the object database is obtained together with the reduction of the nodes determined in the previous stage. If we call the initial object database **B**, the base obtained after comparing the eigen values will be $\mathbf{B}^{cp} \subset \mathbf{B}$, and the nodes for each object $\mathbf{N}_i^{cp} \subset \mathbf{N}_i^{cc}$.

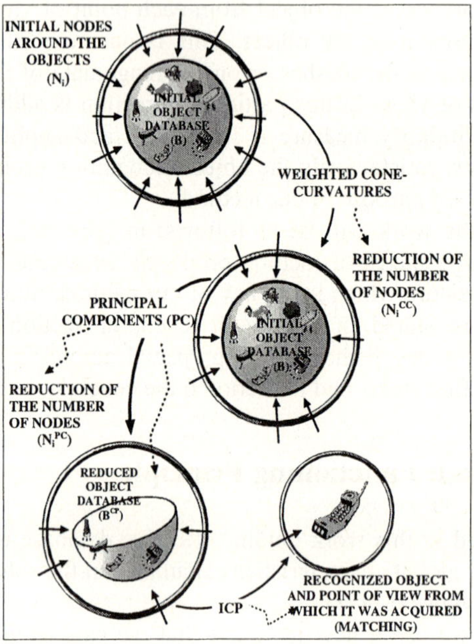

Fig. 1. Scheme of the different stages of the method for object recognition from partial views:graphical representation

The eigen vectors will allow a first approximation to be done to the rotation existing between the partial view and each one of the objects of $\mathbf{B}^{cp}$, which will be used in the last stage when the *Iterative Closest Point (ICP)* algorithm is applied. This allows the matching to be done between the range data, and the convergence error of the algorithm will indicate the object to which the partial view belongs.

The last two stages of the method are based on conventional techniques, whereas the first one represents a novel way of dealing with this problem. Therefore, only this key stage of the applied method will be detailed in next section.

3 First Stage: Robust Determination of the Point of View

As it has been mentioned, in this stage of the recognition method the possible points of view from which the partial view has been acquired are estimated. For this task a new characteristic is proposed. Some preliminary concepts must be introduced previously to present this feature. It is calculated from partial spherical model, which we will call T', created from the range data of a given partial view. The partial spherical modeling technique is not covered in this work. After, a mesh adjusted to the range data is obtained whose patches are hexagonal or pentagonal. Each of the nodes of the mesh has a connectivity of 3 except for those nodes that are in the contour with connectivity less than 3. Fig, 2 shows the intensity image of an object and the spherical model for a partial view of the object.

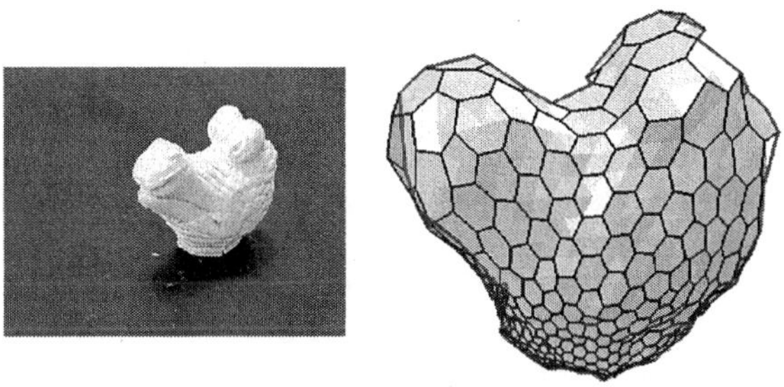

Fig. 2. Intensity image of an object and spherical model for a partial view of the object

A structure called *Modeling Wave Set (MWS)* [2] can be created on the spherical model, which is generated from a simpler structure called *Modeling Wave (MW)*. Any node of the complete spherical mesh T can be a *focus* and a MW can therefore be generated from it. Thus, a tessellated sphere with a number of nodes n–$ord(T)$ will contain n MW's. Fig. 3 shows two MW's on the tessellated sphere and the axes of vision defined by the focus and origin of coordinates. Notice that each MW is composed of several *Wave Fronts* (F^j).

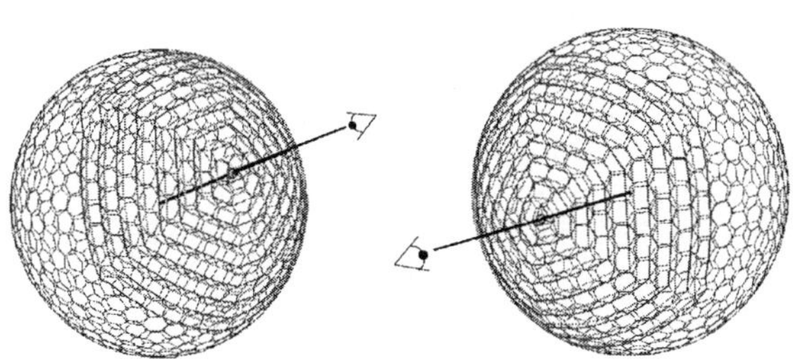

Fig. 3. Representation of two different modeling wave on the tessellated sphere

In this point the concept of Cone-Curvature (CC) is used. The CC is a characteristic calculated for each node of the mesh from the MWS. Its definition and main features are stated in [1]. For each wave front F^j it determines an angle α^j and its range of values is [-π/2, π/2]. Negative values indicate the existence of concave areas; values near to zero correspond to flat surfaces, and positive values to convex areas. Fig. 4 illustrates the definition of Cone Curvature.

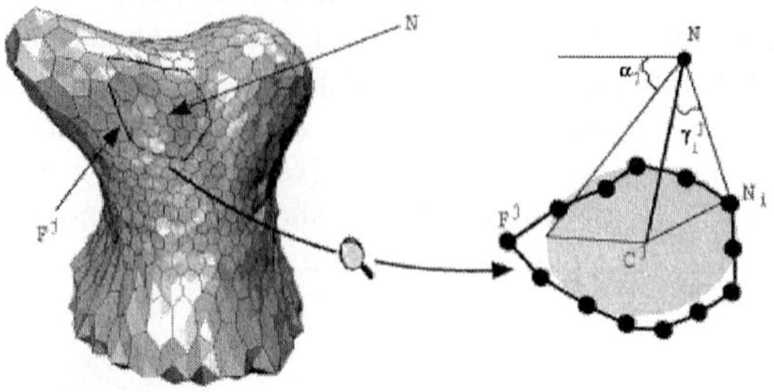

Fig. 4. Definition of the j-th Cone Curvature (CC) for a given focus *N*

Given a focus *N*, there exists a set of *q* wave fronts which define the CC's for this focus $\{\alpha^1, \ldots, \alpha^q\}$ and which provide complete information about the curvature of the existing object from the point of view that determines *N*. Finally, *q*, which is known as *front order*, can have values from 2 (case q=1 does not make sense) to the maximum number of fronts that the object has. As we want to work with partial models, the maximum order will be calculated for a number of wave fronts equal to the number of complete fronts in our partial model.

Main properties of CC's are their uniqueness (sufficient distant values for different objects), invariance to affine transformations- translation, rotation and scaling- (same values map for the same object shape) and robustness (higher orders CC's converge whereas important noise rates appearing in the model generation process). A deeper analysis of these properties can be found in [1], and it can be deduced that they are especially adequate to be applied to recognition tasks.

3.1 Weighted Cone-Curvature (WCC)

In this work we propose to use more compact information from the CC's with the purpose of reducing their dimensionality. This can be done by replacing each vector $\{\alpha^1, \ldots, \alpha^q\}$ calculated from $N' \in T'$ with a scalar linear combination of their components, denoted as c^w, that will characterize the object from this node. We will call this new global characteristic *Weighted Cone-Curvature (WCC)* and it is the key parameter to implement the reduction in the number of nodes.

To evaluate quantitatively if the reduction proposed is possible, the correlation existing in the CC's was calculated. This is shown in gray scale in Fig. 5 (white for high values and black for low values), and it has been calculated as the mean value of all the correlation coefficients of the meshes in the database. From analysis of the figure, and as we had envisaged, it can be concluded that there is a high correlation between fronts of near orders, which increases as this order increases.

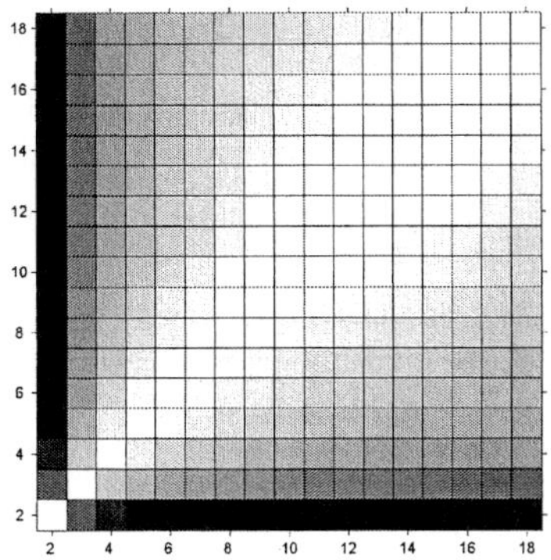

Fig. 5. Illustration of the correlation existing between the Cone-Curvatures of the wave fronts of orders 2 to 18 in the database

If we denote the WCC for each $N' \in T'$ as c^w, the linear combination will be:

$$c^w = \sum_{j=1}^{q} v^j c^j \quad (1)$$

where v^j are the coordinates of the eigen vector associated with the eigen value of greater value of the covariance matrix for the q initial variables.

This eigen vector was determined empirically by evaluating the principal components on the Cone-Curvatures of all the mesh nodes. As regards the orders considered, we studied three possibilities:

1. Wave fronts from $q = 2$ to $q = 18$.
2. Wave fronts from $q = 4$ to $q = 18$.
3. Wave fronts from $q = 4$ to $q = 9$.

Fig. 6 represents, for the object that we are analyzing, the Weighted Cone-Curvatures in the three cases, plotted over the object mesh and using a color code to express the range from negative to positive values. We can see that the Cone-Curvatures for the first and second cases are very similar.

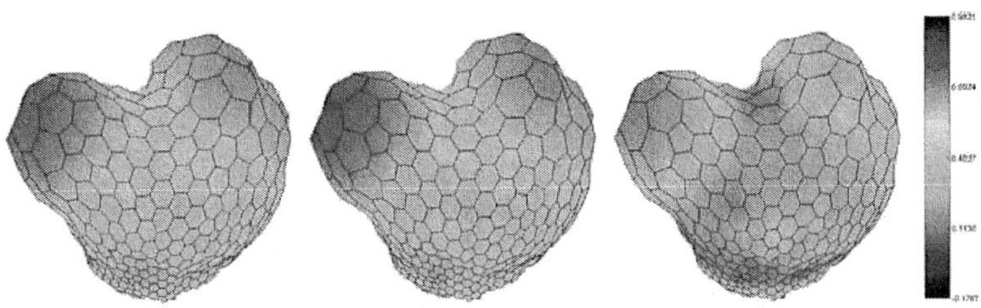

Fig. 6. Representation in color of the Weighted Cone-Curvatures of each mesh node for cases (1), (2) and (3) (left to right). A bar is shown where the colors can be seen for the maximum, mean and minimum Weighted Cone-Curvatures of the object.

3.2 Application of WCC to Partial Views Recognition

In order to apply the WCC's to the recognition of partial views several factors must be taken into acount due to the nature of the handled meshes:

1. The number of complete wave fronts in a partial view is variable.
2. The surface represented by a set number of wave fronts can vary between a partial model and its complete model.
3. The mean length of the internode distance is different for the partial model and the complete model in the same object.

These questions imply that the CC's cannot be used as they are since the partial view and total view wave fronts cannot be compared because of the differences existing between the partial and total meshes. Therefore, we will define a measurement of error based on the WCC's:

Definition 1. *Let $N' \in T'$ be the node of the partial mesh T' which is the nearest to the axis of vision. The error or distance of comparison of weighted cone-curvatures for each $N \in T_i$, where T_i is the i-th total model of the object database is defined as:*

$$e_j(N) = \left| c^{w'}(N') - c^{w}(N_j) \right| \tag{2}$$

where the subscript j extends from 1 to the maximum number of nodes existing in T_i and $|\cdot|$ represents the absolute value.

The fact of conditioning the reduction of nodes around T_i to just one measurement of error can cause significant errors in this reduction. Therefore, in order to reinforce the reduction, for each $N \in T_i$ two errors will be measured. The first will consider the WCC's to the furthest fronts generated from N'. We will call this error *deep error* and give it the symbol $e_j^p(N)$. The second will consider the nearest fronts generated from N'. This time we will call the error *superficial error* and give it the symbol $e_j^s(N)$.

In both instances a set of errors equal to the number of nodes existing in T_i is obtained, and from these errors the nodes $\mathbf{N}_i^{cc}$ of the mesh that will be passed to the next stage of the algorithm will be determined. If we call $\mathbf{N}^p$ to the set of nodes of T_i with less e_i^p values, and $\mathbf{N}^s$ to the set of nodes of T_i with less e_i^s values, $\mathbf{N}_i^{cc}$ will be:

$$\mathbf{N}_i^{cc} = \mathbf{N}^p \cup \mathbf{N}^s \tag{3}$$

4 Principal Components and ICP Stages

In this section the last two stages of the recognition algorithm will be commented on for matching the partial views on complete models. These are the principal components and ICP stages.

In the principal components stage the method proposed is based on calculating the principal components on the range data that we employed to obtain the model T' used in the previous stage. If we call these data $\boldsymbol{X}$, the principal components are defined as the eigen values and eigen vectors $\{(\lambda_i, \vec{e}_i) \quad i = 1, \cdots, m\}$ of the covariance matrix.

The eigen values are invariant to rotations and displacements and the eigen vectors to displacements. The eigen vectors conform a reference system linked to the data. This means that the eigen values can be used to evaluate what part of the range data of the complete model correspond to the scene, and the eigen vectors to calculate a first approximation to the transformation of the partial data to be matched on the total data. This approximation will only reflect the rotation sub matrix of the total transformation, since the origins of the two frames will coincide.

To apply this technique it is necessary to evaluate, before the recognition process, all the possibly existing partial views on the range data of the complete object. For this, the space of the possible points of view existing around the object was discretized, and a method was developed for generating *virtual partial views (VPV's)* based on the z-buffer algorithm. From each of these VPV their principal components will be calculated and used in the matching stage as explained earlier.

Comparison of the eigen values gives information about the possible areas where the partial view can be matched, but this information is global and, as we have said, only gives information about the rotation.

Thus it will be necessary to do a final calculation stage to refine the matching and to calculate the definitive transformation. For this we will use the ICP algorithm on a number of possible candidates marked in the eigen value comparison stage. The ICP must start from an approximation to the initial transformation, which in our case corresponds to the transformation given in the matching of the eigen vectors. The ending error in the ICP algorithm will measure the exactness of the definitive transformation and the correctness of the area where the view will be matched.

The comparison of the eigen values of the partial view and the virtual partial views is done by measuring an index of error given in the following expression:

$$e_i^{cp}(N) = \left\| \Lambda_i^v(N) - \Lambda^r \right\| \quad (4)$$

where $N \in \mathrm{N}_i^{cc}$ is the node from where we generated the VPV, $\Lambda_i^v(N)$ is the vector formed by the eigen values of the VPV generated from the node N of the i th object of the object database ($i=1,\dots, K$), $\Lambda^r = \{\lambda_1^r, \lambda_2^r, \lambda_3^r\}$ is the vector formed by the eigen values of the real partial view and $\|\cdot\|$ is the Euclidean distance.

After the error has been calculated for all the $\mathbf{N}_i^{cc}$ nodes and all the objects in the object database, we obtain a list of these errors, e_i^{cp} ($i=1,\dots, K$), ordered from least to great. If we compare the first error (least error for a set object) in all the lists, an ordering of the different objects in the object database will be obtained. Thus in the last stage we can apply the ICP algorithm on a subset of the object database, just $\mathbf{B}^{cp}$, and for each of the objects using the transformations associated with the subset of nodes that have produced these errors.

For the resolution of the ICP it is necessary to determine an approximation to the transformation matrix between the partial view and the object in the object database R_1. This is calculated bearing in mind that the eigen vectors are orthonormal, and therefore:

$$\mathbf{R}_1 = \mathbf{E}^r(\mathbf{E}_i^v(N))^{-1} = \mathbf{E}^r(\mathbf{E}_i^v(N))^T \quad (5)$$

where $\mathrm{E}_i^v(N)$ are the eigen vectors of the VPV generated from $N \in \mathrm{N}^{cp}$ of the i-th model of the object database B^{cp}, and E' are the eigen vectors of the partial view.

5 Experimental Results

The method proposed in this work was tested on a set of 20 objects. Range data of these objects have been acquired by means of a GRF-2 range finder sensor which provides an average resolution of approximately 1 mm. Real size of the used objects goes from 5 to 10 cm. height and there are both polyhedral shaped and free form objects (see Fig. 7). MWS Models have been built by deforming a tessellated sphere with 1280 nodes.

Fig. 7. Set of objects used to test the presented method

The recognition was done for three partial views per object, except in one of them where after the determination of its partial model it was seen that it did not have enough wave fronts to be able to compare the weighted cone-curvatures. This means that recognition was done on a total of 59 partial models. The success rate has been the 90%, what demonstrates the validity of the method. The average computation time invested by the whole process was 90 seconds, programmed over a Pentium 4 at 2.4 GHz. computer under Matlab environment. A more detailed analysis of these results are next.

As it has been explained, in the first stage the weighted cone-curvatures of the partial model were compared for a node with a maximum number of wave fronts. From this comparison $\mathbf{N}_i^{cc}$ was determined (equation (3)). In the considered experiments, the maximum value of the number of nodes that form the sets $\mathbf{N}^p$ (deep search) and $\mathbf{N}^s$ (superficial search) was 32 each. Since the mesh used to obtain the complete model T_i was 1280, the minimum reduction of the space search in this stage was 95%. The reduction can be even bigger as long as there are nodes coinciding in $\mathbf{N}^p$ and $\mathbf{N}^s$. This step was carried out for all the objects of the initial database **B** and took an average of 7.95 seconds.

Concerning the second stage, it started from these nodes and the eigen values were compared, which allowed us to achieve the first reduction of the database ($\mathbf{B}^{cp}$ database). Reduction of the nodes obtained in the previous stage is also accomplished ($\mathbf{N}_i^{cp}$ set). It was determined experimentally that $\mathbf{B}^{cp}$ consists of approximately 35% of the objects of **B** and $\mathbf{N}_i^{cp}$ of approximately 8% of the nodes of $\mathbf{N}^{cc}$ per object, which represent very satisfactory reduction rates of the stage. This process spent around 1 sec.

Finally, the ICP algorithm was applied on seven objects (the mentioned 35% remaining in the $\mathbf{B}^{cp}$ database) and three nodes (corresponding to the mentioned 8%) for each $\mathbf{N}_i^{cp}$ object. As can be deduced, practically the most part of the time consumed for the algorithm was in this stage.

Fig. 8 shows some examples of recognition concerning to different shaped objects of the database. For each object, left side of this figure contains the range data corresponding to the partial view to recognize. Right side plots the range data of the partial view and the complete range data of the recognized object matched together in the position obtained after application of the algorithm.

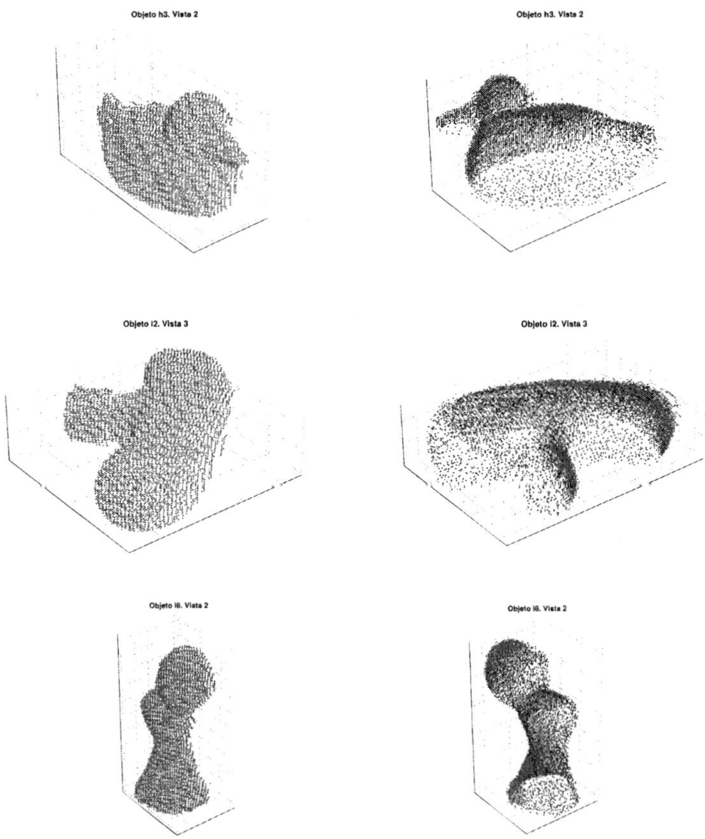

Fig. 8. Recognition results on free-form objects. On the left in each row the partial view to be recognized is shown and on the right the result obtained after applying the algorithm (both partial view and complete object range data).

6 Conclusions

This work has described a method for the recognition of free-form objects from their partial views. The method is divided into three stages: Weighted Cone-Curvatures stage, principal components stage, and ICP stage. Due to its novelty the first one has been described in more detail. The new feature WCC has been defined and analyzed. It exhibits the right properties for applying in recognition and positioning tasks. WCC's are calculated on the spherical models of the objects. These characteristics allow to achieve important reductions in the number of nodes that define the possible axes of vision from which the partial view has been acquired. The validity of the full method was proven with the recognition of 59 partial views in an object database of 20 objects. The success rate was 90%.

We are currently working with a single view in real complex scenes where a hard and difficult task that frequently implies previous processes or steps must be solved before accomplishing recognition. In this case an effective 3D segmentation on the scene is essential to apply the recognition method presented in this paper.

Acknowledgements

This research has been carried out under contract with the Spanish CICYT through the DPI2002-03999-C02 project..

References

1. Adán, A., Adán, M.: A flexible similarity measure for 3D shapes recognition. *IEEE Transactions on Pattern Analysis and Machine Intelligence*, 26(11):1507–1520, November 2004.
2. Adán, A., Cerrada, C., Feliu, V.: Modeling wave set: Definition and application of a new topological organization of 3D object modeling. *Computer Vision and Image Understanding*, 79(2):281–307, August 2000.
3. Adán, A., Cerrada, C., Feliu, V.: Global shape invariants: a solution for 3D free-form object discrimination/identification problem. *Pattern Recognition*, 34(7):1331–1348, July 2001.
4. Campbell, R.J., Flynn, P. J.: Eigenshapes for 3D object recognition in range data. In *Proc. of the IEEE Conference on Computer Vision and Pattern Recognition*, volume 2, pages 2505–2510, Fort Collins, Colorado, June 1999.
5. Hebert, M., Ikeuchi, K., Delingette, H.: A spherical representation for recognition of free-form surfaces. *IEEE Transactions on Pattern Analysis and Machine Intelligence*, 17(7):681–690, July 1995.
6. Johnson, A. E., Hebert, M.: Using spin images for efficient object recognition in cluttered 3d scenes. *IEEE Transactions on Pattern Analysis and Machine Intelligence*, 21(5):433–449, May 1999.
7. Skocaj, D., Leonardis, A.: Robust recognition and pose determination of 3-D objects using range image in eigenspace approach. In *Proc. of 3DIM'01*, pages 171–178, 2001.
8. Stein, F., Medioni, G.: Structural indexing: Efficient 3-D object recognition. *IEEE Transactions on Pattern Analysis and Machine Intelligence*, 14(2):125–145, February 1992.
9. Yamany, S., Farag, A.: Surfacing signatures: An orientation independent free-form surface representation scheme for the purpose of objects registration and matching. *IEEE Transactions on Pattern Analysis and Machine Intelligence*, 24(8):1105–1120, August 2002.

Automatic Braille Code Translation System

Hamid Reza Shahbazkia, Telmo Tavares Silva, and Rui Miguel Guerreiro

Universidade do Algarve,
Laboratório de Sistemas Funcionais Alternativos,
Campus de Gambelas, 8005-139 Faro-Portugal
{hshah, a17145, a14104}@ualg.pt

Abstract. This paper reports the results obtained in the implementation of an Optical Braille Recognizer (O.B.R.), as well as the construction of a keyboard for the Braille code. This project was developed with the objective of enabling teachers of blind people, who do not know the Braille code, to visualize the texts written by their students. An electronic keyboard, less noisy and less expensive than the traditional mechanical ones was built too. To achieve these objectives, the "Compendium of the Braille code for the Portuguese Language" was used. The final program translates plain text, mathematics and chemistry sheets written in Braille code. It's also possible to write plain text, mathematics or chemistry using the developed keyboard. The program is written in Java and the keyboard communicates with it through serial port.

1 Introduction

This project appeared as the result of the educational politic of mixing blind pupils in the normal school classrooms. The Optical Braille Recognizer is therefor intended for teachers, who don't understand Braille language, for visualization of texts written by their blind students in normal mechanical emboss machines. The keyboard is mainly intended for the blind students, as the common mechanical Braille keyboards are very noisy and expensive, so the creation of a new, low noise and low cost became crucial. To accomplish this objectives, the project has been split into several tasks, which are:

1. Locating the Braille points that form the text;
2. Segmenting the image into Braille text lines;
3. Processing of the points found to extract the text;
4. Creating the parsers representing the language;
5. Constructing the keyboard and connection to the parsers;
6. Integrating the text to speech system;
7. User interface

This project is still under development, although there are interesting results, which will be discussed from now on in this article.

In the beginning of the current project there were the following constraints:

M. Lazo and A. Sanfeliu (Eds.): CIARP 2005, LNCS 3773, pp. 233–241, 2005.

1. Translate single sided Braille sheets;
2. The system should be low cost;
3. The system should be platform independent;
4. Should run in a mid range computer;
5. Use of free software;
6. Simplicity of system circuits to allow a low skilled person to assemble the keyboard (possibly in an electronics class).

2 Location of the Points

In Braille code each character is represented by six points, 3 per column and 2 per row, having standard distances between them [1]. The distance between points is 2.5mm. The distance between characters is 3.5mm in the horizontal and 5mm in the vertical. These distances define the braille cells. The characters are formed by embossed dots in any position of the cell. These are the points to be located in the scanned image, as they represent the Braille text.

The location of the points is the first stage of the project. It is very important to have a good input image. The image can be scanned with any scanner, but it should be in high resolution. The input image is crucial for the success of the Optical Braille Recognition (O.B.R.), as in a bad image the points will be fuzzy and difficult to locate.

In Figure 1 it is possible to see distinct zones in the represented points, as this is a partial scanned test image. One zone is brilliant, above the point, and the other zone is darker, under the point [2]. This is due to the emboss of the points, illuminated by the oblique light source from the scanner. This discrepancy has to be enhanced to locate the points more precisely, reducing the probability to detect false points, introduced by eventual noise in the image. Thresholding [4] twice using the Otsu method, accomplished some results, which weren't very reliable with different background colors. A more accurately method was develop that calculates the threshold points based on a given percentage of

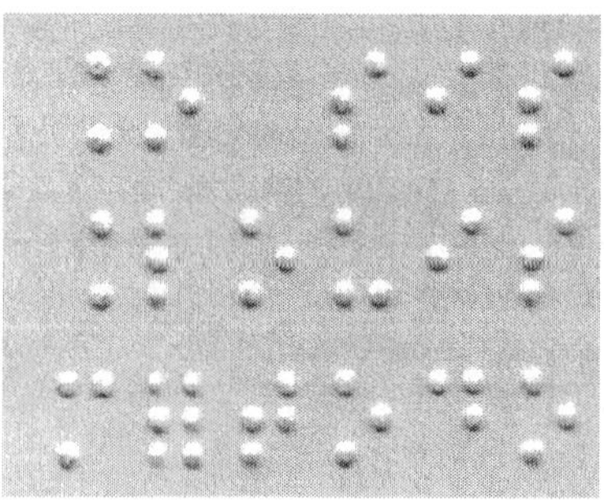

Fig. 1. Partial image of Braille Scanned sheet

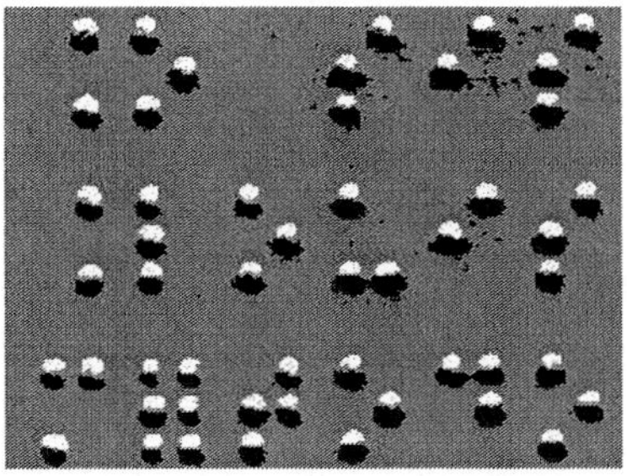

Fig. 2. Partial image after threshold process

the histogram peak[1]. This method was observed to be efficient has it permitted to work with different color sheets. Each zone, brilliant or dark, is isolated by one threshold.

After the threshold process, the image will be composed by three different color regions, as represented in the Figure 2. Now the points have to be located and marked to segment the image. A white zone, with a black zone under, is searched to locate the points. Grouping the regions this way, there is a small probability of detecting a false point. This process has some errors, as some points will not be detected because the white zone, or the black one, may not exist for all points. Although this may happen, it happens to few points, only the ones that are not well embossed by the Braille printer, or those that may be perforated.

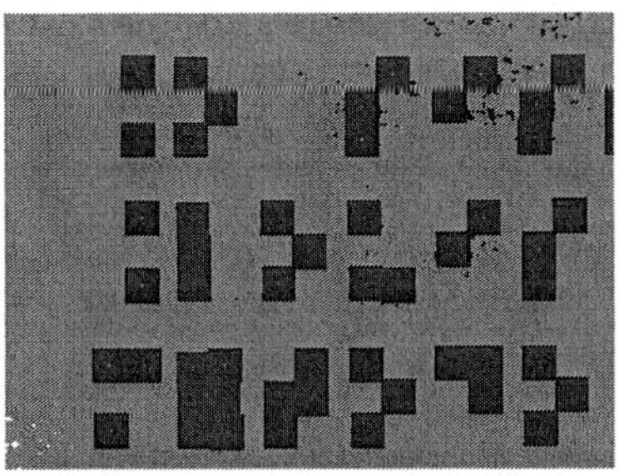

Fig. 3. Partial image after locating the points

The point's center is determined with a very simple approach, the center of mass of the point is computed. After finding the center, a blob is drawn representing the located point, as shown in Figure 3.

[1] The histogram peak represent the background of the image.

3 Isolation of the Lines of Text(Segmentation)

At this point, the text lines are isolated, so the text can be translated. The lines that do not have any blob represented are searched and marked, securing the segmentation in text lines. These will be discarded for a more efficient computing of the translations. Figure 4 represents the image after segmentation.

Fig. 4. Partial image after segmentation

4 Processing of the Points

With the points detected and the image segmented, the next task is to get the Braille characters. In this approach there is no need to segment the image vertically [3]. For each line of text, the first center is found. Having it's coordinates, it's position inside the cell is searched. This is done examining the distance between the current point and the next point center found. This gives the horizontal position, as the vertical one is found dividing the text line into three regions. The coordinates of the center and it's position are stored in a linked list. The rest of the line is computed, ending up with a linked list of centers and positions. The linked list is then parsed and, according to the information it holds, a mask is adjusted to each Braille character, ending up with a line of characters coded into 1's and 0's, representing respectively, position is a point and position is not a point.

This procedure is repeated for every line of text, ending up with the entire page coded.

5 Creation of the Parsers

The parsers are created to translate the text from the coded file. Three parsers were defined, one for text, one for mathematics and one for chemistry. These parsers were created for the Portuguese Braille code. There are many Braille Codes, and even inside one Braille Code there are characters that represent one character in plain text and another in e.g. mathematics. That's why three different parsers have been created.

The parsers were created using Javacc that allowed a more efficient integration with the developed application.

The parsers make use of the Unicode char set, and not the ASCII one. This solution was adopted for the use of the mathematical symbols, since most of these are not available in the ASCII set.

The input of these parsers is a string coded into 1's and 0's and the output is an HTML coded page. The use of HTML tables were very useful to enable printing of mathematical or chemical expressions.

6 Construction of the Keyboard

6.1 Motivations

The will to construct the electronic Braille keyboard came mainly from two reasons:

1. The high price of the mechanical Braille emboss machines;
2. The noisy environment created by students using mechanical machines;

6.2 Hardware Overview

For a cost effective solution the existing school computers were thought to be used, if possible the most downgraded, that are also the most expendable ones. Having this into account the serial port was chosen to be the communication interface between the computer and the keyboard. This interface was widely used in the past and nowadays it is usually used in instrumentation and in several electronic devices, so cheap hardware and free software solutions could be created and used.

After some research [10,5] the PIC 16F628 [6] from Microchip® was chosen. This is a mid-range micro-controller, it has better specs than the widely used PIC 16F84 and the advantage that it is cheaper. The 16F PIC series is FLASH memory based and so can be erased and reprogrammed electrically. This feature allows a faster software development comparing to the UV-erasable micro-controllers. It is a RISC micro-controller with Harvard architecture, 14-bit wide instructions and 8-bit wide data word. It has 2048x14 FLASH program memory, a 224x8 RAM data memory and a 128x8 non-volatile EEPROM data memory. Contains an 8 bit ALU and working register. A total of 35 instructions are available, all are executed in one clock cycle except for program branches that take 2 cycles. The 16F628 architecture also contains some special features that can simplify the circuit system by eliminating the need of external components, reducing the cost and power consumption, and improving reliability. In the system two of these interesting specs were used: the 4MHz internal oscillator, and the USART for serial communication.

To convert the output voltage levels of the micro-controller's USART to TIA/EIA-232 (serial port protocol) a MAX232 converter chip was used.

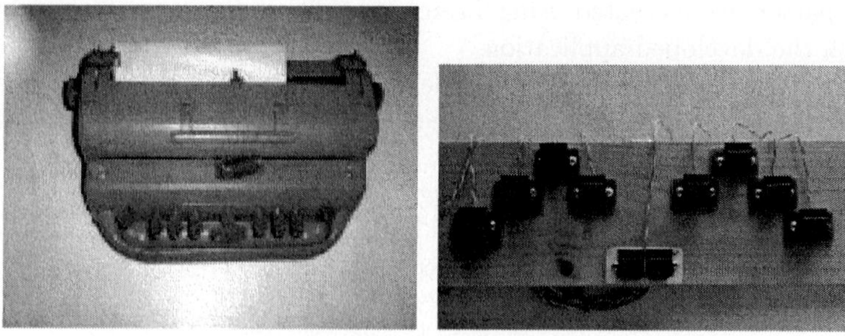

(a) Perkins Brailler. (b) Keyboard layout.

Fig. 5. Keyboard layouts

Microchip® provides PIC programmers that transfer the developed code into the chip's memory, but these don't accomplish the low cost objective of the project and so a cheaper solution was used, the JDM PIC Programmer 2 (JDM). Jens Dyekjær Madsen [7] created this simple, efficient and low cost programmer. It is well documented on the World Wide Web by himself and many other hardware developers, including a small circuit alteration that allows compatibility with the PIC 16F6XX series. The communication interface of JDM programmer is also the serial port.

The layout of a Perkins Brailler mechanical embosser, like the one in Figure ??, was followed maintaining the sequence but dislocating vertically the keys for a more ergonomic positioning, as can be seen in Figure 6.2. This way the Braille students would rapidly adapt to the keyboard.

6.3 Hardware Programming Software

For software development Microchip® provides an integrated development environment called MPLAB® IDE Software. It is MS Windows® based but there are Linux alternatives.

The programmer software used to load the code into the micro-controller was IC-Prog [8], a free MS Windows® based software developed by Bonny Gijzen. There are software alternatives for Linux.

6.4 Keyboard Assembly

The first stage was assembling the JDM programmer, as seen in Figure ??. This was a very important step for the production of the keyboard, so after it was built it was tested with IC-Prog to assert it was a reliable programmer.

The keyboard circuit was mounted on a test board to allow the PIC's programming and testing.

The code was written in assembly language, using MPLAB® for writing and debugging the program. The main routine of the program needed to simultaneously debounce all keys, since a Braille character can be produced by simultaneously pressing until 6 keys. If a pooling approach had been chosen a

Fig. 6. JDM programmer circuit

very long, complicated and possibly ineffective program would be obtained. Instead, a routine by Scott Dattalo [9] that makes use of the notion of vertical counters was adapted. Using two 8-bit registers, grouping them in 2-bit counters in such way that e.g. the two LSBits form a counter, associating a key entry to each counter in such way that if the state of the key is maintained after 4 iterations the state is filtered. If it doesn't maintain the logical value, the 2 bit counter resets. One register accumulates key presses until no key is being pressed, in that moment the composed value of all valid key presses is sent via the PIC's USART.

After loading the final program to the PIC's memory all the components were mounted in a PCB circuit board, as can be seen in Figure 7, and the keyboard assembly was completed.

To finalize, the application developed for O.B.R. was linked to read from the serial port. This application needs to have an active parser mode, so a keyboard

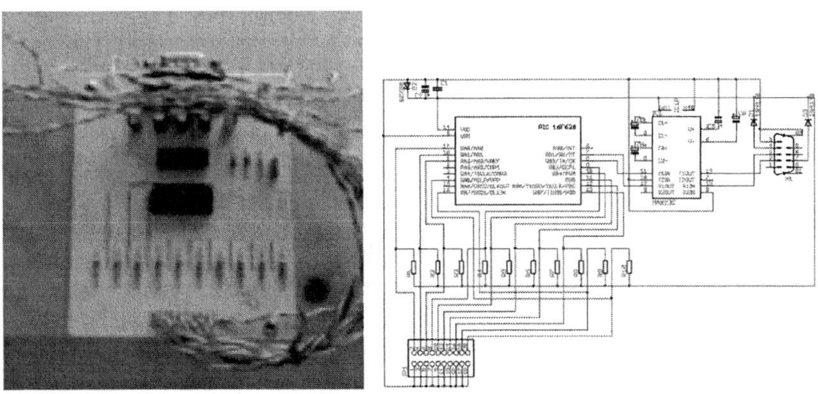

(a) Final keyboard circuit. (b) Final keyboard schematic.

Fig. 7. Final keyboard circuit and schematic

user must send a code composed by the space, the delete, and one letter keys simultaneously pressed. The letter codes are "m" for mathematics (matemática), "q" for Chemistry (química) and "t" for text (texto).

7 Text to Speech System

A Text to Speech System was linked to the developed O.B.R. software. This has been done to enable the user of the software to hear what is being typed in real time. This system had already been developed in a former work [11]. Originally developed for the Linux platform, the program code was changed to compile also under Microsoft Windows®. Some changes have been made so the program could function more accordingly to our objectives.

The software can only synthesize text. For a more complete system, the rules of the text to speech program should be altered. This may be difficult to implement since this system was originally developed for plain text.

8 User Interface

The user interface has been programmed in Java. It permits the user to open the scanned image, and select an area of the image to be converted, also selecting the text, mathematics or chemistry

parser. It permits to get the input from the developed keyboard, allowing the user to type and hear the text. The final user interface program can be seen in Figure 8.

9 Conclusion

Some good results have been obtained so far. The developed software can translate quite accurately the texts in the Braille sheets. However some errors may occur because of bad input image. Some points don't have the white zone or the black one, which will produce bad results in the detection. The input image is very important for the success of the translation, so a good color high resolution image should be obtained. It is also expected that some scanners performed better than others because of different illumination conditions.

A text to speech software system was adapted to the program. This solution is limited since it was developed for plain text, however is very useful, because the user can't feel the output like in a mechanical embosser.

An efficient low cost keyboard was successfully developed. A mechanical embosser would cost about 1000 Euros in Portugal, while the construction of the keyboard and the PIC programmer would only cost about 50 Euros.

At this moment, the software translates an entire page of plain text under 15 seconds in an AMD Athlon 1.41 GHz. It can translate successfully plain text, mathematics and chemistry. However further work should improve the parser's rules, possibly with the aid of Braille teachers and students.

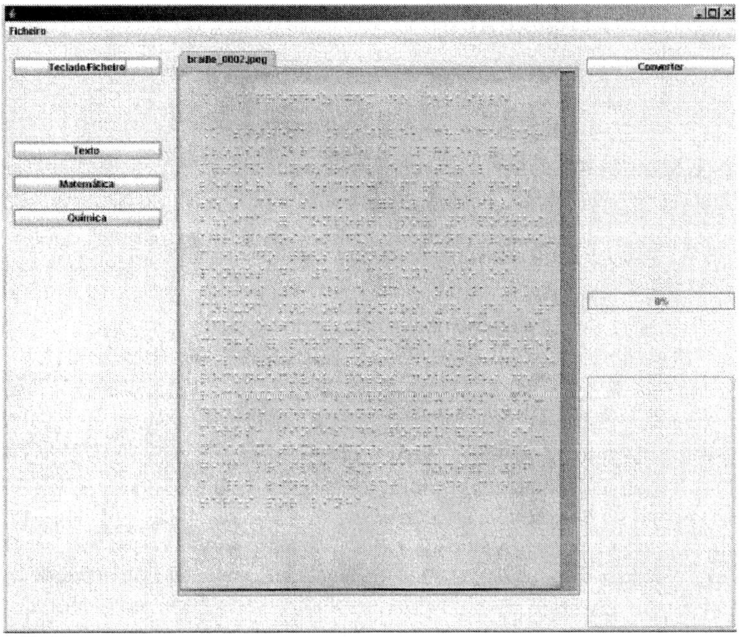

Fig. 8. User interface

References

1. Hermida, X. F., Rodriguez, A. C., Rodriguez, F.M.: Braille O.C.R. for Blind People. Proceedings of ICSPAT-96 (1996).
2. Ritchings, R.T., Antonacopoulos, A., Drakopoulos, D.:Analysis of Scanned Braille Documents. Document Analysis Systems (1995) 413-421.
3. Wong, L., Abdulla, W., Hussman, Stephan: A Software Algorithm Prototype for Optical Recognition of Embossed Braille. 17th International Conference on Pattern Recognition (2004)
4. Russ, J. C.: The Image Processing Handbook. 3rd edition (1998).
5. Microchip: www.microchip.com.
6. 16F628 PIC Datasheet: ww1.microchip.com/download/en/DeviceDoc/40300c.pdf.
7. Madsen, J. D.: www.jdm.homepage.dk.
8. IC-PROG: www.ic-prog.com.
9. Dattalo, S.: www.dattalo.com.
10. PicList: www.piclist.com.
11. Tomaz, F.: w3.ualg.pt/~ftomaz.

Automatic Extraction of DNA Profiles in Polyacrilamide Gel Electrophoresis Images

Francisco Silva-Mata[1], Isneri Talavera-Bustamante[1], Ricardo González-Gazapo[1], Noslén Hernández-González[1], Juan R. Palau-Infante[1], and Marta Santiesteban-Vidal[2]

[1] Advanced Technologies Applications Center, MINBAS, Cuba
{fjsilva, italavera, rgazapo, nhernandez, jpalau}@cenatav.co.cu
http://www.cenatav.co.cu/
[2] Central Criminologist Laboratory, Cuba
gordillo@mn.mn.co.cu

Abstract. In this paper is presented a method for the automatic DNA spots classification and extraction of profiles associated in DNA polyacrilamide gel electrophoresis based on image processing. A software which implements this method was developed, composed by four modules: Digital image acquisition, image preprocessing, feature extraction and classification, and DNA profile extraction. The use of different types of algorithms as: C4.5 Decision Trees, Support Vector Machines and Leader Algorithm are needed to resolve all the tasks. The experimental results show that this method has a very nice computational behavior and effectiveness, and provide a very useful tool to decrease the time and increase the quality of the specialist responses.

1 Introduction

DNA profiling has attracted a good deal of public attention in the last years. The practical application of DNA technology to the identification of biological material has had a significant impact on forensic biology, because it enables much stronger conclusions of identity or non-identity to be made [1].

For human identity, scientists use Short Tandem Repeat ("STR") loci [2]. Each STR locus exhibits variation in DNA molecule length. One person will inherit two specific lengths from their parents, which is likely to be different from the pair of lengths of another person. STR locus of an individual has two "alleles," each corresponding to a true DNA. To form a DNA profile, scientists generate and analyze STR data. Such data is derived from a blood (or other) sample taken from a person or obtained from the crime scene. It is common to build a DNA profile using 10 STR loci (20 alleles). Therefore, when (for example) ten loci are used, it is extremely improbable that the 20 numbers (i.e., 10 length pairs or alleles) from one individual will identically match the 20 numbers of an unrelated individual. This uniqueness serves as a "fingerprint" of genetic identity [3].

During laboratory data generation, the forensic scientist conducts experiments to transform these unknown DNA lengths into observable data [4]. This process has 3 main steps: 1) Perform polymerase chain reaction ("PCR") amplification on the DNA sample to transform the STR lengths into PCR products.2) Size separates the

M. Lazo and A. Sanfeliu (Eds.): CIARP 2005, LNCS 3773, pp. 242 – 251, 2005.

amplified PCR products on a DNA sequencer to form electrophoretic bands (two bands per loci one band for each allele). The locations of these bands are related to their size.3) Detect the bands to acquire data. Each band in loci has a number, related to its side; therefore we obtain a pair of numbers per loci, to build at last de DNA profiles per samples.

There are two chemical techniques in order to take to end the two last steps [5], one using the Capillary Electrophoresis Analysis, and the other applying Electrophoresis on Polyacrilamide Gels with tintion reagents. The first is a very expensive technique, and no many laboratories have the possibilities to apply it. An automatic module for the data processing based on signal processing accompanies the system. The second is a more common analysis, as an output, is obtained DNA sequencers in the form of electrophoretic bands on a Polyacrilamide Gel plate, the bands are visualized with a tintion reagent, one of them is the silver tintion reagent, and in this case we detect the DNA bands as black spots.

There is a standardized method to manually detect the spots of DNA and make the numbers designations of the pair alleles per loci, but it is a very tedious, inefficient and inhuman form to do the task if we have under consideration that only one plate can contain more than 32 samples, plus 12 loci, plus 2 alleles per loci, 768 measurements are necessary to obtain the correspondent profiles.

In this article an automatic solution is presented for DNA profile extraction in Polyacrilamide Gel Electrophoresis Images, integrating image processing, pattern recognition techniques and the associated image acquisition module.

2 Image Acquisition Module

To acquire the images a digital camera Sony DSC-F717 was place on a controllable illumination system. The Polyacrilamide gel plate is placed in a mobile gate between a diffuser plate and the digital camera and the light sources are in the bottom, below the diffuser plate. Figure 1, shows a view of different parts of the module.

The light sources are conformed by Leuci Lamps 8 watt cool-white 4500 ^{0}K.To obtains a uniform illumination in the acquire images, the fulfillment of the equation (1), is necessary [6]:

$$E=(I_i \cos\lambda_i)*r_i^{-1} \tag{1}$$

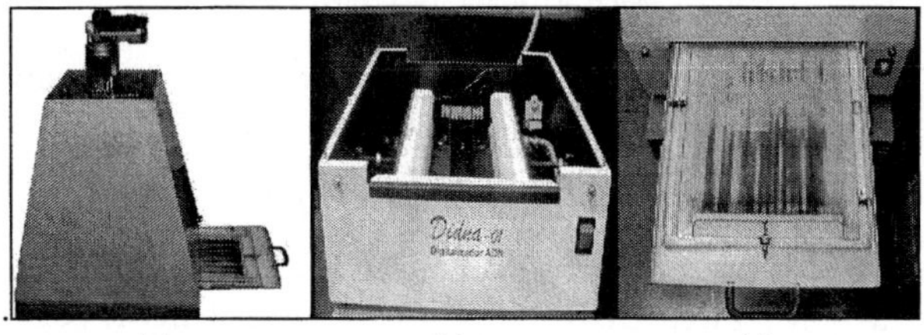

(a) (b) (c)

Fig. 1. Acquisition module: (a) General view, (b) Light Sources, (c) Mobile gate

Where E is the light emission of set light sources, I_i the Light intensity, λ_i the angle between the direction of the luminous flux and the normal to the surface and r_i the distance to the surface.

This condition guarantees that the dimension of the luminous bundle emitted for the source of illumination is little in relation to the distance that separates the diffusion plate from the lamps, and as a result a uniform illumination is obtained.

3 Image Preprocessing

Data artefact can be introduced at every step of the data generation process. There are dozens potential artefacts, some include: Low-level intensity spots, contaminating DNA material, bands reflexion, shifts in the baseline, colour background of the gels and other size distortions. Some of them can be corrected at a preprocessing step in order to enhance the image quality [7].

First, the source image obtained from the acquisition system is RGB, but colour, does not give us any useful information; therefore a conversion to halftones is convenient.

One of the main tasks of preprocessing is the removal or reduction of noise. In order to find the best suited one for this kind of images some linear and non-linear filtering methods, and also filtering methods in the wavelet domain [8] were tested. The best results were obtained using a Homomorphic Filtering [9, 10]. In our case, this filter acts to reduce the low frequency multiplicative noise that it is produced as a result of a non homogeneity illumination or a non homogeneity developed chemical process.

The application of the Fourier transform to the logarithm of the image, gives:

$$F\,\{ln\ I(x, y)\} = F\,\{ln\ L(x, y)\} + F\,\{lnR(x, y)\}. \tag{2}$$

Where L is the luminance and R the reflectance. This can be written as the sum of two functions in the frequency domain as:

$$Z(u, v) = F_L(u, v) + F_R(u, v). \tag{3}$$

F_R is composed of mostly high frequency components and F_L of mostly low frequency components. Z can be convolved with a filter of transfer function $H(u, v)$ that reduces the low frequencies and amplifies high frequencies, thus improving contrast and compressing dynamic range,

$$H(u,v).Z(u,v) = H(u,v).F_L(u,v) + H(u,v).F_R(u,v). \tag{4}$$

The processed image can be found by inverse Fourier transforming the previous equation and taking the exponential,

$$I'(x, y) = e^{F^{-1}}\{[H(u, v).Z(u, v)]\}. \tag{5}$$

Next step contemplates the process of spots segmentation. In order to carry out this task, we apply a Sobel Edge Detector; it uses a special mask [11] to approximate digitally the first derivatives Gx and Gy. In other words, the gradient at the center point in a neighbourhood is computed as follows:

$$g = [Gx^2 + Gy^2]^{1/2} \tag{6}$$

$$g = \{[(z_7 + 2z_8 + z_9) - (z_1 + 2z_2 + z_3)]^2 + [(z_3 + 2z_6 + z_9) - (z_1 + 2z_4 + z_7))]^2\}^{1/2}$$

Where $z_1.....z_9$ conform the image neighbourhood.. Then we say that a pixel at location(x, y) is an edge pixel if $g \geq T$ at that location, where T is a specified threshold.

The segmentation process finished applying automatically a Global Threshold following the iterative procedure proposed by González and Woods [11].

4 Feature Selection

Once finished the spot's segmentation, the next step is to represent and describe them in a form suitable for further computer processing. A representation using 14 boundary and region descriptors was chosen: Area, Complementary area, Perimeter, Rectified perimeter, Compacness, Maximum width, Maximum Height, 2-D moment invariants (φ_1, φ_2, φ_3, φ_4, φ_5), θ (angle of the principal axis), and Height-Width ratio. An automatic tool was developed to assign the descriptor at each spot in the image gel after segmentation.

To know which of these descriptors or features are the most significant to describe DNA spots, a data set formed of 4 images gels with more than 1890 spots were marked by an expert selecting only DNA spots according his experience, at last 965 DNA from the total of spots was marked . A C4.5 Decision tree [12] was used to do the task. Decision trees classify instances by sorting them down the tree from the root to some leaf node, which provides the classification of the instance. Each node in the tree specifies the test of some feature of the instance, and each branch descending from that node corresponds to one of the possible values for this feature. An instance is classified by starting at the root node of the tree, testing the feature species by this node, then moving down the tree branch corresponding to the value of the feature in the given example. This process is then repeated for the sub tree rooted at the new node. The features that are situated in the roots nodes of the tree will be the most significant.

After the training, a decision tree with an effectiveness of 94.7% in the classification among DNA spots and No-DNA spots are obtained. The most significant features probe to be: φ_3, φ_1, φ_4, and area.

5 Classification

In our method all spots present on the polyacrilamide gel images, are described automatically, using the most significant features obtained in section 4. For the profile extraction only DNA spots are useful, therefore a two–class classification problem among DNA spots and No-DNA spots is necessary to solve. In order to realize the classification process with a high velocity, effectiveness, and robustness, a Support Vector Machine$_s$ classifier was selected.

Supports Vector Machines (SVM$_s$) are kernel based learning algorithm introduced by Vapnik [13, 14]. SVM$_s$ classifiers are introduced to solve two-class pattern recognition problems using the Structural Risk Minimization principle. Burges; Cristianini

& Shawe-Taylor [15, 16] worked given a training set in a vector space, SVM_s find the best decision hyperplane that separates two classes. The quality of a decision hyperplane is determined by the distance (i.e. hard or soft margin) between two hyperplanes defined by the support vectors. The best decision hyperplane is the one that maximizes this margin. The mapping to higher dimensional spaces is done using appropriate kernels such as Gaussian kernel and polynomial kernel [17]. SVM_s lend themselves well to accurate non-linear modelling and are very powerful and rapid learners. Good results in the application of SVM_s for different classification task of DNA were reported by Xu and Buckles [18].

In our case a non-linear SVM_s using a radial kernel offered the best results.

6 DNA's Profile Extraction

After the Classification process, an image with only DNA spots is obtained. For the profile extraction, first it is necessary to determine the regions in the image that contains the STR loci patterns, remember that usually we need twelve STR loci patterns in order to obtain the profiles. These patterns contain all the posibles alleles presents in a population and are possible to visualize them in the image as a sequence of DNA black spots for each STR loci. It is used to put the set of these 12 STR loci patterns more than one time in the plate intercalating the set each four samples investigated.

For the determination of these regions the first step is the detection of the candidate's regions according to the intensities histogram along the x axis. The second step is the determination inside of these regions of the periodic sequence of the image according the characteristics of the patterns. The third step is the validation of the results in correspondence with the data position given by the specialist and we finish assigning the coordinates at start and ending of the regions founded and it is marked in the image.

Using as reference the coordinates contributed by the patterns, the next step is the division of the image in lanes, each lane contains one sample or the set of STR loci patterns according to the distribution above mentioned. Normally we have more or less 32 lanes per image.

Inside the pattern's lanes we have different STR loci each of them have a specific sequence of spots always with the same quantity of spots, each of them have assigned a number, it is necessary the determination of these sub regions in the image each of them contains one STR loci with their spots. To solve this task a Sequential Leader algorithm was used [19]. It performs in two basic steps:

1. Chose a cluster threshold value.
2. For every new sample vector (DNA spot centroid that appears in patterns lanes):
   - Compute the distance between the new vector and every cluster's codebook vector.
   - If the distance between the closest codebook vector and the new vector is smaller than the chosen threshold, then recomputed the closest codebook vector with the new vector.
   - Otherwise, make a new cluster with the new vector as its codebook vector.

Sometimes as a consequence of a malfunction of the classification algorithm, or by difficulties in the electrophoresis chemical process, one or more spots inside a sequence of a STR loci pattern were missing and in other cases two of them join up. A restoration of the sequence of spots in the pattern is essential in order to obtain, in next steps, the DNA profiles of samples .To restore the missing spots a new algorithm was developed, which can be described as follows:

```
1) Comment: In the initial conditions the clustered spots in the STR LOCI PATTERN
            sequence are DNA spots and all spots for this analysis are in the same
            lane, therefore for all clustered spots the value of Cluster.Spot.DNA is
            true
2) Comment: Sort the clustered DNA spots in ascendant order by 'y' coordinate value
            of its centroide.
3) Cluster. Sort ();
4) Comment: We denote the clustered spots as spotc, and the others as spot
5) for (all clustered spots) do
6)   Comment: There is a hole (DNA spot not present)
7)   if (distance (spotc[i].centroid. y), spotc[i+1].centroid. y) ≥ threshold) do begin
8)      Comment (Case 1): At this point when a spot is not clustered it means that is
                          not DNA, therefore we want to know which spots not
                          clustered are between spotc[i] and spotc[i+1]
9)      for (all pair (spot[j], spot[k]), not clustered)
10)        Comment: Case 1: There is a spot divided in two neighbouring spots
                    (spot[j] & spot[k]) situated between (spotc[i] & spotc[i+1])
11)        if (((spot[j].centroid. y > spotc[i].centroid. y) &
              (spot[k].centroid. y > spotc[i ].centroid. y) &
             ((spot[j].centroid. y < spotc[i+1].centroid. y) &
              (spot[k].centroid. y < spotc[i+1].centroid. y)))
12)           if ((Abs (spot[j].centroid. y- spot[k].centroid. y) <=2) & ((spot[j].area +
                 spot[k].area)>=area threshold)) do begin
13)              Comment: join the spot[j] & spot[k] into one and eliminate them
14)              Cluster. Add (newElement (spot[j], spot[k]));
15)              Cluster. Sort ();
16)              Delete (spot[j], spot[k]);
17)              end;
18)     for (all not clustered spot)
19)        Comment (Case 2): There are some spots (spot[j]) between spotc[i] &
                             spotc[ i+1] that are not divided (NOT Case1), but they
                             are near enough of spotc[i], in this case the solution is
                             adding to the cluster the most similar of all of them
20)        if ((spot[j].centroid. y > spotc[i].centroid. y) &
              (spot[j].centroid. y < spotc[i+1].centroid. y) &
              (distance (spot[j].centroid. y), spotc[i].centroid. y) < threshold)) do
              begin
21)           Distance[j] =EuclideanDistance between spot[j].featurevector and
                           spotc[i].featurevector]
22)           if ( Distance[j] < distance threshold) do begin
23)              K=index of the minimal Distance[j]
24)              Cluster. add (newElement(spot[k]))
25)              Cluster. Sort ();
26)              end;
```

```
        end;
    end;
Comment: if the restoration of STR Loci Pattern was not completely possible
if (Cluster. count < total )
    ErrorMessage ("STR LOCI NOT COMPLETED")
```

The joined spots are separated by means of the detection of Freeman's chain typical segments of the contour [20], for example: 033332...03332...2110...21110..., the calculation of the horizontal dividing halfback line among them, permits an effective separation.

The final step is to assign the corresponded number to the spots that represents the two alleles per STR loci to conform the DNA profile of each sample (24 pair of numbers are obtained per sample). To solve this task, it is necessary first the layout of the horizontal lines that join the centroide of each spot in the sequence of the STR loci patterns with their matches distributed in the plate, remember that each of these spots in a sequence of a STR loci has a unique number, that is specific for each STR loci pattern, therefore all the spots in the same line have the same number assigned. Applying the formula of distance of one point to a straight line, it is possible to evaluate the distance from the centroid of each spots, (alleles), to the lines of the patterns spots nearest to them. The number assigned to the alleles are the same assigned to the lines of the patterns whose distances are the minors to them.

7 Data Set

A set of 20 DNA polyacrilamide gel electrophoresis plates, containing 200 real samples investigated by the National Forensic Laboratory of Cuba were used for the experimentation. The Plates have been directly recorded with the acquisition module, and the images obtained were automatically store in the computer for the process.

8 System Implementation

For the preprocessing step, we used software in C# based on the algorithms and procedures proposed by Rafael Gonzalez [11].. The feature selection using the Decision Tree C4.5 was implemented by the pack of classes that offers Software WEKA [12] specifically Weka classifier tree J48. As this software is programmed in Java # a DLL that permits the conversion to Visual Studio C# was developed in order to guarantee the compatibility with our method. Classifications with SVMs were done using SVM. NET Version 0.8b[21].

9 Results and Discussion

The SVM_s were training to classify the spots obtained after the electrophoresis process on the gel in DNA and No-DNA spots. For training the same data set used for the feature selection was employed, for testing we used the data set explained in point 7.

The classification accuracy was calculated by taken the number of correctly classified spots by the SVMs, and divided by the total number of samples into the test data set. Table 1 shows the results obtained in the classification.

Table 1. DNA spot classification

Type of spots	#of spots	Confusion matrix		Classification
		ADN	NoADN	
ADN	2019	**1997**	22	
NoADN	4201	101	**4100**	
Total	**6220**			**98.02%**

The good results obtained in the classification task demonstrated the advantages attributed in the literature to the SVM_s as a two class classifier. The training process was very fast, only 30 sec. fundamentally because their structure is automatically determined on the basis of the training data and relatively few parameters are needed; in the other hand training involves optimisation of a function that relates to a quadratic convex programming problem, hence generating a completely reproducible solution (a major drawback of Neural Networks); overfitting can be avoided without using a validation set.

The set of the original plates, were processed by the expert using the standardized manual procedure and the results of the profile extraction were compare with the results obtained applying the automatic method taking into account the success rate and the time of response. Table 2 shows the results obtained in this comparison.

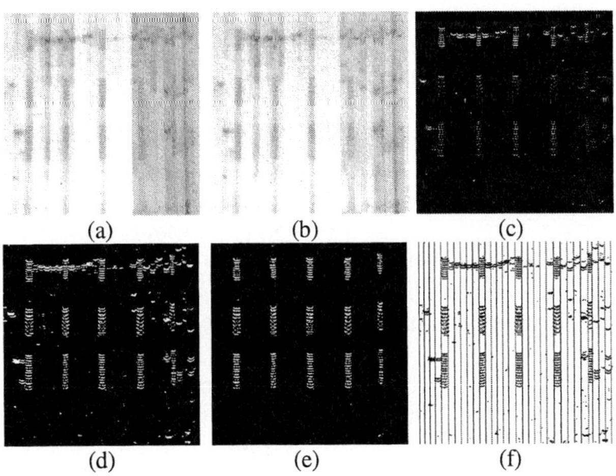

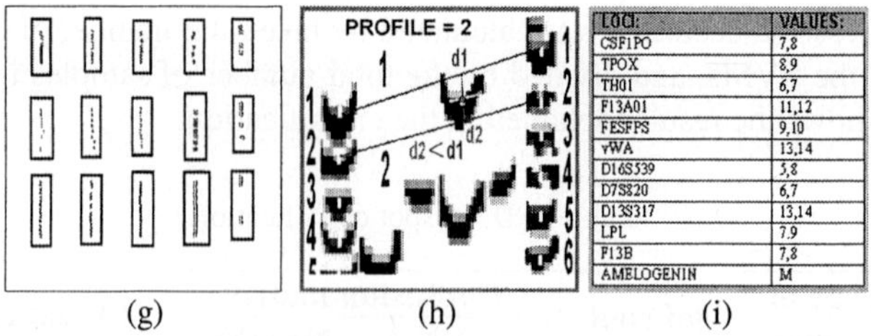

Fig. 2. (a) Original image, (b) Homomorphic filtering, (c) Sobel edge detector, (d) Global threshold, (e) STR loci patterns regions, (f) Division in lanes, (g) Determination sub regions, (h) Assigning number to alleles, (i) DNA profile

Table 2. Automatic Profile extraction results vs. manual method results

# of samples	Profiles detected by expert	System success	Success rate	Time of response	
				Expert	Automat.
200	204	199	97.54%	20 days	15 min

Added to the previous tables only 5 profiles was not possible to extract, 4 caused by the presence of mix samples (DNA of two persons are present in the same sample) with 4 different alleles present in each STR Loci causing that it is not possible to determine, which of the 6 pairs of alleles is the correct by the automatic method. The other one was caused by misclassification errors in the lanes corresponded to the samples, given that the misclassification errors in the lane of the patterns are restored by the algorithm developed for this purpose.

Another significant result is the decrease in the time's response of the task that influences not only in the increase of the available time of the expert but also in the decrease of the cost of the analysis. Fig.2 (a-i) shows a set of images representatives of all the process.

10 Conclusions

The development and implementation of an effective method for the automatic DNA spots classification and extraction of profiles associated in DNA polyacrilamide gel electrophoresis, combining image process and pattern recognition techniques are obtained.

Different types of algorithms as: C4.5 Decision Trees, Support Vector Machines, Leader Algorithm and the contribution with a new one for restoration purposes are used to resolve all the tasks.

The experimental results show that this method has a very nice computational behavior and effectiveness, and provide a very useful tool to decrease the time and increase the quality of the specialist responses.

References

1. Gill, P. Urquhart, A., Millican E., Oldroyd, N., Watson, S. Sparkers.: Criminal intelligence Databases and interpretation of STR_s Advances in Forensic Haemogenetics, 1996; 6:235-42.
2. Lander, E.S.: DNA fingerprinting: The NRC report, Science, vol.260, pp 1221. (1993).
3. Lewontin, R.C., Hartl, D.L.: Population genetics in forensic DNA typing, Science, vol. 254, pp. 1745-1750. (1991).
4. Weber, J., May, P.: Abundant class of human DNA polymorphisms which can be typed using the polymerase chain reaction. Am.. J. Hum. Genet. 1989:44; 388-96.
5. Estrada, C.: Techniques for DNA analysis in forensic genetics. http//: www.ugr.es/~ eianez biotecnología/forensetec.htm#1.(2001).
6. Shortley, G.. Dudly, W. Elements of Physics. B.E.E, Third Ed. (1966), Chap.24 Illumination and Photometry, pp 506.
7. Kacmazmarek, B.Walczak, B., Jong, S. Vandeginste, B.G.M.: Preprocessing of 2-D gel electrophoresis images, Analytical Chemistry, 75 (2003) 3631-3636.
8. Kacmazmarek, B.Walczak B., Jong, S. Vandeginste, B.G.M: Enhancement of images from 2-D gel electrophoresis. Proceedings 9th International Conference, CAC 2004.pp.171.
9. Stockham, T.G.: Image processing in the context of a Visual Model. Proc, IEEE, vol.60, No. 7, pp 828-842, (1972).
10. Short, J., Kittler, J., Messer, K. A comparison of photometric normalization algorithms for face verification. Proceedings of the Sixth IEEE International Conference on Automatic Face and Gesture Recognition.(FGR'04) 2004.
11. Gonzalez, R., Woods, R. "Digital Image Processing using MATLAB" Prentice Hall, Second Ed. (2004), pp 385-387.
12. Quinlan, R. J. C4.5: Programs for Machine Learnig (Morgan Kaufmann Series in Machine Learning). Paperback- January 15, (1993).
13. Vapnik, V., Chervonenkis, A.: Theory of Pattern Recognition. Nauka, Moscow, (1974).
14. Vapnik, V.: The nature of Statistical Learning Theory.. New York: Springer Verlag (1995).
15. Burges, C. J. C.: A Tutorial on Support Vector Machines for Pattern Recognition. Data Mining and Knowledge Discovery 2(2): 121-167 (1998).
16. Cristianini., Shawe-Taylor, J.: An introduction to Support Vector Machine. Cambridge University Press. (2000).
17. Scholkopf, C., Burges, J., Smola, A.: Advances in Kernel methods: Support Vector Learning. MIT. Press. (1999).
18. Xu, Z., Buckles, B.: DNA Sequence Classification by using Support Vector Machine. EECS, Tulane University..
19. Hartigan J.: "Clustering Algorithm". John Wiley and Sons. New York, (1975).
20. Alvarez, A. Ruiz J., Sanchiz, M.: Typical Segment Descriptors: A new method for shape description and classification. LNCS 2905, pp. 512–520, (2003).
21. Ching-Huei, Tsou: A.NET Implementation of Support Vector Machine.IESL MIT Version 0.8b October 25, (2004).

The Use of Bayesian Framework for Kernel Selection in Vector Machines Classifiers

Dmitry Kropotov[1], Nikita Ptashko[2], and Dmitry Vetrov[1]

[1] Dorodnicyn Computing Centre, Vavilova str. 40, Moscow, 119991, Russia
{DKropotov, VetrovD}@yandex.ru
http://dkropotov.narod.ru, vetrovd.narod.ru
[2] Moscow State University, Vorob'evy gory, Moscow, 119234, Russia
Ptashko@inbox.ru

Abstract. In the paper we propose a method based on Bayesian framework for selecting the best kernel function for supervised learning problem. The parameters of the kernel function are considered as model parameters and maximum evidence principle is applied for model selection. We describe a general scheme of Bayesian regularization, present model of kernel classifiers as well as our approximations for evidence estimation, and then give some results of experimental evaluation.

1 Introduction

Support Vector Machines [1] are one of the most popular algorithms for solving regression and classification problems. They have proved their good performance on numerous tasks. The main reasons for the success of SVM are the following. Vapnik's idea of optimal hyperplane construction led to maximal margin principle [2] which provides better generalization ability. Another useful property of SVM is the so-called "kernel trick" which allows linear methods of machine learning to build non-linear surfaces. However, there are some aspects which remain unclear when one starts using SVM. The concrete form of the kernel function should be defined by the user so as regularization coefficient C. As there are several parametric families of kernel functions it is not clear what family and what function from that family will lead to the best performance of SVM. Coefficient C limits the values of weights for the support vectors, thereby giving the algorithm different degrees of flexibility. Usually the parameters of kernel function and coefficient C are defined using a cross-validation procedure. This may be too expensive from computational point of view. Moreover the cross-validation estimates of performance, although unbiased [2], have large variance due to the limited size of the sample. Recently Tipping proposed an SVM-like algorithm, which used Bayesian regularization for best weights selection [4]. It was called Relevance Vector Machines (RVM). In this algorithm the weights of the so-called relevance vectors are interpreted as random values with gaussian prior distribution centered in zero. In this approach there is no need to set a regularization coefficient C to restrict the values of the weights. Large weights are penalized

M. Lazo and A. Sanfeliu (Eds.): CIARP 2005, LNCS 3773, pp. 252–261, 2005.

automatically during training. In the paper we propose an extension of this idea - Generalized Relevance Vector Machines (GRVM) which allows furthermore selecting the best kernel function from the given family for the particular problem. In the next section we give general scheme of Bayesian regularization of machine learning algorithms. Section 3 briefly describes the RVM concept and in section 4 we present the GRVM algorithm for classification tasks. Some numerical aspects of its realization are given in section 5. The last section contains experimental evaluation and discussion.

2 Bayesian Learning and Maximal Evidence Principle

The paradigm of Bayesian learning allows for choosing the most appropriate model for the given training data. The term model in this context means a set of classifiers with fixed number of parameters and their prior distributions. Suppose that we have a set of models (either finite, countable or continuum) $W(\boldsymbol{\alpha})$, $\boldsymbol{\alpha} \in A$. Here $\boldsymbol{\alpha}$ defines the family of classifiers, the structure of their parameters $\boldsymbol{w}$, and their prior distributions $P(\boldsymbol{w}|\boldsymbol{\alpha})$. Denote by $P(D_{train}|\boldsymbol{w})$ the likelihood of the training data description with given values of $\boldsymbol{w}$. As the hyperparameters $\boldsymbol{\alpha}$ do not have direct influence on the training data we may write

$$P(D_{train}|\boldsymbol{w}, \boldsymbol{\alpha}) = P(D_{train}|\boldsymbol{w}) \tag{1}$$

This means that $\boldsymbol{\alpha}$ affects the likelihood of the training data description only by means of its influence on $\boldsymbol{w}$. A classical way of classifier training is based on maximal likelihood principle, that is finding

$$\boldsymbol{w}_{ML} = \arg\max_{\boldsymbol{w}} P(D_{train}|\boldsymbol{w})$$

The probability of new data D_{test} given the training set is then just

$$P(D_{test}|D_{train}) = P(D_{test}|\boldsymbol{w}_{ML})$$

An alternative way of classifier training is to use Bayesian estimation of the posterior probability of $\boldsymbol{w}$

$$P(\boldsymbol{w}|D_{train}) = \frac{P(D_{train}|\boldsymbol{w})P(\boldsymbol{w})}{\int_W P(D_{train}|\boldsymbol{w})P(\boldsymbol{w})d\boldsymbol{w}}$$

Then

$$P(D_{test}|D_{train}) = \int_W P(D_{test}|\boldsymbol{w})P(\boldsymbol{w}|D_{train})d\boldsymbol{w}$$

Such inference can be done within one model. Now suppose we have several (or even continuum) models $W(\boldsymbol{\alpha})$ of different nature, complexity etc. The question is what model is preferable. To answer it we should estimate the so-called evidence

$$P(D_{train}|\boldsymbol{\alpha}) = \int_{W(\boldsymbol{\alpha})} P(D_{train}|\boldsymbol{w})P(\boldsymbol{w}|\boldsymbol{\alpha})d\boldsymbol{w} \tag{2}$$

The known principle of maximal evidence [3] states that we should choose that model which has the greatest value of evidence or, in other words, where the rate of "good" classifiers is the highest. This principle is a compromise between the complexity of a model and classifier's performance on the training sample. Taking into account (1) the likelihood of the test data is calculated in the following way:

$$P(D_{test}|D_{train}) = \int_A \int_{W(\boldsymbol{\alpha})} P(D_{test}|\boldsymbol{w}, \boldsymbol{\alpha}) P(\boldsymbol{w}, \boldsymbol{\alpha}|D_{train}) d\boldsymbol{w} d\boldsymbol{\alpha} = \tag{3}$$

$$\int_A \int_{W(\boldsymbol{\alpha})} P(D_{test}|\boldsymbol{w}) P(\boldsymbol{w}|\boldsymbol{\alpha}, D_{train}) P(\boldsymbol{\alpha}|D_{train}) d\boldsymbol{w} d\boldsymbol{\alpha},$$

where

$$P(\boldsymbol{\alpha}|D_{train}) \propto P(D_{train}|\boldsymbol{\alpha}) P(\boldsymbol{\alpha}),$$

i.e. in case of absence of any prior assumptions on $\boldsymbol{\alpha}$, $P(\boldsymbol{\alpha}|D_{train})$ is proportional to evidence. Integration over A is often intractable that is why $P(\boldsymbol{\alpha}|D_{train})$ is usually approximated by $\delta(\boldsymbol{\alpha}_{MP})$ where $\boldsymbol{\alpha}_{MP} = \arg\max_{\boldsymbol{\alpha}} P(D_{train}|\boldsymbol{\alpha})$. Then equation (3) turns into

$$P(D_{test}|D_{train}) \approx \int_{W(\boldsymbol{\alpha}_{MP})} P(D_{test}|\boldsymbol{w}) P(\boldsymbol{w}|\boldsymbol{\alpha}_{MP}, D_{train}) d\boldsymbol{w} \tag{4}$$

3 Relevance Vector Machines

Here we briefly consider the idea proposed by Tipping on using Bayesian framework in kernel methods [4]. Henceforth we consider the classification problem. Let $D_{train} = \{\boldsymbol{x}, \boldsymbol{t}\} = \{x_i, t_i\}_{i=1}^m$ be training sample where x_i are feature vectors in an n-dimensional real space and t_i are class labels taking values in $\{-1, 1\}$. Consider the family of classifiers $y(x) = \text{sign}(\sum_{i=1}^m w_i K(x, x_i) + w_0) = \text{sign}(h(x, \boldsymbol{w}))$. Establish prior distribution on the weights $P(w_i|\alpha_i) \sim N(0, \alpha_i^{-1})$. The set of parameters $\boldsymbol{\alpha}$ determines the model in which the posterior distribution is looked for. Define the likelihood of training sample as

$$P(D_{train}|\boldsymbol{w}, \boldsymbol{\alpha}) = P(D_{train}|\boldsymbol{w}) = \prod_{i=1}^m \frac{1}{1 + \exp(-t_i h(x_i, \boldsymbol{w}))}$$

Then the evidence of model is given by (2). Our goal is to find $\boldsymbol{\alpha}$ which maximizes evidence and then to get posterior distribution $P(\boldsymbol{w}|D_{train}, \boldsymbol{\alpha})$. As direct calculation of (2) is impossible due to the intractable integral, Tipping used Laplace approximation for its estimation. He approximated $L_{\boldsymbol{\alpha}}(\boldsymbol{w}) = \log(P(D_{train}|\boldsymbol{w})P(\boldsymbol{w}|\boldsymbol{\alpha}))$ by quadratic function using its Taylor decomposition with respect to $\boldsymbol{w}$ at the point of maximum $\boldsymbol{w}_{MP}$. Such approximation can be integrated yielding

$$P(D_{train}|\boldsymbol{\alpha}) \approx \exp(L_{\boldsymbol{\alpha}}(\boldsymbol{w}_{MP})) \mid \Sigma \mid^{1/2}, \tag{5}$$

where $\Sigma = (\nabla_{\boldsymbol{w}} \nabla_{\boldsymbol{w}} L(\boldsymbol{w}) \mid_{\boldsymbol{w}=\boldsymbol{w_{MP}}})^{-1}$. Differentiating the last expression with respect to $\boldsymbol{\alpha}$ and setting the derivatives to zero gives the following iterative re-estimation equation

$$\alpha_i^{new} = \frac{1 - \alpha_i^{old} \Sigma_{ii}}{w_i^{MP}} \tag{6}$$

The training procedure consists of three iterative steps. First we search for the maximum point $\boldsymbol{w_{MP}}$ of $L(\boldsymbol{w})$. Then we make approximation according to (5) and use (6) to get the new values of $\boldsymbol{\alpha}$. The steps are repeated until the process converges.

After the training is finished the integral (4) can be approximated by setting $P(\boldsymbol{w}|D_{train}, \boldsymbol{\alpha}) \approx \delta_(\boldsymbol{w_{MP}})$ resulting in the expression

$$P(D_{test}|D_{train}) = P(D_{test}|\boldsymbol{w_{MP}})$$

It was shown [4] that RVM provides approximately the same quality as SVM with the same kernel function and best value of C selected by cross-validation but does not require the regularization coefficient C to be set by the user. Moreover it appeared that RVM is much more sparse, i.e. the rate of non-zero weights (relevance vectors) is significantly less than the rate of support vectors. This happens because most of the objects are treated as irrelevant and the corresponding α tend to infinity.

4 Generalized Relevance Vector Machines

Model selection via maximal evidence principle allows for avoiding the direct setting of weight constraints in RVM. Nevertheless, making a choice on a kernel function is still needed. The question is whether it is possible to use analogous approach and to treat the kernel function type as meta-parameter using Bayesian framework to define it. Henceforth we consider one of the most popular parametric kernels $K(x, z) = \exp(-\frac{||x-z||^2}{2\sigma^2})$. Our goal is to find the best σ value without cross-validation using maximal evidence principle.

It is easy to see that equation (5) presents a compromise between the accuracy on the training sample (the first item) and some kind of stability with respect to changes of the algorithm's weights (second item). Small values of σ lead to overfitting and hence to high accuracy on the training sample. On the other hand second item of formula (5) does not penalize such σ due to the following reason. Small σ means that almost all objects from the training set have non-zero weights and the influence from the neighboring objects can be neglected. But changes in object's weight just change the height of the corresponding gaussian still keeping its center in the object. The likelihood after such weight changes is still very high and the second term in (5) even encourages small σ. At the same time if we start changing the position of the gaussian center the likelihood of the training object changes dramatically (see fig.1). So small σ make classification unstable with respect to shifts of the kernel centers. Hence it is necessary to extend RVM model allowing kernels to be located at arbitrary point (relevant point) of objects space.

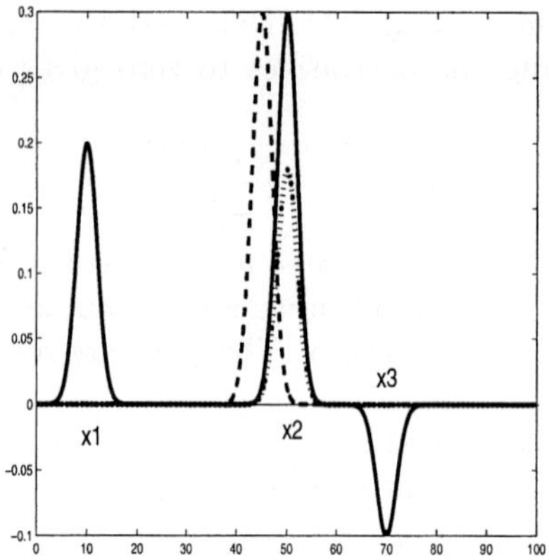

Fig. 1. The likelihood of the training sample is a product of likelihoods in each training object $x1, x2, x3$. Narrow Gaussians centered in training objects have nearly no influence on the other objects from the training set. Small weight change still keeps the likelihood of the corresponding object high enough (dotted line) while small shifts of a relevant point (gaussian center) make likelihood catastorphically low in case of small σ (dashed line).

Let $M(\boldsymbol{\alpha}, \sigma)$ be the model that defines the family of classifiers $y(x) = \text{sign}(\sum_{i=1}^{p} w_i K(x, z_i) + b) = \text{sign}(h(x, \boldsymbol{w}, \boldsymbol{z}))$. Here z_i is the center of ith kernel function (in our case this function is a gaussian). We call it a relevant point. Then the likelihood of the training sample is given by

$$P(D_{train}|\boldsymbol{w}, \boldsymbol{z}) = \prod_{j=1}^{m} \frac{1}{(1 + \exp(-t_j h(x_j, \boldsymbol{w}, \boldsymbol{z})))}$$

We have no prior knowledge about $\boldsymbol{z}$ so that we assume improper uniform distribution across the whole space of objects. Then the evidence is expressed by

$$P(D_{train}|\boldsymbol{\alpha}, \sigma) \propto \int_W \int_{R^n} P(D_{train}|\boldsymbol{w}, \boldsymbol{z}) P(\boldsymbol{w}|\boldsymbol{\alpha}) d\boldsymbol{w} d\boldsymbol{z} \tag{7}$$

Again we will use Laplace approximation for the expression under the integral. Denote $L_{\boldsymbol{\alpha},\sigma}(\boldsymbol{w}, \boldsymbol{z}) = \log(P(D_{train}|\boldsymbol{w}, \boldsymbol{z}) P(\boldsymbol{w}|\boldsymbol{\alpha}))$. Then the integral (7) can be evaluated analytically yielding

$$P(D_{train}|\boldsymbol{\alpha}, \sigma) \approx \exp(L_{\boldsymbol{\alpha},\sigma}(\boldsymbol{w}_{\boldsymbol{MP}}, \boldsymbol{z}_{\boldsymbol{MP}})) det(\nabla_{\boldsymbol{w},\boldsymbol{z}} \nabla_{\boldsymbol{w},\boldsymbol{z}} L_{\boldsymbol{\alpha},\sigma}(\boldsymbol{w}, \boldsymbol{z}) |_{\substack{\boldsymbol{w}=\boldsymbol{w}_{\boldsymbol{MP}} \\ \boldsymbol{z}=\boldsymbol{z}_{\boldsymbol{MP}}}})^{-1/2}$$

Since σ is a scalar we may use direct search methods for its estimation by evaluating

$$E(\sigma) = \max_{\boldsymbol{\alpha}} P(D_{train}|\boldsymbol{\alpha}, \sigma) \tag{8}$$

Then the training process can be presented in the following way:

1. Start with some initial values of $\boldsymbol{w}, \boldsymbol{z}, \boldsymbol{\alpha}, \sigma$.
2. Maximize $P(D_{train}|\boldsymbol{w}, \boldsymbol{z})P(\boldsymbol{w}|\boldsymbol{\alpha})$ with respect to $\boldsymbol{w}$.
3. Re-estimate $\boldsymbol{\alpha}$ according to formula (6).
4. Go to step 2 until the process converges. Otherwise go to step 5.
5. Maximize $P(D_{train}|\boldsymbol{w}, \boldsymbol{z})$ with respect to $\boldsymbol{z}$.
6. Go to step 2 until process converges. Otherwise get $E(\sigma)$ according to (8).
7. Change σ in order to maximize $E(\sigma)$.

Note that there is no need to make additional optimization with respect to $\boldsymbol{\alpha}$ in step 6 as it has been already optimized during steps 2-5. We may use $\boldsymbol{z} = \boldsymbol{x}$ as initial estimation. As the most of α will tend to infinity to the step 5, the number of relevant points to be optimized will be relatively small and we may utilize a gradient descent method.

5 Numerical Realization and Approximations

To implement the algorithm described in the previous section we have to deal with problems connected with high dimensionality of the $(\boldsymbol{w}, \boldsymbol{z})$ space. Its dimension is $p(n+1)+1$. Large number of relevance points (large value of p) is typical in case of small σ. We have to make some assumptions to reduce the computation time. First of all we will set all mixed derivatives $\frac{\partial^2 L_{\boldsymbol{\alpha},\sigma}(\boldsymbol{w},\boldsymbol{z})}{\partial w_i \partial x_{jk}}$ to zero. Then the Taylor decomposition of $L_{\boldsymbol{\alpha},\sigma}(\boldsymbol{w}, \boldsymbol{z})$ at the point of maximum $(\boldsymbol{w_{MP}}, \boldsymbol{z_{MP}})$ will turn to

$$L_{\boldsymbol{\alpha},\sigma}(\boldsymbol{w}, \boldsymbol{z}) \approx L_{\boldsymbol{\alpha},\sigma}(\boldsymbol{w_{MP}}, \boldsymbol{z_{MP}}) + \frac{1}{2}(\triangle w^T H_w \triangle w + \triangle z^T H_z \triangle z)$$

Here Hessian H_w is responsible for the selection of $\boldsymbol{\alpha}$ i.e. for stability with respect to weight changes and Hessian H_z is responsible for the selection of σ i.e. for stability with respect to shifts of relevant points.

Hessian H_z is still difficult to compute as its size is $pn \times pn$. So another approximation is to interpret each relevance point z_k as a single variable. Our goal is to estimate the measure of unsteadiness at the point, not its direction. Differentiating formally with respect to z_k as a single variable we get

$$\frac{\partial}{\partial z_k} L_{\boldsymbol{\alpha},\sigma}(\boldsymbol{w}, \boldsymbol{z}) = \frac{\partial}{\partial z_k} \sum_{i=1}^{p} \log(1 + exp(-t_i h(x_i, \boldsymbol{w}, \boldsymbol{z}))) =$$

$$- \sum_{i=1}^{p} \frac{t_i w_k}{1 + exp(t_i h(x_i, \boldsymbol{w}, \boldsymbol{z}))} \frac{\partial h(x_i, \boldsymbol{w}, \boldsymbol{z})}{\partial z_k}$$

$$\frac{\partial^2}{\partial {z_k}^2} L_{\boldsymbol{\alpha},\sigma}(\boldsymbol{w}, \boldsymbol{z}) = \sum_{i=1}^{p} \left[-\frac{exp(t_i h(x_i, \boldsymbol{w}, \boldsymbol{z}))}{(1 + exp(t_i h(x_i, \boldsymbol{w}, \boldsymbol{z})))^2} \left(\frac{\partial h(x_i, \boldsymbol{w}, \boldsymbol{z})}{\partial z_k} \right)^2 + \right.$$

$$\left. \frac{t_i}{1 + exp(t_i h(x_i, \boldsymbol{w}, \boldsymbol{z}))} \frac{\partial^2 h(x_i, \boldsymbol{w}, \boldsymbol{z})}{\partial {z_k}^2} \right]$$

where

$$\frac{\partial h(x_i, \boldsymbol{w}, \boldsymbol{z})}{\partial z_k} = w_k \frac{||z_k - x_i||}{\sigma^2} K(z_k, x_i);$$

$$\frac{\partial^2 h(x_i, \boldsymbol{w}, \boldsymbol{z})}{\partial {z_k}^2} = w_k \left(\frac{||z_k - x_i||^2}{\sigma^4} - \frac{1}{\sigma^2} \right) K(z_k, x_i)$$

In this Hessian the off-diagonal elements are several orders smaller than the diagonal elements, so we may neglect them getting a diagonal Hessian

$$\hat{H}_z = \mathrm{diag}(\frac{\partial^2 L_{\boldsymbol{\alpha},\sigma}(\boldsymbol{w}, \boldsymbol{z})}{\partial z_1^2}, \ldots, \frac{\partial^2 L_{\boldsymbol{\alpha},\sigma}(\boldsymbol{w}, \boldsymbol{z})}{\partial z_p^2})$$

6 Experimental Evaluation and Discussion

To illustrate the performance of GRVM we made several experiments using datasets taken from the UCI repository [5]. Each data table were split randomly into training (67% of objects) and test sets. We used gaussian kernel function and selected its width via leave-one-out procedure both for SVM and RVM as well as regularization coefficient C in SVM. The use of cross-validation methods is typical for searching the best kernels for the given task and widely used both for SVMs and RVMs. Our task was to check whether our approach can lead to better kernels. So we used GRVM for evidence estimation. The value of σ which corresponded to the maximum of evidence was then used for training usual RVM. Actually we could continue using GRVMs with obtained kernel but our experiments showed that RVM had slightly better performance on all tasks. The results of experiments are shown in table 1. The first three columns

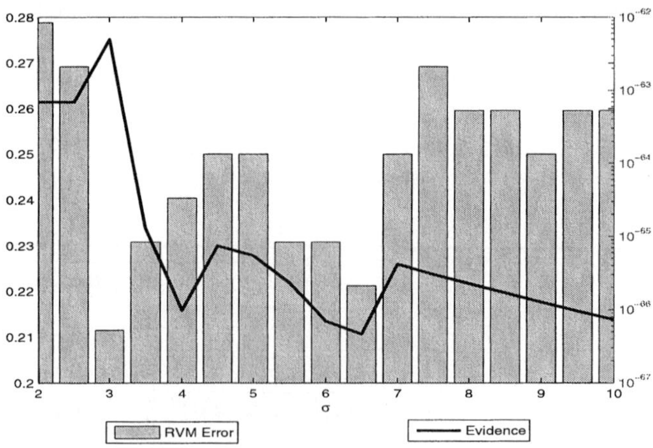

Fig. 2. Maximum of evidence most often corresponds to the minimum of test error

Table 1. Testing results of kernel function selection procedure. Column N contains number of objects in learning sample, other columns contains error rate and number of support[relevant] vectors for RVM and SVM with Leave-One-Out and Maximal Evidence kernel parameter selection procedure (RVM LOO, SVM LOO and RVM ME correspondingly).

		Errors			Vectors		
Data set	N	RVM LOO	SVM LOO	RVM ME	RVM LOO	SVM LOO	RVM ME
AUSTRALIAN	482	14.9%	11.54%	10.58%	37	188	19
BUPA	241	25%	26.92%	21.15%	6	179	7
CREDIT	482	16.35%	15.38%	15.87%	57	217	36
HEPATITIS	108	36.17%	31.91%	31.91%	34	102	11
PIMA	537	22.08%	21.65%	21.21%	29	309	13

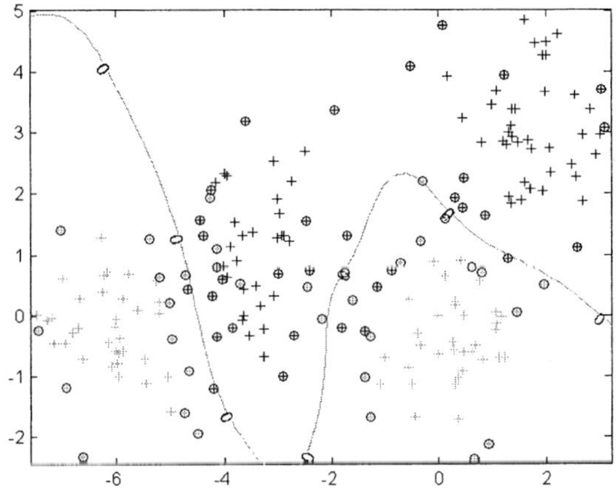

Fig. 3. Example of SVM classifier performance. Data consists of 200 objects of two classes generated from mixture of Gaussian distributions. Parameters of the classifier are: $C = 1, \sigma = 1$. Encircled objects are support vectors. In this case there are 65 support vectors.

(Errors) contain test errors of RVM with kernel selected via leave-one-out procedure, SVM with kernel obtained in the similar way and RVM with kernel which maximizes evidence respectively. The last three columns (Vectors) present number of non-zero weights. It is easy to see that maximum evidence principle selects generally better kernels than leave-one-out procedure. RVM with kernel that was selected by the proposed method outperforms state-of-art SVM classifier with kernel selected by cross-validation. Another important aspect is sparseness of obtained RVM. It is illustrated by last columns of the table. It is known that RVM is more sparse than SVM as extra non-zero weights are penalized through training. Application of maximum evidence principle to kernel determination leads to even more sparse models. A typical relation between test error and evidence value with respect to different σ values is shown in Fig. 2. Evidence is

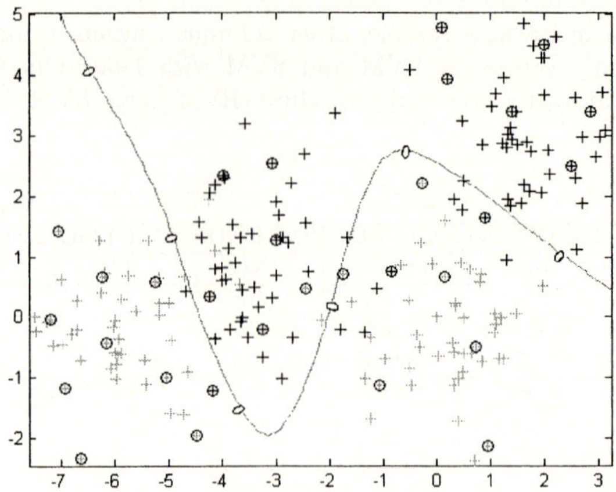

Fig. 4. Example of RVM classifier performance. Data consists of 200 objects of two classes generated from mixture of Gaussian distributions. Encircled objects are relevant vectors.

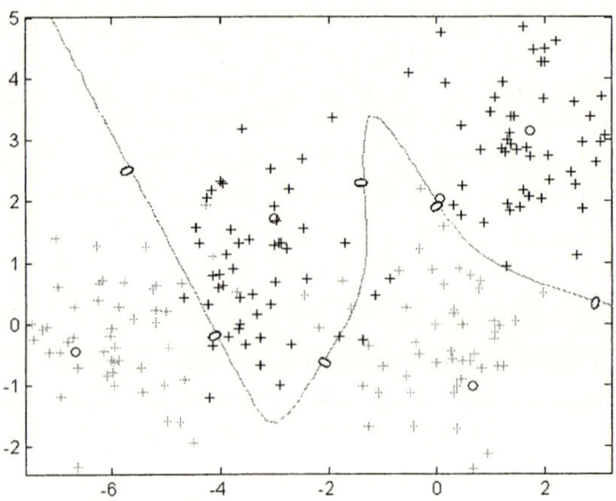

Fig. 5. Example of GRVM classifier performance. Data consists of 200 objects of two classes generated from mixture of Gaussian distributions. Black circles are relevant vectors. There are only 5 relevant vectors.

shown in logarithmic scale. It can be seen that it reaches its maximum on the same σ where test error has minimum. Although it is not necessarily so for all samples, in general this approach works better than traditional cross validation methodology.

GRVM classifier tends to be even more sparse in comparison with RVM and SVM. Figures 3, 4 and 5 illustrate performance of three classifiers on simple data. Data consists of 200 objects of two classes generated from mixture of Gaussian distributions. In all cases σ equals 1. It can be seen that decision surface of SVM is determined by more than 60 support vectors while for RVM the correspondent parameter - number of relevance vectors - is near to 30. Accuracy of GRVM is comparable with those of SVM and RVM, but number of relevant points is only 5. Extension of RVM model allowing kernels to be located at arbitrary points of feature space and optimization of log-likelihood function with respect to kernels centres provide simplier decision models with little amount of relevant points.

7 Conclusions

Success of RVM classifiers shows that Bayesian regularization can be effectively used for optimal determination of models parameters. But simple application of this approach for kernel selection task is not reasonable since classifiers with narrower kernels are more stable with respect to weights variances. Inclusion of kernels centres to model parameters leads to sophisticated optimization procedures which nevertheless can be rather effectively implemented using some approximations.

Series of experiments using data from UCI repository show that maximum of evidence generally better corresponds to the minimum of test error than leave-one-out error. GRVM as well as RVM with kernel parameters selected according to maximal evidence tends to be more sparse. Maximization of evidence can improve the performance in many cases for both RVMs and SVMs. Moreover it allows us to carry out more sophisticated optimization, e.g. setting different σ_i for different features. Creation of effective procedure of evidence gradient estimation is still open question but seems to be a solvable task.

Acknowledgements

This work was supported by the Russian Foundation for Basic Research (projects No. 05-07-90333, 04-01-00161, 04-01-08045, 03-01-00580) and INTAS (YS 04-83-2942).

References

1. Burges, C.J.S: A Tutorial on Support Vector Machines for Pattern Recognition. Data Mining and Knowledge Discovery **2** (1998) 121–167
2. Vapnik, V.N.: The Nature of Statistical Learning Theory. Springer-Verlag New York (1995)
3. MacKay, D.J.C.: Information Theory, Inference, and Learning Algorithms. Cambridge University Press (2003)
4. Tipping, M.E.: Sparse Bayesian Learning and the Relevance Vector Machines. Journal of Machine Learning Research **1** (2001) 211–244
5. Murphy, P.M., Aha, D.W.: UCI Repository of Machine Learning Databases [Machine Readable Data Repository]. Univ. of California, Dept. of Information and Computer Science, Irvine, Calif. (1996)

Genetic Multivariate Polynomials: An Alternative Tool to Neural Networks

Angel Fernando Kuri-Morales[1] and Federico Juárez-Almaraz[2]

[1] Instituto Tecnológico Autónomo de México
[2] Universidad Nacional Autónoma de México
Río Hondo No.1, México 01000, D.F.
akuri@itam.mx

Abstract. One of the basic problems of applied mathematics is to find a synthetic expression (model) which captures the essence of a system given a (necessarily) finite sample which reflects selected characteristics. When the model considers several independent variables its mathematical treatment may become burdensome or even downright impossible from a practical standpoint. In this paper we explore the utilization of an efficient genetic algorithm to select the "best" subset of multivariate monomials out of a full polynomial of the form $F(v_1,\ldots,v_n) = \sum_{i_1=0}^{g_1} \ldots \sum_{i_n}^{g_n} c_{i_1\ldots i_n} v_1^{i_1} \ldots v_n^{i_n}$ (where g_i denotes the maximum desired degree for the i-th independent variable). This regression problem has been tackled with success using neural networks (NN). However, the "black box" characteristic of such models is frequently cited as a major drawback. We show that it is possible to find a polynomial model for an arbitrary set of data. From selected practical cases we argue that, despite the restrictions of a polynomial basis, our Genetic Multivariate Polynomials (GMP) compete with the NN approach without the mentioned limitation. We show how to treat constrained functions as unconstrained ones using GMPs.

1 Introduction

One of the basic goals of the scientific endeavor is to (try to) identify patterns in apparently chaotic data given a (necessarily) finite sample which reflects selected characteristics in the system under study. In this paper we explore the utilization of an efficient genetic algorithm to select the "best" subset of multivariate monomials out of a full polynomial. Such multivariate regression problem has been tackled with success using neural networks (NN) whose "black box" nature is frequently cited as a major drawback. We show that it is possible to find a polynomial model for an arbitrary set of data and give evidence that, despite the restrictions of a polynomial basis, our Genetic Multivariate Polynomials (GMPs) compete with the NN approach without the mentioned "black box" limitation.

1.1 Statistical Systems

Statistical systems are a relatively modern approach to automated machine learning (AML). They rely on the overall analysis of data representing the behavior of the

M. Lazo and A. Sanfeliu (Eds.): CIARP 2005, LNCS 3773, pp. 262 – 270, 2005.

system. No previous knowledge about the system is assumed and, indeed, they do achieve AML with a certain amount of success depending on how one measures it.

1.1.1 Neural Networks

Perhaps the most representative systems in this category are the so-called neural networks (NN). The basic idea is that simple computing elements (which we will refer to as "units"), individually displaying little computing power, when arranged in richly interconnected networks, may embody the essence of the system they model. The term "neuron" arises from suggestive analogies where the units purportedly simulate the behavior of the neuron of a living being. Every connecting path between units has an associated weight. It is in these weights that knowledge, tacitly (as opposed to the explicit rules of the classical AI approach) is stored in a "trained" network. In supervised mode the NN is "shown" the data repeatedly and, via an iterative algorithm, it modifies the initial (typically random) value of the weights so that the NN's outputs replicate the known ones for every element in the data. NNs have evolved from the initial animal-neuron-inspired approach into sophisticated entities in which units are determined by their mathematical properties.

The statistical nature of the learning process has been given solid theoretical foundation by the work of many researchers, outstanding that of Vapnik [VV95]. It has been proven that a feedforward strongly interconnected network of units (perceptrons) constitutes a universal approximator [SH99]. Furthermore, analogous NNs are able to represent the data in the best possible way given a set of data [BB92]. Notice that the proper selection of the data is not an issue here; data is assumed to have been properly selected (a fact which we will take for granted in what follows). In conclusion, NNs are able to extract knowledge, given an arbitrary set of data, fully and optimally. However, a drawback of NNs is that the process by which they arrive at their conclusions is not explicit and, upon presentation of a larger (possibly richer) set of data the learning process has to be repeated or, at best, continued from the previous one. Nevertheless, the NN methodology yields a tool which is able to tackle complex multivariate regression effectively.

1.1.2 Multivariate Polynomials

An obvious alternative is to attempt such regression appealing to a functional representation (such as the one in (1)) where the known response of the system to a set of input stimulae is expressed explicitly.

$$F(v_1,...,v_n) = \sum_{i_1=0}^{g_1} ... \sum_{i_n}^{g_n} c_{i_1...i_n} v_1^{i_1}...v_n^{i_n} \tag{1}$$

In (1) v_i corresponds to the *i-th* independent variable and g_i is the highest allowed power for v_i. In order to find $F(v_1,...,v_n)$ one must device a method to approximate the data in a typically overdetermined system for a given metric. We must also overcome the curse of dimensionality inherent to this approach[1]. In what follows we give a

[1] For instance, consider a problem where n=10 and $g_1=g_2=...=g_n=4$. The number of coefficients in (1) is easily calculated as $C = 5^{10} = 9{,}765{,}625$ which implies that we must have, at least, those many elements in our sample.

method which allows us to solve both problems. In part 2 we expound the method. In part 3 we make a comparison of a representative set of problems tackled with GMPs and NNs. In part 4 we offer our conclusions.

2 Genetic Multivariate Polynomials

To approximate the data vectors we have chosen the minimax or L_∞ norm for reasons that will become apparent in what follows. In L_∞ one seeks an F(x) that minimizes ε_θ, where $\varepsilon_\theta = \max |F(\mathbf{v}_i) - d_i|$; $\mathbf{v}_i$ denotes the *i-th* independent variable vector and d_i the *i-th* desired output. The original data set is found in matrix **O** of dimensions $(n+1) \times s$; where *n* denotes the number of independent variables and *s* the number of elements in the sample. In order to find the approximator of (1) we map the vectors of **O** to a higher dimensional space yielding matrix **V** of dimensions $p \times s$, where $p = \Pi_{i=1}^{n}(1+g_i)$.

2.1 Minimax Approximation to a Set of Size *m*

To illustrate minimax approximation we arbitrarily select a submatrix of **V** of size $m \times m$ (call it **V'**), where $m=p+1$; then, we solve the system of (2).

$$\begin{bmatrix} \eta_1 & (v_1^0 \ldots v_n^0)_1 & \ldots & (v_1^{g_1} \ldots v_n^{g_n})_1 \\ \eta_2 & (v_1^0 \ldots v_n^0)_2 & \ldots & (v_1^{g_1} \ldots v_n^{g_n})_2 \\ \ldots & \ldots & \ldots & \ldots \\ \eta_m & (v_1^0 \ldots v_n^0)_m & \ldots & (v_1^{g_1} \ldots v_n^{g_n})_m \end{bmatrix} \begin{bmatrix} \varepsilon_\theta \\ c_1 \\ \ldots \\ c_m \end{bmatrix} = \begin{bmatrix} d_1 \\ d_2 \\ \ldots \\ d_m \end{bmatrix} \tag{2}$$

Denoting the approximation error for the *i-th* vector as ε_i we may define $\varepsilon_i = \eta_i \varepsilon_\theta$; clearly, $\eta_i \varepsilon_i \le \varepsilon_\theta$. We also denote the elements of row *i*, column *j* of (2) as δ_{ij} and the *i-th* cofactor of the first column as κ_i. From Cramer's rule, we immediately have:

$$\varepsilon_\theta = \frac{\begin{vmatrix} d_1 & \ldots & \delta_{1m} \\ \ldots & \ldots & \ldots \\ d_m & \ldots & \delta_{mm} \end{vmatrix}}{\eta_1 \kappa_1 + \ldots + \eta_m \kappa_m} \tag{3}$$

To minimize ε_θ we have to maximize the denominator of (3). This is easily achieved by a) Selecting the maximum value of the η_i's and b) Making the signs of the η_i's all equal to the signs of the κ_i's. Obviously the η_i's are maximized iff $\eta_i = 1$ for *i=1,...,m* which translates into the well known fact that the minimax fit corresponds to approximation errors of equal absolute size. On the other hand, achieving (b) simply means that we must set the signs of the η_i's to those of the cofactors. Making σ_i=sign(κ_i) system (2) is simply re-written as

$$\begin{bmatrix} \sigma_1 & \dots & \delta_{1m} \\ \dots & \dots & \dots \\ \sigma_m & \dots & \delta_{mm} \end{bmatrix} \begin{bmatrix} \varepsilon_\theta \\ \dots \\ c_m \end{bmatrix} = \begin{bmatrix} d_1 \\ \dots \\ d_m \end{bmatrix} \quad (4)$$

Once having all the elements in (4) it suffices to solve this system to obtain both the value of ε_θ an the coefficients $c_1,...,c_m$ which best fit the elements of **V'** in the minimax sense. To find the minimax coefficients for **V** we apply the next algorithm.

2.2 Exchange Algorithm

1. Set i ← 1.
2. Select an arbitrary set (of size m) of rows of matrix **V**; this set is called M_i.
3. Determine the signs of the ε_i which maximize the denominator of (3).
4. Solve the system of (4). Denote the resulting polynomial by P_i.
5. Calculate the value of $\varepsilon_\phi = \max(|P_i - d_i|)\ \forall\ \mathbf{v}_i \notin M_i$.
6. If $\varepsilon_\phi \le \varepsilon_\theta$ end the algorithm; the coefficients of P_i are those of the polynomial which best approximates **V** in the minimax sense.
7. Set i ← i+1.
8. Exchange the row corresponding to ε_ϕ for the one in M_i which preserves its sign and makes $(\varepsilon_\theta)_{i+1} > (\varepsilon_\theta)_i$.
9. Go to step 4.

□

The exchange algorithm will end as long as the consecutive systems of (4) satisfy Haar's condition while, on the other hand, the cost of its execution (in FLOPs) is of $O(m^6)$. There are implementation issues which allow to apply this algorithm even in the absence of Haar's condition and which reduce its cost to $O(m^2)$. The interested reader is referred to [KG02].

2.3 Genetic Algorithm

The basic reason to choose a minimax norm is that the method outlined above is not dependent on the origin of the elements in **V**. We decided them to be the monomials of a full polynomial. But it makes no difference to the exchange algorithm whether the $\mathbf{v}_i$ are gotten from a set of monomials or they are elements of arbitrary data vectors. This is important because, as stated above, the number of monomials and coefficients in (2) grows geometrically. One way to avoid the problem of such coefficient explosion is to define a priori the number (say μ) of desired monomials of the approximant and then to properly select which of the p possible ones these will be. There are $\binom{p}{\mu}$ possible combinations of monomials and even for modest values of p and μ and exhaustive search is out of the question. This optimization problem may be tackled using a genetic algorithm (GA), as follows.

The genome is a binary string of size *p*. Every bit in it represents a monomial. If the bit is '1' it means that the corresponding monomial remains while if it is a '0' it means that such monomial is not to be considered. All one has to ensure is that the number of 1's is equal to μ. Assume, for example, that $\mathbf{v} = (v_1, v_2, v_3)$ and that $g_1=1$, $g_2=2$, $g_3=2$; if $\mu = 6$ the genome 110000101010000001 corresponds to the polynomial in (5).

$$P(v_1,v_2,v_3)=c_{000}+c_{001}v_3+c_{020}v_2^2+c_{022}v_2^2v_3^2+c_{112}v_1v_2v_3^2+ c_{122}v_1v_2^2v_3^2 \quad (5)$$

It is well known that any elitist GA will converge to a global optimum [GR94]. It has also been shown that a variation of GA called Vasconcelos Genetic Algorithm (VGA) shows superior behavior on a wide range of functions [AK00]. VGA uses a) Deterministic parenthetical selection, b) Annular crossover, c) Uniform mutation [KV98]. All results reported are based on VGA's application.

Therefore, the initial population of the GA is generated randomly. It consists of a set of binary strings of length *p* in which there are only μ 1's. Then the GA's operators are applied as usual. The fitness function is the minimax fitness error as per the exchange algorithm. This error is minimized and, at the end of the process, the polynomial exhibiting the smallest fit error is selected as the best approximant for the original data set.

3 Neural Networks and GMPs

As we already pointed out, NNs have been proven to be able to synthesize the knowledge contained in an arbitrary set of data. Particularly, when the units are the well known perceptrons [SH99], any continuous function may be approximated by a three layer NN, such as the one shown in figure 1.

In figure 1 we show a NN with 6 input variables and one output variable, i.e., one dependent variable and 6 independent ones. The **b** neuron is the so-called bias and its input is canonically set to +1. It is easy to see that there are $w = 33$ $(6 \times 4+4\times 1+4+1)$ weights in this network. The number of neurons in the input and output neurons is determined by the number of input and output variables respectively. The number of neurons in the hidden layer (H) was estimated from the heuristic rule of equation (6).

$$H \approx \frac{S-3O}{3(I+O+1)} \quad (6)$$

Here, S is the number of elements in the data sample; I and O are the number of input and output neurons, respectively. What equation (6) says is that the number of weights should equal, roughly, 1/3 of the size of the sample. With these convention we tackled the problem of approximating a set of constrained functions of which a small fraction is shown in table 1.

In every case, we sampled the independent variables randomly and selected those values which complied with the constraints. Equalities were treated as closely bounded inequalities. For example, the first constraint of function 6 was actually transformed into: $x_1^2 + x_2^2 + x_3^2 + x_4^2 + x_5^2 \geq 9.9999$ and $x_1^2 + x_2^2 + x_3^2 + x_4^2 + x_5^2 \leq 10.0001$. The samples represented the actual values of interest of every one of the functions and the resulting NN, in fact, constitutes an alternate non-constrained version of the original one.

Table 1. A Set of Constrained Functions

No	Function	Constraints
1	$(x_1 - x_2)^2 + (x_2 - x_3)^4 + 1$	$x_1 + x_1 x_2^2 + x_3^4 = 3$
2	$x_1^2 + 4x_2^2$	$\frac{3}{5}x_1 + \frac{4}{5}x_2 \geq \frac{13}{5}$
3	$9 - 8x_1 - 6x_2 - 4x_3 + 2x_1^2$ $+ 2x_2^2 + x_3^2 + 2x_1x_2 + 2x_1x_3$	$x_1 \geq 0; x_2 \geq 0; x_3 \geq 0$ $-x1 - x2 - x3 + 3 \geq 0$
4	$1000 - x_1^2 - 2x_2^2 - x_3^2 - x_1x_2 - x_1x_3$	$x_1^2 + x_2^2 - x_3^2 - 25 = 0$ $8x_1 + 14x_2 + 7x_3 - 56 = 0$ $x_i \geq 0 \quad i = 1,2,3$
5	$100(x2 - x_1^2) + (1 - x_1^2)^2 + 90(x_4 - x_3^2)^2$ $+ (1 - x_3)^2 + 10.1[(x_2 - 1)^2 + (x4 - 1)^2]$ $+ 19.8(x_2 - 1)(x_4 - 1) + 1$	$-10 \leq x_i \leq +10$
6	$\exp(x_1x_2x_3x_4x_5)$	$x_1^2 + x_2^2 + x_3^2 + x_4^2 + x_5^2 = 10$ $x_2x_3 - 5x_4x_5 = 0$ $x_1^3 + x_2^3 = -1$ $-2.3 \leq x_i \leq +2.3 \quad i = 1,2$ $-3.2 \leq x_i \leq +3.2 \quad i = 3,4,5$

Our thesis may be resumed as follows:

a) The domain of a constrained function may be sampled in such a way that the resulting sample represents adequately the domain of a constrained function.

b) Any set of data may be re-expressed as a trained NN.

c) If a GMP is able to duplicate the workings of a NN it is possible to work with the resulting algebraic expression.

d) The optimization process can be performed on the polynomial with traditional calculus' tools.

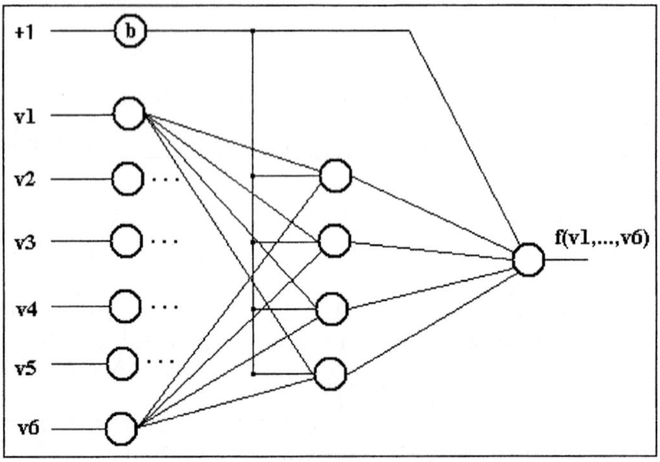

Fig. 1. Three-layered Perceptron Network

3.1 Experiments

Data was divided in two sets: a training set and a test set. The training set encompasses 80% of the data; the test set consists of the remaining 20%. Both NNs and GMPs were trained using the training set. Then both methods were tested for performance on the test set, which they had not previously "seen". The number of weights for the NNs were calculated from (6); the number of monomials in the GMP was set accordingly. In the following table we show the actual errors found from the trained NNs and GMPs for the selected functions. Eight types of error were compiled: a) Maximum training error for NNs and GMPs; b) RMS training error for NNs and GMPs; c) Maximum test error for NNs and GMPs; d) RMS test error for NNs and GMPs.

Table 2. Error Comparison for Selected Functions (NN and GMP)

	Maximum Training Error		RMS Training Error		Maximum Test Error		RMS Test Error	
	NN	GMP	NN	GMP	NN	GMP	NN	GMP
Function								
1	0.0915	0.0745	0.0318	0.0338	0.0668	0.0600	0.0456	0.0400
2	0.5419	0.1593	0.1015	0.0978	0.3310	0.2319	0.0906	0.0393
3	0.0955	0.0919	0.0218	0.0465	0.1381	0.1861	0.0354	0.0618
4	0.2069	0.0724	0.0742	0.0466	0.1872	0.0960	0.0731	0.0480
5	0.2654	0.2148	0.0616	0.0849	0.3695	0.2589	0.1337	0.1249
6	0.0014	0.0003	0.0002	0.0001	0.0328	0.1805	0.0070	0.0280

4 Conclusions

Table 2 shows the remarkable performance of NNs and GMPs for this set of problems. For instance, the RMS test error was always of O(0.1) which directly bears on the generalization properties of the model. NNs behavior was expected but GMP's was not as obvious: with two exceptions, GMPs showed better generalization capabilities than their neural counterparts.

That maximum errors were smaller for GMPs may be explained easily, since the norm focuses on their minimization. That, in the majority of cases, GMPs RMS errors were comparable was not so clear, particularly since the number of monomials and weights were the same. In the perceptron networks the underlying functions (based on a sigmoidal transformation of the local induced field) are much more complex and, in principle, richer than linear combinations of monomials. However, as attested by the results, the VGA does a fine job in finding the best such combinations.

The polynomial expression shows explicitly which powers of the independent variables bear on the behavior of the function and to what extent. It also allows for simple algebraic manipulation of the different terms. For instance, finding the partial derivatives with respect to any of the input variables is trivial and allows for the simple analysis of the function's behavior.

On the other hand, given the reliable representation of the original data, the method suggests a general algorithm to tackle constrained optimization problems as follows:

a) Sample the feasible domain of the constrained function
b) Synthesize the function appealing to a GMP
c) Optimize utilizing traditional algebraic or numerical tools.

We do not claim that the optimization process proposed herein will be able to deliver a global optimum. However, in general, it will certainly approach one or more (depending on the starting VGA's population) local optima. These may be utilized to refine the search using other techniques.

Finally, we would like to emphasize the fact that GMPs are not limited to use simple monomials as units. Other basis are applicable and it only remains to see whether the extra computational cost implied in more complex units yields cost effective results.

References

[VV95] Vapnik, V., "The Nature of Statistical Learning Theory", Springer-Verlag, 1995.

[SH99] Haykin, S., "Neural Networks. A Comprehensive foundation", 2nd Edition, Prentice Hall, 1999.

[BB92] Boser, B. E., I.M. Guyon and V. N. Vapnik, "A training algorithm for optimal margin classifiers", *Proc. 5th Annual ACM Workshop on Computational Learning Theory*, pp. 144–152, 1992.

[KG02] Kuri, A., Galaviz, J., "Algoritmos Genéticos", Fondo de Cultura Económica, México, 2002, pp. 165-181.

[GR94] Rudolph, G., "Convergence Analysis of Canonical Genetic Algorithms", *IEEE Transactions on Neural Networks*, 5(1):96-101, January, 1994.

[AK00] Kuri, A., "A Methodology for the Statistical Characterization of Genetic Algorithms", Lectures Notes in Artificial Intelligence No 2313, pp. 79-89, Coello, C., Albornoz, A., Sucar, L., Cairó, O., (eds.), Springer Verlag, April 2000.

[KV98] Kuri, A., Villegas, C., "A Universal Genetic Algorithm for Constrained Optimization", *EUFIT '98, 6th European Congress on Intelligent Techniques and Soft Computing*, Aachen, Germany, 1998.

Non-supervised Classification of 2D Color Images Using Kohonen Networks and a Novel Metric

Ricardo Pérez-Aguila, Pilar Gómez-Gil, and Antonio Aguilera

Departamento de Ingeniería en Sistemas Computacionales,
Centro de Investigación en Tecnologías de Información y Automatización (CENTIA),
Universidad de las Américas – Puebla (UDLAP),
Ex-Hacienda Santa Catarina Mártir,
Cholula, Puebla, México 72820
{ricardo.perezaa, mariap.gomez, antonio.aguilera}@udlap.mx

Abstract. We describe the application of 1-Dimensional Kohonen Networks in the classification of color 2D images which has been evaluated in Popocatépetl Volcano's images. The Popocatépetl, located in the limits of the State of Puebla in México, is active and under monitoring since 1997. We will consider one of the problems related with the question if our application of the Kohonen Network classifies according to the total intensity color of an image or well, if it classifies according to the connectivity, i.e. the topology, between the pixels that compose an image. In order to give arguments that support our hypothesis that our procedures share the classification according to the topology of the pixels in the images, we will present two approaches based a) in the evaluation of the classification given by the network when the pixels in the images are permuted; and,b) when an additional metric to the Euclidean distance is introduced.

1 Introduction

It is well known the application of 1-Dimensional Kohonen Networks in the non-supervised classification of data with an elevated redundancy degree [5]. On the other hand, non-supervised image classification is an important vision task where images with similar features are grouped in classes. Many processing tasks (description, object recognition or indexing, for example) are based on such a preprocessing [8]. In this paper, we take in account these ideas in order to apply the methods associated to Kohonen Networks to provide solutions to automatic classification of images. The remainder of this paper is organized as follows: Section 1 describes the basis of the 1-Dimensional Kohonen Networks, Section 2 describes some procedures to take in account in order to avoid training bias, Section 3 describes the procedures and applications related to the classification of 2D color images through Kohonen networks and our results and discussion, finally Section 4 presents conclusions and future work.

M. Lazo and A. Sanfeliu (Eds.): CIARP 2005, LNCS 3773, pp. 271 – 284, 2005.

2 Fundamentals of the 1-Dimensional Kohonen Networks

2.1 Classifying Points Embedded in a n-Dimensional Space Through a 1-Dimensional Kohonen Network

A Kohonen Network with two layers, where the first one corresponds to n input neurons and the second one corresponds to m output neurons ([4] and [7]) can be used to classify points embedded in a n-dimensional space in m categories. The input points will have the form $(x_1, \ldots, x_i, \ldots, x_n)$. The total number of connections of the neurons from the input layer to the neurons in the output layer will be $n \times m$ (See Figure 1). Each neuron j, $1 \leq j \leq m$, in the output layer will have associated a n-dimensional weights vector which describes a representative of class C_j. All these vectors will have the form:

$$\text{Output neuron 1: } W_1 = (w_{1,1}, \ldots, w_{1,n})$$
$$\vdots$$
$$\text{Output neuron } m\text{: } W_j = (w_{j,1}, \ldots, w_{j,n})$$

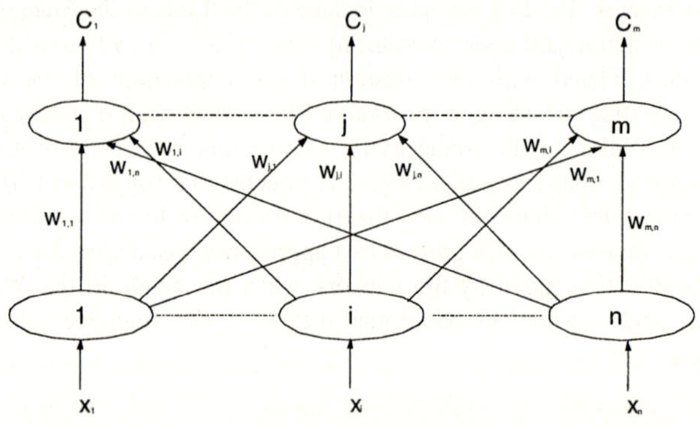

Fig. 1. Topology of a 1-dimensional Kohonen Network [5]

2.2 Training the 1-Dimensional Kohonen Network

A set of training points are presented to the network T times. According to the literature [5], all the values of the weights vectors can be initialized with random values. In order to determine a winner neuron in the output layer in presentation t, $0 \leq t < T$, it is selected that neuron whose weights vector W_j, $1 \leq j \leq m$, is the most similar to the input point P^k. Such selection is based according to the squared Euclidean distance. The selected neuron will be that with the minimal distance between its weight vector and the input point P^k:

$$d_j = \sum_{i=1}^{n} \left(P_i^k - w_{j,i}\right)^2 \qquad 1 \leq j \leq m$$

Once the j-th winner neuron in the t-th presentation has been identified, its weights are updated according to:

$$w_{j,i}(t+1) = w_{j,i}(t) + \frac{1}{t+1}\left[P_i^k - w_{j,i}(t)\right] \qquad 1 \leq i \leq n$$

When the T presentations have been achieved, the final values of the weights vectors correspond to the coordinates of the 'gravity centers' of the points, or clusters of the m classes.

3 Redistribution in the n-Dimensional Space of Kohonen Network's Training Set

To avoid training bias, the training data needs to be redistributed. Consider a set of points distributed in a 2D subspace defined by rectangle $[0,1] \times [0,1]$. Moreover, this set of points is embedded in a sub-region delimited, for example, by rectangle $[0.3,0.6] \times [0.3,0.6]$ (Figure 2).

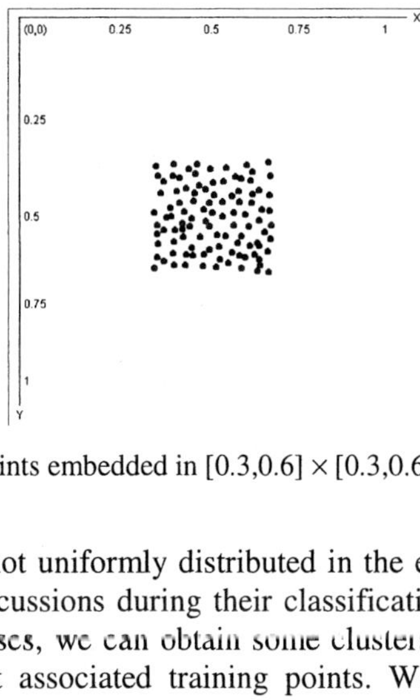

Fig. 2. A set of points embedded in $[0.3,0.6] \times [0.3,0.6] \subset [0,1] \times [0,1]$

Because the points are not uniformly distributed in the exemplified 2D space, we can expect important repercussions during their classification process. For example, for a given number of classes, we can obtain some clusters that coincide with other clusters or classes without associated training points. We will describe a simple methodology to distribute uniformly the points of a training set for the general case of a n-dimensional space.

Consider a unit n-dimensional hypercube H where the points are embedded in their corresponding minimal orthogonal bounding *hyper-box* h such that $h \subseteq H$. The point with the minimal coordinates $P_{\min} = (x_{1_{\min}}, x_{2_{\min}}, \ldots, x_{n-1_{\min}}, x_{n_{\min}})$ and the point with the maximal coordinates $P_{\max} = (x_{1_{\max}}, x_{2_{\max}}, \ldots, x_{n-1_{\max}}, x_{n_{\max}})$ will describe the main diagonal of h. We proceed to apply to each point $P = (x_1, x_2, \ldots, x_{n-1}, x_n)$ in the training set, including $P_{\min}$ and $P_{\max}$, the geometric transformation of translation given by:

$$x_i' = x_i - x_{i_{\min}} \qquad 1 \le i \le n$$

By this way, we will get a new *hyper-box* h' and the points that describe the main diagonal of h' will be $P'_{\min} = \underbrace{(0,\ldots,0)}_{n}$ and $P'_{\max} = (x'_{1_{\max}}, x'_{2_{\max}}, \ldots, x'_{n-1_{\max}}, x'_{n_{\max}})$. See Figure 3.

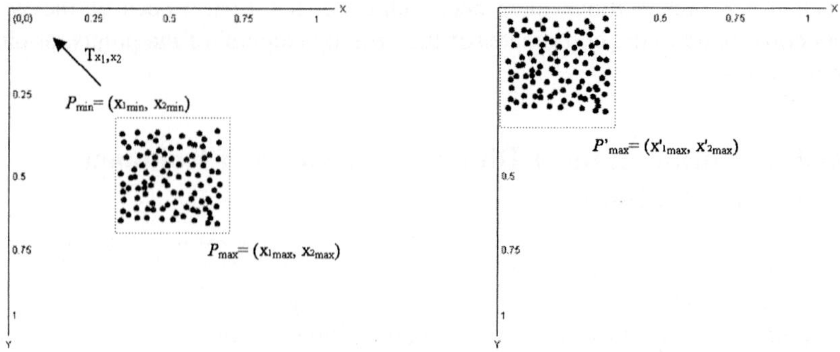

a) b)

Fig. 3. a) A training set and its minimal orthogonal bounding hyper-box *h*. b) Translation of *h* and the training points such that P'_{min} is the origin of the 2D space.

The second part of our procedure will consist in the extension of the current *hyper-box h'* to the whole *n*-dimensional hypercube *H*. The scaling of a point $P=(x_1,x_2,...,x_{n-1},x_n)$ is given by multiplying their coordinates by the factors S_1, S_2, ..., S_n each one related with x_1, x_2, ..., x_n respectively in order to produce the new scaled coordinates x_1', x_2', ..., x_n' [6]. Because we want to extend the bounding *hyper-box h'* and the translated training points to the whole unit hypercube *H*, we have that by scaling the point $P'_{\max}=(x'_{1_{\max}},x'_{2_{\max}},...,x'_{n-1_{\max}},x'_{n_{\max}})$ we must obtain the new point $\underbrace{(1,...,1)}_{n}$.

That is to say, we define the set of *n* equations:

$$1=x'_{i_{\max}}\cdot S_i \qquad 1\le i\le n$$

Starting from these equations we obtain the scaling factors to apply to all points included in the bounding *hyper-box h'* (see Figure 4):

$$S_i=\frac{1}{x'_{i_{\max}}} \qquad 1\le i\le n$$

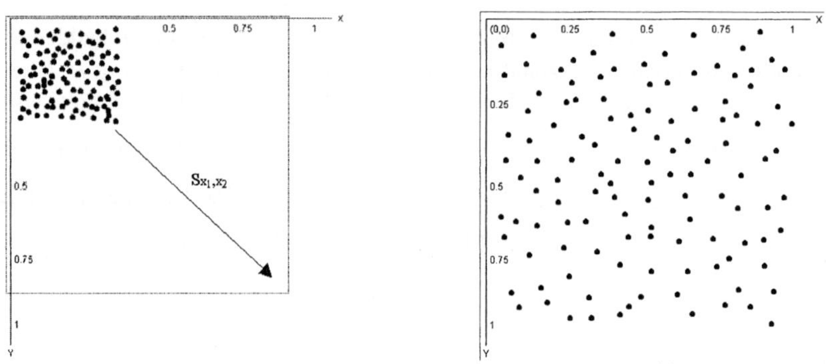

a) b)

Fig. 4. a) Applying to the translated training set scaling factors such that it will be (b) redistributed to the whole 2D space

Finally, each one of the coordinates in the <u>original</u> points of the training set must be transformed in order to be redistributed in the whole unit n-dimensional hypercube $[0,1]^n$ through:

$$x'_i = (x_i - x_{i_{\min}}) \cdot \left(\frac{1}{x'_{i_{\max}}} \right) \qquad 1 \le i \le n$$

4 Image Classification Through 1-Dimensional Kohonen Networks

4.1 Representing Images Through Vectors in $\Re^n$

Let m_1 (rows) and m_2 (columns) be the dimensions of a two-dimensional image. Let $n = m_1 \cdot m_2$. Each pixel in the image will have associated a 3-dimensional point (x_i, y_i, RGB_i) such that $RGB_i \in [0, 16777216]$, $1 \le i \le n$, where RGB_i is the color value associated to the i-th pixel (assuming that the color of pixels are based in the color model RGB). The color values of the pixels will be normalized such that they will be in [0.0, 1.0] through the transformation:

$$normalized\_RGB_i = \frac{RGB_i}{16777216}$$

Basically, we will define a vector in the n-Dimensional space by concatenating the m_l rows in the image considering for each pixel its normalized color RGB value. By this way each image is now associated to a vector in the n-dimensional Euclidean space. Because of the color values normalization the scalars in such vectors will be in [0.1]. By this way, a set of training images to be applied in a Kohonen Network will be embedded in an unit n-Dimensional hypercube once they have been transformed to their respective associated vectors.

4.2 Classifications Results

Our training set contains 148 images selected from *CENAPRED* [3] files. These images represent some of the Popocatépetl volcano fumaroles during the year 2003. The volcano is located in the limits of Puebla state in México; and it is active and under monitoring since 1997. The selected images have an original resolution of 640×480 pixels and 24-bits color under format compression JPG.

We have implemented three 1-Dimensional Kohonen Networks with different topologies (in each case, we applied an scaling to the 148 original images):

- Network Topology τ_0:
  - Images Resolution: 112×64
  - Input Neurons: $n = 112 \times 64 = 7{,}168$
  - Output Neurons (classes): $m = 20$
  - Presentations: $T = 10$
- Network Topology τ_1:
  - Images Resolution: 56×32
  - Input Neurons: $n = 56 \times 32 = 1{,}792$
  - Output Neurons (classes): $m = 30$
  - Presentations: $T = 1{,}000$
- Network Topology τ_2:
  - Images Resolution: 260×180
  - Input Neurons: $n = 260 \times 180 = 46800$
  - Output Neurons (classes): $m = 25$
  - Presentations: $T = 500$

The set of 148 training points (images) were presented the number of times according to the corresponding topologies. The training procedures were applied according to section 2. All the weights vectors' were initialized to 0.5.

Figure 5 shows the classification of the training images using the three proposed topologies. In the figures are also presented the distribution of the 148 training images in each one of the classes. Table 1 presents some images that are representative of each class in Network Topology τ_0 (these images were selected from each class in an arbitrary way).

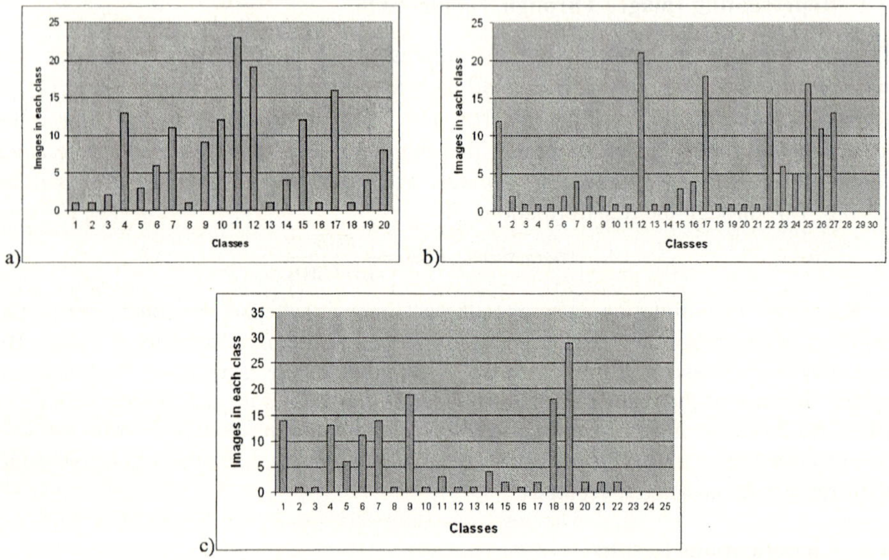

Fig. 5. Classification of the 148 training images according to Network Topology a) τ_0, b) τ_1 and c) τ_2

4.3 Intensity Based Classification vs. Classification Based in the Topology of Pixels in the Images

One of the problems to consider is related with the question if our implementations of the Kohonen Networks classify according to the total intensity color of an image or well, if they classify according to the connectivity, i.e. the topology, between the pixels that compose an image. In order to give arguments that support our hypothesis that our procedures share the classification according to the topology of the pixels in the images, we have developed two approaches:

- An approach (section 3.3.1) based in a classification of the training images but when their pixels are attached to an specific permutation. If our implementation classify by color intensity, then we can expect a distribution of the images in the classes which would be similar to the distributions presented in Figures 5.

Table 1. Representative images of each class in Network Topology τ_0

- An approach (section 3.3.2) based in the distances between the weights vectors associated to each output neuron. The clusters themselves are 2D color images if we apply in an inverse way the procedure described in section 3.1. For example, see in the Table 2 the 2D images corresponding to the clusters in Network Topology τ_2. In this approach we will use an additional metric that guarantee the comparison of images only by their color intensity. According to the Kohonen Network training process, the clusters (classes representatives) have been distributed uniformly in an unit n-Dimensional hypercube. Such distribution implies, in an implicit way, the fact that each cluster has itself specific characteristics that allow to distinguish its respective class among other classes. By applying the new proposed metric, we can expect that the distances provided by it indicate us a considerable proximity between clusters, hence, they have similar color intensities. Moreover, this last result should establish a considerable distinct distribution respect to the distribution indicated by the Euclidean metric. In the case that our Kohonen Network classify only by color intensity, then the clusters distribution reported by both metrics should be similar.

4.3.1 Permutation of Pixels in the Training Images

(See Table 3 for examples of the permutations we describe here.)

- P_1: Random permutation of all the pixels in the image.
- P_2: Division of the image in 25 rectangular regions and random permutation of the pixels in each region.

Table 2. Visualization of clusters in Network Topology τ_2

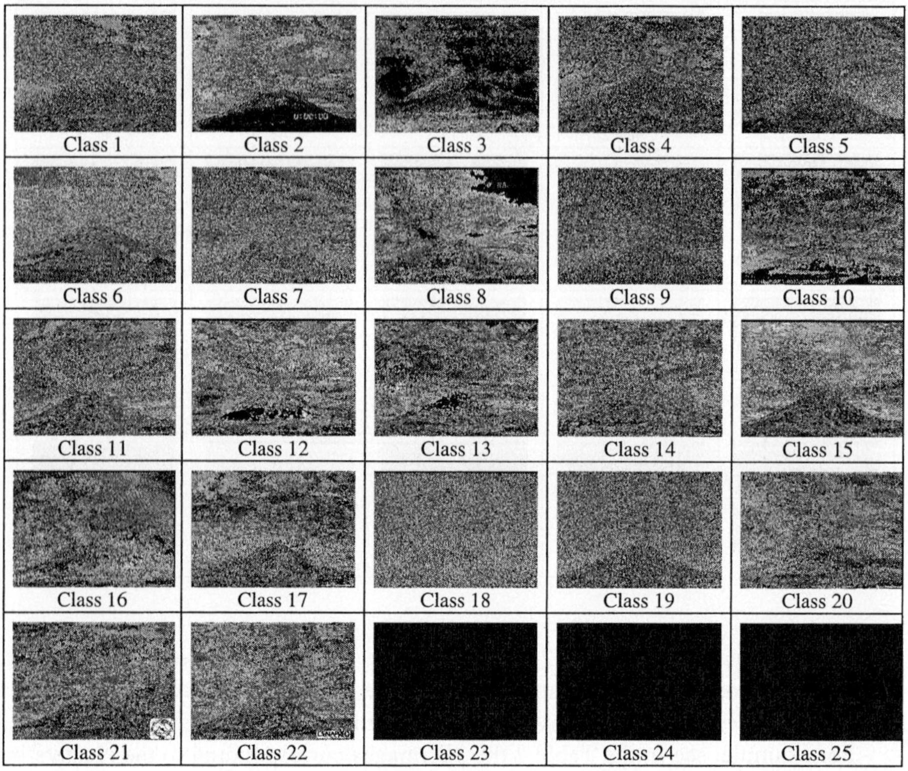

- P_3: Division of the image in 25 rectangular regions and random permutation of such regions.
- P_4: Division of the image in 25 rectangular regions and random permutation of the pixels in each region and random permutation of the regions.

Consider to network topology τ_1. In the cases of permutations P_1, P_3 and P_4, we can observe in their corresponding charts (Table 4) the fact that once the training process has finished two classes grouped the 80% of training images. The case of permutation

Table 3. Permutations of pixels applied to the training images

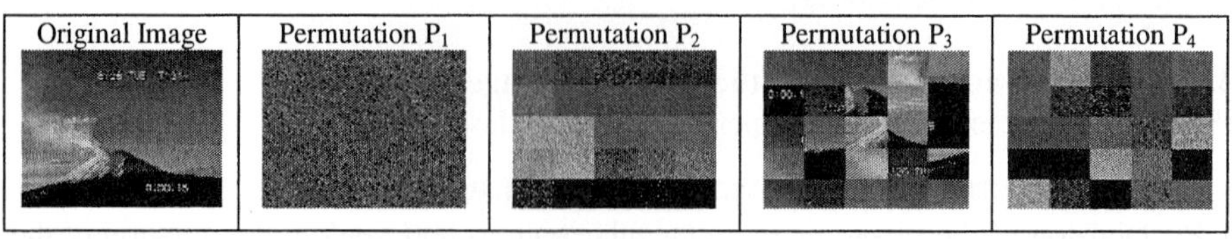

Table 4. Distribution of the training images in the classes of network topology τ_1

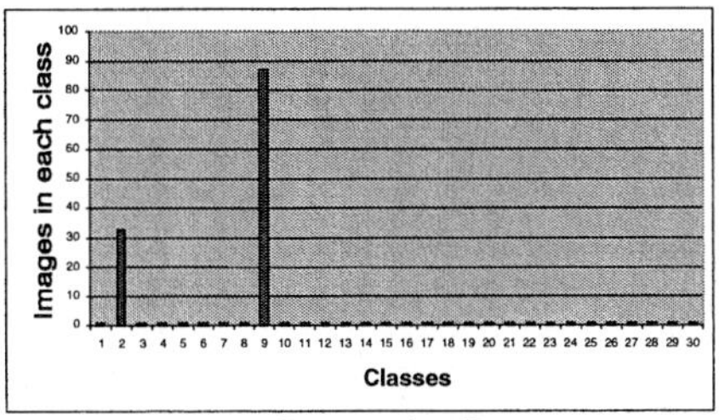 Permutation P_1	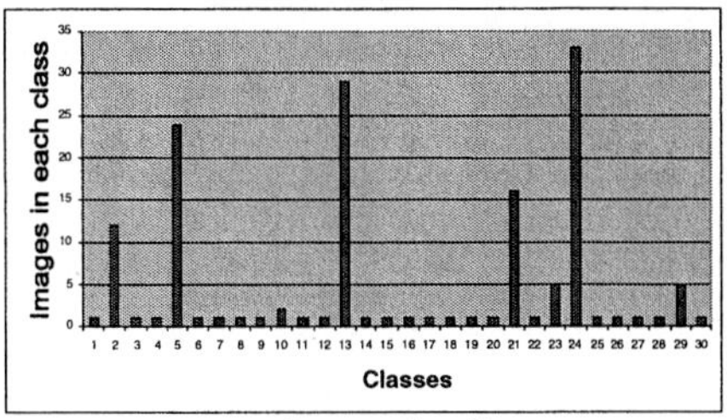 Permutation P_2
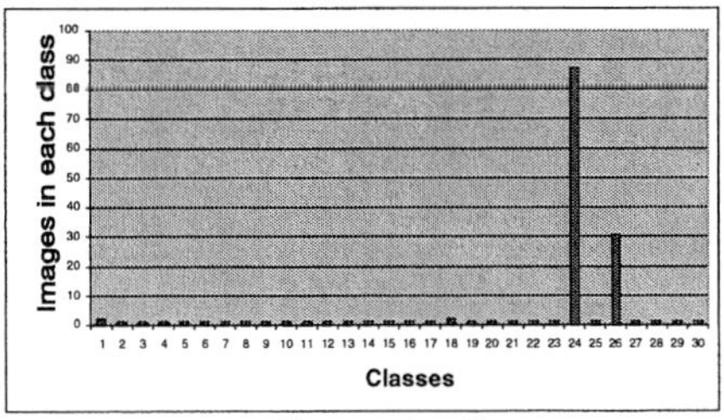 Permutation P_3	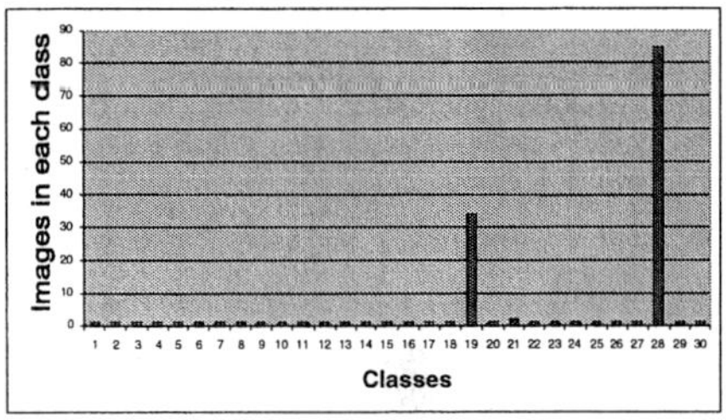 Permutation P_4

τ_2 differs from the others by the property that the 80% of training images is grouped in seven classes with more than 5 images each one. From an informal point of view, permutation P_2 can be considered visually as a permutation that preserved, compared with the remaining permutations, the connectivity of the pixels respect to the original training images. This is because if we increment the number of rectangular regions (more regions than those in permutation P_2) and permute its corresponding pixels, as the number of regions increase the corresponding image will approximate to the original image. In fact, the original images can be seen as images divided in regions with only one pixel each one, obviously, the permutation of the pixel in each region leave to the image in its original state.

4.3.2 Analysis Based in an Additional Metric over $\Re^+$

Definition 1 ([1] & [2]): Let x, y ∈ $\Re^+$. Let ρ be the function described as

$$\rho(x,y)=\begin{cases}1-\dfrac{x}{y} & if \quad x<y\\ 1-\dfrac{y}{x} & if \quad y<x\\ 0 & if \quad x=y\end{cases}$$

We will show in Theorem 1 that such function is a metric over $\Re^+$. Appendix A contains the propositions that support our proof.

Theorem 1: Let x, y ∈ $\Re^+$. Therefore ρ(x, y) is a metric over $\Re^+$.
Proof: Let x, y, z ∈ $\Re^+$.

- We will show that $\rho(x, y) = \rho(y, x)$.
  - If $x = y \Rightarrow \rho(x, y) = 0 = \rho(y, x)$.
  - If $x < y \Rightarrow \rho(x, y) = 1 - x/y = \rho(y, x)$.
  - If $y < x \Rightarrow \rho(x, y) = 1 - y/x = \rho(y, x)$.

  $\therefore (\forall x, y \in \Re^+)(\rho(x, y) = \rho(y, x))$
- By definition of ρ: $(\forall x \in \Re^+)(\rho(x, x) = 0)$.
- By definition of ρ, if $\rho(x, y) = 0 \Rightarrow x = y$.
- By property A.1, $(\forall x, y \in \Re^+)(\rho(x, y) \geq 0)$.
- We will show that $\rho(x, z) \leq \rho(x, y) + \rho(y, z)$.
  - If $x = y = z \Rightarrow \rho(x, z) = 0 \leq \rho(x, y) + \rho(y, z) = 0$
  - If $x = z, x \neq y \Rightarrow \rho(x, z) = 0 \leq \rho(x, y) + \rho(y, z)$
  - If $x = y, x \neq z \Rightarrow \rho(x, z) = \rho(y, z)$
  - If $y = z, x \neq y \Rightarrow \rho(x, z) = \rho(x, y)$
  - If $x < y < z \Rightarrow$ By lemma A.1, $\rho(x, z) < \rho(x, y) + \rho(y, z)$
  - If $x < z < y \Rightarrow$ By lemma A.2, $\rho(x, z) < \rho(x, y) + \rho(y, z)$
  - If $z < x < y \Rightarrow$ By lemma A.3, $\rho(x, z) < \rho(x, y) + \rho(y, z)$
  - If $z < y < x \Rightarrow$ By lemma A.4, $\rho(x, z) < \rho(x, y) + \rho(y, z)$
  - If $y < x < z \Rightarrow$ By lemma A.5, $\rho(x, z) < \rho(x, y) + \rho(y, z)$
  - If $y < z < x \Rightarrow$ By lemma A.6, $\rho(x, z) < \rho(x, y) + \rho(y, z)$

  $\therefore (\forall x, y, z \in \Re^+)(\rho(x, z) \leq \rho(x, y) + \rho(y, z))$

$\therefore$ ρ is a metric over $\Re^+$. ◻

Let I be an image. We know that each one of its pixels p_i will have associated a vector (x_i, y_i, RGB_i), $i \in [1, n]$, $RGB_i \in [0, 16777216]$. Lets assume that the dimensions of each pixel are equal to one. We will define to the Total Intensity of I, denoted by T(I), as follows:

$$T(I) = \sum_{i=1}^{n} RGB_i$$

Let I_A and I_B two images with the same geometrical dimensions. Let $T(I_A)$ and $T(I_B)$ their corresponding Total Intensities. Because $T(I_A), T(I_B) \in \Re^+$ we can determine its distance through the metric ρ.

Now, we will define the similarity between images I_A and I_B according to the value of $\rho(T(I_A), T(I_B))$. Let $0 \leq \varepsilon < 1$ be an arbitrary value such that we will establish

$$I_A \text{ is similar to } I_B \Leftrightarrow \rho(T(I_A), T(I_B)) < \varepsilon$$

A classification based in metric ρ will not take in account the connectivity between the pixels in the images. For example, for the images presented in Figure 6 we have that $\rho(T(I_A), T(I_B)) = 0$.

The Kohonen Network we implemented uses as part of its processes of training and classification the Euclidean metric over $\Re^n$. Because each one of the representatives of the classes (clusters) in the network are themselves vectors in $\Re^n$, then we can determine the Euclidean distance between any pair of clusters.

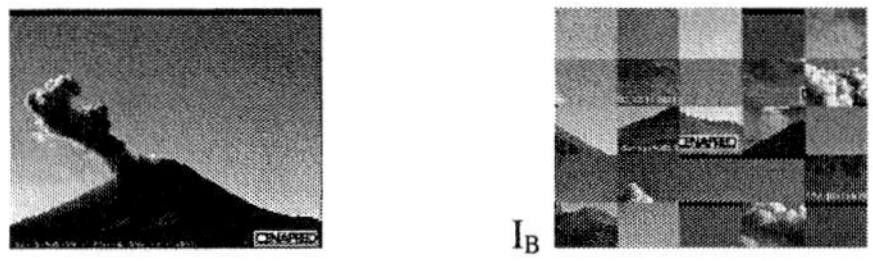

I_A I_B

Fig. 6. An example where $\rho(T(I_A), T(I_B)) = 0$. I_B is image I_A with permutation P_3.

We will define a false color map that will represent the distribution of the clusters in the subspace $[0, 1]^n$. The maximal Euclidean distance between any two clusters will be $d_{\max} = \sqrt{n}$ while in the other hand the minimal distance will be $d_{min} = 0$. Every Euclidean distance between two clusters will be associated with a color in the grayscale through $\frac{d}{d_{\max}} \cdot 256$. By this way if $d = 0$ then it will have associated the black color while if $d = d_{max}$ then it will have associated the white color.

Moreover, we will define a false color map that represent the distances between the clusters in the subspace $[0, 1]^n$ under our metric ρ. For any clusters a and b, $\rho(a, b)$ will be associated with the grayscale through $\rho(a, b) \cdot 256$. If $\rho(a, b) = 0$ then $a = b$ and therefore such distance will be represented through the black color. On the other hand, $\rho(a, b) \cdot 256 \to 256$ while $\rho(a, b) \to 1$.

Consider Network Topology τ_0. The false color maps associated to the distances between the clusters under the Euclidean metric and ρ metric are presented in Table 5. It can be observed in the map under metric ρ that the 47% of the distances between clusters are less than 0.20. This indicates that according this metric an important

Table 5. False Color Maps that show the distances between clusters in Network Topology τ_0

Distances according to Euclidean Metric

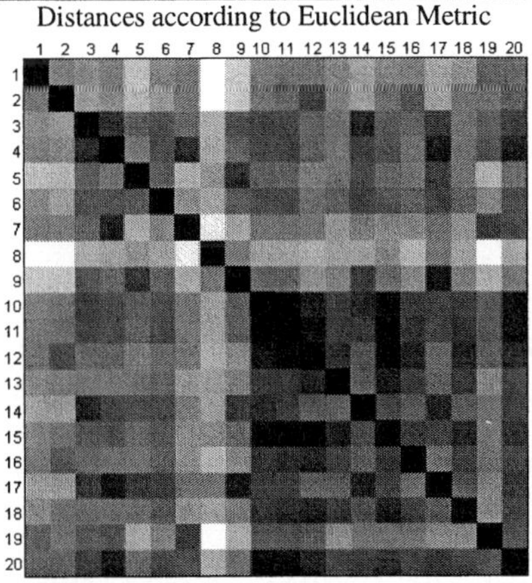

Distances according to ρ Metric

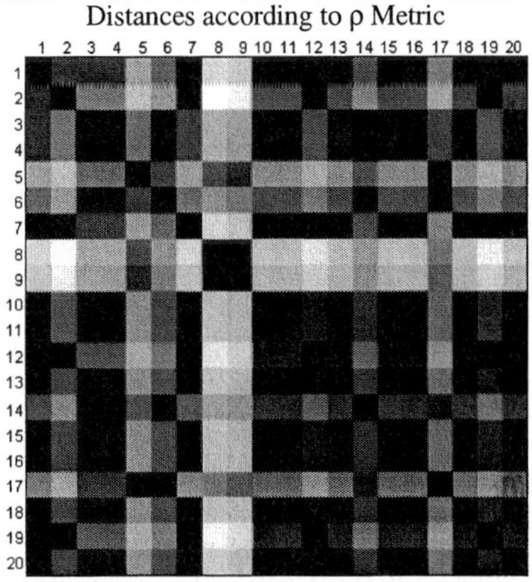

In both maps:

Maximum Distance

Minimum Distance

number of clusters are similar with $\varepsilon = 0.20$ (in fact the mean distance in this metric was 0.2542 with variance 0.0373 and standard deviation 0.1933). In the other hand, we have that for topology τ_0 $n = 7168$, hence, $d_{max}=\sqrt{7168} = 84.66$. Analogously we consider the number of distances whose value is less than the 20% of d_{max}. By this way, the map based in the Euclidean metric reports that only the 19% of the distances between clusters are lower than 16.9328 (the mean distance under Euclidean metric was 24.2119 with variance 94.7531 and standard deviation 9.7341). In conclusion, both metrics report different distributions of the clusters which makes visible the differences between a classification based in topology of pixels, by the Kohonen Network, and a classification based in color intensities of the images.

5 Conclusions

According to the results provided by the approaches discussed in sections 3.3.1 and 3.3.2 we can infer that image classification based in a 1-Dimensional Kohonen Network groups an images set according to features based in the connectivity between pixels, i.e., their topology. As part of our future work, we will analyze in a detailed way the images contained in each one of our classes and their respective neighborhoods in order to determine some features shared by these images. By identifying these features, in our images domain, we will analyze the possible application of our classifications in the prediction of events of Popocatépetl volcano.

Another objective, with respect to future work, considers the comparison of our presented procedures, based in a non-supervised classification, with other techniques that allow the automated retrieval and classification of images such as Case Based Reasoning (CBR) and Image Based Reasoning (IBR).

References

1. Aguilera, Antonio; Lázzeri Menéndez, Santos Gerardo & Pérez-Aguila, Ricardo. Image Based Reasoning Applied to the Comparison of the Popocatépetl Volcano's Fumaroles. Proceedings of the IX Ibero-American Workshops on Artificial Intelligence, Iberamia 2004, pp. 3-8. ISBN: 968-863-783-6. November 22 to 23, 2004. National Institute of Astrophysics, Optics and Electronics (INAOE), Puebla, México.
2. Aguilera, Antonio; Lázzeri Menéndez, Santos Gerardo & Pérez-Aguila, Ricardo. A Procedure for Comparing Color 2-Dimensional Images Through their Extrusions to the 5-Dimensional Colorspace. Proceedings of the 15th International Conference on Electronics, Communications, and Computers CONIELECOMP 2005, pp. 300-305. Published by the IEEE Computer Society. ISBN: 0-7695-2283-1. February 28 to March 2, 2005. Puebla, México.
3. CENAPRED (Centro Nacional de Prevención de Desastres), México. Web Site: http://www.cenapred.unam.mx (April 2003).
4. Davalo, Eric & Naïm, Patrick. Neural Networks. The Macmillan Press Ltd, 1992.
5. Hilera, José & Martínez, Victor. Redes Neuronales Artificiales. Alfaomega, 2000. México.

6. Pérez Aguila, Ricardo. The Extreme Vertices Model in the 4D space and its Applications in the Visualization and Analysis of Multidimensional Data Under the Context of a Geographical Information System. Thesis for the Master's Degree in Sciences. Universidad de las Américas - Puebla. Puebla, México, 2003.
7. Ritter, Helge; Martinetz, Thomas & Schulten, Klaus. Neural Computation and Self-Organizing Maps, An introduction. Addison-Wesley Publishing Company, 1992.
8. Zerubia, Josiane; Yu, Shan; Kato, Zoltan & Berthod, Mark. Bayesian Image Classification Using Markov Random Fields. Image and Vision Computing, 14:285-295, 1996.

Appendix A: Properties of ρ Function

Property A.1: Let $x, y \in \Re^+$. Therefore $\rho(x, y) \in [0, 1)$.

Proof: We consider three cases,

- If $x = y \Rightarrow \rho(x, y) = 0$.
- If $x < y \Rightarrow 1 > x/y > 0 \Rightarrow -1 < -x/y < 0 \Rightarrow 0 < 1 - x/y < 1 \Rightarrow 0 < \rho(x, y) < 1$.
- If $x > y \Rightarrow 1 > y/x > 0 \Rightarrow -1 < -y/x < 0 \Rightarrow 0 < 1 - y/x < 1 \Rightarrow 0 < \rho(x, y) < 1$.

$\therefore (\forall x, y \in \Re^+)(\rho(x, y) \in [0,1))$. $\square$

Lemma A.1: Let $x, y, z \in \Re^+$ such that $x < y < z$. Then $\rho(x, z) < \rho(x, y) + \rho(y, z)$.

Proof: By definition 1 and considering the established hypothesis we have that

$$\rho(x, y) = 1 - x/y \qquad \rho(y, z) = 1 - y/z \qquad \rho(x, z) = 1 - x/z$$

Because by hypothesis, $x < y \Rightarrow x/z < y/z \Rightarrow -x/z > -y/z \Rightarrow 1 - x/z > 1 - y/z$
$\Rightarrow \rho(x, z) > \rho(y, z)$.

Because by hypothesis, $y < z \Rightarrow x/y > x/z \Rightarrow -x/y < -x/z \Rightarrow 1 - x/y < 1 - x/z$
$\Rightarrow \rho(x, y) < \rho(x, z)$.

Due to $1 > \rho(x, z) > \rho(y, z)$ and $1 > \rho(x, z) > \rho(x, y)$
$\Rightarrow 2 > 2\rho(x, z) > \rho(x, y) + \rho(y, z) = 2 - (x/y + y/z) \Rightarrow 2 > 2 - (x/y + y/z)$
$\Rightarrow 1 > 1 - (x/y + y/z) \Rightarrow 2 > \rho(x, y) + \rho(y, z) > 1 > 1 - (x/y + y/z)$
$\Rightarrow \rho(x, y) + \rho(y, z) > 1 \Rightarrow \rho(x, y) + \rho(y, z) > 1 > \rho(x, z)$.
$\therefore \rho(x, z) < \rho(x, y) + \rho(y, z)$. $\square$

Lemma A.2: Let $x, y, z \in \Re^+$ such that $x < z < y$. Then $\rho(x, z) < \rho(x, y) + \rho(y, z)$.

Proof: By definition 1 and considering the established hypothesis we have that

$$\rho(x, y) = 1 - x/y \qquad \rho(y, z) = 1 - z/y \qquad \rho(x, z) = 1 - x/z$$

Because by hypothesis, $x < z \Rightarrow x/y < z/y \Rightarrow -x/y > -z/y \Rightarrow 1 - x/y > 1 - z/y$
$\Rightarrow \rho(x, y) > \rho(y, z)$.

Because by hypothesis, $z < y \Rightarrow x/z > x/y \Rightarrow -x/z < -x/y \Rightarrow 1 - x/z < 1 - x/y$
$\Rightarrow \rho(x, z) < \rho(x, y)$.

Due to $\rho(x, z) < \rho(x, y)$ and $\rho(y, z) < \rho(x, y)$ $\therefore$ $\rho(x, z) < \rho(x, y) + \rho(y, z)$. $\square$

Lemma A.3: Let $x, y, z \in \Re^+$ such that $z < x < y$. Then $\rho(x, z) < \rho(x, y) + \rho(y, z)$.

Proof: By definition 1 and considering the established hypothesis we have that

$$\rho(x, y) = 1 - x/y \qquad \rho(y, z) = 1 - z/y \qquad \rho(x, z) = 1 - z/x$$

Because by hypothesis, $x < y \Rightarrow z/x > z/y \Rightarrow -z/x < -z/y \Rightarrow 1 - z/x < 1 - z/y$
$\Rightarrow \rho(x, z) < \rho(y, z) \Rightarrow \rho(x, z) < \rho(y, z) < \rho(x, y) + \rho(y, z)$
$\therefore \rho(x, z) < \rho(x, y) + \rho(y, z)$. $\square$

Lemma A.4: Let x, y, z $\in \Re^+$ such that $z < y < x$. Then $\rho(x, z) < \rho(x, y) + \rho(y, z)$.

Proof: By definition 1 and considering the established hypothesis we have that

$$\rho(x, y) = 1 - y/x \qquad \rho(y, z) = 1 - z/y \qquad \rho(x, z) = 1 - z/x$$

Because by hypothesis, $z < y \Rightarrow z/x < y/x \Rightarrow -z/x > -y/x \Rightarrow 1 - z/x > 1 - y/x$
$\Rightarrow \rho(x, z) > \rho(x, y)$.

Because by hypothesis, $y < x \Rightarrow z/y > z/x \Rightarrow -z/y < -z/x \Rightarrow 1 - z/y < 1 - z/x$
$\Rightarrow \rho(y, z) < \rho(x, z)$.

Due to $1 > \rho(x, z) > \rho(y, z)$ and $1 > \rho(x, z) > \rho(x, y)$
$\Rightarrow 2 > 2\rho(x, z) > \rho(x, y) + \rho(y, z) = 2 - (y/x + z/y) \Rightarrow 2 > 2 - (y/x + z/y)$
$\Rightarrow 1 > 1 - (y/x + z/y) \Rightarrow 2 > \rho(x, y) + \rho(y, z) > 1 > 1 - (y/x + z/y)$
$\Rightarrow \rho(x, y) + \rho(y, z) > 1 \Rightarrow \rho(x, y) + \rho(y, z) > 1 > \rho(x, z)$
$\therefore \rho(x, z) < \rho(x, y) + \rho(y, z)$. ◻

Lemma A.5: Let x, y, z $\in \Re^+$ such that $y < x < z$. Then $\rho(x, z) < \rho(x, y) + \rho(y, z)$.

Proof: By definition 1 and considering the established hypothesis we have that

$$\rho(x, y) = 1 - y/x \qquad \rho(y, z) = 1 - y/z \qquad \rho(x, z) = 1 - x/z$$

Because by hypothesis, $y < x \Rightarrow y/z < x/z \Rightarrow -y/z > -x/z \Rightarrow 1 - y/z > 1 - x/z$
$\Rightarrow \rho(y, z) > \rho(x, z) \Rightarrow \rho(x, z) < \rho(y, z) < \rho(x, y) + \rho(y, z)$
$\therefore \rho(x, z) < \rho(x, y) + \rho(y, z)$. ◻

Lemma A.6: Let x, y, z $\in \Re^+$ such that $y < z < x$. Then $\rho(x, z) < \rho(x, y) + \rho(y, z)$.

Proof: By definition 1 and considering the established hypothesis we have that

$$\rho(x, y) = 1 - y/x \qquad \rho(y, z) = 1 - y/z \qquad \rho(x, z) = 1 - z/x$$

Because by hypothesis, $y < z \Rightarrow y/x < z/x \Rightarrow -y/x > -z/x \Rightarrow 1 - y/x > 1 - z/x$
$\Rightarrow \rho(x, y) > \rho(x, z) \Rightarrow \rho(x, z) < \rho(x, y) < \rho(x, y) + \rho(y, z)$
$\therefore \rho(x, z) < \rho(x, y)$. ◻

Data Dependent Wavelet Filtering for Lossless Image Compression

Oleksiy Pogrebnyak, Pablo Manrique Ramírez,
Luis Pastor Sanchez Fernandez, and Roberto Sánchez Luna

Instituto Politecnico Nacional, CIC-IPN, Av.Juan de Dios Batiz s/n,
Colonia Nueva Industrial Vallejo, C.P. 07738, Mexico D.F.
olek@pollux.cic.ipn.mx, pmanriq@cic.ipn.mx

Abstract. A data dependent wavelet transform based on the modified lifting scheme is presented. The algorithm is based on the wavelet filters derived from a generalized lifting scheme. The proposed framework for the lifting scheme permits to obtain easily different wavelet FIR filter coefficients in the case of the (~N, N) lifting. To improve the performance of the lifting filters the presented technique additionally realizes IIR filtering by means of the feedback to the already calculated wavelet coefficients. The perfect image restoration in this case is obtained employing the particular features of the lifting scheme. Changing wavelet FIR filter order and/or FIR and IIR coefficients, one can obtain the filter frequency response that match better to the image data than the standard lifting filters, resulting in higher data compression rate. The designed algorithm was tested on different images. The obtained simulation results show that the proposed method performs better in data compression for various images in comparison to the standard technique resulting in significant savings in compressed data length.

Keywords: image processing, wavelets, lifting scheme, adaptive compression

1 Introduction

In the past decade, the wavelet transform has become a popular, powerful tool for different image and signal processing applications such as noise cancellation, data compression, feature detection, etc. Meanwhile, the aspect of wavelet decomposition/reconstruction implementation, especially for image compression applications, now continues to be under consideration.

The first algorithm of the fast discrete wavelet transform (DWT) was proposed by S.G.Mallat [1]. This algorithm is based on the fundamental work of Vetterli [2] on signal/image subband decomposition by 1-D quadrature-mirror filters (QMF), and orthonormal wavelet bases proposed by I.Daubechies [3]. Then, W.Sweldens [4] proposed the lifting scheme based on polyphase factorization of known wavelets that now is widely used (for example, in JPEG2000 standard) for lossless image/signal compression based on DWT. To enhance the energy compaction characteristics of the DWT, different methods basing on an adaptive lifting scheme [4 - 8], principal

M. Lazo and A. Sanfeliu (Eds.): CIARP 2005, LNCS 3773, pp. 285 – 294, 2005.

components filter banks [9] and signal-dependent wavelet/subband filter banks [10-12] were developed recently.

In this paper, we present an algorithm for lossless image compression that is based on a subclass IIR wavelet filters. These filters are derived from the generalized FIR wavelet lifting filters [8, 13] introducing poles in the prototype FIR filters. Performing causal filtering at the analysis and anticausal filtering of the time-inverted data at the synthesis stages, one can obtain the perfect image restoration with the presented IIR filters. Varying the order of the filter and the filter coefficients depending on the image data statistical/spectral properties, the decompositions can be optimized to achieve a minimum of the entropy in the wavelet domain.

2 Generalization of the Lifting Scheme

The lifting scheme [3] is widely used in the wavelet based image analysis. Its main advantages are: the reduced number of calculations; less memory requirements; the possibility of the operation with integer numbers. The lifting scheme consists of the following basic operations: splitting, prediction and update.

Splitting is sometimes referred to as the lazy wavelet. This operation splits the original signal $\{x\}$ into odd and even samples:

$$s_i = x_{2i}, \quad d_i = x_{2i+1}. \tag{1}$$

Prediction, or the dual lifting. This operation at the level k calculates the wavelet coefficients, or the details $\{d^{(k)}\}$ as the error in predicting $\{d^{(k-1)}\}$ from $\{s^{(k-1)}\}$:

$$d_i^{(k)} = d_i^{(k-1)} + \sum_{j=-\tilde{N}}^{\tilde{N}} p_j \cdot s_{i+j}^{(k-1)}, \tag{2}$$

where $\{p\}$ are coefficients of the wavelet-based high-pass FIR filter and $\tilde{N}$ is the prediction filter order.

Update, or the primal lifting. This operation combines $\{s^{(k-1)}\}$ and $\{d^{(k)}\}$, and consists of low-pass FIR filtering to obtain a coarse approximation of the original signal $\{x\}$:

$$s_i^{(k)} = s_i^{(k-1)} + \sum_{j=-N}^{N} u_j \cdot d_{i+j}^{(k)}, \tag{3}$$

where $\{u\}$ are coefficients of the wavelet-based low-pass FIR filter and N is the prediction filter order.

The inverse transform is straightforward: first, the signs of FIR filter coefficients $\{u\}$ and $\{p\}$ are switched; the inverse update followed by inverse prediction is calculated. Finally, the odd and even data samples are merged.

A fresh look at the lifting scheme first was done in [13], where the FIR filters that participate in the prediction and update operation are described in the domain of Z-transform. According to this approach, the transfer function of the prediction FIR filter can be formulated as follows [8]:

$$H_p(z)=1+p_0\left(z+z^{-1}\right)+p_1\left(z^3+z^{-3}\right)+\ldots+p_{\tilde{N}-1}\left(z^{2\tilde{N}-1}+z^{-2\tilde{N}+1}\right), \tag{4}$$

The $H_p(z)$ must has zero at $\omega=0$, i.e., at $z=1$. It can be easily found [5] that this condition is satisfied when

$$\sum_{i=0}^{\tilde{N}-1} p_i = -\frac{1}{2}. \tag{5}$$

When the condition (5) is satisfied, $H_p(-1)=2$ and $H_p(0)=1$ that means the prediction filter has gain 2 at $\omega=\pi$ and unit gain at $\omega=\frac{\pi}{2}$.

Following this approach, the transfer function for update filter can be obtained in the terms of $H_p(z)$ [8]:

$$H_u(z)=1+H_p(z)\left\{u_0\left(z+z^{-1}\right)+u_1\left(z^3+z^{-3}\right)+..+u_{N-1}\left(z^{2N-1}+z^{-2N+1}\right)\right\}. \tag{6}$$

Similarly, $H_u(z)$ must has zero at $\omega=\pi$, i.e., at $z=-1$. It can be easily found [8, 13] that this condition is satisfied when

$$\sum_{i=0}^{N-1} u_i = \frac{1}{4}. \tag{7}$$

When the condition (7) is satisfied, $H_u(1)=1$ and that means the prediction filter has gain 1 at $\omega=0$.

An elegant conversion of the formulas (5), (7) in the case of (4,4) lifting scheme was proposed in [13] to reduce the degree of freedom in the predictor and update coefficients. With some modifications, the formulas for the wavelet filters coefficients are as follows:

$$p_0=-\frac{128+b_p}{256},\quad p_1=\frac{b_p}{256},\, u_0=\frac{64-b_u}{256},\, u_1=\frac{b_u}{256}, \tag{8}$$

where b_p and b_u are the parameters that control the DWT properties. The correspondences between these control parameters and the conventional (non-lifted) biorthogonal wavelet filters can be found in reference [13].

Using the generalization of the lifting scheme (4)- (7), we found by simulations that the coefficients of the lifting filters of an arbitrary order higher than 4 can be found according to (8) and the recursive formulas [8]:

$$p_2 = -\frac{p_1}{c_p},\, p_1 = p_1 - p_2,\, \ldots,\, p_{\tilde{N}} = -\frac{p_{\tilde{N}-1}}{c_p},\, p_{\tilde{N}-1} = p_{\tilde{N}-1} - p_{\tilde{N}}$$

$$u_2 = \frac{u_1}{c_u},\, u_1 = u_1 - u_2,\, \ldots,\, u_N = \frac{u_{N-1}}{c_u},\, u_{N-1} = u_{N-1} - u_{\tilde{N}} \tag{9}$$

where the parameters c_p, c_u controls the filter characteristics. This way, the lifting wavelet filters of an arbitrary order can be derived [8].

In the formula (8) the parameters b_p, b_u control the width of the transition bands and the new parameters c_p, c_u in (9) control the smoothness of the pass and stop bands to prevent the appearance of the lateral lobes: with greater values of b_p, b_u the values of c_p, c_u tend to be greater [8]. In practice, one can use predictor (4) and update filter (6) with $\tilde{N} = 6$, $N = 6$, $b_p = 20, b_u = 8$, $c_p = 6, c_u = 6$ to achieve narrow transition bands [8].

3 Proposed IIR Lifting Scheme

Considering generalized lifting scheme (4), (6) that these all-zeros systems can be modified to obtain rational transfer functions of a special form containing zeros and poles as following:

$$H_p(z) = \frac{1 + p_0\left(z + z^{-1}\right) + p_1\left(z^3 + z^{-3}\right) + \ldots + p_{\tilde{N}-1}\left(z^{2\tilde{N}-1} + z^{-2\tilde{N}+1}\right)}{1 + a_{2p} z^{-2} + a_{4p} z^{-4} + \ldots}, \tag{10}$$

$$H_u(z) = \frac{1 + H_p(z)\left\{u_0\left(z + z^{-1}\right) + u_1\left(z^3 + z^{-3}\right) + \ldots + u_{N-1}\left(z^{2N-1} + z^{-2N+1}\right)\right\}}{1 + a_{2u} z^{-2} + a_{4u} z^{-4} + \ldots}. \tag{11}$$

In (10), (11) the denominators contain only even powers of z because the outputs of predictor and update stages indirectly realize data subsampling (because of splitting (1)) and the presented transfer function are expressed in terms of input data sampling rate.

A specific condition to lifting predictor is that it must have a fixed gain to fulfill condition (7), i.e., to prevent bias in the output of the update filer at $\omega = 0$. This can be done introducing normalization by factor $1 - a_{2p} - a_{4p} - \ldots$ in (11):

$$H_u(z) = \frac{1 + H_p(z)\left\{u_0\left(z + z^{-1}\right) + u_1\left(z^3 + z^{-3}\right) + \ldots + u_{N-1}\left(z^{2N-1} + z^{-2N+1}\right)\right\}}{\left(1 - a_{2p} - a_{4p} - \ldots\right)\left(1 + a_{2u} z^{-2} + a_{4u} z^{-4} + \ldots\right)}. \tag{12}$$

Another problem arises when implementing inverse transform with IIR lifting. The wavelet analysis/synthesis filters must provide the perfect restoration of the original data that is especially important for lossless data compression. In the traditional dyadic wavelet decompositions/restorations technique, special care is took to design orthonormal filter banks where each filter satisfies Nyquist constraint $\left|H_k\left(e^{j\omega}\right)\right|_{\downarrow 2}=1$ [9]. In difference, the lifting scheme has a potential to design biorthogonal IIR wavelet filters in simpler way: in the restoration stage, one can use inverse predictor and inverse update filter that operates upon rearranging the input signal elements (wavelet coefficients) backward

$$\mathbf{s}^{BT}(n)=[s(n-N),s(n-N-1),...,s(0)],$$
$$\mathbf{d}^{BT}(n)=[d(n-N),d(n-N-1),...,d(0)]. \tag{13}$$

and then filtering them with the inverse filters

$$H_u(z)=\frac{1-H_p(z)\left\{u_0\left(z+z^{-1}\right)+u_1\left(z^3+z^{-3}\right)+..+u_{N-1}\left(z^{2N-1}+z^{-2N+1}\right)\right\}}{\left(1+a_{2p}+a_{4p}+...\right)\left(1-a_{2u}z^{-2}-a_{4u}z^{-4}-...\right)}, \tag{14}$$

$$H_p(z)=\frac{1-p_0\left(z+z^{-1}\right)-p_1\left(z^3+z^{-3}\right)-...-p_{\tilde{N}-1}\left(z^{2\tilde{N}-1}+z^{-2\tilde{N}+1}\right)}{1-a_{2p}z^{-2}-a_{4p}z^{-4}-...}, \tag{15}$$

for synthesis and next time performing rearranging of the data: $\{\cdot\}^B$.

Next, we want to proceed with integer calculus whereas it is possible. For this purpose, we use normalized coefficients a_{2p}, a_{2u} as in (8):

$$a_{ip}=\frac{A_{ip}}{256},\ a_{iu}=\frac{A_{iu}}{256}. \tag{16}$$

Taking into account all before mentioned results and restrictions, we can formulate the integer-to-integer IIR lifting steps as following.

Analysis stage:

- prediction:

$$d_i^{(k)}=d_i^{(k-1)}+\left\lfloor\frac{A_{2p}d_{i-2}^{(k-1)}+A_{2p}d_{i-4}^{(k-1)}+(b_p-128)\left(s_{i-1}^{(k-1)}+s_{i+1}^{(k-1)}\right)+b_p\left(s_{i-3}^{(k-1)}+s_{i+3}^{(k-1)}\right)+...}{256}\right\rfloor \tag{17}$$

- update:

$$s_i^{(k)}=s_i^{(k-1)}+\left\lfloor\frac{A_{2u}s_{i-2}^{(k-1)}+A_{4u}s_{i-4}^{(k-1)}}{256}+\frac{(64-b_u)\left(d_{i-1}^{(k)}+d_{i+1}^{(k)}\right)+b_u\left(d_{i-3}^{(k)}+d_{i+3}^{(k)}\right)+...}{256-A_{2p}-A_{4p}}\right\rfloor \tag{18}$$

Synthesis stage:
- inverse update:

$$s_i^{B(k)} = s_i^{B(k-1)} - \left\lfloor \frac{A_{2u}s_{i-2}^{B(k-1)} + A_{4u}s_{i-4}^{B(k-1)}}{256} + \frac{(64-b_u)\left(d_{i-1}^{B(k-1)} + d_{i+1}^{B(k-1)}\right) + b_u\left(d_{i-3}^{B(k-1)} + d_{i+3}^{B(k-1)}\right) + \ldots}{256 - A_{2p} - A_{4p}} \right\rfloor \quad (19)$$

- inverse prediction:

$$d_i^{B(k)} = d_i^{B(k-1)} - \left\lfloor \frac{A_{2p}d_{i-2}^{B(k-1)} + A_{2p}d_{i-4}^{B(k-1)} + (b_p - 128)\left(s_{i-1}^{B(k)} + s_{i+1}^{B(k)}\right) + b_p\left(s_{i-3}^{B(k)} + s_{i+3}^{B(k)}\right) + \ldots}{256} \right\rfloor \quad (20)$$

In formulas (17)-(18), $\lfloor \cdot \rfloor$ denotes the operation of rounding to the nearest lower integer value.

The coefficients $\{b_p\},\{b_u\}$ are that satisfy to (5), (7). Additionally, $\{b_p\},\{b_u\}$, $\tilde{N}, N$ and especially $\{A_p\},\{A_u\}$ are adjusted in such a manner that the filters (17), (18) match to the spectral properties of the image data to minimize the well known first order entropy of the wavelet coefficients

$$\min_{\{b_p\},\{b_u\},\tilde{N},N,\{A_p\},\{A_u\}} \left\{ H(d) = -\sum_i p_i \log(p_i) \right\} \quad (21)$$

where p_i denotes the probability of the different values of wavelet coefficients d. The problem of optimization can be formulated as the problem to minimize the following errors:

- the square error of prediction

$$\varepsilon_p = \sum_i \left[d_i^{(k)}\right]^2 ; \quad (22)$$

- the square error of "update first" prediction

$$\varepsilon_u = \sum_i \left[\varepsilon_i^u\right]^2 , \quad (23)$$

where $\varepsilon_i^u = s_i^{(k-1)} - \left\lfloor \frac{A_{2u}s_{i-2}^{(k-1)} + A_{4u}s_{i-4}^{(k-1)}}{256} + \frac{(64-b_u)\left(\tilde{d}_{i-1}^{(k)} + \tilde{d}_{i+1}^{(k)}\right) + b_u\left(\tilde{d}_{i-3}^{(k)} + \tilde{d}_{i+3}^{(k)}\right) + \ldots}{256 - A_{2p} - A_{4p}} \right\rfloor$,

and $\tilde{d}_i^{(k)} = d_i^{(k-1)} - \left\lfloor \frac{A_{2p}d_{i-2}^{(k-1)} + A_{2p}d_{i-4}^{(k-1)} + (b_p - 128)\left(s_{i-1}^{(k-1)} + s_{i+1}^{(k-1)}\right) + b_p\left(s_{i-3}^{(k-1)} + s_{i+3}^{(k-1)}\right) + \ldots}{256} \right\rfloor$

is the output of "update first" low-pass filter.

Thus, one can obtain the optimal solution finding

$$\min_{\substack{\{b_p\},\{b_u\},\\ \{A_p\},\{A_u\},\\ \{c_p\},\{c_u\}}} \{\varepsilon_p + \varepsilon_u\}$$

at each level of decomposition. Unfortunately, it is difficult to obtain an analytical solution for the optimal $\{b_p\},\{b_u\}$, $\tilde{N}, N$, $\{A_p\},\{A_u\}$ values due to complexity of the expressions (22), (24).

4 Experimental Results

The described in the previous section algorithm were tested on a set of 512x512 standard images "Lena", "Baboon", "Barbara", "Boats", "Goldhill", "Peppers", "Bridge" shown in Fig. 1 (these images are available, for example, at http://sipi.usc.edu/database/).

Fig. 1. Set of standard test images: "Lena", "Baboon", "Barbara", "Boats", "Goldhill", "Peppers", "Bridge" v

Table 1 presents the entropy values in bits per pixel (bpp) obtained for these images by applying standard lifting decomposition (1) – (3) and CDF(1,1) wavelet (Haar wavelet) with $\tilde{N}=1$, $N=1$, $a=0$, $b=0$, CDF(2,2) wavelet with $\tilde{N}=2$, $N=2$, $a=16$, $b=8$ (this wavelet is used by JPEG2000 for lossless image compression), and IIR lifting (17)-(20) with the same FIR parameters and various $\{A_p\},\{A_u\}$ values. The values of $\{A_p\},\{A_u\}$ are those that minimize the first order entropy of the wavelet coefficients in the first level of decompositions, in higher levels they were chosen to be 0.

Table 2 presents the entropy values in bits per pixel (bpp) obtained for the test images by applying generelazid lifting decomposition (4), (6) and IIR lifting (17)-(20). The values of FIR part of the lifting scheme were varied and the values $\{A_p\},\{A_u\}$ were the same parameters as in the previous simulations (see Table 1).

Analyzing the simulation results presented in Table 1 and Table 2, one can conclude that the proposed IIR lifting transform performs better, providing lower entropy values for all test images in comparison to the FIR lifting. Increasing FIR lifting orders $\tilde{N}, N$ and varying FIR coefficients b_p, b_u, c_p, c_u without using IIR coefficients ($\{A_p\}=\vec{0}, \{A_u\}=\vec{0}$), one can obtain higher data compression. The difference between FIR and IIR performance is small sometimes (for example, for Lena image), but in all cases, the IIR technique gives the best compression results.

Table 1. Entropy values in bpp for different techniques, $\tilde{N}=2$, $N=2$, $b_p=16$, $b_u=8$ in cases of CDF(2,2) and IIR lifting with the correspondent $\{A_p\},\{A_u\}$ values

Technique	Image						
	Baboon	Lena	Barbara	Boat	Bridge	Peppers	Goldhill
CDF(1,1) lifting	6.163	4.405	5.087	5.014	3.789	4.715	4.898
CDF(2,2) Lifting	6.137	4.361	4.940	4.976	3.793	4.711	4.885
IIR Lifting	**6.128**	**4.355**	**4.914**	**4.966**	**3.792**	**4.686**	**4.871**
A_{2p}	19	11	28	-11	0	-26	15
A_{4p}	7	-4	11	-3	0	9	16
A_{2u}	9	3	8	-19	3	5	-2
A_{4u}	-8	0	-8	-3	-5	3	-7

Table 2. Entropy values in bpp for different techniques, $\tilde{N}=8$, $N=8$, $\{A_p\},\{A_u\}$ are those from Table 1, b_p, b_u, c_p, c_u were varied to achieve the minimum bpp

Technique	Image						
	Baboon	Lena	Barbara	Boat	Bridge	Peppers	Goldhill
Generalized lifting	6.134	4.359	4.825	4.972	3.792	4.701	4.885
IIR Lifting	**6.125**	**4.351**	**4.817**	**4.963**	**3.791**	**4.678**	**4.869**
b_p	20	20	29	18	11	9	15
b_u	13	9	18	11	8	11	4
c_p	6	6	2	5	4	4	6
c_u	5	6	2	6	9	6	3

5 Conclusions

The novel algorithm of data-dependent DWT based on the generalized IIR lifting scheme is presented. The proposed algorithm requires only four additional integer sums and one floating point multiplication per pixel in comparison to the standard lifting decomposition. The presented previous results show that the derived algorithm provides lossless image compression and the highest data compression rate comparing to the standard wavelet lifting technique. The simulations were performed for the case when the IIR filtering is applied for the first level of decomposition only and at higher levels the generalized FIR lifting was used, because of the difficulties dealing with finding the optimal filter coefficients. One can expect even better energy compaction, and, thus, higher compression rate with the presented algorithm optimizing the filter coefficients for each wavelet decomposition. This aspect of global/local optimization according to (23), (24) to find the optimal filter coefficients b_p, b_u, c_p, c_u, $\{A_p\}, \{A_u\}$ is a subject of future work.

Acknowledgements

This work was supported by by Instituto Politécnico Nacional as a part of the research project CGPI#20051850.

References

1. S.G.Mallat, A theory for multiresolution signal decomposition: The wavelet representation, *IEEE Trans. Pattern Recognition. Machine Intell., Vol. 11*, No. 7, p.p.674-693, 1989.
2. Martin Vetterli, Multi-dimensional sub-band coding: some theory and algorithms, *Signal Processing, Vol. 6*, pp.97-112, 1984.
3. I.Daubechies, Orthonormal bases of compactly supported wavelets, *Commun. Pure Appl. Math., Vol. 41*, p.p. 909-996, Nov. 1998.
4. W.Sweldens, The lifting scheme: A new philosophy in biorthogonal wavelet constructions, *Wavelet Applications in Signal and Image Processing III, A.F.Laine and M.Unser, editors,Proc. SPIE 2569,* p.p. 68-79, 1995.
5. R.Claypoole, R.Baraniuk, and R.Nowak, Adaptive wavelet transforms via lifting, *Proc. IEEE Int. Conf. Acoust., Speech, and Signal Proc.*, May 1998.
6. G. Piella and H. J. A. M. Heijmans, "An adaptive update lifting scheme with perfect reconstruction," *Proc. ICIP'01*, pp. 190 - 193, October 2001.
7. G.C.K. Abhayaratne, "Spatially adaptive wavelet transforms: An optimal interpolation approach", Third International Workshop on Spectral Methods and Multirate Signal Processing (SMMSP) 2003, pp. 155-162, Barcelona, Spain, 12-13 Sept. 2003.
8. Oleksiy Pogrebnyak, Pablo Manrique Ramírez "Adaptive wavelet transform for image compression applications" Proc. SPIE Vol.5203, Applications of Digital Image Processing XXVI, Andrew G. Tescher Chair/Editor, 5- 8 August 2003, San Diego, USA. p.p. 623-630, ISBN 0-8194-5076-6 , ISSN: 0277-786X.
9. P. P. Vaidyanathan and S. Akkarakaran, ``A review of the theory and applications of principal component filter banks," Applied and Computational Harmonic Analysis (invited paper), vol. 10, no. 3, pp. 254-289, May 2001.
10. J. O. Chapa and R. M. Rao, "Algorithms for designing wavelets to match a specified signal," *IEEE Trans. Signal Processing,* vol. 48, pp. 3395 - 3406, December 2000.
11. P. P. Vaidyanathan, ``Theory of optimal orthonormal subband coders", IEEE Trans. Signal Proc., vol. SP. 46, pp. 1528--1543, June 1998.

12. P. Moulin, M. Anitescu, and K. Ramchandran, "Theory of rate-distortion-optimal, constrained filterbanks--Application to IIR and FIR biorthogonal designs," *IEEE Trans. Signal Processing,* vol. 48, pp. 1120 - 1132, April 2000
13. Hoon Yoo and Jechang Jeong, A Unified Framework for Wavelet Transform Based on The Lifting Scheme, *Proc. of IEEE International Conference on Image Processing ICIP2001*, Tessaloniki, Greece, October 7-10, p.p.793-795, 2001.

A Robust Matching Algorithm Based on Global Motion Smoothness Criterion

Mikhail Mozerov[1] and Vitaly Kober[2]

[1] Institute for Information Transmission Problems of RAS,
19 Bolshoi Karetnii, Moscow, Russia
mozer@iitp.ru
[2] Department of Computer Science, Division of Applied Physics, CICESE,
Km 107 Carretera Tijuana-Ensenada, Ensenada 22860, B.C., México
vkober@cicese.mx

Abstract. A new robust matching algorithm for motion detection and computation of precise estimates of motion vectors of moving objects in a sequence of images is presented. Common matching algorithms of dynamic image analysis usually utilize local smoothness constraints. The proposed method exploits global motion smoothness. The suggested matching algorithm is robust to motion discontinuity as well as to noise degradation of a signal. Computer simulation and experimental results demonstrate an excellent performance of the method in terms of dynamic motion analysis.

1 Introduction

Extraction of motion information is an essential part of any video processing system. Such popular tasks as relative depth from motion, 3-D shape recovery, autonomous vehicle or robot navigation, and moving object detection usually involve various motion analysis techniques. Many techniques analyzing motion from optical flow computation have been proposed in the past two decades [1-7]. However, reliable optical flow estimation remains a difficult problem when smoothness constraint is violated. Furthermore, algorithms based on the optical flow concept are also very sensitive to large values of sought motion vectors (more than one pixel) and to noise degradation of a signal. Among a wide variety of approaches, there exist three main categories of motion estimation methods: gradient-based methods [1], frequency-based methods [2], and matching techniques [4]. In this work we remain in framework of matching concept that aims to solve the correspondence problem. It is well known that the correspondence problem is inherently ambiguous, and some additional information must be added to solve it. Various approaches have been suggested for solving the correspondence problem [8-12]. The identification of correspondence between the same points in consecutive images is often formulated as a local (area-based) optimization problem, or shortest-path technique [9]. On the other hand, the correspondence between the same points in neighbor images can be considered as a global optimization problem [11-12]. So the matching is carried out between 2-D arrays of images. A drawback of this approach is owing to contradictions between the

M. Lazo and A. Sanfeliu (Eds.): CIARP 2005, LNCS 3773, pp. 295 – 301, 2005.

smoothness constraint of motion vectors between adjacent pixels and a real signal discontinuity at borders of object segments. In this paper, the local motion smoothness constraint is replaced by a global motion smoothness criterion. The latter yields a high performance in optical flow based techniques. We suggest a new matching algorithm, which is based on dynamic programming and global smoothness criterion. Computer simulation with various image sequences shows that the proposed algorithm is robust to motion discontinuity and to noise degradation of a signal. Experimental results with real dynamic images illustrate a very good performance of the method in terms of motion vector accuracy.

2 Optical Flow Constraint and Global Optimization Technique

A common assumption in dynamic image analysis is that the intensity of a point keeps constant value along its trajectory. More precisely, let $f(x,y,t)$ denote the intensity of the pixel at the coordinates (x,y) and time t. Starting from the point (x_0,y_0) at time t_0, we define the trajectory of this point in time as $(x_0+u_x\delta t, y_0+u_y\delta t, t_0+\delta t)$ with

$$f(x_0, y_0, t_0) = f(x_0 + u_x\delta t, y_0 + u_y\delta t, t_0 + \delta t), \tag{1}$$

where $u = (u_x(x_0,y_0,t_0), u_x(x_0,y_0,t_0))$ is the velocity vector (called the flow vector) of a point (x_0,y_0) at time t_0 and δt is called the interframe interval.

In motion analysis common algorithms usually work if some conditions are fulfilled. For instance gradient-based methods [1] are subject to that the motion vector $(\delta r_x = u_x\delta t, \delta r_y = u_y\delta t)$ and the interframe interval δt are small. Therefore Taylor's expansion may be applied to Eq. (1),

$$f(x+\delta r_x, y+\delta r_y, t+\delta t) = f(x, y, t) + \frac{\partial f(x, y, t)}{\partial x}\delta r_x + \frac{\partial f(x, y, t)}{\partial y}\delta r_y + \frac{\partial f(x, y, t)}{\partial t}\delta t, \tag{2}$$

and finally

$$\frac{\partial f(x, y, t)}{\partial x}u_x + \frac{\partial f(x, y, t)}{\partial y}u_y + \frac{\partial f(x, y, t)}{\partial t} = 0. \tag{3}$$

Note that Eq. (3) is not sufficient for computing the components of velocity field. Another drawback of optical flow approach is a severe restriction for sought values of motion vectors. In general for a sampled signal (digital image), Eq. (3) holds only if motion vector values equal or less than one pixel (image sampling interval). Actually, the sign "=" in Eq. (3) must be replaced by "≈". This means that the time interval in the most cases is a fixed value.

We propose a new method that is based on matching techniques. With the help of matching techniques Eq. (1) can be rewritten as

$$a(x, y) = g(x + r_x(x, y), y + r_y(x, y)), \tag{4}$$

where *a(x,y)* is the intensity function of anchor frame (snapshot at t_0) and g(x,y) is the intensity function of the target frame (snapshot at $t_0 + \delta t$).

We use the following dissimilarity function

$$E_{i,j,k,l} = \left| g_{i+k\delta r,\, j+l\delta r} - a_{i,j} \right|^n \tag{5}$$

as a local feature of correspondence matching as well as a local error function to compute the optical flow. In a sampled space the dissimilarity function values can be described by a 4-D array $\{E_{i,j,k,l};\ i=0,\dots,\ I-1;\ j=0,\dots,\ J-1;\ k=-K,-K+1\dots,\ K;\ l=-L,-L+1,\dots,\ L\}$. Here, I and J are the size of images, and K, L are reasonable values to carry out the correspondence matching, *a(i,j)* and *g(i,j)* are the sampled intensity functions of the anchor and the target frames, respectively. Suppose that the motion vectors possess subpixel values, n equals to 1 or 2, and, finally, the vector's sampling interval belongs to the interval $0<\delta r\leq 1$ that means a subpixel accuracy of the vector estimation in Eq. (4).

Now we need additional constraints to solve the problem. The common approach is that motion vectors possess small signal variations. So absolute differences between all adjacent elements of the motion vector field are assumed to be bounded by values δv:

$$\left|\Delta \mathbf{r}_{i,j}\right| \equiv \left(\left|k_{i,j} - k_{i\pm1,j\pm1}\right|, \left|l_{i,j} - l_{i\pm1,j\pm1}\right| \right) \leq \delta v \,. \tag{6}$$

Now, for a sampled signal the global optimization problem is formulated as follows: find the motion vector field $\{\mathbf{r}_{i,j}\} \equiv \{k_{i,j}, l_{i,j}\}$ with the local smoothness constraint in Eq. (6) in such a way to minimize the sum of the dissimilarity function Eq. (5) evaluated over all elements of images:

$$\left(\mathbf{r}_{i,j}\right) = \underset{\left(r_{i,j}\right),\ \left|\Delta \mathbf{r}_{i,j}\right| \leq \delta v}{ARG\ MIN} \left(\sum_{i=0}^{I-1} \sum_{j=0}^{J-1} E_{i,j,\mathbf{r}} \right), \tag{7}$$

where $\left|\Delta \mathbf{r}_{i,j}\right| \leq \delta v$ denote the smoothness constraint in Eq. (6).

On the other hand, the most successful methods based on optical flow concept utilize the global motion smoothness criterion. In this case the objective function is a combination of the dissimilarity function and the squared values of gradients. So Eq. (7) can be rewritten as

$$\left(\mathbf{r}_{i,j}\right) = \underset{\left(r_{i,j}\right)}{ARG\ MIN} \left(\sum_{i=0}^{I-1} \sum_{j=0}^{J-1} \left(E_{i,j,\mathbf{r}} + w \left|\Delta \mathbf{r}_{i,j}\right|^2 \right) \right), \tag{8}$$

where w is a regularizing parameter.

The method proposed in [11] optimizes Eq. (7) by means of modified dynamic programming. The problem in Eq. (8) can be also solved withy modified dynamic programming:

$$
\begin{aligned}
&O^I\left(E_{i,j,\mathbf{r}}\right)=E^I_{i,j,\mathbf{r}}=S^{I+}_{i,j,\mathbf{r}}+S^{I-}_{i,j,\mathbf{r}}-E_{i,j,\mathbf{r}}\,,\\
&S^{I\pm}_{i,j,\mathbf{r}}=MIN\left(S^{I\pm}_{i\pm k,j,\mathbf{r}}+E_{i,j,\mathbf{r}}+w\left|k_{i,j}-k_{i\pm 1,j}\right|^2\right),\\
&S^{I+}_{0,j,\mathbf{r}}=E_{0,j,\mathbf{r}},\; S^{I-}_{I-1,j,\mathbf{r}}=E_{I-1,j,\mathbf{r}},\\
&O^J\left(E^I_{i,j,\mathbf{r}}\right)=E^{JI}_{i,j,\mathbf{r}}=S^{J+}_{i,j,\mathbf{r}}+S^{J-}_{i,j,\mathbf{r}}-E^I_{i,j,\mathbf{r}}\,,\\
&S^{J\pm}_{i,j,\mathbf{r}}=MIN\left(S^{J\pm}_{i,j\pm l,\mathbf{r}}+E^I_{i,j,\mathbf{r}}+w\left|l_{i,j}-l_{i,j\pm 1}\right|^2\right),\\
&S^{J+}_{i,0,\mathbf{r}}=E^I_{i,0,\mathbf{r}},\; S^{J-}_{i,J-1,\mathbf{r}}=E^I_{i,J-1,\mathbf{r}}.
\end{aligned}
\tag{9}
$$

Finally, the solution can be found by simple procedure,

$$
\left(\mathbf{r}_{i,j}\right)=\underset{\mathbf{r}_{i,j}}{MIN}\left(O^J\left[O^I\left(E_{i,j,\mathbf{r}}\right)\right]\right),
\tag{10}
$$

where O^I and O^J are two consecutive transforms with the use of the recurrence operator in Eq. (9) along I and J axis, respectively.

Note, that after one transform (O^I, e.g.) the solution is equal to the optimal path that can be calculated with conventional dynamic programming. However the global optimization in Eq. (8) requires 2D optimization, whereas conventional dynamic programming solves only 1D optimization problem. After the second transform O^J the necessary optimization is obtained.

So, the proposed algorithm consists of the following steps.

- Form the initial 4D matrix $E_{i,j,\mathbf{r}}$ of the dissimilarity function using Eq. (5).
- Perform two consecutive transforms with the use of the recurrence operator in Eq. (9) along I and J axes, respectively.
- Extract motion information with the help of Eq. (10).

3 Computer Experiments

Computer experiments are carried out to illustrate and compare the performance of conventional matching and proposed algorithms. We are also interested in understanding how well the proposed matching behaves if a signal distorted due to additive noise. In our computer experiments matched pair of images are generated using known test motion vector fields. In our case, the conventional representation of resultant motion vectors by needle diagrams is not effective visual tool. We illustrate matching results by scalar maps. The gray-scale map presentation requires scalar values of motion vector fields. Generated test fields are also scalar (like horizontal disparity in stereo images).

Fig. 1 (a) shows the pair of matched test images. The scalar valued map of a known vector field is given in Fig. 1 (b). Figs. 1 (c) and (d) show the scalar valued maps obtained by matching with local smoothness constraint and with global smoothness criterion, respectively. The visual comparison of the resultant maps shows that the performance of the proposed algorithm is obviously much better.

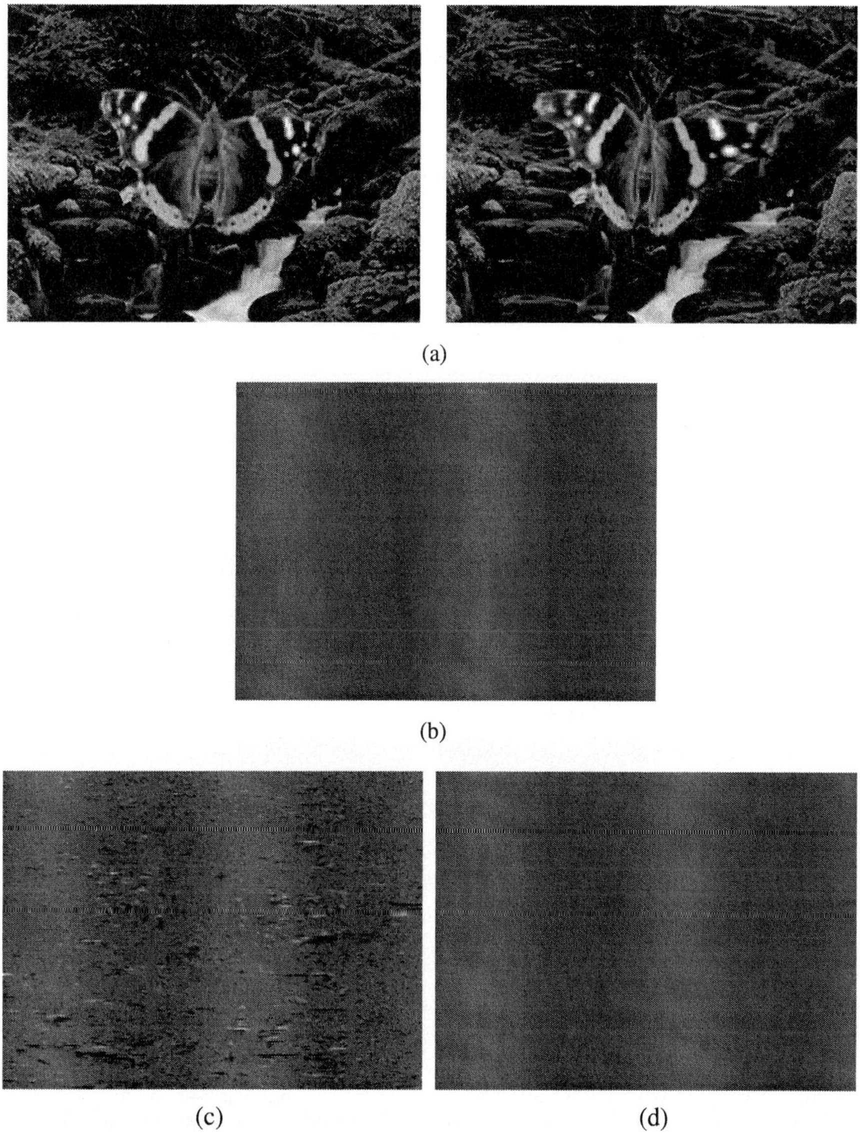

Fig. 1. (a) Test pair of matched images. (b) The scalar valued map of a known vector field. (c), (d) The scalar valued maps obtained by matching with local smoothness constraint and with global smoothness criterion, respectively.

Next we carry out experiments with test images that are degraded using additive Gaussian noise. Fig. 2 (a) shows the pair of matched test images degraded due to the noise. The map of a known vector field is given in Fig. 2 (b). Figs. 2 (c) and (d) show the resultant maps obtained by matching with local smoothness constraint and with global smoothness criterion, respectively. The visual and numerical analysis of the resultant depth maps shows that the proposed matching algorithm is robust to the noise degradation of a signal.

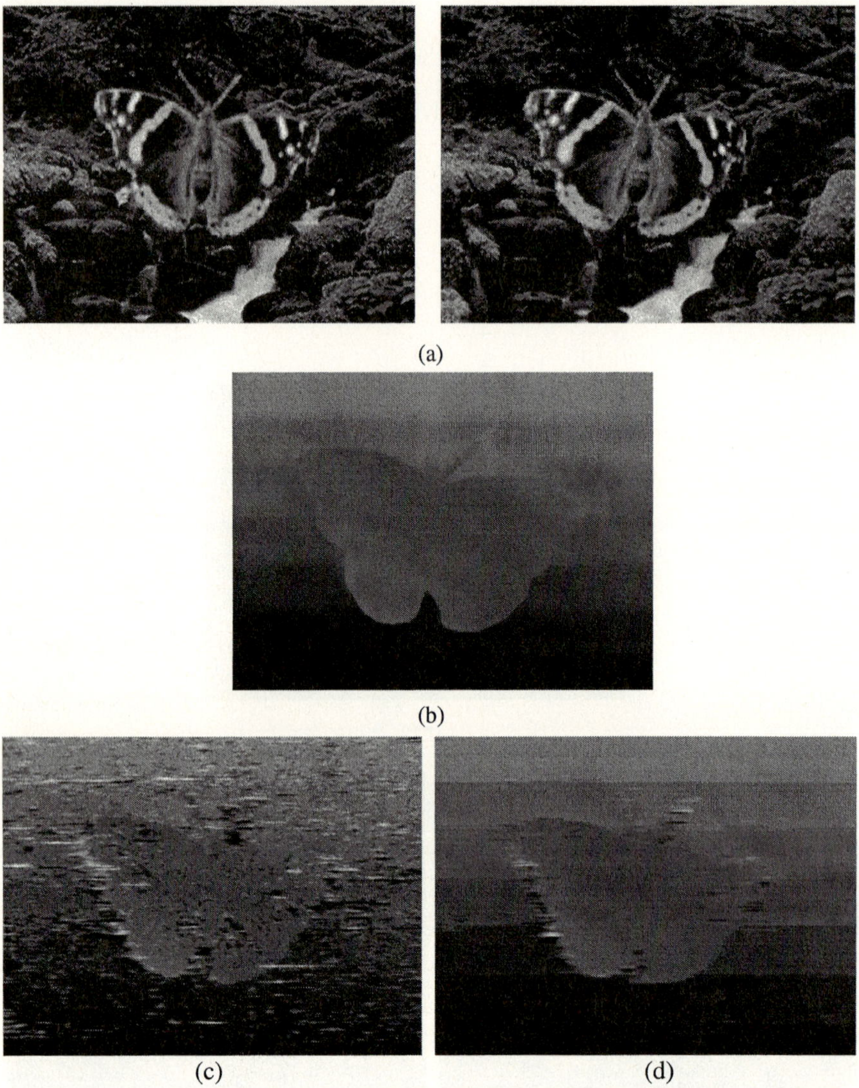

Fig. 2. (a) Test pair of matched images degraded due to additive Gaussian noise.(b) The scalar valued map of a known vector field. (c), (d) The resultant scalar valued maps obtained by matching with local smoothness constraint and with global smoothness criterion, respectively.

The proposed operator in Eq. (9) includes a smoothness parameter w that must be defined during matching process. With the help of many computer experiments we found that this parameter can be represented as follows:

$$w = 1.5\frac{\sum_{i=0}^{I-1}\left|a_{i,j} - a_{i+1,j}\right|}{I}, \tag{11}$$

where $a_{i,j}$ is the image intensity value of the anchor frame.

In other word, the sought parameter is proportional to the mean absolute value of signal gradient along the chosen axis (in Eq. (11) it is the horizontal axis of matched images).

We carried out many computer experiments with different simulated motion vector fields, motion fields, and degradation of matched images. So numerical analysis on the base of the mean squared errors (MSE) criterion shows that the proposed algorithm has advantage over conventional matching algorithms.

4 Conclusion

In this paper, a new motion estimation method based on dynamic programming matching and global motion smoothness criterion has been proposed. The method demonstrates much better results than those obtained with the use of local smoothness constraints. The proposed method is robust to additive noise.

References

1. Horn B.K.P., Schunck B.G., Determining optical flow. Artificial Intelligence, Vol. 17, (1981), 85-204.
2. Watson A.B., Ahumada A.J., Motion: Perception and Representation. In: Tsotsos, J.K., (ed.), (1983), 1-10.
3. Ohta Y.and Kanade T., Stereo by intra- and inter-scanline search using dynamic programming, IEEE Trans. Pattern Anal. Machine Intell., Vol.7, (1985), 139-154.
4. Anandan P., Measuring Visual Motion from Image Sequences. PhD thesis, Univ. of Massachusetts, Amherst (1987).
5. Heitz F., Bouthemy P., Multimodal estimation of discontinuous optical flow using Markov random fields. IEEE Transactions on Pattern Analysis and Machine Intelligence, Vol. 15, (1993), 1213-1232.
6. Kanade T. and Okutomi M., A Stereo Matching Algorithm with an Adaptive Window: Theory and Experiment, IEEE Trans. Pattern Analysis and Machine Intelligence, Vol. 16, pp. (1994), 920-932.
7. Cedaras C., Shah M., Motion based recognition: A survey. Image and Vision Computing, Vol. 13, (1995), 129-154.
8. Anthony Y.K.H., and Pong T.C., Cooperative fusion of stereo and motion, Pattern Recognition, Vol. 28, (1995), 553-562.
9. Chung H.Y., Yung N.H.C., Cheung P.Y.S., Fast motion estimation with search-center prediction, Optical Engineering, Vol. 40, (2001), 952-963.
10. Petrakis E.G.M., Diplaros A., and Milios E., Matching and retrieval of distorted and occluded shapes using dynamic programming, IEEE Trans. Pattern Anal. Machine Intell., Vol.24, (2002), 1501-1516.
11. Mozerov M., Kober V., Tchernykh A., Choi T. S., Motion estimation with a modified dynamic programming, Optical Engineering, Vol. 41, (2002), 2592-2598.
12. Mozerov M., Kober V., Motion Estimation Based on Hidden Segmentation, IEICE Transaction on Fund., Vol. E88-A, (2005), 376-381.

Dynamic Hierarchical Compact Clustering Algorithm

Reynaldo Gil-García[1], José M. Badía-Contelles[2], and Aurora Pons-Porrata[1]

[1] Center of Pattern Recognition and Data Mining,
Universidad de Oriente, Santiago de Cuba, Cuba
{gil, aurora}@app.uo.edu.cu
[2] Universitat Jaume I, Castellón, Spain
badia@icc.uji.es

Abstract. In this paper we introduce a general framework for hierarchical clustering that deals with both static and dynamic data sets. From this framework, different hierarchical agglomerative algorithms can be obtained, by specifying an inter-cluster similarity measure, a subgraph of the β-similarity graph, and a cover algorithm. A new clustering algorithm called *Hierarchical Compact Algorithm* and its dynamic version are presented, which are specific versions of the proposed framework. Our evaluation experiments on several standard document collections show that this algorithm requires less computational time than standard methods in dynamic data sets while achieving a comparable or even better clustering quality. Therefore, we advocate its use for tasks that require dynamic clustering, such as information organization, creation of document taxonomies and hierarchical topic detection.

1 Introduction

Managing, accessing, searching, and browsing large repositories of text documents requires efficient organization of the information. In dynamic information environments, such as the World Wide Web or the stream of newspaper articles, it is usually desirable to apply adaptive methods for document organization such as clustering.

Hierarchical clustering algorithms have an additional interest, because they provide a view of the data at different levels of abstraction, making them ideal for people to visualize and interactively explore large document collections. Besides, clusters very often include subclusters, and the hierarchical structure is indeed a natural constraint on the underlying application domain.

Static clustering methods mainly rely on having the whole collection ready before applying the algorithm. Unlike them, the incremental methods are able to process new data as they are added to the collection. In addition, dynamical algorithms have the ability to update the clustering when data are added or removed from the collection. These algorithms allow us dynamically tracking the ever-changing large scale information being put or removed from the web everyday, without having to perform complete reclustering.

M. Lazo and A. Sanfeliu (Eds.): CIARP 2005, LNCS 3773, pp. 302–310, 2005.

Several incremental clustering algorithms have been proposed (e.g. see [6]). However, these algorithms do not create cluster hierarchies. On the other hand, various hierarchical algorithms have been used for clustering [11], but all of them are static algorithms. Finally, there are a few algorithms that update the cluster hierarchy when a new object arrives, such as GALOIS [3], Charikar's algorithm [5] and DC-tree [10]. These algorithms have several of the following drawbacks: its time complexity is exponential with the dimension of the objects, the number of clusters is fixed a priori, the obtained clusters depend on the data order, they require tuning several parameters and they impose restrictions to the representation space of the objects and to the similarity function.

In this paper we introduce a general hierarchical framework that deals with both static and dynamic data sets. From this framework, different hierarchical agglomerative algorithms can be obtained, by specifying an inter-cluster similarity measure, a subgraph of the β-similarity graph, and a cover algorithm. We also propose a new clustering algorithm called *Hierarchical Compact Algorithm*, which is a specific variant of this framework. This algorithm is compared with other hierarchical clustering methods using four standard document collections. Our evaluation experiments show that this algorithm requires less computational time in dynamic data sets than standard methods while achieving a comparable or even better clustering quality.

2 Static Hierarchical Clustering Algorithm

We call β-similarity graph the undirected graph whose vertices are the clusters and there is an edge from vertex i to vertex j, if the cluster j is β-similar to i. Two clusters are β-similar if their similarity is greater or equal to β, where β is a user-defined parameter. Analogously, i is a β-isolated cluster if its similarity with all clusters is lesser than β.

The clustering algorithms based on graphs involve two main tasks: the construction of a certain graph and a cover routine of this graph that determines the clusters. In this context, a cover for a graph $G = (V, E)$ is a collection $V_1, V_2, ..., V_k$ of subsets of V such that $\cup_{i=1}^{k} V_i = V$, each one representing a cluster.

Our hierarchical clustering algorithm is an agglomerative method and it is based on graph too. It uses a multi-layered clustering to produce the hierarchy. The granularity increases with the layer of the hierarchy, with the top layer being the most general and the leaf nodes being the most specific. At each successive layer of the hierarchy, vertices represent subsets of their parent clusters. The process in each layer has two steps: the construction of a graph and a cover routine of this graph. The general framework is shown in Figure 1.

In our framework, a similarity measure to compare the objects and an inter-cluster similarity measure are required. The algorithm starts with each object being considered a cluster. Then, it constructs a subgraph of the β-similarity graph. The set of vertices of this subgraph must equal to the set of vertices of the graph. A cover routine is applied to this subgraph in order to build the clus-

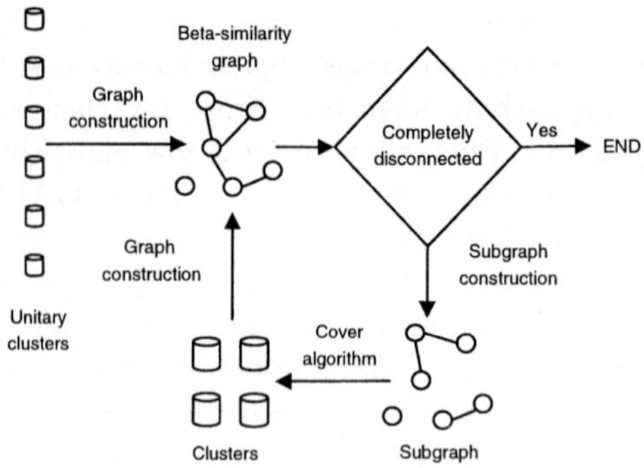

Fig. 1. General framework

ters in the bottom layer. From the obtained clusters, the algorithm constructs a new β-similarity graph and its corresponding subgraph. Then, the cover routine is applied again to obtain the clusters in the next layer. This process is repeated until the β-similarity graph is completely disconnected, that is, all vertices (clusters) of the graph are β-isolated. In our framework, the cover routine should not depend on the order of the incoming objects. This requirement guarantees the order independence of the framework. Notice that we use the same β value and a unique subgraph type in all levels of the hierarchy.

We can obtain disjoint or overlapped clusters at each level of the hierarchy, depending on the cover routine used. It is worth noticing that if we change the type of subgraph, the similarity measures or the cover routine in this general framework, different hierarchical agglomerative algorithms are obtained. In our algorithm, unlike the traditional hierarchical agglomerative algorithms, several clusters can be merged in the same level. Also, since our stopping criterion is that the graph is completely disconnected, the top level of the hierarchy does not necessarily consist of one cluster.

Traditional hierarchical agglomerative algorithms can be obtained as particular cases of the previous general framework if we choose $\beta = 0$, the subgraph should be the mutual nearest neighbour subgraph of the β-similarity graph, and the cover routine should find the connected components in this subgraph.

2.1 Hierarchical Compact Algorithm

In this paper we propose a specific variant of the abovementioned framework. We will call it *Hierarchical Compact Algorithm* (*HCA*). This algorithm assumes the following issues:

1. The group-average as inter-cluster similarity measure.
2. The subgraph is the maximum β-similarity graph [4] disregarding the orientation of its edges (namely undirected $max - S$ graph).
3. The cover routine finds the connected components of the undirected $max - S$ graph, that is, the compact sets [9].

The main steps of the method are shown in the Algorithm 1.

Algorithm 1 Static Hierarchical Compact Algorithm.

---

1. Put each object in a cluster on its own.
2. *level* = 0.
3. Construct the β-similarity graph, G_{level}.
4. While G_{level} is not completely disconnected:
   (a) Construct the undirected $max - S$ graph (subgraph of G_{level}).
   (b) Find the connected components of this subgraph.
   (c) Construct a new β-similarity graph, $G_{level+1}$, where each vertex represents a connected component and the inter-cluster similarity is group-average.
   (d) $level = level + 1$

The proposed algorithm can produce clusters with arbitrary shapes and the generated set of clusters at each level of the hierarchy is unique, independently on the arrival order of the objects. Also, since we use the maximum β-similarity graph, the algorithm produces cohesive clusters. In our algorithm, the number of clusters is not fixed. Besides, it requires a unique parameter and therefore it reduces the problem of tuning the parameter values to suit specific applications. The computational complexity of the *HCA* algorithm is $O(n^2)$.

3 Dynamic Hierarchical Clustering Algorithm

Our dynamic general framework can be defined in a similar way to the static framework explained above. The main difference is that the construction of the graphs and the cover routine must be dynamic. Given a hierarchy of clusters previously built by the algorithm, each time a new object arrives (or is removed), the clusters at all levels of the hierarchy must be revised. The steps of the method are shown in Algorithm 2.

As it can be noticed, the dynamic algorithm comprises the updating of the graphs and the updating of the cover at each level of the hierarchy. The updating of the β-similarity graph is trivial. The details of the other updating processes are described below, focusing in the *Dynamic Hierarchical Compact Algorithm* (DHCA). In this particular case, we need to update the undirected $max - S$ graph and its connected components at each level of the hierarchy.

When a new object arrives, a new unitary cluster is created and the β-similarity graph of the bottom level is updated. Then, the undirected $max - S$ graph is updated too, which can produce a new vertex and can also produce new edges and remove others (see Algorithm 3). Every time an edge is removed from the undirected $max - S$ graph, the cluster (connected component) to which the vertices of this edge belong can become unconnected. Therefore, that cluster must be reconstructed. On the other side, every time an edge is added to the undirected $max - S$ graph, the clusters of its vertices are merged if they are

Algorithm 2 Dynamic general framework.

1. Arrival of an object to cluster (or to remove).
2. Put the new object in a cluster on its own (or remove the cluster to which the object belongs).
3. $level = 0$.
4. Update the β-similarity graph, G_{level}.
5. While G_{level} is not completely disconnected:
   (a) Update the subgraph of G_{level}.
   (b) Update the cover of this subgraph.
   (c) Update the β-similarity graph, $G_{level+1}$.
   (d) $level = level + 1$
6. If there exist levels greater than $level$ in the hierarchy, remove them.

different. The updating of the connected components produces new clusters and removes others (see Algorithm 4). When clusters are created or removed from a level of the hierarchy, the β-similarity graph of the next level must be updated. This process is repeated until this graph is completely disconnected. It is possible that the β-similarity graph became completely disconnected before the top level of the hierarchy is reached. In this case, the next levels of the hierarchy must be removed.

Algorithm 3 Undirected $max - S$ graph updating.

1. Let N be the set of vertices to add to the undirected $max - S$ graph and R the set of vertices to remove from it.
2. Let M be the set of vertices for which a vertex of R is its most β-similar vertex.
3. Remove all vertices of R from the undirected $max - S$ graph and add all vertices of N to it.
4. Find the most β-similar vertices of each vertex of $M \cup N$ and add the corresponding edges to the $max - S$ graph.
5. Find the vertices for which a vertex of N is its most β-similar vertex and update the corresponding edges.

4 Experimental Results

The performance of the Dynamic Hierarchical Compact Algorithm has been evaluated using four document collections, whose general characteristics are summarized in Table 1. Human annotators identified the topics in each collection. The smallest of these datasets contains 695 documents and the largest contains 10369 documents. To ensure diversity in the datasets, we obtained them from different sources.

The AFP collection is from the TREC-5 conference [1] and it contains some articles published by the AFP agency in 1994 year. The ELN collection contains

Algorithm 4 Connected component updating.

1. Let N be the set of vertices added to the undirected $max - S$ graph and R the set of vertices removed from it. Let, also, NE be the set of edges added to the undirected $max - S$ graph and RE the set of edges removed from it.
2. Let Q be a queue with the vertices to be processed, $Q = \emptyset$.
3. Remove all vertices of R from their clusters. Put the remaining vertices of these clusters into Q. Put, also, all vertices of the clusters where at least one edge of RE is incident to a vertex of the cluster into Q. Remove these clusters from the list of the existing clusters.
4. Put all vertices of N into the queue Q.
5. Build the connected components from the vertices in Q and add them to the list of existing clusters.
6. For each edge of NE, merge the clusters to which its vertices belong.

Table 1. Description of collections

Collection	Source	Documents	Terms	Topics
AFP	TREC-5	695	12575	25
ELN	TREC-4	5829	84344	50
TDT	TDT2	9824	55112	193
REU	Reuters-21578	10369	35297	120

a set of "El Norte" newspaper articles dated from 1994. Both collections are in Spanish. We also use the TDT2 dataset, version 4.0 [2]. This corpus consists of 6 months of news stories from the January to June 1998. The news stories were collected from six different sources. Human annotators identified a total of 193 topics in the TDT2 dataset. 9824 English stories belong to one of these topics, the rest are unlabeled. Finally, from Reuters-21578 [8] we selected the documents that are assigned one or more topics and have <BODY> and </BODY> tags.

In our experiments, the documents are represented using the traditional vectorial model. The terms of documents represent the lemmas of the words appearing in the texts. Stop words, such as articles, prepositions and adverbs are disregarded from the document vectors. Terms are statistically weighted using the term frequency (TF). To account for documents of different lengths, the vector is normalized using the document length. We use the traditional cosine measure to compare the documents.

There are many different measures to evaluate the quality of clustering. We adopt a widely used external quality measure: the *Overall F-measure* [7]. This measure compares the system-generated clusters with the manually labelled topics and combines the precision and recall factors. The higher the overall F-measure, the better the clustering is, due to the higher accuracy of the clusters mapping to the topics.

Our experiments were focused on evaluating the quality of the clustering produced by other well known hierarchical clustering methods: Average-link,

Complete-link and Bisecting K-Means. We compare these algorithms with our Dynamic Hierarchical Compact Algorithm.

The results for the various document collections and methods are shown in Table 2. In our algorithm we only evaluated the top level of the hierarchy and the parameter β that produced the best results was chosen. On the contrary, in the other algorithms we consider the flat partition produced by the best level of the hierarchy.

As it can be noticed, our method is either the best or always near to the best solution. It is worth mentioning that our algorithm obtains these results with both less total number of clusters and levels.

Table 2. Quality results obtained by different clustering algorithms

Data	Algorithm	Levels	Clusters in hierarchy	Clusters in best level	F-Overall
AFP	Average-link	695	1389	40	0.84
	Complete-link	695	1389	29	0.83
	Bisecting K-Means	695	1389	13	0.69
	DHCA($\beta = 0.12$)	3	226	45	0.82
ELN	Average-link	5829	11658	170	0.41
	Complete-link	5829	11658	80	0.41
	Bisecting K-Means	5829	11658	42	0.36
	DHCA($\beta = 0.10$)	4	1033	73	0.46
TDT	Average-link	9824	19645	165	0.77
	Complete-link	9824	19645	255	0.50
	Bisecting K-Means	9824	19645	122	0.40
	DHCA($\beta = 0.12$)	4	2636	136	0.76
REU	Average-link	10369	20737	100	0.53
	Complete-link	10369	20737	180	0.37
	Bisecting K-Means	10369	20737	101	0.23
	DHCA($\beta = 0.12$)	4	2095	101	0.52

Figure 2 shows the time spent by the DHCA algorithm and the three classical hierarchical algorithms mentioned above. Each curve represents the time spent to cluster the document sub-collections of size 1000, 2000 and so on. Since the dynamic nature, our algorithm needs to update the cluster each time a new document arrives, which clearly increases its cost (see curve DHCA-T). However, in a dynamic environment we have a collection partially clustered and some new documents arrive. In this case the static algorithms have to cluster the whole collection again, whereas the DHCA algorithm only needs to update the existing clusters. DHCA-P represents the time spent by our algorithm to update the clusters when adding 1000 documents every time. For example, the value shown with 7000 documents represents the time spent to add 1000 new documents to the clustering when we have already clustered 6000 documents. As we can observe, in this case the DHCA clearly overcomes the static algorithms.

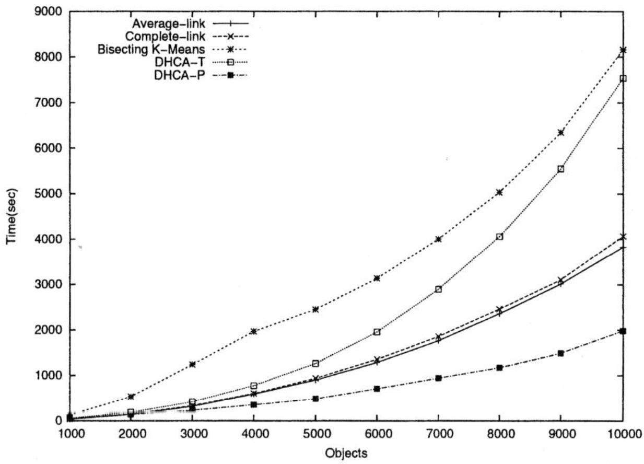

Fig. 2. Time performance

5 Conclusions

In this paper a hierarchical clustering framework, both static and dynamic, has been introduced. This framework is based on the β-similarity graph (relies only on pair-wise document similarity information). Different hierarchical agglomerative algorithms can be obtained from it, by specifying an inter-cluster similarity measure, a subgraph of the β-similarity graph, and a cover algorithm of this subgraph. The traditional hierarchical agglomerative methods can be seen as particular cases of this general framework.

Since in our framework several clusters can be merged at the same level and it stops when the graph is completely disconnected, we can obtain a cluster hierarchy composed by few levels.

A specific variant of the proposed framework, called Hierarchical Compact Algorithm is also introduced. This algorithm obtains cohesive clusters with arbitrary shapes. Another advantage of HCA is that the number of clusters is not fixed and the algorithm requires a unique parameter.

The dynamic version of the Hierarchical Compact Algorithm can be used to organize dynamic data, such as the creation of document taxonomies and the hierarchical topic detection task. Its most important novelty is that it is a dynamic clustering algorithm able to build a cluster hierarchy independent on the data order.

This algorithm was compared with other clustering algorithms in four standard document collections. The experimental results show that our algorithm achieves a comparable or better clustering quality. Moreover, the algorithm achieves better time performance than other traditional hierarchical clustering algorithms in dynamic collections.

Finally, though we employ our algorithm to cluster document collections, it can be also applied to any problem of Pattern Recognition with mixed objects.

Acknowledgements. This work has been partially supported by the research projects Bancaixa (PI-1B2001-14) and CICYT (TIC2002-04400-C03-01).

References

1. Text REtrieval Conference (TREC). http://trec.nist.gov.
2. TDT2 collection, version 4.0, 1998. http://www.nist.gov/speech/tests/tdt.html.
3. C. Carpineto and G. Romano. A lattice conceptual clustering system and its application to browsing retrieval. *Machine Learning 24*, (2):95–122, 1996.
4. J. A. Carrasco-Ochoa, J. Ruiz-Shulcloper, and L. A. De la Vega-Doria. Sensitivity analysis for beta0-compact sets. In *VI Iberoamerican Symposium on Pattern Recognition*, pages 14–19, 2001.
5. M. Charikar, C. Chekuri, T. Feder, and R. Motwani. Incremental clustering and dynamic information retrieval. In *29th Annual Symposium on Theory of Computing*, pages 626–635, 1997.
6. K. M. Hammouda and M. S. Kamel. Efficient phrase-based document indexing for web document clustering. *IEEE Transactions on Knowledge and Data Engineering*, 16(10):1279–1296, 2004.
7. B. Larsen and C. Aone. Fast and effective text mining using linear-time document clustering. In *KDD'99*, pages 16–22, 1999.
8. D. Lewis. Reuters-21578 text collection, version 1.2. http://kdd.ics.uci.edu.
9. A. Pons-Porrata, R. Berlanga-Llavori, and J. Ruiz-Shulcloper. On-line event and topic detection by using the compact sets clustering algorithm. *Journal of Intelligent and Fuzzy Systems*, 3-4:185–194, 2002.
10. W. Wai-chiu and A. Wai-chee Fu. Incremental document clustering for web page classification. In *IEEE 2000 International Conference on Information Society in the 21st Century: Emerging technologies and new challenges*, 2000.
11. Y. Zhao and G. Karypis. Evaluation of hierarchical clustering algorithms for document datasets. In *International Conference on Information and Knowledge Management*, pages 515–524, 2002.

A Robust Footprint Detection Using Color Images and Neural Networks

Marco Mora[1] and Daniel Sbarbaro[2]

[1] Department of Computer Science, Catholic University of Maule,
Casilla 617, Talca, Chile
marco.mora@enseeiht.fr

[2] Department of Electrical Engineering, University of Concepcion,
Casilla 160-C, Concepcion, Chile
dsbarbar@die.udec.cl

Abstract. The automatic detection of different foot's diseases requires the analysis of a footprint, obtained from a digital image of the sole. This paper shows that optical monochromatic images are not suitable for footprint segmentation purposes, while color images provide enough information for carrying out an efficient segmentation. It is shown that a multiplayer perceptron trained with bayesian regularization backpropagation allows to adequately classify the pixels on the color image of the footprint and in this way, to segment the footprint without fingers. The footprint is improved by using a classical smoothing filter, and segmented by performing erosion and dilation operations. This result is very important for the development of a low cost system designed to diagnose pathologies related to the footprint form.

1 Introduction

When the foot is planted, not all the sole is in contact with the ground. The footprint is the surface of the foot in contact with the ground. The characteristic form and zones of the footprint are shown in figure 1(a). Zones 1, 2 and 3 correspond to regions in contact with the surface when the foot is planted; these are called anterior heel, posterior heel and isthmus respectively. Zone 4 does not form part of the surface in contact and is called footprint vault [18]. These footprints play a key role in the detection of different foot's diseases.

The sole image can be acquired either in gray scale or color format. The segmentation of gray scale images can be done using standard techniques [7]. However, there are some problems with the segmentation of gray scale images produced by shadows, surface curvature and metamerism [21]. Taking in account the previous problems, segmentation techniques in color images have been developed. There are studies where the operators for edge detection have been extended from gray scales to color images [3], [8]. In other cases, segmentation techniques based on neural networks and statistical classifiers have been developed [1]. Good reviews of segmentation techniques based on color images can be found in [4] and [5].

M. Lazo and A. Sanfeliu (Eds.): CIARP 2005, LNCS 3773, pp. 311–318, 2005.

Among segmentation methods relevant for this study is the use of neural networks. In particular, the multilayer perceptron (MLP) and the training algorithm called backpropagation [9] have been successfully used in classification and functional approximation. An important characteristic of MLP is its capacity to classify patterns grouped in classes not linearly separable. Besides that, it has been shown that a one-hidden-layer perceptron (or two-layer perceptron) is an universal function estimator [19].

The first disadvantage of the backpropagation algorithm is its speed of convergence, this has led to the use of more sophisticated optimization methods. A good summary of these optimization methods is found in [13], and the application of such methods to the training of neural networks can be found in [17].

A second disadvantage of MLP trained with error backpropagation is that it may classify by mistake patterns not participating in the training process; i.e. it lacks of generalization. Generalization means that the neural network correctly classifies unknown patterns.

A technique to improve the generalization is called regularization, and consists in building a cost function from the sum of a function for error measurement (typically the average quadratic error) and a function representing the network complexity. Different regularization methods propose different functions for representing the network complexity, as example: weight decay [6], weight elimination[11] and approximate smoother [22]. A current technique is the bayesian regularization, which uses the weight decay as the cost function, the Levenberg-Marquardt optimization algorithm [10], and a bayesian approach for defining the regularization parameters [2]. Among the advantages of the bayesian regularization technique are: (1) by using the Levenberg-Marquardt optimization algorithm, the speed of the learning process is improved, and (2) it provided the effective parameters the network is using. By using the network effective parameters, it is possible to define the amount of neurons in the hidden layer according to the procedure described in [10].

The data set used in this work, containing more than 200 images, was obtained using a prototype designed and built to capture sole images. Matlab, the Image Processing Toolbox and the Neural Networks Toolbox were used as platform for carrying out most of data processing work. The structure of this paper is as follows. Section 2 describes the problem of capturing footprints using gray scale images, shows the footprint segmentation using color images and neural networks, and describes the segmentation improvements. Section 3 shows a quality measurement of the footprint segmentation. Finally, Section 4 provides some conclusions.

2 Footprint Segmentation Using Color Images and Neural Networks

A first attempt to solve the segmentation problem considered gray scale images, since the use of this type of image allows the use of simple algorithms for its

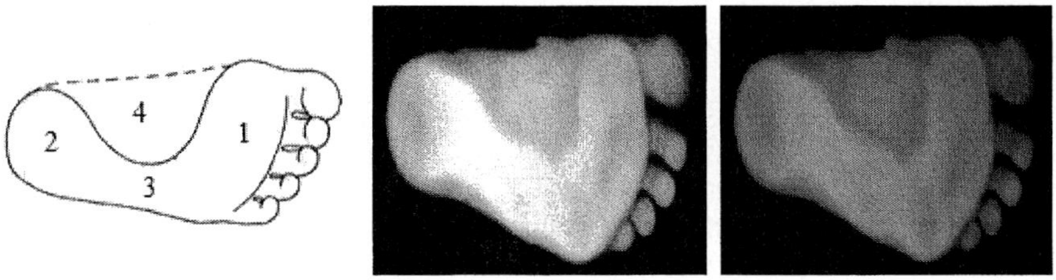

(a) Zones of the sole (b) Gray level image (c) Color image

Fig. 1. Images of the sole

segmentation. Figure 1(b) shows a gray-scale footprint image. It can be seen at first sight that there are patterns of the vault of the foot which have the same level of gray as others of the posterior heel. This means that different regions reflect the same amount of light (i.e. having the same gray values, whereas being differently colored), this phenomenon is known as metamerism [21]. Thus, for this application, a segmentation based on gray scale is not adequate to separate the pixels of the footprint from the rest of the image by a simple threshold method.

Because of the metamerism problem in gray scale images, the use of color images is proposed. Color model means the specification of a system of three-dimensional coordinates and a subspace of this system in which every color is represented by only one point [7]. The RGB color model has been used in this study. Figure 1(c) shows a color footprint image.

This work proposes the use of NN for footprint segmentation. The network acts as a pixel classifier [1],[15], and by the training process, it learns the pixel classes of the training set. In addition, by its generalization capabilities, it can also adequately classify pixels from the same image but not belonging to the training set and also pixels belonging to other images.

The neural network has three inputs corresponding to the RGB coordinates of the particular color. In the color footprint image in figure 1(c) it is clearly shown the existence of 3 pixel classes: the one from the image background, the one from the vault, and the one from the footprint. The network has an output assuming the value 1 for background pixels, 0 for the footprint, and -1 for the vault. The training set considers 709 samples selected from just one image, the 26% correspond to the background, 38% to the vault and 36% to the footprint. The size of each sample image is 434x342 pixels. The training of the multi-layer perceptron has the following characteristics:

- A hidden-layer MLP was used.
- Number of inputs: 3.
- Number of outputs: 1.
- A bayesian regularization backpropagation as training algorithm.
- Learning in batch modality, where weights are updated at the end of each stage.

Table 1. Determining the amount of neurons in the hidden layer for the footprint segmentation by using MLP

NNCO	Epochs	SSE	SSW	Effective parameters	Total parameters
1	142/3000	130.657/0.001	55.7698	3.14e+000	6
2	45/3000	0.00029/0.001	8221.40	1.09e+001	11
3	18/3000	0.00067/0.001	6425.98	1.44e+001	16
4	36/3000	0.00048/0.001	7446.65	1.93e+001	21
5	125/3000	0.00064/0.001	3680.94	2.33e+001	26
6	66/3000	0.00073/0.001	3023.94	2.76e+001	31
7	113/3000	0.00080/0.001	3267.58	3.31e+001	36
8	329/3000	0.00091/0.001	3047.76	3.65e+001	41
9	104/3000	0.00098/0.001	2636.46	4.00e+001	46
10	150/3000	0.00097/0.001	2790.33	4.31e+001	51
11	140/3000	0.00079/0.001	2618.23	4.77e+001	56
12	292/3000	0.00099/0.001	2272.81	4.90e+001	61
13	194/3000	0.00096/0.001	2269.79	5.52e+001	66
14	218/3000	0.00090/0.001	2327.66	5.85e+001	71
15	182/3000	0.00099/0.001	2325.35	5.51e+001	76
16	225/3000	0.00093/0.001	2287.15	5.96e+001	81
30	261/3000	0.00099/0.001	2212.30	5.94e+001	151

- The initial network weights were generated by the Nguyen-Widrow method [12] because it increases the convergence speed of the training algorithm [10].
- The initial regularization parameters a and b were 0 and 1 respectively.
- Successive trainings were done increasing progressively the amount of neurons in the hidden layer.

To determine the amount of neurons of the hidden layer, the procedure described in [10] was used. The details of this procedure are shown in table 1, where NNCO corresponds to the number of neurons in the hidden layer, SEE is the sum of the quadratic errors and SSW is the sum of the weight squares.

From the previous table it can be seen that from 13 neurons in the hidden layer, the SSE, SSW and the effective parameters stay practically constants. As a result, 13 neurons are considered in that layer. The evolution of SSE, SSW and the effective parameters are shown in figure 2. Figure 3 shows the classification results. The classification errors in the footprint edge can be improved by carefully choosing with more detail the training set in this zone.

Because the detection of pathologies related to the footprint shape requires the capture of the footprint without toes, the previous result is improved by smoothing the footprint and by eliminating the toes.

The improvement steps are the following: (1) binarization, (2) footprint erosion in order to disconnect the toes if it is necessary, (3) smoothing of the footprint by median filter or a low pass filter in the frequency domain, (4) discharging the toes by ticketing and segmentation by size, and (5) image dilation in order to recover the size. The techniques previously noted are described in [7]. To visualize the improvements, the binarization is shown in figure 4(a), erosion is

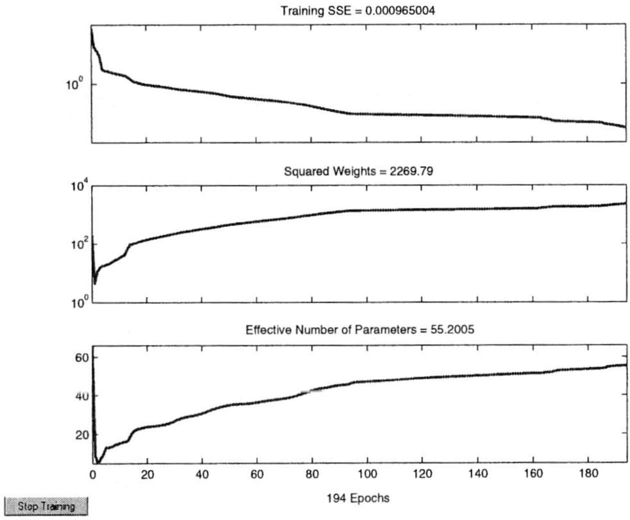

Fig. 2. MLP training

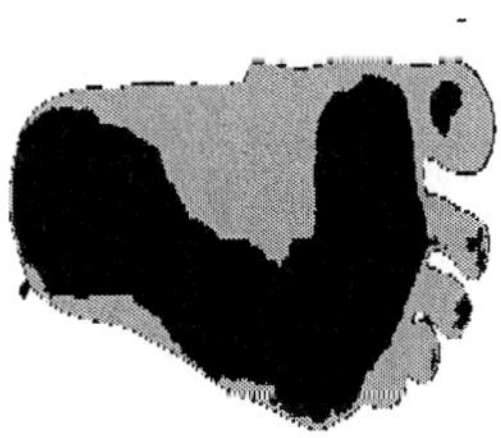

Fig. 3. Sole image classification

shown in figure 4(b), toe elimination is shown in figure 4(c), smoothing is shown in figure 4(d), dilation in figure 4(e), and the final result of the surrounding over the color image in figure 4(f).

3 Quality Assessment of the Footprint Segmentation

In the literature there are few methods to assess the quality of segmentation [14],[20], because the main reference is the one done by the human brain. Hence it is common in segmentation problems to compare the results obtained by the proposed algorithm with the human segmentation [15].

In order to assess the quality of the segmentation carried out by the MLP, a human-assisted segmentation was carried out for 10 footprint images and they are compared with the ones obtained by MLP. The results of such comparison are given in table 2, also the human segmentation of the footprint, the segmen-

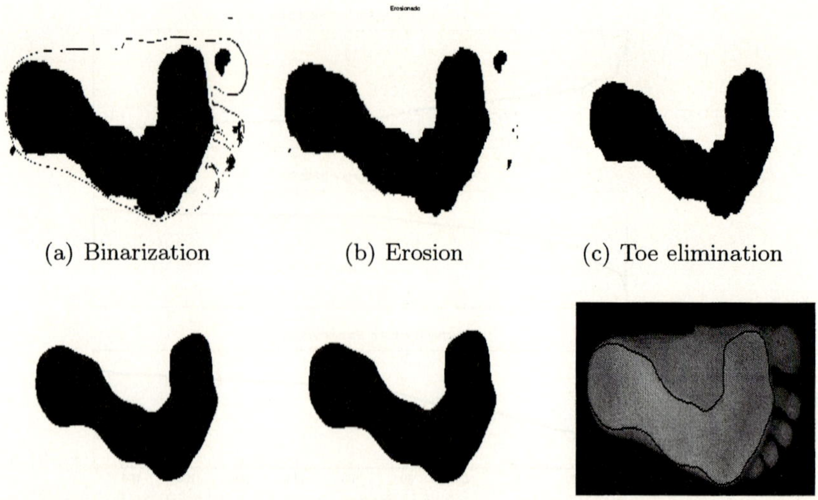

(a) Binarization (b) Erosion (c) Toe elimination

(d) Smoothing (e) Dilation (f) Final edge

Fig. 4. Improvements in the footprint segmentation

Table 2. Quality assessment of the segmentation

N	Size of images	Different colors	Pixels bad classified	Percent pixels good classified
1	324x139	12518	1827	95,94
2	260x112	8741	1000	96,56
3	260x115	8567	1335	95,46
4	268x121	10008	1304	95,97
5	280x118	10626	1029	96,87
6	300x138	13062	1515	96,34
7	280x118	7586	1005	96,96
8	264x113	9903	709	97,62
9	260x118	8244	1335	95,58
10	294x124	10492	1337	96,25

tation done by MLP and its errors are shown respectively in figures 5(a), 5(b) and 5(c). The figures show that the classification errors are concentrated in the borders. It must be noted that the footprint edges are not well defined and there is a small transition zone, where it is not possible to have a perfect human segmentation. It is possible to improve these results by using a training set with more samples corresponding to the edge zone. It is important to remark that the error introduced by the presence of toes is completely eliminated by the process described in the previous section.

(a) Manual segmentation (b) MLP segmentation (c) Segmentation error

Fig. 5. Segmentation quality

4 Conclusions

This work has illustrated that the footprint segmentation using gray scales is not possible due to the problem known as metamerism, and the use of color image is then required.

The multilayer perceptron trained with bayesian regularization backpropagation not only enables to learn a training set representing the task of pixels classification but also to classify adequately pixels of other images.

Future work will consider a comparative study among different automatic segmentation algorithms, such as: non-parametric and non-supervised statistical classifier [23], self-organized neural networks [16], and the use of techniques for edge detection in color images [3],[8].

The results of this study are promising and they have established a very simple and fast method for footprint automatic detection with no toes. It is foreseen on the near future the development of an automatic and real time diagnosis system of pathologies related with the footprint shape.

References

1. E. Littmann and H. Ritter, "Adaptive Color Segmentation: A Comparison of Neural Networks and Statistical Methods", IEEE Trans. on ANN, 8 1 , pp. 175-185, 1997.
2. D. Mackay. "Bayesian Interpolation", Computation and Neural System, California Institute of Technology, 1992.
3. T. Carron and P. Lambert, "Color Edge Detector Using Jointly Hue, Saturation and Intensity", in Proceedings IEEE International Conference on Image Processing, pp. 977-981, October 1994.
4. H. Cheng, X. Jiang, Y. Sun and J. Wang, "Color Image Segmentation: Advances and Prospects", Pattern Recognition, 34, pp. 2259-2281, 2001.
5. L. Lucchese and S. Mitra, "Color Image Segmentation: A State-of-the-Art Survey", (invited paper) Image Processing, Vision, and Pattern Recognition, Proc. of the Indian National Science Academy (INSA-A), New Delhi, India, 67A 2, pp. 207-221, 2001.
6. G. Hinton, "Connectionist Learning Procedures", Artificial Intelligence, vol. 40, pp. 185-234, 1989.

7. R. Gonzalez and R. Woods, "Digital Image Processing", Addison-Wesley, 1992.
8. R. Dony and S. Wesolkowski, "Edge Detection on Color Images Using RGB Vector Angle", in Proceedings of IEEE CCECE'99, Edmonton, Canada, 1999.
9. Rumelhart, McClelland, PDP group. "Explorations in Parallel Distributed Processing". The MIT Press. Vol. 1 y 2, 1986.
10. D. Foresee and M. Hagan, "Gauss-Newton Approximation to Bayesian Learning", Proceedings of the International Joint Conference on Neural Networks, 1997.
11. A. Weigend, D. Rumelhart and B. Huberman, "Generalization by Weigth-Elimination with Applications to Forecasting", Advances in Neural Information Processing System, vol. 3, pp. 875-872, 1991.
12. D. Nguyen and B. Widrow, "Improving the Learning Speed of 2-Layer Neural Networks by Choossing Initial Values of the Adaptive Weights", Proceedings of the IJCNN, vol. 3, pp. 21-26, 1990.
13. D. Luenberger, "Linear and Nonlinear Programming", second edition, Adisson-Wesley, 1984.
14. J. Liu, Y.-H. Yang, "Multiresolution Color Image Segmentation", IEEE Trans. On PAMI, 16(7),pp. 689-700, 1994.
15. J. Moreira and L. Da Fontuora, "Neural-Based Color Image Segmentation and Classification", Anais do IX SIBGRAPI, Brasil, 1996.
16. S. Haykin, "Neural Networks. A Comprehensive Foundation", second edition, Prentice Hall, 1999.
17. H. Demuht and M. Beale, "Neural Networks Toolbox for Use with Matlab: User Guide Version 4", 2003.
18. V. Valenti, "Orthotic Treatment of Walk Alterations", Panamerican Medicine, (in spanish)1979.
19. K. Funahashi. "On the Aproximate Realization of Continuous Mappings by Neural Network". Neural Networks, 2, 183-192, 1989.
20. M. Borsotti, P. Campadelli and P. Schettini, "Quantitative Evaluation of Color Image Segmentation Results", Patt. Rec. Lett., vol.19, 741-747, 1998.
21. T. Gevers and F. Groen, "Segmentation of Color Images", in Proceedings of 7th Scandinavian Conference on Image Analysis, 1991.
22. J. Moody and T. Rogntvalddson, "Smothing Regularizers for Proyective Basis Function Networks", Advances in Neural Information Processing System, vol. 9, pp. 585-591, 1997.
23. T. Hastie, R. Tibshirami and J. Friedman, "The Elements of Statistical Learning", Springer, 2001.

Computing Similarity Among 3D Objects Using Dynamic Time Warping

A. Angeles-Yreta and J. Figueroa-Nazuno

Centro de Investigación en Computación, Instituto Politécnico Nacional,
Unidad Profesional "Adolfo López Mateos" –Zacatenco- México, D.F.
malberto@sagitario.cic.ipn.mx, jfn@cic.ipn.mx

Abstract. A new model to compute similarity is presented. The representation of a 3D object is reviewed; sequence of vertices and index of vertices are the basic information about the *shape* of any 3D object. A linear function called *Labeling* is introduced to create a new sequence or time series from a 3D object. A method to create *randomly* 3D objects is also described. Experimental results show viability to compute similarity among 3D objects using the extracted sequences and the Dynamic Time Warping algorithm.

1 Introduction

The problem of defining and computing similarity among objects (concepts, time series, images, 3D objects, etc.) is the essence of many *Data Mining* applications.

Most of the methods of similarity search among 3D objects use a *feature extraction* technique [1]. A transformation from a 3D object to a *feature vector* is involved. The goal is to preserve, discover or select some property. This feature vector can be handled as a *time series.* Other methods consider 3D objects as images sequences (*2D view based methods*); afterward, models of similarity search among images. Also, there are methods based on histograms, even though they can be a particular case of feature extraction based methods, usually belong to another class (*Histogram based methods*). Finally, hybrid methods exist. In this work a new model to compute similarity among 3D objects is presented.

This work is organized as follow. In section 2, the *Dynamic Time Warping* algorithm used to compute similarity among sequences is described. In section 3, the *3D Object Representation* is discussed. In section 4, a linear function called *Labeling* is presented. This function *converts* the 3D object representation (sequence of vertices and index of these vertices) to a new sequence or time series useful to the properties of the Dynamic Time Warping algorithm. In section 5, a method to create *randomly* 3D objects is introduced. In section 6, *A Model to Compute Similarity* is presented. In section 7 results of *Experimental Test* that show viability of the model are presented. Finally, *Conclusions* of this work are presented in section 8.

2 Dynamic Time Warping

The Dynamic Time Warping algorithm has been applied in automatic speech recognition; is fundamentally a feature-matching scheme [2].

M. Lazo and A. Sanfeliu (Eds.): CIARP 2005, LNCS 3773, pp. 319 – 326, 2005.

Given two sequences $\boldsymbol{Q}$ and $\boldsymbol{C}$ (1), to accomplish the *alignment* (feature-match) is build a matrix of size n by m, where the (i,j) element of the matrix contains the metric $d(q_i, c_j)$ (2), in this case the Euclidean metric:

$$Q = q_1, q_2, q_3, \dots, q_i, \dots, q_n; \quad C = c_1, c_2, c_3, \dots, c_j, \dots, c_m \tag{1}$$

$$d(q_i, c_i) = \sqrt{(q_i - c_i)^2} \tag{2}$$

The objective of the Dynamic Time Warping algorithm is to find a relation $i = \omega(j)$ that produces a warping path.

Definition 1. *Warping path*: A warping path W, is a contiguous set of matrix elements that defines a relation between two sequences, The k_{th} element of W is defined as $w_k = (i,j)_k$, so we have:

$$W = w_1, w_2, \dots, w_k, \dots, w_K \quad \max(m, n) \le K < m + n - 1 \tag{3}$$

Until now, the time and space complexity of the Dynamic Time Warping algorithm is $O(nm)$ [3]. Several constraints has been proposed to reduce the complexity:

1. **Endpoint Constraints.** Requires that the endpoints match exactly; any path begin at (q_1, c_1), and end at (q_n, c_m). Another approach automatically locates endpoints .
2. **Monotonic.** The warping path should be monotonic, that is, $q_{k-1} \le q_k$ and $c_{k-1} \le c_k$. The features of a sequence Q must never match to features already matched in the sequence C.
3. **Global Constraints.** They imply allowed regions in the matrix; no warping path must be outside this area, even if optimal. Itakura parallelogram (left-side Fig. 1) constrains a warping path for maximum compression and expansion factors of two [2], the Window band (right-side Fig. 1) defines a **windows width** r to compress or expand the search space of a warping path. In this work the Itakura parallelogram is used.
4. **Local Constraints.** Determine alignment flexibility. In this work the warping path search is in 0°, 45° and 90°, Fig. 2 depicts this local constraint.

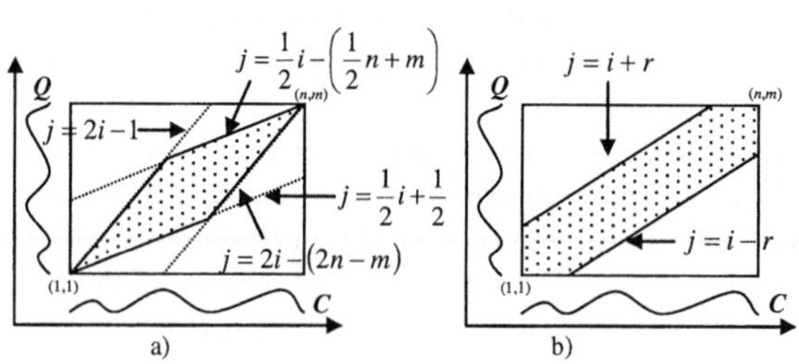

Fig. 1. a) Itakura parallelogram, and b) Window band are the most common global constraints for Dynamic Time Warping

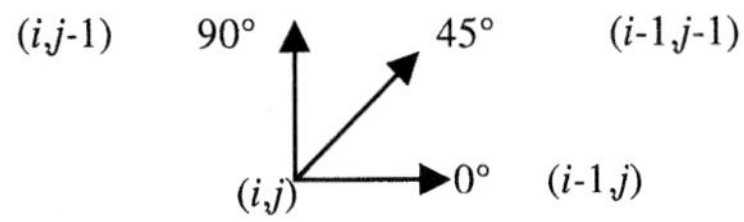

Fig. 2. The local constraint used in this work. It establishes the vicinity in the warping path search.

To avoid an exponential number of warping paths, we use only the warping path that minimizes the cost:

$$DTW(Q,C) \equiv \min\left\{ \sqrt{\sum_{k=1}^{K} w_{ki}} \,/\, K \right. \tag{4}$$

The denominator K is used for the fact that warping paths may have different lengths; the sequence with the lowest match score is declared the most similar. The warping path can be found using dynamic programming, specifically:

$$\gamma(i,j) = d(q_i, c_i) + \min\{\gamma(i-1,j-1), \gamma(i-1,j), \gamma(i,j-1)\} \tag{5}$$

In Fig. 3 an example of two sequences before and after alignment, is shown, the reference (continuous line) and the sample (dotted line).

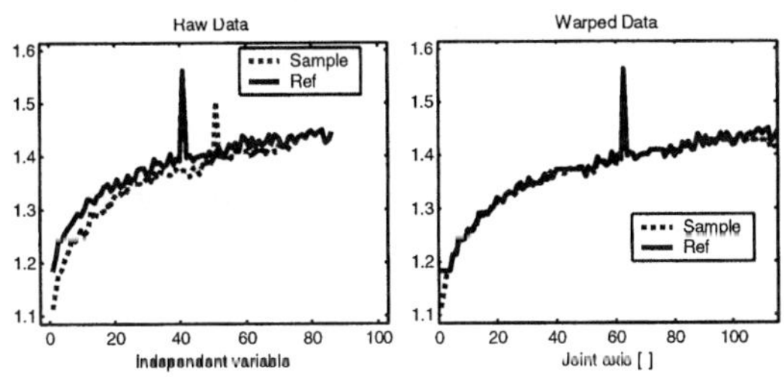

Fig. 3. Example of two sequences. Reference and sample are aligned using Dynamic Time Warping.

3 3D Object Representation

A 3D object can be represented as a graph; a graph is represented by an adjacency matrix. Most of the file formats used to represent 3D objects use an approximation of an adjacency matrix, that is, a sequence of vertices (6) and an index of vertices (7).

$$V = (v_1, v_2, \ldots, v_k), \text{ where } v_i = (x_i, y_i, z_i) \text{ and } x_i, y_i, z_i \in \Re \tag{6}$$

$$F = (v_{f_1}, v_{f_2}, \ldots, v_{f_n}), \text{ where } f_j \in [1,k] \tag{7}$$

Sequence of vertices $\boldsymbol{V}$ composes the graph nodes in a 3D space. The index of vertices $\boldsymbol{F}$ implies the order in which vertices must be drawn, and therefore the graph

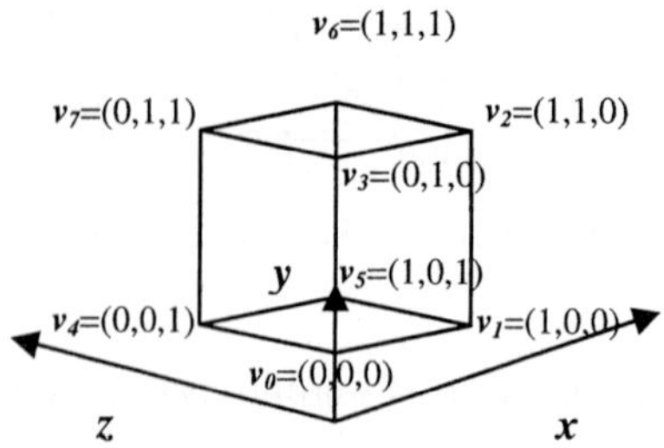

Fig. 4. The figure shows a cube, eight vertices are defined (v_0-v_7), the index of vertices is: v_0, v_1, v_2, v_3, -1, v_2, v_6, v_7, v_3, -1, v_6, v_5, v_4, v_7, -1, v_1, v_2, v_6, v_5, -1, v_0, v_4, v_7, v_3, -1, v_1, v_5, v_4, v_0

edges. Additional information such as position, rotation, cameras location, textures, etc., is ignored. Only the 3D object **shape** is considered when similarity is computed.

In Fig. 1 a cube in VRML format [4] is presented. Vertices are 3D points, the presence of -1 in the index of vertices means that the **face** sequence is almost complete and an extra vertex has to be added. For example, the first face composed by (v_0, v_1, v_2, v_3, -1), -1 has to bee substituted by v_0, that is, the first vertex in the face sequence. Several representations (file formats) uses this representation. Small modifications in index of vertices are detected. In this work this basic information is used (sequence of vertices and index of vertices). Graphics libraries, like OpenGL [5] agree this shape representation. The next code shows how to draw a 3D Object (polygon) defined by means of a sequence of vertices and an index of vertices

```
glBegin(GL_POLYGON);
  for (int i=0; i < length(F); i++)
    glVertex3f(V[F[i]].x, V[F[i].y, V[F[x].z);
glEnd();
```

The `glVertex3f` primitive puts a 3D point (vertex) in floating type. The ***F*** array is the index of vertices (7), and the structure ***V*** is the array of vertices or sequence of vertices (6). The next section presents a linear function to create another sequence or time series **based** on sequence of vertices and index of vertices.

4 Labeling 3D Objects

The Dynamic Time Warping is an excellent metric that **can be indexed** [3]. Given a sequence of vertices ***V*** and index of vertices ***F*** of any 3D object, a linear **function** (`Labeling`) is presented to create a **new** sequence. These sequences can be used to compute similarity among 3D objects using *Dynamic Time Warping* advantages.

```
Function Labeling(V, F):Q
  for (int i=0; i < length(F); i++)
    Q[i]=V[F[i]].x + V[F[i]].y + V[F[i]].z;
  return Q;
```

Parameters of the linear function (**`Labeling`**) are sequence of vertices ***V*** (6) and index of vertices ***F*** (7). The output is a **sequence** or **time series** ***Q*** that reflexes the

Table 1. A polyhedron of four vertices and a vertex index of length 16, the plot shows sequence ***Q***

Vertices	***Q***
$v_1 = (0, 1.081, 1.529)$	2.61
$v_2 = (1.529, -1.081, 0)$	0.448
$v_0 = (0, 1.081, -1.529)$	-0.45
$v_1 = (0, 1.081, 1.529)$	2.61
$v_2 = (1.529, -1.081, 0)$	0.448
$v_3 = (-1.529, -1.081, 0)$	-2.61
$v_0 = (0, 1.081, -1.529)$	-0.45
$v_2 = (1.529, -1.081, 0)$	0.448
$v_3 = (-1.529, -1.081, 0)$	-2.61
$v_1 = (0, 1.081, 1.529)$	2.61
$v_0 = (0, 1.081, -1.529)$	-0.45
$v_3 = (-1.529, -1.081, 0)$	-2.61
$v_3 = (-1.529, -1.081, 0)$	-2.61
$v_2 = (1.529, -1.081, 0)$	0.448
$v_1 = (0, 1.081, 1.529)$	2.61
$v_3 = (-1.529, -1.081, 0)$	-2.61

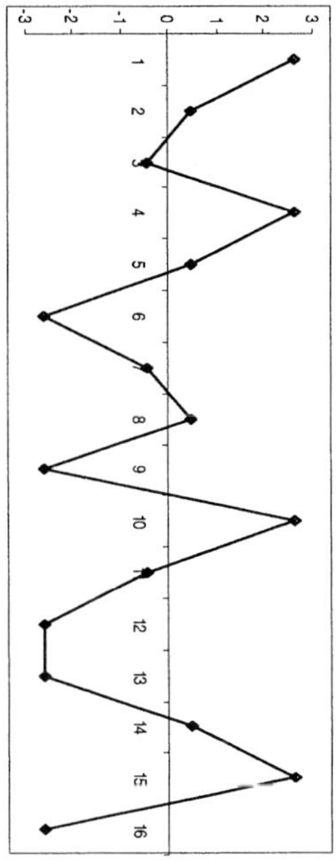

movements of drawing a 3D object, the object vertices have been *labeled* with the x, y, and z addition. In Table 1 a polyhedron of four vertices (v_0-v_3) is considered.

5 Random Modifications of 3D Objects

To show the efficiency of the model (computing similarity among 3D objects using Dynamic Time Warping), a method to create 3D objects is described. Given a 3D object, cube, pyramid, etc., called **base**, random modifications to the sequence of vertices ***V*** (6) are made. The algorithm is sketched in the next code.

```
bool CObject3D::RetriveVRML(char *filename) {
 if (wml.Open(filename))    //VRML file (.wml)
  if(wml.Retrive(&V, &F)) return true;
  else return false;
 else return false; }
```

The **CObject3D** contains basic information (see section 3), that is, a sequence of vertices called ***V*** and an index of vertices called ***F***. **RetriveVRML** method accepts a 3D object **base** (cube, prism, etc.) in VRML format, it can be modified to accept other grammar that define a sequence of vertices and an index of vertices (.3ds-The 3D Studio Format, .dfx-Autodesk's/AutoCAD, .off-Object File Format, etc.).

```
CObject3D::RandomModify(int nModify) {
 int list[V.Length]={0}; // Vertices to be modified
```

```
int count=0;                    // Number of modifications
double x, y, z, min, max;
min = V.GetMin();   max = V.GetMax();

for(int i=0; i < nModify; i++)
 list[(int)myRand.IRandom(0, vertices.Length)]++;
for(i=0; i < V.Length; i++)
 if(list[i]>0) {
   count++;
   x = myRand.IRandom(min, max);
   y = myRand.IRandom(min, max);
   z = myRand.IRandom(min, max);
   V.ModifyVertix(i, x, y, z); }
   wml.SaveVRML(&V, &F, count);       }
```

RandomModify method defines a vertex list called **list** with the candidates to be modified using a pseudo-random number generator with uniform distribution and period of $2^{19,937}$-1 [6] (Mersennne Twister). Uniform distribution warranties equal probability to each vertex to be modified. **nModify** parameter gives indirect control of modifications number made to a sequence of vertices. Finally, **ModifyVertix**, updates the x, y, and z component of $v_i(6)$. Fig. 1 depicts this idea.

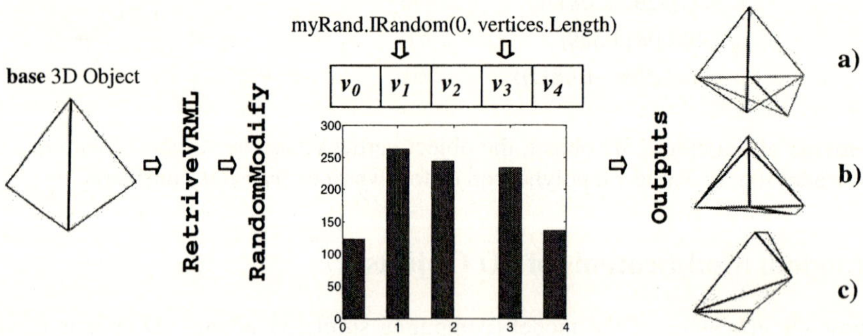

Fig. 5. A 3D Object *base* is the input to generate new 3D Objects with **a) one** modification, **b) two** modifications, and **c) three** modifications

Given a new data set of 3D Objects *randomly* created, a **Labeling** function (see section 4) can be computed over this data set to compute their similarity.

6 A Model to Compute Similarity

To compute similarity among 3D objects, a stage of pre-processing is required. The **Labeling** function creates sequences from 3D objects (see section 4), and these sequences are used to calculate a match score among these 3D objects. Fig 6 shows the model to compute similarity among 3D objects. An advantage of Dynamic Time Warping is that can be **indexed**. Future work presents results of indexing techniques.

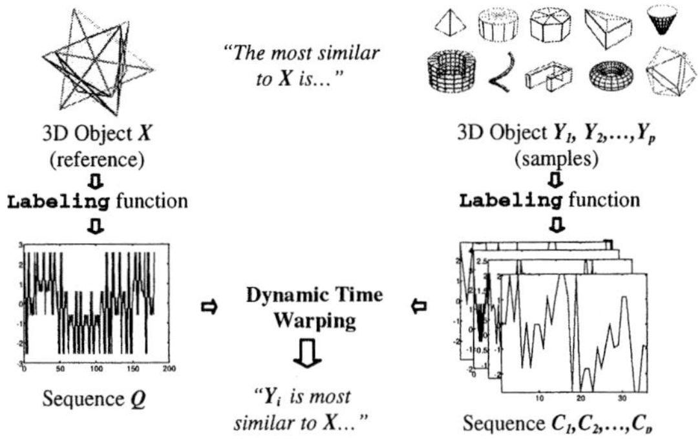

Fig. 6. For each 3D object in the database a sequence is created (see section 4). Using Dynamic Time Warping a similarity distance among 3D objects can be computed.

7 Experimental Tests

Two data sets were used in this work: 3D objects created with a typical *Computer Design System* CAD (specifically, 3D Studio Max 6) and 3D objects *randomly* created (see section 5), the pre-processing stage using the **`Labeling`** function (see section 4) was applied to all 3D objects, finally, Dynamic Time Warping metric was computed for each reference sequence (extracted from a 3D object) against every sample in the database.

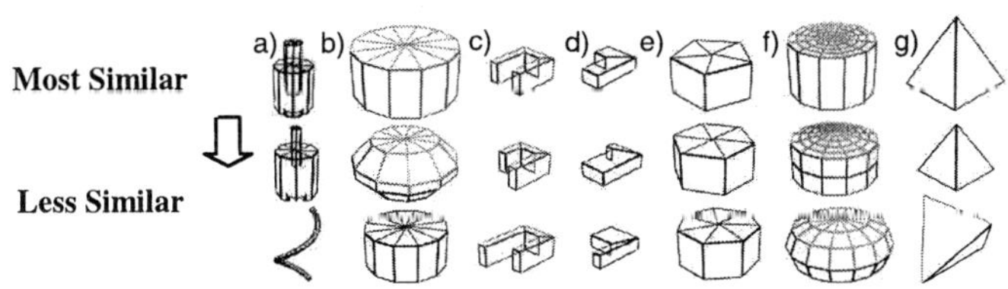

Fig. 7. a) SockAbsorber02, b) ChafCil01, c)Ext_C01, d)Ext_L01, e)Gengon01, f) Huso01, g)Pyramid01 and their two most similar 3D objects

Fig. 7 shows partial results. In Fig. 7 the less similar 3D objects to b), f) and g) respectively (marked with *), were created as part of another class (specifically, Gengon03, ChafCil05, and Polyhedron03), the proposed model can distinguish their similarity; this can be seen in Table 2.

Table 2. Dynamic Time Warping distance, ordered to most similar to less similar

ShockAbsorber02	DTW Distance	ChafCil01	DTW Distance	Ext_C01	DTW Distance	Ext_L01	DTW Distance	Gengon01	DTW Distance	Huso01	DTW Distance	Piramide01	DTW Distance
ShockAbsorber01	118.861	ChafCil02	106.2858	Ext_C02	6.672	Ext_L05	5.0388	Gengon02	13.7403	Huso02	130.4449	Piramide02	8.684
Muelle01	227.2536	**Gengon05**	120.635	Ext_C03	7.5414	Ext_L03	5.7651	Gengon03	20.4739	**ChafCil05**	205.8659	**Polyhedron03**	21.508

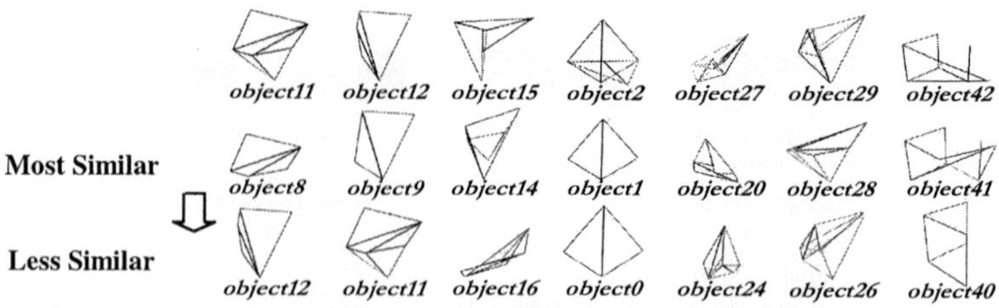

Fig. 8. 3D objects *randomly* created; *object11*, *object8*, and *object12* have 4 modifications, *object2*, *object1*, *object0*, has 1, 1, and 0 modifications respectively, the number of modifications can influence the Dynamic Time Warping distance

8 Conclusions

Experimental results show the efficiency of computing similarity among 3D objects, a linear function is required to *convert* a 3D object into a sequence and then compute Dynamic Time Warping distance among sequences. Two kinds of data sets were used in experimental test, the first one, created with a typical CAD; the other one was created from *base* 3D objects (cube, prism, and pyramid). There is not a true classification per se; the similarity between objects has to be recognized by humans. The proposed model to compute similarity among 3D objects is simpler than other approaches [1], and the results show this idea. An advantage of this model is that has been proved that Dynamic Time Warping technique can be indexed [3].

References

[1] Hlavaty, T., Skala, V.: A Survey of Methods for 3D Model Feature Extraction, *bulletin of the seminar of Geometry and Graphics in Teaching Contemporary Engineer*, Szczyrk, Poland, 2003, No: 13/03. pp. 5-8.

[2] Angeles-Yreta, A., Solís-Estrella, H. Landassuri-Moreno, V. Figueroa-Nazuno, J.: Similarity Search In Seismological Signals. *Fifth Mexican Internacional Conference on Computer Science.* Colima, México. September 2004, pp. 50-56.

[3] E. Keogh, Ratanamahatana C.: Exact indexing of dynamic time warping. *In 28th International Conference on Very Large Data Bases*, pages 406--417, 2002.

[4] Hartman, J., Wernecke, J. The VRML 2.0 handbook: building moving worlds on the web, *Addison-Wesley*, 1996.

[5] Leech, J. Brown, P. (eds.).The OpenGL Graphics System: A Specification, *Silicon Graphics Press*, October 2004.

[6] Makoto Matsumoto, Takuji Nishimura, Mersenne Twister: a 623-dimensionally equidistributed uniform pseudo-random number generator, *ACM Transactions on Modeling and Computer Simulation*, ACM Press, Vol. 8, 1998, pp. 3-30.

Estimation of Facial Angular Information Using a Complex-Number-Based Statistical Model

Mario Castelan* and Edwin R. Hancock

Department of Computer Science, University of York, York Y01 5DD, UK

Abstract. In this paper we explore the use of complex numbers as means of representing angular statistics for surface normal data. Our aim is to use the representation to construct a statistical model that can be used to describe the variations in fields of surface normals. We focus on the problem of representing facial shape. The fields of surface normals used to train the model are furnished by range images. We compare the complex representation with one based on angles, and demonstrate the advantages of the new method. Once trained, we illustrate how the model can be fitted to brightness images by searching for the set of parameters that both satisfy Lambert's law and minimize the integrability error.

1 Introduction

The problem of acquiring surface models of faces is an important one with potentially significant applications in biometrics, computer games and production graphics. There are many ways in which surface models can be acquired, and these include the use of range-scanners, stereoscopic cameras and structured light sensors. However, one of the most appealing methods is to use shape-from-shading (SFS), since this is a non-invasive process which mimics the capabilities of the human vision system. Shape-from-shading aims to recover surface orientation, and hence surface height by solving the image radiance equation. In general, though, SFS is an under-constrained problem since the two degrees of freedom for surface orientation (slant and tilt), must be recovered from a single measured intensity value. In contrast to the human visual system[3], it seems that computer vision systems encounter more difficultly in estimating the tilt of a surface from a single image than its slant (see Figure 1).

One way to overcome the problems with general purpose SFS is to draw on a domain specific model that can be used to constrain the directions of the surface normals. This approach has proved to be particularly effective in the analysis of faces. Attick et al.[1] were the among the first to build 3D statistical shape models of faces for use in conjunction with SFS. Working with cylindrical coordinates they develop an eigenmode model (referred to as eigenheads) for surface height. In fitting the model to data, they impose an image irradiance constraint using the shape coefficients of the model. Later, Vetter et al.[9] decoupled the effects of

* Supported by National Council of Science and Technology (CONACYT), Mexico, under grant No. 141485.

M. Lazo and A. Sanfeliu (Eds.): CIARP 2005, LNCS 3773, pp. 327–338, 2005.

texture and shape on facial appearance. Assuming that full facial correspondence information is to hand, they perform PCA separately on the texture and shape components. Thus they develop a statistical model that can be fitted to image brightness data. These methods deliver accurate and photo-realistic results, but at the expense of considerable computational overheads and simplicity of implementation. This is largely due to the brute force search method used to adjust the model parameters to fit the input image data. Recently, Dogvard and Basri[2] have combined statistical models with symmetry constraints. The model relies on a Cartesian representation of the surface height. Surface gradient is expressed in terms of a set of deformation coefficients, and this allows the symmetric SFS equation to be transformed into a linear system of equations. The linear system can be efficiently solved and used to estimate surface height. Their results show that accuracy is sacrificed for a gain in computational efficiency.

The aim in this paper is to explore whether angular representations can be used to construct statistical models that can be used in conjunction with shape-from-shading. This is a natural approach since it is surface orientation and not surface height that is responsible to the perceived image brightness. Angular data is more difficult to model than Cartesian data since angles wrap around. Hence, small differences in distance on a sphere can correspond to large differences in angles. The classical example here is a short walk across one of the poles of a sphere, when large differences in longitude correspond to small differences travelled. In shape from shading the surface normal is determined by the azimuth and zenith angles. When the surface is illuminated in the direction of the viewer and if the surface reflectance is Lambertian, then the arc-cosine of the zenith angle is determined by the normalized image brightness. The azimuth angle, on the other hand, must be determined using additional constraints provided by smoothness or the occluding boundary. The aim in this paper is to develop a statistical model that can be used to model the distribution of azimuthal direction in faces. To overcome the problems with the representation of angular data, we use complex numbers. Our idea is to encode the azimuth angles as complex numbers and to capture their distribution by adapting the Sirovich snapshot method to deal with complex eigenvectors. We show how the model can be trained using range images and fitted to brightness images using constraints on surface normal direction provided by Lambert's law and surface integrability.

2 Statistical Information for Angular Data

In this paper, we aim to construct a statistical model for the angular variation in surface normal direction. We train our model on surface normals extracted from range images. We aim to recover surface normals from image brightness data by fitting the model to facial images using constraints provided by Lambert's law and integrability.

To construct the statistical model, we represent the surface normal data extracted from the range data as long-vectors. The range data is vectorized by stacking the image columns. If the range images contain M columns and N rows,

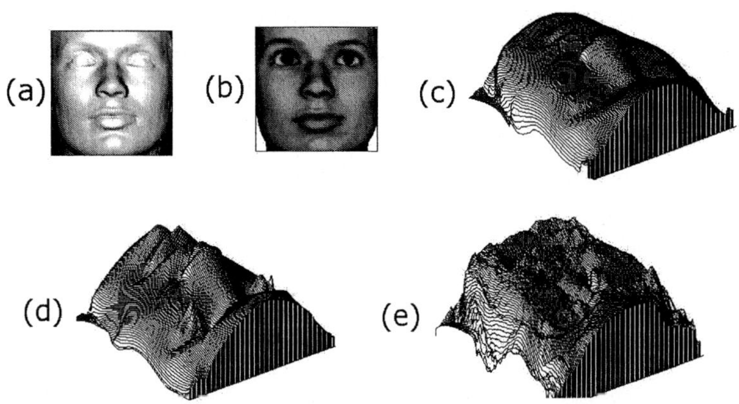

Fig. 1. Effect of incorrectly calculated azimuth and zenith angle in face shape recovery: (a) orthogonal Lambertian (constant albedo) image, (b) true irradiance (non-constant albedo) image, (c) ground-truth surface, (d) surface preserving true azimuth angle but with its zenith angle estimated through SFS and (e) surface preserving true zenith angle, but with its azimuth angle estimated through SFS. Note how the effect of wrongly estimated tilt angle cause a severe deterioration on the recovered surface.

then the pixel with column index j_c and row index j_r corresponds to the element indexed $j = (N-1)j_c + j_r$ of the long-vector. Let $n_j^k = \frac{1}{\sqrt{(p_j^k)^2+(q_j^k)^2+1}}(p_j^k, q_j^k, 1)^T$ be the surface normal at the pixel indexed j of the kth training image. Here $p = \frac{\partial h}{\partial x}$ and $q = \frac{\partial h}{\partial y}$ are the partial derivatives of the surface height h in the x and y directions. The zenith and azimuth angles of the surface normal are respectively $\theta_j^k = \arctan\sqrt{(p_j^k)^2 + (q_j^k)^2}$ and $\phi_j^k = \arctan\frac{q_j^k}{p_j^k}$. Here we use the four quadrant arc-tangent function and therefore $-\pi \leq \phi_j^k \leq \pi$. Unfortunately the angles can not be used to construct statistical models. The reason for this is that statistical calculations performed on angular data can be biased by the angle *cut* point (see Figure 2). To illustrate this problem consider two points on a unit circle placed just above and just below the cut-line. Although the two points are close to one another on the unit circle, when the difference in angles is computed then this may be close to 2π.

Our idea in this paper is to overcome this problem by working with a complex number representation of the azimuth angles of the surface normal. We encode the azimuth angle using the complex number

$$z_j^k = \exp(i\phi_j^k) = \cos\phi_j^k + i\sin\phi_j^k, \tag{1}$$

where $i = \sqrt{-1}$. The azimuth angle is hence given by the real (Re) and imaginary (Im) components of the complex number, i.e.

$$\phi_j^k = \arctan\frac{\text{Im } z_j^k}{\text{Re } z_j^k}. \tag{2}$$

The azimuth angle ϕ_j^k is therefore the principal argument (a unique angle value from $-\pi$ to π) of z_j^k. At the image location indexed j, the mean complex number (center of mass) over the training set is given by

$$\hat{z}_j = \frac{1}{K}\sum_{k=1}^{K} z_j^k. \tag{3}$$

The azimuth angle associated with this complex number (mean direction) and its moduli are, respectively

$$\hat{\phi}_j = \arctan\frac{\text{Im } \hat{z}_j}{\text{Re } \hat{z}_j} \qquad \text{and} \qquad \hat{r}_j = \sqrt{(\text{Im } \hat{z}_j)^2 + (\text{Re } \hat{z}_j)^2}. \tag{4}$$

Note that the cartesian coordinates of the points of $\hat{z}_j$ on the complex plane are defined by the average of the cosines (x-axis) and sines (y-axis) of all of the observations ϕ_j^k of the training set, therefore

$$\text{Re } \hat{z}_j = \hat{r}_j \cos\hat{\phi}_j = \frac{1}{K}\sum_{k=1}^{K} \cos\phi_j^k \quad \text{and} \quad \text{Im } \hat{z}_j = \hat{r}_j \sin\hat{\phi}_j = \frac{1}{K}\sum_{k=1}^{K}. \tag{5}$$

Unfortunately, although this allows us to overcome the problems of representing the azimuth angle statistics, it yields complex numbers that no longer have unit modulus. In fact r_j can fluctuate between 0 and 1. However, r_j is an important measure of the concentration of the azimuth angles in the training data. If the directions of the azimuth angles in the training set are strongly clustered, then r_j will tend to be 1. If, on the other hand, they are scattered then r_j will tend to 0.

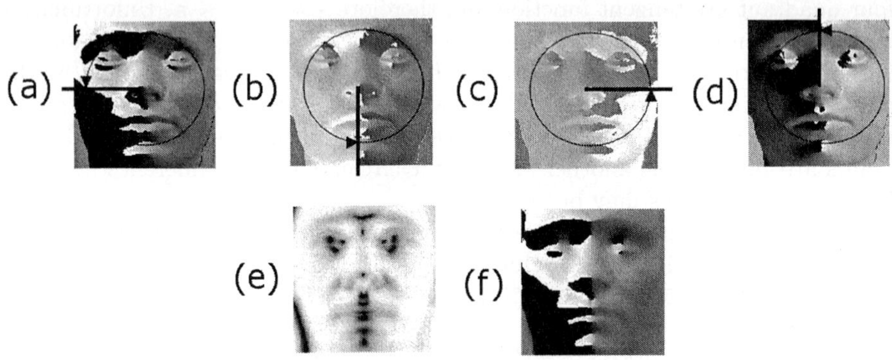

Fig. 2. In the top row, different arguments for one training set example z^k are shown as intensity maps. From left to right, $(-\pi, \pi]$(a), $(-\frac{\pi}{2}, \frac{3\pi}{2}]$ (b), $(0, 2\pi]$ (c) and $(\frac{-3\pi}{2}, \frac{\pi}{2}]$ (d). The mean direction $\hat{\phi}$ (e) and the mean resultant length $\hat{r}$ (f) are presented in the bottom row, from left to right, as intensity plots. Note how $\hat{r}$ demonstrates that the directions of the angles are widely dispersed through the regions where the zenith angle is close to 0, i.e. tip of the nose, centers of the eyes and mouth, and forehead.

Although the mean resultant length $\hat{r}_j$ is a very important measure of dispersion, for purposes of comparison with data on the line we should consider measures of dispersion based on circular data, like the sample circular variance $v_j = 1-\hat{r}_j$, $0 \leq v_j \leq 1$. Following [5], if $1-\cos(\alpha_1-\alpha_2)$ is a measure of distance between two angles α_1 and α_2, then the dispersion of the angles $\phi_j^1, \phi_j^2, \ldots, \phi_j^K$ about a given angle β is

$$D(\beta) = \frac{1}{K}\sum_{k=1}^{K}\{1 - \cos(\phi_j^k - \beta)\}. \tag{6}$$

For any set of angular data, the dispersion of its mean direction over the set is equal to its circular variance, i.e., $D(\hat{\phi}_j) = v_j = 1 - r_j$. In Figure 2(e) and (f), the mean arguments $\hat{\phi}$ and moduli of the center of mass $\hat{z}$ are shown as intensity maps.

3 Construction of the Statistical Models

In their work on eigenfaces, Turk and Pentland were among the the first to explore the use of principal components analysis for performing face recognition [8]. This method can be rendered efficient using the technique described by Sirovich et al.[7] which shows how to avoid explicit covariance matrix computation for large sets of two-dimensional images of objects of the same class.

We convert each image in the training set into a long-vector. Two encodings are investigated. In the first of these the long-vector has the measured azimuth angles as components. Hence, the jth component of the long-vector for the training image indexed k is $V_\phi^k(j) = \phi_j^k$. The second encoding involves using the complex number representation. Here the jth component of the long-vector for the training image indexed k is the complex number $V_z^k(j) = z_j^k$. We center the long-vectors by computing the mean

$$\hat{V} = \frac{1}{K}\sum_{k=1}^{K} V^k. \tag{7}$$

From the centered long-vectors we construct the data matrix

$$X = (\hat{V}^1|\hat{V}^2|...|\hat{V}^K). \tag{8}$$

In the case of the real-valued azimuth angle data the covariance matrix is $\Sigma_\phi = \frac{1}{K}X_\phi X_\phi^T$. For the complex representation the covariance matrix is $\Sigma_z = \frac{1}{K}X_z X_z^\dagger$, where $\dagger$ denotes the transpose of the complex conjugate matrix. The resulting covariance matrices Σ_ϕ and Σ_z are respectively symmetric and Hermitian. We follow Atick et al.[1] and use the numerically efficient method of Sirovich [7] to compute the eigenvectors of Σ. For the real valued azimuth angle data this involves computing the eigen-decomposition of the matrices

$$Y_\phi = X_\phi^T X_\phi = U_\phi \Lambda_\phi U_\phi^T, \tag{9}$$

where the ordered eigenvalue matrix Λ_ϕ and eigenvector matrix U_ϕ are both real. Similarly, for the complex representation we compute the eigen-decomposition

$$Y_z = X_z^\dagger X_z = U_z \Lambda_z U_z^T. \tag{10}$$

In this case the ordered eigenvalue matrix Λ_z is real, but the elements of the eigenvector matrix U_z are complex. The eigenvectors of the matrices $X_\phi X_\phi^T$ and $X_z X_z^\dagger$ (or eigen-modes) are respectively the real matrix $\hat{U}_\phi = X_\phi U_\phi$ and the complex matrix $\hat{U}_z = X_z U_z$.

We deform mean long-vectors in the directions defined by the eigen-mode matrices. If $\tilde{U}_L$ is the result of truncating U after the L leading eigenvectors then the deformed long vector is

$$V = \hat{V} + \sum_{l=1}^{L} \tilde{U}_l b_l, \tag{11}$$

where $b = [b_1, b_2, ..., b_L]^T$ is a vector of real valued parameters of length L and $\tilde{U}_l$ is the lth column of matrix $\tilde{U}$. Suppose that V_o is a centered long-vector of measurements to which we wish to fit the statistical model. We seek the parameter vector b that minimizes the squared error. The solution to this least-

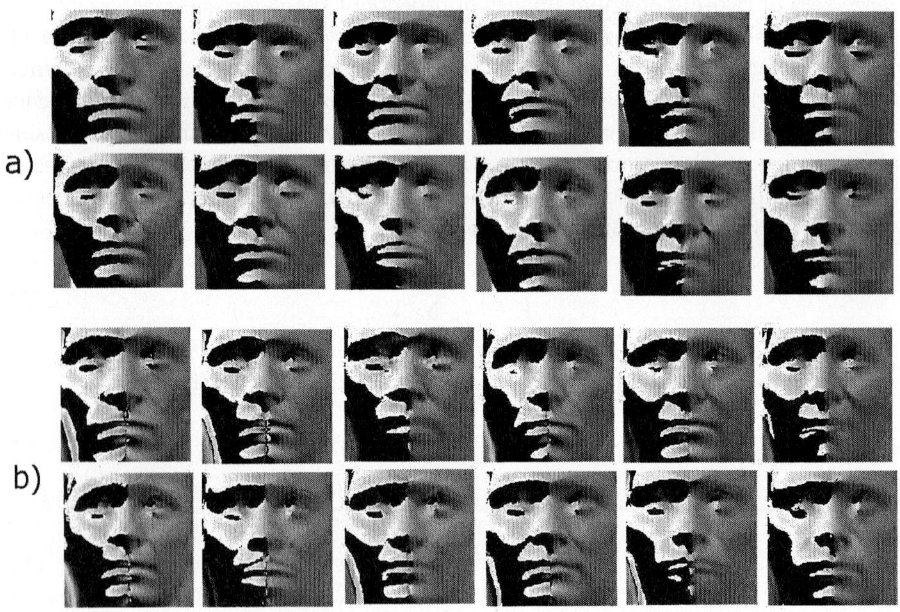

Fig. 3. From left to right, the first six eigen-modes of $\tilde{U}_z$ (a) and $\tilde{U}_\phi$ (b). The two first rows represent, respectively, $\hat{V}_z + \sqrt{3\Lambda_z}\hat{U}_z$ and $\hat{V}_z - \sqrt{3\Lambda_z}\hat{U}_z$. The variations $\hat{V}_\phi + \sqrt{3\Lambda_\phi}\hat{U}_\phi$ and $\hat{V}_\phi - \sqrt{3\Lambda_\phi}\hat{U}_\phi$ are shown in the two rows of (b).

squares estimation problem is $b^* = \tilde{U}^T V_o$. The best fit long-vector allowed by the model is $V_o^* = UU^T V_o$. In the case of both the real and complex representations, the parameter vectors are real.

In Figure 3 we compare the eigen-modes obtained using the real and complex representations. The rows of the figure show the first six eigen-modes. In the top two rows we show the five eigen-modes for Σ_z. The first row is the result of the displacement $\tilde{V}_z = \hat{V}_z + \sqrt{3}\Lambda_z\hat{U}_z$, and the bottom row the result of the displacement $\tilde{V}_z = \hat{V}_z - \sqrt{3}\Lambda_z\hat{U}_z$. We display the azimuth angles $\tilde{\phi}_z(j) = \arctan\frac{\text{Im }(\tilde{V}_z(j))}{\text{Re }(\tilde{V}_z(j))}$ at the pixel location indexed j. In the third and fourth rows, we repeat this analysis for the real-representation. Here we show the eigenmodes of Σ_ϕ The third row shows the result of displacement $\tilde{V}_\phi = \hat{V}_\phi + \sqrt{3}\Lambda_\phi\hat{U}_\phi$, and the bottom row the result of the displacement $\tilde{V}_\phi = \hat{V}_\phi - \sqrt{3}\Lambda_\phi\hat{U}_\phi$. We display the azimuth angles $\tilde{\phi}_z(j) = \tilde{V}_\phi(j)$ at the pixel location indexed j. In general, both models seem to encapsulate the same facial features though the complex model $\hat{U}_z$ shows less noise than the real model $\hat{U}_\phi$. These errors are most evident where $\hat{r}(j)$ is near zero. This suggests that the complex representation $\tilde{U}_z$ is profiting of the inherent accuracy attached in the center of mass $\hat{z}_j$, which might be sacrificed by being projected onto the unit circle while calculating the mean direction $\hat{\phi}_j$.

4 Fitting the Model to Brightness Data

In brief SFS aims to solve the image irradiance equation, $I(x, y) = R(p, q, \mathrm{s})$, where I is the intensity value of the pixel with position (x, y), R is a function referred to as *the reflectance map* [6]. The reflectance map uses the surface gradients $p - \frac{\partial Z(x,y)}{\partial x}$ and $q - \frac{\partial Z(x,y)}{\partial y}$ together with the light source direction vector s to compute a brightness estimate which can be compared with the observed one using a measure of error. If the surface normal at the location (x, y) is $n = [p, q, -1]$, then under Lambertian reflectance model, the image irradiance equation becomes $I(x, y) = n \cdot s$. Surface information can also be decoupled in azimuth (tilt) and zenith (slant) angles (φ and ϑ respectively), related to the surface normal by $n = [\cos\varphi\sin\vartheta, \sin\varphi\sin\vartheta, \cos\vartheta]$.

Let I_j be the normalized image brightness at the pixel indexed j. From Lambert's law, the zenith angle for this pixel is $\vartheta_j = \arccos I_j$. Let $\tilde{\phi}_j = \arctan\frac{\text{Im }\tilde{V}(j)}{\text{Re }\tilde{V}(j)}$ be the azimuth angle at the pixel j obtained by fitting the complex model $\tilde{V}_z = \hat{V}_z + \tilde{U}_z b$. From the surface normal at the pixel j, $n_j = [\cos\phi_j \sin\vartheta_j, \sin\phi_j\sin\vartheta_j, \cos\vartheta_j]^T$, we compute a numerical estimate of the Hessian matrix using first-differences. We are interested in the off-diagonal elements of this matrix $H_{xy}(j) = \frac{\partial n_j^x}{\partial y}$ and $H_{yx}(j) = \frac{\partial n_j^y}{\partial x}$.

Our aim is to fit the complex-model to brightness data so as to minimize the integrability error for the recovered field of surface normals. The error is defined to be

$$\mathrm{Err}(b) = \sum_{j=1}^{MN} |H_{xy}(j) - H_{yx}(j)|. \tag{12}$$

Our algorithm for finding the best-fit parameter vector b is one based on search and involves varying its elements over equally divided intervals between $-\sqrt{3}\Lambda_z e$ and $+\sqrt{3}\Lambda_z e$ where $e = (1, 1, ..., 1)^T$ is the all-ones vector of length L. Briefly, the algorithm is as follows: We initially zero all the components of the parameter vector b. Commencing from the first component, i.e. the one corresponding to the largest eigenvalue of Σ_z, we vary this component in S steps between $-3\sqrt{\Lambda_z(1)}$ and $+3\sqrt{\Lambda_z(1)}$ until $\text{Err}(b)$ is minimized. For each parameter setting, we recompute the field of surface normals so that the integrability error can be calculated. When the best-fit value of $b(1)$ is found it is fixed, and then we repeat the procedure for each of the remaining components of b in turn.

5 Experiments

In this section we present experiments with our statistical model for surface normal data. We commence by showing how the model can be trained on range data, and then fitted to out-of-sample range images. The second strand to the study is to show how the model can be fitted to brightness images to recover surface normals subject to Lambertian reflectivity and integrability constraints.

The face database used for constructing the surface models was provided by the Max-Planck Institute for Biological Cybernetics in Tuebingen, Germany. As described in [9], this database was constructed using Laser scans ($Cyberware^{TM}$) of 200 heads of young adults, and provides head structure data in a cylindrical representation as well as ground-truth surface gradient for each of the face examples. We used $K = 150$ examples of size $M \times N = 150 \times 150$ pixels.

The results of fitting the model to out-of-sample range data (i.e. data not used in training) are shown in Figure 4. In the top row we show the result of

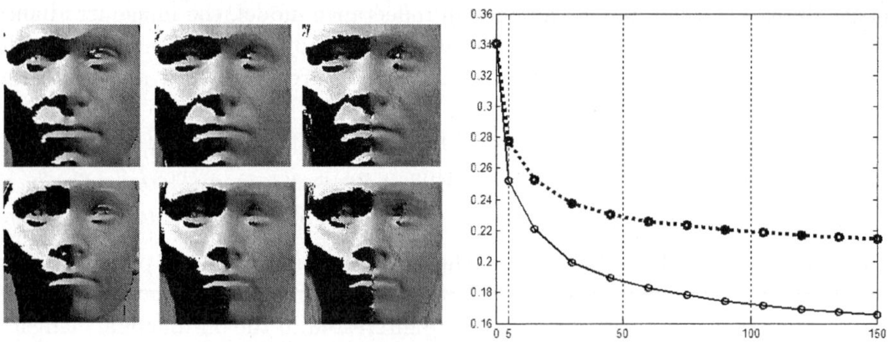

Fig. 4. Out-of-sample recovery analysis. From left to right: the first three columns show the ground truth azimuth angle, recovered azimuth angle using $\tilde{U}_z$ and recovered azimuth angle using $\tilde{U}_\phi$. The rightmost diagram shows the angular difference averaged over 50 out-of-sample data as a function of number of eigenmodes used for $\tilde{U}_z$ (solid line) and $\tilde{U}_\phi$ (dashed line).

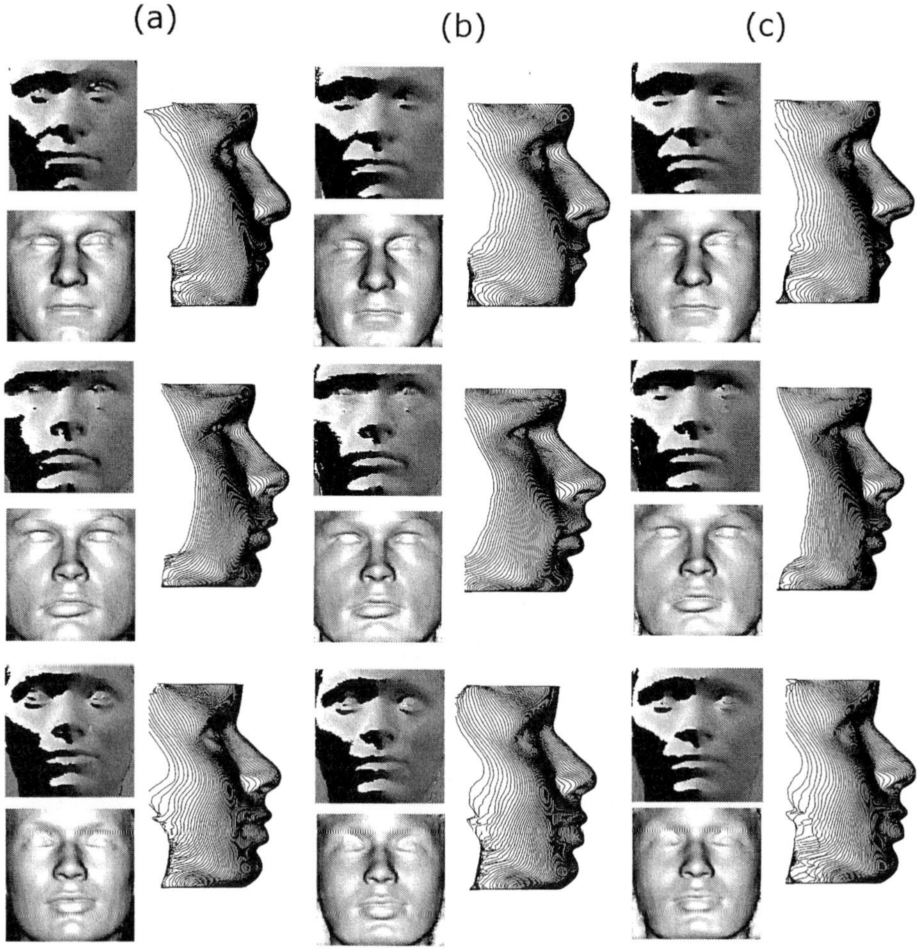

Fig. 5. Fitting the parameters to brightness data. We present three row-wise blocks representing different subjects. The results are organized in individual three-elements panels containing the following attributes: azimuthal angle (at the top), integrated surface (big surface at the right) and frontal re-illumination from integrated surface (at the bottom). Three column-wise blocks show true azimuth angles (a), best fit from true azimuth angles (b), fit from a Lambertian image using integrability constraints (d).

fitting the model to a male subject and the bottom row shows the result of fitting the model to a female subject. We show two panels of results. In the left panel we present the ground truth data, the result of fitting the complex model and the result of fitting the real model. The main feature to note from the panel is that the complex model achieves more accuracy on regions where the zenith angle is small, which in the estimation from the real model can be appreciated as small perturbations. In the rightmost diagram we show the absolute angular

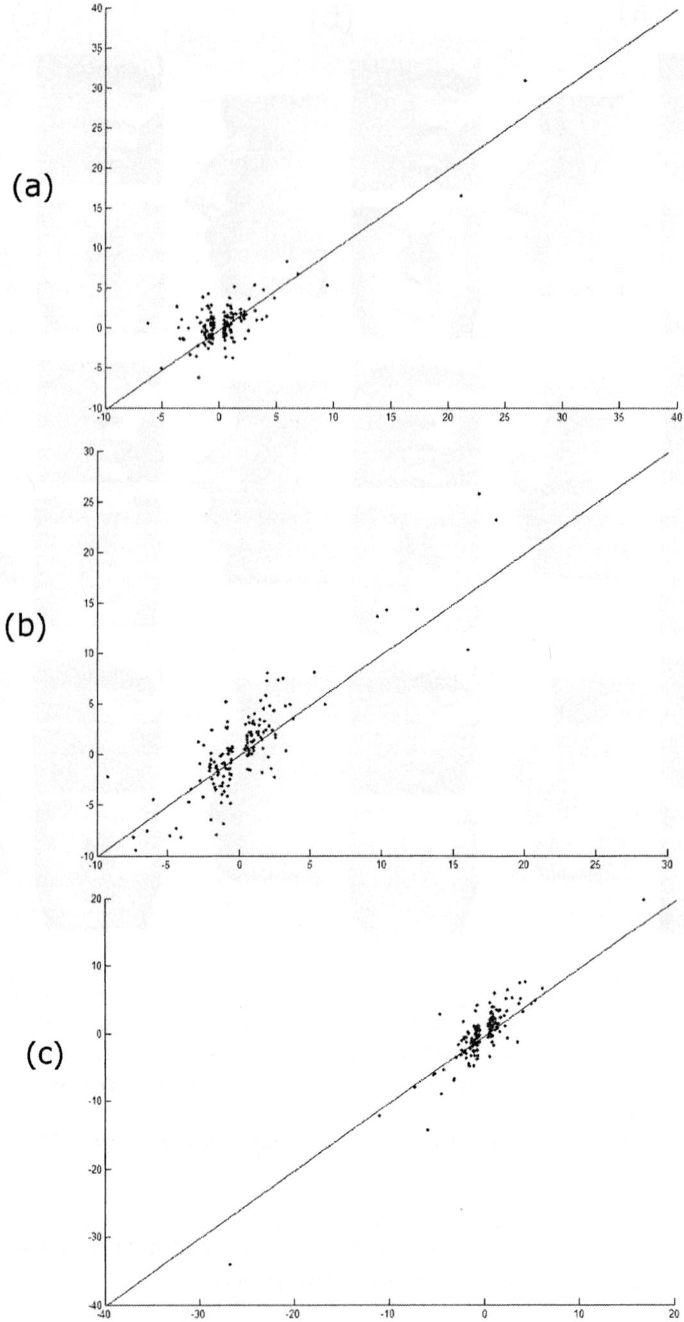

Fig. 6. The scatter plots show the relation between the best-fit parameters (y-axis) and the integrability-based adjustment (x-axis). We show three examples corresponding to the ones presented in Figure 5.

difference[1] averaged over 50 out-of-sample examples as a function of the number of eigen-modes used for $\tilde{U}_z$ and $\tilde{U}_\phi$. From the diagram it is clear that the complex model $\tilde{U}_z$ outperforms the real model. The behavior of both models is similar, and the gap between the lines can be explained as a consequence of the badly recovered regions by the real model.

The result of applying the fitting algorithm outlined in Section 4 to three Lambertian images are shown in Figure 5. We used $L = 150$ parameters and $S = 10$ equally spaced values for making rough estimates of the parameter vector b. The results for each subject are organized into three row-wise blocks. Each block presents: (a) the results obtained from the ground truth surface normals, (b) the results obtained from the best fit to the ground truth azimuth angles, and (c) the results obtained by fitting to brightness information using the lambertian reflectance model and the integrability constraint. Three-elements Individual panels show the following attributes: the estimated azimuth angles (top), profile view of the surface reconstructed by integrating the recovered field of surface normals using the Frankot and Chellappa integration method[4] (bigger surface at the right), and the result of re-illuminating the reconstructed surface in the frontal viewer direction (bottom). We Note that there seems to be no significant differences between the results shown for the best adjustment and the ones shown for the integrability-constrained adjustment.

In Figure 6, the relationship between the best fit parameters and the parameters estimated by the integrability-constrained algorithm are shown as scatter plots, for the three examples explained above. Note how the scatters show a tendency to form a line, revealing a good correlation with the best-fit parameters.

6 Conclusions

We have explored the use of complex numbers as means of representing angular statistics for surface normal data. The reason for doing this is the difficulties encountered in representing surface normal information when attempting to fit statistical shape models to face images using shape-from-shading. We show how the complex valued model can be trained on surface normals delivered by range data and fitted to image brightness data. The fitting to brightness data is effected so as to satisfy Lambert's law and minimize an integrability error. For future work we are planning to experiment with textured images as well as adding different attributes for developing constraints (i.e. irradiance, variable albedo, curvature).

References

1. Atick, J., Griffin, P. and Redlich, N. (1996), Statistical Approach to Shape from Shading: Reconstruction of Three-Dimensional Face Surfaces from Single Two-Dimensional Images, *Neural Computation*, Vol. 8, pp. 1321-1340.

[1] The angular difference between the angles α and β, in radians, can be defined as $\pi - \|\pi - \|\alpha - \beta\|\|$.

2. Dovgard, R. and Basri, R. (2004), Statistical symmetric shape from shading for 3D structure recovery of faces, *European Conf. on Computer Vision (ECCV 04)*, Prague, May 2004.
3. Erens, R.G.F., Kappers, A.M.L. and Koenderink, J.J. (1993), Perception of Local Shape from Shading. *Perception and Psychophysics*, Vol. 54, No. 2, pp. 145 - 156.
4. Frankot, R.T. and Chellapa, R. (1988), A Method for Enforcing Integrability in Shape from Shading Algorithms, *IEEE Trans. Pattern Analysis and Machine Intelligence*, Vol. 10, No. 4, pp. 438 - 451.
5. Mardia, K. V. (1972), Statistics of Directional Data, *Academic Press London and New York.*
6. Horn, B.K.P. (1977), Understanding Image Intensities, *Artificial Intelligence*, Vol. 8, pp. 201-231.
7. Sirovich, L. and Everson, Richard. (1992), Management and Analysis of Large Scientific Datasets,*The International Journal of Supercomputer Applications*, Vol. 6, No. 1, pp. 50 - 68.
8. Turk, M.A. and Pentland, A.P. (1991), Face Recognition Using Eigenfaces,*Proceedings of the IEEE Conference on Computer Vision and Pattern Recognition*, pp. 586 - 591.
9. Blanz, V. and Vetter, T. (1999), A Morphable model for the synthesis of 3D Faces,*Proceedings of SIGGRAPH '99*, pp. 187 - 194.

An Efficient Path-Generation Method for Virtual Colonoscopy

Jeongjin Lee[1], Helen Hong[2,*], Yeong Gil Shin[1], and Soo-Hong Kim[3]

[1] School of Electrical Engineering and Computer Science, Seoul National University,
San 56-1 Shinlim 9-dong Kwanak-gu, Seoul 151-742, Korea
{jjlee, yshin}@cglab.snu.ac.kr
[2] School of Electrical Engineering and Computer Science,
BK21: Information Technology, Seoul National University
hlhong@cse.snu.ac.kr
[3] Dep't of Computer Software Engineering, Sangmyung University,
San 98-20, Anso-Dong, Chonan, Chungnam, Korea
soohkim@smu.ac.kr

Abstract. Virtual colonoscopy is a non-invasive method for diagnosing colon diseases such as diverticulosis and cancer using digitized tomographic images to produce 3D images of the colon. In virtual colonoscopy, it is crucial to generate the camera path rapidly and accurately for an efficient examination. Most of the existing path-generation methods are computationally expensive since they require preliminary data structures and the 3D positions of all path points should be calculated. In this paper, we propose an automated path-generation method that secures visibility by emulating ray propagation through the colon conduit. The proposed method does not require any preliminary data preprocessing steps, which takes several minutes and it also dramatically reduces the number of points needed to represent the camera path. The experimental result is a perceivable increase in computational efficiency and a simpler approach to colon navigation. The proposed method can also be used in other applications that require efficient virtual navigation.

1 Introduction

Colon cancer is one of leading causes of cancer deaths. Periodic examination for early detection of colonic polyps is crucial for effective treatment of colonic cancer. Optical endoscopy and barium enema are colonic polyp detection methods that are widely used for periodic examinations.

Optical endoscopy is an invasive method in which an optical probe is inserted into the colon. The physician examines the inner surface of the colon by manipulating a small camera at the tip of the optical probe. Controlling the camera requires great skill and precision, and the examination of the entire colon takes a long time. Because it is an invasive method, it requires an uncomfortable and lengthy preparation step for the patient and has negative side effects of contagion and bleeding [1-2]. Barium enema is a method in which the physician injects white contrast media into the colon and

* Corresponding author.

M. Lazo and A. Sanfeliu (Eds.): CIARP 2005, LNCS 3773, pp. 339 – 347, 2005.

examines the contrast media adhered to the colon wall using X-ray radiographs taken from different angles. This method requires a large amount of the patient's efforts, but its sensitivity is less than that of optical endoscopy.

Virtual colonoscopy has been developed to increase the sensitivity and specificity of the examination while reducing patient discomfort and the amount of time required for the examination [3-6]. Furthermore, the recent introduction of the multidetector CT, which generates 16 images in 0.5 seconds, reduces the time of CT taken required for virtual colonoscopy and increases sensitivity, enabling it to detect small polyps [7]. Virtual colonoscopy is a computerized, non-invasive method. Unlike optical endoscopy, an optical probe does not need to be inserted, and therefore, virtual colonoscopy causes no pain to the patient. Also, virtual colonoscopy can examine any region using the free movements of a virtual camera, improving the efficiency of diagnosis, whereas optical endoscopy can only examine along the moving direction of an optical probe[8].

Since the average length of a colon is 1.5 meters, it is difficult for a physician to use virtual colonoscopy to manually examine the inside of an entire colon. Therefore, the center-line of a colon needs to be pre-defined to determine the path of the virtual camera. There are several methods that have been developed for this purpose. The physician indicates the center positions of the colonic section on 2D axial images, and these positions are interpolated for virtual navigation. The problem, however, is that it takes a very long time to define all the center positions in the entire colon. Topological thinning eliminates the outermost layer of the segmented colon consecutively until the center-line voxels are left [3][9]. While the path defined by this method is accurate in the geometrical sense, it takes a long time to carry out all the necessary calculations. The navigation path is calculated using Dijkstra's shortest path algorithm [10] with a 3D distance map generated in the preprocessing step. However, the preprocessing step and the search for all the points on the path requires a lot of time [11-13]. The current approaches to the path-generation method for virtual colonoscopy still need progress to improve computational efficiency for clinical applications.

In this paper, we propose an efficient path-generation method, which determines the navigation path by emulating the propagation of rays in ray casting [14]. Our method does not require any data preprocessing steps and rather than generating all points of the path, it generates only a small number of control points representing the path to increase computational efficiency. Since the path is determined using visibility, the virtual camera will follow a path on which the navigator can inspect the colon with the least eye-strain.

The organization of the paper is as follows. In Section 2, we propose a visibility-based automatic path-generation method for virtual colonoscopy. In Section 3, experimental results illustrate how our method efficiently generates an optimal path in a short amount of time. This paper concludes with a brief discussion of the results from Section 4.

2 A Path-Generation Method

Determining the optimal path for virtual colonoscopy is composed of following steps. First, a sequence of 2D axial CT images of the patient's abdomen must be acquired, as shown in Fig. 1(a). Second, the colon is segmented and reconstructed from axial

CT images by a 3D-seeded region growing method [15], as shown in Fig. 1(b). Finally, the examination can be performed by moving a virtual camera along the navigation path to diagnose polyps inside the colon, as shown in Fig. 1(c). The optimal path for virtual colonoscopy is the critical factor in determining the amount of time the examination would take as well as the accuracy of the examination. Without the optimal path, a physician needs to control a virtual camera manually, and it would take a lot of time and effort. If the optimal path is pre-defined, the physician can rapidly examine the entire colon and determine suspicious regions that should be manually examined for a closer look.

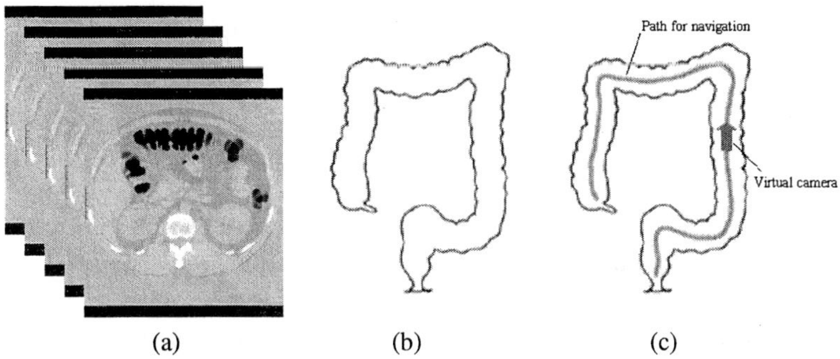

Fig. 1. The procedure for virtual colonoscopy (a) axial CT images (b) segmented colon (c) a virtual camera along the optimal path

Our method for optimal path-generation consists of the following steps. First, the seed point is provided by the physician on a 3D volume rendered image and the starting position and direction of the initial reference ray is found. Next, control points of the optimal path are found continuously using visibility until the end of the colon has been reached. Finally, the optimal path is generated by interpolating these control points.

2.1 The Initialization of the Reference Ray

For a path-generation, the starting position and direction of the initial reference ray must be determined, and used to search for the next control point. First, the physician defines the seed point, $P_{image} = (x_i, y_i, z_i, 1)$ on the 2D screen-projected image of a colon. A 2D image coordinate of this point should is then transformed into a 3D object coordinate by propagating a ray along the perpendicular direction to the image plane. The two intersection points, $P_{\text{int}1}$ and $P_{\text{int}2}$ between the ray and the colon wall are calculated. The center point, P_{center} between $P_{\text{int}1}$ and $P_{\text{int}2}$, is the optimal starting position of the initial reference ray. A ray is progressed by increasing the image depth, z_i from 0. When a viewing matrix is M_{view}, a point P_{image} on a 2D image coordinate can be transformed into a point P_{object} on a 3D object coordinate as follows.

$$P_{object} = M_{view}^{-1} P_{image} . \tag{1}$$

After the starting position has been found, the direction of the initial reference ray must be determined. Rays are progressed in all visible directions from the starting position and the intersection position between the ray and the colon wall is calculated. The direction having the maximum distance to the colon wall along a ray is regarded as the direction having the highest visibility from the starting point. This direction is determined as the direction of the initial reference ray, $R_{d0}(\theta_0, \phi_0)$. If the starting point is not at the end of the colon, a second path is generated along the opposite direction of the initial reference ray and the final navigation path will be composed of two sub-paths.

2.2 The Procedure of the Path-Generation

Control points representing the path are successively calculated by applying procedures shown in Fig. 2. The preliminary preparation of this procedure is generating the starting position and direction of the reference ray as described in Section 2.1. In the first step, the direction having the maximum visibility is found with respect to the starting point, P_0, along the ray R. The ray R is modeled as follows.

$$R = P_0 + l \cdot R_d(\theta, \phi) , \tag{2}$$

where R_d is the direction of the ray in a polar coordinate, and l is the propagated length of the ray. R is, then, progressed around a reference ray, $R_{d0}(\theta_0, \phi_0)$ in the following range.

$$\theta_0 - k_1 \le \theta \le \theta_0 + k_1 , \ \phi_0 - k_1 \le \phi \le \phi_0 + k_1 , \tag{3}$$

where the parameter k_1 represents the field of view. As the ray R is progressed around the reference ray, the intersection point between R and the colon wall is determined. The intersection point having the maximum distance from the starting point is regarded as the point having the maximum visibility. In other words, this position is where the viewer can see the farthest from the viewpoint. In Fig. 2(b), P_{max} has the maximum visibility with respect to P_0 and R_{d0}.

As previously stated, the parameter k_1 from Eq. (3) represents the field of view. When k_1 is large, the field of view becomes broader because visibility is determined with a larger range of view directions. However, the path-generation time gets longer. When k_1 is small, the field of view becomes narrower because visibility is determined with a smaller range of view directions, but the path-generation time is faster. Therefore, the optimal value of k_1 needs to be determined experimentally to increase computational efficiency without losing accuracy.

In the next step, $P_{candidate}$ is selected on the line between P_0 and $P_{\max}$, as shown in Fig. 2(c). This procedure is modeled as follows.

$$P_{candidate} = P_0 + k_2 \cdot (P_{\max} - P_0) \ . \tag{4}$$

The parameter k_2 controls the distance between neighboring control points. When k_2 is large, a smaller number of control points is used to represent the whole colon for faster path-generation. However, a less accurate path is generated in narrow regions of the colon since a single control point represents a larger range of the colon. When k_2 is small, a larger number of control points represent the whole colon, and generates a more accurate path since one control point represents a smaller range of the colon. However, the path-generation time increases when k_2 is small. Therefore, the optimal value of k_2 needs to be determined experimentally to increase computational efficiency without losing accuracy.

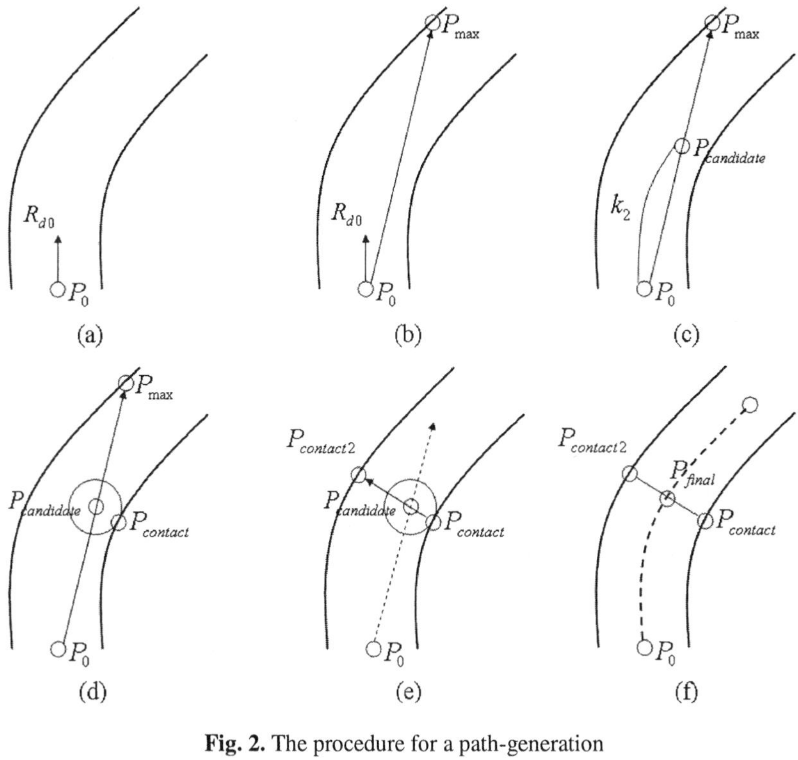

Fig. 2. The procedure for a path-generation

The accuracy of the point determined by the visibility criterion, $P_{candidate}$, is improved by the following procedure. First, a virtual sphere is expanded around $P_{candidate}$ to find intersection points between the expanding sphere and the colon wall, as shown in Fig. 2(d). After finding a set of contact points by expanding a sphere, we progress a ray from each contact point in the set, $P_{contact}$, through $P_{candidate}$ to the colon wall on the opposite side. This is done to find a new intersection point, $P_{contact2}$, between this ray and the colon wall, as shown in Fig. 2(e). A set of midpoints can be determined using each set of $P_{contact}$ and $P_{contact2}$. Finally, the control point for the navigation path, P_{final}, is determined by finding the average of this set of middle points. The next control point is generated with the new starting point, P_{final}, and new reference ray direction $P_{final} - P_0$ by applying the set of steps illustrated in Fig. 2. When the control point at the end of the colon is generated, the cubic spline [16] is interpolated using the determined control points as the final navigation path for virtual colonoscopy.

3 Experimental Results

The implementation and tests have been performed using Intel Compiler 5.0 on an Intel Pentium IV PC containing 2.4 GHz CPU and 1.0 GB of main memory. The method has been applied to four CT scans, whose properties are described in Table 1.

Table 1. Properties of experimental datasets

Subject #	Image size	Slice #	Number of voxels in a segmented colon
1	512 x 512	213	2.84 MB
2	512 x 512	253	2.53 MB
3	512 x 512	368	3.34 MB
4	512 x 512	579	4.85 MB

Based on several experiments, optimal parameters k_1 (= 30°), k_2 (= 0.5) were determined to increase computational efficiency without losing accuracy. Using these parameters, the path-generation time on each dataset is shown in Table 2. The high speed of our path-generation algorithm has dramatically reduced total processing time from minutes [15-16] to seconds.

Fig. 3 shows the automatically generated control points and the interpolated path. The control points are equally distributed near the colon center-line to model the

Table 2. Total processing time for a path-generation

Subject #	1	2	3	4	Average
Time [sec]	19	17	25	40	25

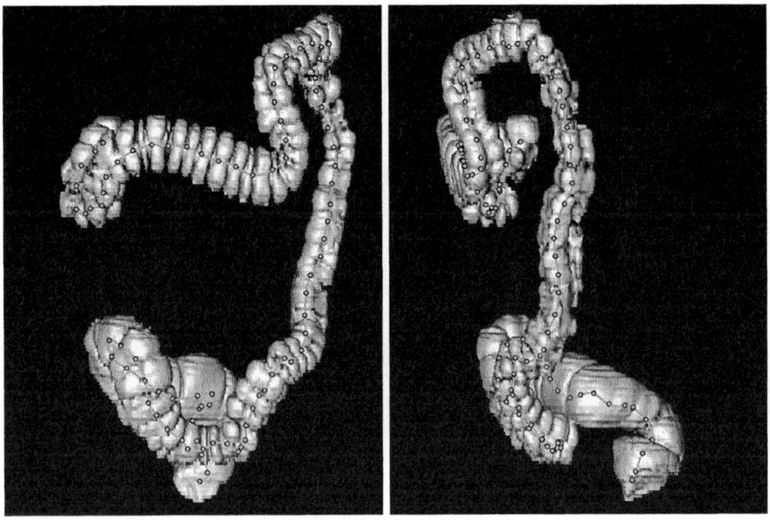

(a) (b)

Fig. 3. Generated control points and the interpolated path of subject 1 (a) in the anterior view (b) in the left view

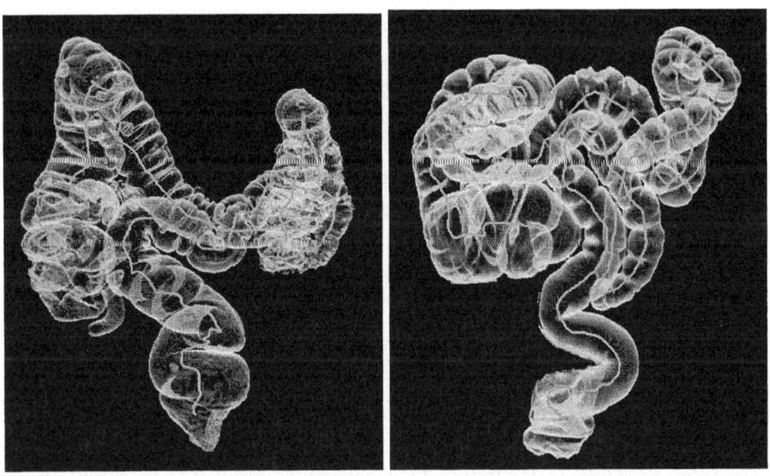

(a) (b)

Fig. 4. The generated navigation path (a) of subject 2 (b) of subject 4

colon shape efficiently and accurately. Fig. 4 shows the automatically generated path. The path generated by our method is located around the center region of the colon.

Fig. 5 shows the result of virtual colonoscopy along the path generated by our method. The path is located at the center of the colon cross section in both a high and low curvature regions. Also, we were able to find a tumor during virtual colonoscopy, as shown in Fig. 5(c). After the detection of the colonic polyp, the diameter should be measured. Polyps having less than 5mm diameter can be regarded as harmless, whereas polyps having more than 8mm diameter are regarded as harmful, and requires follow-up colonoscopy. Other polyps, having 6 ~ 7 mm diameter, require a regular follow-up virtual colonoscopy.

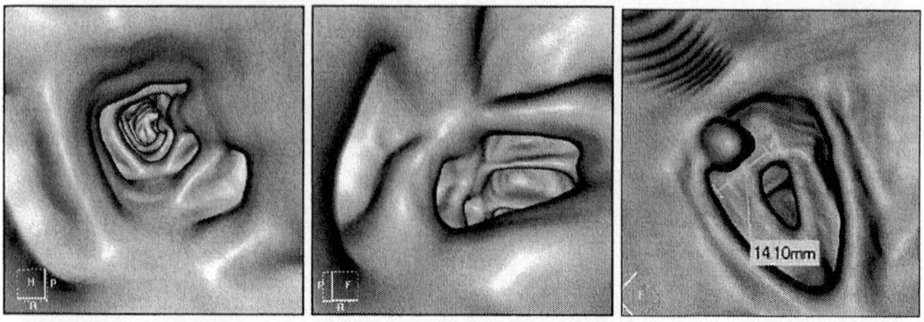

(a) (b) (c)

Fig. 5. Virtual colonoscopy of subject 1 (a) in a low curvature region (b) in a high curvature region (c) in a region with a tumor

4 Conclusion

In this paper, we proposed a noble technique of generating the navigation path for virtual colonoscopy, determined by using visibility. Our method does not require any preliminary data processing steps, such as generating a 3D distance map, which takes several minutes. Also, to increase computational efficiency, our method generates a small number of control points representing the whole navigation path instead of generating all the points of the path. Because this path is generated using visibility, the position of the virtual camera is guaranteed to be on a visually comfortable position. The experimental results on four clinical datasets show that the navigation path is generated rapidly and that the path is located in the center of the colonic section for an effective clinical examination. Our method can be successfully applied to a wide range of applications that require path-generation for virtual navigation.

References

1. Dogramadzi, S., Allen, C. R., Bell G. D., Computer Controlled Colonoscopy, Proceedings of IEEE Instrumentation and Measurement Technology Conference Vol. 1 (1998) 210-213
2. Phee, S. J., Ng, W. S., Chen, I. M., Seow-Choen, F., Davies, B. L., Automation of Colonoscopy. II. Visual control aspects, IEEE Engineering in Medicine and Biology Magazine Vol. 17, No. 3 (1998) 81-88
3. Hong, L., Kaufman, A., Wei, Y., Viswambharan, A., Wax, M., Liang, Z., 3D Virtual Colonoscopy, Proceedings of IEEE Biomedical Visualization (1995) 26-32
4. Lee, T. Y., Lin, P. H., Lin, C. H., Sun, Y. N., Lin, X. Z., Interactive 3-D Virtual Colonoscopy System, IEEE Transactions on Information Technology in Biomedicine Vol. 3, No. 2 (1999) 139-150
5. Hong, L., Muraki, S., Kaufman, A. E., Bartz, D., He, T., Virtual Voyage: Interactive Navigation in the Human Colon, Proceedings of ACM SIGGRAPH (1997) 27-34

6. Rubin, G., Beaulieu, C., Argiro, V., Ringl, H., Norbash, A., Feller, J., Dake, M., Jeffey, R., Napel, S., Perspective Volume Rendering of CT and MR Images: Applications for Endoscopic Imaging, Radiology Vol. 199, No. 2 (1996) 321-330
7. Pickhardt, P. J., Choi, J. R., Hwang, I., Butler, J. A., Puckett, M. L., Hildebrandt, H. A., Wong, R. K., Nugent, P. A., Mysliwiec, P. A., Schindler, W. R., Computed Tomographic Virtual Colonoscopy to Screen for Colorectal Neoplasia in Asymptomatic Adults," The New England Journal of Medicine Vol. 349 (2003) 2191-2200
8. Vining, D., Gelfand, D., Bechtold, R., Scharling, E., Grishaw, E., Shifrin, R., Technical Feasibility of Colon Imaging with Helical CT and Virtual Reality, Annual Meeting of American Roentgen Ray Society (1994) 104
9. Paik, D. S., Beaulieu, C. F., Jeffery, R. B., Rubin, G. D., Napel, S., Automated Flight Path Planning for Virtual Endoscopy, Medical Physics Vol. 25, No. 5 (1998) 629-637
10. Dijkstra, E. W., A Note on Two Problems in Connexion with Graphs, Numerishe Mathemetik Vol. 1 (1959) 269-271
11. He, T., Hong, L., Reliable Navigation for Virtual Endoscopy, IEEE Nuclear Science Symposium Vol. 3 (1999) 1339-1343
12. Zhou, Y., Kaufman, A. E., Toga, A. W., Three-dimensional Skeleton and Centerline Generation Based on an Approximate Minimum Distance Field, The Visual Computer Vol. 14 (1998) 303-314
13. Bitter, I., Kaufman, A. E., Sato, M., Penalized-distance Volumetric Skeleton Algorithm, IEEE Transactions on Visualization and Computer Graphics Vol. 7, No. 3 (2001) 195-206
14. Levoy, M., Efficient Ray Tracing of Volume Data, ACM Transactions on Graphics Vol. 9, No. 3 (1990) 245-261
15. Dehmeshki, J., Amin, H., Wong, W., Dehkordi, M. E., Kamangari, N., Roddie, M., Costelo, J., Automatic Polyp Detection of Colon using High Resolution CT Scans, Proceedings of the 3rd International Symposium on Image and Signal Processing and Analysis Vol. 1 (2003) 577-581
16. Bartels, R. H., Beatty, J. C., Barsky, B. A., An Introduction to Splines for Use in Computer Graphics and Geometric Modelling, Morgan Kaufmann (1998) 9-17
17. Bitter, I., Sato, M., Bender, M. McDonnel, K., Kaufman, A., Wan, M., CEASAR: A Smooth, Accurate and Robust Centerline Extraction Algorithm, Proceedings IEEE Visualization (2000) 45-52
18. Wan, M, Dachille, F., Kaufman, A., Distance-field Based Skeletons for Virtual Navigation, Proceedings of IEEE Visualization (2001) 239-246

Estimation of the Deformation Field for the Left Ventricle Walls in 4-D Multislice Computerized Tomography

Antonio Bravo[1], Rubén Medina[2], Gianfranco Passariello[3], and Mireille Garreau[4]

[1] Grupo de Bioingeniería, Universidad Nacional Experimental del Táchira, Decanato de Investigación, San Cristóbal 5001, Venezuela
abravo@unet.edu.ve

[2] Grupo de Ingeniería Biomédica, Universidad de Los Andes, Facultad de Ingeniería, Mérida 5101, Venezuela
rmedina@ula.ve

[3] Grupo de Bioingeniería y Biofísica Aplicada (GBBA), Universidad Simón Bolívar, Sartenejas, Caracas 39000, Venezuela
gpass@usb.ve

[4] Laboratoire Traitement du Signal et de L'Image, Université de Rennes 1, Rennes 35042, France
mireille.garreau@univ-rennes1.fr

Abstract. This paper describes a method for estimating the deformation field of the Left Ventricle (LV) walls from a 4–D Multi Slice Computerized Tomography (MSCT) database. The approach is composed of two stages: in the first, a 2–D non–rigid correspondence algorithm matches a set of contours on the LV at consecutive time instants. In the second, a 3–D curvature–based correspondence algorithm is used to optimize the initial approximate correspondence. The dense displacement field is obtained based on the optimized correspondence. Parameters like LV volume, radial contraction and torsion are estimated. The algorithm is validated on synthetic objects and tested using a 4–D MSCT database. Results are promising as the error of the displacement vectors is 2.69 ± 1.38 mm using synthetic objects and, when tested in real data, local parameters extracted agree with values obtained using tagged magnetic resonance imaging.

1 Introduction

Heart motion studies are a sensitive indicator of heart disease, in consequence, the estimation of cardiac motion and wall deformation are important parameters for understanding the cardiac function. In particular, the evidence of reduced transmural strain and left ventricle (LV) torsion are both important indicators of myocardial ischemia [1,2]. The detailed deformation analysis of the heart has been performed using highly invasive approaches based either on radiopaque or sonomicrometer markers implanted in the myocardium [3,4]. In these approaches,

M. Lazo and A. Sanfeliu (Eds.): CIARP 2005, LNCS 3773, pp. 348–359, 2005.

implantation of markers may by themselves alter the pattern of deformation [5]. More recently, non-invasive techniques based on tagged Magnetic Resonance Imaging (MRI) has been used to provide accurate estimations [6,7].

Several methodologies have been proposed for image analysis and for extracting parameters describing the ventricular dynamics, thus increasing the frontiers of clinical diagnoses and research on cardiovascular diseases [8]. The complete modeling of mechanical properties of cardiac structures is a problem that remains open, however, several approaches have been proposed for the description of motion and deformations of the myocardial structure based in different cardiac imaging modalities [8,9,10,11]. Clinical and research applications of cardiac image analysis are considerably extensive [12]. However, these applications still have to overcome problems like robustness, computational complexity, 3–D interaction and clinical validation.

Different techniques have been used for describing and quantifying the non–rigid motion of the heart. Non–rigid motion analysis is a difficult problem because the motion implies a varying shape and possibly a varying topological structure. Optical flow has been used for detecting the endocardial motion by analysis of changes in intensity in MRI images [6]. However, the displacement field is usually estimated from 2–D projections of a 3–D object, hence it is approximate. A set of physics–based models have been proposed recently, based in the space-time analysis (3–D + time) of images, which have provided a more realistic representation of cardiac chambers shape [7,11,13]. These models use geometry, kinematics, dynamics and material properties in order to model physical objects and their interactions with the physical world. The success of these approaches relies in considering a priori-knowledge about the LV, shape and motion, to predict ventricular dynamics. Simon *et. al.* introduced two approaches: one is based on a surface matching process [9] and the other is based on a 3–D surface/volume matching process [14]. The first approach provides 3–D displacement vectors between two surfaces for consecutive time instants. The matching procedure between surfaces is performed according to an energy function composed of two terms: a data term and a regularization term. A simulated annealing is used to perform a global optimization of correspondences. The estimated displacement field can represent accurate information related to LV motion.

In this paper, a method for estimating the deformation field for the left ventricle walls from sequences of three-dimensional cardiac images is presented. An efficient non–rigid shape–based correspondence algorithm is applied to the left ventricular surfaces extracted from 4–D imaging databases. The obtained correspondence maps enable the accurate estimation of functional local wall motion indexes.

2 Left Ventricle Geometrical Representation

Our geometrical representation of the left ventricle is constructed from 3–D data points located in the endocardial and epicardial walls of the left ventricle. These points $\mathbf{p}(x, y, z)$ are detected from the 4–D image dataset during the segmentation stage. Endocardial and epicardial walls are manually segmented in each slice of a 4–D MSCT database. Each segmented contour, is parameterized using a 2–D b–spline which is sampled to generate a discrete set of evenly distributed points that are considered as primary contours.

An interpolation algorithm is used with the objective of generating an iso-sampled set of points in three dimensions. This interpolation process is necessary because the resolution along the longitudinal axis (z) is lower than resolution in axial plane (x-y) of the MSCT database. Each 3-D point $\mathbf{p}(x, y, z)$ in the LV wall is located with respect to the coordinate system Γ (Fig. 1.a). The LV wall is a surface that can be represented in the intrinsic reference system Π known as the material coordinate system where each point $p(u, v)$ is defined in the domain $\Omega = [0, 1]$. In this reference system the u axis goes from the apex to the base of the LV while the v axis begins in a point located in the ventricular septum and goes along the equatorial line of the shape arriving to the departing point (Fig. 1.b). Using this representation each point of the LV surface can be expressed in the coordinate system Γ as $\mathbf{p}\,(x(u, v), y(u, v), z(u, v))$.

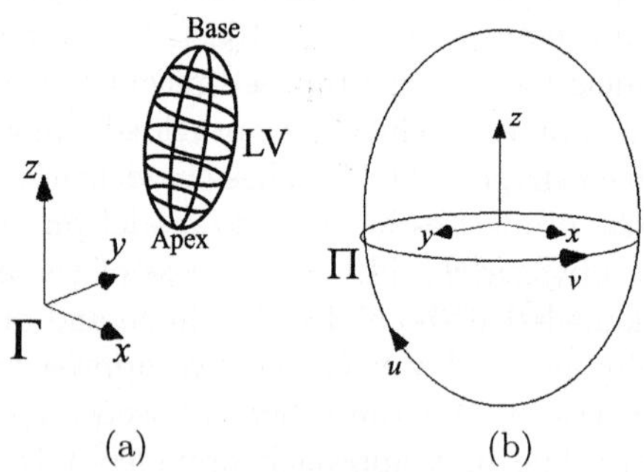

Fig. 1. Reference systems used in the geometrical representation of the LV shape. (a) Γ coordinate reference system. (b) Material coordinate system Π.

The LV is represented as a continuous surface $s(u, v)$ using interpolation based in a set of contour points (u_k, v_l) included in a given neighborhood. The resulting parametric surface is given as the convolution of the discrete samples with a B-spline 2-D interpolation kernel $h(u, v)$ [15]. Such surface is represented as:

$$s(u, v) = \sum_k \sum_l s(u_k, v_l) \cdot h(u - u_k, v - v_l) \ , \qquad (1)$$

where k, l define a neighborhood of 7×7 points. The continuous surface obtained is resampled at the desired sampling distance with the objective of generating new contours (secondary contours) between the given primary contours. The left ventricle endocardial and epicardial surfaces are represented by the set of original and interpolated contours. The primary and secondary contours for the endocardial wall are shown in Fig. 2.

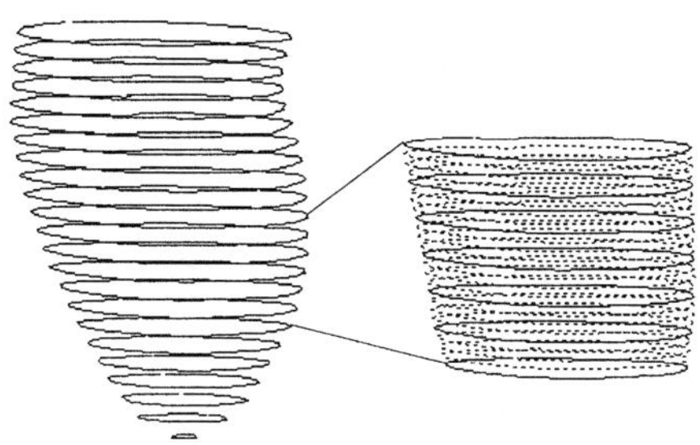

Fig. 2. Endocardial contour stacks. Left figure: the segmented contours. Rigth figure: the complete contours set (including both primary and secondary contours).

3 Shape–Based Correspondence Algorithm

Since the LV is in motion, points $\mathbf{p}(x, y, z)$ at time t will move to a new position $\mathbf{p}'(x', y', z')$ at time $t + 1$. Thus, for non–rigid motion analysis, the problem of shape–based correspondence is to find the Euclidean transformation Q that for all time instants converts the point $\mathbf{p}$ into point $\mathbf{p}'$:

$$Q(\mathbf{p}, t) = \mathbf{p}' \ . \tag{2}$$

The shape–based correspondence algorithm has two stages: the first stage corresponds to the generation of an initial estimate of correspondence based on a set of critical points [16], where the local curvature is maximum, extracted from the primary LV contours at consecutive time instants. Then, in the second stage the algorithm optimizes the initial correspondence in the 3–D space using both primary and secondary contours.

3.1 2–D Non–rigid Correspondence Algorithm

In the first stage we use a 2–D approach based on tracking a set of Critical Points in the primary contours of the LV geometrical representation, using the non–rigid correspondence algorithm proposed by Hill *et al.* [17]. This algorithm transforms a discretized contour $\mathbf{A} = \{\mathbf{A}_i; 1 \leq i \leq n_A\}$ (a primary LV contour at time t), onto some other contour $\mathbf{B} = \{\mathbf{B}_i; 1 \leq i \leq n_B\}$ (a primary LV contour at time $t + 1$), where n_A and n_B are the number of points in contours $\mathbf{A}$ and $\mathbf{B}$ respectively. The algorithm produces two new shapes $\mathbf{A}' = \{\mathbf{A}_{\alpha_i}; 1 \leq i \leq n_\Phi\}$ and $\mathbf{B}' = \{\mathbf{B}_{\beta_i}; 1 \leq i \leq n_\Phi\}$ that are in correspondence and represent sparse subpolygons of $\mathbf{A}$ and $\mathbf{B}$ respectively. The sparseness is related to the fact that each contour has less points than the original thus increasing the distance between each pair of points. The correspondence is defined by a set of ordered pairs $\Phi = \{\phi_i = (\alpha_i, \beta_i); 1 \leq i \leq n_\Phi\}$, where integer values $\{\alpha_i\}$ index the points of $\mathbf{A}$ and $\{\beta_i\}$ index points of $\mathbf{B}$ that are in correspondence.

The Hill's non–rigid correspondence algorithm comprises three parts:

1. Generation of shape approximations to both **A** and **B**, ($\mathbf{A}''$ and $\mathbf{B}''$ respectively). These approximate shapes only contain $n_{A''}$ critical points of **A** and $n_{B''}$ critical points of **B** (usually $n_{A''} \neq n_{B''}$). In this stage no correspondence is established. The critical point detection (CPD) algorithm described by Zhu and Chirlian [18] is used. This CPD algorithm does not require explicit curvature estimation, the algorithm is also reproducible, reliable, invariant, and symmetric.
2. Generation of an initial correspondence between $\mathbf{A}'$ and $\mathbf{B}'$. The path–matching algorithm is used. A reference of correspondence is established ($\alpha_0 = 1, \beta_i = i$). The path–length spacing of the points defining $\mathbf{A}''$ (with respect to $\mathbf{A}_1$) are projected onto **B** (with respect to $\mathbf{B}_i$) and also the path–length spacing of the points defining $\mathbf{B}''$ (with respect to $\mathbf{B}_i$) are projected onto **A** (with respect to $\mathbf{A}_1$). This process generates $[(n_{A''} + n_{B''}) * n_B]$ possible sets of correspondences. The best correspondence will be reached when the pixel $\mathbf{B}_i$ that matches the pixel $\mathbf{A}_1$ is identified by minimizing the following cost function:

$$\min E_i^2 = \sum_{j=1}^{n_{A''}+n_{B''}} \|\mathbf{A}_{\alpha_j} - Q\left(\mathbf{B}_{\beta_j}\right)\|^2, \tag{3}$$

where Q represent the Euclidean transformation $Q(\mathbf{p}) = s\mathbf{R}\mathbf{p}+\mathbf{t}$, s is a scale factor, **R** is a rotation matrix, and **t** is a traslation. This patch–matching algorithm produces a set of correspondences $\Phi = \{\phi_i; 1 \leq i \leq (n_{A''}+n_{B''})\}$. For each pair of correspondence points $(\mathbf{A}_{\alpha_i}, \mathbf{B}_{\beta_i})$, the value T_i is calculated:

$$T_i = \max\left(\text{Area}(\mathbf{A}_{\alpha_{i-1}}, \mathbf{A}_{\alpha_i}, \mathbf{A}_{\alpha_{i+1}}), \text{Area}(\mathbf{B}_{\alpha_{i-1}}, \mathbf{B}_{\alpha_i}, \mathbf{B}_{\alpha_{i+1}})\right), \tag{4}$$

where $Area(\cdot)$ computes the area of a triangle whose vertices are three consecutive points (for instance, $\mathbf{A}_{\alpha_{i-1}}, \mathbf{A}_{\alpha_i}, \mathbf{A}_{\alpha_{i+1}}$). The ϕ_i for which T_i is minimum is deleted repeatedly until $n_\Phi = (n_{A''} + n_{B''})/2$ correspondences are obtained.
3. An iterative local optimization scheme is used to refine the initial set of correspondence by minimizing a cost function. The cost function E is expressed as:

$$E = \lambda E_S + (1 - \lambda)E_R \ , \tag{5}$$

where the first term E_S measures the difference in shape between $\mathbf{A}'$ and its corresponding polygon $\mathbf{B}'$, represented as a mean distance error. The second term E_R ensures that the manner in which $\mathbf{A}'$ differs from **A** is as similar as possible to the manner in which $\mathbf{B}'$ differs from **B** and it is expressed as a mean distance error. The parameter λ expresses the relative contribution of each of the terms included in the cost function and their value is taken based in the experimental results obtained by Hill *et al.* [17].

The method for non–rigid correspondence proposed by Hill, is used in the framework for automatic landmark identification in a set of 2-D shapes representing an object. Within this framework the objective is to obtain a mean shape that represents the set of 2-D shapes based on the information provided by the method of non–rigid correspondence. With this purpose, Hill *et al.* [17] proposed an algorithm that constructs a binary tree whose root is the mean shape. In our application the goal is to establish the correspondence between primary contours, at consecutive time instants, describing the 4-D LV shape. Thus, the correspondence during the entire cardiac cycle could be modeled as a transformation defined by the composition of several time-consecutive transformations as the LV motion is small and varies between two consecutive time instants [7]. The algorithm proposed by Hill *et al.* for constructing the binary tree is modified. In this application the construction of the matrix of correspondence values, considers only pairs of contours that are consecutive in time. The rest of steps of the algorithm are followed to arrive to the mean representative shape located in the root of the tree. In the mean shape the critical point detection algorithm is applied and then, these critical points are projected back along the tree towards the leaves to arrive to the optimal correspondence between primary contours.

3.2 Curvature Based Correspondence Optimization

The non–rigid correspondence algorithm described in the previous section, gives a set of correspondences for all primary contours extracted from the MSCT database. If $\mathbf{p}_1(x_1, y_1, z_1)$ is a point on a primary contour of the LV surface s_1 at time t_1 and $\mathbf{p}_2(x_2, y_2, z_2)$ its corresponding point on the LV surface s_2 at time t_2, then the displacement vector for the point $\mathbf{p}_1$, $\mathbf{v}(\mathbf{p}_1)$ is given by:

$$\mathbf{v}(\mathbf{p}_1) = \mathbf{p}_2 - \mathbf{p}_1 \ . \tag{6}$$

Since all points of a primary contour are on the same axial plane, the non–rigid correspondence method does not consider the through–plane component of the 3–D motion field. Considering that the motion of the heart is sufficiently small between consecutive 3–D images (10–18 images acquired for a cardiac cycle) [7], we can track the evolution of curvature in selected regions or patches of the LV geometrical representation [13]. We use the shape–based tracking algorithm proposed by Shi [19]. This algorithm tries to match points on successive surfaces using a shape similarity metric. Such a metric (ϵ) is based on the difference in principal curvatures k_1 and k_2.

$$\epsilon = \frac{[k_1(\mathbf{p}_1) - k_1(\mathbf{p}_2)]^2 + [k_2(\mathbf{p}_1) - k_2(\mathbf{p}_2)]^2}{2} \ . \tag{7}$$

The shape–based tracking verifies if a point near $\mathbf{p}_2$ ($\hat{\mathbf{p}}_2$) exists, where the shape similarity metric achieves a minimum. The set of neighbor points $\{\hat{\mathbf{p}}_{2,\mathrm{i}}\}$, consist of all points on s_2 that have a distance less than a threshold δ from $\mathbf{p}_2$ on s_2. The euclidean distance metric is used and δ is fixed at 0.3125 mm. The geometrical representation of the LV s_2 at time t_2, considers the primary and secondary contours. The shape similarity metric (7), measures the difference between the principal curvatures of a single point $\mathbf{p}_1$ on s_1 and the neighbor points to $\mathbf{p}_2$ on s_2. Then the point $\hat{\mathbf{p}}_2 \in \{\hat{\mathbf{p}}_{2,\mathrm{i}}\}$ which has the minimum value

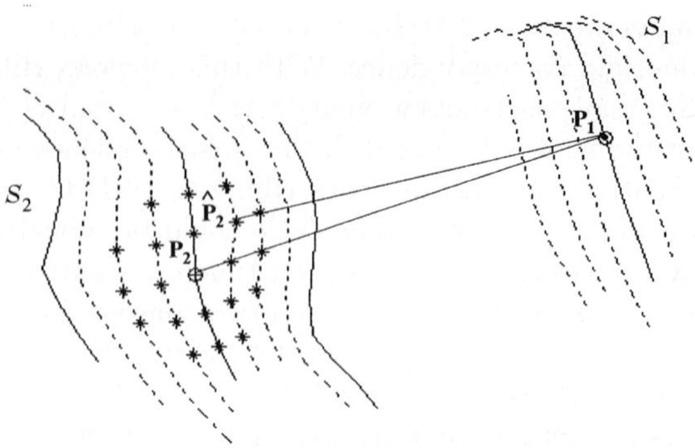

Fig. 3. Search of the new point in correspondence

of ϵ (most similar shape-properties to $\mathbf{p}_1$) is selected as the new correspondence point. This is illustrated in Fig. 3. Principal curvatures are estimated using the method proposed by Sander and Zucker [20].

4 Results

4.1 Validation Using Synthetic Data

An ellipsoidal model is used for validation of the algorithm of motion estimation. With this purpose a 3-D ellipsoidal model is deformed considering five types of motion: translation, radial contraction, longitudinal shortening and torsion. An algorithm based on Free Form Deformations (FFD) [21,22] is used for deforming the initial shape leading to a deformed shape according to a predefined set of motion parameters. In each deformation stage using the FFD algorithm, the points $\mathbf{p}_1(x_1, y_1, z_1)$ before the transformation, and $\mathbf{p}_2(x_2, y_2, z_2)$ after the transformation are known, thus the displacement field is accurately obtained using (6). This motion field is compared with the motion field obtained using the algorithm of motion estimation. In this case the distance between vector endpoints is considered as a measure of errors in the motion estimation. The error obtained (*mean* $\pm$ *standard deviation*) using a population of 42 deformations is 2.69 ± 1.38 mm with a minimum value of 1.06 mm and a maximum value of 5.54 mm. This is close to the value of 2.00 mm obtained by Chandrashekara et al. [7] using 2-D slices in tagged MRI.

4.2 Results on Real Data

The motion estimation algoritm is also tested using real data corresponding to a 4–D MSCT human heart database. In this database the left ventricle endocardial and epicardial walls are extracted using manual segmentation from 18 3-D images corresponding to time instants evenly spaced along the cardiac cycle. In these images, the portion above the mitral valve is excluded because the goal,

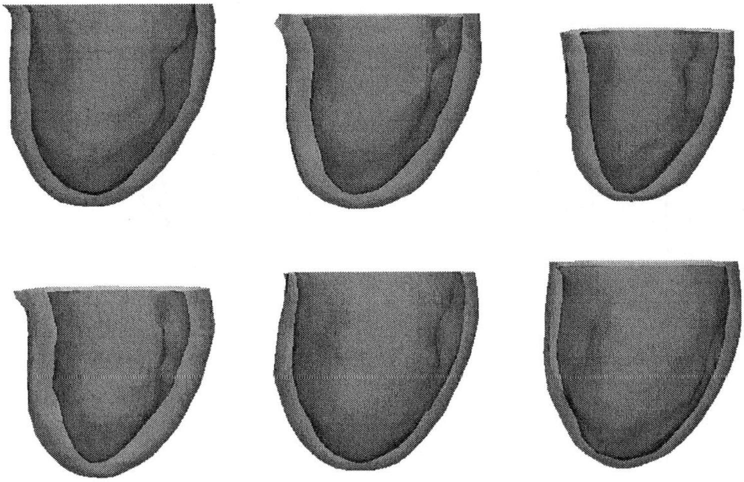

Fig. 4. Shape of the left ventricle for several time instants of the cardiac cycle

in this research, is to study only the Left Ventricular motion. Figure 4 shows the resulting LV shape for six time instants of the cardiac cycle. The longitudinal shortening that is one of the components of ventricular motion is apparent in the images shown. The motion estimation algorithm is applied to the entire 4-D sequence considering the shape correspondence algorithm and the optimization stage based in curvatures. As a result the estimated motion field for the MSCT database is obtained. Figure 5 shows a plot of the motion vectors for the endocardial wall considering three time instants of the cardiac cycle corresponding to end–diastole, 50 % of diastole and end systole. Observe that the magnitude of motion increases as the time approaches the end-systole instant, this is due to the endocardial contraction. The torsion is also apparent in the end-systole instant. Estimation of the motion field for the LV endocardial wall

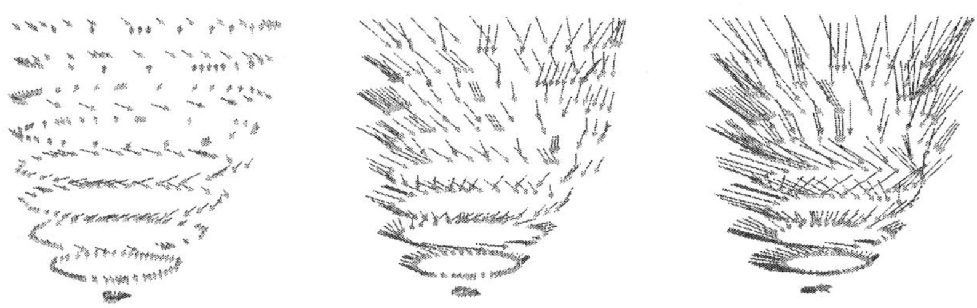

(a) (b) (c)

Fig. 5. Displacement vectors plot. (a) End–diastole. (b) 50 % diastole. (c) End–systole

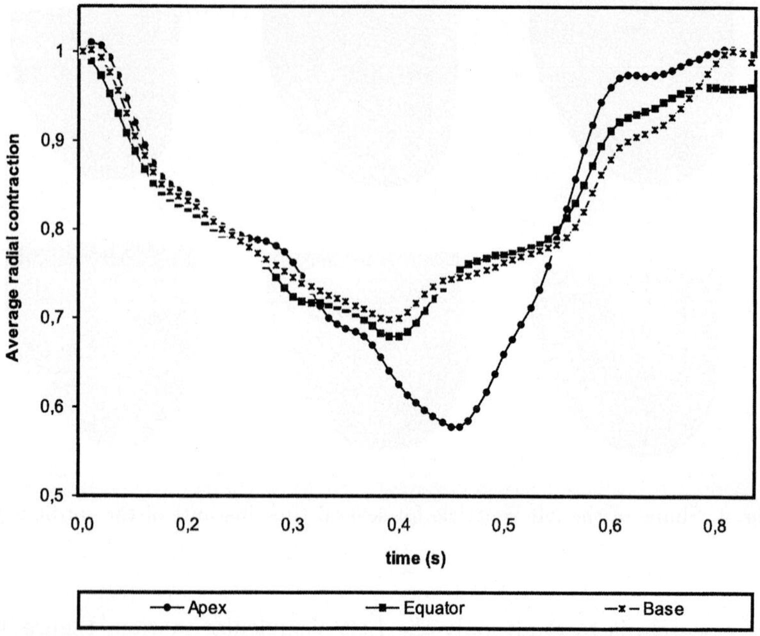

Fig. 6. Average radial contraction of the endocardial wall

enables the calculation of several local mechanical parameters associated with the ventricular motion. These parameters are the average radial contraction and torsion. The average radial contraction represents the average of radial lengths for the endocardial wall in a given axial plane. Figure 6 shows the endocardial LV radial contraction over three axial planes as a function of time. The apex plane is located 10 mm above the actual endocardial apex, the equator axial plane is located in the middle of the distance between the actual apex and the base. The base plane is located 10 mm below the actual base. The average radial contraction index is expressed normalized with respect to the value obtained in end-diastole. Results obtained for the average radial contraction are alike to the values obtained in other research works performed in tagged magnetic resonance imaging like these reported by Allouche *et al.* [10] and Sermesant [23] or in 3–D echocardiography as reported by Gérard *et al.* [11]. Using the proposed method the average radial contraction in the endocardium varies between 30.20 % and 42.22 % while Allouche *et al.* [10] obtained values between 28 % and 38 % using tagged MRI. Figure 7 shows the torsion value obtained over the entire cardiac cycle for the apex, equator and base plane. The torsion angle is defined as the angle between a radial line traced joining the gravity center of the slice and a endocardial contour point at time t and the radial line joining the gravity center and the corresponding endocardial contour point for the $t+1$ time instant. In this case, the torsion value is higher in the apex than in the base of the endocar-

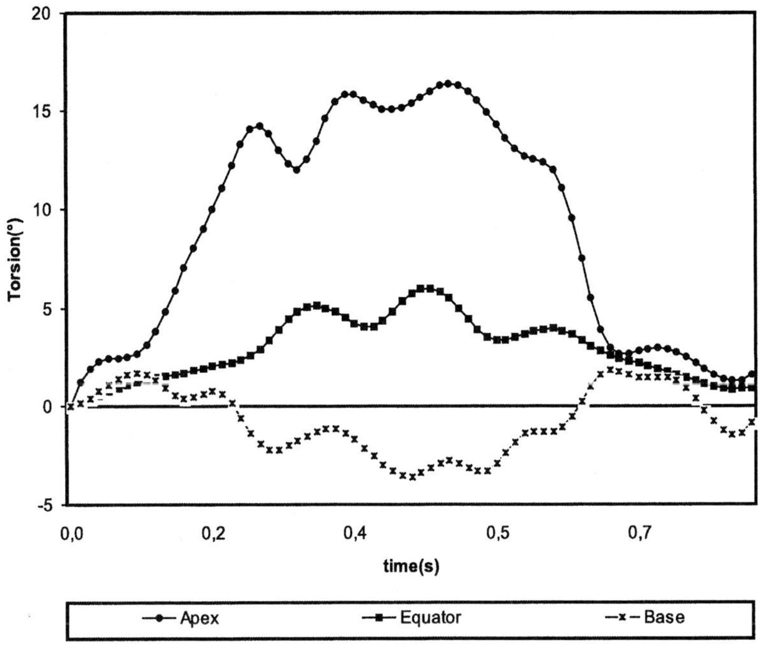

Fig. 7. Endocardial wall torsion

dial wall. Additionally, the torsion angle is opposite between the base and the apex. These features of LV motion are considered normal in healthy subjects [24]. The torsion obtained is also alike to the results reported by Allouche *et al.* [10], Sermesant [23] and by Gérard *et al.* [11]. Using the proposed method the minimal torsion value (−3.60 °) occurs at the base and the maximal torsion value (16.40 °) occurs at the apex while Allouche *et al.* [10], using tagged MRI, obtained a minimum value at the base of −2.5 ° while the maximum value of 12 ° is obtained at the apex.

5 Conclusions

A method for the quantification of LV deformations have been presented. The approach presented considers local geometrical features based in curvature analysis and the assumption that the LV motion is smooth during the entire cardiac cycle. It uses local information of the shapes with the objective of providing an accurate correspondence between consecutive time instants.

Validation of the method considering synthetic data provides low error values for the distances of the vector endpoints of the estimated motion field. Test on real data shows that LV estimated motion during the cardiac cycle is consistent with the LV motion reported by the literature concerning normal subjects. The estimated displacement field reproduces the contraction and relaxation of the normal LV accurately. Additionally, the method enables the calculation of several global and local parameters that are useful for the assessment of cardiac motion like the volume, the average radial contraction and the torsion index. Results obtained on real data agree with other research works based on tagged MRI.

A more complete clinical validation including healthy subjects as well as subjects cursing illnesses affecting the cardiac motion is necessary. The validation should also compare results using other modalities like tagged MRI. Future research will consider the incorporation of motion information extracted from the gray level information of the MSCT database.

Acknowledgment

The authors would like to thank the Investigation Dean's Office of Universidad Nacional Experimental del Táchira, the Parallel Computer Center (CeCalCULA) and CDCHT from Universidad de Los Andes, and the University Sector Planning Office (OPSU) through its Program Alma Mater for its support of this project. Authors would also like to thank Hervé Le Breton and Dominique Boulmier from the Centre Cardio–Pneumologique in Rennes, France for providing the human MSCT database.

References

1. L. Opie. Mechanics of cardiac contraction and relaxation. In E. Braunwald, D. Zipes, and P. Libby, editors, *Heart Disease: A Textbook of Cardiovascular Medicine*, pages 443–478. W. B. Saunders, 6 edition, 2001.
2. T. Arts, S. Meerbaum, and R. Reneman. Torsion of the left ventricle during the ejection phase in the intact dog. *Cardiovasc. Res.*, 18:183, 1984.
3. N. Ingels, G. Daughters, E. Stinson, and E. Alderman. Evaluation of methods for quantitating left ventricular segmental wall motion in man using myocardial markers as a standard. *Circ.*, 61(5):966–972, 1980.
4. F Villarreal, L. Waldman, and W. Lew. Technique for measuring regional two-dimensional finite strains in canine left ventricle. *Circ. Res.*, 62(4):711–721, 1988.
5. T. Fenton, J. Cherry, and G. Klassen. Transmural myocardial deformation in the canine left ventricle wall. *Am. J. Physiol. Heart Circ. Physiol.*, 235(4):H523–H530, 1978.
6. L. Dougherty, J. C. Asmuth, A. S. Blom, L. Axel, and R. Kumar. Validation of an optical flow method for tag displacement estimation. *IEEE Trans. Med. Imag.*, 18(4):359–363, 1999.
7. R. Chandrashekara, R. Mohiaddin, and D. Rueckert. Analysis of 3–D myocardial motion in tagged MR images using nonrigid image registration. *IEEE Trans. Med. Imag.*, 23(10):1245–1250, 2004.
8. A. J. Frangi, D. Rueckert, and J. S. Duncan. Three–dimensional cardiovascular image analysis. *IEEE Trans. Med. Imag.*, 21(9):1005–1010, 2002.
9. A. Simon, M. Garreau, D. Boulmier, J.-L. Coatrieux, and H. Le Breton. Cardiac motion extraction using 3D surface matching in multislice computed tomography. In *Medical Image Computing and Computer-Assisted Intervention MICCAI 2004*, number 3217 in Lecture Notes in Computer Science (LNCS), pages 1057–1059, Springer, 2004.

10. C. Allouche, S. Makram, N. Ayache, and H. Delingette. A new kinetic modeling scheme for the human left ventricle wall motion with MR–tagging imaging. In *Functional Imaging and Modeling of the Heart (FIMH01)*, number 2230 in Lecture Notes in Computer Science (LNCS), pages 61–68, Springer, 2001.
11. O. Gérard, A. C. Billon, J.-M. Rouet, M. Jacob, M. Fradkin, and C. Allouche. Efficient model–based quantification of left ventricular function in 3–D echocardiography. *IEEE Trans. Med. Imag.*, 21(9):1059–1068, 2002.
12. A. J. Frangi, W. J. Niessen, and M. A. Viergever. Three–dimensional modeling for functional analysis of cardiac images: A review. *IEEE Trans. Med. Imag.*, 20(1):2–25, 2001.
13. X. Papademetris, A. J. Sinusas, D. P. Dione, R. T. Constable, and J. S. Duncan. Estimation of 3–D left ventricular deformation from medical images using biomechanical models. *IEEE Trans. Med. Imag.*, 21(7):786–800, 2002.
14. A. Simon, M. Garreau, D. Boulmier, J.-L. Coatrieux, and H. Le Breton. A surface/volume matching process using a markov random field model for cardiac motion extraction in MSCT imaging. In *Functional Imaging and Modeling of the Heart (FIMH05)*, Lecture Notes in Computer Science (LNCS), Barcelona, Spain, June 2005. Accepted for publication.
15. T. Lehmann, C. Gönner, and K. Spitzer. Survey: Interpolation methods in medical image processing. *IEEE Trans. Med. Imag.*, 18(11):1049–1073, 1999.
16. A. Yuille and T. Poggio. Scaling theorems for zero crossings. *IEEE Trans. Pattern Anal. Machine Intell.*, 8(1):15–25, 1986.
17. A. Hill, C. Taylor, and A. Brett. A framework for automatic landmark identification using a new method of nonrigid correspondence. *IEEE Trans. Pattern Anal. Machine Intell.*, 22(3):241–251, 2000.
18. P. Zhu and P. Chirlian. On critical point detection of digital shapes. *IEEE Trans. Pattern Anal. Machine Intell.*, 17(8):737–748, 1995.
19. P. Shi. *Image Analysis of 3D Cardiac Motion Using Physical and Geometrical Models*. PhD thesis, Yale University, May 1996.
20. P. Sander and S. Zucker. Inferring surface trace and differential structure from 3–D images. *IEEE Trans. Pattern Anal. Machine Intell.*, 12(9):833–854, 1990.
21. T. Sederberg and S. Parry. Free–form deformation of solid geometric models. *Comput. Graph.*, 20(4):537–541, 1986.
22. A. Bravo, R. Medina, G. Passariello, and M. Garreau. Deformable parametric model for left ventricle wall motion simulation. In *Proceedings of the 14th IASTED International Conference on Applied Simulation and Modelling ASM 2005*, ACTA Press, pages 24–29, Benalmádena, Spain, june 2005.
23. M. Sermesant. *Modéle électromécanique du cœur pour l'analyse d'image et la simulation.* PhD thesis, Université de Nice Sophia–Antipolis, Institut National de Recherche en Informatique et Automatique (INRIA), France, 2003.
24. A. Sniderman, D. Marpole, and E. Fallen. Regional contraction patterns in the normal and ischemic left ventricle of man. *Amer. J. Cardiol.*, 31(4):484–489, 1973.

Edition Schemes Based on BSE*

J. Arturo Olvera-López, J. Fco. Martínez-Trinidad, and J. Ariel Carrasco-Ochoa

Computer Science Department,
National Institute of Astrophysics, Optics and Electronics,
Luis Enrique Erro No. 1 Sta. María Tonantzintla, Puebla, CP: 72840, México
{aolvera,fmartine,ariel}@inaoep.mx

Abstract. Edition is an important and useful task in supervised classification specifically for instance-based classifiers because edition discards from the training set those useless or harmful objects for the classification accuracy and it helps to reduce the size of the original training sample and to increase both the classification speed and accuracy. In this paper, we propose two edition schemes that combine edition methods and sequential search for instance selection. In addition, we present an empirical comparison between these schemes and some other edition methods.

1 Introduction

Supervised classifiers work on a training set *T* or sample, that is, a set of objects previously assessed and labeled to classify a new object *O*. However, it is common that *T* contains objects with a null or even negative contribution for classification accuracy, these objects could be:

• *Noisy Objects.* These objects come from wrong measurements and they do not contribute to improve the classification accuracy because they lead wrong classification since the features values that describe the objects are not correct at all.

• *Superfluous Objects.* These objects have the characteristic that another object in *T* can generalize their description, that is, the superfluous objects are unnecessary objects.

These kinds of objects (noisy and superfluous) are useless or even harmful for the classification process. Therefore, it is convenient to consider only objects from the training set which are useful to obtain higher accuracy, that is, to apply an edition method to the training set.

The edition is defined as: given a training set *T*, choosing objects from *T* which contribute to improve the classification accuracy. The goal of edition methods is to find a training sample $S \subset T$ such that the classification accuracy using *S* would be higher than using *T*.

When a subset *S* from *T* is searched, we can proceed in three directions [1]:
Incremental. An incremental search begins with $S=\varnothing$ and in each step adds objects that fulfill the selection criteria.

* This work was financially supported by CONACyT (México) through the project J38707-A.

M. Lazo and A. Sanfeliu (Eds.): CIARP 2005, LNCS 3773, pp. 360–367, 2005.

Decremental. This search begins with $S=T$ and removes from S objects that do not fulfill the selection criteria.

Batch. This search involves deciding if each object fulfills the removal criteria before removing any of them. Then all those objects that fulfill the criteria are removed at once, that is, this strategy does not remove one object at each step, it removes sets of objects.

In this paper, we will refer to edition schemes as those edition methods that are based on two steps; the first one consists of applying a pre-processing over the training set and the second one consists of editing the subset obtained in the first step.

In this paper, we propose two edition schemes, which reduce the runtimes of the decremental method *Backward Sequential Edition* (*BSE*) [2] and present an empirical comparison between these edition schemes and some other edition methods.

The structure of this paper is as follows: in section 2, the related work about edition methods is presented. Section 3 describes our proposed edition schemes. Section 4 presents some experimental results and finally in section 5 the conclusions and future work are given.

2 Related Work

In this section, some previous works related to edition methods are reviewed.

Wilson [3] introduced an edition method called *Edited Nearest Neighbor Algorithm (ENN)*, this method removes from S objects that do not agree with the majority of their k nearest neighbors. Wilson suggested a small and odd value for k, the *ENN* method uses $k=3$.

Wilson and Martínez [1] introduced the *DROP1,..., DROP5* methods (*Decremental Reduction Optimization Procedure*). The *DROP1* method is based on the rule: *remove an object O if at least as many of its associates in S would be classified correctly without O.* In this rule, an associate is an object such that O is one of its nearest neighbors. *DROP2* method considers the effect in T of removing an object in S, that is, *DROP2* removes the object O if its associates in T would be classified correctly without O. *DROP3* uses a noise-filtering step before applying *DROP2*; the noise filter used is similar to *ENN.*

DROP4 differs from *DROP3* in the filtering criterion since it is different to *ENN.* In this case, an object is removed only if it is misclassified by its k nearest neighbors and it does not hurt the classification of any other object. *DROP5* is similar to *DROP2* but *DROP5* starts with objects that are nearest to their nearest enemy, that is, nearest neighbors with different output class.

Brighton and Mellish [4] introduced the batch edition method *Iterative Case Filtering (ICF)*, this edition method is based on the *Reachable(O)* and *Coverage(O)* sets, which are based on the neighborhood and the set of associates of an object O. The edition rule is: *remove objects that have a Reachable set size greater than the Coverage set size*, that is, an object O is removed when some other objects could generalize the information from O. *ICF* starts applying *ENN* as noise filter.

In [2] the *Backward Sequential Edition* (*BSE*) was introduced, this method is based on backward sequential search; the *BSE* method starts from the original training sample *T* and finds a subset *S*. At each step, *BSE* removes the object (*WorstO*) with the smallest contribution for the subset quality, in terms of the accuracy of a classifier, which is calculated by the *Classifier()* function. In [2], *k-Nearest Neighbors (k-NN)* with *k*=3 is used as *Classifier()* function. The *BSE* method is depicted in figure 1.

```
BSE( Training set T ): Object set S
    Let S=T
    BestEval = Classifier(S)
    Repeat
        WorstO = null
        For each object O in S
            S' = S – {O}
            If Classifier(S') ≥ BestEval then
                WorstO = O
                BestEval = Classifier(S')
        If WorstO ≠ null then
            S = S – {WorstO}
    Until WorstO == null or S == ∅
    Return S
```

Fig. 1. *BSE* Method

In *BSE*, if there is more than one object with the smallest contribution, only the last is removed.

In [5] three edition methods were introduced: *Depuration, k-NCN* and iterative *k-NCN. Depuration* is based on the *generalized editing*, in which two parameters *k* and *k'* have to be defined, using the parameters the objects are removed or re-labeled (the original class label is changed). *k-NCN* editing is a modification of *ENN* and it consists of using the *k-NCN* (*Nearest Centroid Neighborhood*) instead of *k-NN*. Iterative *k-NCN* consists of applying repeatedly *k-NCN* until no more objects are removed.

In [6] the *NNEE* (*Neural Network Ensemble Editing*) method was proposed. It constructs a neural network ensemble from the training set *T* and changes the class label of each object in *T* to the class label predicted by the ensemble. *NNEE* does not remove objects, just changes class labels in order to increase the classification accuracy.

3 Proposed Schemes

In this section, we introduce two edition schemes in order to reduce the runtimes of *BSE* without a significant reduction in the classification accuracy. These schemes consist of a pre-processing over the training set before applying *BSE*.

It is very common that a training set contains noisy and/or superfluous objects. These objects are useless or harmful for the classification process because noisy objects lead to wrong predictions by classifiers and it is not necessary to store superfluous objects in the training set. Therefore, it is convenient to detect and discard those objects before starting the classification process.

The edition schemes proposed in this section are based on two main steps; the first one pre-processes the sample in order to detect and discard the objects above described, in this way, the size of the original sample is reduced. The second step edits the resultant pre-processed sample in order to increase the classification accuracy.

In the pre-processing step our proposed schemes uses either a noise filter method (remove noisy objects) or an edition method (remove superfluous objects). In the edition step we use *BSE* because according the results shown in [2], *BSE* reduce significantly the number of objects and increases the classification accuracy.

The first edition scheme (*ENN+BSE*) consists of applying *ENN* as noise filter in order to remove those useless noisy objects in the sample and after the clean subset is edited using *BSE*. When a set have been cleaned (filtered) the amount of comparisons in the classification process is reduced because a filtered set contains fewer objects than an unfiltered set. We use *ENN* as noise filter because it is a typical noise filter used in other edition schemes such as *ICF* and *DROP3.*

This scheme supposes that there are noisy objects in the training set, which can be removed in order to obtain a sample reduction in the pre-processing step. If there is not any noisy object, the scheme becomes the *BSE* method.

The second scheme (*DROP+BSE*) is based on editing an edited sample because after editing a sample, it is possible that some objects in the edited set do not contribute for the accuracy in the classification process (superfluous) because other objects in the edited set can generalize their description. This scheme consists of re-editing an edited sample in order to increase the classification accuracy. Our scheme uses *DROP3-DROP5* methods in the pre-processing step because these are the best *DROP* edition methods according to results reported in [1] and [2]. Finally, this scheme uses *BSE* to edit the edited sample.

In contrast to *ENN+BSE,* the sample reduction in *DROP+BSE* does not depend on the kind of objects in the original sample because the edition methods used in the pre-processing step remove some objects before the editing step.

The kind of objects preserved before the editing step depend on the method used in the pre-processing step, for example: *ENN* just removes noisy objects, *DROP3* and *DROP4* remove noisy and some other unnecessary objects, *DROP5* removes central, nosy and border objects.

4 Experimental Results

In this section, we present some experiments in order to compare the *BSE* method against *ENN+BSE* and *DROP+BSE* schemes. In addition, we compare these schemes against *DROP3, DROP4* and *ICF* methods because these methods could be considered as edition schemes since they apply a pre-processing step. Each method was tested on 10 datasets taken from the Machine Learning Database Repository at the University of California, Irvine [7].

The distance function for the experiments was the *Heterogeneous Value Difference Metric* (*HVDM*) [1], which is defined as:

$$HVDM(x,y) = \sqrt{\sum_{a=1}^{F} d_a^{\,2}(x_a, y_a)} \tag{1}$$

where $d_a(x,y)$ is the distance for the feature a and it is defined as:

$$d_a(x,y) = \begin{cases} 1 & \text{if } x \text{ or } y \text{ is unknown} \\ vdm_a(x,y) & \text{if } a \text{ is nominal} \\ \dfrac{|x-y|}{4\sigma_a} & \text{if } a \text{ is numeric} \end{cases} \tag{2}$$

where σ_a is the standard deviation of the values occurring for feature a and $vdm_a(x,y)$ is defined as:

$$vdm_a(x,y) = \sum_{c=1}^{C} \left(\frac{N_{a,x,c}}{N_{a,x}} - \frac{N_{a,y,c}}{N_{a,y}} \right)^2 \tag{3}$$

Where $N_{a,x}$ is the number of times that the feature a takes value x in the training set; $N_{a,x,c}$ is the number of times that the feature a takes value x in the class c; and C is the number of classes.

In each experiment, 10 fold cross validation was used. The dataset was divided into 10 partitions and each edition algorithm was applied to T which is built with 9 of the 10 partitions (90% of the data) and the left partition (10% of the data) was the testing set. Each partition was used as testing set, so 10 tests were made with each dataset.

In Table 1, the results obtained with *k-NN* considering 100% of the data, *BSE* method and *ENN+BSE, DROP+BSE* schemes are shown. For each method, there are two columns; the left one (acc.) is the average classification accuracy and the right one (stor.) shows the percentage of the original training set that was retained by the edition method.

Based on the results shown in Table 1, we can see that the average accuracy of *ENN+BSE* and *DROP+BSE* schemes was higher than such obtained using the original set. On the other hand, the schemes accuracy was slightly smaller than *BSE*'s but the schemes had a lower average number of retained objects.

The schemes *ENN+BSE* and *DROP+BSE* do not improve the accuracy obtained with *BSE,* but the main advantage in these schemes is that their runtimes are shorter than the *BSE* runtimes since *BSE* is an expensive method because it analyses the accuracy impact of leaving out each object at each edition step.

In Table 2, average runtime results for *BSE, ENN+BSE* and *DROP+BSE* are shown. From Table 2 it could be noticed that the *ENN+BSE* and *DROP+BSE* runtimes are shorter than the spent by *BSE*. The complexity of *BSE* is $O(N^4F)$ where N is the total number of objects in the sample and F is the number of features.

The complexity of *ENN+BSE* and *DROP+BSE* schemes is also $O(n^4F)$ which is the same than *BSE*'s but applied with $n < N$ for *ENN+BSE* and $n << N$ for *DROP+BSE*. According to this, the proposed schemes do not reduce the complexity even though they reduce the runtimes.

Table 1. Accuracy and retention percentage for: *k-NN* with 100% of the data, *BSE* method and *ENN+BSE, DROP+BSE* schemes

Dataset	*k*-NN		BSE		ENN+BSE		DROP3+BSE		DROP4+BSE		DROP5+BSE	
	acc.	stor.	acc.	stor.	acc.	stor.	acc.	stor.	acc.	stor.	acc.	stor.
Breast Cancer(WI)	96.28	100	98.71	2.09	96.58	1.25	98.13	0.84	97.27	0.82	97.28	0.89
Cleveland	82.49	100	97.35	15.04	95.01	9.70	91.74	7.29	92.73	7.44	91.39	6.78
Glass	71.90	100	89.67	13.18	81.64	9.45	79.30	8.56	80.32	8.25	77.94	8.30
Hepatitis	80.62	100	97.41	9.24	92.87	4.08	82.20	3.22	89.04	3.58	86.41	3.43
Hungarian	79.55	100	94.27	14.88	91.13	4.64	86.72	3.40	91.12	4.95	91.09	5.29
Iris	94.67	100	99.33	6.14	98.66	5.55	99.30	5.85	98.66	5.03	96.66	5.03
Liver(Bupa)	65.22	100	96.52	12.69	91.58	14.20	90.45	7.85	91.63	9.34	89.02	9.31
Pima Indians	72.79	100	94.27	9.33	90.76	5.45	89.45	4.78	92.31	5.85	91.79	7.40
Thyroid	95.39	100	97.70	3.61	96.29	3.25	97.25	3.61	97.70	3.46	97.70	3.36
Zoo	94.44	100	97.77	10.86	93.33	10.24	91.11	21.36	95.56	8.27	96.82	8.64
Average	**83.33**	**100**	**96.30**	**9.70**	**92.78**	**6.78**	**90.56**	**6.67**	**92.63**	**5.69**	**91.61**	**5.84**

Table 2. Runtimes spent by *BSE,* and *ENN+BSE, DROP+BSE* schemes (*hrs.* = hours, *min.* = minutes and *sec.* = seconds)

Dataset	BSE	ENN+BSE	DROP3+BSE	DROP4+BSE	DROP5+BSE
Breast Cancer(WI)	6.9 hrs.	5.9 hrs.	18.4 sec.	45.5 sec.	59 sec.
Cleveland	7.2 hrs.	4.6 hrs.	40.6 sec.	1.19 min.	1.95 min.
Glass	6.5 min.	2.2 min.	19.9 sec.	39.3 sec.	22.5 sec.
Hepatitis	38.5 min.	24.4 min.	2.0 sec.	3.6 sec.	2.0 sec.
Hungarian	4.9 hrs.	3.4 hrs.	1.1 min.	58.8 sec.	2.2 min.
Iris	1.4 min.	1.2 min.	2.5 sec.	2.8 sec.	2.9 sec.
Liver(Bupa)	29.2 min.	8.4 min.	1.21 min.	1.29 min.	2.0 min.
Pima Indians	0.1 hrs.	3.1 hrs.	3.0 min.	7.1 min.	6.6 min.
Thyroid	18.7 min.	8.3 min.	2.8 sec.	4.2 sec.	2.3 sec.
Zoo	5.1 min.	2.8 min.	3.2 sec.	4.1 sec.	3.0 sec.

A second experiment was a comparison among the proposed schemes, *DROP3*, *DROP4* and *ICF*. The results are shown in Table 3.

From Table 3 we can see that schemes accuracy was better than the obtained with *ICF* and even with *DROP3*, which was better than *DROP4*. With *DROP4+BSE* were obtained both results: almost the best accuracy and the lowest percent of retention.

Finally, the proposed schemes were compared against other kind of edition methods: *Depuration* method (the best edition method reported in [5]) and the *NNEE* method. The results obtained are shown in Table 4 using the results reported in [6] for *Depuration* and *NNEE*. Here also, 10 fold cross validation was used.

In all cases the proposed schemes had better accuracy than *NNEE* and *Depuration*. *ENN+BSE* and *DROP+BSE* schemes have the advantage that they do not change the original distribution of the objects among the classes as *Depuration* and *NNEE* do.

Table 3. Accuracy and retention percentage for: *ICF, DROP3, DROP4* and *ENN+BSE, DROP3+BSE, DROP4+BSE* schemes

Dataset	k-NN		ICF		ENN+BSE		DROP3		DROP3+BSE		DROP4		DROP4+BSE	
	acc.	stor.	acc.	stor.	acc.	Stor.	acc.	stor.	Acc.	stor.	acc.	stor.	acc.	stor.
Breast Cancer(WI)	96.28	100	96.42	18.53	96.58	1.25	95.42	3.26	98.13	0.84	95.99	3.70	97.27	0.82
Cleveland	82.49	100	91.44	43.63	95.01	9.70	78.89	11.44	91.74	7.29	79.53	13.53	92.73	7.44
Glass	71.90	100	68.39	32.91	81.64	9.45	66.28	24.35	79.30	8.56	67.77	29.39	80.32	8.25
Hepatitis	80.62	100	77.95	18.71	92.87	4.08	81.87	7.81	82.20	3.22	78.75	9.75	89.04	3.58
Hungarian	79.55	100	84.58	29.63	91.13	4.64	80.84	12.76	86.72	3.40	78.19	15.26	91.12	4.95
Iris	94.67	100	94.00	45.03	98.66	5.55	95.33	15.33	99.30	5.85	94.67	15.26	98.66	5.03
Liver(Bupa)	65.22	100	59.68	27.63	91.58	14.20	67.82	26.83	90.45	7.85	66.41	33.11	91.63	9.34
Pima Indians	72.79	100	75.43	32.52	90.76	5.45	72.91	16.44	89.45	4.78	71.23	21.70	92.31	5.85
Thyroid	95.39	100	92.05	53.22	96.29	3.25	93.98	9.77	97.25	3.61	93.51	10.39	97.70	3.46
Zoo	94.44	100	81.22	16.54	93.33	10.24	90.00	20.37	91.11	21.36	91.11	21.36	95.56	8.27
Average	**83.33**	**100**	**82.12**	**31.84**	**92.78**	**6.78**	**82.33**	**14.83**	**90.56**	**6.67**	**81.71**	**17.34**	**92.63**	**5.69**

Table 4. Accuracy classification percentage for*: Depuration (Dep.), NNEE and ENN+BSE, DROP+BSE* schemes

Dataset	Dep.	NNEE	ENN + BSE	DROP3 + BSE	DROP4 + BSE	DROP5 + BSE
Glass	59.90	67.94	**81.64**	79.30	80.32	77.94
Iris	95.67	95.47	98.66	**99.30**	98.66	96.66
Liver	57.28	64.06	91.58	90.45	**91.63**	89.02
Pima Indians	72.42	75.57	90.76	89.45	**92.31**	91.79
Wine	94.94	96.05	**99.44**	**99.44**	**99.44**	**99.44**
Zoo	90.75	94.48	93.33	91.11	95.56	**96.82**
Average	**78.49**	**82.26**	**92.57**	**91.51**	**92.99**	**91.95**

5 Conclusions

The main disadvantage in instance-based classifiers is that they are expensive because the classification cost depends on the amount of objects in the training set and it is common that a training set contains useless or harmful objects for the classification accuracy. Therefore, it is necessary editing the training set in order to detect useful objects.

According to results shown in [2], *BSE* is a good edition method but a disadvantage of *BSE* is its high complexity. Our schemes reduce significantly the runtimes edition and the accuracy results are not too low with respect to *BSE.*

From the obtained results, we can conclude that our edition schemes are good options for solving edition problems since they obtained higher accuracy than *ICF, DROP3*, *DROP4* and even than *Depuration* and *NNEE.*

We used *ENN* and *DROPs* in the pre-processing step, but our edition schemes have not been proposed particularity to work only using these methods, some other methods can be used for pre-processing/pre-editing the sample before applying *BSE*.

Based on our experimental results, the main advantages of our schemes over other edition methods are: better accuracy results and low runtimes. In addition, our schemes do not change the original label of the objects as *Depuration* and *NNEE* do.

As future work, we will propose and test some edition schemes that do not depend on the *k-NN* rule and they do not hurt on both classification accuracy and edition runtimes.

References

1. Wilson, D. Randall and Martínez, Tony R. Reduction Techniques for Instance-Based Learning Algorithms. *Machine Learning*, vol 38, pp. 257-286, 2000.
2. Olvera-López, José A., Carrasco-Ochoa, J. Ariel and Martínez-Trinidad, José Fco. Sequential Search for Decremental Edition. Proceedings of the *6th International Conference on Intelligent Data Engineering and Automated Learning, IDEAL 2005*. Brisbane, Australia, vol 3578, pp. 280-285, LNCS Springer-Verlag, 2005.
3. Wilson, D. L. Asymptotic Properties of Nearest Neighbor Rules Using Edited Data. *IEEE Transactions on Systems, Man, and Cybernetics,* vol. 2(3), pp. 408-421, 1972.
4. Brighton, H. and Mellish, C. Advances in Instance Selection for Instance-Based Learning Algorithms. *Data Mining and Knowledge Discovery,* 6, pp. 53-172, 2002.
5. Sánchez, J. S., Barandela, R., Marqués, A. I., Alejo, R., Badenas, J. Analysis of new techniques to obtain quality training sets. *Pattern Recognition Letters,* 24-7, pp. 1015-1022, 2003.
6. Jiang Y., Zhou, Z.-H. Editing training data for kNN classifiers with neural network ensemble. In: *Advances in Neural Networks,* LNCS 3173, pp. 356-361, Springer-Verlag, 2004.
7. Blake, C., Keogh, E., Merz, C.J.: UCI repository of machine learning databases [http://www.ics.uci.edu/~mlearn/MLRepository.html], Department of Information and Computer Science, University of California, Irvine, CA, 1998.

Conceptual K-Means Algorithm with Similarity Functions *

I.O. Ayaquica-Martínez, J.F. Martínez-Trinidad, and J.A. Carrasco-Ochoa

National Institute of Astrophysics, Optics and Electronics,
Computer Science Department, Luis Enrique Erro # 1,
Santa María Tonantzintla, Puebla, Mexico, C.P. 72840
{ayaquica,fmartine,ariel}@inaoep.mx

Abstract. The conceptual k-means algorithm consists of two steps. In the first step the clusters are obtained (aggregation step) and in the second one the concepts or properties for those clusters are generated (characterization step). We consider the conceptual k-means management of mixed, qualitative and quantitative, features is inappropriate. Therefore, in this paper, a new conceptual k-means algorithm using similarity functions is proposed. In the aggregation step we propose to use a different clustering strategy, which allows working in a more natural way with object descriptions in terms of quantitative and qualitative features. In addition, an improvement of the characterization step and a new quality measure for the generated concepts are presented. Some results obtained after applying both, the original and the modified algorithms on different databases are shown. Also, they are compared using the proposed quality measure.

1 Introduction

The conceptual clustering concept surged at 80's with the Michalski's works [1]. The conceptual clustering consists on finding, from a data set, not only the clusters but an interpretation of such clusters.

There are some algorithms to solve the conceptual clustering problem [1,2]; one of them is the conceptual k-means algorithm [2].

The conceptual k-means algorithm, proposed by Ralambondrainy in 1995, is a method that integrates two algorithms: 1) an extended version of the well known k-means clustering algorithm for determining a partition of a set of objects described in terms of mixed features (*aggregation step*), and 2) a conceptual characterization algorithm for the intentional description of the clusters (*characterization step*).

In the aggregation step, a distance function to simultaneously deal with qualitative and quantitative features is defined. The distance between two objects is evaluated as a weighted sum of the distance among the quantitative features, using the normalized Euclidean distance, and the distance among the qualitative features, using the chi-square distance.

* This work was financially supported by CONACyT (México) through the project J38707-A.

M. Lazo and A. Sanfeliu (Eds.): CIARP 2005, LNCS 3773, pp. 368–376, 2005.

This way to define the distance function is inappropriate because it requires transforming of each qualitative feature in a set of Boolean features. The values of these new features are codes but they are deal as numbers, which is incorrect. For this reason, in this paper, we propose to use a different strategy to obtain the clusters.

In the characterization step, it is necessary to define, for each feature, a generalization lattice, which defines a relation among the values of the feature. We consider that the lattice defined for the quantitative features is incorrect, because it does not satisfy the definition of a generalization lattice. Therefore, we propose a new generalization lattice. The definition of a generalization lattice is given in section 2.2.

This paper is structured in the following way: in section 2, a description of the conceptual k-means algorithm is presented. In section 3, a new conceptual k-means algorithm using similarity functions is proposed. In section 4, the results obtained after applying both algorithms over different databases are shown. In section 5, conclusions and future work are presented.

2 Conceptual K-Means Algorithm (CKM)

In this section, a description of the Ralambondrainy's conceptual k-means algorithm is presented. As we have mentioned above, the CKM algorithm consists of two steps: the aggregation and the characterization steps. These steps are described in sections 2.1 and 2.2 respectively.

2.1 Aggregation Step

The goal of the aggregation step is to find a partition $\{C_1,\ldots,C_k\}$ in k clusters of the data set Ω. This algorithm is based on an extension of the well known k-means algorithm in order to allow working with objects described in terms of mixed features.

As a comparison function between objects, a distance function is defined, which is given by a weighted sum of the normalized Euclidean distance (for quantitative features):

$$\delta^2_{1/\sigma^2}(O,O') = \sum_{1 \le i \le p} \frac{(x_i(O) - x_i(O'))^2}{\sigma_i^2}$$

where σ_i denotes the standard deviation of the ith feature. And the chi-square distance (for qualitative features). In order to apply the chi-square distance, a transformation of each qualitative feature in a set of Boolean features to deal them as numbers, is carried out. Therefore, the chi-square distance is given as follows:

$$\delta^2_{\chi^2}(O,O') = \sum_{1 \le j \le q} \frac{(x_j(O) - x_j(O'))^2}{\eta_j}$$

where $q = \sum_{i=1}^{s} |D_i|$ and η_j is the number of objects taking the value 1 in the jth modality. This distance gives more importance to rare modalities than to frequent ones.

Then, in order to work with mixed data, the following distance was proposed:

$$d^2(O,O')=\pi_1\delta^2_{1/\sigma^2}(O,O')+\pi_2\delta^2_{\chi^2}(O,O')$$

where π_1 y π_2 are weights for balancing the influence of quantitative and qualitative features. In [3] a strategy to select the values for the weights π_1 and π_2 is shown.

This algorithm requires transforming the qualitative features in sets of Boolean features. The values of these new features are codes (0 or 1) but they are dealt as numbers, which is incorrect because the codes 0 and 1 are not in the real space.

In addition, this algorithm always uses this distance to manipulate mixed data, not giving the flexibility of using the comparison function which is more suitable for the problem that is being solved.

On the other hand, the centroids obtained by the algorithm are elements that cannot be represented in the same space in which the objects of the sample are represented, the averages obtained by k-means for the qualitative features are real values not 0's and 1's, so that, it is not possible to return to the original representation space.

For this reasons, we propose to use a different strategy in the aggregation step, which is presented in section 3.1.

2.2 Characterization Step

In order to apply the characterization step, a generalization lattice is associated to each feature. A generalization lattice is defined as follows: a generalization lattice is a structure $L = (E,\leq,\vee,\wedge,*,\varnothing)$, where E is a set of elements called *the search space*, $\leq$ is a partial order relation "*is less general than*", which redefines the inclusion relation as follows: $\forall e, f \in E, e \leq f \Rightarrow e \subseteq f$, the symbol * denotes the greatest member of E and it is interpreted as "*all values are possible*" and $\varnothing$ denote the minimal element of E and it is interpreted as "*impossible value*". Every (e,f) has a least upper bound that is denoted by $e\vee f$ called also the generalization of e and f, and a greatest lower bound of e and f denoted by $e\wedge f$ [2].

The generalization lattice for the qualitative features is defined by the user from the available background knowledge. While for the quantitative features, a code or transformation into qualitative features through a partition of the values domain is carry out.

For each cluster C obtained in the aggregation step, a value r of x is typical for this cluster if it satisfies:

$$\mu_x-\sigma_x\leq r\leq\mu_x+\sigma_x$$

where μ_x is the mean of the feature x in the cluster C and σ_x is the standard deviation of x in the cluster C.

Therefore, a coding function $c:\Re\rightarrow\{inf, typical, sup\}$ is defined as:

$$c_r=\begin{cases} inf & if \quad r\leq\mu_x-\sigma_x \\ typical & if \quad \mu_x-\sigma_x\leq r\leq\mu_x+\sigma_x \\ sup & if \quad \mu_x+\sigma_x\leq r \end{cases} \tag{1}$$

The generalization lattice for the quantitative features, associated to the search space $E = \{inf, typical, sup\}$, is shown in figure 1 a).

The values of μ_x and σ_x are calculated with the objects of the cluster. This fact originates a problem when the predicate $\hat{A}_C$ is compared with the counterexamples, because the values *inf*, *typical* and *sup* are syntactically similar but semantically different among clusters. In other words, these values represent different intervals depending on the cluster that is analyzed. For this reason, in this paper, some modifications to this step are proposed. These modifications are presented in the section 3.2.

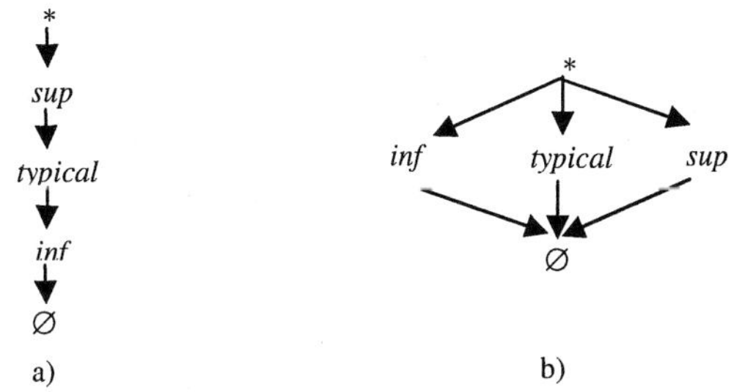

Fig. 1. a) Generalization lattice for the conceptual k-means, b) generalization lattice for the conceptual k-mans with similarity functions

3 Conceptual K-Means Algorithm with Similarity Functions (CKMSF)

In this section, some modifications to the CKM algorithm are presented. In section 3.1, the new strategy to obtain clusters is described and in section 3.2, we propose a new generalization lattice for the quantitative features in characterization step.

3.1 Aggregation Step

In this paper, we propose to use the k-means with similarity functions algorithm (KMSF) [4], for the aggregation step, instead of the original strategy used by the CKM algorithm.

This algorithm allows working in a more natural way (without transforming the space) with mixed features. For each feature, in order to compare its values, a comparison function is defined, which is denoted by $C: D_i \times D_i \rightarrow [0,1]$. This function is given in dependence of the nature of the feature.

The similarity function, used in this paper, to compare two objects is:

$$\Gamma(O_i, O_j) = \sum_{x_t \in R} C_t(x_t(O_i), x_t(O_j)) \Big/ |R|$$

where $C_t(x_t(O_i), x_t(O_j))$ is the comparison function defined for the feature x_t.

The similarity functions are more appropriate than the defined distance function for the aggregation step of the CKM algorithm, because this function does not require transforming features. In addition, they could be defined in terms of comparison functions, which allow expressing how the values of the features are compared in the problem to solve. It is more reasonable than using a fixed function for all the problems.

On the other hand, the KMSF algorithm, selects the centroids of the clusters as objects of the sample instead of centroids, which are in a different representation space, as occur in the k-means algorithm. Considering an object of the sample as the centroid of the cluster is more reasonable than using an element that cannot be represented in the same space.

3.2 Characterization Step

The generalization lattice given by Ralambondrainy [2], for the qualitative features does not satisfy $\forall e, f \in E, e \leq f \Rightarrow e \subseteq f$, because $inf \leq typical$ does not imply that the interval of values represented by the *inf* label are contained in the interval of values represented by the *typical* label and $typical \leq sup$ does not imply that the interval of values represented by the *typical* label are contained in the interval of values represented by the *sup* label; because these intervals are excluding (see expression (1)). Then, the concepts obtained with this generalization lattice do not represent appropriately the objects in the clusters. Therefore, we propose to use the generalization lattice shown in figure 1 b).

This generalization lattice satisfies that $\forall e, f \in E, e \leq f \Rightarrow e \subseteq f$, because $inf \leq * \Rightarrow inf \subseteq *$, $typical \leq * \Rightarrow typical \subseteq *$ and $sup \leq * \Rightarrow sup \subseteq *$, which allows working in a more appropriate way with the quantitative features.

As we have mentioned above, the values of μ_x and σ_x depend of the cluster. Therefore, it is not appropriate to only take the labels *inf*, *typical* and *sup*, but it is also necessary to verify if the value for the feature *x*, for the object that is being analyzed, is inside the range of values for the label of the feature *x* into the cluster.

Another way to define the coding function for the quantitative features is using the mean μ_x and the standard deviation σ_x as global. This allows measuring the range of values of the feature with respect to the total sample of objects. In addition, in this case verifying if an object is covered by the generated concept; it is equivalent to take the labels or the ranges of the labels, because these values do not depend on the cluster.

We consider that taking μ_x global and σ_x local or μ_x local and σ_x global does not make sense, because this values would be evaluating in different levels, i.e., one value is evaluated with respect to the cluster and the other one is evaluated with respect to the whole sample of objects.

Therefore, the proposed conceptual k-means algorithm uses, in the aggregation step, a similarity function given in terms of comparison functions which allows expressing how the features are compared depending on the problem to solve. Also, the centroids are objects in the sample and not elements that cannot be represented in the same space where the objects of the sample are represented.

On the other hand, in the characterization step a new generalization lattice for the quantitative features was introduced.

Finally, we consider that it is important to have a way to evaluate the quality of the concepts. Ralambondrainy [2] proposed to take as quality measure for the concepts the percentage of objects of the cluster that are recognized by the concept. However, it is also necessary to take into account the objects outside the cluster that are recognized by the concept. Therefore, we propose the following quality measure:

$$quality = \sum_{i=1}^{c} examples_i \Big/ total + \sum_{i=1}^{c} counterexamples_i$$

where:

examples$_i$: is the number of objects in the cluster C_i that are covered by the concept;
counterexamples$_i$: is the number of objects outside of the cluster C_i that are covered by the concept;
total: is the number of objects in the sample.

This function obtains higher values if the number of examples covered by the concept increases and the number of counterexamples covered by the concept decreases. And vice versa, the function obtains lower values if the number of examples covered by the concept decreases and the number of counterexamples covered by the concept increases.

4 Experimentation

Initially, some tests with the aggregation step were carried out. The k-means algorithm and the KMSF were applied over different databases and the obtained results were compared. The Iris, Glass, Ecoli, Tae, Hayes, Lenses and Zoo databases were used for the tests; these databases are supervised and they were taken from the UCI repository [5].

Table 1. Percentages of classification obtained by both algorithms over different databases

		k-means algorithm		KMSF algorithm	
Data-bases	**Number of objects**	**% of objects well classified**	**% of objects bad classified**	**% of objects well classified**	**% of objects bad classified**
Iris	150	85.33%	14.67%	90.67%	9.33%
Glass	214	34.11%	65.89%	45.79%	54.21%
Ecoli	336	33.04%	66.96%	42.26%	57.74%
Tae	151	36.42%	63.58%	61.59%	38.41%
Hayes	132	36.36%	63.64%	46.97%	53.03%
Lenses	24	41.67%	58.33%	41.67%	58.33%
Zoo	101	71.29%	28.71%	79.21%	20.79%

In table 1, the results obtained in the aggregation step after applying the k-means and the KMSF algorithms over the databases are shown. The obtained clusters were compared against the original classification.

In table 1, we can observe that the classification obtained by the KMSF algorithm has more well classified objects, in most of the cases, than the classification obtained by the k-means algorithm. This is due to the form in which the objects are compared with the centroids, also that the centroids are objects in the sample instead of being in a different representation space.

Later some tests with the characterization step, using the Iris, Glass, Ecoli and Tae databases were carried out. These databases contain quantitative data. The tests were made taking the global mean and standard deviation and taking the local mean and standard deviation. The characterization step was applied over the clusters obtained in the aggregation step by the k-means and the KMSF algorithms

In addition, an analysis of the parameters α (maximum number of counterexamples that could be covered by a predicate) and β (minimum number of examples that must be covered by a predicate) was carried out. In this analysis, we observed that for small values of β more objects of the cluster are covered by the concept but the concepts are larger and therefore, more difficult to understand. While, for big values of β it could happen that for some clusters any concept could be generated.

In figure 2 a), the results obtained after applying the characterization step over the clusters created by the k-means algorithm taking σ_x global and σ_x local, and both lattices, the original and the new, are shown. In figure 2 b), the results obtained after applying the characterization step over the clusters obtained by the new conceptual k-means algorithm taking σ_x global and σ_x local, and both lattices, the original and the new, are shown. The results shown in figure 2 are for those values of α and β, which obtain the highest concept quality.

In figure 2, we can observe that for σ_x global, the obtained concepts using the new lattice are better than the obtained concepts using the original lattice, according to the proposed quality measure.

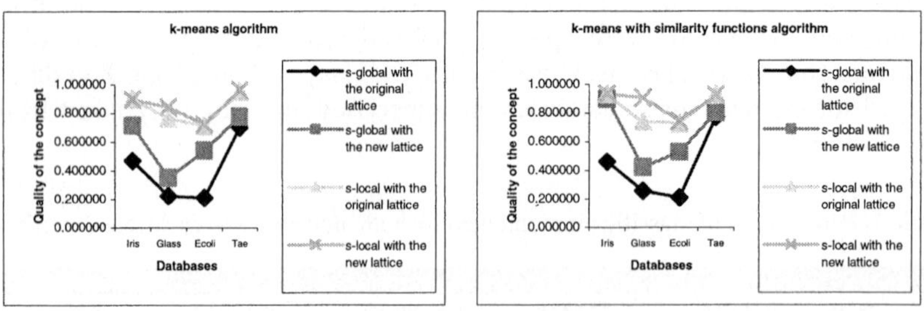

a) b)

Fig. 2. Results obtained in the characterization step: a) for the CKM algorithm and b) for the CKMSF

When the σ_x local is taking, this improvement in the concept quality is not so clear (see figure 2). However, with the new lattice, the concept quality does not depend so much of the parameters α and β, because for any value of α and β the concepts obtain a high quality (see figure 3), which does not occur when the original lattice is used (see figure 4). In that case, it was necessary to do a good selection of the parameters α and β, to obtain concepts with high quality.

Only the results obtained using the Iris database are shown (figures 3 and 4). However, the Glass, Ecoli and Tae databases have a similar behavior.

In addition, some tests with the Hayes, Lenses and Zoo databases, that contain only qualitative information, were carried out. In this case, we only compare the concept quality obtained by the CKM and the CKMSF algorithms because the new generalization lattice for quantitative features does not influence in the qualitative features. Only the results obtained with the Hayes database are shown (figure 5). However, the Lenses and Zoo databases have a similar behavior.

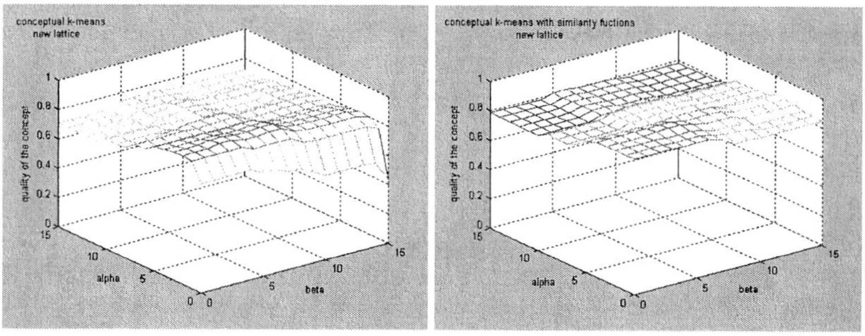

Fig. 3. Results obtained by the characterization step of both algorithms applied over the Iris database, using the new lattice and for values of α and β between 0 and 15

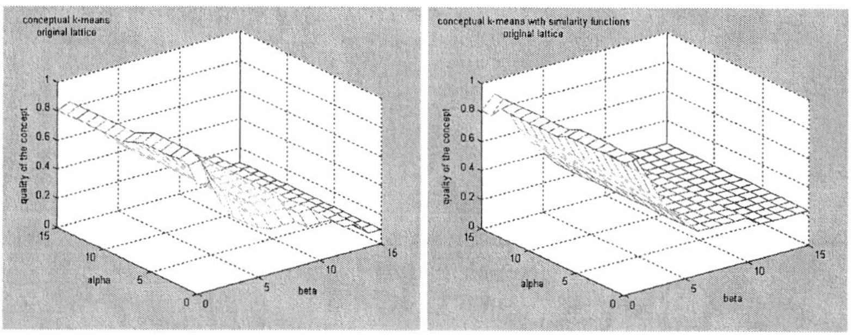

Fig. 4. Results obtained by the characterization step of both algorithms applied over the Iris database, using the original lattice and for values ovf α and β between 0 and 15

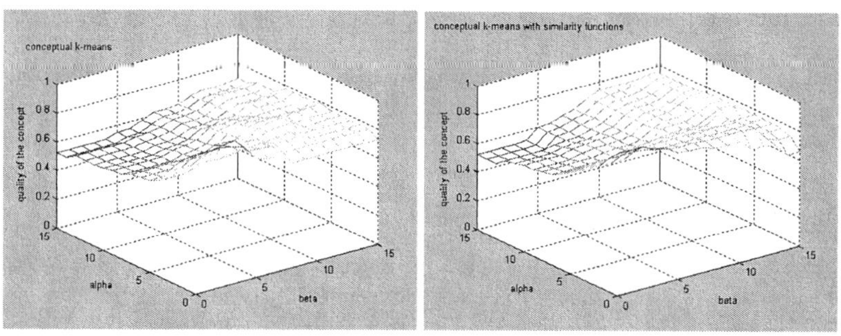

Fig. 5. Results obtainedin th e characterization step, applied over both algorithms, using the Hayes database, for values of α and β between 0 and 15

In figure 5, we can observe that the concepts obtained for the CKMSF have similar quality than those obtained by the CKM even when the clusters obtained, in the aggregation step, by the k-means algorithm are different than the clusters obtained by the KMSF.

5 Conclusions and Future Work

In this paper, we proposed a new conceptual k-means algorithm using similarity functions, which allows dealing in a more natural way with objects described in terms of mixed features.

This algorithm uses, in the aggregation step, the k-means algorithm with similarity functions (KMSF). The KMSF uses a similarity function defined in terms of comparison functions for features, which allow expressing how the values for the features are compared, in the problem to solve. Also, this function does not require transforming the features.

In addition, the centroids of the clusters are objects in the sample instead of elements that cannot be represented in the same space where the objects of the sample are represented.

On the other hand, in the characterization step, we proposed a new generalization lattice, which allows dealing with quantitative features in a more appropriate way.

Besides, we proposed a function to evaluate the quality of the concepts. This function takes into account both the objects into the cluster that are covered by the concept and the objects outside the cluster that are covered by the concept.

Based on the experimentation, we observed that using the new lattice we obtained concepts with a high quality, independently of the values for the parameters α and β, which did not happen when the original lattice was used. In this case, it is necessary to do a good selection of the parameters to obtain concepts with high quality.

As future work, we are working in other way to obtain the characterization of the clusters and in a fuzzy version of the conceptual k-means algorithm with similarity functions.

References

1. Hanson S.J. Conceptual clustering and categorization: bridging the gap between induction and causal models. In Y Kodratoff and R.S. Michalski, editors, Machine Learning: an artificial intelligence approach, vol. 3, pp. 235-268. Morgan Kaufmann, Los Altos CA. (1990).
2. Ralambondrainy H., A conceptual version of the K-means algorithm, Pattern Recognition Letters 16, pp. 1147-1157 (1995).
3. Ralambondrainy H., A clustering method for nominal data and mixture of numerical and nominal data. Proc. First Conf. Internat. Federation of Classification Societies, Aachen (1987).
4. García Serrano J.R. and Martínez-Trinidad J.F., Extension to k-means algorithm for the use of similarity functions. 3rd European Conference on Principles of Data Mining and Knowledge Discovery Proceedings. Prague, Czech. Republic, pp 354-359. (1999).
5. http://www.ics.uci.edu/pub/machine-learning-databases/

Circulation and Topological Control in Image Segmentation

Luis Gustavo Nonato, Antonio M. da Silva Junior,
João Batista, and Odemir Martinez Bruno

Universidade de São Paulo, ICMC, São Carlos, SP, C.P. 668, 13560–970 Brazil
{gnonato, antonio, jbatista, bruno}@icmc.usp.br
http://www.icmc.usp.br

Abstract. In this paper we present an image segmentation technique based on the concepts of circulation and topological control. Circulation is a mathematical tool widely used for engineering problems, but still little explored in the field of image processing. On the other hand, by controlling the topology it is possible to dictate the number of regions in the segmentation process. If we take very small regions as noise, the mechanism can be seen as an efficient means for noise reduction. This has motivated us to combine both mathematical tool in our algorithm. As a result, we obtained an automatic segmentation algorithm that generates segmented regions bounded by simple closed curves; a desireable characteristic in many applications.

1 Introduction

Segmentation plays an important role in image processing especially for edge and object detection, coding and analysis. The spectrum of applications in which segmentation is to be found is quite wide, ranging from medical imaging to robot vision. Over the years a great number of approaches have been proposed, led by the fact that the efficiency of segmentation methods are heavily domain-oriented: the particularities of a problem found in a certain domain may demand the development of techniques with characteristics that are not necessarily suitable for other domains.

In this work we present a new segmentation technique that automatically decomposes an image into a set of regions whose boundaries are Jordan's curves, while keeping the topology of these regions under control. Three-dimensional reconstruction and object recognition (in which the topology of the object under investigation is normally known and where simple closed curves - Jordans curves - bounding the regions can be handled geometriacally) are examples of applications where such feature is desirable.

Making use of a vector field derived from image data, our approach employs the concept of circulation for such a field to decide which adjacent regions must be glued, as expected in region growing methods. The gluing is conducted by a mathematical framework capable of controlling the topology during the entire process.

M. Lazo and A. Sanfeliu (Eds.): CIARP 2005, LNCS 3773, pp. 377–391, 2005.

A consequence of the methodology above is that the segmentation process can be controlled by thresholding the circulation between adjacent regions as well as by the topological properties of the objects in the image. This flexibility makes our approach an interesting segmentation technique, which can be useful in many applications.

This paper is organized as follows: section 2 presents a brief description of prior work in image segmentation. In section 3 we review definitions and some properties necessary to figure out the next sections. The theoretical background for our algorithm is described in section 4. The algorithm itself is presented in section 5. Results are discussed in section 6. Section 7 contains our conclusions and further work.

2 Related Work

The problem of image segmentation has received considerable attention in the literature [12,16]. Several methodologies have been proposed to tackle this problem, and the majority of them fall into two major approaches widely used in this context: edge-based-like [8,7,15] and region-based-like [3].

Region-based segmentation methods group pixels of similar properties (specific to a particular application domain), providing closed regions, which in turn give the boundaries. In edge-based approaches, on the other hand, discontinuities are extracted and the segmentation is guided by contours. The two approaches are complementary, and one may be preferred to the other for some specific applications or domain.

Compared to region-based segmentation techniques, however, edge detection has some very appealing properties. Usually, the algorithms are based on derivative calculations and can be implemented as a simple control structure and regular operators like convolution and, thus, lend themselves to an efficient implementation on special purpose image processors and parallel computers. In addition, edge detection techniques are able to localize surface boundaries more precisely in general.

In this paper, we add three different "functional views" or "perspectives" in which image processing techniques could be categorized, according to the role played in the application domain. They are: degree of automation, topological control and local/global information usage.

Under the first perspective, image processing techniques are classified according to the degree of automation provided. For some domains, like medical imaging, user-free segmentation techniques are highly desirable, as some modalities (CT, MRI) produce multidimensional data sets and require the interpretation of various slices. From this perspective, several semi-automatic and automatic methods for segmenting images have been proposed. Semi-automatic methods are those which require some degree of information, usually entered by the user interactively, either in the beginning or during the process. Various classes of algorithms fall into this category. One typical example are the deformable models such as snakes [5], in which an initial snake (mostly outlined manually around an object of interest) is deformed under internal (bending) and external forces (lines and edges, mainly), converging to a final form to reach an equilibrium energy state.

On the other hand, automatic methods do not require user interaction. Some edge- and region-based approaches can be categorized according to this functionality. Signal Processing techniques (Fourier Transform [1], Wavelets [9]) and some statistical methods - if one considers segmentation as a pixel classification problem - such as Fuzzy [13] and Clustering [4], can lead to segmentation with no human intervention.

A second, but nonetheless important perspective, is the control over the image topology while carrying out segmentation. Few methods are to be found in the literature that are capable of, simultaneously, keeping track of topology while splitting an image into regions of interest. In practical terms, by controlling the topology one can dictate the number of nested segmented regions. This is a very desirable feature for certain domains like segmentation of medical images in which different anatomical structures are sought. For example, the segmentation of an axial image of the brain with Euler number equal to 1 could produce a single contour of the skull (assuming this is the most external anatomical structure present). But, if Euler number is set to values smaller than 0, other internal structures (along with the skull itself) would appear as the result of the segmentation [11].

The third perspective takes into account the usage of either local or global information to reach segmentation. Local information based algorithms use the pixel neighborhood and pixel connectivity as input of the segmentation process. Several families of algorithms belong to this class: classic edge detection[8], mathematical morphology [14], convolution-based techniques, etc. Algorithms based on global information, on the other hand, consider information from an image region or a larger set of pixels, as opposed to a pixel and its near neighborhood. In general, approaches based on global information are used on region segmentation, texture algorithms and active contours.

Both local and global information-based approaches hold important information of the image nature and are functionally complementary. Techniques that explore both local and global features may be very promissing. Methods based on Markov Random Fields (MRF) [6,2], for example, fall in this category. MRF models represent an image through local characteristics, by defining the dependency of each pixel value with its neighbouring pixels. This dependency is expressed in terms of a conditional probability defined globally.

To our knowledge there is no method that combines the three functional view altogether. The majority of the techniques available concentrate on a single view alone and some combines two of them. The method described in this paper encompasses characteristics from the three functional views presented above. It is an automatic approach with full control over topology and, moreover, combines both local and global information.

3 Basic Concepts

This section presents the basic definitions and notation that will be used throughout this paper. The approach undertaken here has been restricted to the two–dimensional Euclidean space $\mathbb{R}^2$.

A **cell** with center (a, b) and radius q is the set of points $(x, y) \in \mathbb{R}^2$ satisfying $\max(|x-a|, |y-b|) \leq q$, i.e., a square with side length $2q$ centered in (a, b). The corners of a cell are called **vertices** of the cell and the four segments bounding the cell are its **edges**.

A **square grid** $\mathcal{G}$ is a cell decomposition of $\mathbb{R}^2$ where each point (a, b), where a and b are integers, is the center of one single cell V (grid cell) with radius equal to $\frac{1}{2}$.

A finite subset of grid cells R is a **region** of $\mathcal{G}$ if for any two cells V_a and V_b in R there is a sequence of grid cells $(V_1, \ldots, V_n)$ in R such that $V_a = V_1$, $V_b = V_n$, and $V_i \cap V_{i+1}$ contains a common edge of V_i and V_{i+1}. From this we can see that each edge in R is contained in either one or two cells of R, which are called **boundary edges** and **interior edges**, respectively. Note from the definion above that each region is a 4-connected set of cells.

Two regions R and S are called **adjacent regions** if $R \cap S = \sigma$, where σ is a set of boundary edges.

Let $\gamma = (e_1, \ldots, e_n)$ be a sequence of distinct boundary edges of a region R such that e_i and e_{i+1} $(e_{n+1} = e_1)$, $i = 1, \ldots, n$, have a vertex in common. γ is said to be a **external boundary curve** of R if γ encloses R and as one "walked" from edge e_i to e_{i+1}, the cells (or cell) in R containing e_i and e_{i+1} are always located on the left of these edges. If γ is enclosed by R and the cells containing its edges are always to the right of the edges, then γ is called a **hole** of R. With the definitions above we stipulate a counter-clock-wise orientation for the boundary of the regions in $\mathcal{G}$, which is essential for the Green's theorem described in next section. The union of the external boundary curve with the holes of R is called the **boundary curve** of R, denoted $B_d(R)$.

Let $\mathcal{U}$ be a subset of $\mathcal{G}$ such that the center (a, b) of each cell in $\mathcal{U}$ satisfies $1 \leq a \leq N$ and $1 \leq b \leq M$. An $N \times M$ digital image, denoted $\mathbb{I}$, is a pair $(\mathcal{U}, I)$, where $I : \mathcal{U} \to \mathbb{R}^+$ is a function that associates each grid cell in $\mathcal{U}$ with a positive value. Note that in our context a digital image can be seen as a set of cells with scalars associated with them.

Let $nc(R)$ and $nh(R)$ be the number of connected components and holes of a region $R \subset \mathcal{G}$, respectively. The **Euler characteristic** of R can be defined by

$$\chi(R) = nc(R) - nh(R). \tag{1}$$

It is worth mentioning that the Euler characterisctic is usually defined either in terms of the number of vertices, edges, and faces or as a difference between the number of connected components and the number of holes in an object. As will be shown in the next section, this last definition is more appropriate in the context of this work.

4 Circulation and Topological Control

In this section we describe the mathematical framework that is the background of our segmentation algorithm. Such a framework is based on two main concepts, namely: circulation through boundary curves and topological control during the gluing process. These concepts are detailed in the following subsections.

4.1 Circulation Through Boundary Curves

Let R be a region in a digital image $\mathbb{I} = (\mathcal{U}, I)$, i.e., each cell in R is associated with a positive scalar, and E the set of the edges in R. Let $F_R : E \to \mathbb{R}^2$ a map that relates each edge $e \in E$ to a two-dimensional vector $F_R(e) = (p, q)$, where $p : \mathcal{N}_{R_e} \to \mathbb{R}$ and $q : \mathcal{N}_{R_e} \to \mathbb{R}$ are real functions from a neighborhood $\mathcal{N}_{R_e}$ of e, in R, to $\mathbb{R}$. Notice that F_R is a vector field defined in R. It is worth mentioning that the vector $F_R(e)$ will depend on the arrangement of the cells in the neighborhood of e as well as the escalar values of these cells.

Proposition 1 below states an important result that is essential for our region-based segmentation algorithm.

Proposition 1. *If $F_R : E \to \mathbb{R}^2$ is constant, i.e., $p = c_1$ and $q = c_2$, for all edge in R then*

$$\oint_{B_d(R)} F_R \, \mathrm{d}s = 0$$

Proof. The proof follows from Green's theorem, as

$$\oint_{B_d(R)} F \, \mathrm{d}s = \iint_R \frac{\partial q}{\partial x} - \frac{\partial p}{\partial y} \, \mathrm{d}x\mathrm{d}y$$

and $\frac{\partial q}{\partial x} = 0$, $\frac{\partial p}{\partial y} = 0$ for all edges in R. □

Proposition 1 deserves some comments. Although Green's theorem is usually defined in the context of continuous vector fields, there are different versions of such a theorem for the discrete case (see [18]). With some manipulation, the proof of Proposition 1 can similarlly be carried out with a discrete version of Green's theorem.

Let's investigate more carefully the relation $\oint_{B_d(R)} F_R \, \mathrm{d}s = \iint_R \frac{\partial q}{\partial x} - \frac{\partial p}{\partial y} \, \mathrm{d}x\mathrm{d}y$, given by Green's theorem in the proof of Proposition 1. The term $\frac{\partial q}{\partial x} - \frac{\partial p}{\partial y}$ on the right double integral represents the z component of the rotational vector of F and it measures the circulation of F_R in each point of the domain. The important fact is that circulation can be seen as a high-pass filter when F_R is properly defined, as illustrated in figure 1. Figure 1b) shows the circulation of figure 1a) for $F_R = (p, q)$ defined as $p = 0.3I_{ij} + 0.25(I_{i+1j} + I_{i-1j}) + 0.1(I_{ij-1} + I_{ij+1})$, $q = 0.3I_{ij} + 0.25(I_{ij-1} + I_{ij+1}) + 0.1(I_{i+1j} + I_{i-1j})$ (we are supposing that R

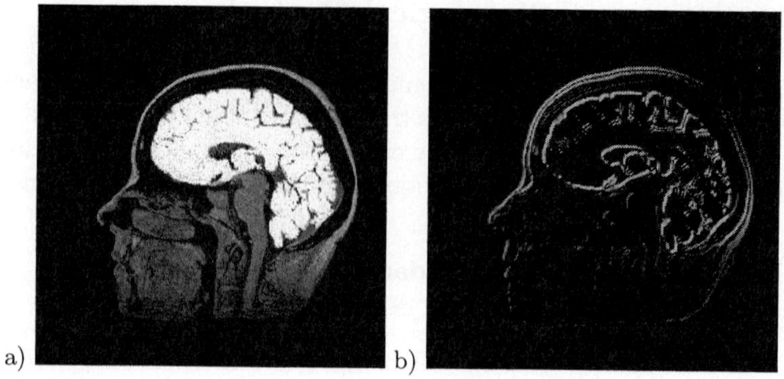

Fig. 1. Circulation as a high-pass filter

is the whole image). Notice from figure 1b) that the high-frequence areas of the image in figure 1a) could be well detected by measuring the circulation of F_R.

Hence, in low-frequence areas, the integral $\iint_R \frac{\partial q}{\partial x} - \frac{\partial p}{\partial y}\, dxdy$ will assume values close to zero, the same happening with $\oint_{B_d(R)} F_R\, \mathrm{d}s$. Thus, by analyzing this last integral we can have an indication whether the region R is crossing or not a high-frequence area. This is an essencial matter in image segmentation. Regions where the integral $\oint_{B_d(R)} F_R\, \mathrm{d}s$ is equal to zero are named **homogeneous regions**. Notice that regions where F_R is constant are always homogeneous. This fact will be important in the development of the segmentation algorithm presented in the next section.

Let R and S be two adjacent regions in a digital image $\mathbb{I} = (\mathcal{U}, I)$ and $\sigma = R \cap S$ be the intersection curve between R and S. In order to analyze the circulation in σ we need to define the vector field in the edges of σ. A natural way to do this is define $F_\sigma = (p, q)$ so that the components p and q, for each edge $e \in \sigma$, are real functions from a neighborhood of e in $R \cup S$.

Next proposition, which is a consequence of the discussion above, tell us how to glue homogeneous regions while keeping the homogeneity.

Proposition 2. *Let R and S be adjacent homogeneous regions and $F_\sigma = (p, q)$ the vector field defined in $\sigma = R \cap S$ as discussed above. If $\frac{\partial q}{\partial x} - \frac{\partial p}{\partial y} = 0$, for each edge in σ, then $R \cup S$ is also homogeneous.*

4.2 Topological Control

In this subsection we shall investigate how to characterize the topology of the union of two adjacent regions. More specifically, we are interested in identifying the Euler characteristic of $R \cup S$ where R and S are two adjacent regions whose topologies are given by $\chi(R)$ and $\chi(S)$, respectively.

In section 2 we defined the Euler characteristic of a region R in terms of its number of connected components and holes, i.e., $\chi(R) = nc(R) - nh(R)$. As in our context regions are always constituted by single connected component, if we characterize the number of holes in $R \cup S$, we shall identify its topology.

Before presenting such a characterization, let us understand the topological behavior of curves generated by intersecting two adjacent regions. If R and S are two adjacent regions then either S is inside R (or vice-versa) or R and S are side by side, as shown in figure 2. In the former, the intersection curve consists in a simple closed curve, as illustrated in figure 2a). Curves generated by intersecting side by side adjacent regions can be formed by a set of disjoint segments. For example, in figure 2b), the intersection between the adjacent regions gives rise to a curve with two connected components.

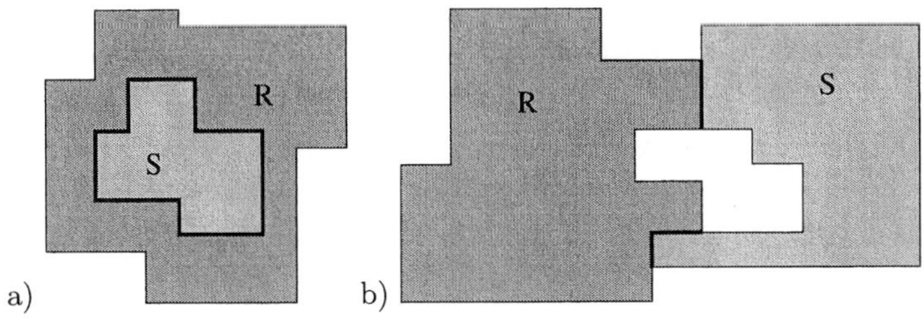

Fig. 2. Intersection of adjacent regions generating: a) a simple closed curve, b) a set of curve segments

Hence, supposing that $\sigma = R \cap S$ is the intersection curve between R and S, we can also compute the Euler characteristic of σ as $\chi(\sigma) = nc(R \cap S) - nh(R \cap S)$, where $nc(R \cap S)$ and $nh(R \cap S)$ are the number of connected components (or segments) and holes in $R \cap S$, respectively. Notice that $nh(R \cap S)$ can only assume value 1 if S is inside R (or R is inside S). Otherwise, $nh(R \cap S)$ becomes 0. Furthermore, if $nh(R \cap S) = 1$ then $nc(R \cap S) = 1$.

Next proposition allows us to quantify, in terms of $\chi(\sigma)$, the number of new holes created when two adjacent regions are unified. We denote this number of new holes by $nh_{\text{new}}(R \cup S)$, i.e., $nh_{\text{new}}(R \cup S) = nh(R \cup S) - nh(R) - nh(S)$.

Proposition 3. *Let R and S be two adjacent regions and $\sigma = R \cap S$ their intersection curve. The number $nh_{\text{new}}(R \cup S)$ of new holes generated by gluing R and S is:*

$$nh_{\text{new}}(R \cup S) = \chi(\sigma) - 1$$

Proof. We know that

$$nh_{\text{new}}(R \cup S) = nh(R \cup S) - nh(R) - nh(S) \tag{2}$$

Additionally, we have that $\chi(R \cup S) = \chi(R) + \chi(S) - \chi(\sigma)$, which from equation 1 becomes

$$nh(R \cup S) = nc(R \cup S) - nc(R) + nh(R) - nc(S) + nh(S) + \chi(\sigma)$$

Substituting equation above in (2) and remembering that $nc(R \cup S) = nc(R) = nc(S) = 1$ we conclude the proposition. □

In the next section we show how the mathematical framework presented above can be handled in order to suit image segmentation effectively.

5 Algorithm

The segmentation algorithm proposed in this work can be divided in three parts, namely: vector field definition, initialization, and region growing. The following subsections are devoted to detailing each of these parts.

5.1 Vector Field Definition

The vector field plays an essential part in our algorithm, as it dictates the behavior and the quality of the segmentation process. Notice that different vector fields can produce distinct results. In our implementation the vector field is defined from weighted mean values in the neighborhood of each edge. More specifically, let R be a region in a $N \times M$ digital image $\mathbb{I} = (\mathcal{U}, I)$ and E the edges of R. We define the vector field $F_R = (p, q)$ as follows:

$$p(e) = \frac{1}{C} \sum_{V_i \in \mathcal{N}_{R_e}} c_i \, I(V_i) \tag{3}$$

$$q(e) = \frac{1}{D} \sum_{V_i \in \mathcal{N}_{R_e}} d_i \, I(V_i) \tag{4}$$

where c_i and d_i are constants satisfying $c_i, d_i > 0, \forall i$ and $C = \sum_{\mathcal{N}_{R_e}} c_i$, $D = \sum_{\mathcal{N}_{R_e}} d_i$. It is important to note that C and D depend on the number of cell in $\mathcal{N}_{R_e}$. The values of c_i and d_i are composed by applying a mask to each edge e. Figure 3a) and 3b) shows the masks for horizontal and vertical edges, which define the values for c_i and d_i, respectively.

If e is either a boundary edge or an edge close to the boundary of R, the values of c_i and d_i are specified by intersecting the mask with R. Figure 4 shows two examples of such an intersection. Notice that the normalization factors C and D are computed as a sum of the mask values in the intersection.

5.2 Initialization

The initialization step aims at starting the segmentation process with a set of regions satisfying proposition 1, i.e., F_R must be constant in each edge of the inicial regions, implying that the line integral of F_R on the boundary curve of each region R is equal to zero.

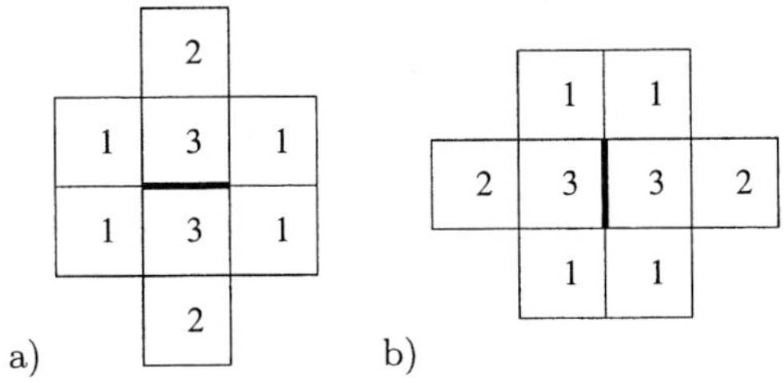

Fig. 3. a) Values of c_i; b) values of d_i

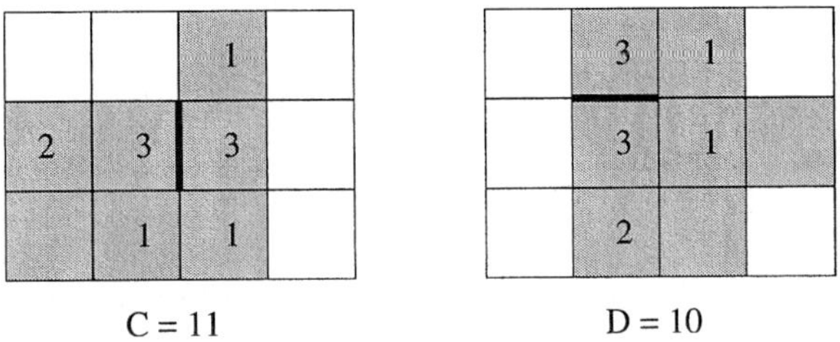

Fig. 4. Examples of the intersection between the mask (applyed in the bold edges) and a region R (gray cells)

An easy way to create these initial regions while ensuring proposition 1, is to make use of the grid cell comprising the whole image as the initial regions. Moreover, since each grid cell of the image is associated with a single scalar, the vector field F_R is constant, thus ensuring proposition 1. The main reason for restraining F_R to be a constant in each initial region is that this property guarantees the homogeneity, i.e., such regions are not crossing a high-frequence area.

After initializing the regions, we compute and store, in a priority queue, the values (and edges) of $\frac{\partial q}{\partial x} - \frac{\partial p}{\partial y}$ evaluated on the boundary edges. The priority queue stores the elements in increasing order and it is used in the growing process to decide which regions must be merged, as discussed in next subsection.

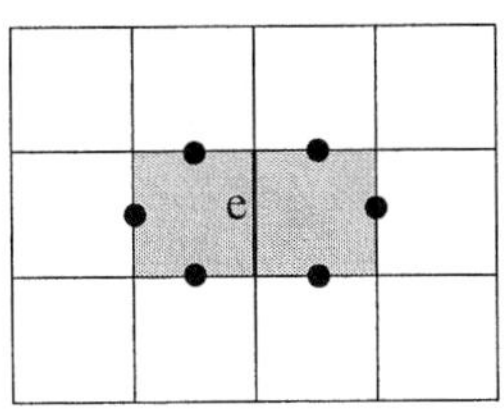

Fig. 5. Least square approximation takes into account the values of p and q in the marked boundary edges

Before presenting the growing process, it is important to discuss how to estimate the derivatives $\frac{\partial q}{\partial x}$ and $\frac{\partial p}{\partial y}$. In our implementation we are making use of least square interpolation to compute second order polynomials from which the derivatives are computed. The least square approximation generates a second order polynomial for each component p and q of the vector field in each boundary edge e, taking into account the values of p and q from the edges of the cells adjacent to e. Figure 5 illustrates which are the the values of p and q involved in the calculation of the polynomials in an edge e.

5.3 Region Growing

The region growing process makes use of the values stored in the priority queue to decide which regions must be glued. The regions adjacent to an edge extracted from the priority queue are merged and the boundary curve of the new region is updated. In order to continue with the growing process it is necessary to compute the circulation on the new boundary curve.

Inspired by proposition 2, we estimate the circulation in each new component of the boundary curve by computing the scalar field line integral

$$\oint_{B_d(R \cap S)} |\frac{\partial q}{\partial x} - \frac{\partial p}{\partial y}|\, dl \tag{5}$$

where R and S are regions that become adjacent after gluing. The computed value is also inserted into the priority queue. For example, suppose that R_1 and R_2 are the regions selected to be merged, as shown in figure 6a). After gluing R_1 and R_2, the new boundary curve component (highlighted as bold in figure 6b)) is updated and the scalar field line integral (5) is computed on it, and the computed value is stored into the priority queue. Therefore, the region growing process aims at merging the regions in an order that preserves homogeneity.

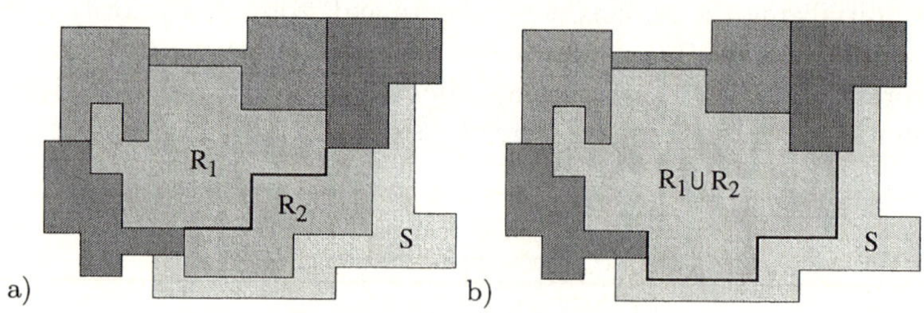

Fig. 6. Keeping the homogeneity in the growing process

The region growing process will have control over the region's topology if proposition 3 is employed, as it allows us to know if new holes are been created during the gluing process. Hence, it is possible to specify, for example, a maximal number of holes in each region. It is also possible to control the size of the holes in a straightforward way. In fact, it is well known that Green's theorem allows us to compute the area of a region through the line integral of the vector field given by $F = (-y, x)$, or similiarly, by computing the summation

$$\frac{1}{2}\sum_{i}^{n} v_x^i v_y^{i+1} - v_y^i v_x^{i+1} \tag{6}$$

where v_x^k and v_y^k are the components x and y of the vertices v^k of a poligonal curve (boundary curve).

As a result, we can estimate the areas of each new hole created by the gluing operation, discarding the ones whose areas are below a desired value. Notice that this procedure can be employed as an alternative tool to noise reduction.

In our implementation we employ two different stopping criteria for the growing region process. The first one ends the process by thresholding the values of the line integral (5). That is, when the priority queue returns a value higher than a threshold, the region growing process stops.

The second stopping criterion takes into account the number of detected regions. In this case the region growing process continues until a desired number of regions is obtained. In our implementation, this criterion does not consider the background of the image as a valid region.

6 Results

In this section we present some results obtained from the framework shown above. The axial MRI image of the brain shown in figure 7 has been used to illustrate our algorithm.

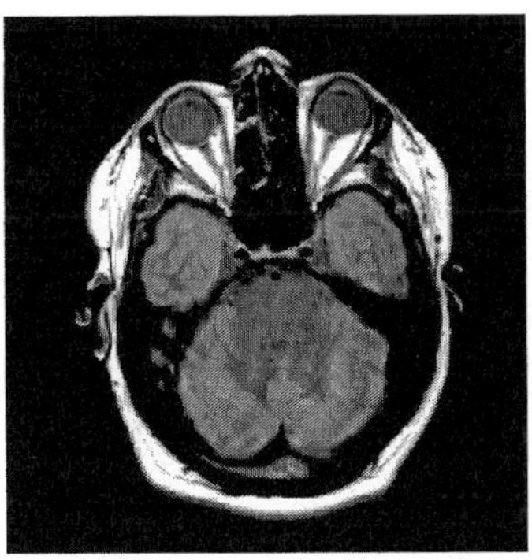

Fig. 7. Axial MRI image used in the segmentation

As mentioned in the previous section, our algorithm considers two different stopping criteria: the line integral thresholding (Eq. 5) and topological properties thresholding. Figure 8 shows the boundary curve of the regions detected by thresholding line integral (5). In this case, the resulting segmentation contains 400 regions approximately and some of them can be accounted on noise. Such noisy regions are not easily removed, since finding an appropriate threshold value to remove them may be a difficult task.

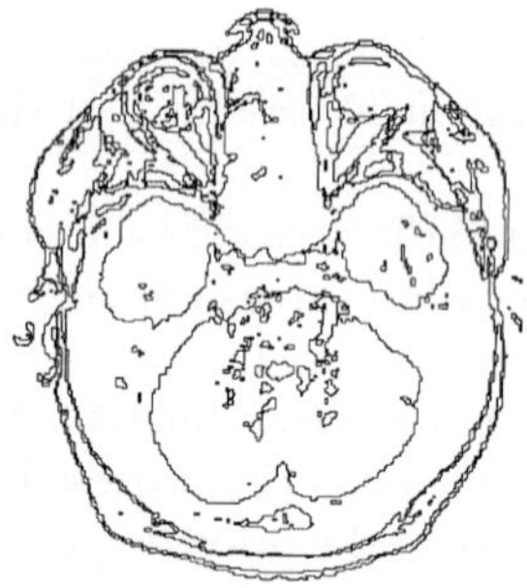

Fig. 8. Boundary curves of the regions dected by thresholding the line integral (5)

The difficulty in removing noisy regions can be overcome by topological thresholding. Some examples are shown in figure 10. Figure 10a) shows the resulting boundary curve when the topological threshold is set to a single region without holes (we are not taken into account the background region). Note that the curve that bounds the head is well detected and the small regions, which are caracterized as holes, are eliminated altogether. Figure 10b) presents the resulting regions (boundary curves) when the topological threshold is set to a single component with a single hole. Figure 10c) shows the resulting regions obtained by setting the number of components to one, the number of holes inside this component to one, and the number of holes within the hole equal two. As the holes are indexed during the growing process, it is straightforward to select some of them in accordance with a desired criterion. In our implementation the holes are chosen from the area, i.e., the holes with the largest areas are selected.

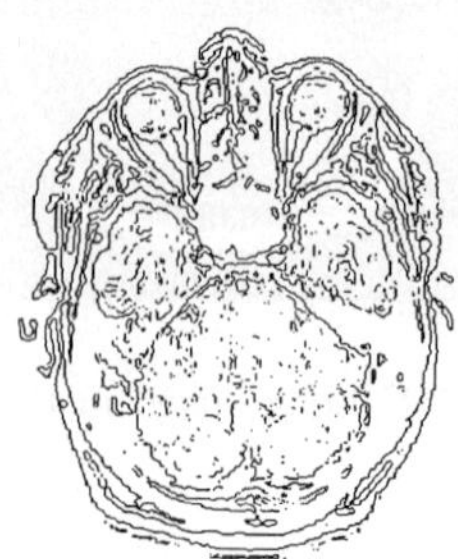

Fig. 9. Segmented image by zero-crossing of the LoG with $\sigma = 1.5$

Figure 9 depicts an edge image obtained by the classical zero-crossing of the Laplacian of the Gaussian (LoG) (with $\sigma = 1.5$). Although this segmentation looks similar to that generated by the proposed method, it does not deal with topological control and, therefore, can not guarantee that edges are closed curves, which define a single region. The topological control provided by the proposed method turns out to be an efficient mechanism to keep noise under control, since the number of regions in the resulting image is defined by a set of parameters when the segmentation begins. This behavior can be observed in figures 8 and 10.

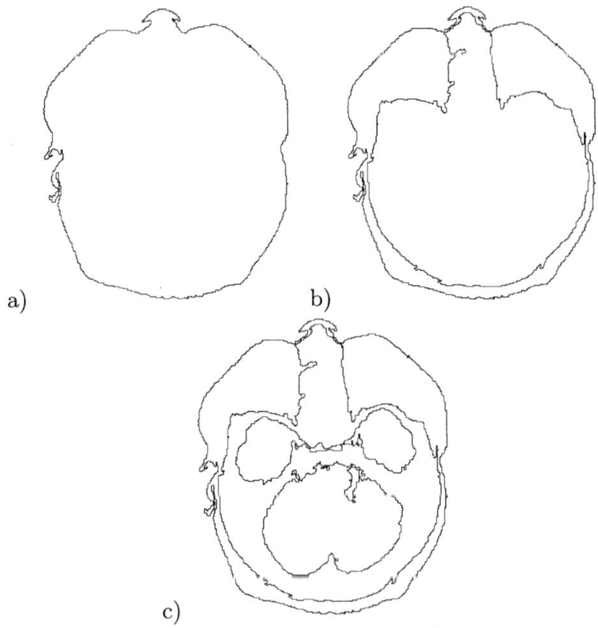

Fig. 10. Regions (and their boundary curves) dected by thresholding the topological properties as: a) a single component; b) a single component with a hole; c) a single component with a hole which has other two holes

To process the image in figure 7, the algorithm took 1.07*s* for the initialization step and 1.77*s* for the region growing (with topological control) stage on a P4 2.4 GHz and 512 MB RAM. This is a satisfactory result when compared with other automatic segmentation techniques described in the literature.

An important property of the algorithm, which can be observed in figure 10, is that the boundary curves produced are Jordan's curves, which are adequate for 3D reconstruction from contours as discussed in [10]. Such feature is not commonly found in other segmentation algorithms.

7 Conclusions and Future Work

This paper presented a new framework to image segmentation that makes use of circulation and topological control during the region growing process. From such a framework we derived an automatic segmentation algorithm capable of detecting regions while keeping their boundaries as Jordan's curves; a desirable property in many applications. The built-in topological control of the algorithm has proven to be an efficient mechanism to reduce noise and enhance the quality of the segmented regions.

The framework is also flexible, as different vector fields (from which the circulation is computed) may produce different segmentations. In fact, this subject is currently under investigation as we are now working on defining a vector field to segment images with texture. We are also investigating how the topological control can be used as a matching creterion. By imposing a certain number of holes in a segmentation process for a single image, we can detect a set of other images with similar characteristis, that is, those which holes are similar in shape or area, for example.

Acknowledgments

We aknowledge Brazilian Funding Agencies FAPESP (proc. # 03/02815-0) and CNPq (proc. # 307268/2003-9) for supporting this work.

References

1. E. Brigham. Fast Fourier Transform and its applications. Englewood Cliffs, NJ: Prentice-Hall, 1988.
2. R. Chellappa and A, Jain (eds.). Markov Random Fields. Academic Press, 1993.
3. X. Jiang. An Adaptive Contour Closure Algorithm and Its Experimental Evaluation. IEEE Trans. Patt. Anal. Mach. Intell., vol 22, no 11, 2000.
4. Kanumgo. An Efficient k-Means Clustering Algorithm: Analysis and Implementation. IEEE Trans. Pattern Anal. Machine Intell., vol. 24, no. 7, pp. 881-892,2002.
5. M. Kass. A. Witkin and D. Terzopoulos. Snakes: Active Contour Models. Int. Journal of Computer Vision, 312-331, 1988.
6. S. Z. Li. Markov random field modeling in computer vision. Springer-Verlag, 1995.
7. Y. Lin, J. Dou, and E. Zhang. Edge Expression Based on Tree Structure. Pattern Recognition, vol. 25, no. 5, pp. 507-517, 1992.
8. W. Ma and B. Manjunath. EdgeFlow: A Technique for Boundary Detection and Image Segmentation. IEEE Trans. on Image Processing, vol. 9, no. 8, 2000.
9. S. Mallat. A Wavelet Tour of Signal Processing, 2nd Edition. Academic Press, 1999.
10. L.G. Nonato, R. Minghim, M.C.F. Oliveira and G. Tavares. A novel approach to Delaunay 3D Reconstruction with a comparative analysis in the light of applications. Computer Graphics Forum., v. 20, n. 2. p. 161-174, 2001.
11. L.G. Nonato, R. Minghim, A. Castelo, J. Batista. Morse Operators for Digital Planar Surfaces and their Application to Image Segmentation. IEEE Transactions on Image Processing, v. 13, n. 2, p. 216-227, 2004.

12. N. Pal and S. Pal. A review on image segmentation techniques. Pattern Recognition, 26: 1277-1294, 1993.
13. M. Rezaee et al. A Multiresolution Image Segmentation Technique Based on Pyramidal Segmentation and Fuzzy Clustering. IEEE Trans. on Image Processing, vol. 9, no. 7, 2000.
14. J. Serra. Image Analysis and Mathematical Morphology. Academic Press, New York, 1982.
15. B. Song and S. Lee. On the Range Image Segmentation Technique Based on Local Correlation. Proc. Second Asian Conf. Computer Vision, pp. 528-532, 1995.
16. M. Sonka et al. Image Processing, Analysis and Machine Vision. PWS Publishing, 1999.
17. C. Xu, D. L. Pham and J. L. Prince. Image Segmentation using Deformable Models. Handbook of Medical Imaging, vol. 2, chapter 3. SPIE Press, 2000.
18. L. Yang and F. Albregtsen. Fast and exact computation of Cartesian geometric moments using discrete Green's theorem. Pattern Recognition, Vol. 29, No. 7, pp. 1061-1073, 1996.

Global k-Means with Similarity Functions*

Saúl López-Escobar, J.A. Carrasco-Ochoa, J.Fco. Martínez-Trinidad

National Institute for Astrophysics, Optics and Electronics,
Luis Enrique Erro No.1 Sta. Ma. Tonantzintla, Puebla, México C. P. 72840
{slopez,ariel,fmartine}@inaoep.mx

Abstract. The k-means algorithm is a frequently used algorithm for solving clustering problems. This algorithm has the disadvantage that it depends on the initial conditions, for that reason, the global k-means algorithm was proposed to solve this problem. On the other hand, the k-means algorithm only works with numerical features. This problem is solved by the k-means algorithm with similarity functions that allows working with qualitative and quantitative variables and missing data (mixed and incomplete data). However, this algorithm still depends on the initial conditions. Therefore, in this paper an algorithm to solve the dependency on initial conditions of the k-means algorithm with similarity functions is proposed, our algorithm is tested and compared against k-means algorithm with similarity functions.

1 Introduction

Clustering is a problem that frequently arises in several fields such as pattern recognition, image processing, machine learning, etc. As is well known, this problem consists in to classify a data set in two or more clusters.

The k-means algorithm is a frequently used clustering algorithm that minimizes an objective function, this algorithm assumes that the number of clusters in which the data set will be classified is known. The algorithm consists in the following steps:

1. Randomly select the initial centers.
2. Each object is assigned to the cluster which the distance of its center to the object is minimum.
3. Re-calculate the centers.
4. Repeat steps 2 and 3 until there is not change in the centers.

This algorithm has the disadvantage that it depends on the initial centers, for that reason; usually the algorithm is executed multiple times in order to find a better clustering.

In order to solve the dependency on the initial conditions of the k-means algorithm, the Global *k*-means algorithm was proposed [1], the basic idea underlying this algorithm is that an optimal solution for a clustering problem with *k* clusters can be obtained using a series of local searches using the *k*-means algorithm. At each local search the *k*-1 clusters centers are always initially placed at their optimal position

* This work was financially supported by CONACyT (Mexico) through project J38707-A.

M. Lazo and A. Sanfeliu (Eds.): CIARP 2005, LNCS 3773, pp. 392 – 399, 2005.

corresponding to the clustering problem with k-1 clusters and the remaining center is searched verifying each object in the data set.

On the other hand, the k-means algorithm only works with numerical variables due to the use of means for calculating the new centers in each iteration. For that reason, the k-means algorithm with similarity functions that allows working with qualitative and quantitative features and missing data was proposed [2], [3]. Problems with this kind of descriptions are very frequent in soft sciences as Medicine, Geology, Sociology, etc. In this kind of descriptions could be not possible to use a distance, only the degree of similarity between objects can be determined, through a similarity function. In this algorithm, the similarity among objects belonging to the same cluster is maximized and the similarity among different clusters is minimized.

As the k-means algorithm, the k-means with similarity functions depends on the initial conditions, therefore in this paper the global k-means with similarity functions is proposed.

This paper is organized as follows: in section 2 the global k-means algorithm is described. Section 3 describes the k-means with similarity functions algorithm. In section 4 we propose the global k-means with similarity functions algorithm. Experimental results are shown in section 5 and finally section 6 provides conclusions and future work.

2 Global *k*-Means Algorithm

The global k-means algorithm was proposed by Aristidis Likas, et al. [1], it constitutes a deterministic effective global clustering algorithm. It does not depend on the initial conditions or any other initial parameter and it uses the k-means algorithm as a local search procedure.

Suppose that a data set $X=\{x_1,\ldots,x_n\}$, $x_i \in R^d$ is given and it is required partitioning it in k clusters $M_1,\ldots,M_k$ such that the following objective function is optimized:

$$J(m_1,\ldots,m_k)=\sum_{i=1}^{n}\sum_{j=1}^{k} I_j(x_i)\partial(x_i,m_j)^2 \quad (1)$$

This function depends on the cluster centers $m_1,\ldots,m_k$., where

$$I_j(x_i)=\begin{cases}1 & if \quad x_i \in M_j \\ 0 & otherwise\end{cases} \quad (2)$$

and

$$\partial(x_i,m_j) = \|x_i - m_j\| \quad (3)$$

To solve a problem with k-clusters we start with one cluster (k'=1) and find its optimal position as the center of the data set. In order to solve the problem with two clusters (k'=2) the first center is placed at the optimal position for the problem with k'=1 and the k-means algorithm is executed n times placing the second center at each object x_i of the data set, x_i must be different to the solution for the problem with one cluster, i=1,...,n. After the n executions of the k-means algorithm we consider the solution for the clustering problem with k'=2 as the solution that minimizes the objective function (1). In general, let ($m_1^*(k$-1),…,$m_{k-1}^*(k$-1)) denote the solution for the problem with (k-1)-clusters. Once the solution for the problem of finding (k-1)-clusters is obtained, this is used to solve the problem with k-clusters executing n times the k-means algorithm where each execution starts with the initial centers: ($m_1^*(k$-1),…,$m_{k-1}^*(k$-1),x_i), $x_i \neq m_p^*(k$-1), p=1,…,k-1, i=1,…,n. The best solution (which minimizes the objective function (1)) after the n executions is considered as the solution for the problem with k-clusters.

3 *k*-Means with Similarity Functions

The k-means with similarity functions algorithm was proposed by Martínez-Trinidad, et al in [2], [3]. It follows the same idea that the k-means algorithm but instead of using a distance for comparing objects, a similarity function is used.

Suppose that a data set $X=\{x_1,\ldots,x_n\}$ is given, where each object is described by a set $R=\{y_1,\ldots,y_s\}$ of features. Each feature takes values in a set of admissible values D_i, $y_i(x_j) \in D_i$ i=1,…,s. We assume that in D_i there is a symbol "?" to denote missing data. Thus, the features can be of any nature (qualitative: boolean, multi-valued, etc. or quantitative: integer, real) and incomplete descriptions of objects are considered. A similarity function $\Gamma:(D_1\times D_2\times\ldots\times D_s)^2\rightarrow[0,1]$, which allows comparing objects is defined. In this work, the similarity function used is:

$$\Gamma(x_i, x_j) = \frac{\left|\left\{y_k \mid C\left(y_k(x_i), y_k(x_j)\right)=1\right\}\right|}{s} \tag{4}$$

where C is a comparison function between features values.

We require partitioning the data set in k clusters M_1,…M_k. In this kind of problems, it could be impossible to calculate means; so objects from the sample, called representative objects x_j^r , are used as centers of the clusters M_j, j=1,…,k.

The data set must be classified according the representative objects of each cluster, i.e., given a set of representative objects, first we obtain the membership $I_j(x_i)$ of the object x_i to cluster M_j, after that, we calculate the representative objects for the new k-partition, this procedure is repeated until there is no change in the representative objects.

So, the objective function is:

$$J(x_1^r,\ldots,x_k^r) = \sum_{j=1}^{k}\sum_{i=1}^{n} I_j(x_i)\Gamma(x_j^r, x_i) \tag{5}$$

where

$$I_j(x_i) = \begin{cases} 1 & \text{if} \quad \Gamma(x_j^r, x_i) = \max\limits_{1\le q\le k}\left\{\Gamma(x_q^r, x_i)\right\} \\ 0 & \text{otherwise} \end{cases} \tag{6}$$

That is, an object x_i will be assigned to the cluster such that x_i is the most similar with their representative objects.

In this case, the objective is to maximize this function.

To determine the representative objects the next expressions are used:

$$r_{M_j}(x_i) = \frac{\beta_{M_j}(x_i)}{(\alpha_{M_j}(x_i) + (1 - \beta_{M_j}(x_i)))} + \eta_{M_q}(x_i) \tag{7}$$

where $x_i \in M_j$ and $q=1,\ldots,k$ $q \neq j$

$$\beta_{M_j}(x_i) = \frac{1}{|M_j| - 1} \sum_{\substack{x_i, x_q \in M_j \\ x_i \neq x_q}} \Gamma(x_i, x_q) \tag{8}$$

$$\alpha_{M_j}(x_i) - \frac{1}{|M_j| - 1} \sum_{\substack{x_i, x_q \in M_j \\ x_i \neq x_q}} \left| \beta_{M_j}(x_i) - \Gamma(x_i, x_q) \right| \tag{9}$$

and

$$\eta_{M_k}(x_i) = \sum_{\substack{q=1 \\ i \neq q}}^{k} \left(1 - \Gamma(x_q^r, x_i)\right) \tag{10}$$

The representative object for the cluster M_j is defined as the object x_r which yields the maximum of $r_{M_j}(x_i)$

$$r_{M_j}(x_r) = \max_{x_p \in M_j} \{ r_{M_j}(x_p) \} \tag{11}$$

4 Global *k*-Means with Similarity Functions Algorithm

The global *k*-means algorithm solves the dependency on the initial conditions of the *k*-means algorithm, but only works with numerical features, therefore we propose an extension to the global *k*-means such that it allows working with mixed and incomplete data.

We consider a problem as the described in section 3. Our algorithm follows the same methodology that the global *k*-means algorithm with the difference that instead using *k*-means algorithm as local search procedure, the *k*-means with similarity functions is used, so it is guaranteed that the obtained centers belong to the data set.

In order to solve a problem with *k*-clusters we start with one cluster ($k'=1$) and we find its optimal position as the representative object of the data set, this is made by finding the object which is the most similar to all the objects of data set. In order to solve the problem with two clusters ($k'=2$) the first center is placed at the optimal position for the problem with $k'=1$ (let x_1^{r*} be the representative object for $k'=1$) and the *k*-means with similarity functions algorithm is executed n-1 times placing the second center at each object x_i of the data set, $x_i \neq x_1^{r*}$, $i=1,\ldots,n$. After the n-1 executions of the *k*-means with similarity functions algorithm, we consider the solution for the clustering problem with $k' = 2$ as the solution that maximizes the error function (5). In general, let ($x_1^{r*}(k-1), x_2^{r*}(k-1),\ldots, x_{k-1}^{r*}(k-1)$) denote the solution for the problem with (*k*-1) –clusters. Once the solution for the problem with (*k*-1)-clusters is obtained this is used to solve the problem with *k*-clusters executing *n*-(*k*-*1*) times the *k*-means with similarity functions algorithm where each execution starts with the initial centers: ($x_1^{r*}(k-1), x_2^{r*}(k-1),\ldots, x_{k-1}^{r*}(k-1), x_i$), $x_i \neq x_p^{r*}$, *p*=1,…,*k*-1, *i*=1,…,*n*. The best solution after the *n*-(*k*-1) executions (which maximizes the error function (5)) is considered as the solution for the problem with *k*-clusters. The proposed algorithm is depicted in Table 1.

Table 1. Global k-means with similarity functions algorithm

```
Input: k = number of clusters
       n = number of objects of the data set
Output: RO [1,…,k] /* Representative Objects */
        OF /* Value of the objective function */
Count = 0
Seeds [1,…,k] = 0
Seeds[1] = most similar object to the data set
for k'=2 to k
   for i=1 to n
      if i ≠ Seeds[1,…,k'-1]
        [SRO,J] = KMeansWithSimilarityFunctions (Seeds[1,…,k'-1],i)
        /* SRO is the set of representative objects */
        /* J is the objective function */
        if J>count then
            count = J
            Seeds = SRO
RO = Seeds
OF = count
```

5 Experimental Results

We have tested the proposed algorithm on several data sets: Iris, Flags, Electro, Machine and Wine [4]. In all data sets we did experiments considering only information of the feature vector and ignoring class labels. The quality of the obtained solutions was evaluated in terms of the objective function (5). The description of each data set is given in Table 2.

Table 2. Data set features

Data set	Objects	Qualitative features	Quantitative features
Iris	150	0	4
Flags	194	3	26
Electro	132	0	11
Machine	209	1	7
Wine	178	0	13

For each data set we did the following experiments:

- One run of the global *k*-means with similarity functions algorithm for the problem with *k*=2,…,15.

- *n* runs (where *n* is the number of objects of the data set) of the *k*-means with similarity functions algorithm for each problem with k=2,…,15 starting with random initial centers. For each data set, the average, the maximum and the minimum of the objective function were calculated.

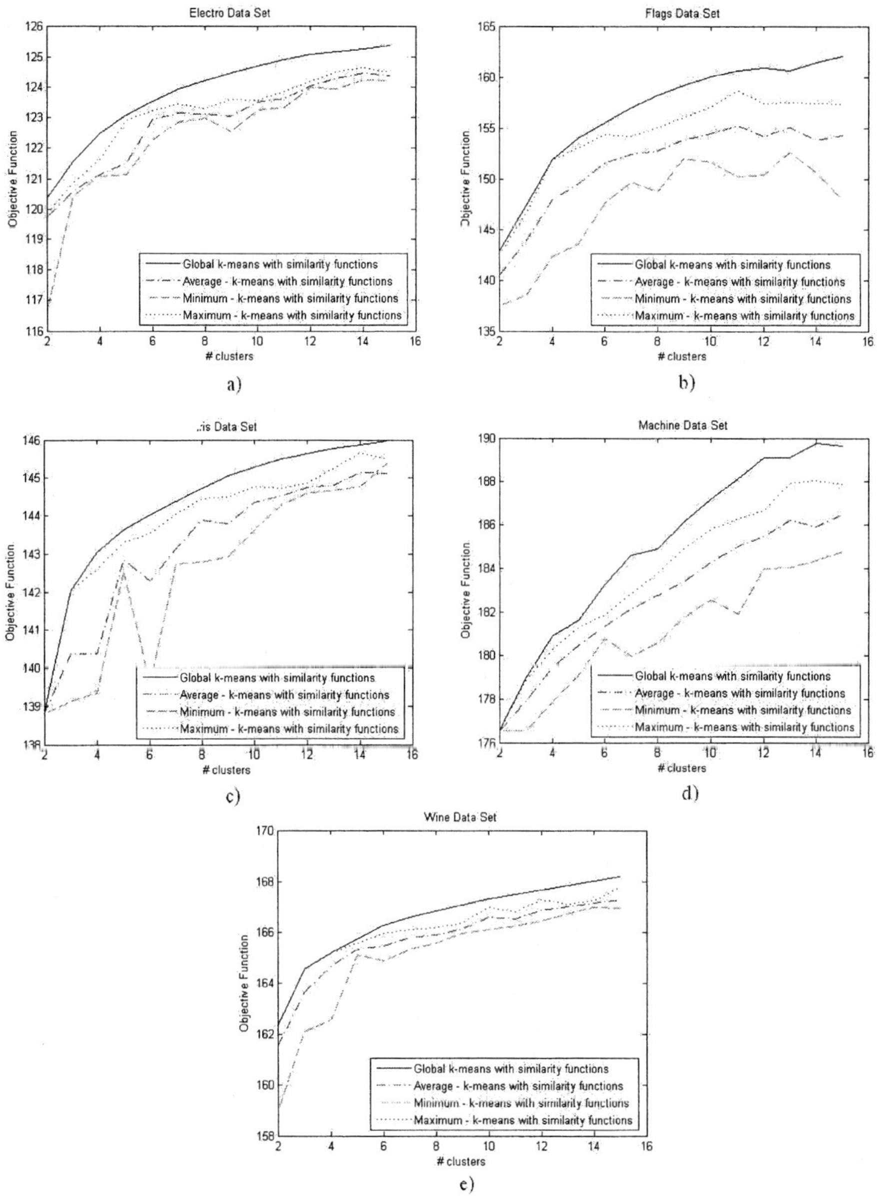

Fig. 1. Experimental results for data sets: a) Electro, b) Flags, c) Iris, d) Machine and e) Wine

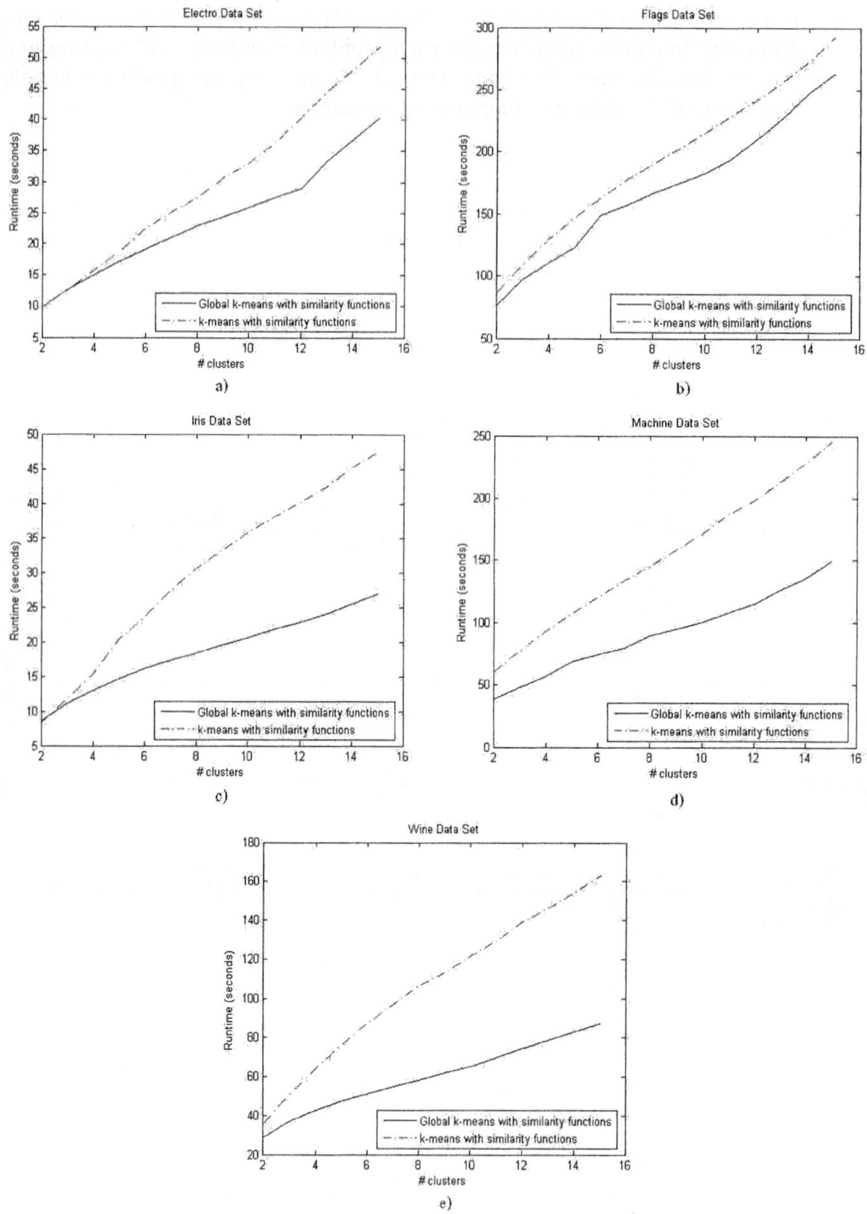

Fig. 2. Runtime for data sets: a) Electro, b) Flags, c) Iris, d) Machine and e) Wine

In figure 1 the value of the objective function obtained from the global *k*-means algorithm with similarity functions is compared against the average, the maximum and the minimum of the *n* values obtained from the runs of the *k*-means with similarity functions algorithm. In our experiments, the Global k-means with similarity functions algorithm obtained better results than the k-means with similarity functions algorithm and in few cases it obtains the same result that the maximum.

In figure 2 the runtime of each experiment is shown. The runtime of the Global k-means algorithm with similarity functions is less than the runtime of the k-means algorithm. This is due because for each value of k we carried out n runs of the k-means with similarity functions algorithm, and the global k-means with similarity functions execute only n-(k-1) runs of the k-means with similarity functions algorithm. Also, each time the global k-means with similarity functions algorithm uses the k-means with similarity functions, it starts with better seeds than the random selection, therefore, it converges faster.

6 Conclusions

In this paper the global k-means with similarity functions algorithm was introduced. Our method is independent of the initial conditions. It was compared against the k-means with similarity functions algorithm.

In our experiments, the global k-means with similarity functions algorithm obtained better clusters in terms of the objective function than the k-means with similarity functions, and only in a few cases, with small values for k, the results were the same that the maximum obtained with the k-means with similarity functions.

The runtimes of our algorithm were less than the time needed for the n executions of the k-means with similarity functions algorithm, and our algorithm's results were better.

As future work, we are going to find a fast global k-means with similarity functions algorithm in order to reduce the computational cost without significantly affecting the quality.

References

1. Aristidis Likas, Nikos Vlassis, and Jakob J. Verbeek, "The global k-means clustering algorithm", *Pattern Recognition 36*, 2003, pp. 451-461.
2. José Francisco Martínez Trinidad, Javier Raymundo García Serrano, and Irene Olaya Ayaquica Martínez, "C-Means Algorithm with Similarity Functions", Computación y Sistemas Vol. 5 No. 4, 2002, pp. 241-246
3. Javier R. García Serrano and J. F. Martínez-Trinidad, "Extension to c-means algorithm for the use of similarity functions", 3rd European Conference on Principles and Practice of Knowledge Discovery in Databases Proceedings. Prague, Czech Rep. (1999). pp. 354-359.
4. C.L. Blake, C. J. Merz, UCI repository of machine learning databases, University of California, Irvine, Departament of Information and Computer Sciences, 1998.

Reconstruction-Independent 3D CAD for Calcification Detection in Digital Breast Tomosynthesis Using Fuzzy Particles

G. Peters[1,3], S. Muller[1], S. Bernard[1], R. Iordache[1],
F. Wheeler[2], and I. Bloch[3]

[1] GE Healthcare Europe, 283, rue de la Minière, 78533 Buc, France
{gero.peters, serge.muller, sylvain.bernard, razvan.iordache}@med.ge.com
[2] GE Global Research, One Research Circle, Niskayuna, NY 12309, USA
wheeler@research.ge.com
[3] Ecole Nationale Supérieure de Télécommunications, CNRS UMR 5141 LTCI, Paris, France
isabelle.bloch@enst.fr

Abstract. In this paper we present a novel approach for microcalcification detection in Digital Breast Tomosynthesis (DBT) datasets. A reconstruction-independent approach, working directly on the projected views, is proposed. Wavelet filter responses on the projections are thresholded and combined to obtain candidate microcalcifications. For each candidate, we create a fuzzy contour through a multi-level thresholding process. We introduce a fuzzy set definition for the class microcalcification contour that allows the computation of fuzzy membership values for each candidate contour. Then, an aggregation operator is presented that combines information over the complete set of projected views, resulting in 3D fuzzy particles. A final decision is made taking into account information acquired over a range of successive processing steps. A clinical example is provided that illustrates our approach. DBT still being a new modality, a similar published approach is not available for comparison and limited clinical data currently prevents a clinical evaluation of the algorithm. .

1 Introduction

Breast cancer continues to be one of the leading causes of cancer mortality among women. Since the underlying causes for this disease remain unknown, early screening is the only means to reduce mortality among the affected population. X-ray mammography is currently the primary method for detecting early breast cancers, reducing the mortality rate by about 30% for women 50 years and older [1]. However, about 30% of breast cancers are still missed by conventional screening mammography. One of the main reasons is the superimposition of tissue that obscures lesions in dense breasts [2]. Digital Breast Tomosynthesis (DBT) [3],[4], is a new three-dimensional (3D) limited-angle tomography breast imaging technique that will substantially overcome the superimposition problem for lesion detection. It then remains important to accu-

M. Lazo and A. Sanfeliu (Eds.): CIARP 2005, LNCS 3773, pp. 400 – 408, 2005.

rately detect and localize microcalcification clusters, which are one of the earliest signs of breast cancer visible in mammograms.

The introduction of DBT brings a variety of new challenges and benefits. Several projected views from different acquisition angles will potentially reduce the number of false positives (FP) caused by summation artifacts as well as the number of false negatives (FN) caused by the masking effect of overlying tissue. At the same time, the dose per acquired image is significantly reduced in comparison to standard 2D mammograms, to maintain a comparable total patient dose per scan. This has a major impact on any processing in the projections, as the characteristics of these images change dramatically, and algorithms developed for 2D mammograms cannot be generally applied without modification.

As DBT systems become available for clinical testing, different strategies for CAD on DBT data are emerging. Chan et al. have presented an approach applying CAD processing on reconstructed slices [6]. A method applying mass detection algorithms directly on the projected views was presented in [7]. Candidates are detected in each projected view separately and afterwards combined in 3D using the acquisition geometry. CAD processing for calcification detection in 3D DBT data has not been made public so far and therefore represents one of the original contributions of this paper. Since DBT is a relatively new modality, 3D reconstruction algorithms for its particular geometry are still not fully optimized. Hence, it is desirable to devise a CAD approach that is independent of the reconstruction algorithm used to generate tomosynthesis slices.

Fuzzy processing has been widely accepted for use in microcalcification detection tasks [8], [9], [10]. In the present work, we propose an original method using fuzzy particles to account for ambiguities in shape and appearance of microcalcifications for the purpose of modeling and identification. The use of a fuzzy set description enables us to maintain the evidence, and the strength of the evidence, gathered from each DBT projection image for each potential finding without making hard decisions in isolation. The final decision as to the presence or absence of calcification is then made in 3D through aggregation of all available information from all projections.

Working directly on DBT projected views offers several advantages. The processing time is reduced compared to the processing of reconstructed slices since they are generally much more numerous than the projected views. The processing is performed on a data space independent of the reconstruction algorithm used to generate 3D images. There are however some issues that need to be addressed. The DBT projected views have a lower Contrast to Noise Ratio (CNR) rendering the detection task in a single image more difficult when using approaches designed for conventional 2D mammograms. It is crucial to delay the detection decision for each candidate particle until information from each view can be jointly considered. With this as our motivation, we develop and present a fuzzy processing operator that aggregates the information extracted from each projected view.

Low-dose projected views contain ambiguities about the objects in the image, including uncertainty about a candidate particle being a microcalcification, imprecision of its position and extent, as well as the incomplete nature of data in the individual projections. We use fuzzy logic to take these ambiguities into account and preserve them up to a point in the processing where we have gathered sufficient information to make a decision that simultaneously utilizes all available information.

The novel approach presented here consists of the following processing steps. We start by detecting candidate particles that potentially are microcalcifications. We then build a fuzzy contour for each candidate particle, based on several extracted attributes and multi-level segmentation. A partial defuzzification is applied, resulting in fuzzy particles better suited for the final aggregation operation. Once information from the entire set of projected views has been aggregated resulting in 3D fuzzy particles, their properties are extracted before the final step deciding whether those particles correspond to microcalcifications or other structures.

2 Candidate Particle Detection

In the initial processing performed on the projected views we extract a map of candidate particles. A "Mexican Hat" wavelet kernel is used to compute the contrast between a structure located in the center of the wavelet and its surrounding neighborhood. Convolving the original image with this kernel creates a band-pass image of sorts that emphasizes small structures in the image. Our implementation incorporates a multi-scale approach to account for the range in size of microcalcifications. The images resulting from the application of wavelets at different scales are combined using a "max" operator resulting in a local contrast image. This image is thresholded against local variance of background noise level. The connected components of this binary image are then labeled as candidates.

This initial step is crucial to all further processing. Any particle missed by the initial detection cannot be recovered later on. A high sensitivity in this step is therefore of utmost importance. To achieve the desired sensitivity we accept an elevated number of false positives (FP), which we will be able to reduce at a later stage with the use of fuzzy particles and the aggregation of information from different projected views.

3 2D Fuzzy Contours

Once the candidate particles have been identified, we create fuzzy contours describing each candidate. Each fuzzy contour accounts for the ambiguities of the original data. For each candidate particle, we compute a set of contour candidates using multi-level thresholding. This ordered set of contours is considered the universe of all possible contours describing a given particle. The prior knowledge about contours of microcalcifications [5] is transformed into a fuzzy set description. Finally, membership values for each contour candidate are calculated.

First, we extract a set of candidate contours for each candidate particle using multi-level thresholding. This is achieved by applying a series of decreasing thresholds to the local contrast image and extracting the level-set. Each candidate particle is treated separately. This processing is applied until either one of the conditions given in Equations (1) and (2) is met

$$A(C) \leq A_{\max} \tag{1}$$

where $A(C)$ is the area enclosed by the contour C and A_{max} is the maximum expected size for the area of a microcalcification

$$G(\rho, C) \geq G(\rho)_{\max} - \Delta G_{\max} \tag{2}$$

where $G(\rho,C)$ is the pixel intensity under the contour C of particle ρ, $G(\rho)_{max}$ is the maximum pixel intensity of particle ρ, and ΔG_{max} is the intensity range expected within a single microcalcification. These two conditions limit the area and intensity range of the candidate particles being extracted to values consistent with actual microcalcifications.

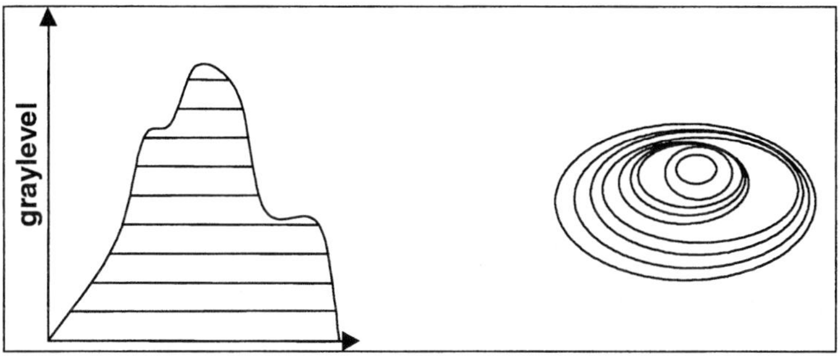

Fig. 1. The function on the left shows a gray level profile of a candidate particle and the thresholds applied. The corresponding extracted contours are shown on the right.

For each candidate particle, we thus obtain a set of candidate contours $\{C_i\}$. In order to create a fuzzy contour we compute, for each contour C_i, the membership value $f_c(C_i)$ to the *microcalcification contour* class.

The fuzzy set corresponding to this class is defined based on prior knowledge about characteristics of microcalcifications, which is summarized by "microcalcifications are small and have a high contrast". This linguistic definition translates to a fuzzy set description using two attributes namely area and gradient shown in Fig. 2.

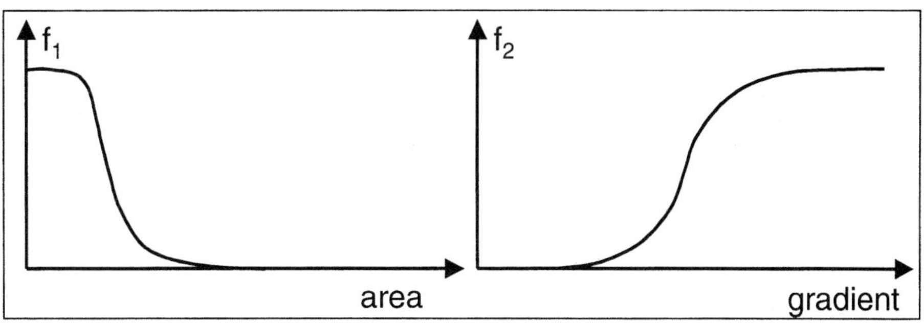

Fig. 2. The above functions correspond to fuzzy set representations of size (size is small) and image gradient under a contour (gradient is high) for particles in the mammography images

The functions depicted in Fig. 2 correspond to fuzzy set representations of size (size is small) and image gradient under a contour (gradient is high). The functions have been designed experimentally in prior work [9].

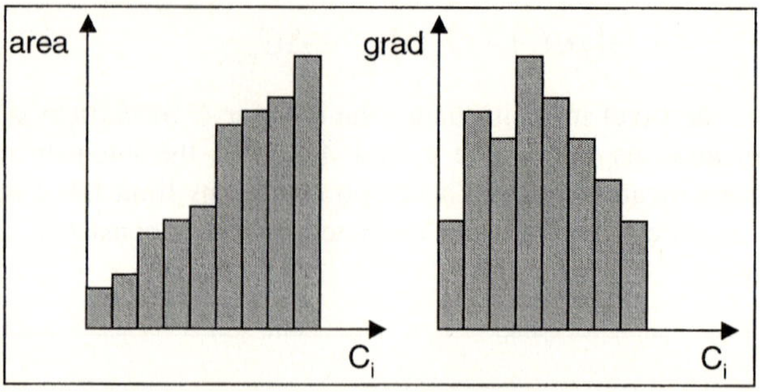

Fig. 3. Values for the fuzzy contour of a given candidate particle for area (left) and gradient under the contour (right)

For each candidate contour C_i, we measure both area A and gradient g values (Fig. 3). We can derive the membership values $f_{area}(C_i)$ and $f_{gradient}(C_i)$ for each contour based on small area and high gradient criteria as

$$f_{area}(C_i) = f_1(A(C_i)); \qquad f_{gradient}(C_i) = f_2(g(C_i)) \tag{3}$$

The conjunction of membership values obtained for each contour based on small area and high gradient provides membership values $f_c(C_i)$ to the class microcalcification contour [9],

$$f_c(C_i) = \wedge\left[f_{area}(C_i), f_{gradient}(C_i)\right] \tag{4}$$

Application of this method for one particular candidate particle is shown in Fig. 4.

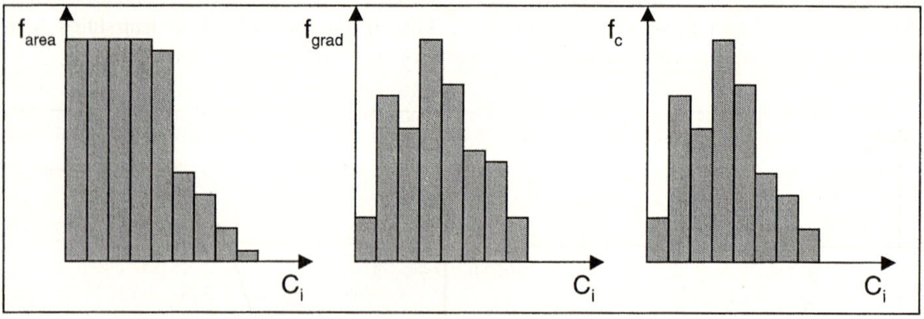

Fig. 4. Membership values for the fuzzy contour of the candidate particle described in Fig. 3 for different criteria: small area (left), large gradient under the contour (middle) using fuzzy sets in Fig. 2, and conjunction of both criteria representing the membership values to the class microcalcification contour (right) for a fuzzy contour corresponding to a single candidate particle

4 Partial Defuzzification

We now build a fuzzy particle for each candidate particle, using the membership function to the *microcalcification contour* class of its respective fuzzy contour. This process will be called partial defuzzification, since it consists in defuzzifying some aspects of the fuzzy contours. To derive a very simple aggregation process in the 3D space of the particles detected on projected views, we transform the fuzzy contours into fuzzy particles in a two-step process.

First, for each candidate contour C_i of a fuzzy contour with a membership function to the *microcalcification contour* class f_c, a connected component C_i is created such as

$$\forall(x, y) \in \dot{C}_i, \quad \dot{C}_i(x, y) = f_c(C_i) \tag{5}$$

where $\dot{C}_i$ denotes the connected component that includes all pixels on or delimited by the contour C_i.

Then, for a projection image P, we generate a fuzzy particle map I such that the value of each pixel is determined by

$$\forall(x, y) \in P \quad I(x, y) = \bigvee_i \left[\dot{C}_i(x, y)\right] \tag{6}$$

In summary, the aim of this partial defuzzification is to create a fuzzy particle map, where each pixel value corresponds to the possibility of that pixel belonging to a microcalcification. Since a single pixel may be enclosed by several different candidate contours, the membership values corresponding to each of these contours are combined in order to obtain the value for this pixel. The "max" operator is the smallest T-conorm and it realizes the equivalent of a union operation on fuzzy sets. It is used here to combine the different membership values corresponding to a given point.

5 Aggregation and Final Decision

After performing separate fuzzy detections in each of the N projection images of the DBT acquisition, the next step consists in aggregating the fuzzy particles by taking into account the acquisition geometry. The goal is to find for each 3D voxel the corresponding information in all of the N fuzzy particle maps that were created.

The aggregation of information gathered in the fuzzy particle maps for a given voxel is expressed as

$$I(x_v, y_v, z_v) = \mathop{\Psi}_{k=1}^{N}\left[I_k(x_k, y_k)\right] \tag{7}$$

where $I(x_v, y_v, z_v)$ is the voxel intensity at position (x_v, y_v, z_v), $I(x_k, y_k)$ is the pixel intensity at position (x_k, y_k) of the kth fuzzy particle map, corresponding to the

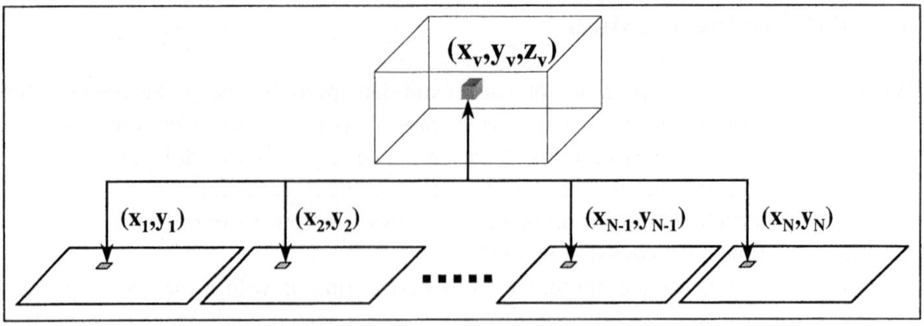

Fig. 5. Information aggregation strategy: For a given voxel (x_v, y_v, z_v) the information from all corresponding pixels (x_k, y_k) is aggregated using the operator Ψ. The position of the pixel (x_k, y_k) corresponding to the projection of a given voxel (x_v, y_v, z_v) is computed using a priori knowledge about the acquisition geometry.

projection of position (x_v, y_v, z_v), and Ψ is the aggregation operator. Fig. 5 illustrates this aggregation operation.

Using the arithmetic mean as aggregation operator, equation (7) can be rewritten as follows:

$$I(x_v, y_v, z_v) = \frac{1}{N}\sum_{k=1}^{N} I_k\left(s_{z,k}\cdot x+\xi_{x,z,k}, s_{z,k}\cdot y+\xi_{y,z,k}\right) \tag{8}$$

where $\xi_{x,z,k}$ and $\xi_{y,z,k}$ are the shift factors in x and y direction and $s_{z,k}$ is the scaling factor. These factors result from the acquisition geometry.

Finally, a defuzzification is applied to the 3D fuzzy particles, taking into account information acquired during the different processing steps, to decide whether particles correspond to microcalcifications. For reasons of simplicity, a simple thresholding was implemented as defuzzification in this preliminary approach.

6 Preliminary Results

In this section we show the result of applying these methods to real DBT data. Fig. 6 shows a projected view and corresponding fuzzy particle map. In Fig. 7 we see the results of aggregating in 3D before and after defuzzification (middle and right) alongside a reconstruction slice (left) that was reconstructed for comparison using Algebraic Reconstruction Technique (ART).

The validity of the proposed approach is illustrated in this example for a cluster of microcalcifications. Microcalcifications of different sizes, shapes and local contrast are detected. Since a clinical database providing ground truth at particle level is hard to come by, a visual sanity check today is the only means to verify our results. As 3D DBT datasets become increasingly numerous, a validation for detection of clusters of microcalcifications on a clinical database should be envisioned.

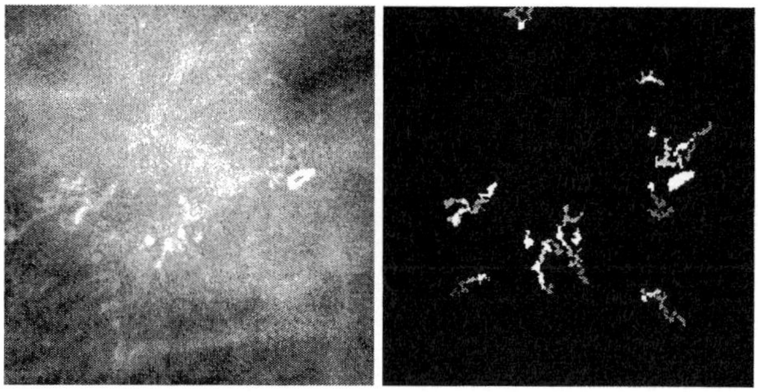

Fig. 6. Selected region of a DBT projected view (left) and the corresponding fuzzy particle map (right) (Tomographic projection data provided courtesy of Dr. D. Kopans, Massachusetts General Hospital, Boston, MA, USA.)

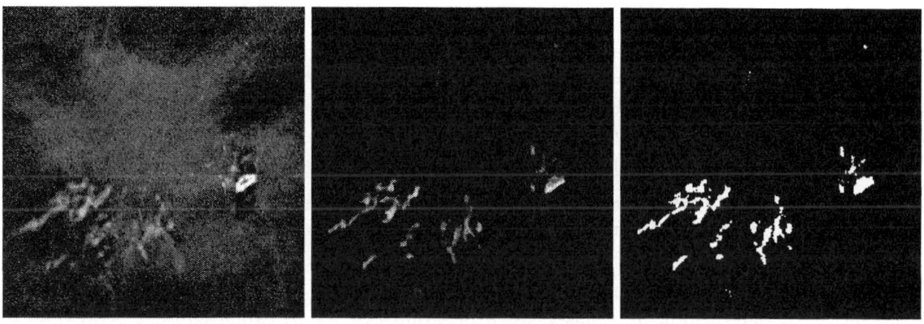

Fig. 7. Selected region of a slice reconstructed with ART (left), the corresponding 3D fuzzy particles in the same slice (middle), and corresponding 3D particles resulting from defuzzification of the 3D fuzzy particles by applying a threshold (right)

7 Conclusion

We have proposed a novel approach to detect microcalcifications in DBT datasets. Our approach exhibits numerous advantages. Working directly on the DBT projected views enables us to work independently of the reconstruction algorithm used to generate the 3D images. In addition, the processing time is expected to be significantly reduced compared to the application of similar operators on reconstructed slices, since they are generally much more numerous than the projected views, and the required 3D processing is sparse.

We have introduced a fuzzy description of the candidate particles to account for the ambiguities in the image data. Another key advantage of combining fuzzy techniques with a detection applied directly on the projected views is that information about each potential microcalcification can be preserved until the aggregation step. A final defuzzification of the aggregated particles allows the reduction of false positives that were accepted at a high level during the initial detection step in the projected views.

The preliminary experiments presented in this paper are quite promising as far as a visual verification is concerned. Nevertheless, an investigation on a clinical database is needed for comparing detection results to state-of-the-art 2D detection algorithms.

References

1. K. Kerlikowske, H. Schipper, In: Fast Facts-Breast Cancer (Epidemiology), Health Press Limited, Oxford, UK, 1998.
2. T. Holland et al, So-called interval cancers of the breast: pathologic and radiographic analysis. Cancer 49, 2527-2533, 1982.
3. Dobbins III, J.T., Godfrey, D.J.: Digital x-ray tomosynthesis: current state of the art and clinical potential. Physics in Medicine and Biology 48, R65-R106, 2003.
4. Wu, T., Stewart, A., Stanton, M., McCauley, T., Phillips, W., Kopans, D.B., Moore, R.H., Eberhard, J.W., Opsahl-Ong, B., Niklason, L., Williams, M.B.: Tomo-graphic mammography using a limited number of low-dose cone-beam projection images. Medical Physics 30, 365-380, 2003.
5. M. Lanyi, In: Diagnosis and Differential Diagnosis of Breast Calcifications, Springer-Verlag Berlin Heidelberg, Germany, 1988.
6. H.-P. Chan, J. Wei, B. Sahiner, E.A. Rafferty, T. Wu, M.A. Roubidoux, R.H. Moore, D.B. Kopans, L.M. Hadjiiski, M.A. Helvie, Computerized Detection of Masses on Digital Tomosynthesis Mammograms - A preliminary Study. In: Proceedings of the 7th International Workshop on Digital Mammography, Chapel Hill, NC, Springer, 2004.
7. I. Reiser, R.M. Nishikawa, M.L. Giger, D.B. Kopans, E.A. Rafferty, R. Moore, T. Wu, A Reconstruction-Independent Method for Computerized Detection of Mammographic Masses in Tomosynthesis Images. In: Proceedings of the 7th International Workshop on Digital Mammography, Chapel Hill, NC, Springer, 2004.
8. H.D. Cheng, Y.M. Lui, R.I. Freimanis, A novel Approach to Microcalcification Detection Using Fuzzy Logic Technique. IEEE Transactions on Medical Imaging, 17 (3) 442-450, 1998.
9. S. Bothorel, B. Bouchon-Meunier, S. Muller, A Fuzzy Logic Based Approach for Semiological Analysis of Microcalcifications in Mammographic Images. International Journal for Intelligent Systems, 12, 819-848, 1997.
10. N. Pandey, Z. Salcic, J. Sivaswamy, Fuzzy Logic Based Microcalcification Detection. Neural Networks for Signal Processing - Proceedings of the IEEE Work-shop, 2 , 662-671, 2000.

Simple and Robust Hard Cut Detection Using Interframe Differences*

Alvaro Pardo[1,2]

[1] DIE, Facultad de Ingeniería y Tecnologías,
Universidad Católica del Uruguay
[2] IIE, Facultad de Ingeniería,
Universidad de la República
apardo@fing.edu.uy

Abstract. In this paper we introduce a simple method for the detection of hard cuts using only interframe differences. The method is inspired in the computational gestalt theory. The key idea in this theory is to define a meaningful event as large deviation from the expected background process. That is, an event that has little probability to occur given a probabilistic background model. In our case we will define a hard cut when the interframe differences have little probability to be produced by a given model of interframe differences of non-cut frames. Since we only use interframe differences, there is no need to perform motion estimation, or other type of processing, and the method turns to be very simple with low computational cost. The proposed method outperforms similar methods proposed in the literature.

1 Introduction

Shot boundary detection algorithms are one of the most basic and important methods for video analysis. They allow the segmentation of the original video sequence into basic units called shots that facilitate high level processing and abstraction of the video signal. Although it may seem a simple task, the automatic and reliable extraction of shot boundaries it has some difficulties, mainly due to the different types of video sequences, which still need to be studied. Even for simple shot transitions like hard cuts (abrupt transition between adjacent frames) there is room for improvements. In particular, one of the possible directions of research is to improve the performance of simple methods. We must remember that a video sequence contains a great amount of data, so in general we should avoid unnecessarily complicated methods. Another direction of work is the study of fully automatic methods that permit to process a wide variety of videos. In this work we will present a simple online method with only a few parameters that performs well for a representative set of testing video sequences.

We can distinguish two types of shot transitions: abrupt transitions, called hard cuts, and gradual transitions. A hard cut is an abrupt change in the frame

* Supported by Proyecto PDT-S/C/OP/17/07.

M. Lazo and A. Sanfeliu (Eds.): CIARP 2005, LNCS 3773, pp. 409–419, 2005.

appearance. Gradual transitions, on the other hand, span over a set of frames and are produced by postproduction effects such as fades, dissolves, morphs and wipes. In this work we will concentrate on hard cut detection.

We can divide the existing techniques for shot boundary detection into the following basic categories: pixel, histogram, block matching, object segmentation and tracking and feature tracking based methods. Some methods proposed in the literature combine some of these basic methods to attain better performances.

Pixel based methods usually compute interframe differences between frames (adjacent or not). The frame difference can be computed in several color spaces. The main drawback of pixel-based methods is their sensitivity to camera and object motion and noise. For this reason filtering is usually applied before computing interframe differences [5]. Regarding the measure of difference, we can make a distinction between distance based methods and thresholding ones. The former ones compute a distance between frames such as the absolute difference, while the later ones compute the number of pixels with a difference above a given threshold. Usually these methods are not very reliable and therefore are mostly used as indicators of probable shot boundaries that are the confirmed by more sophisticated methods [6].

Histogram based methods compare the histograms of a pair of frames using a suitable histogram distance [4]. In contrast to pixel based methods, histogram based methods are robust against camera and object motions since the histograms do not contain any spatial information. Unfortunately, the main critic and limitation is that frames of different shot can have similar histograms and in this way these methods will fail. In addition, like pixel-based methods, these methods are not robust against lighting changes.

Block-matching methods divide each frame into blocks and then match a given set of features of blocks (pixel colors, histograms, and so on) between frames. That is, the best match for each block in the source frame is found in the destination frame (This is the methodology applied in MPEG-like video coding techniques) and the similarity of these block is used as an indicator for shot boundary existence [4,5].

Segmentation and object tracking are typically computational demanding. The underlying idea behind these methods is that frames within a shot contain the same objects. Therefore, they use algorithms for object tracking and segmentation to achieve shot boundary detection.

Feature tracking methods detect shot transitions when there is an abrupt change in the number of features tracked. For example, if the frame edges have strong variations [5]. In [8] the authors propose feature tracking as a measure of frame dissimilarity. Instead of tracking edges, they propose to track fine grained features as corners and textures. Hard cuts are then detected as points with high interframe feature loss.

Nearly all of the previous methods rely on a set of thresholds in order to decide whether there is a shot boundary in a given frame. In the case of the pixel base methods we need a threshold to decide if the interframe distance is enough to declare a shot boundary. For histogram based methods the threshold is applied to the histogram distances. The problem of selection of the right threshold is a key point that has big influence in the overall system performance. Unfortunately it has received little attention in the literature [5] and most of the authors propose heuristics for their selection. Furthermore, it has been demonstrated that global thresholds led to sub optimal methods, with too many false positives or false negatives [5]. To solve this problem adaptive thresholds have been proposed. However, life is never so straight forward, and when using adaptive thresholds we must design an updating rule based on, for example, the statistics of non-boundary frames. This introduces additional problems concerning the correct estimation of this statistical information. Traditionally the problem is solved introducing a learning stage where several video sequences are processed to obtain the desired statistics.

In this paper we introduce a simple method for the detection of hard cuts using only interframe differences. The method is inspired in the works of Computational Gestalt [2,3]. The key idea in this framework is to define the meaningful event as large deviation from the expected background process. That is, an event that has little probability to occur given a probabilistic background model. In our case we will define a hard cut when the interframe differences have little probability to be produced by a given model of interframe differences of non-cut frames. Since we only use interframe differences, there is no need to perform motion estimation, or other type of processing, and the methods turns to be very simple with low computational cost.

In the first step of the algorithm we compute a measure of hard cut probability, or meaningfulness. Then in a second stage we apply an adaptive thresholding technique that only uses the information of the video sequence being processed to find the hard cuts. This contrasts with other methods that need a supervised learning step to obtain the thresholds. This makes our methods very simple and fast.

Since we will use only interframe differences for adjacent frames we assume that the videos are contain mainly smooth transitions. From another point of view, we assume a reasonable temporal sampling. As we said above these methods have problems with strong camera or object motions. If a strong motion or a lightning change occurs, the method may produce a false positive. Even though these restrictions, we will show that the results of the proposed method are very robust and perform well for a wide variety of videos.

2 Proposed Method

Lets suppose we have the probability, $P_\mu = P(e(x) > \mu)$, that the error, $e(x) = |I(x;t) - I(x;t-1)|$ at pixel x, exceeds the threshold μ. Within a video shot segment we expect the frame differences to be small and therefore there would be a small chance for a big number of pixels exceeding a reasonable threshold. Below we will address the threshold selection. If we fix the threshold μ we can compute the error image and the number of pixels, N_μ, exceeding the threshold μ. In order to assess the meaningfulness of this event we must compute its probability of occurrence given the apriori information of interframe differences, P_μ. This can be done computing the probability of at least N_μ pixels exceeding the threshold μ by using the Binomial distribution:

$$B(N, N_\mu, P_\mu) = \sum_{k=N_\mu}^{N} C_k^N P_\mu^k (1 - P_\mu)^{N-k}$$

Using this probability, and following the ideas of the computational gestalt theory, we say that the previous event is meaningful if its probability is very low given the statistics of past frame differences [1]. This means that we say that the event is meaningful if it is a large deviation of what is expected given past information.

Abrupt changes in interframe differences can be produced by hard cuts, fast motion and deformation, but also by slow motions, freezing or frame repetition. Therefore, we must also detect these events. Applying the same idea, given a threshold λ and the probability $P_\lambda = P(e(x) \leq \lambda) = 1 - P(e(x) > \lambda)$, we compute the probability of at least N_λ pixels being below the threshold.

$$B(N, N_\mu, P_\mu) = \sum_{k=N_\lambda}^{N} C_k^N P_\lambda^k (1 - P_\lambda)^{N-k}$$

So far we have presented the basic method for the assessment of the meaningfulness of the events abrupt change and slow change. Now we are going to explain the selection of the thresholds, the combination of the previous measurements for the detection of hard cuts, and the estimation of the probabilities P_μ and P_λ.

The meaningfulness of each of the events is obtained as the minimal probability over a set of fixed thresholds. That is, the meaningfulness of the event abrupt change is obtained as:

$$M_a = \min_{\mu_i} B(N, N_{\mu_i}, P_{\mu_i})$$

where each term corresponds to a threshold $\mu_i \in \{\mu_1, ..., \mu_n\}$. In the same way, the meaningfulness of a slow change is obtained as:

$$M_s = \min_{\lambda_i} B(N, N_{\lambda_i}, P_{\lambda_i})$$

with $\lambda_i \in \{\lambda_1, ..., \lambda_m\}$. The domain of variation of λ_i is set to detect slow changing frames, hence we set $\lambda_i \in \{1, ..., 10\}$. In the same way, since with the threshold μ_i we expect to detect abrupt changes we set $\mu_i \in \{10, ..., 100\}$. The upper limit is set to a reasonable high value and does not play an important role in the algorithm. The upper limit for λ_i and lower limit of μ_i has been set to 10 as a conservative value. We did several experiments changing these values and

[1] In the computational gestalt theory instead of working only with the probabilities the authors propose to estimate the expectation via multiplying the probability by the number of test performed [3].

we didn't encounter differences in the final results. However, it is still an open problem the tuning of it.

To conclude the description of the first step of the algorithm we now present the estimation of probabilities P_μ and P_λ. These probabilities are obtained from the error histogram of past frames. To cope with non-stationary statistics, we use a buffer, Buf, of size n of non-cut histograms and a $\alpha - \beta$ filter. The histogram of errors is updated with the following rule:

$$h_t = \text{Histogram}(|I(x;t) - I(x;t-1)|)$$
$$h = \alpha\text{mean}(Buf) + (1-\alpha)h_t$$

with $\alpha = 0.9$ and $n = 12$. The value for n was chosen to hold in the buffer half second of video (assuming 24 fps).

As said before, we the previous rule we track non-cut error histogram. That means that we must have a rule to decide whether a frame is hard cut or not. To do so we use the measure $H = M_a/M_s$. If $H < 1$ the probability of occurrence of an abrupt change given the previous non-cut probability distributions is smaller, more meaningful, than the occurrence of a slow change.

Algorithm

For all frames $t \geq 2$:

1. Compute interframe differences:

$$e(x) = |I(x;t) - I(x;t-1)|$$

2. Find the meaningfulness of the events abrupt and slow change:

$$M_a = \min_{\mu_i} B(N_{\mu_i}, N, P_{\mu_i})$$

$$M_s = \min_{\lambda_i} B(N_{\lambda_i}, N, P_{\lambda_i})$$

   The probabilities P_{μ_i} and P_{λ_i} are computed using the histogram h [2].
3. If $M_a < M_s$ (there is a probable hard cut), do not introduce the histogram of $e(x;t)$ into the buffer, else, update the histogram with:

$$h_t = \text{Histogram}(|I(x;t) - I(x;t-1)|)$$
$$h = \alpha\text{mean}(Buf) + (1-\alpha)h_t$$

   and introduce h_t in the buffer.

For the computation of the binomial distributions we use the Hoeffding approximations [1] to obtain an upper bound for the logarithm of M_a and M_s using:

$$\log(B(k,n,p)) \leq k\log(pn/k) + n(1-k/n)\log\left(\frac{1-p}{1-k/n}\right) \quad \text{for } k/n \geq p$$

[2] Initially h is computed using first and second frames.

Since both, M_a and M_s, can attain extremely small values is numerically impossible to work directly with them. For this reason we compute their logarithms and use $\log(H) = \log(M_a) - \log(M_s)$ in our method.

As we said in the introduction we propose an online method, therefore, we must decide the occurrence of a hard cut using only past values. In fact we introduce a delay in the system response in order to consider while judging frame t also the results from frames $t+1, ..., t+4$. In the second step of processing we consider a window, $W = [t-4, ..t+4]$ centered in t. We will say that there is a hard cut at frame t if the following conditions are fulfilled:

$$\log(H)(t) = \min_{s \in W} \log(H)(s) \tag{1}$$

$$\log(H)(t) < \min_{s \in \{t-4,..,t-1\}} 4 \log(H)(s) \text{ or } \log(H)(t) < \min_{s \in \{t+1,..,t+4\}} 4 \log(H)(s) \tag{2}$$

$$\log(H)(t) < \text{Threshold}(t) \tag{3}$$

where Threshold(t) is an adaptive threshold that is computed using only the accumulated values of $\log(H)$ for non-cuts X [5]:

$$\text{Threshold}(t) = \text{mean}(X) - 5 * \text{std}(X)$$

This is a simple method of template matching to obtain only prominent peaks. We must mention that we are assuming that hard cuts are separated at least four frames (As we will see in next section some video sequences do not fulfill this hypothesis).

For processing color video sequences we apply the previous method by adding up the meaningfulness $\log(H)$ for the three color channels. In this work we use the YUV color space.

3 Results and Evaluation

We are going to test our algorithm against a set of videos used in [8]. In figures 1 and 2 we show the first frame of each video together with $\log(H)$. As we can see there are set of well defined peaks that correspond to the hard cuts. In table 3 we present the results for all the sequences together with the numerical results obtained in [8]. As in [8] we measure the performance of out method using precision (Prec), recall (Rec) and F1 defined as:

$$\text{Precision} = \frac{\text{True Positives}}{\text{True Positives} + \text{False Positives}}$$

$$\text{Recall} = \frac{\text{True Positives}}{\text{True Positives} + \text{False Negatives}}$$

$$\text{F1} = \frac{2 \times \text{Precision} \times \text{Recall}}{\text{Precision} + \text{Recall}}$$

The proposed method outperforms on average the precision the feature tracking method and the pixel based one, while performs worse than the histogram based one. It has similar recall capabilities than the feature tracking based method. From these number we can conclude that the proposed methods has less false positives than the other three reported methods while achieving similar number of false negatives with respect with the feature tracking method. Summing up the F1 measure is the best among the four methods tested.

Looking at the individual sequences, the proposed method outperforms the feature tracking method three cases while loses precession in two cases (B and H). This is mainly due to strong motions that are not satisfactory resolved in the proposed method. Also, in the case of sequence C, it contains very close hard cuts that are missed due to our restriction of cuts separated in time at least four frames. This sequence has a poor temporal sampling rate On the other hand the proposed method has always better recall perform that then feature tracking one.

Finally, at the bottom of the table 1 we present the average, variance and standard deviation of the results to show that the results are stable.

To show the advantages of the proposed method against other well-known interframe difference methods we are going to compare the output of our method against the output of standard frame difference in the YUV space. For the comparison we normalize both results dividing each one by the maximum difference. The results are presented in figure 3 for videos A (Lisa) and B (Jamie). As we can see the results are less noisy and the peaks at hard cut positions are clearly separated from non-cut ones. This contrast with results obtained with traditional frame difference methods. However, we can also see, especially for the results on Jamie sequence, that the peaks have strong variations. Nevertheless, from this plots we can conclude that an offline hard cut detection would be much easier using $\log(H)$ than the traditional pixel differences as the hard cut peaks are clearly separated from the non-cut ones.

Table 1. Results obtained for sequences in figures 1 and 2

	Proposed Method			Feature tracking [8]			Pixel based [8]			Histogram based [7]		
Seq	Prec	Rec	F1	Prec	Rec	F1	Prec	Rec	F1	Prec	Rec	F1
A	1	1	1	1	1	1	1	1	1	1	1	1
B	.800	1	.889	1	1	1	.825	.825	.825	1	.375	.545
C	.941	.906	.923	.595	.870	.707	.764	.778	.771	.936	.536	.682
D	1	1	1	1	1	1	1	1	1	1	.941	.969
E	1	.840	.913	.938	1	.968	.867	.867	.867	.955	.700	.808
F	1	1	1	1	1	1	0	0	0	1	1	1
G	.882	.938	.909	.810	.944	.872	.708	.994	.809	1	.666	.800
H	.760	.950	.844	.895	.895	.895	.927	1	.962	.971	.895	.932
I	1	1	1	1	1	1	1	1	1	1	.500	.667
Average	.932	.959	.942	.915	.968	.938	.788	.829	.804	.985	.735	.823
Variance	.009	.003	.004	.019	.003	.010	.099	.104	.099	.001	.055	.027
Std dev	.095	.057	.059	.137	.052	.100	.314	.323	.315	.025	.234	.165

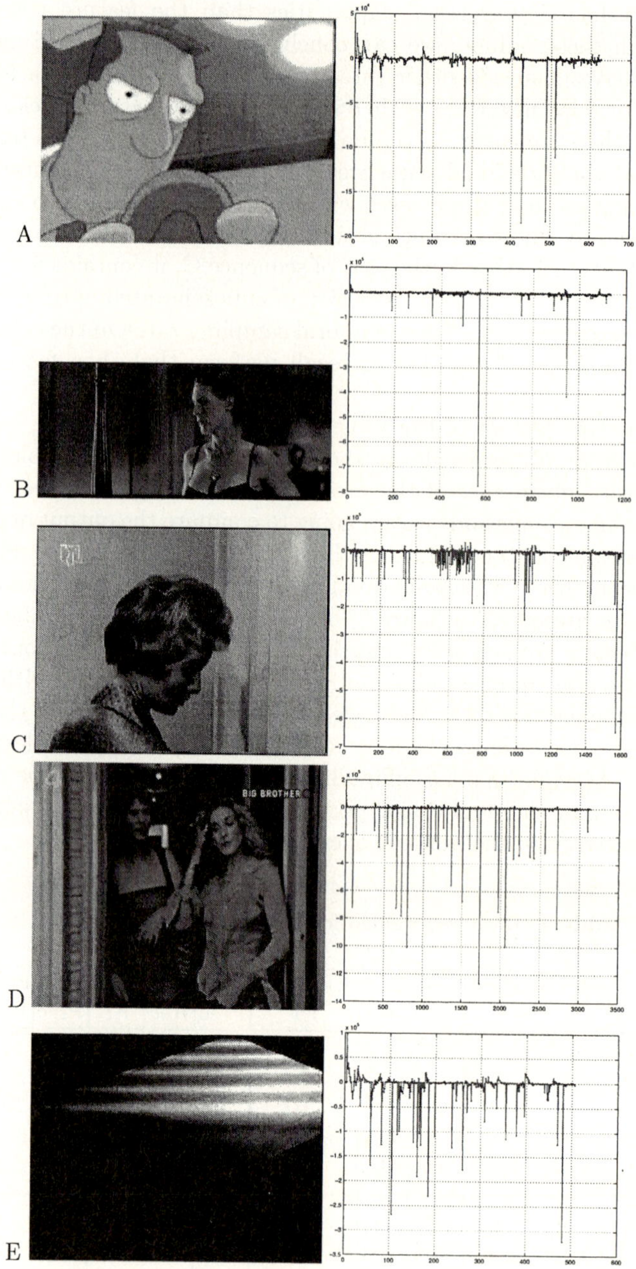

Fig. 1. Left: First frame from the sequence. Right: $\log(H)$ for the sequence. A(Lisa): Cartoon video with substantial object motion. B(Jamie): Strong motions. C(Psycho): Black and white movie with substantial action and motions and many close hard cuts. D(Sex in the city): High quality digitalization TV show. E(Highlander): Low quality digitalization of TV show.

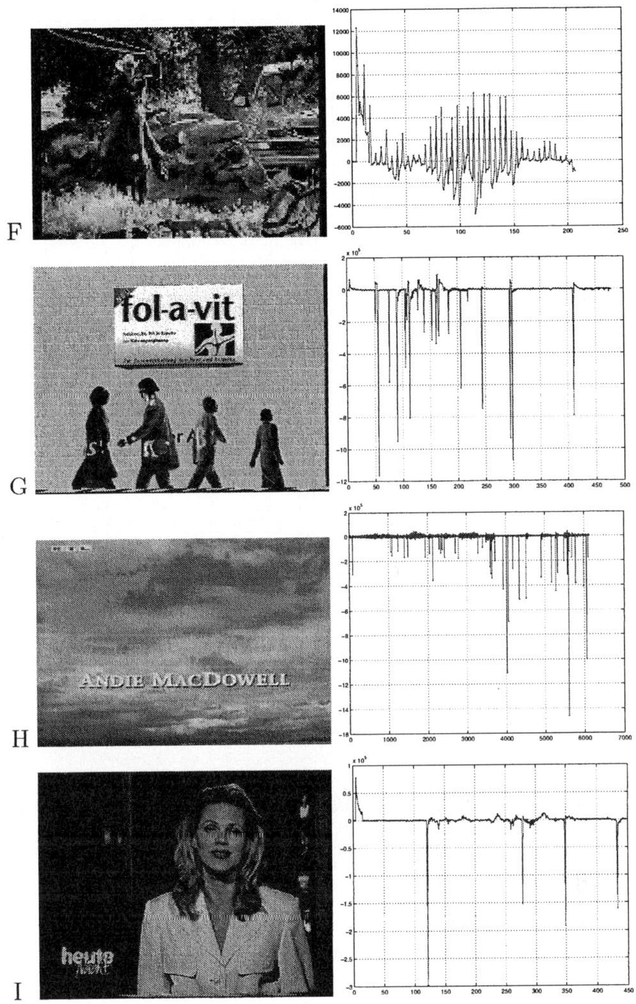

Fig. 2. Left: First frame from the sequence. Right: $\log(H)$ for the sequence. F(Commercial2): Contains no cuts but it has a low of postproductions effects that can be misclassified as cuts. G (Comemrcial1): Commercial sequence. H(Video): Its contains passages of strong motions. I (News): TV news.

4 Conclusions and Future Work

We have presented a simple method that uses only interframe differences that improves the results of previously reported methods. The method obtains a measure for hard cut meaningfulness with clear peaks at hard cut positions. This allows for simpler adaptive threshold and offline detection methods.

We formulated the problem inspired in the computational gestalt theory and presented a novel method to compute hard cuts based on simple interframe

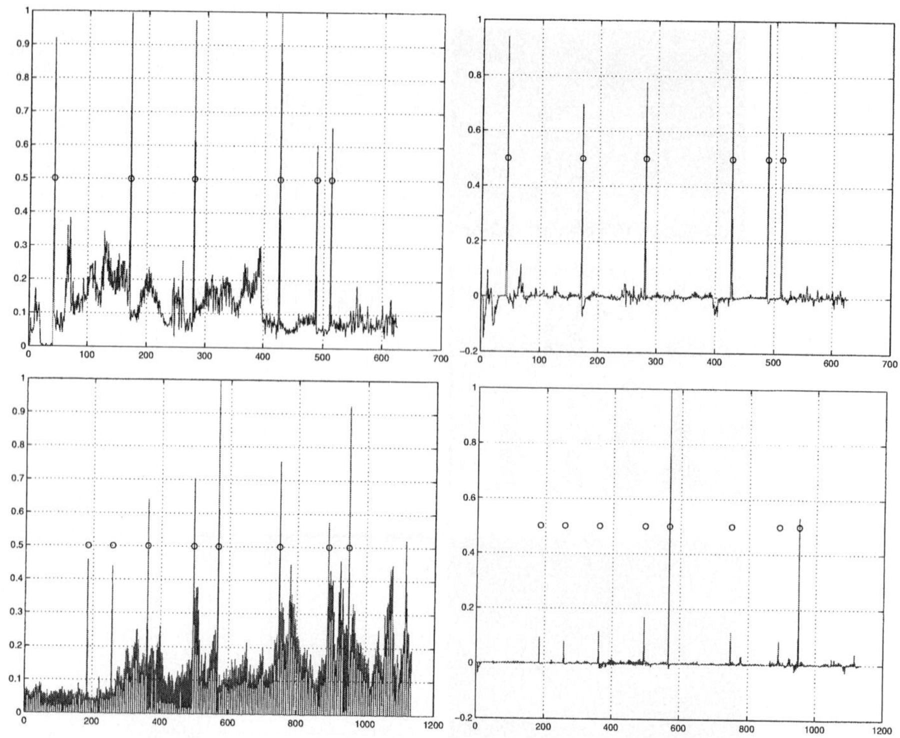

Fig. 3. Left: Results of a tradition pixel base difference method. Right: Results of the proposed algorithm. The black dots indicate the true hard cuts. Top: Results for Lisa sequences. Bottom: Results for Jamie sequence.

differences. We believe this direction of work can provide better results and particularly more formal methods with less heuristics behind them.

In future work we will address the limitation of the method with respect to strong motions and lightning changes, and also we will try to obtain bounds on M_a and M_s to improve the adaptive thresholding technique. This will be important to normalize the peaks in the response ($\log(H)$).

References

1. A. Desolneux. *Evnements significatifs et applications l'analyse d'images.* PhD thesis, ENS-Cachan, France, 2000.
2. A. Desolneux, L. Moisan, and J.-M-Morel. A grouping principle and four applications. *IEEE Transactions on Pattern Analysis and Machine Intelligence*, 25(4):508–512, April 2003.
3. A. Desolneux, L. Moisan, and J.-M-Morel. Maximal meaningful events and applications to image analysis. *The Annals of Statistics*, 31(6):1822–1851, December 2003.

4. Ullas Gargi, Rangachar Kasturi, and Susan H. Strayer. Performance characterization of video-shot-change detection methods. *IEEE Transactions on Circuits and Systems for Video Technology*, 2000.
5. Alan Hanjalic. Shot-boundary detection: Unraveled and resolved. *IEEE Transactions on Circuits and Systems for Video Technology*, 2002.
6. Chung-Lin Huang and Bing Yao Liao. A robust scene-change detection method for video segmentation. *IEEE Transactions on Circuits and Systems for Video Technology*, 2001.
7. S. Pfeiffer, R. Leinhart, G. Kuhne, and W. Effelserberg. The MoCa Project - Movie Content Analysis REsearch at the University of Mannheim.
8. A. Whitehead, P. Bose, and R. Laganiere. Feature based cut detection with automatic threshold selection. In *Proceedings of the International Conference on Image and Video Retrieval*, pages 410–418, 2004.

Development and Validation of an Algorithm for Cardiomyocyte Beating Frequency Determination

Demián Wassermann and Marta Mejail

Universidad de Buenos Aires,
Facultad de Ciencias Exactas y Naturales,
Intendente Güiraldes 2160, Ciudad Universitaria, C1428EGA,
República Argentina
{dwasser, marta}@dc.uba.ar

Abstract. The Chagas disease or *Tripanosomiasis Americana* affects between 16 and 18 million people in endemic areas. This disease affects the beating rate of infected patients' cardiomyocytes. At the Molecular Biology of Chagas Disease Laboratory in Argentina the effect of isolated patient's serum antibodies is studied over rat cardiomyocyte cultures. In this work an image processing application to measure the beating rate of this culture over video sequences is presented. This work is organized as follows. Firstly, a preliminary analysis of the problem is introduced, isolating the main characteristics of the problem. Secondly, a Monte Carlo experiment is designed and used to evaluate the robustness and validity of the algorithm. Finally, an algorithm of order $O(T(N \log N + N))$ for tracking cardiomyocyte membranes is presented, where T is the number of frames and N is the maximum area of the membrane. Its performance is compared against the standard beating rate measure method.

1 Introduction

The Chagas disease or *Tripanosomiasis Americana* affects between 16 and 18 million people in endemic areas. That can be found between 42°N and 46°S parallels, ranging from USA to Argentina and Chile [1]. The annual death rate caused by this disease reaches the number of 45.000 people [2]. Chagas disease is considered a typical socioeconomic illness, inseparable from poverty and underdevelopment. It has been noticed that this disease affects the beating rate of infected patients' cardiomyocyte, a human or mammal cardiac cell. At the Molecular Biology of Chagas Disease Laboratory at INGEBI-CONICET Argentina, the effect of isolated and purified patient's serum antibodies is studied over neonatal rat cardiomyocyte cultures; the neonatal rat cardiomyocytes behave like human cardiomyocytes, in the case of the studied chagas antibodies [3]. The effects of these antibodies over the culture is studied on an inverted microscope connected to a digital camera. The study can be divided in two steps. In the first step the beating rate of the cardiomyocytes is measured, and according to it a volume of antibodies is inoculated to the culture. After a lapse of time a new measure of the beating rate is taken in order to measure the effect of the antibodies.

In this work a technique to measure the beating rate of the cardiomyocytes from a digital video is developed. This algorithm needs to be fast enough to produce the results

M. Lazo and A. Sanfeliu (Eds.): CIARP 2005, LNCS 3773, pp. 420–430, 2005.

in a few minutes (short response-time) because the cardiomyocytes in the culture are dying and this affects the measures and results of the biological study. A preliminary study of the videos is performed as a first stage, a filter is applied to each video frame in order to reduce the image noise and enhance the edges. Then a set of cardiomyocyte cell membranes are manually selected and tracked over the video sequence. The results of this tracking are analyzed to measure the feasibility of extracting the beating rate of the culture from the video sequence. Once the main characteristics of the tracked objects are identified, a Monte Carlo experiment is designed to validate the procedure. Finally a short response-time algorithm based on active contours, more precisely the *fast marching* method (see [4,5]), is developed in order to track the cardiomyocyte cell membranes. This algorithm is developed in order to produce a software tool for an end-user working at the mentioned laboratory.

This work is structured as follows: In Sect. 2 a preliminary study of the cardiomyocyte culture is performed and its main characteristics isolated. Furthermore a technique to infer the beating rate is proposed. in Sect. 3 a Monte Carlo experiment is designed in order to validate the proposed technique and its results are presented. In Sect. 4 a more automated tracking technique based on active contours is presented in order to develop a short response-time software tool. Finally, in Sect. 5 the conclusions of this work are presented.

2 Preliminary Studies

In this section, image preprocessing of the cardiomyocyte culture and a technique for preliminary analysis are described, and several features of the video are characterized.

In order to find the beating frequency in the cardiomyocyte culture in a robust manner, cardiomyocyte cell membranes are tracked over a video sequence. In Fig. 1 the membranes are circled. The centroid norm and area variations over time are calculated as two one dimensional signals: $cd(t)$ and $a(t)$, where t is the frame number. The Fourier transform of these signals is then computed in order to find the beating frequency, which will be the frequency with the greater amplitude.

The first task of the preliminary analysis is the segmentation of the membranes. Here the image is convolved with a Gaussian kernel, and then thresholded. This process is illustrated in Fig. 1, where Fig. 1(a) is the original culture image and Fig. 1(c) is the image after filtering and thresholding. A region of interest (ROI) was selected for each membrane analyzed in a way such that membrane is the only object over the threshold in each ROI in every frame of the sequence. These ROIs are automatically analyzed above the video sequences by calculating the centroid and area of the pixels above the threshold in each ROI for each frame. Then the norm of the centroid and the area are normalized as follows:

$$cd_n(t) = \|cd(t)\| - \frac{\sum_{i=0}^{N-1} \|cd(i)\|}{N}, \; 0 \leq t \leq N-1$$

$$a_n(t) = a(t) - \frac{\sum_{i=0}^{N-1} a(i)}{N}, \; 0 \leq t \leq N-1$$

where $cd(t)$ is the centroid of the tracked object in frame t, $a(t)$ is the area of the tracked object in frame t and N is the number of frames. In Fig. 2 the normalized norm of the

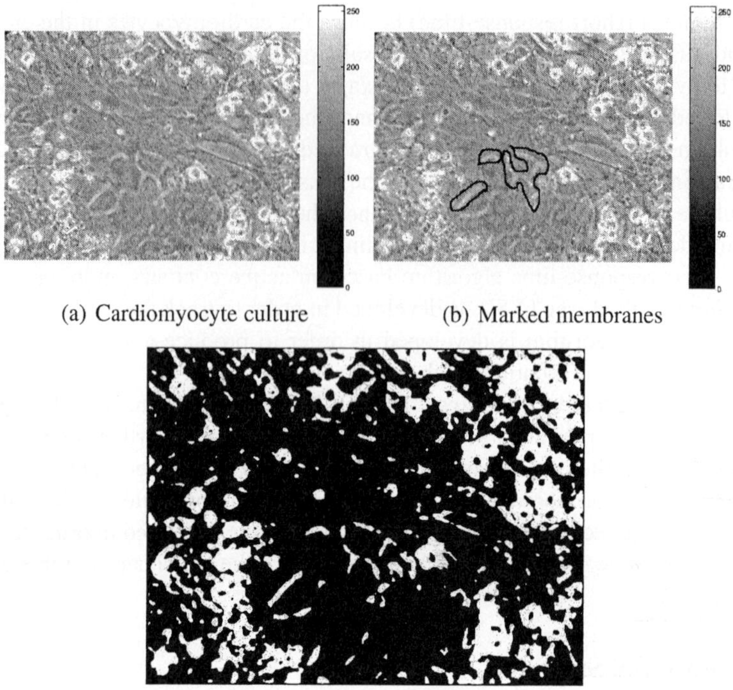

(a) Cardiomyocyte culture (b) Marked membranes

(c) thresholded image

Fig. 1. In (a) a frame of the cardiomyocyte video sequence is shown. In (b) the same frame is shown with some membranes marked. In (c) frame is shown again after it has been filtered and thresholded, the membranes marked in (b) are over the threshold and ready to be segmentated.

centroid, $cd_n(t)$, and the normalized area $a_n(t)$, functions are plotted along with their Fourier transforms. Analyzing the Fourier transform of these functions presented on Fig. 2(c) and Fig. 2(d), it can be noticed that $cd_n(t)$ is composed of several frequencies, but also there are two dominant frequencies, F_0 and F_1 where $F_1 > F_0$. The lower frequency, which also appears on the Fourier transform of $a(t)$, is a consequence of the microscope's light intensity frequency and can be eliminated by normalizing the mean grey level of all the frames in the sequence. Eliminating F_0 and discarding the low amplitude frequencies, the following characteristics can be inferred:

- There is a center of contraction and dilation in the culture. In this work this point will be referred as *beating center*.
- The normalized centroid norm, $cd_n(t)$, has a dominant frequency which indicates the beating rate: F_1.
- The area, $a_n(t)$, suffers no meaningful alteration.
- The topology of the tracked object can change in a periodic way. (i.e.: if the tracked object splits, it will merge again in the following frames.)

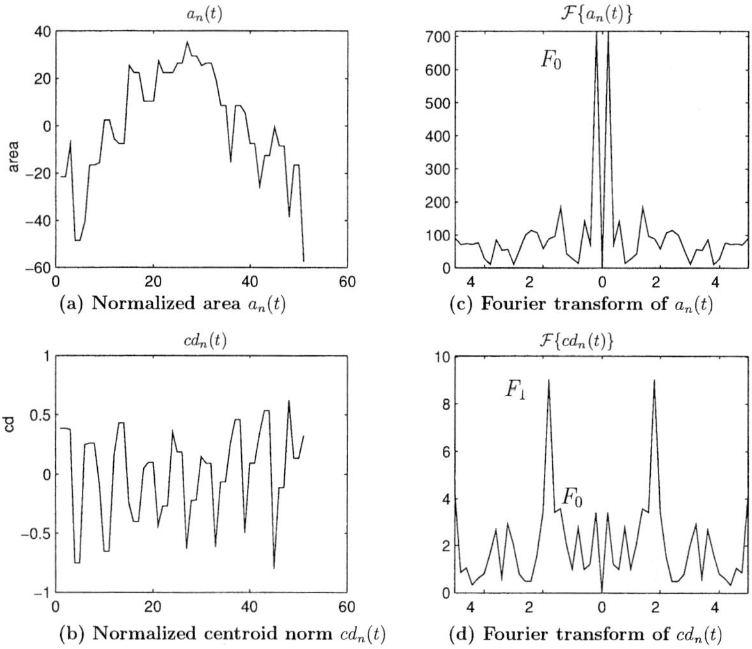

Fig. 2. Normailzed centroid norm $cd_n(t)$ and area $a_n(t)$ functions (Figures (a) and (b)) where t is the video frame number. Fourier transform of the normalized centroid norm $\mathcal{F}\{cd_n(t)\}$ and normalized area $\mathcal{F}\{a_n(t)\}$ (Figures (c) and (d)).

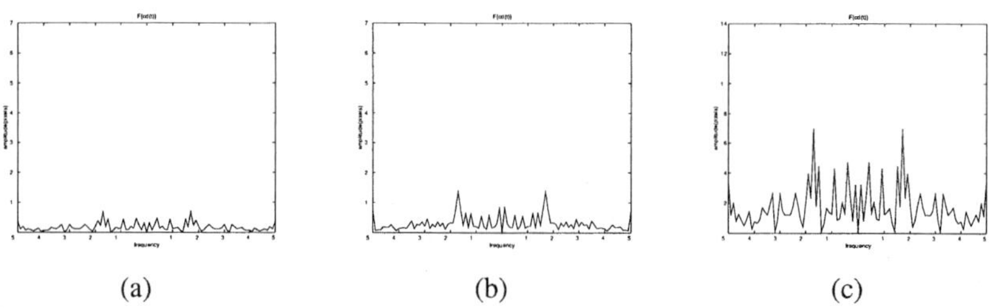

Fig. 3. Fourier transform of the normalized centroid norm of three membranes, (a) near the beating center (20 pixels or less), (b) middle distance from the beating center (between 40 and 60 pixels) and (c) far from the beating center (more than 200 pixels)

On the other hand, analyzing objects with several distances to the beating center, an increment on the amplitude of $cd_n(t)$ can be noticed when the object is near the beating center but no alteration on the beating frequency is registered. This analysis is illustrated in Fig. 3, where the Fourier transform of the normalized centroid norm of three membranes is shown. The first membrane 3(a) is less than 20 pixels far from the beating center, the second membrane 3(b) is between 40 and 60 pixels far from the beating center and the third membrane 1(c) is more than 200 pixels far from it.

3 Synthetic Data Processing and Model Validation

In this section the design and results of a Monte Carlo experiment based on the previously inferred characteristics of the problem are presented. This experiment is used to validate the procedure that finds the beating rate, taking into account the following characteristics of this particular problem:

- Each tracked object has an ondulatory movement along a line. The frequency of this movement is the application's goal.
- The amplitude of each ondulating object's movement is different proportionally with its distance from the beating center.
- The amplitude of each ondulating object's movement suffers slight variations in the same sequence (ie: noise).
- Each tracked object does not follow the previously mentioned line precisely. In fact, each object has slight displacements from the line (ie: noise).
- The area of each tracked object does not have meaningful ondulatory variations.

3.1 Monte Carlo Experiment Design

According to the presented characteristics, a Monte Carlo experiment was designed. This experiment, given the image dimensions, the number of frames to be generated, a beating center and a frequency, generates a number of non-overlapping circular particles. Each particle has a fixed area and moves in an ondulatory manner over a line orientated towards the beating center. This movement has a fixed amplitude, which can be different for each particle. Furthermore, a noise component is added to the position and frequency of each particle. The area the covered by the particles is between 20% and 80% of the image. The frame sequences are generated by Algorithm 1. The random variables used in the algorithm are the following:

- $X_c \sim \mathcal{N}(\frac{w}{2}, 0.6w)$
- $Y_c \sim \mathcal{N}(\frac{h}{2}, 0.6h)$
- $X_p \sim \mathcal{U}(0, w-1)$
- $Y_p \sim \mathcal{U}(0, h-1))$
- $Amplitude \sim \mathcal{N}(0.001, 0.05)$
- $Area \sim \mathcal{U}(minArea, maxArea)$
- $X_n \sim \mathcal{N}(0, 0.05w)$
- $Y_n \sim \mathcal{N}(0, 0.05h)$

where $\mathcal{N}$ and $\mathcal{U}$ represent normal and integer uniform distributions.

Once the Monte Carlo frame sequence is generated, a ROI is inferred for each particle in the same manner that the ROI for every tracked membrane on Sect. 2 was described. The centroid of each particle is tracked and analyzed as presented in Sect. 2.

3.2 Monte Carlo Results

Using the algorithm described on Sect. 3.1, 10000 frame sequences were generated with the following characteristics:

- 50 frames.
- 640×480 pixels per frame.
- The number of particles ranged from 8 to 20 with a uniform integer distribution.
- The beating frequency is a random variable $freq \sim \mathcal{N}(\frac{148}{60}, \frac{20}{60})$ where a common beating frequency is $148\frac{beats}{minutes}$.

Algorithm 1 Monte Carlo frame sequence generation

w, h dimensions of the image I.
nf the number of frames to be generated.
qty the quantity of non-overlapping particles.
$freq$ the beating frequency.
$c \leftarrow (X_c, Y_c)$ is the beating center.
▷ pattern signal generation
$s_t \leftarrow sin\left(2\pi \frac{t}{nf} freq\right), t = [0 \ldots nf]$ is the discretized pattern signal.
▷ minimum and maximum areas for the particles
$minArea \leftarrow \min\left(\frac{(0.2) w\, h}{qty}, 2\right)$
$maxArea \leftarrow \max\left(\frac{(0.8) w\, h}{qty}, 4\right)$
▷ generation of the particles
$P \leftarrow \emptyset$
repeat
    $pos(p) \leftarrow (X_p, Y_p)$
    generate a particle p at (x, y).
    $area(p) \leftarrow Area$
    $amp(p) \leftarrow \min(w, h) Amplitude$ is the amplitude of p's movement.
    $dir(p) \leftarrow \frac{pos(p) - c}{|pos(p) - c|}$ is the unit vector which represents the direction of the p's movement.
    if $(\forall p' \in P)$ p does not touch p' while they're moving **then**
        add p to P.
    end if
until $|P| = qty$
▷ sequence generation
Set every frame $f^t, t \in [1 \ldots nf]$ black.
for every frame f^t **do**
    for every particle $p \in P$ **do**
        draw a white circle of area $area(p)$
        at $pos(p) + dir(p) amp(p) s_i + (X_n, Y_n)$
    end for
end for

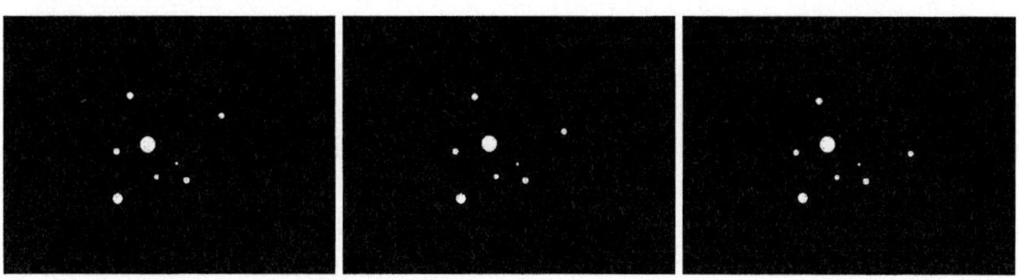

Fig. 4. Three frames of a Monte Carlo frame sequence generated with the algorithm 1 and the parameters specified in Sect. 3.1

Three frames from a Monte Carlo frame sequence generated with the stated parameters and algorithm 1 are shown in Fig. 4. The frequency measurement error for the n-th Monte Carlo experiment is calculated as follows. For each particle $p \in P^n$ is calculated, where P^n is the set of particles of the n-th Monte Carlo experiment and $|P^n|$ the number of particles in the set the main frequency $F_1^{n,p}$ is calculated as stated in Sect. 2:

$$e^n = \sum_{p \in P^n} \frac{(F_1^{n,p} - freq^n)^2}{|P^n|}$$

Then, the mean square difference between the true beating frequency $freq^n$ of the experiment and the frequency $F_1^{n,p}$ is calculated. A histogram presenting the frequency measuring error for each Monte Carlo experiment is presented in Table 1 where it can be seen that the error more than 94% of the experiments is zero.

Table 1. Table presenting the frequency measurement error for each Monte Carlo experiment. It can be seen that the error in more than 94% of the cases, ranges to 0.

Frequency measurment error(e)	Percentage of cases
00	94.46
04	1.23
08	0.88
12	0.80
16	0.94
20	1.16
24 and more	0.53

4 Real Data Processing

The proposed tracking algorithm based on the *fast marching* method presented in [4,5] and applied to image segmentation in [6] is presented in this section. This algorithm is developed in order to relax the restrictions placed on the algorithm presented in Sect. 2, where a ROI in which the membrane to be tracked had to be the only object over the threshold in every frame of the sequence. The short response-time requirement for the application stated in Sect. 1 makes the choice of a tracking algorithm critical. A comprehensive review of tracking techniques is presented in [7], nevertheless the techniques reviewed in that work are bounded by a high-computational cost or by topology dependence; none of these characteristics can be afforded in this work due to the non-functional requirements on the application and the possibility of a topology change in the thresholded tracked membrane. A tracking algorithm based on the *fast marching* algorithm is presented in this section.

4.1 Fast Marching Algorithms

In this section the algorithm introduced in [6,4] is briefly described. Let Γ be the initial position of a curve and let F be its speed in the normal direction. In the level set perspective [8], Γ is viewed as the zero level set of a higher dimensional function $\psi(x, y, z)$ and its movement equation is:

$$\psi(\Gamma(t), t) = 0$$

where $\Gamma(t)$ is the Γ curve in instant t. Then, by chain rule,

$$\psi_t + \nabla\psi(\Gamma(t), t) \cdot \Gamma'(t) = 0$$

and taking F as the speed in the outward normal direction

$$F = \Gamma'(t) \cdot \frac{\nabla\psi}{|\nabla\psi|},$$

an evolution equation for the moving surface can be produced [8,4], namely

$$\psi_t + F|\nabla\psi| = 0. \tag{1}$$

Consider the special case of a surface moving with speed $F(x, y) > 0$. Now, let $T(x, y)$ be the time at which the curve Γ crosses a given point (x, y). The function $T(x, y)$ then satisfies the equation

$$|\nabla T(x, y)|F(x, y) = 1; \tag{2}$$

this simply says that the gradient of arrival time is inversely proportional to the speed of the surface. The way of approximating the position of the moving curve in the *fast marching* approach is to explicitly construct the solution function $T(x, y)$ from equation (1). The algorithm which presents this function reconstruction is presented on [6,4].

Implementation of the Algorithm. In order to solve equation (2) an approximation to the gradient given by [8,4,5],

$$\begin{bmatrix} max(D_{ij}^{-x}, 0)^2 + min(D_{ij}^{+x}, 0)^2 \\ +max(D_{ij}^{-y}, 0)^2 + min(D_{ij}^{+y}, 0)^2 \end{bmatrix}^{\frac{1}{2}} = \frac{1}{F_{ij}}, \tag{3}$$

is used, where D^- and D^+ are the backward and forward difference operators for $T(x, y)$. The central idea behind the *fast marching* method is to systematically construct the solution T using only upwind values. Observe that the upwind difference structure of equation (3) allows to propagate information "one way", that is from smaller values of T to larger values. Plainly speaking no point in T can be affected by points of T containing larger values, taking this "causality principle" [5] into account, a method for calculating the values of T is presented in the algorithm 2.

By implementing the $Trial$ set with a particular heap sort structure [4] this algorithm takes $O(N \log N)$ computations, where N is the number of points in the grid.

4.2 Segmentation Using the Fast Marching Method

Given an image function $I(x, y)$ the objective in segmentation is to separate an object from the background. This can be done applying an image-based speed function $k_I >$

Algorithm 2 *fast marching* algorithm

Given a grid with the initial values of T where the points in the initial curve have a known value and every other point has an ∞ value.
Tag all points in the initial boundary value as *Known*.
Tag all points with a neighbor in *Known* as *Trial*.
Calculate the value of T for each point tagged as *Trial* with equation (3)
Tag all other grid points as *Far*
while there are points in $Trial$ **do**
    Let A be the $Trial$ point with the smallest value.
    Add A to $Known$ and remove it from $Trial$.
    Tag as $Trial$ all points that are not $Known$. If the neighbor is in Far, remove.
    Recompute the values of T at all $Trial$ neighbors of A according to equation (3).
end while

0 such that it controls the outward propagation of the initial curve in a way that it stops in the vicinity of shape boundaries. Mathematically this corresponds to solving equation (2) where $F_{ij} = k_{I\,ij}$:

$$|\nabla T| = \frac{1}{k_{I\,ij}},$$

where $k_{I\,ij}$ approaches to 0 as it gets closer to shape boundaries; in every other case it approachos to 1. In the case of this particular work where $I(x, y)$ is a thresholded binary image $k_{I\,ij}$ can be defined as

$$k_{I\,ij} = \frac{1}{I_{ij} + \epsilon}, \quad \epsilon > 0,$$

where I_{ij} is 1 inside the object to be segmentated and 0 outside of it.

4.3 Tracking by Fast Marching Methods

The *fast marching* method presented on Sect. 4.1 propagates a curve. The segmentation task, introduced in Sect. 4.2, is performed by manually selecting a set of initial curves or points inside the objects to be segmentated and then propagating these curves until the border of the object is reached. This process is illustrated on Fig. 5

The facts that the area of the objects do not suffer a meaningful variation and the displacement performed by the objects between frames is bounded were stated in Sect. 2. Thus, the initialization of the propagating curve inferred from the previously segmented frame is obtained eroding the resulting curve with a circular kernel, see Fig. 5(d), obtaining an initialization curve that can change its topology. For each segmented membrane, the normalized centroid norm $cd_n(t)$ for the video sequence is calculated in order to find the beating rate of the membrane. This is done by analyzing the Fourier transforms of these functions and taking the frequency F_1 as stated in Sect. 2.

The overall cost of processing a membrane in a frame can be calculated as the cost of segmenting the membrane $O(N \log N)$ plus the erosion $O(Nk)$, where N is the area of the segmented membrane and k is the size of the erosion kernel. The cost of calculating the centroid is $O(N)$ -linear in the area of the membrane-, then the overall cost of processing a frame is $O(N \log N + Nk + N) = O(N \log N + N)$.

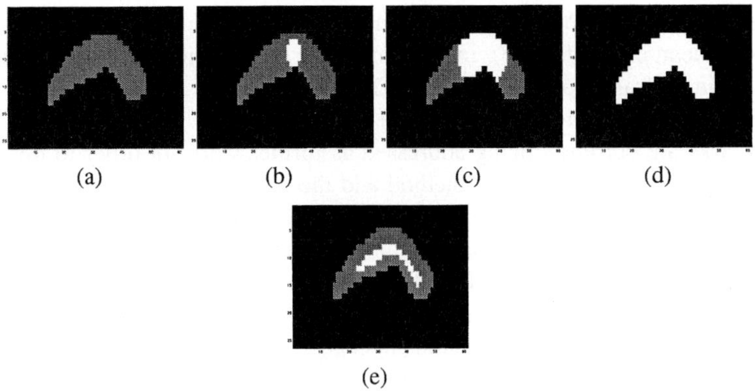

Fig. 5. Segmentation of a membrane using the *fast marching* method. The membrane to be segmentated is shown in (a). An initial curve is selected and propagated until it reaches the border of the object. The evolution of the segmentation progress is shown in (b),(c) and (d). In (b) The membrane to be segmentated in grey and the initial curve in whitem in (c) the evolving curve-white- growing inside the membrane-grey-. In (d) curve has grown to fill the membrane. After the segmentation, the obtained figure is eroded in order to initialize the next frame, shown in white in (e), is used as the initial curve for the next frame.

4.4 Real Data Processing Results

The algorithm described in Sect. 4.3 was applied over several rat cardiomyocyte culture frame sequences with a sampling frequence of 25 frames per second and 10 frames per second. Several membranes were tracked in each video. The results were compared with the measures obtained with the standard method by the staff of the Molecular Biology of Chagas Disease Laboratory at INGEBI-CONICET Argentina. Their method consists of a trained member of the staff who measures the beating rate with a cronometer by looking at the culture over a microscope. The mean measuring difference was of $0.1Hz$ in the 25 frames per second videos and of $0.77Hz$ in the 10 frames per second videos. This measuring difference are one order of magnitude smaller than the measured beating rates.

5 Conclusions and Further Work

In this work the base for an image processing application to measure the beating rate of a rat cardiomyocyte culture is presented. It can be divided in three stages. In the first stage, a preliminary analysis of the problem is introduced, isolating the main characteristics of the problem. In the second stage, a Monte Carlo experiment is designed using this characteristics to evaluate the robustness and validity of the algorithm which attains a rate above 87% of measurements with zero measurement error. Finally, a short-response time $O(T(N \log N + N))$ algorithm for tracking cardiomyocyte membranes is presented, where N is the maximum surface of the tracked membrane in pixels and T is the number of frames in the video sequence. This algorithm is implemented in a testbed application and the beating rate measures obtained with it were compared against the measures obtained by the standard procedure over several videos. This comparison resulted in a mean error of $0.1Hz$ in 25 frames per second videos and in a mean error of $0.77Hz$ in 10 frames per second videos representing a measuring error one order of magnitude smaller than the measures taken by both methods.

Two tasks are currently being addressed as further work: In order to improve the comparison between the standard method and the testbed application more video sequences are being generated and measured by the Chagas Disease Laboratory, the results of this measures will be compared against the measures of the proposed application using the Bland and Alman method [9]. Furthermore this algorithm will be implemented in an end-user application for its use at the Molecular Biology of Chagas Disease Laboratory at INGEBI-CONICET Argentina in Chagas' disease investigation.

The authors want to acknowledge Gabriela Levy and Dr. Mariano Levin for providing the cardiomyocyte culture videos and the manual beating rate measures and Msc. Daniel Acevedo for his support.

References

1. Bonomo, R., Salata, R.: American Trypanosomiasis (Chaga's Disease: Trypanosoma cruzi). In: Nelson Textbook of Pediatrics. W. B. Saunders (2000)
2. Kirchhoff, L.: Trypanosoma species (American Trypanosomiasis, Disease): Biology of Trypanosomes. In: Principles and Practice of Infectious Diseases. Churchhill Livingstone (2000)
3. Levin, M.: Proyecto genoma de trypanosoma cruzi asociado al proyecto de genoma humano. In: V Muestra de Ciencia y Técnica, IX Jornadas de Becarios. (1996)
4. Sethian, J.A.: A fast marching level set method for monotonically advancing fronts. Proc. Nat. Acad. Sci. **93** (1996) 1591 1595.
5. Sethian, J.A.: Level Set Methods and Fast Marching Methods. second edn. Cambridge University Press (1999)
6. Malladi, R., Sethian, J.A.: An o(n log n) algorithm for shape modeling. Proc. Nat. Academy of Sciences, USA **93** (1996) 9389–9392
7. Paragios, N.: Geodesic Active Regions and Level Set Methods: Contributions and Applications in Artificial Vision. PhD thesis, INRIA Sophia Antipolis (2000)
8. Osher, S., Sethian, J.A.: Fronts propagating with curvature-dependent speed: Algorithms based on Hamilton-Jacobi formulations. Journal of Computational Physics **79** (1988) 12–49
9. Bland, J.M., Altman, D.G.: Measuring agreement in method comparison studies. Statistical Methods in Medical Research **8** (1999) 135–160

A Simple Feature Reduction Method for the Detection of Long Biological Signals*

Max Chacón[1], Sergio Jara[1], Carlos Defilippi[2],
Ana Maria Madrid[2], and Claudia Defilippi[2]

[1] Departamento de Ingeniería Informática, Universidad de Santiago de Chile,
Av. Ecuador 3659, PO Box 10233, Santiago, Chile
mchacon@diinf.usach.cl, stjara@nt.entel.cl
[2] Hospital Clínico, Universidad de Chile,
Av. Santos Dumont 999, Santiago, Chile
cdefilippi@med.uchile.cl, amadrid@ns.hospital.uchile.cl

Abstract. Recent advances in digital processing of biological signals have made it possible to incorporate more extensive signals, generating a large number of features that must be analyzed to carry out the detection, and thereby acting against the performance of the detection methods. This paper introduces a simple feature reduction method based on correlation that allows the incorporation of very extensive signals to the new biological signal detection algorithms. To test the proposed technique, it was applied to the detection of Functional Dyspepsia (FD) from the EGG signal, which is one of the most extensive signals in clinical medicine. After applying the proposed reduction to the wavelet transform coefficients extracted from the EGG signal, a neuronal network was used as a classifier for the wavelet transform coefficients obtained from the EGG traces. The results of the classifier achieved *78.6%* sensitivity, and *92.9%* specificity for a universe of 56 patients studied.

1 Introduction

The incorporation of more extensive biological signals and of new transformation methods to represent those signals produces a large number of features which are difficult to analyze by the classifying algorithms that allow the detection of a pathology. To overcome these problems there are feature extraction methods such as Principal Component Analysis and Feature Selection by Mutual Information [1-2]. But these methods require a number of cases (at least equivalent to the features to be selected) to carry out the extraction. On the other hand, the incorporation of new pathologies with long signal registers makes it difficult to obtain test subjects for the analyses, decreasing the number of examples. To solve this problem, use of a simple method is proposed that allows a reduction of the number of redundant features according to the degree of correlation existing between them.

To carry out an evaluation, a problem of great clinical interest has been chosen, which also generates a signal made up of very extensive electric registers.

* This work was supported by FONDECYT project N° 1050082.

M. Lazo and A. Sanfeliu (Eds.): CIARP 2005, LNCS 3773, pp. 431 – 439, 2005.

Functional Dyspepsia (FD) is a complex syndrome which can not be detected by clinical examination and affects 25% of the population. At present, the precise nature of the mechanisms that produce this symptomatology is unknown, but it seems unlikely that a single mechanism can explain the variety of discomforts that comprise this syndrome [3].

The lack of knowledge regarding the specific mechanisms that give origin to this syndrome, the necessity of ruling out a variety of alterations, added to the high degree of incidence in the population, highlight the importance of having recourse to efficient diagnostic mechanisms for the detection of FD. The methodology used at present for the identification of FD consists of following the so called Rome protocol based on the systematic elimination of possible organic alterations [4]. This results in costly procedures and long periods during which patients must live with this condition.

A different approach in order to establish minimal motor alterations in these patients came to light about a decade ago, and involves the study of the electric activity of the digestive tract. These studies are based on the analysis of the graphs of electro-gastric activity over time, obtained from surface electrodes placed on the patient's abdomen. The resulting record, which is similar to an electroencephalogram, is called an electrogastrogram (EGG)[4-8].

Spectral analyses carried out by means of a Fourier transformation are the methods most often used for extracting information from electro-gastric activity. The difficulty in recording these signals has resulted in the design of new methods in order to improve the signal/noise ratio of the EGG [3,9]. The long signal records (approximately 2 hours) require block processing which produces undesired averaging effects in the spectra. In order to avoid this problem, special processing techniques have been developed based on adaptive and mobile media models which achieve a significant improvement in the quality of the record [9].

In several papers attempts have been made to evaluate gastric activity by means of an EGG, but these refer to pathologies other than FD, and they focus on the methods of classification (such as the use of neuronal networks), in which the first steps include the use of a classic Fourier analysis or the extraction of parameters from this transform [10-11].

The main disadvantage of analyses based on Fourier transforms for the diagnosis of FD is that they do not have the ability to temporarily locate the phenomenon of interest. This is due to the fact that Fourier theory only possesses frequency ability, and thus, although it is possible to determine the total number of frequencies that make up a signal, it is impossible to determine the time at which they occur. [12]. This problem becomes especially relevant in the study of EGGs related to FD because it is necessary to analyze the gastric system in its different states: *pre-prandial* (before the ingestion of food), *prandial* (during the ingestion of food), and *post-prandial* (after ingestion of food), which results in records that are too long to only analyze frequencies.

In order to solve the problem of time resolution, a variety of solutions have been developed that attempt to provide, to a greater or lesser degree, a simultaneous improvement in time and frequency resolution. Some of these are spectral methods that vary in time, spectro-temporal methods, and time-scale methods. Most of these solutions are based on segmentation of the signal, thus transforming the problem into a search for the optimal segment.

Among the different alternatives, wavelet transformation stands out because it avoids the problems of segmenting the signal by using windows based on functions that can be completely scaled and modulated. This is called a multiresolution analysis [13]. This type of transform is a powerful alternative for the analysis of non-stationary signals whose spectral characteristics change in time, such as biomedical signals in general [14] and EGG in particular.

Thus, this work consists of pre-processing an EGG signal in order to select the segment that contains FD information, calculating the coefficients of the wavelet transform, and subsequently using them as input for a neuronal classifier which will discriminate between healthy and dyspeptic patients.

2 Methods

2.1 Foundations

In order to avoid the segmentation of the signal required for the Fourier windowing calculation, the wavelet transformation (WT) uses a different alternative that consists of using a window that moves through the signal allowing the spectral calculation of each position. Then we iterate by gently increasing or decreasing the size of the window, thus obtaining a complete set of time-frequency representations at different resolutions.

The WT decomposes the signal into a set of base functions that correspond to a family. Families are generated by dilation and translation of a basic wavelet, called the "mother" wavelet, which is a function of time denoted by decomposes the signal ncy representations at different resolutions..ncreasing or decreasing the size of the window, obtai $\psi(t)$. The translation of ψ provides temporal resolution, and the dilation provides scaling. There are two important conditions that a wavelet must fulfill: i) the function must decay in time $\lim_{t\to\infty}|\psi(t)| = 0$. ii) The function must oscillate so that $\int \psi(t)dt = 0$. In order to implement these functions there are various alternatives, among which the ones most used are those of Haar, Daubechies and Morlet, which are shown in Figure 1.

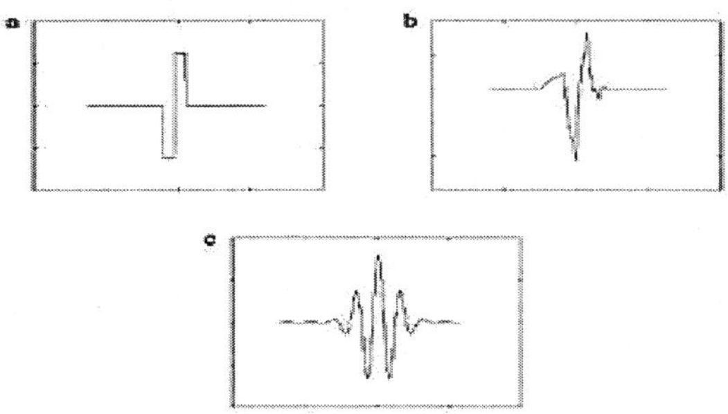

Fig. 1. Wavelets of Haar (a), Daubechies (b) and Morlet (c)

For applications that involve the digital processing of signals, the discrete wavelet transformation (DWT) is used. The result of DWT is a multilevel decomposition in which the coefficients that determine a high degree of resolution correspond to the high frequency components of the signal, while the low resolution levels correspond to the low frequency components.

For the implementation of DWT, beyond the base wavelets that act as bandpass filters, scaling functions, are used to establish upper limits for scaling factors.

The base wavelets in conjunction with the scaling functions form a bank of filters that are applied to the signal to be transformed. The low pass filters formed by the scaling functions limit the spectrum of the base wavelets on the basis of a given scale, covering the lower frequency functions. The output of the filter bank comprises the wavelet coefficient series.

The division of the spectrum is carried out by means of a multiresolution analysis which divides the spectrum in two. The details of the high frequency portion of the signal are kept, while the half corresponding to the lower frequencies can be again subdivided as often as necessary, and is limited only by the available information. Figure 2 below illustrates this type of treatment.

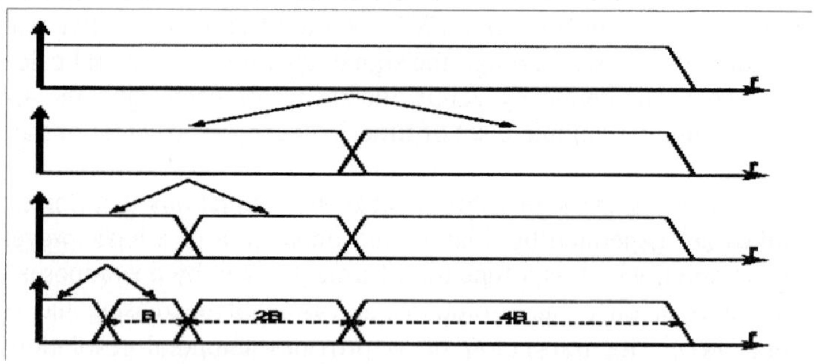

Fig. 2. Division of the spectrum by means of multiresolution analysis

2.2 Data Collection

The original data set corresponds to a total of 150 EGG exams carried out on subjects most of whom suffered from diverse gastric disorders, and among which there is a control group of 14 healthy patients. From the total of sick patients, 42 were selected that fit the Rome protocol; adding the healthy patients to these, a final set of 56 exams is generated for analysis. These exams were carried out between the years 2000 and 2002 in the Clinical Hospital of the Universidad de Chile, using a computational tool known as Polygram Version 5.0 developed by Gastrosoft Inc. [15] for recordring, processing and storing data. The signals obtained were stored digitally with a sampling frequency of 8 Hz for subsequent processing by Matlab version 6.1, using the signal processing, wavelet and neuronal network toolboxes.

Each exam consists of a 2.5-hour record. After a 10 minute relaxation period, the *pre-prandial* stage is initiated under fasting conditions and lasts approximately one hour. Subsequently, a light meal is given to the patient for ingestion, thus initiating the *prandial* stage which lasts between 20 and 30 minutes. Finally, the *post-prandial* stage begins which lasts approximately one hour.

2.3 Process and Pre-processing

The data obtained from the Polygram equipment presents a very high rate of sampling because the maximum frequencies in the stomach correspond to tachygastric episodes and reach 0.15 Hz or 9 cycles per minute (cpm). Frequencies between 9 and 12 cpm correspond to activity in the small intestine. These signals have frequency components that are outside the range of gastric activity, and include a great deal of noise.

In order to focus the process on the relevant information, a subsampling process is carried out followed by a filtering of the signal. The exam is separated into its three stages (*pre-prandial*, *prandial* and *post-prandial*), in order to calculate the wavelet transform coefficients. The complete process is illustrated in Figure 3.

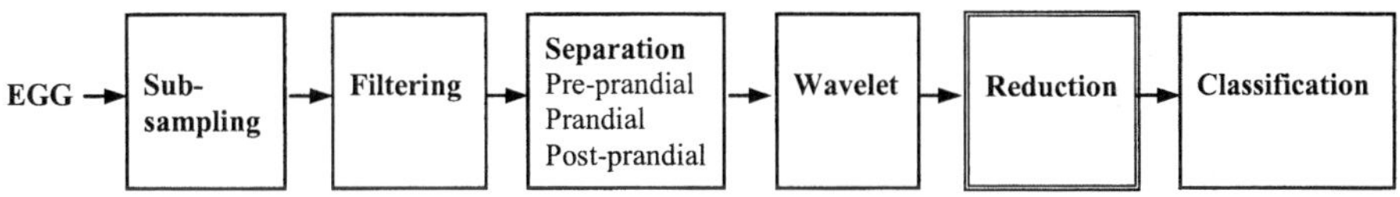

Fig. 3. Pre-processing and classification of EGG

Once the wavelet transform coefficients have been obtained, very little relevant information exists in the low frequency bands (flat responses) and high frequency bands, and these are therefore discarded. After obtaining the coefficients and deleting the high and low frequencies, there still remain a great deal of coefficients for each period which contain redundant information. With this large number of coefficients, and only 56 cases, it is not possible to carry out a Principal Component Analysis or Feature Selection by Mutual Information [1-2].

2.4 Feature Reduction

The reduction method from the generated wavelet coefficients is the following:

i) Create groups of correlated coefficients (given a correlation interval, e.g. 0.05). For that purpose the quantity and kind of wavelet coefficients having a correlation greater than 0.95 are calculated, then those greater than 0.90, and so on successively until a low correlation (e.g. 0.2) is reached. Each calculation begins with the total set of wavelet coefficients. This leads to pairs (c,r), where c represents the number of wavelet coefficients (features) that have a correlation greater than the value indicated by r.

ii) Create a correlation curve, with the correlation index r on the abscissa, with $r \in [0.2, 0.95]$, and the number of coefficients having a correlation coefficient greater than r on the ordinate.

iii) The choice of an adequate point for the reduction will always be a compromise between the reduction of coefficients (features) and the elimination of information. The idea is to try and decrease as much as possible the number of components without decreasing the information considered in the analysis. More than one point can be chosen and evaluated with the classifier. The points that are candidates to be evaluated will be those that show the largest drop along the curve from right to left.

2.5 Classification

Classification is carried out by means of a static neuronal network which uses the backpropagation method for training. The input layer uses the reduction of the wavelet coefficients, and for the hidden layers zero to two layers are tested. For the output layer two output neurons were evaluated: the implementation of a classic classifier, and an output neuron for which a threshold must be calculated.

Different training methods were evaluated such as backpropagation with momentum, resilient backpropagation, secant and second order methods (Levenberg-Marquardt) [16]. In order to evaluate the training of the network, a cross validation process was used [17] which consisted in separating the initial set into seven groups. Each group consisted of the exams of six dyspeptic and two healthy patients. Training was carried out with six groups, and the seventh was reserved for evaluation. This process was carried out seven times in order to evaluate all groups.

3 Results

3.1 Pre-processing

The process is initiated by subsampling the signal which selects one sample for every 20 original samples, thus obtaining a sampling frequency of 24 cpm.

The signal filtering is carried out with a Butterworth low-pass fifth-order filter with a cutoff frequency of 10 cpm. The purpose of this cut-off frequency is to eliminate small intestine activity (9 cpm to 12 cpm), without damaging the signals that correspond to gastric activity.

The EGG record is divided into the three previously mentioned sections, which are analyzed separately. At this stage it is necessary to ensure that the length of each segment is the same for each patient as a way of normalizing the input to the neuronal classifier.

3.2 Feature Extraction

For the calculation of the DWT, the three base wavelets shown in Figure 1 were tested. Daubechies' wavelet shows the best results. An analysis of variability between subjects shows that low and very high frequency signals do not carry any useful information, and thus these coefficients were discarded as shown in Figure 4 below.

Figure 5 shows the graph of correlation versus coefficients obtained according to section 2.4 for the *prandial* stage. It is seen that there are four points at which the curve has more pronounced drops. These points were evaluated by the neuronal classifier, and the best result was obtained with the point having the coordinates (0.65, 80).

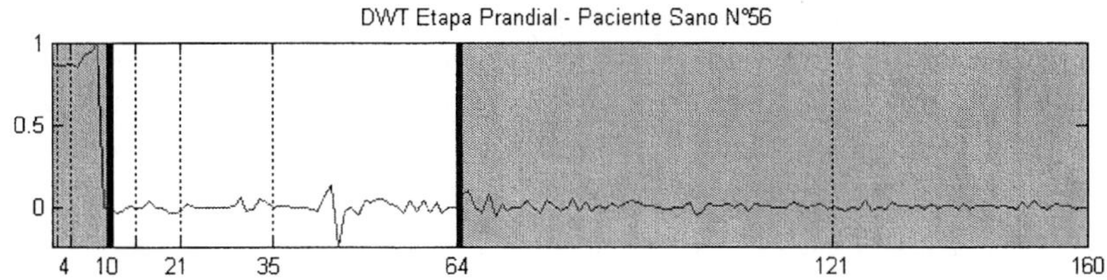

Fig. 4. Elimination of coefficients that do not carry information (shaded regions)

The total coefficient reduction achieved for the *prandial* stage was from 160 to 80, and that for the *pre* and *post-prandial* stages was from 1070 to 300.

3.3 Classifications

Different neuronal classifiers were implemented for each of the exam stages, and the four training methods mentioned in Section 2.5 were evaluated. Sigmoid neurons were used for the hidden layer, and linear and sigmoid neurons were tested for the output layer.

By means of the cross validation process, models with one and two hidden layer were evaluated first, and acceptable results were obtained. However, these results are achieved with reduced numbers of neurons in the hidden layer. Due to this fact, it was decided to eliminate the hidden layer, thus transforming the classifier into a linear discriminator which uses a single output neuron with a sigmoid activation function.

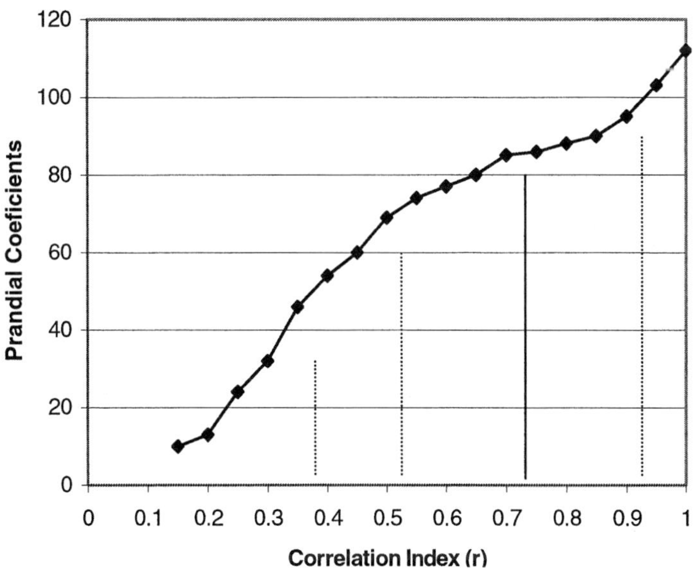

Fig. 5. Feature reduction graph, *prandial* stage (chosen point, solid line)

The best results were obtained for the *prandial* stage with 80 input coefficients, one output neuron, and the resilient backpropagation training method. The threshold value is adjusted in order to improve classification while using only training data, thus achieving *82.1%* accuracy (*17.9%±6%* error, with $p<0.005$), with *78.6%* sensitivity and *92.9%* specificity.

4 Conclusions

Time-frequency analysis methods make it possible to obtain important features for identifying biological signals. When the signals are extensive, however, the number of features generated by these methods prevent an adequate classification of the signals. This paper presents a simple method for extracting important features that make it possible to classify satisfactorily very extensive biological signals. The method has been evaluated using one of the most extensive signals known in clinical practice, that of EGG records (2.5 hours per patient) for the detection of FD.

Attempts to diagnose gastric electrical abnormalities in FD by studying the frequencies generated by the spectral analysis of segments of the EGG signal are not satisfactory. Attempts to systematically extract EGG characteristics for their subsequent classification have generated adequate results in other gastric pathologies [10], but the vast majority of these methods are based purely on a frequency analysis, and complex indices must be developed in order to characterize the different phenomena.

The time-frequency analysis based on the wavelet transform generated more than 1000 coefficients for identifiable sections of EGG signals. Attempts to classify directly these coefficients did not allow an adequate discrimination between healthy patients and those suffering from FD. Only after applying the proposed feature reduction the cases were separated adequately, achieving 82.1% accuracy. In this particular case, application of the feature extraction allowed the complexity of the classification to be reduced to a linear separation problem that was implemented by a neuronal network without hidden layer.

The proposed feature reduction introduced here can be extended to other problems of identification of long biological signals such as those of sleep-wakefulness EEGs [18], or signals of blood pressure and flow for the analysis of the autoregulation of brain blood flow [19].

References

1. Blum A. Langley P. Selection of relevant feature and examples in machine learning, Art. Intell. **97** (1997) 245-71.
2. Duda R. Hart P. Patter Classifications, Wiley, 2nd Eds. (2001).
3. Wai-Man W., Cheng C., Chu-Yu B., Chun-Yu Wong B., Wai-Mo H., Non-Ulcer dyspepsia, Med Progress **2** (2003) 1-8.
4. Drossman D., "ROME II – The Functional Gastrointestinal Disorder". 2nd edition, Degnon Associates, Mc Lean, VA, USA. (2000).
5. Liang J., Chen J., What can be measured from surface electrogastrography (computer simulations). Dig Dis Sci **42** (1997) 1331-43.

6. Verhagen M., Van Schelven L., Samsom M., Smout A., Pitfalls in the analysis of electrogastrographic recording, Gastroenterology **117** (1999) 453-460.
7. Akin A., Sun H., Non-invasive gastric motility monitor: fast electrogastrogram (fEGG). Phys. Measu **23** (2002) 505-519.
8. Chen J., McCallum R., Electrogastrography: Measurement, analysis and prospective application, Med Biol Eng Comput **29** (1991) 339-350.
9. Zhiyue L, Chen J. D. Z, Parolisi S., Shifflett J., Peura D., McCallum R., Prevalence of Gastric Myoelectrical Abnormalities in Patients with Non-Ulcer Dyspepsia and Helicobacter Pylori Infection, Dig Dis Sci **46** (2001) 739-745.
10. Chen, J. Lin, Z. and McCallum, R, A Noninvasive feature-based detection of delayed gastric emptying in humans using neural networks. IEEE Trans Biomed Eng **49** (2000) 409-412.
11. Chen, J. A Computerized data analysis system for electrogastrogram. Comput Biol Med 22 (1992) 45-58.
12. Graps A., An Introduction to Wavelets, IEEE Comput Sci Eng **2** (1995) 2-17.
13. Mallat S., A Theory for Multirresolution Signal Decomposition: The Wavelet Representation, IEEE Trans Patter Anal **11** (1989) 674-93.
14. Torrence Ch. Compo G. A Practical Guide to Wavelet Analysis, Am Meteorol Soc **79** (1998) 61-78.
15. Gastrosoft Inc, Polygram – Software reference manual. Lower GI Edition. USA (1990).
16. Prince J., Euliano N., Lefebre W., Neural and Adaptive System. John Wiley & Sons Inc., New York. (2000).
17. Bishop C. Neural Networks for Pattern Recognition, Oxford Claredon Press. (1995).
18. Flexer A., Gruber G., Dorffner G. A reliable probabilistic sleep stager based on a single EEG signal. Artif Intell Med **33** (2005) 199-207.
19. Panerai R. Assessment of cerebral pressure autoregulation in humans - a review of measurement methods. Physiological Measurement **19** (1998) 305-38.

A Fast Motion Estimation Algorithm Based on Diamond and Simplified Square Search Patterns

Yun Cheng[1,2], Kui Dai[2], Zhiying Wang[2], and Jianjun Guo[2]

[1] Department of Information Engineering, Hunan Institute of Humanities, Science and Technology, 417000 Loudi, China
{chengyun,daikui}@chiplight.com.cn
[2] College of Computer, National University of Defense Technology, 410073 Changsha, China

Abstract. Based on the directional characteristic of SAD(Sum of Absolute Difference) distribution and the center-biased characteristic of motion vectors, a fast BMA(block-matching motion estimation algorithm), DSSS(Diamond and Simplified Square Search), is proposed in this paper. DSSS employs line search pattern(LP), triangle search pattern(TP), or square pattern(SP) adaptively according to the distance between the MBD(Minimum Block Distortion) and SMBD(Second MBD) points to locate the best matching block with large motion vector, and diamond search pattern(DP) to refine the motion vector. Although the proposed DSSS may also be trapped in local minima, the experimental results show that it is faster than DS(Diamond Search) and DTS(Diamond and Triangle Search), while its encoding efficiency is better than DS and it is almost the same as that of DTS.

1 Introduction

Motion Compensated Predictive Coding can improve the encoding efficiency greatly by eliminating the temporal redundancy between successive frames and it was adopted by many video coding standards such as MPEG-1/2/4, H.261, H.263 and H.264/AVC[1], etc. The basic algorithm for motion compensated predictive coding is the block-matching motion estimation(BMME), and the most basic BMA(BMME Algorithm) is the full search (FS). Although FS can find out the best matching block by exhaustively testing all the candidate blocks within the search window, its computation is too heavy, for example, experimental results show that the time of the BMME consumed by FS in H.264/AVC is about 80% of the total. In order to speed up the BMME in the process of video encoding, many researchers have been working hard and have proposed many kinds of fast BMAs.

Most of the fast BMAs find the best matching block (or point) by using some special search patters. For example, TDLs(Two-Dimensional Logarithmic Search) uses "+" search pattern[2]; CSA (Cross-Search Algorithm)[3] and DSWA(Dynamic Search-Window Adjustment) [4] adopt "X" and "+" search patterns; TSS(Three-Step Search), NTSS (New TSS) [5], 4SS (Four-Step Search) [6], and BBGDS(Block-Based Gradient Descent Search)[7] employ square search pattern; DS(Diamond

M. Lazo and A. Sanfeliu (Eds.): CIARP 2005, LNCS 3773, pp. 440 – 449, 2005.

Search) exploits diamond search pattern [8]; HEXBS(Hexagon-Based Search) adopts hexagon search pattern [9]; OCTBS uses octagon search pattern [10]; etc. Some improved fast BMAs usually use two different search patterns in the searching procedure of motion vector, for example, CBHS adopts "X" and diamond patterns [11]; CDS and its improved algorithms use "+" and diamond pattern [12,13,14]; DTS employes diamond and triangle search patterns[15]; etc.

Based on the directional characteristic of SAD distribution and the center-biased characteristic of motion vectors, we proposed a fast BMA, DSSS(Diamond Simplified Square Search), in this paper.

The rest of this paper is organized as follows. Section 2 introduces our previous work briefly. The proposed DSSS is described in Section 3. Experimental results are presented in Section 4. Finally, conclusions are given in Section 5.

2 The Previous Work

In [15] we proposed a fast motion estimation algorithm based on diamond and triangle search patterns(DTS). The DTS algorithm adopts two search patterns adaptively in the process of motion search. The first pattern, called DP(Diamond Pattern, as shown in Fig.1(a)), comprises five checking points from which four points surround the center one to compose a diamond shape. The second pattern consisting of three checking points and covering the MBD point obtained in the previous search step(as shown in Fig.1(b)) forms a triangle shape, called TP(Triangle Pattern). In the process of motion search, DP is used to refine the motion vectors and it is necessary no matter how the motion vector being small or big, while TP is used to locate the best matching block with large motion vector approximately and it can be disused if the motion vector is '0'.

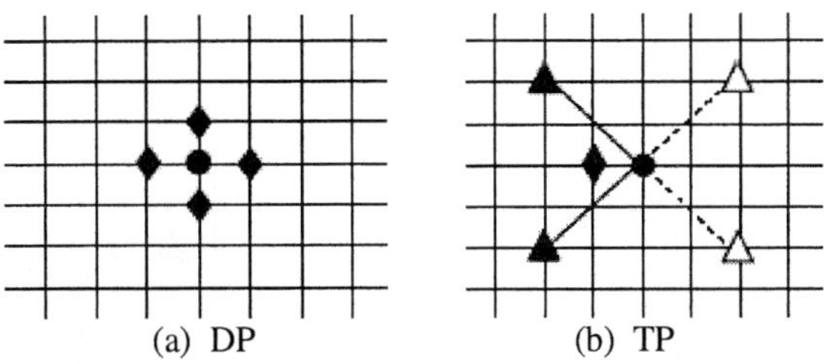

Fig. 1. Two search patterns employed in the proposed DTS algorithm

The DTS algorithm has the following technical characteristics. Firstly, the initial search center is formed according to the predicted motion vector of the current block by the adjacent blocks. Secondly, DP and TP are adaptively employed according to the motion extents of macro blocks.

By analyzing the DTS algorithm, we found that its speed of encoding is not so high for some video sequences, so we developed the proposed DSSS in the following.

3 The Proposed Diamond and Simplified Square Search Algorithm

3.1 DSSS Patterns

The proposed DSSS algorithm employs four search patterns adaptively in the process of motion search. The first pattern is called DP(as shown in Fig.2(a)). The second pattern consisting of two checking point forms a line shape, called LP(Line search Pattern) if the MBD(Minimum Block Distortion) and the SMBD(Second MBD) points obtained in the previous search step are located in different directions(as shown in Fig.2(b)). The third pattern consisting of three checking points and covering the MBD point forms a triangle shape, called TP(Triangle search Pattern) if the MBD and the SMBD points obtained in the previous search step are located in the same direction and the distance of the two points is only one pixel(as shown in Fig.2(c)). The fourth pattern consisting of four checking points forms a square shape, called SP(Square search Pattern) if the MBD and the SMBD points obtained in the previous search step are located in the same direction and the distance of the two points equals two pixels(as shown in Fig.2(d)). In the searching process of motion estimation, DP is

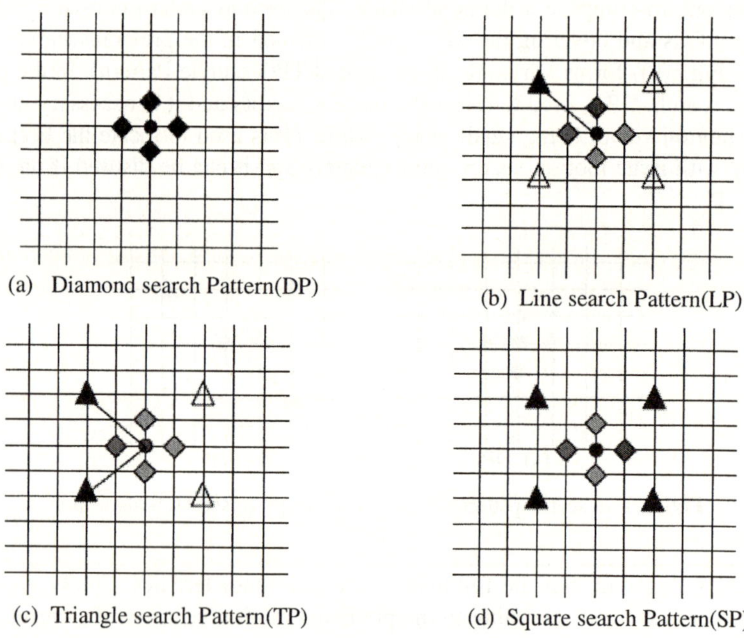

Fig. 2. Four search patterns employed in the proposed DSSS algorithm, only the solid black icons are the new checking points where the computational of block-distortion measurement is required, while the blank triangles are the skipped points, where '◆' and '◆'or '●' represent the MBD and SMBD point found in the previous search step respectively

used to refine the motion vectors and it is necessary no matter how the motion vector being small or big, while LP, TP or SP is used to locate the best matching block with large motion approximately and it can be discarded if the motion vector is '0'.

3.2 Description of the Proposed DSSS Algorithm

The proposed DSSS algorithm mainly comprises 4 stages. In the first stage, in order to reduce the search points for the best matching block with large motion, we use the median motion value of the adjacent blocks (as shown in Fig.3) to predict the motion vector of the current block. The median prediction is expressed as Eq. (1).

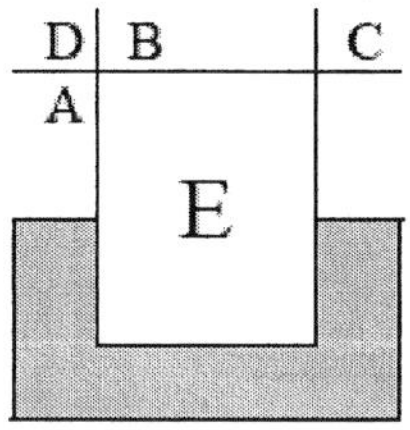

Fig. 3. Reference block location for predicting motion vector

$$pred\_mv = median(mv\_A, mv\_B, mv\_C) \tag{1}$$

In the second stage, in order to find the best matching block with zero or small motion vector efficiently, DP is selected as the search pattern. If the MBD point is located at the search center, then the motion search process terminates immediately and the best matching motion vector is equal to the predicted one. Assume that $P_0(x_0, y_0)$, $P_1(x_1, y_1)$ are the MBD and SMBD (Second MBD) points found in the current search step respectively, the searching pattern for the next search step can be decided by the distance from P_1 to P_0, which is defined by Eq.(2).

$$P_1P_0 = (\Delta x_1, \Delta y_1) = (x_0 - x_1, y_0 - y_1) \tag{2}$$

In the third stage, the proposed DSSS algorithm selects a search pattern from LP, TP, and SP adaptively according to the distance between P_1 and P_0. In the fourth stage, the proposed DSSS algorithm uses DP repeatedly until the new MBD point occurs at the center of DP or DP and LP/TP/SP alternately according to the position of the new MBD point found in the previous search step.

The block diagram of the proposed algorithm is depicted in Fig.4, and the proposed algorithm is summarized as follows.

Step1: Eq. (1) is used to predict the initial motion vector of the current block, and the initial search center point is set according to the predicted value.

Step2: DP is disposed at the search center, and the 5 checking points of DP(as shown in Fig.2(a)) are tested. If the minimum block distortion (MBD) point calculated is located at the center position of DP, then it is the final solution of the motion vector, goto **step5**. Otherwise, the new MBD point is re-positioned as the search center point, goto **step3**.

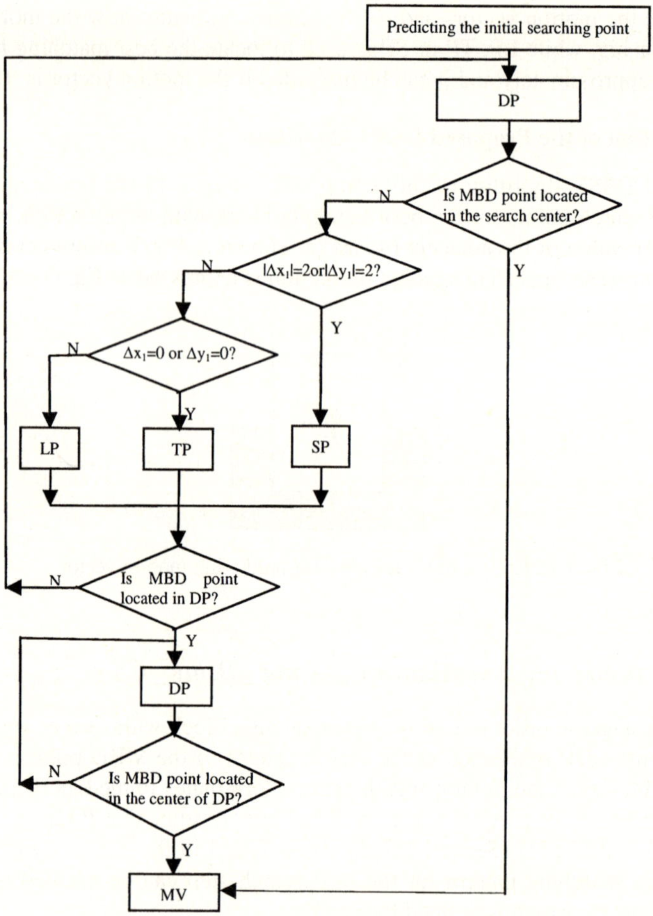

Fig. 4. The block diagram of the proposed algorithm

Step3: If((| Δx_1|=2) or (| Δy_1|=2))
{
SP is disposed at the new search center, and 4 checking points of SP (the 4 black squares as shown in Fig.2 (d)) are tested.
}
Else if((Δx_1=0) or (Δy_1=0))
{
TP is disposed at the new search center, and 2 checking points of TP (the 2 black squares as shown in Fig.2 (c)) are tested.
}
Else

{
LP is disposed at the new search center, and 1 checking points of LP (the 1 black squares as shown in Fig.2 (b)) are tested.
}

If the MBD point is refreshed, the new MBD point is re-positioned as the search center, goto **step2**, otherwise, goto **step4**.

Step4: DP is disposed at the search center, and the 3 checking points of DP are tested according to the position of the MBD point. If the MBD point calculated is located at the center position, goto step5, otherwise, recursively repeat this step.

Step5: Stop searching. The center point is the final solution of the motion vector which points to the best matching block.

3.3 Analysis of the Proposed DSSS Algorithm

For BMME, computational complexity could be measured by average number of search points required for each motion vector estimation. According to the statistical distribution

Table 1. Comparison of least search points near the initial search center for DS,DTS and DSSS

	the best matching point is located in the			
	center	Circular area with a Radius of 1 pixel	Circular area with a Radius of $\sqrt{2}$ pixels	Circular area with a Radius of 2 pixels
DS	13	13	16	18
DTS	5	10	12	13
DSSS	5	9	11	12

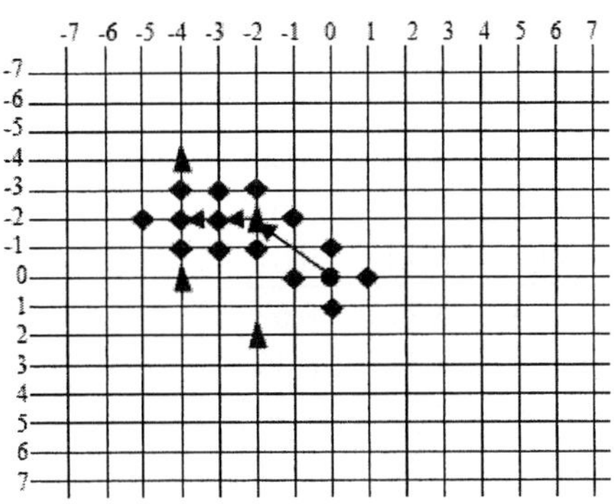

(a) DTS uses six search steps—two times of TP and four times of DP. There are 19 search points in total—taking five, two, four, two, three, and three search points at each step, sequentially.

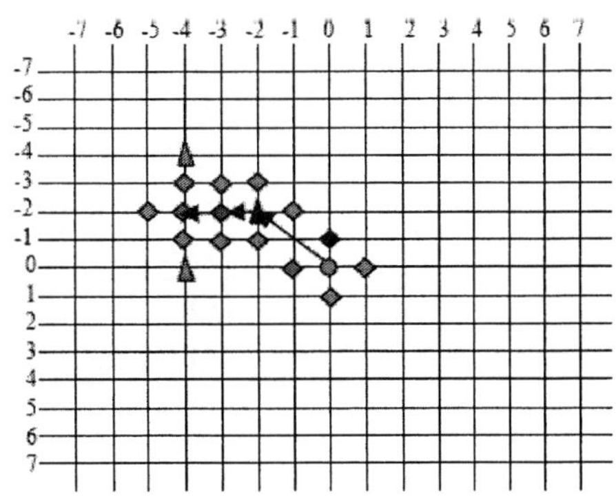

(b) DSSS uses six search steps—one time of LP, one time of TP, and four times of DP. There are 18 search points in total—taking five, one, four, two, three, and three search points at each step, sequentially.

Fig. 5. Search path example which leads to the motion vector (-4,-2) for DTS and DSSS law of motion vectors in different images sequences, assume that the best matching point is located in a circle area with a radius of 2 pixels around the initial search point, the least search points needed for DS, DTS, and DSSS are listed in Table.1.

From Table.1 we observe that the least search points needed for DSSS is always less than that of DS, and the reduced search points is always 3~8. If the MBD point is not located in the initial search center, DSSS can reduce one search point comparing with that of DTS.

If the best matching point is located outside the circular area with a radius of 2 pixels, the least search points needed for DSSS is still less than that of DTS. This could be seen from the practical search path. Fig.5 gives a search path example which leads to the motion vector (-4,-2) for DTS and DSSS.

4 Experimental Results

Our proposed DSSS algorithm was integrated within version 7.6 of the H.264 software [16], and it is compared versus FS, DS, and DTS. Even though many image sequences are tested in the experiment, only four of them are selected out to be compared. The CABAC(Context-Adaptive Binary Arithmetic Coding) entropy coder[17] was used for all of our tests, with quantization parameter (QP) values of 28, 32, 36, and 40, a search range of ±16, and 2 references.

Table 2. The Average number of Search Points per macro-block

		FS	DS	DTS	DSSS
akiyo	QP=28	1089	13.04	5.14	5.12
	QP=32	1089	13.05	5.18	5.16
	QP=36	1089	13.10	5.22	5.20
	QP=40	1089	13.18	5.37	5.32
foreman	QP=28	1089	15.07	8.34	7.96
	QP=32	1089	15.12	8.40	8.00
	QP=36	1089	15.09	8.44	8.04
	QP=40	1089	14.99	8.42	8.01
coastguard	QP=28	1089	14.73	8.81	8.67
	QP=32	1089	14.72	8.54	8.39
	QP=36	1089	14.68	8.13	7.96
	QP=40	1089	14.51	7.80	7.65
mobile	QP=28	1089	14.57	8.81	8.59
	QP=32	1089	14.46	8.72	8.54
	QP=36	1089	14.56	8.77	8.51
	QP=40	1089	14.68	8.94	8.68

The four selected sequences are akiyo(Quarter Common Intermediate Format, QCIF), foreman(QCIF), coastguard(QCIF), and mobile(CIF). The former 100 frames of every sequence are tested, and only the first frame was encoded as I-frame, while the remainders are encoded as P-frames. Although H.264 provides seven different block-sizes for inter-frame coding, we have only used the 16×16 mode so as to compare the speed of motion search accurately. To simplify our comparison, we have used ASP(Average number of Search Points per macro-block) and RD(Rate Distortion) performance plot as shown in Table 2 and Fig.6 respectively.

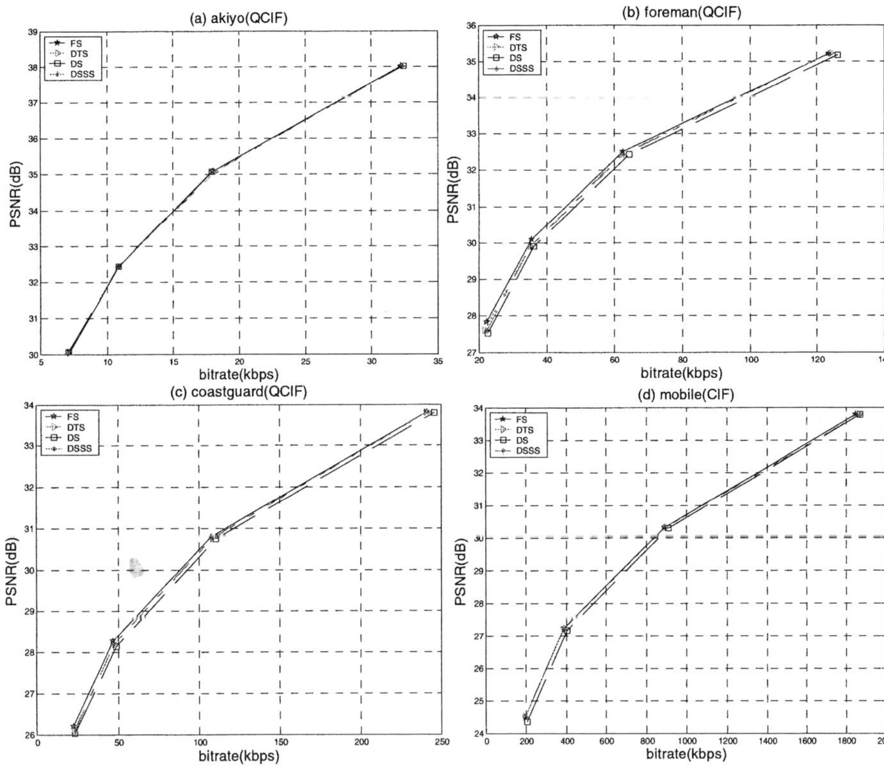

Fig. 6. RD performance plot for sequences (a) akiyo, (b) foreman, (c) coastguard, and (d) mobile

From Table 2 we can observe that the average number of search points per macro-block needed for DS, DTS, and DSSS are 13.04~15.12, 5.14~8.94, and 5.12~8.68 respectively. It's obvious that DSSS is faster than DS and DTS. From Fig.5 we can observe that the encoding efficiency of DSSS is better than DS and it is almost the same as that of DTS.

5 Conclusions

Based on the directional characteristic of SAD distribution and the center-biased characteristic of motion vectors, a fast BMA, DSSS, is proposed in this paper. DSSS employs DP to refine the motion vectors, and LP, TP or SP adaptively according to the distance between the MBD and SMBD point so as to locate the best matching block with large motion vector approximately. Although the proposed DSSS may also be trapped in local minima, experimental results show that it is faster than DS and DTS, while its encoding efficiency is better than DS and it is almost the same as that of DTS.

Acknowledgements. This work was supported by Grant No.04B055 from the Scientific Research Fund of Hunan Provincial Education Department and Grant No. 04JJ6032 from the Provincial Natural Science Foundation of Hunan.

References

1. T. Wiegand and G. Sullivan.: ITU-T Rec. H.264|ISO/IEC 14496-10 AVC, Final Draft, Document JVT-G050, 7th Meeting: Pattaya, Thailand, March 2003
2. J.Jain and A. Jain.: Displacement measurement and its application in interframe image coding. IEEE Transaction on Communication, vol. 29, pp.1799-1808, 1981
3. M. Ghanbari.: The cross-search algorithm for motion estimation. IEEE Transaction on Communication, vol. 38, pp. 950–953, July 1990
4. L. W. Lee, J. F. Wang, et al.: Dynamic search-window adjustment and interlaced search for block-matching algorithm. IEEE Transaction on Circuits and Systems for Video Technology, Vol. 3, pp.85–87, 1993
5. R.Li, B. Zeng, et al.: A new three-step search algorithm for block motion estimation. IEEE Transaction on Circuits and Systems for Video Technology, vol. 4, pp. 438–442, Aug. 1994
6. L. M. Po and W. C. Ma.: A novel four-step search algorithm for fast block motion estimation. IEEE Transaction on Circuits and Systems for Video Technology, vol. 6, pp. 313–317, June 1996
7. L. K. Liu and E. Feig.: A block-based gradient descent search algorithm for block motion estimation in video coding. IEEE Transaction on Circuits and Systems for Video Technology, vol. 6, pp. 419–423, Aug. 1996
8. S. Zhu and K. K. Ma.: A new diamond search algorithm for fast block matching motion estimation. IEEE Transaction on Image Processing, vol. 9, pp.287–290, Feb. 2000
9. C. Zhu, X. Lin, and L.P. Chau.: Hexagon-based search pattern for fast block motion estimation. IEEE Transaction on Circuits and Systems for Video Technology, vol.12, pp.349-355. May 2002
10. L. P. Chau and C. Zhu.: A fast octagon-based search algorithm for motion estimation. Signal Processing, vol. 83, pp.671-675, 2003
11. Sung-Chul Shin, Hyunki Baik, et al.: A center-biased hybrid search method using plus search pattern for block motion estimation. IEEE International Symposium on Circuits and systems, Geneva, Switzerland, vol. IV, pp. 309-312, May, 2000
12. Chun-Ho Cheung and Lai-Man Po.: A novel cross-diamond search algorithm for fast block motion estimation. IEEE Trans. Circuit syst. video technol, vol. 12, pp. 1168-1177, Dec. 2002.
13. Chun-Ho Cheung and Lai-Man Po.: A novel small-cross-diamond search algorithm for fast video coding and videoconferencing applications. IEEE ICIP, vol. I, pp.681-684, 2002.

14. Chi-Wai Lam, Lai-Man Po, et al.: A new cross-diamond search algorithm for fast block matching motion estimation. IEEE Int. Conf. Neural Networks & Signal Processing, pp. 1262–1265, Nanjing, China, 2003.
15. Y. Cheng, Z.Y. Wang, et al.: A fast motion estimation algorithm based on diamond and triangle search patterns. IbPRIA 2005, LNCS 3522, pp.419-426, 2005
16. http://bs.hhi.de/~suehring/tml/download/old_jm/jm7.6, June 2004
17. D. Marpe, H. Schwarz and T. Wiegand.: Context-Based Adaptive Binary Arithmetic Coding in H.264/AVC Video Compression Standard. IEEE Transaction on Circuits and Systems for Video Technology, vol.13, pp. 620–636, July 2003

Selecting Prototypes in Mixed Incomplete Data

Milton García-Borroto[1] and José Ruiz-Shulcloper[2]

[1] Bioplants Center, UNICA, C. de Ávila, Cuba
mil@bioplantas.cu
http://www.bioplantas.cu
[2] Advanced Technologies Applications Center, MINBAS, Cuba
jshulcloper@cenatav.co.cu
http://www.cenatav.co.cu/

Abstract. In this paper we introduce a new method for selecting prototypes with Mixed Incomplete Data (MID) object description, based on an extension of the Nearest Neighbor rule. This new rule allows dealing with functions that are not necessarily dual functions of distances. The introduced compact set editing method (CSE) constructs a prototype consistent subset, which is also subclass consistent. The experimental results show that CSE has a very nice computational behavior and effectiveness, reducing around 50% of prototypes without appreciable degradation on accuracy, in almost all databases with more than 300 objects.

1 Introduction

Supervised classifiers need a good training matrix for classifying with effectiveness. This "goodness" is usually achieved by expert criterion, but sometimes even experts make this selection arbitrarily. These classifiers typically compare a new unclassified object with all stored classified ones to make a decision. This can make them prohibitively costly for large training sets. One possible solution to these problems is to reduce the cardinality of the object descriptions sample, while simultaneously insisting that the decisions based on the reduced data set perform as well, or nearly as well, as the decisions based on the original data set. This process is known as finding prototypes.

There are two different goals approached while finding prototypes:

- Minimize the size of the training set (condensing methods).
- Reduce the size of the training set obtaining classification accuracy never worse than with the initial training matrix (editing methods).

On the other hand, in order to solve practical real problems, especially in soft sciences, we have to deal frequently with description of objects that are *non-classical*, that is, the features are not exclusively numerical or categorical. Both kinds of values can appear simultaneously, and a special symbol is necessary to denote the absence of values (missing values). A *mixed and incomplete description* of objects should be used in this case (MID). Many examples of real problems with this sort of objects can be found [1, 2] and also in the UCI Repository of Machine Learning Databases [3].

M. Lazo and A. Sanfeliu (Eds.): CIARP 2005, LNCS 3773, pp. 450–459, 2005.

Although the terms distance and dissimilarity have been widely exchanged, it is not true that a dissimilarity function is always dual to a distance function. There are many practice applications that use non-reflexive and/or non-symmetrical dissimilarities, which their duals are evidently not distances [4, 5].

Most prototype selection algorithms were developed to deal with distances defined in metric spaces, which almost never is possible to use while working with MID. Some of them may be trivially extended to work with MID (Hart's CNN [6], Wilson's ENN [7], Random [8]) and many others do not, because use properties of distances and metric spaces for working (Construction of new prototypes [9], proximity graphs [10]).

2 Basic Concepts

Let U a universe of objects, structured in $K_1, \ldots, K_r$ classes, described in terms of a finite set of features $R=\{x_1, \ldots x_n\}$. Each of these features has associated a set of admissible values M_i, which include de value '*' for the case of unknown value. Over M_i no algebraic, topologic of logic structure is assumed. Then be $U=M_1\times\ldots\times M_n$, the Cartesian product of the admissible values sets of features of R. Let $O=(x_1(O), x_2(O), \ldots, x_n(O))$, where $x_i:U\rightarrow M_i$. A *comparison criterion* $\varphi_i:M_i\times M_i\rightarrow L_i$ is associated to each x_i, where L_i is a totally ordered set. A *similarity function* is a function Γ as be defined in [11]. $\Gamma(O_1,O_2)$ is an evaluation of the degree of similarity between any two descriptions of objects belonging to U. Any restriction of Γ to any subset of R will be called a *partial similarity function*. Besides, this function is characterized by the following properties: the partial similarity relationships between any pair of objects are preserved when the total similarity between these objects is considered. Also, the maximum value of similarity is reached when the same part of the same object for any non-empty subset of R is considered, including the case of whole R.

There are many pattern recognition algorithms for either numerical data processing or categorical data processing, that can be extended for the case of MID. These extensions are scarce and non trivial because it is necessary to face several problems. One of the simplest is the assumption of a distance for the comparison of MID.

Nearest neighbor rule can not be applied with similarities which are non-dual to distances because the term "near" is associated with distances, while the term "most similar" is associated with analogies.

Let $\alpha(O)=(\alpha_1(O),\ldots, \alpha_r(O))$ the membership t-uple of O in which $\alpha_i(O)$ means the grade of membership of O to the class K_i, i=1,..,r. For example, it could have $\alpha_i(O)=\{0,1\}$ with the obvious interpretation. Let $Q=\bigcup_{i=1}^{r} K_i'$, $K_i'\subset K_i$, $i=1,\ldots r$, a training set.

Let $O\in U\backslash Q$, the *most similar neighbor rule* (MSN) for classifying O is to assign it the membership t-uple $\alpha(O)$ in the following way:

A) Assuming Γ as just a similarity function

If $\max\left\{\max_{O_i\in Q}\{\Gamma(O,O_i)\}, \max_{O_i\in Q}\{\Gamma(O_i,O)\}\right\}=\Gamma(O,O')$ or $\Gamma(O', O)$ then $\alpha(O)=\alpha(O')$

B) Assuming Γ as symmetric similarity function
If $\max_{O_i \in Q}\{\Gamma(O,O_i)\} = \Gamma(O,O')$ then $\alpha(O) = \alpha(O')$, with $O' \in Q$

Observe that in these cases MSN rule does not require that K be a partition neither a hard structuralization of U.

We say that O_i, $O_j \in U$ are *β_0-similar objects* if $\Gamma(O_i, O_j) \geq \beta_0$. In the same way O_i is a *β_0-isolated object* if $\forall O_j \neq O_i \in U \;\; \Gamma(O_j, O_i) < \beta_0$. The β_0 threshold value can be used to control how similar a pair of objects must be in order to be considered β_0-similar.

Definition. $NU \subseteq U$, $NU \neq \varnothing$ is a *compact set* if: [11]

– $\forall O_j \in U \left[O_i \in NU \wedge \max_{\substack{O_t \in U \\ O_t \neq O_i}} \{\Gamma(O_i, O_t)\} = \Gamma(O_i, O_j) \geq \beta_0 \right] \Rightarrow O_j \in NU$

– $\left[\max_{\substack{O_i \in U \\ O_i \neq O_{pi}}} \{\Gamma(O_p, O_i)\} = \Gamma(O_p, O_t) \geq \beta_0 \wedge O_t \in NU \right] \Rightarrow O_p \in NU$

– $|NU|$ is minimal.

– Every β_0-isolated object is a compact set (degenerated).

The compact set criterion induces a unique partition for a given data set, which has the property that one object x and all its most similar neighbors belongs to the same cluster and also, those objects for which x is its most similar neighbor.

In many classification problems, a class is not uniformly formed. Consider, for example, in the universe of all humans we can define two classes: S is the class of all who are sick, and H is the class of all who are healthy. In the class S are grouped together many different objects with many different diseases, which compose *subclasses* inside the outer class. Intuitively, if an object belongs to a subclass its most similar neighbor must be in the same set, so it is obvious that a subclass should be considered as a union of compact sets.

Consider now the problem of selecting a set of prototypes which describes this problem. We face two important difficulties:

1. Selecting the number of prototypes per subclass (and obviously per class) can not be done *a priori*, because it depends on the inner structure of each subclass, which can only safely be inferred from data.
2. If the subclass structure of the class is not preserved someway it may be a serious degradation on accuracy, and it may be whole subclasses without a single representative. That is why it is important to introduce a new kind of consistency.

Let $Q \subset U$ a training matrix of a set of classes $K=\{K_1, K_2,\ldots, K_r\}$, $Cf(LM, x)$ a classifier with learning matrix LM and $\mathrm{MSN}_R(x)$ the most similar neighbor of object x in set R.

Following Hart [6] $R \subset Q$ is a *prototype consistent* subset with respect to (wrt) *Cf* and *Q* iff $\forall x \in Q[Cf(Q,x) = Cf(R,x)]$

Definition. *Let* Φ *a partition of Q in subclasses, such that* $\forall i \in I[\Phi_i \in \Phi\ x_1, x_2 \in \Phi_i \Rightarrow \alpha(x_1) = \alpha(x_2)]$ *and* $R_i \subset \Phi_i$, *a set of representatives associated to each subclass.* $R = \bigcup_{i \in I} R_i$ is *subclass consistent wrt* Φ iff:

$$\forall i \in I\, \forall x \in Q[(x \in \Phi_i \Rightarrow MSN_R(x) \in \Phi_i]$$

3 Compact Set Editing (CSE) Algorithm

Inputs:

- β_0-compact sets in a maximal similarity graph (oriented graph each edge from vertex *a* to vertex *b* means that *b* is the most β_0-similar element of *a*) described by a set of edges C and a set of vertexes V.
- $\alpha(x)$: class associated with vertex *x*

Output:

- Subset of selected prototypes *R*

Notations:

- $S(x) = \{b \in V / (x, b) \in C\}$, set of the successors of vertex *x* in graph *V*. The presence of these elements in *K* guarantee the good classification of *x*
- $A(x) = \{a \in V / (a, x) \in C\}$, set of the predecessors of vertex *x* in graph *V*.

0. $R = \varnothing$
1. Let associate each vertex *x* in *V* with a quadruple (S'_x, E_x, S_x, $Flags_x$), where:
   $S'_x = |\{y \in S(x) / \alpha(x) \neq \alpha(y)\}|$
   $E_x = |\{y \in A(x) / \alpha(x) = \alpha(y)\}|$
   $S_x = |\{y \subset S(x) / \alpha(x) = \alpha(y)\}|$
   $Flags_x \subset V$, $Flags_x = \varnothing$
2. $R' = \{ x \in V / S'_x > 0\}$
3. If $R' = \varnothing$ go to step 6
4. $C \leftarrow C \setminus \{(x, y) \in C / x \in R' \wedge \alpha(x) \neq \alpha(y)\}$
5. For each element $x \in R'$ execute Move(*x*).
6. $\forall x \in V [(S_x = 0) \Rightarrow$ execute Move(*x*)]
7. $\forall x \in V\, \forall y \in Flags_x \left[y \notin \bigcup_{z \in V \setminus \{x\}} Flags_z \Rightarrow \text{execute Move(x)} \right]$
8. Sort the elements of V with the following order relation:
   $x \prec y \Leftrightarrow E_x < E_y \vee (E_x = E_y \wedge S_x < S_y) \vee (E_x = E_y \wedge S_x = S_y \wedge |Flags_x| > |Flags_y|)$
9. Execute Discard(x_1), where x_1 is the first vertex of V ($\prec$)
10. If $V = \varnothing$ end, else go to step 6

Move(x)	**Discard(x)**
m1. Calculate A(x) and S(x) with the current set of vertexes V.	d1. Calculate A(x) and S(x) with the current set of vertexes V.
m2. $\forall\, y \in$ A(x) $[S_y \leftarrow \infty]$	d2. $\forall\, y \in$ S(x) $[Flags_y \leftarrow Flags_y \cup \{x\}]$
m3. $\forall\, y \in$ S(x) $[E_y \leftarrow E_y - 1]$	d3. $\forall\, y \in$ S(x) $[E_y \leftarrow E_y - 1]$
m4. $\forall\, y \in V\, [Flags_y \leftarrow Flags_y \setminus Flags_x]$	d4. $\forall\, y \in$ A(x)$[S_y \neq \infty \Rightarrow S_y \leftarrow S_y$ - 1
m5. $V \leftarrow V - \{x\}, R \leftarrow R \cup \{x\}$	d5. $V \leftarrow V - \{x\}$
m6. $C \leftarrow C \setminus \{(a, b) \in C \,/\, a = x \vee b = x\}$	d6. $C \leftarrow C \setminus \{(a, b) \in C \,/\, a = x \vee b = x\}$

The indexes calculated in step 1 are the core of the later decision of which vertex to select and which to discard. Steps 2-6 break the compact sets eliminating the edges connecting vertexes with different classes, leaving "pure" components (*v. gr.* in figure 1b eliminating edges c-d, d-c and e-d). To guarantee consistency predecessors nodes in this edges are moved to R, because they would be bad classified if do not (its MSN have a different class).

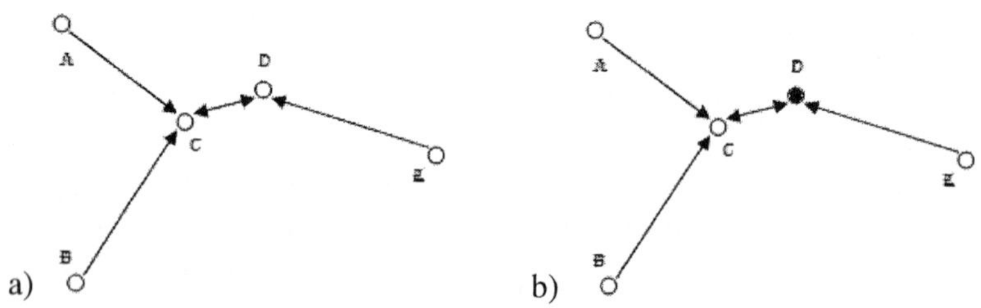

Fig. 1. Maximal similarity graph with a single class (a) and a couple of classes (b)

Let see how the algorithm decides what objects should be included in the result set. Suppose that the graph represented in Figure 1 is associated with a real problem. As you can see nodes C and D are more important than nodes A, B and E, because their presence in the result set guarantee the good classification of the rest of the nodes. The order relation defined assures that nodes with low importance are removed first from the set, and an additional process is done to keep consistency: if a node is discarded one of its MSN must to stay. This is done "flagging" all the successors of x with a non-simultaneous elimination mark (step d2). In step 7 if an object is the last having such "flag", it is automatically moved to R. After each modification in the graph, the indexes are updated. If the good classification of some node x is already assured, its S_x is assigned the value infinite, meaning that this information is no longer necessary for that object.

In the example, node A is the first discarded, flagging C as its only successor. Node C is moved to result set because is the only one to have the "A" flag. So, nodes B and D have S_x equal infinite. All indexes are recalculated, and the process is repeated again. Finally the result set is nodes C and D. Note that this set is prototype consistent, no matter the distribution of the other objects in the space, because of the use of maximal similarity graph.

Let demonstrate some properties of the algorithm.

Proposition 1. *Let Cf the classifier defined by the MSN rule. We have:*
($R \subset Q$ is prototype consistent) $\Leftrightarrow \forall x \in Q[\alpha(x) = \alpha(MSN_R(x))]$

Proof. If $R \subset Q$ is prototype consistent, then by definition we have $\forall x \in Q[Cf(Q,x) = Cf(R,x)]$ (1).
$Cf(Q, x) = \alpha(MSN_Q(x)) = \alpha(x)$, because x is its own MSN (2).
$Cf(R, x) = \alpha(MSN_R(x))$, because the definition of MSN (3).
Substituting (2) and (3) in (1) we have $\forall x \in Q[\alpha(x) = \alpha(MSN_R(x))]$.
The back implication is also obvious.

Proposition 2. *If a set of prototypes $R \subset Q$ is subclass consistent wrt a partition Φ, then it is prototype consistent wrt Q.*
Proof.
This is obvious based on the fact that the partition Φ is such that two elements in the same subclass have the same class.

Theorem 1. *The result set of the algorithm CSE is subclass consistent wrt the partition induced by the β_0-connected subgraphs.*
Proof. Basically the CSE algorithm, for each $x \in Q$ decides if $x \in R$ or not (and then its most similar neighbor $MSN_Q(x) \in R$), so we have

$$\forall x \in Q\lfloor x \in R \vee MSN_Q(x) \in R \rfloor$$

Let $x \in R$ and $x \in V_i$, then $x \in R \cap V_i = R_i$ (1)
$x \in R$ implies that $MSN_R(x) = x$, because x is its own MSN in R. (2)
By (1) and (2) we have that $MSN_R(x) \in R_i$, and then $MSN_R(x) \in V_i$ (3)
Let $MSN_Q(x) \in R$ and $x \in V_i$ (4)
$x \in V_i$ implies that $MSN_Q(x) \in V_i$, because V_i is a β_0-compact set (5).
From (4) and (5) we have:
$MSN_Q(x) \in R$ and $MSN_Q(x) \in V_i$, so $MSN_Q(x) \in R \cap V_i = R_i$, and then, because $R_i \subset R$ and $R \subset Q$, we have $MSN_R(x) \in R_i$, and finally $MSN_R(x) \in V_i$. (6)
By (3) and (6) we have:

$$\forall x \in Q\lfloor x \in R \vee MSN_Q(x) \in R \rfloor \Rightarrow \forall i \in I \forall x \in Q[x \in V_i \Rightarrow MSN_R(x) \in V_i]$$

what prove the theorem.

4 Experimental Results

Traditionally all prototypes selection methods have been defined in $\Re^n$ with distances functions. Many of them can not be extended to deal with MID, because they need properties of metric spaces, for example, the existence of an addition and multiplication operator. We have trivially extended some methods, originally enounced for working in metric spaces, allowing the comparisons with CSE. These methods are: AllKnn [12], Hart's CNN [6], IB2 [13], Dasarathy's MCS [14], Random [8], Relative neighbor editing [10], Random Mutation Hill Climbing (RMHC) [15], Shrink [16] and Wilson's ENN [7].

We use 27 databases from UCI Repository of Machine Learning with mixed and incomplete object description. Each database was split randomly, taking 30% for training (training matrix) and 70% for testing (control matrix). To reduce the influence of the randomness in partition, we repeat the process 5 times, and average the results. We measure the accuracy (# correct classification / # of objects) of each method by the difference of the accuracies over the training matrix and the edited matrix with respect to the control matrix, respectively.

A MSN classifier was used for testing, without weighing the features, because we are only interested in the differences between the selection methods, more than finding a best classifier for a particular example.

Table 1 shows the databases used in the experiments, the size of those databases and the list of methods that outperforms CSE in both, compression ratio and accuracy

Table 1. Databases used in the experiments

Number	UCI name	Objects	Outperforms CSE
1.	Annealing	257	MCS
2.	Audiology	64	-
3.	Breast cancer 1	230	Random
4.	Breast cancer 2	182	Random
5.	Breast cancer 3	69	RMHC
6.	Credit-screening	228	Random, RMHC
7.	Heart-disease Cleveland	94	Random, RMHC
8.	Heart-disease Hungarian	91	Random, RMHC
9.	Heart-disease Long Beach	63	MCS, ENN
10.	Heart-disease Switzerland	37	AllKnn, MCS, Random, RMHC, Shrink, ENN
11.	Hepatitis	56	-
12.	Horse-colic	96	MCS, Random
13.	Monks-problems 1	186	Shrink
14.	Monks-problems 2	194	AllKnn, IB2, Random, RMHC
15.	Monks-problems 3	184	MCS
16.	Mushroom	2655	MCS
17.	Soybean large	95	MCS
18.	Thyroid-disease Allbp	903	-
19.	Thyroid-disease ann	2399	-
20.	Thyroid-disease dis	1243	-
21.	Thyroid-disease hyper	936	-
22.	Thyroid-disease hypo	1233	-
23.	Thyroid-disease hypothyroid	1049	-
24.	Thyroid-disease new-thyroid	72	-
25.	Thyroid-disease rep	1246	-
26.	Thyroid-disease sick	1268	-
27.	Thyroid-disease sick-euthyroid	1055	-

difference. In the 27 databases evaluated, twelve of them CSE had the best behavior, in eight cases was outperformed by only one of the nine methods (not always the same) and in the remainder cases in which was outperformed by other methods, the databases were small.

We can also observe that gaining in compression ratio by other classifiers above CSE will lead to a drastic reduction in classification accuracy, as shown in **Table 2** and **Table 3** (bolded rows). Random based and evolutive methods (Random and RMHC) have a good performance in small databases [8], but are usually slow and inaccurate for big ones. MCS exhibit good performance for medium size database, but for big ones is always worse than CSE.

Table 2. Results of prototype selection for "thyroid-disease ann" database

Method Name	Acc. Difference &	Comp. Ratio	Time(sec)
CSE	-1,75	53,9	151,93
RMHillClimb	-0,43	50,1	670,91
RelativeNeighborEditor	**-5,10**	**79,37**	**3738,04**
MCS	**-5,54**	**83,74**	**487,32**
IB2	**-13,99**	**85,16**	**10,95**
Shrink	**-28,45**	**88,70**	**81,07**
AllKnn	1,98	8,71	1173,69
WilsonENN	1,70	5,04	148,54
CNN	-6,99	8,63	115,64

We have to note than the Time result shown in tables are only useful for comparisons, because the absolute value is highly dependant on the computer where they are executed.

Table 3. Results of prototype selection for "thyroid-disease dis" database

Method Name	Acc. Difference &	Comp. Ratio	Time
CSE	-0,42	58,25	57,1418
RMHillClimb	-0,22	50,52	248,1506
MCS	**-2,54**	**95,58**	**121,0522**
IB2	**-6,33**	**95,09**	**1,5004**
CNN	-2,31	35,32	38,7486
Wilson ENN	0,25	1,21	55,376
AllKnn	0,28	1,85	443,863
Shrink	**-21,71**	**97,35**	**28,3314**

The compression ratio of the method is around 50% of the prototypes in almost all databases, and the reduction of accuracy for medium and big databases is usually lower than 1. The behavior of the remainder methods is not so stable, and is more dependent to the data nature.

5 Conclusions

Many practical pattern recognition problems, especially many of those appearing in soft sciences (medicine, geosciences, criminology, and others), make a necessity to work with MID. Training set prototype selection is a core issue for improving the efficiency and efficacy of many supervised classifiers. To face those problems, firstly we have extended the well known NN rule to MSN, for allowing to work with similarity functions non necessarily dual to distances and with object representation spaces different to metric spaces, which is usual while working with MID. We have defined subclass consistency property, to preserve the subclass structure of the data set while selecting a subset of prototypes.

A new prototype selection method has been introduced (CSE). It works with MID and more general similarities (even non-symmetric or non-positive defined). It produces a subclass consistent subset. We have shown that this algorithm has a good performance compared to other prototype selection algorithms that can be used also with MID after a trivial extension. The new method is neither a pure condensing method nor a pure editing method, having desirable properties of both. Also the method leverages the user to spend time in selecting the training matrix, doing the selection automatically.

Based on preliminary experiments and the results shown, CSE seems to be very adequate for synergy of editing methods with mixed incomplete data, in which we are actually working.

References

1. F. Martínez-Trinidad and A. Guzmán-Arenas. The logical combinatorial approach to Pattern Recognition, an overview through selected works. *Pattern Recognition*, 34: 741-751, 2001.
2. J. Ruiz-Shulcloper and M. A. Abidi. Logical combinatorial pattern recognition: A Review. In S. G. Pandalai, editors, Recent Research Developments in Pattern Recognition. Transword Research Networks, USA.
3. C. J. Merz and P. M. Murphy. UCI Repository of Machine Learning Databases. Technical report, University of California at Irvine, Department of Information and Computer Science, 1998.
4. M. Sato and Y. Sato. Extended fuzzy clustering models for asymmetric similarity. In B. Bouchon-Meunier, R. Yager, and L. Zadeh, editors, Fuzzy logic and soft computing. World Scientific.
5. H. Chen and K. J. Lynch. Automatic construction of networks of concepts characterizing document databases. *IEEE Transactions on systems, man and cybernetics.*, 22: 885-902, 1992.
6. P. E. Hart. The condensed nearest neighbor rule. *IEEE Trans. on Information Theory*, 14: 515-516, 1968.
7. D. L. Wilson. Asymptotic properties of nearest neighbor rules using edited data. *IEEE Transactions on systems, man and cybernetics*, SMC-2: 408-421, 1972.
8. L. I. Kuncheva and J. C. Bezdek. Nearest prototype classification: clustering, genetic algorithms or random search. *IEEE transactions on systems, man and cybernetics. Part C*, 28: 160-164, 1998.

9. S.-W. Kim and J. B. Oommen. A brief taxonomy and ranking of creative prototype reduction schemes, in IEEE SCM Conference, 2002.
10. G. T. Toussaint. Proximity Graphs for Nearest Neighbor Decision Rules: Recent Progress, in 34 Symposium on Computing and Statistics INTERFACE-2002, 2002.
11. J. F. Martínez-Trinidad, J. Ruiz-Shulcloper, and M. S. Lazo-Cortés. Structuralization of universes. *Fuzzy sets and systems*, 112: 485-500, 2000.
12. I. Tomek. Two modifications of CNN. *IEEE Transactions on systems, man and cybernetics*, SMC-6: 769-772, 1976.
13. D. W. Aha, D. Kibler, and M. K. Albert. Instance-based learning algorithms. *Machine Learning*, 6: 37-66, 1991.
14. B. D. Dasarathy. Minimal consistent set (MCS) identification for optimal nearest neighbor decision systems design. *IEEE Transactions on systems, man and cybernetics.*, 24: 511-517, 1994.
15. D. B. Skalak. Prototype and Feature Selection by Sampling and Random Mutation Hill Climbing Algorithms, in Eleventh International Conference on Machine Learning, 1994.
16. D. Kibler and D. W. Aha. Learning representative exemplars of concepts: An initial case study., in Fourth international workshop on Machine learning, pages 24-30, 1987.

Diagnosis of Breast Cancer in Digital Mammograms Using Independent Component Analysis and Neural Networks

Lúcio F.A. Campos, Aristófanes C. Silva, and Allan Kardec Barros

Laboratory for Biologic Information Processing,
University of Maranhão, Av. dos portugueses,
s/n, Campus do Bacanga
lucio@dee.ufma.br, ari@dee.ufma.br, akbarros@ieee.org

Abstract. We propose a method for discrimination and classification of mammograms with benign, malignant and normal tissues using independent component analysis and neural networks. The method was tested for a mammogram set from MIAS database, and multilayer perceptron neural networks, probabilistic neural networks and radial basis function neural networks. The best performance was obtained with probabilistic neural networks, resulting in 97.3% success rate, with 100% of specificity and 96% of sensitivity.

Keywords: Mammogram, breast cancer, independent component analysis, neural networks, computer aided diagnosis.

1 Introduction

Breast cancer is the major cause of death by cancer in the female population. It is know that the best prevention method is early diagnosis, which lessens the mortality and enhances the treatment [1]. Therefore, a great effort has been made to improve the early diagnosis techniques. Among them, the most used is the mammogram, for it is low cost and easy access. However, mammogram has a high error value for medical diagnosis, ranging from 10 to 25%, resulting in a great number of false-positives diagnostics, which causes unneeded biopsies, or false-negatives, which delays the cancer diagnosis. The medical diagnosis using mammography can be aided by image processing and computational vision algorithms, combined with artificial intelligence for features extraction. Those algorithms are able to decrease the error and make the mammograms more reliable [2].

The breast cancer is originated by an exaggerated and disordered cell multiplication, forming a lesion. This lesion is called malignant when its cells have the capacity to cause metastases, that is, invade other healthy cells around them. If those malignant cells reach the blood circulation, they could get into contact with other parts of the body, invading new cells and originate new tumors [3].

On the other hand, the benign lesions do not have this capacity. Their growth is slower, until a maximum fixed size, and they cannot spread to other organs. These kind of lesion is common in the breasts [4].

M. Lazo and A. Sanfeliu (Eds.): CIARP 2005, LNCS 3773, pp. 460–469, 2005.

The mammography of benign tumors are well-defined, circular, with homogeneous texture. The malignant tumors, however, have speculated shape, frequently asymmetric, and less homogeneous than the benign lesions [5].

There are yet structures that can lead to medical misdiagnosis, as calcifications that arise as circular white spots [6].

CAD (Computer-Aided Diagnosis) systems can aid radiologists by providing a second opinion and may be used in the first stage of examination. For this to occur, it is important to develop many techniques to detect and recognize suspicious lesions and also to analyze and discriminate them. Some methods of lesion diagnosis in mammograms images have been reported. In [7], a system based in density-weighted contrast enhancement (*DWCE*) was used, obtaining 82.33% of success. In [8] mammograms are classified by support vector machines (SVM). The system sensibility was 84%. Christoyianni *et al* [9] compared three methods: Gray level histogram moments (GLHM), Spacial Gray Level Dependence Matrix (SGLD) and Independent Component Analysis (ICA). Accordingly to the authors, ICA had a better performance, with 88% of successful discrimination between normal and abnormal lesions, and 79.31% between benign and malignant lesions.

The proposed method is based on feature extraction by Independent Component Analysis. This technique is applied to many situations, as signal processing in cocktail-party environments [10], and pattern recognition in ECG and MEG [11], [12], [13].

Into this work, an image is taken as a linear combination of basis images, mutually statically independents, found using ICA. Such an basis image are extracted through the FastICA algorithm, from a preselected set of region of interest (ROI) of benign, malignant or normal tissues.

The objective of this work is to classify a ROI as normal, benign or malignant from the coefficients (features) extracted using ICA. Then, those features are used as input parameters to a Neural Network do the classification.

We divide this work as follows. Into section 2 we show the techniques for feature extraction and classification of ROI. In Section 3 we present the results and discuss about the application of the techniques under study. Finally, Section 4 presents some concluding remarks.

2 Methods

The block diagram of the proposed method is shown in figure 1. It consists of the selection of ROIs, the extraction of features using ICA, reduction of insignificants features using the *forward-selection* technica and the classification of the ROIs through neural networks.

2.1 Independent Component Analysis

Let us assume that an image is the sum of basis images $s_1,.., s_n$, mutually statistically independent. The image is then composed by the combination of n basis images, where we have n coefficients $a_1 \dots a_n$ [9], [14], such that

$$x_i = a_{i1}.s_1 + a_{i2}.s_2 + \dots + a_{in}.s_n \qquad \forall_i = 1, \cdots n \tag{1}$$

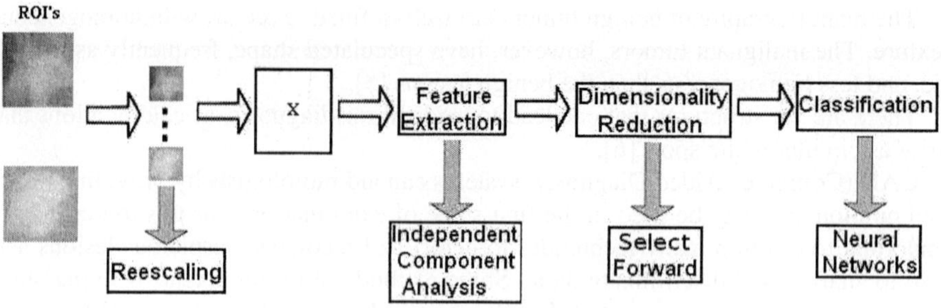

Fig. 1. Block diagram of the proposed method

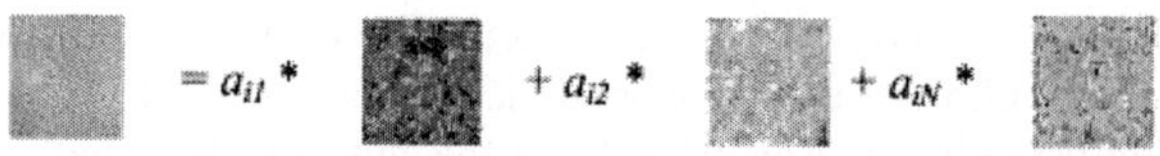

Fig. 2. Region of interest as a linear combination of its basis image mutually statistically independent

In equation 1, only the variables x_i are known, and from them we estimate the coefficients a_{ij} and the independent components s_j, that is:

$$X = A.S \tag{2}$$

Where ***X*** is an mixture matrix, the columns of ***A*** are the basis functions and ***S*** are the basis images.

2.1.1 FastICA Algorithm

The FastICA algorithm is used to solve the blind source separation (BSS) problem, where we want to estimate the basis images and the basis functions of the image **X**. This algorithm is based on fixed-point iteration [15], [16], [17]. In [15], a fixed-point algorithm was introduced using kurtosis, and in [16]-[17], the FastICA algorithm was generalized for general contrast functions [16]. For sphered data, the one-unit FastICA algorithm has the following form:

$$w(k) = E\{x.g(w(k-1)^T.x)\} - E\{g'(w(k-1)^T.x)\}w(k-1) \tag{3}$$

Where the weight vector ***w*** is also normalized to unit norm after every iteration, and

$$w^{-1} = A \tag{4}$$

The function *g* is the derivative of the function *G* used in the general contrast function in equation 5.

$$J_{G(y)} = \left| E_y\{G(y)\} - E_v\{G(v)\} \right|^p \tag{5}$$

Where v is a standardized Gaussian random variable, y is assumed to be normalized to unit variance, and the exponent p=1,2 typically. The subscripts denote expectation with respect to y and v.

The basic form of the FastICa algorithm is as follows [14]:

1. Choose an initial (e.g. random) weight vector **w**.
2. Let $w^{+} = E\{xg(w^{T}.x)\} - E\{g'(w^{T}x)\}w$
3. Let $w = w^{+} / \|w^{+}\|$
4. If not converged, go back to 2.

The expectations are estimated, in practice, using sample averages over a sufficiently large sample of the input data. Units using this FastICA algorithm can then be combined, just as in the case of neural learning rules, into systems that estimate several independent components. Such systems may either estimate the independent component one-by-one using hierarchical decorrelation (deflation), or they may estimate all the independent components [16]-[17].

2.2 Neural Networks

In this work, we use a Multilayer Perceptron Neural Network (MLP), Probabilistic Neural Network (PNN) and Radial Basis Functions Neural Network (RBFNN) to classify malignant, benign and normal tissues.

2.2.1 Multilayer Perceptron Neural Networks

The Multilayer Perceptron (MLP), a feed-forward back-propagation network, is the most frequently used neural network technique in pattern recognition [18], [19].

Speaking, MLPs are supervised learning classifiers that consist of an input layer, an output layer, and one or more hidden layers that extract useful information during learning and assign modifiable weighting coefficients to components of the input layers. In the first (forward) pass, weights assigned to the input units and the nodes in the hidden layers and between the nodes in the hidden layer and the output, determine the output. The output is compared with the target output. An error signal is then back propagated and the connection weights are adjusted correspondingly. During training, MLPs construct a multidimensional space, defined by the activation of the hidden nodes, so that the three classes (malignant, benign and normal tissue) are as separable as possible. The separating surface adapts to the data.

2.2.2 Probabilistic Neural Network

The probabilistic neural network (PNN) is a direct continuation of the work on Bayes classifiers. The PNN learns to approximate the *pdf* of the training examples [19].

More precisely, the PNN is interpreted as a function which approximates the probability density of the underlying example

The PNN consists of nodes allocated in three layers after the inputs:

- *pattern layer*: there is one pattern node for each training example. Each pattern node forms a product of the weight vector and the given example for classification, where the weights entering a node are from a particular example. After that, the product is passed through the activation function:

$$exp[\ (\ x^T w_{ki}\text{-}1\ )\ /\ \sigma^2\ ] \tag{6}$$

Where

- x: Data input
- W_k: Weight
- σ: Smothing adjust

- *summation layer*: each summation node receives the outputs from pattern nodes associated with a given class:

$$\Sigma_{i=1}^{Nk} \exp[\ (\ \mathbf{x}^T \mathbf{w}_{ki}\text{-}1\ )\ /\ \sigma^2\ ] \tag{7}$$

- *output layer*: the output nodes are binary neurons that produce the classification decision

$$\Sigma_{i=1}^{Nk} \exp[\ (\ \mathbf{x}^T \mathbf{w}_{ki}\text{-}1\ )\ /\ \sigma^2\ ] > \Sigma_{i=1}^{Nj} \exp[\ (\ \mathbf{x}^T \mathbf{w}_{kj}\text{-}1\ )\ /\ \sigma^2\ ] \tag{8}$$

2.2.3 Radial Basis Functions Neural Networks

Successful implementation of the Radial Basis Functions Neural Network (RBFNN) can be achieved using efficient supervised or unsupervised learning algorithms for an accurate estimation of the hidden layer [20]-[21].

In our implementation, the k-means unsupervised algorithm was used to estimate the hidden layer weights from a set of training data containing the features from malignant, benign and normal tissue. After the initial training and the estimation of the hidden layer weights, the weights in the output layer are computed using Wiener-filter, for example, by minimizing the mean square error (MSE) between the actual and the desired output over the set of samples.

The RBFNN have a faster learning rate and have been proved to provide excellent discrimination in many applications.

2.3 Selection of Most Significant Features

Our main objective is to identify the effectiveness of a feature or a combination of features when applied to a neural network. Thus, the choice of features to be extracted is important.

Forward selection is a method to find the "best" combination of features (variables) by starting with a single feature, and increasing the number of used features, step by step [22]. In this approach, one adds features to the model one at a time. At each step, each feature that is not already in the model is tested for inclusion in the model. The most significant of these feature is added to the model, so long as P-value is below some pre-selected level.

2.4 Evaluation of the Classification Method

Sensitivity and specificity are the most widely used statistics to describe a diagnostic test. Sensitivity is the proportion of true positives that are correctly identified by the test and is defined by ***S = TP/(TP+FN).*** Specificity is the proportion of true negatives that are correctly identified by the test and is defined by ***TN/(TN+FP).*** Where **FN** is false-negative, **FP** is false-positive, **TN** is true negative and **TP** is true positive diagnosis.

3 Experimental Results and Discussions

Here are describe the results obtained using the method proposed in the previous section.

3.1 Mammogram Database

The database used into this work is the *Mammographic Institute Society Analisys* (MIAS) [23]. The mammograms have a size of 1024 x 1024 pixels, and resolution of 200 micron. This database is composed of 332 mammograms of right and left breast, from 161 patients, where 53 were diagnosed as being malignant, 69 benign and 206 normal. The abnormalities are classified by the kind of found abnormality (calcification, circumscribed masses, architectural distortions asymmetries, and other ill-defined masses) .

This database contains a file lists the mammograms in the MIAS database and provides appropriate details, for example, the class of abnormality, xy image-coordinates of centre of abnormality, and approximate radius (in pixels) of a circle enclosing the abnormality.

From this database, we selected 100 abnormal (50 benign and 50 malignant mammograms) and 100 normal from each group, summing up 200 mammograms. To each mammogram, a ROI was manually selected, containing the lesion, in the case of the benign and malignant mammograms. The ROIs was found through of xy images coordinates of centre of abnormality, contained in file list of MIAS database . To the normal mammograms, was randomly selected the ROI. Only the pectoral muscle was not considered as a possible ROI, although tissue and fatty tissue were. If the tissues had different sizes, it was rescaled each ROI. Therefore, they were resized to 24x24 *pixels*. Figure 3 exemplifies the ROI selection of a mammogram diagnosed as benign, malignant and normal, respectively.

3.2 ICA Application

X of Equation 2 was represented using the chosen ROIs. The images with ROI were rescaled and transformed into a one-dimensional vector

$$P = P_x x P_y \tag{9}$$

where $\boldsymbol{P_x}$ is a rows and $\mathbf{P_y}$ is a colunns of $\boldsymbol{P}$ and $\boldsymbol{P}$ has dimension 1x 576.

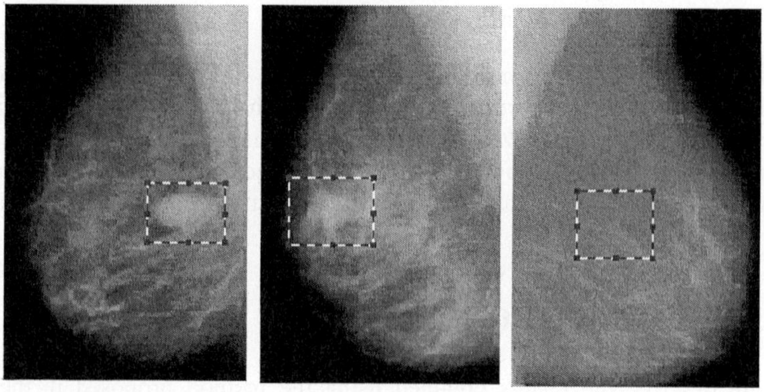

Fig. 3. Chosen region of interest (ROI) of mammograms diagnosed as benign (a), malignant (b) and normal (c)

Each sample represents one row of the mixture matrix. The matrix **X** is represented by the samples into the dimension of **P**, that is, 1x576. Thus, each row of the matrix **A** correspond to a ROI, and each column correspond to an attributed weight to a base image, i.e., an input parameter to the neural network [9].

Using the FastICA algorithm and the matrix *X*, we obtain the basis function matrix **A,** which contains the features of each sample.

Figure 4 exemplifies the basis image found using the basis functions of the malignants, benigns and normal ROIs, respectively. We can clearly observe the differences between the basis images of each kind. Thus, the basis functions of the benign tissue are different of those of the malignant tissue.

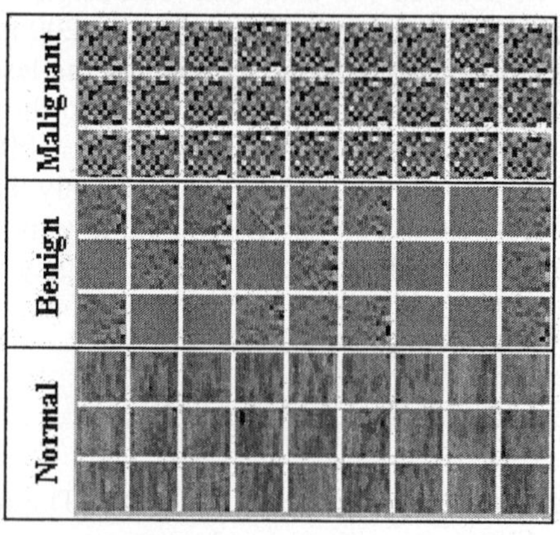

Fig. 4. Basis image sample produced from the ROIs basis functions for normal, benign and malignant tissue

3.3 Neural Networks

Using the *forward-selection* algorithm, basis functions were selected as being the most significant features. The chosen features (a_i) are the input to the Neural Network. For each Neural Networks (MLP, PNN, RBFNN) the algorithm selected the most significant features.

We carried out tests with different Neural Network architetures to find the bests MLP, PNN and RBF Neural Networks.

In order to carry out the tests, we divided a sample in 200 ROIs: 100 for training and 100 for tests.

3.4 Results

Table 1 shows the Neural Networks architecture, the performance of the application of the ICA technique with each Neural Network for discrimination tissues (ROI).

Table 1. Neural Networks architecture and classification of malignant, benign and normal ROI

N.Networks	Arquiteture	TP	TN	FP	FN	(%)		
						Specificity	Sensitivity	Accuracy
PNN	50:76-3:1	96	100	0	4	100	96	97.3
RBF	44:15-3:1	93	98	2	7	98	93	94.6
MLP	44:21:3	90	98	2	9	98	90.91	92.6

Based on the Table 1, the best results was obtained with Probabilistic Neural Networks. The PNN obtained a success rate of 97.3 % on discriminating malignant, benign and normal tissues. The found specificity was 100 % and the sensitivity, 96%. The PNN obtained 96 true positives diagnosis, 100 true negatives, 0 false positives and 4 false negatives.

4 Conclusion

The presented results demonstrate that Independent Component Analysis and Neural Networks is a useful tool to discriminate malignant, benign and normal tissues.

Furthermore, the Probabilistic Neural Network obtained the best performance, classifying those tissues, with a success rate of 97.3%, specificity of 100 % and sensitivity of 96%. It can decrease the number of unneeded biopsies and late cancer diagnosis.

Based on these results, we have observed that such features provide significant support to a more detailed clinical investigation, and the results were very encouraging when tissues were classified with ICA and Neural Networks.

Acknowledgements

To all my co-workers in the Laboratory for Biological Information Processing, specially Denner Guilhon, André Cavalcante and Fausto Lucena.

References

1. INCa, Internet site address: http://www.inca.gov.br/acessed in 04/05/2005.
2. U. Bick, M. Giger, R. Schmidt, R. Nishikawa, D. Wolverton and K. *Doi.Computer-* aided breast cancer detection in screening mammography. Digital Mammogr'9Chicago, *IL* (1996), pp. 97–103.
3. J. G. Elmore, C. K. Wells, C. H. Lee, D. H. Howard, and A. R. Feinstein, \Variability in radiologists' interpretations of mammograms," New England Journal of Medicine, vol. 331, no. 22, pp. 1493{1499, December 1994.
4. L. W. Bassett, V. P. Jackson, R. Jahan, Y. S. Fu, and R. H. Gold, Diagnosis of Diseases of the Breast. W. B. Saunders Company, 1997.
5. D. B. Kopans, The positive predictive value of mammography," American Journal of Roentgenology, vol. 158, no. 3, pp. 521{526, March 1993.
6. L. Tabar and P. B. Dean, Teaching Atlas of Mammography. Georg ThiemeVerlag, 2nd revised ed., 1985.
7. Nicholas Petrick, Berkman Sahiner, HeangPing Chan, Mark A. Helvie, Sophie Paquerault, and Lubomir M. Hadjiiski. Breast Cancer Detection: Evaluation of a Mass-Detection Algorithm for Computer-aided Diagnosis—Experience in 263 Patients· Radiology 2002;224:217-224.
8. Campanini Renato, Bazzani Armando, et al. A novel approach to mass detection in digital mammography based on Support Vector Machines (SVM). In proceedings of the 6th International workshop in digital Mammography (IWDM), pages 399-401, Bremem, Germany, 2002, Springer Verlag.
9. Christoyianni I., Koutras A., Kokkinakis G., "Computer aided diagnosis of breast cancer in digitized mammograms", *Comp. Med. Imag. & Graph.*, 26:309-319, 2002.
10. B. Arons, A review of cocktail party, Cambridge, MA: MIT laboratory, 1990
11. R. Vigário, Extraction of ocular artifacts form ecg using independent components analysis, Eletroenceph. Clin. Neurophysiol., 103 (3) : 395-404, 1997
12. R.vigário. V. Jousmaki, M. Hamalaien R. Hari, and E. Oja, Independent component analysis for identification of artifacts in magnetoencephalographic recordings, In andvances in neural information processing 10 (Proc. NIPS'97), 229-235, Cambridge, Ma, MIT press, 1998
13. S. Makeig, A. J. Bell, T-P. Jung, and T.J. Sejnowski, Indepent component analysis of electroencephalographic data, In Advances in neural information processing systems 8, 145-151. MIT press, 1996.
14. Hyvärinen, A., J. Karhunen, and E. Oja, Independent Component Analysis, John Wiley & Sons, New York, 2001.
15. A. Hyvärinen and E. Oja. A fast fixed-point algorithm for independent component analysis. Neural Computation, 9(7):1483-1492, 1997.

16. A. Hyvärinen. A family of fixed-point algorithms for independent component analysis. In *Proc. IEEE Int. Conf. on Acoustics, Speech and Signal Processing (ICASSP'97)*, pages 3917-3920, Munich, Germany, 1997.
17. A. Hyvärinen. Fast and robust fixed-point algorithms for independent component analysis. *IEEE Trans. on Neural Networks*, 1999.
18. Duda, R.O., Hart, P.E.: Pattern Classification and Scene Analysis. WileyInterscience Publication, New York (1973)
19. Bishop, C.M.: Neural Networks for Pattern Recognition. Oxford UniversityPress, New York (1999)
20. Christoyianni I, Dermatas E, Kokkinakis G. Fast detection of masses in computer-aided mammography. IEEE Signal Process Mag 2000; 17(1):54–64.
21. Christoyianni I, Dermatas E, Kokkinakis G. Neural classification of abnormal tissue in digital mammography using statistical features of the texture. IEEE Int Conf Electron, Circuits Syst 1999;1:117–20.
22. Fukunaga, K.: Introduction to Statistical Pattern Recognition. 2 edn. AcademicPress, London (1990)
23. J Suckling *et al* (1994): The Mammographic Image Analysis Society Digital Mammogram Database Exerpta Medica. International Congress Series 1069 pp375-378.

Automatic Texture Segmentation Based on Wavelet-Domain Hidden Markov Tree

Qiang Sun, Biao Hou, and Li-cheng Jiao

Institute of Intelligent Information Processing, Xidian University,
710071 Xi'an, China
qsun@mail.xidian.edu.cn

Abstract. An automatic texture segmentation approach is presented in this paper, in which wavelet-domain hidden Markov tree (WD-HMT) model is exploited to characterize the texture features of an image, an effective cluster validity index, the ratio of the overlap degree to the separation one between different fuzzy clusters, is used to determine the true number of the textures within an image by solving the minimum of this index in terms of different number of clusters, and the possibilistic C-means (PCM) clustering is performed to extract the training sample data from different textures. In this way, unsupervised segmentation is changed into self-supervised one, and the well-known HMTseg algorithm in the WD-HMT framework is eventually used to produce the final segmentation results, consequently automatic segmentation process is completed. This new approach is applied to segment a variety of composite textured images into distinct homogeneous regions with satisfactory segmentation results demonstrated. Real-world images are also segmented to further justify our approach.

1 Introduction

Image segmentation is an important and hard problem in image analysis. Among others, texture plays an important part in low level image analysis. The image segmentation based on textural information is termed as texture segmentation, which involves the identification of non-overlapping homogeneous regions in an image.

Typically, the first step of texture segmentation is texture feature characterization, which has been discussed through various approaches by far. In this paper, wavelet-domain hidden Markov tree (WD-HMT) model is exploited to characterize texture features. The WD-HMT model [1], proposed first by Crouse *et al.* as a type of wavelet-domain statistical signal models to characterize signals through capturing the inter-scale dependencies of wavelet coefficients, has gained more and more attention from image processing and analysis communities due to its effectiveness in performing image denoising [2, 3], segmentation [4 ,5, 6], texture classification [6], texture synthesis [6] and texture retrieval [7] *etc.*.

Based on the WD-HMT model, one supervised image segmentation algorithm, HMTseg [4], was presented by Choi *et al.* to solve the image segmentation problem. Later, HMTseg algorithm was improved to apply to synthetic aperture radar (SAR)

M. Lazo and A. Sanfeliu (Eds.): CIARP 2005, LNCS 3773, pp. 470–480, 2005.

image segmentation where the "truncated" HMT model [8] was proposed to reduce the effect of speckle present at fine scales.

More recently, a variety of unsupervised segmentation algorithms [9, 10, 11, 12] have been proposed one after another to extend the supervised algorithm [2] to the unsupervised one based on WD-HMT models. Zhen [9] integrated the parameter estimation and classification into one by using one multi-scale Expectation Maximization (EM) algorithm to segment SAR images on the coarse scales. In [10], Song exploited HMT-3S model [6] and the joint multi-context and multi-scale (JMCMS) approach [5] to give another unsupervised segmentation algorithm in which K-means clustering was adopted to extract the appropriate training samples for the unknown textures based on the likelihood disparity of HMT-3S model. Subsequently, Sun [11] utilized an effective soft clustering algorithm, possibilistic C-means (PCM) clustering, to further improve the unsupervised segmentation performance. Alternatively, Xu [12] has also given one unsupervised algorithm, where the dissimilarity between image blocks was measured by the Kullback-Leibler distance (KLD) between different WD-HMT models, followed by a hierarchical clustering of the image blocks at the selected scale. It should be noted that all the unsupervised segmentation algorithms above are implemented under the assumption that the number of the textures in an image is provided *a priori*, which is unpractical for automatically segmenting images in many particular application areas, such as the content-based image retrieval.

In this paper, we present an automatic texture segmentation approach based on the WD-HMT model [1]. Firstly, one global WD-HMT model is trained with the special EM algorithm in [1] with the whole image to be segmented as one texture. This model contains information from all distinct regions, and the different goodness of fit between the global model and local texture regions exists. Secondly, the true number of textures is obtained by finding the minimum of index $v_{os}(c,U)$ [13] over $c = 2,\cdots,C_{\max}$ for the likelihood results of image blocks. Thirdly, PCM clustering [14] is used to extract the training sample data based on the true number of textures. Finally, WD-HMT models for different textures are re-trained with the extracted sample data, and the supervised procedures of HMTseg [4] are performed to achieve the final results with one adaptive context based fusion scheme.

The paper is organized as follows. In Section 2, WT-HMT model is briefly reviewed. Supervised Bayesian image segmentation algorithm, HMTseg, is outlined in Section 3. Automatic segmentation approach is detailed with three main procedures in Section 4. Experimental results on composite and real images are demonstrated in Section 5. Section 6 concludes this paper.

2 Wavelet-Domain Hidden Markov Tree Model

It is well known that the discrete wavelet transform (DWT) is an effective multi-scale image analysis tool due to its intrinsic multi-resolution analysis (MRA) characteristics, which can represent different singularity contents of an image at different scales and subbands. In Fig.1 (a), one quad-tree structure of wavelet coefficients is shown, which demonstrates the dependencies of wavelet coefficients at three subbands, *HL*, *LH*, and *HH*.

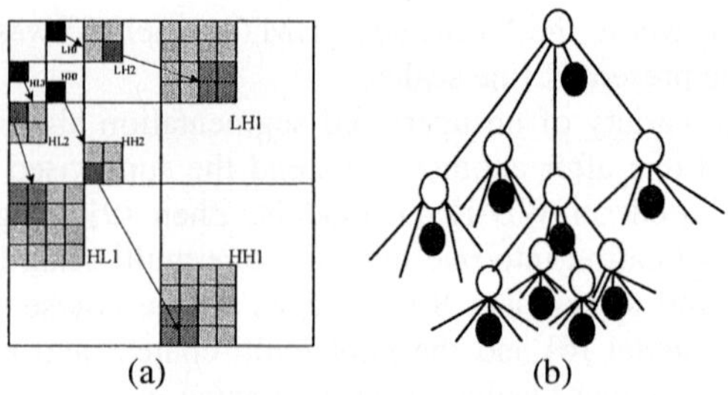

Fig. 1. (a) Quadtree structure of 2-D discrete wavelet transforms. (b) 2-D wavelet-domain hidden Markov tree model for one subband. Each wavelet coefficient (black node) is modeled as a Gaussian mixture model by a hidden state variable (white node)

For multi-scale singularity characterization, one statistical model, hidden Markov tree (HMT) model [1], was proposed to model this structure. The HMT is a multidimensional Gaussian mixture model (GMM) that applies tree-structured Markov chains across scales to capture inter-scale dependencies of wavelet coefficients [6], as shown in Fig.1 (b). In this tree-structured probabilistic model, each wavelet coefficient W is associated with a *hidden* state variable S, which decides whether it is "large" or "small". The marginal density of each coefficient is then modeled as one two-density GMM: one large-variance Gaussian for the large state and one small-variance Gaussian for the small one. Thus, GMM can closely fit the non-Gaussian marginal statistics of wavelet coefficient.

Grouping the HMT model parameters, i.e. state probabilities for the root nodes of different quad-trees, state transition probabilities and variances for two mixtured Gaussians, into one vector $\mathbf{\Theta}$, the HMT can be considered as one high-dimensional yet highly structured Gaussian mixture model $f(W|\mathbf{\Theta})$ that approximates the joint probability density function (pdf) of wavelet coefficients W. For each wavelet coefficient, the overall pdf $f(w)$ can be expressed as

$$f_W(w) = \sum_{m=1}^{M} p_S(m) f_{W|S}(w|S=m), \tag{1}$$

where, M is the number of states and S state variable. The model parameters in $\mathbf{\Theta}$ are estimated by the EM algorithm in [1].

It should be noted that HMT model has one nesting structure that corresponds to multi-scale representation of an image, as shown in Fig. 2. Each subtree of the HMT is also an HMT, with the HMT subtree rooted at node i modeling the statistical characteristics of the wavelet coefficients corresponding to the dyadic square $\boldsymbol{d}_i$ in the original image.

3 Bayesian Image Segmentation Using WD-HMT

One Bayesian segmentation algorithm, HMTseg [4], was proposed to implement supervised segmentation in which the WD-HMT model [1] is exploited to characterize

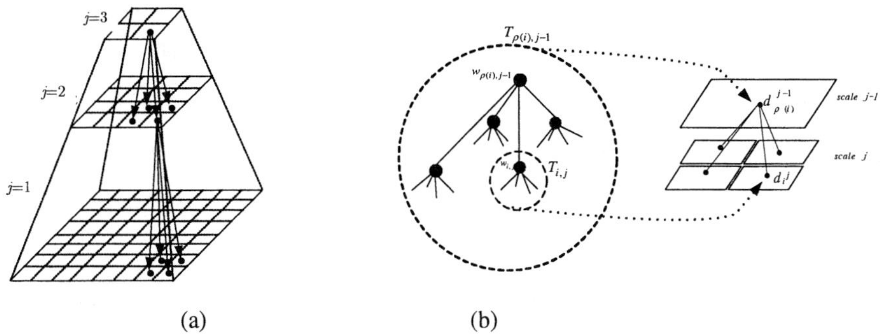

Fig. 2. Multi scale representation of an image; (b) Correspondence of quad-tree structure of wavelet coefficients with multi-scale representation of an image

texture features and context labeling tree is built to capture the dependencies of the multi-scale class labels.

In multi-scale segmentation framework, the dyadic image squares at different scales can be obtained by recursively dividing an image into four equal sub-images. HMTseg can capture the features of these dyadic squares by the WD-HMT model. Moreover, contextual information on each dyadic square is described by one vector $\boldsymbol{v}^j$, which is derived from the labels of dyadic squares at its parent scale. Denote a dyadic square and its class label by d_i^j and c_i^j respectively, and j is the scale index. In HMTseg [], each context vector $\boldsymbol{v}_i^j$ consists of two entries, the value of the class label of the parent square and the majority vote of the class labels of the parent plus its eight neighbors.

The HMTseg algorithm relies on three separate tree structures: the wavelet transform quad-tree, the HMT, and a labeling tree [4]. As for a complete procedure, it includes three essential ingredients, i.e. HMT model training, multi-scale likelihood computation, and fusion of multi-scale maximum likelihood (ML) raw segmentations. The three main steps are summarized as follows. We refer the interested readers to Section IV in [4] to further get the knowledge on the HMTseg algorithm.

1) Train WD-HMT models for each texture using their homogeneous training images. Furthermore, Gaussian mixture is fit to the pixel values for each texture and the likelihood of each pixel is calculated to obtain the pixel-level segmentation,.

2) Calculate the likelihood of each dyadic image square d_i^j at each scale. The conditional likelihoods $f(d_i^j | c_i^j)$ for each d_i^j are obtained in this step, on which ML raw segmentation results are achieved based.

3) Fuse multi-scale likelihoods using context labeling tree to give the multi-scale maximal *a posterior* (MAP) classification. Choose a certain suitable starting scale J such that a reliable raw segmentation can be obtained at this scale. The contextual vector $\boldsymbol{v}^{J-1}$ is calculated from the class label set $\boldsymbol{c}^J$ at the J-th scale. Also, the EM algorithm [4] for context labeling tree is utilized to find $p(c_i^{J-1} | v_i^{J-1})$ by maximizing

the likelihood of the image given the contextual vector $\boldsymbol{v}^{J-1}$. In this step, each iteration updates the contextual posterior distribution $p(c_i \mid d_i, \boldsymbol{v}_i)$. When the process of iteration converges, determine c_i which maximizes the probability $p(c_i \mid d_i, \boldsymbol{v}_i)$. The fusion is repeated in next finer scale with the contextual vector $\boldsymbol{v}^{J-2}$ computed from the label set $\boldsymbol{c}^{J-1}$ at scale $J-1$. Continue the fusion process across scales until the finest scale is reached.

4 Automatic Segmentation

Automatic image segmentation using texture information means identifying all the non-overlapping homogenous regions in an image with the texture features and the number of textures unavailable. Our proposed segmentation method is made up of three steps: the determination of the number of textures utilizing v_{os} index in [13], the extraction of training sample data from different textures via the PCM clustering [14] and the supervised segmentation algorithm, HMTseg [4].

4.1 Determining the Number of Texture Categories

In this paper, the true number of textures in an image is not assumed a priori, which is different from the segmentation methods [9, 10, 11, 12], but determined using the likelihood values of image blocks at a certain suitable scale J through an effective cluster validity index for the fuzzy c-means (FCM) algorithm, v_{os} index in [13], which exploits an overlap measure and a separation measure between clusters to correctly recognize the optimal cluster number of a given data set.

Let $X = \{x_1, x_2, \cdots, x_n\}$ denote a pattern set, and $x_i = [x_{i1}, x_{i2}, \cdots, x_{im}]^T$ represent the m features of the ith sample. The FCM algorithm classifies the collection X of pattern data into c homogeneous groups represented as fuzzy sets $(\tilde{F}_i, i = 1, \cdots, c)$. The objective of FCM is to obtain the fuzzy c-partition in terms of both the data set X and the number c of clusters by minimizing the following function

$$J_m(U,V) = \sum_{i=1}^{c}\sum_{j=1}^{n} u_{ij}^m \left\|x_j - v_i\right\|^2, \quad subject\ to \sum_{i=1}^{c} u_{ij} = 1 \quad for\ all \quad j. \tag{2}$$

In (2), $V = (v_1, \cdots, v_c)$ is a c-tuple of prototypes, i.e. a vector of cluster centroids of the fuzzy cluster $(\tilde{F}_1, \tilde{F}_2, \cdots, \tilde{F}_c)$, n is the total number of feature vectors, c is the number of classes, and $U = \left[u_{ij}\right]$ is a $c \times n$ matrix, called fuzzy partition matrix. Here, u_{ij} is the membership degree of the feature point x_j in the fuzzy cluster $\tilde{F}_i$ and can be denoted as $\mu_{\tilde{F}i}(x_j)$, and $m \in [1, \infty)$ is a weighting exponent, called the fuzzier, typically taken as 2.

The v_{os} index consists of two elements, an overlap measure $Overlap(c,U)$ and a separation one $Sep(c,U)$. The former measure indicates the degree of overlap between fuzzy clusters and can be obtained by calculating an inter-cluster overlap. This measure is defined as

$$Overlap(c,U) = \frac{2}{c(c-1)} \sum_{p=1}^{c-1} \sum_{q=p+1}^{c} \sum_{\mu \in [0.1,0.5]} \sum_{j=1}^{n} \delta(xj, \mu : \tilde{F}_p, \tilde{F}_q) \times w(x_j) , \tag{3}$$

where $\delta(x_j, \mu : \tilde{F}_p, \tilde{F}_q) = \begin{cases} 1 & \text{if } (\mu_{\tilde{F}_p}(x_j) \geq \mu) \text{ and } (\mu_{\tilde{F}_q}(x_j) \geq \mu) \\ 0 & \text{otherwise} \end{cases}$ =, and $w(x_j)$ is empirically given a value of 0.1($\mu_{\tilde{F}i}(x_j) \geq 0.8$), 0.4($0.7 \leq \mu_{\tilde{F}i}(x_j) \leq 0.8$), 0.7($0.6 \leq \mu_{\tilde{F}i}(x_j) \leq 0.7$), 0 otherwise for any $\tilde{F}_i$. A small value of $Overlap(c,U)$ implies a well-classified fuzzy c-partition. Whereas, the latter measure $Sep(c,U)$ indicates the distance between fuzzy clusters and is defined as

$$Sep(c,U) = 1 - \underbrace{\min}_{p \neq q} \left[\underbrace{\max}_{x \in X} \min(\mu_{\tilde{F}_p}(x), \mu_{\tilde{F}_q}(x)) \right] . \tag{4}$$

A large value of $Sep(c,U)$ could tell one a well-separated fuzzy c-partition.

Then, the $v_{os}(c,U)$ index is expressed as the ratio of the normalized overlap measure to the separation one, i.e.

$$v_{os}(c,U) = \frac{Overlap(c,U) \Big/ \underbrace{\max}_{c} Overlap(c,U)}{Sep(c,U) \Big/ \underbrace{\max}_{c} Sep(c,U)} . \tag{5}$$

A small value of $v_{os}(c,U)$ indicates a partition in which the clusters are overlapped to a less degree and more separated from each other. So, the optimal value of c can be determined by minimizing $v_{os}(c,U)$ over $c = 2, \cdots, C_{\max}$.

In this paper, the data set to be clustered is the likelihood values of image blocks. The true number of textures can be obtained by finding the minimum of $v_{os}(c,U)$ for the likelihood results.

4.2 Extraction of Sample Data from Different Textures

The key step for a fully unsupervised segmentation is the extraction of sample data for training different textures to obtain their HMT models used for the following supervised procedure. The input is the true number of textures in an image obtained by the cluster validity index $v_{os}(c,U)$ above. Herein, an effective soft clustering algorithm, PCM clustering [14], is exploited to extract the sample data of different textures. The objective function of the algorithm is formulated as

$$J_m(U,V) = \sum_{k=1}^{N} \sum_{l \in \Gamma_k} (u_{ij})^m \left\| f(y_{k,l}^{(J)} | \Theta) - f(y_k^{(J)} | \Theta) \right\|^2 + \sum_{k=1}^{N} \eta_i \sum_{l \in \Gamma_k} (1 - u_{ij})^m , \tag{6}$$

where U,V and m have the same meanings as those in (2), η_i is a certain positive number, and $f(y_k^{(J)}|\Theta)$ is the likelihood mean of class k at the suitable scale J, $f(y_{k,l}^{(J)}|\Theta)$ the likelihood of an image block l regarding the class k. The updated equation of u_{ij} is

$$u_{ij} = \frac{1}{1+\left(\frac{\left\| f(y_{k,l}^{(J)}|\Theta) - f(y_k^{(J)}|\Theta)\right\|^2}{\eta_i}\right)^{\frac{1}{m-1}}}, \tag{7}$$

where η_i is defined as

$$\eta_i = \frac{\sum_{j=1}^{N} u_{ij}^m \left\| f(y_{k,l}^{(J)}|\Theta) - f(y_k^{(J)}|\Theta)\right\|^2}{\sum_{j=1}^{N} u_{ij}^m}. \tag{8}$$

PCM clustering differs from the K-means and FCM clustering algorithms since the membership of one sample in a cluster is independent of all other clusters in the algorithm. In this clustering, the resulting partition of data can be interpreted as degrees of possibility of the points belonging to the classes, i.e., the compatibilities of the points with the class prototypes [14]. Generally, more reliable and stable clustering results can be obtained with this algorithm.

The complete procedure for the PCM algorithm to implement the extraction of image sample data is listed in [14].

4.3 Adaptive Context-Based Fusion of Multi-scale Segmentation

Effective modeling of contexts for each dyadic square $\boldsymbol{d}_i$ is crucial to effectively fuse the raw segmentations from coarse scale to fine one to obtain a satisfactory result in the multi-scale fusion step. In the original HMTseg method [4], the context $\boldsymbol{v}_i^j$ is specified as a vector of two entries consisting of the value of class label $C_{\rho(i)}$ of the parent square and the majority vote of the class labels of the parent plus its eight neighbors, as illustrated in Fig.3 (a). This simplified context is typically effective for images consisting of separate large homogeneous textures since it focuses on the information of class labels at coarse scales. However, the segmentation results might be unsatisfactory when complicated structures occur in an image, such as most real-world images. In [5], Fan proposed a joint multi-context and multi-scale (JMCMS) approach to Bayesian image segmentation using WD-HMT models, where three contexts (context-2, context-3 and context-5 shown in Fig. 3) are exploited sequentially to fuse the raw segmentation results across scale. However, the computation cost is too expensive, which renders this approach unpractical in real-time image segmentation applications. Herein, one adaptive context model, as shown in Fig. 3(d), is given to fully incorporate both the information of the class labels at the coarse scale and the information at the fine scale to further improve the segmentation performance. In this context model, the context vector for each image block contains two entries of which the first element V1 is defined in the same way with [4], whereas the other one V2 is obtained by the compromise between the coarse scale and fine scale. Generally speaking, if the dominant label $\Omega 1$ at the coarse scale is identical with $\Omega 2$ at the fine scale, V2 is established like context-2; otherwise, V2 is assigned $\Omega 2$. In this way, the new context could adaptively make a trade-off between the parent-scale ML classification results and those at the child scale. It is expected that better segmentation results could be achieved.

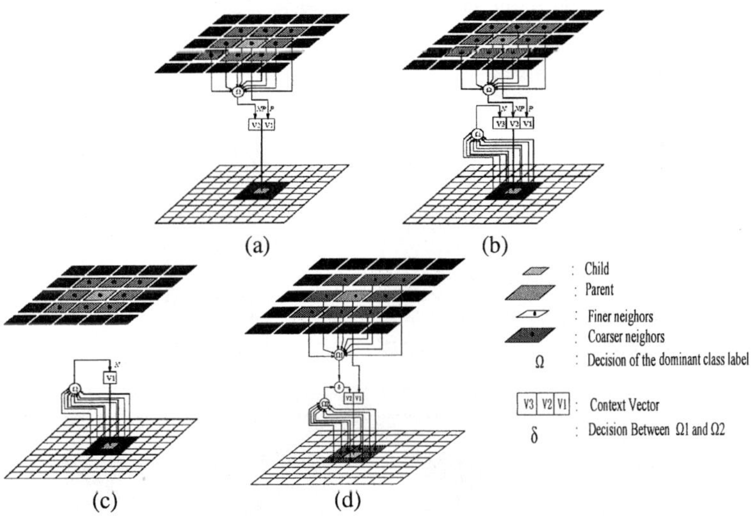

Fig. 3. Context models for inter-scale raw segmentation fusion. (a) Context-2 in [2]; (b) Context 3 in [11]; (c) Context 5 in [11]; (b) Context proposed.

5 Experimental Results

We testified our approach on composite texture images with the size of 256×256 pixels, which are made up of the original textures from Brodatz album [15]. Here, four composite textured images, consisting of 2, 3, 4 and 5 classes of homogeneous textures respectively, are shown in Fig. 4.

Originally, all the textured images are decomposed into four levels by discrete wavelet transform (DWT). The true number of the textures is determined by the disparity of the likelihoods for different image blocks using the cluster validity index $v_{os}(c,U)$ at the suitable, $J=4$ here, which is the coarsest scale. The number of cluster goes through from 2 to 10 ($C_{\max}$), and the optimal (true) number of the textures in an image is found by evaluating the minimum of $v_{os}(c,U)$. Then, the PCM clustering of the model likelihoods is conducted at the scale J .

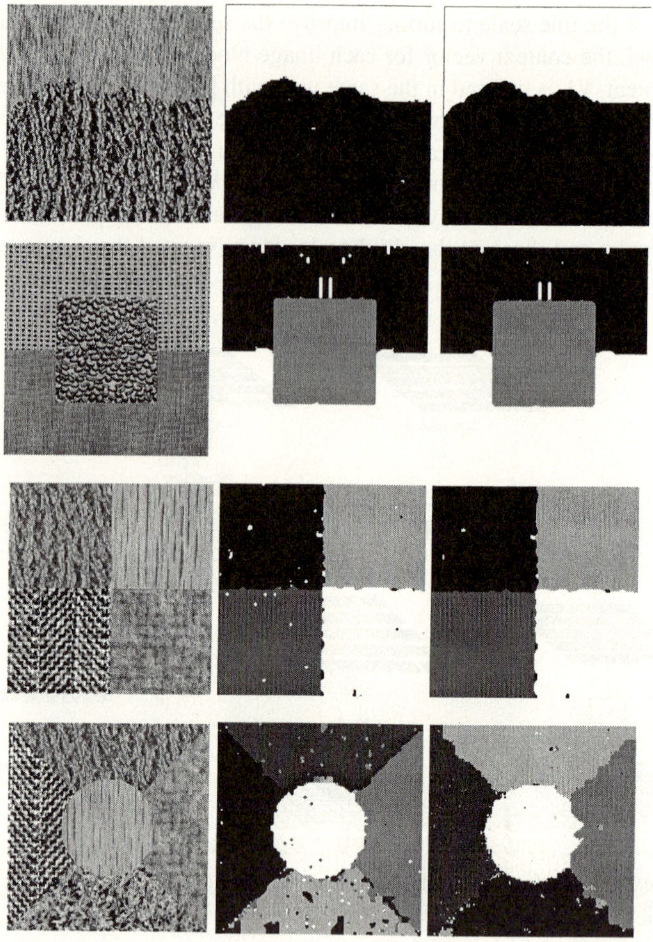

Fig. 4. Four composite texture images and their segmentation results with the proposed approach (the second column) and supervised HMTseg algorithm [4] (the third row)

In Table 1, the values of $v_{os}(c,U)$ in terms of different c for the four composite textured images in Fig. 4 are tabulated, of which the minimum of $v_{os}(c,U)$ is marked with boldface. It can be seen that all the true number of textures in these images have been correctly determined. Moreover, we also applied our method to other composite textures with a return of over 70% correctly detected number of textures obtained.

Fig. 4 also demonstrates the final segmentation results for the four composite textures with the proposed approach and the supervised HMTseg algorithm in [4]. The results demonstrate that the segmentation performance of our approach is basically satisfactory and favorably compares with the results with HMTseg. The rate of misclassified pixels for the four images is given in Table 1. Our approach gives the error percentage of below 8% for all tested composite textured images, which is basically feasible for practical applications. Meanwhile, the segmentation results for real-world images are shown in Fig. 5 with similar performances with the HMTseg algorithm [4].

Table 1. Values of $v_{os}(c,U)$ in terms of different c for the four composite textured images in Fig. 4 and their rate of misclassified pixels

Image	Number of textures	Values of $v_{os}(c,U)$ for c=2,...,10	Rate of misclassified pixels
Composite-2	2	**0.0931(2)**,0.1257(3),0.1969(4), 0.3150(5),0.2500(6),0.3950(7), 0.6881(8),1.2424(9),1.0168(10)	0.59%
Composite-3	3	1.9374(2),**0.0308(3)**,0.3746(4), 0.2774(5),0.1936(6),0.1184(7), 0.0908(8),0.0659(9),0.0586(10)	4.65%
Composite-4	4	1.7898(2), 1.0708(3), **0.0623(4)**, 0.1634(5), 0.1089(6), 0.1226(7), 0.1049(8), 0.0770(9) 0.0996(10)	3.52%
Composite-5	5	1.9502(2),0.0460(3),0.0131(4), **0.0111(5)**,0.0642(6),0.0353(7), 0.0231(8),0.0659(9),0.0868 (10)	6.79%

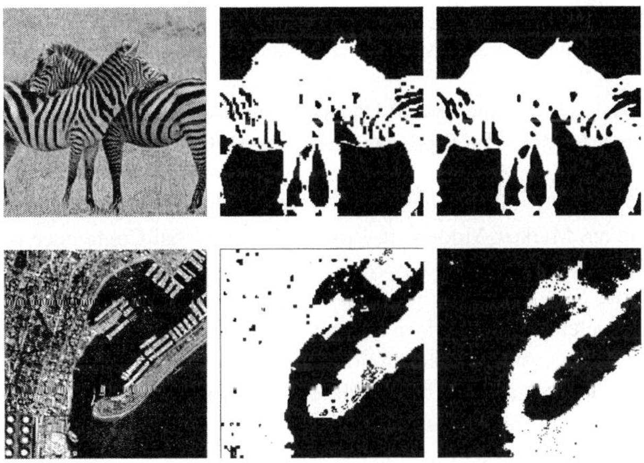

Fig. 5. Real-world images (Zebra and aerial-photo images) and their segmentation results with the proposed approach (the second column) and the HMTseg algorithm [4] (the third row)

6 Conclusions

In this paper, an automatic texture segmentation is developed by characterizing the texture features using WD-HMT model, determining the number of textures with the cluster validity index v_{os}, and extracting the sample data from different textures by means of PCM clustering. Experimental results demonstrated that the proposed method can detect correctly the number of textures and provide good segmentation results on textured images. The further work is concerned with the use of more accurate statistical model describing texture feature, such as HMT-3S model [6].

References

1. Crouse, M.S., Nowak, R.D., Baraniuk, R.G.: Wavelet-Based Signal Processing Using Hidden Markov Models. IEEE Trans. on Signal Processing. 46 (1998) 886–902
2. Romberg J.K., Choi, H., Baraniuk, R.G.: Bayesian Tree-structured Image Modeling Using Wavelet-Domain Hidden Markov Models. IEEE Trans. on Image Processing. 10 (2001) 1056–1068
3. Fan, G.L., Xia, X.G.: Image Denoising Using Local Contextual Hidden Markov Model in the Wavelet Domain. IEEE Signal Processing Letters. 8 (2001) 125–128
4. Choi, H., Baraniuk, R.G.: Multi-scale Image Segmentation Using Wavelet-Domain Hidden Markov Models. IEEE Trans. on Image Processing. 10 (2001) 1309–1321
5. Fan, G.L., Xia, X.G.: A Joint Multi-Context and Multi-Scale Approach to Bayesian Image Segmentation. IEEE Trans. on Geoscience and Remote Sensing. 39 (2001) 2680–2688
6. Fan, G.L., Xia, X.G.: Wavelet-Based Texture Analysis and Synthesis Using Hidden Markov Models. IEEE Trans. on Circuits and Systems. 50 (2003) 106–120
7. Do, M.N., Vetterli, M.: Rotation Invariant Texture Characterization and Retrieval Using Steerable Wavelet-Domain Hidden Markov Models. IEEE Trans. on Multimedia. 4 (2002) 517–527
8. Venkatachalam, V. , Choi, H. , Baraniuk, R.G.: Multi-scale SAR Image Segmentation Using Wavelet-Domain Hidden Markov Tree Models. In Proc. of SPIE, 4053 (2000) 1605–1611
9. Zhen, Y., Lu, C.C.: Wavelet-Based Unsupervised SAR Image Segmentation Using Hidden Markov Tree Models. In Proc. of International Conference on Pattern Recognition. 2(2002) 729–732
10. Song, X.M., Fan, G.L.: Unsupervised Bayesian Image Segmentation Using Wavelet-Domain Hidden Markov Models. In Proc. of International Conference on Image Processing. 2 (2003) 423–426
11. Sun, Q., Gou, S.P., Jiao, L.C.: A New Approach to Unsupervised Image Segmentation Based on Wavelet-Domain Hidden Markov Tree Models. In Proc. of International Conference on Image Analysis and Recognition. 3211 (2004) 41–48
12. Xu, Q., Yang, J., Ding, S.Y.: Unsupervised Multi-scale Image Segmentation Using Wavelet Domain Hidden Markov Tree. In Proc. of the 8th Pacific Rim International Conferences on Artificial Intelligence. 3157 (2004) 797–804
13. Kim, D.W., Lee, K.H., Lee, D.: On Cluster Validity Index for Estimation of the Optimal Number of Fuzzy Clusters. Pattern Recognition. 37 (2004) 2009–2025
14. 14.Krishnapuram, R., Killer, J.M.: A Possibilistic Approach to Clustering. IEEE Trans. on Fuzzy System. 1 (1993) 98–110
15. Brodatz, P.: Textures: A Photographic Album for Artists & Designers. Dover Publications, Inc., New York, 1966

Reward-Punishment Editing for Mixed Data*

Raúl Rodríguez-Colín, J.A. Carrasco-Ochoa, and J.Fco. Martínez-Trinidad

National Institute for Astrophysics, Optics and Electronics,
Luis Enrique Erro No. 1 Sta. Ma. Tonantzintla, Puebla, México C. P. 72840
{raulrc, ariel, fmartine}@inaoep.mx

Abstract. The KNN rule has been widely used in many pattern recognition problems, but it is sensible to noisy data within the training set, therefore, several sample edition methods have been developed in order to solve this problem. A. Franco, D. Maltoni and L. Nanni proposed the Reward-Punishment Editing method in 2004 for editing numerical databases, but it has the problem that the selected prototypes could belong neither to the sample nor to the universe. In this work, we propose a modification based on selecting the prototypes from the training set. To do this selection, we propose the use of the Fuzzy C-means algorithm for mixed data and the KNN rule with similarity functions. Tests with different databases were made and the results were compared against the original Reward-Punishment Editing and the whole set (without any edition).

1 Introduction

The k-nearest neighbor rule (KNN) has been widely used in many pattern recognition problems. Given a set of n training objects, when a new object is going to be classified, the KNN rule identifies the k nearest neighbors in the training set and the new object is labeled with the most frequent class among the k nearest neighbors.

However, some of the data in the training set do not provide useful information to classify new objects; therefore, it is necessary to edit the sample in order to get a better training set which would contribute to obtain better classification rates. In the sample edition area, several methods have been developed [1-3].

The Reward-Punishment Editing method (R-P Editing) is based on two selection criteria: A local criterion rewards each pattern that contributes to classify its neighbors correctly (using the KNN rule), and punish the others; the second criterion rewards each pattern that is classified correctly (using the KNN rule) with a set of prototypes extracted from the training set. Based on these criteria, a weight is assigned to each pattern in the training set. If the weight is smaller than a predefined threshold, the pattern is eliminated from the training set.

In order to select prototypes, the Reward-Punishment Editing method uses the Fuzzy C-means algorithm. This does not guarantee that the selected prototypes belong to the sample, because the prototypes in the classical Fuzzy C-means are computed as the mean of the cluster. Therefore, we propose to use the Fuzzy C-means for mixed

* This work was financially supported by CONACyT (Mexico) through the project J38707-A.

M. Lazo and A. Sanfeliu (Eds.): CIARP 2005, LNCS 3773, pp. 481 – 488, 2005.

data, which guarantees that the selected prototypes belong to the sample. In addition, using the KNN rule with similarity functions allows working with object descriptions through qualitative and quantitative features.

This paper is organized as follows: in section 2 a description of the most similar neighbor method (KNN with similarity functions) is presented, in section 3 the Fuzzy C-means algorithm for mixed data is described, in section 4 the R-P Editing for mixed data algorithm is introduced, in section 5 the obtained results are reported. Finally, in section 6 some conclusions are given.

2 The Most Similar Neighbor

When we talk about the KNN rule with similarity functions, we are talking about the k-most similar neighbor (K-MSN). For that reason, we have to define a similarity comparison function for comparing feature values and establishing its similarity moreover, it is needed to define a similarity function for comparing objects in the data set.

Let us consider a set of n objects $\{O_1,O_2,\ldots,O_n\}$, each object in this set is described by a set $R = \{x_1,\ldots,x_m\}$ of features. Each feature x_i takes values in a set D_i, $x_i(O) \in D_i$, i=1,...,m. Thus, features could be qualitative or quantitative.

For each feature x_i, i=1,...,m, we define a comparison function C_i:D_i×$D_i \rightarrow L_i$ with i=1,2,…,m. where L_i is a totally ordered set such that C_i gives us the similarity between two values of the feature x_i, for i=1,…,m.

Based on the C_i it is possible define a similarity function between objects.

Let Γ: $(D_1 \times \ldots \times D_m)^2 \rightarrow [0,1]$ be a similarity function. $\Gamma(O_j,O_k)$ gives the similarity between O_j and O_k, and satisfies:

$\Gamma(O_j,O_k) \in [0,1]$ for $1 \le j \le n$, $1 \le k \le n$;
$\Gamma(O_j,O_j) = 1$for $1 \le j \le n$;
$\Gamma(O_j,O_k) = \Gamma(O_k,O_j)$for $1 \le j \le n$, $1 \le k \le n$;
$\Gamma(O_i,O_j) > \Gamma(O_i,O_k)$means that O_i is more similar to O_j than to O_k

In this work, we used the following similarity functions.

$$\Gamma(O_i,O_j) = \frac{\left|\left\{x \in R \wedge C\left(x(O_i),x(O_j)\right)=1\ \right\}\right|}{m} \tag{1}$$

Where the comparison functions used in this work are:
For qualitative data:

$$C(x(O_i),x(O_j)) = \begin{cases} 1 & \text{if } x(O_i) = x(O_j) \\ 0 & \text{otherwise} \end{cases} \tag{2}$$

For quantitative data:

$$C(x(O_i),x(O_j)) = \begin{cases} 1 & \text{if} \left| x(O_i) - x(O_j) \right| < \varepsilon \\ 0 & \text{otherwise} \end{cases} \tag{3}$$

The value for ε is introduced by the user based on the data set.

Based on the definitions described above, we can work on databases with numerical information, described in terms of qualitative and quantitative features.

The K-MSN is similar to the KNN rule, but the K-MSN identifies the k most similar neighbors of the new object in the training set, after that, the new object is labeled with the most frequent class among the k most similar neighbors.

3 Fuzzy C-means for Mixed Data

The use of Fuzzy C-means for mixed data allows working with object descriptions in terms of qualitative and quantitative features.

The objective is to obtain fuzzy clusters with the characteristic that the similarity among the objects that belong to the same cluster is high, and at the same time, the similarity among different clusters is low.

In order to obtain this type of clusters, given a group of objects to classify, the Fuzzy C-means for mixed data algorithm randomly selects c objects, which will be the initial representative objects (centers) of the clusters. With the representative objects, the algorithm classifies the rest of the objects in the dataset. After this classification, it calculates the new representative objects. This procedure is repeated until we obtain the same representative objects in two consecutive iterations.

The problem is reduced to optimize the next objective function:

$$J_m(\vartheta)=\sum_{k=1}^{n}\sum_{i=1}^{c}u_{ik}\left(1-\Gamma\left(O_k,O_i^*\right)\right) \tag{4}$$

Where ϑ is a representative object set, one for each cluster M_i, $\Gamma(O_k,O_i^*)$ is the similarity between the object O_k and the representative object O_i^* of M_i and u_{ik} is the membership degree of the object O_k to the cluster M_i. Thus the solution to this problem consists in minimizing $J_m(\vartheta)$. The next formulas are used to calculate u_{ik} and O_i^* respectively.

The degree of membership of the object O_k to M_i is computed via (5).

$$u_{ik}=\frac{1}{\sum_{j=1}^{c}\left[\frac{(1-\Gamma(O_k,O_i^*))}{(1-\Gamma(O_k,O_j^*))}\right]^2} \tag{5}$$

Finally, we use (5) to calculate the representative objects for the clusters M_i, $i=1,\ldots,c$.

$$O_i^* = \min_{q\in M_{i_\alpha}}\left\{\sum_{k=1}^{n}u_{ik}\left(1-\Gamma\left(O_k,O_q\right)\right)\right\} \tag{6}$$

Where

$$M_{i_\alpha} = \left\{ O_k \;\middle|\; \underset{M_i}{u(O_k)} = \max_{j=1,\dots,c} \left\{ \underset{M_j}{u(O_k)} \right\} \right\} \tag{7}$$

4 Reward-Punishment Editing for Mixed Data

The R-P Editing for mixed data is similar to the method proposed in [3] but using the k-most similar neighbor rule and the Fuzzy C-means for mixed data algorithm.

The algorithm is divided in two parts, in the first part, the method rewards and punishes patterns in the training set using the k-most similar neighbor (K-MSN) rule. Each pattern is rewarded if it contributes to the correct classification of another pattern in the training set, in this case the weight *WR* is increased, in the same way; a pattern is punished if it contributes to the wrong classification of another pattern, also in the training set, and the weight *WP* is increased. This part of the method is shown in figure 1.

In the second part, the method selects from the sample a prototype set using the Fuzzy C-means for mixed data and applies the K-MSN rule to classify the patterns in the sample, using the selected prototype set like a training set. These selected prototypes belong to the sample.

```
RPEMD(TS, CL)
    WR = WP = WPR = 0
    for each xi ∈ TS
        // Find the k-most similar neighbor of the pattern xi
        [L, c] = K-MSN(xi, TS, k)
        // Is the pattern correctly classified?
        if CL(i) = c then
            // Reward of the patterns that contributed to the correct classification
            for j = 1 to k
                if CL(L(j)) = c then
                    WR(L(j))= WR(L(j))+ 1
        else
            // Punishment of the patterns that contributed to the wrong classification
            for j = 1 to k
                if CL(L(j)) = c then
                    WP(L(j)) = WP(L(j))+ 1
```

Fig. 1. Part 1 of Reward-Punishment Editing for Mixed Data

Each pattern is rewarded if it is classified correctly using the selected prototypes set, that is, the weight *WPR* is increased. In the second part of this algorithm (fig 2) the variable *np_max* determines the number of elements, for each class, in the selected prototype set.

The *WR*, *WP*, *WPR* values are used to determine if a pattern within the training set will be eliminated.

```
for np = 1 to np_max
    //Generation of np prototypes for each class
    PR = CREATEPROTOTYPES(TS, CL, np)
    for pk = 1 to np step 2
        for each x_i ∈ TS
            //Classification of each pattern
            [L, c] = K-MSN(xi, PR, pk)
            if CL(i) = c then
                WPR(i) = WPR(i) + 1
NORMALIZE(WP, WR, WPR)
OPTIMIZE(TS, CL, A, B, Γ, et)
// Computation of the final weight and Editing
for each xi ∈ TS
    c = CL(i)
    WF(i) = αc·WR(i) + βc·(1-WP(i)) + γc·WPR(i)
    if WF(i) < et then
        TS = TS - { xi }
```

Fig. 2. Part 2 of Reward-Punishment Editing for Mixed Data

The procedure CREATEPROTOTYPES (*TS*, *CL*, *np*) generates a set of prototypes (*PR*) from the training set. For each class, the Fuzzy C-means for mixed data algorithm is used to determine *np* clusters; the *np* representative objects (these objects belong to the original training set) computed by the Fuzzy C-means for mixed data will be the prototype set. Those patterns that are classified correctly (using the K-MSN) with the selected prototype set are rewarded.

Based on *WR, WP* and *WPR* a final weight (*WF*) is computed, if this final weight is lower than a predefined threshold *et*, the pattern is eliminated from the training set. After that, the objects in the dataset are classified using the K-MSN rule with the edited training set.

5 Experimental Results

In this section, we present the results obtained with the Reward-Punishment Editing for mixed data and compare them against the original algorithm and the whole set (without any edition) results.

In our experiments, the training and test sets were randomly constructed. The average classification accuracy from 10 experiments using 10 fold cross validation were calculated. In each experiment k=3 (for K-MSN) and *np_max*=10 were used. Four datasets taken from [5] were used; the description of these databases is shown in Table 1.

Table 1. Databases used in the experiments

Database	Instances	Features	Classes
Iris	150	4	3
Wine	178	13	3
Credit	690	15	2
Bridges	105	11	6

In table 2, the amounts of quantitative and qualitative features are shown for each database.

Table 2. Quantitative and qualitative features for each used database

Datasets	Quantitative features	Qualitative features
Iris	4	0
Wine	13	0
Credit	6	9
Bridges	4	7

Tests with different thresholds were made. The best results were obtained with *et*=0.2 and *et*=0.3. The obtained results for each datasets are showed in figure 3 and figure 4.

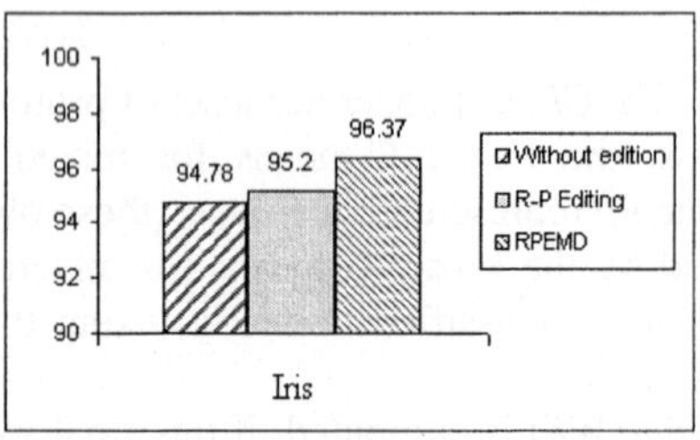

a)

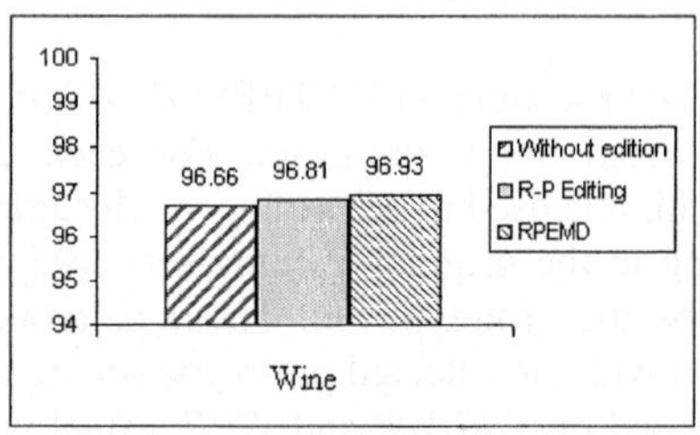

b)

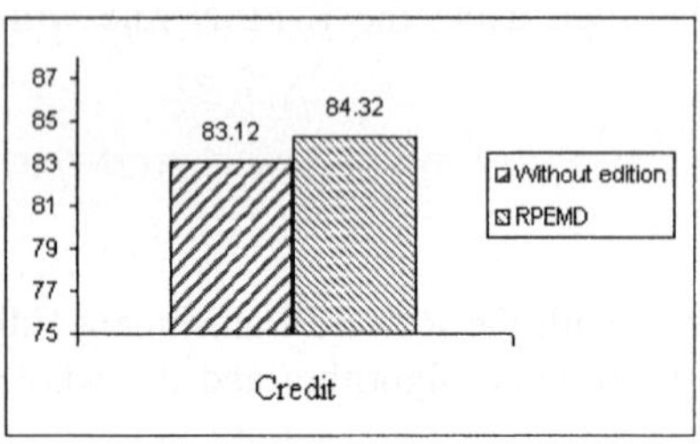

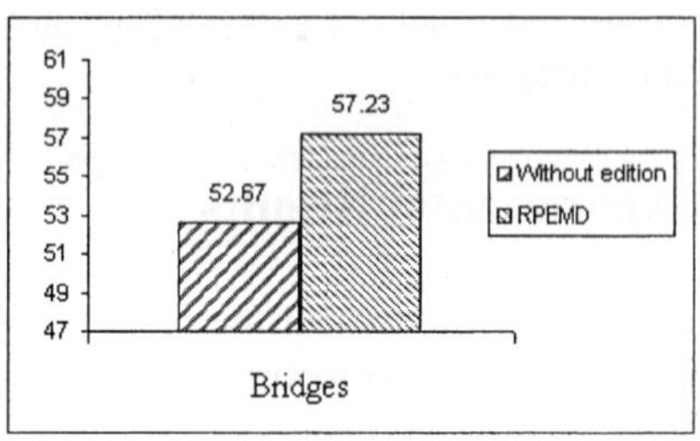

c) d)

Fig. 3. Classification accuracy on a) Iris, b) Wine, c) Credit and d) Bridges using a threshold *et*=0.3 for editing the training set

Notice that the original R-P Editing could not be applied on Credit and Bridges datasets because they have qualitative features.

In all the experiments, we can see that the classification rates obtained with Reward-Punishment Editing for Mixed Data (RPEMD) are better than the rates obtained with the original R-P Editing method and the whole set without any edition.

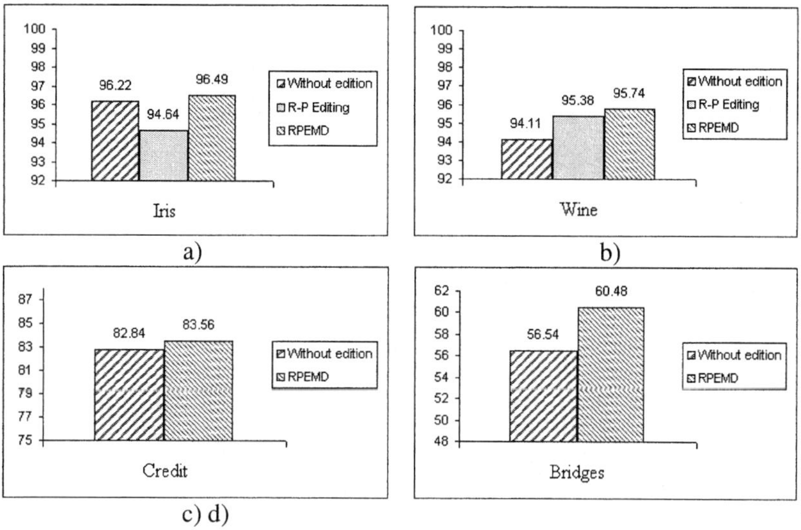

Fig. 4. Classification accuracy on a) Iris, b) Credit, c) Wine and d) Bridges using a threshold *et*=0.2 for editing the training set

Table 3. Size of the Training set after the edition, using *et*=0.2 as threshold of edition

Database	Without Edition	RP-Editing	RPEMD
Iris	100 %	95 %	94 %
Wine	100 %	96 %	93 %
Credit	100 %	-----	95 %
Bridges	100 %	-----	93 %

Table 4. Size of the Training set after the edition, using *et*=0.3 as threshold of edition

Database	Without Edition	RP-Editing	RPEMD
Iris	100 %	94 %	92 %
Wine	100 %	95 %	93 %
Credit	100 %	-----	95 %
Bridges	100 %	-----	92 %

6 Conclusion and Future Work

In supervised classification, the training set quality is very important because it is the basis of the training process. However, in practical cases, there could be irrelevant objects; therefore, it is necessary editing the training sample.

The use of Fuzzy C-means for mixed data and KNN rule with similarity functions in RPEMD allows us to work with object descriptions with mixed data, i.e. quantitative and qualitative features. These characteristics allow applying the new algorithm in many classification problems where the R-P Editing cannot be applied.

The obtained results show that the use of Fuzzy C-means for mixed data and the KNN rule with similarity functions in RPEMD allows getting better accuracy in the classification process.

As future work, we are going to extend the algorithm in order to use other classifiers.

References

1. Wilson, D. Randall and Tony R. Martínez: Reduction Techniques for Instance-Based Learning Algorithms. Machine Learning, Vol. 38. (2000) 257-286.
2. R. Paredes, T. Wagner: Weighting prototypes, a new approach. In the proceedings of International Conference on Pattern Recognition (ICPR), Vol II. (2000) 25-28.
3. A. Franco, D. Maltoni y L. Nanni: Reward- Punishment Editing. In the proceedings of International Conference on Pattern Recognition (ICPR). (2004) (In CD).
4. Irene O. Ayaquica-Martínez and J. Fco. Martínez-Trinidad: Fuzzy C-means algorithm to analyze mixed data. In the proceedings of the 6th Iberoamerican Symposium on Pattern Recognition. Florianópolis, Brazil. (2001) 27-33.
5. C.L. Blake, C.J. Merz: UCI Repository of machine learning databases. [http://www.ics.uci.edu/~mlearn/MLRepository.html] Irvine, CA: University of California, Department of Information and Computer Science. (1998).

Stable Coordinate Pairs in Spanish: Statistical and Structural Description*

Igor A. Bolshakov[1] and Sofia N. Galicia-Haro[2]

[1] Center for Computing Research (CIC),
National Polytechnic Institute (IPN), Mexico City, Mexico
igor@cic.ipn.mx
[2] Faculty of Sciences,
National Autonomous University of Mexico (UNAM),
Mexico City, Mexico
sngh@fciencias.unam.mx

Abstract. Stable coordinate pairs (SCP) like *comentarios y sugerencias* 'comments and suggestions' or *sano y salvo* 'safe and sound' are rather frequent in texts in Spanish, though there are only few thousands of them in language. We characterize SCPs statistically by a numerical Stable Connection Index and reveal its unimodal distribution. We also propose lexical, morphologic, syntactic, and semantic categories for SCP structural description — for both a whole SCP and its components. It is argued that database containing a set of categorized SCPs facilitates several tasks of automatic NLP.. The research is based on a set of ca. 2200 Spanish coordinate pairs.

1 Introduction

In all European languages, coordinate constructions are rather frequent in common texts. For example, in the Internet version of a Mexican newspaper *La Jornada* a coordinated construction is on an average in each fourth sentence. We name word combination of two content words (or content word compounds) linked by a coordinative conjunction Stable Coordinate Pair (SCP), if the occurrence rates of the whole entity and its components satisfy a statistical criterion introduced below. One component in a SCP more or less predicts another. In other words, one component restricts the other both lexically and semantically: *café y té* 'coffee and tea', *guerra y paz* 'war and peace', *ida y vuelta* 'roundtrip'.

Notwithstanding frequent occurrence of SCPs, general linguistics gave them scant attention [1, 7]. Our works [4, 5] seem insufficient either.

The objective of this paper is to describe SCPs in more detail. To characterize them statistically, we propose Stable Connection Index similar to Mutual Information Index well known in statistics [8]. To categorize both whole SCPs and their components, we introduce parameters of lexical, morphologic, syntactic, semantic, and pragmatic nature. It is argued that gathering a set of fully characterized SCPs into a database facili-

* Work done under partial support of Mexican Government (CONACyT, SNI) and CGEPI-IPN, Mexico.

M. Lazo and A. Sanfeliu (Eds.): CIARP 2005, LNCS 3773, pp. 489 – 497, 2005.

tates a variety of NLP applications. The research is based on ca. 2300 Spanish coordinate pairs (2165 stable ones after testing).

2 Stability of Coordinate Pairs

SCP as a whole plays the syntactic role of any major part of speech: noun, adjective, verb, or adverb. SCP occurs in a text as a contiguous segment, with its components that vary morphologically depending on the intra-sentence context. The surface syntactic structure of SCPs can be of two shapes [9]:

- In frequent cases the structure is $P_1 \rightarrow C \rightarrow P_2$ where components P_1 and P_2 are linked with unique conjunction C equal to *y/e* 'and', *o* 'or', or *pero* 'but.'
- In rarer cases the structure contains disjoint conjunctions *y* ... *y* 'both ... and', *ni* .... *ni* 'neither ... nor', *o bien* ... *o bien* 'either ... or':

$$c_1 \rightarrow P_1 \qquad c_2 \rightarrow P_2$$

During the recent years we have gathered a set of ca. 2300 Mexican coordinate pairs intuitively considered stable. Then the problem arose to formally define and to numerically test their stability, in order to filter off the scratch set. We did not take the criterion based only on frequencies of the entire would-be SCPs met in some corpus, since these frequencies depend on the corpus size S while the frequencies of the components P_i taken apart are not considered. A possible solution is to involve Mutual Information well known in statistics [8]

$$\mathrm{MI}(P_1, P_2) \equiv \log \frac{\mathrm{S} \times \mathrm{N}(P_1, P_2)}{\mathrm{N}(P_1) \times \mathrm{N}(P_2)},$$

where N() is frequency of the entity in parentheses met through the corpus. Regrettably, only a limited part of our set proved to be in the text corpus compiled by us from Mexican newspapers [6].

The Web search engines are incomparably richer, but they deliver statistics on queried words and word combinations measured in Web-pages. We can re-conceptualize N() as numbers of relevant pages, and S as the page total managed by the engine. However, now N()/S are not empirical probabilities of occurrences: the same words occurring in a page are counted only once, while the same page is counted repeatedly for each word included. Thus, MI is not now a strictly grounded statistical measure for words. Since *MI* depends on $\mathrm{N}(P_1,P_2)$ and $\mathrm{N}(P_1) \times \mathrm{N}(P_2)$, we may construe other similar criteria from the same 'building blocks.' Among those we have preferred Stable Connection Index

$$\mathrm{SCI}(P_1, P_2) \equiv 16 + \log_2 \frac{\mathrm{N}(P_1, P_2)}{\sqrt{\mathrm{N}(P_1) \times \mathrm{N}(P_2)}},$$

where the constant 16 and the logarithmic base 2 are chosen quite empirically: we tried to allocate a majority of SCI values in the interval [0...16]. To calculate SCI, we do not need to know the steadily increasing total volume S under the search engine's control. SCI reaches its maximally possible value 16 when P_1 and P_2 always go together. It retains its value when N(P_1), N(P_2), and N(P_1,P_2) change proportionally. This is important since all measured values fluctuate quasi-synchronously in time.

Computing SCI values for the available set by means of Google, we have plotted a unimodal (= single-peaked) statistical distribution with the mean value M = 7.2 and standard deviation D = 2.8 (Fig. 1). While dividing the SCP set into three groups, the lower (SCI < $M - D$), the middle ($M - D \leq$ SCI < $M + D$), and the upper one (SCI $\geq M + D$), their relative proportions are 23:57:21.

Hereafter a coordinate pair is considered stable if the following formula is valid:

$$\text{SCI} \geq 0.$$

Taking into account the shape of the distribution and the negligible number of the pairs that did not pass the test on positivity, the threshold seems adequate.

Examples of SCPs with maximal possible SCI values are given in Table 1. One can see than they are of three types: idioms (*a diestra y siniestra* 'to the right and to the left'); usually inseparable geographic names (*América Latina y el Caribe* 'Latin America and the Caribbean') or office names (*Hacienda y Crédito Público* 'Treasury and Public Credit'); fixed everyday-life expressions, also rather idiomatic (*un antes y un después* 'somewhat before and somewhat after', *a tontas y a locas* 'without thinking or reasoning' (lit. 'to idiots and crazies'). The non-idiomatic pairs (*pequeño y mediano* 'small and medium,' *lavadoras y secadoras* 'washing machines and dryers,' *términos y condiciones* 'terms and conditions,' etc.) are rather rare within the upper group. Except for the proper names and the fixed formulas like *una de cal y otra de arena* 'changing one's mind' (lit. 'one of lime and other of sand'), these SCPs can be also used in the inverse order, but with significantly lower SCI values (cf. the figures after '/' sign in the middle column).

The most numerous middle group is illustrated by the following SCPs with SCI in the interval 7.0 to 8.0: *trabajadores y sindicatos* 'workers and trade unions,' *normas y políticas* 'norms and policies,' *casa y jardín* 'house and garden,' *previsible y evitable*

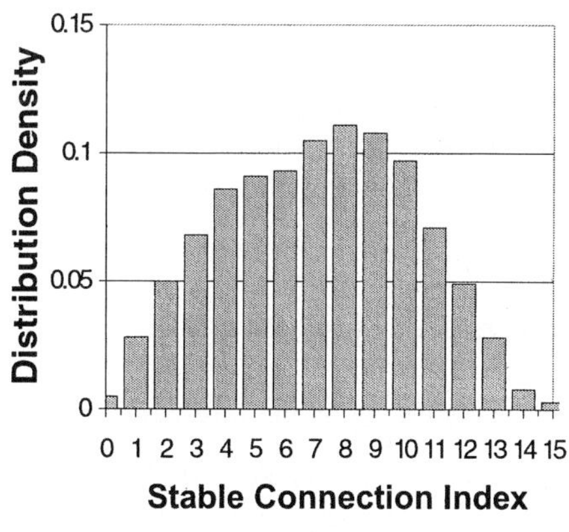

Fig. 1. Distribution of SCI values for the SCP set

Table 1. Several SCPs of the upper group

Spanish SCP	*SCI* (dir/inv)	Translation
a tontas y a locas	**16.8/7.3**	without thinking or reasoning
monedas y billetes	**16.1/11.5**	coins and currency
ayudas y subvenciones	**16.0/11.9**	aid and subventions
un antes y un después	**15.8/4.1**	somewhat before and somewhat after
pequeño y mediano	**15.3/7.7**	small and medium
una de cal y otra de arena	**15.2/-**	changing one's mind
todos para uno y uno para todos	**14.9/11.7**	all for one and one for all
en las buenas y en las malas	**14.9/9.8**	for better or worse
las mil y una noches	**14.9/1.3**	thousand and one night
a diestra y siniestra	**14.8/4.9**	hobnob
lavadoras y secadoras	**14.5/2.9**	washing machines and dryers
escuelas y universidades	**14.4/8.7**	schools and universities
bebés y niños	**14.4/9.6**	babies and children
imagen y sonido	**14.3/10.4**	image and sound
lo público y lo privado	**14.3/11.6**	public and private domains
carteles y edictos	**14.2/-**	posters and proclamations
comentarios y sugerencias	**14.1/11.3**	commentaries and suggestions
Hacienda y Crédito Publico	**14.1/-**	Treasury and Public Credit
términos y condiciones	**14.0/8.7**	terms and conditions
América Latina y el Caribe	**14.0/3.8**	Latin America and the Caribbean

'foreseeable and evitable,' *autobuses y tractores* 'buses and tractors,' *negocios y comercios* 'shops and services,' *cartón y cartoncillo* 'board and chipboard.' Nearly all of them are non-idiomatic with commonly used words as components.

SCPs with the lowest positive SCI values can be illustrated as follows: *servicio y equipo* 'service and equipment,' *noticias y foros de opinión* 'news and opinion polls,' *señores y niños* 'gentlemen and children,' *concentrados y sabores* 'concentrates and flavors,' *granito y concreto* 'granite and concrete.' Mostly, these are commonly used non-idiomatic expressions with components occurring apart much more frequently than the components of the middle group pairs.

The pairs with negative SCI values (ca. 6%) were removed from the initial set so that the total of actual set is now ca. 2200. Most of them were morphological variants of the same SCPs. For example, the pair *acción y proyecto* 'action and project' has negative SCI, while its plural *acciones y proyectos* 'actions and projects' has the SCI value 7.4.

3 External Categorization of SCPs

As a whole, SCP can be characterized by the following categories.

Part of speech is determined by its syntactic role of a SCP in a sentence: SCP can be a noun group (NG, 85% of our set), adjective group (AjG, 7%), adverb group (AvG, 5%), or verb group (VG, 3%). E.g., *embajadas y consulados* 'Embassies and Consulates' is NG, *infantil y juvenil* 'infant and juvenile' is AjG, *comer y beber* 'to eat and drink' is VG, *por arriba y por abajo* 'by above and below' is AvG. Some prepositional groups can play the role of both AjG and AvG, e.g., *en cuerpo y alma* 'in body and soul' is AjG when modifying *hermosa* 'beautiful' or is AvG when modifying *apoyar* 'to help.' We consider these roles as separate SCPs.

Number is relevant only for NGs. Usually it is plural, independently of number of the components P_1 and P_2. Indeed, both *padre y madre* 'father and mother' and *padres y madres* 'fathers and mothers' can be substituted by *they*. However, in cases when P_1 and P_2 refer to the same person, the SCP is externally singular (cf. Sect. 4).

Sphere of usage can be subdivided as follows, without strict borders between the branches:

- Official documentation entries and mass media clichés, including the names of well known organizations: *pérdidas y ganancias* 'losses and gains'; *mayoreo y menudeo* 'wholesale and retail'; *Hacienda y Crédito Público* 'Treasury and Public Credit';
- Common business notions including the names of common shops, workshops or store departments: *frutas y verduras* 'fruits and vegetables'; *vinos y licores* 'wines and liquors';
- Everyday life clichés: *dimes y diretes 'squabble'*; *noche y día* 'night and day';
- Sci-tech terms: *temperatura y presión* 'temperature and pressure'; *hidráulica y mecánica* 'hydraulics and mechanics'; *álgebra y geometría* 'algebra and geometry'
- Cultural and religious terms: *Sansón y Dalila* 'Samson and Delilah'; *Adán y Eva* 'Adam and Eva';
- Official geographic names: *Bosnia y Herzegovina, Trinidad y Tobago.*

External semantic correspondences of an entire SCP are usually their synonyms in the form of:

- A single word: *padre y madre* = *padres* (father and mother = parents);
- The same SCP given in the reverse order. In the examples *hospitales y clínicas* (SCI = 11.8) = *clínicas y hospitales* (SCI = 11.6) 'clinics and hospitals'; *industrial y comercial* (10.2) = *comercial e industrial* (10.3) 'industrial and commercial' SCI values are comparable, and there is no reasons to prefer any order except of a mere habit. There are also cases when the opposite order changes communicative organization of the expression: *México y el mundo* means approximately 'México and its relations with the world', whereas *el mundo y México* means 'the world and its relations with México.' Such oppositions do not seem fully synonymous, even if their SCI values are close to each other.
- A SCP with components synonymous to the corresponding components of the source SCP (one component may be the same). Such SCPs can have comparable SCI values: *colegios e institutos* (12.0) ≈ *escuelas y universidades* (14.4) 'schools and universities'; *astronomía y física del espacio* (11.7) ≈ *astronomía y ciencias del cosmo* (11.6) 'astronomy and space science'. In the case when the options differ in SCI more significantly (*ida y vuelta* (12.4) = *ida y venida* (8.4) 'go and return'; *docentes y estudiantes* (9.6) ≈ *maestros y discípulos* (6.1) 'teachers and pupils') it is recommendable to prefer more stable synonym.

Style is a pragmatic parameter for us: the speaker addresses the given expression to a specific audience. The style can be elevated (very rare: *alfa y omega* 'alpha and omega'), neutral (standard in speech and texts and without any labels in dictionaries), colloquial (used by everybody addressing everyone, very frequent in everyday speech, and given in dictionaries with the *colloq* label), and coarse colloquial (commonly used by men addressing men, not so rare in speech but rarely represented in dictionaries).

4 Internal Categorization of SCPs

Internally, SCPs can be characterized as follows.

Inflectionality. A SCP is inflectional if at least one its component changes its morphologic form depending on the syntactic governor of the SCP and/or of its semantically-induced morphologic characteristics (like tense of verb).

Noun SCPs that at the first glance have both singular and plural forms frequently do not correspond to each other as usual grammatical numbers. We consider each number as a separate SCP, e.g., *bar y cantina* 'bar and canteen' vs. *bares y cantinas* 'bars and canteens'.

Concerning the articles, the situation is different. We adopt the modern Mel'čuk's point of view [10] that the pairs *bar y cantina* and *el bar y la cantina* are grammatical forms of the same pair with variants differing in definiteness. The fact that the purely grammatical feature is represented by a separate auxiliary word is irrelevant for us. Indeed, in some other languages (e.g., Romanian, Bulgarian or Swedish) the definite article is suffixal part of the corresponding noun. So we compute SCI separately for each member of 'morphological' paradigms {*bar y cantina* 'bar and canteen,' *el bar y la cantina* 'the bar and the canteen'}, {*bares y cantinas* 'bars and canteens,' *los bares y las cantinas* 'the bars and the canteens'} and take the maximal SCP in a paradigm to characterize it as a whole. Conventionally, the paradigm may be represented by the version without articles. Note that if there occur in texts also indefinite form of a given coordinate pair like *un bar y una cantina* 'a bar and a canteen', the third member is added to the paradigm proposed, and the maximum is searched among the three variants.

Spanish adjectives change in gender (masculine and feminine) and in number (singular and plural), having totally four combinations. We compute SCI values for each member of the morphologic paradigm, e.g., {*activo y saludable, activos y saludables, activa y saludable, activas y saludables*} ('active and healthful') and then take the maximal value to characterize the whole. By usual convention, the {masculine, singular} form is taken as dictionary representation of the whole paradigm.

Hence we initially had ca. 5400 various forms of coordinate pairs, and after evaluations and unifications the total has reduced to ca. 2300 SCPs.

Semantic link between components can be of the following types:

- Synonyms, quasi-synonyms, and mere repetitions (2% in our set): *presidente y director* 'president and director'; *cine y artes audiovisuales* 'movies and audiovisual arts'; *más y más* 'more and more';

- Co-hyponyms in an unspecified genus–species hierarchy (86%): *maestría y doctorado* 'magister and doctorate degrees'; *axiomas y teoremas* 'axioms and theorems'; *ginecología y obstetricia* 'gynecology and obstetrics.' The degree of the meaning intersection between quasi-synonyms or co-hyponyms is rather vague.
- Antonyms, quasi-antonyms, conversives, and opposite notions (7%): *material y espiritual* 'material and spiritual'; *más o menos* 'more or less'; *a dios y al diablo* 'to God and to devil'; *compra y venta* 'purchase and sale'; *frío y caliente* 'cold and hot'.
- Co-participants or actions in a situation (5%): *gerencia y presupuesto* 'management and budget'; *productos y servicios* 'products and services'.

The latter type is the most complicated semantically. Some subtypes of the situation are as follows:

- In *muerto y enterrado* 'died and buried' there is a time sequence of actions, with the time of P_1 preceding that of P_2.
- In *fabricación y venta* 'manufacturing and sale', *crimen y castigo* 'crime and punishment', *arbitraje y mediación* 'arbitration and mediation', there is a material cause-consequence link: fmanufacturring brings about a product to sell, crime leads to official punishment, and arbitration entails mediation.

Idiomaticity. A SCP is called idiom if its meaning is not just a sum of its components' meanings. Idioms whose meaning does not contain meanings of any of their component are complete phrasemes [10], e.g., *una de cal y otra de arena* 'changing one's mind' (lit. 'one of lime and other of sand'); *ni con melón ni con sandía* 'neither pro nor contra' (lit. 'neither with melon nor with watermelon'). The majority of SCPs are non idiomatic.

Irreversibility of SCP components could be induced by a temporal or causative sequence mentioned above. However many SCPs are reversible, maybe with change of SCI (cf. Sections 2 and 3).

Lexical peculiarity means that at least one component is not used separately. For example, in *toma y daca* 'give and take' word *daca* is peculiar (compare with the word *fro* in *to and fro*).

Coreferentiality. In very rare cases, P_1 and P_2 co-refer to the same person: *padre y esposo* 'father and husband', *madre y amiga* 'mother and wife'. This parameter determines morpho-syntactic agreement in number: such NGs are considered singular.

5 Stable Coordinate Pairs in Natural Language Processing

If we supply each SCP of the available set with all parameters introduced above, including the corresponding syntactic subtree, semantic interpretation (for idioms), and SCI value, the resulting SCP dictionary becomes a database very useful for various applications. Let us give their synopsis.

Referencing in text editing is needed while preparing a new text or editing an already existing one. Indeed, even a native speaker can feel uneasiness while selecting a convenient expression for a given case, SCPs being among such expressions. The appropriate SCP could be found by means of any its component or a one-word synonym of the whole SCP (if any).

Learning foreign language is greatly facilitated with the SCP database. A student should know that *ida y vuelta* is more preferable than *ida y venida* (both are 'round-trip') and *docentes y estudiantes* is much more preferable than *maestros y discípulos* (both are 'teachers and pupils').

Word sense disambiguation. Out of context, a component of a SCP can have different meanings. In our set about 20% of SCPs contain at least one ambiguous word. Nearly all SCPs resolve this ambiguity, selecting only one sense. E..g., in *centros y departamentos* 'centers and departments', the noun *center* has at least two senses: 'midpoint' and 'institution', and the SCP selects the second one; in *pacientes y familiares* 'patients and relatives', the noun *pacientes* ('sick person' or 'object of an action') resolves to the first sense. We suppose that all SCP components in the database are labeled by their sense numbers.

Parsing. Since the DB with SCPs contains their partial parses, the parsing of the embedding sentence is facilitated: the parser finds the sequence of words corresponding to the SCP and copies its dependency subtree from the DB to the dependency tree of the sentence under parsing. For Spanish this operation includes lemmatization. E.g., the textual expression *sanas y salvas* 'safe and sound'$_{\text{FEM,PL}}$ should be reduced to the standard dictionary form *sano y salvo* labeled with FEM,PL. In many cases, the subtree substitution resolves morphological and lexical homonymy. For example, *entre el cielo y la tierra* 'between the heaven and the earth' contains *entre* that can be a form of the verb *entrar* 'enter', so that the sequence permits the false interpretation 'should enter the heaven and the earth'. The finding of the word chain in the SCP dictionary resolves such ambiguities at once.

Detecting and correcting malapropisms. Malapropisms are semantic errors replacing one content word by another, similar in sound but different in meaning. Syntactic links of a malapropos word with its contextual words often remain the same. In [3] semantic text anomalies are detected by noting that malapropisms, as a rule, destroy the collocation(s) that the mutilated word would be in. We can apply the same idea to SCPs. Suppose that the program of malapropism detection and correction finds in a text the syntactically correct coordinate pair *vivito y boleando* 'alive and shoe shinning' with ultimately negative SCI value. By few editing operations on both components, a special subprogram finds the unique similar SCP *vivito y coleando* 'alive and kicking,' thus indicating both the error and its possible correction.

Linguistic steganography is automatic concealment of digital information in rather long orthographically and semantically correct texts. In [2] a steganographic algorithm replaces words by their synonyms, taking into account the context. However, only few SCPs do have synonyms, while the rest permits synonymous paraphrases of neither the whole pair nor its components. This knowledge is quite important for steganography.

6 Conclusion

A convenient numerical measure of stability—Stable Connection Index—is proposed for coordinate pairs and on this ground the notion of a stable coordinate pair is introduced. Various lexical, morphologic, syntactic, semantic, and pragmatic features are proposed, for both entire SCPs and their components. So far, as many as 2200 Spanish SCPs passed the test on positive SCI. Supplied with all categorial information proposed, the set of SCPs forms a useful database. Such DB facilitates several modern applications of NLP. All our examples and calculations were done for Spanish, but our earlier work [5] shows that all our classifications description are applicable also to some other European languages.

References

[1] Bloomfield, L. *Language*. Halt, Rinehart and Winston, 1964.
[2] Bolshakov, I.A. A Method of Linguistic Steganography Based on Collocation-Verified Synonymy. In: J. Fridrich (Ed.) *Information Hiding* (IH 2004), Revised Selected Papers. Lecture Notes in Computer Science, N 3200, Springer, 2004, p. 180–191.
[3] Bolshakov, I.A. An Experiment in Detection and Correction of Malapropisms through the Web. In: A. Gelbukh (Ed.). *Computational Linguistics and Intelligent Text Processing*. (CICLing-2005). Lecture Notes in Computer Science, N 3406, Springer, 2005, p. 803–825.
[4] Bolshakov, I.A., A.N. Gaysinski. Slovar' ustojčivyx sočinennyx par v russkom jazyke (in Russian). *Nauchnaya i Tekhnicheskaya Informatsiya*. Ser. 2, No. 4, 1993, p. 28–33.
[5] Bolshakov, I.A., A. Gelbukh, S.N. Galicia-Haro. Stable Coordinated Pairs in Text Processing. In: V. Matoušek, P. Mautner (Eds.) *Text, Speech and Dialogue* (TSD 2003). Lecture Notes in Artificial Intelligence N 2807, Springer, 2003, p. 27–34.
[6] Galicia-Haro, S. N. Using Electronic Texts for an Annotated Corpus Building. 4th *Mexican International Conference on Computer Science* (ENC-2003), 2003, p. 26–33.
[7] Malkiel, Y. Studies in Irreversible Binomials. *Lingua*, v. 8, 1959, p. 113–160.
[8] Manning, Ch. D., H. Schütze. *Foundations of Statistical Natural Language Processing*. MIT Press, 1999.
[9] Mel'čuk, I. Dependency Syntax: Theory and Practice. SUNY Press, NY, 1988.
[10] Mel'čuk, I. Phrasemes in Language and Phraseology in Linguistics. In: M. Everaert *et al.* (Eds.) *Structural and Psychological Perspectives*. Hillsdale, NJ / Hove, UK: Lawrence Erlbaum Associates Publ., p. 169–252.

Development of a New Index to Evaluate Zooplanktons' Gonads: An Approach Based on a Suitable Combination of Deformable Models

M. Ramiro Pastorinho[1], Miguel A. Guevara[2], Augusto Silva[3], Luis Coelho[3], and Fernando Morgado[1]

[1] Biology Department, University of Aveiro, 3810 – Aveiro, Portugal
{pastorinho, fmorgado}@bio.ua.pt
[2] Computer Sciences Faculty, University of Ciego de Avila, Ciego de Avila 69450, Cuba
mguevaral@yahoo.com
[3] IEETA, University of Aveiro, 3810 -193 Aveiro, Portugal
{lcoelho, asilva}@ieeta.pt

Abstract. *Acartia tonsa* was used as model to establish an index for oocyte maturity determination in zooplankters based in citometry and histochemical evaluation of gonadic masses. Biometry was performed using an ocular micrometer and nucleus/cytoplasm ratios were obtained characterizing each of the three identified stages: Immature, Vitellogenic and Mature. This paper presents a novel approach since it joins (and, indeed, reinforces) the index framework with the evaluation of the same biological samples by a suitable combination of deformable models. Nucleus contour is identified through Active Shape Models techniques, and cytoplasm contour's detected through parametric Snakes, with prior image preprocessing based on statistical and mathematical morphology techniques. Morphometric parameters such as nucleus and cytoplasm area and ratio between them are then easily computed. As a result the dataset validated the applied methodology with a realistic background and a new, more accurate and ecologically realistic index for oocyte staging emerged.

1 Introduction

It's in the oceans that the gross majority of primary biomass is produced by phytoplankton (the world's largest plant crop). When grazing upon these primary producers, zooplankters constitute a crucial link to higher trophic levels which begin with fish and, most of the time, culminate in man [1]. Copepods often represent 80-95% of the mesozooplankton, a fact which considering continuously dwindling yields in fisheries catapults the understanding of their recruitment to an imperious necessity in order to characterize and quantify energetic flux in aquatic environments [1,2,3]. *Acartia tonsa* Dana (Copepoda: Calanoida) was used as model organism (given its dominance in zooplanktonic communities) to establish an index determining oocyte maturity stage (including inter-seasonal variance) in zooplankters [4]. Based in

M. Lazo and A. Sanfeliu (Eds.): CIARP 2005, LNCS 3773, pp. 498 – 505, 2005.

citometry (measurements using an ocular micrometer and thus calculating N/C ratios = area of the Nucleus / area of the Cytoplasm in percentage) and histochemical evaluation of the gonadic masses (identification of chemical constituents) consisted in the division of the oocytes in three stages: Immature, vitellogenic and mature, and in a finer pattern recognizing differences between months of high (H) and low (L) abundance (were reproductive strategies differ [2,5]) within each stage [4]. Roughly by the same time a novel method based in deformable models was being developed to evaluate histological sections [6].

This paper presents a novel approach by fusing both concepts: re-evaluate the same biological material using a suitable combination of deformable models (Active Shape Models [7] and Snakes [8]) in order to either confirm or, by weight of evidence, build a new index. Nucleus contours are identified through Active Shape Models (ASM) techniques, and the cytoplasm contours are detected through parametric deformable models (Snakes), with a prior preprocessing based in statistical and mathematical morphology techniques. Smoothed instances of the final contours (nucleus and cytoplasm) are then obtained through ASM and spline approximation based on the detected cytoplasm edge points, respectively. Morphometric parameters such as nucleus and cytoplasm area and ratio between them are then easily computed.

The outcoming results are the amplification of the index to four development stages and enhanced capability of information gathering regarding oocyte biometry, leading to the clarification of inter-seasonal differences in the reproductive cells of these essential elements for energy transduction in aquatic ecosystems.

In section 2, we describe the details related with material and methods of our technique. Section 3 discusses the results and presents the new characterization index established for the determination of oocyte maturity. Section 4 concludes with a short summary of our work.

2 Material and Methods

For details on biological material collection and processing see Pastorinho et.al. [4].

2.1 Computer Technique

Our method to evaluate gonadic cell masses consists on four well differentiated stages: Initial Image Processing, Initial Segmentation, Final Segmentation and Feature Extraction, which are discussed below.

2.1.1 Initial Image Processing

Initial image processing is carried out to prepare images for objects differentiation and is divided in two steps: initial image preparation and image enhancing.

Initial Image Preparation. The presence of noise in images may represent a serious impairment for subsequent automated quantitative evaluation tasks. This median filter has been used extensively for image noise reduction and smoothing. The filter preserves monotonic image features that fill more than half the area of the transform window. Examples are constant regions, step, edges, or ramp edges of sufficient extent. Median filters are especially good at removing impulse noise from images [9]. Initial image preparation consists on building the median image M (image denoising), which is achieved applying the median filter to the input image I (see Fig.1(B1)) (a 256 gray level image), with a window size of 9x9 pixels. Figure 1(B2) show the median image.

Image Enhancement. Mathematical morphology is a shape-oriented technique for image processing and analysis, based on the use of simple concepts from set theory and geometry [10]. Images under study contain gonadic cells of diverse shape and sizes, in which nucleus appear in different positions with respect to cytoplasm. Due to this, to increase the potential for future object discrimination was used a suitable combination of mathematic morphology (top-hat and bottom-hat) operations. We evaluated structuring elements of different shapes and sizes, obtaining the best results when an octagonal structuring element is used. A flat octagonal structuring element K was created computing the radius of the maximum diagonal diameter in the biggest cell's nucleus of the image under study (see Fig.1(B3)). The mathematical formulation to enhance image M to obtain image E is:

$$
\begin{aligned}
&E = A - B \quad \text{where E is the enhanced image} \\
&A = M + T \\
&T = M - \gamma(M) \quad \text{top-hat of M} \\
&\gamma(M) = M \circ K = [(M \ominus K) \oplus K] \quad \text{open M with the structuring element K} \\
&B = \varphi(M) - M \quad \text{bottom-hat of M} \\
&\varphi(M) = M \bullet K = [(M \oplus K) \ominus K] \quad \text{close M with the structuring element K} \\
&\text{where} \\
&\qquad M = \text{Median image} \\
&\qquad K = \text{Structuring element} \\
&\qquad \ominus = \text{erode operator} \\
&\qquad \oplus = \text{dilate operator}
\end{aligned}
$$

2.1.2 Initial Segmentation

The initial segmentation process is carried out to differentiate objects (gonadic cells) from background and includes two steps: primary image segmentation through thresholding and object's edge detection.

Thresholding. Histogram analysis reveals heuristically that the black pixels were in the interval (0,109) and the white pixels were in the interval (110,255). Mathematical formulation to achieve objects differentiation (image BW) is the following:

$$
BW_{(i,j)} = \begin{Bmatrix} 255 & \forall E'_{(i,j)} > (\rho_2 - d) \\ 0 & \end{Bmatrix}
$$

ρ_2 maximum local peak of white area in the frequency histogram of E'

$\rho_2 \in [110,255]$

ρ_1 minimum local peak of black area in the frequency histogram of E'

$\rho_1 \in [0,109]$

$d = |\rho_2 - \rho_1|/10$

$E' = E - E^C$; E^C complement of E'; E' image enhanced

Edge Detection. This is a critical step, since edge information is a major driving factor in subsequent deformable models performance. Several techniques were tested such as a combination of noise suppression by average and median filtering, with different masks and thresholding, followed by binarization and edge tracking [11]. We've also tried with edge maps detectors [12], but these methods fail where a gonadic cell's edge is not completed and closed. However we found that applying a local median average, as we propose in [6], produces a more suitable set of nucleus and cytoplasm edges (see Fig.1(B4)). The mathematical formulation used to detect edges is:

E_{map} ouput image

$$E_{map}(i,j) = \frac{1}{(2M+1)^2} \sum_{(k,l)\in[-M,M]} |X(i_0+k, j_0+l) - \varpi|$$

ω *N x N windows centered on pixel* (i_0, j_0)

$$M = \frac{N-1}{2}$$

ϖ median of ω

BW input image

2.1.3 Final Segmentation (Deformable Models)

Mathematical foundations of deformable models represent the confluence of geometry, physics, and approximation theory. Geometry is used to represent object shape, physics inflict constraints on how the shape may vary over space and time, and optimal approximation theory makes available the formal underpinnings of mechanisms for fitting the models to measured data. We use a suitable combination of two kinds of deformable models: Active Shape Models (ASM) proposed by Cootes et. al. [7] to identify the nucleus contour and hereafter the Gradient Vector Flow (GVF) Snake proposed by Xu and Prince [8] to identify the cytoplasm boundary.

Active Shape Model. The ASM uses the point distribution model (PDM) and the principal component analysis (PCA) for modeling objects. The implementation of ASM is characterized by the following stages: labeling of training set; alignment of training set; capturing of statistics of a set of aligned shapes, and finally the application of the model to search shape in image. In order to model a nucleus, we represent it by a set of points. The labeling of the points (landmarking) is important, and these can be placed manually or semi-automatically. Each labeled point represents a particular part of the object or its boundary. We can describe each object of the training set by the vector $Xi = [x_{i0}, y_{i0}, x_{i1}, y_{i1}, ..., x_{in-1}, y_{in-1}]$, where n is the number of points that define each object and i is the object identifier. As a result of labeling the training set we have a set of N_s vectors. In order to study a variation of the position of each landmark throughout the set of training images, it's necessary to align all the shapes to each other. The alignment is done by changing the pose (scaling, rotating, and translating) of the shapes. That is made in order to minimize the weighted sum of squares of distances between equivalent points on different shapes. After the alignment of the training set, it there is a diffuse "cloud" around each landmark. These "clouds" represent the variability of object. We can use principal component analysis (PCA) to determine the variation modes of the object. If we assume that the first t principal components explain a sufficiently high percentage (96%) of the total variance of the original data, any shape in the training set can be approximated using the mean shape and the weighted sum of the deviations obtained from the first t modes:

$$X = \overline{X} + Pb$$

$\overline{X}$ mean shape

$P = [p_1 \ p_2 \dots p_3]$ matrix of the first t eigenvectors

$b = (b_1 \ b_2 \dots b_3)^T$ vector of weights

The suitable limits for bk are typically of the order of $-3\sqrt{\lambda_k} \leq b_k \leq 3\sqrt{\lambda_k}$, where λk is the kth eigenvalue derived by PCA. Now we can apply this model to search a shape in image, but first we have to initialize the model over the image. Then, we examine the neighborhood of the landmarks of our estimate, trying to find the better locations for each landmark. Hereafter, we change the shape and the pose of our estimate to better fit the new locations for the landmarks. Each iteration produces a new acceptable shape. The system finishes the search when the shape has insignificant changes over successive iterations (when the desired movement for each landmark has a small value). In our study we assume this value equal to 8 pixels. The desired movement or adjustment of each landmark is obtained from modeling the gray level statistics around each landmark, in order to better fit of the object to the image.

Gradient Vector Flow Snake. For details on GVF model see our previous work Guevara et.al. [6]. But here we first use ASM to segment the nucleus, and then, based on the nucleus edge points the initial snakes for cytoplasm contours are automatically created. We use the parametric equation of the line formed with the nucleus centroid and the maximum radius between the centroid and the nucleus edges took in angles of 20°, in order to obtain the intersection points with the cytoplasm edges. Initial snakes were obtained with spline approximation over the set of this intersection points (see Fig.1 (A)), then the GVF snake deformation is carried out to produce the final snakes. In the snake deformation process to compute the cytoplasm edges we needed to increase rigidity and pressure force weighs, due to the shape variability of gonadic cells. The parameters used in the snake deformation process were: elasticity (0.05), rigidity (0.1), viscosity (1), external force weight (0.6) and pressure force weight (0.2). Figure 1(B5) show the final snakes representing nucleus and cytoplasm contour.

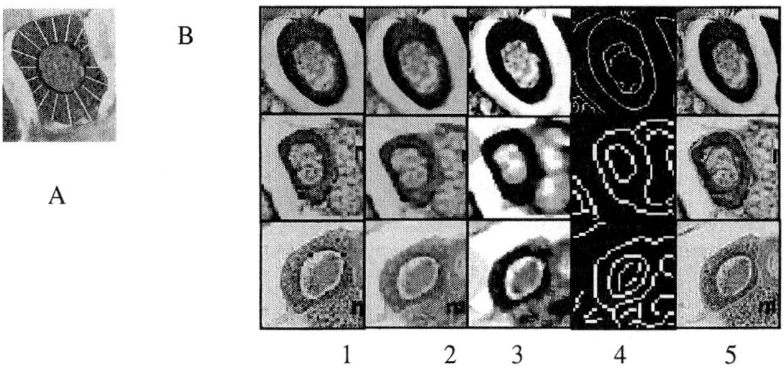

Fig. 1. (A) Spline approximation to create the cytoplasm initial snake; (B) 1-Original image, 2-Enhanced, 3-Segmented, 4-Edges, 5-Final cytoplasm and nucleus edges

2.1.4 Feature Extraction

Morphometric features express the overall size and shape of objects. For these features only the object mask O and its border ς are needed, not the actual gray scale image [13]. We compute nucleus and cytoplasm areas and the ratio between them to evaluated gonadic cells. To do this we use as input the final snakes deformations (the arrays of edge points of nucleus and cytoplasm). Mathematical formulation and computational sequence of measurements are the following:

O_N nucleus pixels

O_C cytoplasm pixels

$\varsigma_N \subset O_N$ set of edge pixels (final snake), contour of O_N

$\varsigma_C \subset O_C$ set of edge pixels (final snake), contour of O_C

$A_N = |O_N|$ area = number of elements of O_N

$A_C = |O_C|$ area = number of elements of O_C

$ratio = (A_N / A_C) * 100$

3 Results and Discussion

This section will only be object of a brief set of considerations given the scope of this article. The original index [8] was divided in three maturity stages: Immature with N/C=73.46 (H=73.02; L=73.91), Vitellogenic with N/C=46.98 (H=52.31; L=41.64) and Mature with N/C= 20.78 (H=19.0; L=22.56). The most significant outcome of this work was the unfolding (significantly different, $p< 0.001$, Table I) of the Vitellogenic stage in two: Primary (N/C= 62.39; H=59.61; L= 65.17) and Secondary (N/C= 29.04; H=23.01; L=35.07). As it would be expected, substantial modifications occurred as well in Immature and mature stages: the latter with N/C=12,29 (H=4.36; L=20.21) and the former with N/C= 121.42 (H=102.38; L=140.45) (significantly different, $p< 0.001$, Table 1). These results fit in ecological models that predict lower parental investment (less offspring, bigger in size) in low abundance epochs (more severe environmental constraints, *e.g.* higher temperature, less available food, enhanced predatorial pressure [14]) in order to enhance viability of the spawned eggs and to assure their own survival [2,3,5].

Table 1. One-way ANOVA tests applied to Oocyte size in the months of September (I) and March (II) and to four stages of oocytical maturation (immature -III; primary vittelogenic –IV; secondary vitellogenic –V, and mature –VI) of *Acartia tonsa.* df = degrees of freedom; MS = Mean square; *Fs* = Test Value; P = Probability value.
I- One way ANOVA of the oocytes size of *Acartia tonsa* distributed by maturation state, for the month of September. The null hypotheses is that the oocyte's size does not differ between maturity status.
II- One way ANOVA of the oocytes size of *Acartia tonsa* distributed by maturation state, for the month of March. The null hypotheses is that the oocyte's size does not differ between maturity status.
III- One-way ANOVA of the Immature (Im) stage of oocytes of *Acartia tonsa* during the period of the study. The null hypotheses is that all the Im cells do not register any variation between samples
IV- One-way ANOVA of the Primary Vittelogenic (PV) stage of oocytes of *Acartia tonsa* during the period of the study. The null hypotheses is that PV the cells do not register any variation between samples.
V- One-way ANOVA of the Secondary Vittelogenic (SV) stage of oocytes of *Acartia tonsa* during the period of the study. The null hypotheses is that SV the cells do not register any variation between samples.
VI- One-way ANOVA of the Mature stage of oocytes of *Acartia tonsa* during the period of the study. The null hypotheses is that all the M cells do not register any variation between samples.

Source of variation	Df	MS	*Fs*	***P***
I-Sample	2	0.008	764.28	$P < 0.001$
II-Sample	2	0.011	752.33	$P < 0.001$
III-Sample	2	0.015	114.17	$P < 0.001$
IV-Sample	2	0.004	78.92	$P < 0.001$
V-Sample	2	0.003	46.23	$P < 0.001$
VI-Sample	2	0.002	36.86	$P < 0.001$

4 Conclusions

We presented an innovative method to segment histological sections based on a suitable combination of deformable models: Active Shape Models and Gradient Vector Flow Snakes, which allowed developing a new index to evaluate Zooplanktons´ gonads. This approach is an extension of our previous work [6], but in this case was include an Active Shape Model to semiautomatically detect the gonad's cell nucleus (N). Afterward, using the set of point of the nucleus contour is built the initial snake to detect automatically cytoplasm (C) contour. The ability of our algorithm was demonstrated on an experimental representative dataset. For present and future biological studies the most significant outcome of this work was the unfolding of the Vitellogenic stage in two: Primary and Secondary. As it would be expected, substantial modifications occurred as well in Immature and mature stages: the latter with N/C=12.29 and the former with N/C=121.42.

Acknowledgment

The authors wish to thank to Research Institute of University of Aveiro Project CTS 2002/22 and to Research Unit 127/94 - IEETA for financial support.

References

1. Runge, J. A.: Should we expect a relationship between primary production and fisheries? The role of copepod dynamics as a filter of trophic variability. Hydrobiol., 167-168 (1988) 61–71.
2. Miralto, A., Ianora, A., Butino, I., Romano, G. and Di Pinto, M.: Egg production and hatching success in north Adriatic sea populations of the copepod *Acartia clausi.* Chemistry and Ecology 18(1-2) (2002) 117–125.
3. Prokopchuk, I.: Mesozooplankton distribution, feeding and reproduction of *Calanus finmarchicus* in the western Norwegian Sea in relation to hydrography and chlorophill *a* in spring. The United Nations University, Final Project (2003).
4. Pastorinho, R., Vieira, L., Ré, P., Pereira, M., Bacelar-Nicolau, P., Morgado, F., Marques, J.C. and Azeiteiro, U.: Distribution, production, histology and histochemistry in *Acartia tonsa* (Copepoda: Calanoida) as means for life history determination in a temperate estuary (Mondego estuary, Portugal). Acta Oecologica 24 (2003) S259–S273.
5. Hairston Jr., N.G. and Bohonak, A. J.: Copepod reproductive strategies: life history theory, phylogenetic pattern and invasion of inland waters. Journal of Marine sysytems 15 (1998) 23-34.
6. Guevara, M.A., Silva, A., Oliveira, H., Pereira, M.L., Morgado, F.: Segmentation and Morphometry of Histological Sections using Deformable Models: A New Tool for Evaluating Testicular Histopathology. Progress in Pattern Recognition, Speech and Image Analysis, Lecture Notes in Computer Science. Vol. 2905 (2003) 282-290.
7. Cootes, T.F., Taylor, C.J., Cooper, D.H., Graham, J.: Active Shape Models – their training and application. Computer Vision and Image Understanding, Vol. 61, n.º 1 (1995) 38-59.
8. Xu, C. and Prince, J.L.: Gradient Vector Flow. A New External Force for Snakes. Proc. IEEE Conf. on Comp. Vis. Patt. Recog. (CVPR), Los Alamitos: Comp. Soc. Press. (1997) 66-71.
9. Senel H.G., Peters R.C.: Topological Median Filters IEEE Trans. Image Processing, Vol.11 (2002) 89-104.
10. 10.-Soille, P. Morphological Image Analysis. Springer-Verlag, Berlin (1999).
11. Guevara, M. A., Rodríguez R.: Knowledge-based vision techniques to classify sugarcane somatic embryos. Proceedings 13th ISPE/IEEE International Conference on CAD/CAM, Robotic and Factories of the Future (CARS & FOF'97). (1997) 388-396.
12. Canny J.F.: A computational approach to edge detection. IEEE Trans. Pattern Anal. Machine Intell. Vol. PAMI-8, (1986) 679-678.
13. Rodenacker K., Bengtsson E.: A feature set for cytometry on digitized microscopic images. Analytical Cellular Pathology IOS Press, Vol. 25 (2003) 1–36.
14. Maffei,C. Vagaggini, D., Zarattini, P., Mura, G.: The dormancy problem for crustacea Anostraca: A rigorous model connecting hatching strategies and environmental conditions. Ecological Modelling 185 (2005) 469–481.

The Performance of Various Edge Detector Algorithms in the Analysis of Total Hip Replacement X-Rays

Alfonso Castro, Carlos Dafonte, and Bernardino Arcay

Dept. of Information and Communications Technologies,
Faculty of Computer Sciences,
University of A Coruña,
Spain
{alfonso,dafonte,cibarcay}@udc.es

Abstract. Most traumatology services use radiological images to control the state and possible displacements of total hip replacement implants. Prostheses are typically and traditionally detected by means of edge detectors, a widely used technique in medical image analysis. This article analyses how different edge detectors identify the prosthesis in X-Rays by measuring the performance of each detection algorithm; it also determines the clinical usefulness of the algorithms with the help of clinical experts.

1 Introduction

Traumatology services spend a considerable amount of time on the follow-up of patients with prostheses or screws in order to check the state of a particular orthopedic device. These follow-ups are usually based on a series of X-rays and comply with standardised protocols [1]. Even so, the medical expert controls the displacement or loosening of the prosthesis with certain measurements that are often subjective and fail to detect small movements that may be significant.

At present, several research groups are developing systems that automatically segment the bone and prostheses and as such provide the expert with quantitative measurements that help him to evaluate the patient's condition. Downing [2] developed a new and accurate method to automatically segment, classify and measure the femoral components of cemented total hip replacement in radiographs; Ozanian [3] described the development of a system that assists the expert in trajectory planning for computer–assisted internal fixation of hip fractures; and Behiels [4] evaluated various image features and different search strategies to apply Active Shape Models (ASM) to bone object boundaries in digitalized radiographs and carry out quantitative measures.

The aim of our group is to build a system that is based on the analysis of X-Rays and automatically segments the bone and the orthopedic device, providing the expert with a series of measurements that improve his diagnosis. The system consists of a module that recommends the most convenient algorithm to evaluate the images, and tries to automate its use as much as possible; the applied algorithm and the values of the different parameters can then be modified by the user in order to enhance the detection [5][6][7].

M. Lazo and A. Sanfeliu (Eds.): CIARP 2005, LNCS 3773, pp. 506 – 517, 2005.

We selected the following algorithms on the basis of their use in the field of medical images analysis: Canny [8], Heitger [9], and the Bezdek fuzzy edge detector [10]. And they have provided results in a range of edge detector studies such as the works of Bowyer [11][12], which are among the best in computerized vision literature. Bowyer's first work presented the results of various algorithms to several observers for evaluation; the second work compared different edge detectors against a heterogeneous set of images by means of ROC curves.

The Canny algorithm is at present considered the reference algorithm in edge detection and has been used in a wide range of image analysis applications. The Bezdek fuzzy edge detector is being used in the development of a system for the detection of tumors in mammographies. We have not found any applications in the field of medical images analysis for the Heitger algorithm, but we nevertheless decided to include it because it provided the best results in Bowyer's edge detectors study [12], which is commonly considered one of the most extensive studies on this technique.

The tests are based on a heterogeneous set of images that presents the most commonly found characteristics: marks made by the expert, sudden contrast changes, etc. The results were contrasted with ground truth masks that present the perfect segmentation carried out by several experts.

In recent years researchers have used techniques based on models for the analysis of X-Ray prosthesis images, i.c. the ASM technique [13]. This technique however requires a considerably "clear" training set (well delimited and with clearly marked areas), it can generate critical outliers in difficult classification areas, and the results are not easily modifiable by the operator. Even though edge detectors do not provide a completely automatic segmentation, we believe that they are better adapted to the characteristics of our system, since their parameters can easily be modified and the results can be corrected with erase and mark tools.

2 Selection of the Test Set

The images used in this study were selected with traditional image processing techniques [14] and with the histogram as a basic tool (see Figure 1). The number of available images amounts to 40.

The available bank of images was analyzed to select a subset of X-Rays that reflected as precisely as possible the different characteristics of the population (artifacts caused by the prosthesis, superpositions, fuzzy edges between the areas, saturation, etc.). We made a visual analysis and histogram exam of the images to decide whether to include or reject the image.

Firstly, as was to be expected in a case of irradiation techniques such as X-Rays, we observed inhomogeneities in the intensity levels of one and the same element, due to the uneven absorption of the radiation by the patient's tissues.

We also noticed that in most cases the histogram is bimodal: one of the modes corresponds to the background in the black area, whereas the other represents the prosthesis with the highest luminosity levels. The transition between the modes is continuous, with a detectable value for the different grey values, which implies that

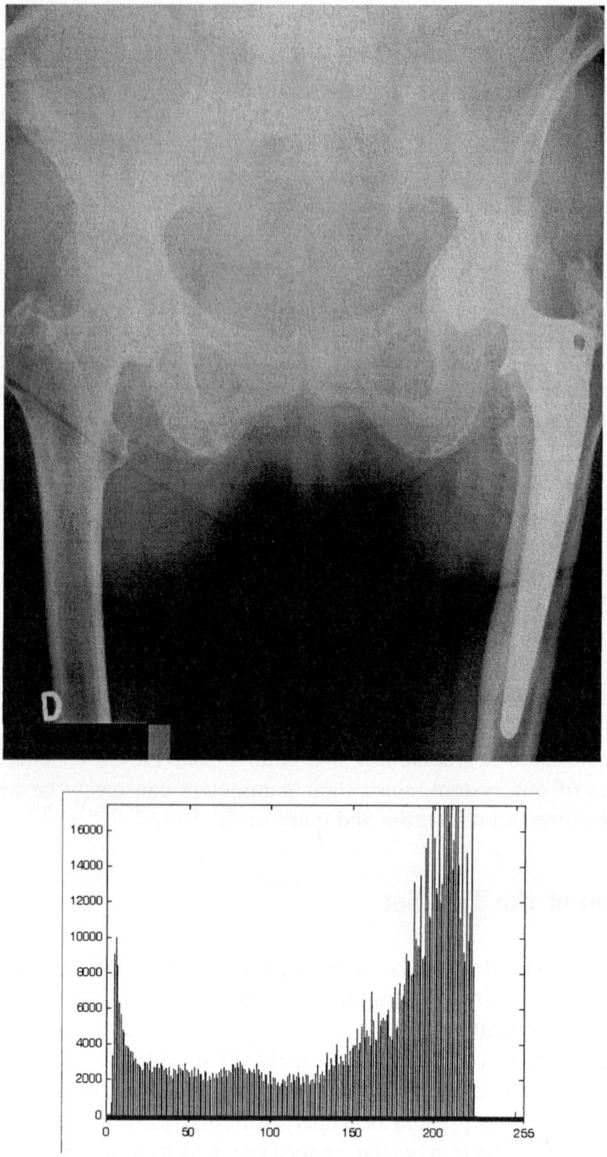

Fig. 1. Image and histogram used in this study

the edges between the elements are fuzzy. The image confirms this. We also observed that the shape of the histogram is similar for all the X-Rays and that the differences are due to the number of pixels between the modes, which varies according to the presence of more or less tissue in the X-Ray.

The images were digitalized with an especially designed scanner; the resolution for the image acquisition was 100 pixels/inch and the number of grey levels 256, which is the highest available value.

Since we observed that most images were similar with regard to the motives that appear and to the intensity levels and their distribution, we finally selected a set of 10 images. The choice of this number was based on the large amount of results that will be obtained from the edge detectors and the fact that the results will be evaluated by experts. An excessively high number of images would make tedious and complicate this evaluation process.

3 Edge Detectors

The algorithms were selected according to two basic criterions: they had to be used in the development of analysis systems for medical images, and they had to apply different techniques for the detection of points that are considered edges.

3.1 Canny Edge Detector

This algorithm was developed by J. Canny [8] as a response to the following requirements:

- Good detection: maximise the probability of marking an edge where there actually is one, and minimise the probability of marking an edge where there is none.
- Good location: the points of the edge that are indicated by the operator should be as close as posible to the edge.
- Unique response: there should be a unique response for each edge.

This algorithm was developed by J. Canny. The detector follows a series of steps:

1. Smoothen the original image with a bidimensional Gaussian function. The width of the function is specified by the user.
2. Calculate the derivation of the filtered image with respect to the two dimensions, in order to calculate the size and direction of the gradient.
3. Find the points of the edge, which correspond with a maximum. Non-maxima must be surpressed: we want to eliminate non-maxima perpendicular to the edge direction, since we expect continuity of edge strength along an extended contour. Any gradient value that is not a local peak is set to zero.
4. Apply tresholding hysteresis. We eliminate those points that are below an inferior limit specified by the user. The points over the superior limit are considered to belong to the edge. The points between the two limits are accepted if they are close to a point with a high response.

3.2 Heitger Edge Detector

The focus of the Heitger edge detector [9] is different from that of Canny in that it tries to solve the weaknesses of algorithms that use asotropic linear operators.

This algorithm uses a logical/lineal operator, based on a set of filters in the quadratic phase (Gabor filters), to detect the interesting elements of the image. The operator is based on the representation of the normal signal in a curve that depicts the edges/line dichotomy.

In order to eliminate possible ambiguities caused by the use of this operator, we apply a phase of suppression and enhancement; the responses of those image points for which the operator does not present an ideal edge or line are suppressed, whereas the responses that do meet the requirements are improved. The suppression is based on the first derivative of the response module, the enhancement on the second directional derivative of the response module.

Finally, we apply a non-maxima suppression phase on which we build a binary image by using a threshold value. The latter is a configurable parameter of the algorithm.

3.3 Bezdek Fuzzy Edge Detector

The edge detector developed by J. Bezdek [9] consists of four phases:

- An enhancement function that is charged with filtering the image in order to facilitate the analysis by the feature detector.
- A feature detection function that applies various filters to the image, in order to detect the points that may correspond to an edge.
- A composition function that combines the results of the different filters, selecting the points that are part of the image edge.
- A thresholding function, whose purpose is to provide a binar background-edge image by using a threshold value.

The algorithm is based on the analysis of the geometrical characteristics that an edge is supposed to have, the development of feature detection functions that allow us to detect these properties in the image, and finally the analysis of the detectors' result by means of a fuzzy function that selects the candidate points. The latter allow us to introduce a certain learning capacity in the selection of the pixels.

The current implementation of the algorithm uses a Sobel filter, in horizontal and vertical direction, as a function for feature detection. The applied function composition is based on the fuzzy rules system of Takagi-Sugeno [15], with a control parameter that checks the fuzziness of the system; this system builds a binary image of edges on a background through a thresholding value that can be fixed as an algorithm parameter.

4 Results

The study was based on the methodology proposed by Bowyer, in which he starts from wide intervals for each parameter and progressively refines the interval by means of ever smaller increases for the values of the parameters that provide the best results.

The parameters that were modified for each algorithm are the following:

- Canny; sigma of the gaussian, inferior and superior hysteresis threshold,
- Heitger: sigma of the gaussian, enhancement factor and thresholding value.
- Bezdek: control parameter of the fuzzy system and thresholding value.

The results were measured with two criteria: the probability of edge detection and the ROC curves. It is indeed very difficult to reflect with only one criterium all the factors that affect the result and correct the deficiencies of each measurement.

The performance of the edge detectors was firstly measured by calculating the edge detection probability [16]. We suppose an image that consists of an edge/background dichotomy: the bigger the probability of correctly classifying an edge pixel, the better the segmentation algorithm, as can be seen in equation 1:

$$D = \frac{N_b + N_h}{N} \qquad (1)$$

N_b: number of pixels that are false positives in the result image
N_h: number of pixels that are false negatives in the result image
N: number of total image points

Figure 2, 3 and 4 shows the best results of this measure for all the X-Ray images for Canny, Heitger and Bezdek.

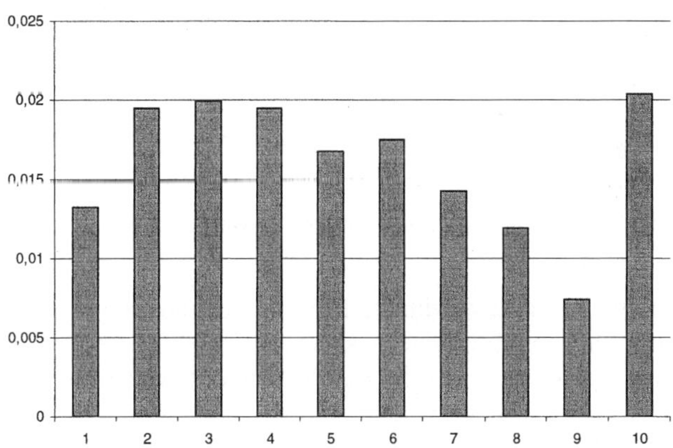

Fig. 2. Discrepancy measurement values for Canny applied to the test set

The most frequently used method to measure the performance of edge detection algorithms are the ROC curves [17]. This method consists in comparing the false positives (points that are erroneously detected as edges) and the true positives (real edge points) in a graphic (Figure 5). If the sampling of the algorithm's parameters space takes place at a sufficiently small interval, we can create a response curve and find the point at which the ratio is optimal, i.e. when the relation between the true and false positives is maximal.

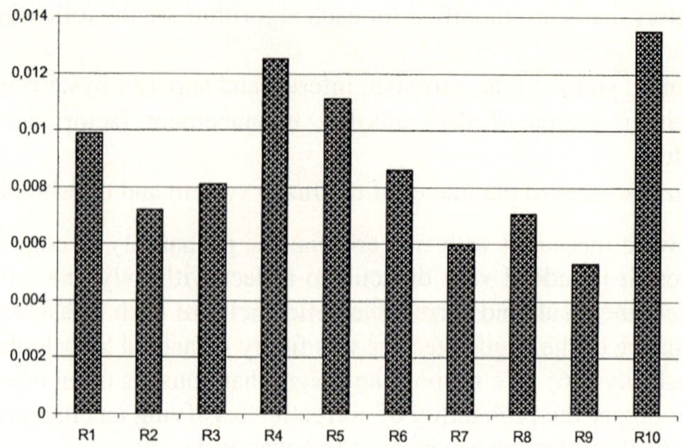

Fig. 3. Discrepancy measurement values for Heitger applied to the test set

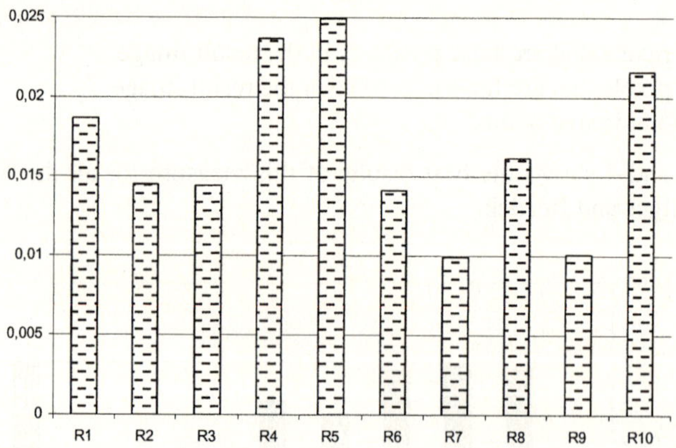

Fig. 4. Discrepancy measurement values for Bezdek applied to the test set

We evaluated the results according to Bowyer's methodology, contrasting the false negatives against the possible false positives (% not detected, % false). The best algorithm is that whose curve has the smallest area; it is usually calculated with the trapezoidal rule.

4.1 Evaluation by Medical Experts

In this phase, the specialists were asked to evaluate the clarity of the elements of the diagnostic image; they were shown the original image with superposition of the detected edges. The final purpose was to evaluate the usefulness of the resulting images during the diagnosis.

We developed a web application that allows the experts to qualify the images in a fast and comfortable manner. Figure 7, 8, and 9 show the experts' punctuations for each algorithm in each category and for each image.

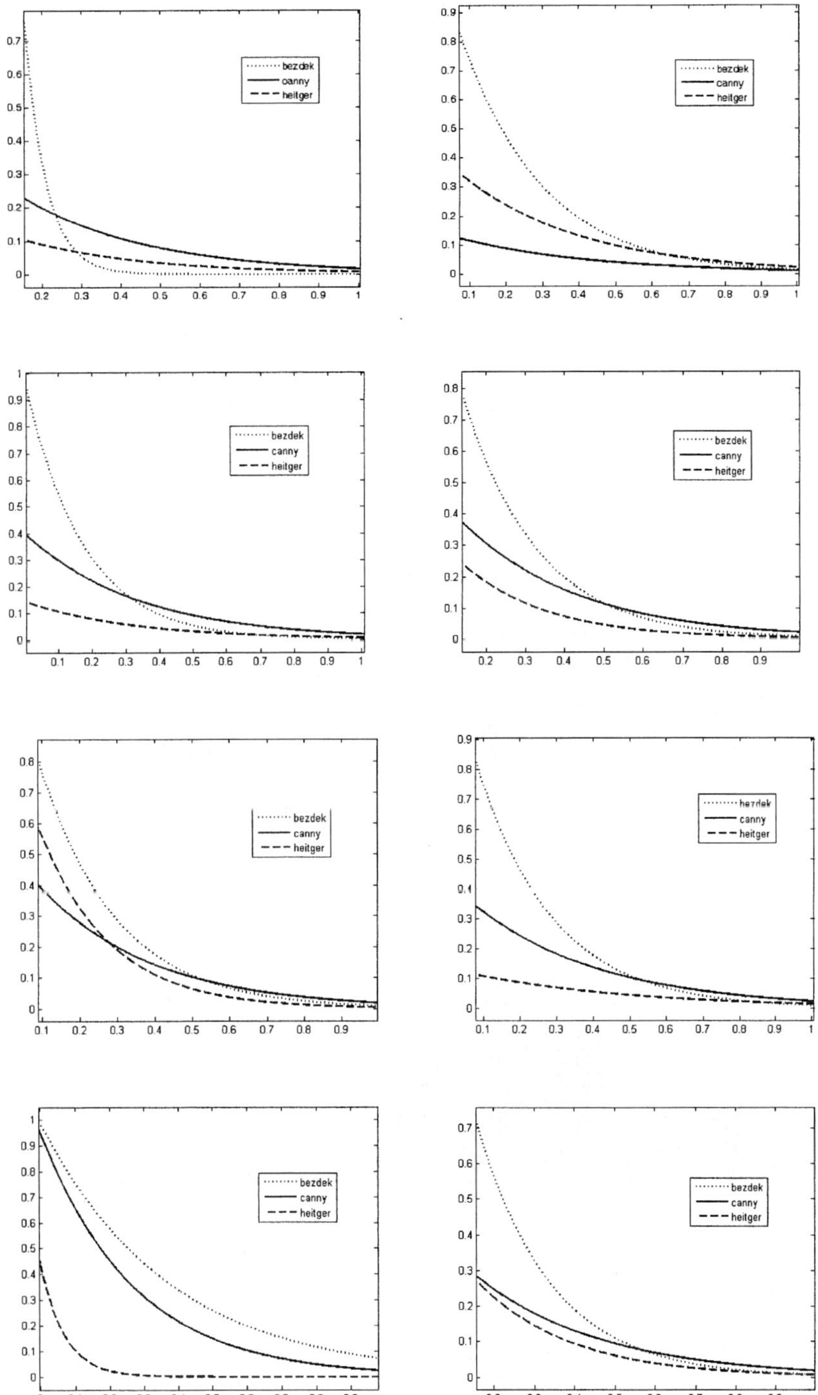
bezdek
canny
heitger

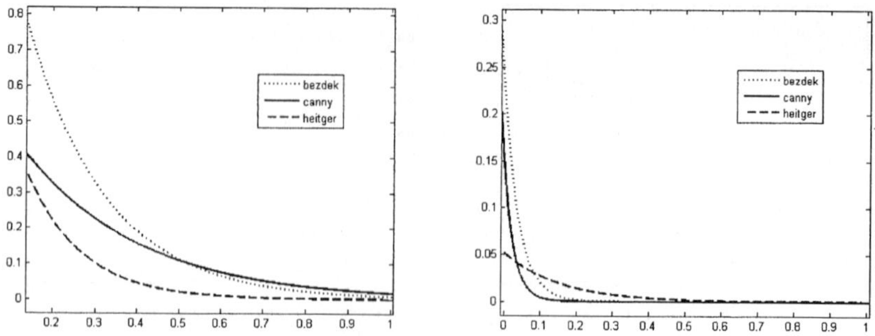

Fig. 5. Curves that represent the different edge detection performances for the X-ray images set. The graphs correspond with the R1-R10 images of left to right and top to down.

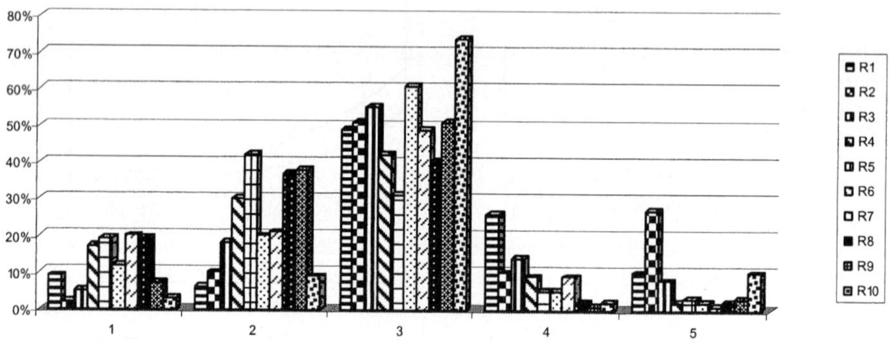

Fig. 6. Qualitative evaluation for Canny

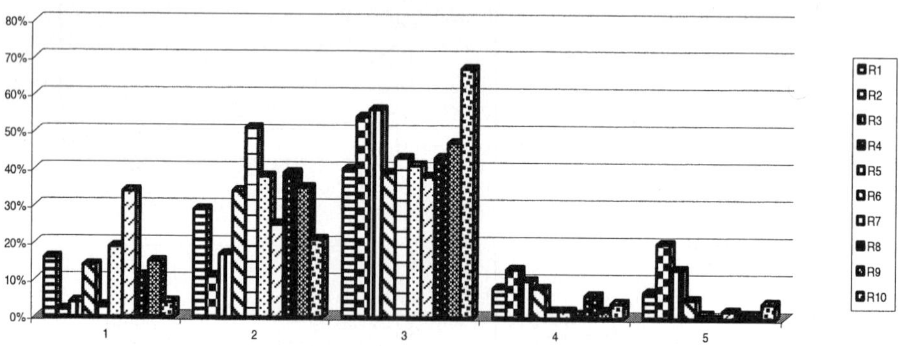

Fig. 7. Qualitative evaluation for Heitger

The evaluation was carried out by four specialists in the field and one resident physician. They worked independently and with anonymous data; there was no contact whatsoever between the evaluators in order to guarantee absolute objectivity.

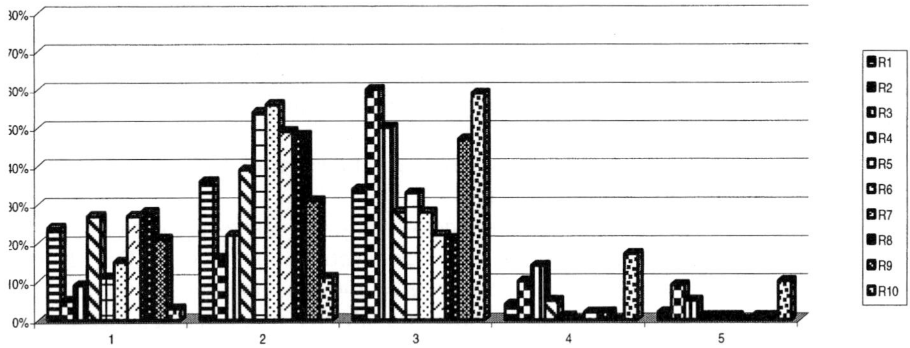

Fig. 8. Qualitative evaluation for Bezdek

Each result was rated with a value between 1 (lowest value) and 5 (highest value). We opted for this interval because the expert can easily associate it with semantic categories (very bad, bad, regular, good, very good).

In order to be considered clinically useful for the specialists, an algorithm must obtain for at least 60% of the results a punctuation of 3 or more. This criterium is based on the assumption that if the punctuation of an image is above 50 %, it is clearly positive. Due to the characteristics of the algorithms and the complexity of the images, the expert will consider a significant part of the results to be of low quality. So if an algorithm obtains an approval percentage that is above 50 %, we can assume that the images provided by the edge detector are really of use to the expert.

5 Conclusions

The study shows that the best results are provided by the Canny and Heitger edge detectors, and that the Bezdek algorithm provides considerably worse results both for the quantitative measures and for the experts. We believe that the main reason for this outcome is the fact that the Bezdek detector uses a Sobel mask in horizontal and vertical for the detection of the candidate points, which provokes the appearance of double edges in the resulting image.

Furthermore, we observe that the Canny algorithm obtains its best results with a low sigma value. High values cause considerable loss of information because of the low signal/noise relationship (mainly in the area where the bone and the iron coincide). The maximal threshold should not have a low value, because too many points are then considered edges, whereas a high minimal threshold makes too many points disappear.

The Heitger algorithm shows the same effect for sigma: since here the most critic parameter is the threshold, small variations in its value create noticeable differences in the result.

The critical parameter for the Bezdek fuzzy edge detector is the control parameter of the fuzzy rules. This means that small variations in its value considerably affect the quality of results.

The quantitative measures by the Heitger and Canny algorithms are very similar but vary according to the analysed image. Also, even though in the analysis of the ROC curves in the global set the Heitger algorithm is more effective, the Canny algorithm provides more stability (interval of the parameters values in which the algorithm gives a result that can be considered good). The experts give the same positive evaluation for both algorithms and their clinical usefulness, but manifest a slight preference for the Canny algorithm.

Although these algorithms do not provide a totally automatic segmentation of the image, we believe that they simplify the edge identification task for the medical expert. We have therefore incorporated both algorithms to the system and are currently trying to determine which algorithm provides the best results on the basis of the image's characteristics.

References

1. Johnson R. C., et al: Clinical and Radiographic Evaluation of Loose Total Hip Reconstruction, a Standard System Terminology for Reporting Results. Journal of Bone and Joint Surgery. 72A (1990) 161-168.
2. Downing M.R., Undrill P.E., Ashcroft P., Hutchison J.D., Hukins D.W.L.: Interpretation of Femoral Component in Total Hip Replacement Radiographs. Image Understanding and Analysis'97. Oxford,UK (1997) 149-152.
3. Ozanian T.O., Phillips R.: Image analysis for computer-assisted internal fixation of hip fractures. Medical Image Analysis. 4 (2000) 137–159.
4. Behiels G., Maes F., Vandermeulen D., Suetens P.: Evaluation of image features and search strategies for segmentation of bone structures in radiographs using Active Shape Models. Medical Image Analysis. 6 (2002) 47–62.
5. Pereira J., Castro A., Ronda D., Arcay B., Pazos A.: Development of a System for Access to and Exploitation of Medical Images. Proceedings of Fifteenth IEEE Symposium on Computer-Based Medical Systems. Maribor, Eslovenia (2002) 309-314.6. Anonymous.
6. Alonso A., Arcay B., Castro A.: Analysis and Evaluation of Hard and Fuzzy Clustering Segmentation Techniques in Burned Patients Images. Image and Vision Computing. 18 (2000) 1045-1054.
7. Pereira J., Castro A., Castro A., Arcay B., Pazos A.: Construction of a System for the Access, Storage and Exploitation of Data and Medical Images Generated in Radiology Information Systems (RIS). Medical Informatics and Internet in Medicine. 27 (3) (2002) 203-218.
8. Canny J.: A computational approach to edge detection. IEEE Trans. on Pattern Analysis and Machine Intelligence. 8 (6) (1986) 679-698.
9. Heitger, F.: Detection using Suppression and Enhancement. Technical report n. 163. Image Science Lab, ETH-Zurich (1995).
10. Bezdek J. C., Chandrasekhar R., Attikouzel Y.: A geometric approach to edge detection. IEEE Transactions on Fuzzy Systems. 6 (1) (1998) 52-75.
11. Heath M.D., Sarkar S., Sanocki T., Bowyer K.W. A Robust Visual Method for Assessing the Relative Performance of Edge-Detection Algorithms. IEEE Transactions on Pattern Analysis and Machine Intelligence 19(12) (1997) 1339-1359.
12. Bowyer K.W., Phillips P.J.: Empirical Evaluation Techniques in Computer Vision. IEEE Computer Press (1998).

13. Kotcheff A.C.W., Redhead A., Taylor C.J., Porter M.L., Hunkins D.W.L.: Shape Model Analysis of THR Radiographs. IEEE Proceedings of ICPR'96. (1996) 391-395.
14. Forsyth D.A., Ponce J.: Computer Vision A Modern Approach. Prentice Hall. (2002).
15. Takagi T., Sugeno M. Fuzzy identification of systems and its application to modeling and control. IEEE Trans. Sys., Man and Cybern 15(1) (1985) 116-132.
16. Lee S.U., Chung S.Y., Park R.H.: A Comparative Performance Study of Several Global Thresholding Techniques for Segmentation. Computer Vision, Graphics and Image Processing. 52 (1990) 171-190.
17. Dougherty S., Bowyer K.W.: Objective Evaluation of Edge Detectors Using a Formally Defined Framework. Empirical Evaluation Techniques in Computer Vision. IEEE Computer Press. (1998) 211-234.

An Incremental Clustering Algorithm Based on Compact Sets with Radius α

Aurora Pons-Porrata[1], Guillermo Sánchez Díaz[2], Manuel Lazo Cortés[3], and Leydis Alfonso Ramírez[1]

[1] Center of Pattern Recognition and Data Mining, University of Oriente, Patricio Lumumba s/n, C.P. 90500 Santiago de Cuba, Cuba
aurora@app.uo.edu.cu, leydis@csd.uo.edu.cu

[2] Center of Technologies Research on Information and Systems, UAEH, Carr. Pachuca-Tulancingo Km. 4.5, C.P. 42084, Pachuca, Hgo., Mexico
sanchezg@uaeh.reduaeh.mx

[3] Institute of Cybernetics, Mathematics and Physics, 15 No. 551 Vedado, C.P. 10400, Havana, Cuba
mlazo@icmf.inf.cu

Abstract. In this paper, we present an incremental clustering algorithm in the logical combinatorial approach to pattern recognition, which finds incrementally the β_0-compact sets with radius α of an object collection. The proposed algorithm allows generating an intermediate subset of clusters between the β_0-connected components and β_0-compact sets (including both of them as particular cases). The evaluation experiments on standard document collections show that the proposed algorithm outperforms the algorithms that obtain the β_0-connected components and the β_0-compact sets.

1 Introduction

In some areas such as finance, banking, engineering, medicine and geosciences the amount of stored data has had an explosive increase [1]. In these areas, there are many instances where the description of objects is non-classical; that is, features are not numerical or exclusively categorical, and sometimes, with missing values (mixed data). Data Mining and Knowledge Discovery on Databases areas process data in order to extract knowledge from data sets [9]. An important tool to extract knowledge is clustering. Several non incremental techniques to obtain clusters of a mixed data set have been proposed [2].

On the other hand, static clustering methods (non incremental algorithms) mainly rely on having the whole object set ready before applying the algorithm. Unlike them, the incremental methods are able to process new data as they are added to the collection. Nowadays, there are many problems that require a clustering of dynamic object collections such as topic detection and tracking, web mining and others.

In the Logical Combinatorial Pattern Recognition approach some clustering criteria have been proposed [6]. These clustering criteria were used to solve

M. Lazo and A. Sanfeliu (Eds.): CIARP 2005, LNCS 3773, pp. 518–527, 2005.

real problems [4], using classical algorithms which generate and store similarity matrix between objects.

However, these algorithms are inapplicable when the data set is large or dynamic. For some of these criteria, incremental algorithms to process large data sets have been developed [8, 7]. The first one finds the β_0-connected components, but it could obtain clusters with low internal cohesion. The second one obtains the β_0-compact sets, but it could generate a great number of cohesive and small clusters.

In this paper, we use the β_0-compact sets with radius α [5]. This clustering criterion allows generating an intermediate subset of clusters between the β_0-connected components and the β_0-compact sets (including both of them as particular cases). Thus a new incremental algorithm in order to generate the β_0-compact sets with radius α of an object collection is introduced.

2 Some Basic Concepts

Let $U = \{O_1, \ldots, O_m\}$ be the universe of objects in study, described in terms of features $R = \{x_1, \ldots, x_n\}$. Besides, let $\beta(O_i, O_j)$ be a similarity function between objects O_i and O_j, and β_0 a similarity threshold defined by the user.

Definition 1. *We say that objects O_i and O_j are β_0-similar if $\beta(O_i, O_j) \geq \beta_0$. If $\forall\, O_j \in U$, $\beta(O_i, O_j) < \beta_0$ then O_j is a β_0-isolated object.*

Notation: Let us denote $\nu_i = max\{\beta(O_i, O_t)/O_t \in U \wedge O_t \neq O_i \wedge \beta(O_i, O_t) \geq \beta_0\}$.

Definition 2. *We say that O_j is α-max β_0-similar to O_i if $\beta(O_i, O_j) \geq \beta_0$ and $\beta(O_i, O_j) \geq \nu_i - \alpha$. In other case, O_i is β_0-isolated and we do not consider ν_i.*

Definition 3. *We call β_0-maximum similarity reduced neighborhood with radius α of an object O_i, and we denote it by $N^0(O_i; \beta_0, \alpha)$, the following set:*

$$N^0(O_i; \beta_0, \alpha) = \{\, O_j \in U : O_j \neq O_i \wedge\ \beta(O_i, O_j) \geq \beta_0 \wedge [\beta(O_i, O_j) \geq (\nu_i - \alpha) \vee \beta(O_j, O_i) \geq (\nu_j - \alpha)] \,\}$$

From definition, $\forall\, O_i \in U, O_i \notin N^0(O_i; \beta_0, \alpha)$. We call *$\beta_0$-maximum similarity neighborhood with radius α of an object O_i*, and we denote it by $N(O_i; \beta_0, \alpha)$, the set $N^0(O_i; \beta_0, \alpha) \cup \{O_i\}$.

The set $N(O_i; \beta_0, \alpha)$ contains to O_i, all its α-max β_0-similar objects, and those objects for which O_i is an α-max β_0-similar object.

From definition 3, an interesting property is the following:

Proposition 1. *$O_i \in N(O_j; \beta_0, \alpha) \equiv O_j \in N(O_i; \beta_0, \alpha)$.*

Proof. It is sufficient with doing explicit the expressions:

$O_i \in N(O_j; \beta_0, \alpha) \equiv \beta(O_j, O_i) \geq \beta_0 \wedge [\beta(O_j, O_i) \geq (\nu_j - \alpha) \vee \beta(O_i, O_j) \geq (\nu_i - \alpha)]$

$O_j \in N(O_i;\beta_0,\alpha) \equiv \beta(O_i,O_j) \geq \beta_0 \wedge [\beta(O_i,O_j) \geq (\nu_i - \alpha) \vee \beta(O_j,O_i) \geq (\nu_j - \alpha)]$

As β is a symmetric function, the equivalence is fulfilled. □

Definition 4. *Let $\delta \subseteq U$, $\delta \neq \emptyset$, δ is a β_0-compact set with radius α with respect to (wrt) β and β_0 if:*

i) $O_i \in \delta \Rightarrow N(O_i;\beta_0,\alpha) \subseteq \delta$.

ii) $\forall O_i, O_j \in \delta\ \exists \{N_{s_1}, N_{s_2}, \ldots, N_{s_q}\} : N_{s_1} = N(O_i;\beta_0,\alpha) \wedge N_{s_q} = N(O_j;\beta_0,\alpha) \wedge N_{s_p} \cap N_{s_{p+1}} \neq \emptyset,\ \forall\, p \in \{1,\ldots,q-1\}$, *being* $\{N_{s_1}, N_{s_2}, \ldots, N_{s_q}\}$ *a set of β_0-maximum similarity neighborhoods with radius α of objects in δ.*

iii) If $\{O_i\} = N(O_i;\beta_0,\alpha)$ then $\delta = \{O_i\}$ is a degenerate β_0-compact set with radius α wrt β and β_0.

The first condition states that each object O_i in δ has its α-max β_0-similar objects and those objects for which O_i is an α-max β_0-similar object in δ. The second condition means that δ is the smallest set that holds the condition i).

We will denote by $\delta(O)$ the β_0-compact set with radius α which the object O belongs.

From now on, we will use the expression (β_0,α)-compact set instead of β_0-compact set with radius α.

For any β_0 and α values, (β_0,α)-compact sets generate a partition of the universe of objects in study.

β_0-compact sets and β_0-connected components [6] are particular cases of (β_0,α)-compact sets, taking $\alpha = 0$ and $\alpha = \beta_M - \beta_0$, being $\beta_M = max\{\nu_i\}_{O_i \in U}$ respectively [5]. For each of them, incremental algorithms have been developed [8, 7].

Definition 5. *We will call graph based on the α-max β_0-similarity according to β to the directed graph $\Gamma_{U,\beta,\beta_0,\alpha}$ whose vertices are the objects of U, and there is an arc from the vertex O_i to the vertex O_j if O_j is an α-max β_0-similar object to O_i. We will denote by $G_{U,\beta,\beta_0,\alpha}$ the undirected graph associated to $\Gamma_{U,\beta,\beta_0,\alpha}$.*

From the previuos definition, we obtain that $N^0(O_i;\beta_0,\alpha)$ coincides with the set of adjacent vertexes to O_i in the graph $G_{U,\beta,\beta_0,\alpha}$.

Proposition 2. *The set of all (β_0,α)-compact sets of U coincides with the set of all connected components of graph $G_{U,\beta,\beta_0,\alpha}$.*

Proof. It is a direct consequence of definitions 4 and 5. Let $\delta = \{O_{i_1}, O_{i_2}, \ldots, O_{i_k}\}$ be a (β_0,α)-compact set of U. If $k = 1$, then $\delta = \{O_{i_1}\}$ is an isolated (β_0,α)-compact set, and $N^0(O_{i_1};\beta_0,\alpha) = \emptyset$, where O_{i_1} is an isolated vertex. Therefore, $\{O_{i_1}\}$ is a connected component in $G_{U,\beta,\beta_0,\alpha}$.

Now, if $k > 1$, where $N^0(O_{i_1};\beta_0,\alpha)$ is the adjacent vertex set of O_{i_1}, condition ii) of definition 4 guarantees that for any pair of objects $O_{i_l}, O_{i_j} \in \delta$, a path in $G_{U,\beta,\beta_0,\alpha}$ that connects these objects exists, and the associated subgraph of δ is connected.

In addition, condition i) of definition 4 guarantees that δ is not a subset of any connected component of graph $G_{U,\beta,\beta_0,\alpha}$, but δ is the same connected component. □

Definition 6. *Let $U' \subset U$ and $\delta \subset U'$ be a (β_0, α)-compact set of U'. Besides, let $O \in U \setminus U'$. We say that object O is connected with δ if there exists some object $O' \in \delta$ such that O is α-max β_0-similar to O' or O' is α-max β_0-similar to O.*

Proposition 3. *Let U', U and O be like above. If object O is not connected with δ, then δ is a (β_0, α)-compact set in $U' \cup \{O\}$.*

Proof. This is immediate from definition 6. As object O is not connected with δ, then $\delta \cup \{O\}$ does not satisfy (β_0, α)-compact set definition. □

Corollary 1. *If O is a β_0-isolated object, then the set of all (β_0, α)-compact sets in $U' \cup \{O\}$ is $\zeta \cup \{\{O\}\}$, where ζ is the set of all (β_0, α)-compact sets in U'. In this case, the graph $G_{U' \cup \{O\},\beta,\beta_0,\alpha}$ and the graph $G_{U',\beta,\beta_0,\alpha}$ differ in only one vertex.*

Let E be the set of edges of graph $G_{U,\beta,\beta_0,\alpha}$.

Proposition 4. *Let U', U, O and δ be like above. If O is connected with δ, and $E_{U',\beta,\beta_0,\alpha} \subset E_{U' \cup \{O\},\beta,\beta_0,\alpha}$ (i.e. new edges appear and no edge of $G_{U',\beta,\beta_0,\alpha}$ was broken by O), then $\delta \cup \{O\}$ is a (β_0, α)-compact set or it is a subset of a (β_0, α)-compact set in $U' \cup \{O\}$.*

Proof. As a consequence of the proposition 2, if δ is a (β_0, α)-compact set in U', then the subgraph associated to δ is a connected component of the graph $G_{U',\beta,\beta_0,\alpha}$. Let $\{O_{i_1}, O_{i_2}, \ldots, O_{i_r}\}$ be the objects connected with O by the new edges in the graph $G_{U' \cup \{O\},\beta,\beta_0,\alpha}$.

If $\{O_{i_1}, O_{i_2}, \ldots, O_{i_r}\} \subseteq \delta$, then O is added to this connected component, and therefore $\delta \cup \{O\}$ is a (β_0, α)-compact set in $U' \cup \{O\}$. Otherwise, if O is also connected with an object $O' \in \delta$, then $O' \in N(O; \beta_0, \alpha)$ and $\delta \cup \{O\}$ is not a (β_0, α)-compact set in $U' \cup \{O\}$, because it does not satisfy condition i) of definition 4. Nevertheless, as the subgraph associated to $\delta \cup \{O\}$ is connected, it is a subset of a (β_0, α)-compact set in $U' \cup \{O\}$. This (β_0, α)-compact set is the union of $\{O\}$ and all (β_0, α)-compact sets in U' to which O is connected. □

3 Incremental Clustering Algorithm

In this paper, we propose a new clustering algorithm that finds incrementally the (β_0, α)-compact sets of an object collection. This algorithm is based on the propositions explained above.

The algorithm stores the maximum β_0-similarity of each object O_i, and the set of objects connected to it in the graph $G_{U',\beta,\beta_0,\alpha}$, that is, the objects belonging to $N^0(O_i; \beta_0, \alpha)$. It stores, also, the similarity values with O_i for each object of $N^0(O_i; \beta_0, \alpha)$.

Every time that new object O arrives, its similarity with each object of existent (β_0, α)-compact sets is calculated and the graph $G_{U',\beta,\beta_0,\alpha}$ is updated. The arrival of O can change the current (β_0, α)-compact sets, because some new (β_0, α)-compact sets may appear, and others that already exist may disappear.

Therefore, after updating the graph $G_{U',\beta,\beta_0,\alpha}$ the (β_0, α)-compact sets are rebuilt starting from O, and the objects in the (β_0, α)-compact sets that become unconnected. The (β_0, α)-compact sets that do not include objects connected with O remain unchanged, by virtue of the Proposition 3. During the graph updating task the algorithm constructs the following sets:

$ClustersToProcess$: A (β_0, α)-compact set is included in this set if it has any object O_j that satisfies the following conditions:

1. The new object O is the most β_0-similar to O_j, and the objects that were α-max β_0-similar to O_j are not anymore; that is, its edges with O_j in the graph $G_{U',\beta,\beta_0,\alpha}$ are broken.
2. O_j had at least two α-max β_0-similar objects, in which its edges are broken, or O_j is α-max β_0-similar to at least another object in this (β_0, α)-compact set.

This set includes the (β_0, α)-compact sets that could lose its compactness when the objects with the previous characteristics are removed from the cluster. Thus, these (β_0, α)-compact sets must be reconstructed.

Example 1: Let be β_0=0.3 and α=0.1. As can be seen in Figure 1, the (β_0, α)-compact set C belongs to the set $ClustersToProcess$, because object O_1 satisfies the conditions mentioned above.

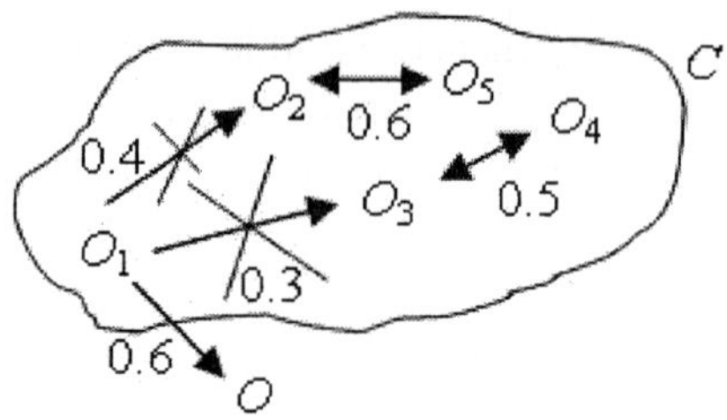

Fig. 1. A cluster that belongs to $ClustersToProcess$

$ObjectsToJoin$: An object O_j is included in this set if it satisfies the following conditions:

1. The new object O is the most β_0-similar to O_j, and the only object that was α-max β_0-similar to O_j is not anymore.
2. O_j is not α-max β_0-similar to any object of its (β_0, α)-compact set.

The objects in this set will be included in the same (β_0, α)-compact set as O, that is, $\delta(O)$. The (β_0, α)-compact set to which O_j belongs continues being a (β_0, α)-compact set when O_j is removed from it.

Example 2: Let be β_0=0.3 and α=0.1. The object O_1 belongs to the set $ObjectsToJoin$, as is illustrated in Figure 2. O_1 will belong to $\delta(O)$ and it must be removed from the (β_0, α)-compact set C. Also $C \backslash \{O_1\}$ is a (β_0, α)-compact set.

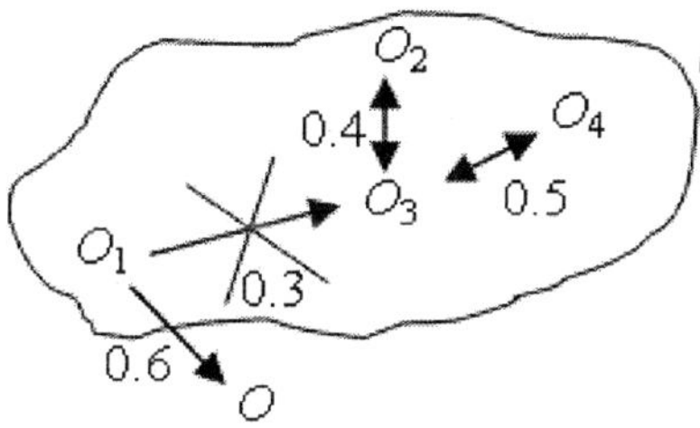

Fig. 2. An example of $ObjectsToJoin$

$ClustersToJoin$: A (β_0, α)-compact set is included in this set if it is not in $ClustersToProcess$ and it has at least one object O_j that satisfies one of the following conditions:

1. O_j is α-max β_0-similar to the new object O.
2. O is α-max β_0-similar to O_j, and no edge of O_j in the graph $G_{U',\beta,\beta_0,\alpha}$ is broken.

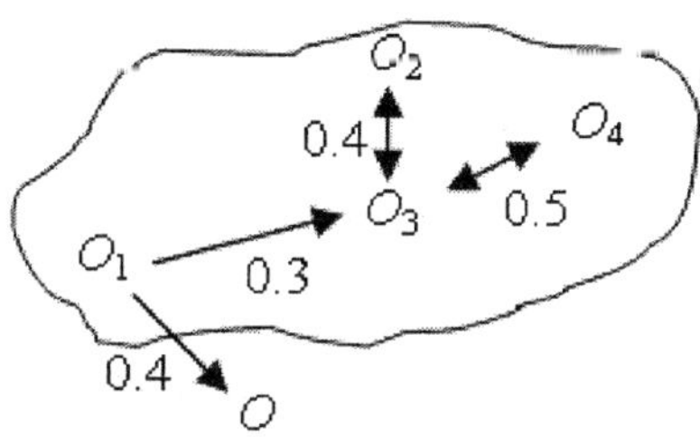

Fig. 3. A cluster that belongs to $ClustersToJoin$

All the objects in $ClustersToJoin$ will be included in the same (β_0, α)-compact set as O. Notice that the clusters in $ClustersToJoin$ are the (β_0, α)-compact sets that satisfy the Proposition 4.

Example 3: Let be β_0=0.3 and α=0.1. As can be seen in Figure 3, the (β_0, α)-compact set C belongs to the set $ClustersToJoin$, because the new object O is connected with it and no edge in C is broken.

3.1 The Incremental Algorithm

The main steps of the algorithm are the following:

1. Arrival of the new object O.
2. Updating of the graph $G_{U',\beta,\beta_0,\alpha}$.
   (a) For each object in the existent (β_0, α)-compact sets, its similarity with O is calculated.
   (b) The maximum β_0-similarity of each object in the graph $G_{U',\beta,\beta_0,\alpha}$, and the set of its α-max β_0-similar objects are updated.
   (c) The maximum β_0-similarity of O, and the set $N^0(O;\beta_0,\alpha)$ are determined.
   (d) The sets $ClustersToProcess$, $ClustersToJoin$ and $ObjectsToJoin$ are built.
   (e) Every time an object is added to $ObjectsToJoin$ it is removed from the (β_0, α)-compact set in which it was located before.
3. Reconstruction of the (β_0, α)-compact sets.
   (a) Let C be a set including O and all the objects included in the (β_0, α)-compact sets in $ClustersToProcess$.
   (b) Build the existing (β_0, α)-compact sets in C, and add them to the existing (β_0, α)-compact set list.
   (c) Add all the objects in $ObjectsToJoin$, and all the objects included in the (β_0, α)-compact sets of $ClustersToJoin$ to $\delta(O)$.
   (d) The (β_0, α)-compact sets in $ClustersToProcess$ and in $ClustersToJoin$ are removed from the existing (β_0, α)-compact set list.

The worst case time complexity of this algorithm is $O(n^2)$, since for each object, all the objects of existing clusters could be checked to find the most similar objects.

4 Evaluation

The effectiveness of the proposed clustering algorithm has been evaluated using four standard document collections, whose general characteristics are summarized in Table 1. Human annotators identified the topics in each collection.

In our experiments, the documents are represented using the traditional vectorial model. The terms of documents represent the lemmas of the words appearing in the texts. Stop words, such as articles, prepositions and adverbs are disregarded from the document vectors. Terms are statistically weighted using the term frequency. To account for documents of different lengths, the vector is normalized using the document length. We use the traditional cosine measure to compare the documents.

The source TREC was obtained of *http://trec.nist.gov*, TDT2 of *http://www.nist.gov/speech/tests/tdt.html*, and finally, Reuters-21578 of *http://kdd.ics.uci.edu*.

Table 1. Description of document collections

Collection	Source	N. of documents	N. of terms	N. of topics	Language
AFP	TREC-5	695	12330	25	Spanish
ELN	TREC-4	1997	39025	49	Spanish
TDT	TDT2	9824	55112	193	English
REU	Reuters-21578	10369	38367	120	English

There are many different measures to evaluate the quality of clustering. We adopt a widely used external quality measure: the Overall F1-Measure [3]. This measure compares the system-generated clusters with the manually labelled topics and combines the precision and recall factors. The higher the overall F1-measure, the better the clustering is, due to the higher accuracy of the clusters mapping to the topics.

Our experiments were focused on evaluating the quality of the clustering produced by GLC [8], Incremental Compact Clustering [7] and the proposed algorithm.

Table 2. Quality results obtained by clustering algorithms

Collection	Algorithm	Parameters	Overall F1-measure
AFP	GLC	$\beta_0 = 0.33$	0.65
	Compact set	$\beta_0 = 0.1$	0.43
	Proposed algorithm	$\beta_0 = 0.25, \alpha = 0.02$	**0.68**
ELN	GLC	$\beta_0 = 0.38$	0.21
	Compact set	$\beta_0 = 0.15$	0.30
	Proposed algorithm	$\beta_0 = 0.22, \alpha = 0.002$	**0.31**
TDT	GLC	$\beta_0 = 0.5$	0.57
	Compact set	$\beta_0 = 0.24$	0.25
	Proposed algorithm	$\beta_0 = 0.45, \alpha = 0.02$	**0.61**
REU	GLC	$\beta_0 = 0.67$	0.32
	Compact set	$\beta_0 = 0.1$	0.14
	Proposed algorithm	$\beta_0 = 0.5, \alpha = 0.04$	**0.49**

The obtained results for each collection are shown in Table 2. Second column contains the values that produce best results. The entries that are boldfaced correspond to the method that performed the best in each document collection.

Several observations can be made by analyzing the results in Table 2. First, in most collections the algorithm GLC obtains better results than Compact algorithm. However, our algorithm overcomes them in all collections. Finally, the best value of β_0 parameter in our algorithm is always greater than the best value of the Incremental Compact Algorithm, but it is always lesser than the β_0 value of the GLC algorithm.

5 Conclusions

In this paper, a new incremental clustering algorithm has been introduced. This algorithm is based on the incremental construction of existing β_0-compact sets with radius α in the object collection. It handles a clustering criterion that generating an intermediate subset of clusters between the β_0-connected components and β_0-compact sets (including both of them as particular cases). In this sense, the proposed algorithm is more restrictive than GLC algorithm, and at the same time, is more flexible than Incremental Compact algorithm.

Our algorithm allows the finding of clusters with arbitrary shapes, the number of clusters is not fixed a priori and it does not impose any restrictions to the representation space of the objects. Another advantage of this algorithm is that the generated set of clusters is unique, independently on the arrival order of the objects.

Our experiments with standard document collections have demonstrated the validity of our algorithm for document clustering tasks. The proposed algorithm overcomes the GLC algorithm and the Incremental Compact algorithm in all document collections.

The new algorithm can be used in tasks such as information organization, browsing, topic tracking and new topic detection. Although we employ our algorithm to cluster document collections, its use is not restricted to this area, since it can be applied to any problem of Pattern Recognition where clustering mixed objects can appear.

As future work, we will study the inclusion of this clustering criterion as clustering routine in a dynamic hierarchical clustering algorithm.

Acknowledgements. This work was financially supported by Institutional Program Research of UAEH (Mexico).

References

[1] Fayyad, U.; Piatetsky-Shapiro, G.; Smyth, P. and Uthurusamy, R.: *Advances in knowledge discovery in databases*, Cambridge, MIT Press, 1996.
[2] Jain, K. and Dubes, R.: *Algorithms for clustering data*, Prentice Hall, 1998.
[3] Larsen, B. and Aone, C.: Fast and Effective Text Mining Using Linear-time Document Clustering. In *Proceedings of KDD'99*, San Diego, California, pp. 16–22, 1999.
[4] Lopez-Caviedez, M.: A cities stratification tool in risk zones for the healt. MSc. Thesis, UAEH, Pachuca, Hgo. Mexico, 2004 (in Spanish).
[5] Lopez-Caviedez, M. and Sanchez-Díaz, G.: A new clustering criterion in pattern recognition. *WSEAS Transactions on Computers* 3(3), pp. 558–562, 2004.
[6] Martínez Trinidad, J. F.; Ruiz Shulcloper, J. and Lazo Cortés, M.: Structuralization of universes. *Fuzzy Sets and Systems* 112 (3), pp. 485–500, 2000.
[7] Pons-Porrata, A.; Berlanga-Llavori, R. and Ruiz-Shulcloper, J.: On-line event and topic detection by using the compact sets clustering algorithm. *Journal of Intelligent and Fuzzy Systems* (3-4), pp. 185–194, 2002.

[8] Sanchez-Díaz, G. and Ruiz-Shulcloper, J.: Mid mining: a logical combinatorial pattern recognition approach to clustering in large data sets. In *Proc. VI Ibero-American Symposium on Pattern Recognition*, Lisboa, Portugal, pp. 475–483, 2000.
[9] Sarker, R.; Abbass, H. and Newton, C.: Introducing data mining and knowledge discovery. *Heuristics & optimization for knowledge discovery*, Idea Group publishing, pp. 1–12, 2000.

Image Registration from Mutual Information of Edge Correspondences

N.A. Alvarez[1] and J.M. Sanchiz[2]

[1] Universidad de Oriente, Santiago de Cuba, Cuba
aime@fastmail.ca
[2] Universidad Jaume I, Castellón, Spain
sanchiz@uji.es

Abstract. Image registration is a fundamental task in image processing. Its aim is to match two or more pictures taken with the same or from different sensors, at different times or from different viewpoints. In image registration the use of an adequate measure of alignment is a crucial issue. Current techniques are classified in two broad categories: pixel based and feature based. All methods include some similarity measure. In this paper a new measure that combines mutual information ideas, spatial information and feature characteristics, is proposed. Edge points obtained from a Canny edge detector are used as features. Feature characteristics like location, edge strength and orientation, are taken into account to compute a joint probability distribution of corresponding edge points in two images. Mutual information based on this function is maximized to find the best alignment parameters. The approach has been tested with a collection of medical images (Nuclear Magnetic Resonance and radiotherapy portal images) and conventional video sequences, obtaining encouraging results.

1 Introduction

Image registration is the process of overlaying two or more images of the same scene taken under different conditions. It is a crucial step of image analysis methods where the final information is obtained from the combination of various data sources. Some applications of registration are found in remote sensing (change detection, environmental monitoring, image mosaicing), medicine (monitoring tissue or injury evolution, treatment verification), cartography (map updating) and computer vision (surveillance systems, motion tracking, ego-motion).

To register two images, a transformation must be found so that each point in one image can be mapped to a point in the second one. It can be assumed that correspondent objects in both images present similar intensity values, and this can be used to accurately estimate the transformation [1]. However, specially in medical imaging modalities, one or both images could be of very low contrast, and significant features should be used instead of intensity values.

A new approach to compute a measure of image alignment was introduced by Viola and Wells [2], and by Maes *et al.* [3]. This measure, *mutual information*,

M. Lazo and A. Sanfeliu (Eds.): CIARP 2005, LNCS 3773, pp. 528–539, 2005.

is based on entropy concepts developed as part of Shannon's information theory. Mutual information is used to measure the statistical dependence between the image intensities of corresponding pixels in two images. The use of mutual information as a criterion for image similarity has been reported quite often in the literature in recent years. It enjoys the reputation of an accurate, robust and general criterion.

We describe a registration method based on ideas of mutual information. But, instead of a joint probability distribution derived from grey levels, used in classical mutual information registration, we propose a joint probability function derived from the spatial localization of features, and features similarity. The possibility of a multifeature approach of mutual information has been introduced by Tomazevic *et al.* [4]. They presented a method that allows an efficient combination of multiple features to estimate the mutual information.

Our work is mainly motivated by improving quality assessment in radiotherapy by performing automatic registration of portal images. Portal images are extremely low contrast images. Although still they show some steady characteristics like bone edges. So, in the method we present edges are used as features and edge points are determined using conventional edge extractors.

In our approach, we define a probability function that two edge points correspond combining three attributes of edges: edge point location, gradient magnitude, and gradient orientation. A joint probability table is computed for all possible correspondences. A minimization of the entropy of this table is applied to obtain the best match, and the registration parameters. The measure we are proposing allows us to incorporate spatial information in the estimation of the joint probability distribution. The lack of this type of information is a drawback in classical mutual information, where only correspondences of intensity values are used. This problem can lead to erroneous results when images contain little information, in the case of poor image quality, low resolution, etc. Our method has been tested with portal images from radiotherapy and from Magnetic Resonance (MR) modalities. It has also been tested with outdoor video sequences.

The structure of this paper is as follows: in Section 2 some related work is discussed. Section 3 describes theoretical aspects of mutual information, and of the approach we are proposing. In Section 4 we present results obtained using our new measure based on mutual information and feature characteristics. Finally, in Section 5 conclusions and further research directions are drawn.

2 Related Work

Registration algorithms have applications in many fields. Currently, research is directed to multimodal registration and to cope with region deformations [5]. A recent study about image registration can be found in the work by Zitova and Flusser [6]. A more specific reference dedicated to the field of medical imaging is the work by Maintz and Viergever [7].

Depending on the information used to bring images into alignment, current techniques are classified in two broad categories: *feature-based* and *pixel-based* approaches. *Feature-based* approaches aim at extracting stable features from the images to be registered. The correspondences among extracted features is found and used to estimate the alignment between the two images. These methods tend to be fast. Leszczynski *et al.* [8] manually selected contours of notable features and used their points for registration using chamfer matching. The introduction of the chamfer distance [9] reduces the computation time, although the method depends on user interaction.

Pixel-based approaches use all the pixels of an image. A Fourier transform-based cross correlation operator was used by Hristov and Fallone [10] to find the optimal registration, accounting for translations and rotations.

In the last decade, a new *pixel-based* approach has been introduced: the mutual information measure. Similarity measures based on this concept have shown to be accurate measures for selecting the best rigid or non-rigid transformation in mono and multi-modal registration. However, being an area-based technique it has limitations, mainly due to the lack of spatial information.

Portal imaging consists of sensing therapeutic radiation applied from electron accelerators in cancer treatment [11]. They are formed when a high energy radiation excites a sensor after being absorbed by anatomical structures as it goes through the body. Due to the high energy of the radiation, there is a poor contrast in portal images compared to x-ray, axial tomography or magnetic resonance images. Detection of patient pose errors during or after treatment is the main use of portal images. Recently, Kim *et al.* [12] reported results on using classical mutual information as the measure of alignment in registration of portal images. Good average accuracies for motion parameters estimation were achieved, but the long computation time of the proposed method makes it difficult to estimate the patient setup error in real time. Since our method deal with a shorter amount of data, only features characteristics, its application in real time would be possible.

Hybrid techniques that combine *pixel-based* and *feature-based* approaches have been proposed. In the work by Rangarajan *et al.* [13] mutual information is computed using feature points locations instead of image intensity. The joint probability distribution required by the mutual information approach is based on distances between pairs of feature points in both images. From this distribution a measure of the correspondence likelihood between pairs of feature points can be derived. The authors report results with autoradiograph images.

Pluim *et al.* [14] extended the mutual information in a different way to include spatial information. The extension is accomplished by multiplying the classical mutual information by a gradient term. This term includes the gradient magnitude and orientation. The method computes a weighting function that favors small angles between gradient vectors. Then, its value is multiplied by the minimum of gradients magnitude. Finally, summation of the resulting product for all pixels gives the gradient term. This combined criterion seems to be more robust than classical mutual information.

The method we propose provides the registration parameters of a pair of images by maximizing the mutual information computed from a joint probability table of feature correspondence feasibility. The probability of correspondence of two edge points is estimated using points attributes. A search of the best registration parameters implies recomputing the joint probability table but not the feature points themselves. The registration parameters giving the lowest entropy, and so the highest mutual information are selected as the best alignment.

3 Registration Based on Feature Characteristics and Mutual Information

3.1 Mutual Information

Mutual Information is a concept from information theory, and is the basis of one of the most robust registration methods [15]. The underlying concept of mutual information is entropy, which can be considered a measure of dispersion of a probability distribution. In thermology, entropy is a measure of the disorder of a system. A homogeneous image has a low entropy while a high contrast image has a high entropy. If we consider as a system the pairs of aligned pixels in two images, disorder or joint entropy increases with misregistration, while in correct alignment the system has a minimum disorder or joint entropy. The mutual information of two images is a measure of the order of the system formed by the two images. Given two images A and B, their mutual information I(A,B) is:

$$I(A, B) = H(A) + H(B) - H(A, B) \ , \tag{1}$$

with H(A) and H(B) being the entropies, and H(A,B) being the joint entropy. Following Shannon's information theory, the entropy of a probability distribution P is computed as:

$$H = -\sum_{p \in P} p \log p \ . \tag{2}$$

In classical mutual information, the joint probability distribution of two images is estimated as the normalized joint histogram of the intensity values [2]. The marginal distributions are obtained by summing over the rows or over the columns of the joint histogram:

$$H(A) = -\sum_{a} p_A^T(a) \log p_A^T(a) \ , \tag{3}$$

$$H(B) = -\sum_{b} p_B^T(b) \log p_B^T(b) \ , \tag{4}$$

where p_A^T and p_B^T are the marginal probability distributions for certain values of the registration parameters T. They are not constant during the registration process because the portion of each image that overlaps with the other changes. The registration parameters T represent a spatial mapping (rigid, affine) that aligns one image with the other.

The mutual information can be estimated with respect to the marginal entropies p_A^T and p_B^T [16] as:

$$I(A,B) = \sum_a \sum_b p_{AB}^T \log \frac{p_{AB}^T}{\sum_a p_A^T \sum_b p_B^T} , \tag{5}$$

where p_{AB}^T represents the joint probability for a given T.

3.2 Including Feature Information

Although successful results are reported when mutual information-based registration is applied, there are cases where it can fail. This may happen in low quality images as we mention in previous section. Some researchers like Papademetris *et al.* [17] have proposed the inclusion of spatial information in the registration process using an approach that integrates intensity and features in a functional with associated weights. Results suggest that this method yields accurate nonrigid registrations.

We propose a new measure of mutual information computed only from features. The use of features for registration seems well suited for images where, like in some medical images, the local structural information is more significant than pixel's intensity information. It also reduces, generally, the amount of data that must be handled during registration. We use edge points as features, and point location, edge strength and edge orientation as feature characteristics. Edge points are a significant source of information for image alignment, they are present in almost every conventional image, as well as in every medical imaging modality like MR, computed tomography (CT) or portal images, so they are useful for intra and inter modality registration. In optimal registration edge points from one image should match their corresponding edge points in location and also in edge strength and orientation.

Let a_1,a_2,...,a_N and b_1,b_2,...,b_M be two sets of feature points in two images A and B. Let D_{ij}^T denote a distance measure between two points a_i and b_j (e.g. Euclidean distance) after applying the transformation T on the set of b_j. When the two images are registered, point a_i will be located close to its matching point b_j. If a joint probability table is built considering the distances from each a_i to all the b_j, with j=1, 2,...,M, in one of the M cells of the i-th column, there will exist the maximum of that column, point b_j, having the biggest likelihood of being the match of a_i. Re-computing the joint probability table for different transformations T, one of the tables obtained will be the best, having the highest likelihood of matched points and so the highest mutual information. Similarly, with the images registered, an edge point a_i will match some b_j having similar edge strength since they represent the same edge point. The edge orientation after the mapping has to be also similar.

Denoting as D_{ij} the distance between a_i and b_j, S_{ij} the difference in edge strength, and O_{ij} the difference in edge orientation after the mapping, we can estimate the mutual information $I(A,B)$ as a function on these feature points characteristics $f(D_{ij}, S_{ij}, O_{ij})$.

The principal modification we propose with respect to the classical mutual information is the use of several feature attributes to estimate the joint probabilities. We use the gradient magnitude at a feature point as an estimation of the edge strength, and the gradient direction as an estimation of the edge orientation:

$$D_{ij}^T = \|a_i - b_j^T\|^2 \ , \tag{6}$$

$$S_{ij} = \Big| |\nabla a_i| - |\nabla b_j| \Big| \ , \tag{7}$$

$$O_{ij}^T = \cos^{-1} \frac{\nabla a_i \nabla b_j^T}{|\nabla a_i||\nabla b_j^T|} \ . \tag{8}$$

Note that S_{ij} does not depend on the registration parameters since the strength difference (gradient magnitude difference) of two edge points remains the same after moving an image. This does not hold for the Euclidean distance D_{ij}^T, or the orientation difference O_{ij}^T, which are affected by translation and rotation. Gradient magnitude at edge points can be different in corresponding edges detected in different images due to the possibly different sensing devices used to take the images. This can be overcome by scaling the gradient magnitude at the edges in both images, giving, for example, a relative measure between zero and one.

To estimate the joint probability of match between two edge points in two images we introduce an exponential function based on the feature attributes, so that if D_{ij}^T, S_{ij} and O_{ij}^T are small, there is a high probability of correspondence between those edge points. The proposed joint probability is expressed as follows:

$$p_{ij}^T = \frac{\exp - (\frac{D_{ij}^T}{\gamma_1} + \frac{S_{ij}}{\gamma_2} + \frac{O_{ij}^T}{\gamma_3})}{\sum_i \sum_j \exp - (\frac{D_{ij}^T}{\gamma_1} + \frac{S_{ij}}{\gamma_2} + \frac{O_{ij}^T}{\gamma_3})} \ , \tag{9}$$

with γ_k being constant weights. Using the probability distribution function given in (9), mutual information is computed as described in (5), but replacing p_{AB}^T with p_{ij}^T.

The main advantage of our approach compared to the classical mutual information is that this latter method does not use the neighbouring relations among pixels at all. All spatial information is lost in the classical approach, while our approach is precisely based on spatial information. Compared to the method reported by Rangarajan *et al.*. [13], we add new feature information in the estimation of the joint probability distribution, so the similarity criterion is improved and this can be particularly effective with images of poor quality, like portal images. With respect to the work reported by Pluim *et al.* [14], our approach is only based on feature points, a smaller amount of data than the classical approach, that uses all the pixels, resulting in a faster estimation of the mutual information. The computation of S_{ij} is done only once at the beginning of the registration as it does not depend on T, O_{ij}^T changes only if the transformation T involves a rotation, while D_{ij}^T is affected by translation and rotation.

It is also possible to control the contribution that each term introduces in the joint probability with the weights γ_1, γ_2 and γ_3.

3.3 Edge Detection

Extraction of edges can be done by several methods, first derivative-based methods (Sobel masks), or second derivative-based, like Laplacian of a Gaussian or Canny [18]. In this work we have used the Canny edge detector, that selects edge points at locations where zero-crossings of the second derivative occur. Since the amount of resulting edge points can be big, a selection of a certain percentage of the strongest ones can be done, using only the selected points for the registration.

3.4 Optimization

Optimization of the registration function is done by exhaustive search over the space of parameters. We assume a rigid transformation to align one image with the other, a rotation followed by a translation, both in 2D, so the search space is three-dimensional. A revision of optimization strategies can be found in the work by Maes *et al.*. [19] where various gradient- and non-gradient-based optimization strategies are compared.

Since the principal purpose of our work is to prove the feasibility of a new form of obtaining the joint probability used for the computation of the mutual information, no analysis on the convenience of using a certain optimization has been made. Exhaustive search is a sufficiently simple method for a bounded three-dimensional search space, and it finds a global optimum, avoiding the main drawback of other optimization algorithms, that may converge to a local optimum.

4 Results

We have tested our approach with a number of pairs of images of different sources: portal images provided from sessions of radiotherapy treatments at the Provincial Hospital of Castellón, Spain, MR images obtained from the internet (http://www.itk.org/HTML/Data.htm) and video sequences. Figure 1 shows pairs of images used in our experiments. Note that pa the pair of MR images, although obtained with the same sensor, are multimodal in the sense that different tissue characteristics are represented. So, we are also testing our method in multimodal registration. We assume that the registration parameters to align the second image with the first one represent a two-dimensional rigid motion. The parameters of this transformation are denoted as θ for the angle of rotation, and as (t_x, t_y) for the translation vector. In portal images, the true image registration parameters were determined by human operators that selected corresponding landmarks in both images. For MR images and video sequences true image registration parameters were available along with the images.

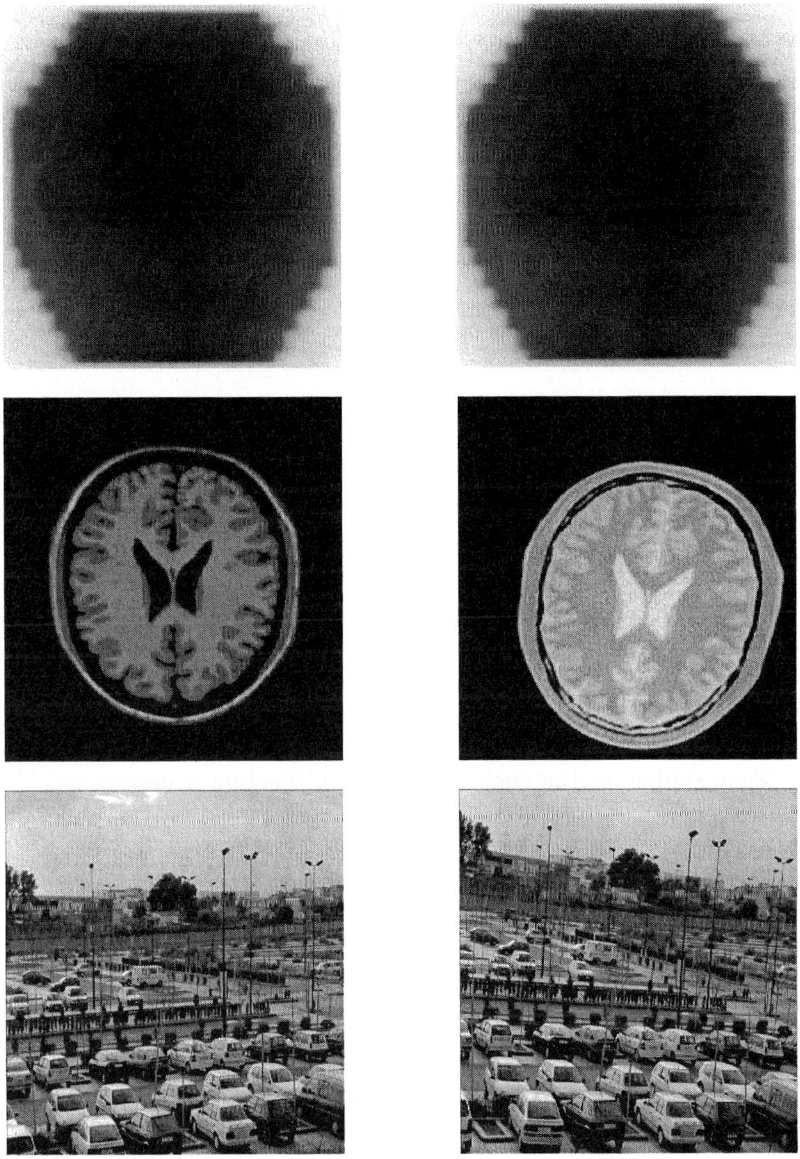

Fig. 1. Pairs of images used in the experiments. Top: portal images obtained in two different sessions. Middle: MR images, T1-weighted (left) and proton-density-weighted (right). Bottom: two images of a video sequence.

Table 1 shows the errors in the estimation of the rigid transform parameters: θ(degrees), t_x and t_y (mm). Results using the classical mutual information (MI) and using our method are presented.

Table 1. Errors in the estimation of rigid transform parameters

	Classical MI			Our method		
	θ	t_x	t_y	θ	t_x	t_y
Portal Images	0.1	2.01	1.93	0.238	0.510	0.396
MR images	0.5	1.12	1.58	0.5	1.35	0.97
Video Sequence	2.02	2.36	2.52	1.30	1.01	1.04
Average	0.87	1.83	2.01	0.68	0.96	0.80
Standard Deviation	1.01	0.64	0.47	0.55	0.42	0.35

Remember that classical MI is based on grey level correspondences at every pixel of two images, where one image has been moved to be aligned with the other. So, to obtain the classical MI registration results, we gave values to the registration parameters aligning an image with the other, we computed the joint histogram of grey levels, which is an estimation of the joint probability that two grey levels correspond, and we selected the registration parameters that provide a maximum of the mutual information.

In the computation of p_{ij}^T the values of γ_1, γ_2 and γ_3 were fixed heuristically. These values are like time constant of the decreasing exponentials that appear in (9). In the zone where the independent variable of an exponential function has a value similar to the time constant, the function decreases quickly. We are interested in quick changes of correspondence probability around values of D_{ij}^T, S_{ij} and O_{ij}^T that are typical in our images. So, we registered some images manually, and we selected the values of γ_1, γ_2 and γ_3 as the mean of the distances (D_{ij}^T, S_{ij}, O_{ij}^T) found between correspondent feature points.

Figure 2 shows the registration results for images in Figure 1. Observe that for the pair of images from a video sequence the mismatch of some edges after registration is still notable. This is due to perspective effects. We assumed a 2D rigid transformation as a motion model, that can not account for real 3D scenes.

Although we assumed a rigid transformation in our tests, there is no a priori restriction to a particular type of transformation, an affine motion model could be used also. Figure 3 shows the joint probability tables of each pair of images after registration using our feature-based method. Low intensity values correspond to high likelihood of correspondence. It can be observed that the information concentrates in an area of the table, as expected.

5 Conclusions and Further Work

The inclusion of spatial information in the computation of the mutual information is a subject under current investigation. In this paper we have proposed a new measure of registration that combines mutual information with spatial

Fig. 2. Sets of edges detected in images of Figure 1 overimposed before the registration in the left column, and after the registration in the right column

information obtained from feature attributes, like edge points. Instead of a joint histogram of grey levels, the classical approach, we estimated a joint probability distribution based on feature points. We introduced a probability estimate that two feature points match based on points similarity. An optimization algorithm

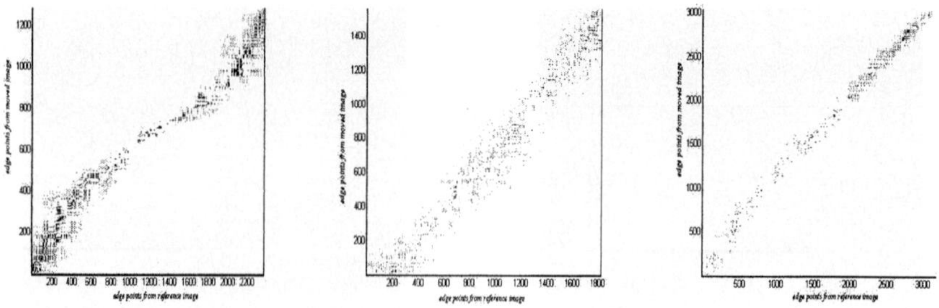

Fig. 3. Joint probability functions computed after registration for portal (left), MR (center) and video sequence (right) images

was then applied to find the best registration parameters where a maximum of the mutual information occurs.

The proposed approach can be used to register images from different sources, multimodal registration, since it can combine different features as needed. A way to compute the probability that two features in two images correspond has to be provided.

Our approach improves the classical mutual information method, which is based only on intensity values, by using feature characteristics. Furthermore, the number of points used to build the probability function is significantly smaller, only feature points, compared to the number used to build the joint histogram, the whole image.

Further work is addressed at investigating the use of other features in the approach, as boundaries of regions in segmented images, or their overlapping area. The key question is which attributes to include in the computation of the joint probability table, and how to combine them. In our work we have used as probability functions a combination of decreasing exponentials that account for differences in location, in edge orientation, and in edge strength, of two feature (edge) points.

Acknowledgments

This work is partially supported by the Spanish Ministry of Science and Technology under Project TIC2003-06953, and by Fundació Caixa Castelló under project P1-1B2002-41.

References

1. Pluim, J.W., Maintz, J.B.A., Viergever, M.A.: Mutual information based registration of medical images: a survey. IEEE Transactions on Medical Imaging **22** (2003) 986–1004
2. Viola, P., Wells, W.M.: Alignment by maximization of mutual information. International Journal on Computer Vision **24** (1997) 137–154

3. Maes, F., Collignon, A., Vandermeulen, D., Marchal, G., Suetens, P.: Multimodality image registration by maximization of mutual information. IEEE Transactions on Medical Imaging **16** (1997) 187–198
4. Tomazevic, D., Likar, B., Pernus, F.: Multi-feature mutual information. In Sonka, M., ed.: Medical Imaging: Image Processing. Volume 5070., SPIE Press (2004) 234–242
5. Lester, H., Arriage, S.R.: A survey of hierarchical non-linear medical image registration. Pattern Recognition **32** (1999) 129–149
6. Zitova, B., Flusser, J.: Image registration methods: a survey. Image and Vision Computing **21** (2003) 977–1000
7. Maintz, J., Viergever, M.A.: A survey of medical image registration. Medical Image Analysis **2** (1999) 1–36
8. Leszczynski, K., Loose, S., Dunscombe, P.: Segmented chamfer matching for the registration of field borders in radiotherapy images. Physics Medicine and Bilogy **40** (1995) 83–94
9. Borgefors, G.: Hierarchical chamfer matching: a parametric edge matching algorithm. IEEE Transactions on Pattern Analysis and Machine Intelligence **10** (1988) 849–865
10. Hristov, D.H., Fallone, B.G.: A gray-level image alignment algorithm for registration of portal images and digitally reconstructed radiographs. Medical Physics **23** (1996) 75–84
11. Langmack, K.A.: Portal imaging. The British Journal of Radiology **74** (2001) 789–804
12. Kim, J., Fessler, J.A., Lam, K.L., Balter, J.M., Ten-Haken, R.K.: A feasibility study of mutual information based setup error estimation for radiotherapy. Medical Physics **28** (2001) 2507–2517
13. Rangarajan, A., Chui, H., Duncan, J.: Rigid point feature registration using mutual information. Medical Image Analysis **3** (1999) 425–440
14. Pluim, J., Maintz, J.B., Viergever, M.A.: Image registration by maximization of combined mutual information and gradient information. IEEE Transactions on Medical Imaging **19** (2000) 809–814
15. West, J., et. al: Comparison and evaluation of retrospective intermodality brain image registration techniques. Journal of Computer Assisted Tomography **21** (1997) 554–566
16. Hill, D.L.G., Batchelor, P.G., Holden, M., Hawkes, D.J.: Medical image registration. Physcis in Medicine and Biology **46** (2001) R1–R45
17. Papademetris, X., Jackowski, A.P., Schultz, R.T., Staib, L.H., Duncan, J.S.: Integrated intensity and point-feature nonrigid registration. In Barillot, C., Haynor, D.R., Hellier, P., eds.: Medical Image Computing and Computer-Assisted Intervention – MICCAI 2004, 7th International Conference Saint-Malo, France, September 26-29, 2004, Proceedings, Part I. Volume 3216., Springer (2004) 763–770
18. Canny, J.: A computational approach to edge detection. IEEE Transactions on Pattern Analysis and Machine Intelligence **8** (1986) 679–698
19. Maes, F., Vandermeulen, D., Suetens, P.: Comparative evaluation of multiresolution optimization strategies for multimodality image registration by maximization of mutual information. Medical Image Analysis **3** (1999) 373–386

A Recursive Least Square Adaptive Filter for Nonuniformity Correction of Infrared Image Sequences *

Flavio Torres[1], Sergio N. Torres[2], and César San Martín[1,2]

[1] Department of Electrical Engineering, University of La Frontera, Casilla 54-D, Temuco, Chile
ftorres@ufro.cl
[2] Department of Electrical Engineering, University of Concepción, Casilla 160-C, Concepción, Chile
sertorre@udec.cl
http://nuc.die.udec.cl

Abstract. In this paper, an adaptive scene-based nonuniformity correction methodology for infrared image sequences is developed. The method estimates detector parameters and carry out the non-uniformity correction based on the recursive least square filter approach, with adaptive supervision. The key advantage of the method is based in its capacity for estimate detectors parameters, and then compensate for fixed-pattern noise in a frame by frame basics. The ability of the method to compensate for nonuniformity is demonstrated by employing several infrared video sequences obtained using two infrared cameras.

Keywords: Image Sequence Processing, Infrared Imaging, RLS.

Topic: Infrared Image and Video Processing, Infrared Sensor-Imaging.

1 Introduction

Infrared (IR) imaging systems employ an IR sensor to digitize the information, and due to its high performance, the most used integrated technology in IR sensors is the Focal Plane Array (FPA). An IR-FPA is a die composed of a group of photodetectors placed in a focal plane forming a matrix of $X \times Y$ pixels, which gives the sensor the ability to collect the IR information.

It is well known that nonuniformity noise in IR imaging sensors, which is due to pixel-to-pixel variation in the detectors' responses, can considerably degrade the quality of IR images since it results in a fixed-pattern-noise (FPN) that is superimposed on the true image. Even more, what makes matter worse is that the nonuniformity slowly varies over time, and depending on the technology used,

* This work was partially supported by Proyecto DIUFRO EP N° 120323 and Grant Milenio ICM P02-049. The authors wish to thank Ernest E. Armstrong (OptiMetrics Inc., USA) and Pierre Potet (CEDIP Infrared Systems, France) for collecting the data.

M. Lazo and A. Sanfeliu (Eds.): CIARP 2005, LNCS 3773, pp. 540–546, 2005.

this drift can take from minutes to hours. In order to solve this problem, several scene-based nonuniformity correction (NUC) techniques have been developed [1,2,3,4,5,6]. Scene-based techniques perform the NUC using only the video sequences that are being imaged, not requiring any kind of laboratory calibration technique.

Our group has been given special attention to NUC methods based on estimation theory. Seeking for more effectiveness in the reduction of NUC, we propose an adaptive scene-based NUC method, based in a RLS (recursive least square) filter [7], to estimate detector parameters and to reduce the FPN in a fast and reliable frame by frame basis. Further, the NUC method based in a RLS algorithm exhibits the advantages of fast convergence rate and unbiased stationary error [8,9].

This paper is organized as follows. In Section 2 the IR-FPA model and the NUC-RLS method is developed. In Section 3 the NUC-RLS technique is tested with video sequences of real raw IR data captured using two infrared cameras. In Section 4 the conclusions of the paper are summarized.

2 The NUC-RLS Algorithm for Infrared Video Sequences

The aim of this paper is to develop a scene-based NUC method for infrared video sequences using fundamental theory in parameters estimation. We begin reviewing the most common model used for IR-FPA technology, and then developing a RLS filter approach for NUC.

2.1 IR-FPA Model

In this paper, we adopt the commonly used linear model for the infrared detector. For the $(ij)^{\text{th}}$ detector in IR-FPA, the measured readout signal Y_{ij} at a given time n can be expressed as:

$$Y_{ij}(n) = g_{ij}(n) \cdot X_{ij}(n) + o_{ij}(n) \tag{1}$$

where $g_{ij}(n)$ and $o_{ij}(n)$ are the gain and the offset of the ij^{th} detector, and $X_{ij}(n)$ is the real incident infrared photon flux collected by the respective detector. Equation (1) is reordered for obtain the inverse model given by:

$$X_{ij}(n) = \frac{1}{g_{ij}(n)} \cdot Y_{ij}(n) - \frac{o_{ij}(n)}{g_{ij}(n)} \tag{2}$$

where this equation performs the NUC correction. The detector parameters have to be estimated using only the measured signal Y_{ij}, and the corrected image is obtained with the inverse model equation.

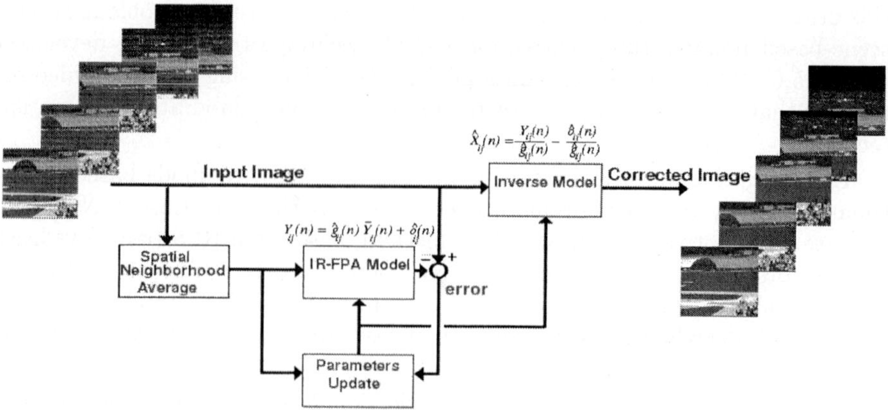

Fig. 1. Scheme of the proposed Scene-Based Non-Uniformity Correction Method

2.2 NUC-RLS Filter Method

We start re-writing equation (1) in a vectorial form:

$$Y_{ij}(n) = \Psi_{ij}^T(n)\Theta_{ij}(n) \tag{3}$$

where, $\Psi_{ij}(n) = [X_{ij}(n), 1]^T$ is the infrared data vector and $\Theta_{ij}(n) = [g_{ij}(n), o_{ij}(n)]^T$, is the detector parameter vector. Because the real incident IR is unknown, the key assumption of this paper is that X_{ij} can be initially estimated from the read-out data Y_{ij}. We propose to initially estimate the real X_{ij} applying a spatial lowpass filter over the corrupted image as follow:

$$\bar{Y}_{ij}(n) = \frac{1}{(2v+1)^2} \sum_{k=i-v}^{i+v} \sum_{l=j-v}^{j+v} Y_{kl}(n) \tag{4}$$

where $\bar{Y}$ is the smoothing version of Y, and only spatio correction is performed. If we supposes that the scene is constantly moving with respect to the detector, $\bar{Y}$ can be assumed as the corrected image and the equation (3) can be used for estimate the detector parameters with $\hat{\Psi}_{ij}(n) = \left[\bar{Y}_{ij}(n), 1\right]^T$, i.e., we suppose that the gain parameters have a spatial normal distribution with unit mean, and the bias have a spatial normal distribution with zero mean. Then, writing equation (2) as:

$$\hat{X}_{ij}(n) = Y_{ij}(n)/\hat{g}_{ij}(n) - \hat{o}_{ij}(n)/\hat{g}_{ij}(n) \tag{5}$$

we can remove the FPN of the corrupted image sequence making it a spatio-temporal NUC method. For a recursive update of the parameters, the RLS algorithm is used and all necessary equations to form the algorithm are:

$$\hat{\Theta}_{ij}(n+1) = \hat{\Theta}_{ij}(n) + \mathrm{K}_{ij}(n+1)\left[Y_{ij}(n+1) - \hat{\Psi}_{ij}^T(n+1)\hat{\Theta}_{ij}(n)\right]$$

$$\mathrm{K}_{ij}(n+1) = \mathrm{P}_{ij}(n)\hat{\Psi}_{ij}(n+1)\left[\lambda - \hat{\Psi}_{ij}^T(n+1)\mathrm{P}_{ij}(n)\hat{\Psi}_{ij}(n+1)\right]^{-1}$$

$$\mathrm{P}_{ij}(n+1) = \left[I - \mathrm{K}_{ij}(n+1)\hat{\Psi}_{ij}^{T}(n+1) \right] \mathrm{P}_{ij}(n) \cdot \frac{1}{\lambda} \tag{6}$$

where, $\hat{\Theta}_{ij}(n) = [\hat{g}_{ij}(n), \hat{o}_{ij}(n)]^T$, is the estimated parameter vector, $\mathrm{K}_{ij}(n)$ is the correction vector, $\mathrm{P}_{ij}(n)$ is the covariance matrix, and λ is the forgetting factor. Varying λ within $0 < \lambda < 1$, we weight the influence of past error values.

The scheme of the proposed RLS-NUC method is shown in Fig. 1. The corrupted image is smoothed using a local spatial neighborhood average filter (4), and the IR-FPA model (3) is used for estimate the gain and offset of each detector with the RLS algorithm. The difference of the readout data and the output of the sensor model evaluated with the estimate real infrared data calculates the error signal. Then, the estimated parameters are introduced into equation (5) for computing the corrected image. On each step, the equation (6) is updated with a new infrared image.

Note that if the scene is not constantly moving with respect to the IR-FPA, on the output of the RLS-NUC method of Fig. 1, the smoothing version of Y is obtained. Therefore, the sensor parameter can not be update and a motion detection algorithm would be required, and it will be develop in future works.

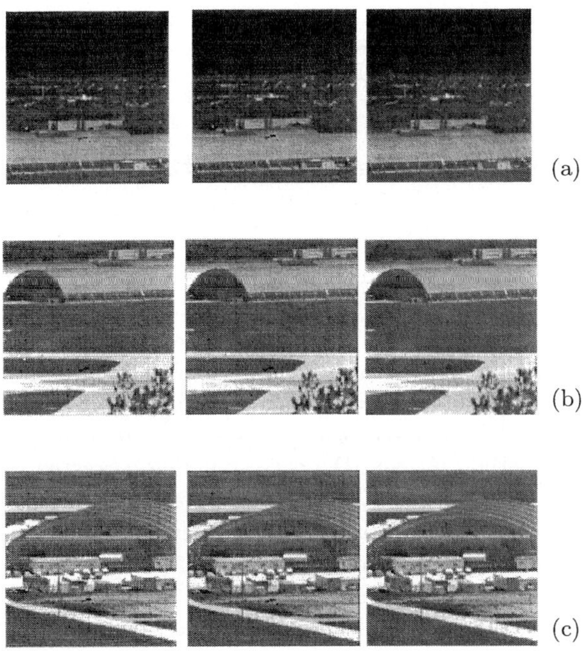

Fig. 2. Performance of the NUC-RLS method under real IR data. (a)(b) (c) The $200-th$ $(1600-th)$ $(2630-th)$ frames of the first set of IR data, at the left the raw corrupted frames, at the right the corresponding frames corrected first by the Scribners method and then by the proposed method.

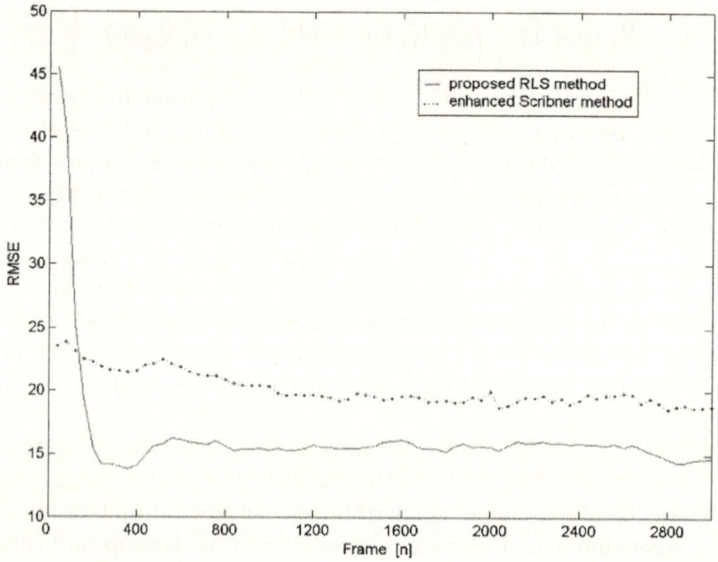

Fig. 3. The evolution of the RMSE between the reference (set 1 calibrated with black bodies) and the corrected frames of IR data set 1. Dashdot line represents the RMSE computed for the enhance Scribners NUC method, and solid line represents the RMSE computed for the proposed NUC-RLS method.

3 Performance Evaluation with Real Infrared Image Sequences

The main goal of this section is to test the ability of the proposed method for reduce nonuniformity on real video data. The algorithm is tested with two real infrared image sequences. The first sequence has been collected using a 128×128 InSb FPA cooled camera (Amber Model AE-4128) operating in the $3-5\mu m$ range. As an example, figure 2 (a)(b)(c) shows from left to right a corrupted readout data frame, the corresponding corrected frame by enhance Scribner NUC method [6], and the corresponding corrected frame by the NUC method proposed in this paper. The NUC performance, in this case, is evaluated employing the index root mean square error (RMSE) computed between a reference (the real IR sequence calibrated with black bodies) and the corrected IR video sequence. Figure 3 shows the calculated RMSE for each frame corrected using enhance Scribner's NUC method and using the proposed method. Further, the average RMSEs computed for the whole infrared sequence are equal to 20.15 and 16.62 for the Scribner NUC method and the NUC-RLS algorithm proposed, respectively. Further, it can be seen in figure 2 using only the naked eye that the non-uniformity is notably reduced by the proposed NUC method.

The second sequence of infrared data has been recorded using a 320×240 HgCdTe FPA cooled camera (CEDIP Jade Model) operating in the $8-12\mu m$

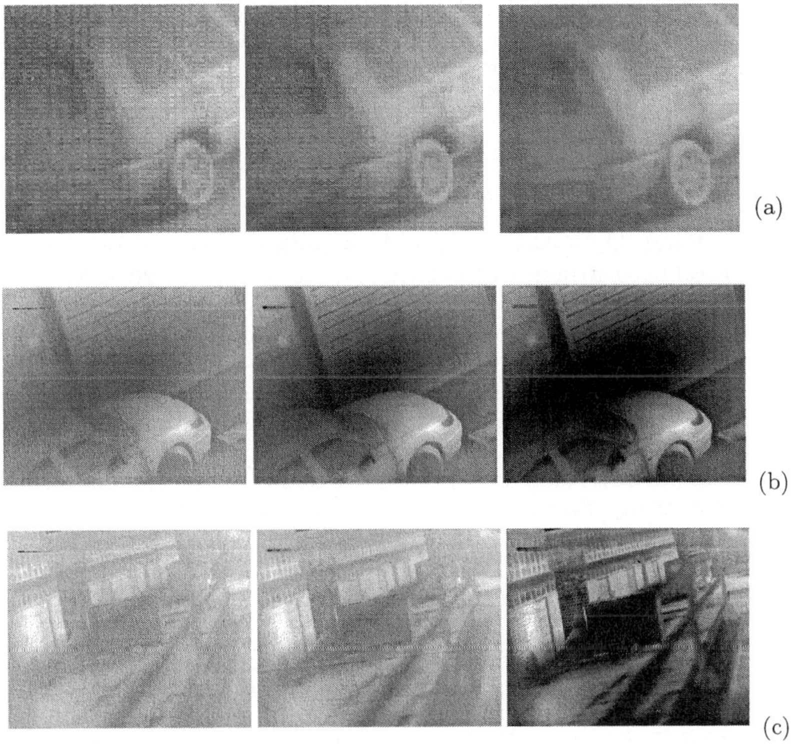

Fig. 4. Performance of the NUC-RLS method under real IR data. (a)(b)(c) The $280-th$ $(500-th)$ $(1000-th)$ frames of the second set of IR data, at the left the raw corrupted frames, at the right the corresponding frames corrected first by the Scribners method and then by the proposed method.

range. As an example, figure 4 (a)(b)(c) shows from the left to right a corrupted readout data frame, the corresponding corrected frame by enhance Scribner NUC method, and the corresponding corrected frame by the NUC method proposed in this paper. Again, it can be seen by only using the naked eye, that the non-uniformity presented in the raw frame has been notably reduced by both NUC method. Thus, we have shown experimentally with real IR data that the proposed scene-based NUC-RLS method has the ability of notably reduces the non-uniformity noise presented in IR-FPA sensors and improve the enhance Scribner NUC method.

4 Conclusions

In this paper a NUC-RLS method is proposed. The main advantage of the method is based in its simplicity using only fundamental parameter estimation theory. The method has the ability of notably reducing the FPN after only processing around 300 frames. The key assumption of the method is that the real infrared data is obtained from the readout data applying an average spatial filter on each step time. It was shown experimentally using real IR data from two technologies that the method is able to reduce the non-uniformity with a faster convergence and low RMSE.

References

1. Torres, S., Hayat, M.: Kalman Filtering for Adaptive Nonuniformity Correction in Infrared Focal Plane Arrays. The JOSA-A Opt. Soc. of America. **20**. (2003) 470–480.
2. Torres, S., Pezoa, J., Hayat, M.: Scene-based Nonuniformity Correction for Focal Plane Arrays Using the Method of the Inverse Covariance Form. OSA App. Opt. Inf. Proc. **42**. (2003) 5872–5881.
3. Scribner, D., Sarkady, K., Kruer, M.: Adaptive Nonuniformity Correction for Infrared Focal Plane Arrays using Neural Networks. Proceeding of SPIE. **1541**. (1991) 100–109.
4. Scribner, D., Sarkady, K., Kruer, M.: Adaptive Retina-like Preprocessing for Imaging Detector Arrays. Proceeding of the IEEE International Conference on Neural Networks. **3**. (1993) 1955–1960.
5. Torres, S., Vera, E., Reeves, R., Sobarzo, S.: Adaptive Scene-Based Nonuniformity Correction Method for Infrared Focal Plane Arrays. Proceeding of SPIE. **5076**. (2003) 130–139.
6. Vera, E., Torres, S.: Fast Adaptive Nonuniformity Correction for Infrared Focal Plane Arrays. To be published in EURASIP Journal on Applied Signal Processing. (2005).
7. L. Ljung and T. Sderstrm: Theory and practice of recursive identification, MIT Press, Cambridge, 1983.
8. E. Eleftheriou, D.D. Falconer, Tracking properties and steady-state performance of RLS adaptive filter algorithms, IEEE Trans. Acoust. Speech Signal Process. ASSP **34** (1986) 1097-1110.
9. E. Ewada, Comparasion of RLS, LMS and sign algorithms for tracking randomly time-varying channels, IEEE Trans. Signal Process. **42** (1994) 2937-2944.

MSCT Lung Perfusion Imaging Based on Multi-stage Registration

Helen Hong[1] and Jeongjin Lee[2,*]

[1] School of Electrical Engineering and Computer Science
BK21: Information Technology, Seoul National University
hlhong@cse.snu.ac.kr
[2] School of Electrical Engineering and Computer Science, Seoul National University,
San 56-1 Shinlim 9-dong Kwanak-gu, Seoul 151-742, Korea
jjlee@cglab.snu.ac.kr

Abstract. We propose a novel subtraction-based method for visualizing segmental and subsegmental pulmonary embolism. For the registration of a pair of CT angiography, a proper geometrical transformation is found through the following steps: First, point-based rough registration is performed for correcting the gross translational mismatch. The center of inertia (COI), apex and hilar point of each unilateral lung are proposed as the reference point. Second, the initial alignment is refined by iterative surface registration. Third, thin-plate spline warping is used to accurately align inner region of lung parenchyma. Finally, enhanced vessels are visualized by subtracting registered pre-contrast images from post-contrast images. To facilitate visualization of parenchymal enhancement, color-coded mapping and image fusion is used. Our method has been successfully applied to four pairs of CT angiography.

1 Introduction

Currently, computed tomography (CT) has become increasingly important in the diagnosis of pulmonary embolism because of the advent of multi-detector row CT scanners providing high spatial and excellent contrast resolution [1-3]. In CT angiography (CTA) images, thrombi are generally recognized as dark regions within enhanced pulmonary arteries. Thus the basis of pulmonary embolism assessment on CT images is the direct visualization of contrast material within the pulmonary arteries. However, it provides only limited information on perfusion defects since lung parenchymal attenuation changes as a result of the injection of contrast material are too faint to be identified on segmental and subsegmental vessels. If lung perfusion can be well visualized, CT may provide more accurate information on pulmonary embolism.

Several methods have been suggested for visualizing perfusion defects in CTA [4]. Mastuni et al. [5] proposed a fully automatic detection method based on segmentation of pulmonary vessels to limit the search space and analysis of several 3D features inside segmented vessel volume. However, several false positive occurs due to flow

* Corresponding author.

M. Lazo and A. Sanfeliu (Eds.): CIARP 2005, LNCS 3773, pp. 547 – 555, 2005.

void and soft tissue between adjacent vessels. Zhou et al. [6] developed a CAD system for detection of pulmonary embolism in CTA images. An adaptive 3D pixel clustering method was developed based on Baysian estimation and Expectation-Maximization (EM) analysis to segment vessels. Then the vessel tree was reconstructed by tracking the vessel and its branches in 3D space based on their geometric characteristics such as the tracked vessel direction and skeleton. Pichon et al. [7] proposed a method to highlight potential pulmonary embolism in a 3D representation of the pulmonary arterial tree. At first, lung vessels are segmented using mathematical morphology. The density values inside the vessels are then used to color the outside of a SSD of the vessel tree. However, pulmonary vessels exhibit a wider distribution of CT values from slice to slice. Thus it is difficult to visualize vessel structures in 3D volume using segmentation-based approach for the pulmonary embolism diagnosis since vessels cannot be accurately segmented and continuously tracked if they are largely or totally clotted by pulmonary embolism. Herzog et al. [8-9] proposed an image post-processing algorithm for visualization of parenchymal attenuation in chest CT angiography, which divided into five steps: lung contour segmentation, vessel cutting, adaptive filtering, color-coding and overlay with the original images. However, the method has a limitation in the direct visualization of emboli by CT angiography alone. Chung et al. [10] evaluated the value of CT perfusion image obtained by 2D mutual information-based registration and subtraction for the detection of pulmonary embolism. However, they evaluated their method using a porcine model under the limited conditions. The 2D registration has a limitation to accurately align three-dimensional anatomy. In addition, the processing time is about 40 seconds for single slice registration. Thus, it is difficult to be useful and acceptable technique for clinical applications in diagnosis of pulmonary embolism.

Current approaches still need more progress in computational efficiency and accuracy for detecting attenuation changes of pulmonary vessels in CTA. In this paper, we propose a novel subtraction-based method for accurately imaging perfusion defects and efficiently detecting segmental and sub-segmental pulmonary embolism in chest CTA images. For the registration of a pair of CTA, a proper geometrical transformation is found through the following steps: First, point-based rough registration is performed for correcting the gross translational mismatch. The center of inertia (COI), apex and hilar point of each unilateral lung are proposed as the reference point. Second, the rough alignment is refined by iterative surface registration. For fast and robust convergence of the distance measure to the optimal value, a 3D distance map is generated by the narrow-band distance propagation. Third, thin-plate spline warping is used to accurately align inner region of lung parenchyma. Finally, enhanced vessels are visualized by subtracting pre-contrast images from registered post-contrast images. To facilitate visualization of parenchymal enhancement, color-coded mapping and image fusion is used.

The organization of the paper is as follows. In Section 2, we discuss how to correct the gross translational mismatch. Then we propose a narrow-band distance propagation to generate a 3D distance map and a distance measure to find an exact geometrical relationship in pre- and post-contrast images of CTA. Finally, nonrigid registration using thin-plate spline warping is described to align deformable and distorted area within lung parenchyma. In Section 3, experimental results show how our registration method accurately and rapidly aligns the lungs. This paper is concluded with brief discussion of the results in Section 4.

2 Lung Perfusion Imaging

Fig. 1 shows the pipeline of our method for lung perfusion imaging in pre- and post-contrast images of chest CTA. In order to extract the precise lung region borders, pulmonary vessels and main airway, we apply the automatic segmentation method of Yim et al. [11] to our experimental datasets. Since our method is applied to the diagnosis of pulmonary embolism, we assume that each CT scan is almost acquired at the maximal inspiration and the dataset includes the thorax from the trachea to below the diaphragm.

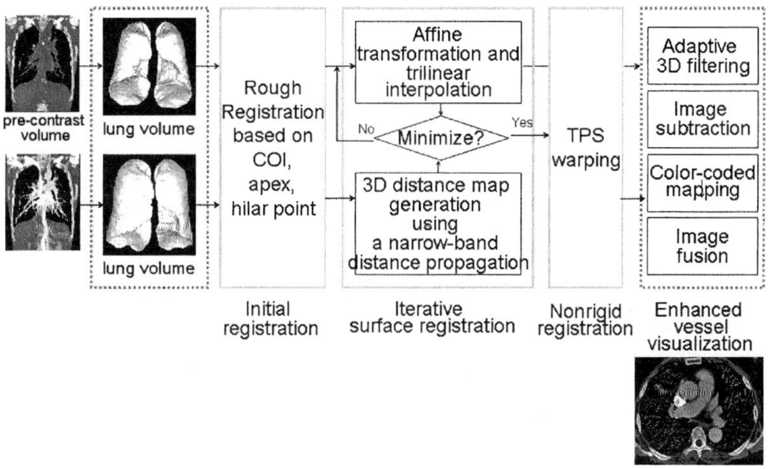

Fig. 1. The pipeline of proposed method for visualization of pulmonary embolism

2.1 Point-Based Rough Registration

Although pre- and post-contrast images of chest CT angiography are acquired at the maximal inspiration, the position of lung boundaries between pre- and post-contrast images can be quite different according to the patient's unexpected respiration and small movement. For the efficient registration of such images, an initial gross correction method is usually applied. Several landmark-based registration techniques have been used for the initial gross correction. To achieve the initial alignment of lung boundaries, these landmark-based registrations require the detection of landmarks and point-to-point registration of corresponding landmarks. These processes much degrade the performance of the whole process.

To minimize the computation time and maximize the effectiveness of initial registration, we propose a point-based rough registration using hilar point and evaluate our method with center of inertia and apex. As shown in Fig. 2(c), hilar point is where the outermost upper lobe vein crosses the basal artery on its way to the left

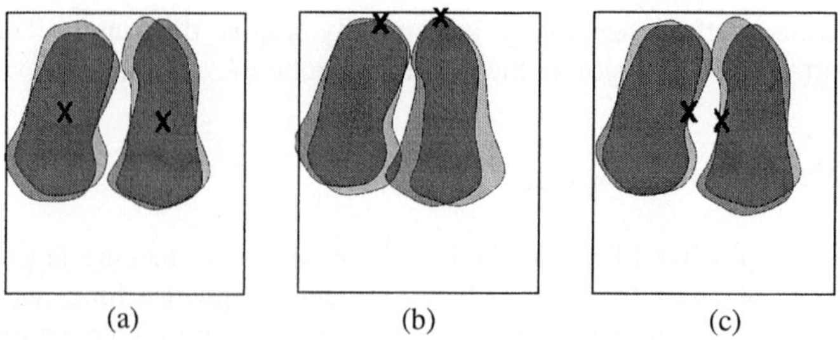

Fig. 2. The effect of point-based rough registration as an initial alignment (a) COI-based registration (b) apex-based registration (c) hilar point-based registration

atrium. The initial registration of two volumes is accomplished by aligning the COI, apex and hilar point, respectively.

The processing time of point-based rough registration is dramatically reduced since it does not require any anatomical landmark detection. In addition, our method leads to robust convergence to the optimal value since the search space is limited near the lungs.

2.2 Iterative Refinement Using Surface Registration

In a surface registration algorithm, the calculation of the distance from a surface boundary to a certain point can be done using a preprocessed distance map based on chamfer matching. Chamfer matching reduces the generation time of a distance map by an approximated distance transformation compared to a Euclidean distance transformation. However, the computation time of distance is still expensive by the two-step distance transformation of forward and backward masks. In particular, when the initial alignment almost corrects the gross translational mismatch, the generation of a 3D distance map of whole volume is unnecessary. From this observation, we propose the narrow-band distance propagation for the efficient generation of a 3D distance map.

To generate a 3D distance map, we approximate the global distance computation with repeated propagation of local distances within a small neighborhood. To approximate Euclidean distances, we consider 26-neighbor relations for 1-distance propagation as shown in Eq. (1). The distance value tells how far it is apart from a surface boundary point. The narrow-band distance propagation is applied to surface boundary points only in the contrast volume. We can generate a 3D distance map very fast since pixels are propagated only in the direction of increasing distances to the maximum neighborhood.

$$DP(i) = \min(\min_{j \in 26-neighbors(i)}(DP(j)+1), DP(i)) \ . \tag{1}$$

The distance measure in Eq. (2) is used to determine the degree of resemblance of lung boundaries of mask and contrast volume. The average of absolute distance difference, *AADD,* reaches the minimum when lung boundary points of mask and contrast volumes are aligned correctly. Since the search space of our distance measure is limited to the surrounding lung boundaries, the Powell's method is sufficient for evaluating *AADD* instead of using a more powerful optimization algorithm.

$$AADD = \frac{1}{N_{mask}} \sum_{i=0}^{N_{mask}-1} \left| D_{\text{contrast}}(i) - D_{\text{mask}}(i) \right| , \tag{2}$$

where $D_{\text{mask}}(i)$ and $D_{\text{contrast}}(i)$ is the distance value of mask volume and the distance value of the 3D distance map of contrast volume, respectively. We assume that $D_{\text{mask}}(i)$ are all set to 0. N_C is the total number of surface boundary points in mask volume.

2.3 Non-rigid Registration Using Thin-Plate Spline Warping

Affine transformation in iterative surface registration is insufficient for accurate modeling of inner lung parenchyma since the lung volumes move in a non-linear way influenced by a combination of body movement, heart beats, and respiration. Thus we use a thin-plate spline warping using 10 control points of vascular structure in each unilateral lung. Our method leads to a non-linear volumetric warping for aligning inner region of lung parenchyma and detecting pulmonary embolism accurately.

Thin-plate splines can be defined as a linear combination of radial basis functions as shown in Eq. (3). A transformation between two volumes can be defined by three separate thin-plate splines.

$$t(x,y,z) = a_1 + a_2 x + a_3 y + a_4 z + \sum_{i=1}^{N} b_i \theta(|\phi_i - (x,y,z)|),\ \theta(s) = |s|, \tag{3}$$

where ϕ_i is *ith* control point. The coefficient a_i characterizes the linear part of the transformation and the coefficient b_i characterizes the non-linear part of the transformation.

2.4 Enhanced Vessel Visualization

A traditional approach for visualizing enhanced vessels after registration is to subtract registered pre-contrast volume from post-contrast volume. However, it is difficult to easily recognize perfusion defects using a traditional subtraction technique when lung parenchymal changes as a result of the injection of contrast material are too small. After subtraction, we apply color-coded mapping to only lung parenchyma and image fusion with original image.

To facilitate visualization of parenchymal enhancement, the subtraction image is mapped onto a spectral color scale, which is interactively controlled by modifying center and width of a spectral color. Then the resulting color-coded parenchymal images are overlaid onto the corresponding slice of contrast volume. For overlaying, all non-parenchymal pixels are replaced by the original pixels of the respective slice position and displayed in the usual CT gray-scale presentation.

3 Experimental Results

All our implementation and test were performed on an Intel Pentium IV PC containing 3.4 GHz and 2.0 GB of main memory. Our method has been applied to four clinical datasets with pulmonary embolism, as described in Table 1, obtained from Siemens Sensation 16-channel multidetector row CT scanner. The image size of all experimental datasets is 512 x 512. The pre- and post-contrast images of chest CT angiography are acquired under the same image conditions excepting the injection of contrast material.

Table 1. Image conditions of experimental datasets

(mm)

Subject #		Image size	Slice number	Pixel size	Slice thickness
1	Pre-contrast	512 x 512	258	0.60 x 0.60	1.5
	Post-contrast	512 x 512	258	0.60 x 0.60	1.5
2	Pre-contrast	512 x 512	175	0.61 x 0.61	1.5
	Post-contrast	512 x 512	175	0.61 x 0.61	1.5
3	Pre-contrast	512 x 512	221	0.69 x 0.69	1.5
	Post-contrast	512 x 512	221	0.69 x 0.69	1.5
4	Pre-contrast	512 x 512	214	0.59 x 0.59	1.5
	Post-contrast	512 x 512	214	0.59 x 0.59	1.5

The performance of our method is evaluated with the aspects of visual inspection, accuracy and total processing time. Fig. 3 shows the results of color-coded mapping and image fusion on original image. Segmental and subsegmental emboli are detected predominantly in the upper lobe of right and left lungs as shown in Fig. 3. We can easily recognize the occlusion of the corresponding segmental and subsegmental arteries as color-coded mapping and fusion.

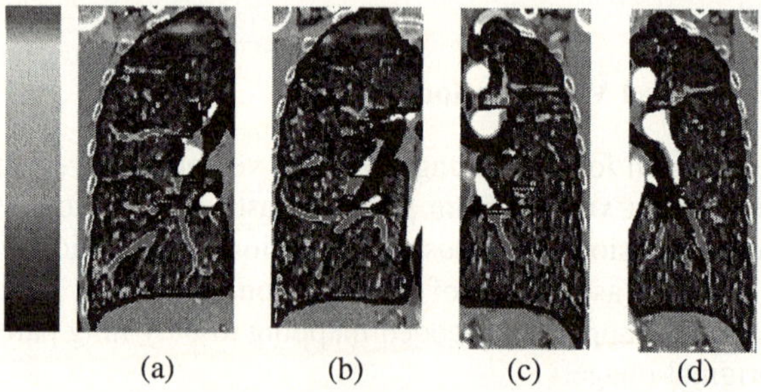

(a) (b) (c) (d)

Fig. 3. The results of color-coded mapping and image fusion in subject 1

Fig. 4 shows how the error, the average of root-mean squared error of corresponding control points, is reduced by our rough registration. The average RMS error reduction of COI- and hilar point-based registration is 0.32mm and 0.27mm, respectively. However, 0.72mm is increased in the average RMS error using apex-based rough registration.

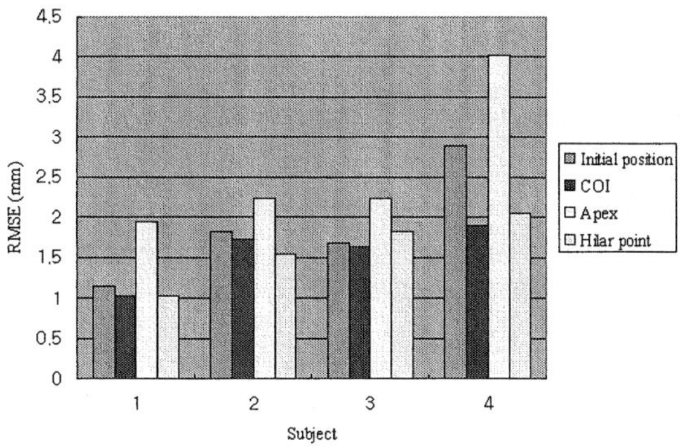

Fig. 4. The accuracy evaluation of corresponding points after rough registration

Fig. 5 shows how the error, the average of absolute distance difference (AADD), is reduced by our rough registration and subsequent iterative surface registration. The COI-, apex- and hilar point-based registration is used as rough registration shown in Fig. 5(a), (b) and (c), respectively. Since positional difference is almost aligned by our rough registration, iterative surface registration rapidly converge to the optimal position. In almost clinical datasets, the AADD errors are less than 0.6 voxels on optimal solution.

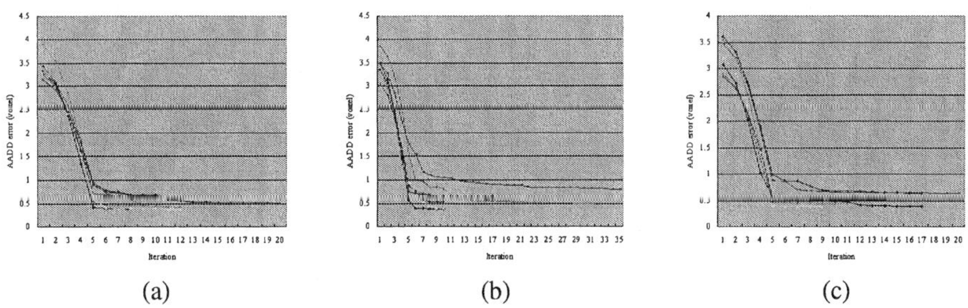

Fig. 5. The accuracy evaluation of corresponding lung boundaries using AADD error per iteration

Fig. 6 shows the results of our method (Method 3) of four patients in comparison with COI-based rough registration (Method 1) and apex-based rough registration (Method 2). The average of RMS errors of Method 1 and Method 3 as shown in Fig. 6 (a) and (c) are all 1.12mm. In contrary to them, the average of RMS error of Method 2 as shown in Fig. 6 (b) is 1.25mm. In conclusion, the average of RMS error is relatively small when COI- or hilar point-based registration is used as the initial alignment. The total processing time is summarized in Table 2 where the execution time is measured for registration. For four subjects, it takes less than 10 minutes.

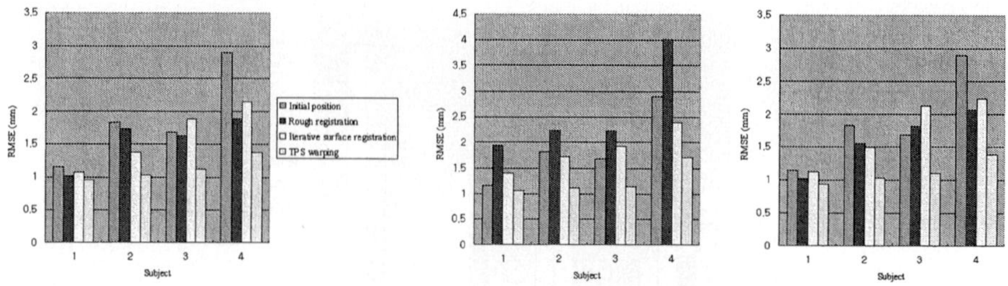

(a) (b) (c)

Fig. 6. The accuracy evaluation of corresponding lung boundaries using AADD error per subject

Table 2. The comparison of processing time for registration

(mm)

Subject #		Iterative surface registration	TPS warping	Enhanced vessel visualization	Total processing time
1	Method 1	80.656	532.906	63.011	676.573
	Method 2	80.716	533.387	62.970	677.073
	Method 3	80.576	533.557	62.921	677.054
2	Method 1	43.833	238.002	39.077	320.912
	Method 2	43.453	237.832	39.116	320.401
	Method 3	43.954	239.935	39.076	322.965
3	Method 1	75.088	374.889	51.194	501.171
	Method 2	74.467	373.758	51.103	499.328
	Method 3	74.847	375.911	51.123	501.881
4	Method 1	71.993	342.663	49.311	463.967
	Method 2	70.591	340.620	49.261	460.472
	Method 3	72.174	341.030	49.231	462.435
Average	Method 1	67.893	372.115	50.648	490.656
	Method 2	67.307	371.399	50.613	489.319
	Method 3	67.888	372.608	50.588	491.084

4 Conclusion

We have developed a new subtraction-based method for visualizing perfusion defects in pre- and post-contrast images of CT angiography. Using the rough registration, the initial gross correction of the lungs can be done much fast and effective without detecting any anatomical landmarks. In the subsequent iterative surface registration, our distance measure using a 3D distance map generated by the narrow-band distance propagation allows rapid and robust convergence to the optimal value. Nonrigid registration using thin-plate spline warping can exactly aligns inner region of lung parenchyma. Our enhanced vessel visualization makes the recognition of attenuation variations within lung parenchyma easily. Four pairs of pre- and post-contrast images of CT angiography have been used for the performance evaluation with the aspects of visual inspection, accuracy and processing time. In visual inspection, we can easily recognize the occlusion of the corresponding segmental and subsegmental arteries. The registration error of our method is less than 1.12mm. All our registration process is finished within 10 minutes. Accurate and fast result of our method can be successfully used to visualize pulmonary perfusion for the diagnosis of pulmonary embolism.

References

1. Schoepf, U.J., Costello, P., CT angiography for diagnosis of pulmonary embolism: state of the art, Radiology, Vol. 230 (2004) 329-337.
2. Patel, S., Kazerooni, E.A., Cascade, P.N., Pulmonary embolism: optimization of small pulmonary artery visualization at multi-detector row CT, Radiology, Vol. 227 (2003) 455-460.
3. Schoepf, U.J., Holzknecht, N., Helmberger, T.K. et al, Subsegmental pulmonary emboli: improved detection with thin-collimation multi-detector row spiral CT, Radiology, Vol. 222 (2002) 483-490.
4. Ko, J.P., Naidich, D.P., Computer-aided diagnosis and the evaluation of lung disease, Journal of Thoraic Imaging, Vol. 19, No. 3 (2004) 136-155.
5. Masutani, Y., MacMahon, H., Doi, K., Computerized detection of pulmonary embolism in spiral CT angiography based on volumetric image analysis, IEEE Trans. on Medical Imaging, Vol. 21, No. 12 (2002) 1517-1523.
6. Zhou C, Hadjiisk LM, Sahiner B. et al., Computerized detection of pulmonary embolism in 3D computed tomographic images: vessel tracking and segmentation technique, Proc. of SPIE Medical Imaging, Vol. 5032 (2003) 1613-1620.
7. Pinchon E, Novak CL, Naidich DP, A novel method for pulmonary emboli visualization from high resolution CT images, Proc. of SPIE Medical Imaging, Vol. 5061 (2004).
8. Herzog, P., Wildberger, J.E., Niethammer, M et al., CT perfusion imaging of the lung in pulmonary embolism, Acad Radiol, Vol. 10 (2003) 1132-1146.
9. Wildberger, J.E., Schoepf, U.J., Mahnken, A.H., et al., Approaches to CT perfusion imaging in pulmonary embolism, Roentgenology (2005) 64-73.
10. Chung, M.J., Goo, J.M., Im, J.G., et al., CT perfusion image of the lung : value in the detection of pulmonary embolism in a porcine model, Investigative Radiology, Vol. 39, No. 10 (2004) 633-640.
11. Yim, Y., Hong, H., Shin, Y.G., Hybrid lung segmentation in chest CT images for computer-aided diagnosis, Proc. of HEALTHCOM 2005 (2005).

Statistical and Linguistic Clustering for Language Modeling in ASR*

R. Justo and I. Torres

Departamento de Electricidad y Electrónica,
Facultad de Ciencia y Tecnología,
Universidad del País Vasco
webjublr@lg.ehu.es, manes@we.lc.ehu.es

Abstract. In this work several sets of categories obtained by a statistical clustering algorithm, as well as a linguistic set, were used to design category-based language models. The language models proposed were evaluated, as usual, in terms of perplexity of the text corpus. Then they were integrated into an ASR system and also evaluated in terms of system performance. It can be seen that category-based language models can perform better, also in terms of WER, when categories are obtained through statistical models instead of using linguistic techniques. They also show that better system performance are obtained when the language model interpolates category based and word based models.

1 Introduction

Automatic Speech Recognition and Understanding (ASRU) Systems are currently based on Statistical Language Modeling. Thus, large amounts of training data are required to get a robust estimation of the parameters of the model. However, the availability of large amounts of training material is not always assured when designing many of usual ASRU applications. As an example, the text corpus needed to train a dialogue system consists of transcriptions of dialogue turns uttered by potential users of the system to be developed. These speakers reproduce the natural behavior of further users including spontaneous, unconstrained and most times noisy speech. This procedure only allows to obtain a limited corpus to train the language model of the ASRU system, smaller than the usual text databases.

One of the ways to deal with sparseness of data is to cluster the vocabulary of the application tasks into a reduced number of categories. Replacing words by the category they belong to entails significant reductions in the number of parameters to be estimated. Thus, smaller training corpora can be used. On the other hand, new words belonging to previously defined categories can be directly added to the vocabulary of the task without changing the training corpus.

* This work has been partially supported by the CICYT proyect TIC2002-04103-C03-02 and by the Universidad del País Vasco under grant 9/UPV 00224.310-13566/2001.

M. Lazo and A. Sanfeliu (Eds.): CIARP 2005, LNCS 3773, pp. 556–565, 2005.

The first issue when generating a category-based language model is the appropriate selection of word classes. Morphosyntactic and/or semantic knowledge is usually applied to manual clustering of linguistic categories (e.g. part of speech POS) [1]. This procedure leads to some perplexity reduction when applied to limited domain tasks. However in less constrained domains these models do not usually improve on word-based language models. Alternatively, iterative clustering algorithms using theoretic information criteria have also been proposed to reduce perplexity in large corpora [2].

In this work the categories obtained through a statistical clustering algorithm are compared with a classical linguistic set of POS. Several category-based language models are evaluated and compared in terms of ASR system performance. Thus, not only the perplexity of a text test set is evaluated but also the WER obtained through the ASR system when different category-based language models are compared. On the other hand, a category-based language model will prove coarser than a word-based model and could lose accuracy in predictions of the next word. In such a case, the language model is only based on relations between word classes and on the probability distribution of words into classes. Alternatively a second approach proposes a language model that interpolates the information associated with the relations between categories and the information associated to the relations between words [3].

These proposals were evaluated through a set of recognition experiments carried out on a Spanish human-machine dialogue system. The experiments carried out shows that category-based language models can also perform better in terms of WER, when categories are obtained through statistical models than for linguistic categories, even for limited domains. They also show that better system performance is obtained when the language model interpolates category-based and word-based models.

Section 2 deals with the method for classifying words into categories. The statistical clustering algorithm is fully explained and the POS categories are presented. In Section 3 the two category-based language model are described and their integration into the decoder is presented. Section 4 deals with experimental evaluation of the proposals and Section 5 presents the main conclusions and suggestions for future work.

2 Classification of Words into Categories

A classical clustering algorithm has been used in this work to automatically obtain a set of categories from a text corpus. The goal of a clustering algorithm is to group samples with high internal similarity. For this purpose, an objective function to be optimized should be defined [4]. This function will also measures the quality of any partition of the data. Thus, the clustering algorithm has to find the partition of the initial set of samples that optimizes the objective function. Section 2.1 fully explains the objective function to be maximized in the clustering algorithm presented in Section 2.2. Finally Section 2.3 presents the linguistic set of categories used for comparison purposes.

2.1 Objective Function: Class Bigram Models

We first describe a class bigram model which is the basis of the objective function to be selected [5]. Suppose a distribution of the W words of the vocabulary into N_C classes using a function $C(\cdot)$, which maps a word w into a class C_w, $C(\cdot) : w \rightarrow C_w$. If each word is assigned to a single class, a word bigram (w_i, w_j) will correspond to the class bigram (C_{w_i}, C_{w_j}).

According to a class bigram model:

$$p(w_j|w_i) = p(w_j|C_{w_j})p(C_{w_j}|C_{w_i}) \tag{1}$$

Given a training corpus and the map function C, $p(w_j|C_{w_j})$ and $p(C_{w_j}|C_{w_i})$ can be estimated taking into account the number of times that particular events have been seen in the training corpus, $N(\ )$.

$$p(w|C_w) = \frac{N(w)}{N(C_w)} \tag{2}$$

$$p(C_{w_j}|C_{w_i}) = \frac{N(C_{w_i}, C_{w_j})}{N(C_{w_i})} \tag{3}$$

The clustering algorithm consist of finding the function C that maximizes the log-likelihood function of the class bigram model described in 1, on the training corpus.

The likelihood is defined as the joint probability of the training samples and using the bigram model is expressed as follows:

$$P(w_1 \ldots w_N) = P(w_1) \prod_{n=2}^{N} P(w_n|w_{n-1}) \tag{4}$$

From equation 4, the function log-likelihood is developed for a bigram class model:

$$F_{bi}(C) = \sum_{n=1}^{T} \log P(\omega_n|\omega_{n-1}) = \sum_{v,w} N(v,w) \log p(w|v) =$$

$$= \sum_{w} N(w) \log \frac{N(w)}{N(C_w)} + \sum_{C_v, C_w} N(C_v, C_w) \log \frac{N(C_v, C_w)}{N(C_v)} =$$

$$= \sum_{C_v, C_w} N(C_v, C_w) \log N(C_v, C_w) - 2\sum_{C} N(C) \log N(C) + \sum_{w} N(w) \log N(w) \tag{5}$$

where each term is defined in 1.

2.2 Clustering Algorithm

The goal of this algorithm is to find the function C , thus, the way the words can be grouped, which maximizes the log-likelihood function of the bigram class

Table 1. Notation for the expression 5

$F_{bi}(\mathcal{C})$	Log-likelihood function for a bigram class model.
T	Training corpus size.
C	Word class.
C_v, C_w	Classes containing the words v and w respectively.
$N(C)$	Number of occurrences of the C class in the training corpus.
$N(C_v, C_w)$	Number of occurrences of the C_v class after C_w class have been seen in the training corpus.
$N(w)$	Number of times w word has appeared in the training.

model, $F_{bi}(\mathcal{C})$ on the training corpus. An iterative clustering algorithm based on sample exchange is used for this purpose [5].

Iterative algorithm.
Start with some initial mapping: N_C classes and $\mathcal{C} : w \rightarrow C_w$.
do
for each w of the vocabulary **do**
for each class k **do**
- tentatively exchange word w from class C_w to class k.
- compute likelihood for this tentative exchange.

exchange word w from class C_w to class k which maximizes the likelihood.
until the stopping criterion is met.

The result of such algorithms strongly depends on the initialization, thus different classes are generated depending on the initial distribution of words into categories.

The initial distribution in [5] is based on placing each of he most frequent words in a single class and the rest in the last class. This technique lets the most frequent words determine the way the words are grouped because they are evaluated first in the process. However, the algorithm used does not permit the use of this technique with the same result because putting each of the most frequent words in a single class means they are unable to leave that class until they are not only word in it. Therefore, a different distribution has been selected [6], consisting of placing each of the most frequent words each in a class, except for the less frequent $N_C - 1$, which are placed in the $N_C - 1$ remaining classes.

2.3 Linguistic Categories

The categories obtained from a text corpus, using classical clustering algorithms, have been compared to the linguistic categories obtained from a morphosyntactic analyzer: "Freeling", in terms of ASR system performance.

"Freeling" is a free software developed in Barcelona's Polytechnic University by the *talp* group. The FreeLing package consists of a library providing language analysis services (such as morphosyntactic analysis, date recognition, PoS tagging, etc.) In this case, only morphosyntactic analysis is used to obtain classes comparable with those obtained automatically. The classes given by the Freeling correspond to the following "eagle" labels: Adjectives, adverbs, determinants, names, verbs, pronouns, conjunctions, interjections, prepositions and another class was defined for the word P, corresponding to silences.

3 Category-Based Language Models into a Speech Recognition System

In this section two category-based language models are defined and then integrated into a speech recognition system.

3.1 A Language Model Based on Category N-Grams

In a first approach, the language model only collects the relations between word groups, "forgetting" the relations between particular words [7].

The probability of a sentence $(w_1, \ldots, w_N)$ can be represented as a product of conditional probabilities:

$$P(w_1, \ldots, w_N) = P(w_1) \prod_{n=2}^{N} P(w_n|w_1 \ldots w_{n-1}) \quad (6)$$

where $P(w_n|w_1 \ldots w_{n-1})$ represents the probability of w_n when the sequence of words $(w_1, \ldots, w_{n-1})$ has been observed.

Assuming that when the categorization process is finished, the set of words in the lexicon belongs to a smaller group of "a priori" defined categories, the probability of w_N conditioned to its $N-1$ predecessors can be defined as follows [7] [8]:

$$P(w_N|w_1 \ldots w_{N-1}) = \sum_{j=1}^{N_c} P(w_N|C_j)P(C_j|C_1 \ldots C_{j-1}) \quad (7)$$

where N_C is the number of different word categories.

The classification algorithm restricts the membership of words to a single class, so a single label corresponding to a category is assigned to a word and the above equation assumes the follows form:

$$P(w_N|w_1 \ldots w_{N-1}) = P(w_N|C_{w_N})P(C_{w_N}|C_{w_1} \ldots C_{w_{N-1}}) \quad (8)$$

The parameters of the distributions of words into categories are calculated as follows:

$$P(w|C) = \frac{N(w,C)}{\sum_{w'} N(w',C)} \quad (9)$$

where $N(w,C)$ is the number of times a word w is labeled by C in the training corpus.

On the other hand, $P(C_{w_N}|C_{w_1}\dots C_{w_{N-1}})$ represents the probability of C_{w_N} being the next class if up to now $C_{w_1}\dots C_{w_{N-1}}$ category sequence has been observed and C_{w_i} represents the class w_i belongs to.

It is important to notice that probabilities are calculated using category n-gram based models, analogous to word n-grams, so the history of an event is reduced to the n-1 previous events, thus:

$$P(w_N|w_1,\dots,w_{N-1}) \cong P(w_N|w_{N-n+1},\dots,w_{N-1}) \quad (10)$$

and expression 8 is rewritten as:

$$P(w_N|w_1\dots w_{N-1}) = P(w_N|C_{w_N})P(C_{w_N}|C_{w_{N-n+1}}\dots C_{w_{N-1}}) \quad (11)$$

An automatic speech recognition system based on the Viterbi algorithm looks for the sequence of states that has the maximum probability given the sequence of acoustic observations, and thus estimates the sequence of words the speaker pronounced

The transition probability between each pair of words is calculated in accordance with expression 11. This model only considers the probability distribution of words into categories and the category n-gram model.

3.2 Interpolating Category and Word N-Gram Models

The category based language model described in the equation 11 does not need so many parameters as the one based on word n-grams. Thus, it may be better estimated, with a higher confidence level. But it fails to capture the relationships between particular words so it is less accurate in predicting the next word.

The hybrid model to be described try to integrate both information sources, i.e. the one relative to relationships between particular words and the one associated with the relationships between groups of words.

This hybrid model is an interpolation of a model based on category n-grams and a model based on word n-grams. It is defined as a linear combination of both models. The probability of the word w_N conditioned to the N-1 previous words, would be represented as follows [3]:

$$\begin{aligned} P(w_N|w_1\dots w_{N-1}) &= \lambda P(w_N|w_1\dots w_{N-1}) + \\ &+(1-\lambda)P(w_N|w_1\dots w_{N-1},M_c) \end{aligned} \quad (12)$$

If n-grams based models are used as in the previous sections:

$$\begin{aligned} P(w_N|w_1\dots w_{N-1}) &= \lambda P(w_N|w_{N-n+1}\dots w_{N-1}) + \\ &+(1-\lambda)\sum_{j=1}^{C} P(w_N|C_j)P(C_j|C_{j-n+1}\dots C_{j-1}) \end{aligned} \quad (13)$$

and assuming that each word belongs to a single class

$$P(w_N|w_1 \ldots w_{N-1}) = \lambda P(w_N|w_{N-n+1} \ldots w_{N-1}) + \\ +(1-\lambda)P(w_N|C_{w_N})P(C_{w_N}|C_{w_{N-n+1}} \ldots C_{w_{N-1}}) \tag{14}$$

In this case the speech recognizer calculates the transition probability between each pair of words taking into account three probability distributions: distribution of words into categories, category n-grams and word n-grams.

4 Experimental Results

Several speech recognition experiments were done using a human-machine dialogue corpus in Spanish, BASURDE [9]. The speakers ask for information about long distances trains schedules, destinations and prices by telephone (8KHz). It was acquired by the "Wizard of Oz" technique and has 227 dialogues uttered by 75 speakers, 43 male and 32 female. The total number of phrases is 1657 and 1340 of them are used for training and the remaining 308 for testing. The starter set of the vocabulary consists of 788 words and the total number of words is 21088.

The language models proposed in this work were evaluated, as usual, in terms of perplexity (PP) of the text corpus. Then they were integrated into an ASR system and evaluated in terms of both, Word Error Rate (WER) and Category Error Rate (CER).

Continuous HMM were used to model a set of context independent units corresponding to the basic set of Spanish phones. These models were previously trained over a task-independent phonetically balanced Spanish corpus (SENGLAR) uttered by 57 speakers and then integrated into the ASR system.

K-testable grammars in the strict sense (K-TSS) were used to get the proposed language models. This formalism is considered as the grammatical approach to the well known n-gram models [10]. The ASR consists finally in a single stochastic automaton integrating acoustic, lexical, word-based and category-based language models along with the required smoothing technique. The search of most probable hypothesis over the full network is based on the Viterbi algorithm.

Category based language models based on 5, 10 and 20 categories, obtained through the clustering algorithm, as well as the language model based on the 10 linguistic classes obtained by "Freeling" were evaluated in these experiments. For comparison purposes a classical word-based language model was also considered. In such a case, the number of classes is equal to the size of the vocabulary, i.e. 788. Table 2 shows the perplexity evaluation for k=2, 3, and 4 models. This table reveals, as expected, important reductions of the PP values for the category-based language models. These PP values increased with the number of categories but similar value was achieved by linguistic and statistical methodologies for equal number of classes.

A first evaluation of the defined categories was achieved using the word sequences obtained through the ASR system. A conventional word-based language model was integrated into the ASR system. Then, once the recognition process

Table 2. Perplexity values for a classical word-based language model (788 classes) and for language models generated using a labeled corpus with 5, 10 and 20 automatically obtained classes on one hand and with 10 linguistic classes on the other hand

PP	without categories	statistical clusterings			linguistic classes
	788 words	5	10	20	10 (9+1)
k=2	29.8	3.06	4.73	7.38	5.15
k=3	27.36	3.02	4.69	7.35	4.64
k=4	27.65	3.03	4.70	7.83	4.36

Table 3. Values of CER when the word based language model is used but the recognized phrases are labeled with the labels corresponding to 5, 10 and 20 automatically obtained categories on one hand and to 10 linguistic categories on the other hand. The value of ($CER \equiv WER$) when the word based language model is used and no categories are considered, i.e. 788 categories, also appears.

	without categories	statistical clustering			linguistic classes
	788 words ($WER \equiv CER$)	5	10	20	10 (9+1)
CER(%)	38.19	27.97	31.43	33.87	39.96

was finished, both the sequences of words obtained by the recognizer and the reference sequences of words were labeled according to the different set of categories defined. Thus, a Category Error Rate (CER) can be calculated. Table 3 shows that CER is clearly lower for statistical categories than for linguistic ones. In this case, CER is similar, even greater, to CER obtained when any clustering was considered. Thus, the confusions, i.e. substitution errors, between words belonging to different cluster seems to be lower for statistical categories than for linguistic ones. Let us note that in certain sense linguistic categories also model the order of the phrase in agreement with the general syntax of the language. However this fact does not seem important in this case, perhaps due to the natural and spontaneous type of speech in the corpus.

For the final evaluation the category based models described in the section above were integrated into the ASR system.

Table 4 shows the WER and CER obtained when the category based language model, defined in section 3.1 was used. Statistical and linguistic categories were compared using corresponding K-TSS language models. Reductions in CER and WER can be seen in the mentioned table when statistical categories were used. However, the integration of the category based language model does not improve the system performance measured in terms of both WER and CER (see table 3 to compare).

Finally the hybrid language model interpolating a category based model and a word based model (see section 3.2) was integrated into the ASR system. Table 5 shows WER and CER obtained when statistical and linguistic categories were considered in the hybrid model. In this table an important reduction in CER and

WER can be seen when compared to Table 4. The interpolation of word-based models and category-based models improves the WER and CER obtained by a simple category category-based language model. Nevertheless, the final performance of the ASR system is similar, maybe a little better, than the reference ASR system which did not consider any category model.

Finally let us note that the objective function used in the statistical clustering algorithm seems to work quite well since the values of CER are quite low for these categories.

Table 4. Values of WER and CER using a category based language model with 5, 10 and 20 statistical clusters on the one hand and 10 linguistic classes on the other one

	statistical clustering			**linguistic classes**
number of classes	**5**	**10**	**20**	**10 (9+1)**
WER (%)	51.06	47.12	46.57	52.42
CER (%)	33.07	36.20	39.63	41.33

Table 5. Values of WER and CER using a hybrid language model where the category based language model has been generated with 5, 10 and 20 statisitcal clusters on the one hand and with 10 linguistic classes on the other one

	statistical clustering			**linguistic classes**
number of classes	**5**	**10**	**20**	**10 (9+1)**
WER (%)	38.34	37.92	38.16	37.67
CER (%)	27.39	30.2	33.02	40.35

5 Conclusions and Future Work

In this work several sets of categories obtained by a statistical clustering algorithm, as well as a linguistic set, were used to design category-based language models. The language models proposed were evaluated, as usual, in terms of perplexity of the text corpus. Then they were integrated into an ASR system and also evaluated in terms of system performance.

The experiments carried out shows that category-based language models can perform better, also in terms of WER, when categories are obtained through statistical models instead of using linguistic techniques, even for limited domains. They also show that better system performance are obtained when the language model interpolates category based and word based models.

These preliminary experiments have shown the power of statistical clustering of words for language modeling, even for limited domain application tasks. However, an in-depth experimentation is required to explore new objective functions and initializations in cluster algorithm. Alternative formalism s to interpolate and integrate models into the ASR system should also be explored.

References

1. Niesler, T.: Category-based statistical language models. PhD thesis, Department of Engineering, University of Cambridge, U.K. (1997)
2. Brown, P.F., deSouza, P.V., Mercer, R.L., Pietra, V.J.D., Lai, J.C.: Class-based n-gram models of natural language. Comput. Linguist. **18** (1992) 467–479
3. Linares, D., Benedí, J., Sánchez, J.: A hybrid language model based on a combination of n-grams and stochastic context-free grammars. ACM Trans. on Asian Language Information Processing **3** (2004) 113–127
4. Duda, R.O., Hart, P.E., Stork, D.G.: Pattern Classification. 2nd edn. Wiley-Interscience (2000)
5. Martin, S., Liermann, J., Ney, H.: Algorithms for bigram and trigram word clustering. Speech Communication **24** (1998) 19–37
6. Barrachina, S.: Técnicas de agrupamiento bilingue aplicada a la inferencia de traductores. PhD thesis, Universidad Jaume I, Departamento de Ingeniería y Ciencia de los Computadores. (2003)
7. Niesler, T.R., Woodland, P.C.: A variable-length category-based n-gram language model. In: IEEE ICASSP-96. Volume I., Atlanta, GA, IEEE (1996) 164–167
8. Nevado, F., Sánchez, J., Benedí, J.: Lexical decoding based on the combination of category-based stochastic models and word-category distribution models. In: IX Spanish Symposium on Pattern Recognition and Image Analysis. Volume 1., Castellón (Spain), Publicacions de la Universitat Jaume I (2001) 183–188
9. Proyecto BASURDE: Spontaneus-Speech Dialogue System in Limited Domains. Comisin Interministerial de Ciencia y Tecnologa TIC98-423-C06 (1998-2001) http://gps-tsc.upc.es/ veu/basurde/Home.htm.
10. Torres, I., Varona, A.: k-TSS language models in speech recognition systems. Computer Speech and Language **15** (2001) 127–149

A Comparative Study of KBS, ANN and Statistical Clustering Techniques for Unattended Stellar Classification

Carlos Dafonte[1], Alejandra Rodríguez[1], Bernardino Arcay[1], Iciar Carricajo[2], and Minia Manteiga[2]

[1] Information and Communications Technologies Department, Faculty of Computer Science, University of A Coruña, 15071, A Coruña, Spain
{dafonte, arodriguezf, cibarcay}@udc.es
[2] Navigation and Earth Sciences Deptartment, University of A Coruña, 15071, A Coruña, Spain
{iciar, manteiga}@udc.es

Abstract. The purpose of this work is to present a comparative analysis of knowledge-based systems, artificial neural networks and statistical clustering algorithms applied to the classification of low resolution stellar spectra. These techniques were used to classify a sample of approximately 258 optical spectra from public catalogues using the standard MK system. At present, we already dispose of a hybrid system that carries out this task, applying the most appropriate classification method to each spectrum with a success rate that is similar to that of human experts.

1 Introduction

This work is part of a global project devoted to the study of the last phases of stellar evolution. Our main purpose is the development of an automatic system for the determination of physical and chemical stellar parameters by means of optical spectroscopy and artificial intelligence techniques. This system can contribute to evolutionary studies in Astrophysics that discover and follow the temporal changes of the physical and chemical conditions of stars.

Spectroscopy is a fundamental tool in the analysis of a star's physical conditions (temperature, pressure, density, etc.) and chemical components (H, He, Ca, K, etc.). In general terms, a stellar spectrum consists of a black body continuum light distribution, distorted by the interstellar absorption and reemission of light, and by the presence of absorption lines, emission lines and molecular bands [1].

We have collected a sample of approximately 400 stellar spectra from astronomical observations carried out by several telescopes. The stellar spectra are collected from telescopes with appropriate spectrographs and detectors. Observers collect the flux distribution of each object and reduce these data to obtain a one-dimensional spectrum calibrated in energy flux (erg-1cms-2s-1Å-1) and wavelength (Å).

In order to extract useful information from the individual spectra and to study the stellar evolution in the whole sample, we must complete a solid and systematic spectral classification in the current Morgan-Keenan system (MK).

M. Lazo and A. Sanfeliu (Eds.): CIARP 2005, LNCS 3773, pp. 566 – 577, 2005.

The MK classification system was firstly proposed in 1943 by Morgan, Keenan & Kellman, and has experienced many revisions ever since [2]. This two-dimensional system is the only one that is widely used for stellar classification. One of its main advantages is that MK classifications are often static, because they are based on the visual study of the spectra and on a set of standard criteria. However, the same spectra can be classified differently by different experts and even differently by the same person at different times. This classification system quantifies stellar temperatures and levels of luminosity. Stars are divided into groups, i.e. spectral types, that are mainly based on the strength of the hydrogen absorption lines and on the presence or absence of some significant lines of Ca, He, Fe, and molecular bands. The temperature of the stars is divided into a sequence called OBAFGKM, ranging from the hottest (type O) to the coolest (type M) stars. These spectral types are further subdivided by a decimal system, ranging from 0 (hottest) to 9.5 (coolest). In addition, a luminosity class (from I to V) is assigned to the star, which depends on the intrinsic stellar brightness.

Table 1 illustrates the main properties of each spectral type in the MK standard classification system.

Table 1. Main spectral features in the MK system

Type	Color	Prominent Lines
O	Bluest	Ionized He
B	Bluish	Neutral He, Neutral H
A	Blue-white	Neutral H
F	White	Neutral H, Ionized Ca
G	Yellow-white	Neutral H, Strongest Ionized Ca
K	Orange	Neutral Metals (Ca, Fe), Ionized Ca
M	Red	Molecules and Neutral Metals

The estimation of the stellar parameters is often carried out by human experts, who analyse the spectra by hand, with no more help than their own experience. These manual analyses usually lead to a MK classification of the spectra. The manual classification techniques are often based on the visual study of the spectra and on a set of standard criteria [1]. Although this manual method of classification has been used by the researchers and the astrophysicists widely and successfully along the years, it is no longer viable because of the spectacular advance of the objects collection technologies, which allow us to obtain a huge amount of spectral data in a relatively short time. Since the manual classification of all the spectra that are currently available would involve a considerable increase in human resources, it is highly advisable to optimise the manual procedure by means of automatic, fast and efficient computational techniques.

In the course of the last 10 years, research in the field of spectral classification has been focused on either the need for the development of automatic tools, or on the revision and improvement of the manual techniques.

As for the application of artificial intelligence techniques to the design of automatic classification systems, some well-known previous works have also applied artificial neural networks to the problem of stellar classification [3], obtaining classifications with diverse resolution grades. Our research team has contributed to this research line with the development of various fuzzy experts systems for the classification of super giant, giant and dwarf stars. A complete description of our previous works can be found in [4].

Our intention is not to test models or techniques that have already demonstrated their suitability in this problem, but rather to integrate several models of artificial neural networks and clustering algorithms with our previous expert systems. Combining all the techniques, we intend to formalise a hybrid system able to determine the most appropriate method for each spectrum type and to obtain on-line MK classifications through an Internet Stellar Database (http://starmind.tic.udc.es).

2 Classification Techniques

The following sections start by describing the spectral data that were used to train and test the automatic classification techniques. Secondly, we describe the morphological analysis algorithms that were applied to the spectra before presenting them to the automatic techniques. Finally, we present the different neural networks and clustering algorithms that were tested and we contrast their results.

2.1 Astrophysical Data

We have chosen a complete and consistent set of spectra in order to design and test the neural networks and clustering algorithms that will be applied to the problem of stellar classification.

The 258 selected spectra proceed from the public catalogues of Silva [4] (28 spectra sampled in the range of 3500 to 8900 Å with 5 Å of spectral resolution), Pickles [1] (97 spectra sampled in the range of 1150 to 25000 Å with 5 Å of spectral resolution) and Jacoby [5] (133 spectra sampled in the range of 3510 to 7426 Å with 1.4 Å of spectral resolution). The selected spectra cover all the types and luminosities of the MK system and are sufficiently representative, because they offer a continuous transition of the spectral features between each spectral type and its adjacent types. These spectra were previously analyzed and corrected by human experts that collaborate in the project.

In order to guarantee the generalization of the designed networks and algorithms, we have built the training set with approximately 50% of the spectra of each spectral type, leaving around 15% of them to validate the training and the remaining 35% to evaluate the classification capability of each model.

The neural networks and the clustering techniques of this experimentation have been designed and tested so as to consider both full spectra and spectral parameters as input patterns. Before presenting the spectra to the automatic techniques, we carry out a morphological analysis of all the spectra in order to obtain the values of the parameters that characterize each spectrum separately.

2.2 Morphological Analysis

The patterns that are presented to both neural networks and clustering algorithms were obtained automatically by using signal processing techniques to measure the spectral peculiarities (absorption and emission lines, spectral energy, molecular bands, etc.).

In particular, we measure the 25 spectral features that are described in Table 2. These spectral parameters can be grouped into three general types:

- Absorption and emission lines: including hydrogen, helium and metallic lines (Ca, K).
- Molecular bands: hydrogen and carbon absorption bands.
- Rates between lines: CH-K rates, He-H rates, etc.

Table 2. Spectral classification parameters

Parameter	Description	Parameter	Description
Band 1	5005 ± 055 Å	**Line H Iδ**	4102 Å
Band 2	6225 ± 150 Å	**Line He I**	4026 Å
Band 3	4435 ± 070 Å	**Line He II**	4471 Å
Band 4	5622 ± 180 Å	**Line H Iβ**	4861 Å
Band 5	5940 ± 135 Å	**Line H Iα**	6563 Å
Band 6	6245 ± 040 Å	**Main Bands**	$\sum_{i=1}^{i=2} Band_i$
Band 7	6262 ± 130 Å	**Secondary Bands**	$\sum_{i=3}^{i=9} Band_i$
Band 8	6745 ± 100 Å	**Rate K-H**	Ca II K / Ca II H
Band 9	7100 ± 050 Å	**Rate CH- H Iγ**	CH band / H Iγ
Line Ca II (K)	3933 Å	**Rate H Iδ - HeI**	H Iδ / He I
Line Ca II (H)	3968 Å	**Rate H Iδ - HeII**	H Iδ /He II
Line CH band	4300 Å	**Energy**	Flux Integral
Line H Iγ	4340 Å	**Line H Iδ**	4102 Å

The signal processing algorithms used to obtain the spectral parameters are mainly based on the spectral continuum estimation and the energy measurement.

From a morphological point of view, an absorption line is a descending (ascending for emission) deep peak that appears in an established wavelength zone. As mentioned, the absorption/emission lines are supposed to appear in a fixed wavelength, but due to the spectrum displacement caused by the measuring instruments, they can be found in the previous or next sample. To accurately calculate the intensity of each line, we carry out an estimation of the local spectral continuum. We smoothen the signal with a low pass filter, excluding the peaks in an interval around the sample where the line was detected. This filter is implemented by a five-point moving average method that selects the five more stable fluxes. That is

$$C_j = \left(\frac{\sum_{j-n}^{j+n} E_i * X_i}{N} \right) \quad (1)$$

where Cj is the estimation of the continuum for sample j, Ei is the flux in sample i, N is the number of values used in the moving average method to calculate the local spectral continuum, and X is a binary vector that indicates the representative fluxes of the spectral continuum in the zone. This means that $Xi = 1$ if Ei is a flux value representative of the local spectral continuum, and $Xi = 0$ if Ei is a peak. The intensity is positive for the absorption lines and negative for the emission lines.

A molecular band is a spectral zone where the flux suddenly decreases from the local continuum during a wide lambda interval. For the molecular bands this means that we only have to measure their energy to decide if they are significant enough. In this case, the upper threshold line for each band is calculated by means of linear interpolation between the fluxes in the limits of the interval defined for each band. Then, the area between this line and the axis of abscissas is calculated with discrete integral; the area that surrounds each band is calculated by integrating the flux signal between the extremes of the band. Finally, the flux of the band is obtained by subtracting both calculated energies. That is

$$B_{lr} = \int_{l}^{r} L(\lambda_i) - \int_{l}^{r} E(\lambda_i) \tag{2}$$

where Blr is the flux of the band between the samples l and r, L is the projection line, E is the flux function, λ the wavelength, l the left limit of the band and r the right limit. Since the obtained value becomes more negative as the band becomes deeper and wider, positive or negative values close to zero are not considered as bands.

The sampling frequency of the input spectra is not limited because we developed a simple algorithm that automatically resamples them; this increases the flexibility and avoids losing spectral resolution because of format reasons.

Although most of the spectra are uniformly sampled, some of them have zones where there is no flux. This lack of information is generally due to the atmospheric effects and to the resolution of the measuring instruments. With the purpose of correcting the spectra and covering all the spectral ranges, we have elaborated an algorithm that reproduces the experts' behaviour in this specific situation. It is based on the interpolation of the energy flux in the wavelengths that belong to void zones.

After having scaled and adapted the spectra, the system carries out an exhaustive analysis of the most relevant spectral features, i.e., molecular bands and absorption/emission lines, using the signal processing algorithms described above. These algorithms have been implemented in a software module, the spectral analyzer, that is equipped with signal processing techniques to extract and measure the main spectral features of each spectrum. It is developed in C++ and integrates ad hoc ActiveX components for the visualization of spectra.

In this module we have also elaborated other algorithms to estimate the flux of some additional spectral features that are not directly considered in the manual process, e.g. the spectral energy. These features have been examined to find out their capacity to classify spectra.

We use both the spectral parameters obtained by the spectral analyzer module and the full spectral data to build the input patterns of the neural networks and clustering techniques.

In order to implement the neural networks we used the Stuttgart Neural Network Simulator (SNNS v.4.1), and we developed the clustering algorithms by using MATLAB v.6.5.1. After analyzing the performance of both techniques, we implemented the best models in C++ by integrating them with the spectral analyzer, which allow us to obtain a unique tool for processing and classifying the optical spectra of stars.

2.3 Knowledge Based Systems

This first approach proposes the implementation of a knowledge-based system that provides the user with a comfortable tool for the processing of stellar spectra. We have integrated signal processing, knowledge-based and fuzzy techniques, obtaining a very satisfactory emulation of the current manual process. This approach results in two classification modalities: spectra with no given luminosity class, and spectra of stars with a well-known luminosity level.

As a previous step towards the design of the expert system, we carried out a sensibility analysis of the classification parameters in order to define the different fuzzy sets, variables and membership functions. In this study, we have analysed the parameters of the spectra from the reference catalogue, using the aforementioned algorithms and determining the different spectral types that each parameter discriminates. Some parameters that seemed to be suitable were discarded, whereas others, which are not explicitly considered in the manual classification, were included, for example the additions of band fluxes: no molecular band, by itself, was found suitable to determine the global temperature (early, intermediate, late) for all the stars in the reference catalogue; however, we found a good discriminant between early, intermediate and late stars, which is the addition of several relevant bands. This new parameter can divide the stars from the catalogue into the three global temperature groups: since some stars that belong to the same group present a greater value in some bands, and in other stars the highest value corresponds to a different band, the addition solves these problems.

As a final result of this analysis, we have defined as many fuzzy variables as classification levels (global, type and subtype) for each luminosity class; we have also defined the fuzzy sets and membership functions determined by the values of the spectral features in the guiding catalogue spectra.

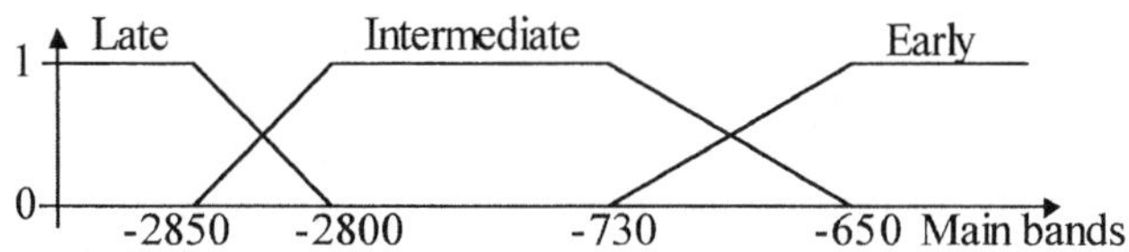

Fig. 1. Membership function for global classification in luminosity 1

The developed expert system stores the information that is necessary to initiate the reasoning process in the facts base. This descriptive knowledge of the spectra is represented by means of frames [8], i.e. objects and properties structured by levels. This model was chosen because it is the simplest and most adequate to transfer the analysis data to the classification module and allows us to establish the equivalence between analysis data and knowledge. The knowledge of the facts base includes general information, such as the names of the stars, and the results of the morphological analysis, i.e. the values of the classification parameters.

The real parameters of spectral classification and the limit values of each type and subtype were included in the expert system in the shape of fuzzy rules. The rules base is that part of the system where the human classification criteria are reproduced. We have adopted IF-THEN production rules for the implementation of this module, because they allow us to manage the uncertainty and imprecision that characterise human reasoning in this field.

The conditions of these rules refer to the values of the parameters stored in the current facts base (working memory). The conclusions allude to three levels of spectral classification: global (late, intermediate, early), spectral type and luminosity, and as such, the module communicates actively with the facts base.

To decide what rule to apply at each moment, we used the Means-End Analysis strategy (MEA) [9]: basically, among the rules that were incorporated last into the working memory, this strategy chooses the not executed rule that has the largest number of patterns. The production rules are linked in a forward reasoning, guided by objectives. The strategy used for the reasoning process combines guided reasoning methods with a method based on truth values. The rules also have associated credibility factors that were obtained from interviews with experts and from the bibliography of this field.

We used the Shortliffe and Buchanan methodology [10] to create an evolution that includes fuzzy sets and membership functions that are contextualized for each spectral type and allow superposition between them. The applied inference method is Max-product, which combines the influence of all the active rules and produces a smooth, continuous output. In our approach, the credibility factor of each rule has also been considered as another truth value. The defuzzification of the data into a crisp output was accomplished by the fuzzy-centroid method [11]. With this mixed strategy, we achieved a remarkable adaptation to human reasoning, able to successfully handle the imprecision and uncertainty implicit in the manual classification process. In addition, we obtained the spectral classification of stars with a probability value that indicates the grade of confidence.

This part of the spectral classifier was developed in OPS/R2 [12] and integrated with the analyzer by means of dynamic link libraries (DLL).

An additional research topic consisted in improving the implemented system by applying the results of the best neural models, and will be described in the next sections. The weights of the output layer units were analyzed so as to determine, for each spectral type, which input parameters have more influence on the output. The normalized values of the higher weights were included in the expert system in the shape of credibility factors of the rules that correspond to the most influential parameters for each spectral type. This modification of the reasoning rules (using the weights values of the trained neural networks) resulted in a slightly significant improvement of the performance of the original expert systems (around 2%).

2.4 Artificial Neural Networks

The neural networks of this approach are based on both supervised and non-supervised learning models. In particular we have implemented Backpropagation,

Kohonen and Radial Basis Functions (RBF) networks. The topologies, the learning functions and the results obtained by these networks are described below.

2.4.1 Backpropagation Networks

Backpropagation is a supervised learning algorithm that belongs to the general feed-forward model. This model is based on two stages of learning: forward propagation and backward propagation.

Training a feed-forward neural network with supervised learning consists of presenting a set of input patterns that are propagated forward by the net until activation reaches the output layer. This constitutes the so-called forward propagation phase. When the activation reaches the output layer, the output is compared with the teaching input (provided in the input patterns). The error, or difference between the output and the teaching input of a target output unit, is then used together with the output of the source unit to compute the necessary changes of the link between both units. In this way the errors are propagated backwards, which is why this phase is called backward propagation [13].

We have tested the backpropagation learning algorithm for the spectral types and luminosity classes. We used both spectral parameters and full spectral data to train the networks.

Table 3. The topologies for backpropagation networks we implemented

Network	Input Patterns	Hidden Layer
Type	Spectral parameters	10
Type	Spectral parameters	5x5
Type	Spectral parameters	10x10
Type	Spectral parameters	10x5x3
Type	659 flux values	100x50x10x3
Luminosity	Spectral parameters	10x10
Luminosity	659 flux values	100x50x10x3

The backpropagation topology that has resulted in a better performance corresponds to a network trained with 25 spectral parameters as input layer and three hidden layers of 10, 5 and 3 units.

In the training phase, we used the topological order to update the weights: first the weights of units in the input layer are updated, then the units in the hidden layers and finally the units in the output layer. The weights are initiated randomly with values in the interval [-1,1].

The number of training cycles, the frequency of validation and the values of the learning parameters were changed during the learning phase of the different implemented topologies. Our observations show that the implemented networks converge when MSE (Mean Square Error) is equal or inferior to 0.05 and the net becomes stable. If the training continues after having reached this rate of MSE, the net is over trained and its performance decreases. In the SNNS simulator, an output greater than 0.5 is equivalent to 1, otherwise to 0. In the analysis of the results, we have not considered the outputs near 0.5 as successes (from 0.45 to 0.55).

2.4.2 Kohonen Networks

The Self-Organizing Map (SOM) algorithm of Kohonen is based on non-supervised learning. SOMs are a unique class of neural networks, since they construct topology-preserving mappings of the training data where the location of a unit carries semantic information [14].

Self-Organising maps consist of two unit layers: a one-dimensional input layer and a two-dimensional competitive layer, organized as a 2D grid of units. Each unit in the competitive layer holds a weight vector that, after training, resembles a different input pattern. The learning algorithm for the SOM networks accomplishes two important goals: the clustering of the input data and the spatial ordering of the map, so that similar input patterns tend to produce a response in units that are close to each other in the grid. In the learning process, the input pattern vectors are presented to all the competitive units in parallel, and the best matching unit is chosen as a winner.

We have tested Kohonen networks for the spectral types and luminosity classes, using two-dimensional maps from 2x2 to 24x24 units. The best results for these networks were achieved by maps of 12x12 units.

2.4.3 RBF Networks

Networks based on Radial Basis Functions (RBF) combine non-supervised learning for hidden units and supervised learning in the output layer. The hidden neurons apply a radial function (generally Gaussian) to the distance that separates the input vector and the weight vector that each one stores, called centroid [13].

We have tested the RBF learning algorithm for the spectral types and luminosity classes. The RFB network that has resulted in a better performance corresponds to a network trained with 25 spectral parameters as input layer and 8 neurons in the hidden layer.

Table 4. The topologies for the implemented RBF networks

Network	Input Patterns	Hidden Layer
Type	Spectral parameters	16
Type	Spectral parameters	8
Type	Spectral parameters	4
Type	659 flux values	124
Luminosity	Spectral parameters	8
Luminosity	659 flux values	124

2.5 Clustering Techniques

In order to refine the classifications of the artificial neural networks, we implemented statistical clustering techniques and applied them to the problem of spectral classification, in particular the K-means, Max-Min and Isodata non-hierarchical clustering methods.

At the initial stage of non-hierarchical clustering, we selected an arbitrary number of clusters or groups. The members of each cluster are checked by means of selected parameters or distance measures, and relocated into the more appropriate clusters with higher separability [15]. The K-means algorithm is based on *k* cluster centers chosen at random, assigning each data item to the closest cluster, recomputing the cluster center (e.g. the centroid of its data items), and looping back to the assignment step if the clusters have not converged. This technique has been applied to large-scale data sets because its time complexity is linear, once the number of clusters *k* and number of passes has been fixed [16]. The Isodata clustering method is a modification of k-means which adds splitting and merging; at each time step, clusters with variance above a fixed threshold are divided and pairs of clusters with centroids closer than another threshold are merged [15].

The Max-min algorithm is based on the heuristic combination of minimum and maximum euclidean distances. At each iterative step, the algorithm verifies the viability of building a new class with an element sufficiently separated of the already existing classes.

As for the application of clustering techniques to the spectral classification of stars, we have used the spectral parameters obtained by means of the morphological analysis algorithms as well as the full spectra. In addition, we have implemented two different versions of each algorithm with 6 and 12 initial clusters.

Although the implemented clustering methods have achieved remarkable success rates in classifying stellar spectra, we have mainly applied this technique to carry out a sensibility analysis of the spectral parameters used to classify stellar spectra.

3 Results

The application of expert systems, clustering techniques and artificial neural networks has allowed us to elaborate a final comparison. We selected the neural models of each type with the best performance and classified, by means of the clustering algorithms and the expert systems, the 100 spectra that were used to test these networks. Figure 1 contrasts the behavior of the three techniques and that of two human experts who collaborated on this project.

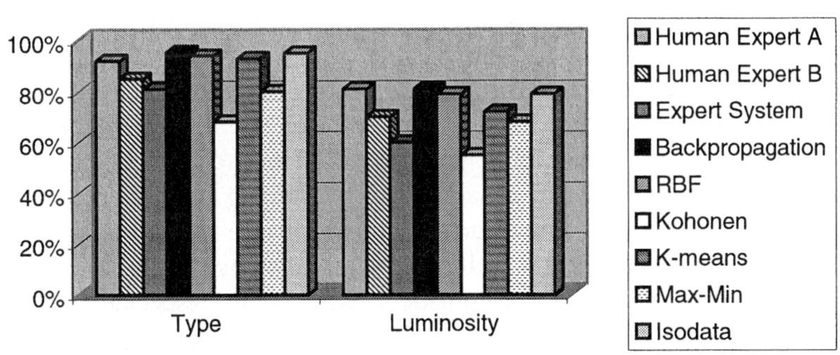

Fig. 2. Final performance for 100 testing spectra

The Backpropagation and RBF networks, as well as K-means and Isodata algorithms, obtained a high success rate of approximately 95%. The Kohonen model obtained a low success rate in all its implementations, which could be due to the size of the training set, since this kind of network has to cluster the data and therefore needs a training set that is big enough to extract similarities and group the data.

Although the final results for the three proposed classification methods seem to be very similar, an exhaustive study has revealed some interesting peculiarities; for example, we have observed that both techniques reached their worst results for B and M spectral types, i.e. the hottest and coolest stars respectively, and indeed, most of the grouping algorithms include these spectra in the same cluster. This fact led us to review the spectral parameters that were being used to train and test the networks and the algorithms: we discovered that B stars usually present great emission lines in zones where a molecular band is expected, so that the automatic techniques are unable to differentiate between them. Our hybrid approach tries to solve these problems by making a previous global classification of the star and then selecting the best method to classify it.

This hybrid strategy consists of choosing, among all the described techniques, those methods that present the best performance for each classification level. The final system is mainly based on an expert system that determines the global type of each star and that, according to the type, sends the spectra to different neural networks or clustering algorithms in order to obtain their spectral type as well as their luminosity level.

The implemented system includes two user-friendly interfaces: a web environment (STARMIND) and another environment under MS-Windows. Both allow the users to select the spectra, visualise them, carry out various analyses and classify as many spectra as they want in a fast, simple and reliable manner.

4 Conclusions

This work has analyzed the classification ability of artificial neural networks, expert system techniques, and statistical clustering techniques applied to stellar spectra. These approaches were integrated into a hybrid system that has resulted in a versatile and flexible automatic technique for the classification of stellar spectra.

Considering the fact that human experts reach an agreement percentage of approximately 87% of the spectra in the course of manual classifications, the success rate of approximately 95% for a sample of 100 testing spectra, obtained by the abovementioned techniques, corresponds to a performance increase of approximately 10%. The additional classification information provided by the clustering techniques refine the parameters used for automatic classifications, especially for cases of spectral types B and M; the implemented clustering techniques make it easier to analyze the sensibility of the spectral parameters used to classify stellar spectra in the neural networks approach.

This research project was made possible thanks to the financial contribution of the Spanish Ministry of Education and Science (AYA2000-1691 and AYA2003-09499).

References

[1] Zombeck M. V.: Handbook of Astronomy and Astrophysics, 2nd. ed. Cambridge University Press (1990)
[2] Morgan W. W., Keenan P. C., Kellman E.: An Atlas of Stellar Spectra with an outline of Spectral Classification, University of Chicago Press (1943)
[3] Weaber W., Torres-Dodgen A.: Neural Networks Classification of the near-infrared spectra of A-type Stars, The Astrophysical Journal, Vol.446 (1995) 300-317
[4] Rodriguez A., Arcay B., Dafonte C., Manteiga M., Carricajo I.: Automated knowledge-based analysis and classification of stellar spectra using fuzzy reasoning, Expert Systems with Applications, Vol.27(2) (2004) 237-244
[5] Silva D. R., Cornell M. E.: A New Library of Stellar Optical Spectra, The Astrophysical Journal Suppl., Vol.81(2), (1992) 865-881
[6] Pickles A. J.: A Stellar Spectral Flux Library. 1150-25000 Å, Publications of the Astronomical Society of the Pacific, Vol 110 (1998) 863-878
[7] Jacoby G. H., Hunter D. A., Christian C. A.:A Library of Stellar Spectra, The Astrophysical Journal Suppl., Vol.56 (1994) 257-281
[8] Sowa J.F.: Knowledge Representation: Logical and Computational, Brooks Cole Publishing Co. (1999)
[9] Valette-Florence, P.: Introduction to Means-End Chain Analysis. Rech. Appl. Mark, Vol.9 (1994) 93-117.
[10] Buchanan, B., Shortliffe, E.: Ruled-based Expert Systems, Adisson-Wesley (1984)
[11] Mendel, J.M. Fuzzy Logic Systems for Engineering: A Tutorial, Proceedings of the IEEE, Vol.83(3) (1995) 345-377
[12] Forgy, C.L.: The OPS/R2 User's Manual. Production Systems Technologies Inc. (1995)
[13] Haykin S.: Neural Networks. A Comprehensive Foundation, MacMillan Coll. Pub. (1994)
[14] Kohonen T.: Self-Organization and Associative Memory, Springer-Verlag, (1987)
[15] Everitt B. et al.:Cluster analysis, Edward Arnold Publishers Ltd. (2001)
[16] Kaufman L., Rousseuw P. J.: Finding groups in Data, Wiley (1990)

An Automatic Goodness Index to Measure Fingerprint Minutiae Quality

Edel García Reyes, José Luis Gil Rodríguez, and Mabel Iglesias Ham

Advanced Technologies Application Center,
7a #21812 e/ 218 y 222, Rpto. Siboney, Playa. C.P. 12200,
Ciudad de La Habana, Cuba
Office Phone number: (+)537.271.4787
Fax number: (+)537.272.1667
{egarcia, jlgil, miglesias}@cenatav.co.cu

Abstract. In this paper, we propose an automatic approach to measure the minutiae quality. When image of 500 dpi is captured, immediately the enhancement, thinning and minutiae extraction processes are executed. The basic idea is to detect the spatial β_0 - Connected minutiae cluster using the Euclidean distance and quantify the number of element for each group. In general, we observe that more than five element in a group is a clue to mark all points in the cluster as bad minutiae. We divide the image in block of 20 x 20 pixels. If one block contains bad minutiae it is mark as a bad block. The goodness quality index is calculated as the proportion of bad blocks respect to the number of total blocks. The proposed index was tested on the FVC2000 fingerprint image database.

1 Introduction

When some agency face the task of make a massive load of card ink fingerprint, to create a large data base, it is necessary to put maximum care in the quality of fingerprint images that will feed the Automatic Fingerprint Identification System (AFIS). It is known that performance of an AFIS relies heavily on the quality of input fingerprint images. Although, it is normal to have a manual quality control, it is desirable that system automatically reject the bad fingerprint that do not accomplish the quality threshold. If each image is storage, with its quality measure associated, it is possible to calculate the average database quality.

Several methods for measuring the quality of fingerprint images were found in the literature [1,2]. In general, they can divide in five categories: methods using standard deviation, methods using directional contrast, methods using Gabor features, methods using local ridge structure, and methods using Fourier spectrum.

The completely path to make fingerprints matching can be segmented in three moments: early steps, middle steps, and last steps. The early steps correspond to the image enhancement and binarization; the middle is associated to thinning, skeleton reconstruction process and the minutiae detection. The last steps in our sequence are the graph based representation of the fingerprint and finally, the graph matching and visual verification. Minutiae extraction corresponds to the middle steps. The basic

M. Lazo and A. Sanfeliu (Eds.): CIARP 2005, LNCS 3773, pp. 578 – 585, 2005.

idea is evaluate the quality in the middle step in this sequence. We propose to detect spatial minutiae clusters using the Euclidean distance and quantify the number of element for each group. In general, the idea is to consider high spatial density of minutiae as a sign of not good automatically minutiae detection. We observe that more than five element in a group is a clue to mark all points in the cluster as bad minutiae. We divide the image in block of 20 x 20 pixels. If one block contains a bad minutiae it is marked as a bad block. The goodness quality index is calculated as the proportion of bad blocks respect to the number of total blocks. With our approach the Goodness index is possible to use it in both sense to evaluate the image enhancement algorithm and the expert visual evaluation of image. The global fingerprint's database quality is the average of all image's quality introduced in it.

The remainder of the paper is organized as follows: Section 2 presents our global workflow to create fingerprint database from card ink impression. Section 3 describes the spatial minutiae cluster algorithm and the goodness quality index. The descriptions of our experiments and results are showed in section 4. Finally, conclusions are presented in section 5.

2 Global Workflow to Create Fingerprint Database from Card Ink Impression

When we have a lot of card ink impression paper that we need to covert in digital format, in order to work with an Automatic Fingerprint Identification System, is very important to guarantee the database quality. This may determine the acceptation of the system by the staff of forensic expert personal.

Load one million of card ink paper may take around six months. This is a great and determinant effort that must be carefully organized, and appropriated software tools are required to reach the quality in the minimum possible time.

First, it is necessary to have an automatic tool to massive scanning of card ink papers with the possibility of an automatic and manual cut of the frames including the image of each finger. Every fingerprint model must have a barcode associated. In this way, the code in the moment that it is scanned is recognized and used as an identifier in the filename of each fingerprint image.

After the cut, it is necessary apply a mask to segment the image in regions which correspond to foreground and background, then a second cut is performed to optimize the followings processes. Immediately, the image enhancement, binarization, thinning, skeleton reconstruction and minutiae extraction are executed. We know that these processes are computational intensive, fundamentally the image enhancement. We enter in a trade of between the calculus time and the quality of the minutiae set.

In this moment, a first calculus of the goodness index is made before to pass the image to visual quality control. The system highlights that finger minutiae set is not reaching the quality threshold. Then, it is possible to examine the automatic cut quality and the quality of minutiae set. May be, some image need a manual cut and edition where some spurious minutiae must be deleted and mark new ones. So, it is necessary a minutiae editor tool. It is the human expert who finally has the responsibility to decide if one fingerprint image could be storage in the database. A second goodness quality index must be calculated to be storage associated to the image in the database after the manual edition. Together with the image and the goodness index, the graph based representation obtained from the minutiae set is also stored.

It is possible to have various scanners to read card ink papers to some repository and other work stations to processing the images. A job manager may distribute the digital images of card models to the processing stations following some priorities. The job manager always has the possibility to examine the average quality of the images stored by a determined operator, or evaluate the average quality of whole database in some determined period of time.

3 Spatial Minutiae Clustering and Goodness Quality Index

In general, the idea is to consider high spatial density of minutiae as a sign of not good automatically minutiae detection. We need to look for the minutiae clusters on the fingerprint image and evaluate its spatial concentration to decide if there is a cluster of bad minutiae. In some cases, when there are singular points like core or delta, it is possible to observe some natural aggregation of point on the fingerprint. In that situation our approach underestimate the fingerprint quality. However, in general, a minutiae cluster is associated with a region of bad image quality where the enhancement algorithm has a bad performance, and the ridge pattern obtained is false. Then, the feature extraction algorithm detect many spurious points near each other.

3.1 Spatial Minutiae Clustering

Every minutia has associated its coordinate x and y. To find spatial minutiae clusters based on its coordinates, it is possible to use an algorithm that operate in a metric space, using a similarity function based on the Euclidean distance. Algorithms *Leader, K-Means*, and *ISODATA* [4] were evaluated and rejected. All of them may obtain different solutions on different order on the input data. In this case, when an impression suffers some geometrical transformation the feature points may change its order. Almost all these algorithms need to know the number of cluster to obtain. Precisely, the goodness quality index proposed is based on the cardinality of the clusters. We need to detect natural points clusters. If a number of cluster if defined previously, all minutiae are distribute between these groups and the membership of some cluster may grow artificially. We prefer an algorithm to detect small connected minutiae groups, regardless the number of cluster obtained.

It is necessary to use some algorithm that detects automatically the number of minutiae clusters in input set. Besides, we are looking for clusters that no necessarily follow an elliptical shape. With these elements in mind, we think about using some algorithm to detect connected component [3].

3.1.1 β_0-Connected Component

Let $O = \{O_1,\ldots,O_m\}$ be set of objects, β a similarity function and β_0 similarity threshold for β.

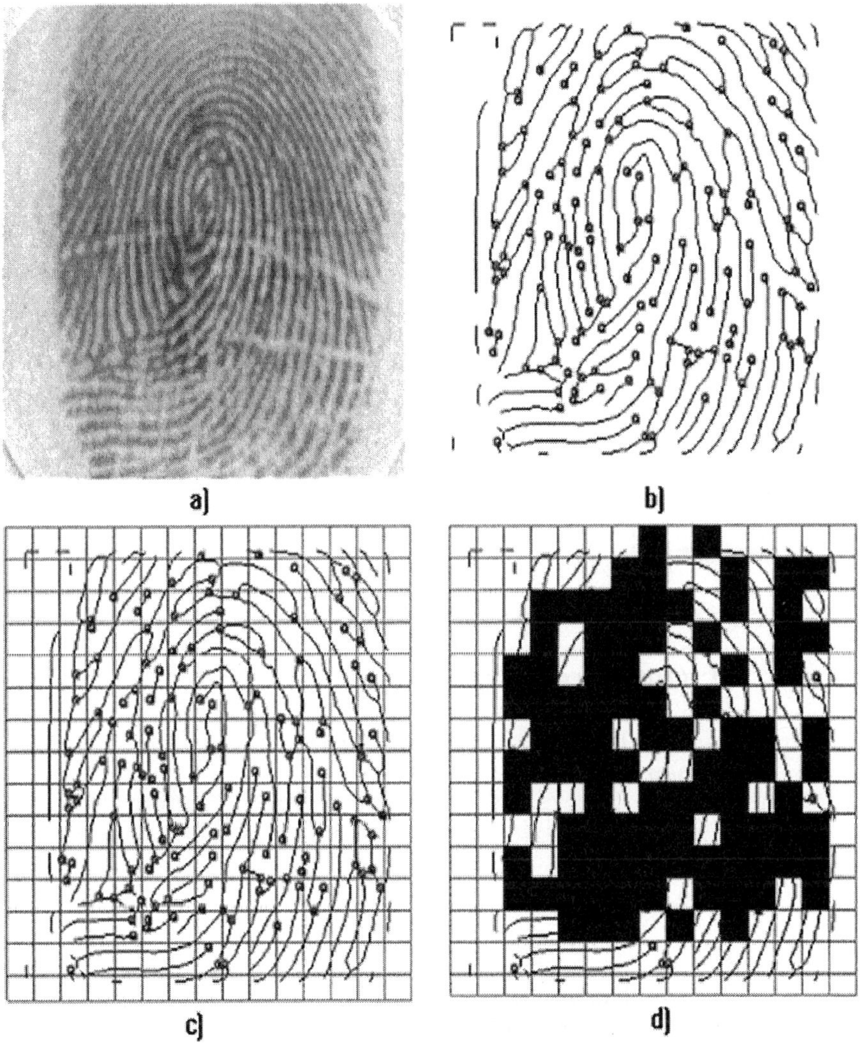

Fig. 1. Goodness quality index = 0.63. a) Bad image from FVC2000 database. b) Minutiae detection. c) Division in block of 20 x 20 pixels. d) Bad block detection.

Definition 1. Two object O_i, O_j are denominated β_0 similar if $\beta(O_i,O_j) \geq \beta_0$.

Definition 2. Let $S \subseteq O$, $S \neq \emptyset$ be β_0-Connected set respect to β iff $\forall\, O_i, O_j \in S$, $\exists \{O_{S1},O_{S2},\ldots,O_{St}\}$ such that $O_i=O_{S1}$, $O_{St}=O_j$ and $\beta(O_{Si-1},O_{Si}) \geq \beta_0$, $i=2,3,\ldots,t$.

It means that for any pair of point in S there is a succession of elements in S beginning in O_i and finishing in O_j such that one is β_0 similar to the next.

```
FindConnectedSet (PairEquivalenceList, m)
{

    for(i=0 ; i < PairEquivalenceList.Count ; i++)
    {
        j = PairEquivalenceList [i].Oj;
        k = PairEquivalenceList [i].Ok;

        while ( AuxPairs[j] > 0 )
            j = AuxPairs[j];

        while ( AuxPairs[k] > 0)
            k = AuxPairs[k];

        if (j != k) AuxPairs[j] = k;
    }

   newlabels = 0;

   for(i=0; i <m ; i++)
   {
      if (AuxPairs[i] == 0)
      {
         FinalPairs[i] = newlabels;
         newlabels++;
      }
   }

   for(i=0; i <m ; i++)
   {
      l = i;
      while (AuxPairs[l] != 0)
          l = AuxPairs[l];

      FinalPairs[i] = FinalPairs[l];
   }

   return FinalPairs;

}
```

Fig. 2. The pseudocode of the main step of the proposed algorithm

3.1.2 Algorithm

Our algorithm to detect β_0-Connected sets is used to observe if there are spatial clusters of minutiae in the image. This algorithm partitions a set of *m* minutiae into *k* disjoint β_0-Connected clusters. A similarity function β that compute the inverse of distance between minutiae is assumed along with a predefined similarly threshold value, β_0.

The algorithm proceeds as follow for a minutiae set O and β_0 threshold. β is the inverse of Euclidean distance:

```
PairEquivalenceList = FindPairNearMinutiae(O,β,β0)

β0-ConnectedSet = FindConnectedSet(PairEquivalenceList,m)
```

To find the equivalence pairs is the similar process to build the adjacency matrix of a graph. A pair of minutiae is included in the *PairEquivalenceList* if they are β_0 similar.

Immediately, the equivalence pair list is processed to obtain the β_0-Connected set following the flow showed in figure 2. For our experiments we found 0.04 as a good threshold for β_0.

3.2 Goodness Quality Index

We use other threshold to classify a cluster as a bad cluster or good cluster. This threshold is related with the number of element in the cluster. If the cluster has more than 5 minutiae it is marked as bad cluster. Then, we divide the fingerprint images in blocks of 20 x 20 pixels. A block is considered to have bad quality if it contains at less one minutia belonging to a bad cluster and otherwise it is considered a good block.

We defined a goodness quality index (*GqI*):

$$GqI = 1 - \frac{number\ of\ bad\ quality\ bocks}{number\ of\ blocks}. \tag{1}$$

4 Experiments and Results

The algorithm described has been implemented and tested. FVC2000 database was used to obtain the quality measure thresholds. FVC2000 is a public database collected using optical sensing techniques. The experts performed a visual pre-selection of four groups of fingerprint images categorized in: good, bad, smudged and dried fingerprint image.

The minutia sets obtained for each fingerprint image were analysed and categorized as good, regular or bad by the experts.

We have found the following quality thresholds (table 1):

Table 1. The thresholds of quality

Thresholds	Description
GqI < 0.78	Bad minutiae set
0.78 ≤ GqI < 0.85	Regular minutiae set
GqI ≥ 0.85	Good minutiae set

The following results (table 2) show the performance of the goodness minutiae index for each fingerprint image category:

Table 2. Goodness quality index for each fingerprint image group from FVC2000 database

	Good	Bad	Smudged	Dried	Total
Number of image	120	40	68	92	320
Average GqI	0.93	0.78	0.87	0.90	0.89

We observed that the goodness quality index not always is consistent with visual human assessment, because our image enhancement and feature detection algorithms are robust and perform very well to obtain the minutiae set, even in some image where there are scars and some level of noise.

We noted that, according to our approach, the FVC2000 database has a goodness quality index of 0.89 relative to our minutiae detection algorithm.

On another hand, the experts made a manual minutia edition of the fingerprint image included in the bad group (GqI = 0.78) and after that it was recalculated the goodness quality index. In this case, the averaged value was elevated to 0.98. It shows that our goodness quality index reach a value near 1 when a good minutiae set is obtained.

5 Conclusion

In this paper we present an approach to measure the minutiae quality that guarantee a control about the average quality of a fingerprint image database.

In general, we observed that our heuristic detect more true bad cluster than false bad cluster. From this point of view it follow a pessimist strategy, because it is possible that an image was stored in the database with some block marked as bad when in reality there was a minutiae concentration due a singularity fingerprint ridge flow.

References

1. Yi-Sheng, M., Patanki, S., Hass, N.: Fingerprint Quality Assessment. Automatic Fingerprint Recognition Systems, Chapter 3 , Ratha, N., and R. Bolle, Editors. Springer-Verlag (2004) 55-66

2. Vallarino, G., Gianarelli, G., Barattini, J., Gómez, A., Férnandez, A., Pardo, A.: Performance Improvement in a Fingerprint Classification System Using Anisotropic Diffusion. Lecture Notes in Computer Science, Springer-Verlag, No. 3287. (2004) 582-588
3. Martínez, F., Ruiz, J., Lazo, M.: Structuralization of Universes. Fuzzy Set and System, Vol. 112/3. (2000) 485-500.
4. Hartigan, J. A.: Clustering Algorithms, New York: John Wiley and Sons (1975)

Classifier Selection Based on Data Complexity Measures*

Edith Hernández-Reyes, J.A. Carrasco-Ochoa, and J.Fco. Martínez-Trinidad

National Institute for Astrophysics, Optics and Electronics,
Luis Enrique Erro No.1 Sta. Ma. Tonantzintla, Puebla, México C. P. 72840
{ereyes, ariel, fmartine}@inaoep.mx

Abstract. Tin Kam Ho and Ester Bernardò Mansilla in 2004 proposed to use data complexity measures to determine the domain of competition of the classifiers. They applied different classifiers over a set of problems of two classes and determined the best classifier for each one. Then for each classifier they analyzed how the values of some pairs of complexity measures were, and based on this analysis they determine the domain of competition of the classifiers. In this work, we propose a new method for selecting the best classifier for a given problem, based in the complexity measures. Some experiments were made with different classifiers and the results are presented.

1 Introduction

Selecting an optimal classifier for a pattern recognition application is a difficult task. Few efforts have been made in this direction; for example STATLOG [1] where several classification algorithms were compared based on some empirical data sets and a metal-level machine learning rule on the algorithm selection was provided. Other example is Meta Analysis of Classification Algorithms [2] where a statistical metamodel to predict the expected classification performance of each algorithm as a function of data characteristics was proposed. They used this information to find the relative ranking of classification algorithms.

In this work we propose an alternative method using the geometry of data distributions and its relationship to classifier behavior. Following [3] the classifier selection depends on the problem complexity, which can be measured based on data distribution. In [3] some data complexity measures were introduced. These measures characterize the complexity of a classification problem, focusing on the geometrical complexity of the class boundary.

In [4] some problems were characterized by nine measures taken from [3] to determine the domain of competition of six classifiers. They made the comparison of their results between two measures. Based on this comparison, they determined the domain of competition of the classifiers. However they did not present the results if more than two measures were compared together.

In this work, we propose a new method for selecting the best classifier for a given problem with two classes (2-class problem). Our method describes problems with

* This work was financially supported by CONACyT (Mexico) through the project J38707-A.

M. Lazo and A. Sanfeliu (Eds.): CIARP 2005, LNCS 3773, pp. 586 – 592, 2005.

complexity measures and labels them with the classifier that gets the best accuracy among five classifiers. After, other classifiers were used to make the selection.

This paper is organized as follows: in section 2 the complexity measures used in this work are described. In section 3 the proposed method is explained, in section 4 some experiments are shown and in section 5 we present our conclusions and future work.

2 Complexity Measures

We selected 9 complexity measures from those defined in [3] which describe the most important aspects of boundary complexity of 2-class problems. The selected measures are shown in table 1.

Table 1. Complexity measures

F1	Fisher's discriminant
F2	Volume of overlap region
F3	Maximum feature efficiency
L2	Error rate of linear classifier
L3	Nonlinearity of linear classifier
N2	Ratio of average intra/Inter class NN distance
N3	Error rate of 1nn classifier
N4	Nonlinearity of 1nn classifier
T2	Average number of points per dimension

These measures are defined as follows:

F1: Fisher's Discriminant

Fisher's discriminant was defined for only one feature. This is measured by calculating, for each class, the mean (μ) and the variances (σ^2) of the feature; and evaluat ing the next expression:

$$\mathrm{F1} = \frac{(\mu_1 - \mu_2)^2}{\sigma_1^2 + \sigma_2^2} \tag{1}$$

For a multidimensional problem, the maximum F1 over all the features is used to describe the problem.

F2: Volume of Overlap Region

This measure takes into account how the discriminatory information is distributed across the features. This can be measured by finding, for each feature (f_i), the maximum $\max(f_i,c_j)$ and the minimum $\min(f_i,c_j)$ values for each class (c_j), and then calculating the length of the overlap region defined as:

$$\mathrm{F2} = \prod_i \frac{MIN(\max(f_i,c_1),\max(f_i,c_2)) - MAX(\min(f_i,c_1),\min(f_i,c_2))}{MAX(\max(f_i,c_1),\max(f_i,c_2) - MIN(\min(f_i,c_1),\min(f_i,c_2)))} \tag{2}$$

F3: Maximum Feature Efficiency

F3 is a measure that describes how much each feature contributes to the separation of the two classes.

For each feature, all points (p) of the same class have values falling in between the maximum and the minimum of that class. If there is an overlap in the feature values, the classes are ambiguous in that region along that dimension. The efficiency of each feature is defined as the fraction, of all remaining points, which are separable by that feature. For a multidimensional problem we use the maximum feature efficiency.

$$\mathrm{F3} = \sum_{p} separable(p)$$

where (3)

$$\mathrm{separable}(p) = \begin{cases} 1 & \text{if } p \text{ is separable by the feature} \\ 0 & \text{otherwise} \end{cases}$$

L2: Nonlinearity of the Linear Classifier

Many algorithms have been proposed to determine linear separability. L2 uses the error rate of the classifier on the training set to describe the nonlinearity of the linear classifier.

$$\mathrm{L2} = error\_rate(linear\_classifier(training\_set)) \tag{4}$$

L3: Nonlinearity of Linear Classifier

L3 describes the nonlinearity of the linear classifier. This metric measures the error rate of the classifier on a test set.

$$\mathrm{L3} = error\_rate(linear\_classifier(test\_set)) \tag{5}$$

N2: Ratio of Average Intra/Inter Class NN Distance

This metric is measured as follows: first compute the average (x) of the Euclidean distances from each point to its nearest neighbour of the same class, and the average (y) of all distances to inter-class nearest neighbors. The ratio of these two averages is the metric N2. This measure compares the dispersion within the classes against the separation between the classes.

$$\mathrm{N2} = \frac{x}{y} \tag{6}$$

N3: The Nearest Neighbor Error Rate

The proximity of points in opposite classes obviously affects the error rate of the nearest neighbor classifier. Thus N3 describes the nonlinearity of the K-nn classifier and it measures the error rate of the K-nn classifier on a test set.

$$\mathrm{N3} = error\_rate(K\_nn(test\_set)) \tag{7}$$

N4: Nonlinearity of the K-nn
Given a training set, a test set is created by linear interpolation between randomly drawn pairs of points from the same class. Then the error rate of the K-nn on this test set is measured. Thus N4 uses the error rate of K-nn with the training set to describe the nonlinearity of the K-nn classifier.

$$\text{N4} = error\_rate(k-nn(training\_set)) \tag{8}$$

T2: Average Number of Points Per Dimension
This metric is measured by calculating the average number of samples per features.

$$\text{T2} = \frac{samples}{features} \tag{9}$$

3 Proposed Method

In this section we describe the proposed method based on data complexity measures to select the best classifier for 2-class.

The idea of our method is to describe the 2-class problem by some complexity measures. The label of each 2-class problem is its best classifier, which is determined testing a set of classifiers, in this way; we will obtain a training set of a supervised classification problem. Therefore a classifier could be used to select the best classifier for a new 2-class problem. Our method works as follow:

1. Given a database set, for each problem with n classes, two or more, C(n,2) 2-class problems are created, taking all possible pairs of classes. This is done because as it was mentioned in section 3, the complexity measures were designed to describe the complexity of 2-class problems.

2. For each 2-class problem created in the previous step

   a) Calculate the nine complexity measures.
   b) Apply the set of classifiers and assign a label that indicates which was the classifier with the lowest error for the 2-class problem.

   Thus, each problem is characterized by its nine complexity measures and labeled with the class of its best classifier. These data conform the training set.

3. Apply a classifier on the training set to make the selection of the best classifier for a new 2-class problem.

This method is depicted in figure 1.

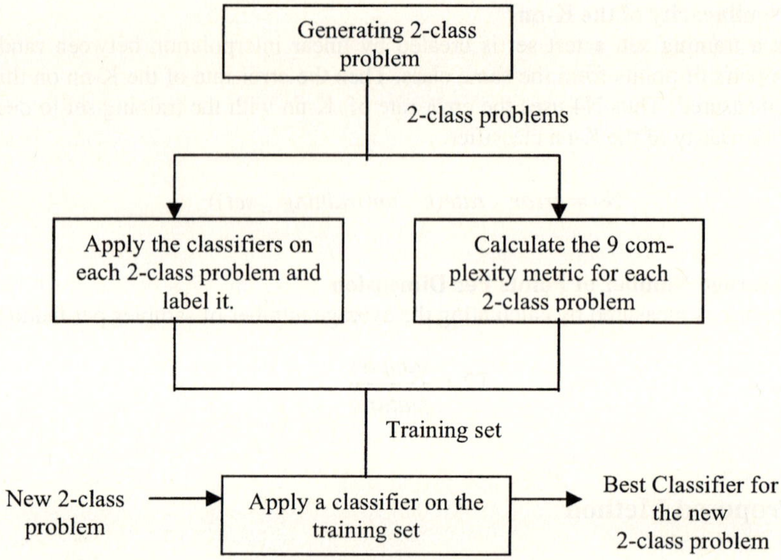

Fig. 1. Proposed method

4 Experimental Results

In order to test our method we selected 5 data sets from the UC-Irving repository [5] (Abalone, Setter, Iris, Pima, Yeast). Following the proposed method, in the first step, for each database, with n classes, C(n,2) 2-class problems were created; thus we had 752 2-class problems (see table 2).

Table 2. 2-class problems for each used database

Databases	Classes	2-class Problems
Abalone	28	378
Iris	3	3
Setter	26	325
Pima	2	1
Yeast	10	45
Total		752

In the second step, for each 2-class problem, the nine complexity measures were calculated. Then, each problem was evaluated with five classifiers. The used classifiers were:

1. K-nn
2. Naive Bayes
3. Lineal regression
4. RBFNetwork
5. J48

RBFNetwork is a normalized Gaussian radial basis function network and J48 is a version of C4.5, both implemented in weka [6].

In our method, we considered the classifier with the lowest error on a 2-class problem as the best method, and then we assign this classifier as the label of the 2-class problem. Table 3 shows how the problems were distributed according their best classifier.

Table 3. Distribution of the problems

Classifier	Problems
K-nn	421
Naive Bayes	208
J48	123

The problems were only distributed in 3 classes (K-nn, Naive Bayes and j48), because the other two classifiers did not obtain a better classification rate for any of the 2-class problems. Thus, we obtained the problems characterized by their nine measures of complexity and labeled with the class of their best classifier. These data form a training set of 752 objects with 9 variables and separated in 3 classes.

Finally, to select the best classifier for a new 2-class problem, we applied three different classifiers (1-nn, J48, RBFNetwork) on the training set. We used ten-fold cross validation to evaluate the accuracy of our method.

From the used classifiers (1-nn, j48 and RBFNetwork). The best was 1-nn, which obtained a classification accuracy of 83.5 %. In table 4 we can appreciate the results.

Table 4. Results for best classifier selection

Classifier	Selection accuracy
1-nn	83.5 %
RBFNetwork	71.6 %
J48	60.2 %

5 Conclusions

In this paper, a new method based on complexity measures for selecting the best classifier of a given 2-class problem was introduced. Our method describes 2-class problems with complexity measures and labels them with the class of their best classifier. After, for making the selection a classifier was used.

We found that the complexity measures are a good set of features to characterize the problems and make the selection of the best classifier. As future work, we will compare our method against other methods. Also, we propose to extend the proposed method for problems with more than two classes by mean of redefining the complexity measures, in order to allow applying them on multiple class problems.

References

1. D. Michie, D. J. Spiegelhalter, and C. C. Taylor: Machine Learning, Neural and Statical Classification. New York: Ellis Horwood, 1994.
2. So Young Sohn: Meta Analysis of Classification Algorithms for Pattern Recognition. IEEE Trans. on PAMI,21,11,Noveber 1999, 1137-1144.
3. T.K. Ho, M. Basu: Complexity measures of supervised classification problem. IEEE Trans. on PAMI, 24, 3, March 2002, 289-300.
4. Ester Bernadó Mansilla, Tin Kam Ho: On Classifier Domains of Competence. ICPR (1) 2004: 136-139
5. C.L. Blake, C.J. Merz: UCI Repository of machine learning databases. [http://www.ics.uci.edu/~mlearn/MLRepository.html] Irvine, CA: University of California, Department of information and Computer Science.
6. Weka: Data Mining Software in Java. [http://www.cs.waikato.ac.nz/ml/weka/]

De-noising Method in the Wavelet Packets Domain for Phase Images

Juan V. Lorenzo-Ginori and Héctor Cruz-Enriquez

Center for Studies on Electronics and Information Technologies, Universidad Central "Marta Abreu" de Las Villas, Carretera a Camajuaní, km 5 ½,
Santa Clara, VC, CP 54830, Cuba
juanl@uclv.edu.cu, hcruz@uclv.edu.cu
http://www.fie.uclv.edu.cu

Abstract. Complex images contaminated by noise appear in various applications. To improve these phase images, noise effects, as loss of contrast and phase residues that deteriorate the phase unwrapping process, should be reduced. Noise reduction in complex images has been addressed by various methods, most of them dealing only with the magnitude image. Few works have been devoted to phase image de-noising, despite the existence of important applications like Interferometric Synthetic Aperture Radar (IFSAR), Current Density Imaging (CDI) and Magnetic Resonance Imaging (MRI). In this work, several de-noising algorithms in the wavelet packets domain were applied to complex images to recover the phase information. These filtering algorithms were applied to simulated images contaminated by three different noise models, including mixtures of Gaussian and Impulsive noise. Significant improvements in SNR for low initial values (SNR<5 dB) were achieved by using the proposed filters, in comparison to other methods reported in the literature.

1 Introduction

Images produced by systems such as Synthetic Aperture Radars (IFSAR), Current Density Imaging (CDI) and Magnetic Resonance Imaging (MRI) appear as arrays of complex numbers and are affected by the presence of noise. These images suffer in many cases from a poor signal to noise ratio (SNR).

Complex images allow the use of both magnitude and phase information, depending on the type of application considered. The presence of noise in the complex images can be originated by numerous causes as can be the noise produced by the acquisition hardware, physiological noise originated from the patients, noisy artifacts provoked by movements during image acquisition (MRI, CDI) and the presence of phase jitter that can appear during the acquisition of signals obtained by IFSAR. In all the previously mentioned cases noise not only produces a deterioration in SNR and loss of contrast in the image, but also it introduces phase residues that will affect negatively the later phase unwrapping process, that is unavoidable in most applications where the analysis is based upon the phase information from the complex image obtained.

M. Lazo and A. Sanfeliu (Eds.): CIARP 2005, LNCS 3773, pp. 593 – 600, 2005.

In this work three noise models were considered. These are combinations of additive white Gaussian (AWGN) and impulsive noise in various proportions. Preliminary results obtained in [1] have been considered as a reference for comparison. The algorithms developed in [2, 3] for magnitude images have been also implemented for comparison for phase images, in order to better show the effectiveness of the filtering methods introduced here. A description of the noise models associated to complex images have been discussed in [2, 3]. Most de-noising algorithms developed for complex images have assumed zero-mean AWGN, which contaminate independently the real and imaginary parts of the complex image. Noise distribution in the magnitude image is usually assumed to have a zero-mean Rician distribution, which behaves as a Gaussian distribution for high SNR and as a Rayleigh one for low SNR. Our main interest is centered in the phase images in low SNR environments.

In a previous work [2], a de-noising algorithm was reported based in a Wiener filter that reduces noise in a very effective way in the magnitude image and it is claimed that it can also make this simultaneously in the phase image. Another approach based in nonlinear filtering was introduced in [1], and de-noising methods using the Wavelet Transform were introduced and tested in [7]. In this work we pursue to show some considerations related to wavelet packets de-noising for phase images that differ in a certain extent from its application to magnitude images and that exhibited some advantage in SNR improvement when compared to the previous cited works.

2 Materials and Methods

2.1 Simulated Image

The complex simulated image was built in similar way as in previous works [1, 2]. This consists in a magnitude image formed as a 64 x 64 pixels square with intensity 210 (bright region) which is centered inside another square of size 128 x 128 with 90 units intensity (dark region). The original unwrapped phase image was defined as the bi-dimensional Gaussian function

$$\varphi_{uv} = A\exp\left(\frac{(u-64)^2}{\sigma_u^2} + \frac{(v-64)^2}{\sigma_v^2}\right), \tag{1}$$

where u and v are the variables associated to the coordinate axes. For the rest of the variables in equation (1), the following values were used: $A = 7\pi$, $\sigma_u^2 = 3500$ and $\sigma_v^2 = 1000$.

The complex image was formed from the magnitude and wrapped phase images. It was contaminated with various proportions of AWGN and impulsive noise, independently for the real and imaginary parts. The various noise models employed here are shown in Table 1. This table shows the standard deviation values for a

Table 1. Noise models

Noise model	σ	P_I, %
1	60	0
2	70	3
3	90	5

Gaussian probability density function with zero mean and the corresponding percentages of impulsive noise.

The impulsive noise was modeled in the same way as in [1], where the probability of occurrence of an impulse for any part, real or imaginary, is given by

$$p = 1 - \sqrt{1 - P_I} \quad . \tag{2}$$

In Table 1 are shown the global percentages P_I of the impulses to be generated. The p value is to be divided evenly for the contribution of positive and negative pulses. Both the image and the noise were modeled considering an 8-bit resolution for the representation of their numerical values.

2.2 Measurement Parameters

In order to demonstrate the effectiveness of the algorithms and compare them with previous works reported in the literature we performed a set of measurements similar to those performed in [1], where we determined the values of SNR, the number of phase residues (RES), the standard deviation (STDV) and the normalized mean square error (NMSE), defined as

$$NMSE = \frac{\sum_i \sum_j \left\| \varphi(i,j) - \hat{\varphi}(i,j) \right\|^2}{\sum_i \sum_j \left\| \varphi(i,j) \right\|^2} \tag{3}$$

where φ is the original unwrapped phase, $\hat{\varphi}$ is the recovered unwrapped phase after filtering and (i, j) are the pixel values in the direction (u, v).

SNR was calculated as

$$SNR = 10 \log_{10} \left(\frac{1}{NMSE} \right) \tag{4}$$

The amount of phase residues that appear both in the noisy and in the de-noised signals were calculated by applying systematically the expression

$$\varphi(r) = \oint_C \nabla \varphi(r) \cdot dr = 2K\pi \tag{5}$$

Here $\varphi(r)$ is the signal phase, $\nabla\varphi(r)$ is the phase gradient and *K* is an integer number that accounts for the phase residues enclosed by the contour *C*.

2.3 De-noising Algorithms

Two new algorithms in the wavelet packets domain were proposed here to increase SNR in phase images. These filtering processes begin with the application of the bi-dimensional Discrete Wavelet Packet Transform (DWPT-2D) to both the real and imaginary parts of the noisy complex image z_n. From this transformation, the noisy DWPT-2D complex coefficients $c_{j,o}^{ch}$ were obtained, where the index *ch* indicates whether the coefficient belongs to the real (*re*) or imaginary (*im*) parts of the complex image, and the terms *j* and *o* indicate the decomposition level and the orientation (horizontal, vertical or diagonal), respectively.

The expression of the transformation *T* for the DWPT-2D is given by

$$c_{j,o}^{ch} = T_{DWPT-2D}\left[z_n\right] \; . \tag{6}$$

After calculating this transformation, the wavelet packet coefficients are appropriately thresholded obtaining { $\hat{c}_{j,o}^{ch}$ }, and the synthesis equation associated to the DWPT equation (6) was applied later, resulting in

$$\hat{z} = T_{DWPT-2D}^{-1}\left[\hat{c}_{j,o}^{ch}\right] . \tag{7}$$

The first filtering method described is based in the classical soft thresholding of the wavelet packet coefficients (called SOFT_WP here). Thresholding was applied independently to the real and imaginary parts, as

$$\hat{c}_{j,o}^{ch}\Big|_{SOFT\_WP} = T_{THR\_SOFT\_WP}\left[c_{j,o}^{ch}\right] = \begin{cases} \operatorname{sgn}\left(c_{j,o}^{ch}\right)\times\left(\left|c_{j,o}^{ch}\right| - thr\right) & \left|c_{j,o}^{ch}\right| \geq thr \\ 0 & \left|c_{j,o}^{ch}\right| < thr \end{cases} \tag{8}$$

where *thr* is the threshold value, whose calculation will be discussed in paragraph 2.4.

The second filtering method (called A_SOFT_WP), thresohlding was applied to the magnitude wavelet packet coefficients, instead of doing this for the real and imaginary parts independently where

$$\left|c_{j,o}\right| = \sqrt{\left(c_{j,o}^{RE}\right)^2 + \left(c_{j,o}^{IM}\right)^2} \; . \tag{9}$$

The filtering transformation was in this case

$$\left|\hat{c}_{j,o}\right|\Big|_{A\_SOFT\_WP} = T_{THR\_SOFT\_WP}\left[\left|c_{j,o}\right|\right] = \begin{cases} \operatorname{sgn}\left(\left|c_{j,o}\right|\right) \times \left(\left|c_{j,o}\right| - thr\right), & \left|c_{j,o}\right| \geq thr_G \\ 0, & \left|c_{j,o}\right| < thr_G \end{cases}, \tag{10}$$

where the threshold is obtained from the thresholds for the real and imaginary parts as

$$thr_G = \left[(thr_{RE})^2 + (thr_{IM})^2\right]^{\frac{1}{2}}.$$

Various other filtering alternatives were devised and tested in the wavelet packet domain, from which we have illustrated here only the most representative cases with which we obtained the best results.

2.4 Threshold Calculation

There exist several methods to obtain the noise standard deviation from noisy data and from this to obtain the threshold values to be used [2, 3]. In most applications noise can be considered uncorrelated and independent from the decomposition level, frequency and orientation. Having this in mind, the best alternative for noise estimation was to apply the DWPT-2D at the finest scale, e. g. the first decomposition level. This is the median absolute deviation (MAD) estimate used in [4], with which the resulting threshold is

$$thr = \frac{median\left(\left|c_{1,o}^{ch}\right|\right)}{0.6745}. \tag{11}$$

Here $median\left(\left|c_{1,o}^{ch}\right|\right)$ is the value of the statistical median of the array formed by the absolute value of the wavelet packets coefficients from the first decomposition level. The global threshold for de-noising is obtained by a wavelet packet coefficients selection rule using a penalization method provided by Birge-Massart [6].

3 Results

Performance evaluation for the filters described above was realized using a simulated complex image as it was described in 2.2. Tables 2 and 3 show the results obtained for the two filters described above, corresponding to SNR and NMSE for two out of the three noise models shown in Table 1. In both filters the wavelet packet *Bior2.6* was employed, with a number $J = 4$ of decomposition levels, which led to good results. As can be observed, in all cases the noisy phase image had SNR values less than 5 dB. This was determined basically because our objective was to improve phase images in low SNR environments. Figure 1 shows in the first column the original (wrapped and unwrapped) simulated images, in the second column the contaminated images (wrapped and unwrapped with an algorithm that does not tolerate phase residues) and in the third column the results obtained once the de-noising process was applied with the filter SOFT_WP. The simulated complex image in this experiment was contaminated with noise model 2 (stdv = 70 and imp = 3%).

Figure 2 shows a comparison between the algorithm proposed here (SOFT_WP) and the best of the previous algorithms published in the literature (A_H_S_U) [7]. In this case the simulated complex image was contaminated with noise model 3 (stdv = 90 and imp = 5%) with the objective of illustrating the effectiveness of the use of wavelet packets in situations of very low signal to noise. The unwrapped phase image shows clearly the improvement obtained with the SOFT_WP filter versus the A_H_S_U filter.

Table 2. Results of filtering in terms of NMSE and SNR, noise models 2 and 3

Image: Image 1 Wavelet: Bior2.6 Noiseless residues: 0 Trials: 20

	Noise model					
	2			3		
filter	NMSE	STDV	SNR	NMSE	STDV	SNR
NONE	0.9144	5.39e-001	0.97	1.2821	7.85e-001	-0.61
A_SOFT_WP	0.0006	4.81e-004	32.88	0.0068	7.17e-003	23.49
SOFT_WP	0.0004	3.50e-005	34.11	0.0027	2.77e-003	27.50

Table 3. Results of filtering in terms of phase residues, noise models 2 and 3

Image: Image 1 Wavelet: Bior2.6 Noiseless residues: 0 Trials: 20

	Noise model			
	2		3	
Filter	Nres	stdv	Nres	stdv
NONE	1396.80	47.75	2149.70	44.17
A_SOFT_WP	0.20	0.62	4.10	2.55
SOFT_WP	0.00	0.00	2.10	2.00

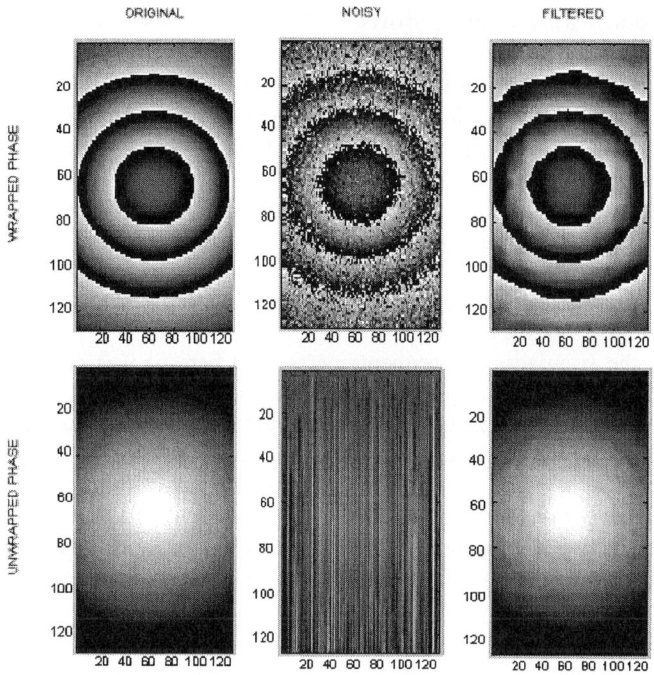

Fig. 1. De-noising of simulated image, wavelet packet Bior2.6, *J*=4, filter SOFT_WP, noise model 2

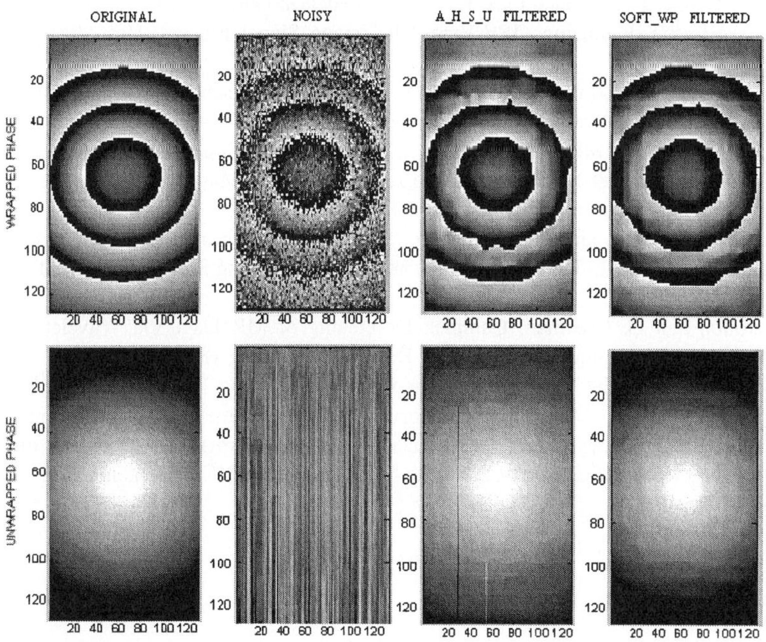

Fig. 2. De-noising of simulated image, wavelet packet Bior2.6, *J*=4, filters A_H_S_U and SOFT_WP, noise model 3

4 Discussion and Conclusions

The proposed methods constitute a new alternative for phase image de-noising that differ from the traditional wavelet-domain methods [2, 3, 4, 5, 7] that are based in Wiener filtering or in soft thresholding and phase preservation of the wavelet coefficients in the wavelet domain.

The use of soft thresholding techniques reduced noise significantly, showing a high and stable SNR gain for all the noise models used in this work. The only drawback present in the wavelet based methods was the poor edge preservation in some regions of interest in the image. The methods based on wavelet packets showed a noticeable reduction of this negative effect.

Through the simulation experiments performed here, it was possible to conclude that it is the magnitude image, and not the phase one, the most sensitive to phase changes in the wavelet packets coefficients. This is because it was observed that the magnitude image was degraded when the real and imaginary parts of the wavelet packet coefficients were filtered independently, while this process led to an improvement of the phase image.

These results indicated a significant noise reduction, which surpass previous results reported in the literature [1, 7] and in this case without the need of an excessive computational burden.

References

1. Lorenzo-Ginori, J. V., Plataniotis, K. N. and Venetsanopoulos, A. N.: Non linear filtering for phase image de-noising.. IEE Proc.-Vis. Image Signal Process, Vol 49(5) 290-296, October 2002.
2. Alexander, M. E. , Baumgartner, R., Summers, A. R., Windischberger, C. , Klarhoefer, M., Moser, E. and Somorjai, R. L,: A Wavelet-based Method for Improving Signal-to-noise Ratio and Contrast in MR Images. Magnetic Resonance Imaging 18 (2000) 169-180.
3. R. D.Nowak: Wavelet-Based Rician Noise Removal for Magnetic Resonance Imaging. IEEE Transactions on Image Processing Vol. 8 (10) 1408-1419, 1999.
4. H.Braunisch, W. Bae-ian, and J. A.Kong,: Phase unwrapping of SAR interferograms after wavelet de-noising. In: IEEE Geoscience and Remote Sensing Symposium, IGARSS 2000. 2 (2000) 752 -754.
5. S. Zaroubi, and G. Goelman: Complex De-noising of MR Data Via Wavelet Analysis: Application to Functional MRI. Magnetic Resonance Imaging 18 (2000) 59-68.
6. M. Misiti *et al*, Wavelet Toolbox user's guide, The MathWorks Inc., Natick, MA, 2000.
7. H. Cruz-Enríquez and J. V. Lorenzo-Ginori, Wavelet-based methods for improving signal-to-noise ratio in phase images, paper accepted in the International Congress on Image Analysis and Recognition ICIAR 2005, (to be published in LNCS), September 28-30, 2005, Toronto, Canada.

A Robust Free Size OCR for Omni-Font Persian/Arabic Printed Document Using Combined MLP/SVM

Hamed Pirsiavash[1,3], Ramin Mehran[2,3], and Farbod Razzazi[3]

[1] Department of Electrical Engineering, Sharif University of Technology, Tehran, Iran
h_pirsiavash@mehr.sharif.edu
[2] Department of Electrical Engineering, K.N.Toosi Univ. of Tech., Tehran, Iran
rmehran@gmail.com
[3] Paya Soft co., Tehran, Iran
razzazi@payasoft.com

Abstract. Optical character recognition of cursive scripts present a number of challenging problems in both segmentation and recognition processes and this attracts many researches in the field of machine learning. This paper presents a novel approach based on a combination of MLP and SVM to design a trainable OCR for Persian/Arabic cursive documents. The implementation results on a comprehensive database show a high degree of accuracy which meets the requirements of commercial use.

1 Introduction

Optical character recognition (OCR) has been extensively used as the basic application of different learning methods in machine learning literature [1, 2]. Consequently, there are also a large number of commercial products available in the market for recognizing printed documents. However, the majority of the efforts are focused on western languages with Roman alphabet and East Asian scripts. Although there has been a great attempt in producing omni-font OCR systems for Persian/Arabic language, the overall performance of such systems are far from perfect. Persian written language which uses modified Arabic alphabet is written cursively, and this intrinsic feature makes it difficult for automatic recognition.

There are two main approaches to automatic understanding of cursive scripts: holistic and segmentation-based [3]. In the first approach, each word is treated as a whole, and the recognition system does not consider it as a combination of separable characters. Very similar to the speech recognition systems, in almost all significant results of holistic methods, hidden Markov models have been used as the recognition engine [4, 5]. The second strategy which owns the majority in the literature, segments each word to containing characters as the building blocks, and recognizes each character then.

In comparison, the first strategy usually outperforms the second, but it needs a more detailed model of the language which its complexity grows as the vocabulary gets larger. In addition, in this method, the number of recognition classes is far more than similar number in segmentation-based methods. Recently, there is also a trend toward hybrid

M. Lazo and A. Sanfeliu (Eds.): CIARP 2005, LNCS 3773, pp. 601 – 610, 2005.

methods which incorporates the segmentation and recognition systems to obtain overall results; these methods are usually called segmentation-by-recognition [6, 7].

One of the main concerns of designing every OCR system is to make it robust to the font variations. Thus, successful examples are omni-font recognition systems with ability to learn new fonts from some tutor. In holistic methods, as the OCR problem is considered on the whole, and the system globally uses learning mechanisms, it is easy to transform it into an omni-font learning system. On the other hand, the segmentation-based systems mainly use learning methods only in recognition process, and to the best of our knowledge, the learning systems are never used for the segmentation process in the literature [8]. Usually, human recognizes unfamiliar words by segmenting them and recognizing each character separately to understand the whole word. With this perspective, in this research, the whole task is broken down into two separate learning systems to gain from reduction of complexity in hierarchy as well as adaptability of learning systems.

The layout of this paper is as follows: Section 2 emphasizes on the characteristics of Persian script that were crucial for the design of OCR systems. In section 3, we will discuss the proposed algorithm. Segmentation and recognition modules are described in separate subsections. Section 4 presents implementation details and results. This is accompanied with conclusive remarks and acknowledgements.

2 Some Notes on Persian/Arabic Script

In this section, we will briefly describe some of the main characteristics of Persian/Arabic script to point out the main difficulties which an OCR system should overcome. As one of the main properties, the script consists of separated words which are aligned by a horizontal virtual line called "Baseline". Words are separated by long spaces and each word consists of one or more isolated segments each of them is called Piece of a Word (PAW). On the contrary, PAWs are separated by short spaces, and each PAW includes one or more characters. If one PAW has more than one character, each of them will be connected to its neighbors along the baseline. Fig. 1 shows a sample Persian/Arabic script where *a* represents the space between two different words, and *b* is the short space between PAWs of the first word which is also shown larger in Fig. 2.

In the latter figure, the first PAW on the right, comprises three characters and the second one, on the left, consists of only a single character, and denotes the pen width value which is heuristically equal to the most frequent value of the vertical projection in each line.

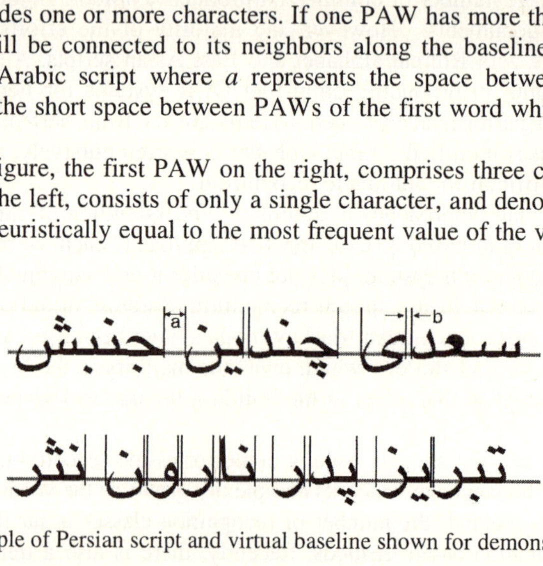

Fig. 1. Sample of Persian script and virtual baseline shown for demonstration only

Fig. 2. An example of a Persian word consists of two PAWs

3 Proposed Algorithm

The overall block diagram of the system is presented in Fig. 3 which depicts layout analysis, post-processing, and natural language processing (NLP) subsystems in addition to recognition and segmentation blocks. The details of the NLP and layout analysis sections are out of scope of this paper and will not be discussed here.

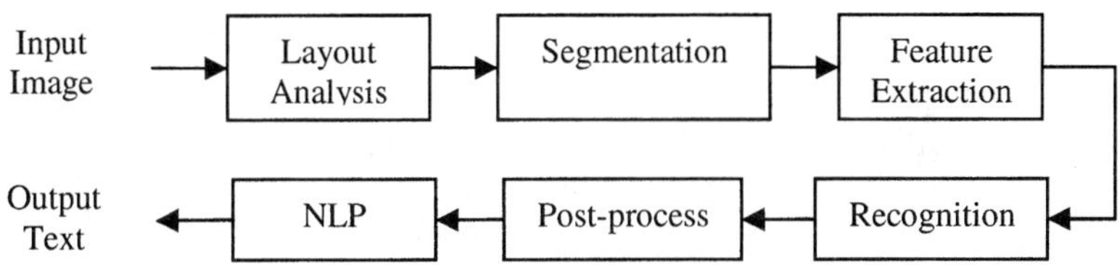

Fig. 3. Overall block diagram

In our design, we exploited the segmentation-based approach, and we considered some measures to overcome the main weaknesses of it. In addition, we examined different methods for segmentation including a system based on If-Then rules, a fuzzy inference system, and an artificial neural network (ANN) system. Finally, we concluded that an ANN approach with extended features provides the best solutions (Section 3.1). In recognition section, we obtained a definite set of features from each segmented symbol which was fed to a support vector machine (SVM) classification engine to obtain the recognized symbol. Using large margin classifiers enables us to achieve high recognition rates which are in coherence with the best results in the literature [2].

We also decomposed each character of Persian script to more primitive symbols called graphemes. This novel decomposition has decreased the complexity of the recognition and segmentation procedures and has improved the overall result. Few different characters could share a single grapheme, and additionally, several joint graphemes could build a single character. Persian language includes many characters which the only difference they have is the number of dots and placement of them.

To finalize the character recognition task, a post-processing section is implemented to combine the result of grapheme recognition and the number of dots. Besides, this section corrects some common grapheme recognition errors using an embedded confusion matrix. Fig. 4 shows the combination of grapheme recognition and post-processing brocks with dot recognition module.

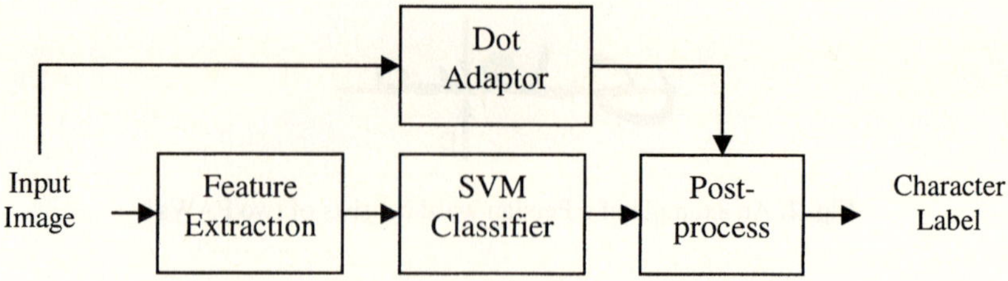

Fig. 4. Grapheme recognition subsystem is combined with dot recognition modules and post-processing blocks to recognize characters

Before proceeding further, we provide concepts of some frequently used terms in this paper for clarification:

Grapheme: In this research, we refer grapheme to any graphical image that would be a character or a part of it which acts as a fundamental building block of words. This resembles the concept of phonemes in speech, but we don't directly choose them in relation to real phonemes.

Pen tip: The vertical position of the pen in the skeleton PAW image.

Junction points: The horizontal position of the grapheme boundary. Thus, cutting the word at junction points results separated graphemes.

3.1 Segmentation

The ultimate goal of the segmentation block is to find the exact junction points in each PAW. In this research, three distinct methods have been used for segmentation of the PAWs. The decision about how segmenting a line is based on specific features which are identical for all of these methods, but the decision maker is different.

1- If Then Rule: In this method, we defined some conditional rules to compare the computed features with some predefined thresholds. The results of these conditions have been combined to determine the junction points. We fine-tuned the rule base and thresholds by observing the test results. The following algorithm, describes how we obtain junction points through this If-Then rules.

Initially, the upper contour of the character image is extracted, and its first derivative is computed (Figures 5 and 6). In order to have robust derivatives, neighboring points should participate in the derivative calculation of each point. This is done by using the convolution of the upper contour signal and h(t) which is defined as follows:

$$h(t)=\begin{cases} t & -n \le t \le n \\ 0 & otherwise \end{cases} \tag{1}$$

As it is depicted in Fig. 6, in junction points, the derivative of the upper contour has a significant peak. Hence, zero crossings of the second derivative of the upper contour are candidate junction points. On the other hand, the pen tip should be near to the baseline in the junction points; therefore, neighboring pixels of the candidate junction points are searched for black pixels near the baseline. Finally, the obtained points are the junction points.

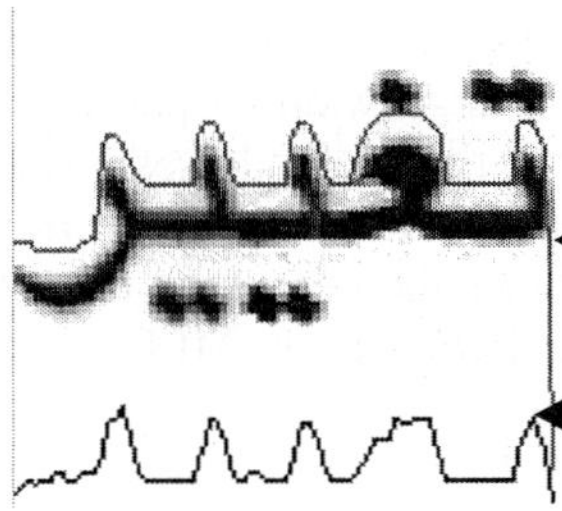

Fig. 5. Sample PAW image with contour and vertical projection

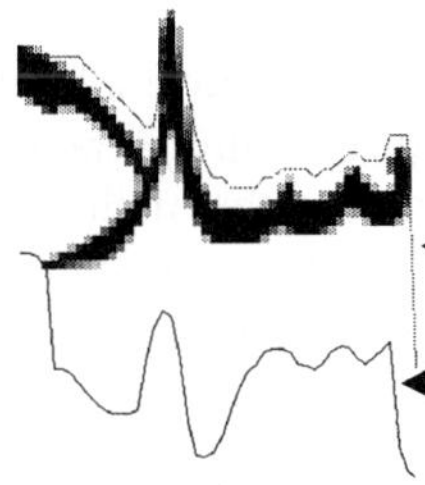

Fig. 6. Sample PAW image with contour (red) and its derivative (gray)

2. Fuzzy Inference System (FIS): As an alternative to the previous method, FIS is used to determine the junction points with increased robustness. The used features in this method are as follows:

a. Vertical projection of the line image (Fig. 5).
b. The first derivative of the upper contour.
c. The distance of the pen tip from the baseline.

The calculation of the first two features is evident, and we will explain the third (f_3) in more details. This feature is computed using the weighted average of the pixel values on each column of the image matrix, where the weights are chosen Gaussian functions.

$$f_3 = \frac{1}{\sqrt{2\pi\sigma}} \sum_y e^{\frac{-(y - baseline)^2}{\sigma^2}} \cdot image(x, y) \qquad (2)$$

$$where\ \sigma = \frac{penwidth}{3}$$

These three features are fed to an FIS which is used as a filter to create zero crossings at the junction points. Thus, applying a zero-crossing detector to the output of the FIS will result the junction points.

3. Artificial Neural Network (ANN): Previously explained systems have a short memory in the derivative calculation. Therefore, the final decision for each point depends on values of a small neighborhood of that very point. It is obvious that using

a larger neighborhood can result in a more accurate decision. Hence, in the neural network method, features of a large window participate in making decision for its center point. On the other hand, this method uses a learning system to find the junction points. In this approach, similar features to the fuzzy system are calculated over a window of width equal to 4 times the pen width to make a feature vector. Resulting vector is fed to a Multi Layer Perceptrons (MLP) with one output neuron that estimates the probability of the center point being the junction point.

Our train set includes labeled junction points. The target vector of the neural network should be equal to one for the junction points and zero for the others. To assist the learning procedure, a Gaussian function with variance equal to 1/6 times the pen width is placed at each junction point. Although this smoothing reduces the accuracy, the results are quite acceptable (Fig. 7).

In practice, our neural network should have a predefined number of inputs; consequently, the input image is normalized with the pen width value in order to have pen width equal to 5 points in all images. In the implementation stage, the neural network window width is set to 20 i.e. 4 times the pen width. Thus, the neural network has 60 neurons in the input layer and 5 hidden neurons.

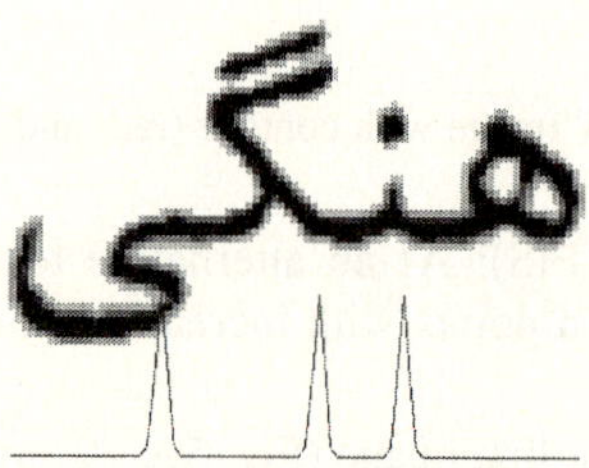

Fig. 7. Sample PAW image neural network target signal, which is used for training procedure

The described neural network uses a hyperbolic tangent sigmoid as the transfer function in all neurons, and it is trained using the standard gradient decent with momentum training algorithm which has adaptive learning rate [9]. In order to facilitate the training process and escape from the local minimums, a simulated annealing algorithm is added to the training process. The peaks of the neural network output are selected as the candidate junction points. Finally, the neighboring points of the candidates are checked for the location of the pen tip, and the final junction points are specified.

3.2 Recognition

The task of this section is to recognize the input grapheme image. In Persian script, every letter can have two to four different shapes in respect to their position in their containing PAW. The four different positions are at the beginning, in the middle, at the end, or character as an isolated word. These positions correspond to the connectivity of the letter from left, both sides, right, or no connection respectively. Table 1 shows the example of four different shapes of character "HEH". This fact is addressed in some previous works [6, 10] as one of unique characteristics of Persian/Arabic scripts which increases the literally available 52 characters of Persian script to 134 different characters in shape. The main idea to overcome this diversity is to recognize the position of characters separately and generate four different recognition systems for each position.

As Table 1 presents, we assigned a group number to each case of character shapes. In contrast to the methods available in the literature, classifiers were designed to recognize graphemes instead of characters in different positions inside words. By introducing graphemes instead of characters, the number of recognition classes reduces from 134 characters to 85 graphemes. Similarly, graphemes have four groups according to their position in the PAW. Meanwhile, a post-processing system is needed to recognize the number and positions of the dots and also the sequence of the graphemes to produce the final recognized characters. As mentioned before, this strategy helps simplifying the segmentation section and decreases the complexity of the classification process significantly.

Table 1. Four possible shapes of a character in a PAW and corresponding character group of each shape and its connectivity direction

Group Number	*1*	*2*	*3*	*4*
Character "HEH"	ﻫ	ﻬ	ﻪ	ﻩ
Connectivity Direction	Left	Both	Right	None

Table 2. Some characteristic features for grapheme recognition

i	*Feature Vector (F_i)*
1-7	Moment invariant Hu features [13, 15].
8	(The variance of the horizontal projection) / (The variance of the vertical projection)
9	(The number of the black pixels in the upper half of the image) / (The number of black pixels in the lower half of the image)
10	(The number of black pixels in the right half of the image) / (The number of black pixels in the left half of the image)
11	(The number of black pixels in the whole image) / (Area of the bounding box of the image)
12	(The width of the bounding box of the image) / (The height of the bounding box of the image)
13	(The variance of the horizontal projection of the upper half of the image) / (The variance of the horizontal projection of the lower half of the image)
14	The 2-D standard deviation of the image
15-34	The elements of the vectors that are extracted from the chain code [14] of the contour of the thinned image [12].
35-37	Quantitative measures of curvatures of the thinned image.

For every grapheme image, a feature vector of length 50 is computed which consists of normalized values of both statistical and structural features. The former is mainly gathered from the statistical distribution of the grapheme skeleton, while the latter is mostly related to the shape and morphological characteristics of Persian script [10, 11].

In addition to some new features specially designed for the printed script recognition, we used a number of features from our previous work on designing a recognition system for isolated handwritten Persian characters [12]. Table 2 provides some of the characteristic features extracted from binary image in brief.

We used an SVM classifier with RBF kernel and parameters listed in Table 3 which are optimized by cross-validation.

Table 3. SVM optimized parameters

Group	Kernel	γ	c	SVs	Classes
1	RBF	0.01	1	1195	13
2	RBF	0.01	2.2	951	12
3	RBF	0.01	2.2	930	20
4	RBF	0.01	1	1664	40

4 Implementation and Results

In order to have confidential results, a comprehensive database of characters is needed, and since there was no standard dataset available for Persian script, we decided to build it from scratch. For our OCR system with segmentation-based strategy which uses learning systems in both recognition and segmentation sections, two different datasets are needed. First set should include the train and test samples of labeled PAWs for neural network which performs segmentation task and the second set should contain labeled graphemes for the SVM classifier. To achieve higher recognition rates, we decided to gather the second set based on the behavior of the neural network segmentation process. Hence, we carried out following procedures to create those two datasets.

At the first move, we designed a primitive segmentation system based on the If-Then rules, and used this system to segment about 40 pages of Persian script from daily newspapers in different font types. Since the results of such segmentation system was not satisfactory, we developed software for manually verifying the results of that primitive segmentation system. Therefore, a labeled dataset has been created for learning perfect segmentation procedure and evaluating different segmentation methods.

On the way to have complete datasets, we trained the segmentation neural network with the first set, and used this system to segment a large number of printed documents in 20 fonts to create four groups of grapheme database. Fig. 8 shows an example of some of these fonts. This dataset is also verified to have a complete multi-font labeled dataset of Persian printed documents. Our database compromises 40,000 sample PAWs for segmentation and 170,000 graphemes. The train and test sets are chosen uniformly random with ratio of 1/3.

A prototype system is implemented in MATLAB environment. The neural networks implementation is based on MATLAB Neural Network toolbox, and the SVM classification is built with the help of OSU-SVM toolbox. To speed up the algorithms and increase the efficiency, the overall system is implemented in Delphi platform. In addition, a modified version of Lib-SVM library is used in Delphi implementations.

Tables 4 to 6 provide the detailed results of our system for segmentation, recognition, and overall results.

Table 4. Correct segmentation rate

Segmentation	Train set	Test set
If Then Rule	-	89%
FIS	-	91%
NN	99.4%	98.7%

Table 5. Grapheme classification rate

Group	Samples	Train set	Test set
1	43521	99.6%	99.5%
2	38562	99.8%	99.3%
3	39452	99.8%	99.6%
4	48521	99.1%	98.3%

Table 6. Overall recognition tate

Type	Train set after NLP	Test set
Character	-	99.2%
Word	95.46%	91.09%

Fig. 8. Example of a Persian script with different font types in each line

5 Conclusion

With the proposed design which uses learning systems in both segmentation and recognition sections, we have achieved a highly accurate OCR system for omni-font free size Persian printed documents. The commercial version of this system will be exploited in Iranian Civil Organization in year 2005. This novel strategy could be extended to other cursive scripts as well with a proper training dataset.

Acknowledgement. The authors would like to thank and acknowledge the Paya Soft co. that sponsored this research.

References

1. A. Amin: Off line Arabic character recognition - a survey. Proceedings of the International Conference on Document Analysis and Recognition, vol.2 (1997) 596-599
2. Y. Lecun,L. Bottou,Y. Bengio,P. Haffner: Gradient-based learning applied to document recognition. Proceedings of the IEEE, vol. 86, no. 11, IEEE, USA (Nov. 1998) 2278-2324
3. B. Al-Badr, RM. Haralick: Segmentation-free word recognition with application to Arabic. Proceedings of the Third International Conference on Document Analysis and Recognition, Part vol.1, IEEE Comput. Soc. Press., Los Alamitos, CA, USA, vol. 1 (1995) 355-359
4. I. Bazzi, R. Schwartz,J. Makhoul: An omnifont open-vocabulary OCR system for English and Arabic. IEEE Transactions on Pattern Analysis & Machine Intelligence, vol. 21, no. 6, IEEE Comput. Soc., USA (June 1999) 495-504
5. AH. Hassin,Tang Xiang-Long,Liu Jia-Feng,Zhao Wei: Printed Arabic character recognition using HMM. Journal of Computer Science & Technology, vol. 19, no. 4, Science Press, China (July 2004) 538-543
6. A. Cheung, M. Bennamoun, NW. Bergmann: An Arabic optical character recognition system using recognition-based segmentation. Pattern Recognition, vol. 34, no. 2, Elsevier, UK. (Feb. 2001) 215-233
7. H. Weissman, M. Schenkel, I. Guyon, C. Nohl, D. Henderson: Recognition-based segmentation of on-line run-on handprinted words: input vs. output segmentation. Pattern Recognition, vol. 27, no. 3, UK. (March 1994) 405-420
8. R. Azmi, E. Kabir: A new segmentation technique for ominifont farsi text. Pattern Recognition Letters, vol. 22, no. 2 (2001) 97-104
9. S. Haykin: Adaptive Filter Theory. 3rd edition, Upper Saddle River, NJ: Prentice-Hall (1996).
10. M. Kavianifar,A. Amin: Preprocessing and structural feature extraction for a multi-fonts Arabic/Persian OCR. Conference on Document Analysis and Recognition, IEEE Computer Soc., pp. 213-216. Los Alamitos, CA, USA (1999)
11. BM. Kurdy,MM. AlSabbagh: Omnifont Arabic optical character recognition system. Proceedings of Int. Conf. on Information and Communication Technologies: From Theory to Applications, IEEE, Piscataway, NJ, USA (2004) 469-70
12. H. Pirsiavash F. Razzazi: Design and Implementation of a Hierarchical Classifier for Isolated Handwritten Persian/Arabic Characters. IJCI Proceedings of International Conference on Signal Processing, Vol. 1, no. 2, Turkey (Sep. 2003)
13. M.K. Hu: Visual Pattern Recognition by Moment Invariants. IEEE Transactions on Information Theory, Vol. IT-8, IEEE (1962) 179-187
14. R.C. Gonzalez ,P. Wintz: Digital Image Processing. Addison Wisely Publishing Company, 2nd Edition (1987) 392-423

A Modified Area Based Local Stereo Correspondence Algorithm for Occlusions

Jungwook Seo and Ernie W. Hill

Department of Computer Science,
University of Manchester,
Manchester M13 9PL, UK
{seoj, ernie.hill}@cs.man.ac.uk

Abstract. Area based local stereo correspondence algorithms that use the simple 'winner takes all' (WTA) method in the optimization step perform poorly near object boundaries particularly in occluded regions. In this paper, we present a new modified area based local algorithm that goes some way towards addressing this controversial issue. This approach utilizes an efficient strategy by adding the concept of a computation skip threshold (CST) to area based local algorithms in order to add the horizontal smoothness assumption to the local algorithms. It shows similar effects to Dynamic Programming(DP) and Scanline Optimization(SO) with significant improvements in occlusions from existing local algorithms. This is achieved by assigning the same disparity value of the previous neighboring point to coherent occluded points. Experiments were carried out comparing the new algorithm to existing algorithms using the standard stereo image pairs and our own images generated by a Scanning Electron Microscope (SEM). The results show that the horizontal graphical performance improves similarly to DP particularly in occlusions but the computational speed is faster than existing local algorithms, due to skipping unnecessary computations for many points in the WTA step.

1 Introduction

The main aim of stereo vision systems is to determine depth between two or more stereo image pairs using an approach which is similar to the human vision system [4]. More recently, a variety of dense stereo correspondence algorithms have been developed for a variety of purposes such as computer vision, robot navigation, intelligent vehicles and so on [11] [13]. These dense stereo matching algorithms can be classified in two categories: namely local and global algorithms. [1] Local algorithms are broadly split into two categories: area based matching and feature based matching. The area based algorithms aggregate costs of pixels in correlated window regions without smoothness assumptions and are fast computationally but exhibit poor performance graphically. Notwithstanding, they have often been used for real time applications. [12] In the feature based matching, two classes have recently received attention: hierarchical feature matching and segmentation matching.

M. Lazo and A. Sanfeliu (Eds.): CIARP 2005, LNCS 3773, pp. 611–619, 2005.

On the other hand global algorithms are based on iterative schemes and minimize the global cost function combining data and smoothness terms. These algorithms such as Graph Cuts(GC) [18] produce better and more accurate disparity maps but the computational costs are often too high. We have attempted to reconstruct the 3D surfaces of specimens from nano-scaled stereo image pairs generated by the SEM at slightly different eucentric tilting angles for a fast nanotechnology application. Initially, we used area based local stereo matching algorithms rather than global ones. However, the results from the existing local algorithms proved not to be accurate enough to reconstruct sufficient detail on the 3D surfaces.

Here, we propose a new modified area based local algorithm by adding the concept of a computation skip threshold (CST) to the basic steps in terms of the horizontal smoothness term. The aim of this approach is to improve graphical performance of existing area based local algorithms particularly for occlusions with speed improvement. Section 2 describes related work. Section 3 presents the new algorithm in detail. Section 4 compares the new algorithm with existing ones and shows all images used and results from experiments. Section 5 contains conclusions.

2 Related Work

The majority of area based local algorithms can be divided into 4 steps as below: [5]

1. Matching cost computations
2. Cost (support) aggregation
3. Disparity computation/optimization(WTA)
4. Disparity refinement

However, some local algorithms combine steps 1 and 2 and use a matching cost based on a correlated area (e.g. normalized cross-correlation [6]). For the matching cost commonly both the squared intensity differences (SD) [10] and the absolute intensity differences (AD) [9] have been used. Recently, there are new robust measures, such as truncated quadratics and contaminated Gaussians [7], which limit the influence of mismatches in the aggregation. However, this paper is concerned with only basic methods (AD and SD). In aggregation, window-based methods aggregate matching cost over a support region in the Disparity Space Image (DSI) [2] C(x, y, d) (three-dimensional in x-y-d space) around a specific pixel of interest; the sum of absolute differences (SAD) or the sum of squared differences (SSD). Additionally, some efficient methods can be used with these techniques. For example, shiftable windows [8] can be used with a separable sliding min-filter. For disparity computation, a straightforward way to determine the best match for a point is to select the point of the other image, which shows the best similarity value within the range of disparities ($d_{min} \leq d \leq d_{max}$). This method is referred to as the 'Winner Takes All' (WTA).

Through the 1980's there has been much interest in feature based techniques due to their efficiency but the interest has declined in the last decade because of improvements in robust global techniques. These methods use symbolic features rather than image intensities. Venkateswar and Chellappa [14] have proposed a hierarchical feature matching algorithm utilizing four types of features: lines, vertices, edges, and surfaces. Matching starts from the highest level of the hierarchy (surfaces) to the lowest (lines). Another feature based approach is to segment the images and then match the segmented regions [16] [15]. Birchfield and Tomasi [16] segment stereo images into small planar patches for which correspondence is determined and introduce an affine transformation model with parameters as bellows:

$$\begin{bmatrix} x_2 \\ y_2 \end{bmatrix} = A \begin{bmatrix} x_1 \\ y_1 \end{bmatrix} + d \tag{1}$$

where $(x_1, y_1) and (x_2, y_2)$ are the coordinates of corresponding points in the left and right images. The vector d defines the translation of a segment between frames and the matrix A defines the in-plane rotation, scale, and shear transformations between frames. The parameters are calculated by spatio-temporal intensity gradients [17].

Global algorithms are formulated by the energy minimization framework [19]. Those methods often skip the aggregation step and intensively work in the disparity computation step to minimizes a global energy shown as follows:

$$E(d) = E_{data}(d) + \lambda E_{smooth}(d) \tag{2}$$

The data term, $E_{data}(d)$ measures how well the disparity function d agrees with the input images. The smoothness term,$E_{smooth}(d)$ encodes the vertical and horizontal smoothness assumptions.

3 A New Modified Algorithm

In this algorithm, a new Computation Skip Threshold (CST) has been added to the cost and disparity computation steps of existing local algorithms in order to determine whether or not the point in the left image should be skipped in the WTA step. In the given stereo pair images; I_L (left) and I_R (right), the pixel intensity value of each point in each epipolar scanline of the I_L will be compared with that of the neighboring previous point in the same scanline of the I_L during the first cost computation step.

$$SKIP_L(x, y) = \begin{cases} 1 \; if \; \|I_L(x, y) - I_L(x-1, y)\| \leq \delta \\ 0 \; if \; \|I_L(x, y) - I_L(x-1, y)\| > \delta \end{cases} \tag{3}$$

In Equation 3, δ is the Computation Skip Threshold (CST) expressed by a pixel intensity value (from 0 to 255). In the first step $SKIP_L$(x,y) of each pixel point is calculated according to Equation 3 before the point is calculated for the AD or SD process. The SKIP function simply marks 1 or 0 in each point but has no influence in existing calculations. In the aggregation step, there is no change in computations. For the first two steps, the new algorithm is exactly the same as existing local algorithms except marking 0 or 1 for each point by the SKIP function. During the third WTA step, if $SKIP_L$(x,y) is 1 the point (x,y) in the left image will be skipped and then the same disparity value of the previous point will be assigned to that point. Conversely, if it is 0 then the point (x,y) will be computed as normal so that the point (x,y) is regarded as where the image intensity is sufficiently changed to be calculated.

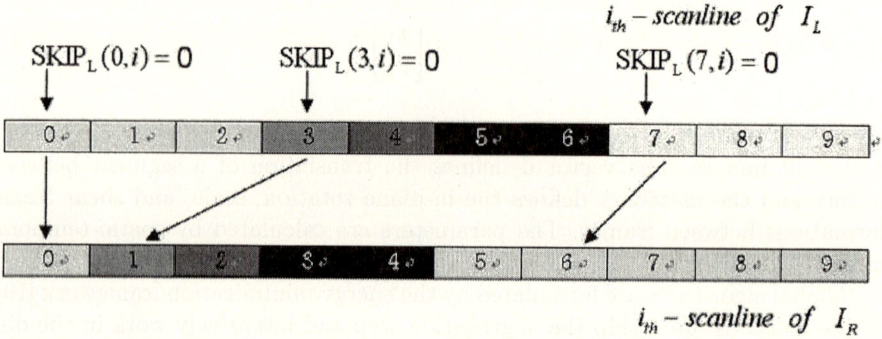

Fig. 1. An example of the i_{th}–scanline in a stereo image pair

Figure 1 illustrates how this method works in each scanline of a stereo image pair. In the cost computation step, $SKIP_L$(x,i) of the first pixel in each scanline is forced to be 0 whereas, that of the remaining ones will be 0 only when the absolute difference between the current pixel value and the previous one in the same scanline of the I_L is bigger than CST. Thus, the value of $SKIP_L(x,i)$ for the three points ($I_L(0,i), I_L(3,i), I_L(7,i)$) where pixel intensity values are changed more than CST from the previous point is 0 and that for the others is 1. In the WTA step, only the three points of the left scanline are computed within the disparity range rather than all of the available 10 points. The disparity value of the remaining seven points will be assigned with that of the previous point of each point. For example, the disparity value of the three points ($I_L(4,i), I_L(5,i), I_L(6,i)$) will be 2 assigned by that of the point $I_L(3,i)$. In this way a large number of computations can be saved. If one assumes that the disparity range is 30 then we can skip 30 x 7 (points) computations but do only 30x3 (points). The aim of this approach is to compute only the points where pixel intensity values are changed in each sacnline more than the CST value so that errors particularly at occlusions have been reduced with the horizontal smoothness term. Consequently, the new method produces an effect similar to that of DP and SO [1], especially for occluded regions by assigning the same disparity cost of the previous point of each point to the occluded points. In the next section, we evaluate the performance of the new algorithm with experiments.

4 Experiments and Results

All work has been done on the basis of the open sources from Scharstein and Szeliski [1] [3]. The experiments were conducted on an AMD Athlon 1.2GHz PC with 1GB RAM to compare the performance and computation speed of the new modified algorithm with those of existing fundamental local algorithms such as SAD+WTA and SSD+WTA. In all experiments, a 9x9 or 5x5 window with min-filter has been used with the commonly used images from Middlebury College [3] such as Map, Sawtooth and Tsukuba (gray level images) with the ground truth maps. The first experiment investigated the role of CST and also compared performances, particularly for occluded regions among three algorithms (Existing, New local algorithms and Dynamic Programming). Two factors such as bad pixel percentages(B) in all area and occluded regions [1] were calculated to evaluate the performance of each algorithm.

$$B = \frac{1}{N} \sum_{(x,y)} (|d_C(x,y) - d_T(x,y)| > \delta_d) \tag{4}$$

where $d_C(x,y)$ is the calculated disparity map and $d_T(x,y)$ is the ground truth map. δ_d is a disparity error tolerance, it is 1 here.

Figure 2 shows that the improved performance of the new algorithm at occluded regions has been simultaneously considered with the bad pixel percentage of the whole area in Map (284x216) and Sawtooth images (434x380). In Figure 2a while the CST increased from 5 to 15, the bad pixel percentage at occluded regions is considerably reduced from 90% in existing algorithms to 60% without increasing bad pixel errors across the image as a whole. Figure 2b also shows more than 30% decrease in error at occlusions. In both images bad pixels have been redueced around 30% but not as much as DP(see Figure 2a). This is for the reason that this algorithm adapts only the horizontal smoothness term but not

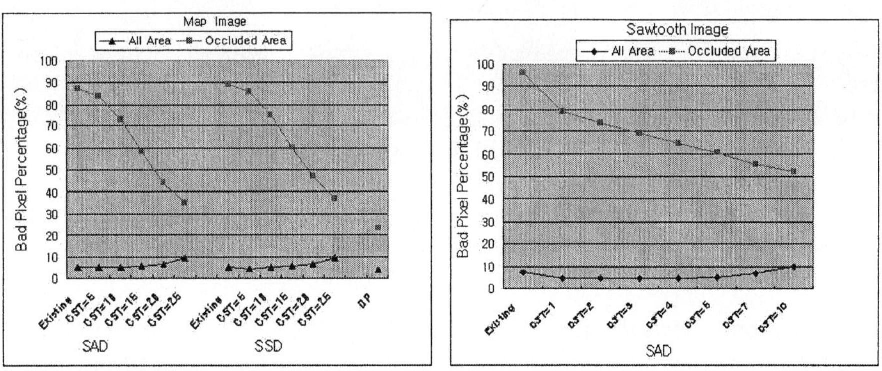

(a) Map Image (b) Sawthooth Image

Fig. 2. Results of performance comparisons between existing and the new algorithms in Map and Sawtooth images with different CSTs

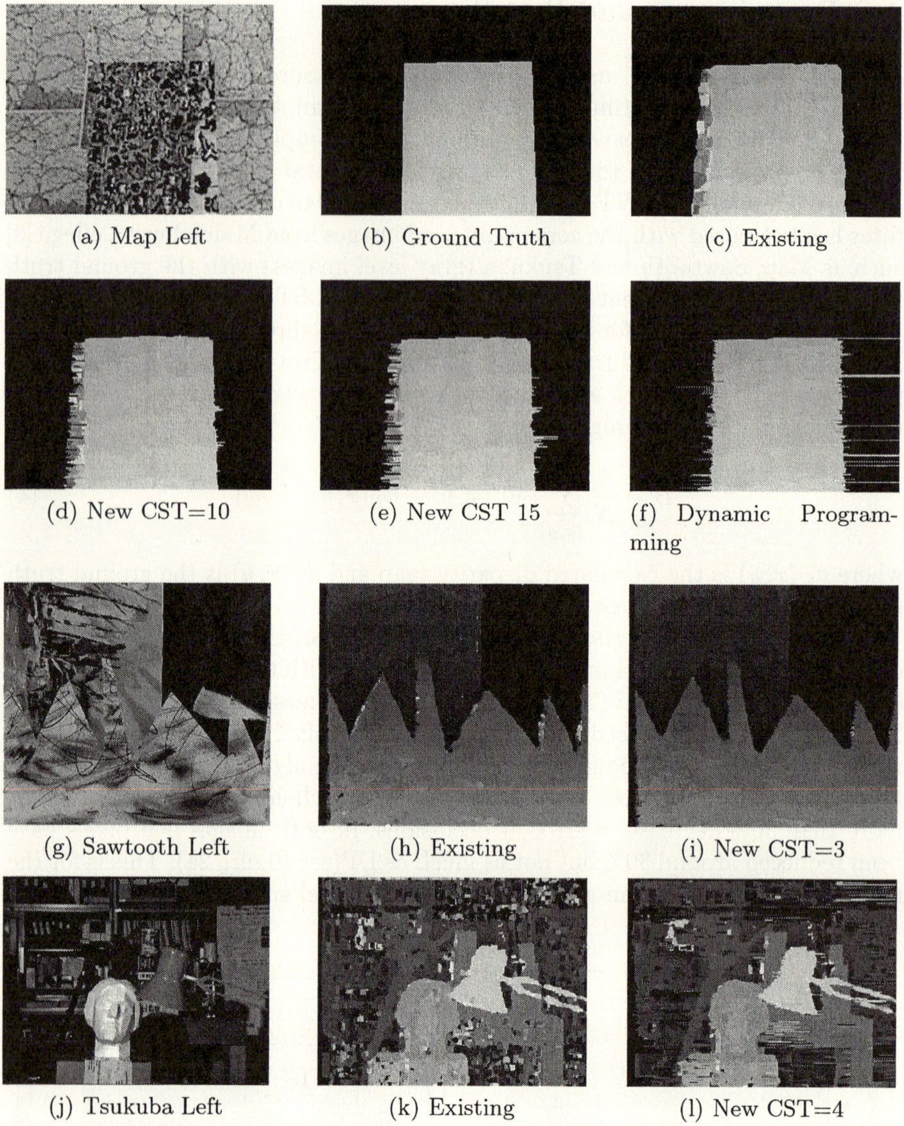

Fig. 3. Experimental images Map,Sawtooth: Window Size=9, Tsukuba: Window Size=5

the vertical one. However, from the points CST=20 in Fingure 2a and CST=5 in Figure 2b the bad pixels in all areas start to be increased so that there seems to be a critical point for the CST. This problem is also the same problem of the difficulty of enforcing consistency causing the horizontal *streaks* in the disparity map of both DP and SO (see Figure 3). Using the map images, the critical CST is 15 (Figure 2a), and in the Sawtooth images the CST is 4 (Figure 2b). With

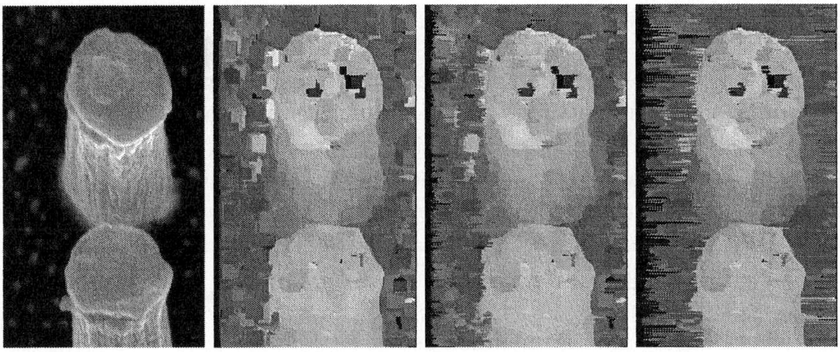

(a) Left image (b) Existing (c) CST=3 (d) CST=4

Fig. 4. Results from a stereo image pair generated by the SEM using a 21x21 window with min filter

Table 1. Results of computation time taken in both images as disparities are increased

Map Image				Sawtooth Image			
Dispa-rity	Improv. (Sec)	Exist. (Sec)	New (Sec)	Dispa-rity	Improv. (Sec)	Exist. (Sec)	New (Sec)
30	0	1.53	1.53	20	0	2.6	2.6
50	0.02	2.56	2.54	40	0.1	3.9	3.8
70	0.04	3.61	3.57	60	0.2	7.9	7.7

an appropriate CST value, the performance of the new algorithm for occluded regions will be between the existing local algorithm shown in the left hand side of Figure 2a and DP shown in the most right hand side.

In the second experiment, a comparison of computation speed between the existing and the new local algorithms in both images has been executed with different disparities. Table 1 shows results of computation time taken. In both images the computation time of the new algorithm is faster than the existing one for all cases. Moreover, in each image the improvement of the computation speed slightly increased as the range of disparities increased. For example, in the Sawtooth image of Table 1 for a disparity range of 20, it is the same speed and for a disparity range of 60, 0.2 seconds faster. Figure 3 shows disparity maps generated by the above experiments. Figure 3c is the map from the existing SSD with a 9x9 adaptive window. It shows bad performance at occluded regions of the left hand side of the object. From Figure 3d, the errors at occluded regions start to be reduced by the new algorithm with CST=10. In Figure 3e with CST=15 shows the best performance. As the value of CST is increased, errors in occluded regions significantly reduced so that the results are going towards those generated by DP (see Figure 3f). In the sawtooth images errors in the left hand side of the sawtooth have been reduced with CST=3(around 30% improvement)as shown

Figure $3g-i$. Also, Tsukuba shows also graphically better results in Figure $3j-l$ with CST=4.

Figure 4 shows another example using smaller objects magnified at a smaller scale. A nano-scaled stereo image pair in high magnification (30,000) is generated by the SEM, using eucentric tilting within slightly different angles (-5 5). It also shows better performance at the occluded regions. Figure 4b is the disparity map generated by the existing SAD algorithm with a 21x 21 window and min-filter. As a result, many errors at occlusions have been generated in the left hand side of each object. In Figure 4c when CST=3, the errors in left hand side of the upper object can be handled and when CST=4 even errors in the left hand side of the bottom object are also handled as shown Figure 4d.

5 Future Work and Conclusion

From all of the experiments, the new modified local algorithm apparently shows approximately a 30% improvement especially in occluded regions due to the added horizontal smoothness term and is moreover faster than existing local ones. The effect of it is similar to that of SO with no occlusion cost necessary and with the lack of the vertical smoothness terms. But both algorithms are different in that SO utilizes DP algorithms to compute the global minimum so as to take much more time than our algortithm. The computing time of the new algorithm is considerably improved when the range of disparities and the size of the images are quite large.

However, the best performance requires an optimized CST value for each image pair as DP also requires a smoothness weight(λ). Fortunately, from our experiments the optimized CST value of all images was 3 or 4 except the map images. It is for the same reason that in DP map images, which are well textured and only have two planar regions, are required for a high value for the smoothness weight(λ) as an input parameter in equation 2 while other images that have many objects at different depth levels are required for smaller values for the parameter [1]. Therefore, the CST value actually works in a similar way to the smoothness weight(λ). If CST is 0, the result of the new algorithm is exactly the same as that of the existing local algorithms. From CST=1 disparity maps of local algorithms start to become smooth up to an optimized CST point(mostly 4) in gray level images without losing the quality of the whole disparity map with speed improvements. This issue of more clearly finding the optimized CST value will be tackled in future work. Finally, we conclude that the new local algorithm adopting the horizontal smoothness can be applied to all kinds of local algorithms, which use the WTA, for a wide range of applications.

References

1. R. Szeliski D. Scharstein: *A taxonomy and evaluation of dense twoframe stereo correspondence algorithms.* IJCV, Vol 47 pp. 7-42, 2002.
2. S. S. Intille A. F. Bobick: *Large occlusion stereo.* IJCV, 33(3):181-200, 1999.

3. http://www.middlebury.edu/stereo.
4. D. Marr: *Vision.* W. H. Freeman and Company, New York, 1982.
5. D. Scharstein: *View Synthesis Using Stereo Vision.* volume 1583 of Lecture Notes in Computer Science (LNCS).Springer-Verlag, 1999.
6. M. J. Hannah R. C. Bolles, H. H. Baker: *The JISCT stereo evaluation.* DARPA Image Understanding Workshop, pages 263-274, 1993.
7. M. J. Black P. Anandan: *A framework for the robust estimation of optical flow.* ICCV, pages 231-236, 1993.
8. M. J. Black and P. Anandan: *A stereo matching algorithm with an adaptive window: theory and experiment.* In Proc. Image Understanding Workshop, pp. 383-389.
9. T. Kanade: *Development of a video-rate stereo machine.* InImage Understanding Workshop, pages 549-557, 1994.
10. T. Kanade L. Matthies, R. Szeliski: *Kalman filter-based algorithms for estimating depth from image sequences.* IJCV, 3:209-236, 1989.
11. D. Gavrila H. Sunyoto, W. Mark: *A Comparative Study of Fast Dense Stereo Vision Algorithms.* IEEE Intelligent vehicles symposium, Parma, Italy, 2004.
12. J.M. Garibaldi H. Hirschmuller, P.R Innocent: *Real-Time Correlation-Based Stereo Vision with Reduced Border Errors.* IJCV,Vol. 47(1/2/3), pp. 229-246, 2002.
13. D. Murray and J. Little: *Using Real-Time Stereo Vision for Mobile Robot Navigation.* Autonomous Robots, Vol. 8 pp. 161-171, 2000.
14. V. Venkateswar and R. Chellappa: *Hierarchical Stereo and Motion Correspondence Using Feature Groupings.* Int'l J.Computer Vision, vol. 15, pp. 245-269, 2000.
15. S. Randriamasy and A. Gagalowicz: *Region Based Stereo Matching Oriented Image Processing.* Proc. Computer Vision and Pattern Recognition, pp. 736-737, 1991.
16. S. Birchfield and C. Tomasi: *Multiway Cut for Stereo and Motion with Slanted Surfaces.* Proc. Int'l Conf. Computer Vision, vol. 1 pp. 489-495, 1999.
17. J. Shi and C. Tomasi: *Good Features to Track.* Proc. Computer Vision and Pattern Recognition, 1994.
18. O. Veksler Y. Boykov and R. Zabih: *Fast approximate energy minimization via graph cuts.* IEEE TPAMI, 23(11):1222.1239, 2001.
19. D. Terzopoulos. *Regularization of inverse visual problems involving discontinuities.* IEEE TPAMI, 8(4):413.424, 1986.

An Evaluation of Wavelet Features Subsets for Mammogram Classification

Cristiane Bastos Rocha Ferreira[1] and Díbio Leandro Borges[2]

[1] Universidade Federal de Goiás,
Instituto de Informática, Goiânia, Go, Brazil
cristiane@inf.ufg.br
[2] BIOSOLO, Goiânia, Go, Brazil
dibio.borges@terra.com.br

Abstract. This paper is about an evaluation for a feature selection strategy for mammogram classification. An earlier solution to this problem is revisited, which constructed a supervised classifier for two problems in mammogram classification: tumor nature, and tumor geometric type. The approach works by transforming the data of the images in a wavelet basis and by using a minimum subset of representative features of these textures based in a specific threshold (λ_T). In this paper different wavelet bases, variation of the selection strategy for the coefficients, and different metrics are all evaluated with known labelled images. This is a suitable solution worth further exploration. For the experiments we have used samples of images labeled by physicians. Results shown are promising, and we describe possible lines for future directions.

1 Introduction

In a pattern recognition approach, the features used to represent the classes must be significative to characterize them with precision and to contribute positively towards the classification process. In the case of images, a transformation of pixels to a different space can help to untangle the meaningful information.

An early diagnostic for medical treatment is very important to total or partial cure. This can avoid the surgical removal of a breast. A common method of diagnosis is by using a Mammogram, which is basically an x-ray of the breast region that displays points with bigger intensities. From the image a trained physician screens it searching for artifacts that could be a sign for the presence of a benign or malign tumor. However suspicious areas appear as almost free shapes and this a challenging for pattern recognition approaches. Besides there are vessels and muscles which are more or less prominent in the images depending on the patient. The variation of images in a class and among considered classes is a factor that will influence directly the problem treated in this paper.

We proposed a solution to this in a previous paper [3] using feature sets with 100, 200, 300 and 500 features to represent each image class. In this paper we report on an strategy to select the wavelet features to be used n the classification, and further it is shown a protocol of tests evaluating the features chosen on two

M. Lazo and A. Sanfeliu (Eds.): CIARP 2005, LNCS 3773, pp. 620–630, 2005.

mammogram classification problems: 1) Type(Benign or Malign) and presence of tumor; and 2) Shape of the Artifacts Distribution in he Mammogram. Considerable advances in this paper are achieved if compared with [3], because of the reduction of the dimensions in space and successful classification rates. This reduction is provided by a new strategy to select the most significant features based on standard deviation of classes by a specific threshold λ_T.

A mammogram classifier is constructed and evaluated using a wavelet decomposition process and a selected subset of representative features. The experiments performed show that successful classification can be achieved, even when we consider the two main problems: 1) Classification between normal, benign, and malign areas; 2) Classification between normal, microcalcifications, radial or spiculated, and circumscribed areas. Section 2 shows the images of typical mammograms and its target classes, along with a revision of literature on mammograms classification. Section 3 defines the problem in terms of a pattern recognition framework and presents a proposed approach for its solution. Section 4 shows experiments on images taken from MIAS [4]. Section 5 gives conclusions and points to future extensions.

2 Mammograms

A mammogram is an x-ray of breast obtained by compression of the breast of patients between two acrylic plates for a few seconds. Thus a typical mammogram is an intensity image with gray levels, showing the levels of contrast inside the breast which characterize normal tissue, vessels, different masses of calcification, and of course noise. This type of image is used by physicians because it is cheap and it allows the discovery of breast cancer that is not perceived in a touch verification. An example of a mammogram and a machine used for obtaining this type of image are shown in Figure 1 a) and b), respectively

Some calcifications can be grouped in classes due their similar geometrical properties. They are usually named radial or spiculated lesions, circumscribed masses lesions and microcalcifications. The radial lesions have a centred region with segments leaving it in many directions. The circumscribed masses lesions are more uniform, resembling a circle, although still irregular. Finally, the microcalcifications constitute small groups of calcified cells without pre-defined form or size.

Another classification adopted by a physician considers the nature of the lesions, such as benign or malign lesions. The distinction between these two classes is very ill-defined in terms of the images themselves, since what usually a physician does is to ask for further analysis including other tests for characterizing the tumor as benign or malign. In terms of an automated classification to be performed by a computer, a strong evidence of a classification in one of these classes will be an important result to achieve. Mammograms without any of the typical artifacts, or abnormalities will be classified as normal cases.

The images used in the experiments were labelled by a physician and they came from the database of MIAS [4] with original size of 1024x1024 pixels, per image, and namely mdbX, where X is a number of the image in the database. However, the images used in the experiments were crops of size 64x64 pixels performed in the original mammograms, whose centers correspond to the centers of the presented abnormalities. The images are irregular textures, and with subtle similarities and differences regarding the classification between radial, circumscribed, microcalcifications, and normal; or between normal, benign, and malign. Figures 5 and 6 show examples of the two classification problems addressed here.

A solution to this whole problem is still a research issue. Some works from the literature either deal only with the segmentation of mammograms in order improve visualization and analysis by a physician, or classify subsets of classes. A review of some work until 1994 can be seen in [9]. We will comment here on some recent works.

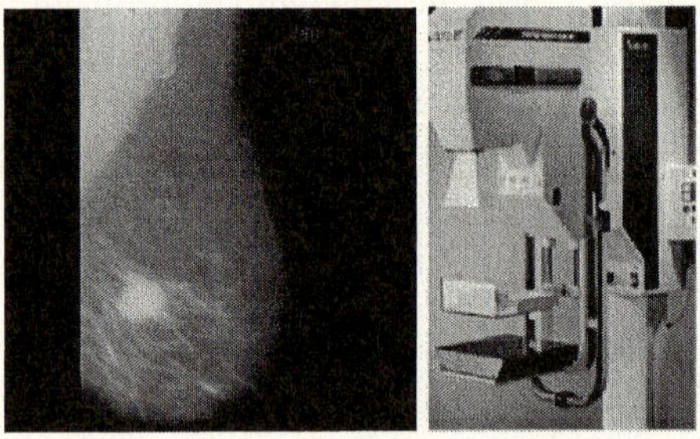

a) b)

Fig. 1. a) Intensity image of a typical mammogram (mdb184) b) Mammogram machine

In [8] is presented a scheme for analyzing mammograms by using a multiresolution representation based on Gabor wavelets. The method is used to detect asymmetry in the fibro-glandular discs of left and right mammograms in order to diagnose breast cancer. The types of lesions are not dealt with as it is the approach taken here. In their work a dictionary of Gabor filters is used and the filter responses for different scales and orientation are analyzed by using the Karhunen-Loève transform, which is applied to select the principal components of the filter responses. They show figures of correct classification for asymmetric, distortion, and normal cases. In [7], thermal texture maps are used in early detection of breast cancer. In this case the relationship between the pattern in each slice and the metabolic activities within a patient's body is revealed and the depth of tumor is estimated by thermal-electric analog and half power point. The conclusion is based on fact that different tissues have different growth patterns and this can distinguished the pixels of tumors and blood vessel. This approach is used to detection of breast cancer and ovarian cancer.

This paper represents the continuity of approach presented in [3] and it shows the constructing and evaluating of classifier for mammogram using a wavelet decomposition process for the feature extracting stage. We evaluate a different strategy for representative feature selecting is presented by using a specific threshold (λ_T), based on standard deviation of classes. The number of features is reduced drastically and results shown have high successful rates.

Section 3 next frames the problem in a pattern recognition framework and presents the details of our approach.

3 The Proposed Approach

In a general way texture can be characterized as the space distribution of the gray levels in a neighborhood, as in [5], that is to say, the variation pattern of the gray levels in a certain area. Texture is a feature that can not be defined for a point, and the resolution at which an image is observed determines the scale at which the texture is perceived. So, texture is a confusion measurement that depends mainly on the scale which the data are observed. There are textures with regularity, deterministic and structured aspects, and others irregular like the mammograms previously shown. In case of regular textures, some measurements can be used like gray-level co-occurrence matrices to capture the spatial dependence of gray-levels values. In addition, entropy, energy, contrast and homogeneity properties can be calculated easily. An autocorrelation function also can be used for images with repetitive texture patterns because it exhibits periodic behavior with a period equal to spacing between adjacent texture primitives. However, in our problem, the images are mammograms with irregular textures, and in addition, the mammogram classes are not homogeneous. Therefore, those measurements will not be representative for the kind of classes we aim to separate in an automated mammogram analysis.

We need first to find what features can be useful, and then select possibly uncorrelated measurements of them. This can be reached by using a wavelet transform in data, because statistical properties of this kind of transformation can help to uncorrelate the data as much as possible without losing their main distinguishable characteristics.

The main contribution of this method is the design and selection of a feature representation of mammogram that can help in the mammogram classification process. We use a wavelet transform in data and we reach a dimensionality reduction. We propose a selecting strategy of main features subsets that have a good representation for the elements of each class and they are more separated in the feature space. A specific threshold (λ_T) based on standard deviation of classes images is used. Extracted and selected features of the decomposed image are used in the construction of the image signature. We believe that this approach can be used in other applications that deal with recognition of irregular textures, like other medical image applications. In order to achieve a separation among image for experiments, the following conventions are adopted: "Basis Image" for mammogram subset with known classification and "Test Image" for mammogram subset with unknown classification, used in test stage.

3.1 Wavelets

The wavelets are functions used as basis for representing other functions, and once a so called mother wavelet is fixed, a family can be generated by translations and dilations of it. If we denote a mother wavelet as y(x), its dilations and translations are

$$\{\psi(\frac{x-b}{a}), (a,b) \in R^{+} \times R\},$$

where $a = 2^{-}j$ and $b = k \times 2^{-}j$, with k and j integers.

The wavelets used in the experiments of this work were implemented following the multiresolution scheme given by Mallat [6].

A bi-dimensional wavelet can be understood as an one-dimensional one along axes x and y. In this way applying convolution of low and high pass filters on the original data, the signal can be decomposed in specific sets of coefficients, at each level of decomposition, as:

- low frequency coefficients ($A_2^d jf$);
- vertical high frequency coefficients ($D_2^1 jf$),
- horizontal high frequency coefficients ($D_2^2 jf$), and
- high frequency coefficients in both directions ($D_2^3 jf$).

The $A_2^d jf$ coefficients represent the entry of next level of decomposition. The decomposition process proposed by Mallat [6] and implemented in our work represents the pyramidal algorithm for a bi-dimensional wavelet transform. Figure 2 represents the wavelet decomposition process and Figure 3 show an example of decomposed mammogram.

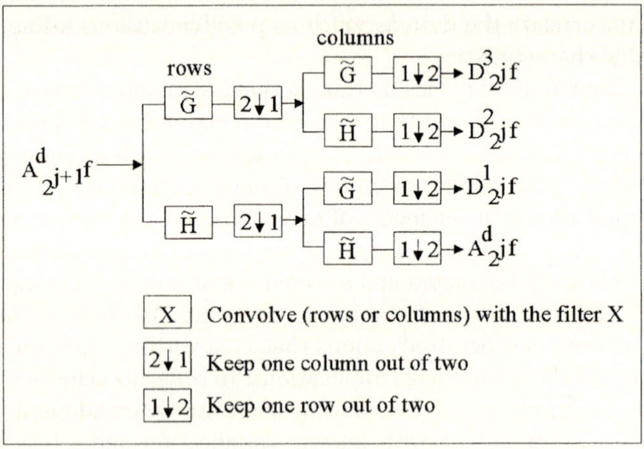

Fig. 2. Decomposition process for computing a wavelet transform

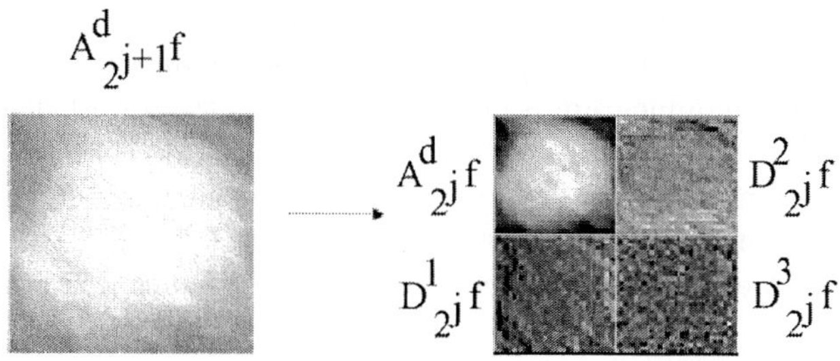

Fig. 3. Example of a decomposed mammogram

By having in mind that decomposing the input image with a Wavelet Transform will be a pre-processing step, the approach can be described then in two main stages as follows.

3.2 First Stage: Building the Classes Signatures

The first stage is based on the Basis Image subset and it is based on the following steps:

- Mammogram images are decomposed with a chosen wavelet basis (W_i);
- Some low frequency coefficients ($CoefClass_j$) are selected, based on their magnitude, in the first decomposition level, considering λ_T as the threshold;
- Signatures of the classes ($ClassSig_j$) are built based on $CoefClass_j$ and on the mean of those coefficients.

The λ_T threshold is calculated using λ [2] defined as:
$\lambda = \frac{\sigma\sqrt{2logn}}{n}$
where σ represents the standard deviation of the class and n represents the number of images in that class.

The λ_T threshold is calculated by a mean of the λ thresholds of j classes, e. g.:

$$\lambda_T = \frac{\sum_{v=1}^{j} \lambda_v}{j},$$

where j represents the number of classes considered.

3.3 Second Stage: Classifying a Mammogram

The second stage is based on the Test Image subset and follows the procedures presented below:

- An unknown mammogram ($Mamo_k$) is decomposed with a chosen wavelet basis (W_i);
- Some low frequency coefficients ($CoefMamo_k$) are selected, based on their magnitude, in the first decomposition level, considering λ_T as a threshold;
- In the second stage, $CoefClass_j$ coefficients represent the unknown mammogram signature ($MamoSig_k$)

- Distances between $MamoSig_k$ and $ClassSig_j$ signatures are calculated by different metrics. D_j are computed for all classes $ClassSig_j$;
- The unknown mammogram is classified based on the lowest distances D_j.

The distance metrics used in order to measure the proximity between unknown mammogram and classes signatures are: Euclidean Distance, Norm in Absolute Value, Mahalanobis Distance and Huffmann Code. The Euclidean Distance is defined by

$$D_{Euclidean} = \sqrt{\sum_{i,j}(A(i,j) - M(i,j))^2}.$$

The Norm in Absolute Value is represented by

$$D_{AbsoluteValue} = \sum_{i,j}(A(i,j) - M(i,j)).$$

A is the matrix that represents the mammogram signature ($MamoSig_k$), M is the class signature ($ClassSig_j$) and the distance is calculated for all $A(i,j) \neq 0$. Mahalanobis Distance is defined by

$$D^2_{Mahalanobis} = (x - m)'C^{-1}(x - m),$$

where x is the features' matrix of mammogram that it is to be classified represented by $MamoSig_k$, m is the matrix of arithmetic mean among all of elements of the same class, represented by $SigClass_j$, and C^{-1} is the covariance matrix of class elements. Huffmann Code is based on the following rules: for an A matrix, for all i and j, we have $A(i,j) = 1$, if $A(i,j) > 0$, and $A(i,j) = -1$, if $A(i,j) < 0$, where i is the number of lines and j is the number of columns of A matrix. Considering that A and B are matrices, the distance between them, using Huffmann Code is calculated by a sum of "1", where the sum is calculated in cases where $A(i,j) = B(i,j)$.

4 Experiments and Analysis of Results

Experiments were accomplished for the two problems: the geometric property of the tumor, and its nature. The first set of experiments took into consideration the geometric property of the tumor, considering four classes: radial lesions, circumscribed lesions, microcalcifications and normal areas. The second experiment took into consideration the nature of the tumors, regardless of geometric property, considering three classes: benign, malign and normal classes.

The images used in this set of experiments are shown by class. Some noisy images were obtained from original ones and used for testing, namely ndbX, rdbX and sdbX. The noisy images were obtained by application of three types of noise: Noisify, Randomize and Spread, corresponding to ndbX, rdbX and sdnX, respectively. The parameter settings were independent, option of gray factor equals 10 to Noisify. In case of Randomize, randomization percentile was 100% and 10 number of repetitions. At last, in case of Spread, both horizontal and vertical spread amount were 10.00.

The images used for constructing the classes are different from the images used for classification. Figures 4(a), 4(b) and 4(c) show benign, malign and normal classes respectively, considering the nature of tumors. Figures 5(a), 5(b), 5(c) and 5(d) show radial lesions, circumscribed lesions, microcalcifications and normal classes, considering the geometric property of tumor.

We consider the variation of two issues: wavelet basis used in the decomposition process, and distance metrics. The wavelet bases tested were Haar, Daubechies 4, Biorthogonal 2.4, Coiflets 2 e Symlets 2. A cross validation process is performed with 75% of images separated for building the classes signatures and 25% of them for testing. Four rounds are tested with all of images considering the mentioned percentages and we present the average results in Tables 3, 4, 5, 6, and 7. Tables 1 and 2 present λ_T threshold values for each test, considering the nature and geometrical properties of tumors, respectively.

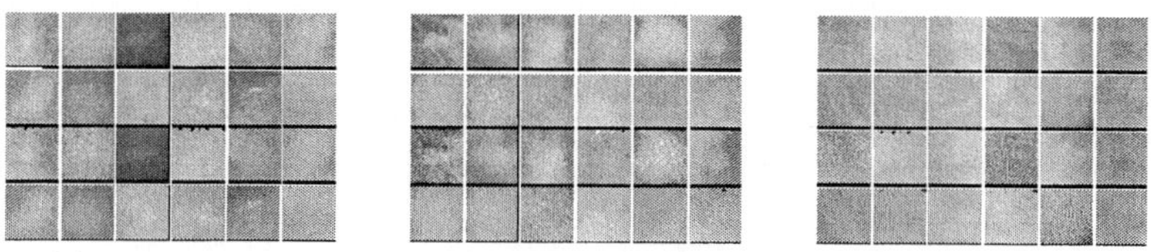

(a) Benign class (b) Malign class (c) Normal class

Fig. 4. Typical images of the classes for the first mammogram classification problem considered in this work (Tumor Nature)

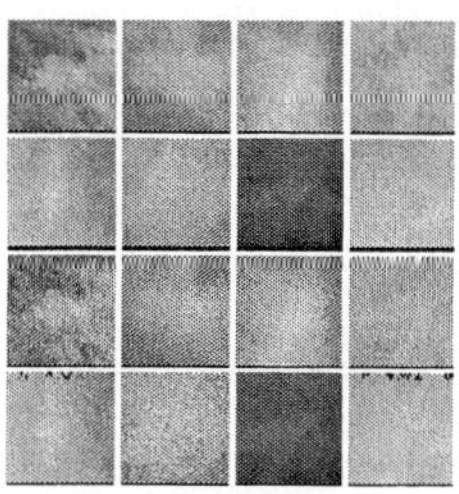

(a) Radial class

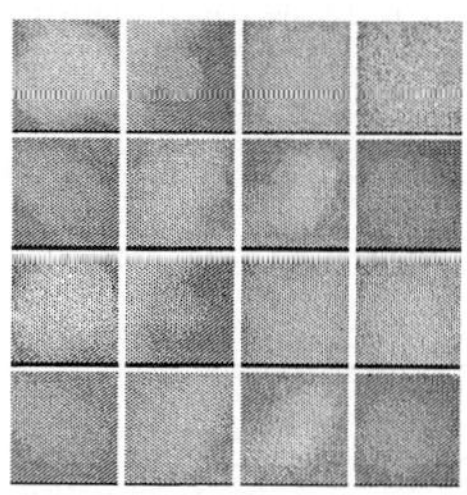

(b) Circumscribed lesion class

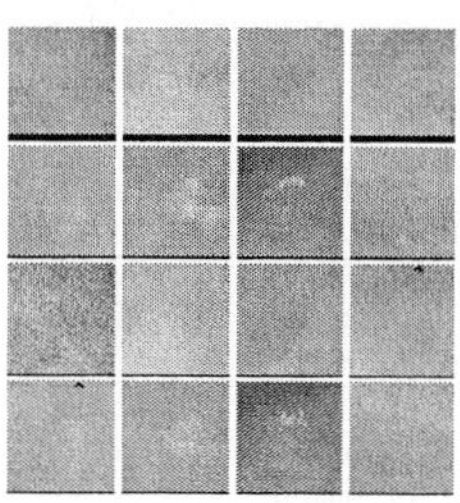

(c) Microcalcification class

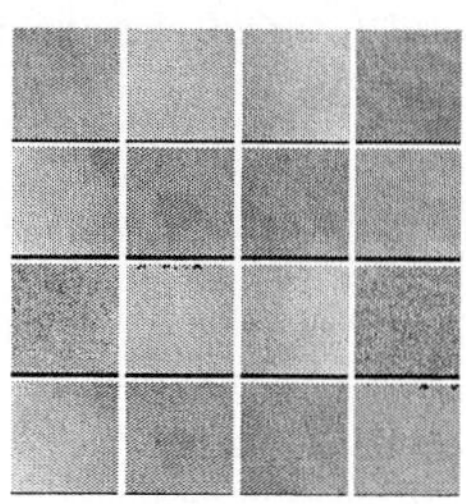

(d) Normal class

Fig. 5. Typical images for the second classification problem (Tumor Geometrical Type)

Table 1. λ_T values, considering nature of the tumors

Round	Daubechies 4	Haar	Biorthogonal 2.4	Coiflets 2	Symlets 2
1	15	15	14	14	15
2	13	14	12	12	14
3	15	15	14	14	15
4	14	14	12	12	14

Table 2. λ_T values, considering the geometrical properties of the tumors

Round	Daubechies 4	Haar	Biorthogonal 2.4	Coiflets 2	Symlets 2
1	15	15	14	14	15
2	17	17	15	15	17
3	15	15	14	14	15
4	17	17	16	16	17

Table 3. Successful rates of classification using Daubechies 4 wavelet basis with normalized data

Class	Euclidean Distance	Norm in Abs. Value	Huffmann Code	Mahalanobis Distance
Benign	95.83	95.83	87.50	95.83
Malign	45.83	33.33	45.83	33.33
Normal	87.50	83.33	87.50	87.50
Radial	56.25	50.00	56.25	50.00
Circumscribed	75.00	75.00	75.00	75.00
Microcalcifications	93.75	93.75	68.75	93.75
Normal	75.00	75.00	87.50	68.75

Table 4. Successful rates of classification using Haar wavelet basis with normalized data

Class	Euclidean Distance	Norm in Abs. Value	Huffmann Code	Mahalanobis Distance
Benign	91.67	91.67	91.87	91.67
Malign	79.17	70.83	79.17	66.67
Normal	95.83	95.83	100.00	95.83
Radial	75.00	75.00	75.00	75.00
Circumscribed	87.50	87.50	87.50	87.50
Microcalcifications	93.75	93.75	93.75	93.75
Normal	93.75	93.75	100.00	100.00

Table 5. Successful rates of classification using Biorthogonal 2.4 wavelet basis with normalized data

Class	Euclidean Distance	Norm in Abs. Value	Huffmann Code	Mahalanobis Distance
Benign	75.00	75.00	66.67	83.33
Malign	50.00	29.17	20.83	29.17
Normal	83.33	83.33	95.83	75.00
Radial	75.00	75.00	62.50	75.00
Circumscribed	62.50	62.50	62.50	62.50
Microcalcifications	75.00	62.50	62.50	56.25
Normal	62.50	56.25	81.25	56.25

Table 6. Successful rates of classification using Coiflets 2 wavelet basis with normalized data

Class	Euclidean Distance	Norm in Abs. Value	Huffmann Code	Mahalanobis Distance
Benign	87.50	87.50	70.83	87.50
Malign	83.33	58.33	54.17	54.17
Normal	87.50	83.33	95.83	83.33
Radial	81.25	81.25	81.25	81.25
Circumscribed	81.25	81.25	81.25	81.25
Microcalcifications	93.75	93.75	93.75	87.50
Normal	81.25	75.00	93.75	75.00

Table 7. Successful rates of classification using Symlets 2 wavelet basis with normalized data

Class	Euclidean Distance	Norm in Abs. Value	Huffmann Code	Mahalanobis Distance
Benign	87.50	87.50	83.33	91.67
Malign	79.17	70.83	75.00	54.17
Normal	95.83	95.83	100.00	95.83
Radial	68.75	62.50	75.00	62.50
Circumscribed	81.25	87.50	81.25	87.50
Microcalcifications	93.75	87.50	93.75	81.25
Normal	93.75	93.75	100.00	100.00

The experiments show that the distance metrics used in the classification process present similar results on average. Euclidean Distance and Norm in Absolute Value show similar successful rates, with the exception of some cases in the malign class. In some cases, Mahalanobis Distance presents inferior rates when compared to other metrics. Haar basis achieves better results considering all the tested classes. The dimensionality of feature space is reduced and the results are promising for the two mammogram classification problems. Selection of features by the λ_T threshold demonstrates its representation capability for choosing the minimum features subset used for building the signatures of classes. The number of features used is about of 1.46% of the low frequency coefficients in the first level of decomposition and 0.37% of total information. Thus relevant information is concentrated in few low frequency coefficients.

5 Conclusions and Future Works

This paper showed an evaluation of a feature selection strategy for two mammogram classification problems. We see this as a practical and important issue to be addressed in medical applications. Variations of the problem, considering tumor nature, and tumor geometric properties are considered. The strategy for the classification was first presented in [3], and in this work we have used a threshold, λ_T, to select the coefficients and have presented experiments in a different number of conditions. The λ_T threshold was capable to choose signatures that conduced to a representation that showed successful rates in classification process, and with λ_T it was possible to use a smaller quantity of features that are useful for mammogram classification problem.

Future extensions of this approach will try to deploy a fully working system in a medical environment. In addition, we suggest the union of this process of decision making of classification with medical inference models of diagnosis.

References

1. P. A. Devijver, J. Kittler *Pattern Recognition: A Statistical Approach* Pretice-Hall, England (1982).
2. D. L. Donoho, I. M. JohnStone, "Ideal spatial adaptation by wavelet shrinkage", *Biometrika*, vol. 81, (1994), 425–455.
3. C. B. R. Ferreira, D. L. Borges, "Analysis of mammogram classification using a wavelet transform decomposition", *Pattern Recognition Letters*, 24, Holand (2003), 973-982.
4. http://www.wiau.man.ac.uk/services/MIAS (Mammographic Image Analysis Society).
5. R. Jain, R. Kasturi, B. Schunck *Machine Vision* McGraw Hill, USA (1995).
6. S. G. Mallat, "A Theory for Multiresolution Signal Decomposition: The Wavelet Representation", *IEEE Transactions on Pattern Analysis and Machine Intelligence*, vol. 11, n. 7, (July 1989), 674–693.
7. H. Qi, P. Kuruganti, Z. Liu, "Early detection of breast cancer using thermal texture maps", em IEEE Symposium on Biomedical Imaging: Macro to Nano, (2002)
8. R. M. Rangayyan, R. J. Ferrari, J. E. L. Desautels, A. F. Frère, "Directional analysis of images with Gabor wavelets", *In: Proceedings of XIII Brazilian Symposium on Computer Graphics and Image Processing, SIBGRAPI*, (2000), 170-177.
9. K. S. Woods, *Automated image analysis techniques for digital mammography*, Ph. D thesis, Dept C. Science and Engineering, University of South Florida, FL, USA (1994).

A New Method for Iris Pupil Contour Delimitation and Its Application in Iris Texture Parameter Estimation

José Luis Gil Rodríguez [1] and Yaniel Díaz Rubio [2]

[1] Advanced Technologies Application Center, MIMBAS,
7a #21812 e/ 218 y 222, Rpto. Siboney, Playa. C.P. 12200,
Ciudad de la Habana, Cuba,
Office Phone Number: (+)537.271.4787, Fax number (+)537.273.0045
[2] Havana University, MES,
San Lázaro y Universidad, Vedado, Ciudad de La Habana, Cuba
jlgil@cenatav.co.cu, verol@ghost.matcom.uh.cu

Abstract. The location of the texture limits in an iris image is a previous step in the person's recognition processes. The iris localization plays a very important role because the speed and performance of an iris recognition system is limited by the results of iris localization to a great extent. It includes finding the iris boundaries (inner and outer). We present a new method for iris pupil contours delimitation and its practical application to iris texture features estimation and isolation. Two different strategies for estimating the inner and outer iris contours are used. The results obtained in the determination of internal contour is used efficiently in the search of the external contour parameters employing a differential integral operator. The proposed algorithm takes advantage of the pupil's circular form using well-known elements of analytic geometry, in particular, the determination of the bounded circumference to a triangle. The algorithm validation experiments were developed in images taken with near infrared illumination, without the presence of specular light in their interior. Satisfactory time results were obtained (minimum 0.0310 s, middle 0.0866 s, maximum 0.1410 s) with 98% of accuracy. We will continue working in the algorithm modification for using with images taken under not controlled conditions.

1 Introduction

Person's recognition using the iris texture has been an active investigation area in last time, because it is considered the most unique phenotypic visible feature in human face that determines their identity and offer biometric feature acquisition without invasion. Person's recognition with iris constitutes one of the main applications of the biometrics at the moment. In this process, the first step to do is the automatic texture iris localization which is characterized by a circular or quasi circular form limited by two borders (iris inner border and outer). The two limits with near circularity form are shown in Fig. 1. The iris inner border coincides with the contour of the eye's pupil and the iris outer border establishes the contact iris-sclera. The iris localization means isolate the iris texture information and play a very important role in the speed and

M. Lazo and A. Sanfeliu (Eds.): CIARP 2005, LNCS 3773, pp. 631 – 641, 2005.

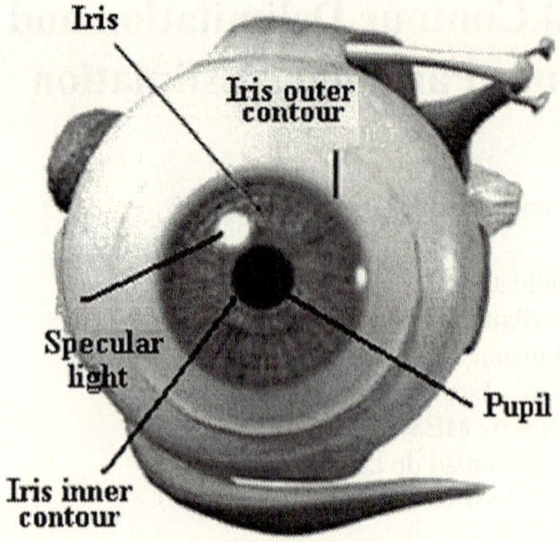

Fig. 1. Circular form of the Iris and pupil. See the iris inner and iris outer boundaries.

performance of an iris recognition system. With the iris texture area delimited we can begin to construct the iris code which is the base of an iris recognition system.

In this paper we present a new method to obtain both, the iris inner and outer border parameters in order to isolate the iris texture information. The proposed method uses different strategies for the parameters estimation of each one of the interest borders, and it uses the results obtained in the determination of the internal contour, in the most efficient search of the external contour parameters.

In order to compute the parameters of the iris inner contour we use the so called "Three Points Method" [1]. It uses well-known elements of analytic geometry and trigonometry, in particular, the determination of the parameters of the circumference bounded to a triangle. To obtain the parameters that define the external contour was used the Daugman's algorithm [2, 3]. This second algorithm receives the output from the first one and after that, search the abrupt gradient changes of a contour integral to find the iris – sclera border.

Portions of the research in this paper use the CASIA iris image database (version 1.0) collected by Institute of Automation, Chinese Academy of Sciences [4]. Our experiments show that the sequential combination of these two algorithms (Three Point Method + Daugman algorithm) during the texture isolation is precise, fast and efficient. The IrisCode formed with the iris texture obtained with our method offer good results during the eye matching applying a test of statistical independence on two coded patterns originated from the same or different eyes.

2 Parameters of the Iris Inner Contour

The iris inner contour coincides with the pupil's external frontier. Since it is assumed that the pupil possesses circular form, the parameters that should be obtained are, the pupil's center coordinates and its radio. To solve this task the algorithm of the three points was designed.

Three points algorithm
The algorithm receives a 256 grey tones image as input (Fig. 2a) and also a precision level P to define the accuracy for finding a point on the pupil contour. P is a threshold used to compare the variation of a texture feature between two points. Particularly, if these two points are located in different regions characterized with different textures, the value P will help us to know the texture change from one region to another.

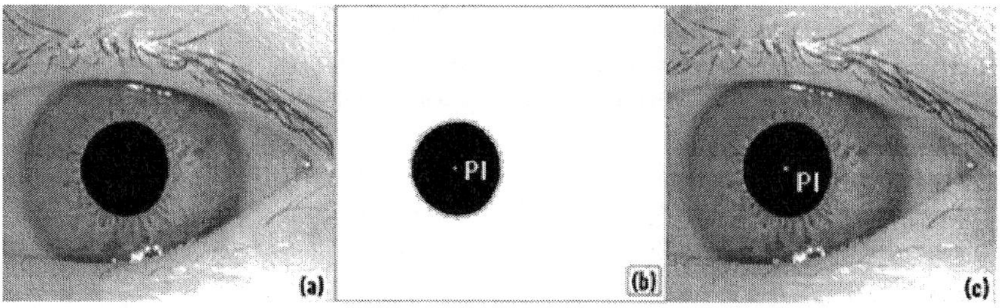

Fig. 2. Process in order to obtain the "interior point" PI using the T*hree points Method.* a) 256 grey tones image as input to the algorithm [3], b) binarized image showing the interior point PI, and c) original image showing the interior point PI already associated.

The general idea is very simple, beginning with an interior point of pupil, we will find three points on the circular contour of the pupil, named P1, P2 and P3 (Fig. 3). With these three points we have a triangle and also a bounded circumference to it. Finally, the bounded circumference parameters are calculated. The mentioned circumference is exactly the pupil's contour. The algorithm steps are as follows:

Step 1: Find the initial point PI located inside the pupil

The original image (Fig. 2a) [3] is binarized to isolate the pupil object from the rest of image. Working with the binarized image we determined which is the row F and the column C with bigger quantity of dark points continuously. A dark point is that whose grey level belongs to the lowest values of the scale [0 .. 255] and it will usually be smaller than 70. The intersection point of the row F and the column C will always be located inside the pupil and we take it as PI (Fig.2b). Taking PI as initial point, the algorithm will begin the search of the points P1, P2 and P3.

This approach is based on the fact that in the eye images, the pupil's grey levels are characterized to have a homogeneous or quasi homogeneous black color, and therefore, its binarization generates a new image with a black stain that represents the pupil on a white background and a grateful method of finding a point inside this stain is the one described above.

Step 2: Find the three points P1, P2 and P3 located on the circumference that defines the iris inner border

The search of these three points begins from the point PI found in the step 1. It is known that there is a very marked texture contrast between the pupil's regions and the iris. For this reason is appropriated to use a quantitative texture feature, as the standard deviation, to detect the frontier between the pupil and the iris. The standard deviation feature is calculated in a point considering a vicinity of 3x3 pixels size which is an habitual procedure in digital image analysis. The standard deviation varies very little inside the pupil, however it will suffer an instantaneous abrupt increasing once the vicinity 3x3 begin to take pixels belonging to the iris region.

The strategy to find the three points P1, P2 and P3 consists on following three trajectories with different addresses whose angles will be 0º, 120º and 240º. On each point of the trajectory we compute the difference between the standard deviation of initial point PI (DSPI) and the points of the trajectory (DSPC). A point whose difference is bigger than threshold P (DSPC - DSPI> P), it will be selected as point belonging to the pupil's contour. The trajectories are taking with these addresses in order to obtain the biggest quantity of information about the contour (Fig. 3).

Step 3: Find the circumference parameters of the iris inner contour

The circumference parameters are the radius and the coordinates of its center. Inside of this circumference the eye pupil is located.

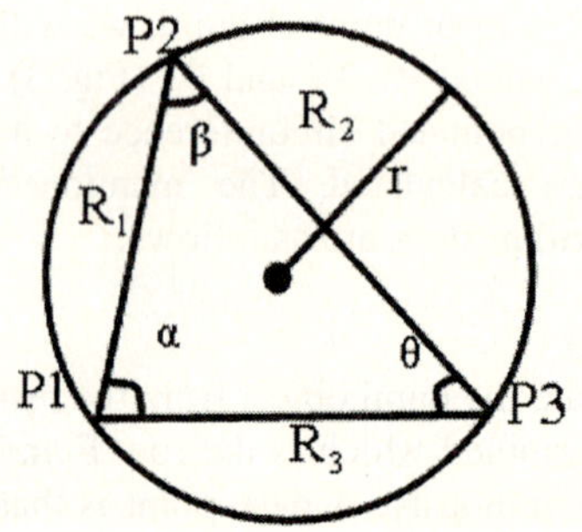

Fig. 3. Circumference bounded to the triangle P1-P2-P3 whose sides are R1, R2 and R3

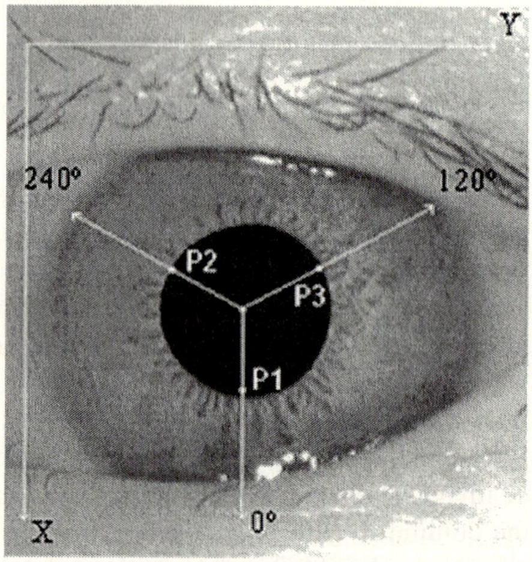

Fig. 4. Image from Fig. 2 (a) showing the points P1, P2 and P3 on the pupil's contour at orientation 0°, 120°, 240°

The points P1, P2 and P3 obtained in the step 2 are not aligned since they belong to the internal contour of the iris which is surrounded by the texture quasi - circular of the iris, that in general possesses irregular form. These three points allow to build a triangle of sides R1, R2 and R3 (Fig. 4) and on that triangle it is possible to define a bounded circumference of radio r that defines the eye's pupil and therefore it determines the extension of iris inner contour that we want to know.

Knowing P1, P2 and P3 the radius r is calculated using the equality settled by the sine law [4] that is enunciated in (1):

$$\frac{\overline{P_1P_2}}{\text{Sen}\ \theta} = \frac{\overline{P_2P_3}}{\text{Sen}\ \alpha} = \frac{\overline{P_3P_1}}{\text{Sen}\ \beta} = 2r \qquad (1)$$

Where,

$\overline{P_1P_2}$: Segment from point P_1 to point P_2 (see Fig. 4).

θ, α and β : angles between the sides of triangle R2,R3; R1,R3 and R1,R2 respectively.

Therefore,

$$r = \frac{\overline{P_1 P_2}}{2 * \text{Sen}\ \theta} \tag{2}$$

If $P_1(x_1, y_1)$ and $P_2(x_2, y_2)$ are the positions coordinates of P_1 y P_2 then the longitude of segment $\overline{P_1 P_2}$ is obtained from (3):

$$\overline{P_1 P_2} = \sqrt{(x_1 - x_2)^2 + (y_1 - y_2)^2} \tag{3}$$

Calculation of angle θ:

The angle θ is comprehend between the segment R2 and segment R3 whose slopes are respectively m_2 and m_3, it can be calculated using the expression (4):

$$\theta = \left| \arctan\left(\frac{(m_2 - m_3)}{(1 + m_2 * m_3)} \right) \right| \tag{4}$$

The slopes m_2 and m_3 are obtained using the well-known formula (5):

$$m = \frac{y_2 - y_1}{x_2 - x_1} \tag{5}$$

When all the necessary data have been calculated, then applying the formula (2), the circumference's radius is obtained. That circumference defines the iris inner contour.

As the circumference is bounded to the triangle P1 P2 P3 (Fig. 4), then its center coincides with the median line intersection point of this triangle. The Fig. 5 shows the circuncenter point. The median line point of the segment $\overline{S}$ is the perpendicular straight line to it, and also crosses by its half point.

The points P1, P2 and P3 define the segments $\overline{P1P2}$ $\overline{P2P3}$ $\overline{P3P1}$. We use two of these segments in order to find the median line M1 and M2 and their interception represents the circumference center.

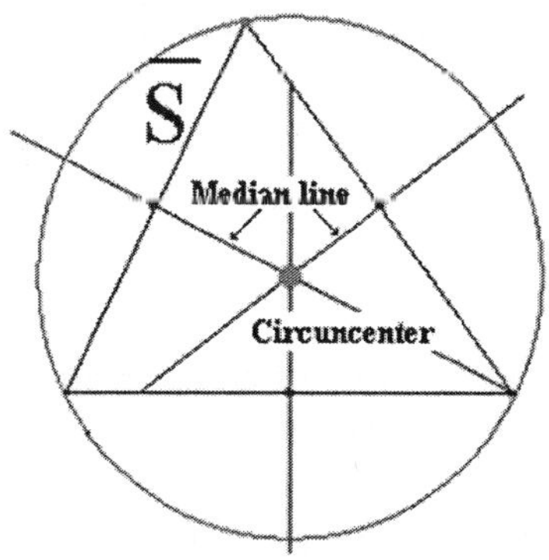

Fig. 5. The circumcenter point is the intersection point of two median line that are sides of a inscribed triangle in a circumference

To define the median lines we must find a point that belongs to each one and also their slopes. A point that belongs to the median line is the half point of segment which cuts it. The half point of a segment $\overline{XY}$ is possible calculate it as,

$$Pm = \left(\frac{x_2 - x_1}{2}, \frac{y_2 - y_1}{2} \right) \quad (6)$$

The slope of a median line is equal to the inverse of the opposed of the slope of the straight line that contains the segment of which is median line. As the straight lines slopes that contain the segment we already found, it is only necessary to calculate the inverse of its opposed one. We need obtain the intersection of two of the three possible median lines, and in that point it is located the circumference center which has the property of being bounded to the shown triangle. This point constitutes the center of the iris inner contour.

3 Parameters of the Iris Outer Contour

In order to obtain the iris external contour parameters we use the values of the iris inner contour parameters already computed above - radius and the circumference center coordinates - which offer an advantageous starting point for the Daugman algorithm expressed in (7).

$$\max_{(r, x_0, y_0)} \left| G_\sigma (r) * \frac{\partial}{\partial r} \oint_{r, x_0, y_0} \frac{I(x, y)}{2\pi r} \partial s \right| \quad (7)$$

The above inequation presents the Daugman' integrodifferential operator for determining the coordinates and radius of the pupil; where I(x, y) is an image such as Fig. 2a containing an eye. The operator searches over the image domain (x, y) for the maximum in the blurred spatial derivative with respect to increasing radius r, of the normalized contour integral of I(x, y) along a circular arc ds of radius r and coordinates (x_0, y_0). The symbol * denotes convolution and $G_\sigma(r)$ is a smoothing function such as a Gaussian of scale σ. The complete operator behaves as a circular edge detector, blurred at a scale set by σ, searching iteratively for the maximal contour integral derivative at successively finer scale of analysis through the three parameter space of center coordinates and radius (x_0, y_0, r) defining a path of contour integration [2].

$$\max_{(r, x_0, y_0)} \left| \frac{1}{\Delta r} \sum_k \left(G_\sigma(r-k) - G_\sigma(r-k-1)\right) \sum_{m=\theta_0}^{\theta_1} I[(r\cos(m) + x_0), (r\sin(m) + y_0)] \right| \quad (8)$$

The final discreet expression (8) describes the process that is used practically in the iris-esclera contact detection with the human eye image.

4 Work of the Integrodifferential Operator

Since the operator behaves as an edge detector, the form of the edge depends on the contour integral used in its expression. In our case an integral of a circular edge detector is used, because the objective is to detect the iris external contour. The operator solves a problem of optimization on three variables: radius r, and the coordinates of the circumference center (x_0, y_0) on the image domain. The operator looks for the maximum of the a partial derived function respect the radius r, a function represented by a circular integral of edge on an arc ds that depends on the radius, the coordinates of the circumference and the angles that limit the arc, and that it is convolved with a Gaussian function which parameter is sigma (scale).

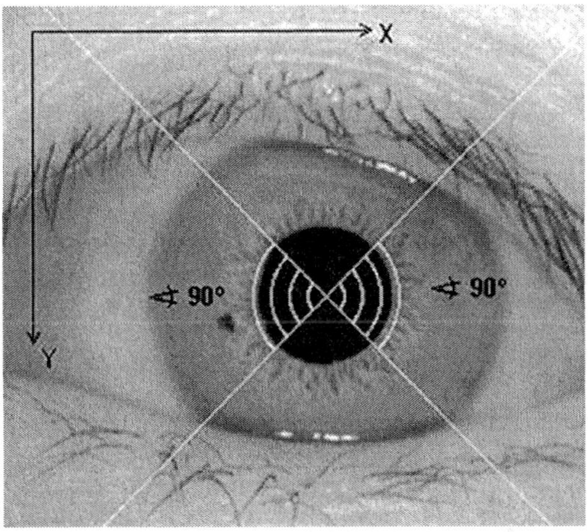

Fig. 6. Iris image showing the contour's integrals. The arches ds are of 90° centred in the axis X with address to positive infinite and negative infinite.

The contour's integral on an arch ds, defines the sector of the contour where it is wanted to find the value of the integral one. In our case, the arches ds are of 90° centred in the axis X with address to positive infinite and negative infinite. The objective of the angles in this address is to avoid the eyelid interference. The Fig. 6 shows the location of the coordinated system, as well as the successive arches that are explored, modifying the radius from inside toward outside, in order to detect the iris's limits.

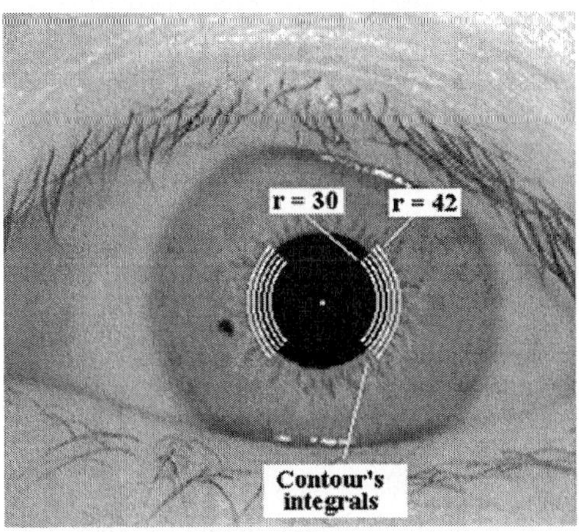

Fig. 7. Iris image showing the contour's integrals computed with r = 30, 33, 36, 39 y 42

The normalization of the contour's integral is applied to have an idea about the intensities half value at the points located on the contour.

The differential of the normalized contour's integral estimates the speed with which it changes their half value, being of interest their maximum values, because they indicate an abrupt change in the averaged intensities of the points among contours of different radios and therefore the sure detection of a border in the radial direction. (See Fig. 7 and Table 1).

The convolution operation with a Gaussian function, whose scale parameter is sigma, has the objective of pondering the obtained values during the differential function evaluation, giving higher importance to the values near to the radius with which the operator is evaluated.

Table 1. Daugman operator values computed from the pupils' center up to the iris border. The abrupt change of the texture properties between the pupil–iris contact and the iris-sclera contact guarantees the iris limits detection.

Radius r	30	33	36	39	42	45
Operator	0	0	20.14	60.41	6.84	6.45

5 The Optimization Problem

The solution to the maximization problem, begins selecting a point inside the pupil that is a center in relation to the iris outer boundary. This initial point is assumed as the pupil's center, previously obtained. Once the initial point is defined, a radius optimization begins. The processes continue changing by approximation, the outer boundary center point, until the max value is obtained.

The radius optimization is implemented increasing the radius in a certain step according to the precision needed to define the outer boundary. The used value is 2 pixels. The strategy for the displacement of the center coordinates is to move it with a certain step, following the vertical and horizontal addresses, 0°, 90°, 180° and 270°. This strategy appears in Fig. 8. The stop condition in the center optimization is the occurrence of three successive iterations without reaching a maximum value of the maximization expression, while in the optimization of the radius the integrals are calculated for all possible radius and selecting the best result.

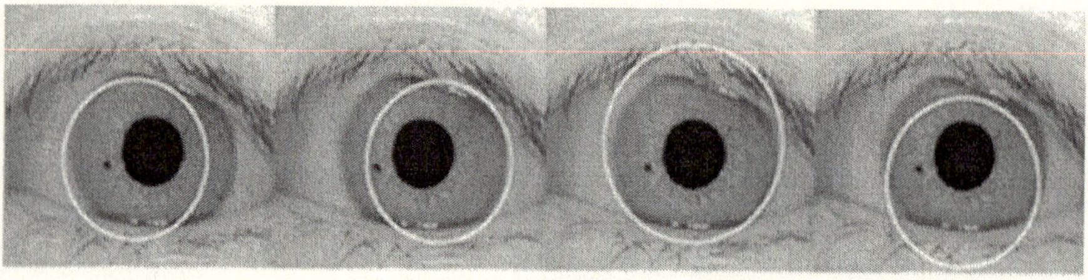

Fig. 8. Iris images belonging to optimization process of the external contour applying Daugman operator. Displayed images show different stages of the not concluded optimization processes.

6 Experimental Results

In order to compare the results of our method with another already published, the CASIA Iris Image Database was adopted. It includes 108 classes and each class has 7 iris images captured in two sessions with a time interval about a month. So there are totally 756 iris images with a resolution of 320x280 pixels. As it is know, in the CASIA iris images some irises are occluded by eyelids and some eyelids are out of the image window. In another way, some eyelash is inside the irises. The experiments are performed in Matlab (version 7) on a PC with P4 2.6 GHz processor and 512Mb RAM.

The Fig. 9 shows an iris images sequence where the inner and outer borders, delimiting the iris's texture, were detected using the Three Point Method combined with the Daugman operator.

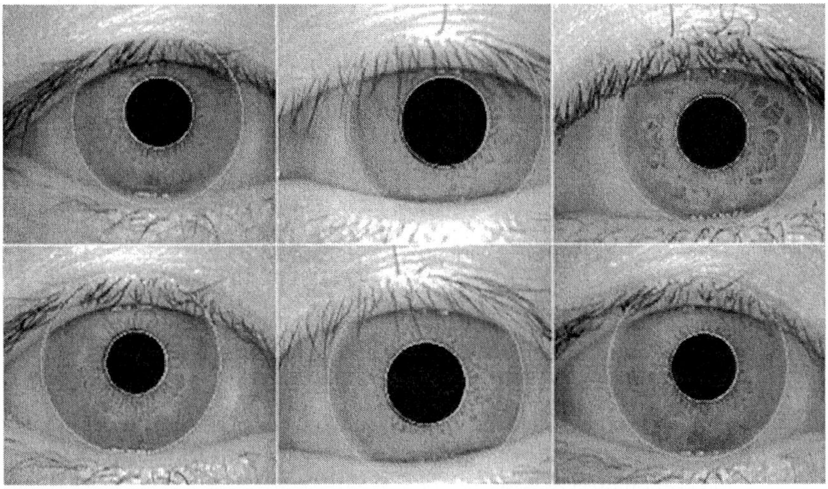

Fig. 9. Results of the proposed method for pupil's circle detection and its combination with the Daugman operator for iris-sclera circle detection

We studied the whole CASIA Iris Image Database in order to obtain the following statistics. In Table 2, the accuracy is the result of eye observations, because we have not developed a method to evaluate quantitatively the boundaries localization results.

Table 2. The localization results of inner and outer iris boundary

Boundary	Accuracy	Mean time	Min. time	Max. time
Inner boundary localization	100%	0.0198 s	0.0150 s	0.0320 s
Inner and outer boundary localization	98%	0.0576 s	0.0160 s	0.3260 s

Observing the accuracy from Table 2, we can see: a) 100% iris inner boundary localization results, this means all the 756 images precisely detected; b) some false localization results that mean several pixel displacement from de true position of contact iris – sclera.

Because there are some special tricks unknown in Daugman, Wildes and Cui' methods, we do not compare with them, but compare the localization results of inner and outer iris boundary published in [5] and the results are listed in Table 3. We also include our results.

Table 3. Comparion with other algorithms

Method	Accuracy	Mean time	Min. time	Max. time
Daugman	98.6%	6.56 s	6.23 s	6.99 s
Wildes 1 [6]	99.9%	8.28 s	6.34 s	12.54 s
Wildes 2 [7]	99.5%	1.98 s	1.05 s	2.36 s
Cui et al. [5]	99.54%	0.2426 s	0.1870 s	0.3290 s
Proposed	98.0%	0.0576 s	0.0160 s	0.3260 s

Note that the accuracy is 98% with the proposed method, lower than the others. However it is the faster, with a 4 times higher speed than the best.

The theoretical reasons of the high speed and robustness of the proposed method are the follows:

1. Pupil detection uses circle fitting, which use the solution of the "Three Point Method". The method makes full use of the local texture variation and doesn't use any optimization procedure. For this reason it can reduce the computational cost greatly.
2. The outer boundary localization combine the output of the "Three Point Method" as input to the integrodifferential operator taking advantage in order to search the abrupt gradient changes of a contour integral to find the iris – sclera border.

Our method combines two different strategies, texture variation (pupil – iris) and edge detection (iris – sclera) to localize the iris zone.

7 Conclusions

Iris localization serves not only computing the position of the iris, but also detecting the important iris texture area, useful to develop the IrisCode information. In this paper we propose an algorithm to localize iris based on pupil and iris texture segmentation. The pupil local texture has a great contrast with the iris texture, this fact is very important for iris localization and at the same time, it is useful to save computational time with our "Three Point Method". The pupil detection using it, provide the initial parameters set (radius, x_0, y_0 of the pupil circle) to the Daugman operator, which takes advantage using these values in order to detect the iris – sclera boundary. The experimental results show the promising performance and robustness of the method. It is fast and we hope a good behaviour in a real time iris recognition system. In the near future, we will continue working to improve the accuracy of the inner and outer boundary localization. We also must do experiments with images taken under not controlled condition, different of CASIA Iris images Database.

Acknowledgements

We want to express thanks to the National Laboratory of Pattern Recognition from Beijing, China for its gracefulness in allowing us the use of the CASIA Iris Images Data Base in our experiments.

References

1. Díaz, Y., J. L. Gil: Algoritmo para la detección del contorno de la pupila del ojo humano. I Conferencia Científica de la Universidad de las Ciencias Informáticas, UCIENCIA 2005. ISBN 959-16-0318-5, (2005).
2. Daugman, J.: High Confidence Visual Recognition of Persons by a Test of Statistical Independence. IEEE Transactions on Pattern Analysis and Machine Intelligence. Vol. 15. No 11. 1148-1160 pp., (1993).
3. Daugman, J.: Demodulation by Complex-Valued Wavelets for Stochastic Pattern Recognition. International Journal of Wavelets, Multiresolution and Information Processing. Vol. 1. No. 1. 1-17 pp., (2003).
4. Center for Biometrics and Security Research (CBSR). CASIA Iris Image Database, http://www.sinobiometrics.com.
5. Cui, J., Y., Wang, T. Tan, L. Ma, Z. Sun: A Fast and Robust Iris Localization Method Based on Texture Segmentation, Center for Biometric Authentication and Testing, National Laboratory of Pattern Recognition. Disponible en internet. (2005)
6. Wildes, R.: Iris Recognition: An Emerging Biometric Technology, Proceedings of the IEEE, Vol. 85, pp.1348-1363, (1997).
7. Camus, T. A., R. Wildes: Reliable and Fast Eye Finding in Close-up Images, Proceedings of the IEEE International Conference on Pattern Recognition, (2002).

Flexible Architecture of Self Organizing Maps for Changing Environments*

Rodrigo Salas[1,2], Héctor Allende[2,3],
Sebastián Moreno[2], and Carolina Saavedra[2]

[1] Universidad de Valparaíso; Departamento de Computación; Valparaíso-Chile
{rodrigo.salas}@uv.cl
[2] Universidad Técnica Federico Santa María; Dept. de Informática,
Casilla 110-V; Valparaíso-Chile
{hallende, smoreno, saavedra}@inf.utfsm.cl
[3] Universidad Adolfo Ibañez; Facultad de Ciencia y Tecnología

Abstract. Catastrophic Interference is a well known problem of Artificial Neural Networks (ANN) learning algorithms where the ANN forget useful knowledge while learning from new data. Furthermore the structure of most neural models must be chosen in advance.

In this paper we introduce a hybrid algorithm called Flexible Architecture of Self Organizing Maps (*FASOM*) that overcomes the Catastrophic Interference and preserves the topology of Clustered data in changing environments. The model consists in K receptive fields of self organizing maps. Each Receptive Field projects high-dimensional data of the input space onto a neuron position in a low-dimensional output space grid by dynamically adapting its structure to a specific region of the input space.

Furthermore the *FASOM* model automatically finds the number of maps and prototypes needed to successfully adapt to the data. The model has the capability of both growing its structure when novel clusters appears and gradually forgets when the data volume is reduced in its receptive fields.

Finally we show the capabilities of our model with experimental results using synthetic sequential data sets and real world data.

Keywords: Catastrophic Interference, Artificial Neural Networks, Self Organizing Maps, Pattern Recognition.

1 Introduction

During this decade a huge amount of real data with highly dimensional samples have been stored for some sufficiently large period of time. Models were constructed to learn this data, but due to the changing nature of the input space, the neural networks catastrophically forgets the previously learned patterns [4].

* This work was supported in part by Research Grant Fondecyt 1040365 and 7050205, DGIP-UTFSM, BMBF-CHL 03-Z13 from German Ministry of Education, DIPUV-22/2004 and CID-04/2003.

M. Lazo and A. Sanfeliu (Eds.): CIARP 2005, LNCS 3773, pp. 642–653, 2005.

In addition, the neural designer has the difficulty to decide in advance the architecture of the model, and if the environment change, the neural network will not obtain a good performance under this new situation. To overcome the architectural design problem several algorithms with adaptive structure have been proposed (See [2], [5], [12] and [13]).

In this paper we propose a hybrid problem-dependent model based on the Kohonen's Self Organizing Maps [8] with the Bauer et al. growing variant of the *SOM* [2], the K-means [11], the Single Linkage clustering algorithm [7] and the addition of new capabilities of gradually forgetting and contracting the net. We call this algorithm Flexible Architecture of Self Organizing Maps (*FASOM*). The *FASOM* is a hybrid model that adapts K receptive fields of dynamical self organizing maps and learn the topology of partitioned spaces [13]. It has the capability of detecting novel data or clusters and creates new maps to learn this patterns avoiding that other receptive fields catastrophically forget. Furthermore the receptive fields with decreasing volume of data can gradually forget by reducing their size and contracting their grid lattice.

The remainder or this paper is organized as follows. The next section we briefly discuss the ANN Catastrophic Interference problem. Then we review the models where our hybrid model is based. In the fourth section, our proposal of the *FASOM* model is stated. Simulation results on synthetic and real data sets are provided in the fifth section. Conclusions and further work are given in the last section.

2 The ANN Catastrophic Interference Problem

Artificial neural networks with highly distributed memory forget catastrophically when faced with sequential learning tasks, i.e., the new learned information most often erases the one previously learned. This major weakness is not only cognitively implausible, as human gradually forget, but disastrous for most practical applications. (See [4] and [10] for a review)

Catastrophic interference is a radical manifestation of a more general problem for connectionist models of memory, the so-called *stability-plasticity* problem [6]. The problem is how to design a system that is simultaneously sensitive to, but not radically disrupted by, new input. A number of ways have been proposed to avoid the problem of catastrophic interference in connectionist networks (see [1], [4]).

3 Review of Unsupervised Clustering and Topology Preserving Algorithms

3.1 Unsupervised Clustering

Clustering can be considered as one of the most important unsupervised learning problem. A cluster is a collection of "similar" objects and they should be "dissimilar" to the objects belonging to other clusters. Unsupervised clustering tries to discover the natural groups inside a data set.

The purpose of any clustering technique [9] is to evolve a $K \times N$ partition matrix $U(\mathcal{X})$ of the data set $\mathcal{X} = \{\underline{x}_1, ..., \underline{x}_N\}$, $\underline{x}_j \in \mathbb{R}^n$, representing its partitioning into a number, say K, of clusters $C_1, ..., C_K$. Each element u_{kj}, $k = 1..K$ and $j = 1..n$ of the matrix $U(\mathcal{X})$ indicates the membership of pattern $\underline{x}_j$ to the cluster C_k. In crisp partitioning of the data, the following condition holds: $u_{kj} = 1$ if $\underline{x}_j \in C_k$; otherwise, $u_{kj} = 0$.

There are several clustering techniques classified as partitional and hierarchical [7]. In this paper we based our model in the following algorithms.

K-means

The K-means method introduced by McQueen [11] is one of the most widely applied partitional clustering technique. This method basically consists on the following steps. First, K randomly chosen points from the data are selected as seed points for the centroids $\overline{z}_k$, $k = 1..K$, of the clusters. Second, assign each data to the cluster with the nearest centroid based on some distance criterion, for example, $\underline{x}_j$ belongs to the cluster C_k if the distance $d(\underline{x}_j, \overline{z}_k) = \|\underline{x}_j - \overline{z}_k\|$ is the minimum for $k = 1..K$. Third, the centroids of the clusters are updated to the "center" of the points belonging to them, for example, $\overline{z}_k = \frac{1}{N_k} \sum_{\underline{x}_j \in C_k} \underline{x}_j$, where N_k is the number of data belonging to the cluster k. Finally, repeat the procedure until either the clusters centroids do not change or some optimal criterion is met.

This algorithm is iteratively repeated for $K = 1, 2, 3, ...$ until some validity measure indicates that partition $U_{K_{opt}}$ is a better partition than U_K, $K < K_{opt}$ (see [9] for some validity indices). In this work we used the F-test to specified the number K of clusters. The F-test measures the variability reduction by comparing the sum of square distance of the data to their centroids $E_K = \sum_{j=1}^{N} \sum_{k=1}^{K} u_{kj} \|\underline{x}_j - \overline{z}_k\|^2$ of K and $K+1$ groups. The test statistic is $F = \frac{E_K - E_{K+1}}{E_{K+1}/(n-K-1)}$ and is compared with the F statistical distribution with p and $p(n-K-1)$ degrees of freedom.

Single Linkage

The Single Linkage clustering scheme, also known as the nearest neighbor method, is usually regarded as a graph theoretical model [7]. It stars by considering each point as cluster of its own. The single linkage algorithm computes the distance between two clusters C_k and C_l as $\delta_{SL}(C_k, C_l) = \min_{\underline{x} \in C_k, \underline{y} \in C_l} \{d(\underline{x}, \underline{y})\}$. If the distance between both clusters is less than some threshold θ then they are merged into one cluster. The process continues until the distance between all the clusters are greater than the threshold θ.

This algorithm is very sensitive to the determination of the parameter θ, for this reason we compute its value proportional to the average distance between the points belonging to the same clusters, i.e., $\theta(\mathcal{X}) \propto \frac{1}{N_k} \sum_{\underline{x}_i, \underline{x}_j \in C_k} d(\underline{x}_i, \underline{x}_j)$. At the beginning θ can be set as a fraction (bigger than one) of the minimum distance of the two closest points. When the algorithm is done, clusters consisting of less than l data are merged to the nearest cluster.

3.2 Topology Preserving Neural Models: The Self Organizing Maps

It is interesting to explore the topological structure of the clusters. The Kohonen's Self Organizing Map [8] and their variants are useful for this task. The self-organizing maps (SOM) neural model is an iterative procedure capable of representing the topological structure of the input space (discrete or continuous) by a discrete set of prototypes (*weight vectors*) which are associated to neurons of the network.

The map is generated by establishing a correspondence between the input signals $\underline{x} \in \mathcal{X} \subseteq \mathbb{R}^n$, $\underline{x} = [x_1, ..., x_n]^T$, and neurons located on a discrete lattice. The correspondence is obtained by a competitive learning algorithm consisting on a sequence of training steps that iteratively modifies the weight vector $\underline{m}_k \in \mathbb{R}^n$, $\underline{m}_k = (m_1^k, ..., m_n^k)$, where k is the location of the prototype in the lattice.

When a new signal $\underline{x}$ arrives every neuron competes to represent it. The best matching unit (bmu) is the neuron that wins the competition and with its neighbors on the lattice they are allowed to learn the signal. The bmu is the reference vector c that is nearest to the input $\underline{x}$, i.e., $c = \arg\min_i\{\|\underline{x} - \underline{m}_i\|\}$.

During the learning process the reference vectors are changed iteratively according to the following adjusting rule,

$$\underline{m}_j(t+1) = \underline{m}_j(t) + \alpha(t)h_c(j,t)[\underline{x} - \underline{m}_j(t)] \qquad j = 1..M$$

where M is the number of prototypes that must be adjusted. The learning parameter $\alpha(t) \in [0,1]$ is a monotonically decreasing real valued sequence. The amount that the units learnt will be governed by a neighborhood kernel $h_c(j,t)$, that is a decreasing function of the distance between the unit j and the bmu c on the map lattice at time t. The neighborhood kernel is usually given by a Gaussian function:

$$h_c(j,t) = \exp\left(\frac{-\left\|\underline{r}_j - \underline{r}_c\right\|^2}{\sigma(t)^2}\right) \tag{1}$$

where $\underline{r}_j$ and $\underline{r}_c$ denote the coordinates of the neurons j and c in the lattice. In practice the neighborhood kernel controlled by the parameter $\sigma(t)$ and is chosen wide enough in the beginning of the learning process to guarantee global ordering of the map, and both its width and height decrease slowly during the learning process. More details and properties of the SOM can be found in [3] and [8].

4 The Flexible Architecture of Self Organizing Maps

The $FASOM$ is a hybrid model that adapts K receptive fields of dynamical self organizing maps and learn the topology of partitioned spaces. It has the capability of detecting novel data or clusters and creates new maps to learn this patterns avoiding that other receptive fields catastrophically forget. Furthermore the receptive fields with decreasing volume of data can gradually forget by reducing their size and contracting their grid lattice.

The learning process has two parts. The first part occurs when the model is created an learn the data for the first time. The second part of the learning process occurs when a new pattern is presented to the trained model. The description of the algorithm follows.

4.1 First Part: Topological Learning Algorithm

First Step: Clustering the data
The purpose of this step is to find the number of clusters presented in the data. To this purpose, first we execute the K-means algorithm, presented in section 3.1, with a very low threshold in order to find more clusters than they really are. Then, the Single Linkage algorithm is executed to merge cluster that are closer and to obtain, hopefully, the optimal number of clusters.

When the number of clusters K and their respective centroids $\underline{z}_k$, $k = 1..K$, are obtained then we proceed to create a grid of size 2×2 for each cluster.

Second Step: Topological Learning
During the learning process when an input data $\underline{x}$ is presented to the model at time t the best matching map (bmm) is found as follows. Let $\mathcal{M}_k$ be the set of prototypes that belong to the map C_k. The best matching units (bmu) $\underline{m}_{c_k}^{[k]}$, $k = 1..K$, of the sample $\underline{x}$ for each of the K maps are detected. The map that contains the closest bmu to the data will be the bmm whose index is given by

$$\eta = \arg \min_{k=1..K} \{ \left\| \underline{x} - \underline{m}_{c_k}^{[k]} \right\|, \underline{m}_{c_k}^{[k]} \in \mathcal{M}_k \} \tag{2}$$

Then all the units that belong to the bmm will be updated iteratively according to the following rule:

$$\underline{m}_j^{[\eta]}(t+1) = \underline{m}_j^{[\eta]}(t) + \alpha(t) h_{c_\eta}^{[\eta]}(j,t) [\underline{x} - \underline{m}_j^{[\eta]}(t)] \qquad j = 1..M_\eta$$

where the neighborhood kernel $h_{c_\eta}^{[\eta]}(j,t)$ is given by equation (1) and the learning parameter $\alpha(t)$ is a monotonically decreasing function through time. For example this functions could be linear $\alpha(t) = \alpha_0 + (\alpha_f - \alpha_0)t/t_\alpha$ or exponential $\alpha(t) = \alpha_0(\alpha_f/\alpha_0)^{t/t_\alpha}$, where α_0 and α_f are the initial and final learning rate respectively, and t_α is the maximum number of iteration steps to arrive α_f

Third Step: Growing the Maps Lattices
In this part we introduce the variant proposed by Bauer et. al. of growing the SOM [2]. If the topological representations of the input space partitions are not good enough, the maps will grow by increasing the number of their prototypes. The quality of the topological representation of each map C_k of the *FASOM* model is measured in terms of the deviation between the units. At the beginning

we compute the quantization error $qe_0^{[k]}$ over the whole data belonging to the cluster $\mathcal{C}_k$.

All units must represent their respective Voronoi polygons of data at a quantization error smaller than a fraction τ of $qe_0^{[k]}$, i.e., $qe_j^{[k]} < \tau \cdot qe_0^{[k]}$, where $qe_j^{[k]} = \sum_{\underline{x}_i \in \mathcal{C}_j^{[k]}} \left\| \underline{x}_i - \underline{m}_j^{[k]} \right\|$, and $\mathcal{C}_j^{[k]} \neq \phi$ are the set of input vectors belonging to the Voronoi polygon of the unit j in the map lattice $\mathcal{C}_k$. The units that not satisfy this criterion require a more detailed data representation.

When the map lattice $\mathcal{C}_k$ is chosen to grow, we compute the value of $qe_j^{[k]}$ for all the units belonging to the map. The unit with the highest $qe_j^{[k]}$, called error unit e , and its most dissimilar neighbor d are detected. To accomplish this the value of e and d are computed by $e = \arg\max_j \left\{ \sum_{\underline{x}_i \in \mathcal{C}_j^{[k]}} \left\| \underline{x}_i - \underline{m}_j^{[k]} \right\| \right\}$ and $d = \arg\max_j \left(\left\| \underline{m}_e^{[k]} - \underline{m}_j^{[k]} \right\| \right)$ respectively, where $\mathcal{C}_j^{[k]} \neq \phi, \underline{m}_j^{[k]} \in \mathcal{N}_e$ and $\mathcal{N}_e$ is the set of neighboring units of the error unit e. A row or column of units is inserted between e and d and their model vector are initialized as the means of their respective neighbors. After insertions, the map is trained again by executing the second step.

4.2 Second Part: Adapting to Changing Environments

The behavior of the input space could change through time, for example, clusters of data could be created, moved, and even vanished. The model should be able to adjust its architecture to the new environment.

Let $FASOM_T$ be the model and $\mathcal{X}_T$ the training dataset, both considered at the training stage T. The adaptation is done as follows.

First step: Detection of strikingly new data
The samples that do not have a good topological representation with the actual model $FASOM_{T-1}$ are identified by computing the influence of the sample $\underline{x}$ to the model $FASOM_{T-1}$ as $\rho(\underline{x}, FASOM_{T-1}) = \left\| \underline{x} - \underline{m}_{c_\eta}^{[\eta]}(t) \right\|$, where $\underline{m}_{c_\eta}^{[\eta]}(t)$ is the *bmu* of the *bmm* η to the data $\underline{x}$. Let $\mathcal{X}_T^{[new]}$ be the set of all the strikingly new data whose influence function are bigger than some threshold θ, i.e., $\rho(\underline{x}, FASOM_{T-1}) > \theta$.

Second Step: Creating Maps for the new data
A new model $FASOM_T^{[new]}$ based on the samples $\mathcal{X}_T^{[new]}$ extracted from the previous step is created. This is accomplished by applying the first step of the previous part (Clustering the data).

Third step: Integration of the maps
Both models are integrated in an unique updated version, i.e.,

$$FASOM_T = FASOM_{T-1} \bigcup FASOM_T^{[new]}$$

Fourth step: Learning the samples
The model $FASOM_T$ learns the whole dataset $\mathcal{X}_T$. This is accomplished by applying second step of the previous part.

Fifth step: Gradually forgetting the old data
Due to the environmental of the input space is not stationary, the clusters behavior change through time, and, for example, either their variance or their data volume can be reduced, or even more, the clusters could be vanished. For this reason, and to keep the complexity of the model rather low we let the maps gradually forget the clusters by shrinking their lattices towards their respective centroids and reducing the number of their prototypes.

Centroid neurons $\overline{m}^{[k]}$ representing the cluster k modelled by the map $\mathcal{C}_k$ are computed as the mean value of the prototypes belonging to the map lattice, i.e., $\overline{m}^{[k]} = \frac{1}{M_k}\sum_{j=1}^{M_k} m_j^{[k]}$, where $m_j^{[k]}$ is the j–th prototype of the grid $\mathcal{C}_k$ and M_k is the number of neurons of that grid.

The map κ will forget the old data by applying once the forgetting rule:

$$\underline{m}_j^{[\kappa]}(T+1) = \underline{m}_j^{[\kappa]}(T) + \gamma[\underline{x} - \overline{m}^{[\kappa]}] \qquad j = 1..M_\kappa$$

where γ is the forgetting rate. $\underline{m}_j^{[\kappa]}(T)$ and $\underline{m}_j^{[\kappa]}(T+1)$ are the values of the prototypes at the end of the stage T and the beginning of stage $T+1$ respectively. The objective is to shrink the maps toward their centroids neurons.

Then, if the units of the map κ are very close, the map is contracted. If the map lattice is a rectangular grid, then we search two rows or columns whose neurons are very close. To accomplish this the value ν is computed by

$$\nu = \underset{e=1..N_r-1;d=1..N_c-1}{\arg\min} \left(\frac{1}{N_c}\sum_{j=1}^{N_c} \left\| \underline{m}_{(e,j)}^{[\kappa]} - \underline{m}_{(e+1,j)}^{[\kappa]} \right\|, \frac{1}{N_r}\sum_{i=1}^{N_r} \left\| \underline{m}_{(i,d)}^{[\kappa]} - \underline{m}_{(i,d+1)}^{[\kappa]} \right\| \right)$$

where $\underline{m}_{(i,j)}^{[\kappa]}$ is the unit located at the position (i,j) in the map lattice κ. N_r and N_c are the number of rows and columns of the map lattice respectively. If the criterion $\nu < \beta$ is met then a row (or a column) of units are inserted between ν and $\nu+1$ and their model vector are initialized as the mean of their respective neighbors. Then the rows (or columns) ν and $\nu+1$ of prototypes are both eliminated. The map is contracted iteratively until no other row or column satisfies the criterion. After contraction, the map is trained again by executing the fourth step.

4.3 Clustering the Data and Evaluation of the Model

To classify the data $\underline{x}_j$ to one of the cluster $k = 1..K$, we find the best matching map given by equation (2) and the data will receive the label of this map η, i.e., for the data $\underline{x}_j$ we set $u_{j\eta} = 1$ and $u_{jk} = 0$ for $k \neq \eta$.

To evaluate the clustering performance we compute the percentage of right classification given by:

$$PC = \frac{1}{N} \sum_{\underline{x}_j, j=1..N} u_{jk} \qquad k = \text{True class of } \underline{x}_j \tag{3}$$

Evaluation of the adaptation quality
To evaluate the quality of the partitions topological representation, a common measure to compare the algorithms is needed. The following metric called the mean square quantization error is used:

$$MSQE = \frac{1}{N} \sum_{\mathcal{M}_k, k=1..K} \sum_{\underline{m}_j^{[k]} \in \mathcal{M}_k} \sum_{\underline{x}_i \in C_j^{[k]}} \left\| \underline{x}_i - \underline{m}_j^{[k]} \right\|^2 \tag{4}$$

5 Simulation Results

To validate the *FASOM* model we apply first the algorithm to computer generated data and then to *El Niño* real data. The models used to compare the results were the K-Dynamical Self Organizing Map *KDSOM* [13] and our model proposal *FASOM* and $FASOM_\gamma$ where the last gradually forgets.

To execute the simulations and to compute the metrics, all the dimensions of the training data were scaled to the unit interval. The test sets were scaled using the same scale applied to the training data (Notice that with this scaling the test data will not necessarily fall in the unit interval).

5.1 Experiment #1: Computer Generated Data

For the synthetic experiment we create gaussian clusters of two-dimensional distribution $\underline{X}_k \sim \mathcal{N}(\mu_k, \Sigma_k)$, $k = 1, ..., K$, where K is the number of clusters, and, μ_k and Σ_k are the mean vector and the covariance matrix respectively of the cluster C_k. The behavior of the clusters change through the several training stages.

The experiment has 5 stages where in the first four we re-train the model. The information about the clusters in the several stages are given in table 1. As can be noted seven clusters were created. The cluster 1 vanishes in the second stage, the cluster 2 decreases the number of data, cluster 3 appears in the second stage, cluster 4 moves from $(0.1, 0.8)$ to $(0.42, 0.56)$, cluster 5 increases its variance and finally the clusters 6 and 7 appear in the third and fourth stage respectively.

The summary of the results is given in table 2. To evaluate the ability of the net to remember past learned information, the model was tested with data of the previous stages, p.e., the model trained after stage four was tested with the data of stage three, two and one. As can be noted, the *FASOM*'s models outperform the *KDSOM*. The $FASOM_\gamma$ shows lower MSQE with less number of prototypes.

Table 1. Summary of the clusters generated for the Synthetic Experiment in the several training stages

Cluster	1	2	3	4	5	6	7	Total
$N_{trainT1}$	250	250	0	250	250	0	0	1000
N_{testT1}	250	250	0	250	250	0	0	1000
μ_{T1}	$[0.9, 0.01]^T$	$[0.8, 0.5]^T$	$[0.6, 0.8]^T$	$[0.1, 0.8]^T$	$[0.2, 0.1]^T$	$[0.5, 0.5]^T$	$[0.01, 0.5]^T$	
Σ_{T1}	$0.05^2 * I_2$	$0.05^2 * I_2$	$0.05^2 * I_2$	$0.05^2 * I_2$	$0.05^2 * I_2$	$0.05^2 * I_2$	$0.05^2 * I_2$	
$N_{trainT2}$	0	250	250	250	250	0	0	1000
N_{testT2}	0	250	250	250	250	0	0	1000
μ_{T2}	$[0.9, 0.01]^T$	$[0.8, 0.5]^T$	$[0.6, 0.8]^T$	$[0.18, 0.74]^T$	$[0.2, 0.1]^T$	$[0.5, 0.5]^T$	$[0.01, 0.5]^T$	
Σ_{T2}	$0.05^2 * I_2$	$0.05^2 * I_2$	$0.05^2 * I_2$	$0.05^2 * I_2$	$0.054^2 * I_2$	$0.05^2 * I_2$	$0.05^2 * I_2$	
$N_{trainT3}$	0	188	250	250	250	750	0	1688
N_{testT3}	0	188	250	250	250	750	0	1688
μ_{T3}	$[0.9, 0.01]^T$	$[0.8, 0.5]^T$	$[0.6, 0.8]^T$	$[0.26, 0.68]^T$	$[0.2, 0.1]^T$	$[0.5, 0.5]^T$	$[0.01, 0.5]^T$	
Σ_{T3}	$0.05^2 * I_2$	$0.05^2 * I_2$	$0.05^2 * I_2$	$0.05^2 * I_2$	$0.0583^2 * I_2$	$0.05^2 * I_2$	$0.05^2 * I_2$	
$N_{trainT4}$	0	125	250	250	250	750	250	1875
N_{testT4}	0	125	250	250	250	750	250	1875
μ_{T4}	$[0.9, 0.01]^T$	$[0.8, 0.5]^T$	$[0.6, 0.8]^T$	$[0.34, 0.62]^T$	$[0.2, 0.1]^T$	$[0.5, 0.5]^T$	$[0.01, 0.5]^T$	
Σ_{T4}	$0.05^2 * I_2$	$0.05^2 * I_2$	$0.05^2 * I_2$	$0.05^2 * I_2$	$0.063^2 * I_2$	$0.05^2 * I_2$	$0.05^2 * I_2$	
$N_{trainT5}$	25	62	250	250	250	750	250	1837
N_{testT5}	25	62	250	250	250	750	250	1837
μ_{T5}	$[0.9, 0.01]^T$	$[0.8, 0.5]^T$	$[0.6, 0.8]^T$	$[0.42, 0.56]^T$	$[0.2, 0.1]^T$	$[0.5, 0.5]^T$	$[0.01, 0.5]^T$	
Σ_{T5}	$0.05^2 * I_2$	$0.05^2 * I_2$	$0.05^2 * I_2$	$0.05^2 * I_2$	$0.068^2 * I_2$	$0.05^2 * I_2$	$0.05^2 * I_2$	

In figure 1 each row of the graphs array corresponds to one model, the first is the *KDSOM*, the second is the $FASOM_\gamma$ and the last is the *FASOM*. Each column of graphs array corresponds to a different training stage. In the figure is easy to note how the *KDSOM* model catastrophically forgets different cluster and tries to model two or three different cluster with the same grid. Instead, the *FASOM* and $FASOM_\gamma$ models learn new cluster in different stages, furthermore, the $FASOM_\gamma$ forgets the cluster with no data as cluster 1, as a consequence the model has a lower complexity.

In figure 2, the models obtained after the fifth stage were tested with data of all previous stages. The graphs show how the models forget previously learned patterns, the *KDSOM* was the most affected model while the *FASOM*'s models obtain comparable results.

5.2 Experiment #2: Real Datasets

In the real dataset experiment we test the algorithm with the *El Niño Data.* The data can be obtained from *http://kdd.ics.uci.edu/databases/el_nino/el_nino.html.* The *El Niño Data* is expected to aid in the understanding and prediction of El Niño Southern Oscillation (ENSO) cycles and was collected by the Pacific Marine Environmental Laboratory National Oceanic and Atmospheric Administration. The data set contains oceanographic and surface meteorological readings taken from a several buoys positioned throughout the equatorial Pacific.

The data consists in the following variables: date, latitude, longitude, zonal winds (*west* < 0, *east* > 0), meridional winds (*south* < 0, *north* > 0), relative humidity, air temperature, sea surface temperature and subsurface temperatures down to a depth of 500 meters. Data taken from the buoys are as early as 1980 for some locations.

The data set was modified by discarding those data with missing values. Finally we obtains 130454 instances of 4 dimensions (meridional winds, relative

Table 2. Summary of the results obtained for the synthetic experiments. The first column **S** indicates the training stage of the experiment, **M** is the neural model where **KD** is the KDSOM, $\mathbf{FS}_\gamma$ and **FS** are the FASOM with and without ($\gamma = 0$) forgetting factor respectively. The column **PC** shows the percentage of the correct classification and **MSQE Test** X is the MSQE error with test data of the stage X but using the trained model of the current stage.

S	M	Neurons	Grids	*MSQE* Train	*PC* Test	*MSQE* Test1	*MSQE* Test2	*MSQE* Test3	*MSQE* Test4	*MSQE* Test5
S1	KD	48	4.0	1.87	100	2.02	–	–	–	–
	FS_γ	47	4.0	**1.51**	100	**1.62**	–	–	–	–
	FS	48	4.0	1.83	100	1.96	–	–	–	–
S2	KD	49	4.0	2.49	75.70	4.13	2.70	–	–	–
	FS_γ	69	5.9	**1.62**	100	**3.32**	**1.77**	–	–	–
	FS	69	5.8	1.95	100	3.62	2.11	–	–	–
S3	KD	49	4.0	5.88	73.34	14.16	6.74	6.31	–	–
	FS_γ	78	7.1	**2.39**	**95.92**	**10.82**	**3.44**	**2.65**	–	–
	FS	87	7.6	2.81	95.66	11.80	4.03	3.05	–	–
S4	KD	49	4.0	7.13	66.01	24.54	12.99	8.69	7.32	7.89
	FS_γ	91	8.3	**2.48**	**95.67**	**18.92**	**8.78**	**4.10**	**2.85**	**3.36**
	FS	101	8.8	2.72	95.52	19.58	9.72	4.55	3.09	3.56

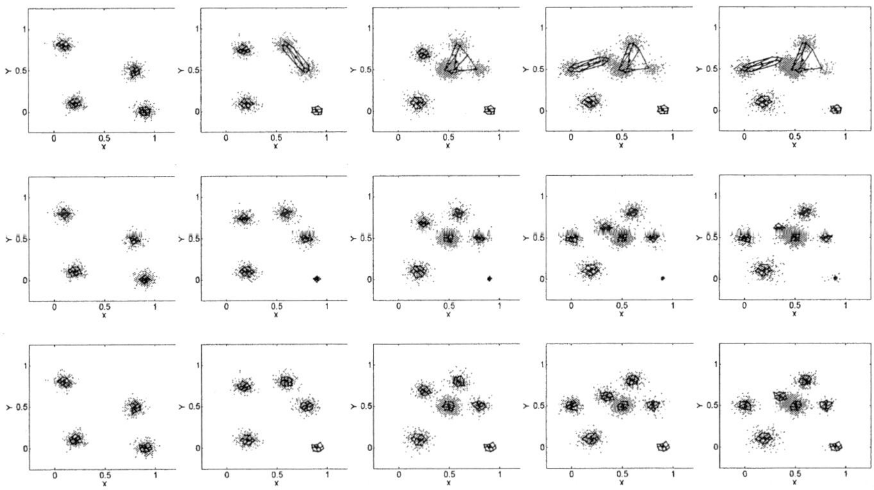

Fig. 1. Synthetic data results: Each column correspond to the training stage. The first row is the KDSOM model, the second is the FASOM_γ with forgetting factor and the last is the FASOM without forgetting.

humidity, sea surface temperature and subsurface temperatures). We divided the dataset according to the years into 19 training sets and one test set with size of 1000 at most for each clusters.

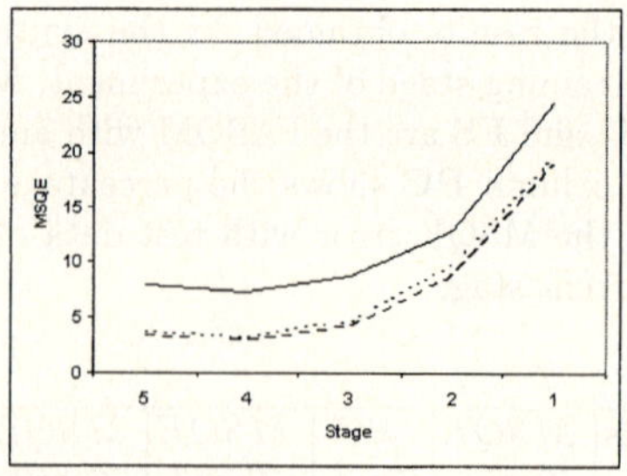

Fig. 2. Synthetic data results: Results obtained with the KDSOM (continuous line), FASOM$_\gamma$ (segmented line) and FASOM (points) models. In the horizontal axis, the stage and in the vertical axis the MSQE of the model trained at stage 4 but evaluated with data of previous stages.

The summary of the results are shown graphically in figure 3. The *FASOM*'s models increase considerably the number of prototypes when new cluster of data are found in stage 4. The *KDSOM* model has the greater MSQE error in train and test set, although it has the lower complexity, the model is not able to adapt when the input space change and forgets the previously learned patterns. It is important to mention that the $FASOM_\gamma$ obtain better performance with less complexity and at the same time it adapts to changing environment.

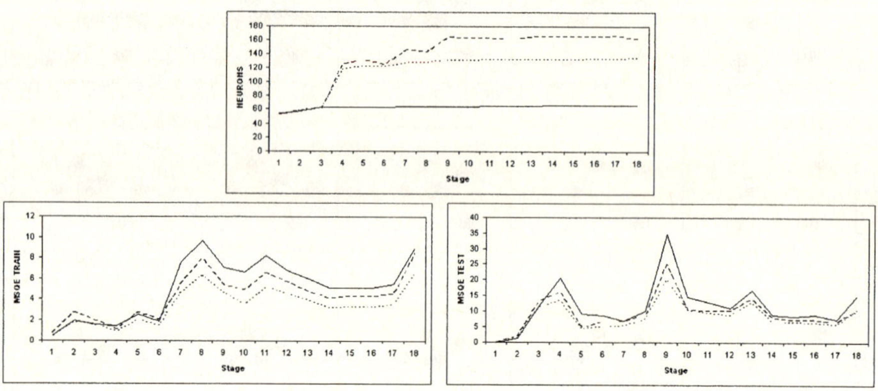

Fig. 3. Real Experiment: Results obtained with the KDSOM (continuous line), FASOM$_\gamma$ (points) and FASOM (segmented line) models. (Up) Number of neurons of the models in each stage. (down-left) MSQE of training for each stage. (down-right) MSQE of the model trained at stage T but evaluated with data of stage $T-1$.

6 Concluding Remarks

In this paper we have introduced the Flexible Arquitecture of Self Organizing Maps (*FASOM*). The *FASOM* is a hybrid model that adapts K receptive fields of dynamical self organizing maps and learn the topology of partitioned spaces. It has the capability of detecting new data or clusters by creating new maps and avoids that other receptive fields catastrophically forget. In addition, receptive fields with few data can gradually forget by reducing their size and contracting their grid lattice.

The performance of our algorithm shows better results in the simulation study in both the synthetic and real data sets. In the real case, we investigated *El Niño* data. The comparative study with the *KDSOM* and *FASOM* without forgetting factor shows that our model the $FASOM_\gamma$ with forgetting outperforms the alternative models while the complexity of our model stays rather low. The *FASOM*s models were able to find the possible number of cluster and learn the topological representation of the partitions in the several training stages.

Further studies are needed in order to analyze the convergence and ordering properties of the maps.

References

1. B. Ans, *Sequential learning in distributed neural networks without catastrophic forgetting: A single and realistic self-refreshing memory can do it*, Neural Information Processing - Letters and Reviews **4** (2004), no. 2, 27–37.
2. H. Bauer and T. Villmann, *Growing a hypercubical output space in a self-organizing feature map*, IEEE Trans. on Neural Networks **8** (1997), no. 2, 226–233.
3. E. Erwin, K. Obermayer, and K. Schulten, *Self-organizing maps: ordering, convergence properties and energy functions*, Biological Cybernetics **67** (1992), 47–55.
4. R. French, *Catastrophic forgetting in connectionist networks*, Trends in Cognitive Sciences **3** (1999), 128–135.
5. B. Fritzke, *Growing cell structures - a self-organizing network for unsupervised and supervised learning*, Neural Networks **7** (1994), no. 9, 1441–1460.
6. S. Grossberg, *Studies of mind and brain: Neural principles of learning, perception, development, cognition, and motor control*, Reidel Press., 1982.
7. A.K. Jain and R.C. Dubes, *Algorithms for clustering data*, Prentice Hall, 1988.
8. T. Kohonen, *Self-Organizing Maps*, Springer Series in Information Sciences, vol. 30, Springer Verlag, Berlin, Heidelberg, 2001, Third Extended Edition 2001.
9. U. Maulik and S. Bandyopadhyay, *Performance evaluation*, IEEE. Trans. on Pattern Analysis and Machine Intelligence **24** (2002), no. 12, 1650–1654.
10. M. McCloskey and N. Cohen, *Catastrophic interference in connectionist networks: The sequential learning problem*, The psychology of Learning and Motivation **24** (1989), 109–164.
11. J. McQueen, *Some methods for classification and analysis of multivariate observations*, In Proceedings of the Fifth Berkeley Symposium on Mathematical Statistics and probability, vol. 1, 1967, pp. 281–297.
12. S. Moreno, H. Allende, C. Rogel, and R. Salas, *Robust growing hierarchical self organizing map*, IWANN 2005. LNCS **3512** (2005), 341–348.
13. C. Saavedra, H. Allende, S. Moreno, and R. Salas, *K-dynamical self organizing maps*, To appear in Lecture Notes in Computer Science, Nov. 2005.

Automatic Segmentation of Pulmonary Structures in Chest CT Images

Yeny Yim[1] and Helen Hong[2,*]

[1] School of Electrical Engineering and Computer Science, Seoul National University
shine@cglab.snu.ac.kr
[2] School of Computer Science and Engineering, BK21: Information Technology, Seoul National University, San 56-1 Shinlim 9-dong Kwanak-gu, Seoul 151-742, Korea
hlhong@cse.snu.ac.kr

Abstract. We propose an automatic segmentation method for accurately identifying lung surfaces, airways, and pulmonary vessels in chest CT images. Our method consists of four steps. First, lungs and airways are extracted by inverse seeded region growing and connected component labeling. Second, pulmonary vessels are extracted from the result of first step by gray-level thresholding. Third, trachea and large airways are delineated from the lungs by three-dimensional region growing based on partitioning. Finally, accurate lung regions are obtained by subtracting the result of third step from the result of first step. The proposed method has been applied to 10 patient datasets with lung cancer or pulmonary embolism. Experimental results show that our segmentation method extracts lung surfaces, airways, and pulmonary vessels automatically and accurately.

1 Introduction

Chest computed tomography (CT) is widely used to evaluate numerous lung diseases, including lung nodules, pulmonary embolism and emphysema [1]. A precursor to all of these applications is the lung segmentation. In particular, since multi-detector row CT scanner routinely generate 300 or more two-dimensional (2D) slices per patient, it is critical to develop an efficient method for automatically segmenting the precise lung boundaries, airways and pulmonary vessels.

Several methods have been suggested for segmentation of lungs in chest CT scans. In Denison [2], manually traced boundaries were used to estimate regional gas and tissue volumes in the lungs of normal subjects. In Hedlund [3], 3D region growing with manually specified seed points was presented for segmenting the lungs. However, these manual and semi-automatic methods are laborious and subject to inter- and intra-observer variations. Brown [4] proposed an automatic, knowledge-based method for segmenting the chest CT images. Anatomic knowledge stored in a semantic network is used to guide the segmentation process. In knowledge-based method, accuracy significantly depends on the level of knowledge. In Armato [5],

* Corresponding author.

M. Lazo and A. Sanfeliu (Eds.): CIARP 2005, LNCS 3773, pp. 654 – 662, 2005.

gray-level thresholding is used to segment the thorax from the background and then the lungs from the thorax. A rolling-ball algorithm is applied to the lung segmentation contours to avoid the loss of juxtapleural nodules. This method was for use as a preprocessing step for automated lung nodule detection and mesothelioma measurement. In Hu [6], gray-level thresholding is used to distinguish between the low density lung regions and denser surrounding tissue. The radiodense pulmonary vessels are excluded from the lung regions through the gray-level thresholding so that holes in the lung surface near the mediastimum are made. To fill these holes, 2D morphological closing is used. However, unsmooth boundaries of lungs are still remained. To solve this problem, Ukil [7] proposed an automatic method for the 3D smoothing of the lung boundaries using 3D morphological closing with an ellipsoidal kernel.

Current approaches still need more progress in computational efficiency and accuracy for segmenting lungs in chest CT scans. In this paper, we describe an automatic segmentation method for accurately identifying pulmonary structures such as lung surfaces, airways, and pulmonary vessels in chest CT images. First, a similar operation to region growing is used to segment the thorax from the background and then the lungs and airways from the thorax. To remove other low-density regions which have similar intensity with the lungs, connected component labeling is used. Second, pulmonary vessels are extracted from the result of first step by gray-level thresholding. Third, trachea and large airways are delineated from the lungs by 3D region growing based on partitioning. Finally, accurate lung regions are obtained by subtracting the result of third step from the result of first step. To evaluate the accuracy, we present results comparing automatically extracted borders by proposed method to manually traced borders from two radiologists. We also compare the results of two automatic segmentation methods: our proposed method and commercial tool Analyze. Experimental results show that our segmentation method extracts pulmonary structures accurately and automatically. Accurate and automatic segmentation would be more useful for clinical applications of pulmonary nodule detection, pulmonary embolism and emphysema analysis.

The organization of the paper is as follows. In Section 2, we discuss how to extract the pulmonary structures from other organs in chest CT images. In Section 3, experimental results show how the method accurately and automatically segments the pulmonary structures in the chest CT images. This paper is concluded with a brief discussion of the results in Section 4.

2 Segmentation of Pulmonary Structures

For the segmentation of the chest CT images, we apply the pipeline shown in Fig. 1. Since our method is applied to the pulmonary nodule matching and pulmonary embolism analysis, we assume that each CT scan is acquired at the maximal inspiration and the dataset includes the thorax from the trachea to the diaphragm.

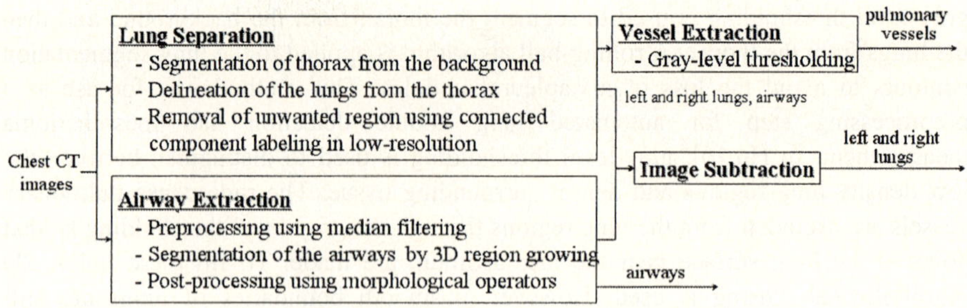

Fig. 1. The pipeline of the automatic lung segmentation

2.1 Threshold Selection Using Optimal Thresholding

For this step, we assume that the image volume contains only two principal brightness regions: 1) high-density regions within the chest wall structures, 2) low-density regions in the lungs. We use optimal thresholding [8] to automatically select a threshold for separating thorax from the lung regions. The segmentation threshold is selected through iterative procedure. We first select the initial threshold T0 and apply T0 to the volume to separate the voxels into high-density and low-density regions. The new threshold for next step is the average of the mean gray-levels of two regions. This threshold update procedure is repeated until there is no change in the threshold. Since the tissue density of CT images varies between subjects according to radiation dose of CT scanner, optimal thresholding allows us to adapt these variations.

2.2 Lung Separation Using 2D Inverse Seeded Region Growing

The goal of this step is to separate voxels of lung tissue from the surrounding anatomy. Generally, thresholding and 3D region growing are used to identify lungs [6]. Since these methods based on difference in attenuation values can produce holes in high-density vessels within the lungs, these holes should be filled by morphological operations such as dilation and erosion [8]. To eliminate the holes, the mask size of these operations has to be larger than the size of holes. However, determining the mask size is difficult to eliminate the holes while distorting the lung region boundaries as little as possible. We propose the 2D inverse seeded region growing (iSRG) method for the automatic lung separation without these limitations in the chest CT images.

The 2D iSRG is used to automatically segment the thorax from the background and then the lung regions from the thorax, as shown in Fig. 2(b) and (c). In first 2D iSRG, the seed pixel is selected at (0, 0) on each 2D slice, which has a gray level smaller than threshold value selected by optimal thresholding. Background air which surrounds the body is extracted by region growing and then thorax is segmented by inverse operation. In second 2D iSRG, the seed pixel is chosen at a pixel of thorax with a gray level larger than the threshold value. As a result of region growing, thorax region which has similar gray level to the seed pixel is extracted. By inverting the result, we can segment the lungs and airways without inner holes and the distortion of

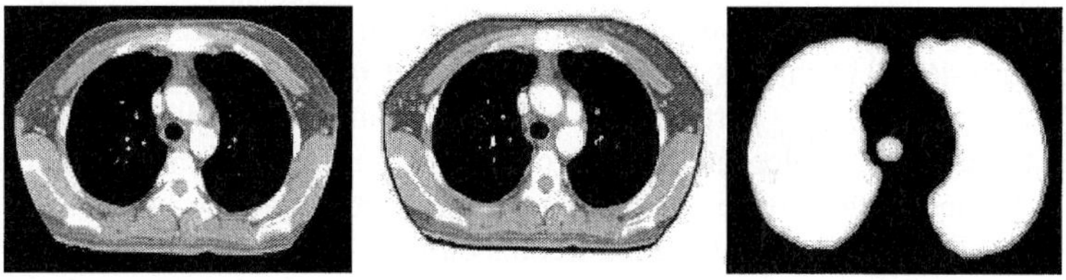

(a) (b) (c)

Fig. 2. The result of lung separation (a) chest CT image (b) thorax extraction from the surrounding anatomy (c) lung delineation from the thorax

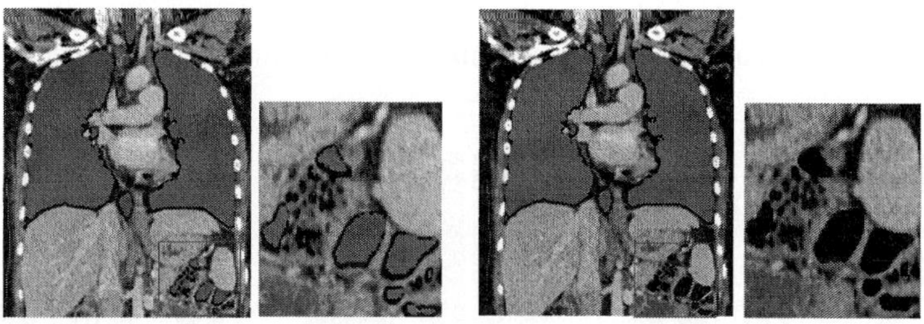

(a) (b)

Fig. 3. The removal of unwanted region (a) the result of 2D iSRG (b) connected component labeling eliminates bowel gas (indicated by square and displayed by enlarged image)

lung boundaries. Binary images are then constructed as shown in Fig. 2(c). The 3D connected component labeling is applied to ensure that non-pulmonary structures, such as bowel gas, are not erroneously identified as lung regions, as shown in Fig. 3.

After the lung separation, pulmonary vessels are extracted from the above result using gray-level thresholding. All pixels with a gray level larger than the threshold value selected by optimal thresholding are identified as pulmonary vessels.

2.3 Airway Extraction Using 3D Region Growing Based on Partitioning

Since the intensities of the trachea and large airways are similar to those of the lungs, the lungs resulting from the lung separation step still contain the trachea and large airways. Thus the airway extraction step segments trachea and large airways by 3D region growing based on partitioning and subtracts the results from the results of lung separation step.

The airway extraction is composed of the following four stages. First, we apply pre-filtering in order to increase robustness of 3D region growing. Due to junctions between the lungs and the airways, the 3D region growing for airway extraction may create an explosion into the lung parenchyma, as shown in Fig. 4(a) and (b). Applying 2D median filter to each slice can make thin these junctions with weak contrast and separate the lungs and the airways, as shown in Fig. 4(c). The mask size for the median filtering is 3×3. Second, threshold value is selected by applying adaptive thresholding. Airway extraction cannot be successful using a single threshold since there are gray-level variations between trachea and large airways. We partition the chest CT images into two parts on the basis of the branching point of trachea. For upper part, a threshold value that is 50% of the difference between the maximum and minimum values in the image is used. For lower part, predefined threshold value is used. Third, 3D region growing with 26-connectivity is applied to the filtered images. The seed point is automatically selected by searching for the large, circular, air-filled region near the center of the first few slices in the dataset. The regions with a gray level smaller than the threshold value are extracted as the trachea and large airways, as shown in Fig. 4(d). Finally, 2D morphological operators are applied to the results of previous step in which high-density airway wall is not included and unwanted cavities are remained. To prevent these occurrences, we apply a 2D binary dilation and closing with a 3×3 mask to each slice repeatedly. We partition the chest CT images into two parts and apply different number of iteration to each part.

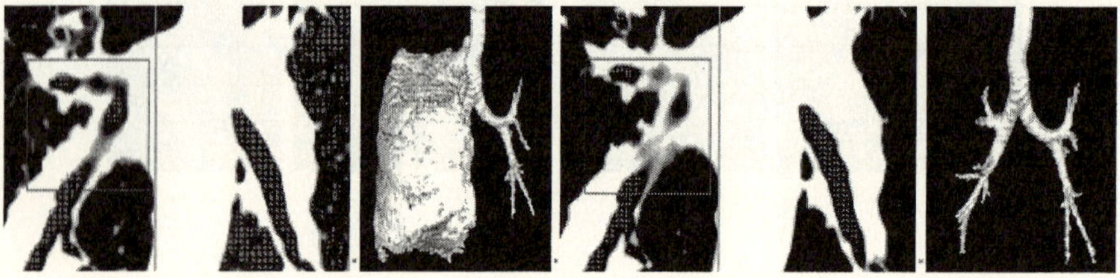

(a) (b) (c) (d)

Fig. 4. The effect of median filtering (a)(b) the result of airway extraction without median filtering (c)(d) the result of airway extraction with median filtering

2.4 Lung Extraction Using Image Subtraction

After the trachea and large airways are extracted, the results are subtracted from the results of the lung separation. Subtracted images contain only the lung regions. Fig. 5 shows the results of lung extraction by image subtraction. Fig. 5(a) and (b) is the results of lung separation and airway extraction, respectively. Fig. 5(c) is obtained by subtracting Fig. 5(b) from Fig. 5(a).

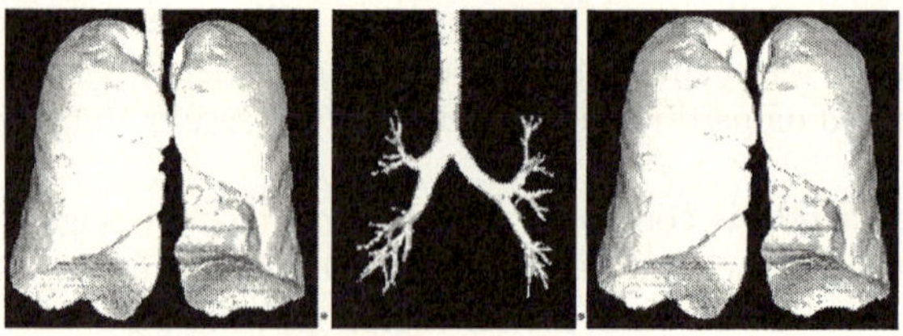

(a) (b) (c)

Fig. 5. The result of lung extraction (a) the result of lung separation (b) the result of airway extraction (c) lungs extracted by image subtraction

3 Experimental Results

All our implementation and test were performed on an Intel Pentium IV PC containing 2.5 GHz and 2.0 GB of main memory. Our segmentation method has been applied to ten patients with pulmonary nodule or embolism of 16-channel chest CT scans whose properties are described in Table 1. The CT images were obtained with a Philips MX8000 multidectector helical CT scanner or Siemens Sensation16 multidectector helical CT scanner. The image size of all patient datasets is 512 x 512. The performance of our method is evaluated with the aspects of visual inspection and accuracy and processing time.

Table 1. Image conditions of experimental datasets

Subject	Slice #	Pixel size (mm)	Slice thickness (mm)	Disease	Subject	Slice #	Pixel size (mm)	Slice thickness (mm)	Disease
1	258	0.6 x 0.6	1.5	PE	6	358	0.64 x 0.64	2.0	PN
2	209	0.77 x 0.77	1.5	PE	7	270	0.57 x 0.57	2.0	PN
3	456	0.61 x 0.61	0.75	PE	8	371	0.6 x 0.6	2.0	PN
4	372	0.68 x 0.68	0.75	PE	9	407	0.62 x 0.62	2.0	PN
5	374	0.61 x 0.61	0.75	PE	10	446	0.55 x 0.55	2.0	PN

(PE: pulmonary embolism, PN: pulmonary nodule)

Fig. 6 shows the results of lung segmentation of subject 1, 6, 7. The first row shows the 2D binary image and the second row shows the 3D display of segmented lungs. These results show our proposed method segments lung boundaries with high curvature precisely.

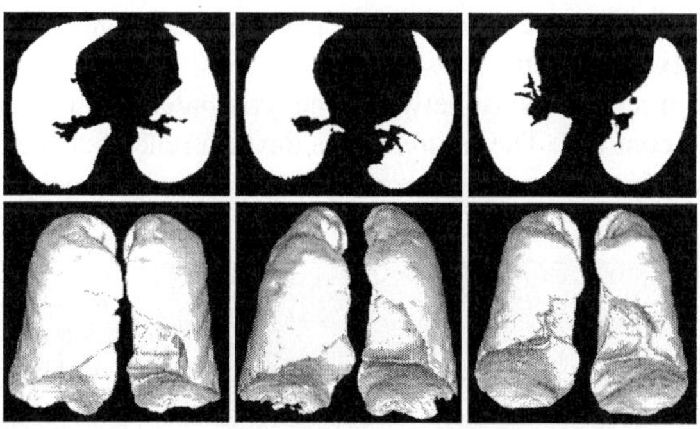

Fig. 6. The results of automatic lung segmentation

Fig. 7 shows the results of airway extraction of subject 1, 3, 6 and pulmonary vessel extraction of subject 3, 6, 8. These results show that our proposed method extracts the airways and pulmonary vessels accurately.

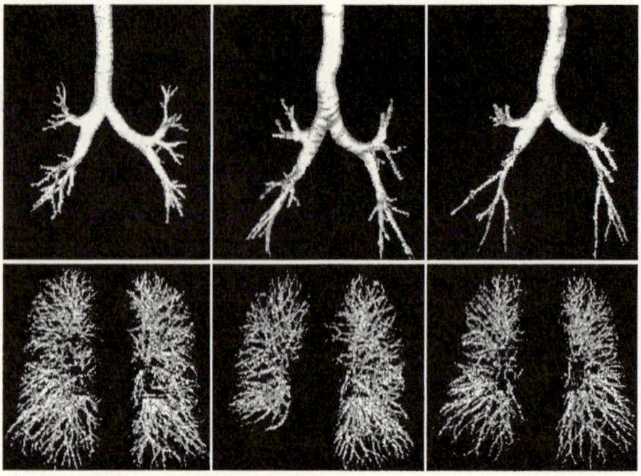

Fig. 7. The results of airway extraction and vessel extraction

To evaluate the accuracy of lung segmentation, we performed two comparisons. First, we compared our method with manual method. Second, considering the manual method as gold standard, we compared our method with commercial tool Analyze (Mayo clinic, Rochester, USA). For manual method, two radiologists manually outlined the left and right lung borders for 10 patient datasets. For the first comparison, the accuracy was measured by computing the mean, rms, and maximum distance between computer-defined contour and the manually-outlined contour. For each pixel on the computer-defined contour, the minimum distance to the manually-outlined contour was computed as

$$d_i = \min_j \left\| X_i^C - X_j^M \right\| \quad (1)$$

where X_i^C is the computer-defined contour pixel location and X_j^M is the manually-outlined contour pixel location.

Fig. 8 shows a comparison between the computer-defined contours and the manually-outlined contours. The figure shows the difference between radiologist1 and

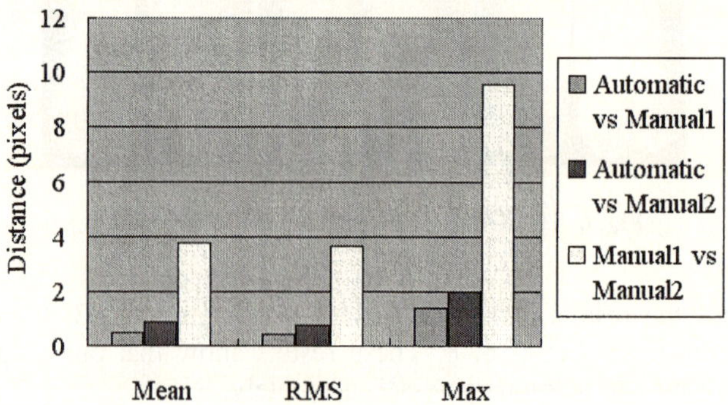

Fig. 8. The accuracy evaluation using distance measure

the computer, and the difference between radiologist2 and the computer. In addition, inter-observer variations are evaluated by computing the distances between the manually-outlined contours. The difference between the radiologists and the computer could be considered not significant since the variations between the computer and any of the radiologists is smaller in magnitude than the variations between two radiologists.

For the second comparison, considering the manual method as gold standard, the accuracy was measured by computing the number of error voxels and error rates of two automatic methods: our method and Analyze. Table 2 shows the average number of error voxels and the error rates of proposed method is much smaller than those of Analyze.

Table 2. Average number of error pixels and error rates

	Analyze	Proposed method
Average number of error voxels	1,607,006	336,975
Error rates	16.21 %	3.16 %

Total processing time is summarized in Table 3 where execution time is measured for lung separation and vessel extraction, airway and lung extraction processes. On average, 22.7 seconds are required to segment 512 x 512 x 352 dataset.

Table 3. Total processing time (sec)

Subject	A	B	Total Processing Time	Subject	A	B	Total Processing Time
1	14.704	2.515	17.219	6	20.391	4.265	24.656
2	7.625	1.922	9.547	7	14.188	2.719	16.907
3	24.063	5.468	29.531	8	19.329	3.468	22.797
4	19.719	4.359	24.078	9	23.047	4.141	27.188
5	20.125	4.937	25.062	10	26.578	3.937	30.515

(A : Lung Separation and Vessel Extraction, B : Airway and Lung Extraction)

4 Conclusion

We have developed an automatic method for accurately identifying pulmonary structures in the chest CT images. Our automatic segmentation extracts accurate lung surfaces, airways and pulmonary vessels. In first step, using 2D iSRG and connected component labeling, the airways and the lungs can be accurately extracted without hole-filling. In particular, connected component labeling in low-resolution can reduce the memory use and computation time. Pulmonary vessels can be identified from the result of first step by gray-level thresholding. In second step, trachea and large airways can be accurately delineated from the lungs by splitting the chest CT image into two parts and applying different threshold values. Accurate lung regions can be identified by subtracting the trachea and large airways from the airways and the lungs. Ten patient datasets with lung cancer or pulmonary embolism have been used for the performance evaluation with the aspects of visual inspection and accuracy and processing time. The results of our method show that lungs with large curvature, airways and pulmonary vessels are accurately extracted. The comparison with manual analysis shows that the root mean square difference between the computer and manual analysis is about 0.8 pixels. The difference could be considered not significant since the variations between the computer and any of the radiologists is smaller in magnitude than inter-observer variations. The comparison with Analyze shows that error rates of our method is 13% smaller than those of Analyze for 10 patient datasets. On average, 22.7 seconds are required to segment 512 x 512 x 352 dataset. Proposed method can be successfully used for lung nodule matching and CT lung perfusion, which are preprocessing step for pulmonary nodule detection and pulmonary embolism analysis, respectively.

Acknowledgements

This work was supported in part by a grant B020211 from Strategic National R&D Program of Ministry of Science and Technology and a grant 10014138 from the Advanced Technology Center Program and the Brain Korea 21 Project. The ICT at Seoul National University provides research facilities for this study.

References

1. Remy-Jardin M., Remy J., Spiral CT of the Chest, Berlin: Springer-Verlag (1996).
2. Denison, D. M., Morgan, M. D. L., Millar, A. B., Estimation of regional gas and tissue volumes of the lung in supine man using computed tomography, Thorax, Vol. 41 (1986) 620-628.
3. Hudlend, L.W., Anderson, R.F., Goulding, P.L., Beck, J.W., Effmann, E.L., Putman, C.E., Two methods for isolating the lung area of a CT scan for density information, Radiology, Vol. 144 (1982) 353-357.
4. Brown, M. S., McNitt-Gray, M. F., Mankovich, N. J., Goldin, J. G., Hiller, J., Wilson, L. S., Aberle, D. R., Method for segmenting chest CT image data using an anatomic model: Preliminary results, IEEE Trans. Medical Imaging Vol. 16, No. 6 (1997) 828-839.
5. ArmatoIII, S.G., Sensakovic, W.F., Automated Lung Segmentation for Thoracic CT: Impact on Computer-Aided Diagnosis, Academic Radiology Vol.11 (2004) 1011-1021.
6. Hu, S., Hoffman, E.A., Reinhardt, J.M., Accurate Lung Segmentation for Accurate Quantitation of Volumetric X-Ray CT Images, IEEE Transactions on Medical Imaging Vol. 20, No. 6 (2001) 490-498.
7. Ukil, S., Reinhardt, J.M., Smoothing Lung Segmentation Surfaces in 3D X-ray CT Images using Anatomic Guidance, In Proc. SPIE Conf. Medical Imaging Vol.5340 (2004) 1066-1075.
8. R.G.Gonzalez, R.E.Woods, Digital Image Processing, 1st Ed. (1993).

Blind Deconvolution of Ultrasonic Signals Using High-Order Spectral Analysis and Wavelets

Roberto H. Herrera[1], Eduardo Moreno[2], Héctor Calas[2], and Rubén Orozco[3]

[1] University of Cienfuegos, Cuatro Caminos, Cienfuegos, Cuba
henry@finf.ucf.edu.cu
[2] Institute of Cybernetics, Mathematics and Physics (ICIMAF), Havana, Cuba
{moreno, hcalas}@icimaf.inf.cu
[3] Central University of Las Villas, Santa Clara, Cuba
rorozco@fie.uclv.edu.cu

Abstract. Defect detection by ultrasonic method is limited by the pulse width. Resolution can be improved through a deconvolution process with a priori information of the pulse or by its estimation. In this paper a regularization of the Wiener filter using wavelet shrinkage is presented for the estimation of the reflectivity function. The final result shows an improved signal to noise ratio with better axial resolution.

1 Introduction

Deconvolution of ultrasonic signals is defined as the solution of the inverse problem of convolving an input signal, known as the transducer impulse response $h(n)$ and medium reflectivity function $x(n)$ and can be represented by [1]:

$$y(n) = h(n) * x(n) + \eta(n) \ . \tag{1}$$

where $y(n)$ is the measured signal, the operator * denotes the convolution operation and $\eta(n)$ is the additive noise. To recover $x(n)$ from the observation $y(n)$ drives to improve the appearance and the axial resolution of the images through the elimination of the dependent effects of the measuring system [1]. The signal $y(n)$ corresponds to A-scan lines of 2-D acoustic image or 1-D signal, where the problem settles down by taking the desired signal $x(n)$ as the input of a linear time invariant system (LTI) with impulse response $h(n)$ [2]. The output of the LTI system is blurred by white Gaussian noise $\eta(n)$ of variance σ^2. In frequency domain from (1) we get:

$$Y(f) = H(f)X(f) + N(f) \ . \tag{2}$$

Where: $Y(f)$, $H(f)$ and $N(f)$ are the Fourier Transform of $y(n)$, $h(n)$ y $\eta(n)$ respectively. If the system frequency response $H(f)$ does not contain zeros an estimation of $x(n)$ can be obtained from:

$$X_1(f) = H^{-1}(f)Y(f) = X(f) + H^{-1}(f)N(f) \ . \tag{3}$$

However where $H(f)$ takes near to zero values, the noise is highly amplified with variance spreading to infinite which leads to incorrect estimates. In this case it is

M. Lazo and A. Sanfeliu (Eds.): CIARP 2005, LNCS 3773, pp. 663–670, 2005.

necessary to include in the inverse filter some regularization parameter which reduces the variance of the estimated signal. The most known case of regularized filter for stationary signals is the Wiener filter [3].

When the signals under analysis shows non stationary properties, as abrupt changes, the Wiener filter based on the Fourier Transform does not give satisfactory results in the estimation, conditioned by the characteristics of Fourier basis (e^{jw}) [1]. A projection into a base that can characterize these non stationary signals and at the same time achieves a better matching with the transmitted pulse, as wavelets, drives to a better localization in time and frequency [3]. Another of the advantages of wavelets is that the signals can be represented with some few coefficients different from zero, what corresponds with the ultrasonic signals, where the trace is only composed by values different from zero in cases of abrupt changes of acoustic impedance, this leads to an efficient methods of compression and noise filtering. R. Neelamani, H. Choi & R. Baranikuk, recently proposed a regularized deconvolution technique based on Wavelet (ForWaRD) [4] which will be used in this paper for the deconvolution of ultrasonic signals as a first step to the conformation of acoustic images by means of Synthetic Aperture Focusing Testing (SAFT).

The initial problem in deconvolution, is the a priori knowledge or not of the system impulse response *h(n)*. Oppenhiem & Shafer have defined the case of estimating *x(n)* from *h(n)* as the well-known homomorphic deconvolution [5], using the real cepstrum for minimum phase signals or the complex cepstrum for the most general case. Another author, Torfinn Taxt in [6], compares seven methods based on the cepstrum for blind deconvolution (without knowing *h(n)*), in the estimation of the reflectivity function in biological media. We select the method of High Order Spectral Analysis (HOSA) because of its immunity to the noise and the not initial conditionality that the transducer's electromechanical impulse response is of minimum phase, something that depends on the construction of the housing of the pieso-electric and of the impedance matching between the transmitter and the ceramic [7].

The paper is structured as follows. Section 2.1 deals with the process of estimating the system function using HOSA. Section 2.2 summarizes the procedure for a first estimate using the Wiener filter. Section 2.3 focuses on the wavelet-based regularized deconvolution. Section 2.4 describes the measurement system and the signals to be processed. Section 3 presents the results with a comparative analysis. Finally Section 4 gives the conclusions of the paper.

2 Materials and Methods

This Section firstly describes the method used for estimating the system function and continues with the wavelet-based deconvolution.

2.1 Estimation of System Function Using HOSA

The system function described in (1) as the transducer's impulse response *h(n)* is a deterministic and causal FIR filter, *x(n)* represents the medium response function that we assume initially, without loss of generality, stationary, zero mean and non Gaussian distribution, this last property guarantees that its third-order cumulant exists, like we will explain later on, on the other hand $\eta(n)$ represents the zero mean Gaussian noise that is uncorrelated with $x(n)$. The third-order cumulant of the zero mean signal $y(n)$ is represented by [1], [8]:

$$c_y(m_1, m_2) = \gamma_x \frac{1}{M} \sum_{k=0}^{M-1} h(k)h(k+m_1)h(k+m_2) \ . \tag{4}$$

where $\gamma_x = E[x^3(n)]$, is a constant equal to the third cumulant of the signal $x(n)$, and E is the operator of statistical average.

By applying the 2-D Z-Transform (Z_{2D}) to (3) we get the bispectrum:

$$C_y(z_1, z_2) = \gamma_x H(z_1)H(z_2)H(z_1^{-1}z_2^{-1}) \ . \tag{5}$$

The bicepstrum $by(m1, m2)$, is obtained as was described in [5], logarithm of the bispectrum and inverse transformation to arrive into the 2-D quefrency domain:

$$b_y(m_1, m_2) = Z_{2D}^{-1}\left[\log(C_y(z_1, z_2))\right] \ . \tag{6}$$

As follows in [1], the cepstrum $\hat{h}(n)$ of $h(n)$ is obtained by evaluating the bicepstrum along the diagonal $m1 = m2$ for all $n \neq 0$:

$$\hat{h}(n) = b_y(-n, n) \qquad \forall n \neq 0 \ . \tag{7}$$

Then from (6) we can estimate $h(n)$ as:

$$h(n) = Z^{-1}\left\{\exp\left[Z(\hat{h}(n))\right]\right\} \ . \tag{8}$$

where Z and Z^{1} are 1-D the direct and inverse Z -Transform respectively.

The bicepstrum is derived from the bispectrum in the same way that the cepstrum is obtained from the spectrum. The main advantage of this estimation method is that the bispectrum of the white Gaussian noise is zero [7], which allows us to estimate $h(n)$ without taking into account the contribution of $\eta(n)$ in (1).

2.2 The Wiener Filter

Having $h(n)$ we can estimate $X_1(f)$ using the Wiener filter:

$$X_1(f) = Y(f)\left[\frac{H^*(f)}{|H(f)|^2 + q}\right] . \tag{9}$$

Where q is a term that includes the regularization parameter and the noise contribution, $H(f)$ is the 1-D Fourier Transform of $h(n)$ and $H^*(f)$ its complex conjugated, the term inside the brackets is the inverse Wiener filter in generic form it is represented by [1]:

$$G(f) = \frac{H^*(f)P_{x_1}(f)}{|H(f)|^2 P_{x_1}(f) + \alpha\sigma^2} . \tag{10}$$

where $Px_1(f)$, is the power spectral density of $x_1(n)$, α is the regularization parameter and σ^2 represents the noise variance. As $Px_1(f)$ is unknown it is necessary to use the iterative Wiener method, in this study we took α=0.01 initially, giving good results in the estimate and σ^2 was calculated as the median of the finest scale wavelets coefficients of $y(n)$ [8], $x_1(n)$ is obtained from $X_1(f)$ by inverse Fourier transformation.

2.3 Wavelet-Based Wiener Filter

The discrete wavelet transform (DWT) represents a 1-D continuous-time signal $x(t)$, in terms of shifted versions of a lowpass scaling function ϕ and shifted and dilated versions of a prototype band-pass wavelet function ψ [4]. As it was demonstrated by I. Daubechies [9], special cases of these functions $\psi_{j,k}(t) = 2^{j/2}\psi(2^j t - k)$ and $\psi_{j,k}(t) = 2^{j/2}\psi(2^j t - k)$ form an orthonormal basis in the $L^2(\Re)$ space, with $j,k \in \mathbb{Z}$. The parameter j is associated with the scale of the analysis and k with the localization or displacement. Signal decomposition at a level J, would be given by [1]:

$$x^J(t) = \sum_{k=1}^{2^{(N-J)}} c(k)\phi_k(t) + \sum_{j=1}^{J}\sum_{k=1}^{2^{(N-J)}} d(j,k)\psi_{j,k}(t) . \tag{11}$$

where $c(k)$ is the inner product $c(k) = \langle x(t), \phi_{j,k}(t)\rangle$ and $d_{j,k} = \langle x(t), \psi_{j,k}(t)\rangle$.

The estimated signal from the Wiener filter is projected into this base, and at each decomposition level the variance σ_j^2 is obtained for noise reduction. The following step is to use the Wiener filter in the wavelet domain where the filtering process is done for the wavelet coefficients. From (10) we have [4]:

$$\lambda_{j,k}^d = \frac{|d_{j,k}|^2}{|d_{j,k}|^2 + \sigma_j^2} \text{ and } \lambda_{j,k}^c = \frac{|c_k|^2}{|c_k|^2 + \sigma_j^2} . \tag{12}$$

By substituting (11) in (10) we obtain the expression of the estimated reflectivity function $\tilde{x}(n)$:

$$\tilde{x}(n) = \sum_{k=1}^{2^{(N-J)}} \lambda_{j,k}^c c(k)\phi_k(n) + \sum_{j=1}^{J}\sum_{k=1}^{2^{(N-J)}} \lambda_{j,k}^d d_{j,k}\psi_{j,k}(n) . \tag{13}$$

2.4 Experimental Setup

The experimental system consisted on the obtaining an acoustic image of 10 bars of acrylic of diameter 5 mm, submerged in water. A data set of 400 RF-sequences has been generated, each RF-sequence containing 9995 sampling points. The RF-lines were sampled at a rate of 50 MHz. An unfocused 3.5 MHz transducer was used in both emission and reception operating in pulse-echo mounted in a scanner controlled by stepping motor with 0.25 mm between A-scan lines.

3 Results and Discussion

The deconvolution process steps, as has been described previously include:

1. Estimate the impulse response from the bicepstrum.
2. Obtain a first estimate of the reflectivity function using the regularized Wiener filter in the domain of the frequency.
3. Apply a noise filtering over the wavelets coefficients.
4. Estimate the reflectivity function with the Wiener filter in the wavelet domain.

3.1 Estimation of the Ultrasound Pulse

The pulse estimation was carried out on a set of 16 zero mean signals. Fig. 1 shows the obtained pulse, using the MatLab® function bicepsf.m of the HOSA Toolbox.

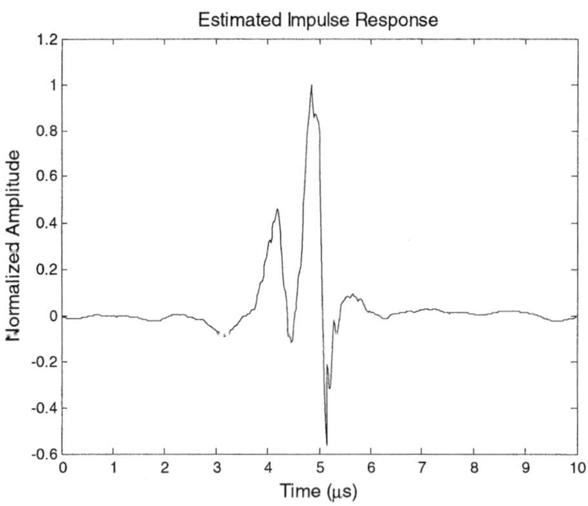

Fig. 1. Estimated impulse response. The normalized pulse width *vs* time in μs.

The spectral content of the obtained pulse includes the same band of the original signal.

3.2 Estimation of the Reflectivity Function

We used an iterative Wiener filter to estimate the power spectral density $Px_l(f)$, as was explained in the section 2.2. After ten iterations the signal $x_l(n)$ was obtained. Fig. 2 shows a segment of the original signal and the estimated one.

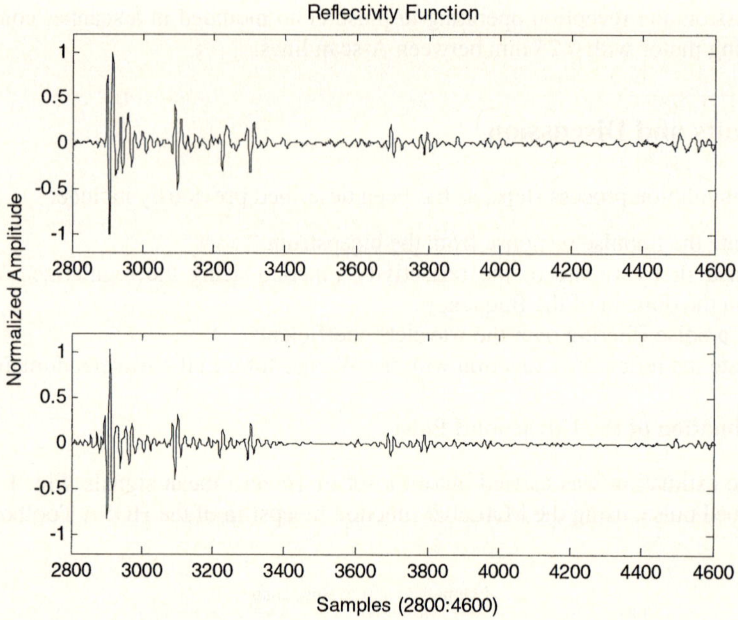

Fig. 2. Estimated reflectivity function obtained by iterative Wiener filter. (upper plot) The original signal $y(n)$; (lower plot) the estimated signal $x_1(n)$.

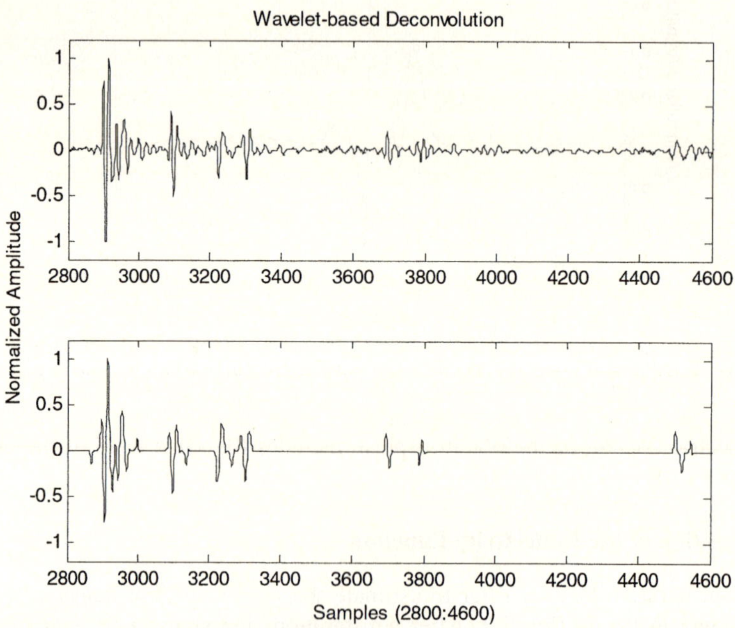

Fig. 3. The Wiener filter applied to the wavelets coefficients. (upper plot) The original signal $y(n)$; (lower plot) the deconvolved signal $\tilde{x}(n)$.

3.3 Noise Filtering

We used a soft threshold over the wavelets coefficients after a decomposition using DB16 and DB10 in the algorithm proposed in [4]. Fig. 3 shows the result of the deconvolution in the wavelet domain.

The estimated signal shows a better spatial localization, which improves the axial resolution.

In accordance with Fig. 4, the deconvolution of the RF signal improves the resolution, quantified as the decrease of the main lobe width of the autocovariance function [7]. The lobe width at half amplitude (-6dB drop) given in samples is 9 samples for the original signal and 4 for estimated one.

We obtained an increment of the axial resolution in a factor of 2.25. The same procedure was applied to the set of 30 signals of a total of 400 to characterize the standard deviation of the values, obtaining a factor of 2.25± 0.36.

This increment of the axial resolution depends of the transducer's spectral properties; consequently it is suggested to prove the method with different frequency bandwidth ratio.

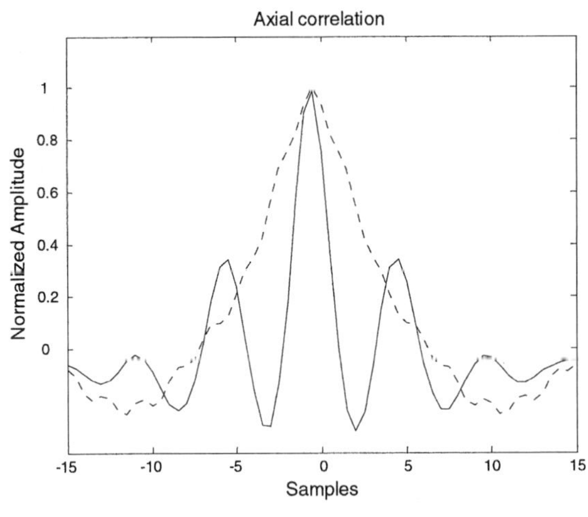

Fig. 4. Autocovariance function of the original signal (*dotted line*) and of the estimated signal (*continuous line*). The amplitude was normalized in both functions and centered in their maximum.

4 Conclusions

This paper establishes a cepstrum-based method using high-order statistics as the first step for the blind deconvolution kernel estimation which is used in the inverse filter design in both Fourier and wavelet domain for the reconstruction of the medium reflectivity function. This procedure results in a significant reduction of the time spatial support, suggesting a significant gain in the axial resolution.

This property is particularly useful in the case of acoustic image generation, where we will apply these results.

References

1. Wan S., Raju B. I. & Srinivasan M. A.: Robust Deconvolution of High-Frequency Ultrasound Images Using Higher-Order Spectral Analysis and Wavelets. IEEE Trans. Ultrason., Ferroelect., Freq. Contr., vol. 50, no. 10 (2003) 1286-1295
2. Herrera R. H.: Procesamiento Digital de Señales Ultrasónicas, M.S. Tesis, CEETI. Fac. Elect., UCLV., Sta. Clara, Cuba (1998)
3. Neelamani R., Choi H. & Baraniuk R.: Wavelet-based deconvolution for Ill-conditioned systems en IEEE Conf. Acoust. Speech, and Signal Processing (ICAASP), vol. 6, (1999) 3241-3244
4. Neelamani R., Choi H. & Baraniuk R.: ForWaRD: Fourier-Wavelet Regularized Deconvolution for Ill-Conditioned Systems, IEEE Trans. Ultrason., Ferroelect., Freq. Contr., vol. 52, no. 2, (2004) 418-432
5. Oppenhiem A. V. & Schafer R. W.: Discrete Time Signal Processing. London: Prentice-Hall (1989)
6. Taxt T.: Comparison of cepstrum-based methods for radial blind deconvolution of ultrasound images, IEEE Trans. Ultrason., Ferroelect., Freq. Contr., vol. 44, no. 3, (1997) 666-674
7. Adam D.: Blind deconvolution of ultrasound sequences using nonparametric local polynomial estimates of the pulse, IEEE Trans. Biomedical Eng., vol. 49, no. 2, (2002) 118-130
8. Donoho D. L.: De-noising by soft-thresholding, IEEE Trans. Inform., Theory, vol. 41, (1995) 613-627
9. Daubechies I.: Ten Lectures on Wavelets. Philadelphia, PA: SIAM (1992)

Statistical Hypothesis Testing and Wavelet Features for Region Segmentation

David Menoti[1], Díbio Leandro Borges[2], and Arnaldo de Albuquerque Araújo[1]

[1] UFMG - Universidade Federal de Minas Gerais,
Grupo de Processamento Digital de Imagens - Departamento de Ciência da Computação,
Av. Antônio Carlos, 6627, Pampulha - 31.270-010, Belo Horizonte-MG, Brazil
{menoti, arnaldo}@dcc.ufmg.br
[2] BIOSOLO, Goiânia - Go, Brazil
dibio@terra.com.br

Abstract. This paper introduces a novel approach for region segmentation. In order to represent the regions, we devise and test new features based on low and high frequency wavelet coefficients which allow to capture and judge regions using changes in brightness and texture. A fusion process through statistical hypothesis testing among regions is established in order to obtain the final segmentation. The proposed local features are extracted from image data driven by global statistical information. Preliminary experiments show that the approach can segment both texturized and regions cluttered with edges, demonstrating promising results. Hypothesis testing is shown to be effective in grouping even small patches in the process.

1 Introduction

Segmentation process is a major bottleneck in applications on Pattern Recognition and Computer Vision areas, and it is kept on the agenda of scientific community. There are several segmentation approaches on literature, however since most of the tests are designed for specific applications, many open problems remain. One which is addressed here in this paper is how to segment regions consistently having images either with highly texturized patches, or artefacts with brightness, or both. Usually the approaches work either for one situation, or another, and in this paper we propose an approach that could work more consistently in both situations.

Segmentation approaches found in the literature could be separated into two main groups: those regarding supervised learning, which take into account knowledge about the application (i.e., training); and those ones regarding unsupervised learning, which relies only in the input image data, or without *a priori* knowledge about the application.

The well known Canny edge detector [1] models boundaries as brightness step edges, which is the most common approach to detect local boundaries. The Canny detector fails wildly inside texturized regions where high contrast edges are present, but usually with no separation between regions. Moreover, it is unable to detect the boundary between textured regions when there is only a subtle change in average image brightness.

M. Lazo and A. Sanfeliu (Eds.): CIARP 2005, LNCS 3773, pp. 671–678, 2005.

A review on image segmentation approaches of the 80's and previous can be found in [2], and an initial guide can be found in [3]. Recently, with availability of computation and memory store devices, more demanding and complex approaches have been proposed.

A highly cited approach was proposed by Shi *et al.* in [4]. The approach extracts the global impression of an image, considering the segmentation task as a graph partitioning problem proposing a global criterion, the normalized cut for segmenting the graph. This criterion can be optimized by an efficient computational technique ($O(N^{3/2})$) based on a generalized eigenvalue problem. In [5], Sharon *et al.* proposed a fast algorithm for image segmentation on multiscale framework based on graph partitioning, and it has a linear time complexity ($O(N)$) in number of pixels presenting results that are at least comparable to the results obtained by the spectral methods [4]. The algorithm is inspired on algebraic multigrid (AMG) solvers of minimization problems of heat and electric networks. In this approach, more measurements were combined in a multiscale framework. The results obtained for some images were better than the ones in [4].

In this paper, we propose a new segmentation algorithm focusing on local features and their consistencies in image data (i.e., an unsupervised approach), which is driven by global statistical information. Patches will be extracted from low and high frequency wavelet coefficients, and new features are devised based on those ones. Brightness and texture are modelled through patch images (e.g. square windows) from these extracted features. Statistic hypothesis testing is then proposed to perform the segmentation, using a fusion process in order to generate more consistent regions according to a control parameter given by the user.

The rest of this paper is organized as follows. In Section 2, the proposed approach is described. The experiments performed for testing and evaluating the algorithm are shown in Section 3. Finally, conclusions and future works for extending the approach in a multi-scale and multiresolution framework are pointed out in Section 4.

2 The Approach

Our proposed approach can be divided into 3 main steps, namely: 1) First, feature extraction by a Wavelet transform is performed. The image I is decomposed into a wavelet space, using Mallat's decomposition algorithm [6] with Haar basis function. This is a non-redundant transformation which leads to four output channels of features, being LL, LH, HL, and HH; 2) New features are devised based on the wavelet coefficients. The output channels of the Wavelet transform are exploited in a windowed (e.g. patches of $k \times k$ elements in size) way in order to generate new features for characterizing brightness and texturized regions; 3) Region growing through statistical hypothesis testing is performed based on information extracted from windowed features, generating consistent region segmentation. A flowchart of the proposed approach can be seen in Figure 1. Details of each step are given in the following subsections.

2.1 Wavelet Transform

A Wavelet transform decomposes data into fundamental building blocks. Its basic difference from Fourier decomposition is that the wavelet functions are well localized in

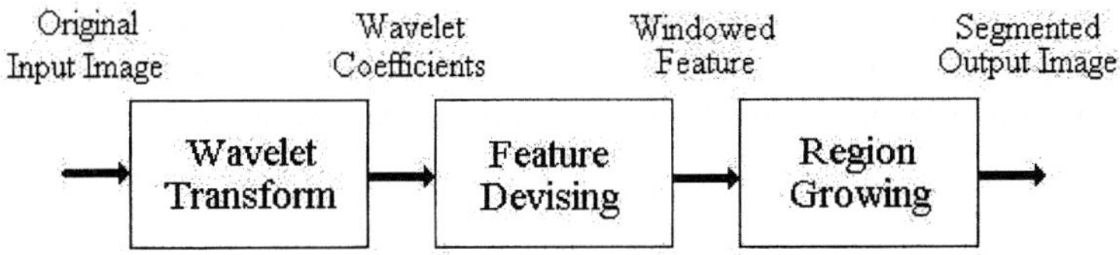

Fig. 1. Flowchart of the proposed approach

time and space, whereas sinusoidal functions used in Fourier transform are not. Since it is possible to design wavelet decompositions with a great variety of basis functions, and also either emphasizing redundancy or eliminating it throughout the levels of decomposition, the literature for such is plenty. Moreover, the Wavelet transform has been used in several fields in Image Processing, Pattern Recognition, and Computer Vision for image denoising and coding, object segmentation, recognition, and characterization.

Here, for our purposes of wavelet feature extraction, a desired decomposition would have to help representing consistently both brightness and texturized regions, eliminating redundancies on scales. We use the well known Mallat's decomposition algorithm [6] with Haar (simpler) basis function (QMF filter pairs: $\widetilde{H} = [\sqrt{2}/2; \sqrt{2}/2]$; $\widetilde{G} = [\sqrt{2}/2; -\sqrt{2}/2]$) for performing the wavelet decomposition, namely Wavelet transform. Given an input image (with $n \times m$ in size), the result of this decomposition process are four output channels of low and high frequency content wavelet coefficients (with $n/2 \times m/2$ elements in size, since it is a downsampling process), e.g. LL, LH, HL, HH. LL is called approximation (low frequency) band, LH, HL, and HH are called horizontal, vertical, and diagonal details (high frequency) bands, respectively. Our first stage then consists of transforming an input image I into four output channels, e.g. LL, LH, HL, and HH.

2.2 Feature Devising

We propose to analyze a region considering what we call a degree of perturbation. In an approximate or complete homogeneous region, changes in brightness are very few or none. On the other hand, in a texturized region it is possible to notice an almost uniform degree of perturbation, or confusion, throughout that region. Therefore, in order to characterize a consistent region we will use this concept of degree of perturbation, namely a consistent region should have a homogeneous degree of perturbation. Thus, different, brightness or texturized, regions will have different degrees of perturbation.

For achieving such an aim, we shall have features allowing us to capture these characteristics from the regions data. Original patches of the image (e.g. square windows) could be the source of these local properties. In this step we devise new features based on the wavelet coefficients, extracted from the latter step. They will be able to represent and capture the degree of perturbation of the patches. In fact, we take square windows of $k \times k$ elements and extract statistics from those, which will be used in the next step for segmentation in a region growing process. Then, the resulting output of this step are statistical matrix images with $n/2k \times m/2k$ elements, having the mean (μ) and variance (σ^2) of the patch windows.

From low and high frequency wavelet coefficients (only first level of decomposition is used) we extract enough information for characterizing consistent regions. Then, we first separate the wavelet coefficients in two kinds of features, e.g.,

$$I\mu_{Low} = \mu(|LL|) = \mu(LL), I\sigma^2_{Low} = \sigma^2(|LL|) = \sigma^2(LL). \quad (1)$$

As the Haar basis function was used in the Wavelet transform, it produces only positive values for LL. Thus, we take them as absolute values. And for high frequency features we have,

$$I\mu_{High} = \mu(\sqrt{(LH)^2 + (HL)^2}), I\sigma^2_{High} = \sigma^2(\sqrt{(LH)^2 + (HL)^2}), \quad (2)$$

HH coefficients are noisy, and usually not reliable for these purposes, and so they are left out.

Those are the proposed new features for the segmentation task, i.e., $I\mu_{Low}$, $I\mu_{High}$, $I\sigma^2_{Low}$, and $I\sigma^2_{High}$. In the next step, those measures extracted from the patches are used as cues for the segmentation. Experiments given here show that those features are enough for characterizing brightness and texturized regions.

2.3 Region Growing Through Statistical Hypothesis Testing

The analysis proposed on mean and variance values makes an important assumption, namely that the features upon which segmentation is based is distributed normally (Gaussian distribution) [7]. The parameter σ^2 is called the variance (i.e., σ is the standard deviation), and it measures the flatness of the distribution. Discrimination between adjacent areas with differing means and standard deviations can be made according to Fischer's criterion [8]:

$$\frac{|\mu_1 - \mu_2|}{\sqrt{\sigma_1^2 + \sigma_2^2}} > \lambda, \quad (3)$$

where λ is a threshold, μ_1, μ_2, σ_1, and σ_2 are averages and variances of respective regions.

In other words, if two regions have good separation in their means, and low variance, then it is possible to discriminate them. However, if the variance becomes high and the mean difference is low it is not possible to separate them.

In order to have a self tuned algorithm, we establish a measure for this purpose. For a better separation, the merging threshold, λ, for the mean intensity for two adjacent regions should be adjusted depending on the expected uniformity of the merged region. Less uniform regions will require a lower threshold to prevent under merging. The uniformity is a function of both intensity mean and variance of the region. A suitable heuristic law for combining both properties into one is [7]:

$$Uniformity = 1 - \sigma^2/\mu^2, \quad (4)$$

where μ and σ^2 are related with the full matrix feature image. Note that the uniformity will be in the range of 0 to 1 for cases where the samples are all positive. The threshold value, λ decreases with the decrease in uniformity as follows:

$$\lambda = (1 - \sigma^2/\mu^2)\lambda_0. \tag{5}$$

This has the advantage that the user need only to supply a single threshold, λ_0. But for our algorithm, we use two features, and so discrimination functions are

$$\frac{|\mu_{Low1} - \mu_{Low2}|}{\sqrt{\sigma^2_{Low1} + \sigma^2_{Low2}}} \geq \lambda_{Low}, \tag{6}$$

$$\frac{|\mu_{High1} - \mu_{High2}|}{\sqrt{\sigma^2_{High1} + \sigma^2_{High2}}} \geq \lambda_{High}, \tag{7}$$

Note that we still need to supply only a single threshold, λ_0 for having λ_{Low} and λ_{High}, since they are dependent on the data by Equation 5. Therefore, for two regions 1 and 2 to be discriminated, they must hold either one of Equations 6 or 7. However, for them to be merged, them can not hold both Equations 6 and 7.

The algorithm is automatically started with chosen seed windows, those ones with more energy on low frequency wavelets coefficients. These seeds are enqueued, and then the region process is started dequeueing window by window. Each dequeued window (i.e., region) is tested with its neighboring windows, merging or generating new regions and putting them on a queue. At this moment the mean and the variance values are updated. The algorithm will evolve until there are no more windows left (i.e., regions) on queue.

3 Experiments

For the experiments, we have used three known images having texturized and britghtness homogeneous regions. They are shown in Figure 2. These images are grayscale and 512 × 512 pixels in size. Parenthesized numbers on captions in Figure 3 and 4 are the percentual significance level in the Gaussian distribution used in statistical hypothesis testing. Resulting images of our proposed algorithm have granularity $2k$, namely each patch image corresponds to $2k \times 2k$ pixels from the original image, where k is the window size and the number 2 comes from the decimation process of the Wavelet transform, i.e., downsampling. Each of the segmented regions on the images in Figures 3 and 4 was fullfilled with its respective average grayscale.

We have performed experiments using different values for λ_0, e.g., 1.28(80%), 1.64(90%), 1.96(95%), in order to verify the algorithm behavior and its extension for other scales. Results are shown in Figure 3, and input images used are those ones in Figure 2. Observing those images, we can notice that segmented regions are more consistent as the λ_0 value increases, namely the images are less oversegmentated. On the other hand, some small regions, which could be dependent on the application or type of scene, are merged together.

Figure 4 shows results from different windows size. For those images we have setup $\lambda_0 = 1.96$, which stands for significance level of 90% in the Gaussian distribution. We have tested two window size, 2, and 4. The images in Figure 4 give an idea of how

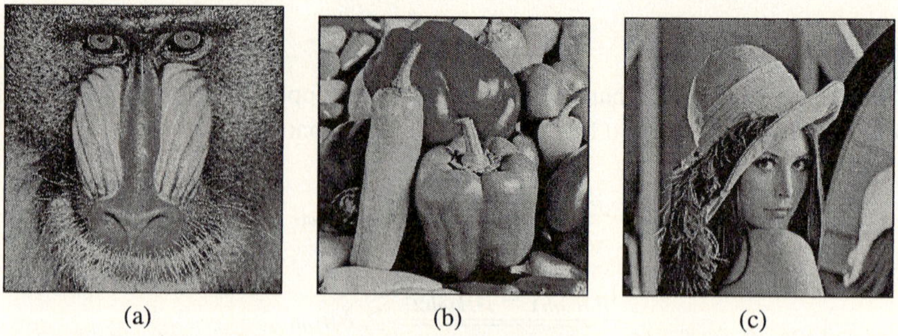

Fig. 2. Images (input) used in our experiments

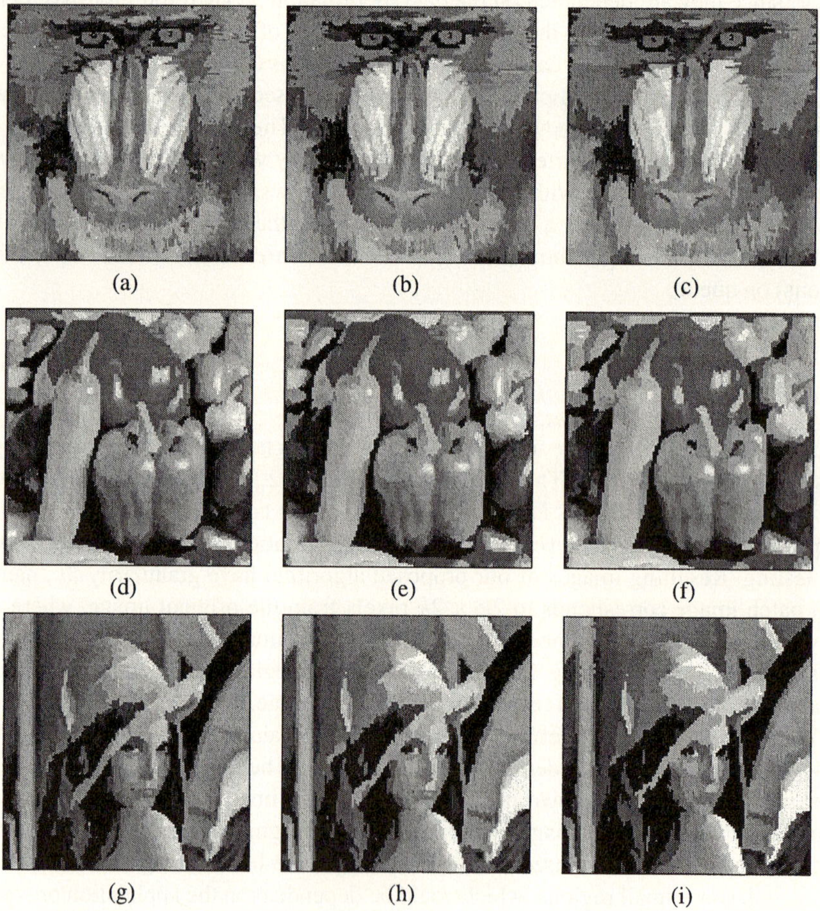

Fig. 3. Experiments used for verifying our proposed approach; using differents values of λ_0 for input images shown in Figure 2. In first col we have (3(a), 3(d), and 3(g)) $\lambda_0 = 1.28(80\%)$, second col (3(b, 3(e), and 3(h)) $\lambda_0 = 1.64(90\%)$, and, in third col (3(c), 3(f), and3(i)) $\lambda_0 = 1.96(95\%)$.

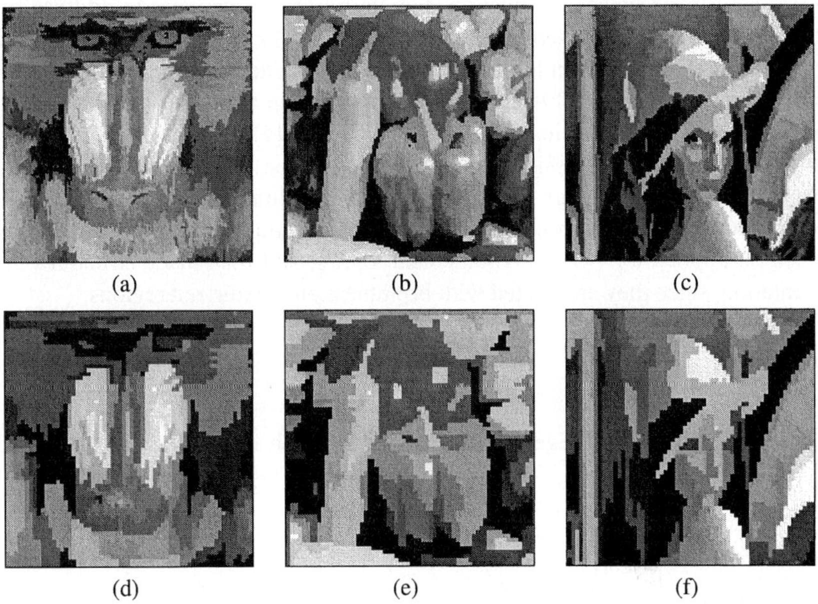

Fig. 4. Experiments used for verifying our proposed approach; using differents values of window size for input images shown in Figure 2. Images on first (4(a),4(b) and 4(c)),second (4(d),4(e)and4(f)) rows are resulting segmented images of our approach using $\lambda_0 = 1.96$, window sizes of $k = 2$ and 4, respectively, related with original ones in Figure 2.

usefull it could be to combine segmentation of several different windows size in order to obtain a more consistent segmentation.

Our algorithm implementation (C++) took less than 5 seconds for segmenting any of those images of 512×512 pixels in size in a Pentium III 1.0 GHz with 512 MB RAM. The time complexity of our proposed algorithm is $O(N)$ considering the number of windows, since region of windows will go to queue only with a new incorporated window, and so, the algorithm will process each window at a maximum of 8 times, i.e., number of neighbors.

4 Conclusions and Future Works

In this paper, we have proposed and tested a new approach for segmenting images into consistent regions. As the experiments show the approach has some advantages, which are to address region segmentation both in texturized regions and regions with brightness, using the same features. Even though one can observe oversegmentation, as for example in images in Figure 4 for small window size (i.e., $k = 2$), it is reasonable to say that these images were segmented in consistent regions, since we do not take into account any *a priori* knowledge or high level perception cue. Thus, the features devised by wavelet coefficients were shown to be a good characterization for both brightness are promising for further investigation. For future works we want to address fusion among scales in order to obtain fine segmentation results, e.g., one pixel wide granularity. Also, a possibility would be to have different window sizes in different scales putting all together in a multi-scale and multiresolution approach. A more extensive comparison with other algorithms, such as the ones in [4], [5], would be necessary in order to confirm our hypothesis that algorithms based on graph cuts perform segmentation without any knowledge about the objects. We think this perception should be driven by other decision process, like intuition for example. Our proposed algorithm can also be applied tor Natural, Biomedical, SARs, and man-made structures image segmentation, since they are related with brightness and texturized regions.

Acknowledgments

We would like to acknowledge support for this research from UFMG, CAPES/MEC, CNPq/MCT.

References

1. Canny, J.F.: A computational approach to edge detection. IEEE Transactions on Pattern Analysis and Machine Intelligence 8 (1986) 679.698
2. Pal, N.R., Pal, S.K.: A review on image segmentation techniques. Pattern Recognition 26 (1993) 1277.1294
3. Haralick, R., Shapiro, L.: Computer and Robot Machine Vision. Addison-Wesley, USA (1992 and 1993)
4. Shi, J., Malik, J.: Normalized cuts and image segmentation. IEEE Transactions on Pattern Analysis and Machine Intelligence 22 (2000) 888.905
5. Galun, M., Sharon, E., Basri, R., Brandt, A.: Texture segmentation by multiscale aggregation of filter responses and shape elements. In: Proceedings of the IEEE International Conference on Computer Vision (ICCV2003), Nice, France (2003) 716.723
6. Mallat, S.: A theory of multiresolution signal decomposition: The wavelet representation. IEEE Transactions on Pattern Analysis and Machine Intelligence 11 (1989) 674.693
7. Montgomery, D.C., Runger, G.C.: Applied Statistics and Probability for Engineers. John Wiley & Sons, Inc., New York - Chichester - Brisbane - Toronto - Singapura (1994)
8. Press, W., Teukolsky, S., Vetterling, W., Flannery, B.: Numerical Recipes in C. 2nd edn. Cambridge University Press, UK (1996)

Evaluating Content-Based Image Retrieval by Combining Color and Wavelet Features in a Region Based Scheme

Fernanda Ramos[1], Herman Martins Gomes[2], and Díbio Leandro Borges[3]

[1] Faculdade de Filosofia, Ciências e Letras de Palmas, Palmas – Pr, Brazil
ramosrs@gmail.com
[2] UFCG - Universidade Federal de Campina Grande,
Departamento de Sistemas e Computação, Av. Aprígio Veloso s/n,
Bodocongó, Campina Grande – Pb, Brazil
hmg@dsc.ufcg.edu.br
[3] BIOSOLO, Goiânia – Go, Brazil
dibio.borges@terra.com.br

Abstract. Content description and representation are still challenging issues for the design and management of content-based image retrieval systems. This work proposes to derive content descriptors of color images by wavelet coding and indexing of the HSV (Hue, Saturation, Value) channels. An efficient scheme for this problem has to trade between being translation and rotation invariant, fast and accurate at the same time. Based on a diverse and difficult database of 1020 color images, and a strong experimental protocol we propose a method that first divides an image into 9 rectangular regions (i.e. zoning), second it applies a wavelet transformation in each of the HSV channels. A subset of the approximation and of detail coefficients of each set is then selected. A similarity measure based on histogram intersection followed by vector distance computation for the 9 regions then evaluates and ranks the closest images of the database by content. In this paper we give the details of the this new approach and show promising results upon extensive experiments performed in our lab.

1 Introduction

Most conventional content-based retrieval systems use color or spatial-color features for characterizing image content [5], [10]. Some interesting works have used additional low-level features that can be computed automatically, i.e., without human assistance, and associated with the color-based features. A promise one is texture. However, even after texture has been widely studied in Psychophysics, as well as in Computer Vision, our understanding of it is still very limited when compared with our knowledge of other features, such as color and shape. A difficult task when using texture is how to represent it or even how to combine it with other features, such as the ones based on color. Most of methods to represent texture are based on co-occurrence statistics, directional filter masks, fractal dimension and Markov Random Fields. Some interesting works have tried to represent texture using visual properties, such as in [4], where texture is characterized by the following features: coarseness, contrast, busyness, complexity and texture strength. In a similar direction, Rao and Lohse [8] have done an experiment to describe texture. They suggest that three perceptual

M. Lazo and A. Sanfeliu (Eds.): CIARP 2005, LNCS 3773, pp. 679 – 690, 2005.

features can describe texture: repetitiveness, directionality and granularity (complexity). Another strategy to characterize texture has been the use of a wavelet transform. In this direction, Brambilla et al. [2] have used multiresolution wavelet transform in a modified CIELUV color space to compute image signatures for use in a content-based image retrieval application. Other approach using wavelet coding on color is [4], where the authors propose a joint coding using texture, color, and shape with statistical moments on the wavelet coefficients. The work we present in this paper is close to those since it also uses a wavelet decomposition to derive descriptors for the images. However, it proposes a different way to represent and select the features, and also to compute and rank the closest matches. We also present a strong experimental protocol showing how they performed so we derived the final features for the approach. There is a large literature on Content Based Retrieval and we point the reader to the survey in [1], and to the works in [2], [5], and [7] for a more detailed covering of the area.

The remaining of this paper is organized as follows. Next, we present in detail our approach that combines color and wavelet features in a region based scheme. An extensive experimental protocol that we used to derive the best features in the three levels of decomposition and the image channels HSV is presented in Section 3. Section 4 summarizes the main results and points to future works.

2 Proposed Method

Figure 1 shows an overview of the proposed method. In the First Stage a signature is computed for each image in the database. It begins by converting the input image from RGB to the HSV color space, such as we could deal directly with perceptually more meaningful information [11]. The second step is used to divide the image into 9 regions. This has shown to be an interesting strategy to associate spatial information to color-based features. The third step corresponds to a Mallat wavelet decomposition [9] using Haar basis function. Finally, the combination of the best features is used as a signature for the input image. To obtain the best features, we have evaluated for each color channel (H, S and V) the sub-images corresponding to the following wavelet coefficients: approximation, horizontal, and vertical, all of them computed on three levels of decomposition. Using the 10% largest coefficients in magnitude for each band, i.e. LL, HL, and LH, has shown to be a sufficient selected set for the best features.

The Second Stage corresponds to the retrieval process in which after computing an intersection of the quantized histograms [11] for each channel and all three bands (i.e. (H,S,V) x (LL,HL,LH) = 9), and for each spatial region of the image, a distance measure computes and ranks the images based on a sum of the intersections.

2.1 Signature Extraction

For each channel (H, S and V), and, respectively, each of the 9 image regions, the wavelet transform is computed using three levels of decomposition for the tests. With the experiments we have noticed that performance was closely the same for the 3rd level of decomposition, so only the 3rd levels with less features were used as features. Of course this will depend upon the initial resolution of the images.

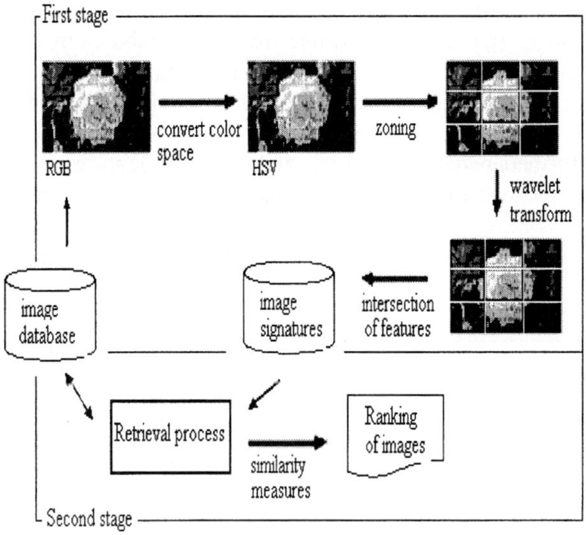

Fig. 1. Overview of the proposed method

Figure 2 shows the composition of the image signature computed. Each histogram used as signature is computed taking into account the coefficients quantized using the mean and standard deviation of each region at each decomposition level. Each histogram contains only 10% of the most significant coefficients of the image region being processed. The best results were obtained by using the combination of the approximation wavelet coefficients calculated on the H and V channel with the vertical coefficients calculated on the S channel, as it will be shown in the experiments.

	Wavelet coefficients	Level of decomposition
For each color channel (H, S and V)	Approximation (LL)	1st
		2nd
		3rd
	Vertical (HL)	1st
		2nd
		3rd
	Horizontal (LH)	1st
		2nd
		3rd

Fig. 2. Image signature structure. Each level of decomposition produces 3 histograms (LL, HL, LH) for each channel (i.e. H, S, and V).

2.2 Retrieval Process

Each image will then have as an index a feature vector of nine (9) histograms (HSV x LL,HL,LH) with 10% of the largest coefficients. All of them are referenced in 9 different spatial regions of the image. Retrieval then consists of measuring a distance for each pair of images (i.e. a query and one from the database) by computing the histogram intersection for each pair of regions and histogram features. A sum of these nine (9) intersection results for each channel (HSV) is computed as a distance and ranking measure in the end. In the experiments we have found a set of the three (3) best features that performed better in the end, and the final feature vector is selected as a combination of those. Table 1 shows the quantities and types of the classes used.

Table 1. Names and quantities of the 27 classes used for the experiments. Total number of images is 1020.

Class	# samples	Class	# samples
1-Water	70	15-Flowers	43
2-Air	53	16-Football	44
3-Animals	55	17-Fruit	19
4-Wires	06	18-Girls	27
5-Trees	103	19-Trees2	55
6-Boxes	15	20-Windows	12
7-Cars	42	21-Foliage	30
8-Christmas	42	22-Mammals	16
9-Cement	14	23-Mosaic	25
10-Buildings	79	24-Mountains	31
11-Sunset	63	25-Bridges	07
12-Ducks	37	26-Sky	43
13-Flags	43	27-Snow	14
14-Texture	32		

3 Experimental Results

The experiments were carried out on 1020 images distributed in 27 classes. Table 1 gives the image classes and their quantities and Figure 3 shows sample images of each class. In the experiments each channel (H, S and V) was evaluated separately. Two sets were separated from each class, being 10% for training and 90% for testing, tests were performed individually for each image of the training set (against the testing set). The successful classification rank was finally computed considering the number of matches between query and result. The confusion graphics show the first classification in red (light gray), where for example a diagonal red (light gray) line would mean perfect matches for all classes. For each image region the wavelet transform is calculated considering three levels of decomposition. Figures 4, 5 and 6 gives the confusion graphics for channels H, S, and V respectively in the first level of decomposition for approximation, horizontal, and vertical coefficients. All the confusion graphics showed in this paper mark (red (light gray) curve in the figures) the respective class that was chosen as the first ranked in the experiment. The complete protocol evaluated the following:

1) In the first set of experiments, each color channel was considered in a separated way. The retrieval process was evaluated based on signatures created

from each of the three channels and considering 3 sub-images generated by the wavelet transform (approximation, horizontal and vertical) at each decomposition level. This totalizes 27 different signatures for each image.

2) The second set of experiments considers the combination of the most promising results of the first experiments, independent of the level of decomposition and trying to get the best results with the coarsest level of decomposition if possible. New signatures were created by combining signatures through the use of intersection of coefficient histograms.

3.1 First Set of Experiments

Independently, each of the 27 possibilities of features (i.e. HSV x 3 coefficients (approximation, horizontal, vertical) x 3 levels of decomposition) was tested in this stage. Ten percent (10%) of the images were separated for validation only, and the results were averaged using a cross-validation scheme. Figure 4 shows confusion graphics related to the experiment on the H channel using the approximation, horizontal and vertical details sub-images in the first decomposition level. Figures 5 and 6 show respectively the results for S and V channels. On the *x* axis the class of the query image is given, and on the *y* axis the class that had the best (highest) score for the classification result. During these experiments, we observed that the best retrieval results when using the channels H (Hue) and V (Value) were obtained from the signatures based on the approximation wavelet coefficients on the third decomposition level. Regarding the S channel best success rates were higher in the third level of decomposition using the vertical detail coefficients. Figures 7, 8 and 9 shows examples of images misclassified according to the labeled database used. Although a general comparison of the success rates obtained here is dependent on the database used, which we know it is not large enough for benchmarking purposes, there is a high correlation between some image classes and the main purpose here would be to design and test a small, however significant and efficient, set of features based on a combination of color and wavelet representations to be used in an image retrieval task. Since it was possible to evaluate out of the 27 sets of features which were the most efficient for retrieval we picked the 3 best ones and performed a second set of experiments in order to find a best combination of them for the final classification.

3.2 Second Set of Experiments

In the second set of experiments the signatures calculated on the channels H and V using the approximation coefficients (LL) and the signatures calculated on the channel S using the vertical coefficients (HL) were combined through the use of intersection of their histograms. No weight was given differently to each signature. In this case, the 10% corresponding to the most significant coefficients are chosen from the resulting histogram after the intersection process. The final results are shown in Figure 10. Only 3 out of 27 classes were not classified correctly as the first choice, which shows an improvement from any of the individual set of features in the first set of experiments.

Fig. 3. Samples representative of the classes. From the top left to the right (1 to 27 as named in Table 1). The complete database has 1020 images.

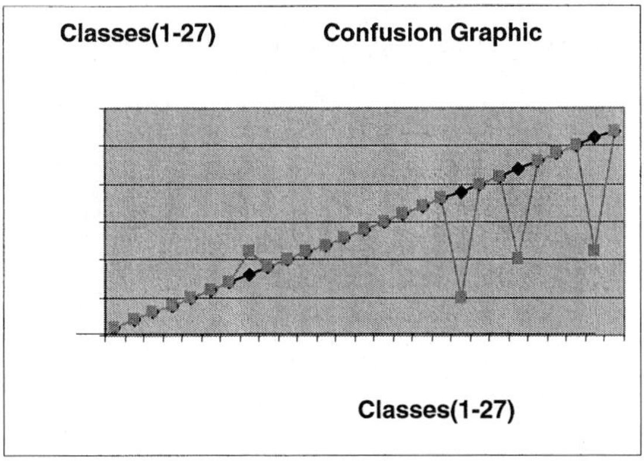

Channel H 1st level (Approximation coef.)

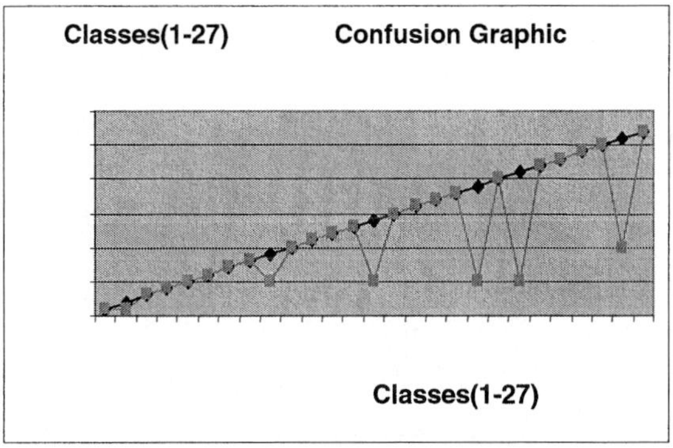

Channel H 1st level (Horizontal coef.)

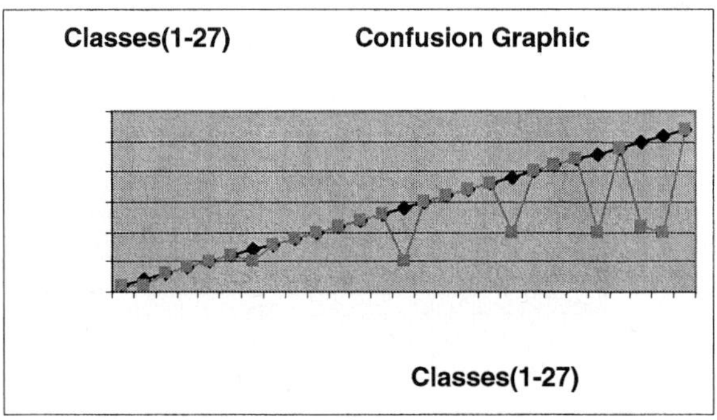

Channel H 1st level (Vertical coef..)

Fig. 4. Confusion graphics: experiment on channel H (Hue Value), all coefficients in the first level of decomposition. (*x* axis is the class of the query image, and *y* axis is the result classification obtained).

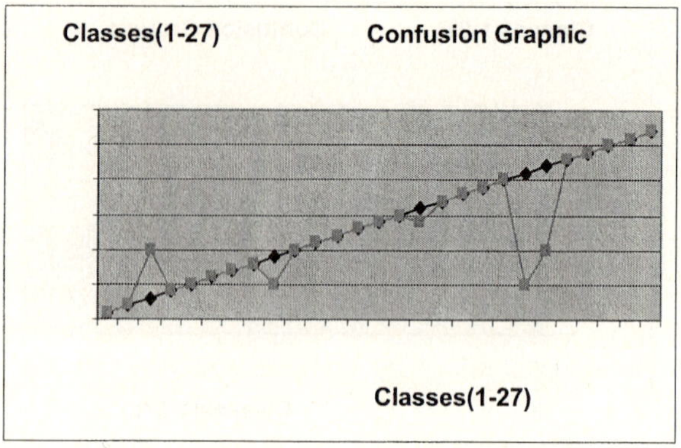

Channel S 1st level (Approximation coef.)

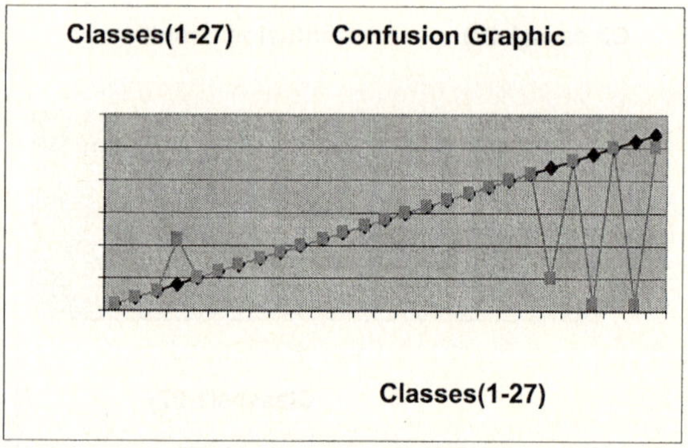

Channel S 1st level (Horizontal coef.)

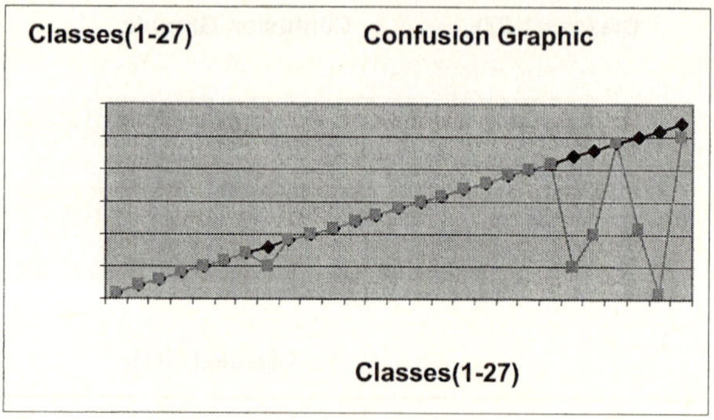

Channel S 1st level (Vertical coef.)

Fig. 5. Confusion graphics: experiment on channel S (Saturation Value), all coefficients in the first level of decomposition. (*x* axis is the class of the query image, and *y* axis is the result classification obtained).

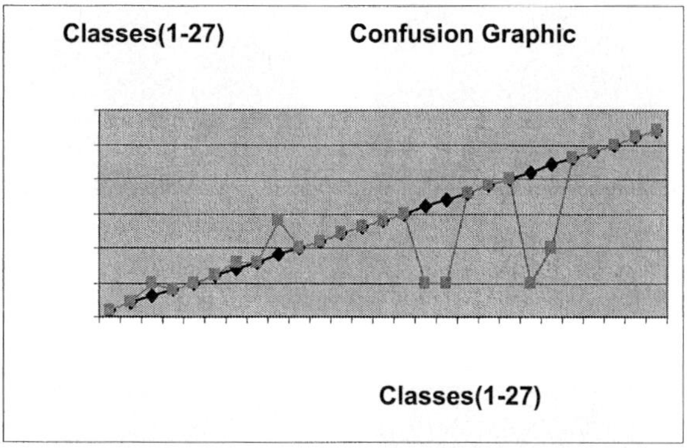

Channel V 1st level (Approximation coef.)

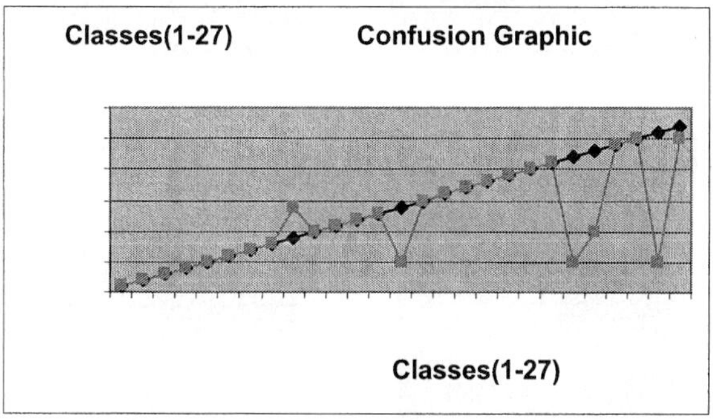

Channel V 1st level (Horizontal coef.)

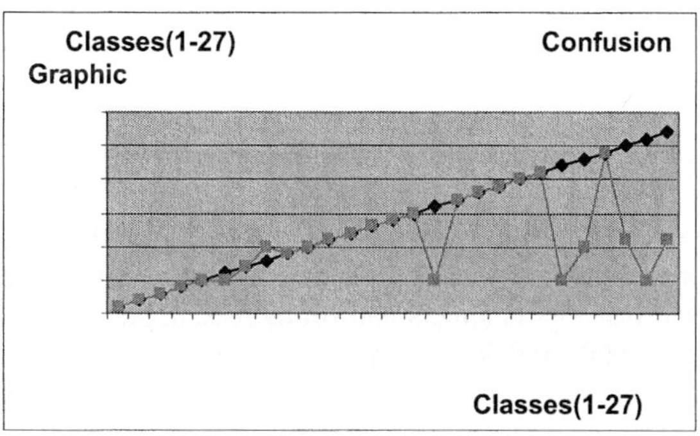

Channel V 1st level (Vertical coef.)

Fig. 6. Confusion graphics: experiment on channel V (intensity Value), all coefficients in the third level of decomposition. (x axis is the class of the query image, and y axis is the result classification obtained).

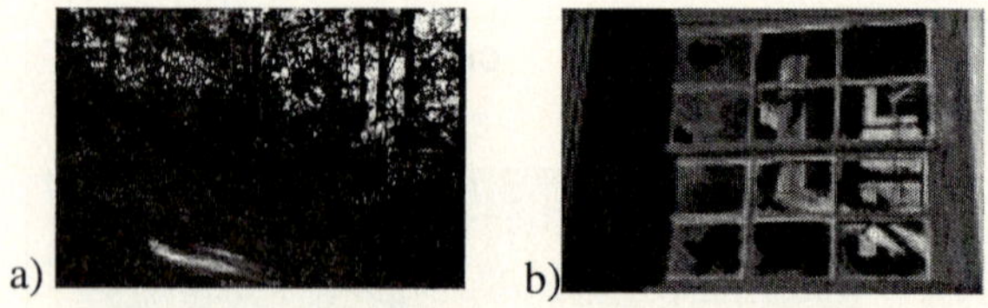

Fig. 7. Examples of misclassification (i.e similar images) occurred in Hue channel a) an image from Class 5 – Trees, and b) an image from Class 19 – Windows

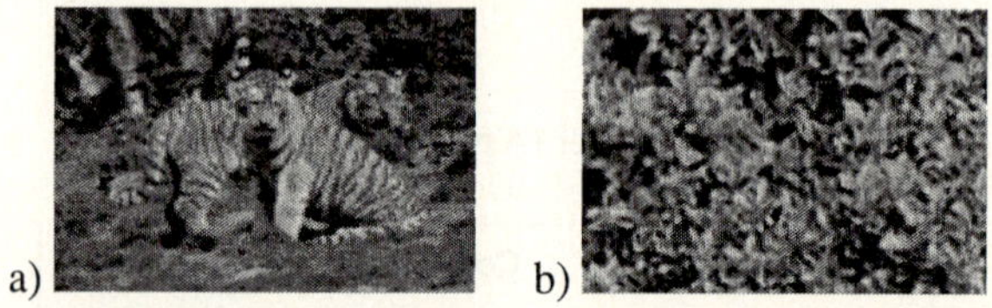

Fig. 8. Examples of misclassification (i.e. similar images) occurred in Value channel a) an image from Class 22 – Mammals, and b) an image from Class 5 – Trees

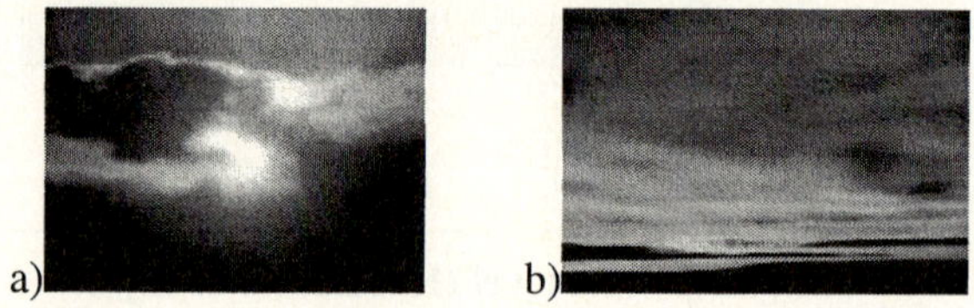

Fig.9. Examples of misclassification (i.e. similar images) occurred in Saturation channel. a) an image from Class 26 – Sky, and b) an image from Class 11 – Sunset.

The main purposes of this work were: 1) first, design a special set of features to be used efficiently as a reduced set of features in image retrieval tasks; 2) evaluate the conditions upon which they could work better and combine the best results in a particular set of features. The first was accomplished with the proposition of a combined set of features based on HSV channels and Mallat decomposition of each channel on approximation, horizontal, and vertical coefficients. A spatial grid, based on 9 regions, to improve localization, and a protocol of experiments using three levels of the decomposition in order to find the most reduced sets were proposed and evaluated. With the best results on those conditions, using 27 different individual sets, we picked the 3 best ones as a useful and efficient reduced set and evaluated the new combined feature. We have found that the new set improved the classification results in the database tested. Those results encourage us to explore further with this feature set, particularly in special purpose image retrieval tasks such as with medical databases, and with feedback relevance schemes where evidence combination together with small sets of features are good characteristics to hold.

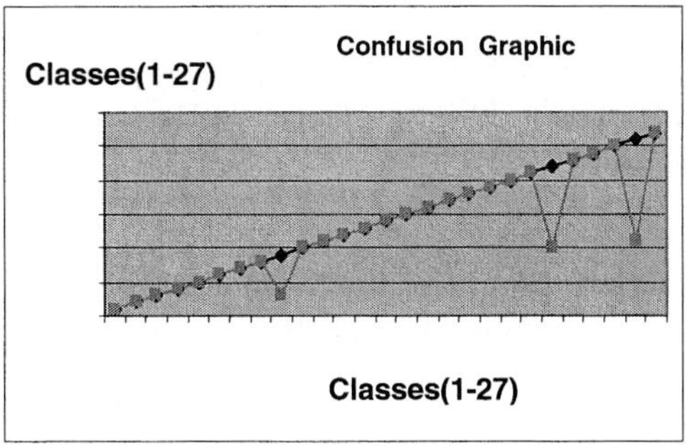

Fig. 10. Confusion graphic: combining the best results (i.e. selected feature set): H, V (approximation coefficients) + S (vertical coefficients), all in the third level of decomposition. (x axis is the class of the query image, and y axis is the result classification obtained).

4 Conclusions

We have presented in this paper an evaluation of a combined set of features to be used in image retrieval tasks. As can be seen from the experiments the combined new feature is an efficient approach to content-based image retrieval that combines color and wavelet coding in a zoning scheme. A set of features is derived from the HSV channels by computing wavelet coefficients in each of them and selecting upon the most significant the ones to index the image. Different than others we did not use global features as moments (e.g. see [1], [2], [6] and [7] for other approaches in image retrieval using wavelet features), but tested to check the combined performance of HSV channels, coarse and detail coefficients in three levels of decomposition using the most significant ones. Extensive testing was done in order to end with only 3 small sets for final similarity measure and rank. One of the difficulties in content-based research is that the databases may have multiple and yet acceptable classifications. Instead of giving only a precision x recall curve we plotted where the misclassifications occurred, considering the voted highest result achieved with all the training set of the images. Of course we do not advocate our approach to be a final word for this, it is still a challenging problem. However we have shown it to be a direct, and generic method (i.e. deal with different types of image classes), and with competitive successful results, not evaluated before, to derive significant features for use in image retrieval. Also, performance measures on a reasonably sized database is given. Although tests were not performed in full using other databases such as Corel, and others with more than 20 thousand images, for the purpose of validating as a useful and reduced set of features the experiments given were meaningful. Future works will deal with relevance feedback for consistent uncertainty treatment [12], special purpose medical databases, and further tests with bigger available databases for benchmarking purposes in image retrieval.

Acknowledgments

This work was partially supported by CAPES/MEC, and CNPq/MCT.

References

[1] E. Albuz, E. Kocalar, ad A. Khokhar," Scalable color image indexing and retrieval using vector wavelets," *IEEE Trans. on Knowledge and Data Eng.*, vol. 13, no. 5, pp. 851-861, Sep. 2001.

[2] Brambilla, C. Ventura, D.A., Gagliardi, I and Schettini R. "Multiresolution Wavelet Transform and Supervised Learning for Content-based Image Retrieval". *IEEE Multimedia Systems 99*, IEEE CS Press, Vol. I, pp. 183-188, 1999.

[3] S.-C. Chen, S. Sista, M.-L. Shyu, and R.L. Kashyap, "An Indexing and Searching Structure for Multimedia Database Systems," IS&T/SPIE Conference on Storage and Retrieval for Media Databases 2000, pp. 262-270, 2000.

[4] Du Buf J.M.H., Kardan M., Spann M. Texture feature performance for image segmentation. *Pattern Recognition*, Vol. 23, pp. 291-309, 1990.

[5] M. Flickner, H. Sawhney, W. Niblack, and J Ashley. Query by image and video content: the qbic system. *IEEE Computer*, 28(9), pp.23--32, Sep. 1995.

[6] Liang, K. and Kuo, C.C. WaveGuide: a joint wavelet-based image representation and description system. *IEEE Transactions on Image Processing*. Vol. 8, n. 11, pp. 1619-1629, 1999.

[7] B. S. Manjunath and W. Y. Ma. Texture features for browsing and retrieval of image data. IEEE Trans. Patt. Anal. Machine Intell., vol.18, pp. 837--842, Aug. 1996.

[8] Rao A.R., Lohse G.L. Identifying High level Features of texture Perception. *CVGIP: Graphic Models and Image Processing*, Vol. 55(3), pp. 218-233, 1993.

[9] Resnikoff, H. and Wells Jr., R. *Wavelet Analysis.* Springer-Verlag, 1998.

[10] Smeulders, A. W.M., Worring, M., Santini, S., Gupta, A., Jain, R. Content-Based Image Retrieval at the End of the Early Years. *IEEE Transactions on Pattern Analysis and Machine Intelligence*. Vol. 22, n. 12, pp. 1349-1380, 2000.

[11] Swain, M. and Ballard, D. Color Indexing. *Int. J. Computer Vision*. Vol. 7, pp. 11-32, 1991.

[12] Yavlinsky, A., Pickering, M., Heesch, D., Ruger, S.: A comparative study of evidence combination strategies. In: *IEEE International Conference on Acoustics, Speech, and Signal Processing*. Volume III, pp 1040—1043, 2004.

Structure in Soccer Videos: Detecting and Classifying Highlights for Automatic Summarization

Ederson Sgarbi[1] and Díbio Leandro Borges[2]

[1] Fundação Faculdades Luiz Meneghel,
Depto. de Informática, Bandeirantes - Pr, Brazil
sgarbi@ffalm.br
[2] BIOSOLO, Goiânia - Go, Brazil
dibio@terra.com.br

Abstract. We propose an automatic framework to detect and classify highlights directly from soccer videos. Sports videos are amongst the most important events for TV transmissions and journalism, however for the purpose of archiving, reuse for sports analysts and coaches, and of main interest to the audience, the considered highlights of the match should be annotated and saved separately. This procedure is done manually by many assistants watching the match from a video. In this paper we develop an automatic framework to perform such a summarization of a soccer video using object-based features. The highlights of a soccer match are defined as shots towards any of the two goal areas, i.e. plays that have already passed the midfield area. Novel algorithms are presented to perform shot classification as long distance shot and others, highlights detection based on object-based features segmentation, and highlights classification for complete summarization of the event. Experiments are reported for complete soccer matches transmitted by TV stations in Brazil, testing for different illumination (day and night), different stadium fields, teams and TV broadcasters.

1 Introduction

With the widespread availability of digital formats for video making, production and TV broadcasting, an important area of technological and scientific interest that has emerged recently is Video Processing. Video Processing is naturally attached to the broad research areas of Computer Vision, Image Processing and Pattern Recognition, although it poses specific challenges concerning domain knowledge and computational resources. Videos are produced as documentaries, news materials, advertisement, movies, shows, TV programs, and sports coverage. Indexing and retrieving such material efficiently require new techniques in content and semantic description, coding and searching unavailable nowadays.

Soccer videos are major products in that industry attracting millions of spectators worldwide. However after a live transmission some plays, or shots of the match carry more interest than others, for example the attacks which came closer

M. Lazo and A. Sanfeliu (Eds.): CIARP 2005, LNCS 3773, pp. 691–700, 2005.

to a goal and of course the goals if any of the two teams scored. Those would be the highlights of the match. Broadcasters have personnel just for producing a logging of a soccer match, which could be then used by analysts in TV programs or as a main source for annotation and further saving in archives. We propose an automatic framework to detect and classify highlights directly from soccer videos. The proposed solution reported here present new algorithms for soccer shot classification, object-based feature segmentation into attack playing fields (i.e. left and right), midfield and stadium audience, and highlights detection and classification. Experiments are shown for more than 7 hours of video, comprising 4 complete matches in different locations, time of playing and teams. More than 94.0 % of the highlights were correctly detected and classified (i.e. recall rate), and the final produced summary is presented with less than 9 min of video instead of the complete 90 min match (i.e. compression rate achieved with summarization is bigger than 90 %).

The following sections of this paper comment on related research found in the literature, present more details of the proposed approach, show and analyze a great deal of experiments in order to evaluate the performance of the system, and draw conclusions about the achievements at this point.

2 Related Works

Sports video summarization research has been a hot topic in the last five years. Reports found in the literature explores sports such as baseball, tennis, and soccer mainly but the list is growing [2]. Worldwide soccer is the main sport attraction, and since a complete match takes more than 90 min, summarizing it including only the highlights is a real necessity for broadcasters and video program makers.

In the literature different features are employed in the attempt to summarize soccer videos. Edges and color are used as features in [4] to detect and recognize the line marks of the field. Motion detection is also used to identify particular camera motion patterns, and along with line marks decide if the scene is part of a highlight or not. The tests shown by the authors use a small number of pre-segmented shots as input and check he correct identification by their system. Their solution rely very much on the line marks detection, and from our experience those features appear occluded and sometimes indistinguishable, especially in shots near the goal area (i.e. highlights) when the players are much closer to each other than in other shots.

A set of fuzzy descriptors is used in [1] to represent and classify the positions of players in the field. Hidden Markov Models are then trained with these descriptors to help identify some subset (penalty, free, and corner kicks) of highlights for classification. Their experiments show only 10 shots pre-segmented for each of the highlights considered and then tested. Tests to show the performance of the players position detection are not given. Identifying the highlights directly from the transmission is a crucial bottleneck in this application, which if not accomplished compromise the whole summarization task.

Other work to use HMMs is [8], however their proposed classification is into "plays" and "breaks" shots only. Motion vectors and color ratios are used as features and a combination of those are trained using HMMs to separate into the two classes: play and break. Their experiments include parts (not complete) of matches and accuracy achieved was around 85 percent. In order to summarize the event a classification into highlights and not only "plays" is necessary.

A combination of color and texture features are used in [6], and [7] in order to identify the players' shirts and track them in a shot. Medium and short distance frames are shown with identification of players with those features. Their proposed system allows tracking of players in a fixed camera situation. From the point of view of a summarization task, classifying highlights, it seems one pre-processing tool yet, because the highlight can not be decided based on these features only.

A summarization soccer system based on cinematic and object-based features is presented in [3]. Color and a spatial ratio mask are used as object-based features in the identification of long, medium and short shots. A cinematic template checking for duration of a break, slow-motion replay and close-ups is a proposed procedure to detect and classify particular events in a match. The events, or the equivalent highlights they propose to detect are: a) goals; b) referee; c) penalty box. Their experiments shown have recall rates of 85.3 % for those mentioned events for 13 hours of soccer video. We argue in this paper that the detection of a referee as an event does not seem to be an interesting highlight of a match, and that their ([3]) penalty box detection relies very much on the line marks and in most attack plays this type of shot is cluttered with players. Actually even that a combination of those events could help identifying a highlight this will be particular to a broadcaster style (e.g. showing a referee in every highlight shot), and the final summary could miss many interesting highlights for not detecting the penalty box.

Our approach presented in this paper addresses those issues, and proposes a complete summarization system for soccer videos based on direct object-based features, and efficient and robust new algorithms for achieving it. We propose to identify highlights as action in the attack fields, not only goals, and we evaluate the performance of the system in more realistic and difficult conditions for 4 complete matches. By more realistic and difficult conditions we mean by using direct transmissions of matches from TV in different stadiums and light (time of the day) conditions. The rest of the paper describe the proposed approach, the experimental protocol, results and conclusions.

3 Structure of a Typical Soccer TV Transmission

Typical transmissions of soccer matches on TV are designed to give a constant view of the main action, close-ups of some shots, and usually when breaks occur some replays. Some broadcasters might even use many different cameras to fill with other viewpoints of the play. Figure.2 shows the three main categories of shots that are used: 1) Long distance shots, 2) Medium distance shots, and 3)

Short distance shots. Important pieces of the game are mostly shown as Long distance shots, since they give a better view of the whole action in a play because the dimensions of the field and number of players in the game.

Semantically we could point two types of plays happening according to developments towards a goal: 1) Action in the midfield, 2) Action in the attack fields (i.e. either right or left). Scoring goals are the main objective of the game, however since it is not so easy to score a goal in soccer highlights of a match will be when the action is placed in the attack fields, i.e. the regions outside the centre circle and closer to the goal areas.

An automatic system to detect and classify the highlights of a soccer video will have to first identify the Long distance shots, then parse the shots as actions in the attack fields (i.e. highlights) and in the midfield. Approaches considering tracking the ball are not robust in practice since it is a very small object in a long distance shot, it is partially occluded in most of the scenes because of the players and marks on the field. Model-based recognition of the goal area using the marks on the field suffer also from the clutter in the scene, and in some fields especially in rainy weather they become indistinguishable.

Our approach will be to propose object-based features to be able to segment the action happening in any of the attack fields, without having to track the ball or follow the marks on the field. As it is shown here with the experiments the solution proved to be very effective and robust to many of the situations encountered in soccer videos.

4 Framework of the Solution Proposed

A functional diagram of the soccer video summarization approach proposed is shown in Figure.1. The video stream is captured from the TV transmission and digitized in color frames, 30 frames per second. The three steps of the approach are: 1) Shot classification, 2) Object-based feature segmentation, 3) Highlights detection and classification. Details of each step are given in the next sections.

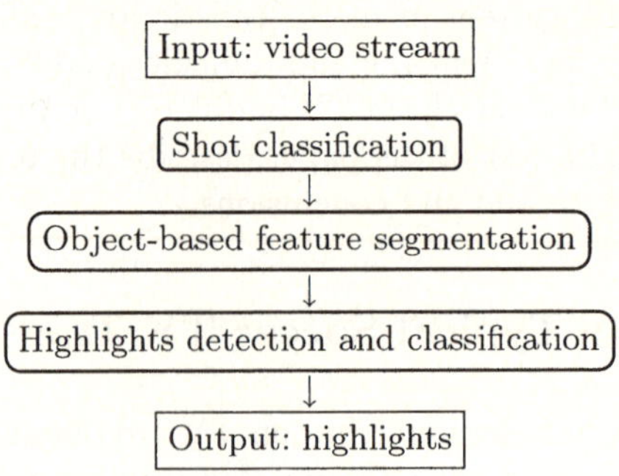

Fig. 1. Main steps of the soccer video summarization approach proposed here

4.1 Shot Classification

Figure 2 shows the three main categories of shots in a soccer video. This step of the approach is aimed to classify the Long distance shots and pass them to the next step of the system. We devise the following algorithm for performing it:

i. Color frame is normalized in RGB, I = (R+G+B)/3;
ii. A histogram is computed for each frame and the dominant bin pixels are selected together with pixels belonging to the 10 % closer bins to the dominant one;
iii. Only frames which have at least 65 % of the pixels selected in the step ii. are picked;
iv. Sequences shorter than 100 frames are classified as Medium distance shots;
v. Sequences longer than 100 frames are classified as Long distance shots;
vi. Other frames which did not pass step iii. above are classified as Short distance shots.

Fig. 2. Three categories of shots commonly found in a soccer TV transmission. (a) Long distance shot, (b) Medium distance shot, (c) Short distance shot.

4.2 Object-Based Feature Segmentation

This step has as input the long distance shots already classified earlier. The aim here will be to design and evaluate object-based features to be able to segment the frames into field and outside areas. Depending upon the concentration of these areas in a frame a decision procedure can be formulated to identify main action in the midfield, or attack fields to the left or to the right.

Upon analyzing the clutter in the long distance shots we devised the following procedure to perform segmentation into either field, or outside areas:

i. Find edges in the image (e.g. Marr-Hildreth filter);
ii. Place a grid of 16x16 cells upon the edge image;
iii. Try to fit a line in each cell by doing a Principal Components Analysis on their values;
iv. Cells will be marked either as "clutter", or "lines" depending on the residuals of the fits ([5]);

v. By checking neighboring cells for region consistency, clean (i.e erase) isolated cells marked as "clutter";

Figure.3 shows snapshots of this step of the approach. This step is performed on each frame of the sequence classified as long distance. Two consistent main regions are given as output of this stage, Figure 3.d) shows an example of the this output.

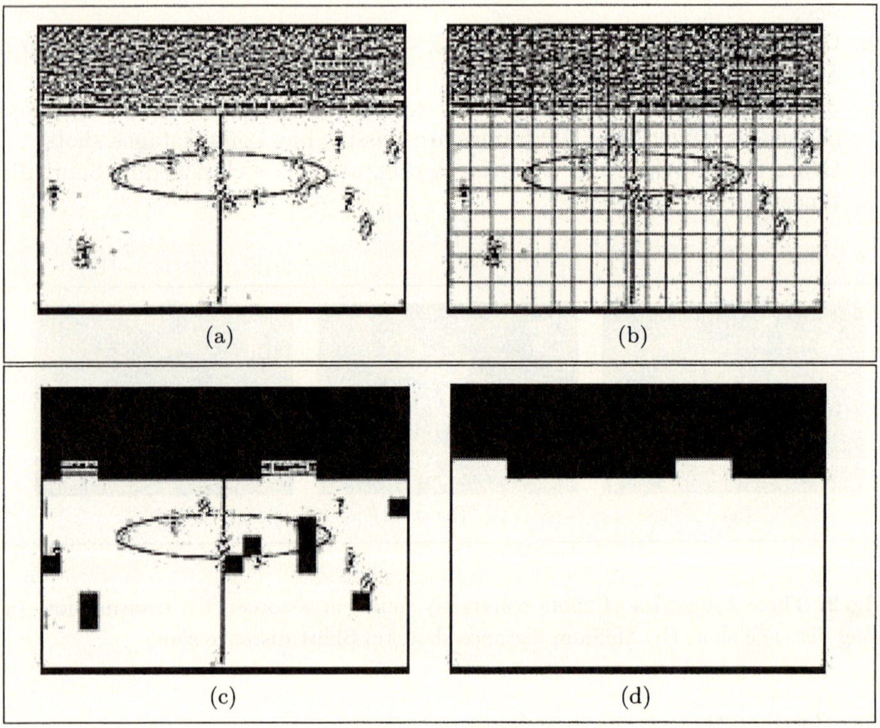

Fig. 3. Typical outputs of the object-based feature segmentation steps. (a) After the binarization, (b) With the grid superimposed to compute the eigenvalues, (c) After the decision on each window about a significant direction, (d) Result after cleaning inconsistent regions.

4.3 Highlights Detection and Classification

The final stage of the approach consists of the decision on highlights detection and classification based on the consistent regions given from the earlier step. The following algorithm performs this stage:

i. Place a 4x4 grid on the two consistent regions image given as input;
ii. Compute the density of black regions on the 16 cells of the grid;

iii. Higher density on the right side cells is classified as "highlight (attack on the right)";
iv. Higher density on the left side cells is classified as "highlight (attack on the left)";
v. Equal or higher density on the middle cells is classified as "not highlight";

Figure.4 shows snapshots of the final highlight classification, from image still with inconsistent regions (4.(a)), after cleaning inconsistent regions (4.(b)), and with grid for density computation placed upon it (4.(c)). The final classification of this example is "highlight (attack on the right)".

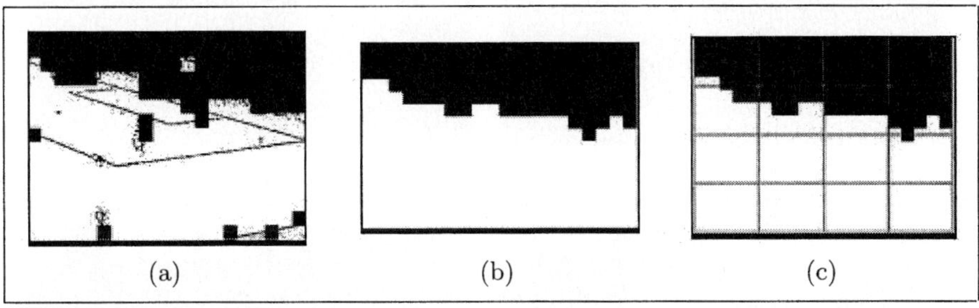

Fig. 4. Three steps on a shot detection and classification. (a) Region classification output before cleaning for inconsistent regions, (b) Final detection for classification, (c) Grid used for classification of highlight, showing an attack to the right.

Next section shows experiments performed for evaluating the approach presented here.

5 Experiments

Some of the works found in the literature of soccer video summarization rely either on the detection of the marks of field, or on cinematic features for processing motion. As we mentioned earlier in this paper those features are not robust in practice, since in most of the TV soccer transmissions (see Figure.5 for example shots) the marks on the field are difficult to recognize with efficiency necessary to perform such a task. On the other hand cinematic features are expensive to compute, and it brings too much burden in this task since 30 frames per second is the acquisition rate to process. The time when the match is played, the Stadium, i.e. the grass conditions of the field, the teams and the transmissions produced by different broadcasters pose realistic conditions to evaluate the approach. Figure.5 shows snapshots of soccer games to illustrate some of these conditions. In order to evaluate the approach proposed here we acquired four (4) complete soccer matches from TV transmissions in different situations: 1) Match G1 "Brazil x Chile", played at night, Conception Stadium, Chile (2004);

2) Match G2 "Figueirense x Flamengo", played at afternoon, O.Scarpelli Stadium, Brazil (2004); 3) Match G3 "Atletico(PR) x Botafogo(RJ)", played at afternoon, J.Americo Stadium, Brazil (2004); 4) Match G4 "Santos x Vasco", played at afternoon, B.Teixeira Stadium, Brazil (2004).

Fig. 5. Shots of four different soccer matches showing different situations to deal with. (a) and (b) are from matches at night, (c) and (d) during the day. All of them are set in different fields (stadiums).

Table.1 shows the compression rates achieved with the summarization approach proposed here for the different soccer matches mentioned G1, G2, G3, and G4. The number of highlights varies of course from match to match, however by detecting the highlights automatically only this information will be handled by TV program editors and placed for further annotation and indexing. The saving in time and computational resources is considerable since the average compression rate is 90.8 % for the 4 matches.

In order to have a ground truth for evaluating the performance of the system we annotated manually every shot in the 4 matches. Table.2 gives the results considering the expected input highlights from the ground truth. It is important to notice in this area that a false detection of a highlight is not of major concern

Table 1. Compression achieved by the soccer highlights detection algorithm in four (4) different games captured from TV transmissions. Data was acquired in full resolution, color, 30 frames per second.

	Input Frames	Highlights	Compression
G1	169200	8035	95.3 %
G2	166074	25958	84.4 %
G3	171513	16792	90.2 %
G4	168455	11611	93.1 %
TOTAL	**675242**	**62396**	**90.8 %**

since they are to be passed to indexing and those could be cleared out. The recall rate, the relative success in detecting the expected highlights is of greater importance. On average the recall rate presented here is 94.6 %. Other works from the literature ([1,3,4]) report recall rates of less than 80 %. Although the test data are not the same we have used similar input size (4 matches), but in much harder conditions such as the field conditions and time of the play.

Table 2. Compression achieved by the soccer highlights detection algorithm in four (4) different games captured from TV transmissions. Data was acquired in full resolution, color, 30 frames per second.

	G1	G2	G3	G4	TOTAL
Input Highlights	190	463	280	280	**1213**
Correct	182	447	263	258	**1150**
Missed	8	19	17	22	**66**
False	82	100	157	169	**508**
Precision	68.9 %	81.7 %	62.6 %	61.4 %	**69.4 %**
Recall	**95.8 %**	**95.9 %**	**94.0 %**	**92.1 %**	**94.6 %**

By analyzing the results we could notice that many of the False highlights detected were due to some texts and logos appearing on the screen during the transmissions. They are usually placed by the broadcasters on either side of the screen cluttering the scene nearby the considered attack fields by the algorithm. Regarding the highlights missed by the system they were mainly due to sudden change of cameras during transmission, cutting from a long distance shot to either medium or short ones. Not many broadcasters use this, and the missed ones were below 5 %, however it would be a point to explore further with more experiments.

6 Conclusions and Future Works

In this paper we have presented an automatic system to detect and classify highlights of soccer videos. A complete summary of the match is achieved making it possible for practical use for annotation, indexing, and video retrieval. We have set a test protocol which includes more than 7 hours of soccer video, i.e. 4 complete matches, with a great variety of circumstances to evaluate the system performance. The summaries obtained produced a compression of 90.8 % from the input data, and a recall rate for the highlights of 94.6 %. This is a higher rate than others seen in the literature [3]. The successful results in such conditions allow us to explore realistic further possibilities of a fully automated soccer video summarization. The missed highlights and the false detected ones from our experiments were mapped to other features to be explored in future work, they are the text and logos appearing during transmission that should be dealt with, and sudden change of cameras in some shots. We are exploring these research lines in our group.

Video processing is an area of growing demand in research and development nowadays. It is a truly research area of Computer Vision and Pattern Recognition with well defined domains shaped with data available and industry demands. The work presented here could be extended to other sports videos as well, since as it was shown exploration of the knowledge of the game is important to predict where the main action will be happening.

References

1. J. Assfalg, M. Bertini, A. Del Bimbo, W. Nunziati, and P. Pala. Soccer highlights detection and recognition using HMMs. In *Proc. IEEE Int. Conf. Mult. and Expo. (ICME)*, pages 825-828, 2002.
2. S. Chang. The holy grail of content-based media analysis. *IEEE Multimedia*, vol.9, pages 957-962, June 2002.
3. A. Eking, A.Tekalp, and R. Mehrotra. Automatic soccer video analysis and summarization. *IEEE Transactions on Image Processing.* vol.12, n.7, pages 796-807, July 2003.
4. Y. Gong, L.T. Sin, C.H. Chuan, H.J. Zhang, and M. Sakauchi. Automatic parsing of TV soccer programs. In *Proc. IEEE Int. Conf. Mult. Comput. Systems*, pages 167-174, 1995.
5. F. Szenberg. *Acompanhamento de cenas com calibração automática de câmeras.* Doctorate Thesis (in Portuguese), Departamento de Informática, PUC-Rio, Rio de Janeiro, Brasil, 2001.
6. N. Vandenbroucke, L. Macaire, C. Vieren, and J. Postaire. Contribution of a color classification to soccer players tracking with snakes. In *Proc. IEEE Int. Conf. Systems, Man, and Cybernetics*, pages 3660-3665, 1997.
7. N. Vandenbroucke, L. Macaire, and J. Postaire. Color image segmentation by pixel classification in an adapted hybrid color space. An application to soccer image analysis. *Computer Vision and Image Understanding.* vol. 90, pages 190-216, 2003.
8. L. Xie, S.F. Chang, A. Divakaran, and H. Sun. Structure analysis of soccer video with Hidden Markov Models. In *Proc. IEEE Int. Conf. Acoustics, Speech, and Signal Processing (ICASSP).* pages 4096-4099, 2002.

Multiscale Vessel Segmentation: A Level Set Approach

Gang Yu, Yalin Miao, Peng Li, and Zhengzhong Bian

School of Life Science and Technology, Xi'an Jiaotong University,
710049 Xi'an, China
yugang@mailst.xjtu.edu.cn

Abstract. This paper presents a novel efficient multiscale vessel segmentation method using the level-set framework. This technique is based on the active contour model that evolves according to the geometric measure of vessel structures. Inspired by the multiscale vessel enhancement filtering, the prior knowledge about the vessel shape is incorporated into the energy function as a region information term. In this method, a new region-based external force is combined with existing geometric snake variation models. A new speed function is designed to precisely control the curve deformation. This multiscale method is more efficient for the segmentation of vessel and line-like structures than the conventional active contour methods. Furthermore, the whole model is implemented in a level-set framework. The solution is stable and robust for various topologic changes. This method was compared with other geometric active contour models. Experimental results of human lung CT images show that this multiscale method is accurate.

1 Introduction

Many diseases are accompanied with the change of vessel shape. Analysis of the vessels that helps identify early features of pathological changes plays an important role in medical diagnosis. Moreover, the vessel segmentation provides a tool to understand the relation between vessels and diseases. Vessel segmentation is an important area in medical image processing.

Early approaches for vessel segmentation include matched filter method [1] and morphological method [2]. In these approaches, all the pixels of the vessels in these approaches should be detected before the whole line shape structures are captured. However, detection accuracy and validity of post processing is always considered, especially for noise or low contrast images. T-snakes method for vessel segmentation was firstly provided in Reference 3, which is topology adaptive, but companied with extensive computational cost. Recently, active contour models [5][7][8][9][10] have become effective tools for extraction of region of interests (ROI), which were widely investigated for overcoming the limitations of traditional methods. Sethian *et al* first introduced the level set method into active contour models for numerical implementation [4]. Reference 5 applied level-set-based active contour methods to vessels extraction, whose corresponding curve evolution is controlled by gradient information. The evolution can be implemented by FastMarching algorithm, because all the speed in the image is defined as the positive or negative speed fields. The following boundary-based approaches added the curvature term and advection term to evolution equation

M. Lazo and A. Sanfeliu (Eds.): CIARP 2005, LNCS 3773, pp. 701 – 709, 2005.

for smoothing the curve and driving the front into the desired boundary. These investigations may improve the segmentation results. However, they are difficult to evolve accurately in weak edge or noise images. Moreover, Most of the methods are sensitive to the initial condition. Region-based methods are more suitable for vessel segmentation because the whole region information, not only boundary gradient information, is considered. Early region-based method is markov random fields-based approach. Recently, many region-based active contour models were presented. Yezzi presented a global approach for image segmentation [8], but it brings too extensive computational cost. The geodesic active region model presented by Nikos [7], who integrates boundary-based with region-based active contour approaches, is more effective region-based snake segmentation methods, because prior knowledge about ROI is introduced.

The important problems in the region-based approaches include the design of region-based models and the combination with the snake energy minimization framework. In this paper, a level-set-based method for vessel segmentation is presented. This method is inspired by multiscale vessel enhancement filtering. The measure of vessel structure as posterior probability estimation is introduced into the energy function. This method is combined with boundary-based snake framework and implemented by level set method. Experimental results on different medical vessel images segmentation demonstrate the performance of the proposed model.

The remainder of the paper is organized as follows. In section 2, a multiscale vessel enhancement method is briefly introduced; in section 3, the proposed energy function is described and the new level set evolution equation is developed; in section 4, experiments on vessels extraction are presented and compared with that of the existing active contour models; finally in section 5, conclusions are reported.

2 Multiscale Vessel Enhancement Filtering

The multiscale vessel enhancement filtering was first presented in Reference 6. The filter depends on the eigenvalues $\lambda_{\sigma,k}\ (k=1,2,3)$ of the Hessian Matrix of the second order image structure. The eigenvectors express three orthonormal directions: $u_{\sigma,1}$ indicates minimum intensity variation, i.e. the direction along the vessel; The ideal tubular structure in a 3D image is: $|\lambda_{\sigma,1}| \approx 0, |\lambda_{\sigma,1}| << |\lambda_{\sigma,2}|, \lambda_{\sigma,2} \approx \lambda_{\sigma,3}$. Two basic ratios and a measure for distinguishing background are defined as:

$$R_B = \frac{\dfrac{\text{Volume}}{(4\pi/3)}}{\left(\dfrac{\text{Largest Cross Section Area}}{\pi}\right)^{\frac{3}{2}}} = \frac{|\lambda_1|}{\sqrt{|\lambda_1 \lambda_2|}}$$

$$R_A = \frac{\dfrac{\text{Largest Cross Section Area}}{\pi}}{(\text{Largest Axis SemiLength})^2} = \frac{|\lambda_2|}{|\lambda_3|}$$

$$S = \|H\|_F = \sqrt{\sum_{j \le D} \lambda_j^2}$$

The first ratio accounts for the deviation from a blob-like structure but cannot distinguish between a line- and a plate-like pattern. The second ratio refers to the largest area cross section of the ellipsoid (in the plane orthogonal to $u_{\sigma,1}$). It is essential for distinguishing between plate-like and line-like structures since only in the latter case it will be zero. The final measure will be low in the background where no structure is present and the eigenvalues are small. The whole vessel-enhancement filter $\nu(x,\sigma)$ at location x and at scale σ is defined as:

$$\nu(x,\sigma) = \begin{cases} 0 & \text{if } \lambda_2 > 0 \text{ or } \lambda_3 > 0 \\ (1-\exp(-\frac{R_A^{\ 2}}{2\alpha^2}))\exp(-\frac{R_B^2}{2\beta^2})(1-\exp(-\frac{S^2}{2c^2})) & \end{cases} \quad (1)$$

The parameters α, β, c are thresholds, which control the sensitivity of the line filter to the measures. Especially, for 2D images, the following vesselness measure can be proposed:

$$v(x,\sigma) = \begin{cases} 0 & \text{if } \lambda_2 > 0 \\ \exp(-\frac{R_B^2}{2\beta^2})(1-\exp(-\frac{S^2}{2c^2})) & \end{cases} \quad (2)$$

The filter is applied at multiple scales that span the range of expected vessel widths according to the imaged anatomy. Multiscale filter is also helpful to improve segmentation in the noise image. The vesselness measure is provided by the filter responses at different scales to obtain a final estimate of vesselness or vessel probability:

$$\nu(x) = \max_{\sigma_{\min} \le \sigma \le \sigma_{\max}} \nu(\sigma, x)$$

Obviously, $\nu(x)$ is between 0 and 1. Equation (1) is given for bright curvilinear structures (MRA and CTA). For dark objects (as in DSA), the conditions (or the images) should be reversed.

3 Vessel Region Information Function and Evolution Equation

3.1 Vessel Region Information Function

The image segmentation can be viewed as an optimization problem with respect to a posteriori partition probability. Usually, the posteriori probability density function is given according to prior probability by the Bayes rule. The vesselness measure is maximal at the center of the vessel and decreases to zero at the vessel boundaries, which is suitable to be used as the vessel probability estimation. For example, if the vesselness measure of a pixel is closer to 1, it is likely that the pixel is in the vessels. Therefore, we define the vessel region information function as:

$$P(I(x)) = \begin{cases} 1 & if\ v(x) \geq a \\ v(x) & if v(x) < a\ and\ v(x) \geq b \\ -(1-v(x)) & if v(x) < b \end{cases} \quad (3)$$

Where $a, b \in [0,1], I(x)$ is the image intensity. a, b are thresholds, which control the sensitivity of region information function. $a = 0.5, b = 0.2$ have proven to be work well in most cases. $P(I(x))$ is a piecewise function, whose values range [-1,1]. When its value is 1 or close to 1, the voxel should be a point in vessels. When its value is much smaller than 1, the voxel may be in or out of vessel. When the value of $P(I(x))$ is negative, the voxel is out of vessels. Moreover, the smaller the function value, the smaller the vessel probability density function. Therefore, $P(I(x))$ is equal to an efficient estimation of the vessel probability density function, which applies not only vessel intensity information, but also the whole line-like structure information of vessels.

3.2 Energy Function and Speed Function

The new vessel region information energy function in 3D space is presented as:

$$E_{vessel} = -\iint_R p(I(x,y,z))dxdydz \quad (4)$$

Where R is the interior fields of the curve (2D) or surface(3D). The integral in equation (4) is to find the boundary of R where E_{vessel} is minimized. The straightforward understanding to the equation is that the boundary of curve or surface should include voxels in the vessels as many as possible. Moreover, E_{vessel} is a region-based energy function and not sensitive to the initial condition.

Integrate it with boundary-based energy function; the whole energy function is described as:

$$E = \alpha E_{vessel} + (1-\alpha)E_{Boundary} \quad (5)$$

where $\alpha \in [0,1]$.

In this paper, we choose geodesic active contour as boundary information energy. It is defined as:

$$E = \alpha E_{vessel} + (1-\alpha)\int_0^1 g\{|\nabla I(C)|\}|C'(p)|dp \quad (6)$$

According to variational theory and gradient descent method, through minimizing E_{vessel}, we can acquire its evolution equation. It is presents as:

$$\frac{\partial C}{\partial t} = p(I(x,y,z)) \cdot \vec{N} \quad (7)$$

Where $\vec{N}$ is the outer normal vector of the curve or surface. When the curve is in the vessels, the vesselness measure is biggish. Therefore, the evolution speed is equal or close to 1, which creates a large expansible force to make the convergence more rapid. When the curve is out of the vessel, the evolution speed is close to -1, which makes the curve shrink rapidly. In other cases, both vessel force and boundary force control the curve evolution.

Reference 11 presented the evolution equation of geodesic active contour. The geodesic active contour evolution model is:

$$\frac{\partial C}{\partial t} = g(|\nabla I|)(c_1 + c_2 k) \cdot \vec{N} - (\nabla g(|\nabla I|) \cdot \vec{N}) \cdot \vec{N} \tag{8}$$

Where k is the curvature of curve, c_1, c_2 is parameters.

From equation (5), (7) and (8), the final speed function is defined as:

$$\frac{\partial C}{\partial t} = \alpha \times p(I(x,y,z)) \cdot \vec{N} + (1-\alpha) \left\{ g(|\nabla I|)(c_1 + c_2 k) \cdot \vec{N} - (\nabla g(|\nabla I|) \cdot \vec{N}) \cdot \vec{N} \right\} \tag{9}$$

3.3 Evolution Equation in Level Set Framework

Assume that the curve C is a level set of a function of $u:[0,a]\times[0,b] \to R$. That is, C coincides with the set of points $u =$ constant ($e.g.\, u = 0$). u is therefore an implicit representation of the curve C. This representation is parameter free, then intrinsic.

If the planar curve C evolves according to

$$\frac{\partial c}{\partial t} = \beta \vec{N}$$

for a given speed function β, then the embedding function u should deform according to

$$\frac{\partial u}{\partial t} = \beta |\nabla u|$$

By embedding the evolution of C in that of u, topological changes of C are handled automatically and accuracy and stability are achieved using the proper numerical algorithm.

Because $\vec{N} = \frac{\nabla u}{|\nabla u|}$, from level set theory, the level set evolution equation is:

$$\frac{\partial u}{\partial t} = \alpha \times p(I(x,y,z)) \cdot |\nabla u| + (1-\alpha) \left\{ g(|\nabla I|)(c_1 + c_2 k) \cdot |\nabla u| - (\nabla g(|\nabla I|) \cdot \vec{N}) \cdot |\nabla u| \right\} \tag{10}$$

Where $k = div(\frac{\nabla u}{|\nabla u|})$.

Equation (10) is the final curve evolution equation, which can be implemented by level set method.

4 Experiments and Results

To demonstrate our vessel segmentation model, the proposed level set evolution equation (10) for vessel extraction is compared with other three conventional methods.

Experiment1: geodesic active contour model presented by reference 11:

$$\frac{\partial C}{\partial t} = g(|\nabla I|)(c_1 + c_2 k)\cdot \vec{N} - (\nabla g(|\nabla I|)\cdot \vec{N})\cdot \vec{N}$$

In the following experiment, $c_1 = 1, c_2 = -0.1$. The values of c_1 and c_2 can work well in most images [11].

Experiment2: The evolution equation presented by Malladi[5]:

$$\frac{\partial C}{\partial t} = g(|\nabla I|)\cdot (c_1 - c_2 k) - \beta(\nabla P \cdot \vec{N})\cdot \vec{N}$$

Where $P = -|\nabla G * I|, \vec{N}$ is outer normal vector. In the following experiment, $c_1 = 1, c_2 = 0.1, \beta = 0.1$. The values of parameters have proven to work in most cases.

Experiment3: fully global approach presented by Yezzi[8]:

$$\frac{\partial C}{\partial t} = (u - v)\cdot (\frac{I-u}{A_u} + \frac{I-v}{A_v})\cdot \vec{N} - \beta \cdot k \cdot \vec{N}$$

Where u, v is the average of interior or exterior intensity of curve, A_u, A_v is interior and exterior area. We set $\beta = 0.1$ in the experiment.

Experiment4: the proposed model in this paper:

$$\frac{\partial u}{\partial t} = \alpha \times p(I(x,y,z))\cdot |\nabla u| + (1-\alpha)$$
$$\left\{g(|\nabla I|)(c_1 + c_2 k)\cdot |\nabla u| - (\nabla g(|\nabla I|)\cdot \vec{N})\cdot |\nabla u|\right\}$$

Where the best results are obtained for $\alpha = 0.6, c_1 = 1, c_2 = -0.1$. In most cases, α should be bigger than 0.5, because the vesselness measure is more efficient than gradient information in noise images. Moreover, the selection of big α makes the segmentation result not sensitive to the initial condition. The selection of c_1 and c_2 is similar to the first experiment.

In the following experiment, we present some segmentation results of 2D medical vessel image. All the methods can be extended to 3D medical image because they are implemented in level set framework. The medical image is pulmonary vessels selected from CT image. The obtained image is low contrast and accompanied by random noise, where many branches are blurry and discontinuous intensity. The first column shows the initial seed curves; the second and the third column show the random middle state of the curves; the fourth column shows the final segmentation result.

Fig1(a)~1(d) are the results of geodesic active contours model, where the big vessel branches can be extracted successfully. However, many narrow or blurry branches fail to be captured because the boundary-based information in these branches is too weak. The results of experiment 2 are Fig2(a)~2(d). Like geodesic active contour model, the only edge-based information is too weak to propagate the front in thin branches. Meanwhile, the boundary-based model is sensitive to the initial condition and all the seeds have to be set nearby branches. Another problem in these approaches is the curves are easy to leak out of weak edges if the improper parameters are selected.

Fig3(a)~3(d) are the results of Yezzi's model. It is not sensitive to the initial condition and all the seeds are set at random. Because it only uses the global intensity information in the evolution equation, many low contrast pixels in vessels are excluded from ROI. Therefore, the result of the experiment is not satisfactory. Fig3 (d) shows the final result, where many thin branches are not captured successfully. Fig4(a)~4(d) are the results of the proposed model in this paper, where the vessels especially narrow thin branches can be extracted successfully. Moreover, many blurry and even broken branches can be captured and connected automatically. Meanwhile, although the intensity of many branches is discontinuous, the vessel region information function is also effective to find them. Fig4(d) shows the final result, which demonstrates the performance of our approach.

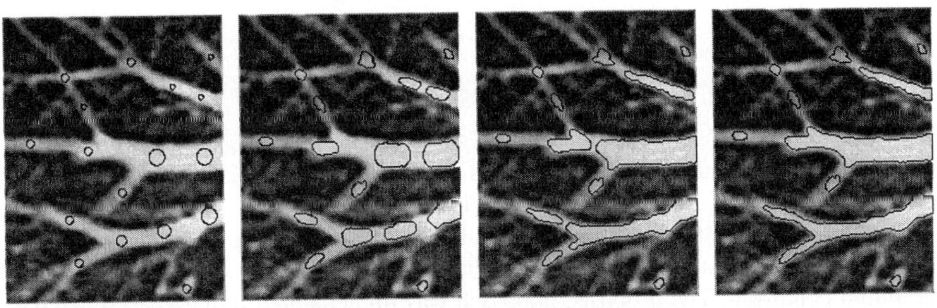

Fig. 1. Geodesic active contour. From left to right, Fig1(a) , Fig1 (b), Fig1 (c), Fig1 (d).

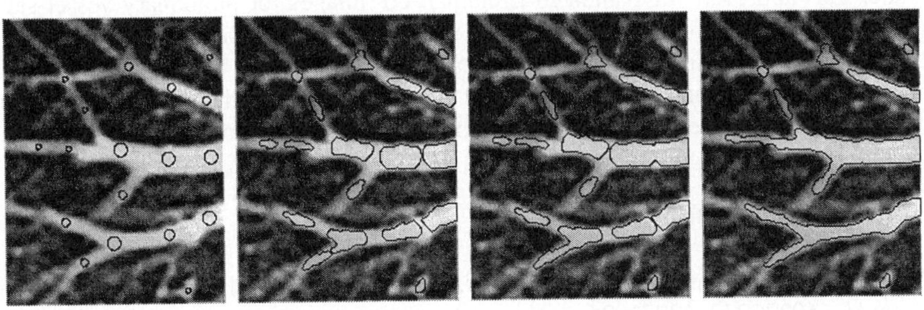

Fig. 2. Malladi's model. From left to right, Fig2(a) , Fig2 (b), Fig2 (c), Fig2 (d).

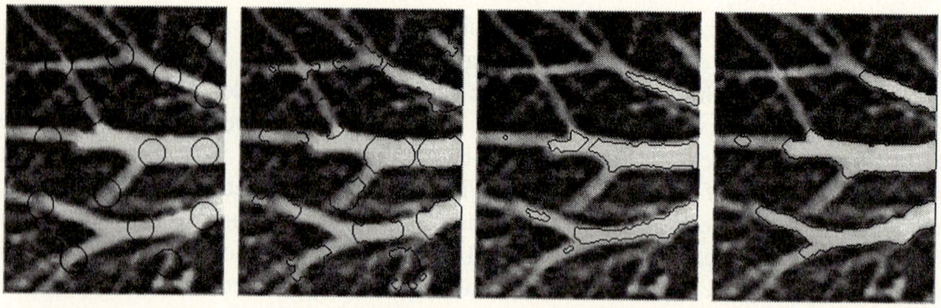

Fig. 3. Yezzi's model. From left to right, Fig3(a) , Fig3 (b), Fig3 (c), Fig3 (d).

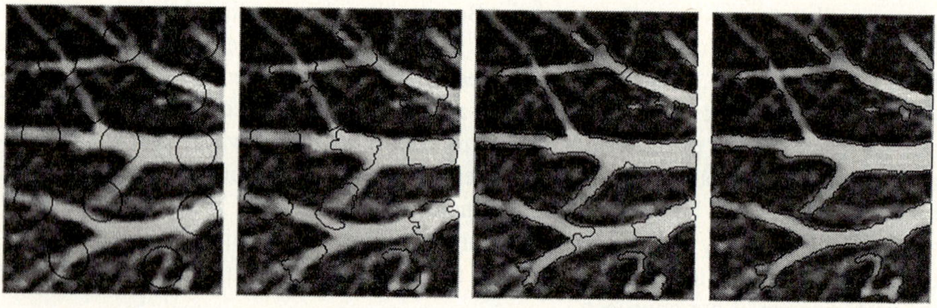

Fig. 4. The proposed model in this paper. From left to right, Fig4(a) , Fig4 (b), Fig4 (c), Fig4 (d).

5 Conclusion

In this paper, we proposed a novel efficient multiscale vessel segmentation method that is based on the curve evolution. In this method, a new regional information function was designed to integrate the multiscale enhancement filter. A new curve evolution model was incorporated with the edge-based speed function. This method is efficient for the segmentation of vessel and other line-like structures. It is not sensitive to the initial condition. The proposed approach was implemented in the level set framework and is suitable for various topologic changes. Moreover, it can be easily extended to 3D images because the multiscale enhancement filter works well in 3D space. This approach was validated in human CT images for pulmonary vessel segmentation. Experiments showed that the new method performs better than the conventional snake models for the segmentation of narrow thin vessel branches. It can automatically analyze line-like structures and works well even when the branches are darker or blurrier. The proposed approach in this paper is very promising.

Acknowledgement

The paper is supported by the National Natural Science Foundation of China under Grant No. 60271022, 60271025.

References

1. Chaudhuri S., Chatterjee S., Katz N., Nelson M., Goldbaum M.: Detection of blood vessels in retinal images using two dimensional matched filters. IEEE Transactions on Medical Imaging 8 (1989) 13-18
2. Thackray B.D., Nelson A.C.: Semi-automatic segmentation of vascular network images using a rotating structuring element (ROSE) with mathematical morphology and dual feature thresholding. IEEE Transactions on Medical Imaging 12(1993) 3-22
3. McInerney T., Terzopou los D.: Snakes T: Topology adaptive snakes. Medical Image Analysis 4(2000)73-91
4. Sechian J.A.: Level Set Methods and Fast Marching Methods. Cambridge University Press, (1999)
5. Malladi R., Sethian J.A., Vemuri B.C.: Shape modeling with front propagation: a level set approach. IEEE Transact ions on Pattern Analysis and Machine Intelligence 17(1995) 2-25
6. Frangi A.F., Niessen W.J., Vincken K.L, Viergever M.A.: Multiscale vessel enhancement filtering. Lecture Notes in Computer Science vol 1496, (1998)130-137.
7. Nikos P.: Geodesic active regions: a new framework to deal with frame partition problems in computer vision. Journal of Visual Communication and Image Representation 13(2002) 249-268.
8. Anthony Yezzi Jr., Andy T., Alan W.: A fully global approach to image segmentation via coupled curve evolution equations. Journal of Visual Communication and Image Representation 13 (2002) 195–216
9. Pascal M., Philippe R., Francois G., Prederic G.: Influence of the noise model on level set active contour segmentation. IEEE Transactions on Pattern Analysis and Machine Intelligence Vol26,No 6(2004)799-803.
10. Ali G., Raphael C.: A new fast level set method. Proceedings of the 6 the Signal Processing Symposium (2004)232-235.
11. Caselles V., Kimmel R., Spairo G.: Geodesic active contours. International journal of Computer Vision 22(1997)61-79.

Quantified and Perceived Unevenness of Solid Printed Areas

Albert Sadovnikov, Lasse Lensu,
Joni-Kristian Kamarainen, and Heikki Kälviäinen

Laboratory of Information Processing, Department of Information Technology,
Lappeenranta University of Technology, P.O.Box 20, 53851 Lappeenranta, Finland
{sadovnik, ltl, jkamarai, kalviai}@lut.fi

Abstract. Mottling is one of the most severe printing defects in modern offset printing using coated papers. It can be defined as undesired unevenness in perceived print density. In our studies, we have implemented two methods known from the literature to quantify print mottle: the standard method for prints from office equipment and the bandpass method specially designed for mottling. Our goal was to study the performance of the methods when compared to human perception. For comparisons, we used a test set of 20 grey samples which were assessed by professional and non-professional people, and the artificial methods. The results show that the bandpass method can be used to quantify mottling of grey samples with a reasonable accuracy. However, we propose a modification to the bandpass method. The enhanced bandpass method utilizes a contrast sensitivity function for the human visual system directly in the frequency domain and the function parameters are optimized based on the human assessment. This results a significant improvement in the correlation to human assessment when compared to the original bandpass method.

1 Introduction

Print quality is an essential attribute when modern printing processes are considered. This is because an increasing proportion of data to be printed are images. If the original of a print is assumed to be ideal, print quality depends on the printability of paper, printing inks, and printing process. Despite major improvements in the before-mentioned factors affecting the quality, there are several undesired effects in prints. One of the most severe defects is mottling which is the uneven appearance of solid printed areas. It is related to density and gloss of print, and it is caused by non-ideal interactions of paper and ink in high-speed printing processes. There are three types of mottling depending on the cause for this defect: back-trap mottle, water-interface mottle, and ink-trap mottle. The causes for these forms of mottling are uneven ink absorption in the paper, insufficient and uneven water absorption of the paper, and incorrect trapping of the ink because of tack, respectively [1]. However, a thorough explanation to this phenomenon is still missing.

M. Lazo and A. Sanfeliu (Eds.): CIARP 2005, LNCS 3773, pp. 710–719, 2005.

Mottling can be defined as undesired unevenness in perceived print density, or more technically as "aperiodic fluctuations of density at a spatial frequency less than 0.4 cycles per millimeter in all directions" [2]. When printing defects are of concern, mottling is generally considered as a stochastic phenomenon. Depending on the cause, however, print unevenness can include several forms of regularity. For example, a regular drift in the printing process causes macro-scale noise in print, whereas structures in the paper formation are random in nature and cause micro-scale noise.

A few methods to quantify mottling by a machine vision system have been proposed. The ISO 13660 standard includes a method for monochrome images. The method is based on computing the standard deviation of small tiles within a larger area [2]. In the standard, the size of the tiles is set to a fixed value, which is a known limitation [3]. The standard method has been improved by using tiles of variable sizes [4]. Other methods relying on clustering, statistics, and wavelets have also been proposed to quantify mottling [5,6,7]. Other approaches to evaluate greyscale mottling have their basis in frequency-domain filtering [8], and frequency analysis [9]. All of the before-mentioned methods are designed for binary or greyscale images. If colour prints were assessed, the performance of the methods would be limited when compared to human assessments.

It is possible to define mottling by using mathematical or physical terms. However, mottling is implicitly related to human perception: If a person looking at a solid print perceives unevenness, mottling is considered as a defect. Thus, a strict definition based on the quantitative sciences can prove to be insufficient. This is why the properties and limits of the human visual system (HVS) must be taken into account in the design of proper methods to quantify mottling. Sensitivity of the HVS to contrast and spatial frequencies of noise in images is independent of luminance within common luminance levels [10]. However, the contrast sensitivity depends on the spatial frequency [11], thus, mottles of different sizes are perceived differently. The peak sensitivity of the HVS is approximately at 3 cycles/degree, and the maximum detected frequency is from 40 cycles/degree (sinusoidal gratings) [12] to over 100 cycles/degree (single cycle) [13].

The purpose of our work was to implement study artificial methods to quantify mottling, and compare the method results to evaluations by humans. Since the grounds of the selected methods are not directly in vision science, we propose a modification to the method which is superior based on the comparison. The modification is in accordance with the psychophysical studies in vision science, and it utilizes the frequency information of the sample images directly.

2 Methods

To study the possibilities of machine vision, we implemented two methods to quantify print mottle: the standard method to assess image quality of printer systems [2], and the bandpass method [8]. The third method described in this work is a modification of the bandpass method accommodating an appropriate contrast sensitivity function (CSF) for the HVS.

2.1 Standard Method

ISO 13660 standard is designed for assessing print quality of office equipment that produce monochrome prints [2]. The attributes of print density for large print areas include graininess and mottling. In the standard, a fixed value has been chosen to separate this two forms of print unevenness. Aperiodic fluctuations of print density at spatial frequencies higher than 0.4 cycles/degree are considered as graininess, whereas frequencies lower than 0.4 cycles/degree are mottling. The standard method is presented in Algorithm 1.

Algorithm 1 *Standard method*

1: Divide the region of interest into tiles.
2: Compute the mean densities within each tile.
3: Compute the standard deviation of the means as the measure of mottling.

The region of interest must be larger than 21.2 mm squared, and it is divided into tiles of size 1.27 mm squared. Within each tile, 900 independent measurements of density are made.

2.2 Bandpass Method

The method is based on applying a set of Gaussian bandpass filters to the image in the frequency domain. The coefficient of variation of reflectance (CV_R) for each spatial image representing a frequency band is computed. Different coefficients represent the variation of reflectance within each band [8]. The coefficients are weighted with the CSF and then summed together as the mottling index. The method is described in Algorithm 2.

Algorithm 2 *Bandpass method*

1: Filter the image with a set of bandpass filters.
2: Compute coefficients of variation from the filtered spatial image for each frequency band.
3: Weight each coefficient with a CSF.
4: Sum the weighted coefficients to get the mottling index.

In Step 1, the image is filtered in the frequency domain with a set of bandpass filters. Five fixed spatial bands are designed to an octave series: 0.5-1, 1-2, 2-4, 4-8, and 8-16 mm (note that we fixed the viewing distance to 30 cm in the human assessments). The band containing the smallest details has been included when compared to [8]. The Gaussian filters are illustrated in Fig. 1. The mean (DC component) is set to 1 so that the mean grey value of the image does not change due to filtering.

In Step 2, the coefficients of variation for each band are computed in the spatial domain. The coefficient of variation is the ratio of standard deviation of reflectance and mean reflectance, i.e.,

$$CV_R = \frac{\sigma_R}{\bar{R}}. \quad (1)$$

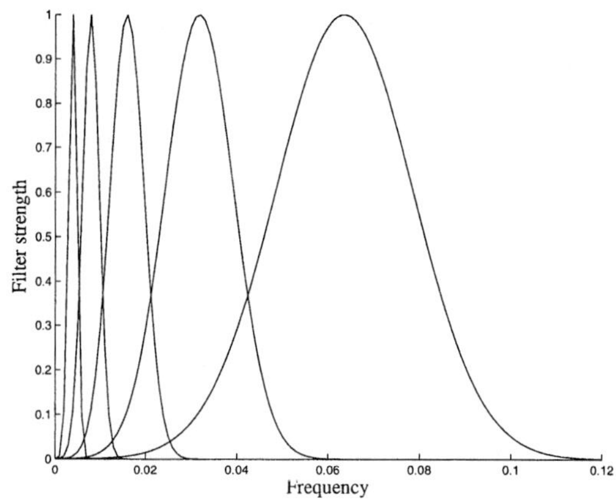

Fig. 1. The filters in 2-D representing the 0.5-1, 1-2, 2-4, 4-8, and 8-16 mm spatial bands

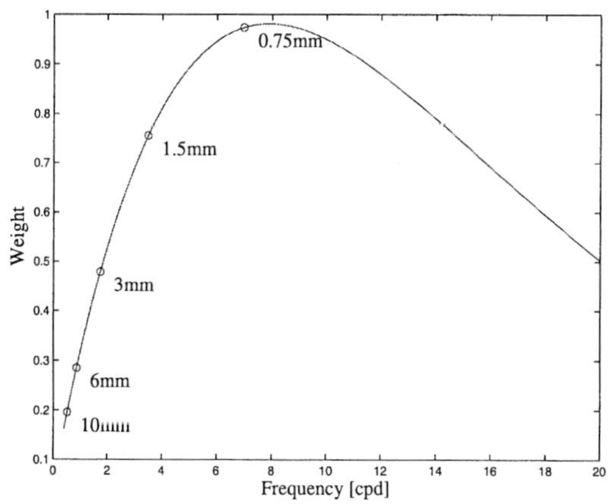

Fig. 2. The Mannos monochrome CSF and the weights corresponding to 0.75, 1, 5, 3, 6, and 10 mm

In Step 3, the coefficients are weighted with a CSF [14] illustrated in Fig. 2. The weights are taken at points representing 0.75, 1.5, 3, 6, and 10 mm.

2.3 Enhanced Method

The idea for this method comes from the bandpass method. Consider a peak in frequency domain which lies in between two bandpass filters, it introduces serious sinusoidal distortion (unevenness) in spatial domain. At the same time, it cannot be detected by a predefined set of bandpass filters, and thus the computed mottling index remains intact. The obvious solution to this bandpass method weakness is to increase number of bandpass filters in order to catch more frequency fluctuations. Finally, increase in the number of filters leads to a limit case, where all the bandpass filters comprise a plane, which has no impact on the values of frequency magnitudes. However, coefficient of variation used as weighted value, makes it complicated for integration in the limit case. We propose to use the following value

$$\overline{\mathrm{CV}}_R = \frac{\sigma_R^2}{R}. \tag{2}$$

to make the result correspond to the bandpass method in the terms of order of magnitude, we take square root inside the integral. In the limit case mottling index will have the form (follows from Parseval's theorem)

$$M = \frac{1}{F(0,0)} \int_{-\infty}^{\infty} \int_{-\infty}^{\infty} CSF(u,v) \sqrt{F(u,v)\overline{F}(u,v)}dudv, \tag{3}$$

where $F(0,0) = R$ is the mean reflectance, $CSF(u,v)$ is a 2-D representation of the CSF, F denotes the Fourier transform of the image, and $\overline{F}$ is the complex conjugate of the transformed image.

Since the frequency for the peak contrast sensitivity of the HVS varies from 2 cpd up to 10 cpd, depending on the type of gratings and its regularity [10], it was decided to introduce the scaling factor into the CSF formulation. The factor scales the function along the frequency axis. It was experimentally found that, for the unevenness type gratings, the peak sensitivity is approximately at 2 cpd. This can be explained by the stochastic nature of mottling and its aperiodicity.

We also studied the effect of orientation sensitivity of the HVS [12]. It is known that human sensitivity is lowest around 45°and 135°and highest at vertical and horizonal directions. However, experiments showed low significance of introducing the orientational scaling. This can also be understood based on the nature of mottling.

2.4 Visual Assessment

To compare the results of the implemented methods to human perception, we collected a set of 20 mottling samples covering a wide range of mottling, and asked human observers to evaluate the perceived mottling. The group of observers consisted of experts from the paper industry, and "laymen" in the area of image processing. The mean of these subjective assessments was used as an initial ground truth for mottling, and the results of all the machine vision methods were compared to this information.

The human assessment consisted of two parts. The first part was a pairwise evaluation of the whole sample set: the observer was asked to select the sample which had less mottling. The main function of this part was to present all samples to the observer, and to give some idea of different forms and levels of mottling. In the second part, each sample was evaluated one at a time, and the observer was asked to rate the level of mottling in a five point Likert scale. Two control questions were used in the assessment: the number of times the person had evaluated mottling, and the time needed for the test. The primary function of the assessment was to quantify the perceived level of mottling of the test set.

The results of the assessments were processed as follows. The people taking the test were divided into two distinct groups based on the control question about the number of times the person had evaluated mottling. The first group was formed by experts who evaluate prints as a part of their work. The second group consisted of people who evaluated mottling for the first time and were not experts in the field of print assessment. Selection criteria for outliers were difficult to design. Each observer had his or her own way of selecting the the use of the scale. The mean and the standard deviation were used as elementary criteria to select outliers. If either one differed from the average of all assessments significantly, the assessment was marked as an outlier.

3 Experiments

We present the results for the set of 20 K70 (70% black) samples (see Fig.3). The original samples are approximately 4.5 cm × 4.5 cm in size. The paper used for printning is 70 g/m^2 LWC (Lightweight Coated) paper, and the samples were printed using heatset offset printing process with round dots. The samples were originally scanned with a flatbed office scanner at 1200 dpi and gamma of 2.2. The gamma value was not altered before applying the machine vision methods. To reduce computing time, the images were re-sampled to 600 dpi because this resolution is more than sufficient in this application when the HVS is concerned.

We inspected mottle sizes ranging from 0.5 to 16 mm while viewing the sample from a distance of 30 cm (spatial frequency range 0.03-1 cycles/mm). Spatially higher- and lower-frequency unevennesses were considered as graininess and banding. The viewing angle of all samples was approximately 8.5°, and the material surrounding each sample was 100% black cardboard. To remove possible defects in images that are not mottling, the inspected contrast of print density was limited to ±10% of the median grey-value of an image.

3.1 Visual Assessment

The results are based on 35 human evaluations. The assessments were made in usual office lighting conditions. However, the conditions were not identical in all evaluations, thus, the human assessment should be considered as an initial one. Evaluators were divided into two groups: experts (12 people) and laymen (23 people). The division was made based on the number of mottling evaluations done prior to this one. As it can be seen from Fig. 4(a), there is only little difference in evaluations between the experts and laymen. This is natural since it would be confusing if the experts evaluated print quality of samples in which mottling is most visible completely distinctly to end-users. However, experts in the printing industry do have a different view of print quality, and there should be representatives from this group in the next and more thorough assessment.

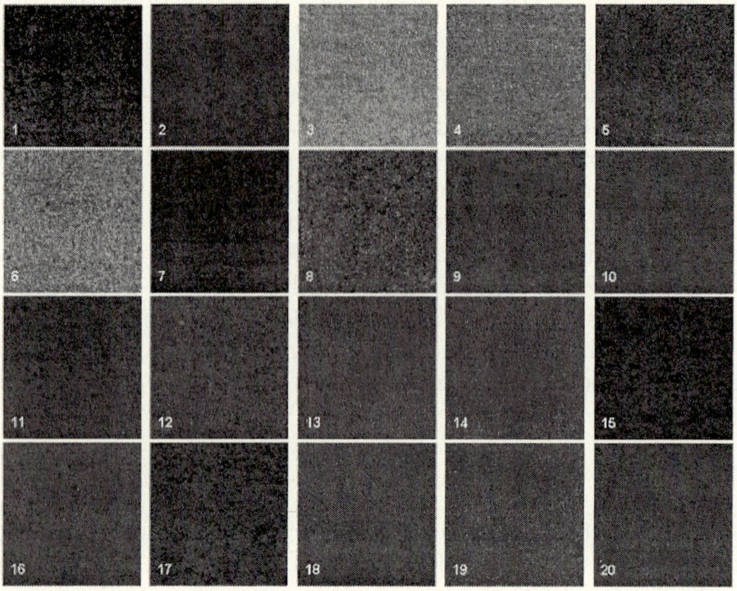

Fig. 3. The set of K70 samples (scaled to fit the figure and altered to enhance the visibility of mottling)

Confidence bounds in Fig. 4(a) show the average results across the whole population ±standard deviation, and show how similar the mottling indices were among all evaluators.

3.2 Machine Vision Assessment

The standard method was implemented as described in the ISO 13660 standard [2]. The implementation of this method is easy and does not require much programming effort. As it was expected, the results produced by the standard method show low correlation to the human assessment (see Fig. 4(b)). In the standard, the size of the tiles is set to a fixed value which is a known limitation [3]. The bandpass method makes use of a few frequency bands to separate information relevant to the HVS. A small number of bands limits the number of spatial classes, and the method becomes similar to a set of low-pass filters used in previous mottling methods. Performance of the method is limited by the resolution of the image and the number of bands. The results of this method can be seen in Fig. 4(c). The increase in the number of bands leads to the enhanced method, which utilizes characteristics of the HVS and outperforms two aforementioned methods (see Fig. 4(d)).

All the artificial methods produced mottling indexes in their own scale. Thus, appropriate scaling was needed for the method comparison. We used simple

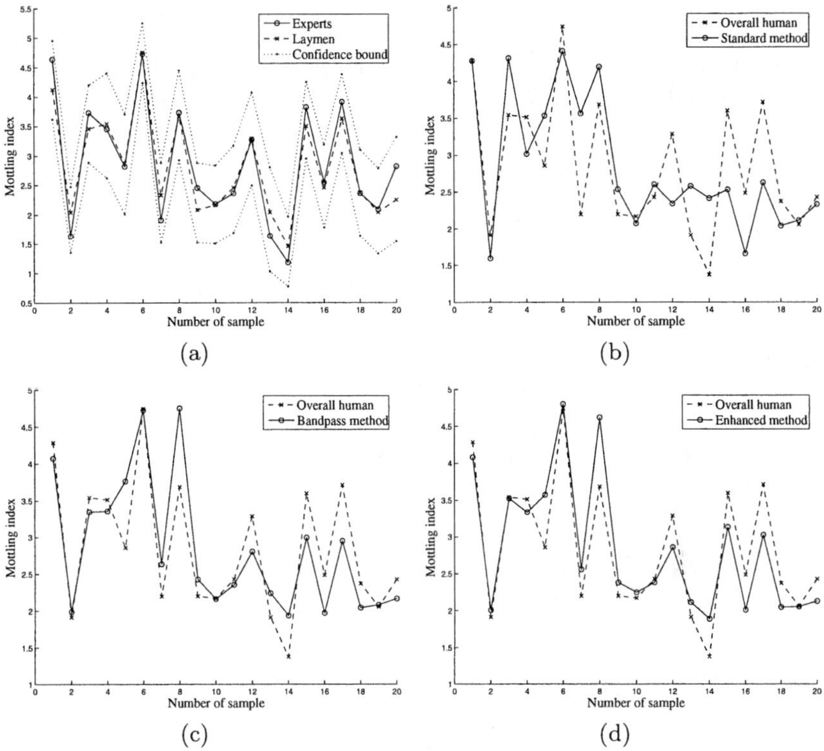

Fig. 4. Mottling assessments: (a) Human evaluation; (b) Standard method; (c) Bandpass method; (d) Enhanced method

normalization which equalizes the mean value and standard deviation of the experimental values across the samples.

3.3 Results Summary

In Table 1, inter-method similarity is presented. Correlation coefficients were used as the similarity measure.

Table 1. Mottling assessment correlations

Methods	Overall	Experts	Laymen	Standard	Bandpass	Enhanced
Overall human	1.0000	0.9848	0.9957	0.6956	0.8579	0.8941
Experts	0.9848	1.0000	0.9644	0.6568	0.8125	0.8516
Laymen	0.9957	0.9644	1.0000	0.7078	0.8715	0.9057
Standard	0.6956	0.6568	0.7078	1.0000	0.8810	0.8755
Bandpass	0.8579	0.8125	0.8715	0.8810	1.0000	0.9949
Enhanced	0.8941	0.8516	0.9057	0.8755	0.9949	1.0000

Fig. 4 shows performance graphs for different assessment approaches.

The collected correlation data allow to state that the enhanced method outperforms the other two methods. It can be also noticed that the machine vision methods correlate better among each other than with human evaluation based data. This leads to the conclusion that all artificial methods have a similar nature and the model of HVS they assume is not accurate.

4 Conclusions

In the presented work, we performed a comparison between the human and machine vision evaluation of mottling. The results of the human evaluation appear to be highly distributed and, thus, a larger number of assessments is needed both in evaluators and in samples. The high deviation in single sample evaluation results leads to the conclusion that a machine vision system modelling an average end-user is necessary. This could bring more precision in delivering printed products of desired quality.

The presented machine vision methods, though having a relatively good correlation with averaged human observation, still need improvement in the sense of modelling of the HVS. The standard method presented can be considered only as a starting point because this method does not model the HVS at all and also it does not have significant correlation with the human mottling evaluation. The bandpass method shows good results, though it should be mentioned, that it is not accurate to use CSF derived for regular sinusoidal gratings for measuring human sensitivity for random reflectance fluctuations. General enhancement for the bandpass method resulted improvement in both computational sense and in precision.

The goals for the future research can be defined as follows: make methods closer to human perception, by involving new knowledge about the HVS, and incorporate mottling evaluation of colour samples. The general conclusion of our research, is that for the implementation of a machine vision solution to the human perception problem, one needs a suitable HVS model and good statistical characteristics of how the humans perceive the phenomenon.

However, the results also show that when assessing low-contrast unevenness of print, humans have diverse opinions about quality.

Acknowledgments

This work was done as a part of Papvision project funded by European Union, National Technology Agency of Finland (TEKES Projects No. 70049/03 and 70056/04), and Academy of Finland (Project No. 204708).

References

1. IGT information leaflet w57: Back trap mottle. WWW:www.igt.nl (2002) [Accessed 2005-02-25]. Available: http://www.igt.nl/igt-site-220105/index-us/w-bladen/GST/W57.pdf.

2. ISO/IEC 13660:2001(e) standard. information technology - office equipment - measurement of image quality attributes for hardcopy output - binary monochrome text and graphic images. ISO/IEC (2001)
3. Briggs, J., Forrest, D., Klein, A., Tse, M.K.: Living with ISO-13660: Pleasures and perils. In: IS&Ts NIP 15: 1999 International Conference on Digital Printing Technologies, IS&T, Springfield VA (1999) 421–425
4. Wolin, D.: Enhanced mottle measurement. In: PICS 2002: IS&T's PICS conference, IS&T (2002) 148–151
5. Armel, D., Wise, J.: An analytic method for quantifying mottle - part 1. Flexo (1998) 70–79
6. Armel, D., Wise, J.: An analytic method for quantifying mottle - part 2. Flexo (1999) 38–43
7. Streckel, B., Steuernagel, B., Falkenhagen, E., Jung, E.: Objective print quality measurements using a scanner and a digital camera. In: DPP 2003: IS&T International Conference on Digital Production Printing and Industrial Applications. (2003) 145–147
8. Johansson, P.Å.: Optical Homogeniety of Prints. PhD thesis, Kunglika Tekniska Högskolan, Stockholm (1999)
9. Rosenberger, R.R.: Stochastic frequency distribution analysis as applied to ink jet print mottle measurement. In: IS&Ts NIP 17: 2001 International Conference on Digital Printing Technologies, IS&T, Springfield VA (2001) 808–812
10. Barten, P.: Contrast Sensitivity of the Human Eye and its Effects on Image Quality. SPIE (1999)
11. Schade, O.H.: Optical and photoelectric analog of the eye. Journal of the Optical Society of America **46** (1956) 721–739
12. Kang, H.R.: Digital Color Halftoning. SPIE & IEEE Press (1999)
13. Campbell, F.W., Carpenter, R.H.S., Levinson, J.Z.: Visibility of aperiodic patterns compared with that of sinusoidal gratings. Journal of Physiology (**204**) 283–298
14. Mannos, J., Sakrison, D.: The effects of a visual fidelity criterion on the encoding of images. IEEE Transactions on Information Theory **20** (1974) 525–536

Active Contour and Morphological Filters for Geometrical Normalization of Human Face

Gabriel Hernández Sierra, Edel Garcia Reyes, and Gerardo Iglesias Ham

Advanced Technologies Application Center, MINBAS,
7a #21812 e/ 218 y 222, Rpto. Siboney, Playa. C.P. 12200,
Ciudad de la Habana, Cuba,
Office Phone Number: (+)537.271.4787,
Fax number: (+)537.272.1667
{gsierra, egarcia, giglesias}@cenatav.co.cu

Abstract. In this paper we resolve the problem of automatically normalize front view photos from a database that contain images of human faces with different size, angle and position. It was used a template with a standardized inter eye distance and dimensions. We are mapping all images to this template applying a geometrical transformation. It is necessary to obtain the eyes positions on image to calculate the transforms parameters. That is not a trivial problem. We use active contour to detect the human face. After that, we apply morphological filters to highlight image signal amplitude in the eyes positions. A set of criterion is applied to select a pair of point with more possibility to be the eyes. Then, a subroutine is feed with eyes coordinates to calculate and apply the geometrical transformation. Our method was applied to 500 photos and it performs very well in the 94% of all cases.

1 Introduction

Face recognition [1, 2, 3, 5] has become an important issue in many applications such as access control, credit card verification and criminal identification. The main task of face recognition is the identification of a given face photo among all the faces stored in an image database. This is our general problem. Our approach need to known the position of eyes to create a face space in which all the faces are geometrically normalized and photometrical correlated [4, 8].

This paper is dedicated to the process of geometrical normalization of human faces. This process is divided in three steps: a) face detection, b) eye detection and c) geometrical normalization [6, 11, 12].

First, it is necessary localize the limit of face using active contour [9, 10]. Then, the eyes are detected searching white spot in a map resulting of apply a combination of morphological filters. Finally, it is performed the geometrical normalization.

The structure of this paper is the following: In section 2, we show the basic concepts about active contour and its employ in face detection. The face and eye detection process are presented in Section 3 and 4 respectively. Section 5 is dedicated to explain the spatial transformation. Section 6 focuses on experimental results of the proposed methodology. Finally, we present some relevant conclusions.

M. Lazo and A. Sanfeliu (Eds.): CIARP 2005, LNCS 3773, pp. 720–728, 2005.

2 Active Contour Model (Snake)

The active contour or snake can be defined as a spline curve that minimize the energy guided by external constraint forces and influenced by image forces that pull it toward feature as lines and edges. In the snake, image and external forces together with the connectivity of contour and the presence of corners will affect the energy function and the detailed structure of the locally optimal contour. The snake has a set of inner forces that serve to put smoothing restrictions to the curve. Also, it has a set of image forces and restrictions imposed by the user. The idea, it is modify an initial elastic curve under the action of such forces until reach the object contour.

The definition of the active energy of the contour is illustrated as

$$E_{snake} = \int_0^1 \alpha E_{internal}(r(s)) + \beta E_{image}(r(s)) + \delta E_{restrictive}(r(s))ds . \quad (1)$$

Where $r(s)$ represent the position of the snake, $E_{internal}$ represents the internal energy of the contour due to bending. Defined as

$$E_{internal}(r(s)) = \|r'(s)\|^2 + \|r''(s)\|^2 . \quad (2)$$

The following approximations are used:

$$\left\|\frac{dr_s}{ds}\right\| \approx \|r_s - r_{s-1}\|^2 \quad \text{and} \quad \left\|\frac{d^2 r_s}{ds^2}\right\| \approx \|r_{s-1} - 2r_s + r_{s+1}\|^2 . \quad (3)$$

Continuity Force: The first derivative $\|r_s - r_{s-1}\|^2$ causes the curve to shrink. It is actually the distance between points. It is evident that a term that facilitates the uniform distribution of the points $d_{pro} - \|r_s - r_{s-1}\|^2$ would much more reflect the wished behavior of contour.

Curvature Force: Since the formulation of the continuity term causes the points to be relatively evenly spaced, $\|r_{s-1} - 2r_s + r_{i+1}\|^2$ gives a reasonable and quick estimate of

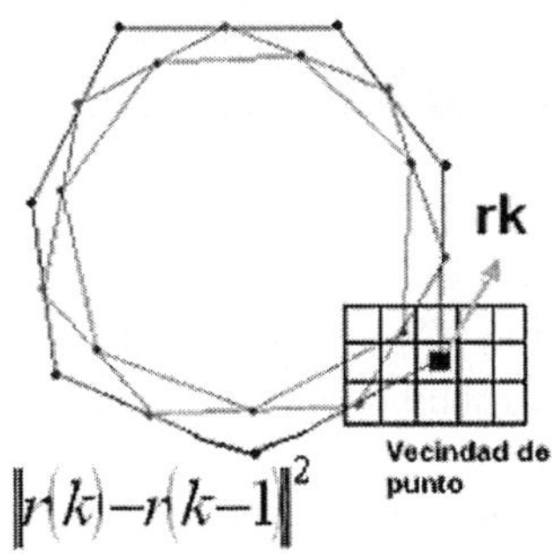

Fig. 1. Continuity forces: Minimizing the distance between points

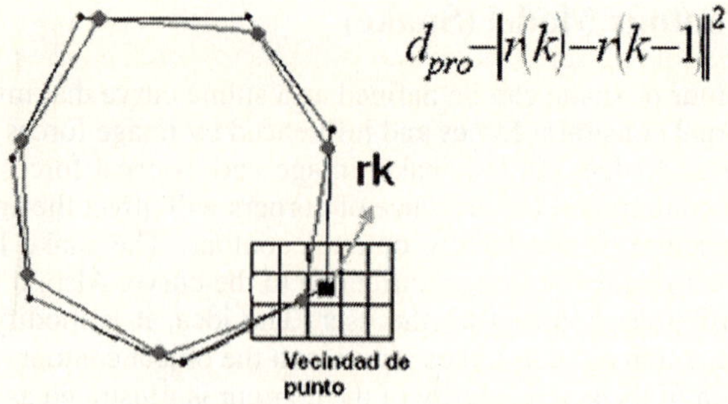

Fig. 2. Continuity forces: Minimizing the difference between the average distance points d_{pro} and the distance between the two points under consideration

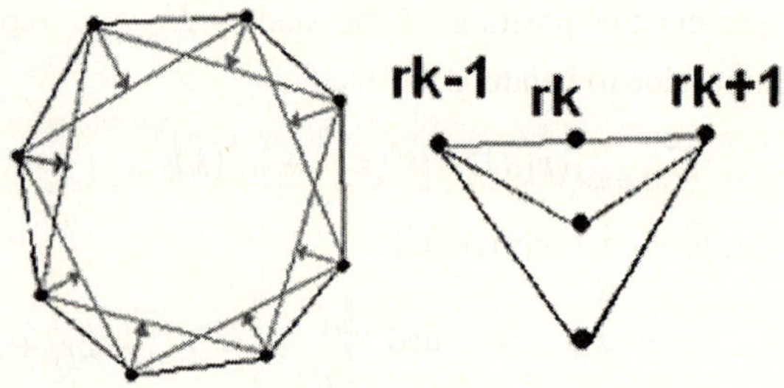

Fig. 3. Curvature Force

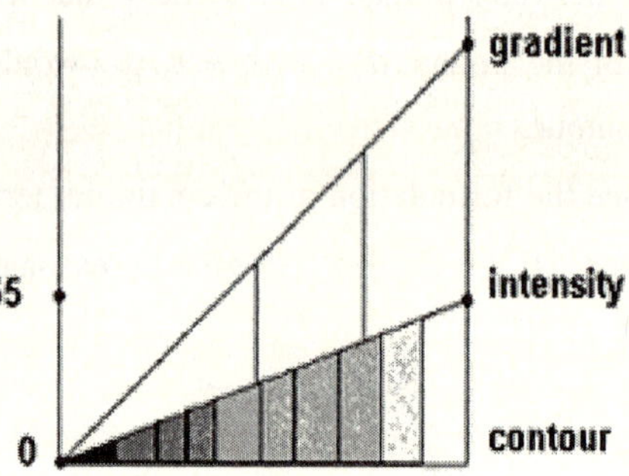

Fig. 4. Image force

the curvature. This term, like the continuity term, is normalized by dividing the largest $d_{\max}$ value in the neighborhood, giving a number between 0 and 1.

Image Force: E_{image} is the image force which is defined taking account the intensity in a point and the gradient of the intensity in a point. We need to select a point in the neighborhood which intensity plus gradient minimize the energy function. When the contour is white it is necessary multiply by -1 this value.

Restrictive Force: It is the distance between an inner points and other on the contour. As the criterion considered is to minimize the energy, the curve will be shrinking. In the case that we are interested to expand the curve, it is necessary to consider multiply by -1 the distance.

3 Face Detection

The basic idea is close a face in a frame to minimize the negative effect of the hair to the algorithm of facial feature extraction. We may initialize a process of expansion of an inner curve searching the face contour applying the snake principle. The problem is to be sure that the initial set of point is internal to the face. To guarantee this condition, it is possibly to apply an active contour to shrink a curve in form of an ellipse to reach the external edges of hair and face. A Sobel filter is applied to the image to facilitate the convergence of snake to the searching edges (see Fig. 5). This way, it is found a previous face approximation closed in a rectangle.

As the snake finish its iterations, it is obtained a set of point most of them over the head contour. Then, a searching is initiated to look up for the two rows and columns with more density of point to form a frame including the face (see Fig. 6).

We position a set of point in the centre of this rectangle to begin a second expanding snake. Initial snake into the face is not a sufficient condition for all points evolve to the

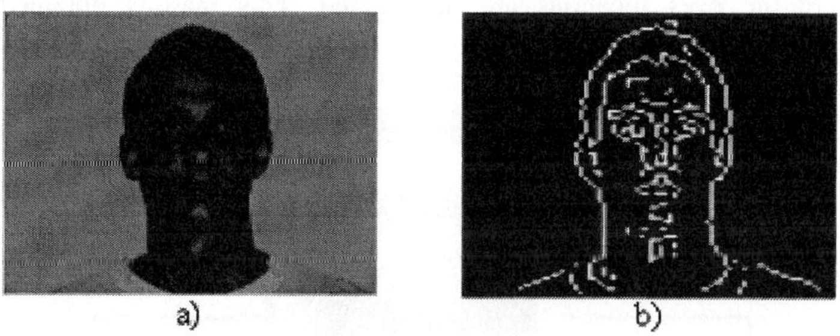

Fig. 5. a) Face image. b) Sobel edges detection.

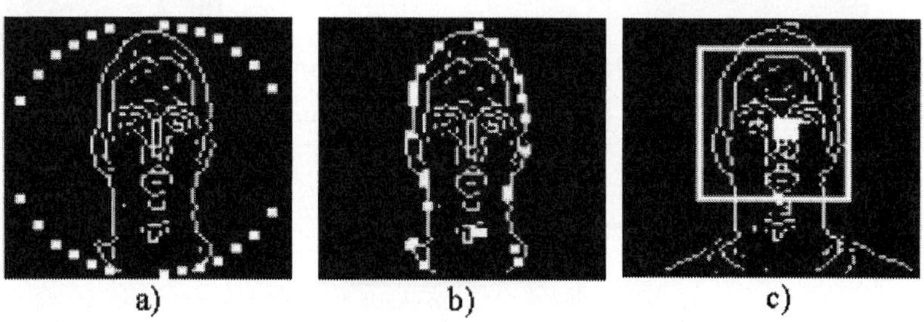

Fig. 6. Shrinking snake evolution. a) Initial elliptical curve, b) Points over the contour, and c) Frame including the face.

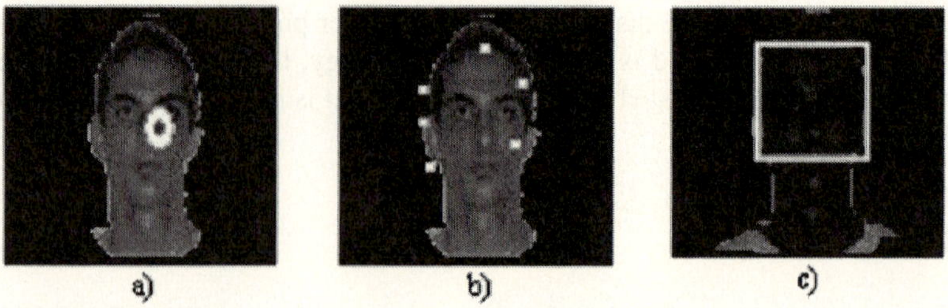

Fig. 7. Expanding snake evolution. a) Initial elliptical curve, b) Points over face contour, and c) Frame including the face.

face contour because some points may be trapped on the eyebrow, eyes and nostril. Only the points over the face contour were taken to build the inner frame (see Fig. 7).

4 Eye Detection

We are interested in highlight the eyes location and eliminate other image elements. Based in the observation that eye images have a combination of white and black pixels, we proposed to utilize dilation filter to amplify the whites pixels and erosion filter to amplify the black one. Then, it is possibly to obtain a map of shade value (*Map*) where the eyes locations are highlighted. This map is obtained by the

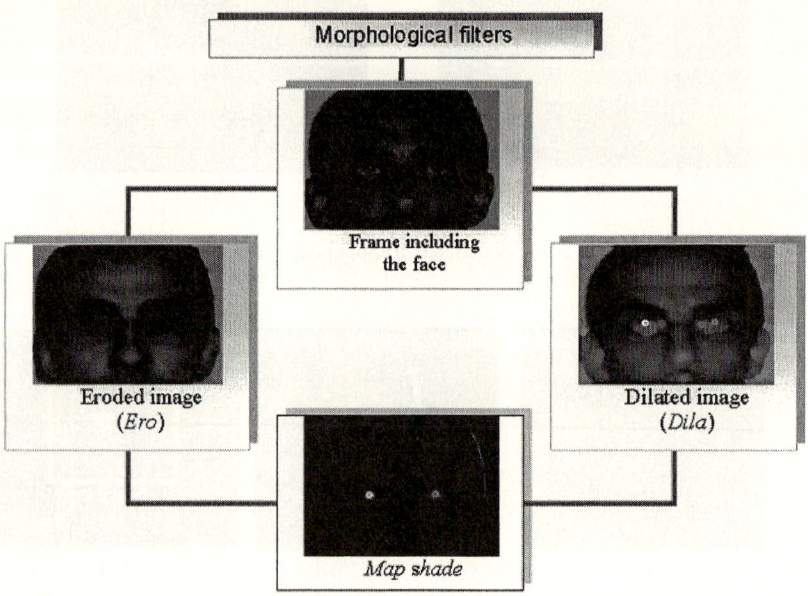

Fig. 8. Morphological operation to obtain the Map shade

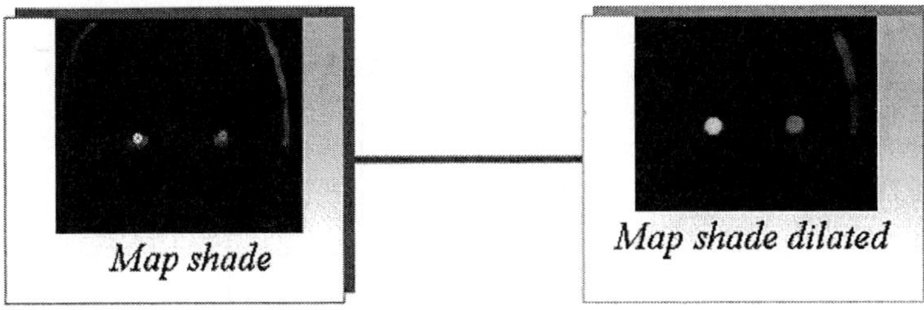

Fig. 9. Map shade dilated

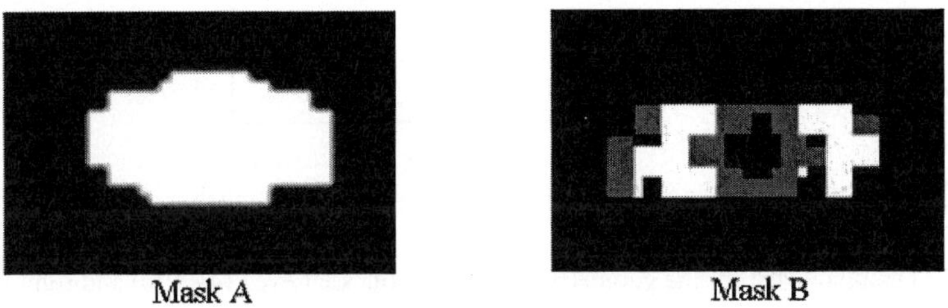

Fig. 10. Masks used to detect eyes positions

subtraction of image dilated (*Dila*) minus image eroded (*Ero*). With this operation we pretend to remark the difference between pixels black and white in both images (see Fig. 8).

$$Map = Dila - Ero\ . \tag{4}$$

After that, a dilate operation is applied to the Map shade to highlight image signal amplitude in the eye position.

On the shade map we select the 10 positions that obtain greater value when matching with Mask A. These points are evaluated in the original image by means of Mask B. The pair of greater score is chosen as the eyes, where the horizontal orientation and the distance between the possible points associated to eyes fulfill the correspondent thresholds.

5 Geometric Normalization

A geometric transformation consists of a spatial transformation, which defines the arrangement of pixels on the image planes and the gray level interpolation, which deals with the assignment of gray levels to pixels in the spatially transformed image. We defined a template with 500 x 400 pixels and the exactly location where is desire to put the eyes of all transformed images (see Fig. 11). This point on the template and the eyes locations are using as *tiepoints*. We used gray level interpolation based on the nearest neighbor concept.

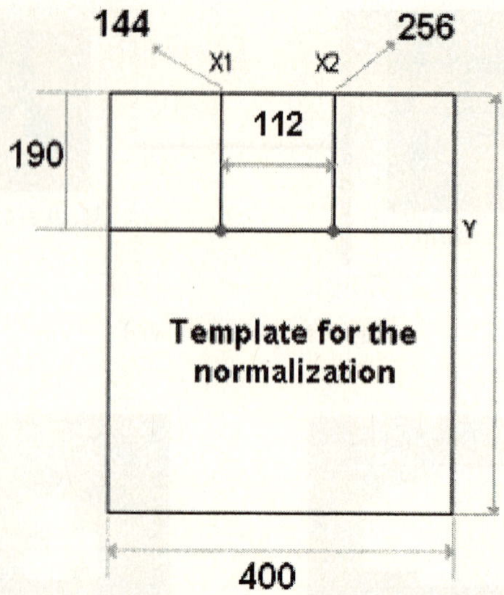

Fig. 11. Template used for the geometric normalization. Left eye (144,190) and right (256,190).

6 Result

In this section, we show some results obtained with our methodology. We selected 500 front view images of students and professors from Havana University, where appear persons with different ages, sex, length of hair, color of skin, head inclination, illumination, color and scale (see Fig. 12 left).

The eyes were correctly detected in 94 percent of images with a probability of more than 9 positive results into 10 images (see Fig. 12 right). Figure 13 show some human faces normalized using the automatic detected coordinates of eyes.

We observed some negative results where the snake does not work very well and the algorithm was affected by earring and glasses with much shine.

7 Conclusions

We present a new methodology for eyes detection that combines active contour, morphological filters and template matching.

We introduce an additional restrictive force in energy function to obligate the snake to evolve to the wanted contour.

We obtained a 94 percent of effectivity when the algorithm was applied to 500 images of faces took in conditions not controlled, corresponding to students of Havana University.

The algorithm presented in this paper resolve the problem of normalization of a set of images mapping all them over a template with standard spatial dimensions, without necessity of manually marking the eyes position.

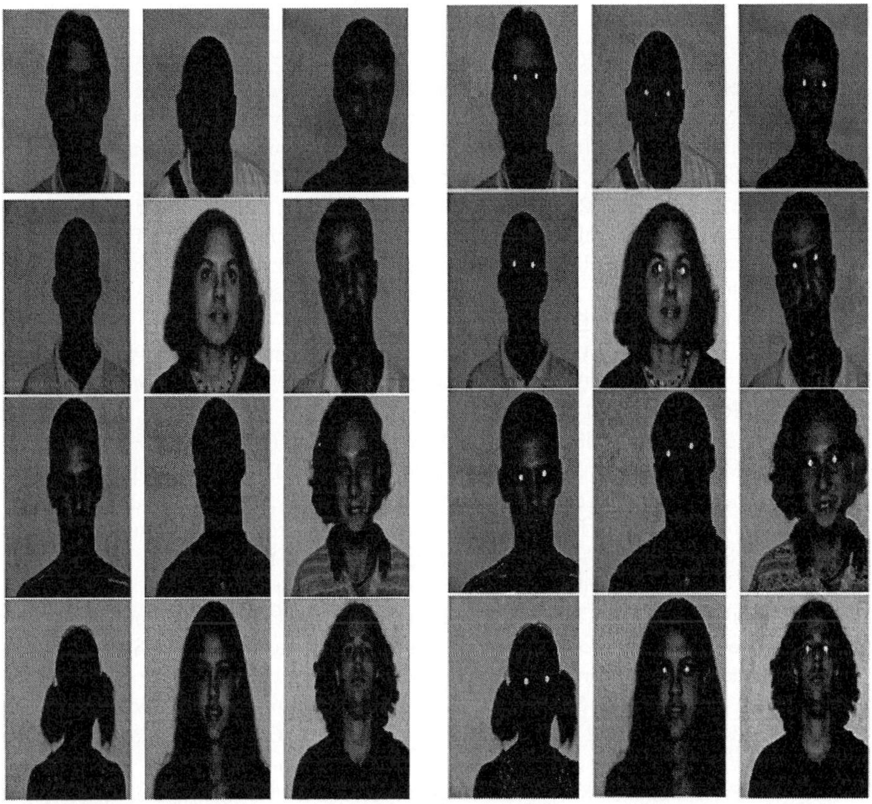

Fig. 12. Some of the photos of the registry. Left: Original photos. Right: Eyes detected.

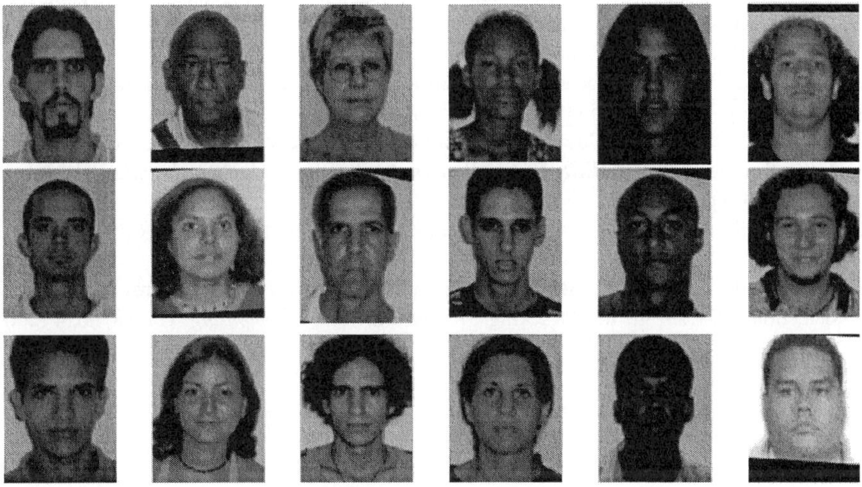

Fig. 13. Examples of normalized images

References

1. García-Mateos, G., Ruiz, A., Lopez-de-Teruel, P.: Face Detection Using Integral Projection Models. In: T. Caelli et al. (eds.): Structural, Syntactic, and Statistical Pattern Recognition: Joint IAPR International Workshops. Lecture Notes in Computer Science, Vol. 2396.Springer-Verlag, Berlin Heidelberg New York (2002) 644-653
2. Graciano, A. B., Cesar, R. M., Bloch, I: Inexact Graph Matching for Facial Feature Segmentation and Recognition in Video Sequences: Results on Face Tracking. In: A. Sanfeliu and J. Ruiz-Shulcloper (eds.): Progress in Pattern Recognition, Speech and Image Analysis. Lecture Notes in Computer Science, Vol. 2935. Springer-Verlag, Berlin Heidelberg New York (2003) 71-78
3. Haddadnia, J., Ahmadi, M., Faez, K.:Human Face Recognition with different statistical feature. In: T. Caelli et al. (eds.): Structural, Syntactic, and Statistical Pattern Recognition: Joint IAPR International Workshops. Lecture Notes in Computer Science, Vol. 2396.Springer-Verlag, Berlin Heidelberg New York (2002) 627-635
4. Hamouz, M., Kittler, J. , Matas, J., Bilek, P.: Face Detection by Learned Affine Correspondences. In: T. Caelli et al. (eds.): Structural, Syntactic, and Statistical Pattern Recognition : Joint IAPR International Workshops. Lecture Notes in Computer Science, Vol. 2396.Springer-Verlag, Berlin Heidelberg New York (2002) 566-575
5. Huang, Y., Tsai, Y.: A transformation-based mechanism for face recognition. In: T. Caelli et al. (eds.): Structural, Syntactic, and Statistical Pattern Recognition: Joint IAPR International Workshops. Lecture Notes in Computer Science, Vol. 2396.Springer-Verlag, Berlin Heidelberg New York (2002) 566-575
6. Huang, W., Sun, Q., Lam, C.-P., Wu, J.-K.: "A robust approach to face and eyes detection from images with cluttered background," *Proc. IEEE Int'l Conf. Pattern Recognition*, vol. 1 (1998) pp. 110–114
7. Jackway, P.T., Deriche, M.: "Scale-space properties of the multiscale morphological dilation-erosion," *IEEE Trans. Pattern Analysis and Machine Intelligence*, vol. 18 (1996) pp. 38–51
8. Ko., J., Kim, E., Byun, H,: Illumination Normalized Face image for Face Recognition In: T. Caelli et al. (eds.): Structural, Syntactic, and Statistical Pattern Recognition : Joint IAPR International Workshops. Lecture Notes in Computer Science, Vol. 2396.Springer-Verlag, Berlin Heidelberg New York (2002) 654-661
9. Lam, K.M., Yan, H.: "Locating and extracting the eye in human face images," *Pattern Recognition*, vol. 29, no. 5 (1996) pp. 771–779
10. Lanitis, A., Taylor, C.J., Cootes, T.F.: "Automatic interpretation and coding of face images using flexible models," *IEEE Trans. Pattern Analysis and Machine Intelligence*, vol. 19, no. 7 (1997) pp. 743–756
11. Sirohey, S., Rosenfeld, A.: "Eye detection," *Technical Report CS-TR-3971, Univ. of Maryland* (1998)
12. Smeraldi, F., Carmona, O., Bigün, J.: "Saccadic search with Gabor features applied to eye detection and real-time head tracking," *Image and Vision Computing*, vol. 18, no. 4 (2000) pp. 323–329

Medical Image Segmentation and the Use of Geometric Algebras in Medical Applications

Rafael Orozco-Aguirre, Jorge Rivera-Rovelo, and Eduardo Bayro-Corrochano

CINVESTAV, Unidad Guadalajara,
López Mateos Sur 590, Zapopan, Jalisco, México
{horozco, rivera, edb}@gdl.cinvestav.mx

Abstract. This paper presents a method for segmentation of medical images and the application of the so called geometric or Clifford algebras for volume representation, non-rigid registration of volumes and object tracking. Segmentation is done combining texture and boundary information in a region growing strategy obtaining good results. To model 2D surfaces and 3D volumetric data we present a new approach based on marching cubes idea however using spheres. We compare our approach with other method based on the delaunay tetrahedrization. The results show that our proposed approach reduces considerably the number of spheres. Also we show how to do non-rigid registration of two volumetric data represented as sets of spheres using 5-dimensional vectors in conformal geometric algebra. Finally we show the application of geometric algebras to track surgical devices in real time.

1 Introduction

When dealing with tumor segmentation in brain images, one way to solve the problem is by using Magnetic Resonance (MR) images because in such images we have different types of them (ie. T1, T2, T1-weighted, T2-weighted, etc.; some of them highlight tumor and other structures), and by combining and differentiating them, the task become more easy and an automatic approach for segmentation become possible (see [1]). Other methods, like the one proposed by [2], use a probabilistic digital brain atlas to search abnormalities (outliers) between the patient data and the atlas. The use of Computer Tomographic (CT) images is less used because they have not such modalities and the development of an automatic algorithm for segmentation is more complicated; however semi-automatic approaches have been proposed (as in [3,4]) using seed points defined manually by the user as initialization, and growing the region by some method. In this work we are interested in segmenting tumors in CT images, so we use a simple but effective algorithm to segment them: a set of 5 *texture descriptors* is used to characterize each pixel of the image by means of 5×1 template or a 5D-vector; then each vector is compared with the typical vector describing a tumor in order to establish an initialization of the tumor in the image (seed points for tumor tissue). Finally, a region growing strategy is used, combined

M. Lazo and A. Sanfeliu (Eds.): CIARP 2005, LNCS 3773, pp. 729–740, 2005.

with boundary information to obtain the final shape of the tumor (this method is explained in section 2).

On the other hand, representation of volumetric objects using primitives like points, lines or planes is a common task. The Union of Spheres proposed in [5] is another possible representation for volumetric data, but it usually needs a large amount of primitives (spheres). This fact aimed us to look a different way to model the object with less primitives but being a good enough representation. In the first approach, the dense Union of Spheres representation is obtained using the Delaunay tetrahedrization and its complexity is $O(n^2)$ in both, time and number of primitives, while our highest number of spheres using our method based on marching cubes is less than $2n$ in the worst case, and some times it is less. We use computer tomography (CT) images to do the experiments, and one of the the surfaces to be modeled is the segmented tumor - n is the number of boundary points in a total of m CT images (slides). This approach is explained in section 4, which uses the concepts explained in section 3.

Some times (ie., when surgeon opens the head and occurs loss of cerebrospinal liquid) tumor and brain structures suffer (non-linear) deformation. In this work (see section 4.2) we present a new approach which uses models based on spheres for using such spheres as the entities to be aligned. This is embedded in the Conformal Geometric Algebra (CGA) framework using the TPS-RPM algorithm but in a 5-dimensional space (see Sect. 4.2). Finally, we show the application of GA for the task of object tracking (section 5).

2 Segmentation

As mentioned in [7,8] segmentation techniques can be categorized in three classes: a) thresholding, b) region-based and c) boundary-based. Due to the advantages and disadvantages of each technique, many segmentation methods are based on the integration information of region and boundary techniques and there are a great variety of methods; some of them working better in some cases, some being more sensitive to noise, etc. This fact make not feasible to determine the best approach to segmentation that integrates boundary and region information because we have not a generally accepted and clear methodology for evaluating the algorithms; additionally, the properties and objectives that the algorithms try to satisfy and the image domain in which they work are different. Interested reader can consult a detailed review of different approaches in [7]. Due to the fact that we are dealing with medical images, we need also to take into account an important characteristic: the texture. Textural properties of the image can be extracted using *texture descriptors* which describe the texture in an area of the image. So, if we use a *texture descriptor* over the whole image, we obtain a new "texture feature image". In most cases, a single operator does not provide enough information about texture, and a set of operators need to be used. This results in a set of "texture feature images" that jointly describe the texture around each pixel.

When segmenting tomographic images, simple segmentation techniques such as region growing, split and merge or boundary segmentation can not be used alone due to the complexity of the brain computer tomographic images, which contain textures of different tissues, similar gray-levels between healthy and non-healthy tissues, and sometimes the boundaries are not well defined. For this reason, we decide to combine not only boundary and region information (as typically it is done), but also to integrate information obtained from texture descriptors and embed that in a region growing strategy. A block diagram of our approach is shown in figure 1.a.

a)

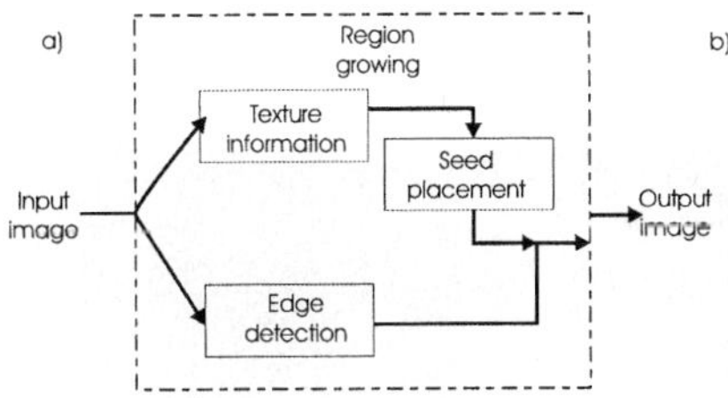

b)

-1	-4	-6	-4	-1
-2	-8	-12	-8	-2
0	0	0	0	0
2	8	12	8	2
1	4	6	4	1

1	-4	6	-4	1
-4	16	-24	16	-4
6	-24	36	-24	6
-4	16	-24	16	-4
1	-4	6	-4	1

-1	-4	-6	-4	-1
0	0	0	0	0
2	8	12	8	2
0	0	0	0	0
-1	-4	-6	-4	-1

-1	-2	0	2	1
0	0	0	0	0
2	4	0	-4	-2
0	0	0	0	0
-1	-2	0	2	1

Fig. 1. a) Block diagram of the approach to segment tumors in CT images (region growing strategy combining texture and boundary information); b) Texture descriptors used to obtain the texture information (4 Laws energy masks)

The first step is to characterize each pixel on images, so we opt for use the texture information provided by some of the Laws's masks to characterize them with a five-dimensional vector (named *texture vector*, V_{ij}, for pixel in coordinates (i,j)). Then, to place automatically the seed points for the region growing strategy, we choose only the pixels having a texture vector for the tissue of interest (in this case we are interested in tumor) and use them as initialization (or seeds) for the region growing strategy; boundary information is used to stop the growing of the region. The construction of V_{ij} is explained as follows: the first element of V_{ij} is only to identify if the pixels corresponds to the background (value set to zero) or to the patient's head (value set to one) - patient's head could be skin, bone, brain, etc.; in order to obtain the texture information, we use a set of four masks of the so called Laws Masks (L5E5, R5R5, L5S5, E5S5 - see 1.b); then we fix the value in a position of V_{ij} with 1's or 0's, depending on if the value is greater than zero or zero, respectively. As a result, each structure (tissue, bone, skin, background) on the medical images used, has the same vector V_{ij} in a high number of its belonging pixels, but not in all of them because of variations in values of neighboring pixels. So we can use the pixels having the texture vector of the object we want to extract to establish them as seed points in a region-growing scheme. Region growing criterions we use are as follows: we compute the mean μ_{seeds} and standard deviation σ_{seeds} of the pixels fixed as seeds; then, for each neighboring pixel being examined to determine if added or not to the region:

$$\text{If } I(x,y) = \pm 2\sigma_{seeds} \text{ and } V_{xy} \neq V_{seed} \text{ at most in 1 element,then } I(x,y) \in R_t$$

where R_t is the region of the tumor. The stopping criterion takes into account the boundaries of the object because the growing of the region is in all directions, but when a boundary pixel is found, the growing in such direction is stopped. Figure 2 shows results of the process explained before: figure 2.a shows one original CT-image; figure 2.b shows the seed points fixed, which have the texture vector of the tumor; figure 2.c shows the final result after the overall process has ended (the tumor extracted). The overall process takes only few seconds per image and it could be used to segment any of the objects; but in our case, we focus our attention on the extraction of the tumor.

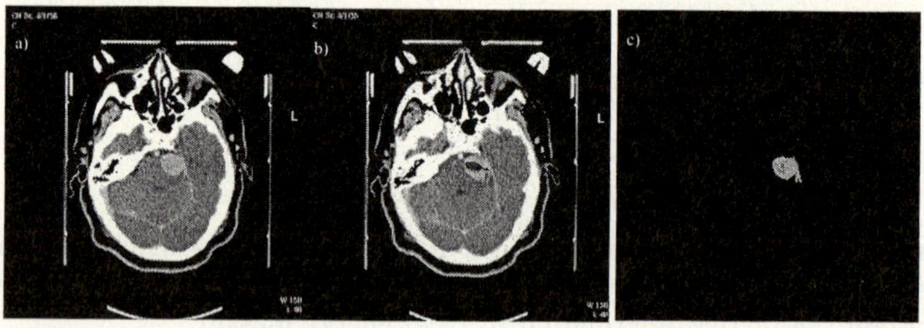

Fig. 2. Results for the segmentation. a) One of the original CT-images; b) Seed points fixed; c) Result for the image of (a) after the whole process (the tumor extracted).

After that, the next step is to model the volumetric data by some method. Due to the fact that tumor can be deformed due to the lost of cefalic liquid once the head of the patient is opened, we need a 3D representation of the tumor which allows us to estimate such deformation to update the shape of the tumor. Next sections explain the basis of our different approach for such modeling as well as a similar method used for comparison. However, first we present how the spheres are represented in conformal geometric algebra (CGA), and then we will show how to build 3D models and register two of them using such entities with TPS-RPM method.

3 Representation of Spheres in CGA

Our objective is not to provide a detailed description of the geometric algebra (GA) and its advantages (interested reader can find very useful material in [10,11]), so we only give a brief introduction and explain how to represent spheres in conformal geometric algebra (CGA) as points in a space of 5 dimensions (because such representation will be used in the non-rigid registration process).

Geometric algebra is a coordinate-free approach to geometry based on the algebras of Grassmann and Clifford. The algebra is defined on a space whose elements are called *multivectors*; a multivector is a linear combination of objects of different grade, e.g. scalars, vectors and k-vectors. It has an associative and fully invertible product called the *geometric* or Clifford product. The existence of such a product and the calculus associated with the geometric algebra endows the system with tremendous power. The Clifford product (or geometric product) ab between two vectors a and b is defined as:

$$ab = a \cdot b + a \wedge b \ . \tag{1}$$

where $a \cdot b$ represents the *dot* or *inner* product and $a \wedge b$ represents the *wedge* or *exterior* product. The geometric algebra $G_{p,q,r}$ is a linear space of dimension 2^n, where $n = p + q + r$ and p, q, r indicate the number of basis vectors which squares to $1, -1, 0$, respectively. This algebra is constructed by the application of geometric product between each two basis vectors e_i , e_j from the base of the vector space $\Re^{p,q,r}$. Thus $G_{p,q,r}$ has elements of grade 0 (scalars), grade 1 (vectors), grade 2 (bivectors), and so on. The CGA $G_{4,1,0}$ is adequate for representing entities like spheres because there is no direct way to describe them as compact entities in $G_{3,0,0}$ (the geometric algebra of the 3D space); the only possibility to define them is given by formulating a constraint equation. However, in CGA the spheres are the basis entities from which the other entities are derived. These basic entities, the spheres $\underline{s}$ with center p and radius ρ are defined by (2).

$$\underline{s} = p + \frac{1}{2}\left(p^2 - \rho^2\right) e + e_0 \ . \tag{2}$$

where $p \in \Re^3$, ρ is a scalar and e, e_0 are defined as in eq. 3 (they are called null vectors), and they are formed with two basis vectors e_-, e_+ additional to the three basis vectors of the 3D-Euclidean space (which have the properties that $e_-^2 = -1; e_+^2 = +1; e_- \cdot e_+ = 0$).

$$e = e_- + e_+; \quad e_0 = \frac{1}{2}(e_- - e_+) \tag{3}$$

In fact, we can think in a conformal point $\underline{x}$ as a degenerate sphere of radius $\rho = 0$. More details on GA and the construction of other entities in CGA can be consulted in [10,11]. We can see eq. 2 as a linear combination: $\underline{s} = \alpha e_1 + \beta e_2 + \gamma e_3 + \delta e_+ + \epsilon e_-$, or represent it as a 5D-vector $\underline{s} = [\alpha \ \beta \ \gamma \ \delta \ \epsilon]^T$. Thus, the sphere in CGA is represented with a 5-dimensional vector, which is an adequate representation to make two sets of 5-vectors, one representing the object and the other the deformed object. These sets are obtained by the method explained in next section (4). Once we have these sets, we will be able to apply the TPS-RPM algorithm in order to do the registration process (see Sect. 4.2). However, let us explain before how the rigid motion is done in GA. In GA, rotations are computed by the so called *rotor*, R, defined as in equation 4, where a is the plane perpendicular to the rotation axis; while translations are computed by the *translator*, T, defined as in equation 5, where t is the translation vector and e is defined as in 3.

$$R = \exp -\frac{1}{2}\theta a \tag{4}$$

$$T = \exp -\frac{t}{2}e \tag{5}$$

To rotate any entity in any dimension, we multiply it by the rotor R from the left and by the conjugate $\tilde{R}$ from the right, $x' = Rx\tilde{R}$. Translations are made in the same way: $y' = Ty\tilde{T}$. If we combine the rotation and the translation, the resulting operator is named *motor* and is expresed as $M = TR$, which is applied in the same way explained: $x' = Mx\tilde{M} = TRx\tilde{R}\tilde{T}$.

4 Volume Representation and Non-rigid Registration

In medical image analysis, the availability of 3D-models is of great interest to medicians because it allows them to have a better understanding of the situation, and such models are relatively easy to build. However, in special situations (as surgical procedures), some structures (as brain or tumor) suffer a (non-rigid) transformation and the initial model must be corrected to reflect the actual shape of the object. For this reason, it is important to have a representation suitable to be deformed, with the minor quantity of primitives involved in such representation as possible to make faster the process. In literature we can find the Union of Spheres algorithm (see [5]), which uses the spheres to build 3D-models of objects and to align or transform it over time. Nevertheless, we use the marching cubes algorithm's ideas to develop an alternative method to build 3D models by using spheres, which has the advantage of reducing the number of primitives needed. For space reasons we do not provide an explanation of the Union of Spheres nor the Marching Cubes algorithms, but it can be found in [5,9].

4.1 3D Models Using Spheres

To build a 3D model of the object of interest using spheres, we are based in the marching cubes algorithm (MCA). The principle of our propposal is the same as in MCA: given a set of m slides (CT images), divide the space in logical cubes (each cube contains eight vertices, four of slide k and four of slide $k+1$) and determine which vertices of each cube are inside (or on) and outside the surface. Then define the number of spheres of each cube according to figure 3 and eq. 6 (where i is the ith sphere of the case indicated by j), taking the indices of the cube's corners as the first cube of such figure indicates. Note that we use the same 15 basic cases of the marching cubes algorithm because the total of 256 cases can be obtained from this basis. Also note that instead of triangles we define spheres and that our goal is not to have a good render algorithm (as intended for Marching cubes algorithm), but have a representation of the volumetric data based on spheres which, as we said before, could be useful in the process of object registration.

$$s^j_{p_i} = c_{p_i} + 0.5(c^2_{p_i} - \rho^2_{p_i})e + e_0 \; ; \; s^j_{m_i} = c_{m_i} + 0.5(c^2_{m_i} - \rho^2_{m_i})e + e_0$$
$$s^j_{g_i} = c_{g_i} + 0.5(c^2_{g_i} - \rho^2_{g_i})e + e_0 \qquad (6)$$

Table 1 is a comparison between the results of the Union of Spheres and our approach for the case of a brain model. The first row shows the worst case with

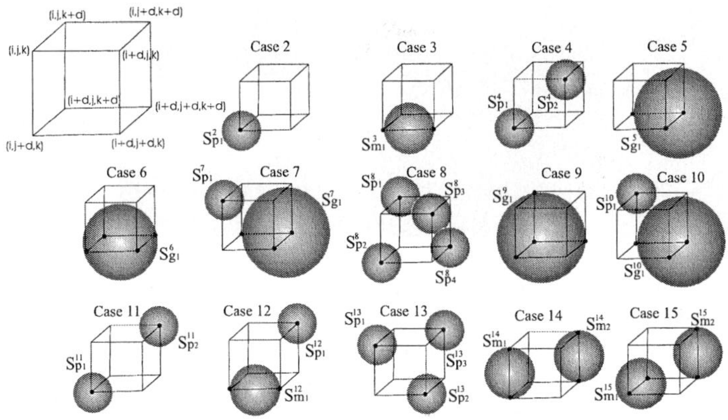

Fig. 3. The basic 15 cases of surface intersecting cubes (defining a different number of spheres with different centers and radius

both approaches; second row shows the number of spheres with improvements in both algorithms (reduction of spheres in DT is done by grouping spheres in a single one which contents the others, while such reduction is done using a displacement of $d = 3$ in our approach). The number of boundary points was $n = 3370$ in both cases. It is obvious the reduction in the number of primitives obtained with our approach, while maintaining clear enough the representation (even in the worst case). Figure 4.a-d shows the results obtained for a set of 36 images of a real patient with a tumor visible in 16 of them (see in figure 4.d the 3D model of the tumor of the real patient).

Table 1. Comparison between number of spheres using approach based on Delaunay tetraherization and our approach based on marching cubes algorithm; n is the number of boundary points; d is the distance between vertices in logical cubes of second approach.)

n/d	Num of spheres with each approach	
	DT approach	Our approach
3370 / 1	13480	11866
3370 / 3	8642	2602

4.2 Registration of Two Models

Suppose you have two points sets and one of them results from the transformation of the other but you do not know the transformation nor the correspondences between the points. In such situation you need an algorithm that find these two unknowns the best as possible. If in addition the transformation is non rigid, the complexity increases enormously. In the variety of registration algorithms

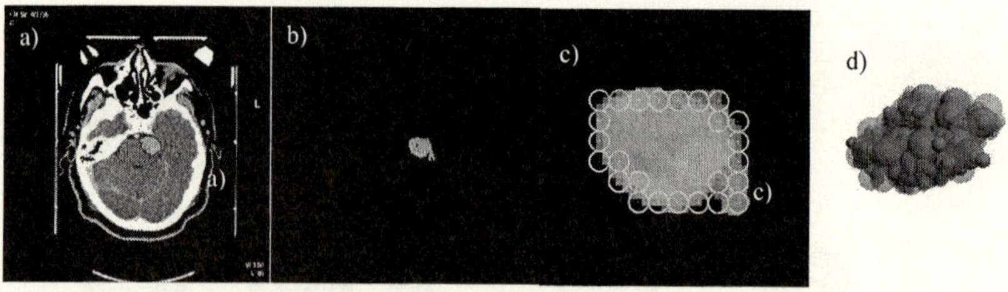

Fig. 4. Real patient: a) Original of one CT slide; b) Segmented object (the tumor); c) Zoom of the approximation by circles according the steps described in section; d) Approximation by spheres of the tumor extracted

existing today, we can find two that solve for correspondence and transformation: Iterated Closest Point (ICP) and Thin plate spline-Robust Point Matching (TPS-RPM). Details of each one of this algorithms can be found in [6]; here we assume, for space reasons, the reader knows them. In a past work we presented a comparison between these algorithms for non-rigid registration and we concluded TPS-RPM gives better results. However, we had used only sets of 2D and 3D points. Now we have spheres as points in a 5D-space modeling the object, and these spheres have not only different centers, but also different radius. So, for the non-rigid registration we follow the simulated annealing process of TPS-RPM explained in [6]. Let be $U_I = \{\underline{s}_j^I\}, j = 1, 2, ..., k$, the initial spheres set; $U_F = \{\underline{s}_i^F\}, i = 1, 2, ..., n$, the final spheres set. To update the matrix M of correspondence for spheres $\underline{s}_j^I$ y $\underline{s}_i^F$, modify m_{ji} as

$$m_{ji} = \frac{1}{T} e^{-\frac{(\underline{s}_i^F - f(\underline{s}_j^I))^\top (\underline{s}_i^F - f(\underline{s}_j^I))}{T}} . \tag{7}$$

for outlier entries $j = k + 1$ and $i = 1, 2, ..., n$:

$$m_{k+1,i} = \frac{1}{T_0} e^{-\frac{(\underline{s}_i^F - f(\underline{s}_{k+1}^I))^\top (\underline{s}_i^F - f(\underline{s}_{k+1}^I))}{T_0}} . \tag{8}$$

and for outliers entries $j = 1, 2, ..., k$ and $i = n + 1$:

$$m_{j,n+1} = \frac{1}{T_0} e^{-\frac{(\underline{s}_{n+1}^F - f(\underline{s}_j^I))^\top (\underline{s}_{n+1}^F - f(\underline{s}_j^I))}{T_0}} . \tag{9}$$

where T is the parameter of temperature which is reduced in each stage of the optimization process beginning at a value T_0 (remember that TPS-RPM use the simulated annealing process). Then, to update transformation we use the QR-decomposition of M to solve eq. 10 (following the same process explained in [6] and omited here for space reasons).

$$E_{tps}(d, w) = \|Y - Vd - \Phi w\|^2 + \lambda_1 (w^T \Phi w) + \lambda_2 [d - I]^T [d - I] . \tag{10}$$

Figure 5.a shows the 3D models as sets of spheres representing the object (the tumor mentioned in figure 4) -one is the initial set (or representation at time t_1);

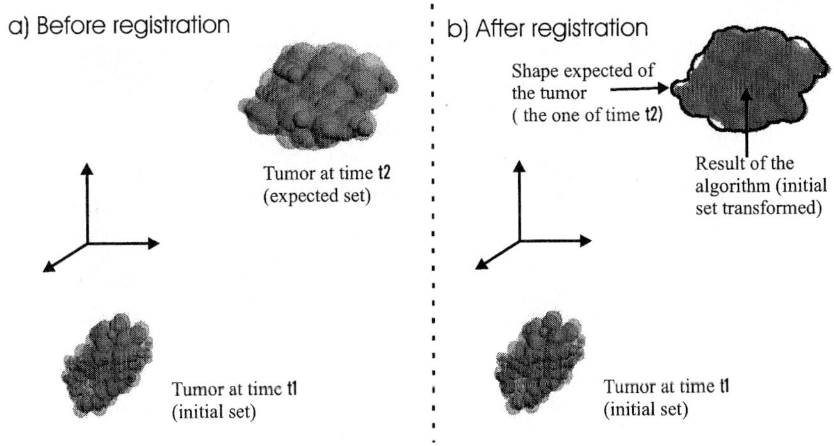

Fig. 5. a) Initial and expected sets (the expected set is obtained by a non-rigid transformation of the initial one); b) Initial and result of applying TPS-RPM to align the sets of spheres, represented as 5D-vectors in conformal geometric algebra. Note that the resulting set has been aligned an looks like the initial one.

the other is the deformed or expected set (or representation at time t_2)- which must be registered. Figure 5.b shows the results of registration process using TPS-RPM algorithm with the spheres as 5D-vectors in conformal geometric algebra. Note that usually, researchers use TPS-RPM with 2D or 3D vectors because they can not go beyond such dimension; in contrast, using conformal geometric algebra we have an homogeneous representation which preserves isometries and uses the sphere as the basic entity. In figure 5, at the left are only the initial and expected sets; at the right the initial and the result of registration but with the shape of the expected set for visual comparison. Note that the algorithm adjusted the radius as expected (this is not possible using only 3D vectors).

5 Object Tracking

Other important task in surgical procedures is the tracking of objects involved in such procedures. For this purpose, some spherical markers are placed on the instruments, and such markers are tracked using the Polaris System (Northern Digital Inc.). To find the transfomation relating the 3D position of the objects being tracked with the virtual model showed on display, we first calibrate the real position of the patient with the 3D-model using the TPS-RPM algorithm (section 4.2). Then we use the so called "motor" (explained in 3), to update the position of the surgical devices in real time. The procedure to track is explained as follows: first, we take two 3D point sets $\{\mathbf{x}_i\}$ and $\{\mathbf{x}'_i\}$ defined in the Euclidean 3D geometric algebra and compute the rotor $\mathbf{R}$ and the translation vector $\mathbf{t}$ which minimize the following equation

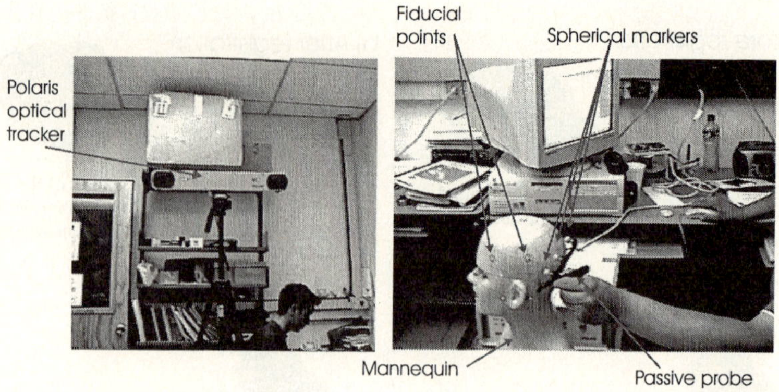

Fig. 6. Scenario for tracking of devices: fiducial points are used to register the 3D model with what is been observed by the polaris system; spherical markers on device are used to track it

$$S = \sum_{i=1}^{n} \left[\mathbf{x}_i' - \mathbf{R}(\mathbf{x}_i - \mathbf{t})\tilde{\mathbf{R}} \right]^2. \tag{11}$$

The equations to compute the rotor and translation vector are obtained using the differentiations of equation (11).

$$F_{\alpha\beta} \equiv \sigma_\alpha \cdot \underline{f}(\sigma_\beta) = \sum_{i=1}^{n} (\sigma_\alpha \cdot \mathbf{u}_i)(\sigma_\beta \cdot \mathbf{v}_i) \tag{12}$$

$$\mathbf{t} = \frac{1}{n} \sum_{i=1}^{n} \left[\mathbf{x}_i - \tilde{\mathbf{R}}\mathbf{x}_i'\mathbf{R} \right] \tag{13}$$

where $\mathbf{u}_i = \mathbf{x}_i - \overline{\mathbf{x}}$ and $\mathbf{v}_i = \mathbf{x}_i'$. By computing the SVD of F we get $F = USV^T$ and using this result we compute the 3×3 rotation matrix $R = VU^T$. Thereafter the translation is computed using equation (13). This method was developed by Lasenby et al. in [12]. The exponential representation of the transformation in our framework reads

$$\mathbf{M} = \mathbf{R} + \frac{\mathbf{t}}{2}\mathbf{R} = e^{\mathbf{l}(\frac{\theta_u}{2} + e\frac{\mathbf{t}_u}{2})} \tag{14}$$

where θ_u is the angle and $\mathbf{t}_u$ the displacement with respect to the screw axis line $\mathbf{l}$. Applying this transformation to each point $\mathbf{x}'$, we can obtain a tracking path as follows:

$$\begin{aligned} \mathbf{x}' = \mathbf{T}\mathbf{R}\mathbf{x}\tilde{\mathbf{R}}\tilde{\mathbf{T}} &= e^{\frac{1}{2}\mathbf{t}e} e^{\frac{\theta_u}{2}\mathbf{n}}\ \mathbf{x}_h\ e^{-\frac{\theta_u}{2}\mathbf{n}} e^{-\frac{1}{2}\mathbf{t}e} \\ &= e^{\mathbf{l}(\frac{\theta_u}{2} + e\frac{\mathbf{t}_u}{2})}\ \mathbf{x}_h\ e^{-\mathbf{l}(\frac{\theta_u}{2} + e\frac{\mathbf{t}_u}{2})} \end{aligned} \tag{15}$$

Figure 7 shows the applicaton of procedure explained before when tracking a "polaris in-line passive probe" with three spherical markers (as the one showed

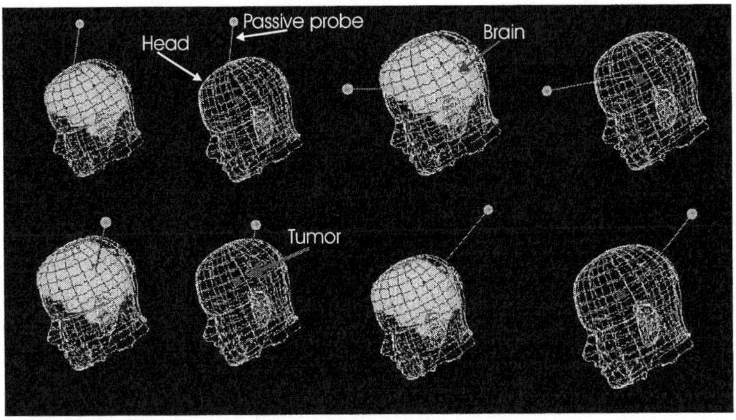

Fig. 7. Images in 3D virtual world of the process of tracking of the surgical device. First and third column: the whole 3D-model (skin + brain +device); second and fourth column: brain hidden to visualize the tumor.

in figure 6:b). The scenario is as follows (see figure 6):a mannequin (in substitution of a real patient); in such mannequin we put nine fiducial markers used to align the "presurgical 3D-model" with the real position when tracking is intended to be. A brain, obtained from a digital atlas, which is segmented and merged with the 3D-model of the mannequin in order to have a more realistic representation in the experiment, together with a tumor (also segmented to visualize in differents views). Figure 7 shows the 3D-model of the mannequin, brain, tumor and the device being tracked; such figure shows different momments while tracking the device. In such figure, the first and third column show the model complete (head+brain+device), the second and fourth one only the the head and the tumor for better visualization of the last one.

6 Conclusions

We have shown the application of GA in three different tasks: volume representation, non-rigid registration of sets of spheres and real time tracking. Also we show at the begining a different approach for medical image segmentation which combines texture and boundary information and embed it into a region-growing scheme, having the advantage of integrating all the information in a simple process. The algorithm proved to be very useful despite the limitations of the used CT images (limitations compared with the facilities given by MRI images, commonly used in similar works). With the GA framework, we show how to obtain a representation of volumetric data using spheres; our approach is based on the ideas exposed in marching cubes algorithm but it is not intended for rendering purposes or displaying in real time, but for reduce the number of primitives modeling the volumetric data and use less primitives in the process of registration. Also, we show how to represent these primitives as spheres in the conformal geometric algebra, which are 5-dimensional vectors that can be used with the principles of TPS-RPM. Experimental results seem to be promising and highlight the potential of GA used in different tasks.

References

1. S. Ho, E. Bullitt, G. Gerig, "Level-set evolution with region competition: automatic 3-D segmentation of brain tumors", *Proceedings of 16th International Conference on Pattern Recognition*, Volume 1, pp. 532-535, 2002.
2. M. Prastawa, E. Bullit, S. Ho and G. Gerig, "A Brain Tumor Segmentation Framework Based on Outlier Detection," *Medical Image Analysis Journal*, 8(3), pp. 275-83, September 2004.
3. M.C. Andrade, "An interactive algorithm for image smoothing and segmentation," *Electronic Letters on Computer Vision and Image Analysis*, **4-1**, pp. 32-48, 2004.
4. P. Lin, C. Zheng, Y. Yang and J. Gu, "Medical Image Segmentation by Level Set Method Incorporating Region and Boundary Statistical Information," *9th Iberoamerican Congress on Pattern Recognition*, National Institute of Astrophysics, Optics and Electronics (INAOE), Puebla, Mexico, pp. 654-660, October 2004.
5. V. Ranjan and A. Fournier, "Union of spheres (UoS) model for volumetric data,", in *Proceedings of the Eleventh Annual Symposium on Computational Geometry*, Vancouver, Canada, 1995, C2-C3, pp. 402-403.
6. H. Chui, A. Rangarajan, "A new point matching algorithm for non-rigid registration". *IEEE Conf. on Computer Vision and Pattern Recognition (CVPR)*, Volume 2, pp. 44-51, 2000.
7. X. Muñoz, "Image segmentation integrating color, texture and boundary information," *Ph.D. Thesis in Computer engineering*, Girona, December 2002.
8. K.S. Fu and J.K. Mui, "A survey on image segmentation," *Pattern Recognition*, 12:395-403, 1980.
9. W. Lorensen and H. Cline, "Marching cubes: a high resolution 3D surface construction algorithm," *Computer Graphics.* **21-4**, 163–169, July 1987.
10. E. Bayro-Corrochano and G. Sobczyk, *Geometric algebra with applications in science and engineering*, Birkhuser, 2001.
11. B. Rosenhahn and G. Sommer, "Pose Estimation in Conformal Geometric Algebra," Technical report 0206, Christian-Albrechts-University of Kiel, November 2002, pp. 13-36.
12. J. Lasenby, A.N. Lasenby, C. Doran and W.J. Fitzgerald, "New geometric methods for computer vision - an application to structure and motion estimation," *International Journal of Computer Vision*, 26(3), pp. 191-213, 1998.

Similarity Measures in Documents Using Association Graphs

José E. Medina Pagola[1], Ernesto Guevara Martínez[2], José Hernández Palancar[1], Abdel Hechavarría Díaz[1], and Raudel Hernández León[1]

[1] Centro de Aplicaciones de Tecnologías de Avanzada (CENATAV), 7ª # 21812 e/ 218 y 228, Rpto. Siboney, CP. 12200, Playa, C. de la Habana, Cuba
{jmedina, jpalancar}@cenatav.co.cu
[2] Instituto Superior Politécnico "José Antonio Echeverria" (ISPJAE), Ave. 114 # 11901, CP. 10390, Marianao, C. de la Habana, Cuba
eguevara@ceis.cujae.edu.cu

Abstract. In this paper we present a new model, designated as Association Graph, to improve document representation, facilitating the ontological dimension. We explain how to generate and use this kind of graph. Also, we analyze different document similarity measures based on this representation. A classical vector space model was used to evaluate this model and measures, investigating their strengths and weaknesses. The proposed model was found to give promising results.

1 Introduction

At the moment, due to vertiginous scientific and technological advances of the last years, institutions have great capacities of creating, storing and distributing their data. This situation, among other things, has increased the necessity of new tools that aid in transforming this vast quantity of data in useful information or new knowledge that can be used in decision making. Data mining systems are examples of this type of tools.

These systems allow us to analyze and to discover interesting patterns in large databases. However, due to the information characteristics contained in traditional databases and data warehouses, data mining systems are not appropriate for the analysis of other types of information less structured like, for example, the one contained in text collections. For this reason, Text Mining arises as an alternative to understand the processing of natural language. Text Mining combines artificial intelligence, statistical, database, and graphic visualization techniques, allowing the comprehension of aspects dealing with the identification, organization and understanding of the knowledge appearing in any text.

Examples of systems that use those techniques, and have gotten some attention in recent years, are pointed out by Yao et al. as RSS (Research Support Systems) and WRSS (Web-based RSS) [1]. They improve current search tools, helping scientists to access, explore, evaluate and use information on digital libraries or on the Web, improving research productivity and quality [2].

M. Lazo and A. Sanfeliu (Eds.): CIARP 2005, LNCS 3773, pp. 741 – 751, 2005.

Text Mining, together with others techniques, such as profiling, collaborative filtering, intelligent agent, etc., should be considered to develop those systems. Text Mining, as many other tasks of text processing, is usually carried out on simple representations of text contents. However, profiling, collaborative filtering and WRSS require more complex semantic relations, usually expressed as semantic graphs [3].

In this paper we propose an approach using Association Graphs, a measure as an alternative representation of documents and a way of measuring their similarities, facilitating their ontological dimensions required by many applications as, for instance, WRSS. In Section 2 we will present general considerations for vector space models in Text Mining. In Section 3 we will analyze the limitations of term correlation for knowledge indexing and representation. In Section 4 we will explain our proposal, as an alternative to improve document representation, facilitating the ontological dimension.

2 Text Mining

Text Mining could be defined as a discovery process of interesting patterns and new knowledge in a text collection; therefore, Text Mining is a specific type of Data Mining applied to documents to discover information not present in any specific one. Hence, its objective is to discover things such as regularities, tendencies, deviations and associations in huge databases in textual form [4].

By applying algorithms of Text Mining to documents stored in different media, for example in WRSS, one may discover patterns and extract knowledge useful to decision-makers, in the example researchers, who are interested in exploratory searching and browsing [1].

The process of Text Mining is carried out in two main stages: a pre-processing stage and a discovery stage. In the first stage, texts are transformed into a kind of structured or semi-structured representation, facilitating their later analysis. In the second stage these representations are analyzed in order to discover interesting patterns or new knowledge [4].

In the pre-processing stage a set of operations is done to simplify and standardize the texts being analyzed. Some of the operations considered are the following:

- Recognizing useful words.
- Ignoring the null words, also known as Stopwords.
- Identifying phrases or terms with multi-words.
- Obtaining the canonical forms of the words, also known as stemming.

As a result of this stage a sequence of distinguished terms is obtained. These terms could be organized in different forms but, in general, they are considered as groups or bags of terms, usually structured using vector models [5]. In these representations, the sequences of the terms, their correlations or syntactical relations are not analyzed; therefore, their mutual independence is supposed. The values of those vectors could be assumed as weights, considering the following interpretations [6]:

- Boolean - Each term is associated with a Boolean value representing if it is present or not in a document.
- TF (Term Frequecy) - Each term is associated with a frequency of appearance in a document, absolute or normalized.
- TF-IDF (Term Frequency - Inverse Document Frequency) - The term is associated with its frequency, adjusted by the inverse of the number of documents containing each term.

These vectors of terms are used in a second stage, among other tasks, to analyze the similarities between documents, or groups of them, using different measures as the Cosine, applied to the angle between the vectors, define as [6]:

$$sim(d_i, d_j) = \cos(d_i, d_j) = \frac{(d_i \bullet d_j)}{\| d_i \| * \| d_j \|} = \frac{\sum w_{ir} * w_{jr}}{\sqrt{\sum w_{ir}^2 * \sum w_{jr}^2}} , \quad (1)$$

where d_i, d_j are the vectors of documents i, j, $\|d_i\|$, $\|d_j\|$ the norms of the vectors, and w_{ir}, w_{jr} are the term weights in the vectors d_i, d_j, respectively.

3 Ontological Requirements

Although, generally, the terms appearing in a document are interrelated and the vector space model, proposed by Salton [7], has been the dominant way to represent and measure document similarities, some authors consider this treatment as an elementary way of the ontological dimension of the information.

While that treatment could be adequate for some applications, in others, like WRSS and collaborative filtering systems, more complex semantic relations are required. Collaborative filtering system, a kind of information filtering, evaluates resources in order to recommend objects preferred by similar users, supposing they are also useful to a particular user [8].

In WRSS, documents are the resources to be evaluated. In this case, the scientific knowledge of documents, or groups of them, and scientific profiles of users should be considered. That knowledge and profiles are usually expressed by semantic graphs constructed generally by users. For that reason, one should evaluate methods for automatic or semi-automatic graph generation, quite difficult to make from a simple vector model.

An alternative approach of the ontological dimension is observed in [9]. In this work the authors use Conceptual Maps to identify potential terms and relationships. So, with this proposal, the user defines his personal Conceptual Maps interactively. Although the author's intention might be the use of Conceptual Maps in an information retrieval process, such approach wasn't discussed in that work.

Other ways to include an ontological dimension are the corpus-based methods in conjunction with lexical taxonomies to calculate semantic similarity between words/concepts. Examples of these methods are those developed over the broad-coverage taxonomy known as Wordnet [10].

Well alternative approaches to the vector space model are the language models. These consider the probabilities of occurrence of a phrase S in a language M, indicated by $P(S/M)$. However, the phrases are usually reduced to one term, assuming again unigrams and independence among them. An example of this model is the Kullback-Leibler Divergence (a variation of the cross-entropy), defined as:

$$D(d_i \parallel d_j) = \sum P(t / d_i) \log \frac{P(t / d_i)}{P(t / d_j)}.$$

This expression could be combined in both directions to obtain a similarity measure, as was pointed out by Feldman and Dagan [11].

An interesting implementation is the proposal of Kou and Gardarin [12]. This proposal is a kind of language model, considering the similarities between two documents as:

$$sim(d_i, d_j) = d_i \bullet d_j = \sum_r w_{ir} w_{jr} + \sum_r \sum_{s \neq r} w_{ir} w_{js} (t_r \bullet t_s),$$

where w_{ir} and w_{js}, using Kou-Gardarin terminology, are the term weights in document vectors d_i, d_j, respectively, and $(t_r \bullet t_s)$ is the a priori correlation between terms t_r and t_s. Actually, the authors included in the first part of the expression the self-correlation in t_r, considering that $(t_r \bullet t_r) = 1$. The authors propose the estimation of the correlation through a training process. As can be noticed, those correlations express the probabilities $P(t_r,t_s/M)$ of phrases containing the terms t_r, t_s in a language M. Besides, that expression could be reduced to the Cosine measure (normalized by the length of the vectors) if the term independence is considered and, for that reason, the correlation $(t_r \bullet t_s)$ is zero.

Although the Kou-Gardarin proposal improves the independence limitation of the vector space model, it considers that two terms are correlated as a tendency, and independent of the documents analyzed in the similarity measure. This assumption underestimates the ontological view of each document.

The approaches mention above are variants of the Generalized Vector Space Model proposed by S.K.M Wong et al. [13]. In their work, they expressed that there was no satisfactory way of computing term correlations based on automatic indexing scheme.

We believe that up to the present time that limitation has not been solved yet. Although several authors have proposed different methods of recognizing term correlations in the retrieval process, those methods try to model the ontological dimension by a global distribution of terms, but not with a local evaluation of documents.

In general, it could be assumed that with a better ontological representation of the information retrieved and discriminated, the better the documents will be mined. Besides, it is expected that a better representation improve the capacity of knowledge comprehension regarding the vector model. These considerations will be developed in more details later on.

4 Association Graphs

It is comprehensible that a same term in two documents could designate different concepts. Besides, two terms could have different relations, according to the subject of each document, and those relations could exist only in the context of some documents, forming a specific group, and independent of the relations in a global dimension or language.

In order to model the relation between two terms in a document, we will consider the shortest physical distance between those terms. So, two documents shall be closer if the number of common terms is greater and the shortest physical distances among those terms are similar. With these assumption we hypothesize that, in order to recognize the semantic relation between two terms, it is enough that they appear together at least once in a small context: a sentence, a paragraph, and so on.

The use of physical distance among terms has been considered in other works. For example, Ahonen et al. has appointed that many documents, especially books and papers, are structured in sections or micro-documents and, logically, terms in a same micro-document are strongly related, but in different micro-documents the physical relation uses to be weak [14]. Although they realized the relevance of the physical relation among terms, the vector model was considered in their work.

Also, many search engines to measure the document's importance or quality consider the proximity among the words of complex equations or queries.

In order to measure the distance between two terms t_r and t_s in a document i, designated by D^i_{rs}, the physical distance in the document between those terms could be defined in different ways. One way could be considering the number of words between them. Although this could be a feasible solution, it ignores the semantic strength in sentences and paragraphs.

Considering the distance by sentence, D^i_{rs} will be $n+1$, where n is the number of intermediate sentences between those containing the terms..

If we consider the distance by paragraph, without ignoring the natural co-occurrence when appearing in the same sentence, and considering: (p_r, n_r), (p_s, n_s), the paragraph and sentence numbers of terms t_r and t_s respectively, the physical distance between these terms is defined as follows:

$$D^i_{rs} = \begin{cases} 1 & (r = s) \vee [(p_r = p_s) \wedge (n_r = n_s)] \\ |p_r - p_s| + 2 & \text{Other case} \end{cases}.$$

Observe that the minimum value of D^i_{rs}, as could be expected, isn't zero, but one in both cases.. This consideration is only a convenient assumption to expressions defined farther on.

Besides, it will be considered in both distance that every term is related to itself, having distance one, in order to include the case two documents have only one term in common.

According to this, a document could be modeled by a graph, where the nodes are the distinguished terms and the arcs are their relations, weighted by their distances. Also, we are considering this is a full connected graph, having any term some relation (stronger or not according to the distance) with the others.

Although the physical relation, in conjunction with the common terms, could be used to evaluate the neighborhood among documents, the weights of the distinguished terms should not be ignored in a similarity measure. To include these values, the document graph could be extended with weighted nodes.

Therefore, a first approximation for a document representation could be seen as a weighted graph by node, considering the weights of the distinguished terms, and by arc, considering the shortest physical distance between the adjacent terms.

As the additional components of these graphs are the arcs, with respect to the vector model, and trying to combine the weights of the terms and the distance between them to express the strength of their association, the vector A^i_{rs}, named *Association Vector*, is proposed as the arc's weight of the related terms t_r, t_s in a document i, defined as:

$$A^i_{rs} = \left(\frac{w^i_r}{\sqrt{D^i_{rs}}}, \frac{w^i_s}{\sqrt{D^i_{rs}}}\right) ,$$

where w^i_r and w^i_s are the weights of the terms t_r and t_s, respectively, in a document i.

As the arc's weight A^i_{rs} is a two-dimensional vector, the strength of the terms's association can be evaluated as the Euclidean norm $\|A^i_{rs}\|$. In this case, the strength is greater if the terms's weights are greater and the distance between the terms is shorter. Besides, the upper value of A^i_{rs} is (w^i_r, w^i_s), when the distance is one, and the lower tends to (0, 0), when the distance is very long.

With these transformations, an *Association Graph* can be defined as a weighted graph by arc, considering as weight of each arc (t_r, t_s) the Association Vector A^i_{rs}.

5 Similarity Measures

Although for a vector model a Cosine measure represents a standard way to evaluate the similarity between two documents, in a graph model (as the Association Graph) other measures should be considered.

As our graph doesn't posses a structural or spatial representation, it is enough to treat it as a set of arcs. Several authors have proposed different matching coefficients for sets, which in general coincide with commonly used measures of association in information retrieval.. Examples of these are: Dice's, Jaccard's and Overlap coefficients, among others [15]. These may all be considered to be normalized versions of the simple matching coefficient of two sets X and Y, defined as: $| X \cap Y|$.

Another version of the simple matching coefficient is the proposal of Pazienza and Vindigni. They define a common coverage of two non-empty sets as the average of the coverage of their intersection with respect to each of them [16].

As we are considering sets of arcs, a first idea for a matching coefficient is trying to define a simple matching-like one. If that were adequate for a common graph, in an Association Graph, where each graph has different association strengths, the coefficient could be better constructed as the Pazienza-Vindigni proposal.

According to the previous idea, and considering the Association Graphs of documents i, j, the *Simple Coverage* as a similarity measure could be used, expressed as:

$$sim(d_i, d_j) = \frac{1}{2}\frac{\sum_{t_r, t_s \in T_{ij}} \| A_{rs}^i \|}{\sum_{t_r, t_s \in T_i} \| A_{rs}^i \|} + \frac{1}{2}\frac{\sum_{t_r, t_s \in T_{ij}} \| A_{rs}^j \|}{\sum_{t_r, t_s \in T_j} \| A_{rs}^j \|}, \qquad (2)$$

where T_i, T_j represent the sets of terms in the Association Graphs of documents *i, j*, respectively, and T_{ij} is the set of the common terms ($T_i \cap T_j$).

Notice that the first part of the expression evaluates the proportion of the total association strength of the common arcs with respect to the total strength in whole document *i*, and the second part the same but in document *j*. The fractions ½ in the formula guarantee that this measure has values in the interval [0, 1].

Although we considered that the Equation 2 is a good first approach, we realized that it doesn't measure the similarities between the vectors associated with the common arcs. In order to include these similarities, we propose the *Weighted Coverage* measure, defined as:

$$sim(d_i, d_j) = \frac{1}{2}\frac{\sum_{t_r, t_s \in T_{ij}} S^{ij}{}_{rs} \| A_{rs}^i \|}{\sum_{t_r, t_s \in T_i} \| A_{rs}^i \|} + \frac{1}{2}\frac{\sum_{t_r, t_s \in T_{ij}} S^{ij}{}_{rs} \| A_{rs}^j \|}{\sum_{t_r, t_s \in T_j} \| A_{rs}^j \|}. \qquad (3)$$

If T_i or T_j are empty sets, the expression is defined as zero. The weight $S^{ij}{}_{rs}$ represents a similarity measure between $A^i{}_{rs}$ and $A^j{}_{rs}$. This weight is defined in this paper as:

$$S^{ij}{}_{rs} = \cos(A_{rs}^i, A_{rs}^j) * (1 - \tfrac{1}{2}(\| A_{rs}^i \| - \| A_{rs}^j \|)^2),$$

where the first part of the expression represents the cosine between those vectors, defined in a similar way as the Equation 1. It can be noticed that the weights defined in this manner include not only the angles between the vectors, but also the differences of their strengths.

This similarity measure could be extended to evaluate the similarities between documents, groups of documents, and user profiles, changing the values ½ of each part of the formula by different fractions. These extensions could be convenient to many applications, as collaborative filtering and WRSS.

6 Experiment and Analysis

In order to evaluate the proposed measure, the data TREC-5 in Spanish (http://trec.nist.gov) was used. From this data, we used 676 news published by AFP during 1994 and classified in 22 topics. Table 1 shows the topics and the quantity of documents for each topic in this data.

The pre-processing stage was done with the library of the system JERARTOP [6], which used the morphological analyzer MACO+, developed by the Natural Language Processing Group of the Polytechnic University of Catalunya, based on extended

Table 1. Topics of TREC-5

Topic	Description	# Doc.
SP51	Ocean's Fish Suplí	75
SP52	Basque Rebels War	13
SP53	Women's status in Latin America	46
SP54	World's Marine Resources	35
SP55	Fate of Carlos Andrés Pérez	108
SP58	Financing of Samper Election	44
SP59	Hoof and Mouth Disease	7
SP60	Methods Narcotraffickers Use to Hide their Drugs	46
SP62	Colombia's Fresh Flower Trade	15
SP63	Drug Trafficking Involvement	5
SP64	Green Iguana Extinction	7
SP65	Raul Castro's Activities	29
SP66	MERCOSUR	68
SP67	Peruvian Fishmeal Industry	8
SP68	AIDS in Argentina	12
SP69	Status of Russian Satellites and Membership in NATO	62
SP70	NATO Peace Force in Bosnia	6
SP71	Status of United States' Certification of Columbia and its War on Drugs	11
SP72	Damage to Mexico's Environment	14
SP73	Illegal Trade of Exotic Animals	12
SP74	Privatization of Major Sectors of Argentina Economy	34
SP75	Heroin in Latin America	19
Total	22 Topics	676

stochastic models ECGI [17]. A detailed description of that analyzer can be found in http://www.lsi.upc.es/~nlp.

A classical vector model was used to evaluate the proposed approach, applying the Cosine measure. The term weights were calculated as TF (*Term Frequency*), normalized by the maximum frequency. K-Nearest Neighbour classifier, with weighted voting by similarity value, was conducted by taking the value of *K* as 5, 10, 15 and 20. A k-fold cross-validation was applied with *k*=10. The results obtained are shown in Table 2, where *simC* and *simG* are the measures obtained by Cosine and Weighted Coverage models respectively.

Precision, Recall and F1 are three commonly used evaluation measures of performance. For a single category or topic, these measures can be defined as [18]:

Precision = "Correctly assigned" / "Assigned to the category"
Recall = "Correctly assigned" / "Belonging to the category"
F1 = 2 * Recall*Precision / (Recall+Precision)

Table 2. Macro-averaged Performance

K	Precision *simC*	Precision *simG*	Recall *simC*	Recall *simG*	F1 *simC*	F1 *simG*
5	0.8175	0.8222	0.7289	0.7356	0.7545	0.7611
10	0.8072	0.8568	0.6663	0.7088	0.6973	0.7414
15	0.8566	0.8482	0.6452	0.7043	0.7079	0.7397
20	0.8425	0.8461	0.6233	0.6813	0.6836	0.7181

Precision, Recall and F1 are three commonly used evaluation measures of performance. For a single category or topic, these measures can be defined as [18]:

Precision = "Correctly assigned" / "Assigned to the category"
Recall = "Correctly assigned" / "Belonging to the category"
F1 = 2 * Recall*Precision / (Recall+Precision)

For evaluating the performance average across categories, there are two conventional methods: Macro-averaging performance and Micro-averaging performance. Macro-averaged performance scores are computed by a simple average of the performance measures for each category. Micro-averaged performance scores are computed by first accumulating the corresponding variables in the per-category expressions, and then using those global quantities to compute the scores. Micro-averaged performance score gives equal weights to every document. Likewise, macro-averaged performance score gives equal weights to every category or topic, regardless of its frequency.

As can be noticed in Table 2, Association Graph model outperforms Cosine similarity model for different *K* values, except for Macro-precision with *K*=15. Besides, as an average, 2.9 % of F1 measure in Weighted Coverage model is bigger than in Cosine model. This proves that the use of physical term association really improves the effectiveness of categorization.

Although these results are only preliminaries, they show that the Association Graph and the proposed measure represent a good model and seem to be better than the Vector-Cosine.

7 Conclusions

Although some approaches have been considered, especially in semi-automatic processing, the vector space model has been the dominant way for document representations, especially as frequency vectors of terms. These representations are relatively easy to build from texts, but cannot express several details of their meanings, having a poor capacity of description. In order to achieve a better representation of the knowledge contained in documents, we have proposed the Association Graphs.

Using this kind of graph, a similarity measure, named Weighted Coverage, is proposed, making it possible to compare and discriminate documents, applying it in different techniques as, for example, clustering and classification algorithms.

Some variations to the proposed measure could be analyzed and other distance measures could be assumed as, for example, limiting the distance to a convenient value.

Nevertheless, the experiment has shown interesting results. Although other experiments must be done, the proposed model was found to give promising results.

References

1. Yao J.T., Yao Y.Y.: Web-based Information Retrieval Support Systems: building research tools for scientists in the new information age. Proceedings of the 2003 IEEE/WIC International Conference on Web Intelligence, (WI 2003), Halifax, Canada (2003).
2. Xu J., Huang Y., Madey G.: A Research Support System Framework for Web Data Mining. Proceedings of WI/IAT 2003 Workshop on Applications, Products and Services of Web-based Support Systems, WSS 2003, Halifax, Canada (2003).
3. Rojo A.: RA, un agente recomendador de recursos digitales de la Web. Master thesis, Universidad de las Américas, Puebla, México (2002). URL: http://www.pue .udlap .mx / ~ tesis/msp/rojo_g_a/.
4. Berry M.: Survey of Text Mining, Clustering, Classification and Retrieval. Springer (2004).
5. Raghavan V., Wong S.: A critical analysis of Vector Space Model for Information Retrieval. Journal of the American Society on Information Science, Vol. 37, No. 5, pp. 279-287 (1986).
6. Pons A.: Desarrollo de algoritmos para la estructuración dinámica de información y su aplicación a la detección de sucesos. Doctoral thesis, University Jaume I, Spain (2004).
7. Salton, G., The SMART Retrieval System - Experiments in Automatic Document Processing. Prentice-Hall, Englewood Cliffs, New Jersey (1971).
8. Ziqiang W., Boqin F.: Collaborative Filtering Algorithm Based on Mutual Information. APWeb 2004, LNCS 3007, pp. 405-415. Springer-Verlag Berlin Heidelberg (2004).
9. Simón A., Rosete A., Panucia K., Ortiz A.: Aproximación a un método para la representación en Mapas Conceptuales del conocimiento almacenado en textos, con beneficios para la Minería de Texto. I Simposio Cubano de Inteligencia Artificial, Convención Informática 2004, Cuba (2004).
10. Budanitsky A., Hirst G.: Semantic distance inWordNet: An experimental, application-oriented evaluation of five measures. Workshop on WordNet and Other Lexical Resources, in the North American Chapter of the Association for Computational Linguistics (NAACL-2000) (2001).
11. Feldman R., Dagan I.: Knowledge Discovery in Textual Databases (KDT). Proceedings of the first International Conference on Data Mining and Knowledge Discovery, KDD'95, Montreal, pp. 112-117 (1995).
12. Kou H., Gardarin G.: Similarity Model and Term Association for Document Categorization. NLDB 2002, LNCS 2553, pp. 223-229, Springer-Verlag Berlin Heidelberg (2002).
13. Wong S.K.M, Ziarko W. and Wong P.C.N.: Generalized Vector Space Model in Information Retrieval. Proc. of the 8th Int. ACM SIGIR Conference on Research and Development in Information Retrieval, New York, ACM 11 (1985).
14. Ahonen H., Heikkinen B., Heinonen O., Klemettinen M.: Discovery of Reasonably sized Fragments Using Inter-paragraph Similarities. Technical Report C-1997-67, University of Helsinki, Department of Computer Science (1997).
15. C. J. van Rijsbergen C.J.: Information Retrieval. London: Butterworths (1979).

16. Pazienza M.T. and Vindigni M.: Agents Based Ontological Mediation in IE Systems. SCIE 2002, LNAI 2700, Springer-Verlag Berlin Heidelberg (2003).
17. Carmona J., et al.: An Environment for Morphosyntactic Processing of Unrestricted Spanish Text. Proceedings of the First International Conference on Language Resources and Evaluation, LREC'98 (1998).
18. Yang Y.: An evaluation of statistical approaches to text categorization. Journal of Information Retrieval, Vol. 1, No. 1/2, pp. 67-88 (1999).

Real-Time Kalman Filtering for Nonuniformity Correction on Infrared Image Sequences: Performance and Analysis*

Sergio K. Sobarzo and Sergio N. Torres

Department of Electrical Engineering, University of Concepción,
Casilla 160-C, Concepción, Chile
{ssobarzo, sertorre}@udec.cl
http://nuc.die.udec.cl

Abstract. A scene-based method for nonuniformity correction of infrared image sequences is developed and tested. The method uses the information embedded in the scene and performs the correction in a frame by frame Kalman Filter approach. The key assumption of the method is that the uncertainty on the input infrared irradiance integrated by each detector is solved using the spatial infrared information collected from the scene. The performance of the method is tested using infrared image sequences captured by two infrared cameras.

Keywords: Infrared Sensor-Imaging, Infrared Focal Plane Arrays, Signal Processing, Kalman Filtering, Image Coding, Processing and Analysis.

1 Introduction

Infrared (IR) imaging systems are widely used in a variety of civilian and military applications such as aerial surveillance, satellite imaging, early fire detection, biology, robotics, and astronomy [1]. An IR Focal-Plane Array (FPA), the heart of an IR imaging system, is an array consisting in a mosaic of photo-detector elements that are placed in the focal plane of the optical imaging system [3].

It is well known that the performance of the whole IR imaging system is strongly affected by the fixed-pattern noise (FPN) [1]. The FPN, also called nonuniformity, is the unequal photoresponse of the detectors in the FPA when an uniform scene is imaged. What makes the FPN even a more challenging problem is that the spatial nonuniformity slowly drifts in time, and depending on the technology used, the drift can take from minutes to hours [1]. The task of any nonuniformity correction (NUC) technique is to compensate for the spatial nonuniformity and updates the compensation as needed to account for the temporal drift in the detector's response [2], [5], [6].

* This work was partially supported by Grant Milenio ICM P02-049. S. Sobarzo acknowledges support from Conicyt. The authors wish to thank Ernest E. Armstrong (OptiMetrics Inc., USA) and Pierre Potet (CEDIP Infrared Systems, France) for collecting the data.

M. Lazo and A. Sanfeliu (Eds.): CIARP 2005, LNCS 3773, pp. 752–761, 2005.

In this paper, a new algorithm for NUC in IR-FPA, based on Kalman filter (KF) theory, is developed and tested. The algorithm operates, per pixel and in a frame by frame basis, assuming that the nonuniformity parameters, the gain and bias, follow a Gauss-Markov model (GMM). As the method operates, the autocorrelation parameters of the gain and bias are fixed to be close enough to one, following GMM's convergence requirements. The per pixel input irradiance parameter is computed on-line using a spatial lowpass filter [4]. The performance of the algorithm is tested using sequences of corrupted IR data captured by two infrared cameras and is compared against the results obtained by using black body radiator corrected data. Further, the algorithm is also tested over a image sequence with artificial nonuniformity. Two performance parameters are computed to check the level of reduction of the nonuniformity.

2 Algorithm

2.1 Mathematical Modelling

The model for each pixel of the IR-FPA is a linear relationship between the input irradiance and the detector response [1,7]. Further, for a single detector in the FPA, the linear input-output relation of the ij-th detector in the k-th frame is approximated by [1]:

$$Y_k^{ij} = A_k^{ij} T_k^{ij} + B_k^{ij} + V_k^{ij} \tag{1}$$

where A_k^{ij} and B_k^{ij} are the ij-th detector's gain and bias, respectively, at the k-th frame. T_k^{ij} represents the average number of photons that are detected by the ij-th detector during the integration time associated with the k-th frame. V_k^{ij} is the additive readout (temporal) noise associated to the ij-th detector for the k-th frame. For simplicity of notation, the pixel superscripts ij will be omitted with the understanding that all operations are performed on a pixel-by-pixel basis.

In this paper, nonuniformity's slow drift between frames is modeled by a Gauss-Markov process for the gain and the bias of each pixel on the FPA. This is:

$$\mathbf{X}_k = \mathbf{\Phi}_{k-1}\mathbf{X}_{k-1} + \mathbf{G}_{k-1}\mathbf{W}_{k-1} \tag{2}$$

where $\mathbf{X}_k$ is the state vector comprising the gain A_k and the bias B_k at the k-th frame and $\mathbf{\Phi}_k$ is the 2×2 transition diagonal matrix between the states at k and $k-1$, with its diagonal elements being the parameters α_k and β_k that represent, respectively, the level of drift in the gain and bias between consecutive frames. $\mathbf{G}_k$ is a 2×2 noise identity matrix that randomly relates the driving (or process) noise vector $\mathbf{W}_k$ to the state vector $\mathbf{X}_k$. The components of $\mathbf{W}_k$ are $W_k^{(1)}$ and $W_k^{(2)}$, the random driving noise for the gain and the bias, respectively, at the k-th frame. A key practical requirement to be set on the model is that, between frames, the drift in the gain and bias is very low; therefore, the drift parameters α_k and β_k have to be set to values closer but not equal to one. All others assumptions are shown and justified in detail elsewhere [7].

Also, in this paper the observation model for a given frame can be cast as:

$$\mathbf{Y}_k = \mathbf{H}_k \mathbf{X}_k + \mathbf{V}_k \tag{3}$$

where $\mathbf{H}_k$ is the observation vector in which the first element contains the input T_k per frame and $\mathbf{V}_k$ is the additive temporal noise. The main assumption in (3) is that the input T_k in any detector is a known parameter. Further, T_k is estimated, for each pixel, using a lowpass spatial filter that can emulate the IR radiation and it lessens the effect of the gain and bias difference between neighboring pixels. The mask size (number of neighboring pixels) must be determined according to the type of the scene imaged and to the amount of nonuniformity.

The $\mathbf{T}_k$ value is estimated averaging the pixel neighborhood. We can assume that a pixel and their near neighbor is illuminating by the same infrared radiance. Averaging the neighboring of a pixel i,j and assuming $\mathbf{A}_{i,j} = 1, \mathbf{B}_{i,j} = 0, \mathbf{V}_{i,j} = 0$ and $T_{i,j} = T$ inside the neighborhood we have:

$$\bar{Y}_k^{ij} = \bar{A}_k^{ij} \bar{T}_k^{ij} + \bar{B}_k^{ij} + \bar{V}_k^{ij} = T_k^{ij} \tag{4}$$

2.2 Kalman Filter Equations

The main idea is to develop an algorithm, based on the KF theory [9], that estimates frame by frame the gain and bias of each pixel using each incoming frame from the read-out data.

The recursive equations of the KF to estimate the parameters (the $\mathbf{X}_k$ vector) are the following [8]:

$$\hat{\mathbf{X}}_k = \left(\mathbf{\Phi}_{k-1} - \mathbf{K}_k \mathbf{H}_k\right) \hat{\mathbf{X}}_{k-1} + \mathbf{K}_k \mathbf{Y}_k \tag{5}$$

where $\hat{\mathbf{X}}_{k+1}$ and $\hat{\mathbf{X}}_k$ are the estimated gain and bias at the k-th and $k-1$-th frame, respectively. $\mathbf{K}_k$ is the Kalman gain vector defined by:

$$\mathbf{K}_k = \mathbf{\Phi}_{k-1} \mathbf{P}_{k-1} \mathbf{H}_k' \mathbf{F}_k^{-1} \tag{6}$$

where $\mathbf{R}_{k-1} = Var(\mathbf{V}_{k-1})$ and $\mathbf{F}_k = \mathbf{H}_k \mathbf{P}_{k-1} \mathbf{H}_k' + \mathbf{R}_{k-1}$

The recursive equation to compute the error covariance matrix $\mathbf{P}_k$ is:

$$\mathbf{P}_k = \mathbf{\Phi}_{k-1} \left(\mathbf{P}_{k-1} - \mathbf{P}_{k-1} \mathbf{H}_k' \mathbf{F}_k^{-1} \mathbf{H}_k \mathbf{P}_{k-1}\right) \mathbf{\Phi}_{k-1}' + \mathbf{G}_{k-1} \mathbf{Q}_{k-1} \mathbf{G}_{k-1}' \tag{7}$$

with $\mathbf{Q}_{k-1} = Var(\mathbf{W}_{k-1})$. The first values that must to feed the recursive equations (5,6,7) are: $\hat{\mathbf{X}}_0 = E(\mathbf{X})$ and $\mathbf{P}_0 = Var(\mathbf{X})$, which must be known.

3 Performance Analysis

The main goal of this section is to test the ability of the proposed NUC method to mitigate nonuniformity as well as to follow the drift in the nonuniformity

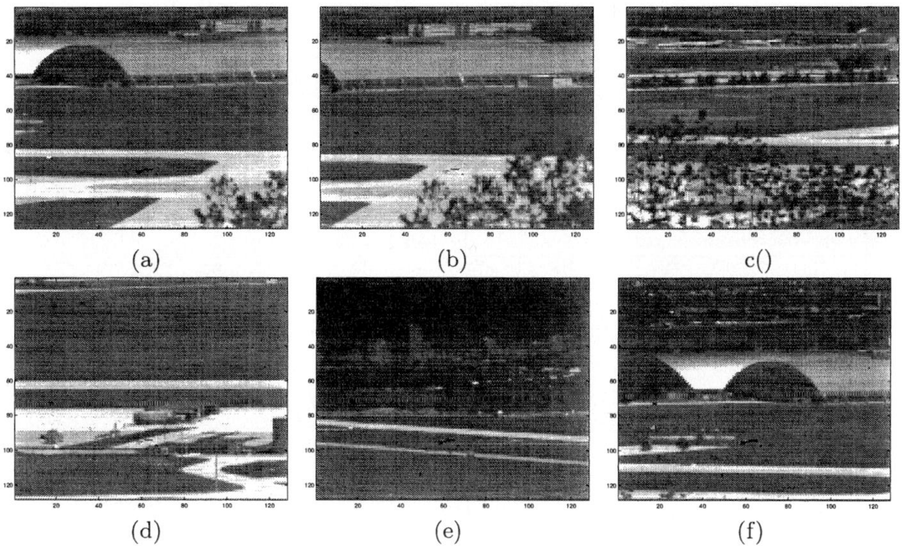

Fig. 1. Six frames of an IR sequence with real NonUniformity. a) The $10-th$ frame. b) The $100-th$ frame. c) The $1000-th$ frame. d) The $2000-th$ frame. e) The $3000-th$ frame. f) The $4000-th$ frame.

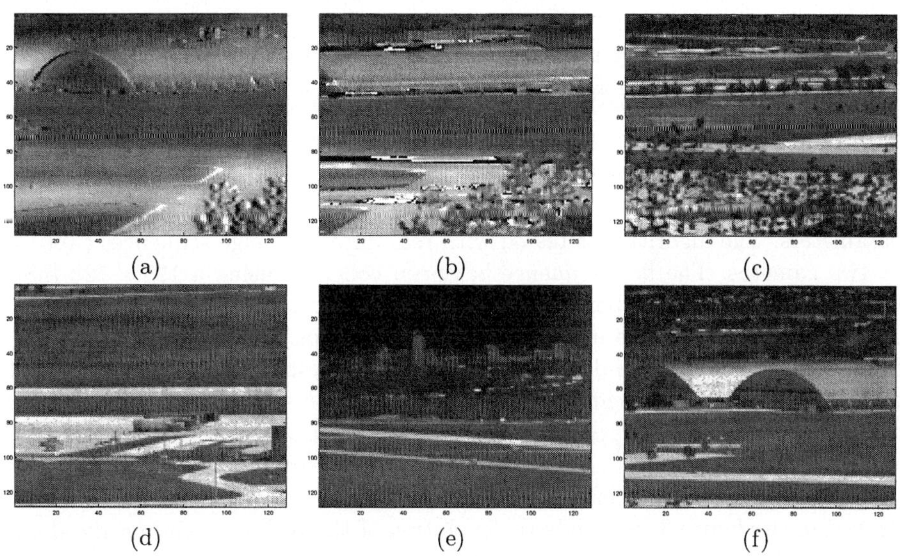

Fig. 2. The six frames of the IR sequence shown in figure 1 corrected using the proposed algorithm. a) The $10-th$ frame. b) The $100-th$ frame. c) The $1000-th$ frame. d) The $2000-th$ frame. e) The $3000-th$ frame. f) The $4000-th$ frame.

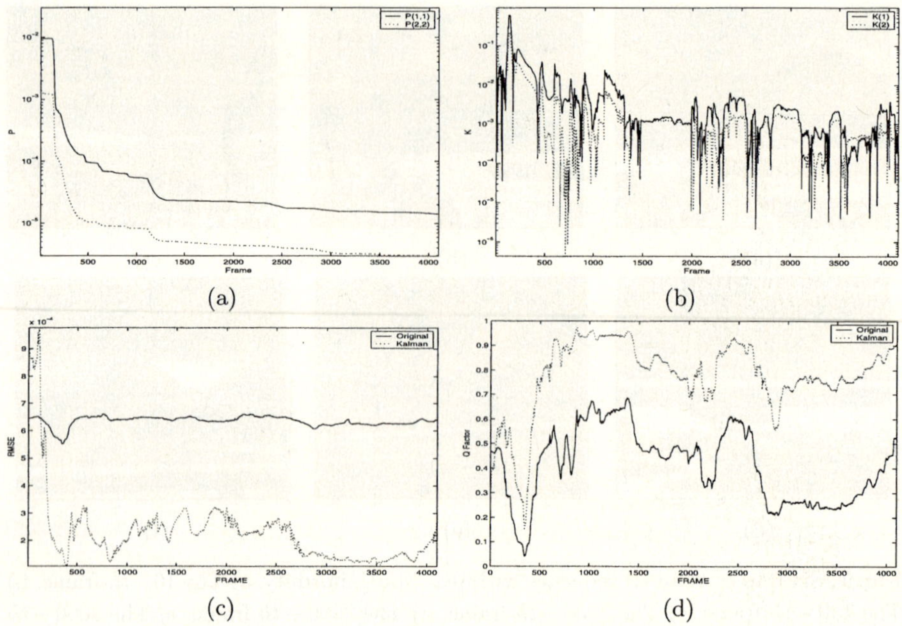

Fig. 3. a) Diagonal elements of the error covariance matrix $\mathbf{P}_k$ versus frame time for the algorithm applied to figure 1 sequence. b) Kalman gain matrix $\mathbf{K}_k$ versus frame time. c) RMSE between the real noisy data and the corrected data with the data corrected with a Black Body technique (true data). d) Q Factor between the real noisy data and the corrected data with the data corrected with a Black Body technique (true data).

parameters. The algorithm is tested with real infrared image sequences capture by two cameras. The first sequence has been collected using a 128×128 InSb FPA cooled camera (Amber Model AE-4128) operating in the $3 - 5\mu m$ range. The collected data is quantized with 16 bits @ 30fps. The figure 1 shows raw frames of the sequence and figure 2 shows the corresponding frames corrected with the proposed algorithm. As expected, it can be seen using the naked eye that the method reach a good nonuniformity correction in the $1000 - th$ frame and after.

The evolution of the error covariance matrix $\mathbf{P}_k$ along the frame time is showed in the figure 3 (a), while the evolution of the Kalman gain matrix along the frame time is shown in the figure 3 (b). As expected, it can be seen a reduction in the diagonal elements of the covariance matrix as long as the method is processing the incoming infrared information, converging therefore to the estimation of the real nonuniformity parameters.

As a numerical measure of the performance of the proposed algorithm, the parameters RMSE [12] and the Q factor [11] are computed between a true image(a one corrected in the laboratory with black bodies radiators) and the real

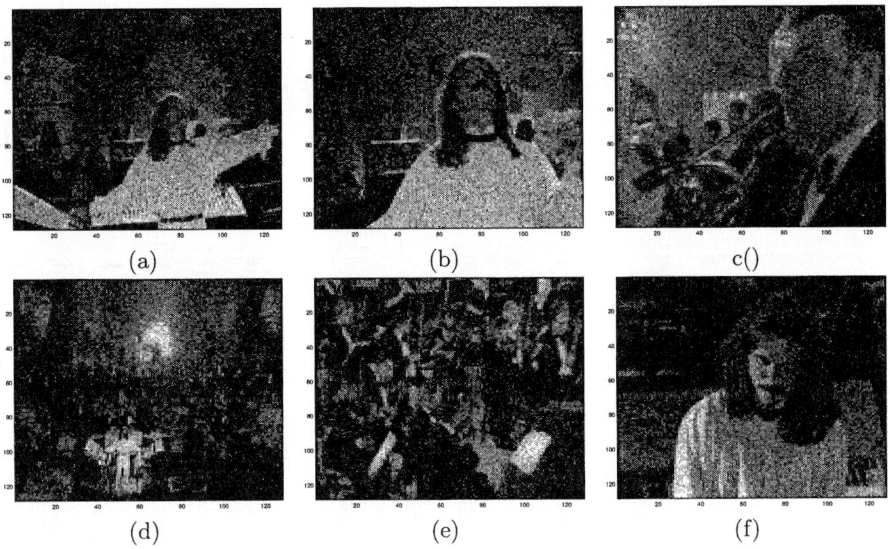

Fig. 4. Six frames of a video sequence with simulated nonuniformity. a) The $10 - th$ frame. b) The $100 - th$ frame. c) The $1000 - th$ frame. d) The $2000 - th$ frame. e) The $3000 - th$ frame. f) The $4000 - th$ frame .

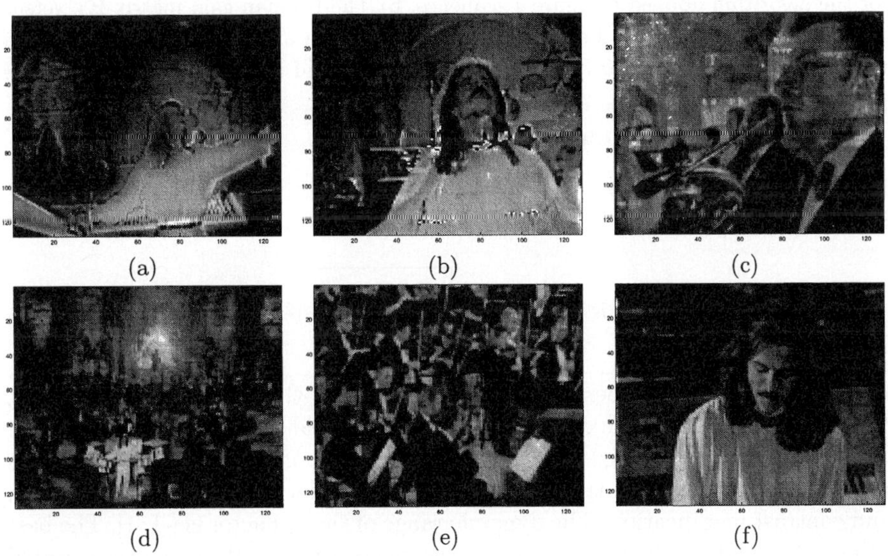

Fig. 5. The frames of figure 4 corrected using the proposed algorithm. a) The $10 - th$ frame. b) The $100 - th$ frame. c) The $1000 - th$ frame. d) The $2000 - th$ frame. e) The $3000 - th$ frame. f) The $4000 - th$ frame.

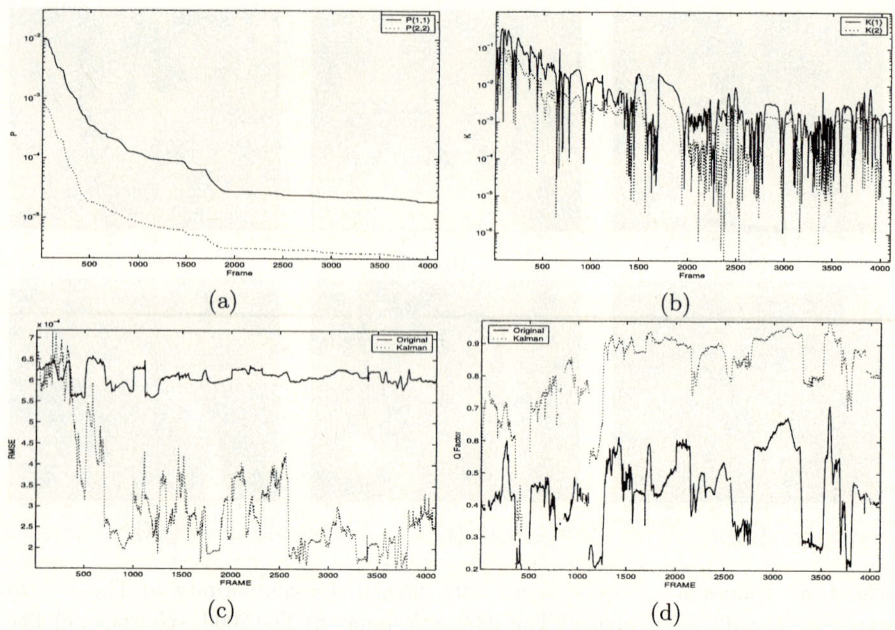

Fig. 6. a) The diagonal elements of the error covariance matrix $\mathbf{P}_k$ versus frame time for the algorithm applied to figure 4 sequence. b) The Kalman gain matrix $\mathbf{K}_k$ versus frame time. c) The RMSE between the the noisy image and the corrected data with the true image. d) Q Factor between the noisy image and the corrected data with the true image.

image (image with FPN) or the image corrected with our method. The RMSE is defined as follow:

$$RMSE = \frac{1}{n}\sqrt{\sum_{i=1}^{n}(Y_i^t - Y_i^c)^2} \tag{8}$$

where n is the total number of pixels, and Y_i^t is the i-th value on the true image. Y_i^c is the i-th value of the corrected image or the real image.

The recently published Q Factor is a measure of three desirable features between two images (the true and corrected): correlation, luminance distortion and contrast modification. The dynamic range of the Q Factor is [-1, 1]. The best value is 1, and it is achieved only if the true image is identical to the compensated image.

$$Q = \frac{\sigma_{Y^tY^c}}{\sigma_{Y^t}\sigma_{Y^c}} \cdot \frac{2\bar{Y^t}\bar{Y^c}}{(\bar{Y^t})^2 + (\bar{Y^c})^2} \cdot \frac{2\sigma_{Y^t}\sigma_{Y^c}}{\sigma_{Y^t}^2 + \sigma_{Y^c}^2} \tag{9}$$

The RMSE and the Q factor between the noisy real sequence and the corrected sequence with the proposed algorithm with a corrected sequence using

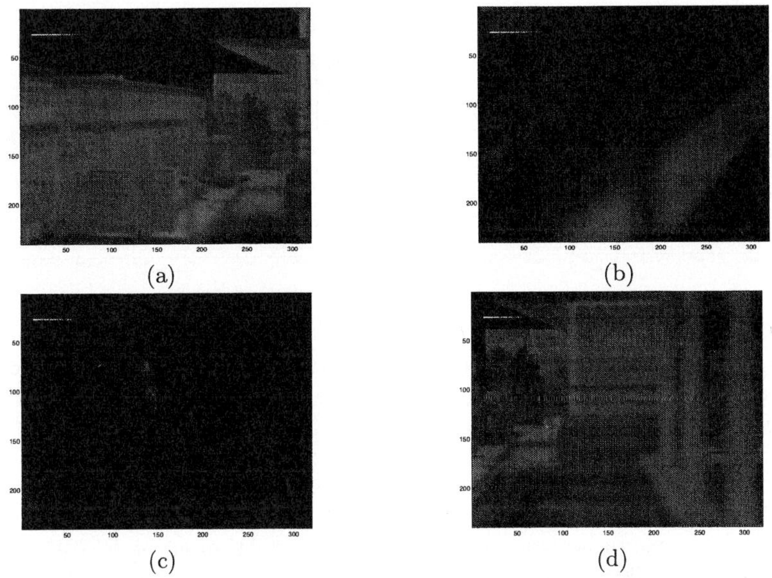

Fig. 7. Four frames with real NonUniformity. a) The $10-th$ frame. b) The $100-th$ frame. c) The $1000-th$ frame. d) The $1500-th$ frame.

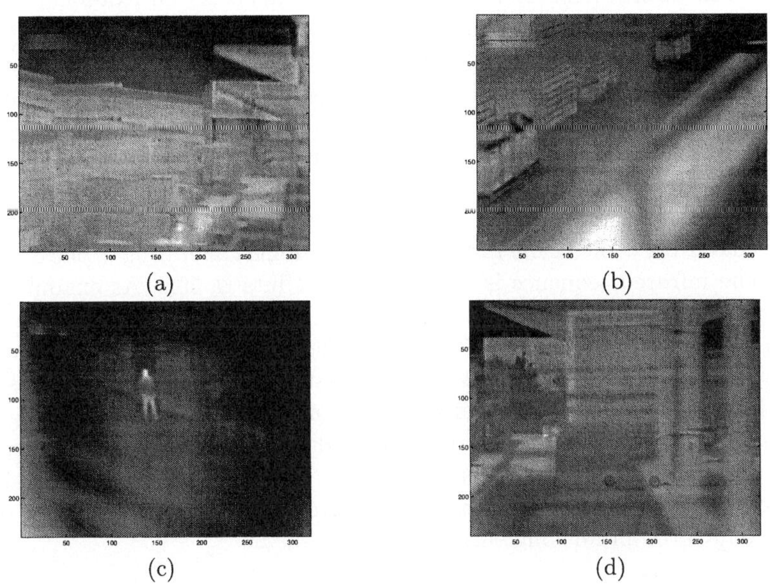

Fig. 8. The four previous frames corrected with the new technique. a) The $10-th$ frame. b) The $100-th$ frame. c) The $1000-th$ frame. d) The $1500-th$ frame .

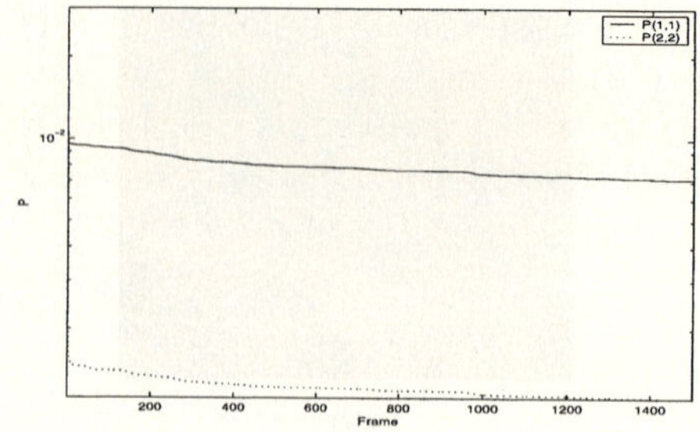

(a)

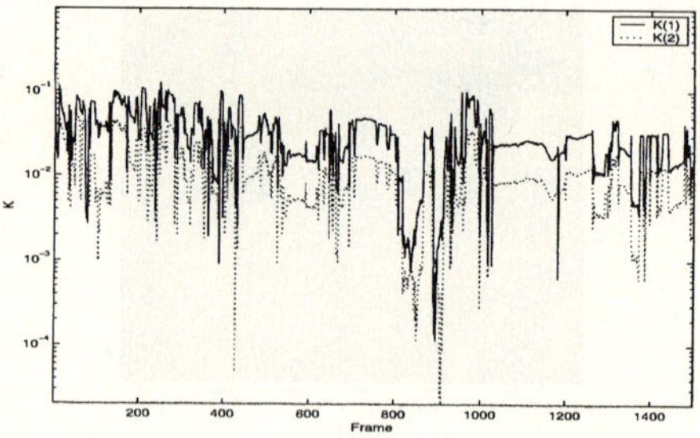

(b)

Fig. 9. a) The diagonal elements of the error covariance matrix $\mathbf{P}_k$ versus the frame time for the algorithm applied to figure 7 sequence. b) The Kalman gain matrix versus the frame time $\mathbf{K}_k$.

a Black Body technique is represented in the figure 3 (c) and the figure 3 (d) respectively. It can be seen a notably numerical reduction in the RMSE after the $500th$ frame. It can be also seen a notably better performance on the Q factor after the $500th$ frame.

The developed algorithm is also applied to an infrared video sequence with simulated nonuniformity. The video sequence was created adding artificial noise to 4100 true frames (frames without nonuniformity). As an example, figure 4 shows images with artificial nonuniformity. The corresponding corrected frames are shown in figure 5. The evolution of $\mathbf{P}_k$, $\mathbf{K}_k$ the RMSE and Q factor is represented in figure 6. The goal of this test is to check the performance of the method with images with a level of nonuniformity more severe that real cases. It can be seen that the method presents a similar performance to the cases tested with real nonuniformity.

Finally, this new technique is applied to infrared data recorded using a 320×240 HgCdTe FPA cooled camera (CEDIP Jade Model) operating in the $8-12\mu m$ range. The infrared sequence is quantized at 14 bits @ 50fs. As examples, the uncorrected and corrected frames are shown in figures 7, 8. The evolution of $\mathbf{P}_k$ and $\mathbf{K}_k$ are shown in the figure 9. Using the naked eye, it can be seen again a good correction of nonuniformity. However, note that a ghosting artifact is presented in the $1500th$ frame. Future works will be oriented to develop methodologies to reduce ghosting artifacts, which are generated when a target has been imaged for some time and then it suddenly is out of the field of view of the camera. Our method could not follow such abrupt change in the operation points of the detectors involved in imaging such target.

4 Conclusions

We have developed and tested a new scene-based NUC method based in standard Kalman filter theory. The algorithm has the advantage to use temporal and spatial data embedded in the develop of the Kalman Filter. The parameters of the algorithm must to be carefully selected according to the specific application and the kind of infrared camera . The foregoing influences the level of nonuniformity and the level of drift in the nonuniformity parameters. It was experimentally demonstrated as well as by using the performance parameters RMSE and Q that the proposed method is able to reach good performance after processing 500 frames.

References

1. Holst, G.: CCD arrays, cameras and displays. SPIE Optical Engineering Press. Bellingham. (1996).
2. D. A. Scribner, K. A. Sarkady, J. T. Caulfield, M. R. Kruer, G. Katz y C. J. Gridley: Nonuniformity correction for staring IR focal plane arrays using scene-based techniques, SPIE, vol. 1308, pp. 224-233, 1990.
3. D. Scribner, M. Kruer and J. Killiany: Infrared Focal Plane Array Technology, IEEE, vol. 79 (1), pp. 66-85, 1991.
4. D. A. Scribner, K. A. Sarkady, M. R. Kruer, J. T. Caulfield, J. D. Hunt, M. Colbert y M. Descour: Adaptive Retina-Like Preprocessing for Imaging Detector Arrays, IEEE, vol. 3, pp. 1955-1960, 1993.
5. M. Schulz y L. Caldwell: Nonuniformity correction and correctability of infrared focal plane arrays, Infrared Physics and Technology, vol 36, pp. 763-777, 1995.
6. John G. Harris, Yu-Ming Chiang: Non Uniformity Correction Using Constant Statics Constraint: Analog and Digital Implementation, Proc. SPIE 3061 pp. 895-905, 1997.
7. Torres, S., Hayat, M.: Kalman filtering for adaptive nonuniformity correction in Infrared Focal Plane Arrays. The Journal of the Optical Society of America A. **20**. (2003) 470–480.
8. Andrew, H. C.: Forecasting, Structural Time Series Models and the Kalman Filter. Cambridge University Press. (1990).
9. R. E. Kalman: A New Approach to Linear Filtering and Prediction Problems, Transactions of the ASME-Journal of Basic Engineering, 82 (Series D), pp. 35-45. 1960.
10. G. Minkler, J. Minkler, Theory and Application of the Kalman Filtering, Magellan Book Company, 1993.
11. Wang, Z., Bovik, A.: A Universal Image Quality Index. IEEE Signal Processing Letters. **20**. (2002) 1–4.
12. Gonzlez, R., Woods, R.: Digital Image Processing. Addison Wesley. (1993).

Maximum Correlation Search Based Watermarking Scheme Resilient to RST

Sergio Bravo and Felix Calderón

Universidad Michoacana de San Nicolás de Hidalgo,
División de Estudios de Posgrado de Ingeniería Eléctrica,
Santiago Tapia 403 Centro,
Morelia, Michoacán, México. CP 58000
sbravo@lsc.fie.umich.mx, calderon@zeus.umich.mx

Abstract. Many of the watermarking schemes that claim resilience to geometrical distortions embed information into invariant or semi-invariant domains. However, the discretisation process required in such domains might lead to low correlation responses during watermarking detection. In this document, a new strategy is proposed to provide resilience to strong Rotation, Scaling and Translation (RST) distortions. The proposed detection process is based on a Genetic Algorithm (GA) that maximises the correlation coefficient between the originally embedded watermark and the input image. Comparisons between a previous scheme, based on Log-Polar Mapping (LPM), and the present approach are reported. Results show that even a simple insertion process provides more robustness, as well as a lower image degradation.

1 Introduction

Multimedia applications are arising, and technological advances afford faster and cheaper forms of copying and distributing multimedia data, with high quality. Hence, digital watermarking has been proposed to provide suitable alternatives to detect copyright infringements, tampering, and so forth. However, any digital signal might suffer a wide set of accidental and incidental distortions that can severely damage and even destroy the embedded watermarks.

In most watermarking schemes, geometrical distortions, applied on content images, usually lead to wrong detection responses due to synchronisation loss between watermarks and detectors.

When the original (non-watermarked) image is available for the detector, synchronisation might be easily restored by using conventional image registration techniques [1], before testing the presence of a watermark. Yet, detectors will seldom be provided the original image in real applications. Thus, different strategies have been proposed to deal with the effects of geometrical distortions in watermarking schemes that do not require the original image during detection.

Some approaches embed either a template (along with the watermark) or a periodic watermark to generate a defined pattern that is used to effectively invert affine transformations in content images before detection [2,3,4,5]. Both

M. Lazo and A. Sanfeliu (Eds.): CIARP 2005, LNCS 3773, pp. 762–769, 2005.

strategies usually provide robustness against geometrical attacks. However, detectors are unable to restore synchronisation if the templates are removed by using specialised attacks, such as collusion and template removal attacks [6,7].

Another proposed strategy is to embed the watermarks into invariant or semi-invariant domains provided by the Fourier-Mellin transform, or Log-Polar Mapping (LPM) [8,9]. Results show those scheme are robust against RST with and without cropping. Unfortunately, stronger attacks might requiere weighter watermarks, which usually cause visible distortions into the watermarked images. In [10] the watermark is inserted in previously normalised versions of the images, and restored to the original form before distribution. The scheme is robust against some geometrical distortions, but the detection is prone to errors when the normalisation parameters change due to cropping. The schemes based on invariant or semi-invariant domains are usually vulnerable to severe geometrical distortions, because of the discretisation and interpolation processes required in the insertion/extraction processes.

A newer strategy is to embed the watermarks into marking regions near to invariant features of the images [11,12]. However, watermarking retrieval highly depends on the accuracy of the used algorithms for detecting points resilient to geometrical changes.

In this paper we propose a strategy to provide resilience to RST, which is based on Maximum Correlation Seach (MCS). The detection scheme might be thought of as an image registration problem [1], where the correlation between the original watermark and the input image is maximised, instead of minimising the difference between two images. This strategy avoids the security problems found in schemes based on template insertion and auto-synchronisation. Moreover, results show that even a simple insertion scheme could significatively improve the discretisation problems found in schemes based on LPM.

The paper is organised as follows. Sections 2 and 3 describe the proposed insertion and detection process, respectively. The specifications of the Genetic Algorithm (GA), used during the detection process, is presented in Sect. 3.1. Section 3.2 describes the proposed whitening filter, and some experiments and comparisons of the present approach with a previous scheme are shown in Sect. 4. Finally, some conclusions and future work are discussed in Sect. 5.

2 Watermark Embedding Process

Let $f(x, y)$ be the pixel intensity of the original image f at (x, y) location, where $0 \leq y \leq M$ and $0 \leq x \leq N$; M and N denote the total number of rows and columns of the image, respectively. The discrete Fourier magnitude, $|F|$, is assessed and a pseudo-random binary watermark, $W_m(x, y) \in \{-1, 1\}$, the same size of the content image, is generated by preserving the symmetry of the Fourier magnitude. Each coefficient of $|F|$ is modified by,

$$|F'(x, y)| = |F(x, y)|\, e^{1+\alpha W_m(x,y)} \ , \tag{1}$$

where α is a user-defined strength parameter (usually set to 0.1), that controls the tradeoff between robustness and image fidelity.

By using (1), we avoid modifying the phase component of the image in order to preserve a better visual quality. Finally, the inverse discrete Fourier transform is assessed from F' to obtain the watermarked image f_w.

3 Watermark Detection Process

Translation attacks are implicitly solved by the well known invariance of the Fourier magnitude [13]. In order to find the rotation angle and scale, we propose a novel detection approach based on a GA that aims to maximise the correlation between the originally inserted watermark, W_m, and the Fourier magnitude logarithm of the input image.

Let $\tilde{f}$ be the input image, and $\log|\tilde{F}|$ the logarithm of its Fourier magnitude. A whitening filter [14] (see Sect. 3.2) is applied to $\log|\tilde{F}|$ and W_m. Then a searching algorithm, based on a GA (see Sect. 3.1), is used to find the scale factor and rotation angle that maximise the correlation between both filtered signals. Finally, a watermark is reported as successfully detected when the best-found correlation value is higher than a predefined threshold τ.

3.1 Genetic Algorithm

Several authors have proposed watermarking schemes where the correlation coefficient is used as a detection measure [15,14]. We propose maximising the correlation between the input image, likely distorted, and the originally inserted watermark, which is computed as,

$$C(\theta, \sigma) = \frac{W_m^T(\theta, \sigma)\, \log|\tilde{F}|}{\log|\tilde{F}|^T\, \log|\tilde{F}|} \quad . \tag{2}$$

The goal is to achieve the values of scaling, σ, and rotation, θ, that might have been applied on the watermarked images by using a MCS based on a GA.

A GA is an evolutive algorithm inspired by a biological process, that attempts to optimise a complex function cost, in such a way that given a random initial population, the GA allows this population to reach a state of maximum fitness in many generations. The general optimisation procedure is: 1) Define a cost function and the chromosome, 2) Create a new population, 3) Evaluate the cost function, 4) Select mates, 5) Mating, 6) Mutate, 7) Check convergence.

Haupt [16] describes those previous steps to minimise a continuous parameters function cost using a GA. In our case, we optimise the function cost, given by (2), which depends on the rotation and the scale parameters. A chromosome $\Phi = [\theta, \sigma]$ is created for each member of the population, where $\theta \in [\theta^{min}, \theta^{max})$ and $\sigma \in [\sigma^{min}, \sigma^{max}]$. Based on the symmetry of the Fourier magnitude we set $\theta^{min} = 0$ and $\theta^{max} = \pi$. In addition, it is well known that scaling in time produces inverse scaling in the Fourier domain [13], hence we set[1] $\sigma^{min} = \frac{1}{1.7}$ and $\sigma^{max} = \frac{1}{0.6}$.

An initial population, of length N_{pop}, is created with chromosomes uniformly distributed over the whole space. In this way, we aim to accelerate the convergence, as we cover the entire space and avoid evaluating the cost of very similar chromosomes in the first generation [16].

Once the first generation is computed, the best half is selected for the paring procedure ($N_{good} = N_{pop}/2$) and the other half is discarded. For paring selection, a weighted probability is computed by using a normalised cost, which is estimated for each chromosome, subtracting the highest cost, of the discarded chromosomes, from the cost of all the chromosomes in the mating pool $C_n = cost_n - cost_{N_{good}+1}$. The probability for each mating chromosome is assessed as,

$$P_n = \left| \frac{C_n}{\sum_{p=1}^{N_{good}} C_p} \right| , \tag{3}$$

note that the higher an individual's cost is, the higher is the probability of having offsprings.

Mating generates two offsprings by mixing the chromosomes of the couples previously selected. Let $\Phi^{(m)} = \{\phi_1^{(m)}, \phi_2^{(m)}\}$ and $\Phi^{(p)} = \{\phi_1^{(p)}, \phi_2^{(p)}\}$ denote the parents selected by the paring procedure. One of the two genes is randomly selected, and then exchanged, whereas the other one is mixed, by,

$$\Phi^{(offspring_1)} = \{\phi_1^{(m)}, \phi_2^{(new_1)}\} \text{ and } \Phi^{(offspring_2)} = \{\phi_1^{(p)}, \phi_2^{(new_2)}\} ,$$

where $\phi^{(new_1)} = \phi_2^{(m)} - \beta_1(\phi_2^{(m)} - \phi_2^{(p)})$ and $\phi^{(new_2)} = \phi_2^{(p)} + \beta_2(\phi_2^{(m)} - \phi_2^{(p)})$, and β_i is randomly selected between the interval [0, 1].

Finally, for the mutation procedure, a percentage of individuals are randomly selected with uniform probability distribution (with the exception of the best individual, which will not be mutated). Then, the gene $j-th$ (randomly selected) of each selected individual is modified by $\phi_j^{(k)} = (\phi_j^{max} - \phi_j^{min})\beta_3 + \phi_j^{min}$.

3.2 Whitening Filter

The correlation measure is an optimum method to detect a signal in Additive White Gaussian Noise (AWGN) channels, but it will be suboptimal in the case of non-AWGN channels. Depovere et al. [14] showed that images might be usually thought of as non-AWGN channels. The authors improved the detection response by applying a simple difference filter, known as *whitening filter*, to the rows of an image in order to remove most of the correlation existing between adjacent pixels. Subsequently, Cox et al. [17] proposed a bidimensional whitening filter (size 11×11), drawn from an elliptical Gaussian distribution, that significatively improved the detection response achieved by Depovere. We propose using a Separable Bidirectional Difference-Whitening Filter (SBD-WF) that computes

[1] We assume that scaling factors out of this range will likely degrade the image quality.

the horizontal and vertical differences. Thus, we aim to decorrelate pixels through both directions, in contrast with the filter proposed by Depovere. In addition, the SBD-WF filter is separable, which can significatively reduce the required computational cost, in comparison with bidimensional Cox's filter.

4 Experimental Results

4.1 Whitening Filter Test

A random watermark was embedded into 1000 diverse nature images, by using (1), and then, it is detected without applying any prior distortion. We applied and compare the performance of the following whitening filters: the filter proposed by Cox et al. [17], an horizontal difference filter, a vertical difference filter, and the proposed SBD-WF . Figure 1(a) shows the correlation values obtained by using the four different whitening filters. Note that there is no significant difference among the correlation values obtained from non-watermarked images. In the watermarked images, the obtained results are similar after applying both the vertical and horizontal difference filters. Higher correlation values are achieved by using Cox's filter and the proposed SDB-WF. However, the computation cost of the SBD-WF is lower than the filter proposed by Cox, which requieres a 2D convolution of the image with a 11 × 11-size kernel.

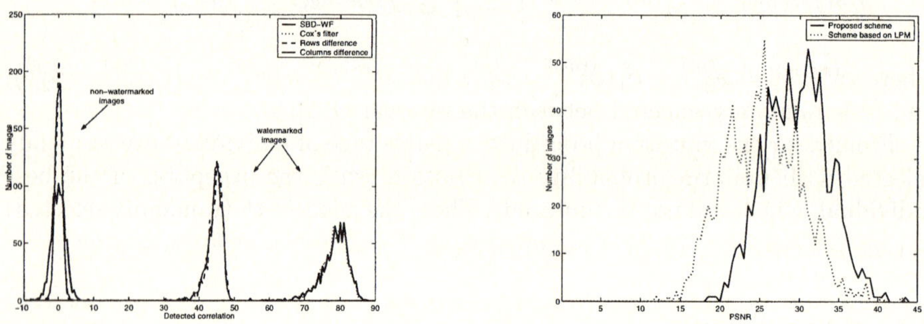

(a) (b)

Fig. 1. Whitening filter and distortion experiments. (a) Correlation detected from 1000 watermarked and non-watermarked by using different whitening filters. (b) Histograms of PSNR values computed from 1000 watermarked images.

4.2 Image Degradation

In order to measure the degradation caused to the watermarked images, 1000 diverse nature test images were watermarked by using the proposed approach (with $\alpha = 0.1^2$) and Lin's scheme [9]. Figure 1(b) depicts a comparison of the

[2] This is the value used in the experiments discussed in the robustness tests.

Peak Signal-to-Noise Ratio (PSNR) values obtained from the images output by both insertion schemes. Results show that Lin's scheme clearly causes more distortion to the images (lower PSNR values) than the proposed approach.

4.3 Robustness

In this section we compare the detection response of Lin's scheme[3] [9] and the proposed approach in images attacked with severe geometrical distortions. We first propose reliable detection thresholds with low false-positive probabilities. Then comparisons between both detection schemes were made.

In this experiment, both detection schemes were applied on 1000 diverse non-watermarked test images. Figures 2(a) and 2(b) show the correlation values detected with the proposed approach and Lin's scheme, respectively. Thus, in order to yield a small false-positive probability, we propose a detection threshold of 9.5 for the proposed scheme and 4.8 for Lin's scheme.

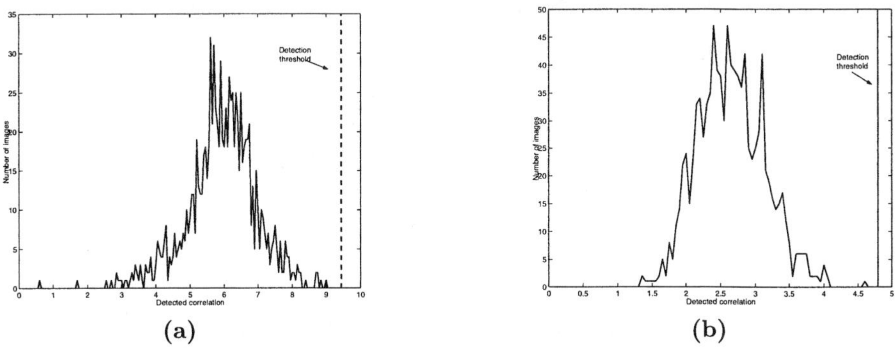

Fig. 2. Correlation detected from 1000 non-watermarked images (a) proposed scheme (b) Lin's scheme.

After defining the detection thresholds, the robustness against strong RST attacks were tested by using the three standard images shown in Figs 3(a)-(c). Figures 3(d)-(e) show the watermarked versions of Lena. Observe that more distortion is perceived when using Lin's scheme. Table 1 shows study cases of the detection responses obtained from both schemes[4], after applying some severe RST attacks on the watermarked test images. Comparatively, the number of faults (printed in bold) detected when using the proposed approach is lower than the faults detected by using Lin's scheme.

Despite the general performance of the proposed scheme is clearly better than Lin's scheme, we think that more robust watermarks and lower impact on human

[3] The original normalised correlation was multiplied by the (constant) watermark magnitude to get higher values.

[4] An initial population of 7,581 was used in our detection scheme, and the reported correlation values required, at most, 15 generations.

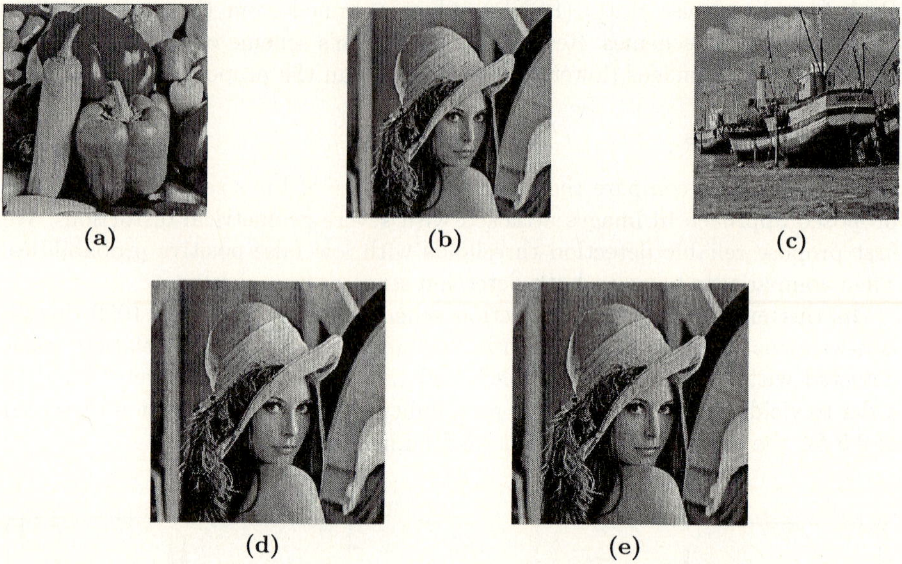

Fig. 3. Watermarked and non-watermarked images. (a), (b) and (c) Standard test images (Peppers, Lena and Ship). (d) Lena image watermarked with the proposed scheme (e) Lena image watermarked with Lin's scheme.

Table 1. Study cases

θ = rotation angle (grades). σ = scale factor.
T_x = horizontal translation. T_y = vertical translation.

	Tests				Lin's scheme			Proposed scheme		
#	θ	σ	T_x	T_y	Peppers	Lena	Ship	Peppers	Lena	Ship
1	45.5,	1.0,	50.0,	50.0,	**3.63**	**3.58**	**3.94**	9.56	**9.08**	9.55
2	10.5,	0.7,	100.0,	100.0,	**3.57**	**3.73**	**3.52**	14.49	11.91	10.75
3	25.5,	1.2,	100.0,	0.0,	**4.02**	**3.88**	**3.83**	10.62	13.73	11.52
4	25.5,	1.0,	0.0,	0.0,	4.84	**4.34**	**4.57**	12.61	13.42	14.38
5	5.5,	1.0,	0.0,	0.0,	5.00	**4.64**	**4.76**	20.83	21.75	25.40
6	0.5,	1.0,	0.0,	0.0,	5.83	5.04	4.87	24.11	25.47	25.40
7	20.0,	0.7,	0.0,	0.0,	8.11	8.03	8.18	11.27	14.74	11.87
8	2.5,	1.5,	0.0,	0.0,	5.63	5.08	5.52	18.67	19.96	13.14

perception is possible by using an embedding process based on Quantisation Index Modulation (QIM).

5 Conclusions

In this paper, a new strategy, based on MCS, is proposed to provide a watermarking scheme resilient to RST. The proposed approach avoid the security problems found in the schemes basd on auto-synchronisation and template insertion. In addition, comparisons were made to show that even a simple insertion scheme could significatively improve the performance of watermarking schemes based on invariant and semi-invariant domains, such as LPM.

Further research is being done to include an optimised embedding scheme, based on QIM, that will provide stronger watermarks with lower impact in human perception. Additionally, a strong feature extraction algorithm is being designed to provide resilience to local geometrical attacks.

References

1. Brown, L.G.: A survey of image registration techniques. ACM Computing Surveys **24** (1992) 325–376
2. Fleet, D.J., Heeger, D.J.: Embedding invisible information in color images. In: IEEE Signal Processing Society 1997 International Conference on Image Processing (ICIP'97), Santa Barbara, CA (1997)
3. Pereira, S., Pun, T.: An iterative template matching algorithm using the chirp-z transform for digital image watermarking. Pattern Recognition **33** (2000) 173–175
4. Kutter, M., Hartung, F.: 5. Computer Security Series. In: Introduction to Watermarking Techniques. 1st edn. Artech House (2000) 97–120
5. Deguillaume, F., Voloshynovskiy, S., Pun, T.: A method for the estimation and recovering of general affine transform. US Patent Application (2002)
6. Craver, S., Periig, A., Petitcolas, F.A.P.: 7. Computer Security Series. In: Robustness of copyright marking systems. 1st edn. Artech House (2000) 149–174
7. Herrigel, A., Voloshynovskiy, S., Rytsar, Y.: The watermark template attack (2001)
8. O' Ruanaidh, J.J.K., Pun, T.: Rotation, scale and translation invariant digital image watermarking. In: Proceedings of ICIP 97, IEEE International Conference on Image Processing, Santa Barbara, CA (1997) 536–539
9. Lin, C.Y., Wu, M., Bloom, J.A., Cox, I.J., Miller, M.L., Lui, Y.M.: Rotation, scale, and translation resilient watermarking for images. IEEE Transactions on Image Processing **10** (2001) 767–782
10. Dong, P., Galatsanos, N.P.: Affine transformation resistant watermarking based on image normalization. In: Proceedings of the IEEE International Conference on Image Processing (ICIP-02), Rochester, NY, USA (2002)
11. Feng, Y., Izquierdo, E.: Robust local watermarking on salient image areas. In F.A.P. Petitcolas, H.K., ed.: Digital Watermarking: First International Workshop, IWDW 2002, Seoul, Korea (2002) 180–201
12. Tang, C.W., Hang, H.M.: A feature-based robust digital image watermarking scheme. Signal Processing **51** (2003) 950–959
13. Zelniker, G., Taylor, F.J.: Advanced Digital Signal Processing: Theory and Applications. Marcel Dekker, Inc., New York, NY, USA (1993)
14. Depovere, G., Kalker, T., Linnartz, J.P.M.G.: Improved watermark detection reliability using filtering before correlation. In: ICIP (1). (1998) 430–434
15. Cox, I., Kilian, J., Leighton, T., Shamoon, T.: Secure spread spectrum watermarking for multimedia. IEEE Transactions on Image Processing **6** (1997) 1673–1687
16. Haupt, R.L., Haupt, S.E.: Practical genetic algorithms. John Wiley & Sons, Inc., New York, NY, USA (1998)
17. Cox, I.J., Miller, M.L., Bloom, J.A.: Digital Watermarking. 1st edn. Morgan Kaufman (2002)

Phoneme Spotting for Speech-Based Crypto-key Generation

L. Paola García-Perera, Juan A. Nolazco-Flores, and Carlos Mex-Perera

Computer Science Department, ITESM, Campus Monterrey,
Av. Eugenio Garza Sada 2501 Sur, Col. Tecnológico,
Monterrey, N.L., México, C.P. 64849
{paola.garcia, jnolazco, carlosmex}@itesm.mx

Abstract. In this research we propose to use phoneme spotting to improve the results in the generation of a cryptographic key. Phoneme spotting selects the phonemes with highest accuracy in the user classification task. The key bits are constructed by using the Automatic Speech Recognition and Support Vector Machines. Firstly, a speech recogniser detects the phoneme limits in each speech utterance. Afterwards, the support vector machine performs a user classification and generates a key. By selecting the highest accuracy phonemes for a a set of 10, 20, 30 and 50 speakers randomly chosen from the YOHO database, it is possible to generate reliable cryptographic keys.

1 Introduction

The key generation based on biometrics is now acquiring more importance since it can solve the problems of traditional cryptosystems authentication. For instance, the automatic speech key generation can be applied for secure telephone calls, file storage, voice e-mail retrieval and digital right management. The necessity of having a key which can not be forgotten, and that can be kept secure is one of the main goals of today key generation. Current biometric authentication uses the intrinsic attributes of the users to provide solution to this security items [12].

For the purpose of this research, speech is the biometric used. It was chosen among the others because it has the flexibility that by changing the uttered sentence, the key automatically changes. Using the Automatic Speech Recognition (ASR) it is possible to obtain the starting and ending time of each phoneme given a utterance and a speech model. Afterwards, a feature adaptation is needed which can convert a set of vectors in a characteristic and final feature. Finally, a user classification task is performed by the Support Vector Machine (SVM).

Monrose *et. al* [6] showed a first method in which a partition plane for the feature vector space was suggested to generate binary biometric keys based on speech. However, a plane that can produce the same key is difficult to find due to the fact that infinite planes are possible. A more flexible way to produce a key - in which the exact control of the assignation of the key values is available - is always attractive. The main challenge of the general research is to find a

M. Lazo and A. Sanfeliu (Eds.): CIARP 2005, LNCS 3773, pp. 770–777, 2005.

suitable method to generate a cryptographic-speech-key that should repeatedly generate the same key every time a user produces the same utterance under certain conditions.

Therefore, the objective of this proposal is to improve the accuracy results in a cryptographic key generation task by using the phoneme spotting. In a similar way ASR uses word spotting to find key words, it is possible to use phoneme spotting [15]. In our case, it is used to make a selection of the highest phoneme accuracies. The phoneme spotting has the ability to locate a set of key phonemes (meaning the phonemes with the highest accuracy) during the training stage. However, selecting the phonemes with highest performance has the drawback that larger pass phrases are required. This issue is not a real problem since the system performs much better, and the pass phrases are not being memorised by the user (the system can give a random sentence that a user can utter).

The system architecture is depicted in Figure 1 and will be discussed in the following sections. The part under the dotted line shows the training phase that is performed offline. The upper part shows the online phase. In the training stage the *speech processing* and *recognition* techniques are used to obtain the model parameters and the starts and ends of the phonemes in each user utterance. Afterwards, using the model parameters and the phoneme segmentation, the feature generation is performed. Next, the *Support Vector Machine* (SVM) classifier and the phoneme selection produces its own new model according to a specific kernel and bit specifications. From all those models, the ones that give the highest results per phoneme are selected and compose the final SVM model. Finally, using the last SVM model the key is generated. The online stage is similar to the training, but a filtering of the unwanted phonemes is also included. This scheme will repeatedly produce the same key if a user utters the same pass phrase.

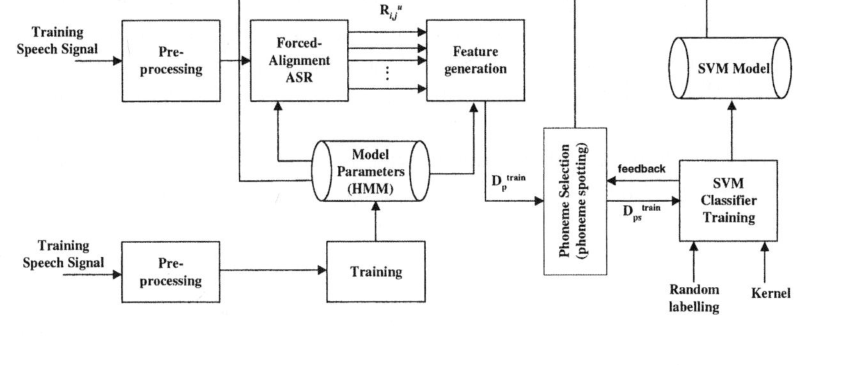

Fig. 1. System Architecture

2 Speech Processing and Phoneme Feature Generation

The ASR is one of the most important parts of our research. Firstly, the speech signal is divided into short windows and the *Mel frequency cepstral coefficients* (MFCC) are obtained. As a result an n-dimension vector, $(n-1)$-dimension MFCCs followed by one energy coefficient is formed. To emphasize the dynamic features of the speech in time, the time-derivative (Δ) and the time-acceleration (Δ^2) of each parameter are calculated [11].

Afterwards, a forced alignment configuration of an ASR is used to obtain a model and the starts and ends of the phonemes per utterance. For this research, the phonemes were selected instead of words since it is possible to generate larger keys with shorter length sentences.

In this training phase the system learns the patterns that represent the speech sound. Depending on the application the units can be words, phonemes, or syllables. The Hidden Markov Model (HMM) is the leading technique for acoustic modelling [10]. An HMM is characterised by the following, see Figure 2:

$A = \{a_{ij}\}, a_{ij} = Prob\{q_j \text{ at } t+1 | q_i \text{ at } t\}$ state transition probability distribution
$B = \{b_j(O_t)\}, b_j(O_t) =$ observation probability distribution
$\pi = \{\pi_i\} = Prob\{q_i \text{ at } t = 1\}$ initial state distribution
$O = \{O_1, O_2, ..., O_T\} =$ observation sequence (input sequence)
$T =$ length of observation sequence
$Q = \{q_1, q_2, ..., q_N\}$ hidden states in the model
$N =$ number of states

The compact notation $\lambda = (A, B, \pi)$ is used to represent an HMM [9]. The parameter set N, M, A, B, and π is calculated using the training data and it defines a probability measure $Prob(O|\lambda)$.

The resulting model has the inherent characteristics of real speech. The output distributions of the HMM are commonly represented by Gaussian Mixture Densities with means and covariances as important parameters, see Figure 3. Depending on the application one or more Gaussians can be included per state. But also, one or more states are also possible for a given reference sound. To determine the parameters of the model and reach convergence it is necessary to first make a guess of their value. Then, more accurate results can be found by optimising the likelihood function and using Baum-Welch re-estimation algorithm.

Assuming the phonemes are modelled with a three-state left-to-right HMM, and assuming the middle state is the most stable part of the phoneme representation, let,

$$C_i = \frac{1}{K} \sum_{l=1}^{K} W_l G_l, \tag{1}$$

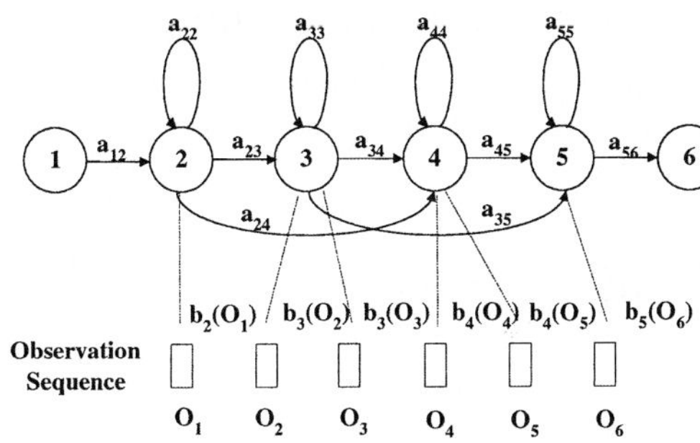

Fig. 2. Left-to-right HMM, *1...6* states, **a** transition probabilities, **b** output probabilities, **O** observation sequence

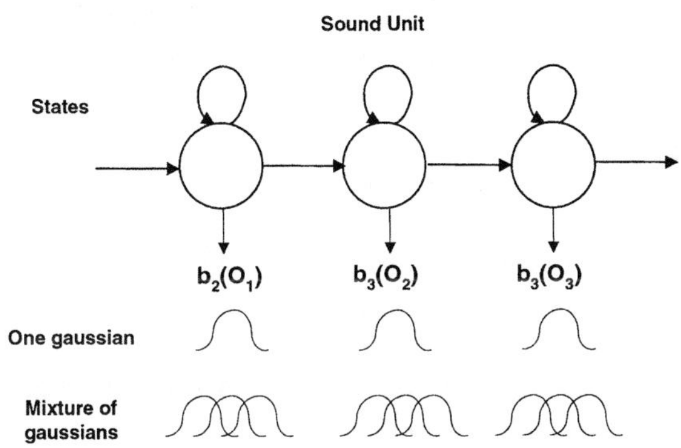

Fig. 3. HMM for a sound unit

where G is the mean of a Gaussian, K is the total number of Gaussians available in that state, W_l is the weight of the Gaussian and i is the index associated to each phoneme.

Given the phonemes' starts and ends, the MFCCs for each phoneme in the utterances can be arranged forming the sets $R^u_{i,j}$, where i is the index associated to each phoneme, j is the j-th user, and u is an index that starts in zero and increments every time the user utters the phoneme i.

Then, the feature vector is defined as

$$\psi^u_{i,j} = \mu(R^u_{i,j}) - C_i$$

where $\mu(R^u_{i,j})$ is the mean vector of the data in the MFCC set $R^u_{i,j}$, and $C_i \in \mathcal{C}_P$ is known as the matching phoneme mean vector of the model. Let us denote the set of vectors,

$$D_p = \{\psi^u_{p,j} \mid \forall\, u, j\}$$

where p is a specific phoneme.

Afterwards, this set is divided in subsets: D_p^{tr} and D_p^{test}. 80% of the total D_p are elements of D_p^{tr} and the remaining 20% form D_p^{test}. Then, $D_p^{train} = \{[\psi_{p,j}^u, b_{p,j}] \mid \forall\ u, j\}$ where $b_{p,j} \in \{-1, 1\}$ is the key bit or class assigned to the phoneme p of the j-th user.

3 Support Vector Machine

The classifier named *Support Vector Machine* (SVM) *Classifier* is a method used for pattern recognition, and was first developed by Vapnik and Chervonenkis [1,3]. Although SVM has been used for several applications, it has also been employed in biometrics [8,7]. For this technique, given the observation inputs and a function-based model, the goal of the basic SVM is to classify these inputs into one of two classes. Firstly, the following set of pairs are defined $\{x_i, y_i\}$; where $x_i \in \mathbb{R}^n$ are the training vectors and $y_i = \{-1, 1\}$ are the labels. The SVM learning algorithm finds an hyperplane (w, b) such that,

$$\min_{x_i, b, \xi} \frac{1}{2} w^T w + C \sum_{i=1}^{l} \xi_i$$

$$\text{subject to } y_i(w^T \phi(x_i) + b) \geq 1 - \xi_i$$

$$\xi_i \geq 0$$

where ξ_i is a slack variable and C is a positive real constant known as a tradeoff parameter between error and margin.

To extend the linear method to a nonlinear technique, the input data is mapped into a higher dimensional space by function ϕ. However, exact specification of ϕ is not needed; instead, the expression known as kernel $K(x_i, x_j) \equiv \phi(x_i)^T \phi(x_j)$ is defined. There are different types of kernels as the linear, polynomial, radial basis function (RBF) and sigmoid. In this research, we study just SVM techinque using radial basis function (RBF) kernel to transform a feature, based on a MFCC-vector, to a binary number (key bit) assigned randomly. The RBF kernel is denoted as $K(x_i, x_j) = e^{(-\gamma||x_i - x_j||^2)}$, where $\gamma > 0$.

The methodology used to implement the SVM training is as follows. Firstly, the training set for each phoneme (D_p^{train}) is formed by assigning a one-bit random label ($b_{p,j}$) to each user. Since a random generator of the values (-1 or 1) is used, the assignation is different for each user. The advantage of this random assignation is that the key entropy grows significantly. Afterwards, by employing a grid search the parameters C and γ are tuned.

The SVM average classification accuracy is computed by the ratio

$$\eta = \frac{\alpha}{\beta}. \tag{2}$$

where α is the number of times that the classification output matches the correct phoneme class on the test data and β is the total number of phonemes to be classified.

By performing the statistics and choosing an appropiate group of phonemes that compute the highest results in the trainning stage, with output D_{ps}^{train}, a key with high performance can be obtained. Just this selection of phonemes will be able to generate the key in the test stage.

Finally a phoneme feature filtering is performed using D_p^{test}. The sets D_{ps}^{test} are computed according to the models obtained in the training phase. This research considers just binary classes and the final key could be obtained by concatenating the bits produced by each selected phoneme. For instance, if a user utters three phonemes: /F/, /AO/, and /R/, and just /F/ and /R/ are selected the final final key is $K = \{f(D_{/F/}), f(D_{/R/})\}$. Thus, the output is formed by two bits.

4 Experimental Methodology and Results

For the purpose of this research the YOHO database was used to perform the experiments [2,4]. YOHO contains clean voice utterances of 138 speakers of different nationalities. It is a combination lock phrases (for instance, "Thirty-Two, Forty-One, Twenty-Five") with 4 enrollment sessions per subject and 24 phrases per enrollment session; 10 verification sessions per subject and 4 phrases per verification session. Given 18768 sentences, 13248 sentences were used for training and 5520 sentences for testing.

The ASR was implemented using the Hidden Markov Models Toolkit (HTK) by Cambridge University Engineering Department [5] configured as a forced-alignment automatic speech recogniser. The important results of the speech processing stage are the twenty sets of mean vectors of the mixture of Gaussians per phoneme given by the HMM and the phoneme segmentation of the utterances. The phonemes used are: /AH/, /AX/, /AY/, /EH/, /ER/, /EY/, /F/, /IH/, /IY/,/K/, /N/, /R/, /S/, /T/, /TH/, /UW/, /V/, /W/. Following

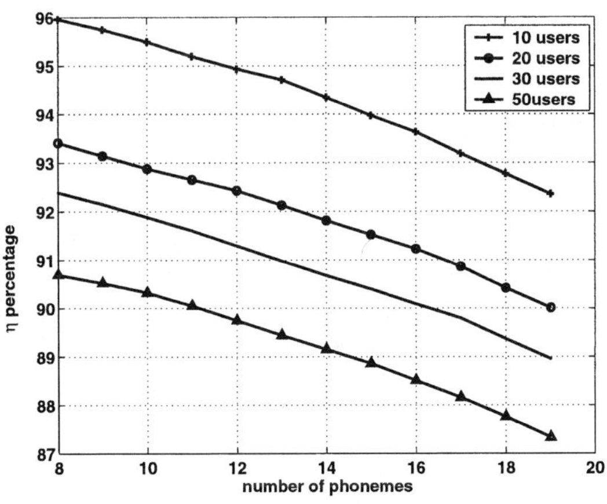

Fig. 4. HMM for a sound unit

the method already described, the D_p sets are formed. It is important to note that the cardinality of each D_p set can be different since the number of equal phoneme utterances can vary from user to user. Next, subsets D_p^{train} and D_p^{test} are constructed. For the training stage, the number of vectors picked per user and per phoneme for generating the model is the same. Each user has the same probability to produce the correct bit per phoneme. However, the number of testing vectors that each user provided can be different.

Following the method a key bit assignation is required. For the purpose of this research, the assignation is arbitrary. Thus, the keys have liberty of assignation, therefore the keys entropy can be easily maximised if they are given in a random fashion with a uniform probability distribution.

The classification of vectors D_{ps}^{train} and D_{ps}^{test} was performed using SVMlight [14]. The behaviour of the SVM is given in terms of Equation 2.

Using the principle of phoneme spotting, the phonemes with the highest accuracy and its SVM model are selected. The accuracy results η are computed for the selected phonemes. The statistics were computed as follows: 500 trials were performed for 10 and 20 users, and 1000 trails were performed for 30 and 50 users. Afterwards, the models that developed the lowest accuracy values are removed. The results for 10, 20, 30 50 users are depicted in Figure 4.

As shown, using phoneme spotting the results become better for all the cases. For instance, for 10 users the key accuracy goes from 92.3% to 95.9%. This is also the behaviour for the different number of users. The most complex experiment was performed using 50 users, but the result shows that 90% accuracy can be achieved.

If less phonemes are taken in account it is possible to compute keys with high accuracies. However, it has the drawback that when just a few phonemes are taken in account the utterances should be larger enough to have cryptographic validity. We have choosen to stop in 8 phonemes, so it is possible to have realiable combinations of phonemes to create the key.

5 Conclusion

We presented an scheme to improve the generation of a cryptographic key from speech signal. With this method we showed that an improvement is possible if just a selection of phonemes (phoneme spotting) is used in the training phase. Results for 10, 20, 30 and 50 speakers, from the YOHO database, were shown.

For future research, we plan to study the clustering of the phonemes to improve the classification task. It is also important to improve the SVM kernel or use artificial neural networks. Moreover, it is important to study the robustness of our system under noisy conditions. Besides, future studies on a M-ary key may be useful to increase the number of different keys available for each user given a fixed number of phonemes in the pass phrase.

Acknowledgments

The authors would like to acknowledge the Cátedra de Seguridad, ITESM, Campus Monterrey and the CONACyT project CONACyT-2002-C01-41372 who partially supported this work.

References

1. Boser, B., Guyon I. and Vapnik V.: A training algorithm for optimal margin classifiers. In Proceedings of the Fifth Annual Workshop on Computational Learning Theory, (1992)
2. Campbell, J. P., Jr.: Features and Measures for Speaker Recognition. Ph.D. Dissertation, Oklahoma State University, (1992)
3. Cortes, C., Vapnik V.: Support-vector network. Machine Learning 20, (1995) 273-297
4. Higgins, A., J. Porter J. and Bahler L.: YOHO Speaker Authentication Final Report. ITT Defense Communications Division (1989)
5. Young,S., P. Woodland HTK Hidden Markov Model Toolkit home page. http://htk.eng.cam.ac.uk/
6. Monrose F., Reiter M. K., Li Q., Wetzel S.. Cryptographic Key Generation From Voice. Proceedings of the IEEE Conference on Security and Privacy, Oakland, CA. (2001)
7. E. Osuna, Freund R., and Girosi F.: Support vector machines: Training and applications. Technical Report AIM-1602, MIT A.I. Lab. (1996)
8. E. Osuna, Freund R., and Girosi F.: Training Support Vector Machines: An Application to Face Recognition, in IEEE Conference on Computer Vision and Pattern Recognition, (1997) 130-136
9. Furui S. Digital Speech Processing, Synthesis, and Recognition. Mercel Dekker,inc. New York, 2001.
10. Rabiner L. R. A tutorial on hidden Markov models and selected applications in speech recognition. Proceedings of the IEEE, 77(2):257–286, February 1989.
11. Rabiner L. R. and Juang B.-H.: Fundamentals of speech recognition. Prentice-Hall, New-Jersey (1993)
12. Uludag U., Pankanti S., Prabhakar S. and Jain A.K.: Biometric cryptosystems: issues and challenges, Proceedings of the IEEE , Volume: 92 , Issue: 6 (2004)
13. Lee K., Hon H., and Reddy R.: An overview of the SPHINX speech recognition system, IEEE Transactions on Acoustics, Speech and Signal Processing, Vol. 38, No. 1, (1990) 35 - 45
14. Joachims T., SVMLight: Support Vector Machine, SVM-Light Support Vector Machine http://svmlight.joachims.org/, University of Dortmund, (1999)
15. Wilcox L., Smith I and Bush M, Wordspotting for voice editing and audio indexing, CHI '92: Proceedings of the SIGCHI conference on Human factors in computing systems, ACM Press, New York, NY, USA(1992), 655–656.

Evaluation System Based on EFuNN for On-Line Training Evaluation in Virtual Reality

Ronei Marcos de Moraes[1] and Liliane dos Santos Machado[2]

[1] UFPB - Federal University of Paraíba - Department of Statistics,
Cidade Universitária s/n, 58051-900, João Pessoa, PB, Brazil
ronei@de.ufpb.br

[2] UFPB - Federal University of Paraíba - Department of Computer Sciences,
Cidade Universitária s/n, 58051-900, João Pessoa, PB, Brazil
liliane@di.ufpb.br

Abstract. In this work is proposed a new approach based on Evolving Fuzzy Neural Networks (EFuNNs) to on-line evaluation of training in virtual reality worlds. EFuNNs are dynamic connectionist feed forward networks with five layers of neurons and they are adaptive rule-based systems. Results of the technique application are provided and compared with another evaluation system based on a backpropagation trained multilayer perceptron neural network.

1 Introduction

Nowadays, with recent technological advances, several kinds of training are made in virtual reality (VR) environments. For example, military combat strategies, surgery and other critical works that involve human risks. So, very realistic VR systems have been developed with training objectives to immerge the user into a virtual world where real situations can be simulated. Simulators based on VR for training need high-end computers to provide realistic haptics, stereoscopic visualization of 3D models and textures [1]. However, it is very important to know the quality of the training and what is the trainees performance. So important as that is the existence of an on-line evaluation coupled to the system, so the trainee can evaluate himself and improve his learning. On-line evaluators must have low complexity to do not compromise simulations performance, but they must have high accuracy to do not compromise evaluation [10]. Because VR worlds are approaches of real worlds, exact measures correspondence between both worlds are not possible in VR simulators. In some applications, data collected from user's interaction cannot be adequated to classical statistical distributions [12].

Some simulators for training already have a method of evaluation. However they just compare the final result with the expected one or are videotape records post-analyzed by an expert [1]. The first models for off-line or on-line evaluation of training were proposed in the year 2000 [4,14]. Since that, statistical models as Hidden Markov Models [11,14], Fuzzy Hidden Markov Models [10], statistical distributions [9] and Fuzzy Gaussian Mixture Models [12] were proposed for training evaluation.

M. Lazo and A. Sanfeliu (Eds.): CIARP 2005, LNCS 3773, pp. 778–785, 2005.

The paper by Rosen *et al.* [13] was proposed for off-line evaluation of training applied to laparoscopic procedures performed in guinea pigs. Using an optoelectronic motion analysis and video records, McBeth *et al.* [9] acquired and compared postural and movement data from experts and residents in different contexts by the use of statistical distributions. Other papers [4,10,11] were proposed for on-line evaluation training in VR simulators. Recently, Machado and Moraes proposed the use of Neural Networks to perform that evaluation [6] to solve the problem of data not adequated to classical statistical distributions.

In 2001 Kasabov [3] proposed a new class of Fuzzy Neural Networks named Evolving Fuzzy Neural Networks (EFuNNs). EFuNNs are structures that evolve according determined principles. EFuNNs have low complexity and high acuracy and, as mentioned before, these features are important to an evaluator from training using VR. In this paper we propose an evaluation system based on EFuNNs for VR simulators and tested it using a bone marrow harvest simulator [5]. Results of the new evaluator are provided and compared with an evaluation system based on a multilayer perceptron (MLP) neural network.

2 VR Simulators and On-Line Evaluation

VR refers to real-time systems modeled by computer graphics that allow user interaction and movements with three or more degrees of freedom [1]. More than a technology, VR became a new science that joins several fields as computer sciences, engineering and cognition. VR worlds are 3D environments created by computer graphics techniques where one or more users are immersed totally or partially to interact with virtual elements. The quality of the user experience in this virtual world is given by the graphics resolution and by the use of special devices for interaction. Basically, the devices stimulate human senses as the vision, the audition and the touch (haptic devices) [1]. There are many purposes for VR systems, but a very important one is the simulation of procedures for training. In medicine, VR based training provides significant benefits over other methods, mainly in critical procedures where a mistake can result in physical or emotional impact on human beings [1].

Some VR simulators for training have a method of evaluation. However they just compare the final result with the expected one or they are videotape records post-analyzed by an expert [1]. It can be not enough to provide a good evaluation. Basically because there are medical procedures where the only sense used is the touch, as in internal exams and minimally invasive surgeries, and the intervention tool trajectory and applied forces inside the body should be known to evaluate the training. In addition, in the second case the student can have forgetten about some details of his training when the evaluation arrives. In these cases, an on-line evaluation system coupled to the VR simulator could supervise the user movements during the internal manipulation of the virtual body and provide the evaluation results to the trainee immediately at the end of the simulation [4].

The VR simulator and the on-line evaluator are independent systems, however they act simultaneously. So, user movements, applied forces, angles, position, torque and other input data can be collected from devices during the simulation to feed the evaluation system [4,13]. Depending on the application, all those variables or some of them will be monitored according to their relevance to the training. It is important to remember that virtual reality based simulators are real time systems. So, the evaluation method requires special attention to do not compromise the simulator performance.

3 Evolving Fuzzy Neural Networks (EFuNNs)

As mentioned before, Evolving Fuzzy Neural Networks (EFuNNs) are structures that evolve according ECOS principles [3]: quick learning, open structure for new features and new knowledge, representing space and time and analyse itself of errors. The EFuNN is a connectionist feed forward network with five layers of neurons, but nodes and connections are created or connected when data examples are presented[3]. The input layer represents input variable of the network as crisp value x. The second layer represents fuzzy quantization of inputs variables. Here, each neuron implements a fuzzy set and its membership function as triangular membership, gaussian membership or other. The third layer contains rule nodes (r_j) which evolve through training. Each one is defined by two connections vectors: $W_1(r_j)$ from fuzzy input layer to rule nodes and $W_2(r_j)$ from rule nodes to fuzzy output layer. These nodes are created during network learning and they represent prototypes of data mapping from fuzzy input to fuzzy output space. In this layer we can use a linear activation function or a Gaussian function. The fourth layer represents fuzzy quantization of the output variables from a function of inputs and from an activation function. The last layer use an activation function to calculate defuzzified values for output variables y.

In the third layer, each $W_1(r_j)$ represents the coordinates of the center of a hypersphere in the fuzzy input space and each $W_2(r_j)$ represents the coordinates of the center of a hypersphere in the fuzzy output space. The radius of the hypersphere of a rule node r_j is defined as $R_j = 1 - S_j$, where S_j is the sensitive threshold parameter for activation of r_j from a new example (x, y). The pair of fuzzy data (x_f, y_f) will be allocated to r_j if x_f is into the r_j input hypersphere and if y_f is into the r_j output hypersphere. For this, two conditions must be satisfied:

a) The local normalized fuzzy distance between x_f and $W_1(r_j)$ must be smaller than R_j. The local normalized fuzzy distance between these two fuzzy membership vectors is done by:

$$D(x_f, W_1(r_j)) = \|x_f - W_1(r_j)\| \,/\, \|x_f + W_1(r_j)\| \tag{1}$$

where $\|a - b\|$ and $\|a + b\|$ are the sum of all the absolute values of a vector that is obtained after vector subtraction $a - b$ or summation $a + b$ respectively.

b) The normalized output error $Err = \|y - y'\| \,/N_{out}$ must be smaller than an error threshold E, where y is as defined before, y' is produced by EFuNN output, N_{out} is the number of outpus and E is the error tolerance of the system for fuzzy output.

If the condictions (a) or (b) are not satisfied, it can be created a new rule node. The weights of rule r_j are updated according to an interactive process:

$$\begin{aligned} W_1(r_j^{(t+1)}) &= W_1(r_j^{(t)}) + l_{j,1}\left(W_1(r_j^{(t)}) - x_f\right) \\ W_2(r_j^{(t+1)}) &= W_2(r_j^{(t)}) + l_{j,2}(A_2 - y_f)A_1(r_j^{(t)}) \end{aligned} \tag{2}$$

where $l_{j,1}$ is the learning rate for the first layer and $l_{j,2}$ is the learning rate for the second layer. In general, it can be assumed they have the same value done by: $l_j = 1/N_{ex}(r_j)$, where $N_{ex}(r_j)$ is the number of examples associated with rule node r_j.

$$A_1(r_j^{(t)}) = f_1(D(W_1(r_j^{(t)}), x_f) \tag{3}$$

is the activation function of the rule $r_j^{(t)}$ and

$$A_2 = f_2(W_2 A_1) \tag{4}$$

is the activation of the fuzzy output neurons, when x is presented. For the functions f_1 and f_2 can be used a simple linear function.

When a new example is associated with a rule r_j, the parameters R_j and S_j are changed:

$$\begin{aligned} R_j^{(t+1)} &= R_j^{(t)} + D\left(W_1(r_j^{(t+1)}), W_1(r_j^{(t)})\right) \\ S_j^{(t+1)} &= S_j^{(t)} - D\left(W_1(r_j^{(t+1)}), W_1(r_j^{(t)})\right) \end{aligned} \tag{5}$$

If exists temporal dependencies between consecutive data, the connection weight W_3 can capture that. The connection W_3 works as a *Short-Term Memory* and a feedback connection from rule nodes layer. If the winning rule node at time $(t-1)$ was $r_{max}^{(t-1)}$ and at time (t) was $r_{max}^{(t)}$, then a link between the two nodes is established by:

$$W_3\left(r_{\max}^{(t-1)}, r_{\max}^{(t)}\right) = W_3\left(r_{\max}^{(t-1)}, r_{\max}^{(t)}\right) + l_3 A_1\left(r_{\max}^{(t-1)}\right) A_1\left(r_{\max}^{(t)}\right) \tag{6}$$

where $A_1\left(r_{\max}^{(t)}\right)$ denotes the activation of a rule node r at a time (t) and l_3 defines a learning rate. If $l_3 = 0$, no temporal associations are learned in an EFuNN.

The EFuNN learning algorithm starts with initial values for parameters [3]. According to mentioned above, the EFuNN is trained by examples until convergence. When a new data example $d = (x, y)$ is presented, the EFuNN either creates a new rule r_n to memorize the new data (input vector $W_1(r_n) = x$ and output vector $W_2(r_n) = y$) or adjusts the winning rule node r_j [3].

4 The Evaluation System

The new methodology proposed in this work was applied in training evaluation over a bone marrow harvest simulator based on VR [4]. The bone marrow is a tissue found inside the bones and used for transplant. Its harvest is a medical procedure performed without any visual feedback except the external view of the donor body. Basically, the physician needs to feel the skin and tissue layers trespassed by the needle to find the bone marrow and then start the material aspiration. Each layer has specific properties as density and elasticity. The bone marrow harvest simulator uses a robotic arm, that offers six degrees of freedom movements and force feedback in the x, y and z axis, to simulate the needle used in a real procedure [5]. So, the goal of the bone marrow simulator is to train the needle insertion stage. The system presents the pelvic region and the robotic arm. The Figure 1 presents the simulator and the layers trespassed by the needle during the bone marrow harvest.

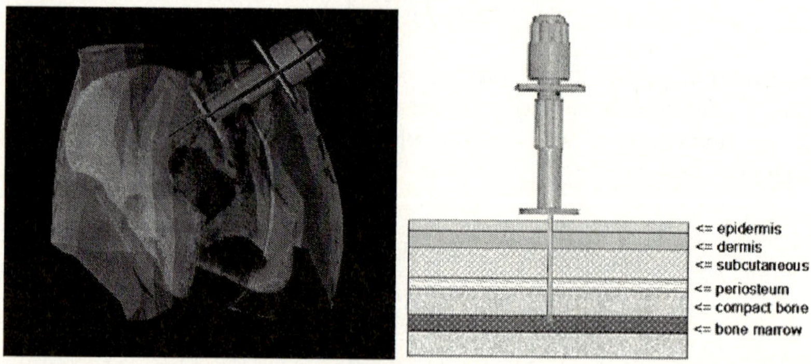

Fig. 1. The Bone Marrow Harvest simulator based on VR and the pelvic tissue layers of human body

An evaluator of performance based on EFuNN and coupled to the bone marrow harvest simulator was implemented. For reasons of general performance of the VR simulator were monitored the following variables: spatial position, velocities, forces and time on each layer. At first moment, the system was calibrated by an expert, according K classes of performance defined by expert. The number of classes of performance was defined as $K = 4$: 1) correct procedures, 2) aceptable procedures, 3) bad executed procedures and 4) very bad executed procedures. So, the classes of performance for a trainee could be: "you are well qualified", "you need some training yet", "you need more training" and "you are a novice". When a trainee uses the system, his performance is compared with each expert classes of performaces and the EFuNN assigns the better class according the trainee's performance. At the end of training, the evaluation system reports to trainee his classification.

To the calibration of EfuNN based training evaluator, an expert executed the procedure approximately a hundred times. The information about performance was acquired using an Evolving Fuzzy Neural Networks and using activation functions done by (3) and (4) for each class. For a controlled and impartial analysis, the procedure was executed hundreds of times by several users. After that, the data collected from these trainings were manually rotuled according to the expert specifications. For each class of performance were selected two hundred cases. These cases were used to validate the evaluation system based on EFuNN. The percentual of correct classification obtained was 98.625% and the Mean Square Error was 0.017956, with 11 misclassifications.

From these data, it was generate the classification matrix showed in the Figure 2. The diagonal of that matrix shows the correct classification. In the other cells, we can observe the mistakes of classifications.

200	0	0	0
0	200	0	0
1	1	189	9
0	0	0	200

Fig. 2. Classification matrix performed by EFuNN based evaluator

It was used the Kappa Coefficient [2] to perform the comparison of the classification agreement. From the classification matrix obtained, the Kappa coefficient for all samples was $K = 98.1667\%$ with variance $\sigma_K^2 = 3.012 \times 10^{-5}$. The Kappa coefficients for each class of performance were: for class 1, $K_1 = 100.000\%$; for class 2, $K_2 = 100.000\%$, for class 3, $K_3 = 92.799\%$ and for class 4, $K_4 = 100.000\%$. That performance is very acceptable and shows the good adaptation of EFuNN in the solution of evaluation problem.

Another important result is the computational performance of the evaluator system: as EFuNN has low computational complexity, other variables could be monitored without degradation of the performance to the virtual reality simulation.

5 Comparison with a MLP Neural Network

A comparison was performed with a Backpropagation trained MLP Neural Network as those proposed by Moraes and Machado [6]. The MLP Neural Network was configured and calibrated by the expert for the same four classes used before. The same eight hundred samples of training (two hundred of each class of performance) were used for a controled and impartial comparison between the two evaluation systems. In this case, after several tests, the better choice was a MLP with four layers with 9, 7, 4, 1 neurons respectively. Nine neurons in the input layer, seven and four in the hidden layers and one in the output layer. The percentual of correct classification obtained was 95.625% and the Mean Square Error was 0.042656, with 35 misclassifications.

191	9	0	0
0	186	14	0
0	2	188	10
0	0	0	200

Fig. 3. Classification matrix performed by MLP Neural Network based evaluator

From the classification matrix obtained (presented in the Figure 3), the Kappa coefficient for all samples was $K = 94.1667\%$ with variance $\sigma_K^2 = 9.293 \times 10^{-5}$. The Kappa coefficients for each class of performance were: for class 1, $K_1 = 94.089\%$; for class 2, $K_2 = 90.713\%$; for class 3, $K_3 = 91.973\%$ and for class 4, $K_4 = 100.000\%$. That performance is good and shows that MLP Neural Network is a competitive approach in the solution of evaluation problem.

We could observe few mistakes in classification performed by MLP Neural Network based evaluator. However, it can see by Figures 2 and 3 and by other information (Kappa coefficients and Mean Square Errors) that the performance of evaluator based on MLP Neural Network is lower than the one of the evaluator based on EFuNN.

About computational performance of evaluator system, some MLP Neural Network tested with 5 or more layers caused performance problems to the VR simulation. However, those MLP neural nets were not the nets with better performance for this task.

6 Conclusions and Further Works

In this paper we presented a new approach to on-line training evaluation in virtual reality simulators. This approach uses an evaluator based on EFuNN and solves the main problems in evaluation procedures. Systems based on this approach can be applied in virtual reality simulators for several areas and can be used to classify the trainee into classes of learning giving him a real position about his performance.

A bone marrow harvest simulator based on virtual reality was implemented to serve as base of the performance tests. The performance obtained by evaluation system based on EFuNN was compared with a backpropagation trained multi-layer perceptron neural network. Based on the obtained data, it is possible to conclude that the evaluation system based on EFuNN presented a superior performance when compared with an evaluation system based on MLP Neural Network for the same case.

By their qualities, this approach could be used for Web-based simulation evaluation also, using plug-ins or agents to collect information about the different variables of user's simulations. In the future, evaluation systems like this can help training in telemedicine.

References

1. Burdea, G. and Coiffet, P., Virtual Reality Technoloy. 2nd ed. New Jersey, Addison-Wesley, 2003.
2. Cohen, J., A coefficient of agreement for nominal scales. Educational and Psychological Measurement, v.20, p.37-46, 1960.
3. Kasabov, N., Evolving Fuzzy Neural Network for Supervised/Unsupervised On-line, Knowledge-based Learning, IEEE Trans. on Man, Machine and Cybernetics, v.31, n.6, 2001.
4. Machado, L. S., Moraes, R. M. and Zuffo, M. K., Fuzzy Rule-Based Evaluation for a Haptic and Stereo Simulator for Bone Marrow Harvest for Transplant. 5th Phantom Users Group Workshop Proceedings, 2000.
5. Machado, L. S., Mello, A. N., Lopes, R. D., Odone Fillho, V. and Zuffo, M. K., A Virtual Reality Simulator for Bone Marrow Harvest for Pediatric Transplant. Studies in Health Technology and Informatics - Medicine Meets Virtual Reality, vol. 81, p.293-297, January, 2001.
6. Machado, L. S.; Moraes, R. M., Neural Networks for on-line Training Evaluation in Virtual Reality Simulators. Proc. of World Congress on Engineering and Technology Education, Brazil, p. 157-160, 2004.
7. Mahoney, D.P. The Power of Touch. Computer Graphics World, v.20, n. 8, p. 41-48, August, 1997.
8. Massie, T., Salisbury, K., The PHANToM Haptic interface: A device for probing virtual objects. ASME Winter Annual Meeting , DSC. v. 55-1. p. 295-300. 1994
9. McBeth, P. B. et al., Quantitative Methodology of Evaluating Surgeon Performance in Laparoscopic Surgery. Studies in Health Technology and Informatics: Medicine Meets Virt. Real., v 85, p. 280-286, Jan., 2002.
10. Moraes, R. M., Machado, L. S., Fuzzy Hidden Markov Models for on-line Training Evaluation in Virtual Reality Simulators. In Computational Intelligent Systems for Applied Research. World Scientific, Singapore, p. 296-303, 2002.
11. Moraes, R. M.; Machado, L. S., Hidden Markov Models for Learning Evaluation in Virtual Reality Simulators. International Journal of Computers & Applications, v.25, n.3, p. 212-215, 2003.
12. Moraes, R. M.; Machado, L. S., Fuzzy Gaussian Mixture Models for on-line Training Evaluation in Virtual Reality Simulators. Anals of the International Conference on Fuzzy Information Processing (FIP'2003). March, Beijing. v. 2, p. 733-740, 2003
13. Rosen J., Richards, C., Hannaford, B. and Sinanan, M., Hidden Markov Models of Minimally Invasive Surgery, Studies in Health Technology and Informatics - Medicine Meets Virtual Reality, vol. 70, p. 279-285, January, 2000.
14. Rosen, J., Solazzo, M., Hannaford, B. and Sinanan, M., Objective Laparoscopic Skills Assessments of Surgical Residents Using Hidden Markov Models Based on Haptic Information and Tool/Tissue Interactions. Studies in Health Technology and Informatics - Medicine Meets Virtual Reality, vol. 81, p. 417-423, January, 2001.

Tool Insert Wear Classification Using Statistical Descriptors and Neuronal Networks

E. Alegre, R. Aláiz, J. Barreiro, and M. Viñuela

Escuela de Ingenierías Industrial e Informática,
Universidad de León, 24071, León, España
{enrique.alegre, rocio.alaiz, joaquin.barreiro}@unileon.es
mavilo92@hotmail.com

Abstract. The goal of this work is to automatically determine the level of tool insert wear based on images acquired using a vision system. Experimental wear was carried out by machining AISI SAE 1045 and 4140 steel bars in a precision CNC lathe and using Sandvik inserts of tungsten carbide. A Pulnix PE2015 B/W with an optic composed by an industrial zoom 70 XL to 1.5X and a diffuse lighting system was used for acquisition. After images were pre-processed and wear area segmented, several patterns of the wear area were obtained using a set of descriptors based on statistical moments. Two sets of experiments were carried out, the first one considering two classes, low wear level and high wear level, respectively; the second one considering three classes. Performance of three classifiers was evaluated: Lp_2, k-nearest neighbours and neural networks. Zernike and Legendre descriptors show the lowest error rates using a MLP neuronal network for classifying.

1 Introduction

Measuring of wear in tools for machining has been in the scope of many studies. Depending on the method for acquiring values and their implementation, methods to wear measuring are classified in direct or indirect, and according to the monitoring in continuous and intermittent [1].

Direct methods measure change of actual parameters values as shape and location of the cutting edge [2] (optical methods: CCD cameras or optic fibber sensors), tool material volumetric loss, electrical resistance at the part-tool interface (voltage measuring of a specific conductive covering), part dimensions (dimensional measuring with optic devices or with micrometers, pneumatic, ultrasonic or electromagnetic transducers) or distance between tool and part.

Indirect methods contrast the wear with process parameters, which are easier of measuring. However, the computational effort later on is bigger. Examples are cutting forces evaluation (effort measuring devices, sensors, piezoelectric plates or rings, bearings with force measuring, torque measuring, etc.), tool or tool-holder vibration (accelerometer), acoustic emissions (transducers integrated in the tool-holder or microphones), current or power consumption in the screw or motor (ammeters or dynamometers), temperature (thermocouples or pyrometers, colour reflectance or chip surface) or roughness of machined surface (mechanical or optical methods) [3].

M. Lazo and A. Sanfeliu (Eds.): CIARP 2005, LNCS 3773, pp. 786–793, 2005.

Continuous or on-line measuring is carried out during the cutting process, while intermittent measuring or off-line is only carried out during predefined intervals. These intermittent measuring generally requires stopping the production. In many cases direct and indirect techniques are used at the same time; for example, an indirect and on-line technique (tool break detection, based on vibration signals) can be combined with a direct and off-line technique (measuring of the wear area with a CCD camera).

Systems for automatic wear monitoring helps to reduce the manufacturing costs, but it is difficult to introduce them in the industrial field. Artificial vision offers many advantages as direct technique of measuring. Although it has already been used with relative success [4], their application is difficult because the results require precision levels in the scope of industrial standards: measuring with quality, integration with the machine tool, handling of tools and advanced techniques of adaptative lighting to obtain optimized images [5,6].

First results obtained carrying out a direct and intermittent wear measuring of the tool inserts using a vision system are showed in this work. The system does not work as continuous method due to the assembly conditions. Disassemble of tool is necessary to obtain images at the end of each machining period. Application of acquisition and pre-processing has been carried out with Matlab. Different wear patterns have been obtained for the different classes analyzed using descriptors, and the results with their errors are showed.

2 Materials and Methods

2.1 Machining and Vision Systems

A CNC parallel lathe has been used for the machining with a maximum turning speed of 2300 rpm. AISI SAE 1045 (20 HB, normalized) and 4140 (34 HB, tempered) steel bars of 250 mm of length and 90 mm of diameter were machined. The tool inserts were of covered tungsten carbide, rhombic, high tough. Different values were used for the cutting parameters: cutting speeds (Vc) between 150 and 300 m/min, feedrate (f) between 0.15 and 0.3 mm/rev and depth of cutting (ap) between 0.5 and 3 mm. After the machining of the part length the tool is disassembled and the insert is located in a tool-fixture; that allows to keeping constant their position in the image for the flank images and also for the crater images. Additionally, roughness and hardness measuring was taken on the machined surface [7].

2.2 Image Acquisition

Images have been acquired [7] using a Pulnix PE2015 B/W camera with 1/3" CCD. Digitalization was carried out with a Matrox Meteor II card. The optical system is composed by a 70XL industrial zoom of OPTEM, with an extension tube of 1X and 0.5X/0,75X/1.5X/2.0X Lens also of OPTEM. The lighting system is composed by a DCR®III regulated light source of FOSTEC that provides an intense cold lighting. A SCDI system of diffuse lighting of NER SCDI-25-F0 is used to avoid shines. The system provides diffuse lighting in the same direction as the camera axis. Positioning of lighting is carried out by means of bundle dual of Fostec.

Acquisition is achieved using a developed Matlab application that uses the Image Acquisition Toolbox. The capture application has three modules: setup of the camera, setup of the sequence and acquisition of the image. These modules let to know the information of the capture device, to choose the resolution, to define the path of information storage and to keep the images.

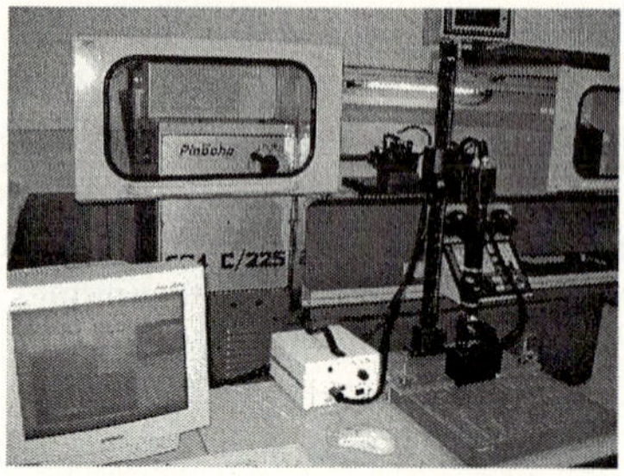

Fig. 1. The camera and the lighting system

2.3 Image Processing

Initially, a low-pass filter was applied to the image for blurring the background and to make easier the segmentation. Later on the region of interest is cropped and the contrast is enhancement by means of a histogram stretching.

Region growing has been used to segment the wear area, selecting the starting points based on the result of a previous threshold. Once the thresholds are obtained, a binary image is generated in which the wear region is set to 1 and the rest one to 0. Later on a median filter is applied to smooth for noise reduction. If the wear region is not effectively closed, a morphological closing is carried out. Finally, the binary image with the wear region is multiplied for the original image, obtaining the area of interest as grey scale perfectly segmented.

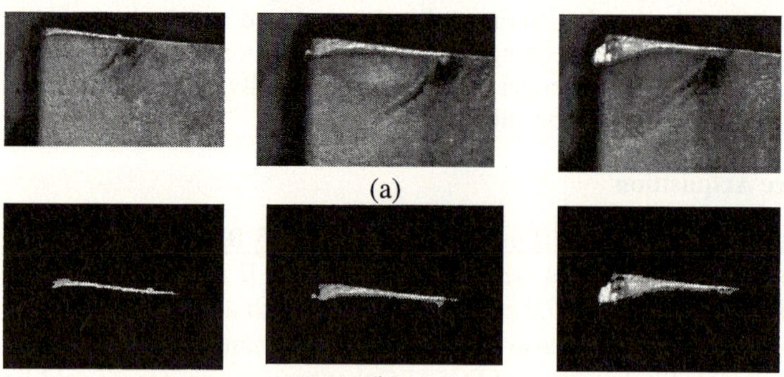

(a)

(b)

Fig. 2. (a) First images in a series showing three wear levels. (b) Segmented images with the wear region in grey scale.

2.4 Samples and Descriptors

Experiments have been carried out using a set of 146 insert images with different wear level in the flank.

Different wear patterns have been obtained for each class, using a different statistical descriptor for each pattern. Table 1 shows the descriptors used.

Table 1. Used descriptors

Pattern #	Descriptor	Details
Pattern 1	Simple moments	9 moments: from m_{00} to m_{22}
Pattern 2	Central moments	9 moments: from mc_{00} to mc_{22}
Pattern 3	Central moments normalized	9 moments: from mcn_{00} to mcn_{22}
Pattern 4	Hu moments	The 7 moments
Pattern 5	Zernike moments	29 moments: all the possible moments until the order 4.
Pattern 6	Legendre moments	9 moments: from ML_{00} to ML_{22}
Pattern 7	Taubín moments	The 8 characteristics of the vector
Pattern 8	Flusser moments	The 6 moments

Additional patterns were also obtained combining diverse moments in the same pattern. The first combination was created with the Zernike and Legendre moments. The second one was created adding simple moments to the Zernike and Legendre moments. The third one was created adding Taubín moments and the last one pattern was created with all the moments.

Finally, the images were divided in two subsets. The first subset, composed by two thirds of the total in each class, was used to obtain the pattern and the second, formed by a third of the images, to carry out the experiments.

2.5 Experiments and Classifiers

Firstly, a supervised classification has been carried out attending to the wear level in each insert. A label has been assigned to each image which indicates its inclusion in one of the three classes settled down by an expert: D001, inserts with low wear; D003, inserts with very high wear; and D002, inserts with medium wear level. A second set of experiments was carried out classifying and labelling images in two classes: D001, or inserts with low wear and D002, or inserts with very high wear.

The minimum Euclidean distance has been used initially to carry out the recognition of these classes, obtaining the prototype of each class by means of the arithmetic media.

Later on a classifier of k nearest neighbours was used, with k=10.

Finally, a neuronal network was evaluated as classifier. A multilayer perceptron neuronal network (MLP) was used, varying the number of training cycles, the number of neurons in the hidden layer and, in some cases, the learning rate. 70% of images in each class were used in the experiments to training the network, and 30% for the test. The medium error and standard deviation have been calculated for the errors. Images for training and test have been chosen in each iteration randomly, and the experiment has been repeated ten times consecutively. Data have also been normalized calculating the media and standard deviation of the training data and then subtracting that media from all the data, so much for training as for test, and dividing them by the previously calculated standard deviation. Finally, a new experiment balancing the data in each class has been carried out, equalling the number of images that are included in each one.

2.6 Results

Three classes and Euclidean distance

Table 2. Error rate: three classes with Lp2

Class	Simple	Cent.	Norm.	Hu	Taub.	Fluss.	Zern	Leg.
1	0.258	0.193	0.548	0.903	0.935	0.968	0.129	0.097
2	0.583	0.583	0.583	0.500	1	0.830	0.250	0.500
3	0.200	0.600	0.200	0	0	1	0.400	0.400

Two classes and neuronal networks

The following tests have been carried out differentiating only between two wear classes, the D001 and the D002. A MLP neuronal network has been used for it, varying the number of training cycles, the number of neurons in the hidden layer and, in some case, the learning rate.

The error results for Zernike and Legendre moments with normalized data are shown next:

Table 3. Error rate: normalized Legendre moments and MLP neuronal network with learning rate 0.1

		500 cycles	3000 cycles	6000 cycles
Without Norm.				
2 N	**D001**	0.124±0.102	0.112±0.059	0.108±0.050
	D002	0.426±0.196	0.274±0.102	0.347±0.143
5 N	**D001**	0.321±0.071	0.100±0.057	0.168±0.079
	D002	0.279±0.114	0.316±0.119	0.353±0.122
12 N	**D001**	0.144±0.078	0.108±0.073	0.112±0.053
	D002	0.279±0.147	0.284±0.099	0.347±0.114

Table 4. Error rate: normalized Zernike moments and MLP neuronal network with learning rate 0.1

		500 cycles	3000 cycles	6000 cycles
Without Norm.				
2 N	**D001**	0.096±0.086	0.124±0.051	0.096±0.078
	D002	0.305±0.135	0.289±0.119	0.315±0.065
5 N	**D001**	0.096±0.057	0.164±0.091	0.148±0.060
	D002	0.389±0.159	0.268±0.094	0.242±0.119
12 N	**D001**	0.140±0.066	0.124±0.066	0.132±0.105
	D002	0.247±0.099	0.310±0.084	0.289±0.087

The following experiments were carried out with *balanced data* and with the normalized Legendre and Zernike descriptors. Results are shown in the tables 5 and 6.

Table 5. Error rate: normalized and balanced Legendre moments and MLP neuronal network with learning rate 0.1

		500 cycles	3000 cycles	6000 cycles
Normalized and Balanced				
2 N	**D001**	0.160±0.128	0.176±0.057	0.188±0.100
	D002	0.263±0.089	0.326±0.098	0.263±0.110
5 N	**D001**	0.156±0.066	0.160±0.065	0.176±0.073
	D002	0.253±0.088	0.263±0.089	0.284±0.071
12 N	**D001**	0.188±0.098	0.188±0.046	0.148±0.059
	D002	0.231±0.103	0.216±0.120	0.310±0.120

Table 6. Error rate: normalized and balanced Zernike moments and MLP neuronal network with learning rate 0.1

		500 cycles	3000 cycles	6000 cycles
Normalized and Balanced				
2 N	**D001**	0.108±0.078	0.144±0.073	0.156±0.100
	D002	0.368±0.113	0.268±0.106	0.258±0.100
5 N	**D001**	0.156±0.079	0.184±0.093	0.140±0.063
	D002	0.273±0.085	0.245±0.119	0.240±0.096
12 N	**D001**	0.180±0.083	0.172±0.068	0.140±0.083
	D002	0.250±0.100	0.247±0.093	0.280±0.107

Combination of moments and neuronal networks

Next, results for the experiment of combining different moments are shown.

Table 7. Error rate: normalized and balanced Zernike and Legendre moments and MLP neuronal network with learning rate 0.1

		500 cycles	3000 cycles	6000 cycles
Normalized and Balanced				
2 N	**D001**	0.136±0.085	0.144±0.087	0.140±0.051
	D002	0.305±0.140	0.242±0.087	0.279±0.056
5 N	**D001**	0.168±0.075	0.140±0.069	0.124±0.078
	D002	0.263±0.110	0.257±0.072	0.242±0.090
12 N	**D001**	0.108±0.108	0.144±0.078	0.152±0.086
	D002	0.274±0.118	0.242±0.079	0.305±0.101

Two classes and 10 nearest neighbours

The following experiment has been carried out using the method of the k-neighbours with two classes, with patterns created with descriptors of Zernike, Legendre and Taubín.

Table 8. Error rate: Zernike, Legendre, Taubín and total moments with 10 nearest neighbours classifier

	Zernike	Legendre	Taubín	Totales
Without Norm				
D001	0.042±0.056	0.074±0.055	0.172±0.084	0.174±0.079
D002	0.368±0.109	0.397±0.116	0.242±0.091	0.195±0.082
Normalized				
D001	0.010±0.022	0.040±0.053	0.174±0.082	0.042±0.042
D002	0.500±0.125	0.463±0.100	0.260±0.079	0.431±0.077

3 Conclusions

The analysis of the obtained results let stay the following conclusions. With the classifier of *minimum Euclidean distance* the descriptors that better discriminate, for both two and three classes experiments, are those of Zernike and Legendre. The other descriptors do not offer reliable results since they provide acceptable results for a class but not for the other ones.

In the case of using a *neuronal network* and two classes the best behaviour is provided again by the moments of Zernike and Legendre, and error is lower when data are normalized.

It has also been confirmed that the use of a pattern composed by several descriptors, as Zernike and Legendre, does not provide significant improvements.

With regard to the neuronal network adjustment, it can be concluded that a learning rate next to 0.1 is the one that better behaviour provides. Variations in the number of training cycles and neurons in the hidden layer do not offer significant differences, although we have observed that it is enough with a network with 5 to 12 neurons in the hidden layer and 3000 to 6000 training cycles.

With the 10 nearest neighbour classifier, the moments of Zernike and of Legendre, the combination of all the moments and, surprisingly, the moments of Taubín, have provided the lower errors. With this classifier the normalization of data worsens the results, contrary to the behaviour observed with neuronal networks.

We can conclude saying that the best results have been obtained with the moments of Zernike and Legendre, normalized and balanced, and a neuronal classifier. The patterns created with combinations of descriptors, whenever the Zernike and Legendre are among them, also provides low error rates.

We believe that the small number of images is the origin of the high error rate obtained with some descriptors. In future works we will carry out new experiments using a bigger number of images and more balanced classes.

References

1. Sick B.: On-Line and indirect tool wear monitoring in turning with artificial neural networks: a review of more than a decade of research. Mechanical Systems and Signal Processing. (2002) 487-546.
2. Reilly, G. A., McCormacka, B. A. O., Taylor, D.: Cutting sharpness measurement: a critical review. Journal of Materials Processing Technology 153 (2004) 261-267.
3. Byrne, G., Dornfeld,D., Inasaki, I., Ketteler, G., Onig, W. K., Teti, R.: Tool condition monitoring (TCM)—the status of research and industrial application. Annals of the CIRP 44 , (1995) 541–567.
4. Jurkovic, J., Korosec, M., Kopac, J.: New approach in tool wear measuring technique using CCD vision system. International Journal of Machine Tools and Manufacture vol. 45, 9 (2005) 1023-1030.
5. Pfeifer, T., Wiegers, L.: Realiable tool wear monitoring by optimised image and illumination control in machine vision. Measurement *28*, (2000) 209-218.
6. Scheffer, C., Heyns, P.S.: An industrial tool wear monitoring system for interrupted turning. Mechanical Systems and Signal Processing 18 (2004) 1219–1242.
7. Hernández, L.K., Cáceres, H., Barreiro, J., Alegre, E., Castejón, M., Fernández, R.A.: Monitorización del desgaste de plaquitas de corte usando visión artificial. In: Proc. VII Congreso Iberoamericano de Ingeniería Mecánica, México (2005).

Robust Surface Registration Using a Gaussian-Weighted Distance Map in PET-CT Brain Images

Ho Lee[1] and Helen Hong[2,*]

[1] School of Electrical Engineering and Computer Science, Seoul National University
holee@cglab.snu.ac.kr
[2] School of Electrical Engineering and Computer Science, BK21: Information Technology, Seoul National University, San 56-1 Shinlim 9-dong Kwanak-gu, Seoul 151-742, Korea
hlhong@cse.snu.ac.kr

Abstract. In this paper, we propose a robust surface registration using a Gaussian-weighted distance map for PET-CT brain fusion. Our method is composed of three steps. First, we segment the head using the inverse region growing and remove the non-head regions segmented with the head using the region growing-based labeling in PET and CT images, respectively. The feature points of the head are then extracted using sharpening filter. Second, a Gaussian-weighted distance map is generated from the feature points of CT images to lead our similarity measure to robust convergence on the optimal location. Third, weighted cross-correlation measures the similarities between the feature points extracted from PET images and the Gaussian-weighted distance map of CT images. In our experiments, we use software phantom and clinical datasets for evaluating our method with the aspect of visual inspection, accuracy, robustness, and computation time. Experimental results show that our method is more accurate and robust than the conventional ones.

1 Introduction

Computed tomography (CT) is a well-established means of diagnosing metastasis of oncology patients and evaluating disease progression and regression during treatment. However, CT has lower sensitivity and specificity than positron emission tomography (PET) in identifying tumors of initial staging or defining their biological behavior and response to therapy, while PET has a limitation in achieving precise lesion size and shape due to the few anatomical structures. Currently, whole body PET-CT fusion using hardware is introduced so as to provide a rough alignment of whole body rapidly. However, it is still critical to develop a registration technique for aligning two different modalities exactly and robustly since images obtained from the PET-CT scanner are acquired with different scan time.

Surface- and voxel-based approaches have been suggested for alignment of functional and anatomical images [1]. In surface-based approach, it requires the delineation of corresponding surfaces in each image. Hongjian et al. [2] used the chamfer distance matching for PET-MR brain fusion. Each rigid surface segmented

* Corresponding author.

M. Lazo and A. Sanfeliu (Eds.): CIARP 2005, LNCS 3773, pp. 794 – 803, 2005.

from PET and MR brain images is aligned by repeatedly minimizing values of each distance map. Maintz et al. [3] proposed a feature-based cross-correlation to search for the optimal location where the number of corresponding points between feature points extracted from both images is a maximum. However, the accuracy of these surface-based approaches is largely affected by the result of surface extraction. In voxel-based approach, it measures the similarity of all geometrically corresponding voxel pairs in overlapping area. Especially, mutual information-based registration [4] shows the accurate results in comparison with other voxel-based approaches and surface-based approach. However, mutual information-based registration requires enormous processing time in comparison with surface-based approaches even though multi-resolution technique or other improvements are used.

Current approaches still need more progress in computational efficiency and accuracy for registration between functional and anatomical images. In this paper, we propose a surface-based registration using Gaussian-weighted distance map (GWDM) to robustly find optimal location even in bad conditions such as blurry and noisy images. Our method is applied to PET and CT brain images, which divided into three steps such as head segmentation and non-head elimination, Gaussian-weighted distance map generation, similarity measure and optimization. In our experiments, we use software phantom and clinical datasets for evaluating our method with the aspects of visual inspection, accuracy, robustness, and computation time.

The organization of the paper is as follows. In Section 2, we discuss how to extract feature points efficiently. Then we propose a robust surface registration using Gaussian-weighted distance map in PET and CT brain images. In Section 3, experimental results show how our method aligns exactly and robustly using software phantom and clinical datasets. This paper is concluded with a brief discussion of the results in Section 4.

2 Surface Registration Using GWDM

Fig. 1 shows the pipeline of our method for the registration of PET and CT brain images. Since CT images have more anatomical information than PET images, CT images are fixed as reference volume and PET images are defined as floating volume. Since rigid transformation is enough to align the head base, we use three translations and three rotations about the *x*-, *y*-, *z*- axis.

2.1 Head Segmentation Using 3D Inverse Region Growing

Since the head segmentation using threshold-based method can produce holes within the head, these holes should be filled by morphological operations such as dilation and erosion. However, we decide the number of iterations of morphological operation in proportion to the size of holes as well as the computation time is increased by the number of iterations. In addition, numerous iterations can produce distortions of edge. Thus we propose a 3D inverse region growing (IRG) for the automatic head segmentation without additional processing such as hole filling in PET and CT brain images.

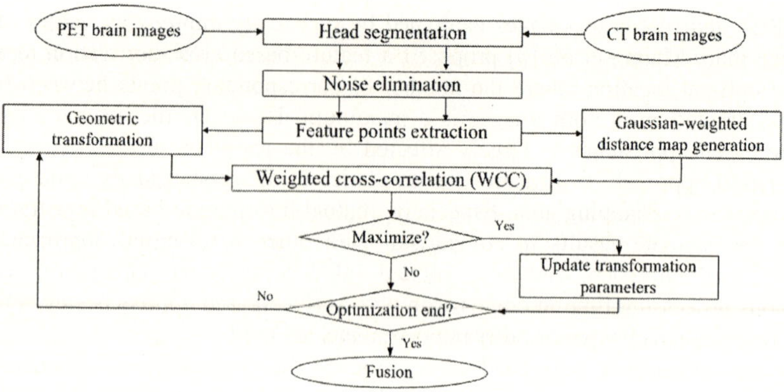

Fig. 1. The pipeline of proposed method using a Gaussian-weighted distance map

First, our 3D IRG starts by choosing a seed voxel at (0, 0, 0) on whole volume and compares seed voxels with neighboring voxels. Region is grown from the seed voxel by adding neighboring voxels that are less than chosen tolerance. When the growth of region stops, this region is background except head. Then we simply segment the head by inverse operation. Thus our 3D IRG segments the head automatically without holes and the distortion of edges by morphological operations in PET and CT images. Fig. 2 shows the comparison of threshold-based method and our 3D IRG method in PET and CT brain images. In Fig. 2(a) and (c), we can easily see holes inside of the head, whereas our method can clearly segment the head without holes as shown in Fig. 2(b) and (d).

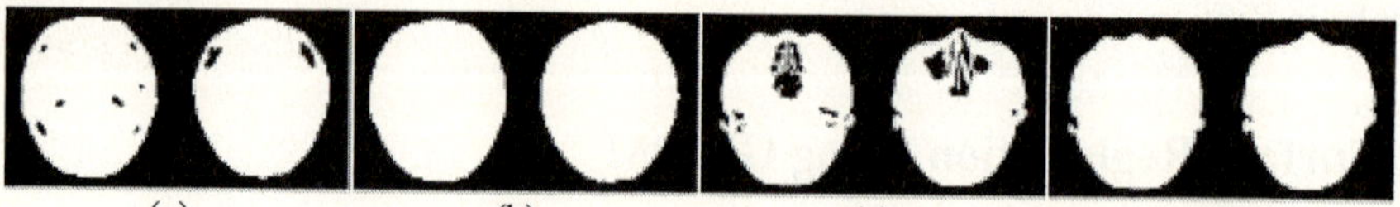

(a) (b) (c) (d)

Fig. 2. The comparison of head segmentation between threshold-based method and 3D IRG method in PET and CT brain images (a) and (c) shows the results of the threshold-based method in PET and CT brain images, respectively. (b) and (d) shows the results of our 3D IRG method in PET and CT brain images, respectively.

2.2 Non-head Elimination Using Region Growing-Based Labeling

Although the 3D IRG segments the head without holes, the non-head regions having the intensities which are similar to the head can be segmented on background area. Since the size of these non-head regions is small in comparison with the head, we propose a region growing-based labeling (RGL) to efficiently eliminate the non- head regions by removing other regions except the largest region.

Our RGL finds the position of 1's voxel for choosing the seed on the binary images while scanning from position at (0, 0, 0) to whole volume size. The region is then grown from the seed voxel by adding neighboring voxels based on connectivity and the voxels of growing region are given to label. When the growth of region stops, we identify the size of label. Since the RGL doesn't require any equivalence table and renumbering of label, Our RGL provides efficient labeling in comparison with a conventional connected component labeling [7] in memory use and time complexity. As shown in Fig. 3(a) and (c), non- head regions are included in PET and CT brain images. Fig. 3(b) and (d) shows the results of the head without the non-head regions removed by the RGL in PET and CT brain images, respectively.

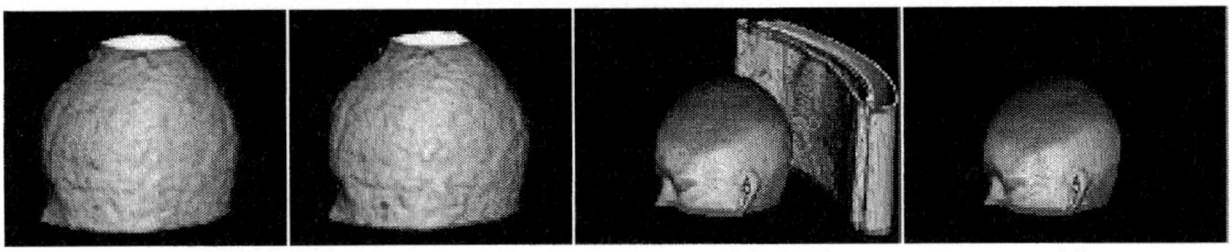

(a) (b) (c) (d)

Fig. 3. The results of the non-head elimination using our RGL method (a) PET brain images (b) the results of non-head elimination in the PET brain image (c) CT brain images (d) the result of non-head elimination in the CT brain image

The feature points are extracted from the binary segmentation images by applying a conventional sharpening filter [7]. Since the holes within head area or the non-head regions in background area are filled or eliminated by 3D IRG and RGL, the feature points are selected from the only head boundary. Fig. 4 shows the feature points of head extracted from PET and CT images, respectively.

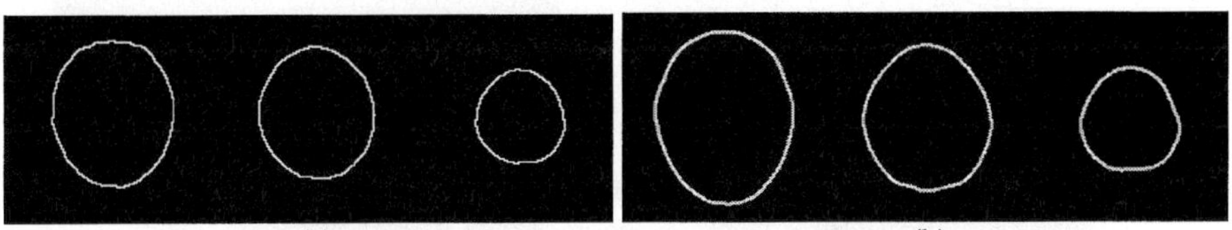

(a) (b)

Fig. 4. The feature points of head extracted from PET and CT images (a) PET slice (b) CT slice

2.3 Feature Points Extraction and Gaussian-Weighted Distance Map Generation

A conventional surface registration is likely to lead the similarity measure to converge on the local optimum near to global optimum since the correspondence of the feature points extracted from PET images can differ from the feature points of CT images. To prevent this occurrence we propose the 2D Gaussian-weighted distance map (GWDM) to robustly converge on global optimum even in blurry and noisy images as well as in a large geometrical displacement.

Our 2D GWDM is generated by assigning the Gaussian-weighted mask to the corresponding feature points. If the current weighting is larger than the weighting of neighbor feature points, the previous weighting is changed to the current one. In our method, GWDM is generated only for CT images. The Gaussian-weighted mask is defined as Eq. (1).

$$G\ (x,y)=\frac{1}{2\pi\sigma^2}e^{-\frac{1}{2\sigma^2}\left\{(x-c_x)^2+(y-c_y)^2\right\}}\approx\lambda e^{-\frac{1}{2\sigma^2}\left\{(x-c_x)^2+(y-c_y)^2\right\}} \qquad (1)$$

where σ is set in proportion to the mask size as a standard deviation. λ is a scaling parameter. c_x and c_y is the center of the Gaussian-weighted mask. The weighting of mask is very large at center, and is reduced in proportion to the distance far from center depending on Gaussian curve. G is the Gaussian-weighted mask.

Fig. 5 shows the process for the generation of GWDM in CT brain image. Fig. 5(a) and Fig. 5(b) show the Gaussian-weighted curve and mask with 13 by 13 size, λ=1, σ=3.0, respectively. Fig. 5(c) shows the extracted feature points. Fig. 5(d) shows the GWDM generated from feature points. Fig. 5(e) shows the weighting of the GWDM in a magnification of Fig. 5(d). The area corresponding to feature points has the brightest intensities while the area far from feature points has dark ones.

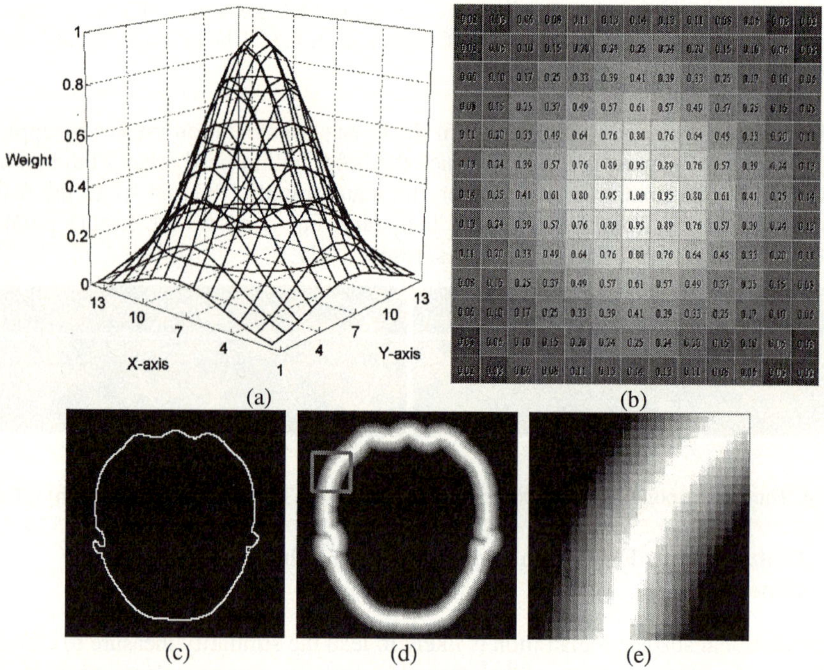

Fig. 5. The generation of a 2D GWDM in CT brain image (a) the Gaussian curve (b) the Gaussian-weighted mask (c) the feature points of head (d) 2D GWDM (e) magnification of (d)

2.4 Weighted Cross-Correlation and Optimization

For similarity measure between the feature points of PET images and the GWDM of CT images, we propose the weighted cross-correlation (WCC). Our approach reduces the computation time because of using the only GWDM of CT images corresponding to the feature points of PET images instead of using whole CT volume. The WCC is defined as Eq. (2).

$$WCC = \frac{1}{\lambda N_{PET}} \sum_{i=0}^{N_{PET}} G_{CT}(Tr(P_{PET}(i))) \tag{2}$$

where N_{PET} and $P_{PET}(i)$ are the total number of feature points and the position of i-th feature point in PET images, respectively. Tr is rigid transformation matrix transforming feature points of PET images into the coordinate system of CT images. G_{CT} is the GWDM of CT images corresponding feature points in PET images. λ is a scaling parameter.

In order to search for the optimal location, we find optimal parameters such as T_x', T_y', T_z', R_x', R_y', R_z' when the WCC reaches maximum as following Eq. (3). Powell's multidimensional direction method is then used to maximize WCC. This method searches for optimal location in the order following T_x, T_y, R_z, R_x, R_y, T_z until WCC doesn't change any more and iterate over constant number.

$$(T_x', T_y', T_z', R_x', R_y', R_z') = \arg\max\,(WCC) \tag{3}$$

3 Experimental Results

All our implementation and test were performed on an Intel Pentium IV PC containing 3.2 GHz CPU and 2.0 GBytes of main memory. Our method has been successfully applied to five clinical datasets and two software phantom datasets, as described in Table 1, for evaluating with the aspects of visual inspection, accuracy, robustness, and computation time.

Table 1. Experimental datasets

Dataset	CT/PET	Image size	Slice number	Voxel Size (mm)	Slice spacing (mm)	Intensity range
Patient1	CT	512×512	158	0.38×0.38	1.0	0 ~ 4095
	FDG-PET	128×128	40	1.95×1.95	3.33	0 ~ 255
Patient2	CT	512×512	35	1.17×1.17	5.00	-976 ~ 1642
	FDG-PET	128×128	82	2.00×2.00	2.00	0 ~ 4095
Patient3	CT	512×512	34	1.17×1.17	5.00	48 ~ 2857
	FDG-PET	128×128	45	4.00×4.00	4.00	0 ~ 4095
Patient4	CT	512×512	28	1.17×1.17	5.00	-976 ~ 1933
	FDG-PET	128×128	80	2.00×2.00	2.00	0 ~ 4095
Patient5	CT	512×512	37	1.17×1.17	5.00	48 ~ 4048
	FDG-PET	128×128	53	4.00×4.00	4.00	0 ~ 4095
Software phantom1	CT	128×128	40	1.95×1.95	3.33	0 ~ 2224
	FDG-PET	128×128	40	1.95×1.95	3.33	0 ~ 4095
Software phantom2	CT	128×128	40	1.95×1.95	3.33	498 ~ 2721
	FDG-PET	128×128	40	1.95×1.95	3.33	0 ~ 4095

As shown in Fig. 6, PET software phantom datasets simulate background, tissue, and brain in the head and are generated by using Gaussian smoothing for blurry properties. The standard deviation of Gaussian smoothing in PET software phantom1 and phantom2 are 1.0 and 2.0, respectively. CT software phantom datasets simulate four areas such as background, tissue, muscle, and skull. In particular, the Gaussian noise with standard deviation 20.0 is added to CT software phantom2. We can see that software phantom2 shown in Fig. 6(c) and (d) are more blurry and noisy than software phantom1 shown in Fig. 6(a) and (b).

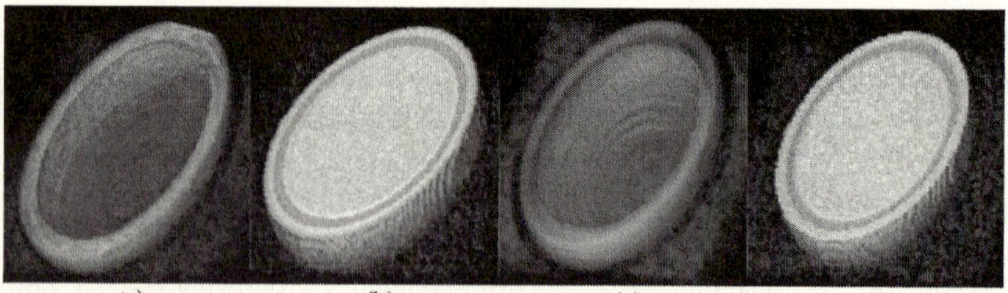

(a) (b) (c) (d)

Fig. 6. Software phantom datasets for accuracy and robust evaluation (a) PET software phantom1 (b) CT software phantom1 (c) PET software phantom2 (d) CT software phantom2

Fig. 7 and Fig. 8 show the comparison of 2D visual inspection and 3D fusion before and after registration. In Fig. 7, the results of 2D visual inspection are displayed by fusing skull edges of CT images and transformed PET brain images in axial, coronal, and sagittal planes together, whereas Fig 8 fuses brain boundary of PET images on the CT images. While the top row of Fig. 7 and Fig. 8 applying scale parameters before registration are misaligned between PET brain images and CT images, the bottom row of Fig. 7 and Fig. 8 applying optimal parameters after registration are well aligned within skull area of CT image. Fig. 7(d) and Fig. 8(d) show the brain in arbitrary 3D view before and after registration. Fig. 9 shows the aligned results in arbitrary 2D plane and 3D view of clinical datasets after registration.

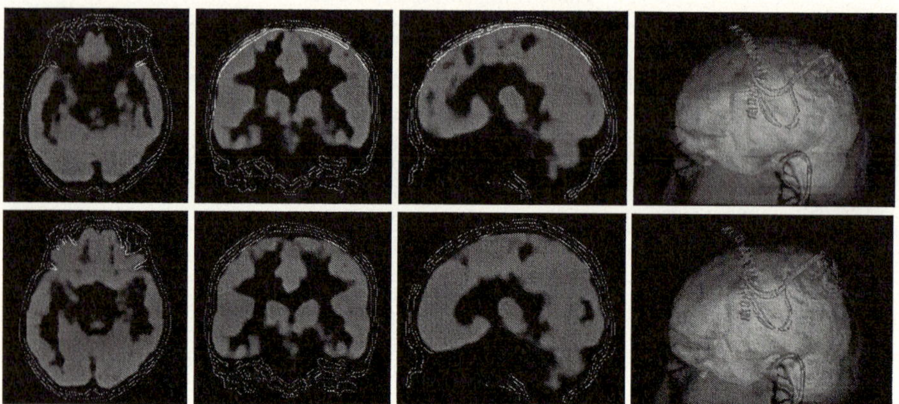

(a) (b) (c) (d)

Fig. 7. The comparison of 2D visual inspection and 3D fusion before and after registration in clinical dataset1 (a) axial plane (b) coronal plane (c) sagittal plane (d) 3D fusion

The registration accuracy of our method is evaluated by comparing with the conventional ones such as mutual information (MI)-based registration, chamfer distance matching (CDM), and feature-based cross-correlation (FCC). For the evaluation, we use the software phantom with the known parameters, called as true transformations. In order to quantify the registration error shown in Table 2, we

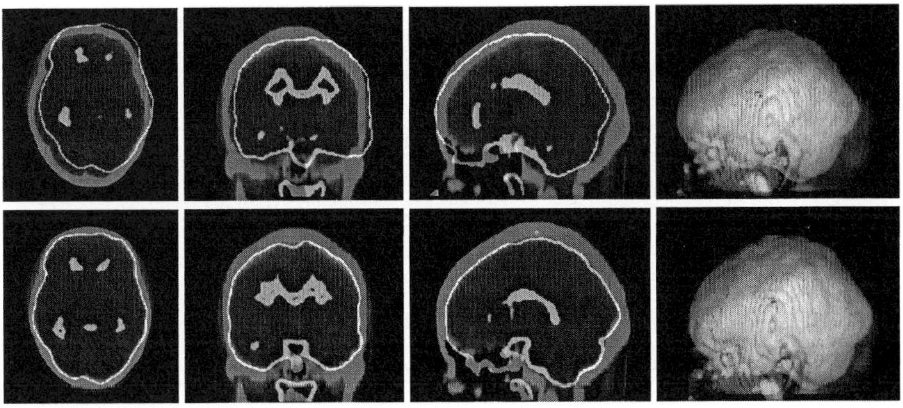

(a) (b) (c) (d)

Fig. 8. The comparison of 2D visual inspection and 3D fusion before and after registration in clinical dataset2 (a) axial plane (b) coronal plane (c) sagittal plane (d) 3D fusion

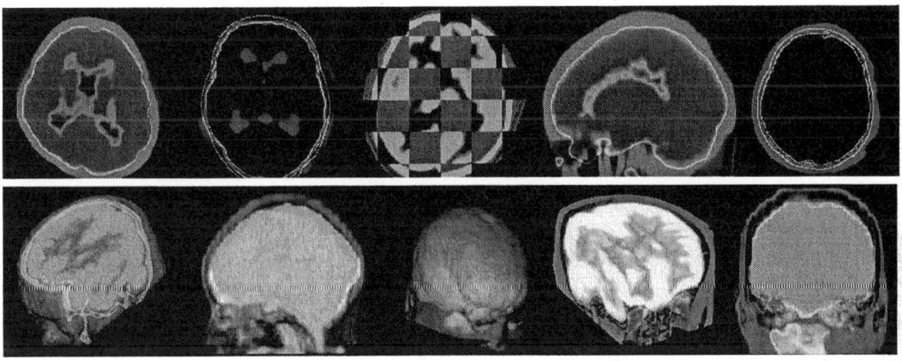

Fig. 9. The results of 2D visual inspection and 3D fusion of clinical datasets after registration

compute each RMSE for translations and rotations as Eq. (4) between estimated parameters and true transformations. At this time, the feature points of head are extracted by applying proposed IRG and RGL for comparing our WCC with CDM or FCC in same environments. The use of MI for accuracy test is restricted to the intensities of whole volume without extracting the feature points of head, and is not included sampling and multi-resolution optimization.

$$T-RMSE=\sqrt{\frac{1}{3}\{(T_x-T_x')^2+(T_y-T_y')^2+(T_z-T_z')^2\}}$$
$$R-RMSE=\sqrt{\frac{1}{3}\{(R_x-R_x')^2+(R_y-R_y')^2+(R_z-R_z')^2\}} \qquad (4)$$

In our method, T-RMSE and R-RMSE are less than 0.1*mm* and 0.4°, respectively in two software phantom datasets and give better accuracy than the conventional ones. In particular, MI shows a large different in software phantom2. This means that MI has a limitation in exact alignment when blurry and noisy images are aligned.

Table 2. Accuracy results using the software phantom with the known parameters

Dataset	Method	T_x (mm)	T_y (mm)	T_z (mm)	R_x (°)	R_y (°)	R_z (°)	T-RMSE (mm)	R-RMSE (°)
Software Phantom 1	TRUE	10.73	12.48	-10.14	-4.8	-5.2	7.3	-	-
	WCC	10.72	12.46	-10.19	-4.74	-5.01	7.21	0.03	0.12
	MI	10.71	12.64	-10.34	-5.31	-5.55	7.67	0.14	0.42
	CDM	11.46	12.07	-9.75	-4.38	-6.13	4.50	0.53	1.72
	FCC	7.87	8.72	-9.09	-5.69	0.67	4.04	2.79	3.91
Software Phantom 2	TRUE	-6.83	-8.58	6.24	4.8	-3.2	-6.3	-	-
	WCC	-6.75	-8.59	6.39	4.43	-2.69	-6.19	0.10	0.37
	MI	-7.80	-8.85	5.85	5.62	-5.46	-7.12	0.63	1.47
	CDM	-6.22	-8.53	6.70	4.19	1.00	-4.88	0.44	2.58
	FCC	-13.07	-2.33	0.76	2.66	-11.98	0.07	5.99	6.38

For robustness test, we evaluated whether the WCC similarity measure searches for optimal location against the noise in software phantom1 with a large geometrical displacement. White zero-mean Gaussian noise with standard deviation 0, 100, 300, and 500 is superimposed onto the only CT software phantom1. As shown in Fig. 10, increasing the noise level does not affect the maximal WCC at optimal location (0*mm* or 0°), as the position of maximal WCC in traces computed for all six optimal parameters is not changed when the amount of noise is increased. This means that our WCC leads to a global maximum using the GWDM even though feature points extracts differently between PET and CT brain images due to blurry or noisy properties.

The total computation time including 3D fusion in two software phantom datasets is measured by comparing our method with conventional ones in Table 3. Our method gives similar computation time to the CDM and FCC and much faster than the MI-based registration.

Table 3. Total computation time

(sec)

	WCC	MI	CDM	FCC
Software-phantom1	8.234	391.843	8.579	8.062
Software-phantom2	8.406	407.734	8.687	7.890

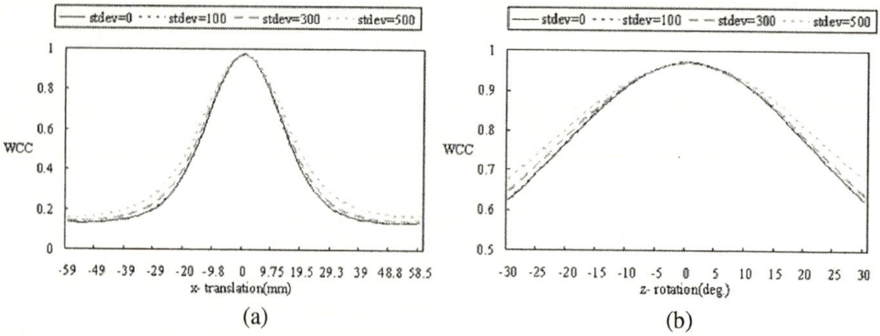

Fig. 10. The robustness test of WCC in software phantom1 added the Gaussian noise with standard deviation 0, 100, 300, 500 (a) translation of x-direction in the range from -60 to 60 *mm* (b) rotation around z-axis in the range from -30 to 30°

4 Conclusion

We have developed an accurate and robust surface registration method using a Gaussian-weighted distance map for brain PET-CT fusion. Our 3D IRG segmented the head without any additional processing such as hole filling. The proposed RGL eliminated efficiently the non-head regions in comparison with the conventional connected component-based labeling. Our GWDM led our similarity measure to robust convergence on the optimal location even though feature points extract differently between PET and CT brain images due to blurry or noisy properties. The WCC rapidly measure the similarities because of considering the GWDM of CT images corresponding to the feature points extracted from PET images instead of using whole volume of CT images. Experimental results showed that our method was much faster than MI and more accurate than conventional registration methods such as MI, CDM, and FCC. In particular, our method was robustly registered at optimal location regardless of increasing noise level.

Acknowledgements

This work was supported in part by a grant B020211 from Strategic National R&D Program of Ministry of Science and Technology and a grant 10014138 from the Advanced Technology Center Program. The ICT at Seoul National University provides research facilities for this study.

References

1. J.B.A.Maintz, M.A.Viergever, A survey of medical image registration, Medical Image Analysis, Vol.2, Iss.1 (1998) 1-36.
2. J.Hongjian, R.Richard A., H.T.Kerrie S., New approach to 3-D registration of multimodality medical images by surface matching, Proc. SPIE, Vol.1808, 196-213
3. J.B.A.Maintz, P.A. van den Elsen, M.A.Viergever, Comparison of edge-based and ridge-based registration of CT and MR brain images, Medical Image Analysis, Vol.1, Iss.2 (1996) 151-161
4. F.Maes, A.Collignon, G.Marchal, P.Suetens, Multimodality Image Registration by maximization of Mutual Information, IEEE Transaction on Medical Imaging, Vol.16, No.2 (1997) 187-198.
5. L.Y.Hsu, M.H.Loew, Fully automatic 3D feature-based registration of multi-modality medical images, Image and Vision Computing Vol.19 (2001) 75-85.
6. E.A.Firle, S.Wesarg, C.Dold, Fast CT/PET registration based on partial volume matching, International Congress Series Vol.1268 (2004) 1440-1445
7. R.G.Gonzalez, R.E.Woods, Digital Image Processing, 1st Ed. (1993)

Optimal Positioning of Sensors in 3D

Andrea Bottino and Aldo Laurentini

Dipartimento di Automatica e Informatica, Politecnico di Torino,
Corso Duca degli Abruzzi, 24 – 10129 Torino, Italy
{andrea.bottino, aldo.laurentini}@polito.it

Abstract. Locating the minimum number of sensors able to see at the same time the entire surface of an object is an important practical problem. Most work presented in this area is restricted to 2D objects. In this paper we present an optimal 3D sensor location algorithms that can locate sensors into a polyhedral environment that are able to see the features of the objects in their entirety. Limitations due to real sensors can be easily taken into account. The algorithm has been implemented, and examples are also given.

1 Introduction

Sensor planning is an important research area in computer vision. It consists of automatically computing sensor positions or trajectories given a task to perform, the sensor features and a model of the environment. A recent survey [15] refers in particular to tasks as reconstruction and inspection. Several other tasks and techniques were considered in the more seasoned surveys [19] and [12]. Sensor panning problems require considering a number of constraints, first of all the visibility constraint. To this effect, the sensor is usually modeled as a point, the vertex of a frustum if the field of view is taken into account, and referred to as a "viewpoint". A feature of an object is said to be visible from the viewpoint if any segment joining a point of the feature and the viewpoint does not intersects the environment or the object itself and lies inside the frustum. A popular 3D solution is locating the viewpoint onto the view sphere, which implicitly takes into account some constraints. Usually the view sphere is discretized, for instance by locating the possible viewpoints at the vertices of some semi-regular polyhedron, as the geodesic dome [4], [21], [22]. In this paper we will deal with a basic visibility problem, that is finding and locating the minimum number of sensors able to see at the same time all points of the surface of an object. The problem arises for tasks as static inspection and surveillance for several kind of sensors, as TV cameras, range sensors, etc. The sensors are supposed to be rotating or omni directional. The problem also arises in the area of image-based modeling and rendering [7]. A related problem is finding an inspection path optimum according to some metric, since according to a popular approach it is constructed joining static sensor positions which guarantee total object visibility [4], [6], [9], [22].

The major contribution of this paper is to present a 3D algorithm for finding a set of zones where a minimal set of viewpoints, able to observe the entire surface of the object, can be independently located. The algorithm works for multiply connected and unconnected general polyhedra, and can locate viewpoints able to observe the interior

M. Lazo and A. Sanfeliu (Eds.): CIARP 2005, LNCS 3773, pp. 804 – 812, 2005.

or the exterior surfaces of the polyhedra. For finding an optimal solution the view space needs not to be discretized, the only restriction being that each face must be completely observed by at least one viewpoint. This complies with the usual definition of feature of an object surface in term of faces or parts of faces, and with the practical requirement of observing a feature in its entirety. It is also worth observing that, if the faces are subdivided into smaller areas, the solution provided by the algorithm converges towards the optimal solution of the unrestricted problem. In the conclusion we will discuss how the approach can be extended in order to take into account additional constraints besides the visibility constraint.

The paper is organized as follows. In section 2 we will deal with the problem in 2D. Section 3 to 7 are devoted to describing the 3D algorithm. In section 6 we will also present some examples. Concluding remarks are contained in Section 8.

2 The Problem in 2D

Although in general the problem addressed is three-dimensional, in some cases it can be restricted to 2D. This is for instance the case of buildings, which can be modeled as objects obtained by extrusion. Much related work in the area of computational geometry stems from the popular Art Gallery Problem. The problem, stated in 1975 refers to the surveillance, or "cover" of polygonal areas with or without polygonal holes. The famous Art Gallery Theorem stated the upper tight bound $\lfloor n/3 \rfloor$ for the minimum number of "guards" (omni directional sensors) for covering any polygon with n edges, metaphorically the interior of an art gallery. The upper tight bound $\lfloor (n+h)/3 \rfloor$ was subsequently found for polygons with n edges and h holes. Many 2D variations of the problem have been considered, as for instance "rectilinear polygons", that is polygons with edges parallel or perpendicular, guards restricted to particular positions, etc. The original problem, as well as several restricted problems, have been found to be NP-hard [6]. For further detail, the reader is referred to the monograph of O'Rourke [13], and to the surveys [16] and [23]. At present, no finite exact algorithm exists able to locate a minimum unrestricted set of guards in a given polygon. In addition, no approximate algorithm with guaranteed approximation has been found.

Let us observe that our problem is similar, but not equal, to the classic Art Gallery problem, since we are interested in observing only the *boundary* of the object. Then, our 2D problem can be called the internal or external edge covering problem. A detailed analysis of the edge covering problem compared with the classic Art Gallery problem is reported in [10]. Among other results, it is shown that in general a minimal set of guards for the Art Gallery problem is not minimal for the interior edge covering, and that also the edge covering problem is NP-hard. However, edge covering admits a restriction which makes practical sense and allows to construct a finite algorithm which supplies a minimum set of viewpoints able to cover internal or external polygonal boundaries. The restriction is that each edge must be observed entirely by at least one guard, and it allows finding one or more sets of regions where a minimal set of viewpoints can be independently located. In addition, the algorithm asymptotically converges to the optimal solution of the unrestricted problem if the edges are subdivided into shorter segments. Finally, the algorithm can easily take into account several constraints. Here we briefly present the essentials of a 2D sensor-positioning algorithm presented in [3]. The steps of the algorithm are as follows.

1. Divide the view space into a partition Π of maximal regions such that the same set of edges is completely visible from all points of a region.
2. Find the dominant zones (a zone Z of Π is dominant if no other zone Z* exists which covers the edges of Z plus some other)
3. Select the minimum number of dominant zones able to cover all the faces.

The idea of partition Π has been also proposed in restricted cases for robot self location in [17], [18]. Step 1), and 2) of the algorithm can be performed in polynomial time (see [10] for the details). Step 3) is an instance of the well-known set covering problem, which in the worst case is exponential. However, covering the edges using the dominant zone only usually substantially reduces the computation complexity. In addition, in many cases several dominant zones are also *essentials*, that is they cover some edges not covered by the other dominant zone, and must be selected. Observe that there could be minimal solutions also including non-dominant zones. However, replacing a non dominant regions with a dominant region covering the same edges plus some others provides multiple coverage of some edges, which is preferable for instance in the case of sensor failure. Some overlapping of the views is also useful for image registration.

3 The 3D Algorithm

The general idea of the 2D algorithm can be extended in 3D:

Step 1- Compute a partition Π of the viewing space into regions Z_i such that:

- The same set $\mathbf{F}_i = (F_p, F_q, \ldots\ldots F_t)$ of faces is completely visible from all points of Z_i $\forall$ i
- The Z_i are maximum regions, i.e. $\mathbf{F}_i \neq \mathbf{F}_j$ for contiguous regions.

The list of the visible faces must be associated to each region of Π.

Step 2- Select the *dominant regions*. A region Z_i is defined to be dominant if there is no other region Z_j of the partition such that $\mathbf{F}_i \subset \mathbf{F}_j$.

Step 3- Select an optimal (or minimum) solution. A minimum solution consists of a set of dominant regions $\mathbf{S}_j = (Z_{j1}, Z_{j2}, \ldots Z_{jk} \ldots)$ which covers $\mathbf{F} = \cup Fi$ with the minimum number of members.

In the following paragraph we will detail the steps of the algorithm. The environment is assumed to consist of simple polygons. Partition Π is built by means of a particular set of surfaces, called the *active visibility surfaces*. Each resulting region will be associated with the list of the faces that are completely visible from that zone. This set can be built traversing the partition graph from an initial region whose set of visible faces is known. Observe that interior inspection is similar, with a polygon enclosing the workspace and defining the outer border.

3.1 Partition Π

A *visibility surface* (VS) relative to a face divides the space into areas where the surface is partially or totally hidden. A VS is an half-open planar surface starting at one of the edges or at a vertex of a face, lying in the half space opposite to the inner side of the face. Also, each potential VS has a positive side, which is the side closer to the originating face. The angle between the normal of this surface and the normal of the originating face is in the range [0,π]. Examples can be seen in **Fig. 1**, where the arrows mark the positive side of the VSs. Each VS can have an *active* and an *inactive* part. Only the active VSs are the effective boundaries of the visibility region of the corresponding surface. A VS is active when:

1. the angle with the normal of the originating face is 0 and the surface is not entering the object in the proximity of the originating vertex or edge (VS of type I)
2. it is tangent to another part of the object (or to another object) and in the neighborhood of this part, the inner side of the object lies on the negative side of the potential VS (that is, the VE surfaces defined in [8]). Those surfaces are defined by a vertex of the object and an edge of the face (VS of type II) or by an edge of the object and a vertex of the face (VS of type III). A surface of the first type is an unbounded triangle starting at the vertex of the object; a surface of the second type is an unbounded trapezoid with the object edge as one of its sides. In both cases, the active part of the VS starts at the intersection point (**Fig. 2**).

We can associate to each active VS an operator ^, where ^j means that the surface is the boundary between a region where face j is hidden and a region where the face j visible, and j is the face the VS relates to. The operator has also a direction, which points to the area where the face is visible (see **Fig. 2**). In the following we will use a result found in [21], that is: if the face is convex (and simply connected), its visibility region is connected. This property is useful in order to avoid more complex situation and allows pruning radically the initial set of potential VSs of a face. Therefore any concave face will be split into convex parts.

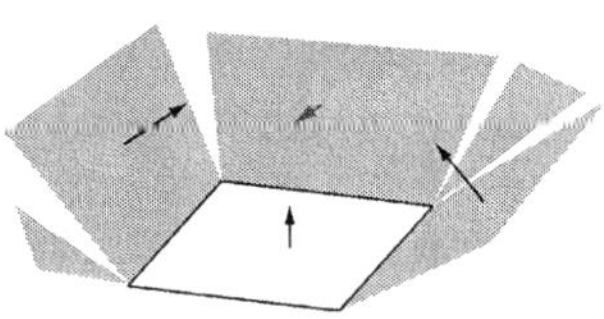

Fig. 1. Example of VSs

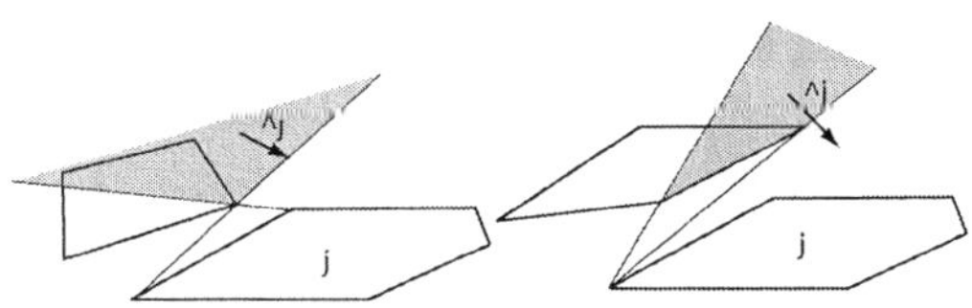

Fig. 2. VS of type II (left) and type III (right)

Finding the active part of a VS

For each initial VS, we must identify the part which is indeed active. In order to construct the active VSs of type I, we must find the regions of the plane P of a face F from where its 2D silhouette is completely visible. Forcing F to be convex, its 2D silhouette from a viewpoint V corresponds to the list of edges of F totally visible from the viewpoint. The active VS of type I can be constructed in the following way:

1. find on P the polygons corresponding to the intersection of the objects with P; let S, the initial active VS, be the union of all the regions in P where the 2D silhouette of F is completely visible;

2. for each edge, define as positive the side of the edge pointing to the internal part of the face; for each edge of the face closed by another face, or by another object intersecting the plane of the face, let H be the half plane in P bounded by the line containing the edge and corresponding to the positive side of the edge. Then S = S∩H (see **Fig. 3**).

Consider **Fig. 3** where a face F and its active VS of type I are shown; edges e_1 and e_2 are closed by other objects, H_1 and H_2 are the half planes bounded by e_1 and e_2.

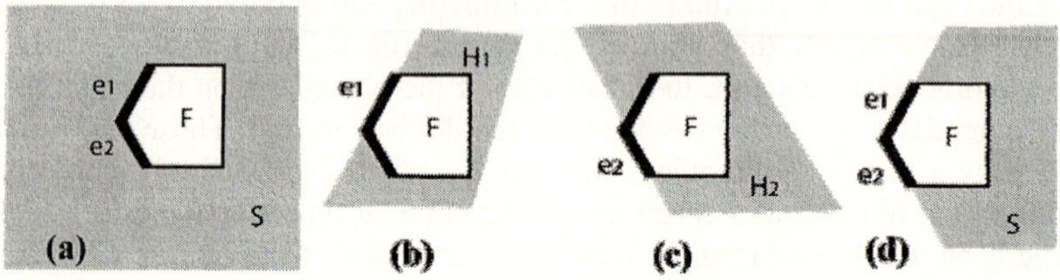

Fig. 3. Active part of the VS of types I

The initial active VS on P can be evaluated using a modified version of the 2D region labeling algorithm of [3].

The active part of a VS of type II can be found determining the parts of the initial unbounded triangular surface where the originating edge is entirely visible. The algorithm is similar to the one used to find the active part of a VS of type I, that is:

1. let P be the initial unbounded VS of type II
2. find on P the polygons corresponding to the intersection of the objects with P; if one of the face is coplanar with P, it must not be considered if its normal is parallel to the positive direction of P
3. let S, the active VS, be the union of all the regions in P where the edge of F is visible

An example can be seen in **Fig. 4**.

Finally, the active part of a VS of type III can be found determining the parts of the initial unbounded trapezoidal surface where the originating vertex of F is visible. The algorithm is similar to the previous one, letting P at point 1 be the initial unbounded VS of type III. An example can be seen in **Fig. 5**.

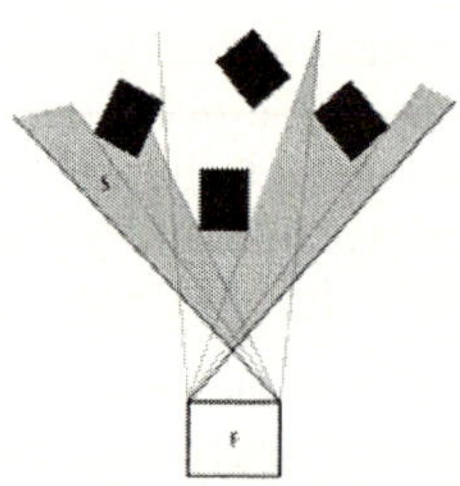

Fig. 4. Active part of a VS of type II

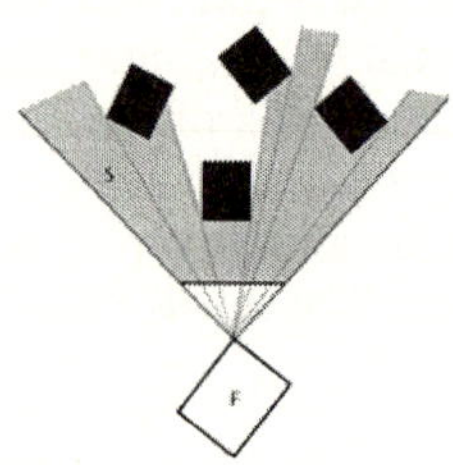

Fig. 5. Active part of a VS of type III

Additional rules for potential VS to be active

Some other conditions must be checked to identify an active VS.

For a potential VS of type II or III, its orientation must be such that the plane containing the surface intersects F only in the originating vertex or on the edges joining the vertex for a surface of type II, on the edge itself for a surface of type III. See for instance **Fig. 6**. The surface S relative to vertex V is lying on the plane P, whose intersection with the face f_1 is the line L. Therefore the surface S is not a potential VS.

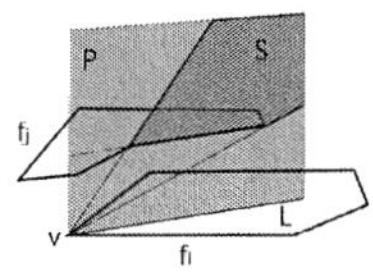

Fig. 6. Surface S is inactive

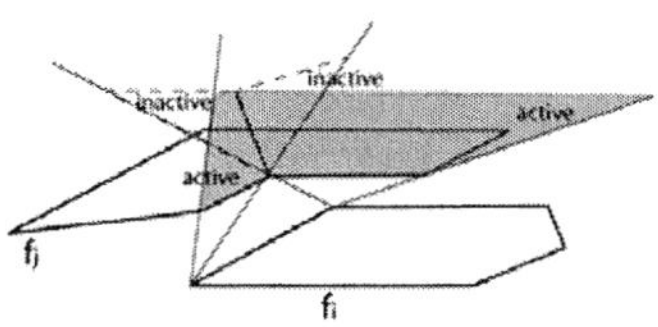

Fig. 7. Only part of these surfaces is active

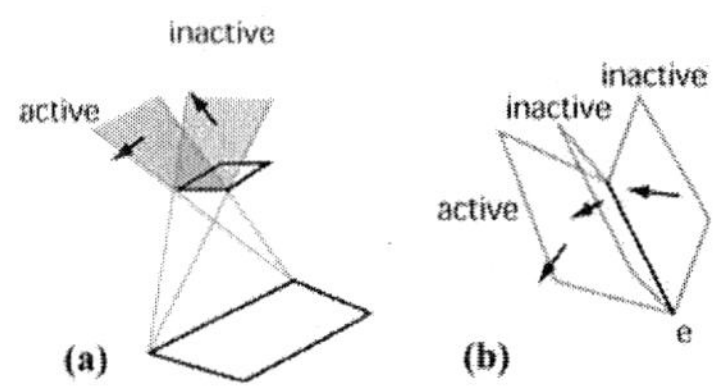

Fig. 8. Only the most external surface is active

Second, when the active parts of two VS relative to elements of the same face intersect somewhere, they both stop at their intersection (see **Fig. 7**). The part of the VS that falls on the negative side of another VS becomes inactive. Finally, consider a set of VS of type III insisting on the same edge e. If one of the VS is found to be on the negative side of another VS, then it is inactive. See for instance **Fig. 8**(a) and (b), where only the outermost surface is active. In (b), e is the edge common to all the VSs. The same rule applies to VSs of type II insisting on the same vertex when previous rules do not apply (that is, when the VSs are not intersecting).

3.2 The Algorithm

Given the definition of VS and operator ^, we can outline a region labeling algorithm:

1. find all the active VSs and the associate operator ^
2. intersect all the active VSs and subdivide the space into regions
3. select one region and compute the set of visibile faces V(f1,…,fn) for that zone
4. visit all the regions and compute their set of visible faces with the following rules:
   a. when crossing a boundary between R1 and R2 in the direction of the operator ^, the operand (j) is added to the set of visible faces of R2
   b. when crossing a boundary between R1 and R2 in the opposite direction of the operator ^, the operand (j) is removed from the set of visible faces of R2

An example of how the algorithm works can be seen in the following pictures. The original object is the L-shaped solid of **Fig. 9** (left). The expression ^(e,f) as a short form for ^e and ^f.

Now, let's imagine to place our viewpoint in the half-plane defined by face 2. The object, the VS surfaces and the corresponding regions as seen from this viewpoint are shown in **Fig. 9** (right). The picture depict also the operators ^ and their sign for the boundaries outgoing the plane of face 2 (the information about other boundaries have been omitted for clarity). Let's choose as starting region the central region of the figure, where the only visible face is 2. If we visit the partition moving southward, we cross a boundary declaring ^1 in the direction of crossing. The operand (1) will become visible, and in the second region 1 and 2 will be visible. Now moving to the right, we cross a boundary declaring ^3 in the direction of crossing. Therefore 3 will become visible in the arrival region. Let's make one more step upward. In the current region 1, 2 and 3 are visible. We cross the boundary in the opposite direction of ^1, therefore 1 will be hidden in the arrival region. By visiting all the regions following the rules specified in step 4 of the algorithm, the final result can be seen in **Fig. 10**.

The algorithm has been implemented. An example of the sensor positioning can be seen in **Fig. 11**, where the white spheres represents the position of the two sensors placed.

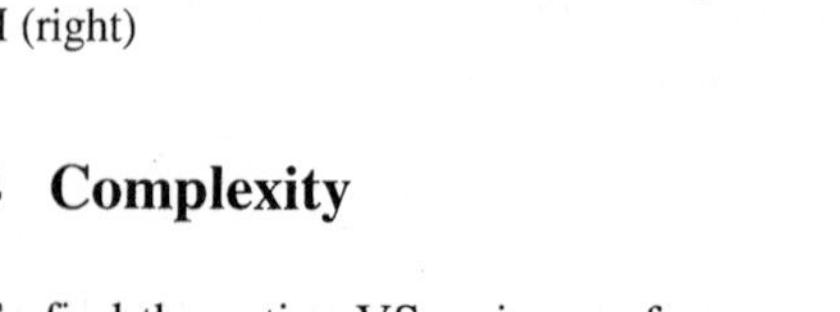

Fig. 9. Object (left) and boundaries of partition Π (right)

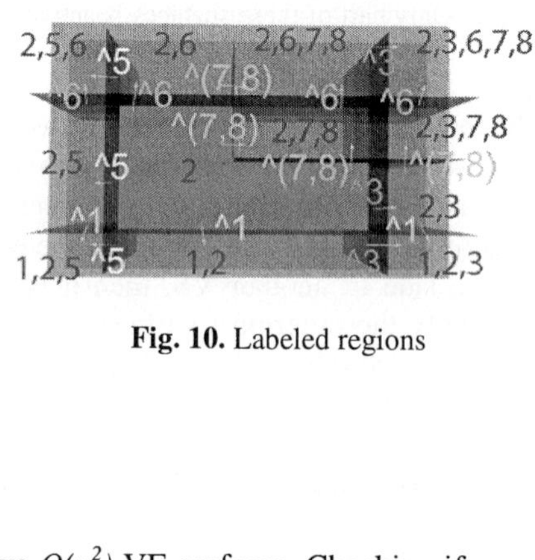

Fig. 10. Labeled regions

4 Complexity

To find the active VSs, given n faces, we have $O(n^2)$ VE surfaces. Checking if a surface intersects the polyhedron at one the edges can be done in constant time. For each surface, checking the extra conditions and finding the active surfaces requires intersecting each surface with any other and sorting the intersections. Overall $O(n^2)$ Vss can be obtained in $O(n^3 \log n)$ time. A classic algorithm can create the partition Π in $O(n^6)$ time. We should stress that this is the asymptotic complexity, while the difference is substantial in real world scenes. For instance, in the example of **Fig. 11**, the faces of the objects are 12, the active VSs after pruning 16, and the regions of the

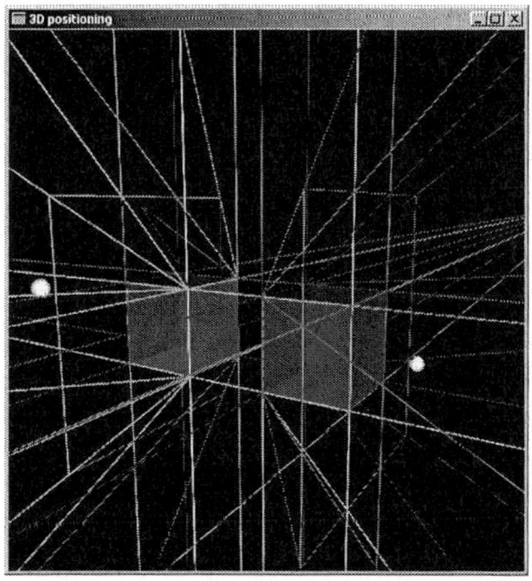

Fig. 11. Objects (blue), boundary lines of partition Π (yellow), and sensor position (white spheres)

partition are 75. Computing the visible surfaces of the starting region takes $O(n^2)$ time [14]. The time required for traversing the partition is $O(p)$ where p is the number of vertices of the partition (regions and edges also are $O(p)$) [2]. To find d dominant zones, we must compare the sets of visible faces of each region. This process can be shortened if we observe that a necessary condition for a region to be dominant is that all the positive crossing directions of the boundaries of the region lead to the interior of the region (except for the faces of the objects). Given c candidate found with this rule, d dominant regions can be found in $O(nc^2)$ time [10]. Step 3 requires, in the worst case, exponential time. However, an interesting alternative could be using a greedy heuristic, which selects the region covering the largest number of uncovered faces each time, requiring polynomial time.

5 Conclusions

In this paper a method for positioning a minimum number of sensors into a 3D polyhedral environment has been presented for some sample cases. With this approach is also simple to take into account additional constraints besides the visibility constraint by adding other rules to the process of generation of the Vss, since for each face f the constraints define a region C(f) of the space where the viewpoint can be located. The approach has been implemented and results have been presented. Future work will be focused on extending the algorithm in order to consider the general case of face covering, and not only its integer face covering restriction. The idea it is to develop an iterative algorithm for the general problem. This requires finding a lower bound for the number of sensors needed. Then we can evaluate the integer solution and check if they match. Otherwise, subdividing some of the initial surfaces and reapplying the integer algorithm can refine the solution. Rules for finding indivisible edges must be studied as well.

References

[1] S. Abrams, P.K. Allen, and K.A. Tarabanis, "Computing camera viewpoints in a robot work-cell," in Proc. 1996 IEEE Int. Conf. Robotics and Autom., pp.1972-1979
[2] Baase S, Computer algorithms. Addison-Wesley, New York, 1988
[3] A. Bottino, A. Laurentini "Optimal positioning of sensors in 2D". Proc. CIARP 2004, Puebla (Mexico)
[4] S.Y. Chen, and Y.F. Li," Automatic sensor placement for model-based robot vision," to appear in IEEE Trans. On Systems, Man ,and Cybernetics
[5] C. K. Cowan and P.D. Kovesi, "Automatic sensor placement from vision task requirements," ," IEEE Trans. Pattern Analysis and Machine Intelligence, Vol.10, no.3, May 1988, pp.407-416
[6] T. Danner and L.E. Kavraki, "Randomized planning for short inspection paths," Proc. 2000 IEEE Int. Conf. Robotics and Autom., pp.971-976, April 2000
[7] S. Fleishman, D. Cohen-Or, and D. Lishinski," Automatic camera placement for image-based modelling," Computer Graphic Forum, June 2000, 101-110
[8] Gigus, J. Canny, R. Seidel, "Efficiently computing and representing the aspect graphs of polyhedral objects", IEEE Trans. PAMI, Vol. 13, no. 6, pp. 542-551, June 1991
[9] G. D. Kazakakis, and A.A. Argyros, "Fast positioning of limited visibility guards for inspection of 2D workspaces," Proc. 2002 IEEE/RSJ Intl. Conf. On Intelligent Robots and Systems, pp.2843-2848, October 2002
[10] A. Laurentini, "Guarding the walls of an art gallery," The Visual Computer, vol.15, pp.265-278, 1999
[11] Nemhauser G. and Wolsey L., Integer and Combinatorial Optimization, John Wiley& Sons, 1988
[12] T.S. Newman and A.K. Jain, "A survey of automated visual inspection," Comput. Vis. Image Understand. , vol.61, no.2, pp.231-262, 1995
[13] J. O'Rourke, Art gallery theorems and algorithms, Oxford University Press, New York,1987
[14] Goodman JE, O'Rourke J, Discrete and Computational Geometry, Chapman and Hall, New York, 2004
[15] Scott W.R, Roth G. "View Planning for Automated Three-Dimensional Object Reconstruction and Inspection". ACM Computing Surveys, 2003, Vol. 35(1), pp. 64–96
[16] T. Shermer, "Recent results in art galleries," IEEE Proc. Vol. 80, pp.1384-1399, 1992
[17] K.T. Simsarian, , T.J. Olson, and N. Nandhakumar, "View-invariant regions and mobile robot self-localization," IEEE Trans. Robot. and Automat., vol. 12, no. 5 , pp. 810 –816, 1996
[18] R.Talluri and J.K.Aggarwal,"Mobile robot self-location using model-image feature correspondence," IEEE Trans. On Robotics and Automation, Vol.12, no.1, February 1996, pp.63-77
[19] K.A. Tarabanis, P.K. Allen, and R. Y. Tsai, "A survey of sensor planning in computer vision," ," IEEE Trans. Robot. and Automat., vol. 11, no. 1 , pp. 86 –104, 1995
[20] K.A. Tarabanis, P.K. Allen, R. Y. Tsai, "The MVP sensor planning system for robotic vision tasks," IEEE Trans. Robot. and Automat., vol. 11, no. 1 , pp. 72 –85, 1995
[21] K. Tarabanis, R.Y. Tsai, A. Kaul, "Computing occlusion-free viewpoint", IEEE Trans. PAMI, Vol. 18, no. 3, pp. 279-292, march 1996
[22] E. Trucco, M. Umasuthan, A.M. Fallace, and V. Roberto," Model –based planning of optimal sensor placements for inspection," IEEE Trans. Robot. and Automat., vol. 13, no. 2 , pp. 182 –194, 1997
[23] J. Urrutia, "Art Gallery and Illumination Problems" Handbook on Computational Geometry, Elsevier Science Publishers, J.R. Sack and J. Urrutia eds. pp. 973-1026, 2000

Automatic Window Design for Gray-Scale Image Processing Based on Entropy Minimization

David C. Martins Jr., Roberto M. Cesar Jr., and Junior Barrera

USP–Universidade de São Paulo,
IME–Instituto de Matemática e Estatística,
Computer Science Department,
Rua do Matão, 1010 - Cidade Universitária,
CEP: 05508-090, São Paulo, SP, Brasil

Abstract. This paper generalizes the technique described in [1] to gray-scale image processing applications. This method chooses a subset of variables W (i.e. pixels seen through a window) that maximizes the information observed in a set of training data by mean conditional entropy minimization. The task is formalized as a combinatorial optimization problem, where the search space is the powerset of the candidate variables and the measure to be minimized is the mean entropy of the estimated conditional probabilities. As a full exploration of the search space requires an enormous computational effort, some heuristics of the feature selection literature are applied. The introduced approach is mathematically sound and experimental results with texture recognition application show that it is also adequate to treat problems with gray-scale images.

1 Introduction

The paper [1] discusses a technique based on information theory concepts to estimate a good W-operator to perform binary image transformations (e.g. noisy image filtering). A W-operator is an image transformation that is locally defined inside a window W and translation invariant [2]. This means that it depends just on shapes of the input image seen through the window W and that the transformation rule applied is the same for all image pixels. A remarkable property of a W-operator is that it may be characterized by a Boolean function which depends on $|W|$ variables, where $|W|$ is the cardinality of W.

Here, the W-operator will be extended to be applied to gray-scale images. For this, instead of considering it as a Boolean function, we will consider it as a function whose domain is a vector of integer numbers (gray levels) and the output is a integer number (one of the considered classes). Then, the method developed in [1] can be extended to deal with this problem in a similar way to the design of W-operators for binary image transformations.

In order to build the training set, the adopted window collects feature vectors (vectors of integer numbers representing gray levels) translating over the input gray-scale images. From this training set, a gray-scale W-operator is estimated.

M. Lazo and A. Sanfeliu (Eds.): CIARP 2005, LNCS 3773, pp. 813–824, 2005.

This task is an optimization problem. The training data gives a sample of a joint distribution of the observed feature vectors and their classification. A loss function measures the cost of a feature vector missclassification. An operator error is the expectation of the loss function under the joint distribution. Given a set of operators, the target operator is the one that has minimum error. As, in practice, the joint distribution is known just by its samples, it should be estimated. This implies that operators error should also be estimated and, consequently, the target operator itself should be estimated. Estimating an operator is an easy task when the sampling of the joint distribution considered is large. However, this is rarely the case. Usually, the problem involves large windows with non concentrated probability mass joint distributions requiring prohibitive amount of training data.

The fact that each pixel in gray-scale images contains more than two possible values worsens the problem of lack of training data. Because of this, an approach for dealing with the lack of training data becomes even more required. By constraining the considered space of operators, less training data is necessary to get good estimations of the best candidate operator [3]. However, depending on how many gray levels exists in an image, the constraint may be so excessive that even the best operator of such space lead to very bad classification results. Therefore, quantization is usually necessary.

In this paper, we discuss how to apply the criterion function used in [1] to estimate an sub-window W^* that gives one of the best operators to perform classification over images with arbitrary number of gray levels and arbitrary number of classes.

The search space of this problem is the powerset of W, denoted $\mathcal{P}(W)$. The criterion to be minimized is the degree of mixture of the observed classes. The mean conditional entropy is adopted as a measure of this degree. The important property of entropy explored here is that when the probability mass of a distribution becomes more concentrated somewhere in its domain, the entropy decreases. This means that when a given feature vector defined in a window has a majoritary label (i.e. it is classified almost always in a same class), its entropy of the conditional distribution should be low. Thus, the optimization algorithm consists in estimating the mean conditional entropy for the joint distribution estimated for each sub-window and choosing the one that minimizes this measure.

Each observed feature vector has a probability and a corresponding conditional distribution from which the entropy is computed. The mean conditional entropy is the mean of the computed entropies, weighted by the feature vector probabilities.

As $\mathcal{P}(W)$ has an exponential size in terms of the cardinality of W, we adopted some heuristics to explore this space in reasonable computational time. The adopted heuristic was the SFFS feature selection algorithm [4].

Following this Introduction, Section 2 recalls the mathematical fundamentals of W-operators design with extension to gray-scale images. Section 3 introduces the definitions and properties of the mean conditional entropy and presents the proposed technique for generating the minimal window and, consequently, choosing a minimal family of operators. Section 4 presents results of the application of the proposed technique to recognize textures with multilevel gray tone. Finally, Section 5 presents some concluding remarks of this work.

2 W-Operator Definition and Design

In this section, we recall the notion of W-operator and the main principles for designing W-operators from training data.

2.1 W-Operator Definition and Properties

Let E denote the integer plane and $+$ denote the vector addition on E. The opposite of $+$ is denoted $-$. An *image* is a function f from E to $L = \{1, ..., k\}$, where k is the number of gray tones.

The *translation* of an image f by a vector $h \in E$ is the image $f(x)_h$. An *image classification* or *operator* is a mapping Ψ from L^E into Y^E, where $Y = \{1, ..., c\}$ is the set of labels (classes).

An operator Ψ is called *translation invariant* iff, for every $h \in E$ and $f \in L^E$,

$$\Psi(f_x) = (\Psi(f))_x \; . \tag{1}$$

Let W be a finite subset of E. A *constraint class* of f over W, denoted $C_{f|W}$, is the family of functions whose constraint to W results in $f|W$, i.e.,

$$C_{f|W} = \{g \in L^E : f|W = g|W\} \; . \tag{2}$$

An operator $\Psi : L^E \to Y^E$ is called *locally defined in the window* W iff, for every $x \in E$, $f \in L^E$.

$$\Psi(f)(x) = \Psi(g), \forall g \in C_{f_{-x}|W} \; . \tag{3}$$

An operator is called a *W-operator* if it is both translation invariant and locally defined in a finite window W. Given a W-operator $\Psi : L^E \to Y^E$, exists one characteristic function $\psi : L^W \to Y$ such that:

$$\Psi(f)(x) = \psi(f_{-x}|W), \forall x \in E \; . \tag{4}$$

2.2 W-Operator Design

Designing an operator means choosing an element of a family of operators to perform a given task. One formalization of this idea is as an optimization problem, where the search space is the family of candidate operators and the optimization criteria is a measure of the operator quality. In the commonly adopted formulation, the criteria is based on a statistical model for the images associated to a measure of images similarity, the loss function.

Let **S** and **I** be two discrete random functions defined on E, i.e. realizations of **S** or **I** are images obtained according with some probability distribution on L^E. Let us model image transformations in a given context by the joint random process $(\mathbf{S}, \mathbf{I})$, where the process **S** represents the input images and **I** the output images. The process **I** depends on the process **S** according to a conditional distribution.

Given a space of operators $\mathcal{F}$ and a loss function ℓ from $L \times L$ to $\Re^+$, the error $Er[\Psi]$ of an operator $\Psi \in F$ is the expectation of $\ell(\Psi(\mathbf{S}), \mathbf{I})$, i.e., $Er[\Psi] = E[\ell(\Psi(\mathbf{S}), \mathbf{I})]$. The *target* operator Ψ_{opt} is the one of minimum error, i.e., $Er[\Psi_{opt}] \leq Er[\Psi]$, for every $\Psi \in \mathcal{F}$.

A joint random process $(\mathbf{S}, \mathbf{I})$ is jointly stationary in relation to a finite window W, if the probability of seeing a given feature vector in the input image through W together with a given value in the output image is the same for every translation of W, that is, for every $x \in E$,

$$P((S|W_x, I(x)) = P(S|W, I(o)) \ , \tag{5}$$

where S is a realization of **S**, I is the function equivalent to a realization of **I**, and o is the origin of E.

In order to make the model usable in practice, from now on suppose that $(\mathbf{S}, \mathbf{I})$ is jointly stationary w.r.t the finite window W. Under this hypothesis, the error of predicting an image from the observation of another image can be substituted by the error of predicting a pixel from the observation of a feature vector through W and, consequently, the optimal operator Ψ_{opt} is always a W-operator. Thus, the optimization problem can be equivalently formulated in the space of functions defined on L^W, with joint random processes on (L^W, Y) and loss functions ℓ from $L \times L$ to $\Re^+$.

In practice, the distributions on (L^W, Y) are unknown and should be estimated, which implies in estimating $Er[\psi]$ and ψ_{opt} itself. When the window is small or the distribution has a probability mass concentrated somewhere, the estimation is easy. However, this almost never happens. Usually, we have large windows with non concentrated mass distributions, thus requiring prohibitive amount of training data.

An approach for dealing with the lack of data is constraining the search space. The estimated error of an operator in a constrained space can be decomposed as the addition of the error increment of the optimal operator (i.e., increase in the error of the optimal operator by the reduction of the search space) and the estimation error in the constrained space. A constraint is beneficial when the constraint estimation error decreases (i.e., w.r.t the estimation error in the full space) more than the error increment of the optimal operator. The known constraints are heuristics proposed by experts.

3 Window Design by Conditional Entropy Minimization

Information theory has its roots in Claude Shannon's works [5] and has been successfully applied in a multitude of situations. In particular, mutual information is a useful measure to characterize the stochastic dependence among discrete random variables [6] [7] [8]. It may be applied to feature selection problems in order to help identifying good subspaces to perform pattern recognition [9] [10]. For instance, Lewis [11] explored the mutual information concept for text categorization while Bonnlander and Weigend used similar ideas for dimensionality reduction in neural networks [12]. Additional works that may also be of interest include [13] [14]. An important concept related to the mutual information is the mean conditional entropy, which is explored in our approach.

3.1 Feature Selection: Problem Formulation

Given a set of training samples T where each sample is a pair $(\mathbf{x}, \mathbf{y})$, a function ψ from L^n to $Y = \{1, ..., c\}$, called a *classifier*, may be designed. Feature selection is a procedure to select a subset Z of $\mathcal{I} = \{1, 2, ..., n\}$ such that $\mathbf{X_Z}$ be a good subspace of $\mathbf{X}$ to design a classifier ψ from $L^{|Z|}$ to Y.

The choice of Z creates a constrained search space for designing the classifier ψ. Z is a good subspace, if the classifier designed in Z from a training sample T has smaller error than the one designed in the full space from the same training sample T.

Usually, it is impossible to evaluate all subsets Z of $\mathcal{I}$. Two different aspects involve searching for most suitable subsets: a criterion function and a search algorithm (often based on heuristics in order to cope with the combinatorial explosion) [15]. There are many of such algorithms proposed in the literature and the reader should refer to [16] for a comparative review.

Next section explains how we explore the mean conditional entropy as a criterion function to distinguish between good and bad feature subsets.

3.2 Mean Conditional Entropy as Criterion Function

Let X be a random variable and P be its probability distribution. The *entropy* of X is defined as:

$$H(X) = -\sum_{x \in X} P(x) log P(x) \ , \tag{6}$$

with $log 0 = 0$. Similar definitions hold for random vectors $\mathbf{X}$. The motivation for using the entropy as a criterion function for feature selection is due to its capabilities of measuring the amount of information about labels (Y) that may be extracted from the features ($\mathbf{X}$). The more informative is $\mathbf{X}$ w.r.t. Y, the smaller is $H(Y|\mathbf{X})$. The basic idea behind this method is to minimize the conditional entropy of Y w.r.t the instances $\mathbf{x_{Z_i}}$ of $\mathbf{X_Z}$.

The criterion function adopted by the algorithm is the mean conditional entropy as described in [1] (Equation 7).

$$\hat{E}[H(Y|X_Z)] = \sum_{i=1}^{|L|^{|Z|}} \frac{\hat{H}(Y|X_{Z_i}) \cdot (o_i + \alpha)}{\alpha |L|^{|Z|} + t} \ , \tag{7}$$

where $\hat{H}(Y|\mathbf{X_{Z_i}})$ is the entropy of the estimated conditional probability $\hat{P}(Y|\mathbf{X_{Z_i}})$, o_i is the number occurrences of $\mathbf{X_{Z_i}}$ in the training set, t is the total number of training samples, $|L|^{|Z|}$ is the number of possible instances of $\mathbf{X_Z}$ and α is a weight factor used to model $P(\mathbf{X_Z})$ in order to circumvent problems when some instances of $\mathbf{X_Z}$ are not observed in the training data. These non observed instances lead to prior entropy of Y ($\hat{H}(Y)$), which is slightly different from the criterion defined by [1] based on the entropy of the uniform distribution (maximum entropy).

Thus, feature selection may be defined as an optimization problem where we search for $Z^* \subseteq \mathcal{I}$ such that:

$$Z^* : H(Y|X_{Z^*}) = min_{Z \subseteq \mathcal{I}}\{\hat{E}[H(Y|X_Z)]\} , \tag{8}$$

with $\mathcal{I} = \{1, 2, ..., n\}$.

Dimensionality reduction is related to the U-curve problem where classification error is plotted against feature vector dimension (for an *a priori* fixed number of training samples). This plot leads to a U-shaped curve implying that an increasing dimension initially improves the classifier performance. Nevertheless, this process reach a minimum after which estimation errors degrades the classifier performance [15]. As it would be expected, the mean conditional entropy with α positive and conditional entropies of non observed instances conveniently treated reflects this fact, thus corroborating its use for feature selection [1].

4 Experimental Results

This section presents a method for texture classification that uses the SFFS algorithm with mean conditional entropy to design W-operators that classify

Fig. 1. Textures with 256 gray levels used in this experiment

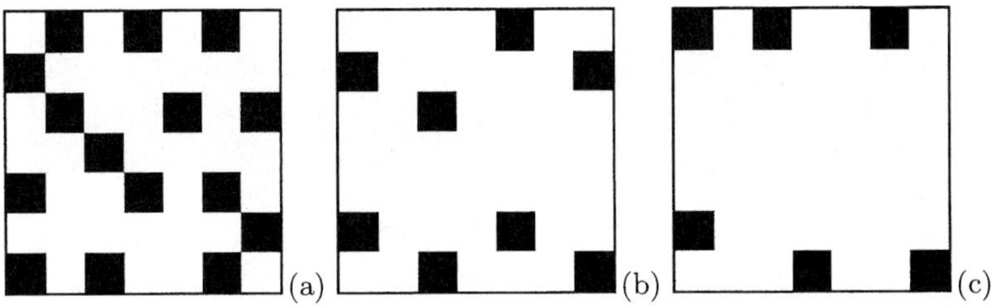

Fig. 2. Typical subwindows obtained using the textures of the Figure 1 to design the W-operator. (a) $k' = 2$, 20% of pixels to form the training set; (b) $k' = 4$, 20% of pixels to form the training set; (c) $k' = 8$, 40% of pixels to form the training set.

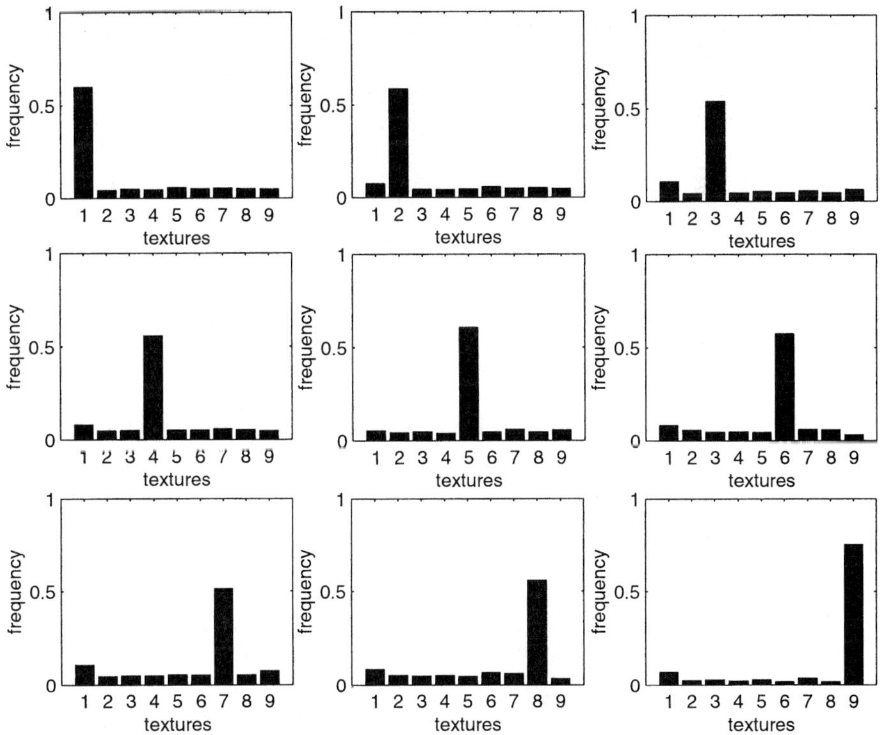

Fig. 3. Histograms of label frequency after the classification performed by the W-operator for each region of the Figure 1 (40% of pixels used to form the training set; $k' = 8$). The textures are numbered from 1 to 9 and the histograms are placed in raster order by these numbers.

gray-scale textures. Figure 1 shows an example containing 9 textures with 256 gray tones ($c = 9$ and $k = 256$).

The training set used to choose the window points and design the W-operator under this window is obtained from input textures. A window of fixed dimen-

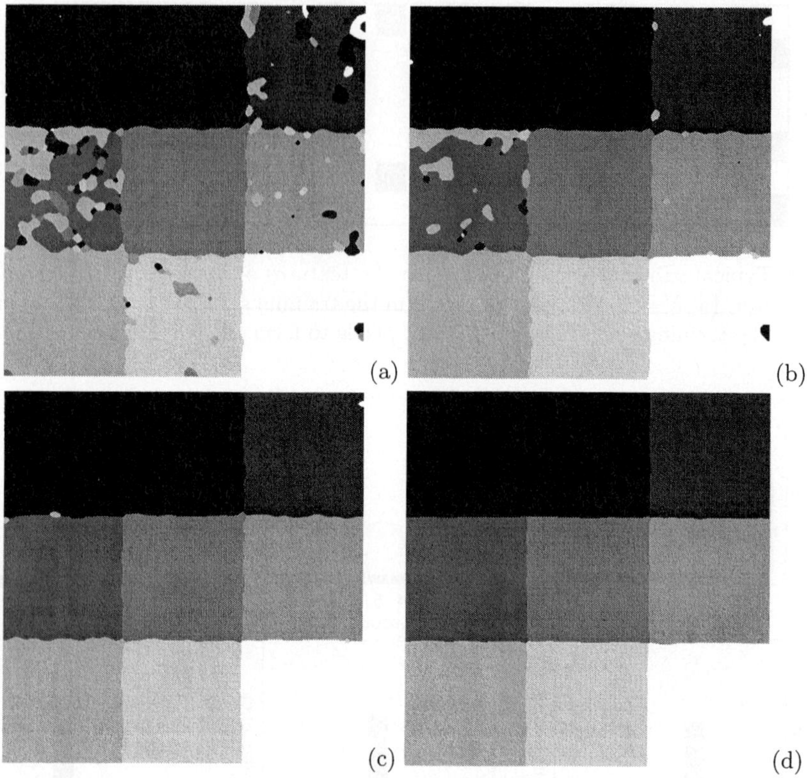

Fig. 4. Final results after applying the mode filters post-processing. (a) $k' = 2$, 10% of pixels to form the training set, MAE = 0.1020; (b) $k' = 2$, 20% of pixels to form the training set, MAE = 0.0375; (c) $k' = 4$, 20% of pixels to form the training set, MAE = 0.0095; (d) $k' = 8$, 40% of pixels to form the training set, MAE = 0.0037.

sions is centered at each selected pixel collecting the feature vector observed and its respective label (texture). Each feature vector is quantized in order to avoid excessive constraining in the space of W-operators that can be estimated adequately. Given a quantization degree $k' < k$, the lowest and highest gray levels observed in the considered feature vector form a interval which is divided in k' intervals of equal size. Then, these intervals are used to do the quantization of the collected feature vector. Thus, each quantized feature vector together with its label form a training sample.

The feature selection algorithm used to choose the window points is the Sequential Floating Forward Selection (SFFS). This algorithm has a good cost-benefit, i.e., it is computationally efficient and returns a very good feature subspace [4]. The criterion function used to drive this method is the mean conditional entropy as defined by Equation 7.

We have analyzed the MAE (Mean Absolute Error) obtained by application of our technique using as input nine textures presented in Figure 1 with increas-

Table 1. Average, standard deviation, minimum and maximum for MAE results after 10 executions for increasing number of training samples (% of pixels) and increasing quantization level k

		Training samples		
		10%	20%	40%
$k' = 2$	avg	0.0899	0.0345	0.0151
	±std	±0.0099	±0.0049	±0.0019
	min	0.0723	0.0281	0.0121
	max	0.1020	0.0420	0.0182
$k' = 4$	avg	0.0711	0.0097	0.0087
	±std	±0.0082	±0.0008	±0.0010
	min	0.0628	0.0085	0.0071
	max	0.0859	0.0110	0.0100
$k' = 8$	avg	0.0270	0.0176	0.0038
	±std	±0.0033	±0.0019	±0.0003
	min	0.0197	0.0157	0.0033
	max	0.0308	0.0218	0.0043

ing quantization degrees k' (2, 4 and 8), increasing number of training samples (10%, 20% and 40% of pixels of each texture randomly chosen) and a 7 by 7 window (49 features in total). The designed W-operator observes and quantizes the feature vectors through a subset of the window points (chosen by SFFS with mean conditional entropy) to label the pixel centered at this window. The results presented here took as the image test, the image of the Figure 1. Typical subwindows obtained are ilustrated by Figure 2.

In all cases, each region correponding to one of the textures received the correct label with significant majority. Figure 3 shows a histogram for pixel classification of the nine considered regions, using $k' = 8$ and 40% of the image to form the training data. These histograms do not take into account the undefined labels.

In order to remove the undefined labels and improve the final texture segmentation, one step of post-processing is proposed. This step is an application of the mode filter multiple times for decreasing window dimensions. The mode filter is a window-based classifier that translates a window over all pixels of the labeled image produced by the designed W-operator and attributes the most frequent label observed to its central pixel. We propose the application of mode filter to windows with the following dimensions in the same order as they appears: 15×15, 13×13, 11×11, 9×9, 7×7, 5×5, 3×3. Assuming that there are many more correct labels than incorrect ones (see Figure 3), this step helps to eliminate errors, although, depending on similarity among textures in certain regions, there is a risk to propagate errors.

Figure 4 presents the final texture segmentation result of the image presented by Figure 1, for 4 distinct pair values (k', % of training samples). Results obtained using the textures of the Figure 1 as input after 10 executions for each considered pair (k', % of training samples) are summarized in the Table 1. Note

Fig. 5. (a) Mosaic of textures obtained from the Figure 1; (b) Correponding template of labels; (c) Final result using $k' = 4$ and 20% of pixels from the textures of Figure 1 (MAE = 0.0380); (d) Corresponding texture segmentation

that the results are satisfactory even taking small training samples to design the W-operators. Also is important to note that quantizations $k' = 4$ and $k' = 8$ lead to better results than those obtained by $k' = 2$, although this last quantization level already presents good results. Finally, a result obtained from the mosaic of the Figute 5(a) using $k' = 4$ and 20% of pixels from the textures of Figure 1 to design the W-operator is ilustrated by Figure 5(c), showing that our method is adequate for segmentation of small textures. Figure 5(b) shows its corresponding template of labels and Figure 5(d) shows the corresponding texture segmentation.

5 Concluding Remarks

This paper presents an extension for the design of W-operators from training data to be applied to gray-scale image analysis. A hypothesis for applying the presented approach is that the conditional probabilities of the studied pattern recognition problem have mass concentrated in one class when the problem has a good solution. Experimental results with texture recognition have been presented.

The proposed technique is general and may be applied in a wide range of image processing problems besides texture segmentation, including document analysis and color image processing.

For the estimation of the conditional entropy it is required the estimation of the conditional probabilities $P(Y|\mathbf{X_Z})$ and the prior distribution $P(\mathbf{X_Z})$. The conditional probabilities are estimated based on simple counting of the observed classifications of a given feature vector. The entropy for $\mathbf{X_Z}$ is computed from the estimated distribution $\hat{P}(Y|\mathbf{X_Z})$. The distribution of $P(Y|\mathbf{X_Z})$ when $\mathbf{X_Z}$ is not observed in training set were considered uniform in [1]. But the conditional entropy $H(Y|\mathbf{X_Z})$ can not be higher than the entropy *a priori* of Y $(H(Y))$, since the information *a priori* about Y cannot decrease.

The parameter α in Equation 7 gives a determined probability mass for the non-observed instances. We have verified empirically that this parameter fixed as 1 leads to a very good balance between error due to noise in feature vector classification and estimation error. However, this parameter could be estimated from the training data in order to obtain better results. We are currently working on this problem to improve the proposed technique.

A branch and bound feature selection algorithm that explores the "U-curve" effect by our mean conditional entropy estimator [1] is under development. The goal is to obtain the optimal feature subspace in reasonable computational time. Results will be reported in due time.

Acknowledgements

The authors are grateful to FAPESP (99/12765-2, 01/09401-0 and 04/03967-0), CNPq (300722/98-2, 52.1097/01-0 and 468413/00-6) and CAPES for financial support. This work was partially supported by grant 1 D43 TW07015-01 from the National Institutes of Health, USA. We also thank Daniel O. Dantas by his complementing post-processing idea (mode filter applied more than once).

References

1. D. C. Martins-Jr, R. M. Cesar-Jr, and J. Barrera. W-operator window design by maximization of training data information. In *Proceedings of XVII Brazilian Symposium on Computer Graphics and Image Processing (SIBGRAPI)*, pages 162–169. IEEE Computer Society Press, October 2004.
2. J. Barrera, R. Terada, R. Hirata-Jr., and N. S. T. Hirata. Automatic programming of morphological machines by pac learning. *Fundamenta Informaticae*, pages 229–258, 2000.
3. E. R. Dougherty, J. Barrera, G. Mozelle, S. Kim, and M. Brun. Multiresolution analysis for optimal binary filters. *J. Math. Imaging Vis.*, 14(1):53–72, 2001.
4. P. Pudil, J. Novovicov, and J. Kittler. Floating search methods in feature selection. *Pattern Recognition Letters*, 15:1119–1125, 1994.

5. C. E. Shannon. A mathematical theory of communication. *Bell System Technical Journal*, 27:379–423, 623–656, July, October 1948.
6. T. M. Cover and J. A. Thomas. Elements of information theory. In *Wiley Series in Telecommunications*. John Wiley & Sons, New York, NY, USA, 1991.
7. S. Kullback. *Information Theory and Statistics*. Dover, 1968.
8. E. S. Soofi. Principal information theoretic approaches. *Journal of the American Statistical Association*, 95:1349–1353, 2000.
9. R. O. Duda, P. E. Hart, and D. Stork. *Pattern Classification*. John Wiley & Sons, NY, 2000.
10. M. A. Hall and L. A. Smith. Feature selection for machine learning: Comparing a correlation-based filter approach to the wrapper. In *Proc. FLAIRS Conference*, pages 235–239. AAAI Press, 1999.
11. D. D. Lewis. Feature selection and feature extraction for text categorization. In *Proceedings of Speech and Natural Language Workshop*, pages 212–217, San Mateo, California, 1992. Morgan Kaufmann.
12. B. V. Bonnlander and A. S. Weigend. Selecting input variables using mutual information and nonparametric density estimation. In *Proc. of the 1994 Int. Symp. on Artificial Neural Networks*, pages 42–50, Tainan, Taiwan, 1994.
13. P. Viola and W. M. Wells, III. Alignment by maximization of mutual information. *Int. J. Comput. Vision*, 24(2):137–154, 1997.
14. M. Zaffalon and M. Hutter. Robust feature selection by mutual information distributions. In *18th International Conference on Uncertainty in Artificial Intelligence (UAI)*, pages 577–584, 2002.
15. T. E. Campos, I. Bloch, and R. M. Cesar-Jr. Feature selection based on fuzzy distances between clusters: First results on simulated data. In S. Singh, N. Murshed, and W. Kropatsch, editors, *Proc. ICAPR'2001 - International Conference on Advances in Pattern Recognition*, volume 2013 of *Lecture Notes in Computer Science, Springer-Verlag Press*, pages 186–195, Rio de Janeiro, Brasil, 2001.
16. A. Jain and D. Zongker. Feature selection - evaluation, application, and small sample performance. *IEEE Transactions on Pattern Analysis and Machine Intelligence*, 19(2):153–158, 1997.

On Shape Orientation When the Standard Method Does Not Work

Joviša Žunić[1,*] and Lazar Kopanja[2]

[1] Computer Science, Exeter University Exeter EX4 4QF, U.K.
J.Zunic@ex.ac.uk
[2] Department of Mathematics and Informatics, Novi Sad University, 21000 Novi Sad, Trg D. Obradovića 4, Serbia and Montenegro
Kopanjal@yahoo.com

Abstract. In this paper we consider some questions related to the orientation of shapes when the standard method does not work. A typical situation is when a shapes under consideration has more than two axes of symmetry or if the shape is n-fold rotationally symmetric, when $n > 2$. Those situations are well studied in literature. Here, we give a very simple proof of the main result from [11] and slightly adapt their definition of principal axes for rotationally symmetric shapes. We show some desirable properties that hold if the orientation of such shapes is computed in such a modified way.

Keywords: Shape, orientation, image processing, early vision.

1 Introduction

The computation of a shape's orientation is a common task in the area of computer vision and image processing, being used for example to define a local frame of reference, and helpful for recognition and registration, robot manipulation, etc. It is also important in human visual perception; for instance, orientable shapes can be matched more quickly than shapes with no distinct axis [8]. Another example is the perceptual difference between a square and a diamond (rotated square) noted by Mach in 1886 [6], which can be explained by their multiple reference frames, i.e. ambiguous orientations [8]. There are situations (see Fig. 1 (a), (b), (c)) when the orientation of the shapes seems to be easily and naturally determined. On the other hand, a planar disc could be understood as a shape without orientation.

Most situations are somewhere in between. For very non-regular shapes it could be difficult to say what the orientation should be – see Fig. 6**(a)**,**(b)**. Rotationally symmetric shapes can also have poorly defined orientation – see Fig 2 (d). Moreover, even for regular polygons (see Fig. 2 (a) and (b)) is debatable whether they are orientable or not. For instance, is a square an orientable shape?

* The author is also with the Mathematical institute of Serbian Academy of Sciences and Arts, Belgrade.

M. Lazo and A. Sanfeliu (Eds.): CIARP 2005, LNCS 3773, pp. 825–836, 2005.

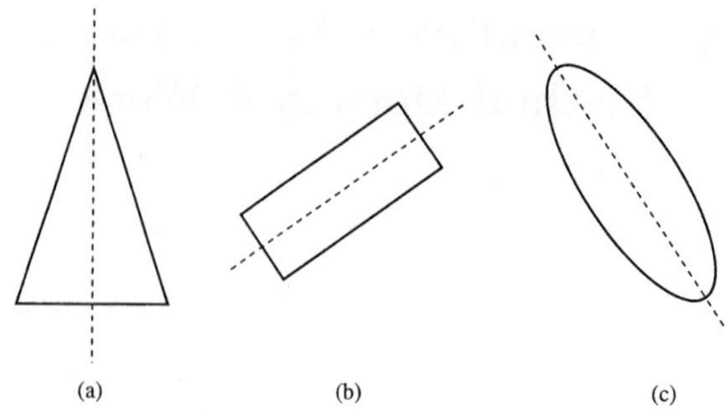

Fig. 1. It is reasonable to say that the orientation of the presented shapes coincide with the dashed lines

The same question arises for any regular n-gon, but also for shapes having several axes of symmetry, and n-fold ($n > 2$) rotational symmetric shapes – see shapes from Fig. 2. It is known ([11]) that the standard method, based on computing the axis of the last second moment, does not suggest any answer what the shape orientation should be if applied to n-fold ($n > 2$) rotationally symmetric shapes.

An compromised answer could be that such shapes are orientable but they do not have the unique orientation. Naturally, if a n-fold rotationally symmetric shape is considered as an orientable shape, than it should be n lines (making mutual angles that are multiplication of $\frac{2\pi}{n}$) that define its orientation. If a shape has n axes of symmetry than it is reasonable to use such axes to represent the shape orientation. Some solutions are proposed in [5,9,11], for example.

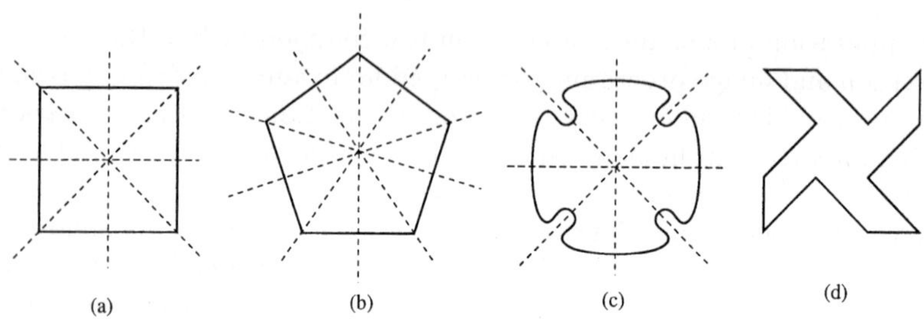

Fig. 2. The dashed lines seem to be reasonable candidates to represent the orientation of the shapes (a), (b), and (c). It is not quite clear what the orientation of 4-fold rotationally symmetric shape (d) should be.

2 Standard Method for Computing Orientation

In this section we give a short overview of the method which is mostly used in practice for computing orientation.

The standard approach defines the orientation by the so called axis of the least second moment ([1,2]). That is the line which minimizes the integral of the squares of distances of the points (belonging to the shape) to the line. The integral is

$$I(\delta, \rho, S) = \iint_S r^2(x, y, \delta, \rho) dxdy \tag{1}$$

where $r(x, y, \delta, \rho)$ is the perpendicular distance from the point (x, y) to the line given in the form

$$x \cdot \cos\delta - y \cdot \sin\delta = \rho.$$

It can be shown that the line that minimizes $I(S, \delta, \rho)$ passes through the centroid $(x_c(S), y_c(S))$ of the shape S where $(x_c(S), y_c(S)) = \left(\frac{\iint_S x dxdy}{\iint_S dxdy}, \frac{\iint_S y dxdy}{\iint_S dxdy}\right)$. In other words, without loss of generality, we can assume that the origin is placed at the centroid. Since required line minimizing $I(S, \delta, \rho)$, passes through the origin we can set $\rho = 0$. In this way, the shape orientation problem can be reformulated to the problem of determining δ for which the function $I(S, \delta)$ defined as

$$I(\delta, S) = I(\delta, \rho = 0, S) = \iint_S (-x \cdot \sin\delta + y \cdot \cos\delta)^2 dxdy^1$$

reaches the minimum.

Further, if the central geometric moments $\overline{m}_{p,q}(S)$ are defined as usually

$$\overline{m}_{p,q}(S) = \iint_S (x - x_c(S))^p \cdot (y - y_c(S))^q \; dx \; dy,$$

and by the assumed $(x_c(S), y_c(S)) = (0, 0)$, we obtain

$$I(\delta, S) \;=\; (\sin\delta)^2 \cdot \overline{m}_{2,0}(S) - \sin(2 \cdot \delta) \cdot \overline{m}_{1,1,}(S) + (\cos\delta)^2 \cdot \overline{m}_{0,2}(S). \tag{2}$$

The minimum of the function $I(\delta, S)$ can be computed easily. Setting the first derivative $I'(x, S)$ to zero, we have

$$I'(\delta, S) = \sin(2\delta) \cdot (\overline{m}_{2,0}(S) - \overline{m}_{0,2}(S)) - 2 \cdot \cos(2\delta) \cdot \overline{m}_{1,1}(S) = 0.$$

That easily gives that the required angle δ, but also the angle $\delta + \pi/2$, satisfies the equation

$$\frac{\sin(2\delta)}{\cos(2\delta)} = \frac{2 \cdot \overline{m}_{1,1}(S)}{\overline{m}_{2,0}(S) - \overline{m}_{0,2}(S)}. \tag{3}$$

Thus, the maximum and minimum of $I(\delta, S)$ are easy to compute.

Let us mention that, when working with digital objects which are actually digitizations of real shapes, then central geometric moments $\overline{m}_{p,q}(S)$ are replaced with their discrete analogue, i.e., with the so called *central discrete moments.*

[1] The squared distance of a point (x, y) to the line $X \cdot \cos\delta - Y \cdot \sin\delta = 0$ is $(-x \sin\delta + y \cos\delta)^2$.

Since the digitization on the integer grid $\mathbf{Z}^2$ of a real shape S consists of all pixels whose centers are inside S it is natural to approximate $\overline{m}_{p,q}(S)$ by the central discrete moment $M_{p,q}(S)$ defined as

$$M_{p,q}(S) = \sum_{(i,j)\in S\cap\mathbf{Z}^2} (i - x_{cd}(S))^p \cdot (j - y_{cd}(S))^q$$

where $(x_{cd}(S), y_{cd}(S))$ is the centroid of the discrete shape $S \cap \mathbf{Z}^2$. For some details about the efficiency of the approximation $\overline{m}_{p,q}(S) \approx M_{p,q}(S)$ see [3].

If the all geometric moments in (3) are replaced with the corresponding discrete moments we have the equation

$$\frac{\sin(2\delta)}{\cos(2\delta)} = \frac{2 \cdot M_{1,1}(S)}{M_{2,0}(S) - M_{0,2}(S)} \tag{4}$$

which describes the angle δ which is used to describe the orientation of discrete shape $S \cap \mathbf{Z}^2$.

So, the standard method is very simple (in both "real" and "discrete" versions) and it comes from a natural definition of the shape orientation. However, it is not always effective. Indeed, if $I(\delta, S)$ is a constant function then the method does not work – i.e., it does not tell us what the angle should be used to define the orientation of S. $I(\delta, S) = contsnt$ can happen for very non regular shapes but perhaps the most typical situation is when the considered shape S has more than two axes of symmetry, or more generally, if S is an n-fold rotationally symmetric shape (with $n > 2$).

The next lemma (it is a particular case of Theorem 1 from [11]) proves easily that the standard method cannot be used if the measured shape has more than two symmetry axes.

Lemma 1. *If a given shape has more than two axes of symmetry then $I(\delta, S)$ is a constant function.*

Proof. From (2) it is obvious that $I(\delta, S)$ can have no more than one maximum and one minimum on the interval $[0, \pi)$ or it must be a constant function. Trivially $I(0, S) = I(\pi, S)$. So, if S has more than two axes of symmetry then $I(\delta, S)$ must be constant since the first derivative $I'(\delta, S)$ does not have more than two zeros on the interval $[0, \pi)$. ∎

Remark 1. Lemma 1 implies $I(S, \delta) = \frac{1}{2} \cdot (\overline{m}_{2,0}(S) + \overline{m}_{0,2}(S))$ (for all $\delta \in [0, \pi)$) if S has more than two symmetry axes. The standard method does not tell us what the orientation should be in such a situation. Obviously, the standard method is limited by the simplicity of the function $I(\delta, S)$.

3 High-Order Principal Axes

In [11] it has been noted that the standard method does not work if applied to n-fold ($n > 2$) rotationally symmetric shapes. As usual, rotationally symmetric shapes are such shapes which are identical to itself after being rotated through any multiple of $\frac{2\pi}{n}$ (the problem of detecting number of folds but also the problem of detecting symmetry axes are well studied – see [4,7,10], for example). So, if a discrete point set S is n-fold rotationally symmetric then it is of the form

$$S = \left\{ (r_i, \theta_{i,j}) \mid i = 1, \ldots, m, \;\; j = 1, \ldots, n, \text{ and } \theta_{i,j} = \theta_{i,1} + (j-1)\frac{2\pi}{n} \right\} \quad (5)$$

where points $(r_i, \theta_{i,j})$ from S are given in polar coordinates.

As mentioned, the function $I(\delta, S)$ is not a strong enough mathematical tool to be used for the defining the orientation of n-fold ($n > 2$) rotationally symmetric shapes. In order to overcome such a problem, the authors of [11] proposed the use of the Nth*-order central moments of inertia.* A precise definition follows.

Definition 1. *Let a shape S whose centroid coincide with the origin. Then, the N-order central moment of inertia, denoted as $I_N(\delta, S)$ about a line going through the shape centroid with slope* $\tan\delta$ *is defined as*

$$I_N(\delta, S) = \sum_{(x,y)\in S} (-x\sin\delta + y\cos\delta)^N. \quad (6)$$

In other words, the authors suggest that a more complex function than (2) should be used. Obviously, if $N = 2$ we have the standard method.

A nice result, related to n-fold rotationally symmetric shapes and their corresponded N^{th}-order central moments has been proven in [11]. The proof presented in [11] is pretty long. Here, we give a very elemental proof.

Theorem 1. *([11]) For an n-fold rotationally symmetric shape S, having the centroid coincident with the origin, its Nth-order central moment of inertia $I_N(\delta, S)$ is constant about any line going through its centroid for all N less than n.*

Proof. Let an n-fold rotationally symmetric shape S, with the centroid placed at the origin. Setting the first derivative of $I_N(\delta, S)$ to be equal to zero, we can derive that there are not more than $2N$ values of δ for which $dI_N(\delta, S)/d\delta$ vanishes, if $I_N(\delta, S)$ is not a constant function. Indeed, starting form

$$\frac{dI_N(\delta, S)}{d\delta} = \sum_{(x,y)\in S} N \cdot (-x\sin\delta + y\cos\delta)^{N-1} \cdot (-x\cos\delta - y\sin\delta) \quad (7)$$

we will distinguish two situations – denoted below by **(i)** and **(ii)**.

(i) – If $\delta = 0$ and $\delta = \pi$ (i.e. $\sin\delta = 0$) are not solution of $dI_N(\delta, S)/d\delta = 0$, then (from (8))

$$\frac{dI_N(\delta, S)}{d\delta} = 0 \quad \Leftrightarrow \quad (\sin\delta)^N \cdot \sum_{(x,y)\in S} (-x \; + y\cot\delta)^{N-1} \cdot (x\cot\delta + y) = 0.$$

Since the quantity

$$\sum_{(x,y)\in S} (-x \ + y\cot\delta)^{N-1} \cdot (x\cot\delta + y)$$

is an N-degree polynomial on $\cot\delta$ it cannot have more than N real zeros

$$\cot\delta = z_1, \ \cot\delta = z_2, \ \ldots, \ \cot\delta = z_k, \qquad (k \le N).$$

In other words, because of $\cot\delta = \cot(\delta+\pi)$ the equation

$$\frac{dI_N(\delta,S)}{d\delta} = 0$$

has no more than $2N$ solutions.

(ii) – If $\delta = 0$ and $\delta = \pi$ (i.e. $\sin\delta = 0$) are solution of $dI_N(\delta,S)/d\delta = 0$, then easily (see (8))

$$\sum_{(x,y)\in S} x \cdot y^{N-1} = 0. \tag{8}$$

But, in such a situation

$$P(\cot\delta) = \sum_{(x,y)\in S} (-x \ + y\cot\delta)^{N-1} \cdot (x\cot\delta + y)$$

is an $(N-1)$-degree polynomial on $\cot\delta$ (see (10), the coefficient of $(\cot\delta)^N$ vanishes). Consequently, $P(\cot\delta)$ cannot have more than $N-1$ real zeros:

$$\cot\delta = z_1, \ \cot\delta = z_2, \ \ldots, \ \cot\delta = z_k, \qquad (k \le N-1),$$

i.e. there are no more than $2(N-1)$ values of δ for which $P(\cot\delta)$ vanishes. So, again, $dI_N(\delta,S)d/\delta = 0$ has at most $2N$ solutions, including $\delta = 0$ and $\delta = \pi$.

Thus, the number of zeros that could have $dI_N(\delta,S)/d\delta$ is not bigger than $2N$.

On the other side, if S is a fixed n-fold rotationally symmetric shape, then $I_N(\delta,S)$ must have (because of the symmetry) at least n local minima and n local maxima (one minimum and one maximum on each interval of the form $[\beta, \beta+2\pi/n)$, or it must be a constant function. That means, $dI_N(\delta,S)/d\delta$ must have (at least) $2n$ zeros $\delta_1, \delta_2, \ldots, \delta_{2n}$.

Since the presumption $N < n$ does not allow $2n$ zeros of $dI_N(\delta,S)/d\delta$ if $I_N(\delta,S)$ is not a constant functions, we just derived a contradiction. Thus $I_N(\delta,S)$ must be a a constant function for all N less than n. ∎

4 Comments on High-Order Principal Axes

The computing orientation is not always easy and straightforward. As shown by Lemma 1, even the orientation of a square cannot be computed if the standard method is applied. Once again, the standard method, if works, gives only one line which should represent the shape orientation. Lemma 1 is related to the shapes having more than two axes of symmetry but there are also irregular shapes whose orientation is not computable by the standard method. Since it is clear that the function (2) (that uses the second degree moments only) is not powerful enough to define the orientation of any shape, [11] involves more complex functions $I_N(\delta, S)$ that should be used to define the orientation of n-fold rotationally symmetric shapes.

Precisely, [11] defines an N-th order principal axis of a degenerate shape S (a shape for which the standard method does not work) as a line going through the centroid of S about which the $I_N(\delta, S)$ is minimized. Then, the orientation of S is defined by one of N-th order principal axes. Of course, for any fixed N there are still shapes whose orientation cannot be computed in this generalized manner – it is enough to consider an n-fold rotationally symmetric shape with $n > N$ (see Theorem 1).

Theorem 1 gives a clear answer that for an n-fold rotationally symmetric shape, the N-th order principal axes cannot be determined for all $N < n$. On the other side, even Theorem 1 says nothing about the existence of minima (maxima) of $I_{N=n}(\delta, S)$ it seems that $N = n$ could be an appropriate choice of the order to define the high order principal axes for an n-fold rotationally symmetric shape. If n-th order principal axes of an n-fold rotationally symmetric shape S exist, then they can be computed easily, as given by the next lemma.

Lemma 2. *([11]) The directions, δ, of the Nth-order principal axes of an n-fold rotationally symmetric S satisfy following equations:*

$$\tan(n\delta) = \begin{cases} \dfrac{n \cdot M_{n-1,1}(S)}{M_{n,0}(S) - (n-1) \cdot M_{n-2,2}(S)} & \text{if } n \text{ is even} \\[2ex] \dfrac{-M_{n,0}(S)}{M_{n-1,1}(S)} & \text{if } n \text{ is odd.} \end{cases}$$

Remark 2. It is important to notice that Lemma 2 does say nothing if S is not n-fold rotationally symmetric.

Some examples of shape orientations obtained by a use of higher order principal axes are given Fig. 3. In the presented cases, the method satisfies the basic request for which it was involved - i.e. it suggests a precise answer what the orientation of n-fold symmetric shapes should be. That could be enough for, let say, an image normalization task. Also, a very nice property is given by Lemma 2 – i.e. in the case when S is an n-fold rotationally symmetric shape (with a known n) then the computation of principal axes is very simple.

On the other side, just looking at the presented example, we can see that sometimes (even case) the orientation coincide with one of symmetry axes, but sometimes (odd case) does not. That could be a strong objection. This disadvantage is caused by the fact that there is no a good enough "geometric" motivation for a use of centralized geometric moments having an odd order. The preference that the shape orientation coincides with one of its symmetry axes (if any) seems to be very reasonable.

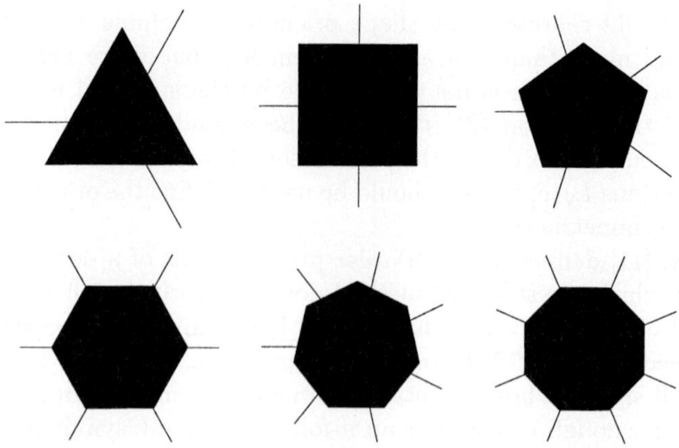

Fig. 3. The principal axes (obtained as suggested in [11]) for regular 3, 4, 5, 6, 7, and 8-gons are presented

The situation is even worse. If a shape S has at least one symmetry axis and if the orientation is computed as the line that minimizes $I_{2k+1}(\beta, S)$ then very likely such a line will not coincide with any axis of symmetry of S. Indeed, let an axis-symetric set S. Without loss of generality we can assume that this axis coincides with the x-axis. So, S is the union of the sets:

- Set A which consists of all points from S that have a positive y coordinate;
- set B which consists of all points from S that have a negative y coordinate;
- set C which consists of all points from S that have y coordinate equal to zero.

Since x-axis is a symmetry axis of S, we have $(x, y) \in A \Leftrightarrow (x, -y) \in B$. Thus, we can write:

$$I_{2k+1}(\delta, S) = \sum_{(x,y)\in A} (-x\sin\delta + y\cos\delta)^{2k+1} + \sum_{(x,y)\in B} (-x\sin\delta + y\cos\delta)^{2k+1}$$

$$+ \sum_{(x,y)\in C} (-x\sin\delta + y\cos\delta)^{2k+1} =$$

$$= \sum_{(x,y)\in A} \left((-x\sin\delta + y\cos\delta)^{2k+1} + (-x\sin\delta - y\cos\delta)^{2k}\right)$$

$$+ \sum_{(x,0)\in C} 2k(-x\sin\delta)^{2k+1}.$$

The first derivative is

$$\frac{dI_{2k+1}(\delta, S)}{d\delta} = \sum_{(x,y)\in A} (2k+1)\cdot(-x\sin\delta + y\cos\delta)^{2k}\cdot(-x\cos\delta - y\sin\delta)$$

$$+ \sum_{(x,y)\in A} (2k+1)\cdot(-x\sin\delta - y\cos\delta)^{2k}\cdot(-x\cos\delta + y\sin\delta)$$

$$+ \sum_{(x,0)\in C} (2k+1)\cdot(-x\sin\delta)^{2k}(-x\cos\delta).$$

From the last equality we obtain

$$\frac{d^2 I_{2k+1}(0,S)}{d\delta^2} = -(4k+2)\sum_{(x,y)\in A} xy^{2k} = -(4k+2)M_{1,2k}(S).$$

Thus, $d^2 I_{2k+1}(0,S)/d\delta^2$ is not necessarily equal to zero and, consequently, a maximum is not guaranteed.

It is interesting to note $d^2 I_{2k+1}(\pi/2,S)/d\delta^2 = 0$. So, if $I_{2k+1}(\delta,S)$ reaches the maximum for an angle δ_0, then it seems to be more reasonable to define the orientation of S by the angle $\pi/2+\delta_0$, rather than by the angle δ_0, as suggested by [11].

5 Modified Use of High Order Principal Axes

Here, we use a modified approach to the problem. We accept that we have to use a more complex method than the standard one. So, we are going to use N^{th}-order central moments with $N > 2$ and will try to make a compromise between the following requests:

- **(c1)** The method should have a reasonable geometric motivation;
- **(c2)** The method should give some answer what orientation should be even for rotationally symmetric shapes;
- **(c3)** The method should give reasonably good results if applied to non regular shapes;
- **(c4)** The orientation should be relatively easy to compute.

If we go back to the standard definition of shape orientation, we can see that it is defined by the line that minimizes the sum of squares of distances of the points to this line. The squared distance (rather than the pure Euclidean distance) has been taken in order to enable an easy mathematical calculation. Following this initial idea and taking into account the problems explained by Theorem 1, we suggest that the orientation should be defined as a line which minimizes the total sum of a (suitably chosen) even-power of distances of the points to the line. We give a formal definition.

Definition 2. *Let a given integer k and let a given shape S whose centroid coincide with the origin. Then, the orientation of S is defined by an angle δ that minimizes*

$$I_{2k}(\delta,S) = \sum_{(x,y)\in S} (-x\sin\delta + y\cos\delta)^{2k}. \tag{9}$$

Now, we show a desirable property of the orientation computed in accordance with Definition 2. Let an axis-symetric set S. Because of the definition of $I_{2k}(\delta, S)$, without loss of generality we can assume that this axis coincides with the x-axis. Again, if S is represented as the union of:

- set A consisting of all points from S that have a positive y coordinate,
- set B consisting of all points from S that have a negative y coordinate,
- set C consisting of all points from S that have y coordinate equal to zero,

and if the x-axis is a symmetry axis of S, we have $(x, y) \in A \Leftrightarrow (x, -y) \in B$. Thus, we can write:

$$\begin{aligned} I_{2k}(\delta, S) = & \sum_{(x,y)\in A} (-x\sin\delta + y\cos\delta)^{2k} + \sum_{(x,y)\in B} (-x\sin\delta + y\cos\delta)^{2k} \\ & + \sum_{(x,y)\in C} (-x\sin\delta + y\cos\delta)^{2k} \\ = & \sum_{(x,y)\in A} \left((-x\sin\delta + y\cos\delta)^{2k} + (-x\sin\delta - y\cos\delta)^{2k}\right) \\ & + \sum_{(x,0)\in C} 2k(-x\sin\delta)^{2k} \end{aligned}$$

$$\begin{aligned} \frac{dI_{2k}(\delta, S)}{d\delta} = & \sum_{(x,y)\in A} 2k(-x\sin\delta + y\cos\delta)^{2k-1}(-x\cos\delta - y\sin\delta) \\ & + \sum_{(x,y)\in A} 2k(-x\sin\delta - y\cos\delta)^{2k-1}(-x\cos\delta + y\sin\delta) \\ & + \sum_{(x,0)\in C} 2k(-x\sin\delta)^{2k-1}(-x\cos\delta). \end{aligned}$$

From the last equality we have that the first derivative of I_{2k} vanishes if $\delta = 0$, but also if $\delta = \pi/2$, i.e.,

$$\frac{dI_{2k}(0, S)}{d\delta} = \frac{dI_{2k}(\pi/2, S)}{d\delta} = 0.$$

The above equality shows that a symmetry axis (if any) has a "good chance" to be coincident with the computed orientation if Definition 2 is applied.

Since naturally defined, the orientation computed in proposed manner should performs well if applied to non regular shapes – that is illustrated by a few examples on Fig. 6.

Of course, the main disadvantage of the modified method is a higher computation complexity caused by the size of coefficient $2k$ from (9). It is not expected that a closed formula (as it is the formula (3) in the case of $2k = 2$) could

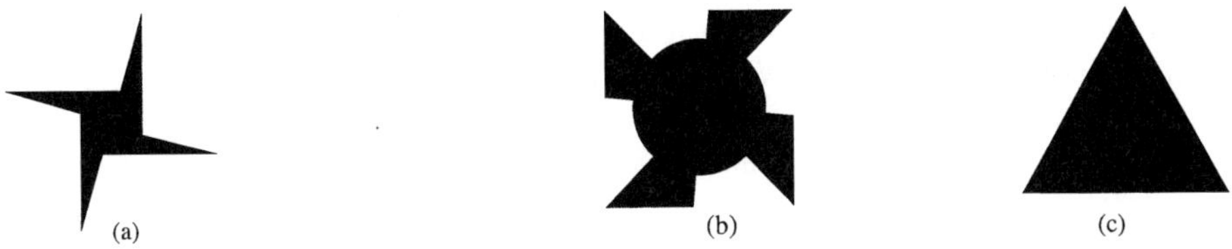

Fig. 4. (a) I_2 is nearly a constant value. The minimum of I_4 is reached for 44 degrees, while I_8 has the minimun for 42 degrees. (b) I_2 is nearly a constant value. The minimum of I_4 is reached for 11 degrees, while I_8 has the minimum for 8 degrees. (c) I_2 and I_4 are nearly constants. The minimum of I_6 is reached for 150 degrees – as preferred.

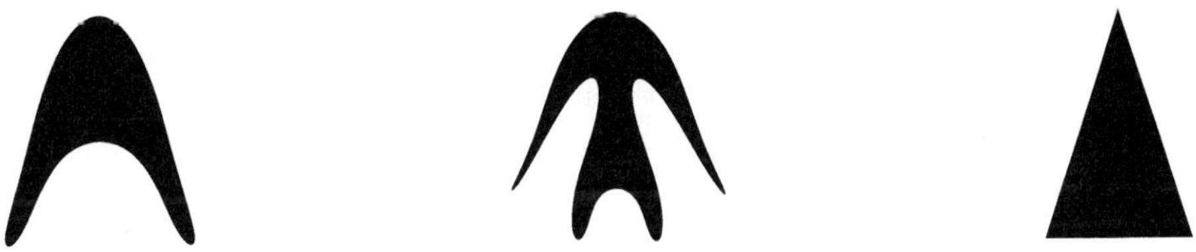

Fig. 5. The presented figures have exactly one axis of symmetry. In all presented cases the minimum of I_2, I_4, I_6, I_8, and I_{10} is obtained to be very close to 90 degrees.

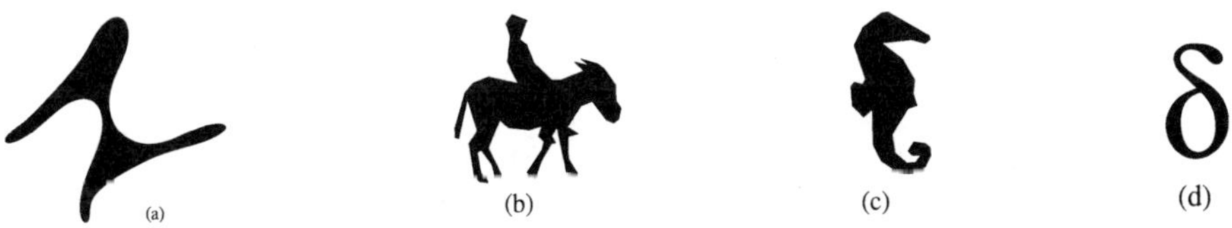

Fig. 6. Minimum values for I_2, I_4, I_6, I_8, and I_{10} are obtained for the following angle values: (a) 48, 56, 61, 63, and 64, respectively. (b) 114, 131, 32, 31, and 31, respectively. (c) 96, 95, 94, 92, and 92, respectively. (d) 87, 88, 88, 88, and 88, respectively.

be derived. But, the formula (9) enables an easy and straightforward numerical computation. Several examples are given on Fig. 4-6.

Rotationally symmetric shapes are presented on Fig. 4. The obtained results are in accordance with the previous theoretical observations. Particularly, the obtained minimum of I_6 says that the orientation of a regular triangle is coincident with one of its symmetry axes.

On Fig. 5 the orientation is measured for shapes having one symmetry axis. In all cases the computed minimal values for I_2, I_4, I_6, I_8, and I_{10} are obtained for an angle of 90 degrees – as preferred.

Fig. 6 displays non symmetric shapes. It may be assumed that the orientation is not well-defined for the shapes presented on Fig. 6 (a) and Fig. 6 (b). Indeed, when measure the orientation as the minimum of I_N we obtain different angle values for different values of N.

On the other side, since the shape on Fig. 6(c) and Fig. 6 (d) seems to be "well orientable" we obtain almost same angle values that should represent the orientation.

6 Concluding Remarks

In this paper we consider some problems related to the shape orientation. The most studied situation when such problems arise, is when working with shapes having many axes of symmetry and with n-fold rotationally symmetric shapes. The paper is mainly based on the results presented in [11]. A very short proof of the main result from [11] is presented. It is clarified that the most of of problems come from the fact that the function (2) is not complex enough to be used to compute orientation of an arbitrary shape. As an solution, a use of higher moments is suggested in [11]. Some disadvantages of such a proposal are discussed here as well. The main of them is that shapes having an odd number of axes of symmetry could have the computed orientation that does not coincide with any of symmetry axes. This paper suggest a modified use of the higher order moments that should avoid this disadvantage.

References

1. B.K.P. Horn, *Robot Vision,* MIT Press, Cambridge, MA, 1986.
2. R. Jain, R. Kasturi, B.G. Schunck, *Machine Vision,* McGraw-Hill, New York, 1995.
3. R. Klette, J. Žunić, "Digital approximation of moments of convex regions," *Graphical Models and Image Processing,* Vol. 61, pp. 274-298, 1999.
4. J.-C. Lin, W.-H. Tsai, J.-A. Chen "Detecting Number of Folds by a Simple Mathematical Property," *Patt. Rec. Letters,* Vol. 15, pp. 1081-1088, 1994.
5. J.-C. Lin, "The Family of Universal Axes," *Patt. Rec.,* Vol. 29, pp. 477-485, 1996.
6. E. Mach, *The analysis of sensations (Beiträge zur Analyse der Empfindungen),* Routledge, London, 1996.
7. G. Marola, "On the Detection of Axes of Symmetry of Symmetric and Almost Symmetric Planar Images," *IEEE Trans. PAMI,* Vol. 11, No. 6, pp. 104-108, 1989.
8. S.E. Palmer, *Vision Science: Photons to Phenomenology,* MIT Press, 1999.
9. D. Shen, H. H. S. Ip, "Optimal Axes for Defining the Orientations of Shapes," *Electronic Letters,* Vol. 32, No. 20, pp. 1873-1874, 1996.
10. D. Shen, H. H. S. Ip, K. K. T. Cheung, and E. K. Teoh, "Symmetry Detection by Generalized Complex (GC) Moments: A Close-Form Solution," *IEEE Trans. PAMI,* Vol. 21, No. 5, pp. 466–476, 1999.
11. W.H. Tsai, S.L. Chou, "Detection of Generalized Principal Axes in Rotationally Symmetric Shapes," *Patt. Rec.,* Vol. 24, pp. 95-104, 1991.

Fuzzy Modeling and Evaluation of the Spatial Relation "Along"

Celina Maki Takemura[1,*], Roberto Cesar Jr.[1,**], and Isabelle Bloch[2]

[1] IME/USP - Instituto de Matemática e Estatística da Universidade de São Paulo, Rua do Matão, 1010, Cidade Universitária 05508-090, São Paulo - SP - Brasil
{cesar, maki}@vision.ime.usp.br

[2] GET - École Nationale Supérieure des Télécommunications, Dept TSI - CNRS UMR 5141 - 46, rue Barrault 75634 Paris Cedex 13, France
isabelle.bloch@enst.fr

Abstract. The analysis of spatial relations among objects in an image is a important vision problem that involves both shape analysis and structural pattern recognition. In this paper, we propose a new approach to characterize the spatial relation *along*, an important feature of spatial configuration in space that has been overlooked in the literature up to now. We propose a mathematical definition of the degree to which an object A is along an object B, based on the region *between* A and B and a degree of elongatedness of this region. In order to better fit the perceptual meaning of the relation, distance information is included as well. Experimental results obtained using synthetic shapes and brain structures in medical imaging corroborate the proposed model and the derived measures, thus showing their adequation with the common sense.

1 Introduction

To our knowledge, the only work addressing *alongness* between objects by giving mathematical definitions was developed in the context of geographic information systems (GIS) [1]. In this work, the relation *along* between a line and an object is defined as the length of the intersection of the line and the boundary of the object, normalized either by the length of this boundary (*perimeter alongness*) or by the length of the line (*line alongness*). In these definitions, the boundary can also be extended to a *buffer zone* around the boundary. Crevier [2] addresses the problem of spatial relationships between line segments by detecting collinear chains of segments based on the probability that sucessive segments belong to the same underlying structure. However this approach cannot be directly extended to any object shape.

Here we consider the more general case where both objects can have any shape, and where they are not necessarily adjacent. For computer vision applications, the considered objects can be obtained for instance from a crisp or fuzzy segmentation of digital images.

* C. M. Takemura is grateful to CAPES (BEX 3402/04-5).

** R. Cesar Jr. is grateful to FAPESP (99/12765-2), to CAPES and to CNPq (300722/98-2 and 474596/2004-4).

M. Lazo and A. Sanfeliu (Eds.): CIARP 2005, LNCS 3773, pp. 837–848, 2005.

The *along* relation is an intrinsically vague notion. Indeed, in numerous situations even of moderate complexity, it is difficult to provide a definite binary answer to the question "is A *along* B?", and the answer should rather be a matter of degree. Therefore fuzzy modeling is appropriate. Now if the objects are themselves imprecisely defined, as fuzzy sets, this induces a second level of fuzziness. In this paper, we propose a fuzzy model of the relation *along* , for both crisp and fuzzy objects. It is based on a measure of elongatedness of the region *between* both objects.

In Section 2 we motivate our work based on a few references to other domains such as psychophysics or linguistics. We propose a mathematical model and a measure of *alongness* between crisp objects in Section 3. Their generalization to fuzzy objects is discussed in Section 4. Experimental results using both synthetic and real objects are shown in Section 5. Some properties and possible extensions are provided in Section 6.

2 Spatial Relations and Motivation for Using Fuzzy Definitions

According to Biederman[3], any object, even the simplest one, may project an infinity of image configurations to the retina considering orientation and, consequently, the bidimensional projection, possible occlusion, texture complexity, or if it is a novel exemplar of its particular category. The hypothesis explored in [3] is that the visual perception may be modeled as a process related to the identification of individual primitive elements, e.g. a finite number of geometrical components. In addition, Biederman claims that the relation between parts is a main feature to the object perception, i.e. two different arrangements of the same components may produce different objects.

Hummel and Biederman, in [4], claim that the majority of the visual recognition models are based on template matching or feature list matching. The two of them present limitations and are not in accordance with the human recognition [3]. In that way, the authors in [4] present a *strutural description* to characterize the object as a configuration of features, sensitive to the attribute structure and indifferent to the image overview.

Kosslyn et al, in [5], re-affirm the importance of relative positions for object and scene recognition. They classify those spatial relationships, psychophysically, according to their visuospatial processing, as absolute coordinate representations (i.e. precise spatial localization) and categorical representations (i.e. association of an interval of position to a equivalence class, e.g. *left of*).

The works in this area started mainly with Freeman's paper [6], and was continued during the 80's by Klette and Rosenfeld [7]. In [6], Freeman presents mathematical-computational formalisms to represent the semantic context of terms (in English) that codify relationships between objects by underlining the necessity of using fuzzy representations for a number of relations. Then several authors proposed fuzzy representations of some spatial relations (see e.g. [8] for a review).

Moreover, when considering works in psycholinguistics, it appears that even if the objects are crisp, the lack of clarity in the concepts related to the relative positions gives the background to the use of fuzzy definitions of these concepts.

3 Modeling the Spatial Relation *Along* for Crisp Objects

In the example of Fig.1(a), it can be said that A is along B, or that B is along A. The intuitive meaning of the relation is polymorphic: some assumptions can be made or not on the objects (at least one should be elongated, or both should), the distance between them should be reduced with respect to the size of the objects (typically we would not say that A is along B in the example of Fig.1(b)). What is quite clear is that the region between A and B, denoted by β, should be elongated, as is the case in Fig.1(a). In our model, we choose to propose a definition that does not necessarily consider the shape of the objects as a whole, that is symmetrical in both arguments, and that involves the region between the objects and their distance. Moreover, as already advocated in [6], defining such relations in a binary way would not be satisfactory, and a degree of satisfaction of the relation is more appropriate. Finally, we want also to be able to deal with situations where the relation is satisfied locally, between parts of the objects only.

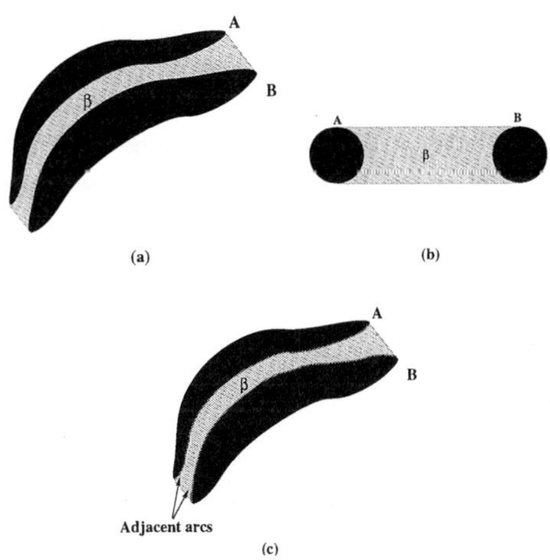

Fig. 1. (a) Example where A is along B, with an elongated region β between A and B. (b) Case where β is elongated but A is not along B. (c) Same example as (a) where adjacent arcs are shown.

Based on these considerations, we propose a mathematical definition of the degree to witch an object A is along an object B, based on the region between A and B [9] . The basic idea to characterize to which degree "A is along B" is based on two steps:

1. calculate the region β between A and B;
2. measure how elongated is β, thus defining the degree to which A is along B.

This approach is interesting because it involves explicitely the *between* region, which is also committed in the usual semantics of the *along* relation, and a good technique to calculate the region between A and B is available and used in our approach. Once the region between A and B is obtained, the issue of how elongated is β may be treated by shape analysis, leading to different measures which may be chosen depending on the application, as explained below.

3.1 Definition of the Region Between Two Objects

Since no assumption on the shapes of the objects is made, some classical ways to define the *between* region may not be appropriate. In particular, if the objects have complex shapes with concavities, a simple definition based on the convex hull of the union of both objects does not lead to a satisfactory result. We have addressed this problem in [9], where new methods are proposed in order to cope with complex shapes. We choose here one of these methods, the visibility approach, which provides results adapted to our aim. In particular, concavities of an object that are not visible from the other one are not included in the *between* area. More formally, this approach relies on the notion of admissible segments as introduced in [7]. A segment $]a, b[$, with a in A and b in B (A and B are supposed to be compact sets or digital objects), is said admissible if it is included in $A^C \cap B^C$[9]. Note that a and b then necessarily belong to the boundary of A and B, respectively. This has interesting consequences from an algorithmic point of view, since it considerably reduces the size of the set of points to be explored. The visible points are those which belong to admissible segments. The region between A and B can then be defined as the union of admissible segments.

(a) (b)

Fig. 2. (a) Region between two objects, calculated by the visibility approach; (b) Analogous to (a), but showing that the concavity of one of the objects is properly excluded from the *between* region by the visibility method.

Here, for the second step, we need to keep the extremities (belonging to the boundary of A or B) of the admissible segments in the *between* region. Therefore we slightly modify the definition of [9] as:

$$\beta = \cup\{[a, b], a \in A, b \in B,]a, b[\text{ admissible}\}. \tag{1}$$

This definition is illustrated in Fig.2 for two different cases. Note that, in contrast to the objects in Fig.2(a), in case of Fig.2(b), there is a concavity in one of the shapes not visible from the other object, and which is properly excluded from the *between* region by the visibility approach.

3.2 Definition of the Degree of Elongatedness

There are different possible approaches to measure how elongated is a region. One of the most popular ones is given by the inverse of compacity, i.e. how elongated is the region with respect to a circle. This can be measured in the 2D case by the elongatedness measure $c = P^2/S$, where P and S represent the perimeter and the area of the region. We have $c = 4\pi$ for a perfect disk, and the more elongated is the shape, the larger is c. In order to normalize this measure between 0 and 1, we propose a first *alongness* measure defined as:

$$\alpha_1 = f_a\left(\frac{P^2(\beta)}{S(\beta)}\right), \tag{2}$$

where $S(\beta)$ and $P(\beta)$ denote the area and perimeter of region β, respectively, and f_a is an increasing function, typically a sigmoid, such as $f_a(x) = (1 - \exp(-ax))/(1 + \exp(-ax))$. This measure α_1 tends towards 1 as β becomes more elongated. Although a is a parameter of the method, it preserves the order between different situations, which is the most important property. Absolute values can be changed by tuning a to enhance the difference between different situations.

However the measure α_1 does not lead to good results in all situations. Indeed it considers a global elongatedness, while the elongatedness only in some directions is useful. Let us consider the example in Fig.1(b). The region between A and B is elongated, but this does not mean that A is along B. On the other hand, the situation in Fig.1(a) is good since β is elongated in the direction of its adjacency with A and B. In order to model this, instead of using the complete perimeter of β, the total arc length $L(\beta)$ of the contour portions of β adjacent to A or to B is used (see the adjacent arcs indicated in Fig.1(c)). Here, with the modified definition of β (Equation 1), these lines are actually the intersections between A and β and between B and β. The new elongatedness measure is then defined as:

$$\alpha_2 = f_a\left(\frac{L^2(\beta)}{S(\beta)}\right). \tag{3}$$

Although this measure produces proper results, it presents the drawback of not taking directly into account the distance between A and B, which is useful in some situations. Also, because α_2 is a global measure over A and B, it fails in identifying if there are some parts of A that are along some parts of B, i.e. it lacks the capability of local analysis.

There is an interesting way of incorporating these aspects in the present approach by considering the distance between the two shapes within the *between* area. Let x be an image point, and $d(x, A)$ and $d(x, B)$ the distances from x to A and B respectively (in the digital case, they can be computed in a very efficient way using distance transforms). Let $D_{AB}(x) = d(x, A) + d(x, B)$. Instead of using the area of β to calculate how elongated it is, we define the volume $V(\beta)$ below the surface $\{(x, D_{AB}(x)),\ x \in \beta\}$, which is calculated as:

$$V(\beta) = \int_\beta D_{AB}(x)dx. \tag{4}$$

In the digital case, the integral becomes a finite sum.

This leads to an *alongness* measure taking into account the distance between A and B:

$$\alpha_3 = \underset{a}{f}\left(\frac{L^2(\beta)}{V(\beta)}\right). \tag{5}$$

The distance $D_{AB}(x)$ may be used in a more interesting way in order to deal with situations where just some parts of A can be considered along some parts of B. In such cases, it is expected that such parts are near each other, thus generating a *between* region with lower values of $D_{AB}(x)$. Let $\beta_t = \{x,\ D_{AB}(x) < t\}$, where t is a distance threshold. Let $L(\beta_t)$, $S(\beta_t)$ and $V(\beta_t)$ be the total adjacent arc length, area and volume for β_t. Two local *alongness* measures, in the areas which are sufficiently near to each other according to the threshold, are then defined as:

$$\alpha_4(t) = \underset{a}{f}\left(\frac{L^2(\beta_t)}{S(\beta_t)}\right), \tag{6}$$

and

$$\alpha_5(t) = \underset{a}{f}\left(\frac{L^2(\beta_t)}{V(\beta_t)}\right). \tag{7}$$

4 Modeling the Spatial Relation *Along* for Fuzzy Objects

Now we consider the case of fuzzy objects, which may be useful to deal with spatial imprecision, rough segmentation, etc. We follow the same approach in two steps as in the crisp case.

The visibility approach for defining the *between* region can be extended to the fuzzy case by introducing the degree to which a segment is included in $A^C \cap B^C$ (which is now a fuzzy region). Let μ_A and μ_B be the membership functions of the fuzzy objects A and B. The degree of inclusion μ_{incl} of a segment $]a, b[$ in $A^C \cap B^C$ is given by:

$$\mu_{incl}(]a, b[) = \inf_{y \in]a,b[} \min[1 - \mu_A(y), 1 - \mu_B(y)]. \tag{8}$$

Let us denote the support of the fuzzy objects A and B by Supp(A) and Supp(B) respectively. The region between A and B, denoted by β_F, is then defined as

$$\beta_F(x) = \sup\{\mu_{incl}(]a, b[); x \in [a, b], a \in \text{Supp}(A), b \in \text{Supp}(B)\}. \tag{9}$$

In order to define *alongness* measures analogous to $\alpha_l, l = 1...5$, it is necessary to calculate the perimeter, area and volume of β_F. Perimeter $P(\beta_F)$ and area $S(\beta_F)$ are usually defined as [10]:

$$P(\beta_F) = \int_{\text{Supp}(\beta_F)} |\bigtriangledown \beta_F(x)| dx, \tag{10}$$

where $\bigtriangledown \beta_F(x)$ is the gradient of β_F, and

$$S(\beta_F) = \int_{\text{Supp}(\beta_F)} \beta_F(x) dx. \tag{11}$$

The extension of α_2 requires to define the adjacency region R_{adj} between the objects and β. In order to guarantee the consistency with the crisp case, we can simply take the intersection between A and β and between B and β and extend L as:

$$R_{adj}(\beta_F, \mu_{A \cup B}) = (\text{Supp}(\beta_F) \cap \text{Supp}(A)) \cup (\text{Supp}(\beta_F) \cap \text{Supp}(B)), \tag{12}$$

where $\mu_{A \cup B}$ represents the union of the fuzzy objects A and B, and:

$$L(\beta_F, \mu_{A \cup B}) = S(R_{adj}(\beta_F, \mu_{A \cup B})). \tag{13}$$

Finally, it is also necessary to calculate the distance of any point x of the *between* region to A and to B. We propose the use of the lenght of the admissible segments:

$$D_{AB}(x) = \inf\{\|b-a\|,]a,b[\text{ admissible}, x \in]a,b[\}, \text{ for } x \in (\text{Supp}(A) \cup \text{Supp}(B))^C \tag{14}$$

Then, we define the volume $V(\beta_F)$ below the surface $\{(x, D_{AB}), x \in \beta_F\}$ by weighting each point by its membership to $\beta_F(x)$, as:

$$V(\beta_F) = \int_{\text{Supp}(\beta_F)} \beta_F(x) D_{AB}(x) dx. \tag{15}$$

In order to keep the fuzzy nature of the model, instead of thresholding the distance function as in the crisp case, we propose to select the closest area based on a decreasing function g of D_{AB}. We thus have $\beta_{F_t}(x) = \beta_F(x) g(D_{AB}(x))$. In our experiments, we have chosen g as:

$$g(t) = 1 - f_{a_1}(t), \tag{16}$$

with $a_1 = 0.3$.

5 Experimental Results

Extensive results with a large number of pairs of shapes have been successfully produced. Some of these results are presented and discussed in this section.

(a) (b)

Fig. 3. Results using the visibility approach to calculate β. (a) Synthetic shapes and the region β between them. The adjacent arcs are also indicated. (b) The distance map $D_{AB}(x)$ in β is represented as grey-levels.

Table 1. *Alongness* values for different shape configurations (synthetic shapes) with parameters $a = 0.125$ and $t = 10$

Shapes	 (a)	 (b)	 (c)
α_1	0.907	0.450	0.874
α_2	0.885	0.431	0.340
α_3	0.172	0.011	0.010
$\alpha_4(10)$	0.834	0.653	0.072
$\alpha_5(10)$	0.165	0.127	0.010

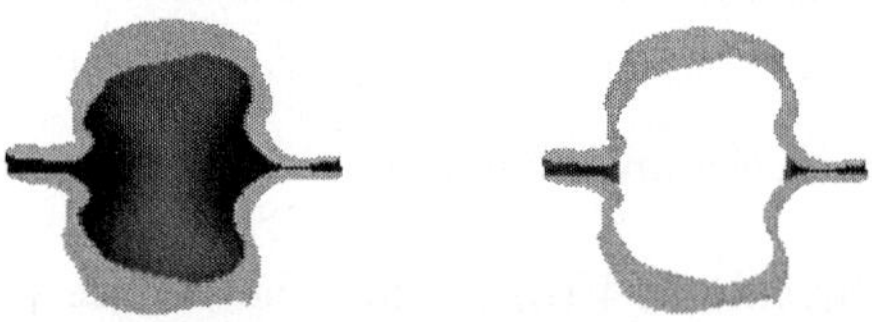

(a) (b)

Fig. 4. Results using the visibility approach to calculate β and β_t. (a) The distance map $D_{AB}(x)$ in β is represented as grey-levels. (b) The thresholded *between* region $\beta_t = \{x,\ D_{AB}(x) < t\}$, indicating that only nearby contour portions are taken into account by this approach.

5.1 Crisp Objects

Table 1 shows some results obtained on synthetic objects illustrating different situations. The adjacent lines and distance values of the object in Table 1(a) are shown in Fig.3 (a) and (b), respectively. High values of $D_{AB}(x)$ correctly indicate image regions where the shapes are locally far from each other.

In the example of Table 1(a), the two objects can be considered as along each other, leading to high values of α_1, α_2 and α_4. However some parts of the objects are closer to each other than other parts. When the distance increases, the corresponding parts can hardly be considered as along each other. This is

Table 2. *Alongness* values for different shape configurations (brain structures from medical imaging) with parameters $a = 0.25$ and $t = 10$

Shapes	(a)	(b)	(c)	(d)
α_1	0.746	0.677	0.487	0.708
α_2	0.746	0.677	0.438	0.289
α_3	0.717	0.611	0.133	0.015
$\alpha_4(10)$	0.746	0.677	0.438	0.001
$\alpha_5(10)$	0.717	0.611	0.133	0.000

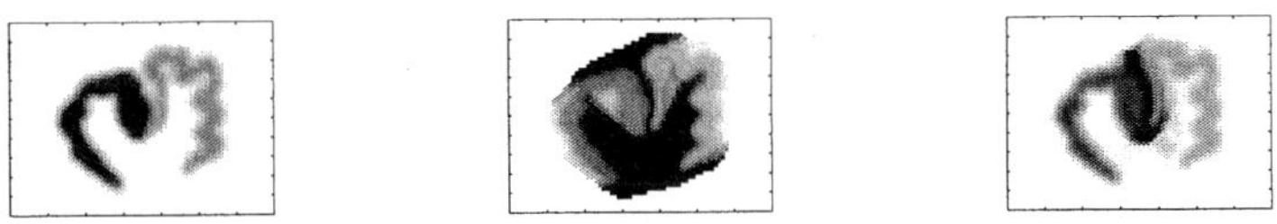

(a) (b) (c)

Fig. 5. Results using the fuzzy visibility approach to calculate β_F and β_{F_t}. (a) Original shapes. (b) Shapes and the region β_F between them. (c) Shapes and the thresholded *between* region $\beta_{F_t}(x) = \{x, D_{AB}(x) < t\}$.

well expressed by the lower values obtained for α_3 and α_5. These effects are even stronger on the example of Table 1(b) where only small parts of the objects can be considered as being along each other. The *between* regions β and β_t (i.e. thresholded) are shown in Fig.4. The third case is a typical example where the region between A and B is elongated, but not in the direction of its adjacency with A and B. This is not taken into account by α_1, while the other measures provide low values as expected: α_2 is much smaller than α_1 and the other three values are almost 0.

Table 2 shows results obtained on real objects, which are some brain structures extracted from magnetic resonance images. Similar values are obtained for all measures in the two first cases where the relation is well satisfied. The third example shows the interest of local measures and distance information (in particular the similar values obtained for α_2 and α_4 illustrate the fact that only the parts that are close to each other are actually involved in the computation of the *between* region for this example), while the last one is a case where the relation is not satisfied, which is well reflected by all measures except α_1, as expected.

5.2 Fuzzy Objects

The experiments concerning the fuzzy approach are based on the construction of synthetical fuzzy objects by a Gaussian smoothing of the crisp ones, only

(a) (b)

Fig. 6. (a) The distance map $D_{AB}(x)$ in β_F of the objects in Figure 5 (a). (b) The decreasing function g of $D_{AB}(x)$.

Table 3. *Alongness* values for different shape configurations (fuzzy synthetic shapes) with parameters $a = 0.50$ and $a_1 = 0.30$

		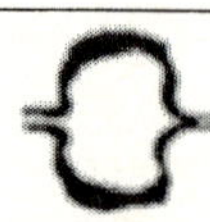	
Shapes	(a)	(b)	(c)
α_{F_1}	0.990	0.815	0.982
α_{F_2}	0.999	0.948	0.881
α_{F_3}	0.879	0.531	0.515
α_{F_4}	0.975	0.755	0.572
α_{F_5}	0.686	0.552	0.508

Table 4. *Alongness* values for different shape configurations (fuzzy brain structures from medical imaging) with parameters $a = 0.25$ and $a_1 = 0.30$

Shapes	(a)	(b)	(c)	(d)
α_{F_1}	0.996	0.997	0.980	0.997
α_{F_2}	0.984	0.965	0.972	0.971
α_{F_3}	0.888	0.840	0.675	0.536
α_{F_4}	0.812	0.764	0.781	0.544
α_{F_5}	0.675	0.643	0.579	0.503

for the sake of illustration. In real applications, fuzzy objects may be obtained from a fuzzy segmentation of the image, from imprecision at their boundaries, from partial volume effect modeling, etc. Figure 5 illustrates an example of fuzzy objects along with the *between* region and the fuzzy regions β_F and β_{F_t}. The distance map and the selected area are depicted in Figure 6.

Some results obtained on fuzzy synthetic shapes are given in Table 3, while some results on fuzzy real objects are given in Table 4. In these tables, α_{F_i} denotes the fuzzy equivalent of α_i.

Results are again in accordance with what could be intuitively expected. This illustrates the consistency of the proposed extension to fuzzy sets.

Since the computation of L, S and V in the fuzzy case is based on the support of the fuzzy objects, which is larger than the corresponding crisp objects, we have to choose a different value for the parameter a, in order to achieve a better discrimination between the different situations. However a has the same values for all objects in each table, for the sake of comparison. Note that in Table 3 as well as in Table 4, the results obtained on fuzzy synthetic and real objects are qualitatively the same as the results obtained on crisp object: in particular, α_{F_3} and α_{F_5} well reflect the distance constraint on the *alongness* degree.

6 Conclusion

We proposed in this paper an original method to model the relation *along* and to compute the degree to which this relation is satisfied between two objects of any shape. Several measures are proposed, taking into account different types of information: region between the objects, adjacency between the objects and this region, distance, parts of objects. The definitions are symmetrical by construction. They inherit some properties of the visibility method for computing the between area such as invariance under translation and rotation. Measures α_1, α_2 and α_4 are also invariant under isotropic scaling. Finally, the proposed measures fit well the intuitive meaning of the relation in a large class of situations, and provide a ranking between different situations which is consistent with the common sense. One of the advantages of the proposed approach is the decomposition of the solution in two parts, i.e. to find the region between the objects and to calculate its elongatedness. The inverse of compacity (sometimes called circularity) has been adopted to measure how elongated is the region between the shapes. This is by no means the unique way of characterizing elongatedness. In fact, if the region between the shapes becomes very complex (e.g. Fig.7), the area starts to increase fast with respect to the perimeter (i.e. space-filling property), and circularity-based measures may produce poor results. In such cases, alternative elongatedness measures may be adapted to replace circularity in our proposed approach (e.g. shape measures that characterize thinness of a shape).

Alternative approaches to the computation of length of the adjacencies and distances can be tested. We can restrict, for example, the adjacent region to the

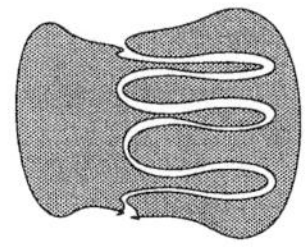

Fig. 7. Complex shapes lead to space-filling *between* region. This may affect the circularity-based elongatedness measure, thus requiring alternative approaches to evaluate how elongated is the *between* region.

watershed line of this intersection, and compute its length in a classical way. On the other hand, instead of using Equation 14, we can calculate $D_{\mu_{A \cup B}}$ with the distances to the α-cuts. The distance $d(x, \mu)$ from a point x to a fuzzy set with membership function μ can indeed be defined by integrating over α the distance from x to each α-cut. Another option is to calculate $d(x, \mu)$ as the distance of x to the support of μ, i.e. $d(x, \mu) = d(x, \mathrm{Supp}(\mu))$. These definitions are useful for implementation purposes since for each α-cut, a fast distance transform can be used.

Extensions to 3D are straightforward: the computation of the *between* relation does not make any assumption on the dimension of space; the measures of elongatedness can be simply performed by replacing lengths by surfaces and surfaces by volumes.

Future work also aims at introducing this relation as a new feature in structural pattern recognition or content-based image retrieval schemes.

References

1. Shariff, A.R., Egenhofer, M., Mark, D.: Natural-language spatial relations between linear and areal objects: The topology and metric of english-language terms. International Journal of Geographical Information Science **12**(3) (1998) 215–246
2. Crevier, D.: A probabilistic method for extracting chains of collinear segments. Computer Vision and Image Understanding **76**(1) (1999) 36–53
3. Biederman, I.: Recognition-by-components: a theory of human image understanding. Psychological Review **94**(2) (1987) 115–147
4. Hummel, J.E., Biederman, I.: Dynamic binding in a neural network for shape recognition. Psychological Review **99**(3) (1992) 480–517
5. Kosslyn, S.M., Chabris, C.F., Marsolek, C.J., Koening, O.: Categorical versus coordinate spatial relations: computational analyses and computer simulations. Journal of Experimental Psychology: Human Perception and Performance **18**(2) (1992) 562–577
6. Freeman, J.: The modelling of spatial relations. Computer Graphics and Image Processing **4** (1975) 156–171
7. Rosenfeld, A., Klette, R.: Degree of adjacency or surroundedness. Pattern Recognition **18**(2) (1985) 169–177
8. Bloch, I.: Fuzzy Spatial Relationships for Image Processing and Interpretation: A Review. Image and Vision Computing **23**(2) (2005) 89–110
9. Bloch, I., Colliot, O., Cesar-Jr., R.M.: Mathematical modeling of the relationship "between" based on morphological operators. In: ISMM 2005, Paris, France (2005) 299–308
10. Rosenfeld, A.: The fuzzy geometry of image subsets. Pattern Recognition Letters **2** (1984) 311–317

A Computational Model for Pattern and Tile Designs Classification Using Plane Symmetry Groups

José M. Valiente[1], Francisco Albert[2], and José María Gomis[2]

[1] DISCA
[2] DEGI , Universidad Politécnica de Valencia, Camino de Vera s/n, 46022 Valencia, Spain
jvalient@disca.upv.es, {fraalgi1,jmgomis}@degi.upv.es

Abstract. This paper presents a computational model for pattern analysis and classification using symmetry group theory. The model was designed to be part of an integrated management system for pattern design cataloguing and retrieval in the textile and tile industries. While another reference model [6], uses intensive image processing operations, our model is oriented to the use of graphic entities. The model starts by detecting the objects present in the initial digitized image. These objects are then transformed into Bezier curves and grouped to form motifs. The objects and motifs are compared and their symmetries are computed. Motif repetition in the pattern provides the fundamental parallelogram, the deflexion axes and rotation centres that allow us to classify the pattern according its plane symmetry group. This paper summarizes the results obtained from processing 22 pattern designs from Islamic mosaics in the Alcazar of Seville.

1 Introduction

The interest of plane symmetry group theory for the design and cataloguing of regular plane segmentations can be seen in works such as [1] or [2]. These works analyze, with mathematical and geometrical rigor, the design patterns used by the ancient Islamic handcraft workers for covering architectural surfaces and walls. In addition, these works have become a key reference for most contributions that, in the form of computer models have analyzed their pattern geometries in recent years. Most of these research works describe design pattern geometry and provide tools ,like Shape Grammars [14], for design pattern generation which are very useful in the world of Computer Graphics. However few of such works analyze pattern designs using computer vision. Nevertheless, from this perspective, there are many works on the analysis of independent symmetries, [3] [4] [5], although few works have studied symmetry groups in images. Among these works, it is worth mentioning the theoretical approaches of [4] and [5], and particularly the computational model proposed by Y. Liu, R.T. Collins and Y. Tsin [6]. This, as opposed to the model presented in this paper, works in image space and thus obtains global symmetries, with no specification of pattern objects and motifs. We have taken it as a reference model for our work.

M. Lazo and A. Sanfeliu (Eds.): CIARP 2005, LNCS 3773, pp. 849 – 860, 2005.

In this paper we propose an alternative computational model which, based on symmetry group theory [1], [2], allows the automatic analysis, decomposition and classification of the digital image of a regular design pattern. To evaluate this model's capacity to analyze historical Islamic design patterns, the authors analyze the tile patterns used in one of the most emblematic Islamic buildings in Spain: the Alcazar of Seville, built between 1364 and 1366. This palace possesses one of the largest and most beautiful patterns in Islamic Art.

2 Design Patterns and Tile Designs: Identification of PSG

Design patterns and tile designs are both the result of a systematic repetition of one given geometrical form. However, each has certain inherent characteristics [3]: in the case of a design pattern, the repeated geometrical form has no constraints, since the result is a set of independent geometrical forms more or less close to each other. In the case of tile designs, the repeated form necessarily requires a given shape to avoid gaps or overlapping. "Geometrical Form" here means what is perceived or seen, and comprises any figure, image or drawing used as unit motif to create a pattern design.

Despite these formal differences between design patterns and tile designs, their classification in terms of compositive syntax, is similar and in accordance with symmetry group theory. This theory states that any 2D pattern can be classified according to the set of geometrical transformations that transforms it into itself. Transformations that preserve distances are known as *isometries*, and the plane isometries are: rotations, translations, reflections and glide reflections. The set of isometric transformations that makes a motif coincide with itself is known as *symmetry group*. Three types or categories of symmetry groups are defined:

- **Point symmetry groups (psg)**: including cyclic and dihedral symmetry groups. The cyclic group C_n has only n-fold rotational symmetry around the center. The dihedral group D_n also includes *n* reflection axes.
- **Frieze symmetry groups (FSG)**: containing only one translational symmetry and other symmetries.
- **Plane symmetry groups (PSG) or Wallpaper groups**: containing two translational symmetries and other symmetries.

The importance of this theory lies in the fact that all design patterns and tile designs can be classified according to the FSG or PSG to which they belong. It is known that there are geometric restrictions, called '*crystallographic constraints*', which limit the number of possible rotations that can be applied to completely fill the plane or frieze [7]. Accordingly, the PSG and FSG are limited to 17 and 7 classes respectively. We only address the problem of PSG identification.

In a previous work [8] we studied the specific aspects used to identify the PSG. Following other works in the literature, we suggested that the basic information on the pattern structure resides in three features:

- **Fundamental Parallelogram (*FP*)**: the smallest part of the pattern that by replicating and displacing is able to generate the whole pattern. The FP is defined by two displacement vectors, the parallelogram sides, which can be used to locate the centre position of all motifs in the pattern. In [6] the FP is known as the *unit lattice*.

- **Design symmetries axes (*DSA*)**: the reflection or glide reflection symmetry axes of motifs present in the pattern.
- **Design rotation centers (*DRC*)**: the points around the motifs can rotate to find another repetition of themselves in the pattern. According with the crystallographic constraints above mentioned, there are a limited number of possible rotations.. The corresponding DRC or *n-fold rotation centers* are featured by an order $n = 2, 3, 4$ and 6 which indicate rotations of 180º, 120º, 90º and 60º respectively.

Thus, we propose using these three features to identify the PSG of a given pattern. Table 1 shows the strict relation between these structural descriptors and each of the 17 PSG. The first column shows standard PSG nomenclature.

Table 1. PSG classification using FP, DSA, and DRC features

PSG	FP	DSA	DRC	DSA and DRC with respect to FP
P1	S,RE, ERO,RO, P	None	None	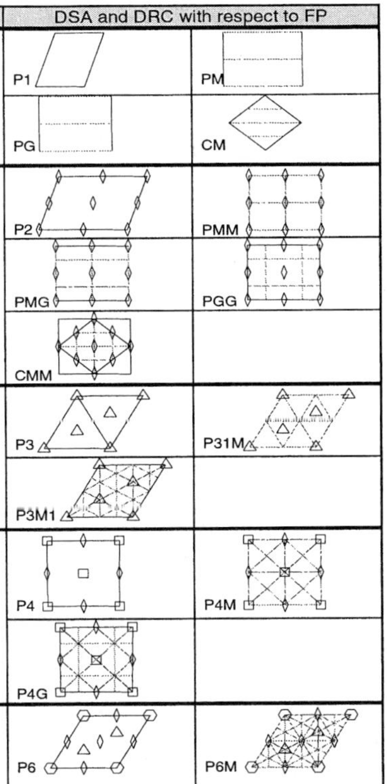
PM	S,RE	RA II FP side		
PG	S,RE	GRA II FP side		
CM	S,RO,ERO	RA II FP diag		
P2	S,RE, ERO,RO, P	None	2-fold (180º) ◊	
PMM	S,RE	RA II FP sides		
PMG	S,RE	GRA II FP side RA II 2nd FP side		
PGG	S,RE	GRA II FP sides		
CMM	S, RO,ROE	RA II FP diag. RA II FP 2nd diag.		
P3	ERO	None	3-fold (120º) △	
P31M	ERO	RA II FP sides RA II FP diag.		
P3M1	ERO	RA _I_ FP sides RA II FP diag,		
P4	S	None	4-fold (90º) □ 2-fold (180º) ◊	
P4M	S	RA II FP sides RA II FP diags		
P4G	S	GRA II FP sides RA II FP diags		
P6	ERO	None	6-fold (60º) ⬡	
P6M	ERO	RA II FP sides RA II FP diags RA _I_ FP sides	3-fold (120º) 2-fold (180º)	
FP = parallelogram (P), square (S), rhombus (RO), rectangle (RE) and equilateral rhombus (ERO)				DSA = reflection axe (RA), glide reflection axe (GRA)

3 A Reference Computational Model

As mentioned above, Y. Liu, R.T. Collins and Y. Tsin have recently proposed a computational model (afterwards **LCT** Model) for periodic pattern perception based on crystallographic group theory [6]. LCT Model input is the image containing 1D or 2D periodic pattern. LCT outputs are the frieze or wallpaper group the image belongs to and its median tile. Figure 1 shows a scheme of the main LCT components.

The model has four main stages: (i) Lattice detection, which is the extraction of two linearly independent vectors that describe the translational symmetry of the pattern. (ii) Median tile, which is a representative tile extracted using the median of pixels in all tile-shaped regions formed by the lattice. (iii) Test symmetries, which extract the rotation and reflection symmetries in the pattern. (iv) Classification, which classifies the pattern in one of the 17 wallpaper or 7 frieze symmetry groups.

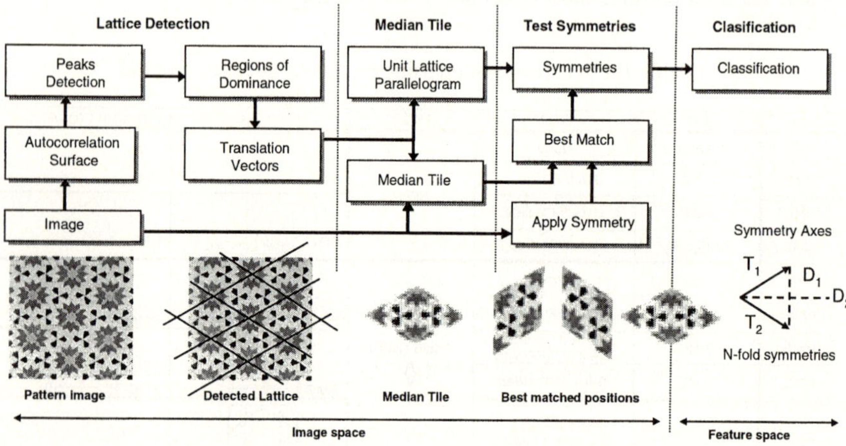

Fig. 1. A schematic workflow of the computational model reported in [6]

To prove this computational model, several synthetic and real-world pattern samples were used. The problems arise from two main causes. Firstly, real-world patterns are very noisy so they depart from ideal frieze or wallpaper patterns. Secondly, symmetry groups have hierarchical relationships among themselves, so they are not mutually exclusive classes. That means a given pattern can be classified in several symmetry groups. To address these problems, the authors propose a modified version of their computational model that uses a measurement of symmetry group distances and Geometric AIC (*Akaike Information Criterion*) [13]. The result is a very robust and successful algorithm only limited by practical issues, such as the use of distorted or damaged samples from the real world.

It is significant that most of the task proposed by the model is performed in the image space using pixel values. Only in the last stage are feature vectors (symmetry scores or group distances) used to classify the pattern. All the other stages require an intensive use of bitmap manipulations, with the subsequent computational requirements.

4 The Proposed Computational Model

We propose an alternative to the LCT model that, with the same aim and scope, attempts to approach the problem from the point of view of the graphic world, rather

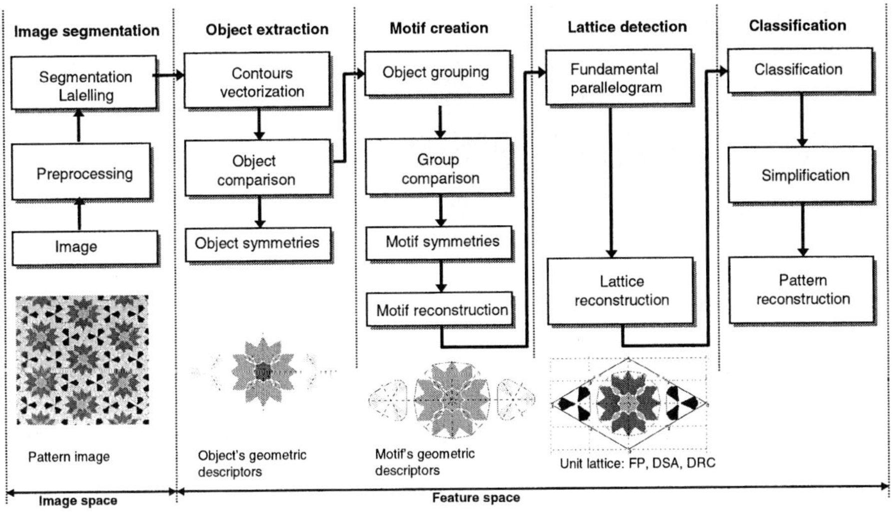

Fig. 2. Main components of the proposed computational model

than the image world. Figure 2 shows a scheme of proposed model's main components.

The underlying idea of our proposal is to reverse the typical process of producing a pattern in contexts such as ceramics, textile or graphic arts. In these contexts, the artist or graphic designer creates graphical entities or motifs using state of the art computer and acquisition tools. Then, they combine these motifs, regularly repeating them using geometric transformations, filling a flat area and producing the pattern design. Similarly, tiling can be produced including the motif inside a tile, with defined geometric form, and repeating the tiles with no gaps or overlapping. As indicated before, only a subset of geometric transformations is possible, as dictated by Symmetry Group Theory.

We propose extracting the motifs from the pattern image in the form of graphic entities, and using these entities to perform most of the work, such as computing geometric features, unit lattice or placement rules and, finally, to classify the pattern according to the symmetry group. In the process, we obtain many graphic objects, in parametric forms, such as Bezier curves or B-splines, which can be stored for later use in re-design tasks.

With this aim, we propose a computational model which has five main stages, depending on the feature space used to represent the data in each case. Below we briefly explain each stage:

Step 1. Image Segmentation. In this first stage the image is acquired and preprocessed to reduce noise and enhance its quality. Then, a colour segmentation algorithm is applied to decompose the image in homogeneous regions differentiated by colour or texture attributes. In [9] we proposed the use of CIE Luv colour spaces and clustering algorithms such as Mean-Shift or K-Means for this purpose. The output is again an image but each region (object) has been properly labelled with an index that differentiates it from the other regions and from the background.

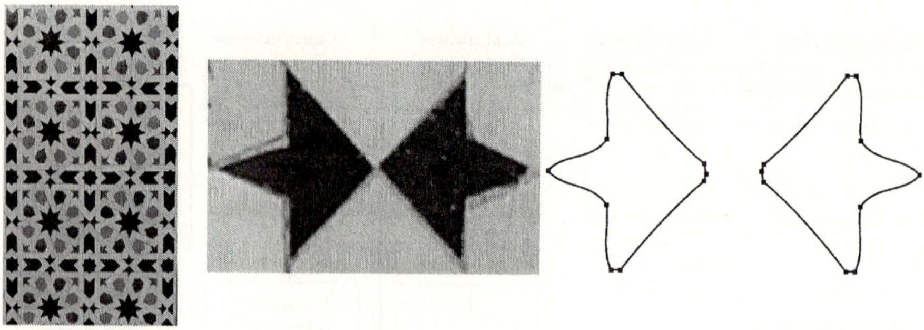

Fig. 3. Illustrative image of a historical tile design (left), detail (centre) and vectorization result (right) showing the Bezier curve nodes.

Step 2. Object Extraction. Using the labelled image as input, a vector data structure is generated. It is formed by a list of objects -which will constitute the output data-, each one of which contains a number of properties (colour, area, etc) and a list of contours (an external one and any number –zero included– of internal contours) that delimit the object's region. The contours are formed by a piece-wise sequence of Bezier curves arranged cyclically. Figure 3 (right) shows the vectorized objects found in the detail of figure 3 (centre). Within this stage there are three clearly differentiated phases:

- *Contour vectorization [10]*: The stage begins with a piecewise primitive approximation of the object contours using Bezier curves, by means of a two pass process: first, to obtain the border pixels sequence with a contour retrieval algorithm, and then, breaking down the point sequence into sub-sequences that are approximated by Bezier curves using a least-square method. This representation is more manageable and compact and allows scale invariance.
- *Object comparison:* The second sub-stage is an object comparison that attempts to obtain similar objects repeated in the image. Each set of similar objects is referred to as an 'object class'. Object comparison is limited to the external contour. To compare contours we use a more manageable feature called normalized signature, which is a representation of a fixed number of re-sampled contour points. The normalized signatures are translation and scale invariant. In [11] we describe the geometric symmetries that can be computed using signatures (reflection, rotations and shifts), and a dissimilarity measure that allows us to compare two contours. The proposed comparison method can indicate if both objects are similar (they do not exceed the similarity threshold), and the geometric transformation which links them. Figure 4 shows an example of object comparison where similar objects are drawn with the same color.
- *Object symmetries*: By comparing one object with itself we obtain its circular or reflected symmetry axis

Step 3. Motif Creation. A motif is a set of objects that are related by perceptual features. They are what humans first detect on visual analysis of a pattern. Even though the use of motifs to perform the PSG classification is not mandatory, we think that these entities provide us with a greater degree of abstraction and allow us to simplify the processing. In addition, they are the valuable graphic entities that users want to recover from a pattern to use in re-design tasks. This could be one of the most interesting contributions of this work.

Using the data structure with the list of objects as input, we can generate a list of groups or motifs, each represented by a number of related objects and a contour (minimal convex polygon that includes such objects). Figure 4 shows an example of object grouping and motif creation. This stage is similar to object extraction, in that first the working units (objects / motifs) are obtained and then compared, although the procedures used are very different:

- *Object grouping*: The related objects are grouped using perceptual criteria (inclusion, contact, co-circularity, co-linearity and overlapping).
- *Group comparison*: The comparison is done at two levels, first it is checked that the groups (motifs) contain a certain percentage of similar objects, and then the transformations relating the objects to the two motifs are compared (displacements, rotations or symmetries). The presence of a predominant transformation indicates that both motifs are formed by similar objects that are equally distributed inside the motif they belong to. Such motifs are considered to be similar, even if there are some disjoint objects, and they are sub-classified as the same class. It is very common for incomplete motifs (in the borders of the image) or motifs with gaps to appear.
- *Motif symmetries:* Global motif symmetries are obtained by comparing the symmetry axes and rotation centres of the objects in each motif class.

Fig. 4. Object comparison (left), motif creation (centre) and final classification (right) showing the fundamental parallelogram (black square), the symmetry axes (broken lines) and the rotation centres (circles)

- *Motif reconstruction:* This is the first moment at which we have enough information to start correcting errors. This correction, or *reconstruction*, covers two different aspects: (i) *Restitution,* which restores missing objects to a motif by bringing them from another motif in the same class and, (ii) *unification,* which unifies different objects located in the same position in their respective class. In [12] we introduced a set of rules to perform these tasks.

Step 4. Lattice Detection. In this stage we obtain the translational symmetry of the pattern. Two operations are carried out:

- *Fundamental parallelogram*: There are motifs in each class related by displacements. We obtain the two unique displacement vectors that, through linear combinations, make them to coincide. These two vectors act as the basis of the vector space defined by the positions of similar motifs. As usually there are several motifs there will be several bases, so we will choose the one with an n-times area, since pattern repeatability is that of the less frequently repeated elements. Such vectors form two sides of the Fundamental Parallelogram or unit lattice: the smallest part able to generate the whole pattern by replicating and displacing.
- *Lattice reconstruction [12]*: While in the case of motif reconstruction we worked with loose objects, now we work with complete motifs. The repetition of fundamental parallelograms will form a mesh where all the motifs located in the same relative position within each mesh cell must be equal. If they are not, we remove some and replicate others to unify the pattern.

Step 5. Classification. In this last stage we perform the whole PSG classification. The operations in this stage are the following:

- *Classification*: Considering the geometry of the FP, the symmetry axes and the rotation centres, the FP is classified in accordance with Table 1.
- *Simplification*: The pattern is simplified, since the content of the FP and its PSG will suffice to define the whole pattern; therefore we can suppress all redundant information without decomposing any objects or motifs.
- *Pattern reconstruction [12]*: Once the plane symmetry group has become available, the defects can be corrected since the reflections and rotations involve the content of the motifs and even the object regions. For this purpose we check that all the objects or motifs related by symmetry axes or rotation centres are equal and following the correct orientation; otherwise, we choose the best alternatives (those which fulfil the symmetry criterion) and any incorrect ones are replaced.

Figure 4 (right) shows the analysis result for the pattern in Figure 3 (left). Only the motifs contained in the FP have been left, without dividing any of them.

5 Experiments and Results

To validate the proposed methodology we have successfully used 22 different tiling patterns, with repetition in two plane directions, from the mosaic collection of Pedro I's Palace in the Alcazar of Seville (Spain). Figure 5 shows an example of such mosaics. Two problems arise: the first one is related to the historical nature of these tiles which were made in the 14th century using handcraft techniques. Consequently, there are inaccuracies in the position and finish of the mosaic tiles. The second problem is the use of a tile design technique widely extended in Islamic decoration of that period, known as "*lacería*" or "*interlace*" (Figure 5 right). They can be defined as figures, built from regular polygons or stars, developed in the form of a band that extend its sides in such a way that they alternatively cross each other, generating a composition of artistically arranged loops.

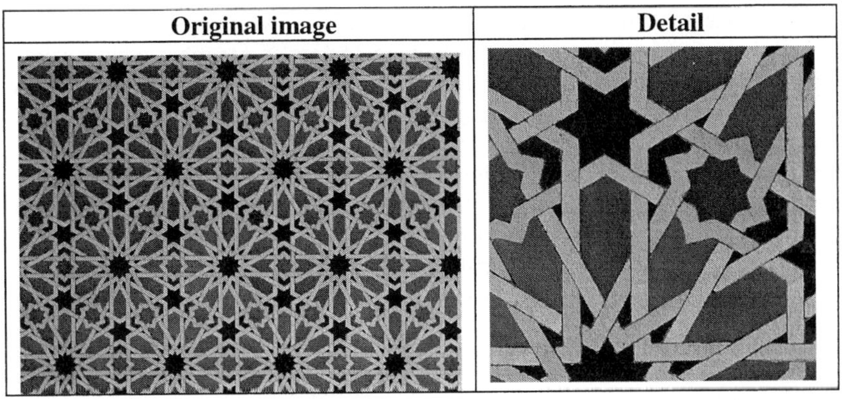

Fig. 5. Original image (left) and detail (right) from a mosaic of the Alcazar of Seville

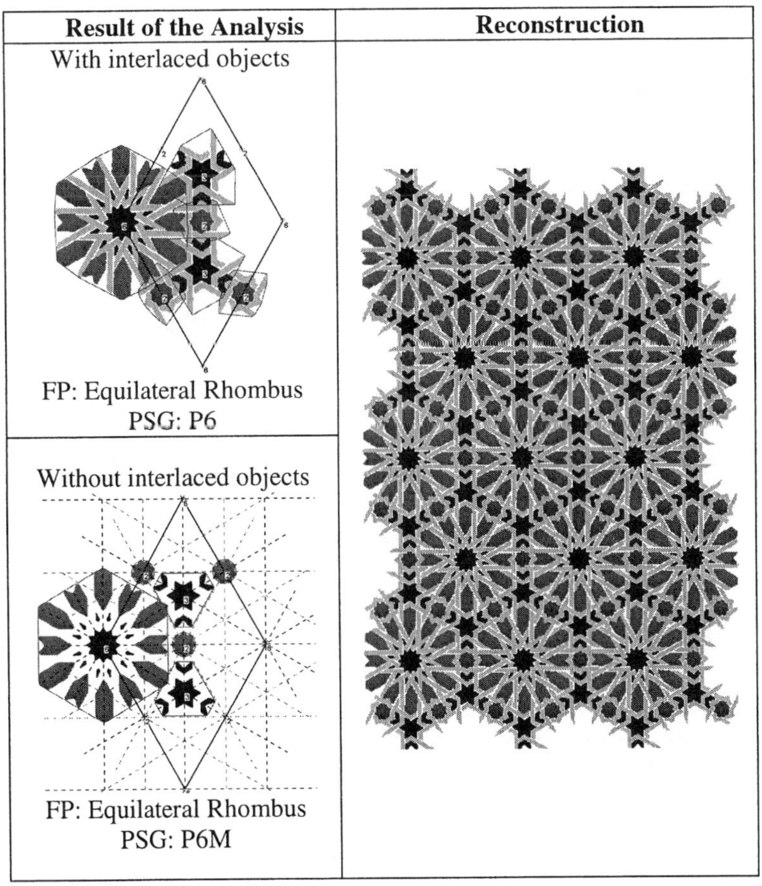

Fig. 6. Simplified result of the analysis (left) with interlaced objects (up) and without them (down), and pattern reconstruction (right) of the original mosaic in figure 5

The treatment of the *lacerias* was twofold. Firstly we increased the color tolerances of the segmentation operator achieving fusion of *lacerias,* which were then considered as background. And secondly, we reduced the color tolerances in such a way that *lacerias* appeared as independent objects. Figure 6 shows the results obtained in both cases. The upper image is the simplified result of the analysis considering all the objects of the pattern, while the lower image is the result without considering the interlaced objects. The fact that the interlaced objects are always arranged circularly, without symmetry axes common to all of them, makes Plane Symmetry Group different in both cases. The image on the right shows the pattern reconstruction from the simplified analysis with interlaced objects, by repetition and displacement using the FP directions.

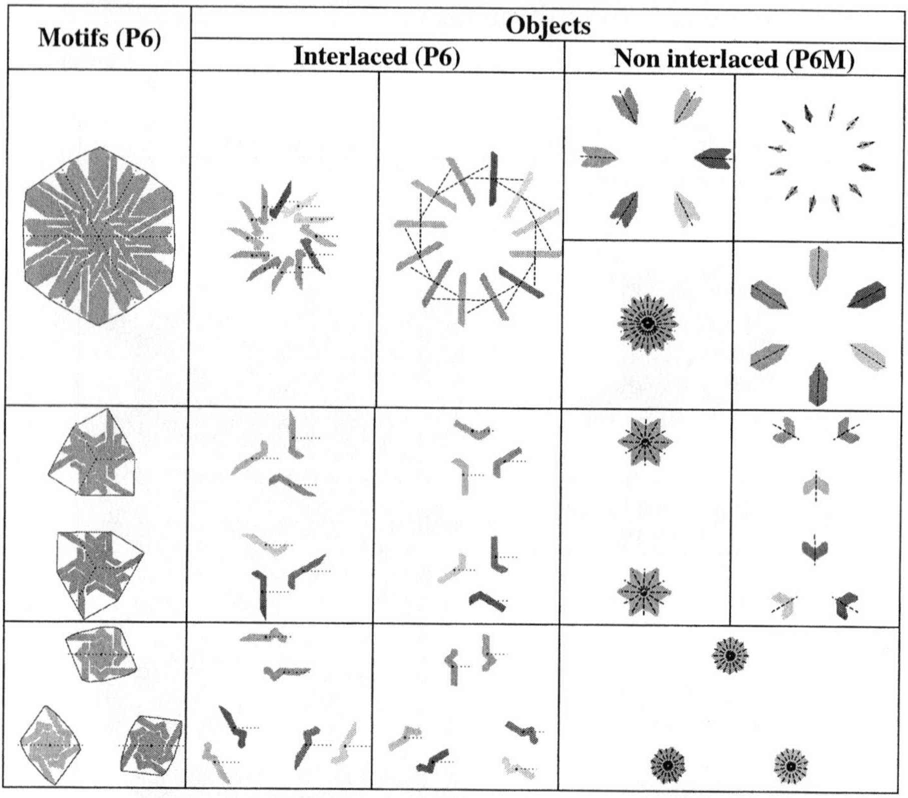

Fig. 7. Motifs and objects obtained after simplification. The interlaced objects have been separated from the rest. Symmetry axes are represented with a dashed black line and different orientations are showed by different colours.

Finally, Figure 7 shows the main motifs and their objects obtained from the analysis, including all symmetry axes. As this figure shows, the interlaced objects either do not have symmetry axes, or they are not common to all, while the other objects have symmetry axes and are common to all, so that the Plane Symmetry Groups of each type of objects, have the same PF and rotation centers, but one has symmetry axes

(P6M) and the other does not (P6). The motifs that contain the interlaced objects have the less restrictive PSG, which is P6.

The experiments show that this computational model satisfactorily reached its objectives with most of the processed images. In some cases, the user must tune system parameters to obtain a correct classification. Figure 8 summarizes the results obtained showing the obtained PSG for the two possible classifications. Observe the high number of P4-P4M tile designs in this kind of mosaics.

Typical processing time is presented in Table 2. In the segmentation stage the time depends on the image size but, in the other stages, it depends heavily on the number of existing objects, (motifs) and their complexity, with the longest time requirement for processing the tiles with interlaced objects.

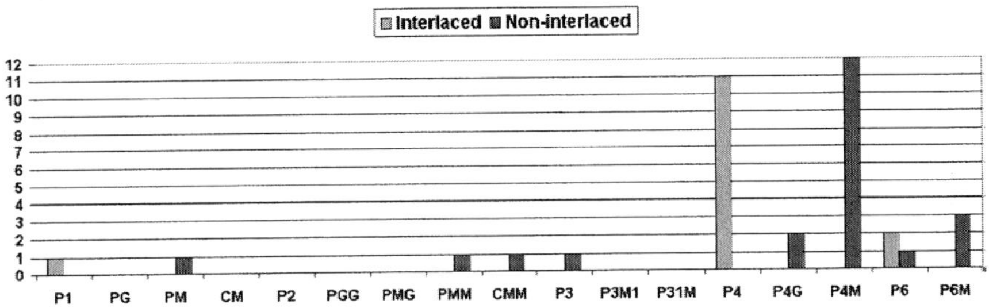

Fig. 8. Number of patterns in each PSG with and without considering interlaced objects

Table 2. Processing time for several examples on a Pentium III 450 MHz computer

	Minimum	Median	Maximum
Time	24''	1'10''	4'26''
Image size	3264x2448	3264x2448	3264x2448
Number of objects	54	162	699

6 Conclusions

This paper presents a computational model for analyzing periodic design patterns. The successful results obtained after analysis of tiling design patterns in the Alcazar of Seville are also reported. The main findings can be summarized as follows:

- All the tiling patterns used were successfully classified. Their structures (fundamental parallelogram and plane symmetry group) and elements (objects and motifs) were obtained in the form of graphic entities.
- The problems derived from the use of interlaced objects in most of the tiles analyzed were solved. From the data obtained, we can conclude that in the case of interlace tile design patterns it is advisable to provide the two possible classifications rather than their more generic classification (without symmetry axes).
- Compression ratios up to 1:1000, with respect to the original image in jpeg format, were obtained. The pattern structure was reduced to its fundamental parallelogram geometry and content and one object/motif per class.

The proposed computational model behaves perfectly with all the mosaic samples used and its output data represents a meaningful and compact design description of the original pattern. This data reduction is very convenient for storing and retrieval purposes in information systems, which are a current issue in the ceramic and textile industries.

Acknowledgements

This paper has received the support of the Spanish Ministry for Science and Technology and the European Union (Project DPI2001-2713). This work has been possible thanks to the collaboration of the *Real Alcázar of Seville* foundation.

References

1. Schattschneider, D. The Plane Symmetry Groups: Their Recognition and Notation. *The American Mathematical Monthly*, vol. 85, pp. 439-450, 1978.
2. Grünbaum, B., Shephard, G.C. *Tilings and Patterns*, W. H. Freeman, New York, 1987.
3. Shubnikov, A. V.; Koptsik, V. A. *Symmetry in Science and Art*, Plenum Press, New York, 1974.
4. Atallah, J.M. "On Symmetry Detection", *IEEE Transactions on Computers*, C-34, pp. 663-666, 1985.
5. Dinggang, S., Ip, H.S.H, Cheung, K.T.K.; T.E. Khwang. Symmetry Detection by Generalized Complex (GC) Moments: A Close-Form Solution, *IEEE Transactions on Pattern Analysis and Machine Intelligence*, vol. 21, pp. 466- 476, 1999.
6. Y. Liu, Y.; Collins, R.T. and Tsin, Y. A Computational Model for Periodic Pattern Perception Based on Frieze and Wallpaper Groups, *IEEE Trans. Pattern Analysis and Machine Intelligence*, vol. 26, no. 3, pp. 354-371, Mar. 2004.
7. Horne C. E. *Geometric Symmetry in Patterns and Tilings*. Woodhead Publishing. Abington Hall, England, 1st edition (2000)
8. Valiente J.M.; Albert, F.; Carretero M. and Gomis J.M.: Structural Description of Textile and Tile Pattern Designs Using Image Processing, *Proceedings of the 17th International Conference on Pattern Recognition (ICPR 2004), IEEE Computer Society Press*, Cambridge (England), Aug. 2004.
9. Valiente, J.M.; Agustí, M.; Gomis, J.M. and Carretero, M.: Estudio de técnicas de segmentación de imágenes en color aplicadas al diseño textil, *Proceedings of the XIII International Congress of Graphics Engineering*, Badajoz (Spain), June 2001.
10. Albert, F.; Gomis, J.M.; Valor, M; Valiente, J.M. and Carretero,M. Análisis estructural de motivos decorativos en diseño textil, *Proceedings of the XIII International Congress of Graphics Engineering*, Badajoz (Spain), June 2001.
11. Van Otterloo, P.J. *A contour-oriented approach to shape analysis*, Prentice-Hall International, 1991.
12. Albert, F., Gomis, J.M.; Valiente, J.M. Reconstruction Techniques in the Image Analysis of Islamic Mosaics from the Alhambra, *Proceedings of the 2004 Computer Graphics International (CGI 2004), IEEE Computer Society Press*, Heraklion, Crete (Grecian), 2004.
13. Kanatane, K. Comments on Symmetry as a Continuous Feature, *IEEE Transactions on Pattern Analysis and Machine Intelligence*, vol. 19, no. 3, pp. 246-247, March 1997.
14. Shape Grammars. http://www.shapegrammar.org/intro.html

Spectral Patterns for the Generation of Unidirectional Irregular Waves

Luis Pastor Sanchez Fernandez[1], Roberto Herrera Charles[2], and Oleksiy Pogrebnyak[1]

[1] Center for Computing Research, National Polytechnic Institute,
Av. Juan de Dios Batiz s/n casi esq, Miguel Othon de Mendizabal, Col. Nueva Industrial,
Vallejo. CP 07738. Mexico City, Mexico
{lsanchez, olek}@cic.ipn.mx
[2] Research and Development Center of Digital Technology,
Tijuana, Baja California, C.P. 22510, Mexico
charles@cic.ipn.mx

Abstract. The wave is a complex and important phenomenon for structures designs in the coastal zones and beaches. This paper presents a novel system for the generation of spectral patterns of unidirectional irregular waves in research laboratories. The system's control basic elements are a linear motor, a servo controller and a personal computer. The used main mathematical tools are a feed forward neural network, digital signal processing and statistical analysis. The research aim is to obtain a system of more accuracy and small response time. This behavior is interpreted, in marine hydraulics, as a fast calibration of experiments. The wave power spectrums are generated in a test channel of rectangular section with dimensions: length 12 m; depth 40 cm; width 30 cm.

1 Introduction

The design of coastal and maritime works is complex. The wave is a main element and its mathematical representation is difficult [1], [2]. The mathematical models make possible to represent the sea disturbance and to calculate its effects, although in many cases, they need a calibration by means of physical modeling on reduced scale [3], [4], [5], [6], [7]. In complex maritime work designs, the physical modeling on reduced scale is essential. This paper presents a system for the generation of spectral patterns of unidirectional irregular waves, in project and research laboratories. The system main elements are digital signal processing, neural network and linear motor.

The research aim is to obtain a system of easy operation and greater efficiency with respect to traditional methods. The traditional methods make a control of open loop and the operator has a fundamental function. In this work, we used a combined neural control [8], [9], [10] that makes shorter the transitory response. This behavior is interpreted, in marine hydraulics, as a fast calibration. In addition, the spectral patterns of the generated wave will have small errors with respect to the reference spectral patterns.

M. Lazo and A. Sanfeliu (Eds.): CIARP 2005, LNCS 3773, pp. 861 – 868, 2005.

2 Technical Support and Schemes of Operation

Fig.1 presents the combined neural control to generate spectral patterns of irregular unidirectional wave, where:

S_T : Target spectrum; S_G : Generated spectrum.

The controlled process is a wave channel and the control final element is a generator formed by a linear motor and a paddle device (see photo in fig 2).

A linear motor [11] is a type of electric motor, an induction motor in which the fixed stator and moving armature are straight and parallel to each other (rather than being circular and one inside the other as in an ordinary induction motor). Linear motors are used, for example, in power sliding doors. There is a magnetic force between the stator and armature; this force has been used to support a vehicle, as in the experimental maglev linear motor train [12].

A controller PI (proportional-integral) and an inverse neural network (INN) form the combined control.

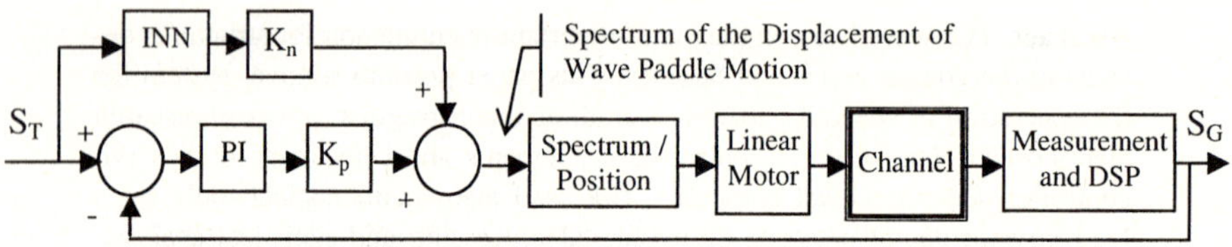

Fig. 1. Combined neural control to generate spectral patterns of irregular unidirectional wave

Fig. 2. Linear motor with paddle device and a channel of irregular and unidirectional wave

3 Wave Generation Theory

Eq. (1) is basic for the spectral analysis of a registry of irregular wave in a fixed station, and this defines the spectral density function *S(f)* [2].

$$\sum_{f}^{f+df} \frac{1}{2} a_n^2 = S(f)df \tag{1}$$

This equation, nevertheless, contains an infinite number of amplitudes a_n of components of the waves and, therefore, is not applicable to practical calculation. For the practical analysis, a wave registry of N points is acquired, with a constant sampling period: $\eta(\Delta t)$, $\eta(2\Delta t)$,…$\eta(N\Delta t)$. Analyzing the harmonics of the wave profile $\eta(t)$, the profile can be expressed as the well-known finite Fourier series [2], [13]:

$$\eta(t) = \frac{A_0}{2} + \sum_{k=1}^{N/2-1} (A_k \cos(\frac{2\pi k}{N} t_*) + B_k \sin(\frac{2\pi k}{N} t_*)) + \frac{A_{N/2}}{2} \cos(\pi t_*) \quad (2)$$

$$t_* = t / \Delta t : t_* = 1, 2, 3, ...N$$

The wave power spectrum can be generated by two general methods: first, in discreet form, with a series of Fourier and the components of power of each harmonic. Second, in the continuous form, with the significant wave height and period and empirical equations of spectrum such as the Mitsuyasu [2], [8], Pierson and Moskowitz, JONSWAP [2], etc., for example, the spectra of wind waves fully- developed in the open sea, can be approximated by the following standard formulas:

$$S(f) = 0.257 H_{1/3}^2 T_{1/3}^{-4} f^{-5} \exp[-1.03(T_{1/3} f)^{-4}] \quad (3)$$

$$S(f) = 0.205 H_{1/3}^2 T_{1/3}^{-4} f^{-5} \exp[-0.75(T_{1/3} f)^{-4}] \quad (4)$$

where $H_{1/3}$: is the significant wave height; $T_{1/3}$: is the significant wave period; f : is the frequency.

Fig 3 presents an example of sea spectrum. The dash-dot line is the result of fitting Eq. (4) with the values of the significant wave height and period of the record. Although some difference is observed between the actual and standard spectra, partly because of the shallow water effect in the wave record which was taken at the depth of 11 m, the standard spectrum describes the features of the actual spectrum quite well.

The wave generator of mechanical type is more useful and simple and it reproduces better the wave forms. The theory of displacement of the beater (paddle) and the characteristics of the generated waves are studied by several investigators [2], [3], [4], [8].

The desired wave power spectrum is multiplied by the transfer function of the wave generator, well-known as the equation of efficiency of the paddle. This transfer function is obtained solving the differential equation for the free boundary conditions (see Eq. 5 and 6)

Piston type:

$$F(f,h) = \frac{H}{2e} = \frac{4\sinh^2(2\pi h / L)}{4\pi h / L + \sinh(4\pi h / L)} \quad (5)$$

Flap type:

$$F(f,h) = \frac{H}{2e} = (\frac{4\sinh^2(2\pi h / L)}{4\pi h / L})(\frac{1 - \cosh(2\pi h / L) + (2\pi h / L)\sinh(2\pi h / L)}{4\pi h / L + \sinh(4\pi h / L)}) \quad (6)$$

where H is the height of the produced wave in the channel; e is the amplitude of wave paddle at the mean water level; f denotes the wave frequency; L is the wavelength; h is the depth of the water at the front of the paddle in the channel.

The Inverse Fourier Transform is applied to product of Eq. (3) or Eq. (4) and Eq. (5) or Eq. (6) to obtain the wave signal in time domain. The Fig.4 presents the process of the preparation of input signal to an irregular wave generator. The control systems, in general of open loop, need a relatively great time for the calibration each experiment in order to generate a wave spectral pattern (target spectrum).

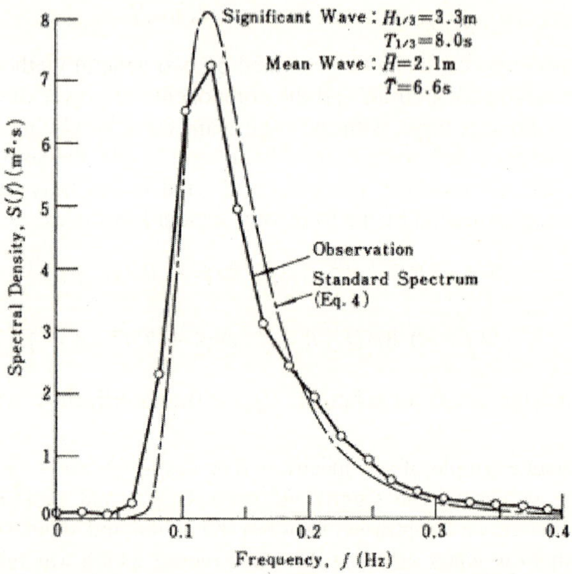

Fig. 3. Example of spectrum of sea waves

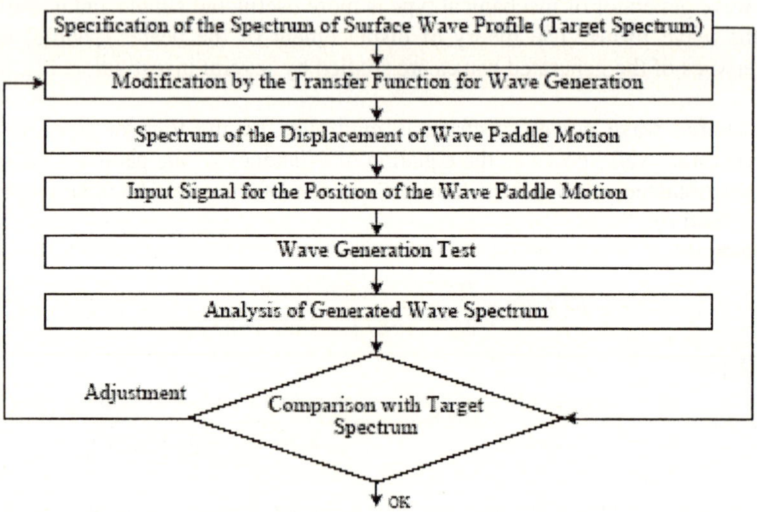

Fig. 4. Process of the preparation of input signal for an irregular wave generator

4 Feed Forward Neural Network

For identification and control systems, an artificial neural network (ANN) with three layers is adequate. A hidden layer is sufficient to identify any continuous function [10], [11], [14], [15]. The input neurons are determined by the number of frequency bands where the spectrum is divided. The tests were made with 128 and 64 inputs. The best results were obtained with 64 (training error and epochs). Another input neuron is added for the different water levels in the channel. The hidden layer uses a sigmoid function. The output layer uses a lineal function. The number of neurons of the output layer is determined by the number of frequency bands, where the generated wave spectrum will be divided (the number of output neurons were taken equal to the number of input neurons).

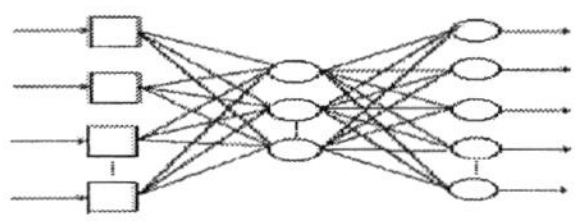

Fig. 5. Neural network topology

4.1 Training Patterns

P^{μ} : Input patterns [f(1), f(2),........f(nf), h]

T_0^{μ} : Output patterns [$f_o(1)$, $f_o(2)$,........$f_o(nf)$]

where f: power spectrum harmonics; h: channel level

Quality factor in spectrum estimation:
Generally, the sea disturbance is simulated by a random (pseudorandom) process. The variability of the sea disturbance spectrum is given by:

$$\hat{S}(f) = S(f)\chi_2^2 \tag{7}$$

The variability of the spectrum is determined by the chi-square distribution with two degrees of freedom, that is the estimation by the periodogram method [2]. In order to reduce the variation, the temporary registry of the wave measurement is divided in a set of M windows. The training patterns for neural network are obtained according to the scheme in Fig. 6.

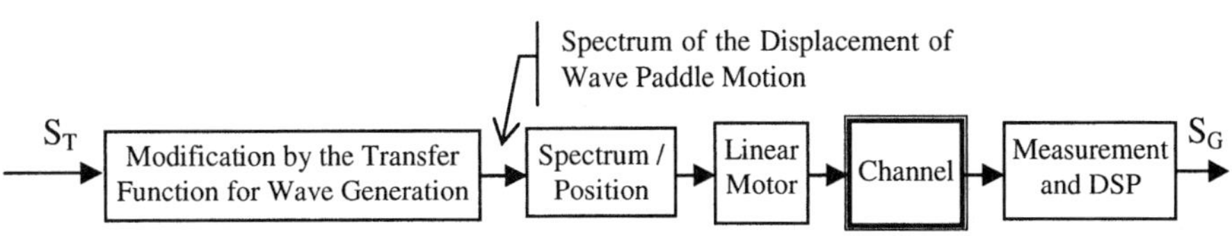

Fig. 6. Acquisition scheme for the neural network training patterns

4.1.1 Patterns and Neural Control Versus Open Loop Control

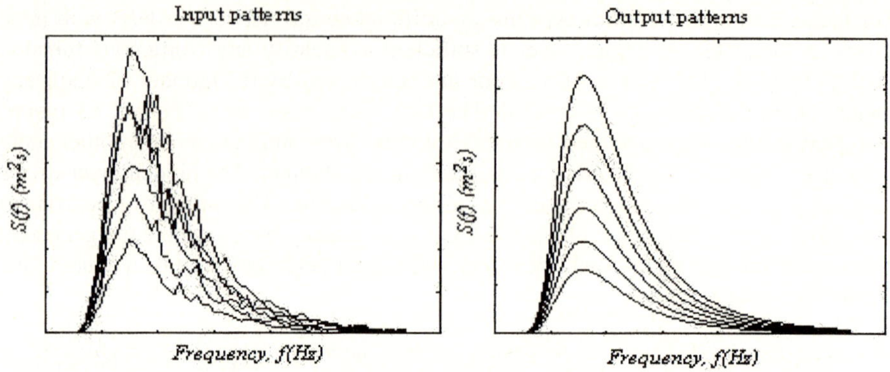

Fig. 7. Example of Patterns .Training performance is 6.97697e^{-10}, Goal is 1e^{-10}. Epochs: 25.

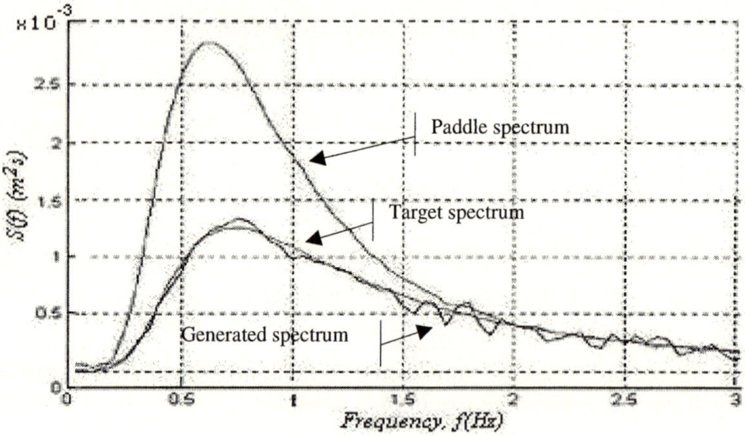

Fig. 8. Example of neural control performance

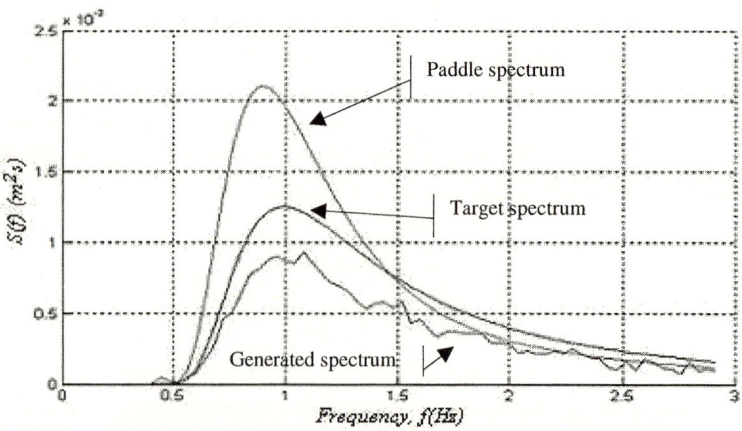

Fig. 9. Example of open loop control performance

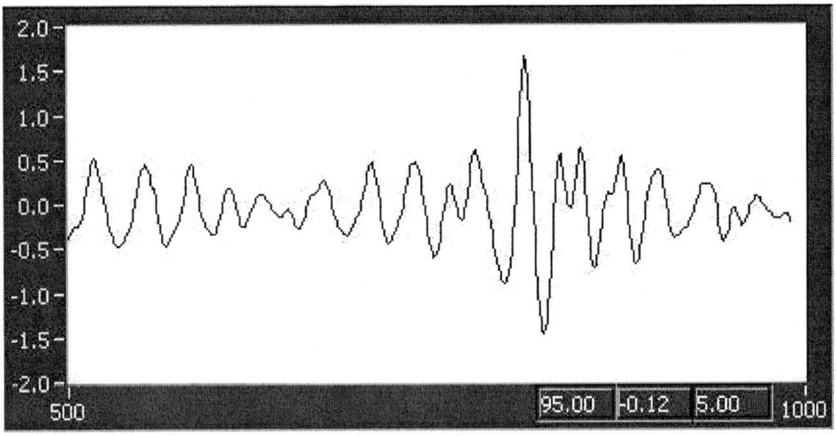

Fig. 10. Example of irregular wave profile. Axis X: samples; Axis Y: water level in cm.

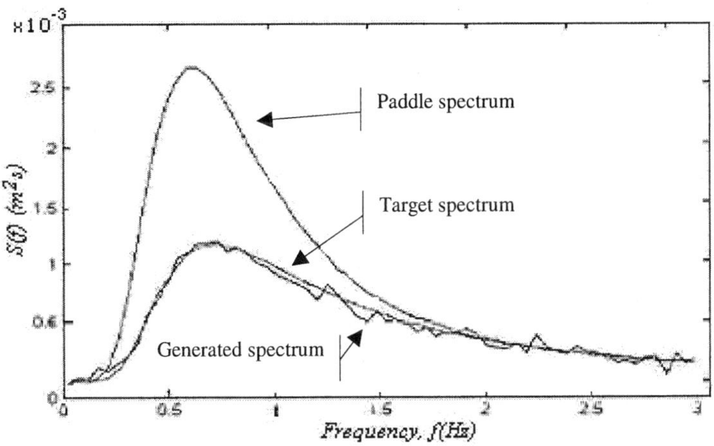

Fig. 11. Neural control performance for the irregular wave profile in Fig. 10

5 Conclusions and Future Work

The coastal and maritime work are complex and highly expensive. The optimal design requires the physical modeling. The sea phenomena are reproduced in the hydraulic research laboratories, this way, the designs can be tested. This works include "pedraplenes", oil platforms, artificial beaches, protective installations of the coasts, conservation of the ecosystem, etc.

The presented work on the spectral patterns for the generation of unidirectional irregular waves creates a novel method that uses linear motors and neural networks to generate irregular wave with high accuracy and fast calibration, obtaining satisfactory results. The combined neural control allows to generate spectrums more exact than the spectrums generated with conventional systems (open-loop control). The system does not require an expert operator in "experiments calibration". The linear motors reduce the mechanical facilities. The hydraulic pistons and complex electro-mechanic devices are unnecessary.

The control is made with a distributed architecture, because the linear motor has a system of independent control.

For the future work, self-learning elements will be introduced. These elements will make possible to create spectral patterns during the operation of the system and to suggest a new training of the neural network, when the conditions of channel operation have large changes.

References

1. Goda, Y. *"Numerical Experiments on Wave Statistics with Spectral Simulation"* Report 9-3 Port and Harbor Research Institute, 1970. pp-197.
2. Goda, Y. *Random Seas and Design of Maritime Structures.* Scientific World, 2000.
3. Bell, Paul S. Shallow water bathymetry derived from an analysis of X-band marine radar images of wave, *Coastal Engineering. Vol. 37* No.3-4. 1999, pp 513-527.
4. Bretschneider, C.L. 1973. *Deep water wave forecasting curves. En: Shore Protection Manual. U.S. Army* Coastal Engineering Research Center. 36-37.
5. Bullock, G. N. and Morton, G. J. "Performance of a Wedge-Type Absorbing Wave Maker" *Journal Waterw. Port Coastal and Ocean Eng. Div.*, ASCE, Enero, pp 1-17, 1989.
6. Carvahlo, M. M. *"Sea Wave Simulation" Recent Advances in Hidraulic Physical Modelling,* R. Martins, Ed. Kluwer Academic, Dordrecht, 1989. pp. 447-502.
7. Lizano, O., Ocampo F. J. et. al. "Evaluación de modelos numéricos de Tercera Generación para el pronóstico del oleaje en Centroamérica y MéxicoTop". *Meteor. Oceanog.*, 8(1):40-49,2001
8. Mitsuyasu H. et al. Observation of the power spectrum of Ocean Waves using a C over eaf Buoy, *JGR. J Geophysics, 1980.*
9. Hertz, J, Krogh, A, Palmer R. G. *Introduction to the Theory of Neural Computation.* Addison-Wesley Publishing Company, 1994.
10. Psaltis, D. et al. A multi layered neural network controller. *IEEE Control System Magazine, 8(3)*:17-21. Abril 1988.
11. Su C. Y. and Stepanenko, Y. Adaptive control of a class of nonlinear systems with fuzzy logic. *IEEE Trans, Fuzzy Systems Vol 2 No. 4* pp. 285-294. 1994.
12. Alter D. M. and Tsao T. C. Control of linear motors for machines tool feed: design and implementation of optimal feedback control, ASME Journal of Dynamics system, Measurement and Control, Vol. 118, 1996. pp649-656.
13. Oppenheim, A.V., Schafer, R.W. and Buck, J.R., *Discrete-Time Signal Processing*, 2nd Edition. Prentice-Hall Int. Ed. 1999.
14. Barrientos, Antonio et. al. *Control de Sistemas Continuos*. McGraw-Hill, España. 1996.
15. Liaw, C. and Cheng, S.. Fuzzy two-degrees-of-freedom speed controller for motor drives. *IEEE Transaction on Industrial Electronics, Vol. 42. No 2,* pp. 209-216. 1996.

Recognition of Note Onsets in Digital Music Using Semitone Bands

Antonio Pertusa[1], Anssi Klapuri[2], and José M. Iñesta[1]

[1] Departamento de Lenguajes y Sistemas Informáticos,
Universidad de Alicante, Spain
{pertusa, inesta}@dlsi.ua.es
[2] Signal Processing Laboratory,
Tampere University of Technology, Finland
klap@cs.tut.fi

Abstract. A simple note onset detection system for music is presented in this work. To detect onsets, a 1/12 octave filterbank is simulated in the frequency domain and the band derivatives in time are considered. The first harmonics of a tuned instrument are close to the center frequency of these bands and, in most instruments, these harmonics are those with the highest amplitudes. The goal of this work is to make a musically motivated system which is sensitive on onsets in music but robust against the spectrum variations that occur at times that do not represent onsets. Therefore, the system tries to find semitone variations, which correspond to note onsets. Promising results are presented for this real time onset detection system.

1 Introduction

Onset detection refers to the detection of the beginnings of discrete events in an audio signal. It is an essential component of many systems such as rhythm tracking and transcription schemes. There have been many different approaches for onset detection, but it still remains an open problem.

For detecting the beginnings of the notes in a musical signal the presented system analyses the spectrum information across 1/12 octave (one semitone) bands and compute their relative differences in time to obtain a detection function. Finally, the peaks in this function that are over a threshold are considered as onsets.

There are several onset detection systems that apply a pre-processing stage by separating the signal into multiple frequency bands. In an onset detector introduced by Klapuri [1], a perceptually motivated filter-bank is used, dividing the signal into eight bands. Goto [2] slices the spectrogram into spectrum strips [3]. Scheirer [4] uses a six band filter-bank and Duxbury *et al* [5] utilizes a filterbank to separate the signal into five bands.

M. Lazo and A. Sanfeliu (Eds.): CIARP 2005, LNCS 3773, pp. 869–879, 2005.

In the well-tempered scale, the one used in western music, the first harmonics[1] of the tuned instrument notes are close to the center frequencies of the 1/12 octave bands. In most instruments these first harmonics are those with the highest amplitudes.

It is not our aim to use a perceptually motivated approach. Instead, a musically motivated filter-bank is utilized. In music, notes are separated by semitones, so it makes sense to use a semitone filterbank to detect their onsets. By using semitone bands the effect of subtle spectrum variations produced during the sustain and release stage of a note is minimized. While a note is sounding, those variations mainly occur close to the center frequencies of the 1/12 octave bands. This means that the output band values for a note will remain similar after its attack, avoiding false positive onsets. And when a new note of a tuned instrument begins, the output band values will increase significantly because the the main energy of its harmonics will be concentrated in the center frequencies of the semitone bands. This means that the system is specially sensitive to frequency variations that are larger than one semitone.

This way, the spectrum variations produced at the beginning of the notes are emphasized and those produced while the notes are sounding are minimized. This makes the system robust against smooth vibratos that are not higher than a semitone. It also has a special feature; if a pitch bend (*glissando*) occurs, a new onset is usually detected when it reaches more than one quarter tone higher or lower than the starting pitch. This kind of detector can be useful for some music transcription systems, those that have the pitch units measured in semitones.

2 Input Data

2.1 Spectral Analysis

From a digital audio file a short-time Fourier transform (STFT) is computed, providing its spectrogram. In order to remove unused frequency components and increasing spectral resolution downsampling from 44,100 Hz to 22,050 Hz sampling rate was done. Thus, the highest possible frequency is $f_s/2 = 11{,}025$ Hz, which is high enough to cover the range of useful pitches.

The STFT is calculated using a Hanning window with $N = 2048$ samples. An overlapping percentage of 50% ($O = 0.5$) is also applied in order to retain the information at the frame boundaries. The time resolution Δt can be calculated as:

$$\Delta t = \frac{(1-O)N}{f_s} \quad . \tag{1}$$

Therefore, with the parameter values described, Eq. 1 yields $\Delta t = 46.4$ milliseconds and the STFT provides 1024 frequency values with a spectral resolu-

[1] A "partial" is any of the frequencies in a spectrum, being "harmonic" those multiples of a privileged frequency called fundamental that provides the pitch of the sounding note.

tion of 10.77 Hz. Concert piano frequencies range from $G\sharp_{-1}$ (27.5 Hz) to C_7 (4186 Hz). We want to use 1/12 octave bands. The band centered in pitch $G\sharp_0$ has a center frequency of 51.91 Hz, and the fundamental frequency of the next pitch, A_0, is 55.00 Hz, so a spectral resolution of 10.77 Hz is not enough to build the lower bands.

To minimize this problem, zero padding was applied for having more points in the spectrum, appending three windows of 2048 zero samples at the end of the input signal in the time domain before doing the STFT. Zero padding does not add spectral resolution, but interpolates. With these values, a resolution of $10.77/4 = 2.69$ Hz is obtained.

2.2 Semitone Bands

In this work, the analysis is performed by a computer software in the frequency domain. Therefore, the FFT algorithm is utilized to compute the narrowband (linear) frequency spectrum. Then, this spectrum is apportioned among the octave bands to produce the corresponding octave spectrum, simulating the response of a 1/12 octave filterbank in the frequency domain.

The spectral bins obtained after the STFT computation are analyzed into B bands in a logarithmic scale ranging from 50 Hz (pitch $G\sharp_0$) to 10,600 Hz (pitch F_8), almost eight octaves. This way, $B = 94$ spectral bands are obtained and their center frequencies correspond to the fundamental frequencies of the 94 notes in that range.

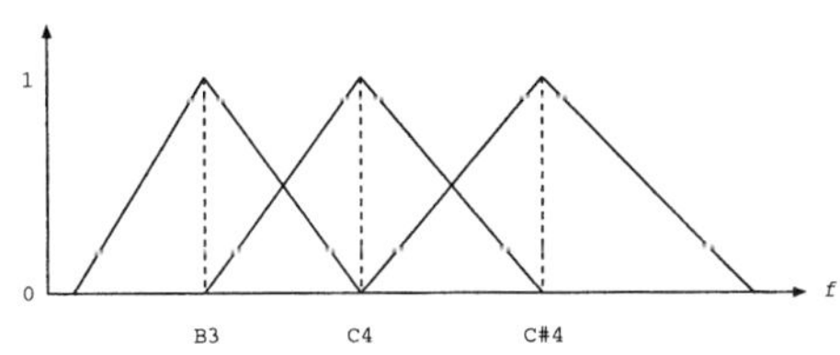

Fig. 1. Example of triangular windowing for pitches B_3, C_4 and $C\sharp_4$

To build the 1/12 octave bands, a set of different sized triangular windows are used (see Fig. 1). There is one window centered at the fundamental frequency of each pitch. For wider windows (those centered in the highest frequencies), many bins are considered but for lower bands only a few bins are used. Therefore, if the input signal is an uniformly distributed noise, wider bands will have higher values than narrower ones. To minimize this problem, a RMS (Root Mean Square) computation is performed, in order to emphasize the highest spectrum values. A simple equation to get each band value $b_k(t)$ at time t can be used;

$$b_k(t) = \sqrt{\sum_{j=1}^{W_k} (X(j,t) w_{kj})^2} \,, \tag{2}$$

being $\{w_{kj}\}_{j=1}^{W_k}$ the triangular window values for each band, W_k the size of the k-th window and X the set of spectrum bins corresponding to that window at time t, with j indexing the frequency bin.

The RMS of the bands is used instead of the energy. This is because small variations in the highest amplitude bands are emphasized, causing false onsets during the sustain stage of some notes. Moreover, some soft onsets could be masked by strong onsets.

3 Note Onset Recognition

3.1 Basic Note Onset Recognition

Like in other onset detection algorithms [2][4][6][7], a first order derivative function is used to pick potential onset candidates. In this work the derivative $c(t)$ is computed for each band k.

$$c_k(t) = \frac{d}{dt} b_k(t) \tag{3}$$

We must combine onset components to yield the onsets in the overall signal. In order to detect only the beginnings of the notes, the positive first order derivatives of all the bands are summed at each time. The negative derivatives are not considered.

$$a(t) = \sum_{k=1}^{B} \max\{0, c_k(t)\}. \tag{4}$$

To normalize the onset detection function, the overall sum of the band values $s(t)$ is also computed:

$$s(t) = \sum_{k=1}^{B} b_k(t) \tag{5}$$

and the sum of the positive derivatives $a(t)$ is divided by the sum of the band amplitudes $s(t)$ to compute a relative difference. Therefore, the onset detection function $o(t) \in [0, 1]$ is:

$$o(t) = \frac{a(t)}{s(t)} \; . \tag{6}$$

The Fig. 2 shows an example of the detection function $o(t)$ for a Mozart real piano melody[2].

A silence threshold μ is applied, in such a way that if $s(t) < \mu$, then $o(t) = 0$. This is done to avoid false positive onsets when the overall amplitude is very low.

The peaks in $o(t)$ are considered as onset candidates and a low level threshold θ is applied to decide which of these candidates are onsets. Due to the fact that

---

[2] RWC-MDB-C-2001 No. 27 from RWC database [8].

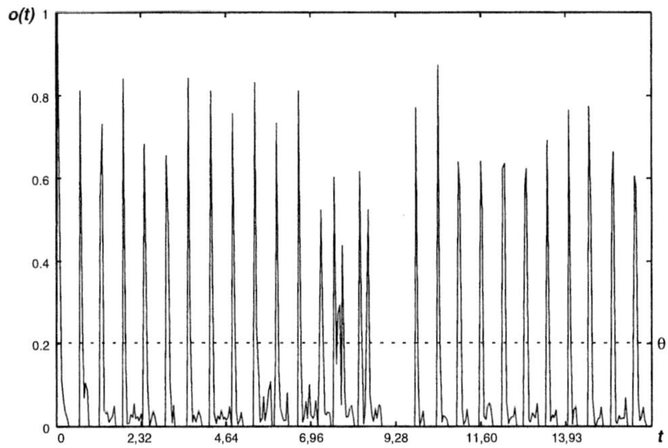

Fig. 2. Example of the onset detection function $o(t)$ for a piano melody. All the detected onsets (peaks over the threshold θ) correspond to actual onsets.

only the peaks are taken into account for onset candidates, two consecutive onsets at t and $t+1$ cannot be detected so the minimum difference in time between two onsets is $2\Delta t = 92.8$ milliseconds.

The human ear cannot distingish between two transients less than 10 ms apart [9]. However, in an onset detector, correct matches usually imply that the target and detected onsets are within a 50 ms window, to allow for the inaccuracy of the hand labelling process [3]. The presented system uses a 46.4 ms window to detect onsets, which is an admisible temporal resolution.

3.2 Note Onset Recognition for Complex Instruments

The previous methodology yields good results for instruments like piano or guitar, having sharp attack envelopes. But for instruments that have a longer attack time, like a church organ, or those with "moving" harmonics as some kind of strings or electric guitars, more time frames should be considered.

The methodology in this case is the same as in the previous subsection, but Eq. 3 is replaced by this one:

$$\tilde{c}_k(t) = \sum_{i=1}^{C} i \cdot [b_k(t+i) - b_k(t-i)] \ , \tag{7}$$

being C the number of considered time frames. This is a variation of an equation (Eq. 5.16) proposed by Young *et al.* in [10] to enhance the performance of a speech recognition system.

The idea of the weighting is that the difference is centered on each particular frame, thus two-side difference (with $C=1$) is used instead of the frame itself. When using $C=2$, the difference is calculated from a longer period, playing i the role of a weight.

An example of the onset detection function for a cello melody[3] is shown in Fig. 3 without considering additional frames (a), with $C = 1$ (b) and with $C = 2$ (c).

Note that the higher C is, the lower is the precision in time for detecting onsets but the system yields better results for complex instruments. For a robust detection, the notes need to have a duration $l \geq \Delta t(C + 1)$. If $C = 2$ and with the utilized parameters, $l = 139.2$ ms, so this method variation is not suitable for very rapid onsets[4].

To normalize $o(t)$ into the range $[0, 1]$ Eq. 5 is replaced by

$$\tilde{s}(t) = \sum_{k=1}^{B} \sum_{i=1}^{C} i \cdot b_k(t + i) \tag{8}$$

when the Eq. 7 is used, because only local loudness is considered in Eq. 5.

4 Results

In this work, the experiments were done using an onset detection database proposed by Leveau *et al.* [11] in 2004. Most of its melodies belong to the RWC database [8].

Rigorous evaluation of onset detection is a complex task [12]. The evaluation results of onset detection algorithms presented in various publications are in most cases not comparable [13], and they depend very much on the database used for the experiments. Unfortunately, at the moment there are not similar works using the Leveau *et al.* database, so in this paper our algorithm is not compared with others. However, our system is currently being evaluated at the MIREX 2005 competition[5], which results will be released soon.

A set of real melodies was used to carry out the experiments. To test the system, some real melodies were selected and listened to detect the actual onsets. New audio files were generated adding "click" sounds where the onsets were detected. The number of false positive and negative onsets was finally counted by analysing the generated wavefiles.

The error metric can be defined in precision/recall terms. The precision is the percentage of the detected onsets that are correct. The recall is the percentage of the true onsets that were found with respect to the actual onsets. A false positive is considered as a detected onset that was not present in the signal, and a false negative as an undetected onset.

The silence threshold μ is not very relevant, because in most of the melodies the values of $s(t)$ are usually over this threshold. It is only useful when silences occur or when the considered spectrogram has a very low loudness, so the system is not very sensitive to the variation of this parameter. The threshold θ can control the precision/recall deviation.

---

[3] RWC-MDB-C-2001 No. 36 from RWC database [8].

[4] 139 ms is the length of a semiquaver when tempo is 107 bpm.

[5] 2nd Annual Music Information Retrieval Evaluation eXchange.

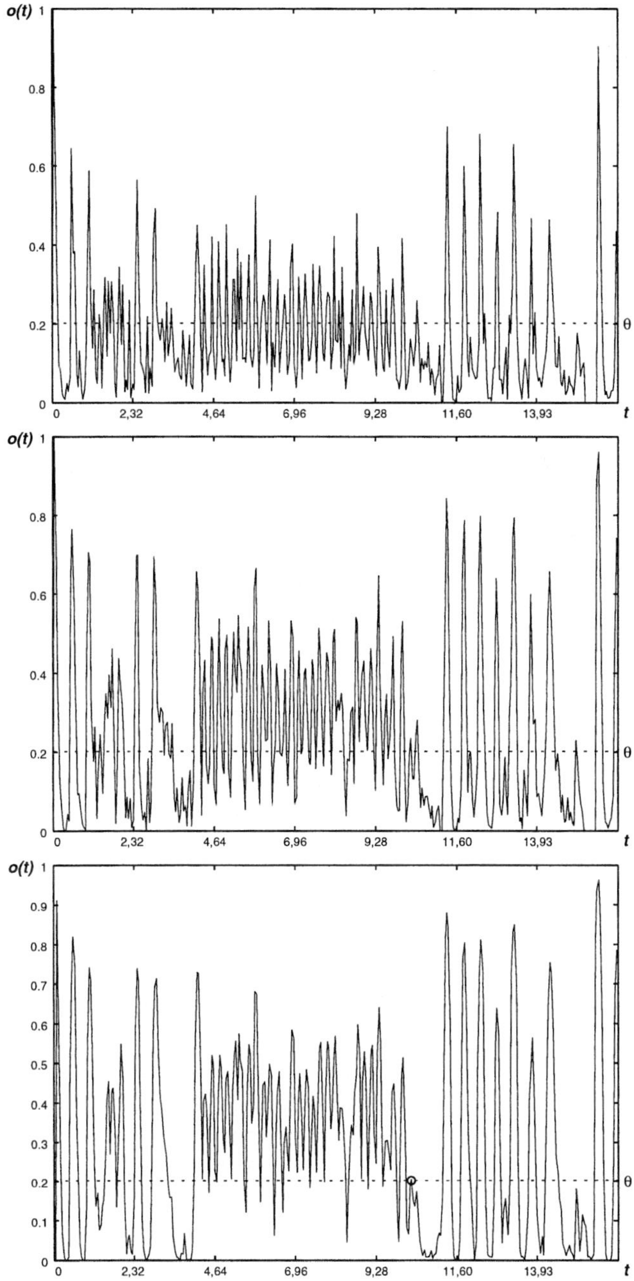

Fig. 3. Onset detection function $o(t)$ for a polyphonic cello melody. (a) Without additional frames; (b) with $C = 1$; (c) with $C = 2$. When $C = 2$, all the onsets were succesfully detected except by one (marked with a circle).

Table 1. Results for the database proposed in [11]. The first columns are the melody name, the duration (secs.), and the number of actual onsets. The next columns are the number of correcly detected onsets (OK), false positives (FP), false negatives (FN), precision (P) and recall (R). The experiments were performed without additional frames (basic detection) and with $C = 2$.

Tested melodies			**Basic detection**					**With C=2**				
Content	Dur (s)	On	OK	FP	FN	P(%)	R(%)	OK	FP	FN	P(%)	R(%)
Solo trumpet	14	60	57	1	3	98.3	95					
Solo clarinet	30	38	38	1	0	97.4	100					
Solo saxophone	12	10	10	4	0	71.4	100					
Solo synthetic bass	7	25	25	1	0	96.2	100					
Solo cello	14	65	49	23	16	68.1	75.4	50	5	15	90.9	76.9
Solo violin	15	79	72	12	7	85.7	91.1					
Solo distorted guitar	6	20	20	3	0	87	100					
Solo steel guitar	14	58	58	2	0	96.7	100					
Solo electric guitar	15	35	31	4	4	88.6	88.6					
Solo piano	15	20	20	0	0	100	100					
Techno	6	56	38	1	19	97.4	67.9					
Rock	15	62	62	21	1	74.7	98.4					
Jazz (octet)	14	52	40	1	12	97.6	76.9					
Jazz (contrabass)	11	52	51	6	1	89.5	98.1					
Classic 1	20	50	49	17	1	74.2	98	50	5	0	90.9	100
Classic 2	14	12	11	15	1	42.3	91.7	11	20	1	35.5	91.7
Pop 1	15	38	32	11	6	74.4	84.2					

4.1 Results Without Additional Frames

The results of the experiments with basic detection are shown in the table 1. They were obtained with a silence threshold $\mu = 70$ and with $\theta = 0.18$.

The system works specially well for the piano melody. In other tested piano melodies results showed that the system is robust for this instrument. It also works well for the tested melodies played by a trumpet, a clarinet, a bass or guitars.

In the melody played by a saxophone a few extra onsets appeared close to the actual onsets. This is due to the nature of this instrument; its attack begins with a small amount of noise, specially evident when it is played legato, like in the tested melody. Its pitch also starts in a frequency slighly lower than the played pitch and it takes a little time to reach the desired pitch. So in some notes both the attack and the moment when the pitch was reached were detected, yielding some false positive onsets.

The cello is a very difficult instrument for onset detection, and the results were not very good when no aditional frames were utilized. Though the violin is another problematic instrument, the results were not bad. Usually, distorted guitars are also a difficult problem for onset detection, but the tested melody yielded good results. More experiments were done with other melodies played by distorted guitars and the system yielded good results too.

In the techno melody, some onsets were not detected probably because they were masked by the strength of the drums. In the rock melody, several false positives appeared when the distorted guitar was played muted. However, in other similar rock melodies the obtained results were very good due to the presence of drums, that are usually helpful for detecting onsets.

The octet jazz melody yielded some false negatives, but most of them belong to very soft onsets produced by the hi-hat of the drumset. The results for the other jazz melody were satisfactory.

In the first classic melody the system obtained good results for the initial notes but, when the singer started, several false positive were achieved. This also happened in another tested singing melodies. The human voice behaviour is different to most of the instruments because of its complex spectral features, so this system do not seem to be the most adequate to deal with this problem.

The second classic melody was very difficult due to the presence of strings, and when no additional frames were considered several false positives appeared. Finally, the pop melody yielded false positives with human voice, and some false negatives corresponding to very soft onsets.

4.2 Results with Additional Frames

As discussed before, for some kind of instruments, like a cello or a church organ, more time frames are needed. In the tested database only three melodies suggest to use additional frames. They are the cello melody and the two classic melodies, and the results with $C = 2$ are in the Tab. 1. The detected onsets considering $C = 1$ were similar to those obtained with basic detection, so they are not shown in the table.

The results with $C = 2$ are not shown for melodies which instrument features do not suggest the use of additional frames. These results are obviously worse considering more time frames than without additional time frames.

The system yielded much better results for the cello and the first classic melodies. However, worse results were obtained for the second classic melody. Obviously, only three examples are not enough to test the performance of the system when $C = 2$ but, unfortunately, in this database only these melodies recommend the use of more frames. In other tested melodies from the RWC database the results improved importantly, for example for the cello melody (in Fig. 3), for an organ and for some classic melodies.

Anyway, in most cases the system yields better results without considering time frames, and more frames should only be utilized for specific instruments.

5 Conclusions and Future Work

In this work, a musically motivated onset detection system is presented. In its basic version, the spectrogram of a melody is performed and 1/12 octave band filters are applied. The derivatives in time are computed for each band and summed. Then, this sum is normalized dividing it by the sum of the band values in the considered time frame. Finally, all the peaks over a threshold are detected onsets. A simple improvement was made by using more time frames in order to make the system more robust for complex instruments.

The system is intended for tuned musical instruments, and the results for these kind of melodies were very satisfactory. It does not seem to be the most adequate for voice or drums, because it is based in the harmonic properties of the musical instruments. However, when drums were present in the tested melodies, the system was robust. With voice, results are worse due to its harmonic properties.

The simplicity of the system makes it easy to implement, and several future work lines can be developed over this basic scheme. An adaptative filterbank could be added for non-tuned instruments, detecting the highest spectrum peak and moving the fundamental frequency of the closest band to that peak.

A dynamic value of C (the number of aditional time frames) depending on the instruments could also be considered. Usually, in the melodies where C must be increased, the detected onsets in $o(t)$ have lower values than they should have. As an example, in Fig. 2 the peaks detected as onsets have higher values than those detected in Fig. 3 (a). This is because cello attacks are softer than piano attacks. Therefore, the analysis of the $o(t)$ function in the first time frames could be performed to tune the value of C.

Acknowledgements

This work has been funded by the Spanish CICYT project TIRIG with code TIC2003-08496-C04, partially supported by European Union-FEDER funds, and the Generalitat Valenciana project with code GV04B-541. Thanks to Jasón Box for migrating the onset detector C++ code into D2K.

References

1. Klapuri, A. "Sound Onset Detection by Applying Psychoacoustic Knowledge", *IEEE Int. Conf. on Acoustics, Speech and Signal Processing, ICASSP*, March 15-19, 1999, Phoenix, USA, pp. 3089-3092
2. Goto, M. and Muraoka, Y. "Beat tracking based on multiple-agent architecture — A real-time beat tracking system for audio signals —" in *Proc. of the Second Int. Conf. on Multi-Agent Systems*, pp.103–110, December 1996.
3. Bello, J.P., Daudet, L., Abdallah, S., Duxbury, C., Davies, M. and Sandler, M.B. "A tutorial on onset detection in music signals", in *IEEE Transactions on Speech and Audio Processing"*, vol. 13, issue 5, pp. 1035 – 1047, Sept. 2005.
4. Scheirer, E.D. "Tempo and beat analysis of acoustic musical signals" *J. Acoust. Soc. Am.*, vol. 103, no.1, pp. 588-601, Jan 1998
5. Duxbury, C., Sandler, M. and Davies, M. "A hybrid approach to musical note onset detection" in *Proc. Digital Audio Effects Conference (DAFX)*, 2002.
6. Goto, M. and Muraoka, Y. "A Real-Time Beat Tracking System for Audio Signals" *Proc. of the 1995 Int. Computer Music Conference*, pp. 171–174, Sep 1995

7. Bilmes, J. "Timing is of the Essence: Perceptual and Computational Techniques for Representing, Learning and Reproducing Expressive Timing in Percusive Rhythm". MSc Thesis, MIT, 1993.
8. Goto, M. "RWC music database", published at http://staff.aist.go.jp/m.goto/RWC-MDB/
9. Moore, B.C.J., "An introduction to the Psychology of Hearing", Academic Press, fifth edition, 1997.
10. Young, S., Kershaw, D, Odell, J., Ollason, D., Valtchev, V. and Woodland, P. "The HTK book (for HTK version 3.1)" *Cambridge University*, 2000.
11. Leveau, P., Daudet, L. and Richard, G. "Methodology and tools for the evaluation of automatic onset detection algorithms in music", *Proc. of the Int. Symposium on Music Information Retrieval (ISMIR)*, Barcelona, 2004.
12. Rodet, X., Escribe, J. and Durignon, S. "Improving score to audio alignment: Percussion alignment and Precise Onset Estimation" *Proc. of the 2004 Int. Computer Music Conference*, pp. 450–453, Nov. 2004.
13. Lerch, A., Klich, I. "On the Evaluation of Automatic Onset Tracking Systems", *White Paper, Berlin, Germany, April 2005.*

Tool-Wear Monitoring Based on Continuous Hidden Markov Models

Antonio G. Vallejo Jr.[1], Juan A. Nolazco-Flores[2], Rubén Morales-Menéndez[2], L. Enrique Sucar[3], and Ciro A. Rodríguez[2]

[1] ITESM Laguna Campus, Mechatronic Dept., Torreón, Coah., México
[2] ITESM Monterrey Campus, Monterrey NL, México
[3] ITESM Morelos Campus, Cuernavaca Mor, México
{avallejo, jnolazco, rmm, esucar, ciro.rodriguez}@itesm.mx

Abstract. In this work we propose to monitor the cutting tool-wear condition in a CNC-machining center by using continuous Hidden Markov Models (HMM). A database was built with the vibration signals obtained during the machining process. The workpiece used in the milling process was aluminum 6061. Cutting tests were performed on a Huron milling machine equipped with a Sinumerik 840D open CNC. We trained/tested the HMM under 18 different operating conditions. We identified three key transitions in the signals. First, the cutting tool touches the workpiece. Second, a stable waveform is observed when the tool is in contact with the workpiece. Third, the tool finishes the milling process. Considering these transitions, we use a five-state HMM for modeling the process. The HMMs are created by preprocessing the waveforms, followed by training step using Baum-Welch algorithm. In the recognition process, the signal waveform is also preprocessed, then the trained HMM are used for decoding. Early experimental results validate our proposal in exploiting speech recognition frameworks in monitoring machining centers. The classifier was capable of detecting the cutting tool condition within large variations of spindle speed and feed rate, and accuracy of 84.19%.

Keywords: Signal Processing and Analysis, Remote Sensing Applications of Pattern Recognition, Hidden Markov Models, Tool-wear monitoring.

1 Introduction

Manufacturing processes are typically complex. High Speed Machining (HSM) systems demand precise and complex operations; operators have to implement complicated operations in these systems too. Computerized numerical controls (CNC) systems demand supervisor and protection functions such as monitoring, and supervising [5]. Also, special software for supporting operators is required [7].

In any typical metal-cutting process, key factors that define the product quality are dimensional accuracy and surface finish. One important part in the

M. Lazo and A. Sanfeliu (Eds.): CIARP 2005, LNCS 3773, pp. 880–890, 2005.

CNC machines is the cutting tool condition, and it is important to constraint the following aspects: progressive tool wear, deflection of cutting tool and the variation of process conditions. We need a cutting tool condition monitoring system in order to reduce operating cost with the same quality, [13].

Tool wear is caused by a combination of various phenomena. Contact with the chip produces a crater in the face of the tool. Flank wear, on the other hand, is commonly due to friction between the tool and the work-piece material. Once the protective coating is removed, sudden chipping of the cutting edges may occur, leading to catastrophic failure of the tool. Recent studies conclude that rake-face wear, flank wear, chipping and breakage are the main modes of tool wear in HSM. One of the main goals in HSM is to find an *appropriate trade-off* among tool wear, surface quality and productivity, considering the cost of the tool, its replacement cost, the cost of maintain the machine in idle time, and so forth.

Safety is fundamental in tool condition monitoring systems; also, accurate data acquisition from sensors are mandatory. Sensors should meet certain requirements ensuring robustness, reliability and non-intrusive behavior under normal working conditions. Almost all sensors present restrictions in the manufacturing industry because the harsh environment. The development of new sensors or technologies for monitoring tool wear are critical in machining business.

In this work, we propose a new recognition approach for tool-wear monitoring using continuous Hidden Markov Models (HMM). The vibration signals between the tool and the workpiece will provide the database. In section 2, we describe the state of the art. In section 3 we present our proposal to solve the problem. In section 4, the experimental set up is described. In section 5, the experimental results are shown. Finally, section 6 concludes the paper.

2 State of the Art

Tool failure represents about 20 % of machine tool down-time, and tool wear negatively impacts the work quality in the context of dimensions, finish, and surface integrity [9]. Using fuzzy logic, artificial neural networks, and linear regression, important contributions for tool-wear monitoring had been proposed, with different sensors (acoustic, electrical, magnetic, accelerometer, etc.) installed in strategic points of the CNC machine.

In [5], Haber and Alique developed an intelligent supervisory system for tool wear prediction using a model-based approach. In order to deal with nonlinear process characteristics, they used an Artificial Neural Network (ANN) output error model to predict online the resultant cutting force under different cutting conditions. First, an ANN model is created considering the cutting force, the feed rate, and the radial depth of the cut. The residual error obtained of the two forces was compared with an adaptive threshold to estimate the tool wear. This method evaluated the behavior of the tool in three states; new tool, half-worn tool, and worn tool.

In [6], Haber *et al.* presented an investigation of tool wear monitoring in a high speed machining process on the basis of the analysis of different signals signatures in the time and frequency domains. They used sensorial information from relevant sensors (e.g., dynamometer, accelerometer, and acoustic emission sensor) to obtain the deviation of representative variables. During the tests measurements at different cutting speeds and feed rates were carried out to determine the effects of a new and worn tool in high speed roughing. Data were transformed from time domain to frequency domain through a Fast Fourier Transformer (FFT) algorithm in order to analyze frequency components. They conducted second harmonic of the tooth path excitation frequency in the vibration signal is the best index for tool wear monitoring. Additionally, the spectrum analysis of acoustic emission (AE) signals corroborates that AE sensors are very sensitive to changes in tool condition. Also, [13] worked with multilayered neural networks for tool condition monitoring in the milling process.

In [10], Owsley *et al.* presented an approach for feature extraction from vibrations during the drilling. Self-organizing feature maps (SOFM's) extract the features. They modified the SOFM algorithm in order to improve its generalization abilities and to allow it to server as a preprocessor for a HMM classifier. The authors used a discrete hidden Markov model. Similar proposals for tool-wear monitoring can be found in [2,15,1,8,14].

3 Tool Wear Monitoring System

Figure 1 shows a flow diagram of the system for monitoring tool-wear using continuous HMM.

The vibration signal in the machining process is considered the input signal. As we can see in Figure 1, the input signal is preprocessed and then it is separated into two branches. The training data branch leads to a HMM model. Given the model and the parameterized signal a decoder produce a transcript of a specific pattern as a result. In this training phase the system learns the patterns that

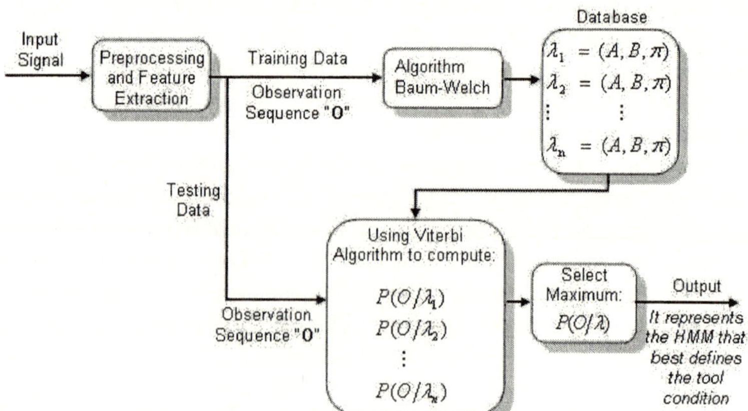

Fig. 1. Flow diagram for monitoring the tool-wear with continuous HMM

represent the vibration signals. The testing branch uses the preprocessed input signal and the HMM model to compute $P(O \mid \lambda)$ using the Viterbi algorithm for each model. The model with higher probability is selected as result. Next, we review the steps and basic concepts of the proposed algorithm.

3.1 Hidden Markov Models

Real world processes produce observable outputs which can be characterized as signals (discrete/continuous, pure/corrupted, etc.). A problem of fundamental interest is characterizing such signals in terms of models (deterministic/statistical). Statistical models use the statistical properties of the signal, such as Hidden Markov Models, [11,3].

Definitions. For completeness we will review some basic definitions. A HMM, as depicted in Figure 2, is characterized by the following:

- N, number of states in the model. We denote the states as $S = S_1, \cdots, S_N$, and the state at time t as q_t.
- M, number of distinct observation symbols per state. We denote the individual symbols as $V = v_1, \cdots, v_M$.
- The state transition probability distribution $A = P[q_t = S_j | q_{t-1} = S_i]$, $1 \leq ij \leq N$
- The observation symbol probability distribution in state j, $B = P[v_k | q_t = S_j], 1 \leq j \leq N, 1 \leq k \leq M$
- The initial state distribution $\pi = P[q_1 = S_i]$, $1 \leq i \leq N$

Given appropriate values of N, M, A, B, and π, the HMM can be used as a generator to give an observation sequence $O = O_1, \cdots, O_T$. Then, a complete specification of an HMM requires specification of two model parameters (N,

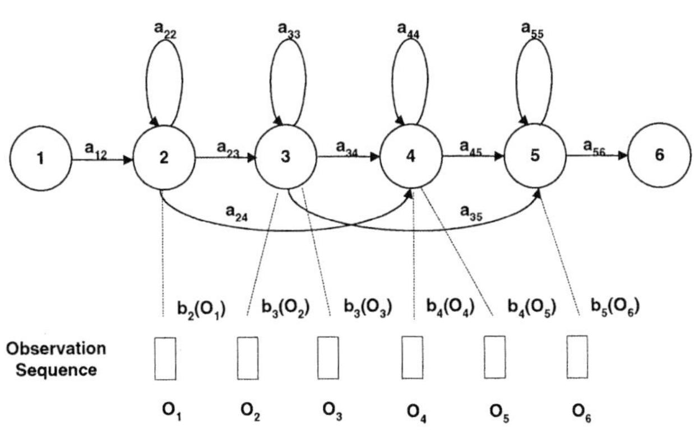

Fig. 2. Elements of a HMM: left-right model, 6 states, and observations per state

and M), specification of observation symbols, and the specification of the three probability measures $\lambda = (A, B, \pi)$. The parameters N, M and λ are learned from data. Given this model and the observation we can compute $P(O|\lambda)$.

3.2 Baum-Welch Algorithm

The well-known Baum-Welch algorithm [11] is used to compute the model parameters (means, variance, and transitions) given the training data. It is an iterative process for parameter estimation based on a training data set for a given model λ. The goal is to obtain a new model $\bar{\lambda}$ where the function

$$Q(\lambda, \bar{\lambda}) = \sum_{Q} \frac{P(O, Q \mid \lambda)}{P(O \mid \lambda)} log[P(O, Q \mid \bar{\lambda})] \quad (1)$$

is maximized. For this algorithm it is need to define a forward and a backward probability as

$$\alpha_t(i) = P(O_1^t, q_t = i \mid \lambda), \quad \beta_t(i) = P(O_{t+1}^T \mid q_t = i, \lambda) \quad (2)$$

Based on this two functions, the probability for changing from state j to state k at time t can be defined as

$$\xi_t(j, k) = \frac{\sum_i \alpha_{i-1}(i) a_{ij} c_{jk} b_{jk}(o_t) \beta_t(j)}{\sum_{i=1}^{N} \alpha_T(i)} \quad (3)$$

where $b_j(o)$ is a continuous output probability density function (pdf) for state j and can be described as a weighted mixture of Gaussian functions, as follow

$$b_j(o) = \sum_{k=1}^{M} c_{jk} N(o, \mu_{jk}, U_{jk}) = \sum_{k=1}^{M} c_{jk} b_{jk}(o, \mu_{jk}, U_{jk}) \quad (4)$$

where c_{jk} is the weight of the gaussian k and $N(o, \mu_{jk}, U_{jk})$ is a single gaussian of mean value μ_{jk} and a covariance matrix U_{jk}. Therefore, the model can be described in terms of μ_{jk},U_{jk} and c_{jk}, and the new set of parameters for model $\bar{\lambda}$ are recalculated using Baum-Welch as follow

$$\bar{\mu}_{jk} = \frac{\sum_{t=1}^{T} \xi(j, k) o_t}{\sum_{t=1}^{T} \xi_t(t, k)} \quad (5)$$

$$\bar{U}_{jk} = \frac{\sum_{t=1}^{T} \xi_t(j, k)(o_t - \bar{\mu}_{jk})(o_t - \bar{\mu}_{jk})^t}{\sum_{t=1}^{T} \xi_t(j, k)} \quad (6)$$

$$\bar{c}_{jk} = \frac{\sum_{t=1}^{T} \xi_t(j, k)}{\sum_{t=1}^{T} \sum_k \xi_t(j, k)} \quad (7)$$

Now, the term b_{jk} can be written as

$$b_{jk}(o_t, \mu_{jk}, \sigma_{jk}) = \frac{1}{\prod_{i=1}^{d} \sqrt{2\pi\sigma_{jki}}} e^{-\frac{1}{2} \sum_{i=1}^{d} (\frac{o_{ti} - \mu_{jki}}{\sigma_{jki}})^2} \quad (8)$$

3.3 Viterbi Algorithm

The Viterbi algorithm [3] is used to find the single best state sequence, $Q = q_1, \cdots, q_T$, for the given observation sequence $O = O_1, \cdots, O_T$, we need to define the quantity

$$P(O|\lambda) = max_{q_1,\cdots,q_{t-1}} P[q_1, \cdots, q_t = i, O_1, \cdots, O_t \mid \lambda] \tag{9}$$

3.4 Feature Extraction

The vibration signals are pre-processed calculating their Mel Frequency Cesptral Coefficient (MFCC) representation [12]. This common transformation has shown to be more robust and reliable than other techniques. The process to calculate the MFCC is shown in Figure 3.

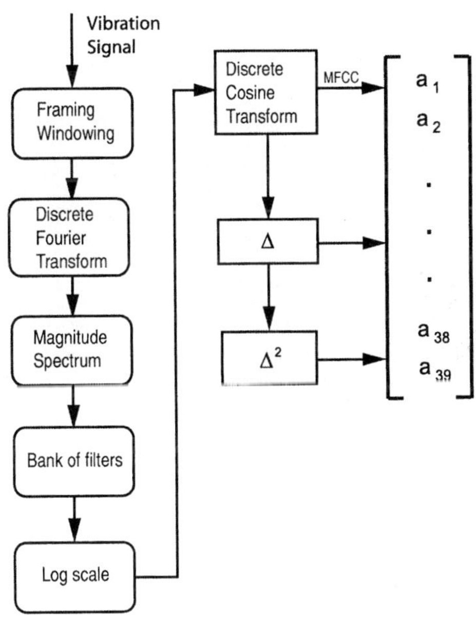

Fig. 3. Feature extraction process

Each signal is divided into short frames. For each frame the amplitude spectrum is obtained using the Discrete Fourier Transform (DFT). Afterwards, the spectrum is converted to a logarithm scale. To smooth the scaled spectrum, bandpass filter banks are used. Finally, the discrete cosine transform is applied to eliminate the correlation between components. The result is a 13-dimension vector, each dimension corresponding to one parameter. We applied similar considerations as in speech recognition [4], where it is common to estimate the time-derivative (Δ) and the time-acceleration (Δ^2) of each parameter. Then, the final representation is a 39 dimension vector formed by 12-dimension MFCC, followed by 1 energy coefficient, 13Δ and 13 Δ^2 coefficients.

4 Experimental Set Up

4.1 CNC Machine

The experimental tests were conducted in a KX10 HURON machining center, with a capacity of 20 KW, three axis, and equipped with a SIEMENS open-Sinumerik 840D controller, left image in Figure 4. This machining center possesses high precision sideways that allow all three axis to reach a speed of up to 30 m/min. The machine has high-rigidity, high-precision features and there is not interference between the workpiece and the moving parts.

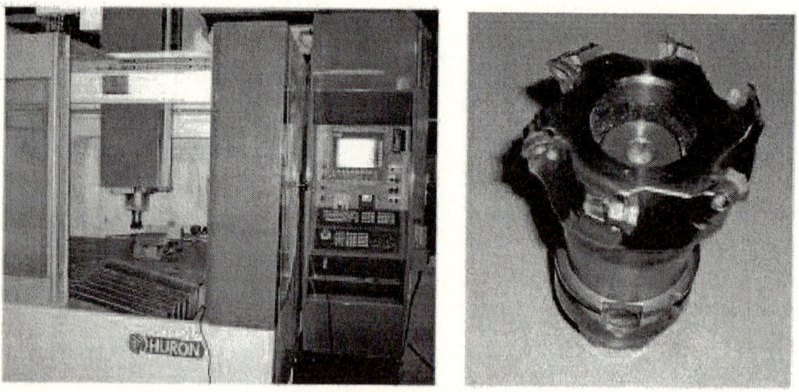

Fig. 4. KX10 Huron CNC-milling center (left), and cutting tool (right)

The cutting tool is an Octomill R220.43-03.00-05 face mill of SECO Carboloy, with a diameter of 80 mm, depth of cut 3.5 mm, and six inserts of the SECO Carboloy OFEX-05T305TN-ME07 T250M type, right image in Figure 4.

4.2 Data Acquisition System

Figure 5 shows a diagram of the experimental set-up. The vibration signal is recorded by using an accelerometer installed on the flat metal support. The vibration signals during the machining process was acquired using a 8 bits analog-digital converter (ADC) sampling at 50 KHz.

The accelerometer has as sensing element a ceramic/shear with ($\pm$20%) 10.2 $mV/(m/s^2)$ sensitivity and a frequency range of 1.2 Hz - 10 KHz. The range of measurement is $\pm$ 490 m/s^2. We recorded the vibration signals for several machining conditions. Spindle speed : $2,000$, $1,500$, and $1,000$ rev/min. Feed

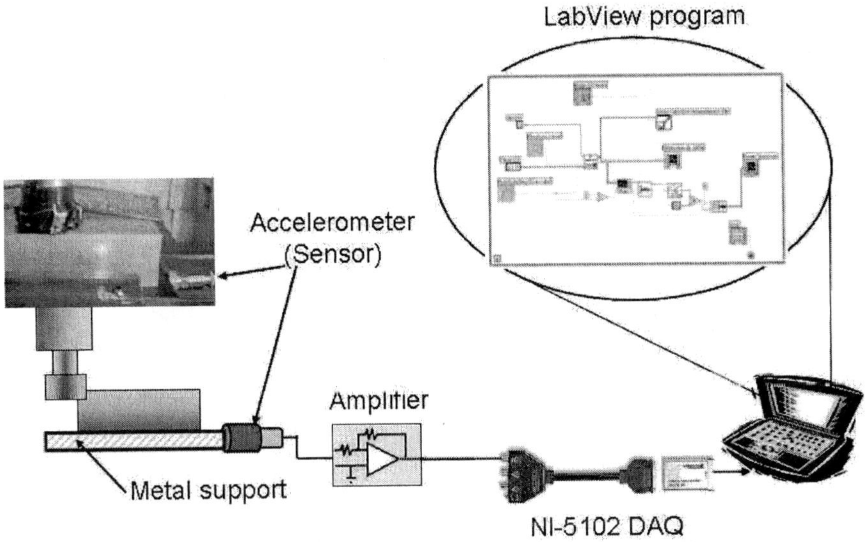

Fig. 5. Experimental Set-up: Acquisition System to record the vibration signals

rate of the tool : 600, 800, and 1,000 mm/min. Depth of the tool: 1 mm. All the experiments were made considering two conditions for the tool: good and worn inserts. We applied a full factorial design to consider all the defined levels for each machining condition. Then, we required 18 different operating conditions, and we reproduced the experiments 9 (tool with good inserts) and 8 (tool with worn inserts) times. We obtained 153 experiments. Figure 6 shows some examples of the vibration signals. The vibration signals on left of the figure represent normal conditions of the tool (inserts in good conditions) at different operating conditions. The vibration signals on the right of the figure were recorded with worn inserts.

5 Results

Our database was built with the vibration signals obtained during the machining process. This database contains 153 experiments under 18 different operating conditions. The first 5 experiments (T_r) were used for training, and last 4 experiments were used for testing (T_s). The data streams are processed using the Sphinx HMM Toolkit developed at Carnegie Mellon University. The toolkit was configured to use several Gaussian, left-right, five states, HMMs. Table 1 presents the accuracy when a signal is processed for the classifier.

We evaluate the performance of the classifier considering the following conditions:

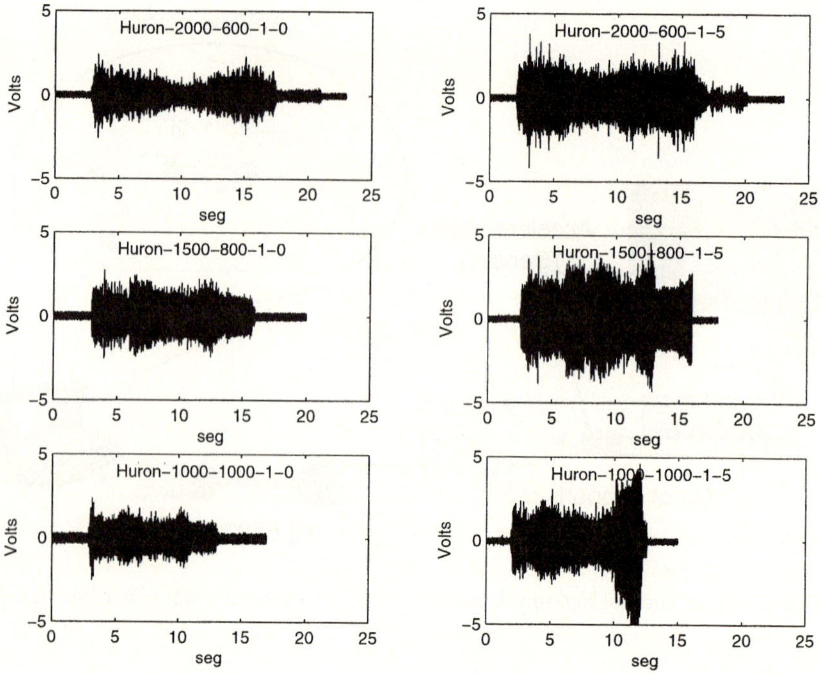

Fig. 6. Vibration Signals. Left signals represent good cutting tool conditions. Right signals were obtained with worn inserts. Each condition is defined by the spindle speed (2000, 1500, 1000 rpm), feed rate (600, 800, 1000 mm/min), depth of the cut (1 mm) and number of damage inserts (0,5).

- First, we train and test the algorithm with the same database, $T_r = T_s$, and we obtain 95% of success, almost all conditions were identified. Note that we have very few data for both training and testing steps.
- Second, we test the algorithm with different database, $T_r \neq T_s$. We obtain 66.70% of success to recognize the pattern. In this case, the parameters of the HMM were obtained using only one Gaussian.
- Third, we compute the parameters of the HMM with different Gaussian. We obtained an 84.10% success with 16 Gaussian. We train and test the algorithm with different database.

We also configured the HMM toolkit for recognition of two states: good and faulty(worn inserts) condition. Table 2 presents the results for each condition using the HMMs with 16 Gaussian. This table also shows the False Alarm Rate (FAR) and the False Fault Rate (FFR) and Expected number of workpieces machining when the fault condition is detected. The FAR is the rate when decoder detects the tool is in fault condition (worn inserts), but the tool is in good condition. The FFR is the rate when decoder detects the tool is in good condition and it is not. The FAR condition is not a problem for the machining process.

Table 1. Accuracy of the model

Experiments for testing	Accuracy
$Tr = Ts$	95 %
$Tr \neq Ts$	66.70 % with 1 Gaussian
$Tr \neq Ts$	68.30 % with 2 Gaussian
$Tr \neq Ts$	79.40 % with 8 Gaussian
$Tr \neq Ts$	84.10 % with 16 Gaussian

However, the FFR condition could be a huge problem when it presents a higher value, because the poor quality of the product and the tool can be broken before being detected.

Given the FFR we can easily obtain the probability to detect the fault condition as follow:

$$E(k) = \sum_{k=1}^{\infty} P(k) \tag{10}$$

From this equation, we can also obtain the expected number of pieces processed before the fault condition is detected, as shown:

$$E[k] = \frac{1}{1 - P_{b,g}} \tag{11}$$

This value is important because it establishes the number of pieces before the fault condition is detected. This number must be small to reduce the number of pieces with a poor quality surface, and to reduce the possibilities that the tool could be broken.

Table 2. Probabilities of the HMMs with the 16 gaussian

Condition	Probability	Description
$P_{g,g}$,$P_{b,b}$	0.841	Success probability
$P_{g,b}$	0.016	False alarm rate $E(k)$ = 1.016
$P_{b,g}$	0.143	False fault rate $E(k)$ =1.167

6 Conclusions and Future Work

In this paper we have proposed an algorithm to monitor the cutting tool-wear condition in a CNC-machining center by using continuous Hidden Markov Models. The speech recognition framework was exploited in this domain with successful results and great potential. A database was built with the vibration signals of different conditions during the machining process of an Aluminium 6061 workpiece. We trained/tested the HMM for each operating conditions, and the results were satisfactory given the limited number of experiments. This is a first stage the development of an intelligent system to monitor, supervise, and control the machining process for a CNC-machining center. We are working in the process to acquire more vibration signals with other sensors installed in different points of the machine. We will use these additional signals to train and test new continuous HMMs and evaluate the accuracy of the classifier with the new conditions.

References

1. O B Abouelatta and J Madl. Surface roughness prediction based on cutting parameters and tool vibrations in turning operations. *Materials Processing Technology*, (118):269–277, 2001.
2. L Atlas, M Ostendorf, and G D Bernard. Hidden markov models for monitoring machining tool-wear. *IEEE*, pages 3887–3890, 2000.
3. Jeff Bilmes. What hmms can do. Technical report.
4. Steven B. Davis and Paul Mermelstein. Comparison of parametric representations for monosyllabic word recognition in continuously spoken sentences. *IEEE Transactions on Acoustic, Speech, and Signal Processing*, 4(28):357–366, 1980.
5. R E Haber and A Alique. Intelligent process supervision for predicting tool wear in machining processes. *Mechatronics*, (13):825–849, 2003.
6. R E Haber, J E Jiménez, C R Peres, and J R Alique. An investigation of tool-wear monitoring in a high-spped machining process. *Sensors and Actuators A*, (116):539–545, 2004.
7. Y Koren, U Heisel, F Jovane, T Moriwaki, G Pritschow, G Ulsoy, and H Van Brussel. Reconfigurable manufacturing systems. *Annals of the CIRP*, 48(2):527–540, 1999.
8. K Y Lee, M C Kang, Y H Jeong, D W Lee, and J S Kim. Simulation of surface roughness and profile in high-speed and milling. *Materials Processing Technology*, (113):410–415, 2001.
9. S Y Liang, R L Hecker, and R G Landers. Machining process monitoring and control: The state-of-the-art. *ASME International Mechanical Engenieering Congress and Exposition*, pages 1–12, 2002.
10. L M D Owsley, L E Atlas, and G D Bernard. Self-organizing feature maps and hidden markov models for machine-tool monitoring. *IEEE Transactions on Signal Processing*, 45(11):2787–2798, 1997.
11. L R Rabiner. A tutorial on hidden markov models and selected applications in speech recognition. *Proceedings of the IEEE*, 77(2):257–286, 1989.
12. L R Rabiner and B H Juang. *Fundamentals of speech recognition.* Prentice-Hall, New-Jersey, 1993.
13. H Saglam and A Unuvar. Tool condition monitoring in milling based on cutting forces by a neural network. *International Journal of Production Research*, 41(7):1519–1532, 2003.
14. Y H Tsai, J C Chen, and S J Lou. An in-process surface recognition system based on neural networks in end milling cutting operations. *Machine Tools and Manufacture*, (39):583–605, 1999.
15. G M Zhang and C Lin. A hidden markov model approach to the study of random tool motion during machining. Technical report.

Hand Gesture Recognition Via a New Self-organized Neural Network

E. Stergiopoulou, N. Papamarkos[1], and A. Atsalakis

[1] Image Processing and Multimedia Laboratory,
Department of Electrical & Computer Engineering,
Democritus University of Thrace,
67100 Xanthi, Greece
papamark@ee.duth.gr

Abstract. A new method for hand gesture recognition is proposed which is based on an innovative Self-Growing and Self-Organized Neural Gas (SGONG) network. Initially, the region of the hand is detected by using a color segmentation technique that depends on a skin-color distribution map. Then, the SGONG network is applied on the segmented hand so as to approach its topology. Based on the output grid of neurons, palm geometric characteristics are obtained which in accordance with powerful finger features allow the identification of the raised fingers. Finally, the hand gesture recognition is accomplished through a probability-based classification method.

1 Introduction

Hand gesture recognition is a promising research field in computer vision. Its most appealing application is the development of more effective and friendly interfaces for human–machine interaction, since gestures are a natural and powerful way of communication. Moreover, it can be used to teleconferencing and telemedicine, because it doesn't require any special hardware. Last but not least, it can be applied to the interpretation and the learning of the sign language.

Hand gesture recognition is a complex problem that has been dealt with many different ways. Huang et al. [1] created a system consisting of three modules: i) model based hand tracking that uses the Hausdorff distance measure to track shape–variant hand motion, ii) feature extraction by applying the scale and rotation invariant Fourier descriptor and iii) recognition by using a 3D modified Hopfield neural network (HNN). Huang et al. [2] developed also another model based recognition system that consists of three stages as well: i) feature extraction based on spatial (edge) and temporal (motion) information, ii) training that uses the principal component analysis (PCA), the hidden Markov model (HMM) and a modified Hausdorff distance and iii) recognition by applying the Viterbi algorithm. Yin et al. [3] used a RCE neural network based color segmentation algorithm for hand segmentation, extracted edge points of fingers as points of interest and matched them based on the topological features of the hand, such as the centre of the palm. Herpers et al. [4] used a hand

M. Lazo and A. Sanfeliu (Eds.): CIARP 2005, LNCS 3773, pp. 891 – 904, 2005.

segmentation algorithm that detects connected skin–tone blobs in the region of interest. A medial axis transform is applied, and finally, an analysis of the resulting image skeleton allows the gesture recognition.

In the proposed method, hand gesture recognition is divided into four main phases: the detection of the hand's region, the approximation of its topology, the extraction of its features and its identification. The detection of the hand's region is achieved by using a color segmentation technique based on a skin color distribution map in the YCbCr space [6-7]. The technique is reliable, since it is relatively immune to changing lightning conditions and provides good coverage of the human skin color. It is very fast and doesn't require post–processing of the hand image. Once the hand is detected, a new Self-Growing and Self-Organized Neural Gas (SGONG) [8] network is used in order to approximate its topology. The SGONG is an innovative neural network that grows according to the hand's morphology in a very robust way. The positions of the output neurons of the SGONG network approximate the shape and the structure of the segmented hand. That is, as it can be viewed in Fig. 1(c), the grid of the output neurons takes the shape of the hand. Also, an effective algorithm is developed in order to locate a gesture's raised fingers, which is a necessary step of the recognition process. In the final stage, suitable features are extracted that identify, regardless to the hand's slope, the raised fingers, and therefore, the corresponding gesture. Finally, the completion of the recognition process is achieved by using a probability–based classification method.

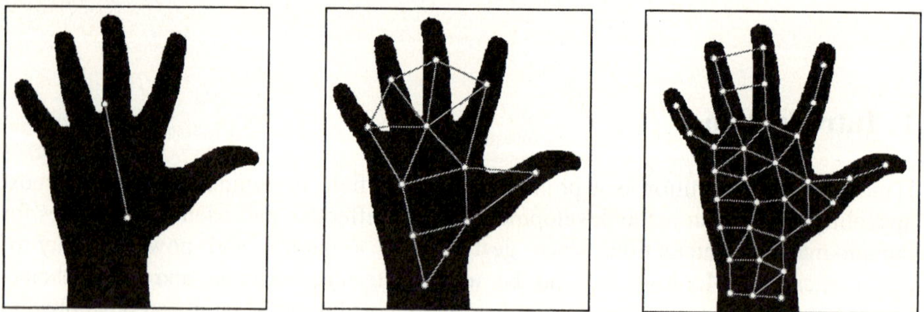

(a) (b) (c)

Fig. 1. Growth of the SGONG network: (a) starting point, (b) a growing stage, (c) the final output grid of neurons

The proposed gesture recognition system has been trained to identify 26 hand gestures. It has been tested by using a large number of gestures and the achieved recognition rate is satisfactory.

2 Description of the Method

The purpose of the proposed gesture recognition method is to recognize a set of 26 hand gestures. The principal assumption is that the images include exactly one hand.

Furthermore, the gestures are made with the right hand, the arm is roughly vertical, the palm is facing the camera and the fingers are either raised or not. Finally, the image background is plain, uniform and its color differs from the skin color.

The entire method consists of the following four main stages:

- Color Segmentation
- Application of the Self-Growing and Self-Organized Neural Gas Network
- Finger Identification
- Recognition Process

Analysis of these stages follows.

2.1 Color Segmentation

The detection of the hand region can be achieved through color segmentation. The aim is to classify the pixels of the input image into skin color and non-skin color clusters. This can be accomplished by using a thresholding technique that exploits the information of a skin color distribution map in an appropriate color space.

It is a fact that skin color varies quite dramatically. First of all, it is vulnerable to changing lightning conditions that obviously affect its luminance. Moreover, it differs among people and especially among people from different ethnic groups. The perceived variance, however, is really a variance in luminance due to the fairness or the darkness of the skin. Researchers, also, claim that the skin chromaticity is the same for all races [5]. So regarding to the skin color, luminance introduces many problems, whereas chromaticity includes the useful information. Thus, proper color spaces for skin color detection are those that separate luminance from chromaticity components.

The proposed color space is the YCbCr space, where Y is the luminance and Cb, Cr the chrominance components. RGB values can be transformed to YCbCr color space using the following equation [6-7]:

$$\begin{bmatrix} Y \\ Cb \\ Cr \end{bmatrix} = \begin{bmatrix} 16 \\ 128 \\ 128 \end{bmatrix} + \begin{bmatrix} 65.481 & 128.553 & 24.966 \\ -37.797 & -74.203 & 112 \\ 112 & -93.786 & -18.214 \end{bmatrix} \begin{bmatrix} R \\ G \\ B \end{bmatrix} \tag{1}$$

Given that the input RGB values are within range [0,1] the output values of the transformation will be [16, 235] for Y and [16, 240] for Cb and Cr. In this color space, a distribution map of the chrominance components of skin color was created, by using a test set of 50 images. It is found that Cb and Cr values are narrowly and consistently distributed. Particularly, the ranges of Cb and Cr values are, as shown in Fig. 2, $R_{Cb} = [80, 105]$ and $R_{Cr} = [130, 165]$, respectively. These ranges were selected very strictly, in order to minimize the noise effect and maximize the possibility that the colors correspond to skin.

Let C_{bi} and C_{ri} be the chrominance components of the i-th pixel. If $C_{bi} \in R_{Cb}$ and $C_{ri} \in R_{Cr}$, then the pixel belongs to the hand region.

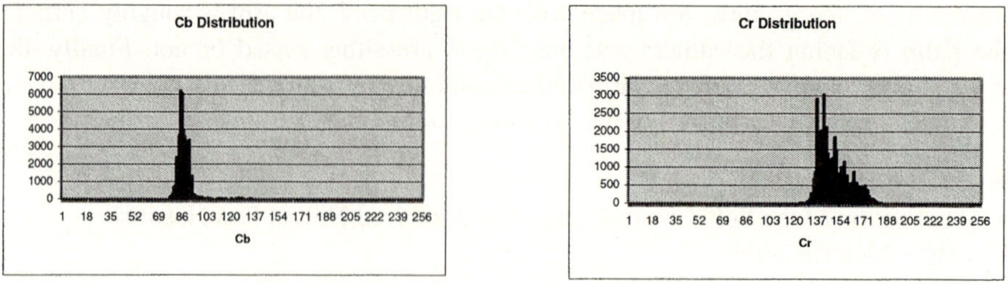

Fig. 2. Distribution of: Cb component and Cr component

Finally, a thresholding technique completes the color segmentation of the input image. The technique consists of the following steps.

- Calculation of the Euclidean distance between the C_{bi}, C_{ri} values and the edges of R_{Cb} and R_{Cr}, for every pixel.
- Comparison of the Euclidean differences with a proper threshold. If at least one difference is less than the threshold, then the pixel belongs to the hand region. The proper threshold's value is taken equal to 18.

The output image of the color segmentation process is considered as binary. As illustrated in Fig. 3 the hand region, that is the region of interest, became black and the background white. The hand region is normalized to certain dimensions so as the system to be invariant of the hand's size. It is worth to underline also, that the segmentation results are very good (almost noiseless) without further processing (e.g. filtering) of the image.

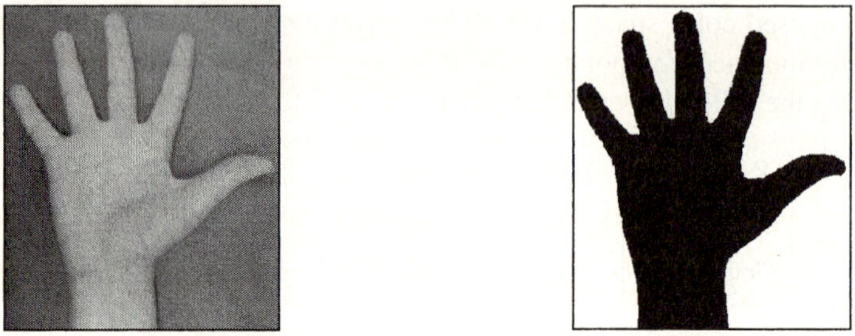

(a) (b)

Fig. 3. (a) Original image, (b) Segmented image

2.2 Application of the Self-growing and Self-organized Neural Gas Network

The next stage of the recognition process is the application of the Self Growing and Organized Neural Gas (SGONG) [8] on the segmented (binary) image.

The SGONG is an unsupervised neural classifier. It achieves clustering of the input data, so as the distance of the data items within the same class (intra-cluster variance) is small and the distance of the data items stemming from different classes (inter-cluster variance) is large. Moreover, the final number of classes is determined by the SGONG during the learning process. It is an innovative neural network that combines the advantages both of the Kohonen Self-Organized Feature Map (SOFM) and the Growing Neural Gas (GNG) neural classifiers.

The SGONG consists of two layers, i.e. the input and the output layer. It has the following main characteristics:

a. Is faster than the Kohonen SOFM,
b. The dimensions of the input space and the output lattice of neurons are always identical. Thus, the structure of neurons in the output layer approaches the structure of the input data,
c. Criteria are used to ensure fast converge of the neural network. Also, these criteria permit the detection of isolated classes.

The coordinates of the output neurons are the coordinates of the classes' centers. Each neuron is described by two local parameters, related to the training ratio and to the influence by the neighbourhood neurons. Both of them decrease from a high to a lower value during a predefined local time in order to gradually minimize the neurons' ability to adapt to the input data. As it is shown in Fig. 1, the network begins with only two neurons and it inserts new neurons in order to achieve better data clustering. Its growth is based on the following criteria:

- A neuron is inserted near the one with the greatest contribution to the total classification error, only if the average length of its connections with the neighbor neurons is relatively large.
- A neuron is removed if no input vector is classified to its cluster for a predefined number of epochs.
- All neurons are classified according to their importance. The less valuable neuron is removed, only if the subsequent increase in the mean classification error is less than a predefined value.
- A neuron is removed, if it belongs to an empty class.
- The connections of the neurons are created dynamically by using the "Competitive Hebbian Learning" method.

The main characteristic of the SGONG is that both neurons and their connections approximate effectively the input data's topology. This is the exact reason for using the specific neural network in this application. Particularly, the proposed method uses the coordinates of random samples of the binary image as the input data. The network grows gradually on the black segment, i.e. the hand region and a structure of neurons and their connections is finally, created that describes effectively the hand's morphology. The output data of the network, in other words, is an array of the neurons' coordinates and an array of the neurons' connections. Based on this information important finger features are extracted.

2.3 The Training Steps of the SGONG Network

The training procedure for the SGONG neural classifier starts by considering first two output neurons ($c = 2$). The local counters N_i , $i = 1,2$ of created neurons are set to zero. The initial positions of the created output neurons, that is, the initial values for the weight vectors W_i, $i = 1,2$ are initialized by randomly selecting two different vectors from the input space. All the vectors of the training data set X' are circularly used for the training of the SGONG network.

The training steps of the SGONG are as follows:

Step 1. At the beginning of each epoch the accumulated errors $AE_i^{(1)}$, $AE_i^{(2)}$, $\forall i \in [1,c]$ are set to zero. The variable $AE_i^{(1)}$ expresses, at the end of each epoch, the quantity of the total quantization error that corresponds to $Neuron_i$, while the variable $AE_i^{(2)}$, represents the increment of the total quantization error that we would have if the $Neuron_i$ was removed.

Step 2. For a given input vector X_k, the first and the second winner neurons $Neuron_{w1}$, $Neuron_{w2}$ are obtained:

$$\text{for } Neuron_{w1} : \|X_k - W_{w1}\| \le \|X_k - W_i\|, \ \forall i \in [1,c] \tag{2}$$

$$\text{for } Neuron_{w2} : \|X_k - W_{w2}\| \le \|X_k - W_i\|, \ \forall i \in [1,c] \text{ and } i \ne w1 \tag{3}$$

Step 3. The local variables $AE_{w1}^{(1)}$ and $AE_{w1}^{(2)}$ change their values according to the relations:

$$AE_{w1}^{(1)} = AE_{w1}^{(1)} + \|X_k - W_{w1}\| \tag{4}$$

$$AE_{w1}^{(2)} = AE_{w1}^{(2)} + \|X_k - W_{w2}\| \tag{5}$$

$$N_{w1} = N_{w1} + 1 \tag{6}$$

Step 4. If $N_{w1} \le N_{idle}$ then the local learning rates $\varepsilon 1_{w1}$ and $\varepsilon 2_{w1}$ change their values according to equations (7), (8) and (9). Otherwise, the local learning rates have the constant values $\varepsilon 1_{w1} = \varepsilon 1_{\min}$ and $\varepsilon 2_{w1} = 0$.

$$\varepsilon 2_{w1} = \varepsilon 1_{w1} / r_{w1} \tag{7}$$

$$\varepsilon 1_{w1} = \varepsilon 1_{\max} + \varepsilon 1_{\min} - \varepsilon 1_{\min} \cdot \left(\frac{\varepsilon 1_{\max}}{\varepsilon 1_{\min}} \right)^{\frac{N_{w1}}{N_{idle}}} \tag{8}$$

$$r_{w1} = r_{\max} + 1 - r_{\max} \cdot \left(\frac{1}{r_{\max}} \right)^{\frac{N_{w1}}{N_{idle}}} \tag{9}$$

The learning rate $\varepsilon 1_i$ is applied to the weights of $Neuron_i$ if this is the winner neuron ($w1 = i$), while $\varepsilon 2_i$ is applied to the weights of $Neuron_i$ if this belongs to the neighborhood domain of the winner neuron ($i \in nei(w1)$). The learning rate $\varepsilon 2_i$ is used in order to have soft competitive effects between the output neurons. That is, for each output neuron, it is necessary that the influence from its neighboring neurons to be gradually reduced from a maximum to a minimum value. The values of the learning rates $\varepsilon 1_i$ and $\varepsilon 2_i$ are not constant but they are reduced according to the local counter N_i. Doing this, the potential ability of moving of neuron i toward an input vector (plasticity) is reduced with time. Both learning rates change their values from maximum to minimum in a period, which is defined by the N_{idle} parameter. The variable r_{wi} initially takes its minimum value $r_{\min} = 1$ and in a period, defined by the N_{idle} parameter, reaches its maximum value r_{max}.

Step 5. In accordance with the Kohonen SOFM, the weight vector of the winner neuron $Neuron_{w1}$ and the weight vectors of its neighboring neurons $Neuron_m$, $m \in nei(w1)$, are adapted according to the following relations:

$$W_{w1} = W_{w1} + \varepsilon 1_{w1} \cdot (X_k - W_{w1}) \tag{10}$$

$$W_m = W_m + \varepsilon 2_m \cdot (X_k - W_m),\ \forall m \in nei(w1) \tag{11}$$

Step 6. With regard to generation of lateral connections, SGONG employs the following strategy. The CHR is applied in order to create or remove connections between neurons. As soon as the neurons $Neuron_{w1}$ and $Neuron_{w2}$ are detected, the connection between them is created or is refreshed. That is

$$s_{w1,w2} = 0 \tag{12}$$

With the purpose of removing of superfluous lateral connections, the age of all connections emanating from $Neuron_{w1}$, except the connection with $Neuron_{w2}$, is increased by one:

$$s_{w1,m} = s_{w1,m} + 1,\ \forall m \in nei(w1),\ \text{with } m \neq w2 \tag{13}$$

Step 7. At the end of each epoch it is examined if all neurons are in *idle state*, or equivalently, if all the local counters N_i, $\forall i \in [1,c]$ are greater than the predefined value N_{idle} and the neurons are well trained. In this case, the training procedure stops, and the convergence of SGONG network is assumed. The number of input vectors needed for a neuron to reach the "*idle state*" influences the convergence speed of the proposed technique. If the training procedure continues, the lateral connections between neurons with age greater than the maximum value α are removed. Due to dynamic generation or removal of lateral connections, the neighborhood domain of each neuron changes with time in order to include neurons that are topologically adjacent.

2.4 Finger Identification

2.4.1 Determination of the Raised Fingers' Number

An essential step for the recognition is to determine the number of fingers that a gesture consists of. This is accomplished by locating the neurons that correspond to the fingertips.

(a) (b)

Fig. 4. (a) Hand image after the application of the SGONG network, (b) hand image after the location of the raised fingers

Observations of the structure of the output neurons' grid leads to the conclusion that fingertip neurons are connected to neighbourhood neurons by only two types of connections: i) connections that go through the background, and ii) connections that belong exclusively only to the hand region. The crucial point is that fingertip neurons use only one connection of the second type. Based on this conclusion, the determination of the number of fingers is:

- Remove all the connections that go through the background.
- Find the neurons that have only one connection. These neurons are the fingertips, as indicated in Fig. 4.
- Find successively the neighbor neurons. Stop when a neuron with more than two connections is found. This is the finger's last neuron (root-neuron).

Find the fingers' mean length (i.e. the mean fingertip and root neuron distance). If a finger's length differs significantly from the mean value then it is not considered to be a finger.

2.4.2 Extraction of Hand Shape Characteristics

Palm Region

Many images include redundant information that could reduce the accuracy of the extraction techniques and lead to false conclusions. Such an example is the presence of a part of the arm. Therefore, it is important to find the most useful hand region, which is the palm.

The algorithm of finding the palm region is based on the observation that the arm is thinner than the palm. Thus, a local minimum should appear at the horizontal projection of the binary image. The minimum defines the limits of the palm region as it is shown in Fig. 5.

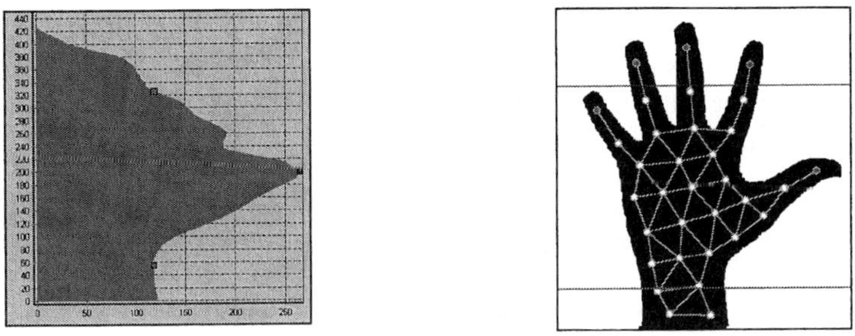

(a) (b)

Fig. 5. (a) Horizontal projection, (b) Palm region

This procedure is as follows:

- Create the horizontal projection of the image *H[j]*:
- Find the global maximum $H\left[j^{\max}\right]$ and the local minima $H\left[j_i^{\min}\right]$ of $H[j]$.
- Calculate the slope of the lines segments connecting the global maximum and the local minima, which satisfy the condition $j_i^{\min} < j^{\max}$. The minimum j_{lower} that corresponds to the greatest of these slopes defines the lower limit of the palm region, only if its distance from the maximum is greater than a threshold value equal to ImageHeight/6.
- The point that defines the upper limit of the palm region is denoted as j_{upper} and is obtained by the following relation:

$$H\left[j_{upper}\right] \leq H\left[j_{lower}\right] \text{ and } j_{upper} > j^{\max} > j_{lower} \tag{14}$$

Palm Centre
The coordinates of the centre of the palm are taken equal to the mean values of the coordinates of the neurons that belong to the palm region.

Hand Slope
Despite of the roughly vertical direction of the arm, the slope of the hand varies. This fact should be taken under consideration because it affects the accuracy of the finger features, and consequently, the efficiency of the identification process. The recognition results depend greatly on the correct calculation of the hand slope.

The hand slope can be estimated by the angle of the left side of the palm, as it can be viewed in Fig. 6(a). The technique consists of the following steps:

- Find the neuron N_{Left}, which belongs to the palm region and has the smallest horizontal coordinate.
- Obtain the set of palm neurons N_{set} that belong to the left boundary of the neurons grid. To do this, and for each neuron, starting from the N_{Left}, we obtain the neighborhood neuron which has, simultaneously, the smallest vertical and horizontal coordinates.
- The first and the final neurons of the set N_{set} define the hand slope line (HSL) which angle with the horizontal axis is taken equal to the hand's slope.

The hand slope is considered as a reference angle and is used in order to improve the feature extraction techniques.

2.4.3 Extraction of Finger Features

Finger Angles

A geometric feature that individualizes the fingers is their, relative to the hand slope, angles. As it is illustrated in Fig. 6(b), we extract two finger angles.

- RC Angle. It is an angle formed by the HSL and the line that joints the root neuron and the hand center. It is used directly for the finger identification process.
- TC Angle. It is an angle formed by the HSL and the line that joints the fingertip neuron and the hand center. This angle provides the most discrete values for each finger and thus is valuable for the recognition.

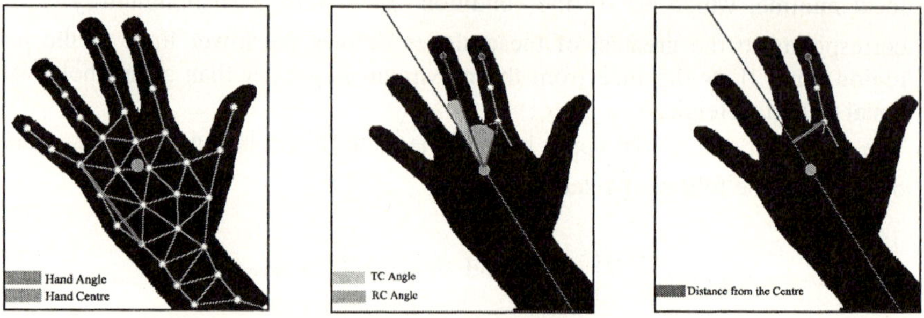

(a) (b) (c)

Fig. 6. (a) Hand slope and centre, (b) Fingers' angles, (c) Distance from the centre

Distance from the Palm Centre

A powerful feature for the identification process is the vertical distance of the finger's root neuron from the line passing through the palm centre and having the same slope as the HSL. An example is illustrated in Fig. 6(c).

3 Recognition Process

The recognition process is actually a choice of the most possible gesture. It is based on a classification process of the raised fingers into five classes (thumb, index, middle, ring, little) according to their features. The classification depends on the probabilities of a finger to belong to the above classes. The probabilities derive from the features distributions. Therefore, the recognition process consists of two stages: the off–line creation of the features distributions and the probability based classification.

3.1 Features Distributions

The finger features are naturally occurring features, thus a Gaussian distribution can model them. Their distributions are created by using a test set of 100 images from different people.

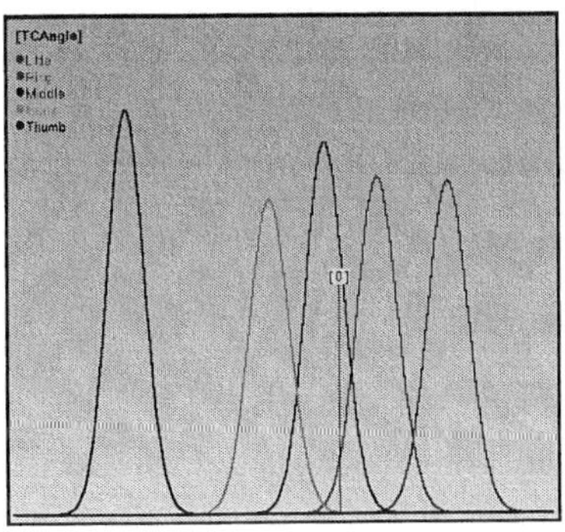

(a)

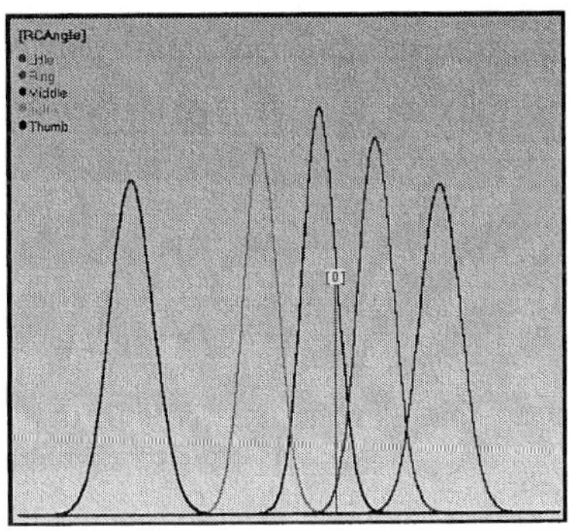

(b)

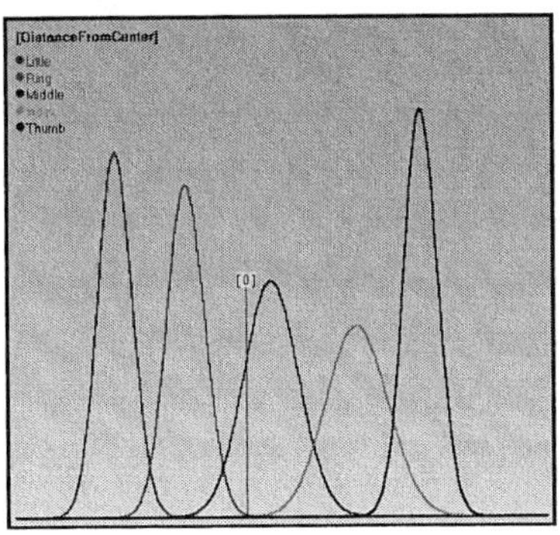

(c)

Fig. 7. Features distributions (a) TC Angle, (b) RC Angle, (c) Distance from the centre

If f_i is the i-th feature ($i \in [1,\ 3]$), then its Gaussian distributions for every class c_j ($j \in [1,\ 5]$) are given by the relation:

$$p_{fi}^{c_j}(x) = \frac{e^{-\frac{\left(x - m_{Pi}^{c_j}\right)^2}{2\sigma^2}}}{\sigma\sqrt{2\pi}} \tag{15}$$

where, $j = 1,...,5$, m_{fi}^{cj} is the mean value and σ_{fi}^{cj} the standard deviation of the fi feature of the cj class. . The Gaussian distributions of the above features are shown in Fig. 7. As it can be observed from the distributions, the five classes are well defined and are well discriminated.

3.2 Classification

The first step of the classification process is the calculation of the probabilities $RPcj$ of a raised finger to belong to each one of the five classes. Let x_0 be the value of the i-th feature fi. Calculate the probability $p_{fi}^{cj}(x_0)$ for $i \in [1,\ 3]$ and $j \in [1,\ 5]$. The requested probability is the sum of the probabilities of all the features for each class

$$RPcj = \sum_{i=1}^{3} p_{f_i}^{c_j} \tag{16}$$

where, $j = 1,...,5$, m_{fi}^{cj} is the mean value and σ_{fi}^{cj} the standard deviation of the fi feature of the cj class. . The Gaussian distributions of the above features are shown in Fig. 7. As it can be observed from the distributions, the five classes are well defined and are well discriminated.

This process is repeated for every raised finger.

Knowing the number of the raised fingers, one can define the possible gestures that can be created. For each one of these possible gestures the probability score is calculated, i.e. the sum of the gesture' s each raised finger to belong to each one of the classes. Finally, the gesture is recognized as the one with the higher probability score.

4 Experimental Results

The proposed hand gesture recognition system, which was implemented in DELPHI, was tested with 158 test hand images 1580 times. It is trained to recognize up to 26 gestures. The recognition rate, under the conditions described above, is 90.45%. Fig. 8 illustrates recognition examples.

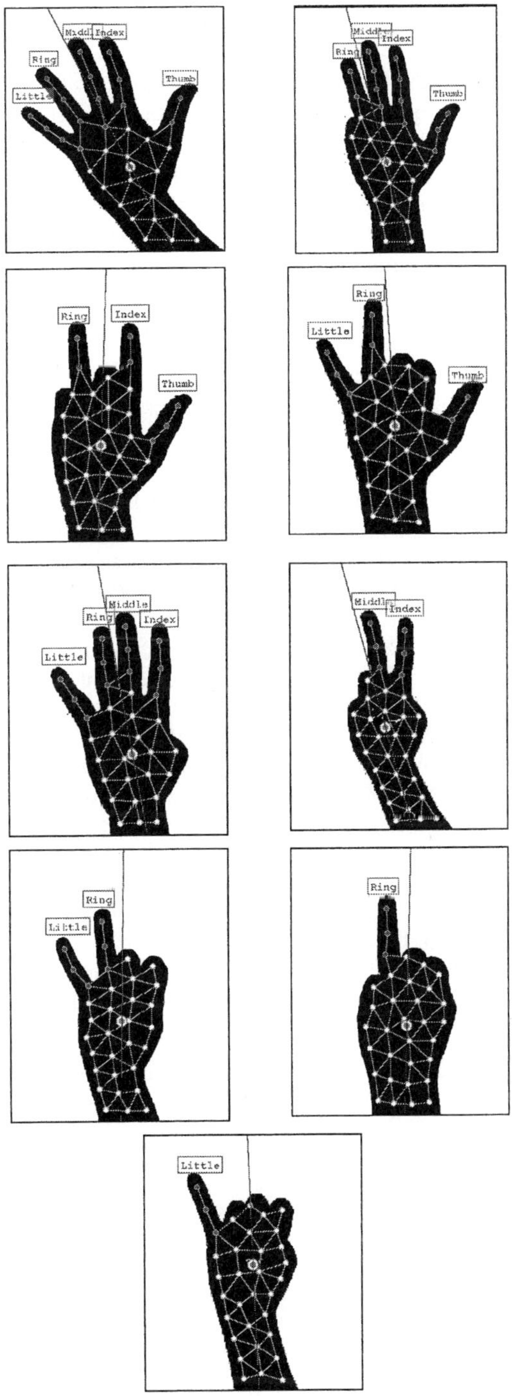

Fig. 8. Gesture recognition examples

5 Conclusions

This paper introduces a new technique for hand gesture recognition. It is based on a color segmentation technique for the detection of the hand region and on the use of the Self-Growing and Self-Organized Neural Gas network (SGONG) for the approximation of the hand's topology. The identification of the raised fingers, which depends on hand shape characteristics and fingers' features, is invariant of the hand's slope. Finally, the recognition process is completed by a probability-based classification with very high rates of success.

References

[1] Huang Chung-Lin, Huang Wen-Yi (1998). Sign language recognition using model-based tracking and a 3D Hopfield neural network. Machine Vision and Applications, 10:292-307. Springer-Verlag.

[2] Huang Chung-Lin, Jeng Sheng-Hung (2001). A model-based hand gesture recognition system. *Machine Vision and Applications*, 12:243-258. Springer-Verlag.

[3] Yin Xiaoming, Xie Ming (2003). Estimation of the fundamental matrix from uncalibrated stereo hand images for 3D hand gesture recognition. *Pattern Recognition*, 36:567-584. Pergamon.

[4] Herpers R., Derpanis K., MacLean W.J., Verghese G., Jenkin M., Milios E., Jepson A., Tsotsos J.K. (2001). SAVI: an actively controlled teleconferencing system. *Image snd Vision Computing*, 19:793-804. Elsevier.

[5] O' Mara David T. J. (2002). Automated Facial Metrology. Ph.D. Thesis, University of Western Australia, Department of Computer Science and Software Engineering.

[6] Chai Douglas, Ngan N. King (1999). Face segmentation using skin color map in videophone applications. *IEEE Transactions on Circuits and Systems for Video Technology,* 551-564.

[7] Chai Douglas, Ngan N. King (Apr. 1998). Locating facial region of a head–and–shoulders color image. Third IEEE International Conference on Automatic Face and Gesture Recognition, Nara, Japan, 124-129 .

[8] Atsalakis Antonis (2004). Colour Reduction in Digital Images. Ph.D. Thesis, Democritus University of Thrace, Department of Electrical and Computer Engineering.

Image Thresholding of Historical Documents Using Entropy and ROC Curves

Carlos A.B. Mello and Antonio H.M. Costa

Department of Computing Systems, Polytechnic School of Pernambuco,
Rua Benfica, 455, Madalena, Recife, PE, Brazil
cabm@dsc.upe.br

Abstract. It is presented herein a new thresholding algorithm for images of historical documents. The algorithm provides high quality binary images using entropy information of the images to define a primary threshold value which is adjusted with the use of ROC curves.

1 Introduction

Thresholding or binarization is a conversion from a color image to a bi-level one. This is the first step in several image processing applications. This process can be understood as a classification between objects and background in an image. It does not identify objects; just separate them from the background. This separation is not so easily done in images with low contrast. For these cases, image enhancement techniques must be used first to improve the visual appearance of the image. Another major problem is the definition of the features that are going to be analyzed in the search of the correct threshold value which will classify a pixel as object or background. The final bi-level image presents pixels whose gray level of 0 (black) indicates an object (or the signal) and a gray level of 1 (white) indicates the background. With document images, the background can be seen as the paper of the document and the object is the ink.

When the images are from historical documents this problem is quite singular. In these cases, the paper presents several types of noise. In some documents, the ink has faded; some of the others were written on both sides of the paper presenting ink-bleeding interference. A conversion into a bi-level image of this kind of documents using a nearest color threshold algorithm does not achieve high quality results. Thus ink and paper separation is not always a simple task.

In this work, we analyze the application of the thresholding process to generate high quality bi-level images from grey-scale images of documents. The images are of letters, documents and post cards from the end of the 19th century and beginning of the 20th century. The Image Processing of Historical Documents Project (DocHist) aims at the preservation of and easy access to the content of a file of thousands of documents.

In the complete file, there are documents written on one side or on both sides of the sheet of paper. In the latter case, two classes are identified: documents with or without back-to-front interference.

M. Lazo and A. Sanfeliu (Eds.): CIARP 2005, LNCS 3773, pp. 905 – 916, 2005.

The second class is the most common and it is easy to reduce the color palette suitably. The bi-level image can be generated from the grayscale one through the application of a threshold filter. A neighborhood filter [15] can also be used to reduce the "salt-and-pepper" noise in the image.

Palette reduction of documents with ink-bleeding interference is far more difficult to address. A straightforward threshold algorithm does not eliminate all the influence of the ink transposition from one side to the other in all cases.

It is presented herein a variation on a previous entropy-based algorithm [12]. It is used to define a primary threshold value which is adjusted using Receiver Operating Characteristic (ROC) curves [13].

2 Materials and Methods

This research takes place in the scope of the DocHist Project for preservation and broadcasting of a file of thousand of historical documents. The bequest is composed of more than 6,500 letters, documents and post cards which amounts more than 30,000 pages.

To preserve the file, the documents are digitized in 200 dpi resolution in true color and stored in JPEG file format with 1% loss for better quality/space storage rate. Even in this format each image of a document reaches, in average, 400 Kb. Although broadband Internet access is a common practice nowadays, the visualization of a bequest of thousand of files is not a simple task. Even in JPEG file format all the bequest must consume Giga bytes of space. There are new mobile devices which are not suitable to access large files as palm tops or PDA´s (Personal Digital Assistants).

A possible solution to this problem is to convert the images to bi-level which is not a simple task. As said before, some documents are written on both sides of the paper creating back-to-front interference; in others the ink has faded. Thus, the binarization by commercial softwares with standard settings is not appropriate. Figure 1 presents a sample document and its bi-level version produced by straightforward threshold algorithms.

Besides compression rates, high quality bi-level images yield better response from OCR tools. This allows the use of text files to make available the contents of the documents instead of its full digitized image.

The problem remains in the generation of these bi-level images from the original ones. For this, an entropy-based segmentation algorithm was proposed and extended with variations in the logarithmic basis [12].

2.1 Thresholding Algorithms

There are several algorithms for thresholding purposes. The first ones were based on simple features of the images or their histograms. The mean of the grayscale histogram is used as cut-off value in the thresholding by mean gray level [15]. Another algorithm is based on the percentage of black pixels desired [15] (10% is the value suggested in [15]). In the two peaks algorithm, the threshold occurs at the low point between two peaks in the histogram [15]. In adaptive algorithms, the iterative selection [17] makes an initial guess at a threshold value which is refined improving this value. The initial guess is the mean gray level which separates two areas and the mean values of these areas are evaluated (Tb and To). A new estimative of the threshold is evaluated as (Tb + To)/2. The process repeats with this new value of threshold until no change is found in the value in two consecutives steps.

It is presented herein some of the most well-known thresholding algorithms, which are classified based on the type of information used. The taxonomy used herein defines three categories of thresholding algorithms based on *histogram entropy*, *maximization or minimization functions* and *fuzzy theory*.

Fig. 1. (left) Grayscale sample document written on both sides of the paper and (right) its bi-level version by a threshold algorithm

Entropy [19] is a measure of information content. In Information Theory, it is assumed that there are *n* possible symbols *s* which occur with probability *p(s)*. The entropy associated with the source S of symbols is:

$$H(S) = -\sum_{i=0}^{n} p[s_i]\log(p[s_i])$$

where the entropy can be measured in bits/symbols. Although the logarithmic base is not defined, [7] and [10] analyze that changes in the base do not affect the concept of entropy as it was explored in [12].

Six entropy-based segmentation algorithms are briefly described herein: Pun [16], Kapur *et al* [6], Johannsen [5], Li-Lee [11], Wu-Lu [20] and Renyi [18].

Pun's algorithm [16] analyses the entropy of black pixels, *Hb*, and the entropy of the white pixels, *Hw*, bounded by the threshold value *t*. The algorithm suggests that *t* is such that maximizes the function *H* = *Hb* + *Hw*, where *Hb* and *Hw* are defined by:

$$Hb = -\sum_{i=0}^{t} p[i]\log(p[i]) \quad \text{(Eq. 1)}$$

$$Hw = -\sum_{i=t+1}^{255} p[i]\log(p[i]) \quad \text{(Eq. 2)}$$

where *p[i]* is the probability of pixel *i* with color *color[i]* is in the image.

In [6], Kapur *et al* defined a probability distribution *A* for an object and a distribution *B* to the background of the document image, such that:

A: p0/Pt, p1/Pt, ..., pt/Pt
B: (pt+1)/(1 – Pt), (pt + 2)/(1 - Pt),..., p255/(1 – Pt)

The entropy values *Hw* and *Hb* are evaluated using Equations 1 and 2 with *p[i]* defined with these new distributions. The maximization of the function *Hw* + *Hb* is analyzed to define the threshold value *t*.

Another variation of an entropy-based algorithm is proposed by Johannsen and Bille [5] trying to minimize the function *Sb(t)* + *Sw(t)*, with:

$$S_w(t) = \log(\sum_{i=t+1}^{255} p_i) + (1/\sum_{i=t+1}^{255} p_i)[E(p_t) + E(\sum_{i=t+1}^{255} p_i)]$$

and

$$S_b(t) = \log(\sum_{i=0}^{t} p_i) + (1/\sum_{i=0}^{t} p_i)[E(p_t) + E(\sum_{i=0}^{t-1} p_i)]$$

where *E(x)=-xlog(x)* and *t* is the threshold value.

The Li-Lee algorithm [11] uses the minimum cross entropy thresholding, where the threshold selection is solved by minimizing the cross entropy between the image and its segmented version.

The basic idea of the Wu-Lu algorithm is the use of the lower difference between the minimum entropy of the objects and the entropy of the background [20]. The method is very useful in ultra-sound images which have few different contrast values.

The Renyi method [18] uses two probability distribution function (one for the object and the other for the background), the derivatives of the distributions and the methods of Maximum Sum Entropy and Entropic Correlation.

Other algorithms are based on the maximization or minimization of functions. Although Kapur and Johannsen algorithms, presented previously, work in the same way, they were classified as Entropy algorithms because of the major importance of this feature in them. For this category of algorithms, five techniques are selected.

The Brink method [8] identify two threshold values (T1 and T2), using the Brink´s maximization algorithm. The colors below T1 are turned to black and the colors above T2 are turned to white. The values between T1 and T2 are colorized analyzing the neighbors of the pixel. A 25x25 area is analyzed and, if there is a pixel in this area which color is greater than T2, then the pixel is converted to white.

In the Minimum Thresholding algorithm, Kittler and Illingworth [9] use the histogram as a measured probability density function of two distributions (object and background pixels). The minimization of a criterion function defines the threshold.

Fisher method [1] consists in the localization of the threshold values between the gray levels classes. These threshold values are found using a minimization of the sum of the inertia associated to the two different classes.

In the Kittler and Illingworth Algorithm based on Yan´s Unified algorithm [22] the foreground and background class conditional probability density functions are assumed to be Gaussian, but in contrast to the previous method the equal variance assumption is removed. The error expression can be interpreted also as a fitting expression to be minimized.

Otsu [14] suggested minimizing the weighted sum of within-class variances of the foreground and background pixels to establish an optimum threshold. The algorithm has its basics in the discriminant analysis. The segmentation is done using the mean values of the foreground and background classes (μ_b and μ_w, for the pixels classified as ink or paper, respectively), of the between-classes variances σ_b^2, within-classes variances σ_w^2 and total variance σ_T^2. Otsu demonstrated that the optimal value of the threshold t^* can be reached by the maximizing the function $\eta(t) = \frac{\sigma_b^2(t)}{\sigma_T^2}$, *i.e.*, the ratio between the variance between-classes and the total variance.

In a fuzzy set, an element x belongs to a set S with probability p_x. This definition of fuzzy sets can be easily applied to the segmentation problem. Most of the algorithms use a measure of fuzziness which is a distance between the original gray level image and the segmented one. The minimization of the fuzziness produces the most accurate binarized version of the image. We can cite three binarization algorithms that use fuzzy theory: C Means [4], Huang [3] and Yager [21].

In addition, there is also the Ye-Danielsson [2] algorithm which is implemented as an iterative thresholding.

Fig. 2 presents the application of these algorithms in the sample document of Fig. 1. It can be observed that some algorithms performance was very poor as some images are completely black or white.

2.2 Entropy-Based Segmentation Algorithm

At first, the algorithm scans the image in search for the most frequent color, t. As we are working with images of letters and documents, it is correct to suppose that this color belongs to the paper. This color is used as an initial threshold value for the evaluation of Hb and Hw as defined in Eq. 1 and 2 before.

As defined in [7], the use of different logarithmic bases does not change the concept of entropy. This base is taken as the area of the image: width by height.

With *Hw* and *Hb*, the entropy, *H*, of the image is evaluated as their sum:

$$H = Hw + Hb . \qquad \text{(Eq. 3)}$$

Based on the value of *H*, three classes of documents were identified, which define two multiplicative factors, as follows:

- $H \leq 0.25$ (documents with few parts of text or very faded ink), then $mw = 2$ and $mb = 3$;
- $0.25 < H < 0.30$ (the most common cases), then $mw = 1$ and $mb = 2.6$;
- $H \geq 0.30$ (documents with many black areas), then $mw = mb = 1$.

These values of *mw* and *mb* were found empirically after several experiments where the hit rate of OCR tools in typed documents (as the one of Fig. 3-left) defined the correct values. With the values of *Hw*, *Hb*, *mw* and *mb* the threshold value, *th*, is defined as:

$$th = mw.Hw + mb.Hb . \qquad \text{(Eq. 4)}$$

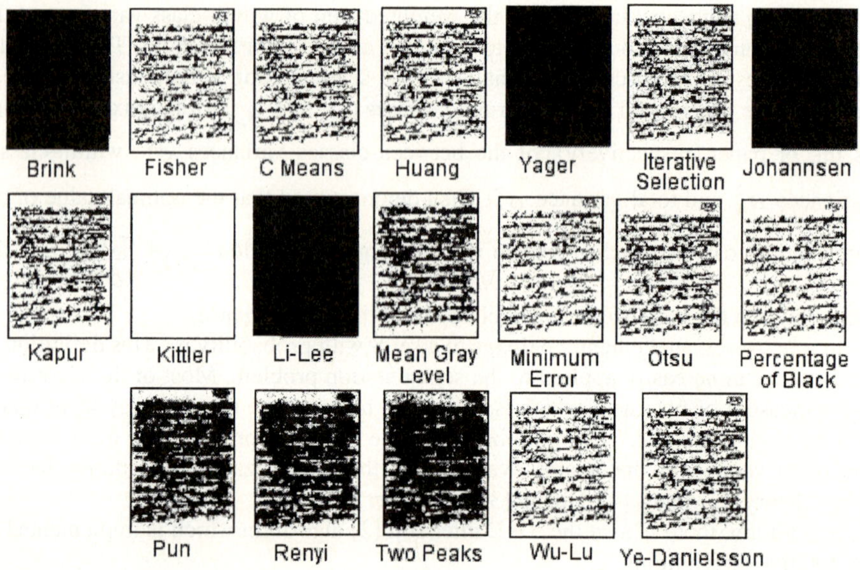

Fig. 2. Application of several thresholding algorithms in document presented in Fig. 1 with back-to-front interference

The grayscale image is scanned again and each pixel i with *graylevel[i]* is turned to white if:

$$(graylevel[i]/256) \geq th \,. \qquad \text{(Eq. 5)}$$

Otherwise, its color remains the same (to generate a new grayscale image but with a white background) or it is turned to black (generating a bi-level image). This is called the *segmentation condition.*

Fig. 3 presents a zooming into a document and its binarized version generated by the entropy-based algorithm.

The problem comes when the images have back-to-front interference. As it can be seen in Fig. 4, the results of the algorithm are not the best, even though it is far better

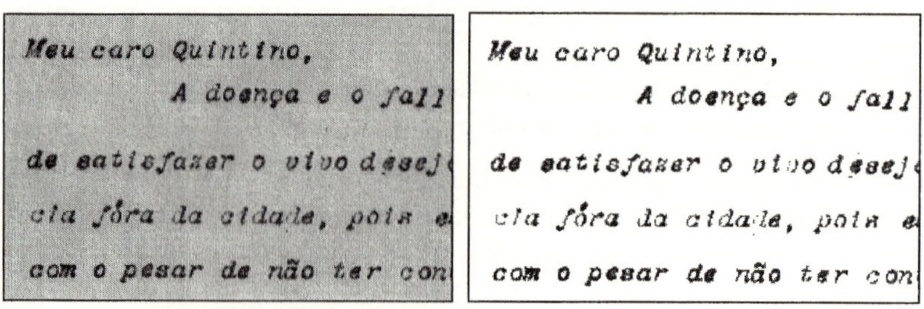

Fig. 3. (left) Sample document and (right) its bi-level version by entropy algorithm

than other ones. It can be noticed in Fig. 4-left that the bi-level image presents some elements of the opposite side of the paper, although its quality is much better than the one created by a straightforward thresholding algorithm (Fig. 4-center). The correction of this threshold value is proposed in the next Section with the use of ROC curves.

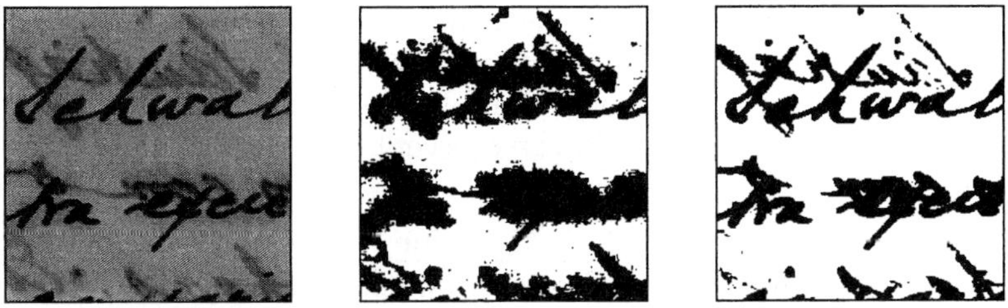

Fig. 4. (left) Sample document with back-to-front interference, (center) binarized image using a nearest color thresholding algorithm with default values and (right) bi-level image generated by new entropy-based algorithm

2.3 Thresholding by ROC Curves

The threshold value defined by the entropy-based algorithm is not always the best value. So, to adjust this value, it used a receiver operating characteristic (ROC) curve from Detection Theory [13]. This is usually used in medical analysis where some tests can generate *true positives* (TP), *false positives* (FP), *true negatives* (TN) and *false negatives* (FN) answers. TP represents the number of patients who have some disease, and have this corroborated by having a "high" test (above some chosen cutoff level). FP represents false positives - the test was wrong, and resulted that non-diseased patients are really ill. Similarly, true negatives are represented by TN, and false negatives by FN.

In elementary statistical texts, some will encounter other terms:

- The sensitivity is how accurate the test is at picking out patients with the disease. It is simply the True Positive. In other words, sensitivity gives us the proportion of cases picked out by the test, relative to all cases that actually have the disease.
- Specificity is the ability of the test to pick out patients who do not have the disease. This is synonymous with the True Negative.

A receiver operating characteristic (ROC) curve shows the relationship between probability of detection (PD) and probability of false alarm (PFA) for different threshold values. The two numbers of interests are the probability of detection (TP) and the probability of false alarms (FP). The probability of detection (PD) is the probability of correctly detecting a Threat user. The probability of false alarm (PFA) is the probability of declaring a user to be a Threat when s/he is Normal. The detection threshold is varied systematically to examine the performance of the model for different thresholds. Varying the threshold produces different classifiers with different (PD) and probability of false alarm (PFA). By plotting PD and PFA for different thresholds values, one can get a ROC curve.

For thresholding applications, this theory can be easily adapted as one can see the TP as the ink pixels correctly classified as object; FP represents background elements classified as object, and so on.

The new proposed algorithm starts with the application of the previous entropy-based algorithm. This initial threshold value (th) is used to define a binary matrix (M) with the same size of the input image. Each cell of this matrix is set to *true* if the corresponding pixel in the input image (IM) is equal to th. This leads to the building of the PD *versus* PFA curve (the ROC curve) according to algorithm 1.

Algorithm 1

n1 ← the number of true elements in M (elements equal to th in IM)
n0 ← the number of false elements in M (elements different to th in IM)
for t = 0 to 255
  pd(t) ← Σ (IM > t **AND** M)/n1
  pfa(t) ← Σ (IM > t **AND** ¬M)/n0
end

For our kind of images, the ROC curve defined by this algorithm is a step like function which has its maximum values equal to 1 for both axes. Different initial threshold values define different ROC curves.

Fig. 5 presents the PD *versus* PFA curve for the sample image of Fig. 4-left. For this document, th = 104 and PFA is equal to 1 when PD is 0.758.

One can see in the bi-level image (Fig. 4-right) that there are still many elements of the ink that is in the other side of the paper. So this cut-off value is not the best one.

It was observed in the handwritten documents that the percentage of ink is about 10% of the complete image. So, the correct ROC curve must grow to 1 when PD values about 0.9. For this, different values of th must be used. This creates different M matrixes leading to new PDxPFA curves. If the curve grows to 1 with PD less than 0.9, then the initial th must decrease; otherwise, it must increase. Fig. 6 presents some resulting images for different th and the PD value which turns PFA equals to 1, starting from the initial th = 104, and PD = 0.758 (present in Fig. 5).

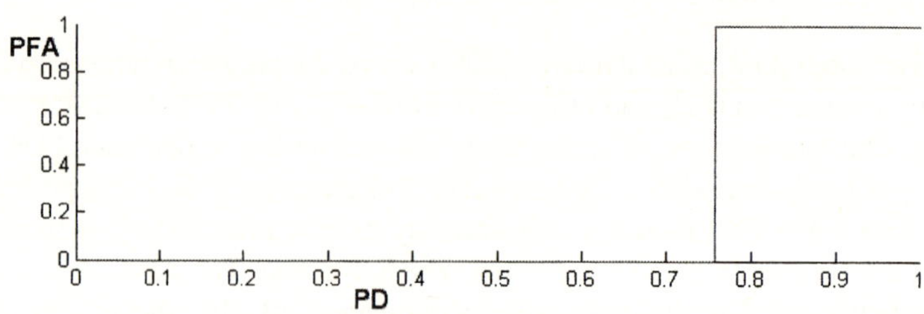

Fig. 5. (top-left) Original document with back-to-front interference. (top-right) Binarized version generated with th = 104. (bottom) PD *versus* PFA graphic; PFA = 1 for PD = 0.756.

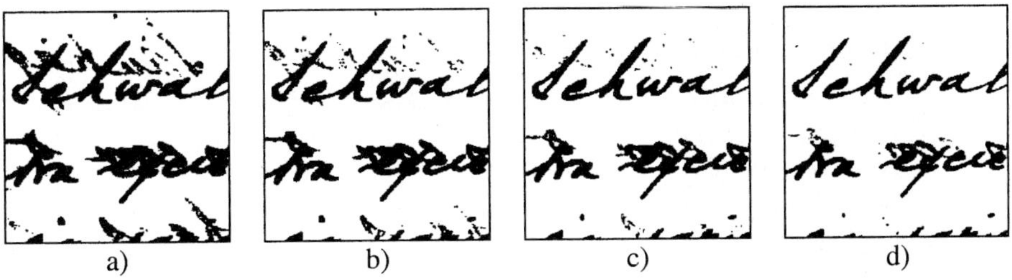

Fig. 6. Bi-level images generated by different threshold values (th) and the corresponding PD value for which PFA turns equal to 1: a) th = 100, PD = 0.771, b) th = 90, PD = 0.8244, c) th = 80, PD = 0.8534 and d) th = 70, PD = 0.8749

3 Results

For the sample document of Fig. 4, the initial threshold value is 104 and, as it could be seen, it did not result a good quality image. For this th, PD is 0.756 (Fig. 5). So, the th value must be decreased until PD equals to 0.9. In fact, a small variation of this PD value is accepted. Changing the th value, PD reaches the value of 0.8983 (when PFA turns from 0 to 1) with th = 57. The final PD *versus* PFA graphic just as the final bi-level image of the sample document of Fig. 4 are shown in Fig. 7.

Fig. 8 presents others sample documents, their bi-level images generated by the entropy-based algorithm with and without the ROC correction and the threshold values defined (initial and final).

As can be seen in Fig. 8, the correction achieved better quality images for all cases. The same happened with images without back-to-front interference. But, in these cases, the difference between the initial threshold value and the final one is smaller. Thus, the correction can be applied to every case.

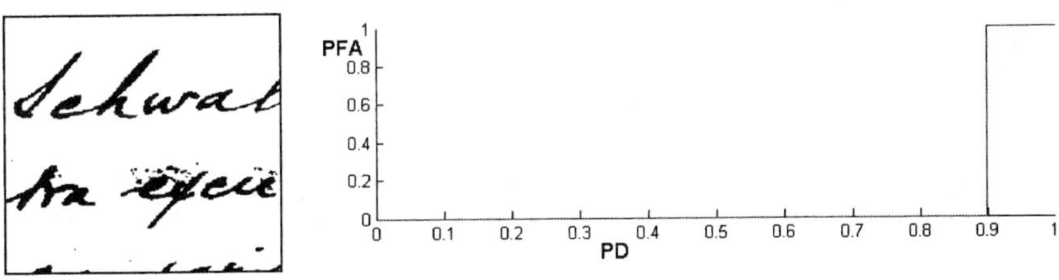

Fig. 7. (left) Final bi-level version of document presented in Fig. 4-top-left after correction by ROC curve. (right) PD *versus* PFA graphic. The threshold value is now 57, with PD = 0.8983.

4 Conclusions

This paper presents a variation of an entropy-based thresholding algorithm for images of historical documents. The algorithm defines an initial threshold value which is adjusted by the use of ROC curves. These adjustments define new cut-off values and they generate better quality bi-level images. The method is quite suitable when

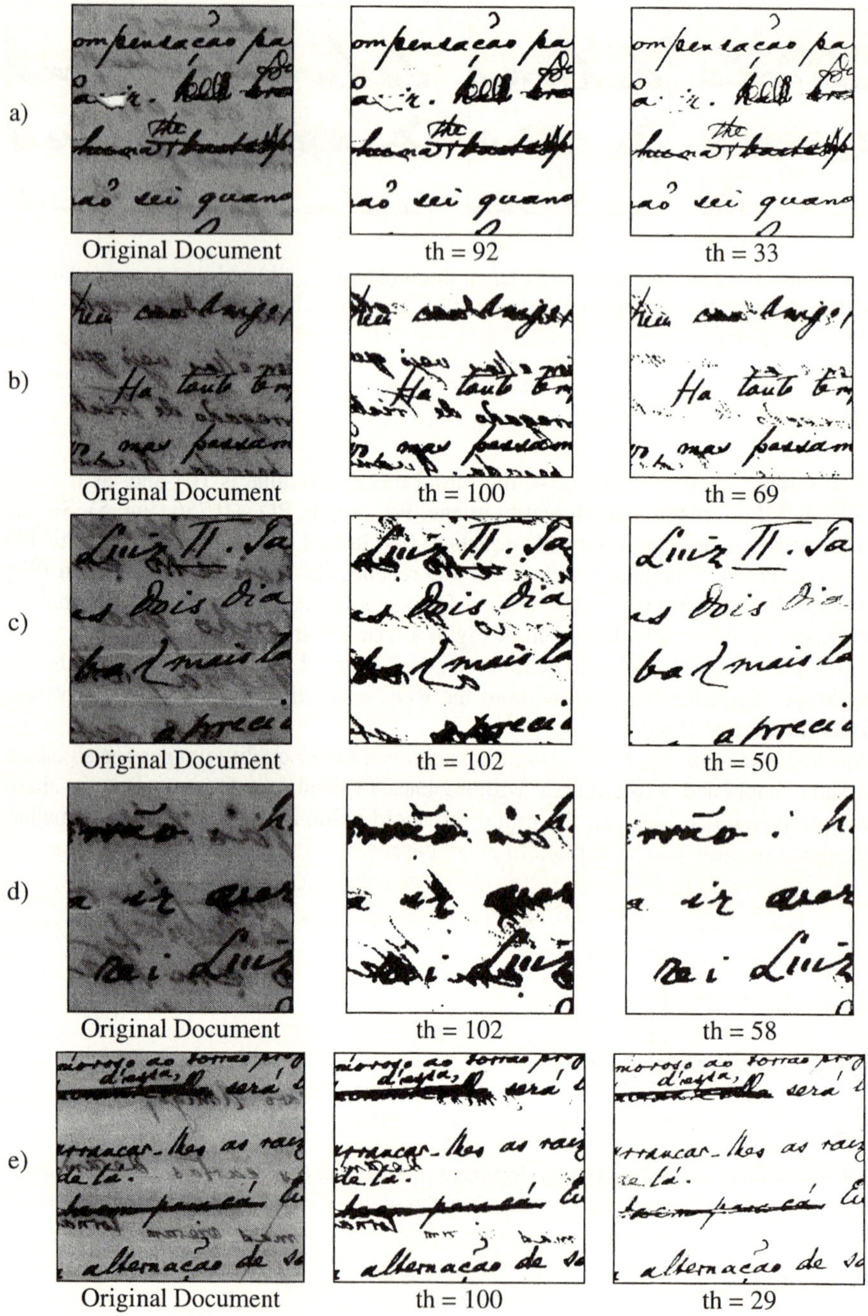

Fig. 8. (left) Sample original documents and bi-level images generated by entropy-based threshold algorithm (center) without and (right) with ROC correction

applied to documents written on both sides of the paper, presenting back-to-front interference. By visual inspection, the binary images are far better than the ones produced by others well-known algorithm.

The monochromatic images can be used to make files of thousand of historical documents more easily accessible by the Internet even through mobile devices which have slower connections.

A MatLab implementation of the proposed algorithm just as a sample image of a document is avaliable at: http://www.upe.poli.br/dsc/recpad/site_hist/throc.htm

Acknowledgments

This research is partially sponsored by CNPq (PDPG-TI 55.0017/2003-8), FACEPE and University of Pernambuco.

References

1. M.S.Chang, S.M.Kang, W.S.Rho, H.G.Kim and D.J.Kim. "Improved binarization algorithm for document image by histogram and edge detection", *Proc. 3rd Intern. Conf .on Document Analysis and Recognition*, pp.636-639, Canada, 1995.
2. C.A.Glasbye, "An Analysis of Histogram-Based Thresholding Algorithm", CVGIP: Graphical Models and Image Processing, nov 1993.
3. L.K.Huang L.K and M.J.Wang, "Image Thresholding by Minimizing the Measures of Fuzziness", Pattern Recognition, 1995.
4. C.V.Jawahar, P.K.Biswas and K.Ray, "Investigations On Fuzzy Thresholding Based On Fuzzy Clustering", Pattern Recognition, 1997.
5. G.Johannsen and J.Bille, "A Threshold Selection Method using Information Measures", *Proceedings, 6th Int. Conf. Pattern Recognition*, Munich, Germany, pp.140-143, 1982.
6. J.N.Kapur, P.K.Sahoo and A.K.C.Wong. "A New Method for Gray-Level Picture Thresholding using the Entropy of the Histogram", Computer Vision, Graphics and Image Processing, 29(3), 1985.
7. J. N. Kapur, *Measures of Information and their Applications*, John Wiley and Sons, 1994.
8. S.W.Katz and A.D.Brink, "Segmentation of Chromosome Images", IEEE, 1993, pp 85-90.
9. J.Kittler and J.Illingworth, "Minimum Error Thresholding", Pattern Recognition, Volume 19, Issue 1, pp 41-47, 1986.
10. S.Kullback. *Information Theory and Statistics*.Dover Publications, Inc.1997.
11. C.H.Li and C.K.Lee, "Minimum Cross Entropy Thresholding", Pattern Recognition, v.26, no 4, pp 616-626, 1993.
12. C.A.B.Mello. "A New Entropy and Logarithmic Based Binarization Algorithm for Grayscale Images". IASTED VIIP 2004, Hawaii, USA, 2004.
13. N.A.McMilan, C.D.Creelman. *Detection Theory*. LEA Pub., 2005.
14. N.Otsu. "A threshold selection method from gray-level histogram". *IEEE Trans .on Systems, Man, and Cybernetics*, vol 8: 62-66, 1978.
15. J.R.Parker, *Algorithms for Image Processing and Computer Vision*, John Wiley and Sons, 1997.
16. T.Pun, "Entropic Thresholding, A New Approach", C.Graphics and Image Proc., 1981.
17. T.W.Ridler and S.Calvard. "Picture Thresholding Using an Iterative Selection Method", *IEEE Trans. on Systems, Man and Cybernetics*, Vol.SMC-8, 8:630-632, 1978

18. P.Sahoo, C.Wilkins and J.Yeager, "Threshold Selection using Renyi's Entropy", Pattern recognition Vol 30, No 1, pp 71-84, 1997
19. C.Shannon. "A Mathematical Theory of Communication". Bell System Technology Journal, vol. 27, pp. 370-423, 623-656, 1948.
20. Lu Wu, Songde Ma, Hanqing Lu, "An Effective Entropic thresholding for Ultrasonic Images", IEEE, pp.1552-1554, 1998.
21. R.R.Yager, "On the Measures of Fuzziness and Negation.Part.1: Membership in the Unit Interval", Int Journal of Gen. Sys, 1979.
22. H.Yan, "Unified Formulation of a Class of Image Thresholding Techniques", Pattern Recognition, Vol. 29, No 12, pp 2025-2032, 1996.

De-noising of Underwater Acoustic Signals Based on ICA Feature Extraction

Kong Wei and Yang Bin

Information Engineering College, Shanghai Maritime University, Shanghai 200135, China
kongwei@sjtu.edu.cn, binyang@cie.shmtu.edu.cn

Abstract. As an efficient sparse coding and feature extraction method, independent component analysis (ICA) has been widely used in speech signal processing. In this paper, ICA method is studied in extracting low frequency features of underwater acoustic signals. The generalized Gaussian model (GGM) is introduced as the p.d.f. estimator in ICA to extract the basis vectors. It is demonstrated that the ICA features of ship radiated signals are localized both in time and frequency domain. Based on the ICA features, an extended de-noising method is proposed for underwater acoustic signals which can extract the basis vectors directly from the noisy observation. The de-noising experiments of underwater acoustic signals show that the proposed method offers an efficient approach for detecting weak underwater acoustic signals from noise environment.

1 Introduction

Recently, independent component analysis (ICA) has been shown highly effective in encoding patterns, including image and speech signals [1-4]. Unlike correlation-based learning algorithm, ICA can extract the higher order statistics from data. And the most informative features of sound signals require higher-order statistics for their characterization. Nowadays, pattern recognition and object detection of underwater acoustic signals are hard works since these signals are non-Gaussian, non-stationary and non-linear complex signals. In this paper, ICA is used in extracting the higher-order statistics of underwater acoustic signals, and the generalized Gaussian model (GGM) was introduced in ICA algorithm to estimate the p.d.f. of coefficients. By inferring only one parameter q, ICA algorithm can extract the efficient basis vectors for different underwater acoustic signals. The time and frequency domain characteristic of the ICA basis and the sparseness of coefficients demonstrate that ICA feature extraction of underwater acoustic signals is efficient.

Based on the ICA features, an extended de-noising method is proposed for noisy underwater acoustic signals. In many ICA-based de-noising works, the de-noising process of noisy signals needs noise-free source data to train the ICA basis vectors as a priori knowledge. Unfortunately, the noise-free signal is always not acquirable in practice. In this paper, the ICA algorithm based on GGM is presented on extracting the efficient basis vectors directly from the noisy signals. At the same time the shrinkage function can be obtained from the p.d.f. of each coefficient. Using the maximum likelihood (ML) method on the non-Gaussian variables corrupted by

M. Lazo and A. Sanfeliu (Eds.): CIARP 2005, LNCS 3773, pp. 917 – 924, 2005.

additive white Gaussian noise, we show how to apply the shrinkage method on the coefficients to reduce noise. The de-noising experiments of the artificial mixtures of underwater acoustic signals show that the short-term zero crossing rate (ZCR) of source signals is improved after de-noising.

2 ICA Feature Extraction Using GGM

ICA assume the observation $\boldsymbol{x}$ is the linear mixture of the independent components $\boldsymbol{u}$, $\boldsymbol{x} = \boldsymbol{A}\boldsymbol{s}$, where the columns of $\boldsymbol{A}$ are described as the basis vectors. An ICA feature extraction algorithm is applied to obtain independent vectors $\boldsymbol{u}$ and weight matrix $\boldsymbol{W}$ from signal segment $\boldsymbol{x}$, $\boldsymbol{u} = \boldsymbol{W}\,\boldsymbol{x}$, then the basis vectors $\boldsymbol{A}$ can be calculated by the relation $\boldsymbol{A} = \boldsymbol{W}^{-1}$. The *infomax* learning rule is used here [1-4]:

$$\Delta W \propto \eta[I - \varphi(s)s^T]W \tag{1}$$

Where the vector $\varphi(s)$ is a function of the prior and is defined by $\varphi(s) = -\frac{\partial \log p(s)}{\partial s}$, here $p(s)$ are the p.d.f.s of vectors $\boldsymbol{s}$. It can be seen that the knowledge of the p.d.f. of the independent components $\boldsymbol{s}$ plays an important role. Here the generalized Gaussian model (GGM) is used in ICA feature extraction of underwater acoustic signals.

The GGM models a family of density functions that is peaked and symmetric at the mean, with a varying degree of normality in the following general form [5, 6]

$$p_g(s \mid \theta) = \frac{\omega(q)}{\sigma}\exp[-c(q) \mid \frac{s-\mu}{\sigma} \mid^q], \qquad \theta = \{\mu, \theta, q\} \tag{2}$$

where

$$c(q) = \left[\frac{\Gamma[3/q]}{\Gamma[1/q]}\right]^{q/2}, \qquad \omega(q) = \frac{\Gamma[3/q]^{1/2}}{(2/q)\Gamma[3/q]^{3/2}} \tag{3}$$

$\mu = E[s]$ and $\sigma = \sqrt{E[(s-\mu)^2]}$ are the mean and standard deviation of the data respectively. $\Gamma[\cdot]$ is the Gamma function. By inferring q, a wide class of statistical distributions can be characterized. The Gaussian, Laplacian, and strong Laplacian distributions can be modeled by putting $q = 2$, $q = 1$, and $q < 1$ respectively. In ICA learning rules, the problem then becomes to estimate the value of q from the data. This can be accomplished by simply finding the maximum posteriori value q. The posterior distribution of q given the observations $\boldsymbol{x}=\{x_1,\ldots,x_n\}$ is

$$p(q \mid x) \propto p(x \mid q)p(q) \tag{4}$$

where the data likelihood is

$$p(x \mid q) = \prod_n \omega(q)\exp[-c(q) \mid x_n \mid^q] \tag{5}$$

and $p(q)$ defines the prior distribution for q. Gamma function $\Gamma[\cdot]$ is used as $p(q)$ here.

In the case of the GGM as the p.d.f of s, the vector $\varphi(s)$ in eq. 1 can be derived as

$$\varphi_i(s_i) = -qc\sigma_i^{-q} \mid s_i - \mu_i \mid^{q-1} sign(s_i - \mu_i) \tag{6}$$

Using the GGM-based ICA learning rule (eq. 1), the basis vectors of ship radiated signals and sea noises are extracted respectively. 40,000 samples of each signal were used and the sample-rates were down-sampled to 500Hz. For each signal, 1000 samples of length 40 (8ms) were generated. Each segment was pre-whitened to improve the convergence speed. The adaptation started from the 40×40 identity matrix and trained through the 1000 data vectors. The learning rate was gradually decreased from 0.2 to 0.05 during the iteration. When W is achieved, the basis vectors of signals can be obtained by $\boldsymbol{A} = \boldsymbol{W}^{-1}$. Figure 1 show the basis vectors of ship radiated signals and sea noise.

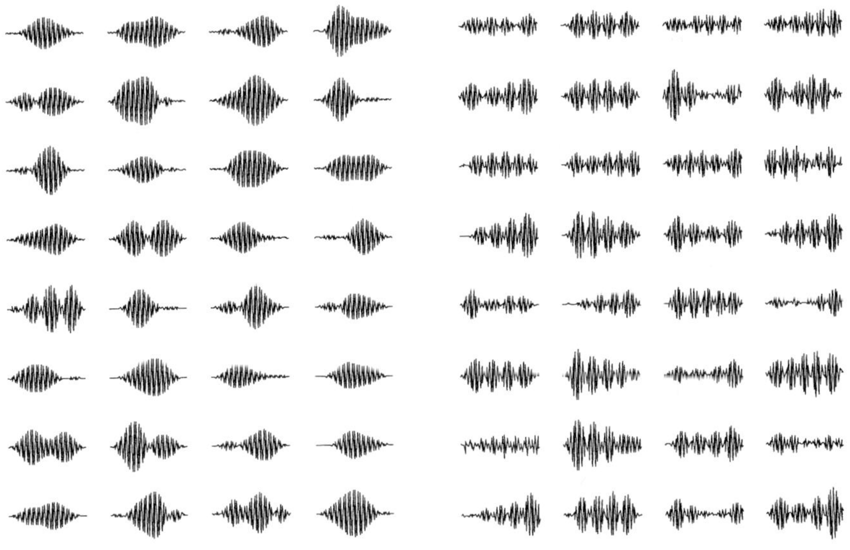

(a) (b)

Fig. 1. (a)-(b) Basis vectors of ship radiated signals and sea noises in time domain

40 basis vectors of ship radiated signals are show in Fig. 1 (a), in which each subfigure denotes one basis vector which is the column vector of $\boldsymbol{A}$, the same as Fig. 1 (b). The basis vectors look like short-time Fourier bases, but are different in that they are asymmetric in time. The basis vectors of ship radiated signals have one or two peaks and are local in time, but those of sea noises have a few peaks, generally four, and cover all time span like Fourier basis. Fig.2 gives the frequency domain characteristic of fig.1.

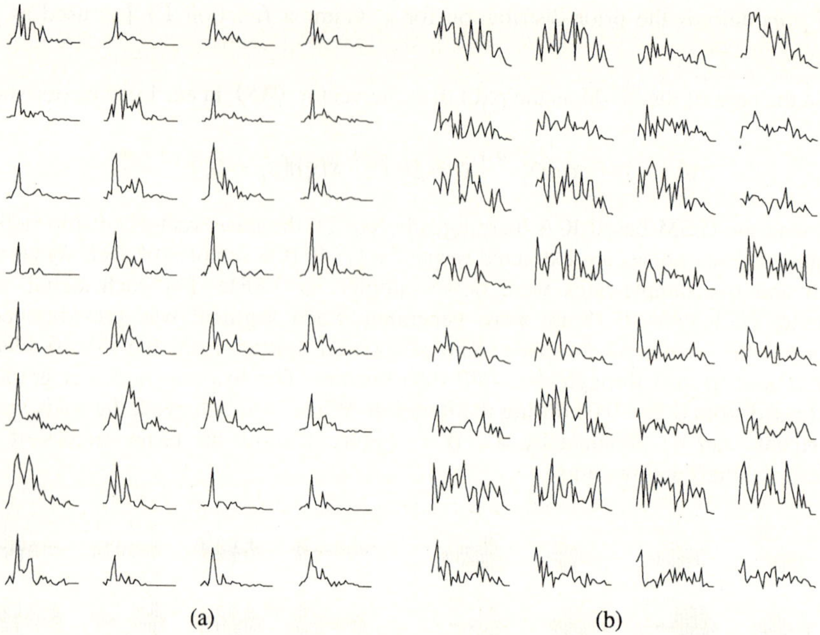

Fig. 2. (a)-(b) The frequency spectrum of fig.1 (a) and (b)

It can be seen that the ICA basis vectors of ship radiated signals are localized both in time (Fig1. (a)) and frequency domain (Fig2. (a)), and not localized in sea noise (Fig1. (b) and Fig2. (b)). The ICA feature of ship radiated signals are focus on low frequency (Fig.2 (b)), and that of sea noises are global in all frequency domain because sea noises are close to Gaussian distribution.

In order to compare the sparseness of the coefficients produced by ICA and other conventional methods, the log-scaled histograms of the coefficients of DFT, DCT,

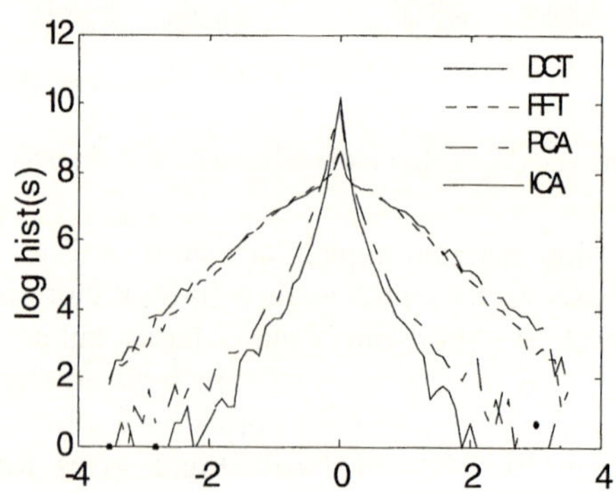

Fig. 3. Histograms of the coefficients of ship radiated signals in different methods

PCA and ICA for ship radiated signals are shown in fig.3. It can be seen that the distribution of the ICA coefficients is peakier than the others, and this characteristic yields greater sparseness in encode efficiency.

3 De-noising Method Based on ICA Feature Extraction

In recently ICA-based de-noising works of speech or image, the de-noising process of noisy signals needs noise-free source data to train the ICA basis vectors as a priori knowledge. Unfortunately, the corresponding noise-free signals are always not acquirable, especially for the underwater acoustic signals. The object ship radiated signals are always submerged in loudly sea noises. In this paper, based on Hyvärinen's maximum likelihood de-noising method [7, 8, 9], an extended method based on GGM-ICA feature extraction is proposed.

In the noise environment, denote y as the noisy coefficient of a basis vector, s as the original noise-free version of coefficient of basis vector, and v as a Gaussian noise with zero mean and variance σ^2. Then the variable y can be describe as

$$y = s + v \tag{7}$$

We want to estimate s from the only observed noisy coefficient y. Denote p as the probability of s, and $f = -\log p$ as its negative log-density, the estimator of s can be obtained by the maximum likelihood (ML) method [7]

$$\hat{s} = \arg\min_{s} \frac{1}{2\sigma^2}(y-s)^2 + f(s) \tag{8}$$

Assuming $f(\bullet)$ to be strictly convex and differentiable, the ML estimation gives the equation

$$\hat{s} = h(y) \tag{9}$$

where the nonlinear function $h(\bullet)$ is called as *shrinkage* function, and the inverse is given by

$$h^{-1}(s) = s + \sigma^2 f'(s) \tag{10}$$

Thus, the estimation of s is obtained by inverting a certain function involving $f'(\bullet)$.

For current ICA-based de-noising works, however, the de-noising process of noisy signals needs noise-free source data to train the ICA basis vectors. When the corresponding noise-free signals are inaccessible, these algorithms are failed. The GGM-based ICA algorithm in last section has been used to extract the basis vectors directly from noisy signals when the noise-free signals cannot be obtained, and the p.d.f. of the coefficients $p(s)$ learned by the GGM can get simultaneously. Since $f(\bullet)$ in eq. 10 is a function of p, the probability of s has been obtained by GGM in ICA feature extraction, so the shrinkage function can be obtained easily.

To recover the de-noised signal from the noisy source three steps are needed. Firstly, by using GGM-based ICA, we can obtain the un-mixing matrix $\boldsymbol{W}$ and the p.d.f. of the corresponding coefficients $p(s)$ at the same time. From the experiments, it shows that the coefficients of the basis vectors extracted from noisy underwater acoustic signals have sparse distributions. Secondly, the shrinkage functions can be estimated by $p(s)$ by eq.10, and the de-noised coefficients can be calculated by $\hat{s} = h(y)$. Finally, recover the de-noised ship radiated signals by $\hat{x} = W^{-1}\hat{s} = A\hat{s}$.

This sparse coding method based on ICA may be viewed as a way for determining the basis and corresponding shrinkage functions base on the data themselves. Our method use the transformation based on the statistical properties of the data, whereas the wavelet shrinkage method chooses a predetermined wavelet transform. And the second difference is that we estimate the shrinkage nonlinearities by the ML estimation, again adapting to the data themselves, whereas the wavelet shrinkage method use fixed threshold derived by the min-max principle.

4 Experiments

We select 4 kinds of the ship radiated signals mixed with sea noises to test the de-noising method. The sampling rate is 500Hz and each mixture has 7800 samples. The first step is the feature extraction of the noisy signals using the GGM-based ICA algorithm described in section 2. The un-mixing matrix **W** was extracted by the learning rule eq. 1, and it was used as the filter in the de-noising processing. To judge the results of the de-noising, the signal-to-noise ratio (SNR) is used

$$SNR_i = 10\log\left|\frac{\sum_{t=1}^{N} Signal(t)^2}{\sum_{t=1}^{N} Noise(t)^2}\right| \tag{11}$$

The ship radiated signals mixed with sea noises with the input SNRs of 16.6680, 6.6346, 0.4932 and -0.6203 respectively. By using the method presented in section 3, we obtain the de-noising results for these 4 kinds of mixtures are 17.7891, 7.7121, 1.9061 and 0.9028dB respectively.

To compare the proposed method and conventional de-noising methods, the results of the mean filter (n=3, n=5) and wavelet filter (db3, n=3) are also given in table 1. Where SNR_{in} denotes the input SNR of the noisy ship radiated signals and SNR_{out} denotes the output SNR of the de-noised signals.

In table 1, the first column denotes the 4 kinds of mixtures with different input SNR. The second and third columns denotes the de-noising results for these 4 kinds of

Table 1. The de-noising results of 4 kinds of mixtures

SNR_{in} of noisy ship radiated signals (dB)	SNR_{out} of mean filter (dB)		SNR_{out} of wavelet filter (dB)	SNR_{out} of our method (dB)
	n=3	n=5		
16.6680	16.3109	11.2377	12.8825	17.7891
6.6346	7.1221	6.0431	7.1446	7.7121
0.4932	1.3909	1.2900	0.9203	1.9061
-0.6203	0.7743	0.7043	0.3306	0.9028

noisy signals using mean filter with n=3, n=5 respectively. The fourth and fifth column are the de-noising results of wavelet filter and our method. For these 4 experiments (each row of the table) we can see that the presented method is efficient and always better than conventional methods. For example, in the second experiment with SNR_{in} =6.6346, the de-noising result of mean filter and wavelet filter are 7.1221 (n=3), 6.0431 (n =5) and 7.7121 respectively, and the results of our method is 7.7121, which is the best in these methods.

Fig. 4 shows the graph of the de-noising results of the second experiment by our method. Fig. 4 (a) is some kind of ship radiated signals, (b) is the sea noises, (c) is the mixture of (a) and (b) with SNR of 6.6346, and (d) is the de-noising result of the mixture. Here we use short-term zero crossing rate (ZCR) to detect the crossing characteristic of the ship. The short-term ZCR is defined as

$$ZCR = \frac{1}{2}\sum_{n=1}^{N-1} | sign[x(n)] - sign[x(n-1)] | \tag{12}$$

where N is the number of samples. The short-term ZCR is an efficient method to detect the crossing characteristic of the ship. The short-term ZCR is very high when ship is far away from sonar because the observed signals are almost sea noises which are close to Gaussian distribution in the frequency of 0~400Hz. However, when ship comes close to sonar it becomes very low because the ship radiated signals present a strong non-Gaussian distribution in 0~400Hz. Fig.5 show the short-term ZCR of fig.4.

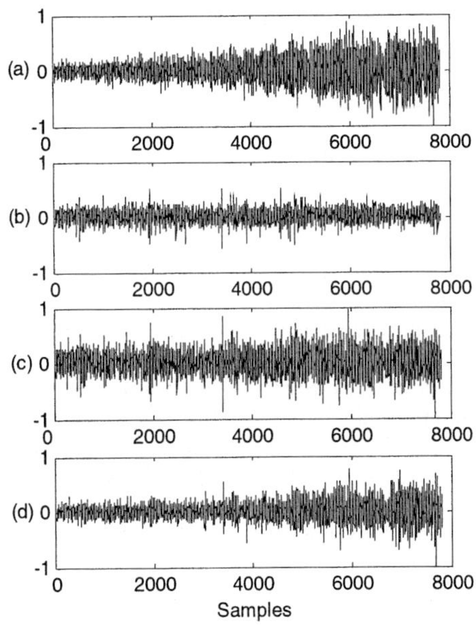

Fig. 4. The de-noising results of noisy ship radiated signals. (a) ship radiated signals, (b) sea noises, (c) the mixture of (a) and (b) with SNR of 6.6346, (d) the de-noising result of (c).

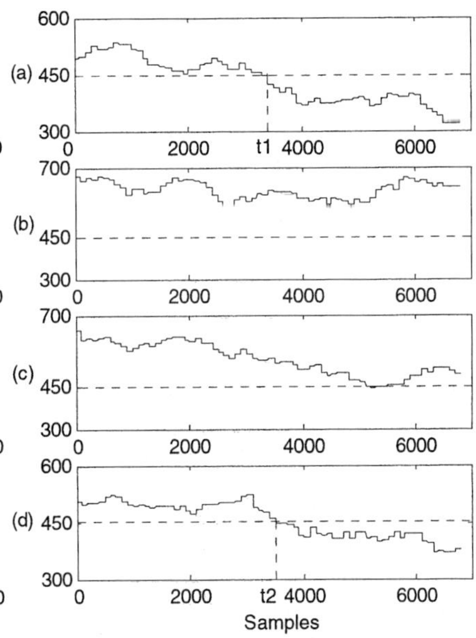

Fig. 5. (a)-(d) The short-time ZCR of the corresponding signals in fig.4 (a)-(d)

Fig.5 (a) is the short-term ZCR of the ship radiated signals (Fig.4 (a)), we can see that the value descended quickly after time t1=3300/500Hz=6.6s, (b) is the short-term ZCR of sea noise. They are higher than that of ship radiated signals. Therefore, we can choose 450 as the threshold to detect ship signals. (c) is the short-term ZCR of noisy signals. From this figure we can see that the short-term ZCR failed to detect the crossing characteristic of ship since the short-term ZCR higher than the threshold. (4) is the short-term ZCR of de-noised signals. It is clear that the values are lower than the threshold after the time t2=3500/500Hz=7s which means that the ship can be detected at time t2.

5 Conclusions

Feature extraction and de-noising are important task of pattern recognition of underwater acoustic signals. This paper presented a method of GGM-based ICA feature extraction for underwater acoustic signals. It is demonstrated that the ICA features of underwater acoustic signals are efficient. Since how to extract efficient basis vectors directly from the observed noisy signals is the key objective of noisy signals, in this paper, a method of extracting the basis vectors directly from noisy data is proposed. Sparse coding is achieved by ICA feature extraction in which the ICA features and the shrinkage functions can be obtained simultaneously. By shrinkage the absolute values of the sparse components towards zero, noise can be reduced. Experiments on ship radiated signals mixed with different intensive sea noises show that the proposed method can efficiently remove the additive white Gaussian noise.

References

1. Te-Won Lee, Gil-Jin Jang, The Statistical Structures of Male and Female Speech Signals, in Proc. ICASSP, (Salt Lack City, Utah), May 2001
2. Jong-Hawn Lee, Ho-Young Jung, Speech Feature Extraction Using Independent Component Analysis, in Proc. ICASP, Istanbul, Turkey, June, 2000,Vol. 3, pp: 1631-1634
3. Anthony J Bell, Terrence J Sejnowski, Learning the Higher-order structure of a nature sound, Network: Computation in Neural System 7 (1996), 261-266
4. Gil-Jin Jang, Te-won Lee, Learning statistically efficient features for speaker recognition, Neurocomputing, 49 (2002): 329-348
5. Miller J. H. & Thomas J. B., Detectors for Discrete-Time Signals in Non-Gaussian noise, IEEE Transactions on Information Theory, Vol IT-18, no. 2, March 1972. Page(s) 241-250
6. Te-Won Lee, Michael S. Lewicki, The Generalized Gaussian Mixture Model Using ICA, in international workshop on Independent Component Analysis (ICA'00), Helsinki, Finland, June 2000, pp: 239-244
7. Hyvärinen A., Sparse code shrinkage: Denoising of nongaussian data by maximum likelihood estimation. Neural Computation, 1999, 11(7):1739-1768
8. Hyvärinen A., Hoyer P., Oja E., Sparse code shrinkage: Denoising by nonlinear maximum likelihood estimation, Advances in Neural Information Processing System 11 (NIPS'98), 1999
9. Hyvärinen A., Hoyer P., Oja E., Image denoising by sparse code shrinkage, Intelligent Signal Processing, IEEE Press, 2000

Efficient Feature Extraction and De-noising Method for Chinese Speech Signals Using GGM-Based ICA

Yang Bin and Kong Wei

Information Engineering College, Shanghai Maritime University, Shanghai 200135, China
binyang@cie.shmtu.edu.cn, kongwei@sjtu.edu.cn

Abstract. In this paper we study the ICA feature extraction method for Chinese speech signals. The generalized Gaussian model (GGM) is introduced as the p.d.f. estimator in ICA since it can provide a general method for modeling non-Gaussian statistical structure of univariate distributions. It is demonstrated that the ICA features of Chinese speech are localized in both time and frequency domain and the resulting coefficients are statistically independent and sparse. The GGM-based ICA method is also used in extracting the basis vectors directly from the noisy observation, which is an efficient method for noise reduction when priori knowledge of source data is not acquirable. The de-nosing experiments show that the proposed method is more efficient than conventional methods in the environment of additive white Gaussian noise.

1 Introduction

Chinese is a typical tonal and syllabic language, in which each Chinese character corresponds to a monosyllable and basically has a phoneme structure with a lexical tone. Each Chinese character has four lexical tones (Tone1, Tone2, Tone 3, and Tone 4) and a neutral tone. There are about 400 toneless Chinese syllables and about 1,300 toned Chinese syllables. How to extract efficient features from Chinese speech signals is a key task of Chinese speech coding, de-noising and recognition.

Nowadays, many efforts have gone into finding learning algorithms to obtain the statistical characteristics of speech and sound signals. However, these commonly used features have the limitations that they are sensitive only to second-order statistics since they all use correlation-based learning rules like principal component analysis (PCA). The failure of correlation-based learning algorithm is that they are typically global and reflect only the amplitude spectrum of the signal and ignore the phase spectrum. The most informative features of sound signals, however, require higher-order statistics for their characterization [1-4]. For this reason, we study the ICA feature extraction method on Chinese speech signals in this paper. The generalized Gaussian model was introduced here to provide a general method for modeling non-Gaussian statistical structure of the resulting coefficients which have the form of $p(x) \propto \exp(-|x|^q)$. By inferring q, a wide class of statistical distributions can be characterized. By comparing the ICA basis with DFT, DCT and PCA basis, it can be seen that the proposed method is more efficient than conventional features.

M. Lazo and A. Sanfeliu (Eds.): CIARP 2005, LNCS 3773, pp. 925 – 932, 2005.

The advantage of GGM-based ICA method is also applied in the de-noising of Chinese speech signals even when the trained priori knowledge of source data is not acquirable. Not only the ICA features but also the de-noising shrinkage function can be obtained from the GGM-based ICA sparse coding. Using the maximum likelihood (ML) method on the non-Gaussian variables corrupted by additive white Gaussian noise, we show how to apply the GGM-based shrinkage method on the coefficients to reduce noise. Experiment of noisy male Chinese speech signals shows that our de-noising method is successful in improving the signal to noise ratio (SNR).

2 ICA Feature Extraction Using GGM

In ICA feature extraction methods, the source speech signal is represented as segments

$$x = As = \sum_{i=1}^{N} a_i s_i \tag{1}$$

Where $\boldsymbol{A}$ is defined as 'basis vector' of source signals, and $\boldsymbol{s}$ is its corresponding coefficient. ICA algorithm is performed to obtain the estimation of independent components $\boldsymbol{s}$ from speech segments $\boldsymbol{x}$ by the un-mixing matrix $\boldsymbol{W}$

$$\boldsymbol{u} = \boldsymbol{W}\boldsymbol{x} \tag{2}$$

where $\boldsymbol{u}$ is the estimation of independent components $\boldsymbol{s}$. Basis functions $\boldsymbol{A}$ can be calculated from the ICA algorithm by the relation $\boldsymbol{A} = \boldsymbol{W}^{-1}$.

By maximizing the log likelihood of the separated signals, both the independent coefficients and the unknown basis functions can be inferred. The learning rules is represented as

$$\Delta W \propto \frac{\partial \log p(s)}{\partial W} W^T W = \eta [I - \varphi(s) s^T] W \tag{3}$$

here $\boldsymbol{W}^T\boldsymbol{W}$ is used to perform the natural gradient, it simplifies the learning rules and speeds convergence considerably. The vector $\varphi(s)$ is a function of the prior and is defined by $\varphi(s) = \frac{\partial \log p(s)}{\partial s}$, and $p(s)$ is the p.d.f. of s. Here we use the GGM as the p.d.f. estimator. The GGM models a family of density functions that is peaked and symmetric at the mean, with a varying degree of normality in the following general form [5]

$$p_g(s \mid \theta) = \frac{\omega(q)}{\sigma} \exp[-c(q) \mid \frac{s-\mu}{\sigma} \mid^q], \qquad \theta = \{\mu, \theta, q\} \tag{4}$$

where

$$c(q) = [\frac{\Gamma[3/q]}{\Gamma[1/q]}]^{q/2} \tag{5}$$

and

$$\omega(q) = \frac{\Gamma[3/q]^{\frac{1}{2}}}{(2/q)\Gamma[1/q]^{\frac{3}{2}}} \tag{6}$$

$\mu = E[s], \sigma = \sqrt{E[(s-\mu)^2]}$ are the mean and standard deviation of the data respectively, and $\Gamma[\cdot]$ is the Gamma function. By inferring q, a wide class of statistical distributions can be characterized. The Gaussian, Laplacian, and strong Laplacian (such as speech signal) distributions can be modeled by putting $q = 2$, $q = 1$, and $q < 1$ respectively. The exponent q controls the distribution's deviation from normal.

For the purposes of finding the basis functions, the problem then becomes to estimate the value of q from the data. This can be accomplished by simply finding the maximum posteriori value q. The posterior distribution of q given the observations $\boldsymbol{x}=\{x_1,\ldots,x_n\}$ is

$$p(q \mid x) \propto p(x \mid q)p(q) \tag{7}$$

where the data likelihood is

$$p(x \mid q) = \prod_n \omega(q)\exp[-c(q) \mid x_n \mid^q] \tag{8}$$

and $p(q)$ defines the prior distribution for q, here Gamma function $\Gamma[\cdot]$ is used as $p(q)$.

In the case of the GGM, the vector $\varphi(s)$ in eq.3 can be derived as

$$\varphi_i(s_i) = -qc\sigma_i^{-q} \mid s_i - \mu_i \mid^{q-1} sign(s_i - \mu_i) \tag{9}$$

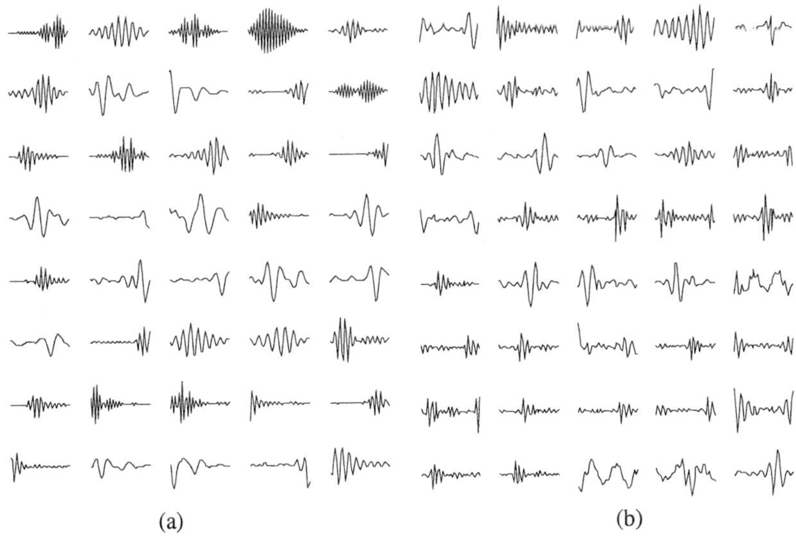

Fig. 1. (a)-(b) Some basis vectors of male and female Chinese speech signals

Using the learning rule eq. 3 the un-mixing matrix $\boldsymbol{W}$ is iterated by the natural gradient until convergence is achieved.

To learn the basis vector, one male Chinese speech signals and one female Chinese speech signals were used. The sampling rates of the original data are both 8kHz. Fig.1 (a) and (b) show some of the basis vector of the male and female Chinese speech

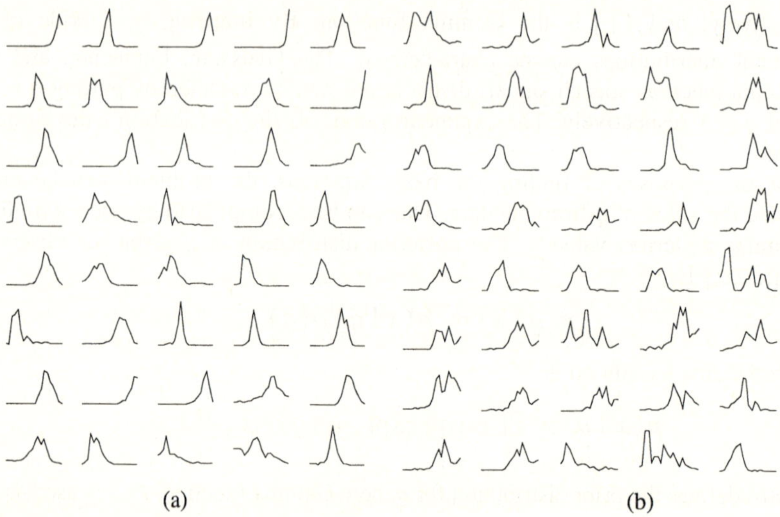

Fig. 2. (a)-(b) The frequency spectrum of fig.1 (a) and (b)

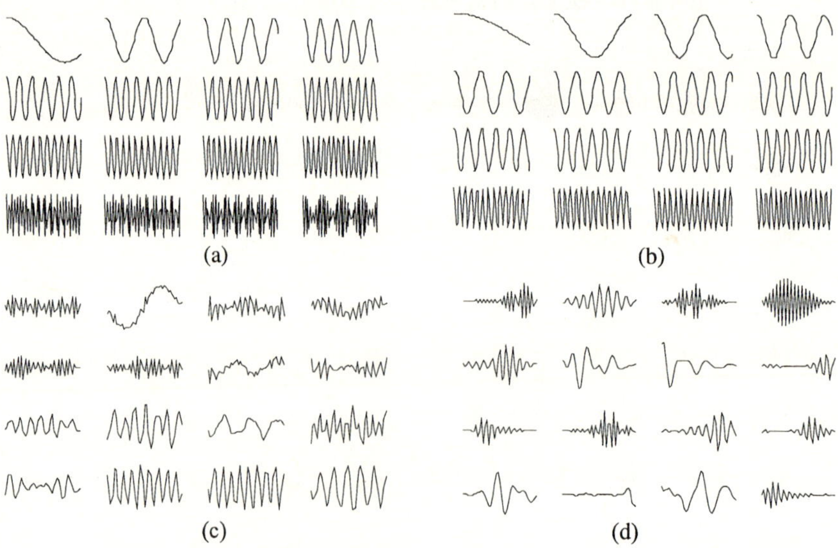

Fig. 3. Comparison of DFT, DCT, PCA and ICA basis vector of male Chinese speech signal, (a) DFT basis vector, (b) DCT basis vector, (c) PCA basis vector, (d) ICA basis vector

signals learned by the GGM-based ICA method. Fig.2 shows the frequency spectrum of fig.1 (a) and (b) respectively. It can be seen that the ICA basis vectors of Chinese speech signals are localized both in time and frequency domain.

For comparison, discrete Fourier transform (DFT), discrete cosine transform (DCT), and principal component analysis (PCA) basis vectors as conventional methods are adopted. Fig.3 compares the waveforms of the DFT, DCT and PCA basis with the ICA basis.16 basis functions of male Chinese speech signals for each method are displayed.

From fig. 3 (a)-(d) we can see that the DFT and DCT basis look similar and they are spread all over the time axis. For different signals the DFT and DCT basis are fixed. PCA basis is data driven and exhibits less regularity and global. However, the ICA basis functions are localized in time and frequency, thus they reflect both the phase and frequency information inherent in the data.

3 Speech De-noising Using GGM-Based ICA

ICA feature extraction is wildly used in de-noising of image and speech signals since ICA is an efficient sparse coding method for finding a representation of data [6, 7]. In these methods, however, the trained basis vectors were needed and applied for the removal of Gaussian noise. In the noise environment, denote y as the noisy coefficient of a basis vector, s as the original noise-free version of coefficient of basis vector, and v as a Gaussian noise with zero mean and variance σ^2. Then the variable y can be describe as

$$y = s + v \tag{10}$$

Denote p as the probability of s, and f = - log p as its negative log-density, we want to estimate s from the observed noisy coefficient y. The estimator of s can be obtained by the maximum likelihood (ML) method

$$\hat{s} = \arg\min_{s} \frac{1}{2\sigma^2}(y-s)^2 + f(s) \tag{11}$$

Assuming $f(\bullet)$ to be strictly convex and differentiable, the ML estimation gives the equation

$$\hat{s} = h(y) \tag{12}$$

where the nonlinear function h(•) is called as *shrinkage* function, and the inverse is given by

$$h^{-1}(s) = s + \sigma^2 f'(s) \tag{13}$$

Thus, the estimation of s is obtained by inverting a certain function involving $f'(\bullet)$. Since $f(\bullet)$ is a function of p.

There are two difficulties in this method. One is: the noise-free source data is needed to train the ICA basis vectors as a priori knowledge. Unfortunately, the corresponding noise-free signals are always not acquirable in practice. The other is how to efficiently estimate the p.d.f. of the coefficient vector s which is the key of estimating $\hat{s}$. To solve these two problems the GGM-based ICA algorithm in section 2 is used to extract the basis vectors directly from noisy speech signals when the noise-free signals cannot be obtained. It is fortunately that the p.d.f. of the coefficients $p(s)$ can be learned by the GGM simultaneously since the parameter q of the GGM is determined during the ICA feature extraction.

To recover the de-noised speech signal from the noisy source three steps are needed. Firstly, extract the ICA basis vector directly from the noisy speech signals by using GGM-based ICA. The p.d.f. of the corresponding coefficients $p(s)$ are obtained at the same time. It is demonstrated that the coefficients of the basis vectors extracted directly from noisy speech have sparse distributions. Secondly, the shrinkage functions can be estimated by $p(s)$ by eq. 13, and the de-noised coefficients can be calculated by $\hat{s} = h(y)$. Finally, recover the de-noised speech signal by $\hat{x} = W^{-1}\hat{s} = A\hat{s}$.

This method is closed related to the wavelet shrinkage method. However, the sparse coding based on ICA may be viewed as a way for determining the basis and corresponding shrinkage functions base on the data themselves. Our method use the transformation based on the statistical properties of the data, whereas the wavelet shrinkage method chooses a predetermined wavelet transform. And the second difference is that we estimate the shrinkage nonlinearities by the ML estimation, again adapting to the data themselves, whereas the wavelet shrinkage method use fixed threshold derived by the mini-max principle.

4 Experiments

Noisy male Chinese speech signals mixed with white Gaussian noise were applied to perform the proposed method. The sampling rate is 8kHz and 64000 samples are used. The first step is the feature extraction of the noisy signals using the GGM-based ICA algorithm described in section 2. For the noisy speech signal, the mean was subtracted (eq.14) and then 1000 vectors of length 64 (8ms) were generated, and each segment was pre-whitened to improve the convergence speed (eq.15).

$$\boldsymbol{x} = \boldsymbol{x} - \boldsymbol{E}\{\boldsymbol{x}\} \tag{14}$$

$$\boldsymbol{v} = \boldsymbol{E}\{\boldsymbol{x}\,\boldsymbol{x}^{T}\}^{-1/2}\boldsymbol{x} \tag{15}$$

This pre-processing removes both first- and second-order statistics from the input data, and makes the covariance matrix of $\boldsymbol{x}$ equal to the identity matrix, where $\boldsymbol{x}$ denoted as the observed noisy signals. The adaptation of the un-mixing matrix $\boldsymbol{W}$ started from the 64×64 identity matrix and trained through the 1000 vectors. The learning rate was gradually decreased from 0.2 to 0.05 during the iteration. The signal-to-noise ratio (SNR) is used to judge the results of the de-noising

$$SNR_i = 10\log\left|\frac{\sum_{t=1}^{N} Signal(t)^2}{\sum_{t=1}^{N} Noise(t)^2}\right| \tag{16}$$

Fig. 4 shows the noisy male Chinese speech signals with the input SNR of 6.3850dB and the de-noising results of wavelet method (db3, n=3) and our proposed method in (b), (c) and (d) respectively. For comparison, the corresponding noise-free signal is given by (a). The SNR of the input noisy signal is 6.3850. The output SNR of wavelet and GGM-based ICA method are 10.5446 and 12.9910 respectively. It can be seen that the de-noising result of the proposed method is better than that of wavelet de-noising method.

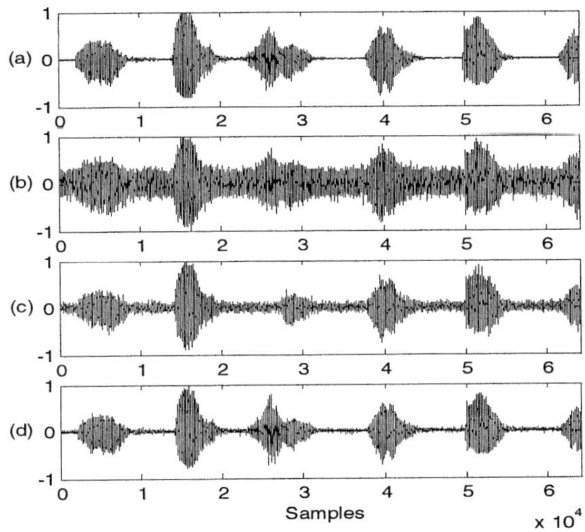

Fig. 4. The de-noising results of male Chinese speech signals, (a) noise-free male Chinese speech signal, (b) noisy male Chinese speech signal, (c) the de-noising result of wavelet, (d) the de-noising result of GGM-based ICA

5 Conclusions

In this paper, we obtained efficient feature extraction method for Chinese speech signals. It is demonstrated that the GGM-based ICA features are localized both in time and frequency domain. This efficient ICA feature extraction method was also applied to the de-noising of Chinese speech signals and demonstrated better performance than wavelet de-noising method. The proposed de-noising method can be directly used in practice since it does not need the noise-free signals to train the priori knowledge. The experiment on noisy male Chinese speech signal shows that the proposed method is efficient to remove the additive white Gaussian noise.

References

1. Te-Won Lee, Gil-Jin Jang, The Statistical Structures of Male and Female Speech Signals, in Proc. ICASSP, (Salt Lack City, Utah), May 2001
2. Jong-Hawn Lee, Ho-Young Jung, Speech Feature Extraction Using Independent Component Analysis, in Proc. ICASP, Istanbul, Turkey, June, 2000,Vol. 3, pp: 1631-1634

3. Anthony J Bell, Terrence J Sejnowski, Learning the Higher-order structure of a nature sound, Network: Computation in Neural System 7 (1996), 261-266
4. Gil-Jin Jang, Te-won Lee, Learning statistically efficient features for speaker recognition, Neurocomputing, 49 (2002): 329-348
5. Te-Won Lee, Michael S. Lewicki, The Generalized Gaussian Mixture Model Using ICA, in international workshop on Independent Component Analysis (ICA'00), Helsinki, Finland, June 2000, pp: 239-244
6. A. Hyvärinen, Sparse code shrinkage: Denoising of nongaussian data by maximum likelihood estimation. Technical Report A51, Helsinki University of Technology, Laboratory of Computer and Information Science, 1998
7. Hyvärinen A., Hoyer P., Oja E., Sparse code shrinkage: Denoising by nonlinear maximum likelihood estimation, Advances in Neural Information Processing System 11 (NIPS'98), 1999

Adapted Wavelets for Pattern Detection

Hector Mesa[1,2]

[1] University of La Habana,
Faculty of Mathematics and Computer Sciences,
10400 La Habana, Cuba
hectormesa@matcom.uh.cu
[2] Paris-Sud XI University, 91400 Orsay, Paris, France
hector.mesa@math.u-psud.fr

Abstract. Wavelets are widely used in numerous applied fields involving for example signal analysis, image compression or function approximation. The idea of adapting wavelet to specific problems, it means to create and use problem and data dependent wavelets, has been developed for various purposes. In this paper, we are interested in to define, starting from a given pattern, an efficient design of FIR adapted wavelets based on the lifting scheme. We apply the constructed wavelet for pattern detection in the 1D case. To do so, we propose a three stages detection procedure which is finally illustrated by spike detection in EEG.

1 Introduction

The fields of application of wavelets grows because of their attractive properties for various purposes. The possibility to construct new wavelets with simplicity is one of the characteristics.

The construction of problem or data dependent wavelets have been undertaken by many authors: for instance, Zhang et al.[1] construct orthonormal wavelets bases which are best suited to represent a given signal, Lucas et al.[2] create orthogonal wavelets to improve the classification accuracy for certain given classes and Du et al.[3] use adapted wavelets for crackle detection.

The main contribution of the present paper is a modification of the Lifting Method to construct adapted wavelets introduced by Sweldens. Such wavelets are particulary well suited for pattern detection what we use for illustration. The modification overcomes the drawback of Sweldens approach concerning the too coarse approximation.

The paper is organized as follows. Section 2 gives some motivations to use pattern-matched wavelets as templates and proposes a three stages procedure to use them for pattern detection problems. In section 3 we propose a lifting based method to construct such pattern-adapted wavelets. Section 4 illustrates the procedure by considering the spike detection problem.

M. Lazo and A. Sanfeliu (Eds.): CIARP 2005, LNCS 3773, pp. 933–944, 2005.

2 Pattern Detection in 1D with Adapted Wavelets

For many applications, detection of known or a priori unknown patterns in signals are required. Those patterns can also be transformed (translated, scaled, etc), so it is usually needed to estimate the parameters of the transformation.

Here, we will suppose that we have to detect some translated and scaled versions of one given pattern. On the matter of this article, the pattern detection problem consists of, given a finitely supported pattern f and a signal S, to find where the signal is similar to a scaled version of the pattern estimating both time-shift and scale factor.

2.1 Why Adapted Wavelets for Pattern Detection

Template matching or pattern matching is used for this purpose [4]. Two methods are commonly used: signal substraction, where the norm of the difference is used as a measure of the dissimilarity, and the correlation, where the scalar product is considered as a measure of similarity. Both methods are equivalent when the template and the signal are normalized so they have zero average and norm 1. But a zero-average 1D finite supported function is close to a wavelet.

On the other hand, the wavelet transforms have efficient implementations and allow to decompose any signal in "frequency" bands. So, why not to use wavelets as templates, this is to use pattern-adapted wavelets.

A wavelet ψ_f approximating any given pattern f allows, by means of the wavelet transform, to estimate the correlation of any signal S, not only with the pattern itself, but with its scaled versions. The continuous wavelet transform (CWT) of a signal S with the wavelet Ψ at scale $a > 0$ and time b is defined as:

$$W_\Psi S(a,b) = \left\langle S, \frac{1}{\sqrt{a}} \Psi(\frac{x-b}{a}) \right\rangle . \tag{1}$$

The values $W_\Psi(a,b)$ are also called the wavelet coefficients of S in (a,b).

The discrete-like transforms –discrete wavelet transform (DWT) and translation invariant wavelet transform (SWT)– are fast algorithms to compute it for dyadic scales ($a_j = 2^j a_0$). It is calculated at scale-dependent shifts by the DWT ($b_{j,k} = b_0 + ja_k$) and at some fixed shifts $b_{j,k} = b_0 + j$ by the SWT.

Also, for any fixed scale $a > 0$, every local maxima of the similarity cause local maxima of the wavelet energy (squared wavelet coefficients), i.e. those pairs (a,b) for which the wavelet energy is locally maximum as a function of b are the only possible values for which the similarity between the signal and the corresponding scaled and translated versions of the pattern is locally maximum.

2.2 A Three Stages Procedure

So, we can search such wavelet energy maxima (called *similarity alert* or simply *alert*) and then to individually test if they are interesting with respect to the problem (true alert) or not (false alert). Then, to know if the alert is true or false it is needed to verify some rules.

The similarity is verified by using rules that are designed only from the pattern – we called them pattern-based rules –. The relevance with respect to the problem is checked by using problem dependent rules. Usually, neural networks are implemented to create such rules automatically from a training set of data [5,6].

Resuming this idea we propose a three stages procedure:

1. *Given the motif f to detect, create the pattern adapted wavelet $\psi_f(x)$.* Without loss of generality we will suppose that $supp(f) = [0,1]$ (so that the scale a represents the size of the corresponding pattern and b the starting time), $\int_0^1 f(x)dx = 0$ and $\|f\|_2 = 1$.
2. *Detect all the alerts on the signal.* This is to search the local maxima of the signal wavelet energy for any b and all possible, for the problem, durations $a > 0$.
3. *Detect and discard all the false alerts.* For this some rules must be applied to decide if each alert is false or not.

3 Pattern Adapted Wavelets

Let us start this section by giving some basic ideas about wavelets. More can be found for example in [7].

Wavelets are sufficiently smooth functions with zero average. The wavelet transform is well localized both in time and in frequency, unlike the Fourier transform.

One important concept on the wavelet theory, is the *Multiresolution Analysis* (MRA). It is the base of discrete decomposition of signals in terms of translates and scaling of a single function and so of the computationally efficient algorithms to compute the DWT and SWT like the Mallat's "a trous" [7] which iteratively computes the wavelet transform for successive scale levels.

The MRA is a family $M = \{V_j\}_{j\in\mathbb{Z}}$ of nested closed subspaces of L^2:

$$\{0\} \subset \cdots \subset V_1 \subset V_0 \subset V_{-1} \subset \cdots \subset L^2 \tag{2}$$

named approximation spaces which satisfy the conditions stated for example in [8] p. 65. It can be defined another family of closed subspaces $\{W_j\}_{j\in\mathbb{Z}}$, called details spaces, such that $V_{j-1} = V_j \oplus W_j$.

The so called scaling function φ and wavelet ψ are so that their linear integer translates spans generate V_0 and W_0 respectively.

One of the most important consequences of the MRA definition is the existence of two filters u and v satisfying the two-scales relations:

$$\begin{cases} \frac{1}{\sqrt{2}}\varphi(\frac{x}{2}) = \sum_k u[k]\varphi(x-k) \\ \frac{1}{\sqrt{2}}\psi(\frac{x}{2}) = \sum_k v[k]\varphi(x-k) \end{cases} . \tag{3}$$

Those filters are known as the two-scales filters.

The fast algorithms take profit of this relation to compute the transform at dyadic scales. The invertibility of the fast algorithms are ensured by a new pairs of filters $\mathring{u}, \mathring{v}$ satisfying the *perfect reconstruction* (PR) property:

$$\begin{cases} u^\vee \star \mathring{u} + v^\vee \star \mathring{v} = 2\delta_0 \\ \widetilde{u}^\vee \star \mathring{u} + \widetilde{v}^\vee \star \mathring{v} = 0 \end{cases} \tag{4}$$

where δ_k is the unit response at time k and where the convolution operator is denoted by $\star$ and the subsampling, upsampling, modulation and transpose of a filter u are denoted by $[u]_{\downarrow_2}$, $[u]_{\uparrow_2}$, $\widetilde{u}$ and $u^\vee$ respectively.

In the case of the existence of a biorthogonal MRA with scaling function $\mathring{\varphi}$ and wavelet $\mathring{\psi}$ in L^2, the associated filters satisfy (4). The second MRA, scaling and wavelet function, and filters will be called dual and denoted by appending a "$\circ$" (e.g. $\mathring{\varphi}$).

3.1 Adapted Wavelet Construction

There are many ways to construct wavelets. Some of those approaches are to create signal (or pattern) adapted wavelets e.g. [9,10].

Abry et al. [11,12,13] propose to construct a time-space matched scaling function or wavelet by projecting the pattern onto the approximation spaces or detail spaces (V_0, W_0 respectively) of some initially given MRA. Then, it is possible to compute the new functions as *admissible* (i.e. invertible) *linear combinations* of the original ones and to compute the associated filters.

Their approach allows to construct four new functions φ, ψ, $\mathring{\varphi}$ and $\mathring{\psi}$ in L^2 satisfying the biorthogonality conditions and generating a pair of biorthogonal MRAs. As said above, the existence of such functions and MRAs, ensures the property (4). The main problem is that in general, when using this approach, the new associated filters may not exist or will have infinite impulse response (IIR), reducing the efficiency of the algorithms. So, truncating the filters is required but it may be the cause of large errors which will grow at each iteration compromising the convergence and the accuracy of the algorithms.

3.2 Lifting Based Methods

Principle. Another approach is the lifting method introduced by W. Sweldens [14,15]. This method allows, starting from four filters u, v, $\mathring{u}$, $\mathring{v}$ satisfying the PR property (i.e. a perfect reconstruction filter bank PRFB), to construct a new PRFB. This method, for instance, allows to create second generation wavelets which are not necessarily translates and dilates of one fixed function [16]. Also, Sweldens shows that any discrete wavelet transform can be decomposed in (primal and dual) lifting steps, giving a new, more efficient, algorithm called fast lifting transform [17].

The idea of wavelet construction with a primal lifting step is, starting from a scaling function φ and wavelet ψ generating a MRA which are associated to u and v, to make

$$\psi_l(x) = \psi(x) + \sum_i l[i]\varphi(x-i) \tag{5}$$

where l is a finite filter with zero average.

The new PRFB would be $(u,\ v^N,\ \mathring{u}^N,\ \mathring{v})$ with

$$u^N = u \ - \ [l]^{\vee}_{\uparrow 2} \star v \tag{6}$$

$$\mathring{v}^N = \mathring{v} \ + \ [l]_{\uparrow 2} \star \mathring{u}\ . \tag{7}$$

The dual lifting step can be obtained by exchanging the primal functions and filters with the dual ones.

Let $f \in L^2$ be a normalized ($\|f\|_2 = 1$) and compactly supported function with zero-average. To approximate f by a wavelet function ψ_f constructed with this method we have to project $f - \psi$ onto V_0 which gives us the lifting filter l^* and so a pattern-matched wavelet

$$\psi_f(x) = \psi(x) + l^* \star \varphi(x)\ . \tag{8}$$

The approximation with this method can be too coarse as shown in Figure 1(b).

A Variant. To circumvent this drawback, we propose to use a dilated version of f ($f_\rho(x) = \frac{1}{\sqrt{\rho}} f(x/\rho)$ where ρ is the dilation coefficient) and a variant of the lifting step.

The dilation coefficient ρ allows to take profit of the good approximation properties of the scaling functions [18] reducing $\|f - \mathbb{P}_{V_0} f\|$, where $\mathbb{P}_{V_0} f$ means the projection of f onto V_0, but ψ is still seen reducing the accuracy of the approximation (see Figure 1(c)).

We propose a variant to the lifting step which reduces the influence of ψ in the constructed wavelet ψ_f. Let l be a finite filter with $\sum_k l[k] = 0$, a real number c such that $|c| > c_{min}$ for some $c_{min} > 0$ and an integer k. The new primal wavelet will be

$$\psi_l(x) = c\psi(x-k) + \sum_i l[i]\varphi(x-i) \tag{9}$$

and the associated filters $(u,\ v^N,\ \mathring{u}^N,\ \mathring{v}^N)$ where

$$v^N = c \cdot v \star \delta_{2k} \ + \ [l]_{\uparrow 2} \star u \tag{10}$$

$$\mathring{u}^N = u \ - \ \frac{1}{c}\delta_{2k} \star [l]^{\vee}_{\uparrow 2} \star v \tag{11}$$

$$\mathring{v}^N = \frac{1}{c}\delta_{2k} \star \mathring{v}\ . \tag{12}$$

The new four filters also satisfy (4).

The use of a small enough c and a convenient k reduce the influence of ψ. The value of c_{min} must be chosen so that the dual filters $\mathring{u}$ and $\mathring{v}$ are not too large.

If $W_0 \perp V_0$ and $\mathbb{P}_{W_0} f \not\equiv 0$, the optimal values of c and k can be obtained from the wavelet decomposition of $\mathbb{P}_{V_{-1}} f$:

As

$$\mathbb{P}_{V_{-1}} f = \mathbb{P}_{V_0} f + \mathbb{P}_{W_0} f \ , \tag{13}$$

then taking c^*, k^* such that

$$k^* = \arg\max_k |W_\psi(0,k)| \ , \tag{14}$$

and

$$c^* = sign(W_\psi(0,k^*)) \max(\ |W_\psi(0,k^*)| \, , c_{min} \ ) \ . \tag{15}$$

where $sign(\cdot)$ denotes the sign function.

If $\mathbb{P}_{W_0} f \equiv 0$ then k^* is free and $c^* = c_{min}$.

When $W_0 \not\perp V_0$ then an optimization problem has to be solved:

$$\min_{\sum_k l[k]=0, \ |c|>c_{min}} \left(\|f - c\psi(x-k) - l \star \varphi(x)\|^2 \right) \ . \tag{16}$$

Resuming, projecting f onto V_0 gives l^* and for the convenient values of c^* and k^* we get the pattern-matched wavelet.

$$\psi_f(x) = c^* \psi(x-k^*) \ + \ l^* \star \varphi(x) \ . \tag{17}$$

An example of a pattern-adapted wavelet computed using this method can be seen in Figure 1(d).

Illustration. Let us consider $f(x) = \sqrt{3}(.5 - 2\,|x - .5|)\mathbb{1}_{[0,1]}$(see Figure 1(a)) as motif. Let us use $Db5$'s MRA, this is the MRA generated by the scaling function and wavelet with 5 vanishing moments obtained by Daubechies [19], for which $V_0 \perp W_0$.

Figure 1(b) shows the wavelet constructed using a classical lifting step. Due to the small support of f ([0, 1]), the new wavelet is not well adapted to the pattern. By approximating f_ρ, a dilated version of f, with $\rho = 16$ we get a much better solution but the influence of the original wavelet is evident.

Now, using our lifting's variant step for $\rho = 16$ (see 1(d)), we get better results. Notice that the original wavelet has almost disappeared.

Properties. This construction method is stable for small variations in the pattern:

Let $g \in L^2$ be a function such that $\|g\|_2 = 1$. Let $f^\varepsilon(x) = f(x) + \varepsilon g(x)$ for any $\varepsilon \in \mathbb{R}$. We have that

$$\left\|\psi_f - \psi_f^\varepsilon\right\|^2 \le \varepsilon^2 \cdot {}^T\sigma_g \left(H\right)^{-1} \sigma_g \ , \tag{18}$$

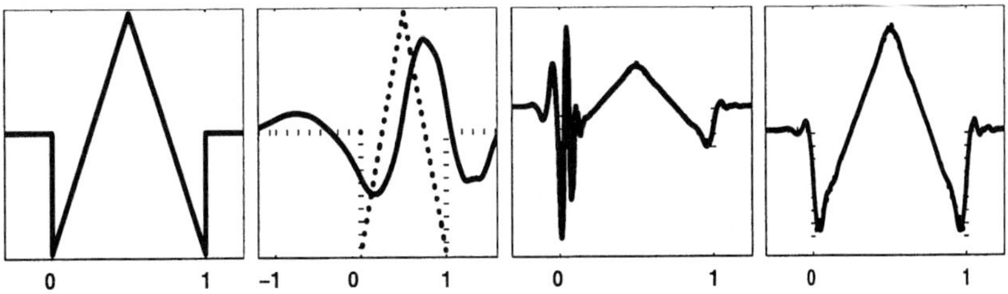

Fig. 1. Example of pattern adapted wavelets construction using lifting-based methods starting from $Db5$'s MRA. (a) the pattern f, (b) the wavelet obtained by an original lifting step, (c) the wavelet obtained by using the original lifting step but f was dilated with $\rho = 16$ and (d) wavelet created by using our variant and $\rho = 16$.

where $\sigma_g[i] = \langle g, \varphi(x-k)\rangle$, $H[i,j] = \gamma[i-j]$ and $\gamma[i] = \langle \varphi, \varphi(x-i)\rangle$ is the sampled autocorrelation function.

Continuity and differentiability properties of the constructed wavelet are ensured by the original scaling function's properties and it is possible to obtain an arbitrary number of vanishing moments by adding some linear constraints, besides the l's null sum restriction, while keeping the stability of the method. Unlike the projection methods, the dual functions may not have finite energy but the PR property hold so the analysis-synthesis algorithms work.

The good behavior of such adapted wavelets for pattern detection to find possible points (in the time-scale plane) of locally maximum similarity is shown in Figure 2(a) where it is represented the CWT of a fragment of an EEG with a wavelet adapted to a simple model of a spike-wave complex (a spike followed by a slower wave) (Figure 3 (a)) which we want to detect.

Three maxima (one with positive coefficient in the center and two negatives on both sides) are present for each complex location but a further analysis shows that the true location is represented by center ones (all for scales between $a = .2$ and .3).

Figures 3(b) and (c) show the scaled and shifted versions of the adapted wavelet for two consecutive local maxima ($b = .0985$ and $b = 1.125$ respectively). They are also multiplied by the estimated amplitude. See that in the first case, although the similarity is high, it is lower than this of the second case (fig 3(c)) where there is an almost perfect match. Those false maxima must be eliminated by selection rules like to check the possible scales or duration (in this example, the complexes have a duration around .22s) or by direct testing if there are only a few of local maxima to check.

4 Real World Example: Spike Detection in EEG

Electroencephalogram (EEG) is an important clinical tool for diagnosing, monitoring and managing neurological disorders related to epilepsy. Spikes correspond to tiny epileptic discharges which last for a fraction of a second. Beyond

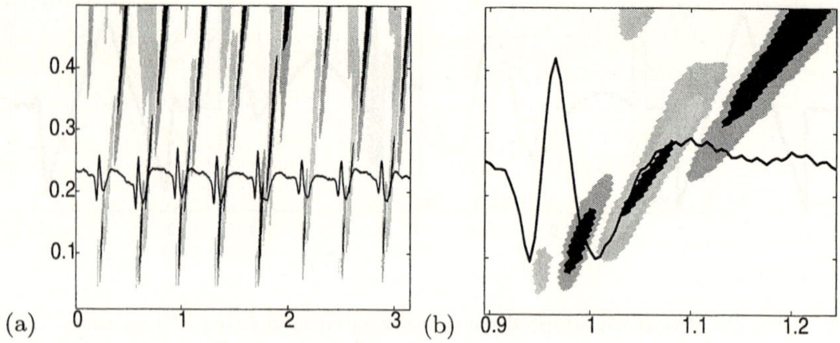

Fig. 2. (a)An EEG fragment and its CWT with the spike-wave complex adapted wavelet. (b)A zoom between .9 and 1.2s shows the existence of three local maxima of the wavelet energy around a spike-wave complex.

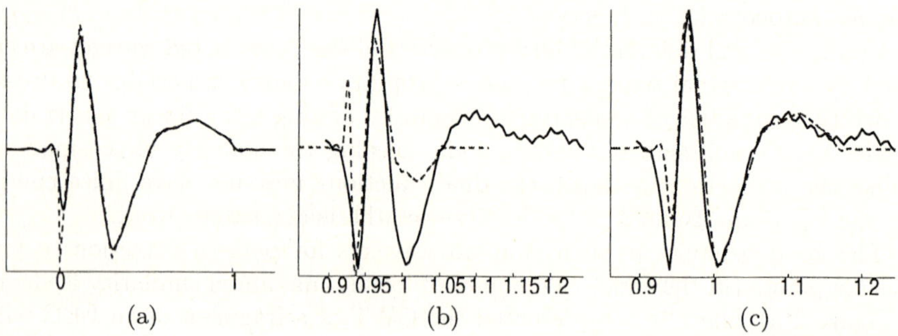

Fig. 3. (a)Spike-wave complex model (dashed line) and the adapted wavelet(solid line). The EEG signal with scaled (a) and shifted (b) adapted wavelet: (b) for $b = .985s$ and $a = .125$, (c) for $b = 1.05s$ and $a = .225$.

of the diagnosis of epilepsy, automatic spike detection helps to make quantitative descriptions of spike density, topology and morphology what could help to determine patient syndrome and surgical outcome [20].

Spike detection is tedious and requires skill to do it well. The noise and the artifacts make this task difficult [21]. That is why there are so many people working on automatic spike detection. We use this problem to illustrate the behavior of this procedure as an example of the use of the pattern-matched wavelets. Let us first describe the problem.

4.1 The Problem

The epileptic spikes on the EEG was loosely defined by Gloor in [22]. He gives three characteristics regarding their form (a restricted triangular transient), its duration (having a duration of $\leq$ 200ms) and the electric field (as defined by involvement of a second adjacent electrode). He says also that the spikes must be clearly distinguishable from background activity and having an amplitude of, at least, twice of the preceding 5s of background activity in any channel of the EEG.

Many works roughly follow this definition and emphasize the local context, morphology and the field of the spike. As local context it is understood the local characteristics of the signal compared with the background activity. The term "background activity" is used to describe the context in which the spikes occurs and it is typically used to normalize the spikes parameters to account for varying electrical output from different patients and determine whether the spike is more than a random variation of the underlying rhythmic activity [20].

As morphology it is understood every attribute used to describe the spike and its background. Relative height, relative sharpness at the apex and total duration are some examples of attributes.

To detect the presence of field it is needed to analyze adjacent electrode signals. Overlapping spikes on different channels are used to create a spike-event [23] so it is used as a rule to discard false alerts.

4.2 The Detection Procedure

First we have to choose the pattern. From the first characteristic given by Gloor, we take a triangular function (Figure 1(a)) as a very simple pattern. We will use *Db*5's as initial MRA, whose wavelet is two times continuously differentiable, and $\rho = 16$. The resulting wavelet is shown in Figure 1(d).

The alert detection process for a signal S consists in the detection of local maxima in b of the wavelet energy $W^2_{\psi_f} S(a,b)$ for every scale $a > 0$. It can be done for dyadic scales, with the DWT or SWT, or for more regularly spaced scales, by using the CWT.

This will give us the times when the spike-alerts occur. To decide the optimum scale a^*(i.e. the duration) for any alert time b^*, it is needed to compare between the adjacent scales for the times b such that the wavelet supports intercept. We will take $\frac{1}{a^3} W^2_{\psi_f}(a,b)$ as an estimation of spikes slopes and will keep those alerts where it is locally maximum as a two-variables function.

4.3 Some Selection Rules

Pattern-Based Rules. Those rules consist of the threshold of upper bounds of the approximated similarity between the pattern and the signal's fragment. Two possible upper bounds of the similarity are

$$corr(a^*,b^*) \leq \left(1 + \frac{\left|W_{\psi_f} S(a,b) - \Gamma^* \cdot W_{\psi_f} S(a^*,b^*)\right|}{\left|W_{\psi_f} S(a^*,b^*)\right| \sqrt{1-\Gamma^{*2}}}\right)^{-1} \tag{19}$$

and

$$corr(a^*,b^*) \leq \left(1 + \left|\frac{a^{*2}\partial^2_{b,b} W_{\psi_f} S(a^*,b^*) + W_{\psi_f} S(a^*,b^*) \left\|\psi'_f\right\|^2}{\left|W_{\psi_f} S(a^*,b^*)\right| \sqrt{\left\|\psi''_f\right\|^2 - \left\|\psi'_f\right\|^2}}\right|\right)^{-1} \tag{20}$$

where $\Gamma^* = \left\langle \psi_f(x),\ \psi_f(\frac{x-(b-b^*)/a^*}{a/a^*}) \right\rangle$ is the correlation function of ψ_f and $\partial_{b,b}$ means the second derivative twice in b. Those bounds can be easily evaluated from some selected values of the pair $(a/a^*, \frac{b-b^*}{a^*})$.

Problem-Dependent Rules. Now, as every pattern-similar event will satisfy those conditions, it is necessary to add some problem-dependent selection rules.

As $supp(f) = [0,1]$, from the characteristics given by Gloor, we have that $a \leq .2$. To discard some possible discontinuities we will keep only all scales $a > .01$ for EEG sampled at 200Hz. Hence the first rule is that the possible scales are in the range $[.01, .2]$, so, adding one scale up and one down of the range in the analysis, we can discard those events whose duration is not in the range: if the estimated slopes for any of those out-of-range scales is larger than those corresponding to the scales in the range, then this alert is discarded.

Other rules are taken from the facts that the spikes must be distinguishable, with an amplitude of at least twice that of the background, must be more than a random event and must cause a field. The first three rules depend on each channel independently and the last include other adjacent channels in the analysis. As a measure of the average background amplitude we can use the average of the locally maximum wavelet energy for $5s$ of signal before the alert-time. The rule consists in normalizing the wavelet energies by the average background amplitudes and comparing it with a threshold $\tau_\sigma >= 4$.

To keep only those events that are not caused by random effects, we take those whose instant wavelet energy is larger than a multiple of the standard deviation σ of the background amplitudes plus its mean μ.

4.4 Spike Detection Results

Here we show some results of the procedure with the described rules. Figures 4 and 5 show two different EEG with the detected spikes. Each figure represents

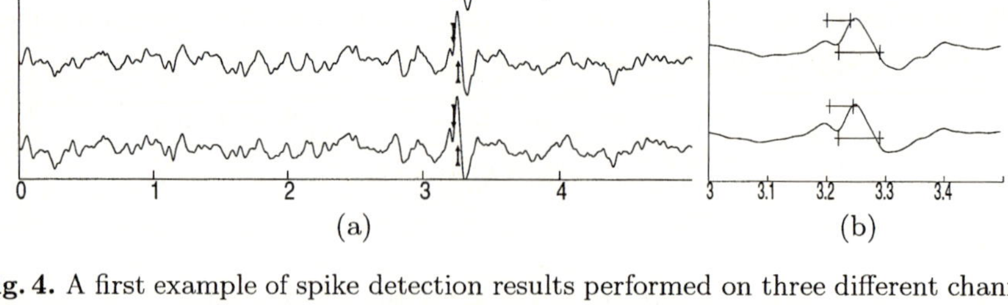

Fig. 4. A first example of spike detection results performed on three different channels independently of each other. (a)The EEG and the detected locations which are signaled by an arrows. (b) Zoom of (a) between 3 and 3.5s. The interval duration of the detected events are marked as line segments limited by two crosses ('+').

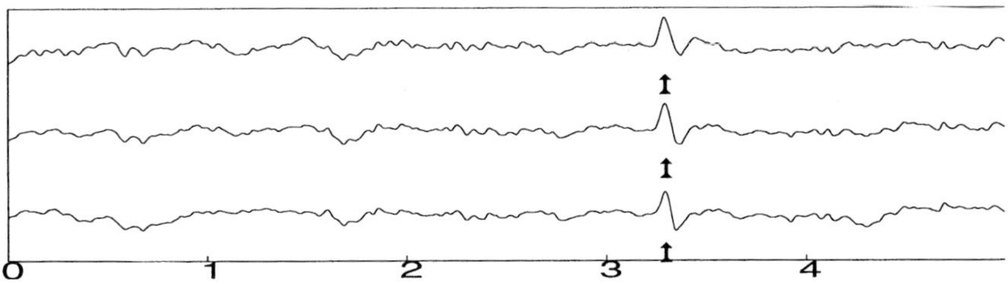

Fig. 5. A second example of spike detection results performed on three different channels independently of each other. The detected locations are signaled by an arrow.

three adjacent channels of the same EEG. Notice that there exists spike events almost simultaneously in various channels, i.e. there exists a field for those spikes.

Figure 4 (b) represents a zoom of Figure 4 (a) between 3 and 3.5s. The interval of duration of the detected events are signaled as line segments limited by two crosses ('+'). Notice the inverted spike-event overlapping the other (larger) spike in the second and third channels represented in Figure 4 by the up-down arrows.

5 Conclusions

To end, let us give some concluding remarks for future work. First, this paper shows how the lifting methods can be used to construct pattern-adapted wavelets. Unlike Abry et al. approach, they always give FIR filters but the dual functions may have infinite energy. An additional analysis must be done when L^2 dual functions are required. Second, as many of the pattern detection problems are for images, the generalization of this method to the 2D case will be done but such pattern-adapted wavelet construction method is more difficult. Since efficient 2D wavelets are associated to MRAs obtained by tensor products of the 1D wavelet filters and many possible patterns cannot be well approximated by such wavelets. Finally, another problem to solve is that, up to now, we start with a pattern given a priori and separately but for many applications such motifs are noisy or have to be taken from some experimental signals [24].

References

1. Zhang, J.K., Davidson, T.N., Wong, K.M.: Efficient design of orthonormal wavelet bases for signal representation. IEEE Transactions on Signal Processing **52** (2004) 1983–1996
2. Lucas, M.F., Hitti, E., Doncarli, C.: Optimisation d'ondelettes pour la classification. 18ième colloque GRETSI sur le traitement du Signal et des Images, Toulouse, France (2001)
3. Du, M., Chan, F.H.Y., Lam, F.K., Sun, J.: Crackle detection and classification based on matched wavelet analysis. In: Engineering in Medicine and Biology Society. Volume 4., Chicago, IL, USA, 19th Annual International Conference of the IEEE (1997) 1638–1641

4. Brunelli, R., Poggio, T.: Template matching: Matched spatial filters and beyond. Pattern Recognition **30** (1997) 751–768
5. Ozdamar, O., Kalayci, T.: Detection of spikes with artificial neural networks using raw EEG. Computers and Biomedical Research **31** (1998) 122–142
6. Kalayci, T., Ozdamar, O.: Wavelet processing for automated neural network detection of EEG spikes. IEEE Med. Engng. Biol. **14** (1995) 160–166
7. Mallat, S.: A wavelet tour of signal processing. Academic Press (1998)
8. Misiti, M., Misiti, Y., Oppenheim, G., Poggi, J.M.: Les ondelettes et leurs applications. Hermes (2003)
9. Chapa, J.O., Rao, R.M.: Algorithms for designing wavelets to match a specified signal. IEEE Transactions on Signal Processing **48** (2000) 3395–3406
10. Fung, C.C., Shi, P.: Design of compactly supported wavelet to match singularities in medical images. Applications of Digital Image Processing XXV (2002) 358–369
11. Abry, P.: Ondelettes et turbulences. Diderot Editeur, Paris (1997)
12. Aldroubi, A., Unser, M.: Families of multiresolution and wavelet spaces with optimal properties. Numer. Funct. Anal. and Optimiz. **14** (1993) 417–446
13. Abry, P., Aldroubi, A.: Designing multiresolution analysis-type wavelets and their fast alghorithm. The journal of Fourier Analysis and Applications. **2** (1995) 135–159
14. Sweldens, W.: The lifting scheme: A new philosophy in biorthogonal wavelet constructions. In Laine, A., Unser, M., eds.: Wavelet Applications in Signal and Image Processing III, Proc. SPIE 2569 (1995) 68–79
15. Sweldens, W.: The lifting scheme: A custom-design construction of biorthogonal wavelets. Appl. Comput. Harmon. Anal. **3** (1996) 186–200
16. Sweldens, W.: The lifting scheme: A construction of second generation wavelets. SIAM J. Math. Anal. **29** (1997) 511–546
17. Sweldens, W., Daubechies, I.: Factoring wavelets transform into lifting steps. J. Fourier Anal. Appl. **4** (1998) 247–269
18. Strang, G., Nguyen, T.: Wavelets and Filters Banks. Wellesley-Cambridge Press (1996)
19. Daubechies, I.: Ten Lectures on Wavelets. 3rd. edn. CBMS-NSF (1994)
20. Wilson, S.B., Emerson, R.: Spike detection: a review and comparison of algorithms. Clinical Neurophysiology **113** (2002) 1873–1881
21. Varsta, M., Heikkonen, J., Millan, J.R.: Epileptic activity detection in EEG with neural networks. Research Reports B3, Laboratory of Computational Engineering, Helsinki University of Technology (1998)
22. Gloor, P.: Contributions of electroencephalography and electrocorticography in the neurosurgical treatment of the epilepsies. Adv. Neurol. **8** (1975) 59–105
23. Wilson, S.B., Turner, C.A., Emerson, R.G., Scheuer, M.L.: Spike detection. Clinical Neurophysiology **110** (1999) 404–411
24. Scott, C., Nowak, R.: TEMPLAR: A wavelet based framework for pattern learning and analysis. IEEE Transactions on Signal Processing **52** (2004) 2264–2274

Edge Detection in Contaminated Images, Using Cluster Analysis

Héctor Allende[1] and Jorge Galbiati[2]

[1] Universidad Técnica Federico Santa María, Departamento de Informática, Casilla 110-V, Valparaíso
hallende@inf.utfsm.cl
[2] Pontificia Universidad Católica de Valparaíso, Instituto de Estadística, Casilla 4059, Valparaíso, Chile
jorge.galbiati@pucv.cl

Abstract. In this paper we present a method to detect edges in images. The method consists of using a 3x3 pixel mask to scan the image, moving it from left to right and from top to bottom, one pixel at a time. Each time it is placed on the image, an agglomerative hierarchical cluster analysis is applied to the eight outer pixels. When there is more than one cluster, it means that window is on an edge, and the central pixel is marked as an edge point. After scanning all the image, we obtain a new image showing the marked pixels around the existing edges of the image. Then a thinning algorithm is applied so that the edges are well defined. The method results to be particularly efficient when the image is contaminated. In those cases, a previous restoration method is applied.

1 Introduction

Edge detection is based on the assumption that discontinuities in the intensity of an image correspond to edges in the image, without disregarding the fact that often changes of intensity are not due only to edges, but can be produced by light effects, like shades or brightness, effects which demand additional treatment.

Among the operators used most frequently for edge detection are gradient operators and compass operators. The first one computes the gradient in two perpendicular directions, which are used to find the module and phase, and the second measures the gradient module in a set of different directions, selecting the one with largest value at each point. Unfortunately the derivative amplifies the noise, for that reason, filters must be used to smooth the images. When there are steep changes of intensity in the image, the gradient and compass operators work well, but don't do so when there are gradual changes in intensity. The Laplace operator is used in these cases, but it is more sensitive to noise so it requires a better smoothing of the image.

The amplification of the noise produced by most of the edge detectors usually result in reporting non existing edges. In this paper we introduce a detector based on cluster analysis for contaminated images, which also filters the image without altering it too much. Is is based on the cluster analysis filter proposed

M. Lazo and A. Sanfeliu (Eds.): CIARP 2005, LNCS 3773, pp. 945–953, 2005.

by [1], to which was added the ability to detect edges, using the same structure of grouping pixels into clusters. The results obtained by this edge detector are compared with known detectors to investigate its effectiveness.

2 Edge Detection Algorithm

The image is analyzed through sliding windows, which move along the image from left to right and from top to bottom, one pixel at a time. These windows consist of a 3x3 pixel square, numbered according to Figure 1. To analyze the central pixel in each window, a cluster analysis algorithm is applied to the eight surrounding pixels to detect groups with similar light intensity. Because of its simplicity, the best algorithm to use is the agglomerative hierarchical algorithm. In each iteration, the two nearest clusters are combined to form one, according to some distance measure previously determined.

The result is a nested or hierarchical series of groups of clusters formed with these eight pixels, starting with eight clusters with one pixel each, followed by seven, etc., ending with one single cluster containing the eight pixels. At each iteration, the distance at which the two closest clusters are grouped is recorded, forming an ascending sequence. A significantly big increase at iteration k + 1, as compared to some threshold value $T_{cluster}$, indicates that the optimum pattern of clusters is the one defined in the k-th step. A value of 25 for the threshold $T_{cluster}$ of in a scale of 1 to 255 has shown empirically to be a good choice [1]. The usual number of clusters is one, which corresponds to a smooth area.

Once the cluster pattern for the surrounding pixels is defined, the central pixel is examined and compared to the average intensity value of each cluster, with the purpose of determining if it belongs to one of them. If it differs too much from all the clusters, then it is considered a contaminated pixel (an outlier). To decide whether it belongs to some cluster, a second threshold value is introduced, T_{member}, to which the distances to the average of each group are compared. Empirical evidence shows that a suitable value for T_{member} is 36 [1].

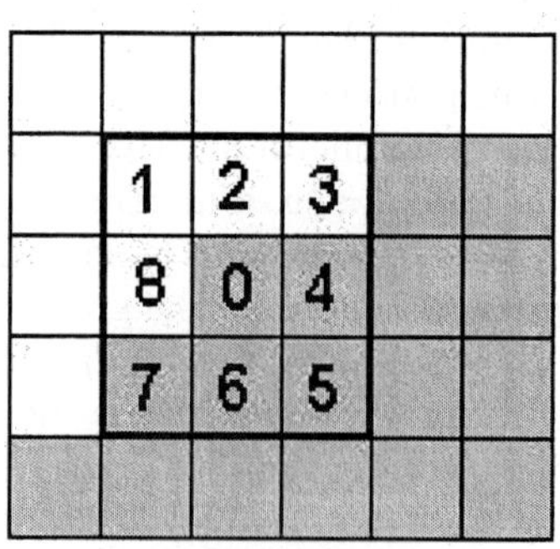

Fig. 1. 3 by 3 pixel window. The central pixel $Px(0)$ is being analyzed, based on the eight pixels $Px(1)$ to $Px(8)$.

If the central pixel is considered to be contaminated, then it is assigned to one of the surrounding clusters. This is done through a probabilistic procedure, favoring the clusters with highest number of pixels, and those that have greater adjacency with the central pixel and those that group more adjacent pixels together [1]. This way it manages to eliminate noise from the image without blurring it, as other well-known filter do. Once that the image has been treated to eliminate the existing noise, a second smoothing is carried out, using a median filter, to improve the definition of each cluster. Then the edge detection procedure is applied. It consists sliding 3x3 pixel windows, in a similar way as was described before. The same cluster analysis algorithm is applied, but this time it is used to keep record of the number of clusters present in each window. If there are more than one cluster in the window, then it means that it contains an edge, so the central pixel is marked as an edge point. Suppose that $Px(0)$ denotes the central pixel which is being analyzed, and $Px(y)$ one of its neighborhood pixels, y=1,2,..,8, numbered as in Figure 1. Let $C_{Px(y)}$ be the cluster containing $Px(y)$. Then $Px(0)$ is marked as a border pixel if in satisfies one of the following conditions:

$$\begin{array}{c} C_{Px(2)} \neq C_{Px(0)} \\ C_{Px(4)} \neq C_{Px(0)} \\ C_{Px(6)} \neq C_{Px(0)} \\ C_{Px(8)} \neq C_{Px(0)} \end{array}$$

When scanning the entire image using the previous method, the resulting edges are not very precise. In order to enhance the border lines, a thinning algorithm is applied. An appropriate algorithm is the one proposed by Nagendraprasad ,Wang and Gupta (1993) based on a previous one due to Wang and Zhang (1989) and improved by Carrasco and Forcecada [2], and it consists of the following:

Let $b(p)$ be the number of neighbors of $Px(0)$ that are marked as borders. We will call these pixels "black", while the ones that are not marked as borders will be referred to as "white". let $a(p)$ be the number of transitions from white to black, of the neighboring pixels, visited in the same order established in Figure 1. Let $c(p)$, $e(p)$ and $f(p)$ be functions defined in the following way:

$$c(p) = \begin{cases} 1, \text{if} \quad Px(2) = Px(3) = Px(4) = Px(7) \quad \text{and} \quad Px(6) = Px(8) \\ 1, \text{if} \quad Px(4) = Px(5) = Px(6) = Px(1) \quad \text{and} \quad Px(8) = Px(2) \\ 0, \qquad \text{in other cases} \end{cases}$$

$$e(p) = (Px(4) + Px(6)) * Px(2) * Px(8)$$

$$f(p) = (Px(8) + Px(2)) * Px(6) * Px(4)$$

We proceed to scan the image iteratively. At each step, if $b(p)$ has a value between 1 and 7 and $a(p)$ or $(1-g) * c(p) + g(p) * d(p) = 1$, with $g = 0$ for odd iterations, $g = 1$ for even iterations. $d(p)$ is defined by

Fig. 2. (a) Original image 50 percent contaminated, standard deviation 20. Edge detection methods:(b) Prewitt (c) Sobel (d) Log (Laplacian of normal) (e) Roberts (f) Zero-cross (g) Canny (h) Proposed.

$$d(p) = \begin{cases} 1, \text{if} \quad Px(3) = Px(6) = Px(7) = Px(8) \quad \text{and} \quad Px(2) = Px(4) \\ 1, \text{if} \quad Px(2) = Px(5) = Px(8) = Px(1) \quad \text{and} \quad Px(4) = Px(6) \\ 0, \qquad\qquad \text{in other cases} \end{cases}$$

If we are in an even number iteration, then if $e(p) = 0$ the $p - th$ pixel is changed to white. If the iteration is odd-numbered, then if $f(p) = 0$, the p-th pixel is turned to white. In other cases, the p-th pixel is not changed. This process is carried out along the entire image. With this procedure we obtain the edges of the image, as connected lines, one pixel wide.

3 Experimental Results

We present several study cases with different levels of contamination, as a percentage P of contaminated pixels, and a standard deviation. A percentage P of pixels is randomly chosen and are contaminated in the following way: Let (i,j) be a chosen pixel and let x_{ij} be its light intensity. A random number Y is generated from a normal random variable with mean 0 and some fixed standard deviation. The intensity is then substituted by x_{ij} +Y, approximated to the nearest integer between 0 and 255. Tests are carried out using the threshold values mentioned

Fig. 3. (a) Original image 25 percent contaminated, standard deviation 40. Edge detection methods:(b) Prewitt (c) Sobel (d) Log (Laplacian of normal) (e) Roberts (f) Zero-cross (g) Canny (h) Proposed.

Fig. 4. (a) Original image 10 percent contaminated, standard deviation 80. Edge detection methods:(b) Prewitt (c) Sobel (d) Log (Laplacian of normal) (e) Roberts (f) Zero-cross (g) Canny (h) Proposed.

earlier for $T_{cluster}$ and T_{member}. The percentage of contamination and the standard deviation were given the values (50,20), (25, 40) and (10, 80). To observe the quality of the resulting edges they were compared to other commonly used edge detectors, like Prewitt [3], Sobel [4], LOG (Laplacian of Gaussian), Roberts, Zero-Cross and Canny.

The Roberts, Sobel and Prewitt edge detectors are based on the gradient of the image, formed by a vector field associated to each pixel. The vector's module is associated to the light intensity, and the direction of the vector to the direction of the major change in intensity. The Zero-Cross, Canny and LOG are based on the Laplacian, which is associated to the second derivative of the light

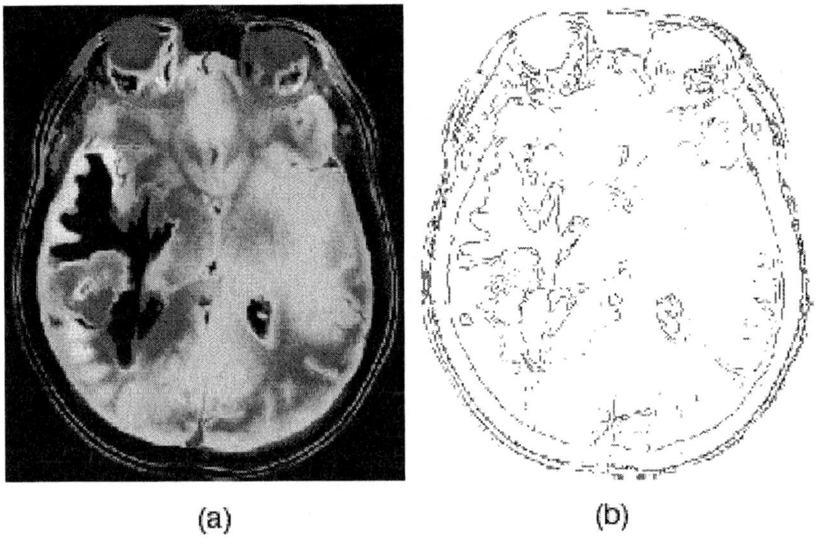

Fig. 5. (a) Original contaminated image. (b) Edge detection using proposed method.

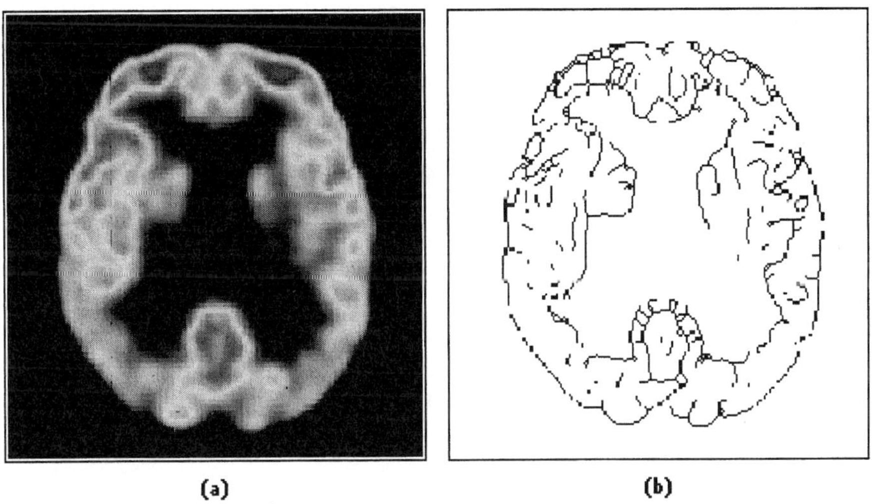

Fig. 6. (a) Original contaminated image. (b) Edge detection using proposed method.

intensity of the image, with which the zero crossings are detected, determining thus, the location of edges. Figures 2 to 4 show the results obtained for each of these detectors and for the one introduced in this article.

The times taken to complete the edge detection process, including smoothing and line enhancing, ranged between 515.5 and 523.4 seconds. For uncontaminated images, times for edge detection and line enhancement ranged between 255.8 and 258.4 seconds.

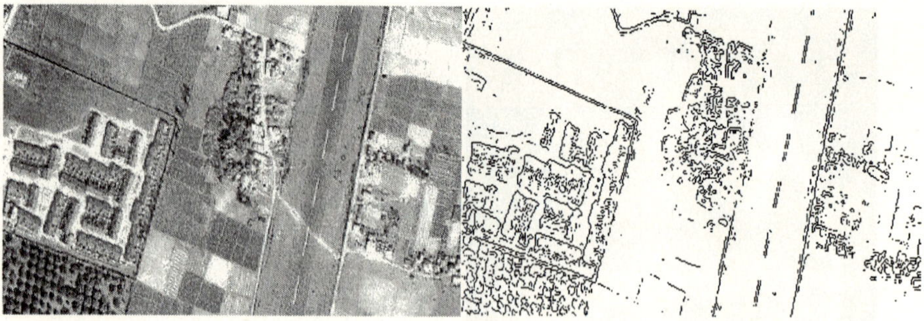

Fig. 7. (a) Original contaminated image. (b) Edge detection using proposed method.

Also, tests were carried out with other type of images, which by their particular way of obtaining the image, are naturally contaminated with noise, like satellite images and medical images. Figures 5 to 7 show the results.

4 Conclusions

The method introduced in this article approaches the problem of detecting edges in contaminated images. As it can be seen from the experimental results shown here, most of the edge detectors behave relatively well when there is a low level of contamination or when the standard deviation of the contamination is small (figure 2), due to the fact that the contaminated pixels are easy to smooth. But when there is a high contamination standard deviation is large (figures 3 and 4) then nonexisting edges appear, because most of the contaminated pixels cannot be smoothed out. In both cases, the proposed edge detector is able to find the proper borders, avoiding to point out contaminated pixels as edges. We can see with the results obtained in figures 5, 6 and 7, the power of the proposed detector to find borders in contaminated images, therefore it is a good alternative for processing medical images and satellite images. Observing the figures we can notice that for different contamination levels, we get similar results, obtaining the proper borders of the image, and not of the contamination.

References

1. H. Allende, J. Galbiati : A non-parametric to filter for digital image restoration, using cluster analysis. Pattern Recognition Letters, Vol 25, (June 2004), pp. 841-847.
2. Rafael C. Carrasco and Mikel L. Forcada : A note on the Nagendraprasad-Wang-Gupta thinning algorithm. Pattern Recognition Letters 16(5), (1995) pp. 539-541.
3. J. M. S. Prewitt: Object enhancement and extraction. In A. Rosenfeld and B. S. Lipkin, editors, Picture Processing and Psychophysics, pp. 75-149. Academic Press, New York (1970).
4. K. K. Pingle: Line of vision perception by to computer. In A. Grasselli, publisher, Automatic Interpretation and Classification of Images, pp. 277-284. Academic Press, New York,(1969).

5. H. Allende, J. Galbiati, R. Vallejos : Digital Image Restoration Using Autoregressive Time Series Models. Proceedings of the Second Latino-American Seminar on Radar Remote Sensing, ESA-SP-434,(1998) pp. 53-59.
6. H. Allende, J. Galbiati, R. Vallejos: Robust Image Modeling on Image Processing. Pattern Recognition Letters, Vol. 22, No. 11,(2001) pp. 1219-1231.
7. H.O. Bustos: Robust statistics in SAR image processing. ESA-SP No. 407, (February 1997), pp. 81-89.
8. C. da Costa Freitas, A. C. Frery, A. H. Correia: Generalized Distributions for Multilook Polarimetric SAR Data under the Multiplicative Model. Technical Report, (June 2002).
9. R.L. Kashyap, K.B. Eom: Robust Image Techniques with an Image Restoration Application. IEEE Transactions on Acoustics, Speech and Signal Processing, Vol. 36, No. 8, pp. 1313-1325 (1988).
10. L. Kaufman, P.J. Rousseeuw : Finding Groups in Data: An Introduction to Cluster Analysis. J. Wiley, N. York (1990).

Automatic Edge Detection by Combining Kohonen SOM and the Canny Operator

P. Sampaziotis and N. Papamarkos

Image Processing and Multimedia Laboratory,
Department of Electrical & Computer Engineering,
Democritus University of Thrace,
67100 Xanthi, Greece
papamark@ee.duth.gr

Abstract. In this paper a new method for edge detection in grayscale images is presented. It is based on the use of the Kohonen self-organizing map (SOM) neural network combined with the methodology of Canny edge detector. Gradient information obtained from different masks and at different smoothing scales is classified in three classes (Edge, Non Edge and Fuzzy Edge) using an hierarchical Kohonen network. Using the three classes obtained, the final stage of hysterisis thresholding is performed in a fully automatic way. The proposed technique is extensively tested with success.

1 Introduction

Changes or discontinuities in an image amplitude attribute such as intensity are fundamentally important primitive characteristics of an image because they often provide an indication of the physical extent of objects within the image. The detection of these changes or discontinuities is a fundamental operation in computer vision with numerous approaches to it.

Marr and Hildreth [3] introduced the theory of edge detection and described a method for determining the edges using the zero-crossings of the Laplacian of Gaussian of an image. Canny determined edges by an optimization process [1] and proposed an approximation to the optimal detector as the maxima of gradient magnitude of a Gaussian-smoothed image. Lily Rui Liang and Carl G. Looney proposed a fuzzy classifier [2] that detects classes of image pixels corresponding to gray level variation in the various directions. A fuzzy reasoning approach was proposed by Todd Law and Hidenori Itoh [8], in which image filtering, edge detection and edge tracing are completely based on fuzzy rules. The use of self-organising map and the Peano scan for edge detection in multispectral images was proposed by P.J. Toivanen and J. Ansamaki [5]. In [10], Pihno used a feed-forward artificial neural of perceptron-like units and trained it with a synthetic image formed of concentric rings with different gray levels. Weller [11] trained a neural net by reference to a small training set, so that a Sobel operator was simulated. In Bezdek's approach [12], a neural net is trained on

M. Lazo and A. Sanfeliu (Eds.): CIARP 2005, LNCS 3773, pp. 954–965, 2005.

all possible exemplars based on binary images, with each windowed possibility being scored by the (normalised) Sobel operator.

Among the various edge detection methods proposed so far, the Canny edge detector is most widely used due to its optimality to the three criteria of good detection, good localization, and single response to an edge.

In this paper a new edge detection technique is proposed which improves the canny edge detection the following way:

- Utilizes edge information extracted not only from one edge detection masks but from a number of different masks.
- Uses Kohonen SOM in order to obtain three main classes of edges (Edge, Fuzzy-Edge, Non-Edge) that are next used to automatically obtain the final edge pixels according to the Canny's hysterisis thresholding procedure.

The proposed technique is extensively tested with many different types of images and it is found that it performs satisfactory even with degraded images.

2 Overview

A typical implementation of the Canny edge detector follows the steps below:

1. Smooth the image with an appropriate Gaussian Filter to reduce noise.
2. Determine gradient magnitude and gradient direction at each pixel.
3. Suppress non edge pixels with non maximum suppression. If the gradient magnitude at a pixel is larger than those at its two neighbors in the gradient direction, mark the pixel as an edge. Otherwise, mark the pixel as the background.
4. Remove the weak edges by hysteresis thresholding.

The first step of the Canny edge detector is the gaussian smoothing. Gaussian filters are low-pass filters and thus apart from filtering the noise they also blur an image. The Gaussian outputs a 'weighted average' of each pixel's neighborhood, with the average weighted more towards the value of the central pixels. The degree of smoothing is determined by the standard deviation of the filter. Filtering an image with a gaussian does not preserve edges. Larger values of standard deviation correspond to images at coarser resolutions with low detail level.

After the image filtering, the next step is the determination of the image gradient. The simplest method to compute the gradient magnitude $G(j,k)$ refers to the combination of row $G_R(j,k)$ and column $G_C(j,k)$ gradient. The spatial gradient magnitude is given by:

$$G(j,k) = \sqrt{G_C(j,k)^2 + G_R(j,k)^2} \tag{1}$$

and the orientation of the spatial gradient with respect to the row axis is:

$$\theta(j,k) = \arctan\left\{\frac{G_C(j,k)}{G_R(j,k)}\right\} \tag{2}$$

The discrete approximation of $G_R(j,k)$ and $G_C(j,k)$ can be given by the pixel difference, separated by a null value [9] :

$$G_R(j,k) = P(j,k+1) - P(j,k-1) \tag{3}$$

$$G_C(j,k) = P(j-1,k) - P(j+1,k) \tag{4}$$

The separated pixel difference is sensitive to small luminance fluctuations in the image and thus it is preferred to use 3×3 spatial masks which perform differentiation in one coordinate direction and spatial averaging in the and orthogonal direction simultaneously. The most widely used masks are the Sobel, Prewitt and Frei-Chen operators. As show in figures 1 and 2 these masks have different weightings, in order to adjust the importance of each pixel in terms of its contribution to the spatial gradient. Frei and Chen have proposed north, south, east, and west weightings so that the gradient is the same for horizontal, vertical, and diagonal edges, the Prewitt operator is more sensitive to horizontal and vertical edges than to diagonal edges and the reverse is true for the Sobel operator.

$$\frac{1}{4}\begin{bmatrix} 1 & 0 & -1 \\ 2 & 0 & -2 \\ 1 & 0 & -1 \end{bmatrix} \text{(a)} \qquad \frac{1}{3}\begin{bmatrix} 1 & 0 & -1 \\ 1 & 0 & -1 \\ 1 & 0 & -1 \end{bmatrix} \text{(b)} \qquad \frac{1}{2+\sqrt{2}}\begin{bmatrix} 1 & 0 & -1 \\ \sqrt{2} & 0 & -\sqrt{2} \\ 1 & 0 & -1 \end{bmatrix} \text{(c)}$$

Fig. 1. Row gradient masks: (a) Sobel (b) Prewitt (c) Frei-Chen

$$\frac{1}{4}\begin{bmatrix} -1 & -2 & -1 \\ 0 & 0 & 0 \\ 1 & 2 & 1 \end{bmatrix} \text{(a)} \qquad \frac{1}{3}\begin{bmatrix} -1 & -1 & -1 \\ 0 & 0 & 0 \\ 1 & 1 & 1 \end{bmatrix} \text{(b)} \qquad \frac{1}{2+\sqrt{2}}\begin{bmatrix} -1 & -\sqrt{2} & -1 \\ 0 & 0 & 0 \\ 1 & \sqrt{2} & 1 \end{bmatrix} \text{(c)}$$

Fig. 2. Column gradient masks: (a) Sobel (b) Prewitt (c) Frei-Chen

Hysterisis thresholding uses a high threshold T_{high} and a low threshold T_{low} which both are user-defined. Every pixel in an image that has gradient magnitude greater than T_{high} or less than T_{low} is presumed to be an edge or a non-edge pixel respectively. Any other pixel that is connected with an edge pixel and has gradient magnitude greater than T_{low} is also selected as edge pixel. This process is repeated until every pixel is marked as edge or non edge pixel. In terms of clustering, by selecting the two thresholds, the image pixels are grouped in three clusters : Edge cluster, non-edge cluster and fuzzy-edge cluster with fuzziness defined by means of spatial connectivity with edge pixels.

The basic idea of this work is to automate the edge map clustering using the Kohonen self-organizing map. As described previously in this section, gradient depends on the size of the gaussian filter and the differentiation operator . Thus it is more robust to create a feature space with gradient information obtained from different masks and at different detail levels of the image and represent the gradient magnitude in a vectorial form and not with a scalar value.

2.1 Kohonen SOM Neural Network

The Kohonen SOM is a neural network that simulates the hypothesized self-organization process carried out in the human brain when some input data are presented [4]. The Kohonen network consists of two layers. The first layer is the input layer and the second is the competition layer in which the units are arranged in a one or two dimensional grid. Each unit in the input layer has a feed-forward connection to each unit in the competition layer. The architecture of the Kohonen network is shown in figure 3. The network maps a set of input vectors into a set of output vectors (neurons) without supervision. That is, there is no a-priori knowledge of the characteristics of the output classes. The training algorithm is based on competitive learning and is as follows :

1. Define of the desired set A of output classes c_i

$$A = \{c_1, \ldots, c_N\} \tag{5}$$

   and the topology of the competition layer neurons.
2. Initialize output units c_i with reference vectors $\mathbf{w}_{c_i}$ chosen randomly from a finite data set $\mathbf{D} = \{\mathbf{d}_1, \ldots, \mathbf{d}_M\}$ and set the time parameter $t = 0$.
3. Present an input vector $\mathbf{d}$ and find the winner output neuron $s(\mathbf{d}) = s$:

$$s(\mathbf{d}) = arg\ min_{c \in A} \|\mathbf{d} - \mathbf{w}_c\| \tag{6}$$

4. Adapt each unit c according to

$$\Delta \mathbf{w}_c = \epsilon(t) h_{sh}(\mathbf{d} - \mathbf{w}_c) \tag{7}$$

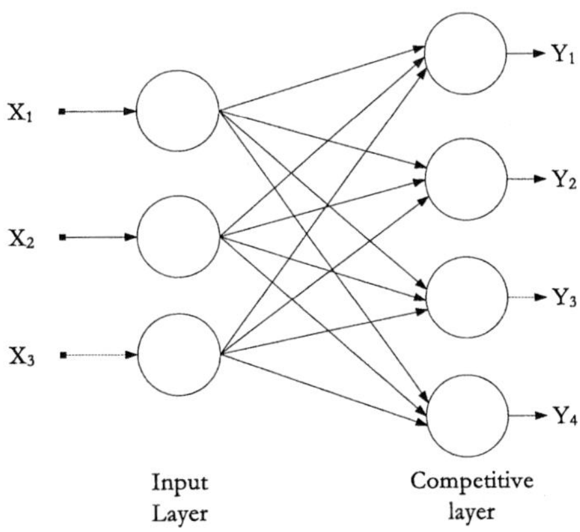

Fig. 3. Architecture of the Kohonen Self-Organising Map

where $\epsilon(t)$ is the function that controls the learning rate and h_{sh} the function that defines the neighborhood units of the winner neuron that will be adapted. For the learning rate in this work we used the function:

$$\epsilon(t) = \epsilon_{initial} \left(\frac{\epsilon_{final}}{\epsilon_{initial}} \right) \tag{8}$$

and as a neighborhood function the gaussian :

$$H_{cs} = exp \left(\frac{-\|c - s\|}{2\sigma^2} \right) \tag{9}$$

with standard deviation varied according to

$$\sigma(t) = \sigma_{initial} \left(\frac{\sigma_{final}}{\sigma_{initial}} \right) \tag{10}$$

.

5. Repeat steps 3 and 4 until all the vectors of the training dataset **D** are presented to the network.
6. Increase the time parameter:

$$t = t + 1; \tag{11}$$

7. If $t < t_{max}$ continue with step 3.

3 Description of the Method

As shown in figure 4 , the proposed edge detection method consists of two parts.

The first one follows the the three first steps of the Canny edge detector. Firstly we smooth the grayscale image I with an appropriate Gaussian Filter of standard deviation $\sigma_{central}$ in order to reduce image noise. We call the smoothed image I_C. Then we calculate gradient magnitude and direction using the Sobel operator and perform non maximum-suppression. Every pixel with gradient magnitude greater than zero is set 0 (edge) and all the other pixels are set to 255 (non-edge). This process leads to a single-pixel width binary edge map M. The second part is the classification of images pixel into three clasees (Edge, Non-Edge, Fuzzy Edge). We separately smooth the original grayscale image I

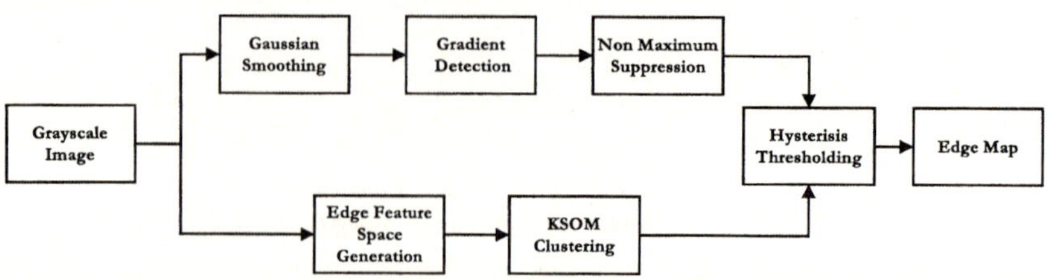

Fig. 4. Flowchart of the proposed method

with a gaussian filter of standard deviation σ_{low} and σ_{high}. The values of σ_{low} and σ_{hight} have a small deviation above and below σ_{center} respectively in order to create different detail levels but also avoid the problem of edge dislocation. For each of these three smoothed images I_L, I_C and I_H, we compute the gradient magnitude using Sobel,Prewitt, Frei-Chen and Separated Pixel Difference operator.

For every pixel P of the image I we assign a 12-component vector. Each vector's element represents gradient magnitude from different combination of smoothing scale and differentiation mask. This process produces a 12-dimension feature space $\mathbf{D}$, which will be sampled in order to train the Kohonen SOM.

As shown in figure 5 we approach the clustering process in a hierarchical way, which has been carried out after a large number of experiments.

At the first level, we use a Kohonen map with three output units connected in line topology. These output units represent three clusters: high,medium and low gradient class. The training dataset for the Kohonen map consists of randomly choosen vectors of the input space $\mathbf{D}$. After the training of the Kohonen network we assign each pixel of the image to one of the output classes according to the euclidean distance between the pixel's vector in feature space $\mathbf{D}$ and the vectors of the SOFM output units.

At the second level, all the pixels that are mapped into the high and medium gradient class are grouped in order to form the Edge Pixel class. The Low Gradient class is splitted in two classes: the Fuzzy-Edge Pixel class and the Non-Edge Pixel class, using a Kohonen map with the same topology as the one at the first

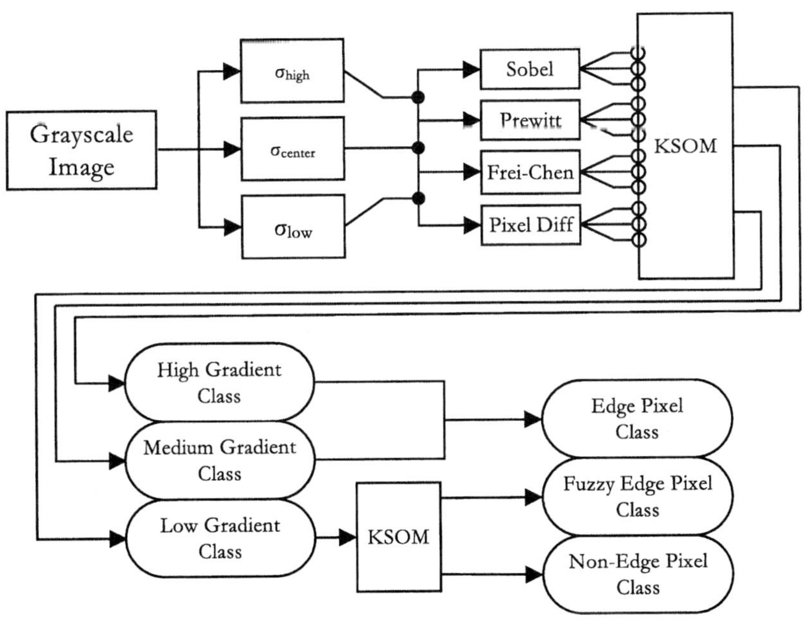

Fig. 5. Flowchart of the clustering process

level but with two output units. All the pixels that were mapped into the Low Gradient class on the first level, are now assigned at these two classes.

The next step of the method is the hysterisis thresholding in a revised way. By integrating the information of the pixel class labeling performed in the previous step, there is no need for the user-defined thresholds T_{low} and T_{high}. Hysterisis thresholding is summarized as follows:

1. Mark as Non-Edge class pixel, every pixel that is marked as non-edge (255) in the binary edge map M.
2. Select a pixel P that belongs to the Edge class.
3. Every pixel that is connected with 8-neighborhood with P and belongs to the Fuzzy-Edge class is marked as edge pixel(0) and it is classified into the Edge class.
4. Repeat step 2 for all pixels of the Edge-class.
5. The remaining Fuzzy-edge class pixels are classified into the Non-edge class and marked as non-edge pixels (255).

4 Experimental Results

The method analysed in this paper is implemented in visual enviroment (Borland Delphi) and tested on several images with satisfactory results. For an AMD Athlon 64 (2GHz) bazed PC with 512 MB RAM, the processing time for a 512×512 image with a Kohonen Som network trained for 300 epochs with 1000 samples, was 2.55 seconds. Edges extracted with the proposed method are shown in figure 6. In 6(b) we have the binary edge map M after gaussian smoothing with $\sigma_{central} = 1$, gradient detection with the sobel operator and non-maximum suppression. In 6(c) we can see the result of the classification using the Kohonen SOM. Pixels classified to the Non-Edge class are shown in black color. Red coloured pixels are the pixels that belong to the Edge class and the pixels of the Fuzzy-edge class are shown in green color. The parametres of the Kohonen maps for these examples are: $\epsilon_i = 0.9$, $\epsilon_f = 0.01$ and $T_{max} = 400$ with training vectors from an input space formed as described previously with $\sigma_{low} = 0.8$ and $\sigma_{high} = 1.2$. The final edges exctracted with automatic hysterisis thresholding are shown in 6 (d). Two additional examples are shown in figures 7 and 8.

In order to have some comparative results, our technique was tested against the results of objective edge evaluation and detector parameter selection method proposed in [6]. In this work, Yitzhak Yitzhaky and Eli Peli propose a statistical objective performance analysis and detector parameter selection method, using detection results produced by different parameters of the same edge detector. Using the correspondence between the different detection results, an estimated best edge map, utilized as an estimated ground truth (EGT), is obtained. This is done using both a receiver operating characteristics (ROC) analysis and a Chi-square test. The best edge detector parameter set (PS) is then selected by the same statistical approach, using the EGT. This method was implemented in Matlab for the canny edge detector.

For the tests we used six ground truth images from the GT dataset used in [7] which is freely available on the internet. In figure 9 we see the test images and corresponding ground truth images. In these manually created GT images black represents edge, gray represents no-edge and white represents dont care. The GT is created by specifying edges that should be detected and regions in which no edges should be detected. Areas not specified either as edge or as no-edge default to dont-care regions. This makes it practical to specify GT for images that contain regions in which there are edges but their specification would be tedious and error-prone (for example, in a grassy area) [7]. The results of the pixel based comparison between the ground truth and the edge images were based on the following values:

- True positives (TP): Number of pixels marked as edges, which coincide with edge pixels in the GT.
- False positives (FP): Number of pixels marked as edges, which coincide with non-edge pixels in the GT.
- True negatives (TN): Number of pixels marked as non-edges, which coincide with non-edge pixels in the GT.
- False negatives (FN): Number of pixels marked as non-edges, which coincide with edge pixels in the GT.

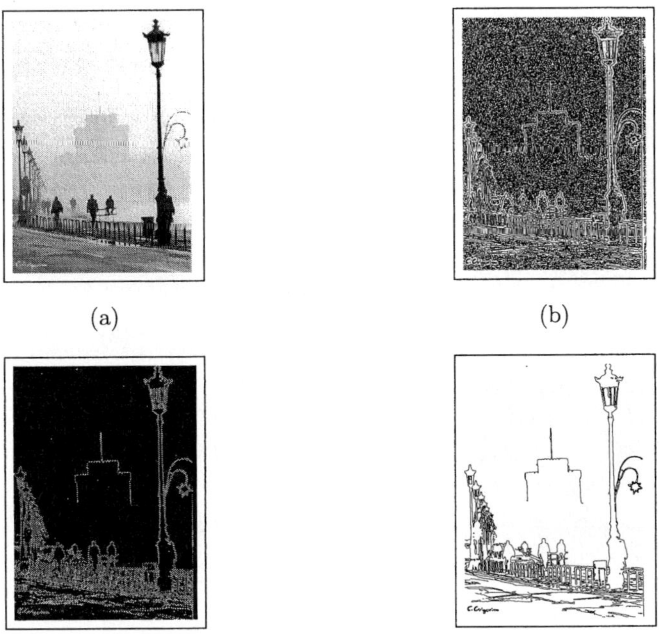

(a) (b)

(c) (d)

Fig. 6. (a) Original grayscale image, (b) Binary edge map M after smoothing differentation and non-maximum suppression, (c) Edge classes obtained by Kohonen SOM (d) Final edge map after automatic hysterisis thresholding

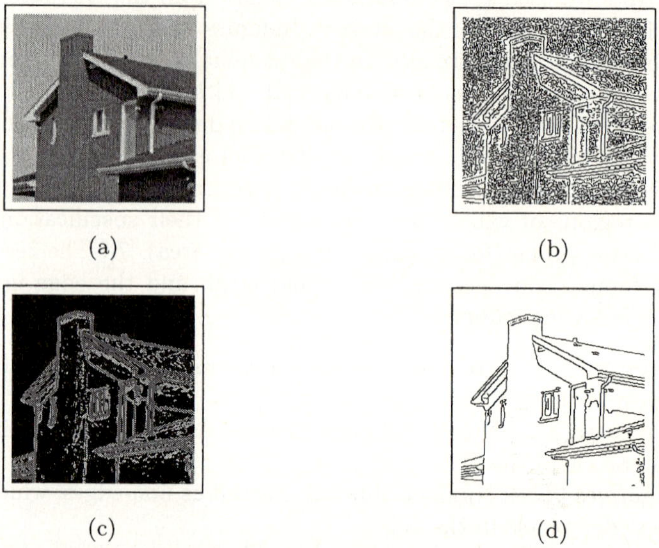

Fig. 7. (a) Original grayscale image, (b) Binary edge map M after smoothing differentation and non-maximum suppression, (c) Edge classes obtained by Kohonen SOM (d) Final edge map after automatic hysterisis thresholding

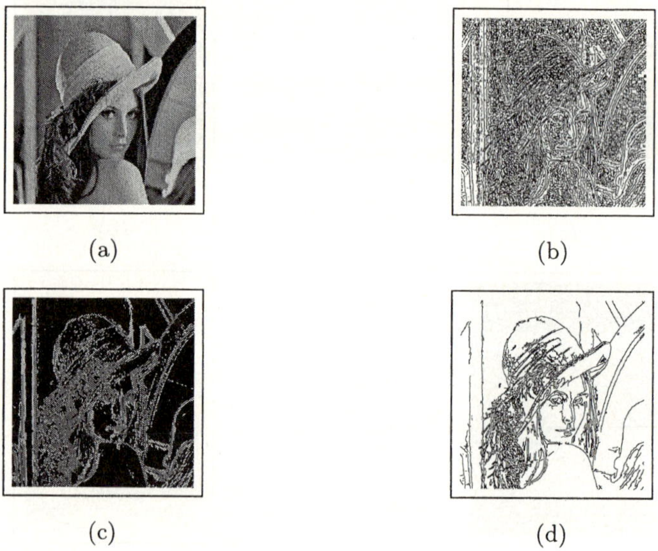

Fig. 8. (a) Original grayscale image, (b) Binary edge map M after smoothing differentation and non-maximum suppression, (c) Edge classes obtained by Kohonen SOM (d) Final edge map after automatic hysterisis thresholding

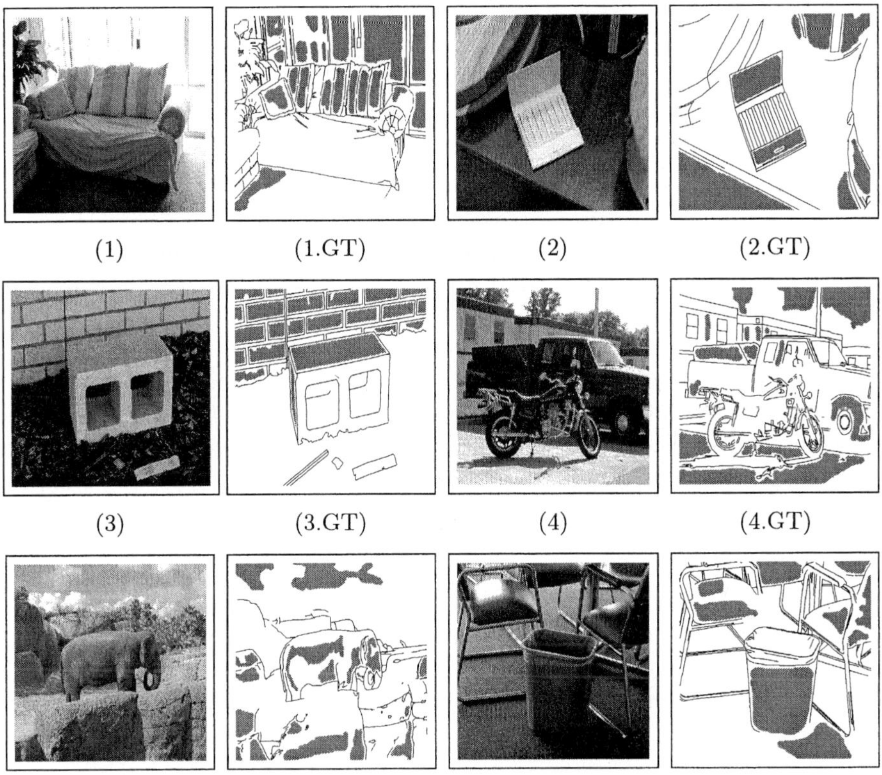

(1) (1.GT) (2) (2.GT)

(3) (3.GT) (4) (4.GT)

(5) (5.GT) (6) (6.GT)

Fig. 9. Images used for pixel-based evaluation

The calculation of these values is performed as follows: if a detector reports an edge pixel within a specified tolerance T_{match} of an edge in the GT, then it is counted as a true positive (TP) and the matched pixel in the GT is marked so that it cannot be used in another match. The Tmatch threshold for tolerance in matching a detected edge pixel to GT allows detected edges to match the GT even if displaced by a small distance [7]. In our test we used a value of Tmatch = 1. If a detector reports an edge pixel in a GT no-edge region, then it is counted as a false positive (FP). Edge pixels reported in a dont care region do not count as TPs or FPs. Background pixels that match pixels in a GT no-edge region are counted as true negatives (TN). Background pixels that match GT edge pixels are counted as false negatives (FN).

For the pixel-based comparison, these similarity measures were used:

– The percentage correct classification (PCC):

$$PCC = \frac{TP + TN}{TP + TN + FP + FN} \tag{12}$$

– The Jaccard Coefficient:

$$Jaccard = \frac{TP}{TP + FP + FN} \tag{13}$$

– The Dice Coefficient:

$$Dice = \frac{2 \times TP}{2 \times TP + FP + FN} \tag{14}$$

These three measures yield different properties: The PCC measure describes the proportion of matches to the total number of (pixels). Jaccard measure is an overlap ratio which excludes all non-occurrences, and, thereby, disregards the information on matches between background pixels. The Dice measure is similar to Jaccord but it gives more weight to occurrences of edge pixels (TPs).

From each test image we extract three edge maps. The first one is obtained using our method. The second and third, using canny edge detection with parameters selected with the process described in [6], with EGT estimated with ROC analysis and best parameter selection (PS) using ROC analysis and Chi-Square test respectively.

In table 1 we present the results of pixel-based comparison to the ground truth images. Larger values of PCC, $Jaccard$ coefficient and $Dice$ coefficient indicate greater similarity to the GT images. From the comparison of the measurments we conclude that for this GT dataset, the method proposed in this paper performs better compared to the method of detector parameter selection proposed in [6].

Table 1. Results of pixel-based evaluation. Larger values indicate better performance.

GT evaluation results				
		Our method	PS: ROC analysis	PS: Chi Square test
Image 1	PCC	0.520055	0.477554	0.484051
	Jaccard	0.111810	0.033120	0.045144
	Dice	0.201133	0.064117	0.086389
Image 2	PCC	0.509625	0,496870	0,497209
	Jaccard	0.065781	0,041458	0,042076
	Dice	0,123443	0,079608	0,080754
Image 3	PCC	0,528503	0,518710	0,520773
	Jaccard	0,127268	0,108964	0,112783
	Dice	0,225799	0,196515	0,202704
Image 4	PCC	0,533181	0,511978	0,511269
	Jaccard	0,156842	0,118467	0,117178
	Dice	0,271156	0,211838	0,209775
Image 5	PCC	0,520935	0,504178	0,510735
	Jaccard	0,092413	0,059962	0,072394
	Dice	0,169191	0,113140	0,135014
Image 6	PCC	0,523620	0,511709	0,515407
	Jaccard	0,120254	0,098250	0,105069
	Dice	0,214691	0,178922	0,190159

References

1. J. Canny: A computational approach to edge detection, IEEE Transactions on pattern analysis and machine intelligence 8 (6) (1986) 679–698.
2. Lily Rui Liang, Carl G. Looney: Competitive fuzzy edge detection. Applied Soft Computing 3 (2003) 123-137
3. D. Marr, E. Hildreth: Theory of edge detection, Proc. Roy. Soc. London B-207 (1980) 187–217.
4. T. Kohonen, Self-Organizing Maps, 2nd edition, Springer, Berlin, 1997.
5. P.J. Toivanen, J. Ansamaki, J.P.S. Parkkinen, J. Mielikainen: Edge detection in multispectral images using the self-organizing map. Pattern Recognition Letters 24 (2003) 2987-2994
6. Yitzhak Yitzhaky, Eli Peli: A Method for Objective Edge Detection Evaluation and Detector Parameter Selection. IEEE Transactions on pattern analysis and machine intelligence 25 (8) (2003) 1027–1033
7. Kevin Bowyerm,Christine Kranenburg : Edge Detector Evaluation Using Empirical ROC Curves. Computer Vision and Image Understanding 84(2001)77-103
8. Todd Law, Hidenori Itoh, Hirohisa Seki: Image Filtering, Edge Detection and Edge Tracing Using Fuzzy Reasoning. IEEE Transactions on pattern analysis and machine intelligence 18 (5) (1996) 481–491
9. William K. Pratt: Digital Image Processing, Third Edition, John Wiley & Sons, Inc. (2001)
10. Armando J. Pinho: Modeling Non-Linear Edge Detectors Using Artificial Neural Networks. Proc. of the 15th Annual Int. Conf. of the IEEE Eng. in Medicine and Biology Soc.,San Diego, CA, U.S.A. October 1993, pp 306-307.
11. S. Weller: Artificial Neural Net Learns the Sobel Operators (and More), Applications of Artificial Neural Networks II , SPIE Proceedings Vol SPIE-1469 pp 69–76, Aug 1991.
12. J.C. Bezdek and D. Kerr: Training Edge Detecting Neural networks with Model-Based Examples, Proc 3rd International Confererence on Fuzzy Systems, FUZZ-IEEE'94, Orlando, Florida, USA. pp 894–901, June 26 - 29, 1994.

An Innovative Algorithm for Solving Jigsaw Puzzles Using Geometrical and Color Features

M. Makridis, N. Papamarkos[1], and C. Chamzas

[1] Image Processing and Multimedia Laboratory,
Department of Electrical & Computer Engineering,
Democritus University of Thrace,
67100 Xanthi, Greece
papamark@ee.duth.gr

Abstract. The proposed technique deals with jigsaw puzzles and takes advantage of both geometrical and color features. It is considered that an image is being divided into pieces. The shape of these pieces is not predefined, yet the background's color is. The whole method concerns a recurrent algorithm, which initially, finds the most important corner points around the contour of a piece, afterwards performs color segmentation with a Kohonen's SOFM based technique and finally uses a comparing routine. This routine is based on the corner points found before. It compares a set of angles, the color of the image around the region of the corner points, the color of the contour and finally compares sequences of points by calculating the Euclidean distance of luminance between them. At a final stage the method decides which pieces match. If the result is not satisfying, the algorithm is being repeated with new adaptive modified parameter values as far as the corner points and the color segmentation is concerned.

1 Introduction

The aim of this paper is to provide an automatic method for jigsaw puzzle solving. Automatic solution of jigsaw puzzles by shape alone goes back to 1967 [1]. Since then numerous papers have been written, yet few take advantage of color information. The majority of the proposed techniques works on curve matching. Some of them [11] divide the contour of each piece into partial curves through breakpoint. 2-D boundary curves are represented by shape feature strings which are obtained by a polygonal approximation. The matching stage finds the longest common sub-string and is solved by geometric hashing. In this paper we introduce a few new ideas about how color information and shape matching can go along in solving jigsaw puzzles.

There are many reasons for someone to work on this subject. Related problems include reconstructing archeological artifacts [2]-[6] and or even fitting a protein with known amino acid sequence to a 3D electron density map [7]. However, what is of most interest is that of simulating the human brain. It is very difficult to create an algorithm as effective as human apprehension yet it is very challenging.

In the proposed method, jigsaw puzzle solving algorithm is divided into three main stages. The inputs of the system are images that contain the pieces of the puzzle

M. Lazo and A. Sanfeliu (Eds.): CIARP 2005, LNCS 3773, pp. 966 – 976, 2005.

over a background color. In the first stage some basic features that can contribute to the final decision, whether two pieces are similar or not, are being extracted. We use an algorithm for detection of high curvature points, named 'IPAN' [12]. This algorithm finds the most significant points along the contour of an image and calculates the angle with a certain way, which is described below. This is the first feature and the most powerful in our method. The other one has to do with color segmentation. Color segmentation is being accomplished by a Kohonen's SOFM (Self Organized Feature Map) based technique proposed by Papamarkos et al. [8]-[10]. In the second phase we examine all the pieces in pairs. For every pair we examine all its corner points and we decide if two points, one for every piece, are similar according to the color of the neighborhood of each point, the angle and the similarity of their neighborhood's points. The algorithm ends if two pairs of corner points are found. Finally if no matching pairs are found the first two phases are being repeated with properly modified parameters, until all pieces are matched or a maximum number of recursions is reached. This technique has been implemented in Delphi 7 and handles with 24-bit depth color images.

2 Description of the Method

The purpose of the proposed technique is to solve the puzzle problem by combining color and geometrical information. Specifically, the technique takes in a number of color pieces (around 10-15) as inputs to reconstruct the original image. There are two principal assumptions. Firstly we define the color of the background (e.g. white), so we are able to distinguish the background from the foreground and the size of the images should be big enough so as IPAN algorithm can find at least 10 to 15 corner points. While we know the color of the background we can achieve binarization and extract the contour of our pieces. Furthermore, none of the pieces should fit wholly inside the contour of another, because the proposed technique handles only with the external contour of its piece. This means that every piece is concerned as a solid object.

The entire method consists of the following five main stages:

- Corner Detection
- Color Segmentation
- Comparing Routine
- Iteration of all stages above if it is needed
- Matching Routine

2.1 Background and Foreground

In order to extract the contour boundary of an image, which is necessary for corner detection, we should first convert our image in a binary one. Since we know the color of the background we can easily perform binarization. Yet, what happens if some pixels of the foreground have the same value of luminance? These pixels could contain useful color information for our algorithm. Having in mind this case we created a function that detects these pixels and works as follows: i.e. we consider background as white. We put the value 0 to all pixels that have not value 255. Then we find the contour be separating black and white pixels. Afterwards we read each row of the image from left to right and after 2 pixels of contour are found, we set the following query: If the second pixel has on the left a 'black' pixel, then set all pixels between them black (foreground), else we consider these pixels as two peaks of the contour and leave them unattached.

2.1.1 Corner Detection (Corner Matching)

At this stage, every piece is being approximated with a polygon. The algorithm, which is used, is called IPAN. It is a two-pass algorithm which defines a corner in a simple and intuitively appealing way, as a location where a triangle of specified size and angle can be inscribed in curve. A curve is represented by a sequence of points p_i in the image plane. The ordered points are densely sampled along the curve and no regular spacing between them is assumed. A chain-coded curve can also be handled if converted to a sequence of grid points. The second pass is a post-processing procedure so as to remove superfluous candidates.

First Pass: In each curve point p the detector tries to inscribe in the curve a variable triangle (p^-, p, p^+) that satisfies the set of following rules:

- $d_{\min}^2 \le \left| p - p^+ \right|^2 \le d_{\max}^2$
- $d_{\min}^2 \le \left| p - p^- \right|^2 \le d_{\max}^2$ (1)
- $\alpha \le \alpha_{\max}$

where $| p - p^+ | = | a |$ is the distance between p and p^+, $| p - p^- | = | b |$ the distance between p and p^-, and $\alpha \in (-\pi, \pi)$ the angle of the triangle. The latter is computed as:

$$\alpha = ar\cos\left(\frac{a^2 + b^2 + c^2}{2ab}\right) \tag{2}$$

Variations of the triangle that satisfy the conditions are called admissible. Search for the admissible variations starts from p outwards and stops if any of the conditions (1) is violated. Among the admissible variations, the least opening angle $\alpha(p)$ is selected.

Second Pass: A corner detector can respond to the same corner in a few consecutive points. Similarly to edge detection, a post-processing step is needed to select the strongest response by discarding superfluous points. A candidate point p is discarded if it has a sharper neighbor p_v: $a(p) > a(p_v)$. A candidate point is a valid neighbor of p if $\left| p - p_v \right|^2 \le d_{\max}^2$

Parameters: $d_{\min}, d_{\max}$ and $\alpha_{\max}$ are the parameters of the algorithm and they are very important for the final stage, which will be discussed below.

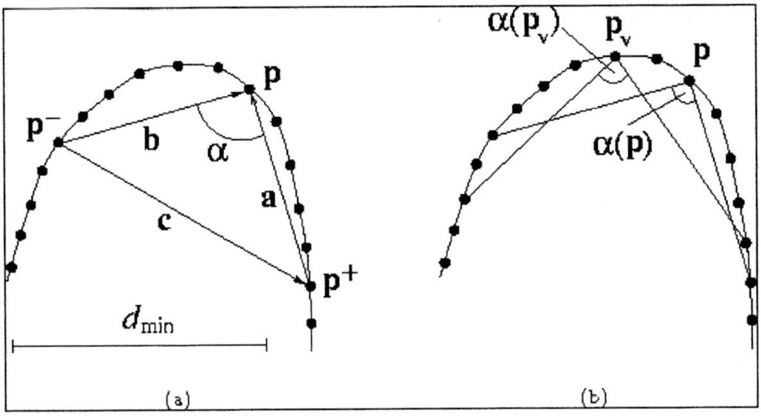

Fig. 1. Detecting High Curvature Points. (a) Determining if p is a candidate point. (b) Testing p in terms of his neighbors.

The parameters of the algorithm contribute to the flexibility of the algorithm by giving us each time a different number of corner points according to their value. Moreover, the angle of every candidate point p is being calculated toward its neighborhood's points and therefore, IPAN is rotationally and scale invariant. Finally, we compute the metacenter of each corner point's inscribed triangle. If metacenter is pixel of background, then the angle is concave, otherwise it is convex. The results of this method are shown in figure 2.

2.1.2 Color Segmentation (Color Similarity)

In the second stage of the technique, a Kohonen's SOFM based color reduction method proposed by Papamarkos et al. [8]-[10] is applied. The metric that uses Kohonen SOFM is the Euclidian color distance. It calculates, therefore, the distance for R, B and G layers of every pixel in order to conclude in which class is this pixel nearer. In order better results to be achieved the number of classes is not constant. It varies between 10 and 30 so as our technique to be effective but not time consuming. Pieces with many similarities, in terms of color information, cannot be distinguished, unless a large number of classes is used. On the other hand, it would be time consuming to apply 30 classes to well distinguished pieces, when the same result can be achieved with only 10.

A problem that we have to deal with here is that only pixels of each piece should be processed and not those of the background. So, we separate the background from the foreground. Samples for the algorithm are taken through each piece, in order to perform unified classes for all the pieces. Although the original color segmentation technique would consider a constant number of randomly taken samples, this would be a drawback for the proposed paper, because each application of the technique would result in different results. Thus, the number of the samples is a percentage of the total number of pixels and moreover we created a function that takes into account specified pixels of every piece, if they contain useful information, which means they are pixels of the foreground. The results are shown in figure 3.

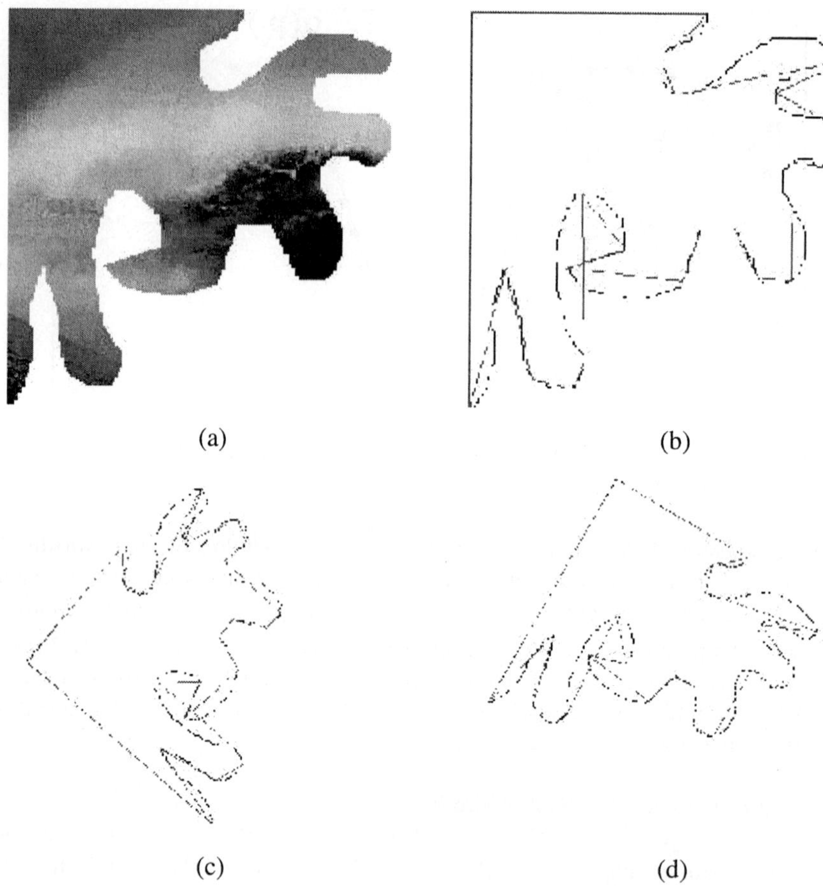

Fig. 2. Polygonal Approximation with a rotationally invariant technique called IPAN. (a) An image piece. (b) Corner points extracted with IPAN. (c) and (d) Ipan extracts certain corner points in the image through its rotation invariance.

2.1.3 Comparing Stage

At this stage we compare couples of pieces and determine whether they are matching or not. From the first stage we concluded to a number of important characteristic points along the contour boundary. We assume that each corner point of the first image corresponds to all corner points of the second. During the comparing stage we discard all corner points that fail to be one with comparing rules. The purpose of this stage is to minimize this number in order to choose 4 points, if it is possible. Having two points from each piece that correspond to precisely two points from the second one, it is easy for us to compute the rotation angle and the shift that is needed for the two pieces to match.

First of all we compare the angle (in degrees) of every point $\alpha(p_{1i})$ of the first image with the angle of every point $\alpha(p_{2i})$ of the second image. If

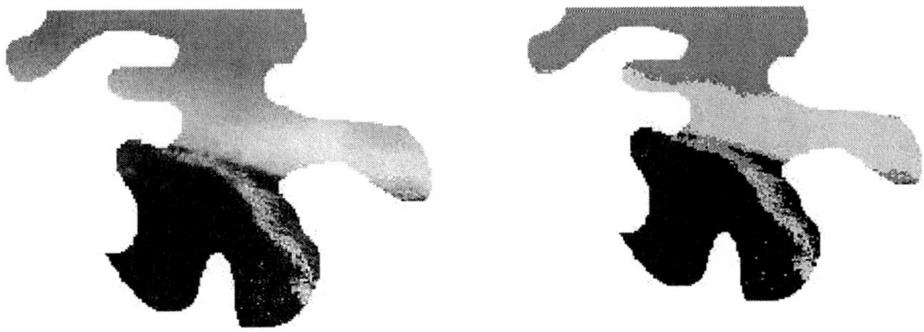

(a) (b)

Fig. 3. Color Segmentation with Kohonen SOFM (a) Original Image (b) Color Segmentation with vector's dimension equals to 3

$|\alpha(p_{1i}) - \alpha(p_{2i})| > 10$, then the corresponding points will be discarded and will not be examined any more.

Then we compare all points left as far as the luminance is concerned. All points with different luminance, after the application of Kohonen's algorithm, will be discarded as well.

The third criterion is a function F that compares the Euclidean distance of luminance between a connected sequence of points from the first image and another from the second one. If $\{c_{1,i-5},...,c_{1,i-1}, p_{1,i}, c_{1,i+1},...,c_{1,i+5}\}$ is a sequence around $p_{1,i}$ of the first image and $\{c_{2,j-10},...,c_{2,j-1}, p_{2,j}, c_{2,j+1},...,c_{2,j+10}\}$ another sequence around $p_{2,j}$ of the other image, where c, pixels of the contour. Then:

$$F = \min\left(\frac{(p_{1i} - p_{2j}) + \sum_{l=-5}^{5} c_{1,i+l} - c_{2,j+l+k}}{11}\right) \quad for\ k = -5,...,5 \tag{3}$$

After finding F, every point $p_{1,i}$ corresponds to 3 at most points $p_{2,j}$, those that minimize function F. All the other points are being discarded.

Furthermore we compare $(p_{1,i-1}, p_{1,i}, p_{1,i+1})$ with $(p_{2,j-1}, p_{2,j}, p_{2,j+1})$ as far as their angles ($|\alpha(p_{1,i}) - \alpha(p_{2,j})| < 10$) and the values of luminance is concerned.

At this point, we introduce two sets of points from both images, each one having five elements as shown in figure 4. Every point p_i of the first set corresponds to another point p_j of the second set. To minimize the chances for a mismatch we test them once more geometrically. As it is shown in figure 4, we compare angle a1 with a2 and part d1 with d3 as well as d2 with d4. All the possible combinations of angles for 5 points are 12. If 10 out of 12 are very similar we conclude that piece *I* and piece *J* match, and the algorithm ends. Otherwise we continue with all the possible combinations of 5-point sequences and in case we run out of combinations we go forward to the next and final stage.

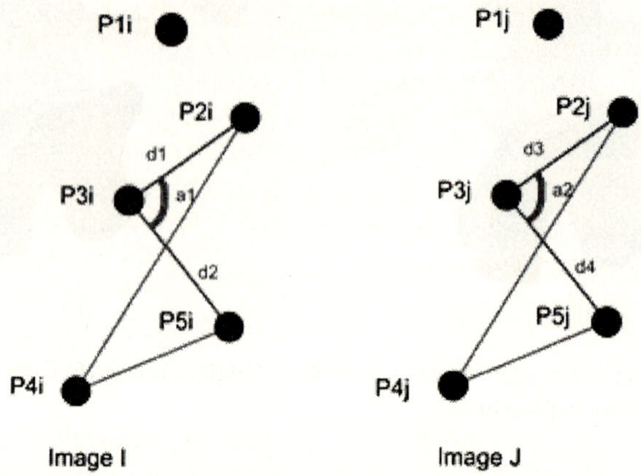

Fig. 4. Comparison of two 5-point sets with each other

2.1.4 Recursion Stage

At this stage what is of most importance are the parameters of stages 1 and 2. If we decrease d_{min} , d_{max} and α_{max} , IPAN algorithm takes out a large number of corner points and our algorithm falls short of speed, yet it can cope with low-analysis images where the search for important corner points should be meticulous in order to be effective. On the other hand, if we increase the values of the parameters we decrease the number of corner points and the algorithm is solving very fast puzzles with high-analysis images. So, the initial values of the parameters are high and if none solution has found the whole method is being repeated automatically with lower values after each recursion. The initial set of parameters is d_{min} =10, d_{max} =12 and α_{max} =160. Additionally Kohonen SOFM is very reliable with 30 classes but faster with 10. The initial value for the Kohonen SOFM is 10. When many recursions are needed is sometimes time-consuming but generally the algorithm is very flexible, as it can cope with various different shaped images. The values of the parameters have been chosen by trial and error. Once our goal is achieved, this stage stops.

2.1.5 Matching Routine

Since has been decided which images are matching together, what is left to do, is to merge the images and show up the results. The rotation and shift phase for all images is being done in terms of one image, which is called reference image. Firstly, if two images fit at points $p_{1,1}$ *and* $p_{1,2}$ and $p_{2,1}$ *and* $p_{2,2}$ respectively, shift and rotation angle are being calculated from the following equations:

$$\begin{aligned} &Shift: && CoordinateX: X_{Shift} = X_{p1,1} - X_{p2,1} \\ & && CoordinateY: Y_{Shift} = Y_{p1,1} - Y_{p2,1} \\ &Rotation: && R_{angle} = \arctan\left(\frac{Y_{p1,1} - Y_{p1,2}}{X_{p1,1} - X_{p1,2}}\right) - \arctan\left(\frac{Y_{p2,1} - Y_{p2,2}}{X_{p2,1} - X_{p2,2}}\right) \end{aligned} \tag{4}$$

However, it is possible that some images don't have common points with the reference image. That is why we created a routine that relates all the images together. So, if for example image 2 fits with the reference image since it has been rotated by angle 'a1' around center point 'c1' and it has been shifted for 'd1' pixels and image 3 fits with the image 2 since it has been rotated by angle 'a2' around center point 'c2' and it has been shifted for 'd2' pixels, we consider that image 3 should be rotated by 'a1' around 'c1' plus 'a2' around 'c2' and it should be shifted by 'd1+d2' so as to fit with the reference image. The whole procedure is being repeated for each image, until all images have been related with the reference one.

3 Experimental Results

The proposed technique for solving jigsaw puzzles, has been implemented in Delphi 7 and tested many images, after they have been cut from 3 to 10 pieces each. The success rate for those images with pieces that were not rotated reaches 90% and 80% for the others. Figure 6 shows the pieces of figure 5(g) image before the application of the technique.

(a)

(b)

(c)

(d)

(e)

(f)

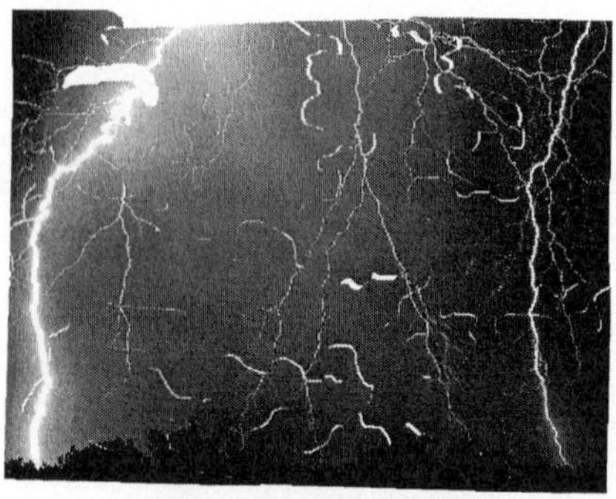

(g)

(h)

(i)

(j)

Fig. 5. Some experimental results. (a) Image reconstruction out of 6 pieces. (b) Image reconstruction out of 8 pieces (c) Image reconstruction out of 6 pieces. (d) Image reconstruction out of 5 pieces (e) Image reconstruction out of 5 pieces. (f) Image reconstruction out of 7 pieces (g) Image reconstruction out of 15 pieces. (h) Image reconstruction out of 9 pieces (i) Image reconstruction out of 8 pieces. (j) Image reconstruction out of 7 pieces.

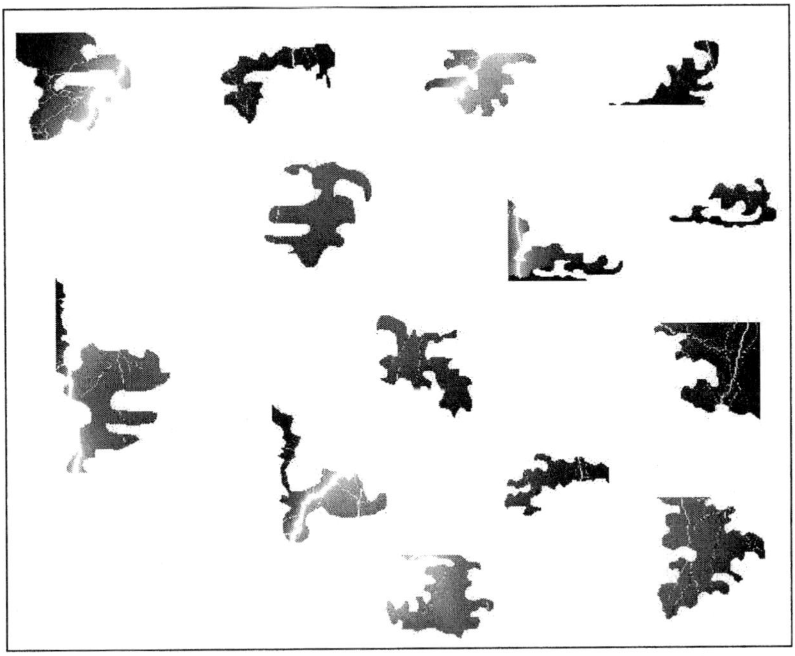

Fig. 6. The pieces of example g in figure 5 before the application of the algorithm

References

[1] H. Freeman and L. Gardner. Apictorial jigsaw puzzles: The computer solution of a problem in pattern recognition. IEEE Trans. on Electronic Computers 13 (1964) 118–127.

[2] W. Kong and B.B. Kimia. On solving 2D and 3D puzzles using curve matching. Proc. IEEE Computer Vision and Pattern Recognition, 2001.

[3] H. C. da Gama Leitao and J. Stolfi. Automatic reassembly of irregular fragments. Tech. Report IC-98-06, Univ. of Campinas, 1998.

[4] H. C. da Gama Leitao and J. Stolfi. Information Contents of Fracture Lines. Tech. Report IC-99-24, Univ. of Campinas, 1999.

[5] K. Leutwyle. Solving a digital jigsaw puzzle. http://www.sciam.com/explorations/2001/062501fresco/

[6] M. Levoy. The digital Forma Urbis Romae project. http://www.graphics.stanford.edu/projects/forma-urbis/

[7] C. Wang. Determining the Molecular Conformation from Distance or Density Data. PhD thesis, Department of Electrical Engineering and Computer Science, MIT, 2000.

[8] N. Papamarkos, A. Atsalakis and C. Strouthopoulos, "Adaptive Color Reduction", *IEEE Trans. on Systems, Man, and Cybernetics-Part B*, Vol. 32, No. 1, pp. 44-56, Feb. 2002.

[9] N. Papamarkos, "Color reduction using local features and a SOFM neural network", *Int. Journal of Imaging Systems and Technology*, Vol. 10, No 5, pp. 404-409, 1999.

[10] A. Atsalakis, N. Papamarkos , N. Kroupis , D. Soudris and A. Thanailakis, "A Color Quantization Technique Based On Image Decomposition and Its Hardware Implementation", IEE Proceedings Vision, Image and Signal Processing, Vol. 151, Issue 6, pp. 511-524, 2004.

[11] H. Wolfson. On curve matching. PAMI, 12:483–489, 1990.
[12] D. Chetverikov and Zs. Szabo. A Simple and E_cient Algorithm for Detection of High Curvature Points in Planar Curves. In M. Vincze, editor, Robust Vision for Industrial Applications 1999, volume 128 of Schriftenreihe der Osterreihicshen Computer Gesellschaft, pages 175,184, Steyr, Austria, 1999. Osterreihicshe Computer Gesellschaft.

Image Dominant Colors Estimation and Color Reduction Via a New Self-growing and Self-organized Neural Gas*

A. Atsalakis, N. Papamarkos[1], and I. Andreadis

[1] Image Processing and Multimedia Laboratory,
Department of Electrical & Computer Engineering,
Democritus University of Thrace,
67100 Xanthi, Greece
papamark@ee.duth.gr

Abstract. A new method for the reduction of the number of colors in a digital image is proposed. The new method is based on the development of a new neural network classifier that combines the advantages of the Growing Neural Gas (GNG) and the Kohonen Self-Organized Feature Map (SOFM) neural networks. We call the new neural network: Self-Growing and Self-Organized Neural Gas (SGONG). Its main advantage is that it defines the number of the created neurons and their topology in an automatic way. Besides, a new method is proposed for the Estimation of the Most Important of already created Classes (EMIC). The combination of SGONG and EMIC in color images results in retaining the isolated and significant colors with the minimum number of color classes. The above techniques are able to be fed by both color and spatial features. For this reason a similarity function is used for vector comparison. To speed up the entire algorithm and to reduce memory requirements, a fractal scanning sub-sampling technique is used. The method is applicable to any type of color images and it can accommodate any type of color space.

1 Introduction

The reduction of the number of colors in digital images is an active research area. True type color images consist of more than 16 million of different colors. The image color reduction is an important task for presentation, transmission, segmentation and compression of color images. The proposed method can be considered as a Color Quantization (CQ) technique. The goal of the CQ techniques is to reduce the number of colors in an image in a way that minimizes the perceived difference between the original and the quantized image. Several techniques have been proposed for CQ which can be classified in the following three major categories. Firstly, there is a class of techniques that are based on splitting algorithms. According to those approaches, the color space is divided into disjointed regions by consecutive splitting up the color space. The methods of median-cut [1] and variance-based algorithm [2] belong to this category. The method of Octree [3] is based on splitting the color space to smaller

* This work is supported by the project PYTHAGORAS 1249-6.

M. Lazo and A. Sanfeliu (Eds.): CIARP 2005, LNCS 3773, pp. 977 – 988, 2005.

cubes. An optimized splitting technique is proposed by Wu [4] who utilizes the principal component analysis to split optimally the original color space. The second major class of CQ techniques is based on cluster analysis. Techniques in this category attempt to find the optimal palette by using vector classifiers. In this category belong methods like ACR [5], FOSART [6], Fuzzy ART [7] and FCM [8]. As it is noticed by Buhmann et al. [9], one of the basic disadvantages of the most classic CQ approaches is the fact that they neglect spatial, i.e. contextual, information. In order to overcome this disadvantage, the color reduction problem must be considered as a clustering problem with the input vectors describing not only the color information but also extra spatial features derived from the neighboring area of each pixel [10-11]. Artificial neural networks are very efficient approaches to create powerful vector classifiers and to solve clustering problems. A well-known unsupervised neural network classifier is the Kohonen SOFM [12]. This network consists of two separate layers of fully connected neurons, i.e. the input and the output layer. Although, the Kohonen SOFM performs topology preserving mapping, there is a major drawback: the dimensions of the input space and the output lattice of neurons are not always identical and, consequently, the structure of the input data is not always preserved in the output layer.

Several implementations of the Kohonen SOFM have been proposed for color reduction. Dekker [13] proposes a color reduction technique which is based on a Kohonen SOFM classifier. According to this approach, equal sized classes are produced. Papamarkos and Atsalakis propose a new technique according to which a Kohonen SOFM neural network is fed not only with the image gray-scale values but also with local spatial features extracted from the neighboring of the sampling pixels [10-11]. An extension to the methods mentioned above, is the Adaptive Color Reduction (ACR) technique [5]. This technique, by applying a tree-driven splitting and merging strategy, decomposes the initial image into a number of color planes. A two-stage color segmentation methodology based on a Kohonen SOFM network is also proposed by Huang et al. [14]. Ashikur et al. [15] propose a CQ technique by combining the SOFM with a supervised counter propagation network. With the exception of the ACR algorithm, all the techniques mentioned above have the same drawback: the final number of colors should be predefined.

The proposed color reduction technique uses a new Self-Growing and Self-Organized Neural Gas (SGONG) network. We develop this neural classifier in order to combine the growing mechanism of the GNG algorithm [16] and the learning scheme of the Kohonen SOFM. Specifically, the learning rate and the influence of neighboring neurons are monotonically decreased with the time. Furthermore, at the end of each epoch, three criteria are applied that improve the mechanism of growing and the convergence efficiency of the network. These criteria define when a neuron must be removed or added to the output lattice. The proposed neural network is faster than the Kohonen SOFM. In contrast with the GNG classifier, a local counter is defined for each neuron that influences the learning rate of this neuron and the strength of its connections with the neighboring neurons. In addition, these local counters are also used to specify the convergence of the proposed neural network. The main advantage of the SGONG classifier is its ability to influence the final number of neurons by using three suitable criteria. Thus, in the color reduction problem, the proper number of the image's dominant colors can be adaptively determined.

An extension to any vector quantization technique is proposed for Estimation of the Most Important of already created Classes (EMIC). In order to function the EMIC technique, a predefined number of classes and a set of vectors representative of data space is required. The proposed technique is based on Comparative Hebbian Rule CHR [17] and no heuristic parameters are adjusted in order to be applied.

Concluding, in this paper

- A new self-growing and self-organized neural network is introduced. This SGONG neural network has the following characteristics:
  - faster than the Kohonen SOFM,
  - the dimensions of the input space and the output lattice of neurons are always identical. Thus, the structure of neurons in the output layer approaches the structure of the input data,
  - criteria are used to ensure fast converge of the neural network, detection is of isolated classes and automatically estimation the number of neurons in the output layer.
- The EMIC method is proposed for choosing efficiently very few numbers of classes in automatic way.
- Even though the quantized image is described with few colors, isolated and small color classes can be detected combining the SGONG and EMIC methods
- Except for color components, the above methods can also be fed by additional local spatial features.
- The color reduction results obtained are better than previous reported techniques.

The proposed color reduction technique was tested by using a variety of images and the results are compared with other similar techniques.

2 Combination of Color and Spatial Features

To simplify our approach, let us consider a digital image of n pixels and the corresponding data set X, consisting of n input vectors (feature vectors) X_k :

$$X_k = [f1_k, f2_k, f3_k, g1_k, g2_k, g3_k, z1_k, z2_k],\ k = 1,...,n \tag{1}$$

where $X_k \in \Re^D$, with D=8 the dimensionality of the input space. Each input vector X_k consists of the pixel's color components $f_k = [f1_k, f2_k, f3_k]$ and additional spatial features $g_k = [g1_k, g2_k, g3_k]$ and $z_k = [z1_k, z2_k]$ extracted from a neighborhood region of this pixel. In color images, using for example the RGB color space, the elements $f1_k$, $f2_k$, $f3_k \in [0,255]$, express the intensity values of red, green and blue color components of the k pixel. Apart from the RGB color space, which is not perceptually uniform, more advantageous and perceptually uniform color spaces like CIE-L*a*b* or CIE-L*u*v*, can be used.

The neighborhood region of each pixel can be defined using a mask of 3×3 or 5×5 dimensions, where the central mask's element expresses the pixel's position.

Depending on the spatial features used, the color of each pixel is associated with the spatial color characteristics of the neighboring pixels. The spatial feature vectors g_k and z_k can be derived from edge extraction, smoothing, noise reduction masks, min and max values, etc. Besides, the coordinates of each pixel can be used as additional features. According to the above analysis, color domain and spatial domain are concatenated in a joint domain of features. The vector X_k combine vectors of different nature and thus their elements take values in different ranges. In order to compare efficiently two different vectors X_k and X_m, $(k,m=1,\ldots n)$ a similarity function $S(X_k,X_m)$ is defined which takes values in range [0,1] [18]. If $S(X_k,X_m)=1$ then the vectors X_k and X_m are considered equal.

$$S(X_k,X_m)=S_f(X_k,X_m)\cdot S_g(X_k,X_m)\cdot S_z(X_k,X_m), \tag{2}$$

$$S_f(X_k,X_m)=e^{-\left\|\frac{f_k-f_m}{h_f}\right\|^2},\quad S_g(X_k,X_m)=e^{-\left\|\frac{g_k-g_m}{h_g}\right\|^2},\quad S_z(X_k,X_m)=e^{-\left\|\frac{z_k-z_m}{h_z}\right\|^2}$$

The parameters h_f, h_g and h_z are normalization factors which are user defined. Usually, these parameters express the scatter of vectors *f, g, z*, respectively.

From equation (2) we have

$$S(X_k,X_m)=e^{-\left(\left\|\frac{f_k-f_m}{h_f}\right\|^2+\left\|\frac{g_k-g_m}{h_g}\right\|^2+\left\|\frac{z_k-z_m}{h_z}\right\|^2\right)}=e^{-\|X'_k-X'_m\|}$$

where $X'_k=\left[\frac{f1_k}{h_f},\frac{f2_k}{h_f},\frac{f3_k}{h_f},\frac{g1_k}{h_g},\frac{g2_k}{h_g},\frac{g3_k}{h_g},\frac{z1_k}{h_z},\frac{z2_k}{h_z}\right]$ the properly normalized vector of X_k.

The proposed technique can be applied to color images without any sub-sampling. However, in the case of large-size images and in order to achieve reduction of the computational time and memory size requirements, it is preferable to have a sub-sampling version of the original image. We choose to use a fractal scanning process, based on the well-known Hilbert's space filling curve [10-11], where scans one area of the image completely before moving to the next. So, the neighborhood relationship between pixels is retained in neighboring samples.

3 The SGONG Neural Network

The proposed SGONG network consists of two separated layers of fully connected neurons, the input layer and the output mapping layer. In contrast with the Kohonen SOFM, the space of the mapping layer has always the same dimensionality with the input space, and also, the created neurons take their position in order the structure of neurons to approximate the structure of the input training vectors. In other words, the topology of the created neurons always approximates the topology of the training vectors. All vectors of the training data set X' are circularly used for the training of the SGONG network. In contrast with the GNG network, where a new neuron is always inserted at the end of each epoch, in the proposed algorithm three new criteria are applied that control the growing of the output lattice of neurons. In summary, we introduce the following three criteria:

- remove the inactive neurons,
- add new neurons,
- and finally, remove the non important neurons.

In accordance with the Kohonen SOFM, the proposed neural network uses the same equations for the adaptation of neuron's position and utilizes a cooling scheme for the learning rates used for weights readjustments. In contrast with the GNG classifier, in the proposed technique, the learning rates are locally defined in such a way that the adaptation ability of each neuron to each training vector is proportionally decreased with the number of vectors classified in the corresponding class. This removes the problem of increased neuron's plasticity or the danger of convergence in local minima, when the constant learning rates are not well adjusted. The proposed strategy makes the convergence faster, compared with the GNG classifier, as the weights of all neurons are stabilized and the network is forced to converge, when a predefined number of vectors have been classified to each neuron.

The adjacency relations between neurons are described by lateral connections between them. The Competitive Hebbian Rule (CHR) [12] is used to dynamically create or remove the lateral connections during the training procedure. This approach improves the data clustering capabilities of the SGONG network, in comparison with the Kohonen SOFM, where the lateral connections are fixed and predefined. Taking into account that the new neurons are inserted in order to support these with the highest error, and that the neuron's lateral connections perfectly describe the topology of the input vectors, we conclude that in contrast with Kohonen SOFM the proposed technique, during the training procedure, always gives a good description of the data structure. In addition, as the new neurons are inserted near these with the maximum accumulated error at the end of a single epoch, the proposed technique is robust to noisy data. The length of each epoch determines the robustness to noisy data. On the other hand, the convergence is not based on optimizing any model of the process or its data, as the proposed neural network shares almost the same weight-update scheme with the Kohonen SOFM neural network.

3.1 The Training Steps of the SGONG Network

The training procedure for the SGONG neural classifier starts by considering first two output neurons ($c = 2$). The local counters N_i, $i = 1,2$ of created neurons are set to zero. The initial positions of the created output neurons, that is, the initial values for the weight vectors W_i, $i = 1,2$ are initialized by randomly selecting two different vectors from the input space. All the vectors of the training data set X' are circularly used for the training of the SGONG network.

The training steps of the SGONG are as follows:

Step 1. At the beginning of each epoch the accumulated errors $AE_i^{(1)}$, $AE_i^{(2)}$, $\forall i \in [1,c]$ are set to zero. The variable $AE_i^{(1)}$ expresses, at the end of each epoch, the quantity of the total quantization error that corresponds to $Neuron_i$, while the variable $AE_i^{(2)}$, represents the increment of the total quantization error that we would have if the $Neuron_i$ was removed.

Step 2. For a given input vector X_k, the first and the second winner neurons $Neuron_{w1}$, $Neuron_{w2}$ are obtained:

$$\text{for } Neuron_{w1}: \; S(X_k, W_{w1}) \geq S(X_k, W_i) \;\; \forall i \in [1,c] \quad (3) \tag{3}$$

$$\text{for } Neuron_{w2}: \; S(X_k, W_{w2}) \geq S(X_k, W_i), \;\; \forall i \in [1,c] \text{ and } i \neq w1 \tag{4}$$

Step 3. The local variables $AE_{w1}^{(1)}$ and $AE_{w1}^{(2)}$ change their values according to the relations:

$$AE_{w1}^{(1)} = AE_{w1}^{(1)} + \left\| X'_k - W'_{w1} \right\| \tag{5}$$

$$AE_{w1}^{(2)} = AE_{w1}^{(2)} + \left\| X'_k - W'_{w2} \right\| \tag{6}$$

$$N_{w1} = N_{w1} + 1 \tag{7}$$

Step 4. If $N_{w1} \leq N_{idle}$ then the local learning rates $\varepsilon 1_{w1}$ and $\varepsilon 2_{w1}$ change their values according to equations (8), (9) and (10). Otherwise, the local learning rates have the constant values $\varepsilon 1_{w1} = \varepsilon 1_{\min}$ and $\varepsilon 2_{w1} = 0$.

$$\varepsilon 2_{w1} = \varepsilon 1_{w1} / r_{w1} \tag{8}$$

$$\varepsilon 1_{w1} = \varepsilon 1_{\max} + \varepsilon 1_{\min} - \varepsilon 1_{\min} \cdot \left(\frac{\varepsilon 1_{\max}}{\varepsilon 1_{\min}} \right)^{\frac{N_{w1}}{N_{idle}}} \tag{9}$$

$$r_{w1} = r_{\max} + 1 - r_{\max} \cdot \left(\frac{1}{r_{\max}} \right)^{\frac{N_{w1}}{N_{idle}}} \tag{10}$$

The learning rate $\varepsilon 1_i$ is applied to the weights of $Neuron_i$ if this is the winner neuron ($w1 = i$), while $\varepsilon 2_i$ is applied to the weights of $Neuron_i$ if this belongs to the neighborhood domain of the winner neuron ($i \in nei(w1)$). The learning rate $\varepsilon 2_i$ is used in order to have soft competitive effects between the output neurons. That is, for each output neuron, it is necessary that the influence from its neighboring neurons to be gradually reduced from a maximum to a minimum value. The values of the learning rates $\varepsilon 1_i$ and $\varepsilon 2_i$ are not constant but they are reduced according to the local counter N_i. Doing this, the potential ability of moving of neuron i toward an input vector (plasticity) is reduced with time. Both learning rates change their values from maximum to minimum in a period, which is defined by the N_{idle} parameter. The variable r_{wi} initially takes its minimum value $r_{\min} = 1$ and in a period, defined by the N_{idle} parameter, reaches its maximum value r_{max} .

Step 5. In accordance with the Kohonen SOFM, the weight vector of the winner neuron $Neuron_{w1}$ and the weight vectors of its neighboring neurons $Neuron_m$, $m \in nei(w1)$, are adapted according to the following relations:

$$W'_{w1} = W'_{w1} + \varepsilon 1_{w1} \cdot (X'_k - W'_{w1}) \tag{11}$$

$$W'_m = W'_m + \varepsilon 2_m \cdot (X'_k - W'_m), \ \forall m \in nei(w1) \tag{12}$$

Step 6. With regard to generation of lateral connections, SGONG employs the following strategy. The CHR is applied in order to create or remove connections between neurons. As soon as the neurons $Neuron_{w1}$ and $Neuron_{w2}$ are detected, the connection between them is created or is refreshed. That is

$$s_{w1,w2} = 0 \tag{13}$$

With the purpose of removing of superfluous lateral connections, the age of all connections emanating from $Neuron_{w1}$, except the connection with $Neuron_{w2}$, is increased by one:

$$s_{w1,m} = s_{w1,m} + 1, \ \forall m \in nei(w1), \text{ with } m \neq w2 \tag{14}$$

Step 7. At the end of each epoch it is examined if all neurons are in *idle state*, or equivalently, if all the local counters N_i , $\forall i \in [1,c]$ are greater than the predefined value N_{idle} and the neurons are considered well trained. In this case, the training procedure stops, and the convergence of SGONG network is assumed. The number of input vectors needed for a neuron to reach the "*idle state*" influences the convergence speed of the proposed technique. If the training procedure continues, the lateral connections between neurons with age greater than the maximum value α are removed. Due to dynamic generation or removal of lateral connections, the neighborhood domain of each neuron changes with time in order to include neurons that are topologically adjacent.

Step 8. At the end of each epoch, three criteria that modify the number of the output neurons c and make the proposed neural network to become self-growing are applied. These criteria are applied in the following order:

- A class (neuron) is removed if for a predefined consecutive number of epochs, none of training samples have classified in this class.
- A new class (neuron) is added near the class with the maximum contribution in total quantization error (with the maximum $AE^{(1)}$), if the average distance of its vectors from neighboring classes is greater than a predefined value. This value is expressed as a percentage (t_1) of the average distance between all classes.

- The class (neuron) with the minimum average distance of its vectors from neighboring classes is removed if this quantity is less than a predefined value. This value is expressed as a percentage (t_2) of the average distance between all classes.

In order to make faster the network convergence it can be defied not to apply the above criteria when the total number of epochs is above a predefined value. This has as a result the rapid passing of all neurons to the "*idle state*" and therefore the finalizing of the training procedure. After the training procedure the de-normalized vectors W_i, $i = 1,2,\ldots c$ expresses the centers of final classes.

4 On the Estimation of Most Important Classes

As it is already mentioned, the EMIC technique requires only a predefined number of classes and a set of vectors representative of data space. It considers the position of given classes in feature space and the number of vectors classified to each class in order to choose automatically the most important classes. Initially the Comparative Hebbian Rule CHR [17] is applied extracting the lateral connections between classes. Then, we consider in the middle of each lateral connection a new class and we apply again the CHR in order to update the lateral connections between all classes. A kind of histogram is defined counting the population of vectors in connected nodes – classes. The EMIC can be considered as finding the peaks in created histogram. A class is denoted as a peak if its height, i.e. the number of classified vectors, is greater of the height of neighboring classes. .

The Image in Fig. 1 is described in RGB color space and only for presentation reasons the color vectors are projected onto the plane defined by the first and the second Principal Component of all color vectors, Fig 1(b). Doing this, each color is represented by a two-dimensional vector. In Fig. 1(c) the main concentrations of 2D-vectors are described by white color. The SGONG classifier with proper settings converges to 16 classes whose centers and their neighboring relations are depicted on Fig. 1(d) with red circles and lines, respectively. We consider in the middle of each connection a new class and we continue the training procedure of SGONG, for only one epoch, considering that all classes are in idle state. This is happening in order to find again the new lateral connections using the CHR procedure that coexists in SGONG. A class is denoted as a peak if the number of vectors which have been classified to it is greater from the number of vectors classified to neighboring classes. As depicted in Fig. 1(e) 13 peaks have estimated which corresponds to the most important classes.

5 Experiments

The proposed method and the CQ methods that are based on the Kohonen SOFM, GNG, and FCM classifiers were implemented in software, called "ImageQuant", and can be downloaded and tested from the site http://ipml.ee.duth.gr/~papamark/ . In this, paper, due to the space limitation, we give only the following two experiments. Both experiments demonstrate the ability of the proposed SGONG neural classifier and the

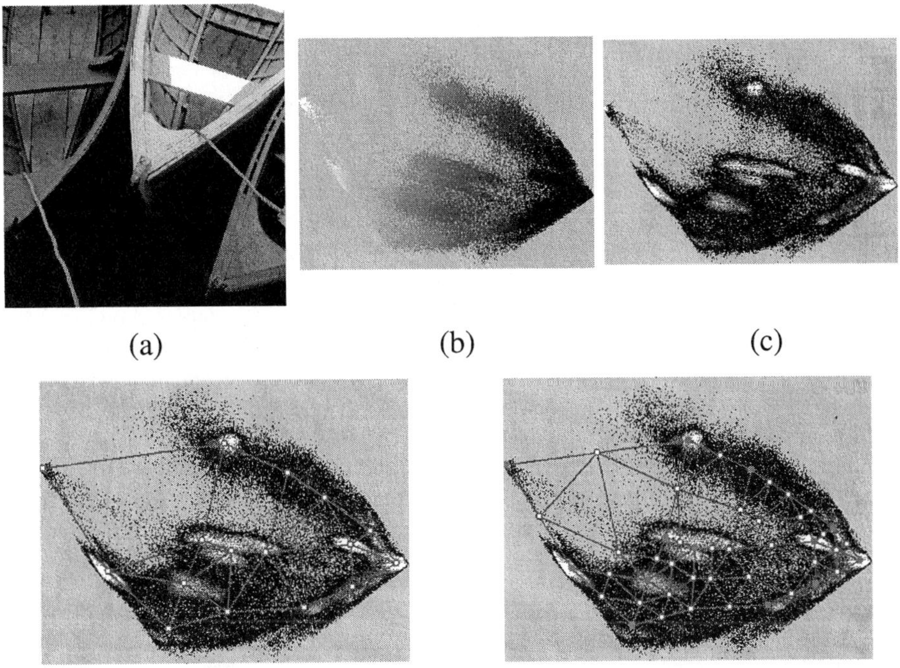

(a) (b) (c)

(d) (e)

Fig. 1. Estimation of dominant colors

EMIC technique to define, in an adaptive way, the number of final classes, i.e. the number of final colors, according to the structure of the input data.

Experiment 1

In the first experiment the original image of Fig. 1 has 113081 unique colors. The proposed SGONG neural classifier converges to 16 unique colors applying the following main settings:

- The maximum number of output neurons is adjusted to 45,
- A new class (neuron) is added near this one with the maximum contribution in quantization error, if the average distance of its vectors from neighboring classes is greater than 30% of the average distance between all classes ($t_1 = 0.3$).
- The class (neuron) with the minimum average distance of its vectors from neighboring classes is removed if this quantity is less than 20% of average distance between all classes ($t_2 = 0.2$).
- The initial values for $\varepsilon 1_{max}$, $\varepsilon 1_{min}$, r_{max} are set to 0.2, 0.0005 and 400 respectively.
- The original image is sub-sampled taking samples from the peaks of Hilbert's fractal. The size of fractal is adjusted to take almost 3000 samples.

– A neuron is getting to “idle state” if 9000 vectors have classified to it ($N_{idle} = 9000$).

The number of most important classes obtained applying the EMIC technique. As depicted on Fig. 1(e) only 13 classes have estimated.

Experiment 2

In the second experiment the test image of Fig 2 has 33806 unique colors. In order to automatically find the number of the image dominant colors, the SGONG classifier uses the same settings as in Experiment 1. The resultant image is depicted on Fig 2 (b) and has only nine colors. The colors can be more reduced by applying the EMIC technique. Doing this, an image of only seven colors is constructed, which depicted on Fig 2(c). Furthermore, for comparison reasons, the CQ techniques based on Kohonen SOFM, the GNG, and the Fuzzy C-Means are applied. In order to have comparative results, the above techniques use exactly the same samples in the same order. Other applied techniques are the Color Quantization method of Dekker [13], and finally, the method of Wu [4]. In all above cases the RGB color model was used.

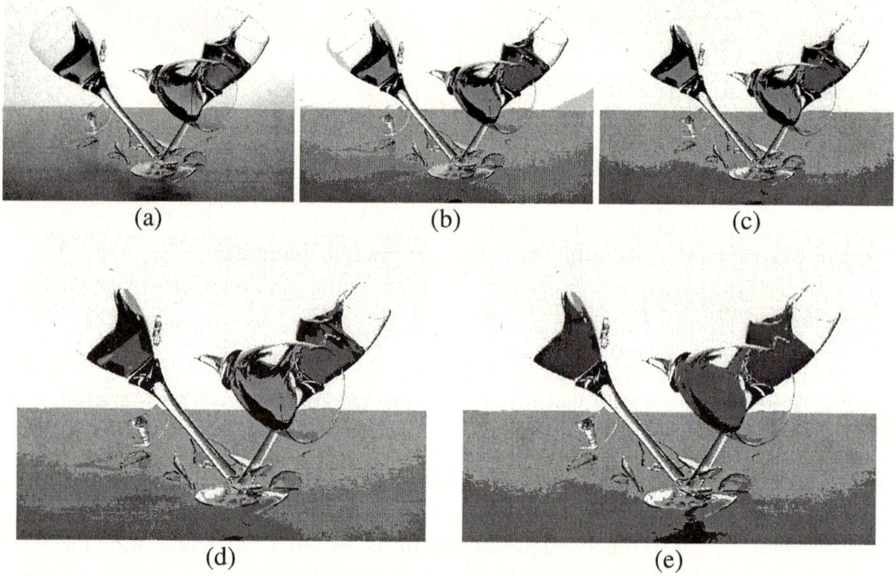

Fig. 2. (a) Initial image of 33806 unique colors. (b) Color quantization using the SGONG technique, the number of classes has automatically estimated to nine with appropriate settings. (c) The EMIC method is applied resulting in an image of only 7 classes. (d) Color quantization using the SGONG technique, the number of classes are predetermined and equal to 7, the criteria that influence the growing of the output lattice of neurons are neglected. (e) The same settings with Fig (d) except of using with R,G,B color components the additional features “a” and “b” of L*a*b* color space.

Table 1. Comparative results

	SGONG & Estimation Fig.2(c)	SGONG Fig.2(d)	FCM	GNG	Dekker	Wu
MSE	694,28	719,38	1107,11	821,39	1972,72	1049,32
ADC	42,51	44,29	52,52	46,6	77,21	54,21
SNR	51,23	50,87	46,56	49,54	40,78	47,1
PSNR	56,38	56,03	51,72	54,7	45,94	52,25

6 Conclusions

This paper proposes a new CQ technique which is based on a new neural network classifier (SGONG). The SGONG network classifier is suitable for CQ applications. Each pixel is considered as a multidimensional vector which contains the color components and additional spatial characteristics derived from the neighborhood domain of each pixel. An efficient way to combine color and feature vectors is used. The main advantage of the SGONG network is that it controls the number of created neurons and their topology in an automatic way. . The convergence speed of SGONG classifier is comparable to the convergence speed of the GNG classifier, while the stability of SGONG classifier is comparable to the stability of Kohonen SOFM classifier. The number of resultant classes can efficiently be reduced more, applying the EMIC technique. The combination the SGONG and EMIC techniques in colored images enable the efficient description of images with very few numbers of colors. In order to speed up the entire algorithm, a fractal sub-sampling procedure based on the Hilbert's space filling curve is applied to initial image, taking samples only from the fractal peaks and their neighboring pixels. The proposed CQ technique has been extensively tested and compared to other similar techniques.

References

[1] Heckbert, P. (1982). Color image quantization for frame buffer display. *Computer & Graphics*, 16:297-307.

[2] Wan, S.J., Prusinkiewicz, P. and Wong, S.K.M. (1990). Variance based color image quantization for frame buffer display. *Color Research and Application*, 15: 52-58.

[3] Ashdown, I. (1994). *Octree CQ, from the book: Radiosity-A Programmer's Perspective*, Wiley, New York.

[4] Wu, X. (1992). CQ by dynamic programming and principal analysis. *ACM Transactions on Graphics*, 11:384–372.

[5] Papamarkos, N., Atsalakis, A. and Strouthopoulos, C. (2002). Adaptive Color Reduction. *IEEE Trans. On Systems, Man, and Cybernetics, Part B*, 32:44-56.

[6] Baraldi, A. and Blonda, P. (1999). A Survey of Fuzzy Clustering Algorithms for Pattern Recognition—Part I&II., *IEEE Trans. On Systems, Man, and Cyb., Part B*, 29:778-801.

[7] Carpenter, G., Grossberg, S. and Rosen, D.B. (1991). Fuzzy ART: Fast stable learning and categorization of analog patterns by an adaptive resonance system. Neural Networks, 4:759-771.

[8] Bezdek, J.C. (1981). *Pattern recognition with fuzzy objective function algorithms*. Plenum Press, New York.

[9] Buhmann, J.M., Fellner, D.W., Held, M., Kettere, J. and Puzicha, J. (1998). Dithered CQ. *Proceedings of the EUROGR.'98*, Lisboa, Computer Graphics Forum 17(3): 219-231.

[10] Papamarkos, N. and Atsalakis, A. (2000). Gray-level reduction using local spatial features. *Computer Vision and Image Understanding*, 78:336-350.

[11] Papamarkos, N. (1999). Color reduction using local features and a SOFM neural network. *Int. Journal of Imaging Systems and Technology*, 10:404-409.

[12] Kohonen, T. (1990). The self-organizing map. *Proceedings of IEEE*, 78: 1464-1480.

[13] Dekker, A.H. (1994). Kohonen neural networks for optimal CQ. *Computation in Neural Systems,* 5:351-367.

[14] Huang, H.Y., Chen, Y.S. and Hsu, W.H. (2002). Color image segmentation using a self-organized map algorithm. *Journal of Electronic Imaging*, 11:136-148.

[15] Rahman, A. and Rahman, C.M. (2003). A new approach for compressing color images using neural network. *Processing of CIMCA*, pp. 12-14, Vienna, Austria.

[16] Fritzke, B. (1995). A growing neural gas network learns topologies. *in Advances in Neural Information Processing Systems*. 7, Tesauro, G., Touretzky, D.S. and Leen, T.K., Eds. Cambridge, MA: MIT Press, pp. 625-632.

[17] T. M. Martinetz and K. J. Schulten, "Topology representing networks," Neural Networks, vol. 7, no. 3, pp. 507-522, 1994.

[18] D. Comaniciu and P. Meer, "Mean Shift: A robust approach toward feature space analysis", IEEE Transactions on Pattern Analysis and Machine Intelligence, vol. 24, no. 5, 2002.

Oversegmentation Reduction Via Multiresolution Image Representation

Maria Frucci, Giuliana Ramella, and Gabriella Sanniti di Baja

Institute of Cybernetics "E.Caianiello", CNR, Pozzuoli (Naples), Italy
{m.frucci, g.ramella, g.sannitidibaja}@cib.na.cnr.it

Abstract. We introduce a method to reduce oversegmentation in watershed partitioned images, that is based on the use of a multiresolution representation of the input image. The underlying idea is that the most significant components perceived in the highest resolution image will remain identifiable also at lower resolution. Thus, starting from the image at the highest resolution, we first obtain a multiresolution representation by building a resolution pyramid. Then, we identify the seeds for watershed segmentation on the lower resolution pyramid levels and suitably use them to identify the significant seeds in the highest resolution image. This is finally partitioned by watershed segmentation, providing a satisfactory result. Since different lower resolution levels can be used to identify the seeds, we obtain alternative segmentations of the highest resolution image, so that the user can select the preferred level of detail.

1 Introduction

Any image analysis task requires a segmentation step to distinguish the significant components of the image, i.e., the foreground, from the background.

A frequently adopted segmentation technique is based on the watershed transformation, [1,2]. Basically, watershed transformation originates a partition of a gray-level image into regions characterized by a common property, such as an almost homogeneous gray-level distribution. The partition regions are then assigned to either the foreground or the background, by taking into account the properties expected to characterize the two sets. If the user perceives as more significant the regions with locally higher (lower) intensity, hence the regions locally lighter (darker), the assignment criterion could be based on the maximal difference in gray-level among adjacent partition regions. This problem is still partially open, especially because its solution is strongly conditioned by the quality of the image partition.

Unfortunately, watershed segmentation is generally affected by excessive fragmentation into regions. This, besides requiring a suitable complex process to reduce the number of seeds from which the partition originates, may bias the successive assignment of the partition regions to the foreground and the background. We think that an effective way to reduce the number of seeds can be found by resorting to multiresolution representation. If a gray-level image is observed at different resolutions, only the most significant regions will be perceived at all resolutions, even if in a more coarse way at lower resolution. Regions that, at the highest resolution image, can be interpreted as noise or constitute fine details are generally not preserved when resolution

M. Lazo and A. Sanfeliu (Eds.): CIARP 2005, LNCS 3773, pp. 989–996, 2005.

decreases. Thus, if the seeds for watershed segmentation of the highest resolution image are identified in a lower resolution level, the resulting partition is expected to be characterized by a reduced number of regions, corresponding to the most significant image parts. In this communication, we face this problem.

Starting from a gray-level image, we create a multiresolution representation by building a resolution pyramid. To this purpose, we modify the algorithm illustrated in [3,4]. Here, we use a different 3×3 mask of weights to compute the gray-level of (parent) pixels at lower resolution, in order to obtain more faithful representations of the original input at all resolutions. Then, we identify the seeds for watershed segmentation at one of the lower resolution levels. These seeds are suitably projected onto the highest resolution level of the pyramid and are used to select among the seeds originally detected at that resolution, only those corresponding to the most significant regions. All other seeds originally found in the highest resolution image undergo a suitable removal process, aimed at merging the corresponding partition regions. The watershed segmentation of the highest resolution image is finally accomplished, by using only the seeds that survived the removal process. Different segmentations are suggested for the same image, depending on the pyramid level used to identify the seeds to be projected and, hence, on the desired detail of information to be preserved.

The paper is organized as follows. In Section 2, we briefly discuss the method to build the resolution pyramid. In Section 3, we illustrate the process that, starting from the seeds identified at a selected lower resolution level, allows us to identify among all seeds at the highest resolution, only those regarded as the most significant. In Section 4, we show the results of the watershed segmentation of the highest resolution image by using seeds computed at lower resolution levels. We also show the results obtained after we apply to the partitioned image a method to distinguish the foreground from the background. Finally, in Section 5 we give some concluding remarks.

2 The Resolution Pyramid

We consider images where the locally darker regions (i.e., those whose associated gray-level is locally lower) constitute the foreground. In our images, gray-levels are in the range [0, 255]. Let G_1 be a $2^n \times 2^n$ gray-level image. If the input image has a different number of rows/columns, a suitable number of rows/columns is added to build G_1. Pixels in the added rows/columns are assigned the maximum gray-level present in the original image, i.e., are seen as certainly belonging to the background. Through this paper, G_1 is interpreted as a 3D landscape, where for every pixel in position (x,y), its gray-level plays the role of the z-coordinate in the landscape. This interpretation is helpful to describe our process in a simple and intuitive way.

A multiresolution image representation is of interest in many contests, since it provides from coarse to fine representations of an input image, always preserving the most relevant features. In this framework, resolution pyramids are among the most common representation systems [5]. We here modify the discrete method [3,4] to build a resolution pyramid. In [3,4], we focused both on shift invariance and topology preservation. Here, we are still interested in shift invariance and aim at a more faithful computation of gray-levels for the parent pixels.

Pyramid construction is based on a recursive subdivision into quadrants of G_1. At each recursion step, resolution decreases by four and, in principle, the process terminates when the image including one single pixel is built. Actually, we do not compute resolution levels including less than 32×32 pixels, as they would give too coarse representations of G_1. For the running example shown in this paper, the base of the pyramid, level 1, is the image G_1 at full resolution (128×128), the next level of the pyramid, level 2, represents the image at a uniformly lower resolution (64×64), and the apex of the pyramid is the 32×32 image, which constitutes level 3. We use a decimation process involving the use of a partition grid. When the grid is placed onto the current resolution image, G_k, the image is divided into blocks of 2×2 children pixels, which correspond to parent pixels at the immediately lower resolution level G_{k+1}. Practically, we inspect in forward raster fashion only pixels belonging to even rows and columns of G_k, meaning that we use the bottom right child pixel in a block to find the coordinates of the parent pixel in G_{k+1}. Let us indicate with (i,j) the pixel in position (i,j). For each inspected pixel (i,j) of G_k, the parent pixel in G_{k+1} will be (i/2,j/2).

4	6	4
6	9	6
4	6	4

Fig. 1. The multiplicative mask of weights used to build the pyramid

To compute the gray-level of the parent pixel (i/2,j/2) in G_{k+1}, we average the gray-levels of (i,j) and of its eight neighbors in G_k. Since, the partition grid could be shifted on G_k and, hence, any pixel in the 3×3 window centered on (i,j) could be the bottom right pixel of the block, we introduce a multiplicative mask of weights to evaluate the contribution given by the nine pixels in the 3×3 window centered on (i,j).

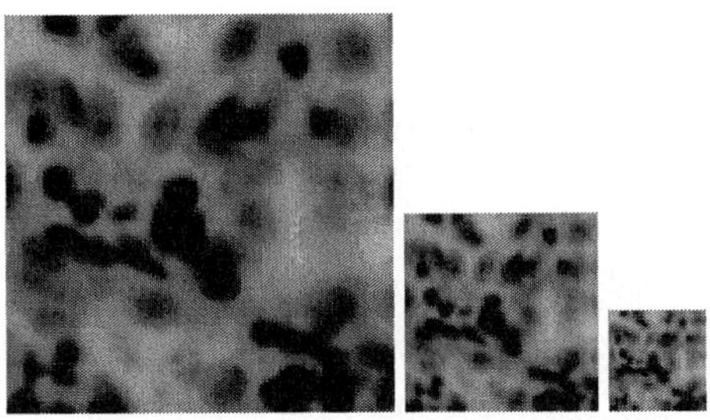

Fig. 2. The three levels of the pyramid computed for a 128×128 input image

In this way, the gray-level of (i/2,j/2) will be computed almost independently of the position of the partition grid. To this aim, we consider the nine 3×3 windows centered on (i,j) and on each of its eight neighbors. Pixel (i,j) is included in all nine windows, its horizontal/vertical neighbors are included in six windows and diagonal neighbors in four windows. The number of windows including a pixel constitutes the corresponding weight for the multiplicative mask. See Fig. 1. It can be noted that the weights in our mask are practically midway between the Gaussian and the uniform weights.

The gray-levels computed by using the mask are then normalized to assume values in the range [0, 255]. Once the computation of G_{k+1} is done, the successive lower resolution level is built by the same procedure. The pyramid built for the running example is shown in Fig. 2.

3 Selection of the Significant Seeds

At each level k, the gradient image ∇_k corresponding to G_k is interpreted as a 3D landscape. This interpretation is useful to illustrate in a simple manner the paradigm on which watershed segmentation is founded. High gray-levels correspond in the landscape to mountains, while low gray-levels correspond to valleys. If the bottom of each valley is pierced and the landscape is immersed in water, then valleys are filled in by water. Filling starts from the deepest valleys and then continues through less and less deep valleys. These begin to be filled as soon as the water level reaches their bottom. A dam (watershed) is built wherever water could spread from a basin into the close ones. When the whole landscape has been covered by water, the basins are interpreted as the parts into which the landscape is partitioned.

The regional minima found in ∇_k are generally used as the seeds starting from which watershed transformation generates a partition of ∇_k (and, hence, of G_k) into regions characterized by some gray-level homogeneity. See Fig. 3, where the watershed lines found by using the regional minima in the three gradient images at the three pyramid levels are shown in white. There are respectively 709, 280, and 116 seeds (and, hence, basins), for pyramid levels 1, 2 and 3. We note that the image at level 1 is affected by excessive fragmentation, caused by the very large number of regional minima. Some (heavy) process is generally accomplished to select among the seeds found in ∇_1 only those that are significant to correctly partition G_1. See, e.g., [6].

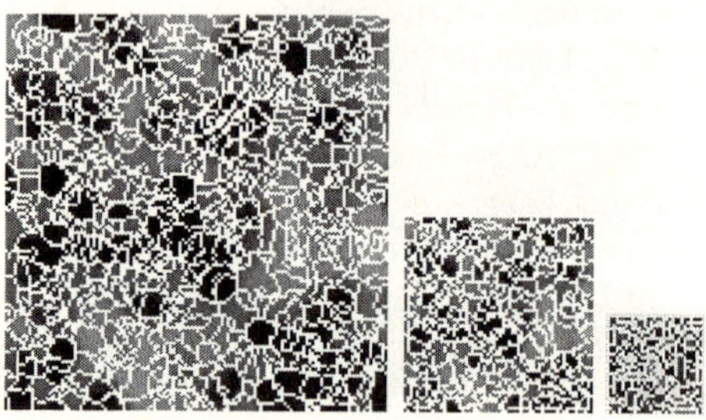

Fig. 3. The watershed lines (white) found at the three pyramid levels starting from the relative regional minima, superimposed on the three gray-level images. The found basins are 709, at level 1, 280, at level 2, and 116, at level 3.

Since G_1 is well represented even at the lowest resolution level of the pyramid (see Fig. 2) and, in turn, the seeds found in ∇_3 are considerably less than those found in ∇_1, we will use the seeds found in ∇_3 to select among the seeds detected in ∇_1 the most significant ones and obtain, in this way, a less fragmented partition of G_1. To this aim, we project the seeds from level 3 to level 1. This is possible due to the fact that our pyramid construction method preserves the links parent-children. Thus, for each pixel at level 3 we can easily identify its descendants at level 1. Obviously, since any parent pixel at level 3 has four children at level 2 and each of these children has in turn four children at level 1, for each seed pixel found in ∇_3 we identify a 6×6 block of descendants in ∇_1. See Fig. 4 middle.

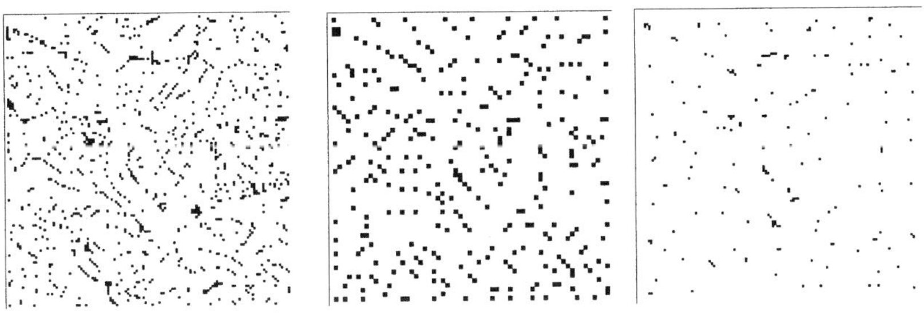

Fig. 4. Seeds found at level 1, left; descendants at level 1 of the seeds found at level 3, middle; descendants remaining after reduction (see text), right

Our idea is to regard as significant a seed originally detected in ∇_1(Fig. 4 left), only provided that its associated partition region (Fig. 3, level 1) includes at least one descendant of the seeds found at level 3 (Fig. 4 middle). All other seeds detected in ∇_1 are regarded as non significant and, by means of a *flooding* process, the corresponding partition regions are merged.

Due to the large size of the sets of descendants originated from the seeds found at level 3, still too many seeds would be preserved at level 1. To reduce their number, we do the following process. Let M be the number of connected components of descendants, CCD_i, found at level 1. In the gradient image ∇_1, we inspect the M sets C_i of pixels with homologous positions with respect to the pixels of the sets CCD_i. In each set C_i, we identify and preserve as seeds only the pixels, whose gray-level is minimal with respect to the gray-levels of the other pixels of C_i. All other descendants are removed (Fig. 4 right). Flooding is then applied at level 1 to merge all partition regions that do not include at least one descendant that survived the removal process.

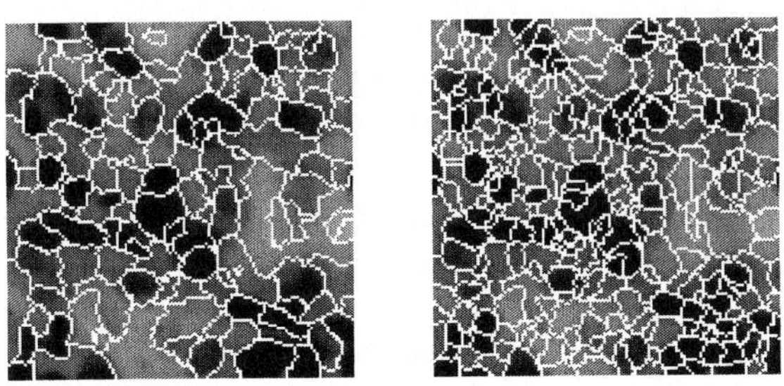

Fig. 5. Partition of G_1 at level 1 into 133 basins, by using the seeds found at level 3, left, and partition of G_1 at level 1 into 284 basins, by using the seeds found at level 2, right

The watershed lines of the partition of G_1, obtained by using the seeds found at level 3 to identify the significant seeds at level 1, are superimposed in white on G_1 in Fig. 5 left. By selecting a different lower resolution level, we can use the seeds found there to identify the significant seeds among those detected at level 1. For example, by sing the seeds found at level 2 and by applying the same process described above, the watershed partition of G_1 shown in Fig. 5 right is obtained.

By comparing the results shown in Figs. 5 and 3, we see that a considerable reduction of the fragmentation is obtained, as expected. To show that the obtained partitions are significant, we briefly illustrate in the following Section a process that allows us to assign to either the background or the foreground the partition regions.

4 Region Assignment to Foreground and Background

The model that we follow to assign the watershed partition regions to either the background or the foreground is inspired by visual perception. In our gray-level images, the foreground is perceived as characterized by locally lower intensity. We assume that the border separating the foreground from the background is placed wherever strong differences in gray-level occur. Assignment is done by means of a process requiring two steps. A more detailed description of this process can be found in [7].

The first step of the process globally assigns to the foreground and to the background the regions characterized by locally minimal and locally maximal average gray-levels (valleys and peaks and in the landscape representation).

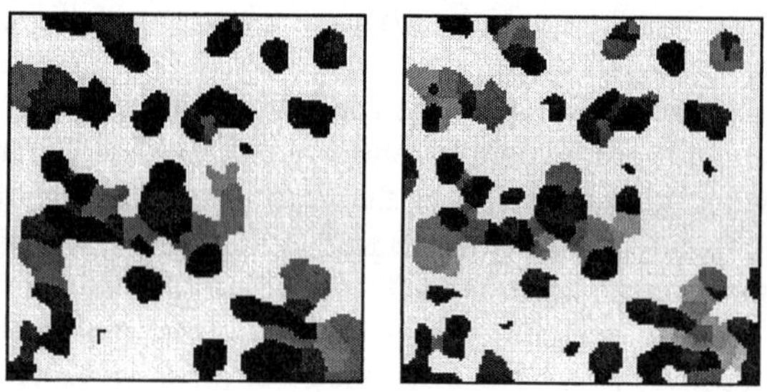

Fig. 6. Foreground components identified in correspondence of the two alternative partitions shown in Fig. 5. Gray-tones are related to the significance of the regions (see text). Darker regions are more significant.

The second step is guided by the maximal gray-level difference Δ between all pairs of adjacent regions. It assigns to the foreground and to the background the partition regions placed along the slopes in the landscape. This step is iterated (with a new Δ computed at each iteration) until all regions are assigned. Two cases are possible depending on the number N of adjacent regions with maximal Δ. If N=1, the darker region in the pair of regions with difference Δ is (locally) assigned to the foreground, while the lighter region is assigned to the background. In fact, in correspondence with these two adjacent regions with difference Δ, we assume that a transition from background to foreground occurs. Based on the same assumption, we (globally) assign to the foreground (background) also all the regions equally dark or darker (equally light or lighter) than the region, in the pair of adjacent regions with difference Δ, assigned to the foreground (background). If N>1, a conflictual assignment is possible if, for any of the pairs characterized by the maximal Δ, say the i-th pair, the darker region, say DR_i, happens to be lighter of the lighter region, say LR_j, in another pair of regions characterized by the maximal Δ, say the j-th pair. In fact, DR_i should be assigned to the foreground, by taking into account the average gray-levels in the i-th pair, but it should be assigned to the background, by taking into account the relation between the average gray-levels of LR_i and DR_j. If this is the case, a local process, still based on the maximal Δ, is accomplished to assign the regions along the slope including DR_i. Once the conflictual cases have been treated and all the pairs with the maximal Δ have been locally assigned, the same global process done for N=1 is safely applied.

A relevance parameter, taking into account the perceptual significance, is also set for the regions assigned to the foreground, which allows us to rank foreground components. The relevance parameter for regions detected during the first step assumes value 1 if the region (i.e., a valley in the landscape representation) has an average gray-level smaller than that characterizing all peaks in the landscape (i.e., all regions assigned to the background). It assumes value 2 otherwise, meaning that such a valley, though assigned to the foreground, has a perceptual significance smaller than that pertaining the other valleys. During the second step, the relevance parameter of a region assigned to the foreground is set to the number of foreground regions in the shortest path, linking that region to the most relevant part in the same foreground component. The result of this process applied to the watershed partitions shown in Fig. 5 is shown in Fig.6, where darker gray-tones correspond to more significant regions.

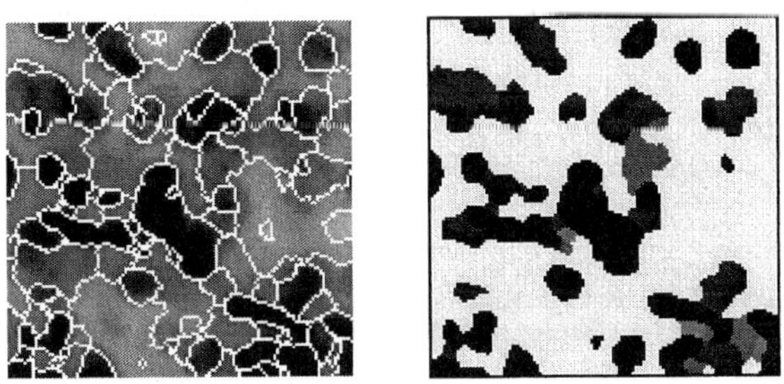

Fig. 7. Result of the segmentation process [6] applied to G_1. The final segmentation into 119 basins, left, and the result of the assignment process to identify the foreground, right.

If we apply to G_1 the high performance, but computationally more expensive, segmentation algorithm [6], we obtain the result shown in Fig. 7. Also in this case, region assignment is done by using the algorithm [7]. We can now compare Figs. 6 and 7, by using Fig. 7 as a reference. We note that even starting from seeds found at low resolution (levels 2 and 3 of the pyramid), the results shown in Fig. 6 are comparable with those in Fig. 7. Obviously, more details are identified if the seeds are taken at level 2, as it is expected because of the higher resolution of level 2 with respect to level 3.

5 Conclusion

We have introduced a method to reduce the excessive fragmentation of gray-level images into regions, when watershed segmentation is used. Our method is based on the use of a multiresolution representation of the input image and on the detection of the most significant seeds for segmenting the highest resolution image, guided by the seeds found at lower resolution. The underlying idea is that the most significant components perceived in the highest resolution image will remain identifiable also at lower resolution. Thus, starting from the highest resolution image, we first build a resolution pyramid. Then, we identify the seeds for watershed segmentation on one of the lower resolution pyramid levels and suitably use them to identify the significant seeds in the highest resolution image. This image is finally partitioned by watershed segmentation, providing a satisfactory result. Since different lower resolution levels can be used to identify the significant seeds at the highest resolution, we obtain alternative segmentations of the highest resolution image, among which the user can select the best suited one for the specific task.

The performance of the method has been shown on a sample image only, but we have tested our procedure on a large set of biological images. The obtained results have been judged as satisfactory by the experts in the field.

References

1. S.Beucher, C.Lantuejoul, "Use of watersheds in contour detection", *Proc. Int. Workshop on Image Processing, Real-Time Edge and Motion Detection/Estimation*, Rennes, France, 1979.
2. S.Beucher, F.Meyer, "The morphological approach of segmentation: the watershed transformation", in *Mathematical Morphology in Image Processing*, E.Dougherty (Ed.) M.Dekker, New York, 433-481, 1993.
3. G.Borgefors, G.Ramella, G.Sanniti di Baja, "Shape and topology preserving multi-valued image pyramids for multi-resolution skeletonization", *Pattern Recognition Letters*, 22, 741-751, 2001.
4. G.Ramella, G.Sanniti di Baja, "Grey level image components for multi-scale representation", in Progress in Pattern Recognition, Image Analysis and Applications, A.Sanfeliu, J.F.Martinez Trinidad, J.A.Carrasco Ochoa (Eds.), LNCS 3287, Springer, Berlin, 574 - 581, 2004.
5. A.Rosenfeld (Ed.), "Multiresolution Image Processing and Analysis", Springer, Berlin; 1984.
6. M.Frucci, "A novel merging method in watershed segmentation", *Proc. 4th Indian Conf. on Computer Vision, Graphics, and Image Processing*, Applied Publishing Private Ltd, Kolkata, India, 532-537, 2004.
7. M.Frucci, C.Arcelli, G.Sanniti di Baja, "Detecting and Ranking Foreground Regions in Gray-Level Images", in "Brain, Vision and Artificial Intelligence", M. De Gregorio, V. Di Maio, M. Frucci, C. Musio (Eds.), LNCS 3704, Springer, Berlin, 2005 (in press).

A Hybrid Approach for Image Retrieval with Ontological Content-Based Indexing

Oleg Starostenko, Alberto Chávez-Aragón, J. Alfredo Sánchez, and Yulia Ostróvskaya

Universidad de las Américas, Puebla,
Computer Science Department, Cholula, Puebla, 72820, Mexico
{oldwall, sp098974, alfredo, yulia}@mail.udlap.mx

Abstract. This paper presents a novel approach for image retrieval from digital collections. Specifically, we describe IRONS (Image Retrieval with Ontological Descriptions of Shapes), a system based on the application of several novel algorithms that combine low-level image analysis techniques with automatic shape extraction and indexing. In order to speed up preprocessing, we have proposed and implemented the convex regions algorithm and discrete curve evolution approach. The image indexing module of IRONS is addressed using two proposed algorithms: the tangent space and the two-segment turning function for shapes representation invariant to rotation and scale. Another goal of the proposed method is the integration of user-oriented descriptions, which leads to more complete retrieval by accelerating the convergence to the expected result. For the definition of image semantics, ontology annotation of sub-regions has been used.

1 Introduction

A typical approach to automatic indexing and classification of images is based on the analysis of low-level image characteristics, such as color, texture or shape [1], [2], but this type of systems does not provide the semantics associated with the content of each image. There are a number of well-known systems for visual information retrieval (VIR). The Query by Image Content system (QBIC) provides retrieval of images, graphics and video data from online collections using image features such as color, texture, and shape for computing the similarity between images [3]. AMORE (Advanced Multimedia Oriented Retrieval Engine) and SQUID systems provide image retrieval from the Web using queries formed by keywords specifying similar images, sketches, and SQL predicates [4]. Whereas the contributions of these systems have been important in the field, they do not provide ways to represent the meaning of objects in the images. In order to overcome this problem, our hypothesis is to apply the machine-understandable semantics for search, access, and retrieval of multimedia information using ontology [5]. The widely used Grubber's definition permits to describe semantics, establishes a common and shared understanding of a domain and facilitates the implementation of user-oriented vocabulary of terms and their relationship with objects in image the [6]. The potential applications of the proposed image retrieval facilities include systems for supporting digital image processing services,

M. Lazo and A. Sanfeliu (Eds.): CIARP 2005, LNCS 3773, pp. 997 – 1004, 2005.

high performance exchange of multimedia data in distributed collaborative and learning environments, digital libraries, etc.

2 Proposed Image Retrieval Method

The proposed method may be described as a combination of specific descriptors based on low-level image preprocessing for extraction of sub-regions (objects) invariant to scale, rotation, and illumination, and the application of ontology concepts for definition of machine-understandable semantics for retrieved images. The main procedures for image preprocessing, indexing, ontological description and retrieval are:

1. In order to divide the image into regions, the SUSAN corner detection method is used by applying the circular mask [7], [8]. The extracted principal corners present the points that define particular positions of objects in the image.

2. The spatial sampling of the original image is provided by computing the average values of color regions via the *I1I2I3* color model, applying slicing *8x8* pixels windows generating the main color descriptor of each region [9].

3. Comparing the proposed method with well-known prototypes, where the description is applied to the whole image, the textual annotations of sub-regions are preferred for the simple definition of their semantic characteristics. Subdivision of image into sub-regions is provided by Convex Regions Preprocessing Algorithm in Images (CORPAI) proposed by the authors [10]. Detected principal corners are used for convex hulls generation providing the vertical slabs algorithm and producing a sorted array that is used to determine the sub-region as a polygon.

4. The frequent problem of shape representation is a great number of necessary vertices for polygon transformation, which may be reduced by the proposed discrete curve evolution process. This technique reduces the set of vertices of a polygon to a subset of vertices containing relevant information about the original outline [10].

5. The next step is indexing of the simplified object (shape, polygon); here two different approaches have been proposed and implemented. One of them is based on an object transform to a tangent space, and the other represents the object as a two-segment turning function.

6. Finally, it is possible to establish the relationship between the object and its formal explicit definition. In such a way, the meaning of an image may be obtained in textual form as a set of annotations for each sub-region related to a particular ontology. The Resource Description Framework (RDF) language to support the ontology management is used in this approach that defines a syntactic convention and a simple data model to implement machine-readable semantics [11]. Using RDF it is possible to describe each web resource with relations to its object-attributes-value based on metadata standard developed by the World Wide Web Consortium [12].

3 Irons Image Retrieval System

The block diagram of the Image Retrieval by Ontological Description of Shapes (IRONS) system implementing the proposed method is shown in Fig. 1. The input for the system may be an image, its shape, or a keyword, which describes the object with a certain degree of similarity. The retrieved images will be the ones with more similarity to the low-level features of the query (if the input is an image or its sub-region) and will have a high degree of matching with the ontology annotations defining the content of the image. Once the user draws a query, the system uses the shape indexing algorithm in order to generate the feature vector for comparison with the other ones in the image database [10]. Then the content-based recognition process is applied to shapes (based on the ontological textual description) in order to find similar ones in the ontology namespace.

The IRONS system consists of four principal modules: query preprocessing, indexing module, feature vector comparison and feedback GUI, and it operates according to the algorithm described in section 2. The query preprocessing module provides the selection of sub-regions containing relevant objects. Once the sub-region is extracted, the object within that sub-region is found by the CORPAI algorithm.

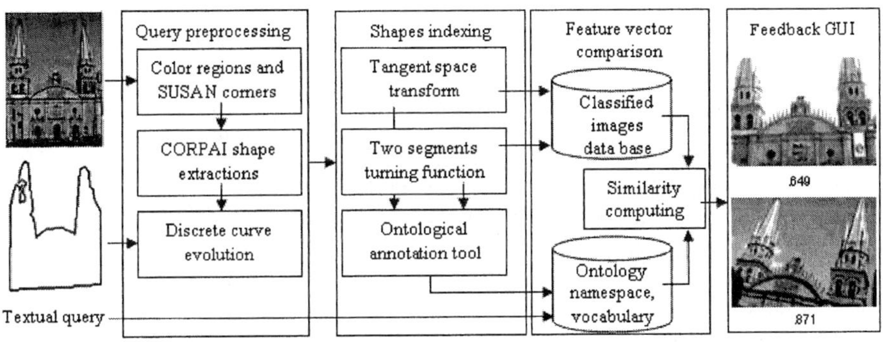

Fig. 1. Block diagram of the proposed IRONS system

The discrete curve evolution process reduces the complexity of the extracted shape. If the query is a keyword, the preprocessing step is not applied. The indexing module generates a feature vector describing low-level image characteristics and content-based annotations. The preprocessed polygon is represented either by tangent space or by two-segment turning function because these techniques are invariant to scaling, rotation, and translation. The ontological annotation tool is used for searching matches in the ontology name space. The images with higher matching are retrieved and visualized on GUI with a certain degree of similarity.

3.1 Query Preprocessing Module

The algorithm for image preprocessing using color and principal corners is described. *Input:* A color image with luminance of pixels *Ic*; *Output:* the region's feature vector

1. *Ig* ⇐ *ComputeLuminance (using Ic)* // it converts color into gray level image
2. *Principal corners* ⇐ *SUSAN operator (Ig)* // detection of object's corners
3. *Scs* ⇐ *SpatialSampling(Ic)* // reduction of image size to an 8x8 pixels window

4. ColorDescriptor ⇐ *ComputeColorDescriptorI1I2I3 (Scs)* // descriptors based on *I1I2I3* color system model
5. FeaturesVector⇐ *ComputeDescriptor (Principal Corners, ColorDescriptor)* // the sub-region descriptor includes a color vector and the principal corner's position.
6. Subregion ⇐ *CORPAI(Ic,Sp)* // applying the CORPAI algorithm over regions *ConvexHulls(points[])* // compute the convex hull
{ if(query_sub-region(image[][])) // apply boundary detection operator to sub-region (operator*(image[][]))}*
7. Ic_{NEW} ⇐ *TransformationFromSubregionToImage (Subregion)* // transformation of the irregular convex sub-region of the original image to a new normalized one
8. FeaturesVector ⇐ *ComputeDescriptor (Principal Corners, ColorDescriptor, ConvexRegions)* // the convex region descriptor is obtained.
9. FeaturesVector ⇐ *DiscreteCurveEvolution (Simplified Polygon)* // removal of the least important polygon vertexes.

Fig. 2. Results of applying the vertical slabs algorithm for extraction of a convex sub-region and the containing object

The last procedure of the preprocessing step is simplification of polygons representing the shape of objects detected by discrete curve evolution. This process removes the least important vertexes of a polygon, computing the relevance measure *K*, where $\beta(s_1,s_2)$ is the turn angle of the common vertex of segments s_1,s_2, and l is the length function normalized with respect to the total length of the polygonal curve *C*.

$$K(s_1, s_2) = \frac{\beta(s_1, s_2) l(s_1) l(s_2)}{l(s_1) + l(s_2)} \qquad (1)$$

The lower value of $K(s_1, s_2)$ corresponds to the least contribution of this curve to a shape. This process of vertexes removal is repeated until we obtain the desired shape simplification using the designed interface presented in Fig. 3.

3.2 Indexing Module

The polygonal representation is not a convenient form for calculating similarity between two shapes, an alternative representation such as the Tangent Space Representation (TSR) is proposed for generation of the feature vector and quantitative comparison of simple shapes. Using TSR, a curve *C* is converted to a step function: the steps on the *x*-axis represent the arc length of each segment in *C*, and the *y*-axis represents the turn angle between two consecutive segments in C. In Fig. 3 indexing module GUI of the TSR is shown where the results of applying the discrete curve evolution and the TSR for selected complexity of the shape are depicted.

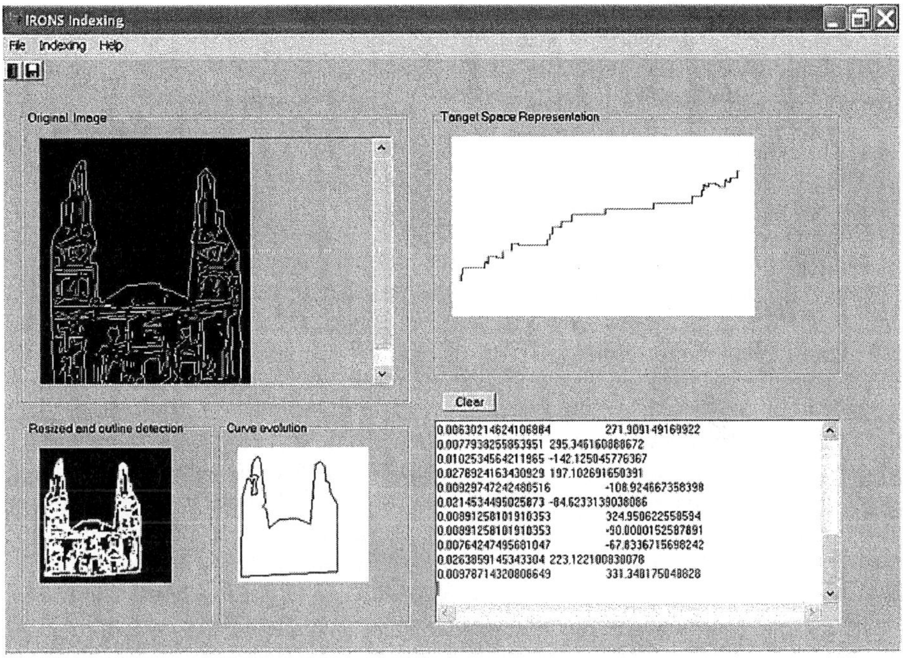

Fig. 3. Tangent space representation of shapes of the IRONS indexing module

Another possible way for shape indexing is to apply the cumulative angle function or turning function, which may speed up the computing the similarity between two shapes. In general, the turning function of a polygon A returns the angle between the counterclockwise tangent and the x-axis as a function of the arc length s $\Theta_A(s)$. This function is invariant to translation and scale of a polygon, but it is not invariant to rotation. If a polygon is rotated by an angle θ, the turning function value changes by the amount of θ. To overcome this problem, we additionally propose an alternative way called two-segment turning function (2STF). With each iteration, the angle between two consecutives edges of a polygon is calculated. As a result, we may analyze the edges with rotation. Now we have the same representation of a shape even though that shape has been rotated. 2STF is calculated by traversing a digital curve in the counterclockwise direction and assigning a certain value of 2STF to each line segment. The x-value (the assigned value) defines the length of the line segment normalized with respect to the length of the complete curve. The y-value is the directional angle of the line segment with respect to its previous segment.

Using the GUI of the IRONS indexing module (Fig. 3), the 2STF may be computed and visualized in the same way as TSR. Once, the efficient way to represent a shape is obtained via TSR or 2STF, the matching strategy to find the degree of similarity between two shapes is applied. Shape representation and matching are considered the most difficult aspects of content-based image retrieval [10]. In this work we use hybrid feature vector which defines such low-level image characteristics as semantic descriptions. This permits to speed up the matching process as well as reduce the number of iterations with non-sensical results. The similarity value between two shapes is based on proposed algorithm:

1. The polygon simplified by curve evolution is transposed into TSR or 2STF.
2. The resulting curves representing the polygon are scaled to the same length.
3. One of the curves is shifted vertically over the second one for a better fit.
4. The area between the two curves is computed.

Now the user may define a threshold value for the computed area as the acceptable degree of similarity between the reference and the analyzed patterns.

3.3 Ontological Annotation Tool

The ontology is described by a directed acyclic graph; each node has a feature vector that represents the concept associated with that node. Concept inclusion is represented by the IS-A inter-relationship. For instance, particular elements of buildings, churches, and so on form specific concepts of shapes defining these buildings, churches, etc. If the query describes an object using this ontology, the system would recover shapes that contain windows, columns, façades, etc. even though, those images have not been labeled as geometric figures for the retrieved object. The feature vectors of each node in the ontology name space consist of keywords linking the previously classified images to the characteristics of the new shape extracted by the TSR or 2STF. The indexing and the ontology annotation processes may be described now as:

1. *FeaturesVector* ⇐ *Shape$_i$(Pentagon, Pi,Ci)* // *Pi* is its TSR or 2STF representation and *Ci* is the compactness of the shape computed as a ratio: square of *RegionBorderLength* and *ShapeArea*.

2. *SaveRelationInOntology(Ic, FeaturesVector of Ic$_{NEW}$, Td)* // update the ontology namespace.

As has been mentioned, two kinds of vector comparison are used: matching the low-level image features and definition of similarity in ontological annotations. The computing of similarity is additionally provided by computing the Euclidean distance d_E to compare feature vectors according to the equation:

$$d_E(\mu,\sigma)=\sqrt{\sum(\mu-\sigma)^2}\,, \tag{2}$$

where μ and σ denote two feature vectors.

The query interface of the IRONS system is shown in Fig. 4 where the images with high degree of matching are shown in downward order. The user may submit a visual example, a sketch, a keyword or a combination of the above.

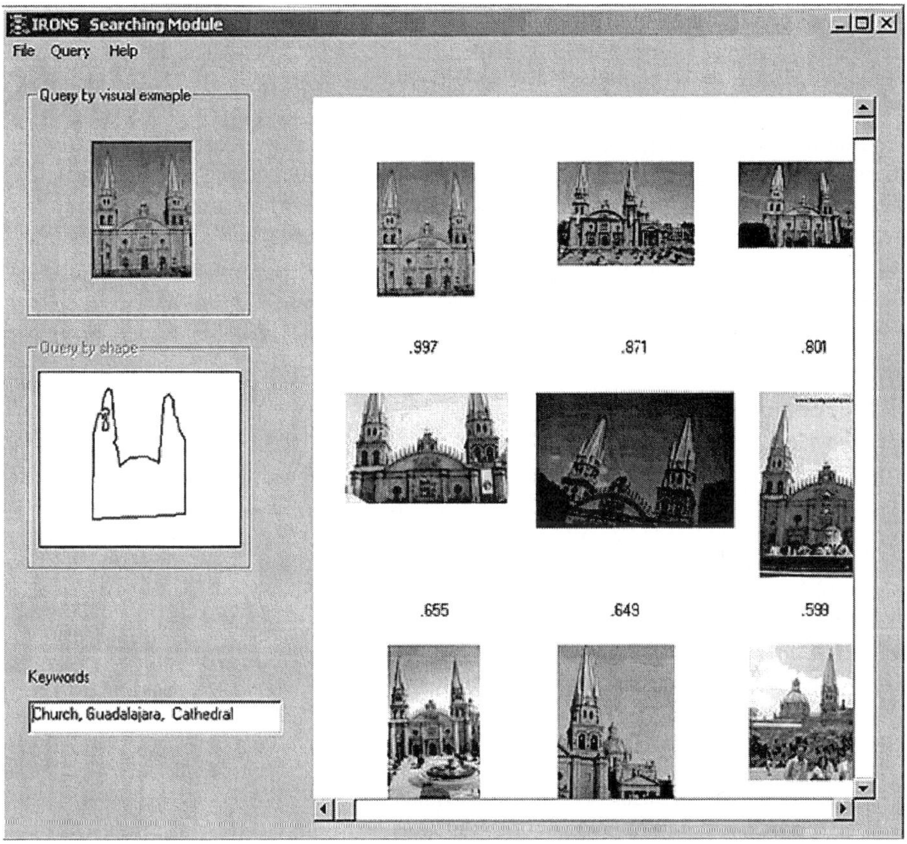

Fig. 4. Image retrieval GUI of the IRONS system

4 Evaluation, Contribution, and Conclusions

Evaluations of the proposed method and testing of the implemented system have been done comparing the results of image retrieval by the IRONS to several well-known systems, particularly, QBIC and AMORE systems. We performed a number of experiments to verify the role of the shape-based and ontology-based indexing in the retrieval process. We test the proposed method using the image collection CE-Shape-1. This database contains approximately 1400 images randomly taken from Internet and divided into 60 different categories with about 20 images per category.

The system performance is better when the image is processed in sub-regions; excessive subdivision does not produce good results. Satisfactory retrieval of expected images is achieved faster through the use of ontological descriptions due to the lower number of iterations in the search process. The analysis of the indexing approaches shows that 2STF is twice as fast as TSR. This occurs because the typical data structures used in indexing tools are hashing tables, which are manipulated with specific keys or signatures representing a shape. The disadvantages of the system are errors in spatial sampling during generation of the image feature vector as well as the required amount of system memory. Factors like tolerance to occlusion and deformation, robustness against noise, and feasibility of indexing are also considered in our approach.

The most important contribution of this research is the proposed hybrid method combining the advantages of low-level image characteristics extraction with textual description of image semantics. The use of ontological annotations allows simple and fast estimation of the meaning of a sub-region and of the whole image. The proposed image retrieval method is robust to partial occlusion and to small changes in the position of the objects. From the obtained experimental results, we can conclude that the method could be considered as an alternative way for the development of visual information retrieval facilities.

References

1. T. Gevers, A.W. Smeulders.: PicToSeek: Combining color and shape invariant features for image retrieval, IEEE Trans. on Image Processing, Vol. 9(1) (2000) 102-119.
2. O. Starostenko, J. Chávez.: Motion estimation algorithms of image processing services for wide community, Proc. of Knowledge/Based Intelligent Information Engineering Systems Conference KES'2001, Japan (2001) 758-763.
3. QBIC (TM). IBM's Query by image content, http://wwwqbic.almaden.ibm.com/.
4. The Amore. Advance multimedia oriented retrieval engine, http://www.ariadne.ac.uk/issue9/web-focus/
5. D. Fensel.: Ontologies: a silver bullet for knowledge management and electronic commerce, USA: Springer (2001).
6. T.R. Gruber, A translation approach to portable ontology specifications, Knowledge Acquisition (1993) 199-220.
7. S.M. Smith, J.M. Brady.: A new approach to low-level image processing. Journal of Computer Vision, 23(1), 1997, 45-78.
8. O. Starostenko, J. Neme.: Novel advanced complex pattern recognition and motion characteristics estimation algorithms, Proc. VI Iber - American Symposium on Pattern recognition, Brazil (2001) 7-13.
9. M.S. Lew.: Principles of visual information retrieval, Advances in pattern recognition USA: Springer-Verlag (2001).
10. J.A. Chávez-Aragón, O. Starostenko, M. Medina.: Convex regions preprocessing algorithm in images, Proc. of III International Symposium in Intelligent Technologies, Mexico (2002) 41-45.
11. D. Fensel.: The semantic web and its languages, IEEE Computer Society Vol. 15(6) (2000) 67-73.
12. D. Beckett.: The design and implementation of the redland RDF application framework, Proc. of the 10th International World Wide Web Conference, WWW (2001) 120-125.

Automatic Evaluation of Document Binarization Results*

E. Badekas and N. Papamarkos[1]

[1]Image Processing and Multimedia Laboratory,
Department of Electrical & Computer Engineering,
Democritus University of Thrace,
67100 Xanthi, Greece
papamark@ee.duth.gr

Abstract. Most of the document binarization techniques have many parameters that can initially be specified. Usually, subjective document binarization evaluation, employs human observes for the estimation of the best parameter values of the techniques. Thus, the selection of the best values for these parameters is crucial for the final binarization result. However, there is not any set of parameters that guarantees the best binarization result for all document images. It is important, the estimation of the best values to be adaptive for each one of the processing images. This paper proposes a new method which permits the estimation of the best parameter values for each one of the document binarization techniques and also the estimation of the best document binarization result of all techniques. In this way, document binarization techniques can be compared and evaluated using, for each one of them, the best parameter values for every document image.

1 Introduction

Document binarization is an active area in image processing. Many binarization techniques have been proposed and most of them have parameters, the best values of which must initially be defined. Although, the estimation of the parameters values is a crucial stage, it is usually missed or heuristic estimated because there is no automatic parameter estimation process exists for document binarization techniques, until now.

In this paper, a Parameter Estimation Algorithm (PEA), which can be used to detect the best values for the parameter set (PS) of every document binarization technique, is proposed. The estimation is based on the analysis of the correspondence between the different document binarization results obtained by the application of a specific binarization technique to a document image, using different PS values. The proposed method is based on the work of Yitzhaky and Peli [1] which is used for edge detection evaluation. In their approach, a specific range and a specific step for each one of the parameters is initially defined. The best values for the PS are then estimated by comparing the results obtained by all possible combinations of the PS values. The best PS values are estimated using a Receiver Operating Characteristics (ROC) analysis and a Chi-square test. In order to improve this algorithm, we use a wide initial range for every parameter and in order to estimate the best parameter

* This paper was partially supported by the project Archimedes of TEI Serron.

M. Lazo and A. Sanfeliu (Eds.): CIARP 2005, LNCS 3773, pp. 1005 – 1014, 2005.

value an adaptive convergence procedure is applied. Specifically, in each iteration of the adaptive procedure, the parameters' ranges are redefined according to the estimation of the best and second best binarization result obtained. The adaptive procedure terminates when the ranges of the parameters values cannot be further reduced and the best PS values are those obtained from the last iteration.

For document binarization, it is important to lead to the best binarization result comparing the binary images obtained by a set of independent binarization techniques. For this purpose, we introduce a new technique that using the PEA leads to the evaluation of the best binarization results obtained by a set of independent binarization techniques. Specifically, for every independent binarization technique the best PS values are first estimated by using the PEA. Next, the best document binarization results obtained are compared using the Yitzhaky and Peli method and the final best binarization result is achieved.

2 Obtaining the Best Binarization Result

When we binarize a document image, we do not know initially the optimum result, that is, which is the ideal result that we must obtain. This is a major problem in comparative evaluation tests. In order to have comparative results, it is important to estimate a ground truth image. By estimating the ground truth image we can compare the different results obtained, and therefore, we can estimate the best of it. This Estimated Ground Truth (EGT) image, can be selected from a list of Potential Ground Truth (PGT) images as proposed by Yitzhaky and Peli [1].

Consider N document binary images D_j $(j=1,...,N)$ obtained by the application of one or more document binarization techniques to a gray-scale document image of size $K \times L$. In order to get the best binary image it is necessary to obtain the EGT image. After this, the independent binarization results are compared with the EGT image using the ROC analysis or a Chi-square test.

The entire procedure is described in the following where with "0" and "1" are considered the background and foreground pixels, respectively.

Stage 1 For every pixel, it is counted how many binary images consider this as foreground pixel. The results are stored to a matrix $C(x,y)$, $x=0,..,K-1$ and $y=0,..,L-1$. The values of the matrix will be between 0 and N.

Stage 2 N PGT_i, $i=1,..,N$ binary images are produced using the matrix $C(x,y)$. Every PGT_i image is defined as the image that has as foreground pixels all the pixels with $C(x,y) \geq i$.

Stage 3 For each PGT_i image, four average probabilities are defined which they assigned to pixels that are:

- Foreground in both PGT_i and D_j images:

$$TP_{PGT_i} = \frac{1}{N}\sum_{j=1}^{N}\frac{1}{K \cdot L}\sum_{k=1}^{K}\sum_{l=1}^{L} PGT_{i_1} \cap D_{j_1} \qquad (1)$$

- Foreground in PGT_i image and background in D_j image:

$$FP_{PGT_i} = \frac{1}{N}\sum_{j=1}^{N}\frac{1}{K \cdot L}\sum_{k=1}^{K}\sum_{l=1}^{L} PGT_{i_1} \cap D_{j_0} \tag{2}$$

- Background in both PGT_i and D_j images:

$$TN_{PGT_i} = \frac{1}{N}\sum_{j=1}^{N}\frac{1}{K \cdot L}\sum_{k=1}^{K}\sum_{l=1}^{L} PGT_{i_0} \cap D_{j_0} \tag{3}$$

- Background in PGT_i image and foreground in D_j image:

$$FN_{PGT_i} = \frac{1}{N}\sum_{j=1}^{N}\frac{1}{K \cdot L}\sum_{k=1}^{K}\sum_{l=1}^{L} PGT_{i_0} \cap D_{j_1} \tag{4}$$

Stage 4 In this stage, the sensitivity TPR_{PGT_i} and specificity $(1 - FPR_{PGT_i})$ values are calculated according to the relations:

$$TPR_{PGT_i} = \frac{TP_{PGT_i}}{P} \tag{5}$$

$$FPR_{PGT_i} = \frac{FP_{PGT_i}}{1-P} \tag{6}$$

where $P = TP_{PGT_i} + FN_{PGT_i}, \forall i$

Stage 5 This stage is used to obtain the EGT image, which is selected to be one of the PGT_i images. There are two measure methods that can be used:

The ROC analysis

It is a graphical method which is using a diagram constituted of two curves (CT-ROC diagram). The first curve (the ROC curve) constituted of N points with coordinates $(TPR_{PGT_i}, FPR_{PGT_i})$ and each one of the points is assigned to a PGT_i image. The points of this curve are the correspondence levels of the diagram. A second line, which is considered as diagnosis line, is used to detect the Correspondence Threshold (CT). This line has two points with coordinates (0,1) and *(P,P)*. The PGT_i point of the ROC curve which is closest to the intersection point of the two curves is the CT level and defines which PGT_i image will be then considered as the EGT image.

The Chi-square test

For each PGT_i, the $X^2_{PGT_i}$ value is calculated, according to the relation:

$$X^2_{PGT_i} = \frac{(sensitivity - Q_{PGT_i}) \cdot (specificity - (1 - Q_{PGT_i}))}{(1 - Q_{PGT_i}) \cdot Q_{PGT_i}} \tag{7}$$

A histogram from the values of $X^2_{PGT_i}$ is constructed (CT-Chi-square histogram). The best CT will be the value of i that maximizes $X^2_{PGT_i}$. The PGT_i image in this CT level will be then considered as the EGT image. Fig.1 shows examples of a CT ROC Diagram and a CT Chi-square histogram, for $N = 9$. In both cases the CT level is equal to five.

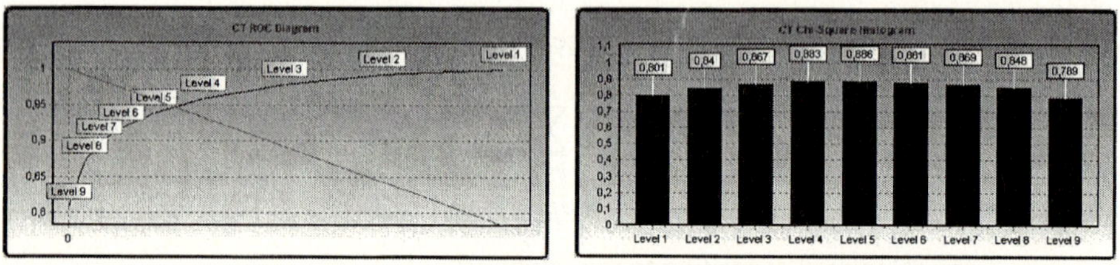

Fig. 1. A CT ROC diagram (left) and a CT Chi-square histogram (right)

Stage 6 For each D_j image, four probabilities are calculated (as in Stage 3), which they assigned to pixels that are: (a) foreground in both D_j and EGT images $TP_{D_j,EGT}$, (b) foreground in D_j image and background in EGT image $FP_{D_j,EGT}$, (c) background in both D_j and EGT images $TN_{D_j,EGT}$, (d) background in D_j image and foreground in EGT image $FN_{D_j,EGT}$.

Stage 7 Stages 4 and 5 are repeated to compare each binary image D_j with the EGT image, using the probabilities calculated in stage 6 rather than the average probabilities calculated in Stage 3. According to the Chi-square test, the maximum value of $X^2_{D_j,EGT}$ indicates the D_j image which is the estimated best document binarization result. Sorting the $X^2_{D_j,EGT}$ values, the D_j images are sorted according to their quality.

3 Parameter Estimation Algorithms

In the first stage of the proposed evaluation system it is necessary to estimate the best PS values for each one of the independent document binarization techniques. This estimation is based on the method of Yitzhaky and Peli [1] proposed for edge detection evaluation. However, in order to increase the accuracy of the estimated best PS values we improve this algorithm by using a wide initial range for every parameter and an adaptive convergence procedure. That is, the parameters' ranges are redefined according to the estimation of the best and second best binarization result obtained in each iteration of the adaptive procedure. This procedure terminates when the ranges of the parameters values cannot be further reduced and the best PS values are those obtained from the last iteration. It is important to notice that this is an adaptive procedure because it is applied to every processing document image.

The stages of the proposed parameter estimation algorithm, for two parameters (P_1, P_2), are as follows:

Stage 1 Define the initial range of the PS values. Consider as $[s_1, e_1]$ the range for the first parameter and $[s_2, e_2]$ the range for the second one.

Stage 2 Define the number of steps that will be used in each iteration. For the two parameters case, let St_1 and St_2 be the numbers of steps for the ranges $[s_1, e_1]$ and $[s_2, e_2]$, respectively. In most of the cases $St_1 = St_2 = 3$.

Stage 3 Calculate the lengths L_1 and L_2 of each step, according to the relations:

$$L_1 = \frac{e_1 - s_1}{St_1 - 1}, \qquad L_2 = \frac{e_2 - s_2}{St_2 - 1} \tag{8}$$

Stage 4 In each step, the values of parameters P_1, P_2 are updated with the relations:

$$P_1(i) = s_1 + i \cdot L_1, \quad (i = 0, \ldots, St_1 - 1) \tag{9}$$

$$P_2(i) = s_2 + i \cdot L_2, \quad (i = 0, \ldots, St_2 - 1) \tag{10}$$

Stage 5 Apply the binarization technique to the processed document image using all the possible combinations of (P_1, P_2). Thus, N binary images $D_j, j = 1, \ldots, N$ are produced, where N is equal to $N = St_1 \cdot St_2$.

Stage 6 Examine the N binary document results, using the algorithm described in Section 2, to estimate the best and the second best document binarization results. Let (P_{1B}, P_{2B}) and (P_{1S}, P_{2S}) be the parameters' values obtained from the best and the second best binarization results, respectively.

Stage 7 Redefine the ranges for the two parameters as $[s_1', e_1']$ and $[s_2', e_2']$ that will be used during the next iteration of the method, according to the relations:

$$[s_1', e_1'] = \begin{cases} \text{if } P_{1B} \neq P_{1S} \text{ then } \begin{cases} \text{if } P_{1B} > P_{1S} \text{ then } [s_1', e_1'] = [P_{1S}, P_{1B}] \\ \text{if } P_{1B} < P_{1S} \text{ then } [s_1', e_1'] = [P_{1B}, P_{1S}] \end{cases} \\ \text{if } P_{1B} = P_{1S} = A \text{ then } [s_1', e_1'] = [\frac{s_1 + A}{2}, \frac{e_1 + A}{2}] \end{cases} \tag{11}$$

$$[s_2', e_2'] = \begin{cases} \text{if } P_{2B} \neq P_{2S} \text{ then } \begin{cases} \text{if } P_{2B} > P_{2S} \text{ then } [s_2', e_2'] = [P_{2S}, P_{2B}] \\ \text{if } P_{2B} < P_{2S} \text{ then } [s_2', e_2'] = [P_{2B}, P_{2S}] \end{cases} \\ \text{if } P_{2B} = P_{2S} = A \text{ then } [s_2', e_2'] = [\frac{s_2 + A}{2}, \frac{e_2 + A}{2}] \end{cases} \tag{12}$$

Stage 8 Redefine the steps St_1', St_2' for the ranges that will be used in the next iteration according to the relations:

$$St_1' = \begin{cases} \text{if } e_1' - s_1' < St_1 \text{ then } St_1' = St_1 - 1 \\ \text{else } St_1' = St_1 \end{cases} \tag{13}$$

$$St_2' = \begin{cases} \text{if } e_2' - s_2' < St_2 \text{ then } St_2' = St_2 - 1 \\ \text{else } St_2' = St_2 \end{cases} \tag{14}$$

Stage 9 If $St_1' \cdot St_2' > 3$ go to Stage 3 and repeat all the stages. The iterations terminate when the calculated new steps for the next iteration have a product less or equal to 3 ($St_1' \cdot St_2' \leq 3$). The best PS values are those estimated during the Stage 6 of the last iteration.

4 Comparing the Results of Different Binarization Techniques

The proposed evaluation technique can be extended to estimate the best binarization results by comparing the binary images obtained by independent techniques. The algorithm described in Section 2 can be used to compare the binarization results obtained by the application of independent document binarization techniques. Specifically, the best document binarization results obtained from the independent techniques using the best PS values are compared through a similar to the Section 2 procedure. That is, the final best document binarization result is obtained as follows:

Stage 1 Estimate the best PS values for each document binarization technique, using the PEA described in Section 3.

Stage 2 Obtain the document binarization results from each one of the independent binarization techniques by using their best PS values.

Stage 3 Compare the binary images obtained in Stage 2 and estimate the final best document binarization result by using the algorithm described in Section 2.

5 Experimental Results

The proposed evaluation technique is used to compare and estimate the best document binarization result produced by seven independent binarization techniques: Otsu [2], Fuzzy C-Mean (FCM) [3], Niblack [4], Sauvola and Pietaksinen's [5-6], Bernsen [7], Adaptive Logical Level Technique (ALLT) [8-9] and Improvement of Integrated Function Algorithm (IIFA) [10-11]. It should be noticed that we use improvement versions for the ALLT and IIFA, proposed by Badekas and Papamarkos [12].

Fig. 2 shows a document image coming from the old Greek Parliamentary Proceedings. For the specific image, the initial range for each parameter and the best

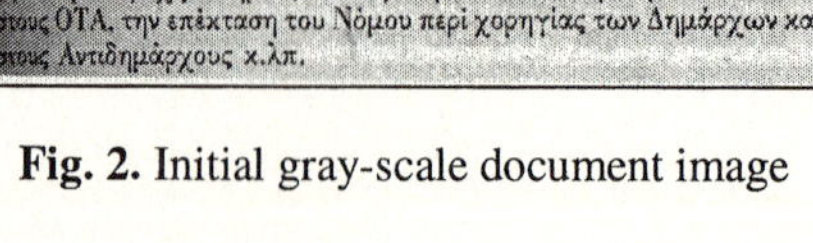

48. Οι Βουλευτές κ.κ. ΝΙΚΟΛΑΟΣ ΓΚΕΛΕΣΤΑΘΗΣ, ΘΕΟΦΙΛΟΣ ΓΑΤΣΟΣ και ΔΗΜΗΤΡΙΟΣ ΒΡΕΤΤΑΚΟΣ κατάθεσαν αναφορά της Τοπικής Ένωσης Δήμων και Κοινοτήτων Νομού Ξάνθης, με την οποία ζητά την παροχή πλήρους διοικητικής και οικονομικής αυτοτέλειας στους ΟΤΑ, την επέκταση του Νόμου περί χορηγίας των Δημάρχων και στους Αντιδημάρχους κ.λπ.

Fig. 2. Initial gray-scale document image

Table 1. The initial ranges and the estimated best *PS* values

	Technique	Initial ranges	Best *PS* values
1.	Niblack	$W \in [3,15]$, $k \in [0.2,1.2]$	$W = 14$ and $k = 0.67$
2.	Sauvola	$W \in [3,15]$, $k \in [0.1,0.6]$	$W = 14$ and $k = 0.34$
3.	Bernsen	$W \in [3,15]$, $L \in [10,90]$	$W = 14$ and $L = 72$
4.	ALLT	$a \in [0.1,0.4]$	$a = 0.10$
5.	IIFA	$T_p \in [10,90]$	$T_p = 10$

Table 2. The five iterations that applied in order to detect the best *PS* values for the binarization techniques of Niblack, Sauvola and Bernsen

Iterations	Niblack	Sauvola	Bernsen
First	1. W=3, k=0.2	1. W=3, k=0.1	1. W=3, L=10
	2. W=3, k=0.7	2. W=3, k=0.35	2. W=3, L=50
	3. W=3, k=1.2	3. W=3, k=0.6	3. W=3, L=90
	4. W=9, k=0.2	4. W=9, k=0.1	4. W=9, L=10
	5. W=9, k=0.7 (1st)	5. W=9, k=0.35 (1st)	5. W=9, L=50 (1st)
	6. W=9, k=1.2	6. W=9, k=0.6	6. W=9, L=90
	7. W=15, k=0.2	7. W=15, k=0.1	7. W=15, L=10
	8. W=15, k=0.7 (2nd)	8. W=15, k=0.35 (2nd)	8. W=15, L=50
	9. W=15, k=1.2	9. W=15, k=0.6	9. W=15, L=90 (2nd)
Second	1. W=9, k=0.45	1. W=9, k=0.22	1. W=9, L=50
	2. W=9, k=0.7	2. W=9, k=0.35	2. W=9, L=70
	3. W=9, k=0.95	3. W=9, k=0.48	3. W=9, L=90
	4. W=12, k=0.45	4. W=12, k=0.22	4. W=12, L=50
	5. W=12, k=0.7 (1st)	5. W=12, k=0.35 (1st)	5. W=12, L=70 (1st)
	6. W=12, k=0.95	6. W=12, k=0.48	6. W=12, L=90
	7. W=15, k=0.45	7. W=15, k=0.22	7. W=15, L=50
	8. W=15, k=0.7 (2nd)	8. W=15, k=0.35 (2nd)	8. W=15, L=70 (2nd)
	9. W=15, k=0.95	9. W=15, k=0.48	9. W=15, L=90
Third	1. W=12, k=0.58	1. W=12, k=0.28	1. W=12, L=60
	2. W=12, k=0.7	2. W=12, k=0.35	2. W=12, L=70
	3. W=12, k=0.82	3. W=12, k=0.42	3. W=12, L=80
	4. W=14, k=0.58	4. W=14, k=0.28	4. W=14, L=60
	5. W=14, k=0.7 (1st)	5. W=14, k=0.35 (1st)	5. W=14, L=70 (1st)
	6. W=14, k=0.82	6. W=14, k=0.42	6. W=14, L=80 (2nd)
	7. W=16, k=0.58	7. W=16, k=0.28	7. W=16, L=60
	8. W=16, k=0.7 (2nd)	8. W=16, k=0.35 (2nd)	8. W=16, L=70
	9. W=16, k=0.82	9. W=16, k=0.42	9. W=16, L=80
Fourth	1. W=14, k=0.64 (1st)	1. W=14, k=0.32	1. W=13, L=70
	2. W=14, k=0.7 (2nd)	2. W=14, k=0.35 (2nd)	2. W=13, L=75
	3. W=14, k=0.76	3. W=14, k=0.38	3. W=13, L=80
	4. W=16, k=0.64	4. W=16, k=0.32	4. W=14, L=70 (2nd)
	5. W=16, k=0.7	5. W=16, k=0.35 (1st)	5. W=14, L=75 (1st)
	6. W=16, k=0.76	6. W=16, k=0.38	6. W=14, L=80
Fifth	1. W=14, k=0.64	1. W=14, k=0.34 (1st)	1. W=14, L=70
	2. W=14, k=0.67 (1st)	2. W=14, k=0.36	2. W=14, L=72 (1st)
	3. W=14, k=0.7 (2nd)	3. W=16, k=0.34 (2nd)	3. W=14, L=74 (2nd)
		4. W=16, k=0.36	

PS values obtained are given in Table 1. The best PS values for all binarization techniques are obtained using five iterations. Tables 2 and 3 give all the PS values obtained during the five iterations and also the best and second best PS values that are estimated in each iteration. The Otsu's technique has no parameters to define and FCM is used with a value of fuzzyfier *m* equal to 1.5. The results obtained by the application of the independent techniques using their best PS values, are compared using the algorithm described in Section 2. Fig.3 shows the binary images obtained by ALLT and Bernsen's technique which are estimated as the best binarization results using the Chi-square test and the ROC analysis, respectively, in order to obtain the EGT image. The corresponding diagrams for these two cases, which are constructed according to the proposed technique to compare the independent binarization techniques, are given in Fig. 4.

Table 3. The five iterations that applied in order to detect the best *PS* values for the ALLT and IIFA

Iterations	ALLT	IIFA
First	1. a=10 (1st) 2. a=25 (2nd) 3. a=40	1. Tp=10 (2nd) 2. Tp =50 (1st) 3. Tp =90
Second	1. a=10 (1st) 2. a=18 (2nd) 3. a=26	1. Tp=10 (2nd) 2. Tp =30 (1st) 3. Tp =50
Third	1. a=10 (1st) 2. a=14 (2nd) 3. a=18	1. Tp=10 (2nd) 2. Tp =20 (1st) 3. Tp =30
Fourth	1. a=10 (1st) 2. a=12 (2nd) 3. a=14	1. Tp=10 (1st) 2. Tp =15 (2nd) 3. Tp =20
Fifth	1. a=10 (1st) 2. a=11 (2nd) 3. a=12	1. Tp=10 (1st) 2. Tp =12 (2nd) 3. Tp =14

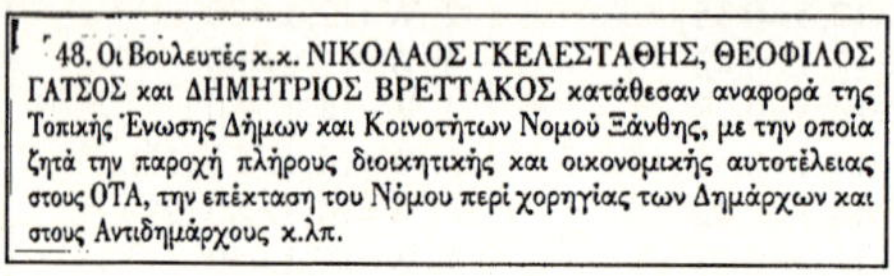
48. Οι Βουλευτές κ.κ. ΝΙΚΟΛΑΟΣ ΓΚΕΛΕΣΤΑΘΗΣ, ΘΕΟΦΙΛΟΣ ΓΑΤΣΟΣ και ΔΗΜΗΤΡΙΟΣ ΒΡΕΤΤΑΚΟΣ κατάθεσαν αναφορά της Τοπικής Ένωσης Δήμων και Κοινοτήτων Νομού Ξάνθης, με την οποία ζητά την παροχή πλήρους διοικητικής και οικονομικής αυτοτέλειας στους ΟΤΑ, την επέκταση του Νόμου περί χορηγίας των Δημάρχων και στους Αντιδημάρχους κ.λπ.

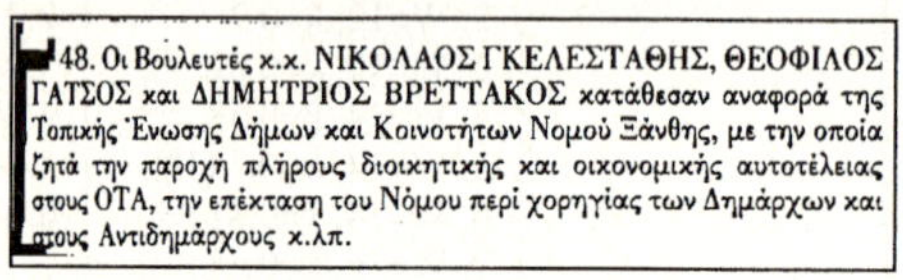
48. Οι Βουλευτές κ.κ. ΝΙΚΟΛΑΟΣ ΓΚΕΛΕΣΤΑΘΗΣ, ΘΕΟΦΙΛΟΣ ΓΑΤΣΟΣ και ΔΗΜΗΤΡΙΟΣ ΒΡΕΤΤΑΚΟΣ κατάθεσαν αναφορά της Τοπικής Ένωσης Δήμων και Κοινοτήτων Νομού Ξάνθης, με την οποία ζητά την παροχή πλήρους διοικητικής και οικονομικής αυτοτέλειας στους ΟΤΑ, την επέκταση του Νόμου περί χορηγίας των Δημάρχων και στους Αντιδημάρχους κ.λπ.

Fig. 3. Binarization result of ALLT (left) and Bernsen's technique (right)

The proposed technique is applied to a large number of document images. For each document image, the binarization results obtained, by the application of the independent binarization techniques, are sorted according to the ordering quality results obtained by the proposed evaluation method. The rating value for a document binarization technique can be between 1 (best) and 7 (worst). The mean rating value for each binarization technique is then calculated and the histogram shown in Fig. 5 is constructed using these values. It is obvious that the minimum value of this histogram is assigned to the binarization technique which has the best performance. The Sauvola's technique gives, in most of the cases, the best document binarization result. These conclusions agree with the evaluation test that has been made by Sezgin and Sankur [13].

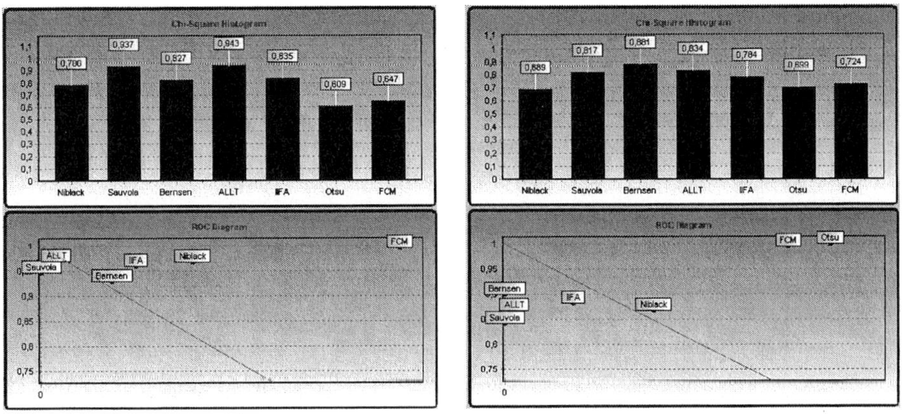

Fig. 4. The Chi-square histogram and the ROC diagram constructed using the *EGT* image calculated from the CT Chi-square histogram (left) and the CT ROC diagram (right)

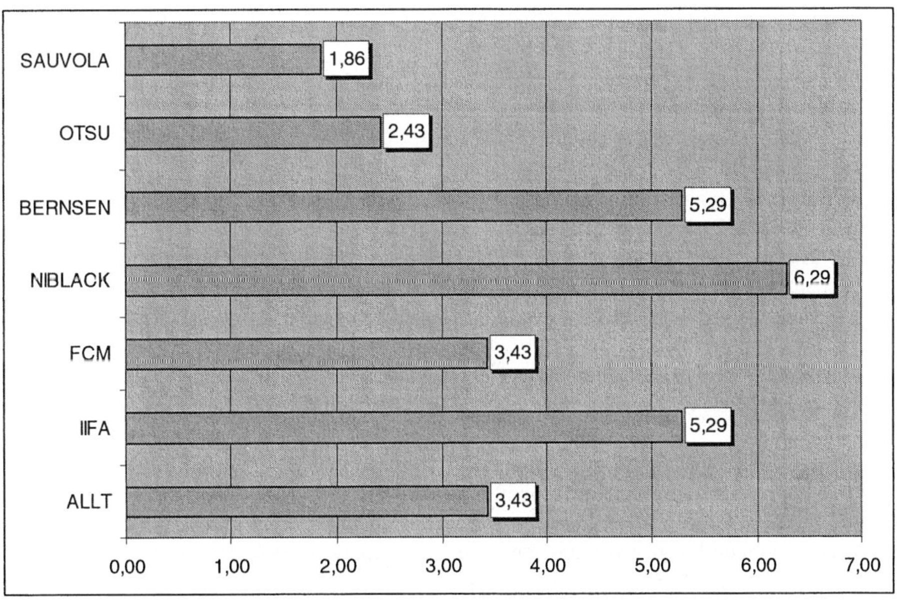

Fig. 5. The histogram constructed by the mean rating values. Sauvola's technique is the binarization technique with the best performance in the examined document image database

6 Conclusions

This paper proposes a method for the estimation of the best PS values of a document binarization technique and the best binarization result obtained by a set of independent document binarization techniques. It is important that the best PS values are adaptively estimated according to the processing document image. The proposed method is extended to produce an evaluation system for independent document binarization techniques. The estimation of the best PS values is achieved by applying an adaptive convergence procedure starting from a wide initial range for every parameter. The entire system was extensively tested with a variety of document images. Many of them came from standard document databases such as the old Greek Parliamentary Proceedings. The entire system is implemented in visual environment using Dephi 7.

References

1. Y. Yitzhaky and E. Peli, A Method for Objective Edge Detection Evaluation and Detector Parameter Selection, IEEE Transactions on Pattern Analysis and Machine Intelligence, 25 (8) (2003) 1027-1033.
2. N. Otsu, A thresholding selection method from gray-level histogram, IEEE Trans. Systems Man Cybernet. SMC-8 (1978) 62-66.
3. Z. Chi, H. Yan, and T. Pham, Fuzzy Algorithms: With Applications to Image Processing and Pattern Recognition, World Scientific Publishing, 1996.
4. W. Niblack, An Introduction to Digital Image Processing, Englewood Cliffs, N.J. Prentice Hall, (1986) 115-116.
5. J. Sauvola, T. Seppanen, S. Haapakoski, and M.Pietikainen, Adaptive Document Binarization, ICDAR Ulm Germany (1997) 147-152.
6. J. Sauvola and M. Pietikainen, Adaptive Document Image Binarization, Pattern Recognition 33 (2000) 225–236.
7. J. Bernsen, Dynamic thresholding of grey-level images, Proc. Eighth Int. Conf. Pattern Recognition, Paris (1986) 1251-1255.
8. M. Kamel and A. Zhao, Extraction of binary character / graphics images from gray-scale document images, CVGIP: Graphical Models Image Process. 55 (3) (1993) 203-217.
9. Y. Yang and H. Yan, An adaptive logical method for binarization of degraded document images, Pattern Recognition 33 (2000) 787-807.
10. J.M. White and G.D. Rohrer, Image segmentation for optical character recognition and other applications requiring character image extraction, IBM J. Res. Dev. 27 (4) (1983) 400-411.
11. O.D. Trier and T. Taxt, Improvement of 'Integrated Function Algorithm' for binarization of document images, Pattern Recognition Letters 16 (1995) 277-283.
12. E. Badekas and N. Papamarkos, "A system for document binarization", 3rd International Symposium on Image and Signal Processing and Analysis ISPA 2003, Rome, Italy.
13. M. Sezgin and B. Sankur, Survey over image thresholding techniques and quantitative performance evaluation, Journal of Electronic Imaging 13(1) (2004) 146–165.

A Comparative Study on Support Vector Machine and Constructive RBF Neural Network for Prediction of Success of Dental Implants

Adriano L.I. Oliveira[1], Carolina Baldisserotto[1], and Julio Baldisserotto[2]

[1] Department of Computing Systems, Polytechnic School of Engineering, Pernambuco State University, Rua Benfica, 455, Madalena, Recife – PE, Brazil, 50.750-410

[2] Faculdade de Odontologia, Universidade Federal do Rio Grande do Sul, Rua Ramiro Barcelos, 2492, Porto Alegre – RS, Brazil, 90.040-060

adriano@dsc.upe.br, carol_baldi@yahoo.com.br, bjulio@ghc.com.br

Abstract. The market demand for dental implants is growing at a significant pace. In practice, some dental implants do not succeed. Important questions in this regard concern whether machine learning techniques could be used to predict if an implant will be successful and which are the best techniques for this problem. This paper presents a comparative study on three machine learning techniques for prediction of success of dental implants. The techniques compared here are: (a) support vector machines (SVM); (b) weighted support vector machines; and (c) constructive RBF neural networks (RBF-DDA) with parameter selection. We present a number of simulations using real-world data. The simulations were carried out using 10-fold cross validation and the results show that the methods achieve comparable performance, yet RBF-DDA had the advantage of building smaller classifiers.

1 Introduction

Dental implants have been used successfully to replace lost teeth with very high success rates [3]. Nevertheless, oral rehabilitation through dental implants presents failure risks related to the different phases of the *osseointegration* process (the integration of the implant to the adjacent bone) [13]. A number of risk factors may be related to the failure of dental implants, such as the general health conditions of the patient, the surgical technique employed, the use of smoke by the patient and the type of implant [12]. In this work, a dental implant is considered successful if it presents characteristics of osseointegration in the different phases of the process, including the prosthetic loading and its preservation. We considered that a failure took place whenever any problem related to the implant motivated its removal.

The features of the patients considered in this work were carefully chosen by an oral surgeon specialist in dental implants. The features considered here were: 1) age of the patient, 2) gender, 3) implant type, 4) implant position, 5) surgical

M. Lazo and A. Sanfeliu (Eds.): CIARP 2005, LNCS 3773, pp. 1015–1026, 2005.

technique, 6) an indication whether the patient was a smoker of not and 7) an indication whether the patient had a previous illness (diabetes or osteoporosis) or medical treatment (radiotherapy). These features are best described in the remaining of the paper. Some of these features, also referred to as *risk factors*, were also considered in a recent studied which used statistical techniques to analyze the risk factors associated with dental implants [12]. The data for the present study were collect between the years 1998 and 2004 by a single oral surgeon. The data set consists of 157 patterns which describe dental implants.

In the period in which data were collected there were implants carried out less than five years before. Therefore, instead of classifying the outcome of an implant simply as success or failure, we have classified our data into seven classes: (1) success confirmed until one year; (2) success confirmed between 1 and 2 years; (3) success confirmed between 2 and 3 years; (4) success confirmed between 3 and 4 years; (5) success confirmed between 4 and 5 years; (6) success confirmed for more than 5 years; and (6) failure. In general, the longer the number of years of confirmed success, the greater is the likelihood of definitive success of an implant.

Nowadays the prediction of success of failure of a dental implant is almost always carried out by the oral surgeons through clinical and radiological evaluation. Therefore, the accuracy of such predictions is heavily dependent on the experience of the oral surgeon. This works aims to help predicting the success or failure of a dental implant via machine learning techniques, thereby hoping to improve the accuracy of the predictions.

We have considered three machine learning techniques for our comparison, namely, (a) support vector machines (SMVs) [7,8,1]; (b) weighted SVMs [10,6]; and (c) RBF-DDA with θ^- selection [17].

SVMs are a recent powerful class of machine learning techniques based on the principle of structural risk minimization (SRM). SVMs have been applied successfully to a wide range of problems such as text classification and optical character recognition [8,18]. Weighted SVM is an extension to SVM more appropriate to handle imbalanced datasets, that is, datasets which have unequal proportion of samples between classes [10,6]. We have considered this extension to SVM here because our dataset is imbalanced, as detailed in section 3. DDA is a fast training method for RBF and PNN neural networks [5,4]. RBF-DDA with θ^- selection uses cross-validation to select the value of parameter θ^- thus improving performance in some classification problems [17]. We decided to use the last classifier in order to assess its performance in a task different from those considered in the paper in which it was originally proposed [17]. Thus this paper also contributes by further exploring this classifier on a different data set.

The classifiers considered in this work were compared using 10-fold cross-validation together with Student paired t-tests with 95% confidence level.

This paper is organized as follows. Next section reviews the machine learning techniques considered in this work. Section 3 describes the experiments carried out along with the results and discussion. Finally, section 4 presents our conclusions and suggestions for further research.

2 The Machine Learning Techniques Compared

2.1 Support Vector Machines

Support vector machine (SVM) is a recent technique for classification and regression which has achieved remarkable accuracy in a number of important problems [7,18,8,1]. SVM is based on the principle of *structural risk minimization* (SRM), which states that, in order to achieve good generalization performance, a machine learning algorithm should attempt to minimize the *structural risk* instead of the *empirical risk* [8,1]. The empirical risk is the error in the training set, whereas the structural risk considers both the error in the training set and the complexity of the class of functions used to fit the data. Despite its popularity in the machine learning and pattern recognition communities, a recent study has shown that simpler methods, such as kNN and neural networks, can achieve performance comparable to or even better than SVMs in some classification and regression problems [14].

The main idea of support vector machines is to built optimal hyperplanes - that is, hyperplanes that maximize the margin of separation of classes - in order to separate training patterns of different classes. An SVM minimizes the first equation below subject to the condition specified in the second equation

$$
\begin{aligned}
\min_{w,b,\xi} \quad & \frac{1}{2} w^T w + C \sum_{i=1}^{l} \xi_i \\
\text{subject to} \quad & y_i (w^T \phi(x_i) + b) \geq 1 - \xi_i, \\
& \xi_i \geq 0.
\end{aligned}
\tag{1}
$$

The training vectors x_i are mapped into a higher (maybe infinite) dimensional space by the function ϕ. Then SVM finds a linear separating hyperplane with the maximal margin in this higher dimensional space. A kernel $K(\vec{x}, \vec{y})$ is an inner product in some feature space, $K(\vec{x}, \vec{y}) = \phi^T(\vec{x})\phi(\vec{y})$. A number of kernels have been proposed in the literature [18,8,1,2]. In this work we use the radial basis function (RBF) kernel, which is the kernel used more frequently. The kernel function $K(x_i, x_j)$ in an RBF kernel is given by $K(x_i, x_j) = \exp(-\gamma||x_i - x_j||^2), \gamma > 0$.

SVMs with RBF kernels have two parameters, namely, C, the penalty parameter of the error term ($C > 0$) and γ, the width of the RBF kernels. These parameters have great influence on performance and therefore their values must be carefully selected for a given problem. In this work, model selection is carried out via 10-fold cross-validation on training data. A grid search procedure on C and γ is performed, whereby pairs of (C, γ) are tried and the one with the best cross-validation accuracy is selected [11]. A practical method for identifying good parameters consists in trying exponentially growing sequences of C and γ. In our experiments, the sequence used was $C = 2^{-5}, 2^{-3}, \cdots, 2^{15}$, and $\gamma = 2^{-15}, 2^{-13}, \cdots, 2^{3}$ [11].

2.2 Weighted Support Vector Machines

Weighted support vector machine (WSVM) was proposed to address two important problems which appear quite often in pattern recognition, namely, (1) classification problems with imbalanced datasets, that is, datasets in which the classes are not equally represented; and (2) classification problems in which a classification error of one type is more expensive or undesirable than other [10].

The idea of WSVM consists in penalizing with higher penalty the most undesirables types of errors [10,6]. For this purpose, WSVMs have one *weight* w_i per class. In WSVMs each class i has a different penalty parameter C_i. This is in contrast to the original SVM, which has only one the penalty parameter of the error term ($C > 0$) (equation (1)), which is used for all classes. The parameter C_i in WSVMs is set to $w_i C$. In practice, higher values of w_i should be used for classes with smaller number of samples.

The motivation for considering WSVMs in our problem is that our dataset is imbalanced, in particular, we have quite few cases of failure of dental implants (as detailed in section 3).

2.3 Constructive RBF Neural Networks

The DDA algorithm is a very fast constructive training algorithm for RBF and probabilistic neural networks (PNNs) [5,4]. In most problems training is finished in only four to five epochs. The algorithm has obtained good performance in a number of problems, which has motivated a number of extensions to the method recently proposed in the literature [17,16,15].

An RBF trained by DDA is referred as RBF-DDA. The number of units in the input layer represents the dimensionality of the input space. The input layer is fully connected to the hidden layer. RBF-DDAs have a single hidden layer. The number of hidden units is automatically determined during training. Hidden units use Gaussian activation functions. RBF-DDA uses 1-of-n coding in the output layer, with each unit of this layer representing a class. Classification uses a winner-takes-all approach, whereby the unit with the highest activation gives the class. Each hidden unit is connected to exactly one output unit. Each of these connections has a weight A_i. Output units uses linear activation functions with values computed by

$$f(\vec{x}) = \sum_{i=1}^{m} A_i \times R_i(\vec{x}) \tag{2}$$

where m is the number of RBFs connected to that output.

The DDA training algorithm is constructive, starting with an empty hidden layer, with units being added to it as needed. The centers of RBFs, $\vec{r_i}$, and their widths, σ_i are determined by DDA during training. The values of the weights of connections between hidden and output layers are also given by DDA.

The complete DDA algorithm for one training epoch is shown in Fig. 1. The algorithm is executed until no changes in the parameters values (number of hidden units and their respective parameters and weights values) are detected. This usually takes place in only four to five epochs [5]. This natural stopping criterion leads to networks that naturally avoid overfitting training data [5,4].

1: // *reset weights:*
FORALL prototypes p_i^k **DO**
  $A_i^k = 0.0$
ENDFOR
2: // *train one complete epoch*
FORALL training pattern $(\overrightarrow{x}, c)$ **DO**
  IF $\exists p_i^c : R_i^c(\overrightarrow{x}) \geq \theta^+$ **THEN**
3: // *sample covered by existing neuron of the same class*
    $A_i^c += 1.0$
  ELSE
4: // *"commit": introduce new prototype*
    add new prototype $p_{m_c+1}^c$ with:
    $\overrightarrow{r}_{m_c+1}^c = \overrightarrow{x}$
    $A_{m_c+1}^c = 1.0$
    $m_c += 1$
5: // *adapt radii*
    $\sigma_{m_c+1}^c = \max_{k \neq c \wedge 1 \leq j \leq m_k} \{\sigma : R_{m_c+1}^c(\overrightarrow{r}_j^k) < \theta^-\}$
  ENDIF
6: // *"shrink": adjust conflicting prototypes*
  FORALL $k \neq c, 1 \leq j \leq m_k$ **DO**
    $\sigma_j^k = \max\{\sigma : R_j^k(\overrightarrow{x}) < \theta^- \}$
  ENDFOR
ENDFOR

Fig. 1. DDA algorithm for one training epoch

The DDA algorithm relies on two parameters in order to decide about the introduction of new prototypes (RBF units) in the networks. One of these parameters is a *positive threshold* (θ^+), which must be overtaken by an activation of a prototype of the same class so that no new prototype is added. The other is a *negative threshold* (θ^-), which is the upper limit for the activation of conflicting classes [5,4].

A trained RBF-DDA network holds the following two equations for every training pattern $\overrightarrow{x}$ of class c [5,4]:

$$\exists i : R_i^c(\overrightarrow{x}) \geq \theta^+ \tag{3}$$

$$\forall k \neq c, 1 \leq j \leq m_k : R_j^k < \theta^- \tag{4}$$

Notice that the above conditions do not guarantee the correct classification of all training patterns, because they hold for hidden units, not for output units.

During training, the DDA algorithm creates a new prototype for a given training pattern $\overrightarrow{x}$ only if there is no prototype of *the same class* in the network whose output $R_i(\vec{x}) \geq \theta^+$. Otherwise, the algorithm only increments the weight A_i of the connection associated with one of the RBFs (of the same class of the training pattern) which gives $R_i(\vec{x}) \geq \theta^+$ (step 3 of Fig. 1). When a new prototype is introduced in the network, its center will have the value of the training vector $\vec{x}$ and the weight of its connection to the output layer is set to 1 (step 4 of Fig. 1). The width of the Gaussian will be chosen in such a way that the outputs produced by the new prototype for existing prototypes of conflicting classes is smaller than θ^- (step 5 of Fig. 1). Finally, there is a *shrink phase*, in which the widths of conflicting prototypes are adjusted to produce output values smaller than θ^- for the training pattern $\vec{x}$ (step 6 of Fig. 1).

Originally, it was assumed that the value of DDA parameters would not influence classification performance and therefore the use of their default values, $\theta^+ = 0.4$ and $\theta^- = 0.1$, was recommended for all datasets [5,4]. In contrast, it was observed more recently that, for some datasets, the value of θ^- considerably influences generalization performance in some problems [17]. To take advantage of this observation, a method has been proposed for improving RBF-DDA by carefully selecting the value of θ^- [17].

In the RBF-DDA with θ^- selection method, the value of the parameter θ^- is selected via cross-validation, starting with $\theta^- = 0.1$ [17]. Next, θ^- is decreased by $\theta^- = \theta^- \times 10^{-1}$. This is done because it was observed that performance does not change significantly for intermediate values of θ^- [17]. θ^- is decreased until the cross-validation error starts to increase, since smaller values lead to overfitting [17]. The near optimal θ^- found by this procedure is subsequently used to train using the complete training set [17]. The algorithm is shown in Fig. 2.

$\theta^-_{opt} = \theta^- = 10^{-1}$
Train one RBF-DDA with θ^- using the reduced training set and test on the validation set to obtain $ValError = MinValError$
REPEAT
  $\theta^- = \theta^- \times 10^{-1}$
  Train one RBF-DDA with θ^- using the reduced training set and test on the validation set to obtain $ValError$
  IF $ValError < MinValError$
    $MinValError = ValError$
    $\theta^-_{opt} = \theta^-$
  ENDIF
UNTIL $ValError > MinValError$ **OR** $\theta^- = 10^{-10}$
Train one RBF-DDA with θ^-_{opt} using the complete training set
Test the optimized RBF-DDA on the test set

Fig. 2. Optimizing RBF-DDA through θ^- selection

3 Experiments

3.1 Data Set

The input variables considered in this work were chosen by an expert (oral surgeon) based on his previous experience. According to the expert, the most important factors which influence the success or failure of a dental implant are those shown in table 1. Some of those factor were also considered in a recent study which used statistical techniques for analyzing dental implant failure [12]. Table 1 shows the input variables together with their possible values in our data set.

Table 1. Input variables

Name	Possible values
Age (years)	from 17 to 74
Gender	{male, female}
Implant position	{ posterior maxilla, anterior maxilla, posterior mandible, anterior mandible }
Implant type	{conventional, surface treatment}
Surgical technique	{conventional, complex}
Smoker?	{yes, no}
Previous illness or medical treatment?	{no, yes (diabetes), yes (osteoporosis), yes (radiotherapy) }

The distribution of the dependent variable in our problem is shown in table 2. This is a classification problem with seven classes. One of the classes indicates failure whereas the remaining six classes indicate success, with a variable period of time. Note that this is an imbalanced dataset, since the number of samples per class is quite different.

Table 2. Distribution of dependent variable

Class	Frequency	Percentage
1 (success - up to 1 year)	2	1.27%
2 (success - from 1 to 2 years)	24	15.29%
3 (success - from 2 to 3 years)	25	15.92%
4 (success - from 3 to 4 years)	21	13.38%
5 (success - from 4 to 5 years)	16	10.19%
6 (success - five years or more)	62	39.49%
7 (failure)	7	4.46%
Total	157	100%

3.2 Experimental Setup

Due to the small number of examples in our data set we have used 10-fold cross-validation in order to compare the machine learning techniques. This is a well known technique widely used to compare classifiers whenever data is scarce [2]. In 10-fold cross-validation the data set is divided in ten disjoints subsets (folds) [2]. Subsequently, the classifier is trained using a data set composed of nine of these subsets and tested using the remaining one. This is carried ten times, always using a different subset for testing. Finally, the cross-validation error is computed as the mean of the ten test errors thus obtained.

In order to improve even more our comparison, we have firstly generated ten versions of our data set by randomly distributing the patterns. Therefore, each data set contains the same patterns yet in different orders. This means that the subsets used in 10-fold cross-validation are different for each random distributed version of our original data set.

We have performed 10-fold cross-validation using each of the ten randomly ordered versions of our data set. Hence, for each classifier, one hundred simulations were carried out (including the training and test phases).

In the case of weighted SVM (WSVM), we have employed the following values for the weights per class: $w_1 = 12$, $w_6 = 0.3$, and $w_7 = 4$. For the remaining classes, $w_i = 1$. These values were selected according to the distribution of the samples per class in our dataset, presented in table 2.

3.3 Results and Discussion

In this study we are interested in comparing the machine learning techniques in our problem regarding the classification error and the complexity of the classifiers, that is, the number of training prototypes stored by each of them. The simulations using RBF-DDA with parameter selection [17] were carried out using SNNS [19], whereas SVM and weighted SVM simulations used LIBSVM [6].

Table 3 compares the classifiers with respect to both 10-fold cross-validation errors and the respective number of training prototypes stored by each classifier. Each line of this table shows the 10-fold cross validation error and number of stored prototypes obtained by each classifier using a different version of our data set (with random order of the patterns). The table also presents the mean and standard deviation of the error and of the number of stored prototypes over the ten versions of our data set obtained by each classifier.

The results of table 3 show that SVM and RBF with θ^- selection achieved equivalent classification performance (around 24% mean error). The best results obtained by RBF with θ^- selection (shown in table 3) used $\theta^- = 0.01$. In spite of the similar accuracies obtained, RBF-DDA was able to build considerably smaller classifiers than SVMs in this problem. Hence, in this problem RBF-DDA with θ^- selection achieved a better trade-off between accuracy and complexity compared to SVM. RBF-DDA with θ^- selection is also much faster to train than SVMs, which can be also an important advantage in practical applications.

Table 3. Comparison of classifiers: 10-fold cross-validation errors and number of prototypes stored

	RBF-DDA with θ^- selection	SVM	weighted SVM ($w_1 = 12, w_6 = 0.3, w_7 = 4$)
Random set 1	26.03% [73.9]	25.64% [111.6]	23.72% [109.2]
Random set 2	22.09% [73.9]	24.36% [101.0]	23.72% [98.8]
Random set 3	23.61% [73.2]	23.08% [108.7]	23.08% [107.3]
Random set 4	24.09% [73.7]	23.08% [102.5]	22.44% [99.1]
Random set 5	22.73% [73.7]	24.36% [106.5]	22.44% [104.2]
Random set 6	24.52% [73.7]	24.36% [101.6]	23.72% [103.4]
Random set 7	24.94% [73.9]	23.72% [101.6]	22.44% [98.8]
Random set 8	26.97% [73.7]	24.36% [97.5]	23.72% [95.1]
Random set 9	26.06% [73.2]	24.36% [107.2]	23.72% [102.5]
Random set 10	24.06% [73.9]	23.08% [102.3]	23.08% [103.4]
mean	24.51% [73.68]	24.04% [104.05]	23.21% [102.18]
st.dev	1.53% [0.27]	0.81% [4.27]	0.59% [4.28]

The use of WSVM in our problem produced a small improvement in performance compared to both RBF-DDA with θ^- selection and SVM, as shown in table 3. WSVM outperformed SVM in our problem and at the same time produced slightly smaller classifiers (table 3 shows that WSVM stored 102.18 prototypes in the mean whereas SVM stored 104.05).

Next, we compared the classifiers regarding both the performance and the number of prototypes stored using Student paired t-test. In order to compare two classifiers using the Student paired t-test, we first perform 10-fold cross-validation using the same training and test sets for each of the classifiers. Subsequently, we compute the collection of test errors, $\{x_i\}$ for the first classifier and $\{y_i\}$ for the second one. Then, we compute $d_i = x_i - y_i$, which is used to compute t as follows

$$t = \frac{\bar{d}}{\sqrt{s_d^2/k}} \tag{5}$$

where $\bar{d}$ is the mean of d_i, s_d is the standard deviation of d_i and k is the number of folds. In our experiments, we have performed 10-fold cross-validation, thus $k = 10$. Moreover, we employ 95% confidence level. For this confidence level, the t-student distribution table with $k - 1 = 9$ gives $z = 2.262$. Hence, for 95% confidence level, the results produced by two classifiers being compared will be considered statistically different only if $t > z$ or $t < -z$.

The results of hypothesis tests using the Student test with 95% confidence level for comparing the classifiers regarding classification errors are shown in table 4. Table 5 compares the classifiers regarding the number of prototypes stored. These results were computed from the results shown in table 3.

Table 4 shows that the difference in performance between the RBF-DDA and SVM classifiers is not statistically significant. Conversely, the results of this

Table 4. Hypothesis tests for classification errors

RBF-DDA (θ^-) sel. × SVM	RBF-DDA (θ^-) sel. × Weighted SVM	SVM × Weighted SVM
$t = 1.02$	$t = 2.91$	$t = 3.88$
not significant	**significant**	**significant**

table shows that the differences in performance between RBF-DDA and weighted SVM as well as between SVM and WSVM are statistically significant.

Table 5 shows that the difference in the number of prototypes stored is statistically significant in the three comparisons performed.

Table 5. Hypothesis tests for number of prototypes stored

RBF-DDA (θ^-) sel. × SVM	RBF-DDA (θ^-) sel. × Weighted SVM	SVM × Weighted SVM
$t = -21.93$	$t = -20.70$	$t = 3.02$
significant	**significant**	**significant**

The results obtained in our simulations confirmed an observation that appeared recently in the literature, namely, that SVMs, despite their strong theoretical foundations and excellent generalization performance in a number of problems, are not the best choice for all classification and regression problems [14]. Simpler methods such kNN and neural networks can achieve performance comparable to or even better than SVMs in some classification and regression problems [14]. In problems, such as the one considered in this paper, where both classifiers obtained the same generalization performance, other performance measures, such as training time, classification time and complexity must be compared. In our case, the simulations showed that RBF-DDA with θ^- selection was better in terms of complexity and consequently in terms of classification time as well. RBF-DDA with θ^- selection certainly outperforms SVMs concerning training time as well, since we need to select just one parameter whereas with SVMs we need to select two parameters.

4 Conclusions

We have presented a comparative study on three machine learning techniques for prediction of success of dental implants. The data set consisted of 157 examples concerning real-world clinical cases. The input variables concerned risk factors for dental implants chosen by an expert (oral surgeon). The simulations were carried out using ten versions of the data set with different random orders of the patterns. For each random data set, the simulations were carried out via 10-fold cross-validation, due to the small size of the data set. The techniques compared were support vector machines (SVMs), weighted support vector machines (WSVMs) and RBF-DDA with θ^- selection.

The classifiers considered in this study achieved similar classification performance (around 24% of mean cross-validation error). Yet RBF-DDA with θ^- selection obtained smaller classifiers (73.68 mean number of prototypes) than SVM (104.05 mean number of prototypes) and WSWVM (102.18 mean number of prototypes) . This can represent an advantage in practice for RBF-DDA with θ^- selection, since the memory requirement and the time to classify novel patterns will be much smaller than those of SVM and WSWM. Nevertheless, WSVM obtained a small improvement in performance (decrease in classfication error around 1%) compared with RBF-DDA which was statistically significant according to a Student paired t-test with 95% confidence level.

Future work includes considering other classifiers for this problem such as the multilayer perceptron (MLP) and SVM with other kernel functions as well as evaluating the classification accuracy per class. Another research direction consists in determining the influence of each risk factor (input) on the classification accuracy, such as was done in [9].

References

1. V. David Sanchez A. Advanced support vector machines and kernel methods. *Neurocomputing*, 55:5–20, 2003.
2. A.Webb. *Statistical Pattern Recognition*. Wiley, second edition, 2002.
3. M. Barry, D. Kennedy, K. Keating, and Z. Schauperl. Design of dynamic test equipment for the testing of dental implants. *Materials & Design*, 26(3):209–216, 2005.
4. M. Berthold and J. Diamond. Constructive training of probabilistic neural networks. *Neurocomputing*, 19:167 183, 1998.
5. Michael R. Berthold and Jay Diamond. Boosting the performance of RBF networks with dynamic decay adjustment. In G. Tesauro et al, editor, *Advances in Neural Information Processing*, volume 7, pages 521–528. MIT Press, 1995.
6. Chih-Chung Chang and Chih-Jen Lin. *LIBSVM: a library for support vector machines*, 2001. Software available at `http://www.csie.ntu.edu.tw/~cjlin/libsvm`.
7. C. Cortes and V. Vapnik. Support-vector network. *Machine Learning*, pages 273–297, 1995.
8. N. Cristianini and J. Shawe-Taylor. *An Introduction to Support Vector Machines*. Cambridge University Press, 2000.
9. Dursun Delen, Glenn Walker, and Amit Kadam. Predicting breast cancer survivability: a comparison of three data mining methods. *Artificial Intelligence in Medicine*, 34(2):113–127, 2005.
10. Federico Girosi Edgar E. Osuna, Robert Freund. Support vector machines: Training and application. Technical Report A.I. Memo 1602, MIT A.I. Lab, 1997.
11. C.-W. Hsu, C.-C. Chang, and C.-J. Lin. *A Practical Guide to Support Vector Classification*, 2004. Available at `http://www.csie.ntu.edu.tw/~cjlin/libsvm`.
12. Donald Hui, J. Hodges, and N. Sandler. Predicting cumulative risk in endosseous dental implant failure. *Journal of Oral and Maxillofacial Surgery*, 62:40–41, 2004.

13. P. Laine, A. Salo, R. Kontio, S. Ylijoki, and C. Lindqvist. Failed dental implants - clinical, radiological and bacteriological findings in 17 patients. *Journal of Cranio-Maxillofacial Surgery*, 33:212–217, 2005.
14. D. Meyer, F. Leisch, and K. Hornik. The support vector machine under test. *Neurocomputing*, 55:169–186, 2003.
15. A. L. I. Oliveira, B. J. M. Melo, and S. R. L. Meira. Improving constructive training of RBF networks through selective pruning and model selection. *Neurocomputing*, 64:537–541, 2005.
16. A. L. I. Oliveira, B. J. M. Melo, and S. R. L. Meira. Integrated method for constructive training of radial basis functions networks. *Electronics Letters*, 41(7):429–430, 2005.
17. A. L. I. Oliveira, F. B. L. Neto, and S. R. L. Meira. Improving RBF-DDA performance on optical character recognition through parameter selection. In *Proc. of the 17th International Conference on Pattern Recognition (ICPR'2004)*, volume 4, pages 625–628. IEEE Computer Society Press, 2004.
18. J. Shawe-Taylor and N. Cristianini. *Kernel Methods for Pattern Analysis*. Cambridge University Press, 2004.
19. A. Zell. *SNNS - Stuttgart Neural Network Simulator, User Manual, Version 4.2*. University of Stuttgart and University of Tubingen, 1998.

A Fast Distance Between Histograms

Francesc Serratosa[1] and Alberto Sanfeliu[2]

[1] Universitat Rovira I Virgili, Dept. d'Enginyeria Informàtica i Matemàtiques, Spain
francesc.serratosa@.urv.net
[2] Universitat Politècnica de Catalunya, Institut de Robòtica i Informàtica Industrial, Spain
sanfeliu@iri.upc.es

Abstract. In this paper we present a new method for comparing histograms. Its main advantage is that it takes less time than previous methods.

The present distances between histograms are defined on a structure called signature, which is a lossless representation of histograms. Moreover, the type of the elements of the sets that the histograms represent are ordinal, nominal and modulo.

We show that the computational cost of these distances is $O(z')$ for the ordinal and nominal types and $O(z'^2)$ for the modulo one, where z' is the number of non-empty bins of the histograms. In the literature, the computational cost of the algorithms presented depends on the number of bins in the histograms. In most applications, the histograms are sparse, so considering only the non-empty bins dramatically reduces the time needed for comparison.

The distances we present in this paper are experimentally validated on image retrieval and the positioning of mobile robots through image recognition.

1 Introduction

A histogram of a set with respect a measurement represents the frequency of quantified values of that measurement in the samples. Finding the distance or similarity between histograms is important in pattern classification or clustering and image retrieval. Several measures of similarity between histograms have therefore been used in computer vision and pattern recognition.

Most of the distance measures in the literature (there is an interesting compilation in [1]) consider the overlap or intersection between two histograms as a function of the distance value but do not take into account the similarity in the non-overlapping parts of the two histograms. For this reason, Rubner presented in [2] a new definition of the distance measure between histograms that overcomes this problem of non-overlapping parts. Called Earth Mover's Distance, it is defined as the minimum amount of work that must be performed to transform one histogram into another by moving distribution mass. This author used the simplex algorithm. Later, Cha presented in [1] three algorithms for obtaining the distance between one-dimensional histograms that use the Earth Mover's Distance. These algorithms compute the distance between histograms when the type of measurements are *nominal*, *ordinal* and *modulo* in $O(z)$, $O(z)$ and $O(z^2)$, respectively, and where z the number of levels or bins.

Often, for specific set measurements, only a small fraction of the *bins* in a histogram contains significant information, i.e. most of the *bins* are empty. This is more frequent

M. Lazo and A. Sanfeliu (Eds.): CIARP 2005, LNCS 3773, pp. 1027 – 1035, 2005.

when the dimensions of the element domain increase. In such cases, the methods that use histograms as fixed-sized structures are not very efficient. For this reason, Rubner [2] presented variable-size descriptions called *signatures*, which do not explicitly consider the empty bins.

If the statistical properties of the data are known *a priori*, the similarity measures can be improved by smoothing projections, as we can see in [3]. In [4] an algorithm was presented that used the *intersection function*, L_1 *norm*, L_2 *norm* and X^2 *test* to compute the distance between histograms. In [5], the authors performed image retrieval based on colour histograms. Because the distance measure between colours is computationally expensive, they presented a low dimensional and easy-to-compute distance measure and showed that this was a lower boundary for the colour-histogram distance measure. An exact histogram-matching algorithm was presented in [6]. The aim of this algorithm was to study how various image characteristics affect colour reproduction by perturbing them in a known way.

Given two histograms, it is often useful to define a quantitative measure of their dissimilarity in order to approximate perceptual dissimilarity as well as possible. We therefore believe that a good definition of the distance between histograms needs to consider the distance between the basic features of the elements of the set i.e. similar pairs of histograms defined from different basic features may obtain different distances between histograms. We call the distance between set elements the *ground distance*.

In this paper we present the distances between histograms whose computational cost depends only on the non-empty bins rather than, as in the algorithms in [1,2], on the total number of bins. The type of measurements are *nominal*, *ordinal* and *modulo* and the computational cost is $O(z')$, $O(z')$ and $O(z'^2)$, respectively, where z' is the number of non-empty bins in the histograms. In [7], we show that these distances are the same as the distances between the histograms in [1] but that the computational time for each comparison is lower when the histograms are large or sparse. We also depict the algorithms to compute them not shown here due to lack of space.

The next sections are organised as follows. In section 2 we define the histograms and signatures. In section 3 we present three possible types of measurements and their related distances. In section 4 we use these distances as ground distances when defining the distances between signatures. In section 6 we address image retrieval problem with the proposed distance measures. Finally, we conclude by stressing the advantage of using the distance between signatures.

2 Histograms and Signatures

In this section, we formally define histograms and signatures. We end this section with a simple example to show the representations of the histograms and signatures given a set of measurements.

2.1 Histogram Definition

Let x be a measurement that can have one of T values contained in the set $X=\{x_1,...x_T\}$. Consider a set of n elements whose measurements of the value of x are $A=\{a_1,...a_n\}$, where $a_t \in X$.

The histogram of the set A along measurement x is $H(x,A)$, which is an ordered list consisting of the number of occurrences of the discrete values of x among the a_t. As we are interested only in comparing the histograms and sets of the same measurement x, $H(A)$ will be used instead of $H(x,A)$ without loss of generality. If $H_i(A)$, $1 \le i \le T$, denotes the number of elements of A that have value x_i, then $H(A)=[H_1(A), \ldots, H_T(A)]$ where

$$H_i(A) = \sum_{t=1}^{n} C_{i,t}^{A} \quad \text{and} \quad C_{i,t}^{A} = \begin{cases} 1 & \text{if } a_t = x_i \\ 0 & \text{otherwise} \end{cases} \tag{1}$$

The elements $H_i(A)$ are usually called *bins* of the histogram.

2.2 Signature Definition

Let $H(A)=[H_1(A), \ldots, H_T(A)]$ and $S(A)=[S_1(A), \ldots, S_z(A)]$ be the histogram and the signature of the set A, respectively. Each $S_k(A)$, $1 \le k \le z \le T$ comprises a pair of terms, $S_k(A)=\{w_k, m_k\}$. The first term, w_k, shows the relation between the signature $S(A)$ and the histogram $H(A)$. Therefore, if the $w_k=i$ then the second term, m_k, is the number of elements of A that have value x_i, i.e. $m_k=H_i(A)$ where $w_k<w_t \Leftrightarrow k<t$ and $m_k>0$.

The signature of a set is a lossless representation of its histogram in which the *bins* of the histogram whose value is 0 are not expressed implicitly. From the signature definition, we obtain the following expression,

$$H_{w_k}(A) = m_k \quad where \quad 1 \le k \le z \tag{2}$$

2.3 Extended Signature

The **extended signature** is one in which some empty bins have been added. That is, we allow $m_i=0$ for some bins. This is a useful structure for ensuring that, given a pair of signatures to be compared, the number of bins is the same and that each bin in both signatures represents the same bin in the histograms.

2.4 Example

In this section we show a pair of sets with their histogram and signature representations. This example is used to explain the distance measures in the next sections. Figure 1 shows the sets A and B and their histogram representations. Both sets have 10 elements between 1 and 8. The horizontal axis in the histograms represents the values of the elements and the vertical axis represents the number of elements with this value.

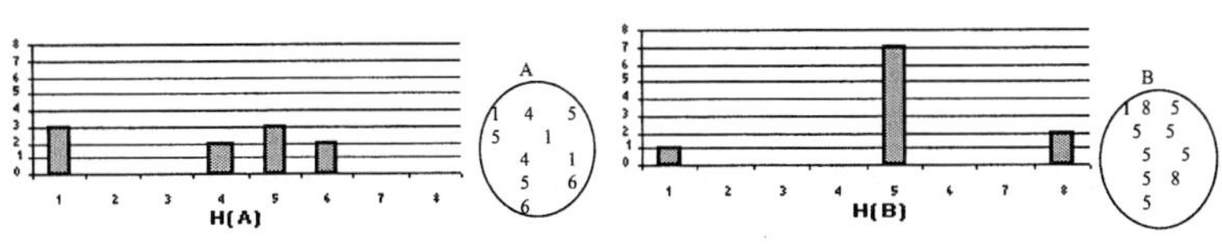

Fig. 1. Sets A and B and their histograms

Figure 2 shows the signature representation of sets *A* and *B*. The length of the signatures is 4 and 3, respectively. The vertical axis represents the number of elements of each bin and the horizontal axis represents the bins of the signature. Set A has 2 elements with a value of 6 since this value is represented by the bin 4 ($W_4^A=6$) and the value of the vertical axis is 2 at bin 4.

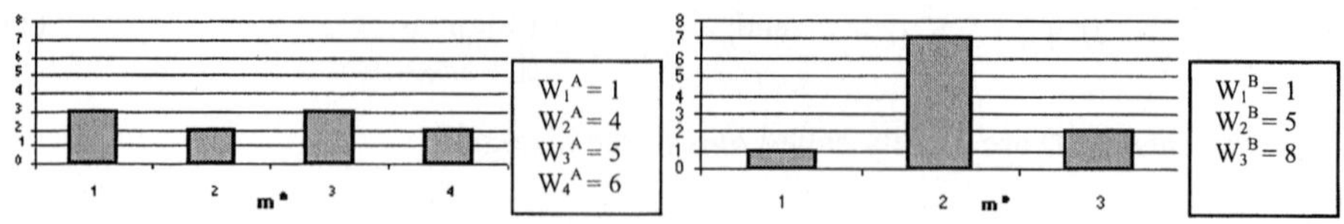

Fig. 2. Signature representation of the sets A and B

Figure 3 shows the extended signatures of the sets *A* and *B* with *5* bins. Note that the value that the extended signatures represents for each bin, w_i, is the same for both signatures.

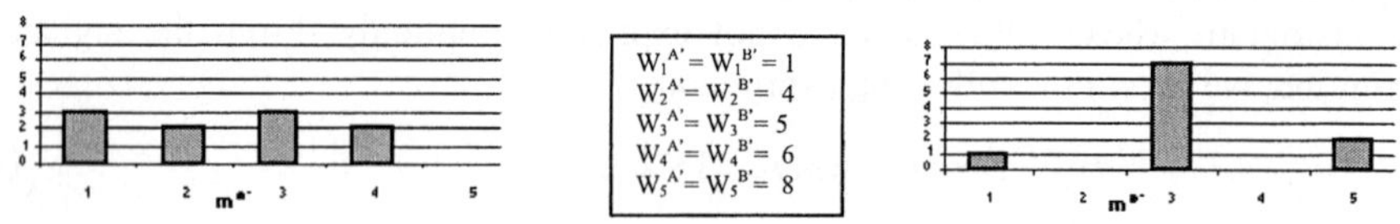

Fig. 3. Extended Signatures A' and B'. The number of elements m_i is represented graphically and the value of its elements is represented by w_i.

3 Type of Measurements and Distance Between Them

We consider three types of measurements, called nominal, ordinal and modulo. In a nominal measurement, each value of the measurement is a name and there is no relation, such as greater than or lower than, between them (e.g. the names of students). In an ordinal measurement, the values are ordered (e.g. the age of the students). Finally, in a modulo measurement, the values are ordered but they form a ring because of the arithmetic modulo operation (e.g. the angle in a circumference).

Corresponding to these three types of measurements, we define three measures of difference between two measurement levels $a \in X$ and $b \in X$, as follows:

a) Nominal distance:

$$d_{nom}(a,b) = \begin{cases} 0 & if \quad a = b \\ 1 & otherwise \end{cases} \tag{3}$$

The distance value between two nominal measurement values is either match or mismatch, which are mathematically represented by 0 or 1.

b) Ordinal distance:

$$d_{ord}(a,b)=|a-b| \tag{4}$$

The distance value between two ordinal measurement values is computed by the absolute difference of each element.

c) Modulo distance:

$$d_{\text{mod}}(a,b)=\begin{cases} |a-b| & \textit{if } |a-b|\le T/2 \\ T-|a-b| & \textit{otherwise} \end{cases} \tag{5}$$

The distance value between two modulo measurement values is the interior difference of each element.

4 Distance Between Signatures

In this section, we present the nominal, ordinal and modulo distances between signatures. For the following definitions of the distances and for the algorithms section, we assume that the extended signatures of *S(A)* and *S(B)* are *S(A')* and *S(B')*, respectively, where $S_i(A')=\{w_i^{A'},m_i^{A'}\}$ and $S_i(B')=\{w_i^{B'},m_i^{B'}\}$. The number of bins of *S(A)* and *S(B)* is z^A and z^B and the number of bins of both extended signatures is z'.

4.1 Nominal Distance

The nominal distance between the histograms in [5] is the number of elements that do not overlap or intersect. We redefine this distance using signatures as follows,

$$D_{nom}(S(A),S(B))=\sum_{i=1}^{z'}\left|m_i^{A'}-m_i^{B'}\right| \tag{6}$$

4.2 Ordinal Distance

The ordinal distance between two histograms was presented in [6] as the minimum work needed to transform one histogram into another. Histogram *H(A)* can be transformed into histogram *H(B)* by moving elements to the left or to the right and the total number of all the necessary minimum movements is the distance between them. There are two operations. Suppose an element *a* that belongs to bin *i*. One operation is *move left (a)*. This result of this operation is that element *a* belongs to bin *i-1* and its cost is 1. This operation is impossible for the elements that belong to bin *1*. Another operation is *move right (a)*. Similarly, after this operation, *a* belongs to bin *i+1* and the cost is 1. The same restriction applies to the right-most bin. These operations are graphically represented by right-to-left arrows and left-to-right arrows. The total number of arrows is the distance value. This is the shortest movement and there is no other way to move elements in shorter steps and transform one histogram to the other. The distance between signatures is defined as follows,

$$D_{ord}(S(A),S(B))=\sum_{i=1}^{z'-1}\left[\left(w_{i+1}^{A'}-w_i^{A'}\right)\left|\sum_{j=1}^{i}\left(m_j^{A'}-m_j^{B'}\right)\right|\right] \tag{7}$$

The arrows do not have a constant size (or constant cost) but depend on the distance between bins. If element a belongs to bin i, the result of operation *move left (a)* is that the element a belongs to bin i-1 and its cost is $w_i - w_{i-1}$. Similarly, after the operation *move right(a)*, the element a belongs to bin i+1 and the cost is $w_{i+1} - w_i$. In equation (7), the number of arrows that go from bin i to bin i+1 is described by the inner addition and the cost of these arrows is $w_{i+1} - w_i$.

4.3 Modulo Distance

One major difference in modulo type histograms or signatures is that the first bin and the last bin are considered to be adjacent to each other. It therefore forms a closed circle due to the nature of the data type. Transforming a modulo type histogram or signature into another while computing their distance should allow cells to move from the first bin to the last bin, or vice versa, at the cost of a single movement. Now, cells or blocks of earth can move from the first bin to the last bin with the operation *move left (1)* in the histogram case or *move left (w_1)* in the signature case. Similarly, blocks can move from the last bin to the first one with the operations *move right (T)* in the histogram case or *move right ($w_{z'}$)* in the signature case.

The cost of these operations is calculated as for the cost of the operations in the ordinal distance except for the movements of blocks from the first bin to the last or vice versa. For the distance between histograms, the cost, as in all the movements, is one. For the distance between signatures, the real distance between bins or the length of the arrows has to be considered. The cost of these movements is therefore the sum of three terms (see figure 4.a): (a) the cost from the last bin of the signature, $w_{z'}$, to the last bin of the histogram, T; (b) the cost from the last bin of the histogram, T, to the first bin of the histogram, 1; (c) the cost from the first bin of the histogram, 1, to the first bin of the signature, w_1. The costs are then calculated as the length of these terms. The cost of (a) is T-$w_{z'}$, the cost of (b) is 1 (similar to the cost between histograms) and the cost of (c) is w_1-1. Therefore, the final cost from the last bin to the first or vice versa between signatures is w_1-$w_{z'}$+T.

Example. Figure 4.b shows graphically the minimum arrows needed to get the modulo distance in (a) the histogram case and (b) the signature case. The distance is

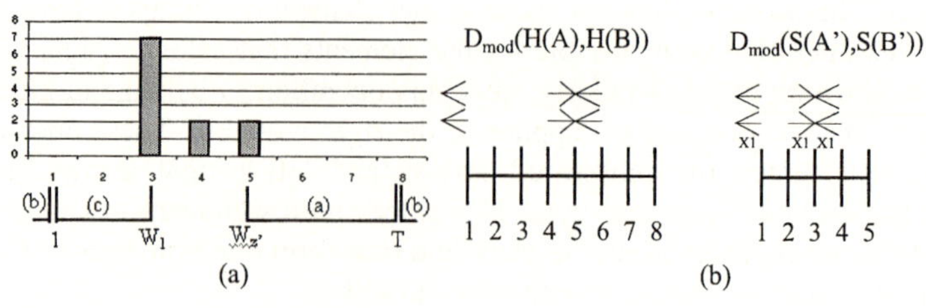

Fig. 4. (a) The three terms that need to be considered in order to compute the cost of moving blocks from the last bin to the first or vice versa in the modulo distance between signatures. (b) Arrow representation of the modulo distance in case of the histograms and signatures.

obtained as in the ordinal example except that the arrows from the first bin to the last are allowed or vice versa. The value of the distance between signatures is 2x1+2x1+2x1=6. In this signature representation, the cost of the two arrows that go from the first bin to the last bin is one. This is because $w_1=1$ (the first bin in the histogram representation) and $w_5=8$ (the last bin in the histogram representation, T=8). This cost is then 1-8-8=1.

Due to the previously explained modulo properties, we can transform one signature or histogram into another in several ways. In one of these ways, there is a minimum distance whose number of movements (or the cost of the arrows and the number of arrows) is the lowest. If there is a borderline between bins that has both directional arrows, they are cancelled out. These movements are redundant, so the distance cannot be obtained through this configuration of arrows. To find the minimum configuration of arrows, we can add a complete chain in the histogram or signature of the same directional arrows and the opposite arrows on the same border between bins are then cancelled out. The modulo distance between signatures is defined as

$$D_{\mathrm{mod}}(S(A),S(B)) = \min_{c}\left\{\sum_{i=1}^{z'-1}\left[\left(w_{i+1}^{A'}-w_{i}^{A'}\right)\left|c+\sum_{j=1}^{i}\left(m_{j}^{A'}-m_{j}^{B'}\right)\right|\right]+\left(w_{1}^{A'}-w_{z'}^{A'}+T\right)|c|\right\} \quad (8)$$

The cost of moving a block of earth from one bin to another is not 1 but the length of the arrows or the distance between the bins (as explained in the ordinal distance between signatures). The cost of the movement of blocks from the first bin to the last or vice versa is $w_1-w_{z'}+T$ and the cost of the other movements is $w^{A'}_{i+1}-w^{A'}_{i}$. The term c represents the chains of left arrows or right arrows added to the current arrow representation. The absolute value of c at the end of the expression is the number of chains added to the current representation. It comes from the cost of the arrows from the last bin to the first or vice versa.

Example. Figure 5 shows five different transformations of signature *S(A)* to signature *S(B)* and their related costs. In the first transformation, one chain of right arrows is added (c=1). In the second transformation, no chains are added (c=0), so the cost is the same as the ordinal distance. In the third to the last transformations, 1, 2 and 3 chains of left arrows are added, respectively. We can see that the minimum cost is 6 and c=-2, the distance value is 6 for the modulo distance and 14 for the ordinal distance.

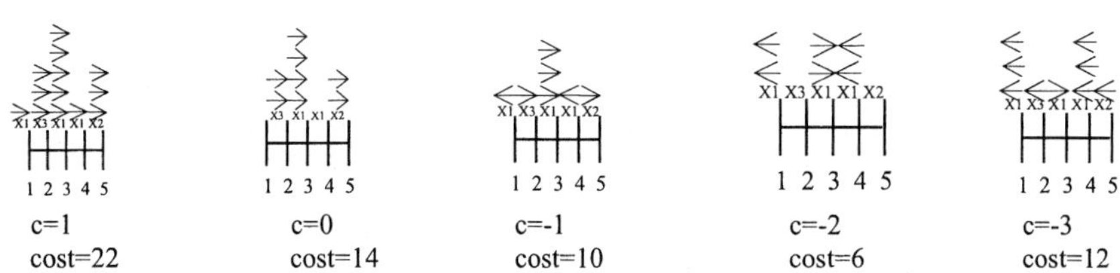

Fig. 5. Five different transformations of signature S(A) to signature S(B) with their related c and cost obtained

5 Experiment with Colour Images

To show the validity of our new method, we first tested the ordinal and modulo distances between histograms and between signatures. We used 1000 images (640 x 480 pixels) obtained from public databases. To validate the ordinal distance, we calculated the histograms from the illumination coordinate with 2^8 levels (table 1) and with 2^{16} levels (table 3). Also, to test the modulo distance, the histograms represented the hue coordinate with 2^8 levels (table 2) and with 2^{16} levels (table 4). Each table below shows the results of 5 different tests. In the first and second rows, the distance between histograms and signatures, respectively, are computed. In the other three rows, the distance between signatures is computed but, in order to reduce the length of the signature (and therefore increase the speed), the bins with fewer elements than 100, 200 or 300 in tables 1 and 2 and fewer elements than 1, 2 or 3 in tables 3 and 4 were removed. The first column shows the number of bins of the histogram (first cell) or signatures (the other four cells). The second column shows the increase in speed if we use signatures instead of histograms. It is calculated as the ratio between the run time of the histogram method and that of the signature method. The third column shows the average correctness. The last column shows the decrease in correctness as a result of using the signatures with filtered histograms, which is obtained as the ratio of the correctness of the histogram to the correctness of each filter.

Tables 1 to 4 show that our method is more useful when the number of levels increases, since the number of empty bins tends to increase. Moreover, the increase is greater when comparing the histograms of the hues, because the algorithm has a quadratic computational cost. Note that in the case of the first filter (third experiment in the tables), there is no decrease in correctness although the increase in speed is greater than with the signature method.

Table 1. Illumination 2^8 bins. Ordinal histogram.

	Length	Increase Speed	Correct.	Decrease in Correct.
Histo.	265	1	78%	1
Signa.	235	1.12	78%	1
Sig100	157	1.68	78%	1
Sig200	106	2.50	69%	0.88
Sig300	57	4.64	57%	0.73

Table 3. Illumination 2^{16} bins. Ordinal histogram.

	Length	Increase Speed	Correct.	Decrease in Correct.
Histo.	65,536	1	81%	1
Signa.	245	267.49	81%	1
Sig. 1	115	569.87	81%	1
Sig. 2	87	753.28	67%	0.82
Sig. 3	32	2048.00	55%	0.67

Table 2. Hue 2^8 bins. Modulo histogram.

	Length	Increase Speed	Correct.	Decrease in Correct.
Histo.	265	1	86%	1
Signa.	215	1.23	86%	1
Sig100	131	2.02	85%	0.98
Sig200	95	2.78	73%	0.84
Sig300	45	5.88	65%	0.75

Table 4. Hue 2^{16} bins. Modulo histogram.

	Length	Increase Speed	Correct.	Decrease in Correct.
Histo.	65,536	1	89%	1
Signa.	205	319.68	89%	1
Sig. 1	127	516.03	89%	1
Sig. 2	99	661.97	78%	0.87
Sig. 3	51	1285.01	69%	0.77

6 Conclusions

We have presented the nominal, ordinal and modulo distance between signatures. We have shown that signatures are a lossless representation of histograms and that computing the distances between signatures is the same as computing the distances between histograms but with a lower computational time. We have validated these new distances with a huge amount of real images and observed an important saving of time since most of the histograms are sparse. Moreover, when we applied filtering techniques to the histograms, the number of bins of the signatures decreased, so the run time of their comparison also decreased.

References

1. S.-H. Cha, S. N. Srihari, "On measuring the distance between histograms" Pattern Recognition 35, pp: 1355–1370, 2002.
2. Y. Rubner, C. Tomasi, and L. J. Guibas, "A Metric for Distributions with Applications to Image Databases" International Journal of Computer Vision 40 (2), pp: 99-121, 2000.
3. J.-K. Kamarainen, V. Kyrki, J. Llonen, H. Kälviäinen, "Improving similarity measures of histograms using smoothing projections", Pattern Recognition Letters 24, pp: 2009–2019, 2003.
4. F.-D. Jou, K.-Ch. Fan, Y.-L. Chang, "Efficient matching of large-size histograms", Pattern Recognition Letters 25, pp: 277–286, 2004.
5. J.Hafner, J.S. Sawhney, W. Equitz, M. Flicker & W. Niblack, "Efficient Colour Histogram Indexing for Quadratic Form Distance Functions", Trans. On Pattern Analysis and Machine Intelligence, 17 (7), pp: 729-735, 1995.
6. J. Morovic, J. Shaw & P-L. Sun, "A fast, non-iterative and exact histogram matching algorithm", Pattern Recognition Letters 23, pp:127–135, 2002.
7. F. Serratosa & A. Sanfeliu, "Signatures versus Histograms: Definitions, Distances and Algorithms", Submitted to Pattern recognition, 2005.

Median Associative Memories: New Results

Humberto Sossa and Ricardo Barrón

Centro de Investigación en Computación-IPN,
Av. Juan de Dios Bátiz, esquina con Miguel Othón de Mendizábal,
Mexico City, 07738. Mexico
hsossa@cic.ipn.mx, rbarron@cic.ipn.mx

Abstract. Median associative memories (MEDMEMs) first described in [1] have proven to be efficient tools for the reconstruction of patterns corrupted with mixed noise. First formal conditions under which these tools are able to reconstruct patterns either from the fundamental set of patterns and from distorted versions of them were given in [1]. In this paper, new more accurate conditions are provided that assure perfect reconstruction. Numerical and real examples are also given.

1 Introduction

An associative memory (**M**) as described in [1] can be viewed as a device that relates input patterns and output patterns: $\mathbf{x} \rightarrow \mathbf{M} \rightarrow \mathbf{y}$, with **x** and **y**, respectively the input and output patterns vectors. Each input vector forms an association with a corresponding output vector. The associative memory **M** is represented by a matrix whose *ij*-th component is m_{ij}. **M** is generated from a finite a priori set of known associations, known as the *fundamental set of associations*, or simply the *fundamental set* (FS). If ξ is an index, the fundamental set is represented as: $\{(\mathbf{x}^{\xi}, \mathbf{y}^{\xi}) \mid \xi = 1,2,\ldots,p\}$ with p the cardinality of the set. Patterns that form the fundamental set are called *fundamental patterns*. If it holds that $\mathbf{x}^{\xi} = \mathbf{y}^{\xi}\ \forall\, \xi \in \{1,2,\ldots p\}$, then **M** is auto-associative, otherwise it is hetero-associative. A distorted version of a pattern $\mathbf{x}$ to be recalled will be denoted as $\tilde{\mathbf{x}}$. If when feeding a distorted version of $\mathbf{x}^{w}$ with $w \in \{1,2,\ldots,p\}$ to an associative memory **M**, then it happens that the output corresponds exactly to the associated pattern $\mathbf{y}^{w}$, we say that recalling is robust, if $\mathbf{x}^{w}$ is not distorted recalling is perfect. Several models for associative memories have emerged in the last 40 years. Refer for example to [3-6].

In [1] we first described an associative model based on the functioning of well-known median operator. Also in this paper was given a first set of formal conditions under which the proposed set of memories operate. In this paper, we provide more accurate conditions for the functioning of these memories. Examples with synthetic and real data are also given.

M. Lazo and A. Sanfeliu (Eds.): CIARP 2005, LNCS 3773, pp. 1036 – 1046, 2005.

2 Basics of Median Associative Memories

Two associative memories are fully described in [1]. Due to space limitations, only hetero-associative memories are described. Auto-associative memories can be obtained simple by doing $\mathbf{x}^{\xi} = \mathbf{y}^{\xi}\ \forall \xi \in \{1,2,\ldots p\}$. Let us designate hetero-associative median memories as HAM-memories. Let $\mathbf{x} \in \mathbf{Z}^n$ and $\mathbf{y} \in \mathbf{Z}^m$ two vectors. To operate HAM memories two operations are required, one for memory training: $\Diamond_{\mathrm{A}}$ and one for pattern recall: $\Diamond_{\mathrm{B}}$.

2.1 Memory Construction

Two steps are required to build the HAM-memory:

Step 1: For each $\xi = 1,2,\cdots,p$, from each couple $\left(\mathbf{x}^{\xi},\mathbf{y}^{\xi}\right)$ build matrix: $\left[\mathbf{y}^{\xi} \Diamond_{\mathrm{A}} \left(\mathbf{x}^{\xi}\right)^t\right]_{m\times n}$ as:

$$\mathbf{y}\ \Diamond_{\mathrm{A}} \mathbf{x}^t = \begin{pmatrix} \mathrm{A}(y_1,x_1) & \mathrm{A}(y_1,x_2) & \cdots & \mathrm{A}(y_1,x_n) \\ \mathrm{A}(y_2,x_1) & \mathrm{A}(y_2,x_2) & \cdots & \mathrm{A}(y_2,x_n) \\ \vdots & \vdots & \ddots & \vdots \\ \mathrm{A}(y_m,x_1) & \mathrm{A}(y_m,x_2) & \cdots & \mathrm{A}(y_m,x_n) \end{pmatrix}_{m\times n} \tag{1}$$

Step 2: Apply the median operator to the matrices obtained in Step 1 to get matrix $\mathbf{M}$ as follows:

$$\mathbf{M} = \operatorname*{\mathbf{med}}_{\xi=1}^{p}\left[\mathbf{y}^{\xi} \Diamond_{\mathrm{A}} \left(\mathbf{x}^{\xi}\right)^t\right] \tag{2}$$

The *ij*-th component $\mathbf{M}$ is given as follows:

$$m_{ij} = \operatorname*{\mathbf{med}}_{\xi=1}^{p} \mathrm{A}\left(y_i^{\xi}, x_j^{\xi}\right). \tag{3}$$

2.2 Pattern Recall

We have two cases:

Case 1: Recall of a fundamental pattern. A pattern $\mathbf{x}^w$, with $w \in \{1,2,\cdots,p\}$ is presented to the memory $\mathbf{M}$ and the following operation is done:

$$\mathbf{M} \Diamond_{\mathrm{B}} \mathbf{x}^w. \tag{4}$$

The result is a column vector of dimension n, with i-th component given as:

$$\left(\mathbf{M}\Diamond_{\mathrm{B}}x^{w}\right)_i = \operatorname*{\mathbf{med}}_{j=1}^{n} \mathrm{B}\left(m_{ij}, x_j^{w}\right). \tag{5}$$

Case 2: Recall of a pattern from an altered version of it. A pattern $\tilde{\mathbf{x}}$ (altered version of a pattern $\mathbf{x}^{w}$ is presented to the HAM memory $\mathbf{M}$ and the following operation is done:

$$\mathbf{M}\Diamond_{\mathrm{B}}\tilde{\mathbf{x}}. \tag{6}$$

Again, the result is a column vector of dimension n, with i-th component given as:

$$\left(\mathbf{M}\Diamond_{\mathrm{B}}\tilde{\mathbf{x}}\right)_i = \operatorname*{\mathbf{med}}_{j=1}^{n} \mathrm{B}\left(m_{ij}, \tilde{x}_j\right). \tag{7}$$

Operators A and B might be chosen among those already proposed in the literature. In this paper we adopt operators A and B used in [6]. Operators A and B are defined as follows:

$$\mathrm{A}(x, y) = x - y \tag{8.a}$$

$$\mathrm{B}(x, y) = x + y \tag{8.b}$$

Conditions, for perfect recall of a pattern of the FS or from an altered version of them, according to [1] follow:

Theorem 1 [1]. Let $\left\{\left(\mathbf{x}^{\alpha}, \mathbf{y}^{\alpha}\right) \mid \alpha = 1,2,\ldots,p\right\}$ with $\mathbf{x}^{\alpha} \in \mathbf{R}^{n}$, $\mathbf{y}^{\alpha} \in \mathbf{R}^{m}$ the fundamental set of an HAM-memory $\mathbf{M}$ and let $\left(\mathbf{x}^{\gamma}, \mathbf{y}^{\gamma}\right)$ an arbitrary fundamental couple with $\gamma \in \{1,\cdots,p\}$. If $\operatorname*{\mathbf{med}}_{j=1}^{n} \varepsilon_{ij} = 0$, $i = 1,\cdots,m$, $\varepsilon_{ij} = m_{ij} - \mathrm{A}\left(y_i^{\gamma}, x_j^{\gamma}\right)$ then $\left(\mathbf{M}\Diamond_{\mathrm{B}}\mathbf{x}^{\gamma}\right)_i = \mathbf{y}_i^{\gamma}, i = 1\ldots m$.

Corollary 1 [1]. Let $\left\{\left(\mathbf{x}^{\alpha}, \mathbf{y}^{\alpha}\right) \mid \alpha = 1,2,\ldots,p\right\}$, $\mathbf{x}^{\alpha} \in \mathbf{R}^{n}$, $\mathbf{y}^{\alpha} \in \mathbf{R}^{m}$. A HAM-median memory $\mathbf{M}$ has perfect recall if for all $\alpha = 1,\cdots,p$, $\mathbf{M}^{\alpha} = \mathbf{M}$ where $\mathbf{M} = \mathbf{y}^{\xi}\Diamond_{\mathrm{A}}\left(\mathbf{x}^{\xi}\right)^{t}$ is the associated partial matrix to the fundamental couple $\left(\mathbf{x}^{\alpha}, \mathbf{y}^{\alpha}\right)$ and p is the number of couples.

Theorem 2 [1]. Let $\left\{\left(\mathbf{x}^{\alpha}, \mathbf{y}^{\alpha}\right) \mid \alpha = 1,2,\ldots,p\right\}$, $\mathbf{x}^{\alpha} \in \mathbf{R}^{n}$, $\mathbf{y}^{\alpha} \in \mathbf{R}^{m}$ a FS with perfect recall. Let $\eta^{\alpha} \in \mathbf{R}^{n}$ a pattern of mixed noise. A HAM-median memory $\mathbf{M}$ has perfect recall in the presence of mixed noise if this noise is of median zero, this is if $\operatorname*{\mathbf{med}}_{j=1}^{n} \eta_j^{\alpha} = 0, \forall\alpha$.

2.3 Case of a General Fundamental Set

In [2], it was shown that due to, in general, a fundamental set (FS) does not satisfy the restricted conditions imposed by Theorems 1 and its Corollary. In [2] it is proposed the following procedure to transform a general FS into an auxiliary FS' satisfying the desired conditions:

TRAINING PHASE:

Step 1. Transform the FS into an auxiliary fundamental set (FS') satisfying Theorem 1:

1) Make $D = cont$, a vector.
2) Make $(\bar{\mathbf{x}}^1, \bar{\mathbf{y}}^1) = (\mathbf{x}^1, \mathbf{y}^1)$.
3) For the remaining couples do {
   For $\xi = 2$ to p {
   $\bar{x}^{\xi} = \bar{x}^{\xi-1} + D$; $\hat{\mathbf{x}}^{\xi} = \bar{\mathbf{x}}^{\xi} - \mathbf{x}^{\xi}$; $\bar{y}^{\xi} = \bar{y}^{\xi-1} + D$; $\hat{\mathbf{y}}^{\xi} = \bar{\mathbf{y}}^{\xi} - \mathbf{y}^{\xi}$.
   }

Step 2. Build matrix **M** in terms of set FS': Apply to FS' steps 1 and 2 of the training procedure described at the beginning of this section.

RECALLING PHASE:

We have also two cases, i.e.:

Case 1: Recalling of a fundamental pattern of FS:

1) Transform $\mathbf{x}^{\xi}$ to $\bar{\mathbf{x}}^{\xi}$ by applying the following transformation: $\bar{\mathbf{x}}^{\xi} = \mathbf{x}^{\xi} + \hat{\mathbf{x}}^{\xi}$.
2) Apply equations (4) and (5) to each $\bar{\mathbf{x}}^{\xi}$ of FS' to recall $\bar{\mathbf{y}}^{\xi}$
3) Recall each $\mathbf{y}^{\xi}$ by applying the following inverse transformation: $\mathbf{y}^{\xi} = \bar{\mathbf{y}}^{\xi} - \hat{\mathbf{y}}^{\xi}$.

Case 2: Recalling of a pattern $\mathbf{y}^{\xi}$ from an altered version of its key: $\tilde{\mathbf{x}}^{\xi}$:

1) Transform $\tilde{\mathbf{x}}^{\xi}$ to $\bar{\mathbf{x}}^{\xi}$ by applying the following transformation: $\bar{\mathbf{x}}^{\xi} = \tilde{\mathbf{x}}^{\xi} + \hat{\mathbf{x}}^{\xi}$.
2) Apply equations (6) and (7) to $\bar{\mathbf{x}}^{\xi}$ to get $\bar{\mathbf{y}}^{\xi}$, and
3) Anti-transform $\bar{\mathbf{y}}^{\xi}$ as $\mathbf{y}^{\xi} = \bar{\mathbf{y}}^{\xi} - \hat{\mathbf{y}}^{\xi}$ to get $\mathbf{y}^{\xi}$.

3 New Results About MEDMEMs

In general, noise added to a pattern does not satisfy the conditions imposed by Theorem 2. The following new results (in the transformed domain) state the conditions under which MEDMEMS present perfect recall under general mixed noise:

Theorem 3. Let $\{(\mathbf{x}^\alpha, \mathbf{y}^\alpha) \mid \alpha = 1,2,\ldots,p\}$, $\mathbf{x}^\alpha \in \mathbf{R}^n$, $\mathbf{y}^\alpha \in \mathbf{R}^m$ a fundamental set $\mathbf{x}^{\xi+1} = \mathbf{x}^\xi + D$, $\mathbf{y}^{\xi+1} = \mathbf{y}^\xi + D$, $\xi = 1,2,\ldots,p$, $D = (d,\cdots,d)^T$, $d = Const$. Without lost of generality suppose that is p odd. Thus the associative memory $\mathbf{M} = \mathbf{y}^\xi \Diamond_{\mathrm{A}} (\mathbf{x}^\xi)^T$ has perfect recall in the presence of noise if less than $\frac{n+1}{2} - 1$ of the elements of any of the input patterns are distorted by mixed noise.

In other words, it is enough that less than 50% of the elements of a pattern of the FS be distorted by mixed noise of any level so that the pattern is perfectly recalled. Let us verify this with an example:

Example 1. Let us suppose the following fundamental set of patterns in the transformed domain, obtained from a general FS as explained in section 2.3:

$$\mathbf{x}^1 = \begin{pmatrix} 2 \\ 1 \\ 0 \\ 3 \\ 1 \end{pmatrix}, \mathbf{y}^1 = \begin{pmatrix} 2 \\ 1 \\ 3 \end{pmatrix}; \mathbf{x}^2 = \begin{pmatrix} 7 \\ 6 \\ 5 \\ 8 \\ 6 \end{pmatrix}, \mathbf{y}^2 = \begin{pmatrix} 7 \\ 6 \\ 8 \end{pmatrix} \text{ and } \mathbf{x}^3 = \begin{pmatrix} 12 \\ 11 \\ 10 \\ 13 \\ 11 \end{pmatrix}, \mathbf{y}^3 = \begin{pmatrix} 12 \\ 11 \\ 13 \end{pmatrix}.$$

According to Corollary 1, one can easily verify that:

$$\mathbf{M} = \mathbf{y}^1 \Diamond_{\mathrm{A}} (\mathbf{x}^1)^T = \begin{pmatrix} 0 & 1 & 2 & -1 & 1 \\ -1 & 0 & 1 & -2 & 0 \\ 1 & 2 & 3 & 0 & 2 \end{pmatrix}.$$

In this case, as $n = 5$, then according to Theorem 3 it is enough that no more than $\frac{5+1}{2} - 1 = 2$ elements of any of the patterns keys is contaminated with mixed noise for perfect recall of its corresponding pattern. Let us verify this with an example. Let us suppose the following distorted version of key $\mathbf{x}^2$, where second and fifth components (underlined) have been highly modified:

$$\tilde{\mathbf{x}} = (7 \quad \underline{33} \quad 5 \quad 8 \quad \underline{12})^T.$$

When applying equations (6) and (7), we have that:

$$\mathbf{M} \Diamond_B \tilde{\mathbf{x}} = \begin{pmatrix} \mathbf{med}(7,34,7,7,13) \\ \mathbf{med}(6,33,6,6,12) \\ \mathbf{med}(8,35,8,8,14) \end{pmatrix} = \begin{pmatrix} 7 \\ 6 \\ 8 \end{pmatrix}$$

As we can appreciate the recalled pattern exactly corresponds to the pattern: $\mathbf{y}^2$.

In case more than 50% of the elements of a key pattern are distorted by mixed noise, the recalled pattern in the transformed domain is an additive multiple of the corresponding pattern $\mathbf{y}^\xi$. Let us verify this with the following example:

Example 2. Let us suppose the following distorted version of key pattern $\mathbf{x}^2$ of example 1, where as reader can appreciate four components (underlined) appear modified:

$$\tilde{\mathbf{x}} = (\underline{9} \quad 6 \quad \underline{7} \quad \underline{10} \quad \underline{8})^T .$$

When applying equations (6) and (7), wc havc:

$$\mathbf{M} \Diamond_B \tilde{\mathbf{x}} = \begin{pmatrix} \mathbf{med}(9,7,9,9,9) \\ \mathbf{med}(8,6,8,8,8) \\ \mathbf{med}(10,8,10,10,10) \end{pmatrix} = \begin{pmatrix} 9 \\ 8 \\ 10 \end{pmatrix}.$$

Note how in this case the recalled version of $\mathbf{y}^2$, $\mathbf{y}^\xi_{recalled}$, in the transformed domain differs in 2 with respect two the original one.

The preceding fact can be formally expressed by the following:

Proposition 1. If a distorted key pattern $\tilde{\mathbf{x}}^\xi$ does satisfies the conditions imposed by Theorem 3, the recalled version, $\mathbf{y}^\xi_{recalled}$, is additive multiple of the corresponding pattern $\mathbf{y}^\xi$.

The following result provides sufficient conditions under which a fundamental pattern has perfect recall if more than 50% of its elements are distorted by mixed noise:

Theorem 4. Let $\{(\mathbf{x}^\xi, \mathbf{y}^\xi) \mid \xi = 1,2,\ldots,p\}$, $\mathbf{x}^\alpha \in \mathbf{R}^n$, $\mathbf{y}^\alpha \in \mathbf{R}^m$ a fundamental set $\mathbf{x}^{\xi+1} = \mathbf{x}^\xi + D$, $\mathbf{y}^{\xi+1} = \mathbf{y}^\xi + D$, $\xi = 1,2,\ldots,p$, $D = (d,\cdots,d)^T$, $d = Const$. Without lost of generality suppose that is p odd. Thus the associative memory $\mathbf{M} = \mathbf{y}^\xi \Diamond_{\mathrm{A}} (\mathbf{x}^\xi)^T$ has perfect recall in the presence of noise if more than $\dfrac{n+1}{2} - 1$ of its components are distorted by noise with absolute magnitude less than $d/2$. The index of its corresponding pattern is given by: $i = \arg\min_l d(m_{1j} \Diamond_B x_j^\xi, y_1^l), \xi = 1,\cdots,p$.

Example 3. The absolute magnitude of the noise added to key pattern $\mathbf{x}^2$ in example 2 is less than $d/2 = 5/2 = 2.5$ unities, thus according to Theorem 4:

$$i = \arg\min_l d\left(m_{1j} \Diamond_B x_j^k, y_1^l\right) = \arg\min_l \left(|9-2|, |9-7|, |9-12|\right) = 2 .$$

Thus, the pattern associated to the distorted key is $\mathbf{y}^2$ as predicted by Theorem 4. A special case of Theorem 4 is given by the following:

Corollary 2. Let $\{(\mathbf{x}^\xi, \mathbf{y}^\xi) \mid \xi = 1,2,\ldots,p\}$, $\mathbf{x}^\alpha \in \mathbf{R}^n$, $\mathbf{y}^\alpha \in \mathbf{R}^m$ a fundamental set $\mathbf{x}^{\xi+1} = \mathbf{x}^\xi + D$, $\mathbf{y}^{\xi+1} = \mathbf{y}^\xi + D$, $\xi = 1,2,\ldots,p$, $D = (d,\cdots,d)^T$, $d = Const.$ Without lost of generality let us suppose that p is odd. Thus the associative memory $\mathbf{M} = \mathbf{y}^\xi \Diamond_A (\mathbf{x}^\xi)^T$ has perfect recall in the presence of noise if all the components of any pattern are distorted but the absolute magnitude of the noise added to them is less than $d/2$. The index of its corresponding pattern is given by: $i = \arg\min_l d\left(m_{1j} \Diamond_B x_j^\xi, y_1^l\right), \xi = 1,\cdots,p$.

Example 4. Let us suppose the following distorted version of key $\mathbf{x}^2$ of example 1 where now all elements have been modified:

$$\tilde{\mathbf{x}} = \begin{pmatrix} 9 & 5 & 3 & 10 & 7 \end{pmatrix}^T .$$

By applying equations (6) and (7), we have:

$$\mathbf{M} \Diamond_B \tilde{\mathbf{x}} = \begin{pmatrix} \mathbf{med}(9,6,5,9,8) \\ \mathbf{med}(8,5,4,8,7) \\ \mathbf{med}(10,7,6,10,9) \end{pmatrix} = \begin{pmatrix} 8 \\ 7 \\ 9 \end{pmatrix} .$$

The index of the corresponding pattern is obtained as:

$$i = \arg\min_l d\left(m_{1j} \Diamond_B x_j^k, y_1^l\right) = \arg\min_l \left(|8-2|, |8-7|, |8-12|\right) = 2 .$$

Thus, the pattern associated to the distorted key is $\mathbf{y}^2$ as expected.

4 Experiments with Real Patterns

In this section, it is shown the applicability of the results given in section 3. Experiments were performed on different sets of images. In this paper we show the results obtained with photos of five famous mathematicians. These are shown in

Figure 1. The images are 51×51 pixels and 256 gray-levels. To build the memory, each image $f_{51 \times 51}(i, j)$ was first converted to a pattern vector $\mathbf{x}^{\xi}$ of dimension 2,601 (51×51) elements by means of the standard scan method, giving as a result the five patterns $\mathbf{x}^{\xi} = \begin{bmatrix} x_1^{\xi} & x_2^{\xi} & \cdots & x_{2601}^{\xi} \end{bmatrix}, \xi = 1,\ldots,5$. It is not difficult to see that this set of vectors does not satisfy the conditions established by Theorem 1 and its Corollary. It is thus transformed into an auxiliary FS by means of the transformation procedure described in section 2.3, giving as a result the transformed patterns: $\mathbf{z}^{\xi} = \begin{bmatrix} z_1^{\xi} & z_2^{\xi} & \cdots & z_{2601}^{\xi} \end{bmatrix}, \xi = 1,\ldots,5$. It is not difficult to see in the transformed domain, each transformed pattern vector is an additive translation of the preceding one.

(a) (b) (c) (d) (e)

Fig. 1. Images of the five famous people used in the experiments. (a) Descartes. (b) Einstein. (c) Euler. (d) Galileo, and (e) Newton. All Images are 51×51 pixels and 256 gray levels.

First pattern vector $\mathbf{z}^1$ was used to build matrix $\mathbf{M}$. Any other pattern could be used due to according to Corollary 1: $\mathbf{M}^1 = \mathbf{M}^2 = \ldots = \mathbf{M}^5 = \mathbf{M}$. To build matrix $\mathbf{M}$, equations 1-3 were used.

4.1 Recalling of the Fundamental Set of Images

Patterns $\mathbf{z}^1$ to $\mathbf{z}^5$ were presented to matrix $\mathbf{M}$ for recall. Equations 6 and 7 were used for this purpose. In all cases, as expected, the whole FS of images was perfectly recalled.

4.2 Recalling of a Pattern from a Distorted Version of It

Three experiments were performed. In the first experiment the effectiveness of Theorem 3 was verified when less than 50% of the pixels of an image was distorted by mixed noise. In the second experiment the effectiveness of Theorem 4 was verified when all pixels of an image were distorted with noise but with absolute magnitude less than $d/2$. In the third experiment, the pixels of an image were distorted in such a way that they do not satisfy Theorems 3 to 4, no perfect recall should thus occur.

4.2.1 Effectiveness of Theorem 3

In this case the five images shown in Figure 1 were corrupted with mixed noise in such a way that less than half of its pixels changed in their values. For each photo several noisy versions with different levels of salt and pepper noisy were generated. Figure 2 shows 5 of these noisy images. Note the level of added distortion. When applying the recalling procedure described in Section 2.3, as specified by Theorem 3 in all cases as shown in Figure 2(b) the desired image was of course perfectly recalled.

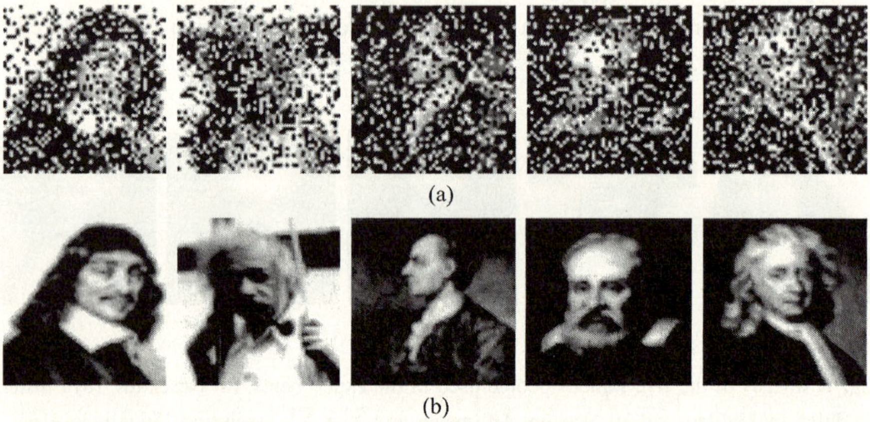

Fig. 2. (a) Noisy images used to verify the effectiveness of Theorem 3 when less than 50% of the elements of patterns are distorted by noise. (b) Recalled images.

4.2.2 Effectiveness of Theorem 4

In this case all elements of the five images shown in Figure 1 were distorted with mixed noise but respecting the restriction that the absolute magnitude of the level of noise added to a pixel is inferior to $d/2$. For each image a noisy version was generated. The five noisy versions are shown in Figure 3(a). When applying the recalling procedure described in section 2.3, as expected in all cases the desired image was perfectly recalled. Figure 3(b) shows the recalled versions.

4.2.3 Results When Recalling Conditions Are Not Satisfied

One experiment was performed. In the case more than 50% of the elements of each pattern were distorted with saturating salt and pepper noise. In this case mainly salt noise was added to the images. One noisy version for each image was generated in each case. Figure 4(b) show the noisy versions for each image. Figure 4(c) show the corresponding recalled versions. As can be appreciated in some cases, the desired image is correctly recalled. In others it is associated to other image.

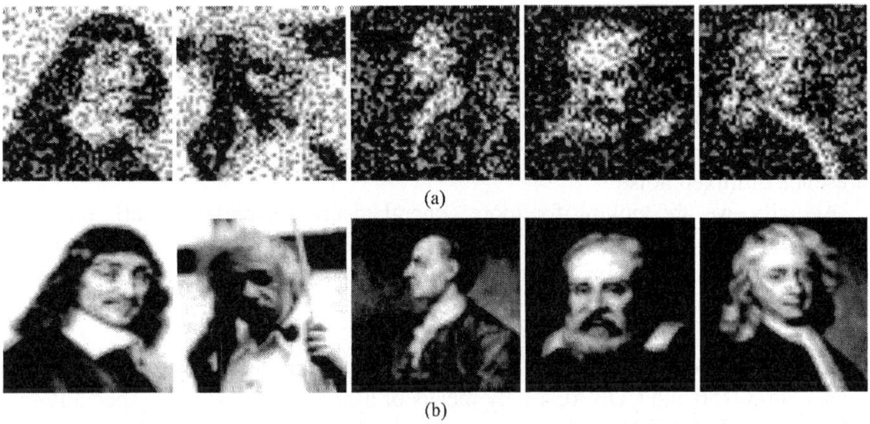

Fig. 3. (a) Noisy images used to verify the effectiveness of Corollary 2 when the absolute magnitude of the noise added to the pixels is less than $d/2$. (b) Recalled versions.

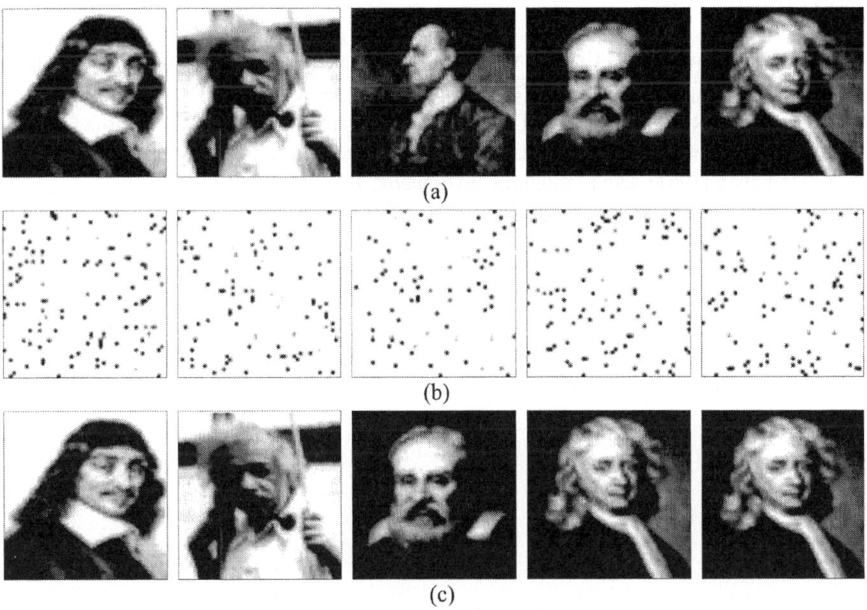

Fig. 4. (a) Original images. (b) Noisy images used to verify the effectiveness of the propositions when more than 50% of the elements of patterns are distorted by noise with absolute magnitude of noise added greater than $d/2$. In this case 99% of the elements of the images were altered. The ratio between salt noise and pepper noise added to the elements was 99 to 1. (c) Recalled images.

5 Conclusions and Present Research

In this paper we have presented some new results about median memories recently introduced in [1]. The new propositions provide new conditions under which the proposed memories can perfectly recalled a pattern of a given fundamental set in the presence of mixed noise.

Actually, we are looking for more general results for perfect recall. We are also investigating the performance of the proposed memories with other operators different form **min**, **max** and **median**. We are also searching for more efficient methods to speed up the learning and recalling procedures.

Acknowledgements. This work was economically supported by CGPI-IPN under grants 20050156 and CONACYT by means of grant 46805. H. Sossa specially thanks COTEPABE-IPN, CONACYT (Dirección de Asuntos Internacionales) and DAAD (Deutscher Akademischer Austauschdienst) for the economical support granted during research stay at Friedrich-Schiller University, Jena, Germany.

References

[1] H. Sossa, R. Barrón and R. A. Vázquez (2004). New Associative Memories to Recall Real-Valued Patterns. LNCS 3287. Springer Verlag. Pp. 195-202.

[2] H. Sossa and R. Barrón (2004). Transforming Fundamental Set of Patterns to a Canonical Form to Improve Pattern Recall. LNAI 3315. Springer Verlag. Pp. 687-696.

[3] K. Steinbuch (1961). Die Lernmatrix, *Kybernetik*, 1(1):26-45.

[4] J. A. Anderson (1972), A simple neural network generating an interactive memory, *Mathematical Biosciences*, 14:197-220.

[5] J. J. Hopfield (1982). Neural networks and physical systems with emergent collective computational abilities, *Proceedings of the National Academy of Sciences*, 79: 2554-2558, 1982.

[6] G. X. Ritter el al. (1998). Morphological associative memories, *IEEE Transactions on Neural Networks*, 9:281-293.

Language Resources for a Bilingual Automatic Index System of Broadcast News in Basque and Spanish

G. Bordel[1], A. Ezeiza[2], K. Lopez de Ipina[3], J.M. López[3], M. Peñagarikano[1], and E. Zulueta[3]

University of the Basque Country,
[1] Elektrizitate eta Elektronika Saila, Leioa
{german, mpenagar}@ehu.es
[2] Ixa taldea. Sistemen Ingeniaritza eta Automatika Saila, Donostia
aitzol.ezeiza@ehu.es
[3] Sistemen Ingeniaritza eta Automatika Saila, Gasteiz
{isplopek, josemanuel.lopez, iepzugue}@ehu.es

Abstract. Automatic Indexing of Broadcast News is a developing research area of great recent interest [1]. This paper describes the development steps for designing an automatic index system of broadcast news for both Basque and Spanish. This application requires of appropriate Language Resources to design all the components of the system. Nowadays, large and well-defined resources can be found in most widely used languages, but there is a lot of work to do with respect to minority languages. Even if Spanish has much more resources than Basque, this work has parallel efforts for both languages. These two languages have been chosen because they are evenly official in the Basque Autonomous Community and they are used in many mass media of the Community including the Basque Public Radio and Television EITB [2].

1 Introduction

Automatic Indexing of Broadcast News is a topic of growing interest for the mass media in order to take maximum output of their recorded resources. Actually, it is a challenging problem from researchers' point of view, due to many unresolved issues like speaker changes and overlapping, different background conditions, large vocabulary, etc. In order to achieve significant results in this area, high-quality language resources are required. Since the main goal of our project is the development of an index system of broadcast news in the Basque Country, our approach is to create resources for all the languages used in the mass media. The analysis of the specific linguistic problematic indicates that both Basque and Spanish are official in the Basque Autonomous Community and they are used in the Basque Public Radio and Television EITB [2] and in most of the mass media of the Basque Country (radios and newspapers). Thus it is clear that both languages have to be taken into account to develop an efficient index system. Therefore, all of the tools (ASR system, NLP system, index system) and resources (digital library, Lexicon) to be developed will be oriented to create a bilingual system in Basque and Spanish.

Spanish has been briefly studied for development of these kind of systems but the use of Basque language (a very odd minority language) introduces a new difficulty to

M. Lazo and A. Sanfeliu (Eds.): CIARP 2005, LNCS 3773, pp. 1047 – 1054, 2005.

the development of the system, since it needs specific tools and the resources available are fewer.

Basque is a Pre-Indo-European language of unknown origin and it has about 1.000.000 speakers in the Basque Country. It presents a wide dialectal distribution, including six the main dialects, and this dialectal variety entails phonetic, phonologic, and morphologic differences.

Moreover, since 1968 the Royal Academy of the Basque Language, Euskaltzaindia [3] has been involved in a standardisation process of Basque. At present, morphology, which is very rich in Basque, is completely standardised in the unified standard Basque, but the lexical standardization process is still going on. The standard Basque, called "Batua", has nowadays a great importance in the Basque community, since the public institutions and most of the mass media use it. Furthermore, people who have studied Basque as a second language use "Batua" as well.

Hence, we have made use of the standard version of Basque as well as the standard Spanish in the development of the resources presented in this work.

The following section describes the main morphological features of the language and details the statistical analysis of morphemes using three different textual samples. Section 3 presents the resources developed. Section 4 describes the processing of the data. Finally, conclusions are summarised in section 5.

2 Morphological Features of Basque

Basque is an agglutinative language with a special morpho-syntactic structure inside the words [4] that may lead to intractable vocabularies of words for a CSR when the size of task is large. A first approach to the problem is to use morphemes instead of words in the system in order to define the system vocabulary [5].

This approach has been evaluated over three textual samples analysing both the coverage and the Out of Vocabulary rate, when we use words and pseudo-morphemes obtained by the automatic morphological segmentation tool AHOZATI [6].

Table 1. Main characteristics of the textual databases for morphologic analysis

	STDBASQUE	NEWSPAPER	BCNEWS
Text amount	1,6M	1,3M	2,5M
Number of words	197,589	166,972	210,221
Number of pseudo-morphemes	346,232	304,767	372,126
Number of sentences	15,384	13,572	19,230
Vocabulary size in words	50,121	38,696	58,085
Vocabulary size in pseudo-morphemes	20,117	15,302	23,983

Table 1 shows the main features of the three textual samples relating to size, number of words and pseudo-morphemes and vocabulary size, both in words and pseudo-morphemes for each database [6].

Figure 1 shows some of the interesting conclusions derived of this analysis. The first important outcome of our analysis is that the vocabulary size of pseudo-morphemes is reduced about 60% (Fig. 1, a) in all cases relative to the vocabulary size of words. Regarding the unit size, Fig. 1 (b) shows the plot of Relative Frequency of Occurrence (RFO) of the pseudo-morphemes and words versus their length in characters over the textual sample named STDBASQUE. Although only 10% of the pseudo-morphemes in the vocabulary have fewer than four characters, such small morphemes have an Accumulated Frequency of about 40% in the databases (the Accumulated Frequency is calculated as the sum of the individual pseudo-morphemes RFO) [7].

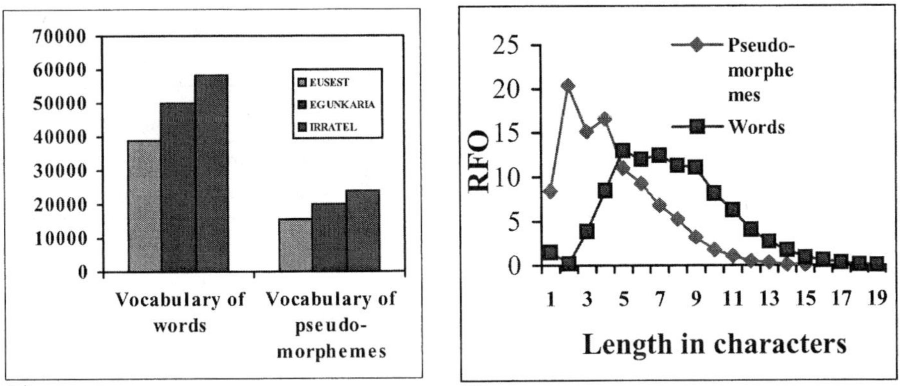

(a) (b)

Fig. 1. (a) Vocabulary size of the words and pseudo-morphemes in the three textual samples and (b) Relative Frequency of Occurrence (RFO) of the words and pseudo-morphemes in relation to their length in characters (STDBASQUE sample)

To check the validity of the unit inventory, units having less than 4 characters and having plosives at their boundaries were selected from the texts. They represent some 25% of the total. This high number of small and acoustically difficult recognition units could lead to an increase of the acoustic confusion, and could also generate a high number of insertions (Fig. 2 over the textual sample EGUNKARIA[8]).

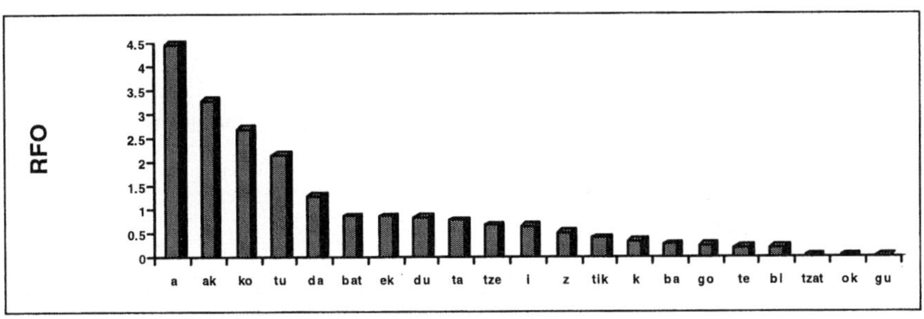

Fig. 2. Relative Frequency of Occurrence (RFO) of small and acoustically difficult recognition units in BCNEWS sample

Finally, Fig. 3 shows the analysis of coverage and Out of Vocabulary rate over the textual sample BCNEWS. When pseudo-morphemes are used, the coverage in texts is better and complete coverage is easily achieved. OOV rate is higher in this sample.

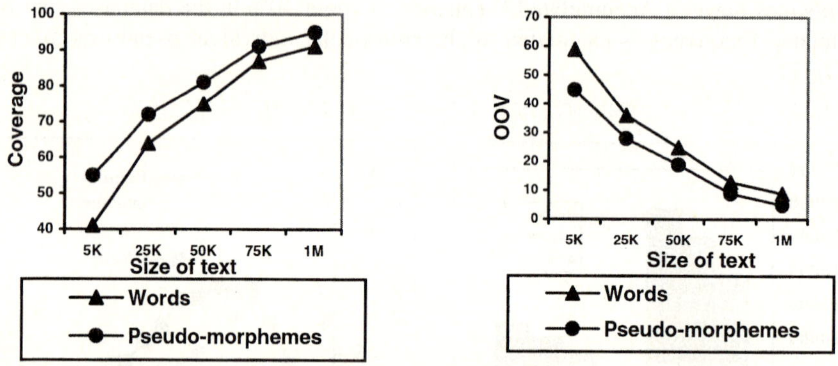

(a) (b)

Fig. 3. Coverage (a) and OOV rate (b) for the textual sample BCNEWS

3 Resources Developed

Resources in Spanish

- 6 hours of video in MPEG4 (WMV 9) format of "Teleberri" program, the daily program of broadcast news in Spanish, directly provided by the Basque Public Radio and Television EITB [2].
- 6 hours of audio (WAV format) extracted from the video (MPEG4) files.
- 6 hours of audio transcription in XML format containing information about speaker changes, noises and music fragments, and each word's phonetic and morphologic information.
- 1 year of scripts, in text format, of the "Teleberri" program. The text is divided in sentences and paragraph.
- 1 year of local newspapers in Spanish Gara [9], in text format. The text is divided in sentences and paragraph.
- Lexicon extracted from the XML transcription files, including morphologic, phonologic and orthographic information.

Resources in Basque

- 6 hours of video in MPEG4 (WMV 9) format of "Gaur Egun" program, the daily program of broadcast news in Basque directly provided by the Basque Public Radio and Television EITB [2].
- 6 hours of audio (WAV format) extracted from the video (MPEG4) files.

- 6 hours of audio transcription in XML format containing information about speaker changes, noises and music fragments, and each word's phonetic and orthographic transcription including word's lemma and Part-Of-Speech disambiguated tags.
- 1 year of scripts, in text format, of the "Gaur Egun" program.
- 1 year of local newspapers in Basque (Euskaldunon Egunkaria [8]), in text format.
- Lexicon extracted from the XML transcription files, including phonologic, orthographic, and morphologic information.

4 Processing Methodology

Processing of the Video Data

The video data used in this work has been provided directly by the Basque Public Radio and Television. The format used to store the broadcast contents is MPEG4 (WMV 9), and the Basque Public Radio and Television has been very kind offering us all these resources.

The ASR system developed doesn't actually use the useful graphical information of the videos, but the images have been used thoroughly during transcription in order to find additional information that could enrich the transcription, as names and descriptions of speakers, translation of foreign speakers' words, description tables and maps, etc.

In the near future some specific image information retrieval techniques could be incorporated to the ASR system.

Processing of the Audio Data

The audio data has been extracted out from the MPEG4 video files, using FFmpeg free software[1]. The audio files have been stored in WAV format (16 KHz, linear, 16 bits).

When the audio data was ready, the XML label files were created manually, using the Transcriber free tool [10]. The XML files include information of distinct speakers, noises, and paragraphs of the broadcast news. The transcription files follow the conventions defined in the COST278 project and they contain extra phonetic and orthographic information of each of the words. Some of the recommendations and features described by the Linguistic Data Consortium in [11] have been also included for a better interpretation of the transcription files.

These features include identification of the dialect used by speakers, correct spelling of mispronounced words, language marks for any inclusion of foreign speech in the transcription, and identification numbers for related topics in both Basque and Spanish Broadcast News.

Table 2 shows a simplified sample of the enriched version of the transcription for Basque. Some of the morphological information has been deleted to easier reading of the example.

---

[1] Available online at http://ffmpeg.sourceforge.net

Table 2. Simplified sample of the output of the Transcriber free tool [10] enriched with morpho-syntactic information of Basque

```
<Sync time="333.439"/>
+horretarako /hortarako/<Word lemma="hori" POS="ADB"/>
+denok /danok/<Word lemma="dena" POS="IZL"/>
lagundu<Word lemma="lagundu" POS="ADI"/>
behar<Word lemma="behar" POS="ADI"/>
dugu<Word lemma="*ukan" POS="ADL"/>
.
</Turn>
<Turn mode="spontaneous" fidelity="high" start-
Time="335.182" endTime="336.065">
<Sync time="335.182"/>
^Batasunak<Word lemma="9batasuna" POS="IZB"/>
```

As Basque is an agglutinative language with very rich inflection variety [4], Basque XML files include morphologic information such as each word's lemma and Part-Of-Speech tag. This information could be very useful in the development of Language Models for the recognition of continuous Speech in this context.

Using this transcribed information, a Lexicon for each language has been extracted. The Lexicon stores information of each different word that appears in the transcription. This information could be very useful for developing speech recognition tools as well as many other NLP applications.

Processing of the Textual Data

There are two independent types of textual resources: The text extracted from the newspapers Gara [9] and Euskaldunon Egunkaria [8]), and the scripts of the "Telebarri" and "Gaur Egun" programs. These last resources are very interesting because they are directly related (date, program) with the texts read in the broadcast news both in Spanish and Basque.

All of them were processed to include morphologic information such as each word's lemma and Part-Of-Speech tag. Using all the information, a Lexicon for each language has been extracted taken into account the context of the word in order to eliminate the ambiguity. The Lexicon stores information of each different word that appears in the transcription, and this information could be very useful for developing speech recognition tools. Table 3 shows some examples of the lexicon information.

The first column of Table 3 shows some example of the words as they have been transcribed from the Broadcast News audio recording. The alternative transcriptions of the word are spotted in second place, and the morphological information is later added, and it includes morpho-syntactic information, lemma information [4] and its corresponding sub-lexical unit segmentation as explained in [6].

Table 3. Sample of the Lexicon for Basque, including information extracted of the morphologic analysis of the transcription

Input	Transcription	Morphological Analysis	LEMA	Morphological segmentation
euskaldunena	ewS.'kal.du.ne.'2na	ADJ IZO DEK GEN MG DEK ABS NUMS MUGM ;	euskaldun	euskaldun=en=a;
		ADJ IZO DEK GEN NUMP MUGM DEK ABS NUMS MUGM ;		euskaldun=en=a;
		ADJ IZO GRA SUP DEK ABS NUMS MUGM		euskaldun=en=a
margolarien	mar.'Go.la.r6i.'2en	IZE ARR DEK GEN NUMP MUGM ;	margolari	margolari=en;
		IZE ARR DEK GEN NUMP MUGM DEK ABS MG		margolari=en
margolaritzan	mar.'Go.la.r6i.'2t&san mar.'Go.la.r6i.'2t&c~an	IZE ARR DEK NUMS MUGM DEK INE	margolaritza	margolaritz=an
margolaritza	mar.'go.la.r6i.'2t&sa	IZE ARR; IZE ARR DEK ABS MG ;	margolaritza	margolaritza;
	mar.'go.la.r6i.'2t&c~a	IZE ARR DEK ABS NUMS MUGM		margolaritza;
				margolaritz=a

5 Concluding Remarks

In this paper a developing system for automatic indexing of bilingual Broadcast News has been presented. Its development entails the compilation of resources for both Basque and Spanish, which are the official languages in the Basque Country, and they are used in the Basque Public Radio and Television EITB [2] and in most of the mass media of the Basque Country.

Resources for Basque have been explained in more detail, since it is a minority language with special problematic. Since it is an agglutinative language, analysis of coverage and words OOV has been carried out in order to develop an appropriate Lexicon.

Finally, we would like to remark that lexicons are enriched using morphologic and phonetic information, not just extracting a word list, so this information could be useful in future development of more sophisticated approaches in ASR systems and transcription of Broadcast News.

Acknowledgements

We would like to thank UZEI for they help extracting information about RFO of phonemes. We thank also all the people and entities that have collaborated in the development of this work: EITB [2], Gara [9] and Euskaldunon Egunkaria [8].

References

1. Vandecatseye, A., J.P. Martens, J. Neto, H. Meinedo, C. Garcia-Mateo, F.J. Dieguez, F. Mihelic, J. Zibert, J. Nouza, P. David, M. Pleva, A. Cizmar, H. Papageorgiou, C. Alexandris, 2004. The COST278 pan-European Broadcast News Database. In Proceedings of LREC 2004, Lisbon (Portugal).
2. EITB Basque Public Radio and Television, *http://www.eitb.com/*
3. Euskaltzaindia, *http://www.euskaltzaindia.net/*
4. Alegria I., Artola X., Sarasola K., Urkia M.: "Automatic morphological analysis of Basque", Literary & Linguistic Computing Vol,11, No, 4, 193-203, Oxford Univ Press, 1996.
5. Peñagarikano M., Bordel G., Varona A., Lopez de Ipina: "Using non-word Lexical Units in Automatic Speech Understanding", Proceedings of IEEE, ICASSP99, Phoenix, Arizona.
6. Lopez de Ipiña K., Graña M., Ezeiza N., Hernández M., Zulueta E., Ezeiza A., Tovar C.: "Selection of Lexical Units for Continuous Speech Recognition of Basque", Progress in Pattern Recognition, pp 244-250. Speech and Image Analysis, Springer. Berlin. 2003.
7. Lopez de Ipina K., Ezeiza N., Bordel. N., Graña M.: "Automatic Morphological Segmentation for Speech Processing in Basque" IEEE TTS Workshop. Santa Monica USA. 2002.
8. Egunkaria, Euskaldunon Egunkaria, the only newspaper in Basque, which has been recently replaced by Berria, online at *http://www.berria.info/*
9. GARA, local Basque Country newspaper in Spanish, online at *http://www.gara.net/*
10. Barras C., Geoffrois E., Wu Z., and Liberman M.: "Transcriber: a Free Tool for Segmenting, Labeling and Transcribing Speech" First International Conference on Language Resources and Evaluation (LREC-1998).
11. Linguistic Data Consortium, Design Specifications for the Transcription of Spoken Language, available online at http://www.ldc.upenn.edu/Projects/Corpus_Cookbook.

3D Assisted 2D Face Recognition: Methodology

J. Kittler, M. Hamouz, J.R. Tena, A. Hilton, J. Illingworth, and M. Ruiz

CVSSP, Surrey University, Guildford, Surrey, GU2 7XH, UK

Abstract. We address the problem of pose and illumination invariance in face recognition and propose to use explicit 3D model and variants of existing algorithms for both pose [Fit01,MSCA04] and illumination normalization [ZS04] prior to applying 2D face recognition algorithm. However, contrary to prior work we will use person specific, rather than general 3D face models. The proposed solution is realistic as for many applications the additional cost of acquiring 3D face images during enrolment of the subjects is acceptable. 3D sensing is not required during normal operation of the face recognition system. The proposed methodology achieves illumination invariance by estimating the illumination sources using the 3D face model. By-product of this process is the recovery of the face skin albedo which can be used as a photometrically normalised face image. Standard face recognition techniques can then be applied to such illumination corrected images.

1 Introduction

Face recognition is considered as one of the major challenges in computer vision. The problem is of interest to the computer vision community because of its importance in personal identity authentication for security applications, in control of physical access to buildings, in personalisation of services, in control of logical access to teleservices, in border control, and for its many other potential uses.

Face recognition differs from a normal task of object recognition in computer vision in the sense that each member of the face category (face of each individual) is considered as a separate entity. In other words, samples of the face population represent different identities. This makes the task of face recognition very difficult as individuals are distinguished by relatively minor differences in face shape and appearance. These minor differences are normally sufficient to discriminate between individuals, provided the reference face image (template) and the probe (test image of unknown identity) are acquired under controlled illumination conditions and in a standard pose, nominally the frontal one. However, in many situations the illumination conditions and the pose are difficult to control and the photometric effect of any illumination and pose changes invariably swamp the subtle differences in shape and texture of face images of two individuals.

One possibility to avoid the pose and illumination problem is to base the face recognition on 3D data rather than 2D. Different 3D sensing technologies

M. Lazo and A. Sanfeliu (Eds.): CIARP 2005, LNCS 3773, pp. 1055–1065, 2005.

have been developed to acquire 3D face images (depth images). These include stripe-based stereo systems (Minolta, Cyberware, etc.), and area-based stereo (3dMD, Surfim, Wicks and Wilson, etc.). The recognition is then accomplished by matching two 3D surfaces, a reference 3D surface (template) and a test 3D face image. This first of all involves 3D surface registration, followed by the extraction of 3D image features and finally decision making. However, the 3D face recognition approach has failed to live up to all expectations. This is partly caused by missing data, inaccuracies in surface registration and most importantly, by not making use of the discriminatory information conveyed by the skin surface texture.

A more promising alternative is to make use of 3D face shape as well as skin texture by simultaneously acquiring 3D and 2D face image. However, this solution requires a relatively expensive sensor system and may not be acceptable in many application scenarios. We propose an approach whereby the recognition, in the operational mode, is based on 2D face images only. However, the recognition process is assisted by a 3D face model. We believe that during the enrolment of a user, it is perfectly feasible to acquire a 3D model of the face using 3D sensing. The 3D model can then be associated with a 2D face template and used for the recognition of 2D test images. Given a 2D image of a face and its 3D model, it is possible to estimate the illumination sources and separate the effect of light and albedo. The albedo image can then be relighted to the same conditions as those used during the user enrolment. The photometrically corrected face image can then provide a better basis for matching.

The above process requires the 3D face model to be registered with the 2D probe image. In principle, once the two types of spatial data sets are registered, the 2D image could also be corrected for pose. However, in this paper we shall assume that the person to be recognised is cooperative and presents himself or herself in the frontal pose. No geometric correction is therefore necessary.

The idea of using a 3D model in conjunction with 2D face data has been explored before. For instance, Zhao and Chellappa [ZC00] investigated a general 3D face model, as well as shape from shading, to improve the recognition performance in an environment with varying illumination. In many respects, our work is similar, but the main difference is that we propose to use client specific 3D face model, rather than a general model. This should lead to a better accuracy in estimating the photometrically corrected image and therefore better performance rates.

In this paper we describe the methodology developed for the proposed 3D assisted 2D face recognition system. In the next section we present a review of the relevant literature. In Section 3.2 we describe the method used for registering 2D face image to a 3D face model. In Section 3.3 we discuss the method of illumination source estimation and the face relighting. Section 4 provides a brief overview of the recognition method, based on Linear Discriminant Analysis. The paper is drawn to conclusion in Section 5.

2 State of the Art

Pose and illumination were identified as major problems in 2D face recognition. Approaches trying to solve these two issues in 2D are bound to have limited performance due to the intrinsic 3D nature of the problem.

Blanz and Vetter [BV03] proposed an algorithm which takes a single image on the input and reconstructs 3D shape and illumination-free texture. Phong's model is used to capture the illumination variance. The model explicitly separates imaging parameters (such as head orientation and illumination) from personal parameters allowing invariant description of the identity of faces. Texture and shape parameters yielding the best fit are used as features. Several distance measures have been evaluated on the FERET and the CMU-PIE databases.

Basri and Jacobs [BJ03] proved that a set of images of a convex Lambertian object obtained under arbitrary illumination can be accurately approximated by a 9D linear space which can be analytically characterized using surface spherical harmonics. Zhang and Samaras [ZS04] used Blanz and Vetter's morphable model together with a spherical harmonic representation for 2D recognition. The method is reported to perform well even when multiple illuminants are present.

Yin and Yourst [YY03] describe their 3D face recognition system which uses 2D data only. The algorithm exploits 3D shape reconstructed from front and profile images of the person using a dynamic mesh. A curvature-based descriptor is computed for each vertex of the mesh. Shape and texture features are then used for matching.

These approaches represent significant steps towards the solution of illumination, pose and expression problems. However there are still several open research problems like full expression invariance, accuracy of the Lambertian model with regard to the specular properties of human skin and stability of the model in presence of glasses, beards and changing hair, etc., that need addressing.

3 Methodology of 3D Assisted Photometric Normalisation

The function of the proposed recognition system can be summarised in the the following steps:

Enrolment:

3D pose normalization $\Longrightarrow$ "3D to 3D" dense registration.

Test:

"3D to 2D" dense registration $\Longrightarrow$ Illumination correction $\Longrightarrow$ 2D recognition.

3.1 3D to 3D Registration

Data coming from the 3D sensor during the enrolment are absolute 3D coordinates relative to sensor's internal coordinate system. Such a coordinate system is typically defined by the calibration chart and is unknown to the user. Assuming that the coordinate system changes whenever the sensor moves/is recalibrated, data coming from the 3D sensor needs to be registered to a common reference coordinate system. This is necessary for subsequent stages as face surfaces of different people need to be manipulated in the same manner.

The registration process can be divided in the two following stages. First, the surface is pose normalised. This is achieved by a LM-ICP variant of Iterative Closest Point algorithm proposed by Fitzgibbon [Fit01], which assumes a rigid transformation and uses robust matching to improve performance in the presence of outliers. For such purposes a generic face surface template is used and the face surface under consideration is rotated and translated to minimize distance between the two surfaces. Practical experience shows that such registration is only approximate. Due to the inter-personal shape differences, there will always be misregistrations which cannot be expressed by a rigid transformation. However we believe that for the purpose of pose normalization, performance of ICP is adequate.

The second stage in the registration process is a fine registration. This is a necessary step in order to obtain dense correspondences between shapes. Dense correspondences are established for a pair of surfaces by finding for each point in one of them a corresponding point in the other. Constructing dense correspondences facilitates learning inter- and intra-personal shape and texture variability. Most existing algorithms solving this problem exploit the fact that although globally different, face surfaces of different people are locally similar. In other words, the deformation leading from one face surface to another can be locally constrained. This enables an efficient search for similar features. A representative method for finding dense correspondences is the method of Mao et al. [MSCA04]. The algorithm is initiated by 5 manually defined landmarks to establish initial mapping of a generic model onto the surface of an individual. Following global registration, the generic shape is further deformed locally to the input data. The similarity measure is based on a combination of curvature, distance and surface normals. The deformation process is then completed by minimizing the overall energy of the generic model. The movement of generic model vertices is restricted.

An example of the output from this algorithm is depicted in Fig. 1.

Given dense correspondences, intra- and possibly inter-personal shape variations can be analyzed. For one person, the variations are down to changes in expression and possibly aging. With textured meshes, correspondences between textures can be directly derived from 3D surface correspondence. This facilitates efficient texture analysis.

3.2 3D to 2D Registration

Given an image of a person for the purpose of verification, the 3D model has to be first registered with the 2D data. In the verification context, the algorithm proposed by Blanz and Vetter [BV03] suffers from several drawbacks. As it attempts to learn both intra- and inter-personal texture and shape variability simultaneously, the number of optimization parameters is high with too few

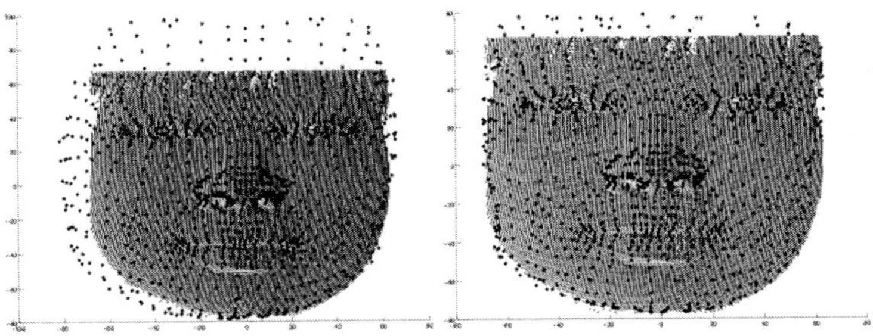

Fig. 1. Examples of registration by Mao et al [MSCA04], initial fit left, final registration right, model surface vertices depicted by dots

constraints and the algorithm often converges to a local minimum. This causes inaccuracies in both the recovered shape and texture and also computational complexity is increased. We believe that using person-specific shape and texture will greatly reduce the number of free parameters in the optimization loop and therefore the accuracy will increase. The shape model will have to capture only the expression variability of the given person and texture model mainly the illumination changes. It is unrealistic to expect that for every person enrolled there will be a huge expression training set available, and thus expression variability will have to be learnt over different people. However, the resulting inaccuracies for the given person will be compensated by introducing person-specific shape in the optimization process. To train such a model, densely registered shape and texture data (described above) are needed. As a part of a score function to be minimized, an illumination factor has to be defined. Recently, Basri and Jacobs [BJ03] have proposed a novel approach for modelling Lambertian reflectance cxploiting 3D information.

3.3 Illumination Model Using Spherical Harmonics

Belhumeur and Kriegman proved that the set of images of an object in fixed pose but under all possible illumination conditions is a convex cone (illumination cone) [BK96]. The cone can be well approximated by a low-dimensional subspace for Lambertian objects. Several training images of the object under varying illumination are needed to reconstruct the cone, which makes it impractical. Basri and Jacobs [BJ03] proved that a set of images of a convex Lambertian object under distant lighting lies close to a 9D linear subspace and this subspace can be analytically characterized using surface spherical harmonics. This stems from the observation that a Lambertian surfaces acts as a low-pass filter for the lighting function and therefore the reflectance can be accurately approximated by low-order spherical harmonics. These findings were directly applied for illumination correction in the approach of Zhang and Samaras [ZS04]. As 3D information is needed, Blanz and Vetter's morphable model was used together with a spherical harmonic representation. This method is applied to 2D face recognition and is reported to perform well even when multiple illuminants are present. Zhang's and Samaras's algorithm for texture recovery is summarized in Alg. 1.

Data : Pixels with corresponding surface normals (shape registered with texture)
Result : Recovered albedo (illumination-free texture)

for *Each pixel of the face* **do**
    Compute the spherical-harmonics basis (9-dimensional vector) using the attached surface normal
end

Iteratively solve equation for $ALBEDO$ and $9D\_LIGHT$:
$INTENSITY = ALBEDO \cdot (BASIS \cdot 9D\_LIGHT)$

where $INTENSITY$ is a vector of gray-scale intensities, $ALBEDO$ is a vector of albedos, $BASIS$ is a [number of pixels] $\times$ 9 matrix representing spherical harmonics basis and $9D\_LIGHT$ is a 9-dimensional illumination vector;

Use $ALBEDO$ as a delit texture;

Algorithm 1. Texture recovery algorithm (for details see [ZS04])

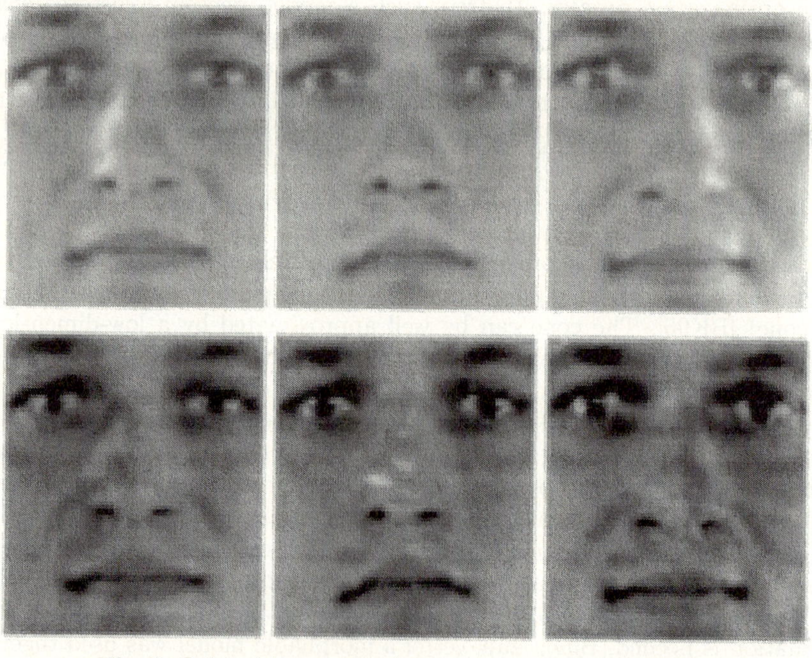

Fig. 2. Original images (top), Recovered albedo (bottom)

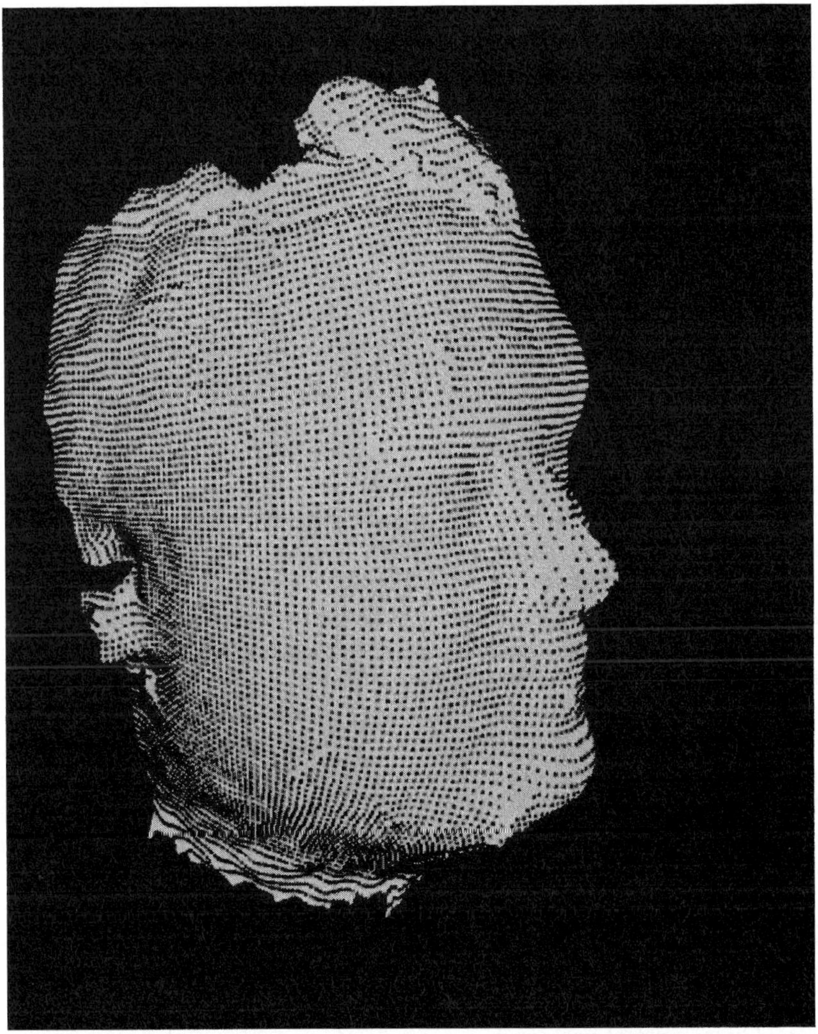

Fig. 3. Face surface produced by the sensor [YHR04]

By using surface normals computed directly from the 3D data instead of the reconstructed normals from the morphable model we believe that recognition accuracy will increase. Fig. 2 shows the example of the recovered albedo using Zhang's and Samaras's algorithm for texture recovery and person specific 3D shape. For each image, 3D shape was acquired using our own active stereo sensor [YHR04]. The shape for the first image is shown in Fig 3. Just to demonstrate the success of the delighting, similarity matrices consisting of correlation coefficients computed directly between the pixels are presented below. The matrix on the left shows the similarity between the original images, the right between delit images. Ideally, all entries in the similarity matrix should be exactly 1.0 as these are images of the same person. The factors like illumination and misregistration however reduce the score to a number smaller than 1.0. The improvement by the proposed illumination correction is clearly noticeable.

$$\begin{pmatrix} 1.0000 & 0.7847 & 0.5872 \\ 0.7847 & 1.0000 & 0.6989 \\ 0.5872 & 0.6989 & 1.0000 \end{pmatrix} \qquad \begin{pmatrix} 1.0000 & 0.8252 & 0.7424 \\ 0.8252 & 1.0000 & 0.7880 \\ 0.7424 & 0.7880 & 1.0000 \end{pmatrix}$$

4 2D-Based Matching

Once a person-specific morphable model is successfully matched to the input image, densely registered illumination free texture can be obtained. Existing 2D recognition algorithms can be used on such data. As the enrolment data includes full view of the head, even partially non-frontal poses can be used for recognition.

A large variety of face recognition methods have been suggested in the literature [ZCPR03]. However, it is well known that in controlled conditions, which we try to emulate by 3D assisted pose and photometric normalisation of the input image, Linear Discriminant Analysis (LDA) provides an effective pattern representation. Although it is designed to extract only first order discriminatory information, in recent experiments in face based personal identity verification, LDA has been shown to outperform both linear and nonlinear boundary Support Vector Machines [JKLM99]. This may be the consequence of the sparseness of training data in this particular application where only a few gallery images are available in the training set for each client. In such situations only the simplest model, defined in terms of the class mean vector, can be inferred for each client distribution and this is exactly what LDA is able to exploit.

The LDA projection maximises the ratio of between class and within class scatters. Given a set of vectors $x_i, i = 1, \ldots, M$, $x_i \in R^D$, each belonging to one of c classes $\{C_1, C_2, \ldots, C_c\}$, we compute the between-class scatter matrix, S_B,

$$S_B = \sum_{i=1}^{c} (\nu_i - \nu)(\nu_i - \nu)^T \tag{1}$$

and within-class scatter matrix, S_W

$$S_W = \sum_{i=1}^{c} \sum_{x_k \in C_i} (x_k - \nu_i)(x_k - \nu_i)^T \tag{2}$$

where ν is the grand mean and ν_i is the mean of class C_i.

The objective of LDA is to find the transformation matrix, W_{opt}, that maximises the ratio of determinants $\frac{|W^T S_B W|}{|W^T S_W W|}$. W_{opt} is known to be the solution of the following eigenvalue problem [DK82]:

$$S_B W - S_W W \Lambda = 0 \tag{3}$$

where Λ is a diagonal matrix whose elements are the eigenvalues of matrix $S_W^{-1} S_B$. The column vectors $\boldsymbol{w_i}$ $(i = 1, \ldots, c-1)$ of matrix W are referred to as *Fisherfaces*.

In high dimensional problems (e.g. in the case where x_i are images and D is $\approx 10^5$) S_W is almost always singular, since the number of training samples M is much smaller than D. Therefore, an initial dimensionality reduction must be carried out before solving the eigenvalue problem in (3). Commonly, dimensionality reduction is achieved by Principal Component Analysis [TP91]; the first $(M - c)$ eigenprojections are used to represent vectors x_i. The dimensionality reduction also allows S_W and S_B to be efficiently calculated. The optimal linear feature extractor W_{opt} is then defined as:

$$W_{opt} = W_{lda} * W_{pca} \tag{4}$$

where W_{pca} is the PCA projection matrix and W_{lda} is the optimal projection obtained by maximising

$$W_{lda} = arg \max_W \frac{|W^T W_{pca}^T S_W W_{pca} W|}{|W^T W_{pca}^T S_B W_{pca} W|} \tag{5}$$

The LDA axes are known to perform prewhitening of the within class covariances. In other words, the within class covariance matrix becomes an identity matrix. The assumption that each client distribution is Gaussian with mean μ_i and an identity covariance matrix underlies the LDA approach. Under this assumption the optimal metric for face image classification is the Euclidean metric. Accordingly, given a probe image, $\mathbf{x}$, in the LDA space, we can compute a matching score s for the probe and the i-th client mean μ_i as the Euclidean distance between the two vectors, i.e.

$$s_E = \sqrt{(\mathbf{x} - \mu_i)^T (\mathbf{x} - \mu_i)} \tag{6}$$

Alternatively we can match the probe to a model using the normalised correlation as a matching score function. The measure is defined as

$$s_N = \frac{||\mathbf{x}^T \mu_i||}{\sqrt{\mathbf{x}^T \mathbf{x} \mu_i^T \mu_i}} \tag{7}$$

The normalised correlation projects the probe vector onto the mean vector of the claimed client identity, emanating from the origin. It effectively uses just one dimensional space onto which the test data is projected. The magnitude of projection is normalised by the length of the mean and probe vectors.

Although normalised correlation is very effective, in many situations it has been outperformed by the gradient metric defined as

$$s_o = \frac{||(\mathbf{x} - \mu_i)^T \nabla P(i|\mathbf{x})||}{||\nabla P(i|\mathbf{x})||} \tag{8}$$

where $\nabla P(i|\mathbf{x})$ is the gradient direction for user i defined as

$$\nabla P(i|\mathbf{x}) = \sum_{\substack{j=1 \\ j \neq i}}^{m} p(\mathbf{x}|j)(\mu_j - \mu_i) \tag{9}$$

and $p(\mathbf{x}|j)$ is j^{th} class probability density function assumed to be Gaussian.

Either of these score functions or their combination can be used for final decision making in the LDA space.

5 Discussion and Conclusion

We addressed the problem of pose and illumination invariance in face recognition and propose an approach which makes use of 3D face models in 2D face recognition. The proposed solution is realistic as for many applications the additional cost of acquiring 3D face images during enrolment of the subjects is acceptable. 3D sensing is not required during normal operation of the face recognition system, as the recognition process is based on standard 2D face imaging.

The proposed methodology achieves illumination invariance by estimating the illumination sources using the 3D face model. This involves modelling the effect of illumination using a low order spherical harmonics model. The by-product of the process is the recovery of the face skin albedo which can be used as a photometrically normalised face image, or can be relit to the same lighting conditions as those used during the enrolment. Standard face recognition techniques can then be applied to such illumination corrected images.

The proposed methodology, which is distinguished from existing techniques by deploying user specific, rather than general, 3D face models, was outlined. Simple experiments confirming the benefits of the proposed photometric normalisation were conducted.

Acknowledgements

This work was supported by EPSRC Research Grant GR/S46543/01 with contributions from EU Project Biosecure and COST 275.

References

[BJ03] Ronen Basri and David W. Jacobs. Lambertian Reflectance and Linear Subspaces. *IEEE Trans. Pattern Anal. Mach. Intell.*, 25(2):218–233, 2003.

[BK96] P. N. Belhumeur and D. J. Kriegman. What is the Set of Images of an Object Under All Possible Lighting Conditions. In *Proc. of IEEE Conference of Computer Vision and Pattern Recognition*, pages 270–277, 1996.

[BV03] Volker Blanz and Thomas Vetter. Face Recognition Based on Fitting a 3D Morphable Model. *IEEE Trans. Pattern Anal. Mach. Intell.*, 25(9):1063–1074, 2003.

[DK82] P. A. Devijver and J. Kittler. *Pattern Recognition: A Statistical Approach.* Prentice Hall, 1982.

[Fit01] A. W. Fitzgibbon. Robust Registration of 2D and 3D Point Sets. In *Proceedings of the British Machine Vision Conference*, pages 662–670, 2001.

[JKLM99] K. Jonsson, Josef Kittler, Yongping Li, and Jiri Matas. Support Vector Machines for Face Authentication. In *BMVC*, 1999.

[KHHI05] J. Kittler, A. Hilton, M. Hamouz, and J. Illingworth. 3D Assisted Face Recognition: A Survey of 3D Imaging, Modelling and Recognition Approaches. In *Proc. of IEEE Workshop on Advanced 3D Imaging for Safety and Security, A3DISS 2005 (CD-ROM of the CVPR 2005)*, 2005.

[MSCA04] Z. Mao, J.P. Siebert, W.P. Cockshott, and A. F. Ayoub. Constructing dense correspondences to analyze 3D facial change. In *Proc.of the 17th International Conference on Pattern Recognition, ICPR'04)*, volume 3, pages 144–148, 2004.

[TP91] M. A. Turk and A. P. Pentland. Eigenfaces for Recognition. *Journal of Cognitive Neuroscience*, 3(1):71–86, 1991.

[YHR04] I.A. Ypsilos, A. Hilton, and S. Rowe. Video-rate Capture of Dynamic Face Shape and Appearance. In *Proc. 6th Int. Conf. on Automatic Face and Gesture Recognition (FGR 2004)*, pages 117–122, 2004.

[YY03] Lijun Yin and Matt T. Yourst. 3D face recognition based on high-resolution 3D face modeling from frontal and profile views. In *WBMA '03: Proceedings of the 2003 ACM SIGMM workshop on Biometrics methods and applications*, pages 1–8. ACM Press, 2003.

[ZC00] WenYi Zhao and Rama Chellappa. SFS Based View Synthesis for Robust Face Recognition. In *FG '00: Proceedings of the Fourth IEEE International Conference on Automatic Face and Gesture Recognition 2000*, page 285, Washington, DC, USA, 2000. IEEE Computer Society.

[ZCPR03] W. Zhao, R. Chellappa, P. J. Phillips, and A. Rosenfeld. Face recognition: A literature survey. *ACM Comput. Surv.*, 35(4):399–458, 2003.

[ZS04] Lei Zhang and Dimitris Samaras. Pose Invariant Face Recognition under Arbitrary Unknown Lighting using Spherical Harmonics. In *Proc. Biometric Authentication Workshop 2004, (in conjunction with ECCV2004), pp. 10–23*, 2004.

Automatic Annotation of Sport Video Content

Marco Bertini, Alberto Del Bimbo, and Walter Nunziati

Dipartimento di Sistemi e Informatica - Universitá degli Studi di Firenze
{bertini, delbimbo, nunziati}@dsi.unifi.it

Abstract. Automatic semantic annotation of video streams allows to extract significant clips for archiving and retrieval of video content. In this paper, we present a system that performs automatic annotation of soccer videos, detecting principal highlights, and recognizing identity of players. Highlight detection is carried out by means of finite state machines that encode domain knowledge, while player identification is based on face detection, and on the analysis of contextual information such as jersey's numbers and superimposed text captions. Results obtained on actual soccer videos shows overall highlight detection rates of about 90%. Lower, but still promising, accuracy is achieved on the very difficult player identification task.

1 Introduction and Background Work

To provide effective archiving and retrieval of video material, video streams must be annotated with respect to its semantic content, producing metadata that is attached to the video data and stored in databases. This will permit, for example, to produce special video summaries for a sport program such those that recollect the best actions occurred during a typical soccer turn, or those where are notable actions of a certain player. In this case the parts of the video containing important highlights must be selected and edited to create a new video sequence. One limitation to the diffusion of this practice is due to the fact that manually summarizing, annotating or tagging video is a cumbersome and expensive process. This has motivated recently the investigation of techniques to extract semantic information automatically from sports video sequences. At semantic level, video annotation regards the identification and recognition of meaningful entities and events represented in the video. Semantic video annotation is obtained combining observed features and patterns, like settings, text captions, people and objects, highlights and events, and domain knowledge. The latter is required in order to reduce the semantic gap between the observable features of the multimedia material and the interpretation that a user have. A good review of multimodal video annotation is provided in [16].

Due to their huge commercial appeal sports videos represent an important application domain for video automatic annotation [20]. Sport shots can be classified into the most common scene types, that are playfield, players' close-ups and crowd, using edges, segments and color information. From playfield shots it

M. Lazo and A. Sanfeliu (Eds.): CIARP 2005, LNCS 3773, pp. 1066–1078, 2005.

is possible to perform sport classification based on the characteristics of the playfield like ground color and lines. Solutions for recognition of specific highlights have been proposed for different sports like soccer, tennis, basketball, volleyball, baseball, American football. Usually these methods exploit low and mid level audio and visual cues, such as the detection of referee's whistle, excited speech, color and edge related features, playfield zone identification, players and ball tracking, motion indexes, etc. and relate them to a domain knowledge of the sports or of the video producers. In the first case knowledge of the sports rules and typical actions are used, in the second case the production rules employed by directors, like the presence of slow motion replays, are used. Good examples are reported in [17]for tennis, in [21] for basketball, in [11] and [13] for football and in [1], [6], [19] for soccer.

Several researchers have also focussed on the identification of people in the video for the purpose of video semantic annotation. Person recognition by means of association of interpreted textual content - extracted from text captions - to faces - automatically detected from skin tone analysis - has been investigated in the context of news video in [14], and more recently in [3] and [4]. Two important recent works for people identification are [7] and [15].

In this paper we present recent results of our research for providing rich annotations of highlights in soccer. The definition of highlights is based on formal methods (using finite state machines) and is detected through a model checking engine. Highlight detection is based on a limited set of visual cues, which are derived from low–level features such as edges, shapes and color. To provide a richer annotation, we add details related to the players who take part in a particular highlight occurrence using information extracted from faces, jersey numbers and superimposed text captions, which are usually present in the video stream.

The paper is organized as follows. In Sect. 2, we briefly introduce peculiarities that can be exploited for modeling highlights in soccer, providing details on estimation of visual cues, and on the model checking algorithm. Detection and recognition of the player is discussed in Sect.3. Players that are not identified in this process are then linked by similarity to one of the labeled faces (3.4). Examples of highlight recognition and superimposed caption extraction and face detection and recognition are shown in Sect.4 and 5, together with indications of results obtained. Conclusions and future work are discussed in Sect. 6.

2 Soccer Video Highlight Detection

Our solution for highlight modeling and detection employs finite state machines (FSMs). States represent main phases in which actions can be decomposed. Events indicate transitions from one state to the other: they capture the relevant steps in the progression of the play and are expressed in terms of a logical combination of a few visual cues, the camera motion, the playfield zone that is framed and the position of soccer players extracted from the video stream. Time constraints, for example a minimum temporal duration, can be applied to state

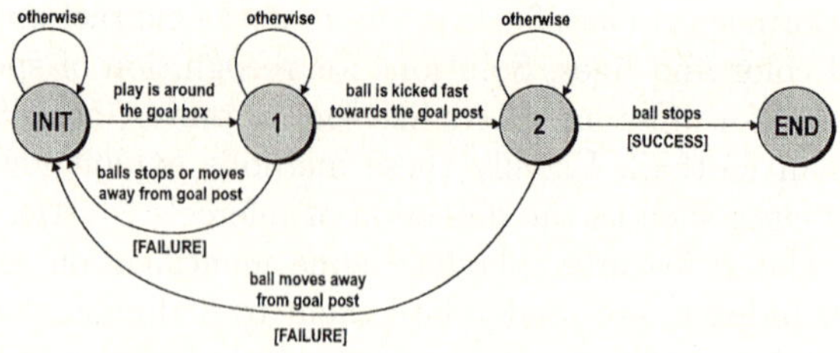

Fig. 1. The informal model of a shot on goal highlight in the soccer domain

transitions [1]. Fig. 1 shows how the essential phases of a shot on goal highlight have been represented as a FSM.

In the following we discuss in detail the solutions adopted for the estimation of the visual cues and the each separate detector and players' annotation.

2.1 Estimation of Visual Cues

Camera Motion. In soccer, ball instantaneous position and motion direction are important cues for the understanting of the play. A well known production rule of soccer videos is that the director uses the main camera to follow the ball and the play. For this reason, we rely on camera motion as a somewhat rough, but reliable estimate of the speed and the direction of the ball. As the main camera is observing the soccer playfield in a fixed position, a 3-parameter image motion estimation algorithm capturing horizontal and vertical translations and isotropic scaling is sufficient to get a reasonable estimate of camera pan, tilt and zoom. Motion estimation algorithm that has been used is an adaptation to the sports videos domain of the algorithm reported in [2], that is based on corner tracking and motion vector clustering. As it works with a selected number of salient image locations, the algorithm can cope with large displacements due to fast camera motion. The algorithm employs deterministic sample consensus to perform a statistical motion grouping. This is particularly effective to cluster multiple independent image motions, and is therefore suitable for the specific case of sports videos to separate camera motion from the motion of individual players.

Playfield Zone Estimation. To estimate playfield zone, the playfield is first partitioned in several, possibly overlapping zones, which are defined so that the change from one to the other indicates a change in the play. In general, a typical camera view is associated with each playfield zone, and we exploit common patterns of these views to recognize which zone is framed. Fig. 2 shows the partition of the playfield that we have used. Each zone is recognized using a dedicated Naïve Bayes classifier, which takes as input a (vector-quantized) descriptor. The descriptor itself is derived from low–level features such as edge, shape and color. Since classifiers have identical structure, large differences in

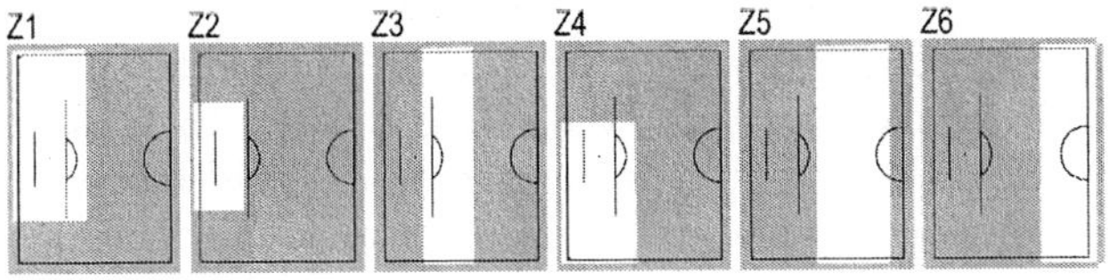

Fig. 2. Playfield partition for soccer

their outputs are likely to be significant, so we choose the classifier with the highest output probability as the one identifying the zone currently framed.

Player Position and Speed. Players' position is instrumental for the recognition of those highlights that are characterized by a typical deployment of players on the playfield, like all "free shots". For these highlights, both camera and players are usually still at the start of the action, allowing a robust estimation of the position of players, so that typical configurations of the deployment can be recognized. We exploited the knowledge of the actual planar model of the playfield to estimate automatically the homography [10] which maps any imaged playfield point (x, y) onto the real playfield point (X, Y). Players are first detected as "blobs" from each frame by color differencing to identify their position on the frame. Bottom-end point of each detected template is remapped onto the playfield model trough the estimated homography. Assuming the pinhole camera projection model, the image-to-playfield transformation has the form of a planar homography. Since we are provided with a set of line segments as the result of image segmentation, the homography is estimated using four line correspondences. If $[a\ b\ c]^T$ such that $ax + by + c = 0$ is the image of a playfield line $[A\ B\ C]^T$, it holds:

$$[a\ b\ c]^T = \mathrm{K}\,[A\ B\ C]^T \ , \tag{1}$$

with $\mathrm{K} = \mathrm{H}^T$, and H is the image–to–model homography.

The output of the registration process is then used to build a compact representation of how the players are deployed, such as the histogram of players' occupation of playfield zones. The presence or absence of players in the areas contributes to discriminate between three classes of free kicks, namely penalty kicks, corner kicks and free kicks with wall.

Motion information of objects and/or athletes that are present in the scene is obtained from the same motion processing and clustering used for camera motion estimation. In fact, we cluster motion magnitude and direction of pixels that are moving independently. This measure is sufficient to detect characteristic acceleration and deceleration of groups of players when actions change somewhat.

2.2 Model Checking

To recognize highlights from the occurrence of the visual cues, operational models are used to perform model checking over the FSMs that model the highlights.

The combination of the measures of the visual cues that are estimated, are checked against each highlight model in parallel. The model checking algorithm works as follows: in the main loop, the visual features that are used to detect the occurrence of highlights (e.g. line segments, players' blobs, playfield color) are extracted from each frame. From these features, descriptors related to the three visual cues previously discussed are computed. Visual cues are discretized: for example, for soccer videos we have 12 possible values for the cue playfield zone, 5 values (both in horizontal and vertical direction) for the camera motion, and 3 different values for the player position descriptor. Hence, a 4-dimensional vector is input in all models at each instant, and the constraints associated with transitions from the current state are checked. If a constraint is verified, the current state is updated, leading either to an advancement in the model evolution, or to a rejection of the current segments (hence resetting the model). Whenever a model progresses from the initial state, the current frame number is stored, to mark the beginning of a possible highlight; if the model succeeds-i.e. a highlight is identified-the current frame number is also stored to mark the end of an actual highlight, otherwise the initial frame number information is discarded.

3 Player Identification

Player identification in sports videos is a complex task, mainly because of player's fast motion and frequent occlusions. Only close-up views are useful for recognition; however also in close–up views players may exhibit large variations in pose and expression, making them sometimes hard to recognize even for a human observer. On the positive side, close-up shots in sports videos have a strong visual appearance. In fact, players wear colored jerseys, usually decorated with some stripes or logos, and most important, showing the player's number. The player's jersey number is unique during an international tournament, and can be used to recognize players identity either analyzing a graphic screen, or checking an existing database, such as those available on the UEFA Euro 2004 website. Superimposed text captions are also shown to point out some interesting details about the player currently framed. They can be used as well to extract important information that is useful for the player identification.

These considerations lead to the fact that, for the purpose of player's identification, face recognition is not the only possible approach. We decided to exploit the information present in close-up shots with frontal faces and superimposed text captions and or the player's jersey number. After this first step, non-identified faces are in turn analyzed in order to understand if a face is similar to any of the faces already annotated using text or jersey's number.

In the following we discuss in detail the solutions adopted for each separate detector and players' annotation.

3.1 Face Detection

Detection of faces is achieved trough an implementation of the algorithm proposed by Viola and Jones [18]. We briefly outline here the algorithm, referring the reader to the original paper by Viola and Jones, and their subsequent work. Basically, the algorithm employs several simple classifiers devoted to signal the presence of a particular feature of the face, like the alignment of the two eyes or the symmetry in frontal views. A large number of these simple features is initially selected. Then, a classifier is constructed by selecting a small number of important features using AdaBoost [8]. A feature is weighted combination of pixel sums of two rectangles, and can be computed for each pixel in constant time using auxiliary images like the *Summed Area Table* (SAT), which is defined as follows:

$$SAT(x,y) = \sum_{i \leq y} \sum_{j \leq x} I(i,j)$$

where I is the original image. Rotated version of the SAT are employed to compute rotated features. The current algorithm uses the templates of Fig. 3 to compute features: Computation of a single feature f at a given position (x, y) requires to subtract the sum of the intensity values of all the pixels lying under the white rectangle of a template (p_w) from the sum of the intensity values of all the pixels lying under the black rectangle (p_b) of the same template: $f(x, y) = \sum_i p_b(i) - \sum_i p_w(i)$.

Fig. 3. Rectangle features by the face and number detection algorithm

In the current implemementation, the algorithm has been trained to detect frontal and quasi-frontal faces. Training has been carried out with a few hundreds of positive examples taken from a standard face dataset, and another 100 examples manually cropped from soccer video sequences. To deal with the problem of false detection we defined a face verification procedure which is run within the bounding box of each hypothesized face. For each detected face, we produce a color histogram of the region immediately below the face bounding box. The histogram is applied to the Hue component in the HSV color space, normalized w.r.t. white, black, and 5 shades of gray. This histogram is clearly dominated by the principal color of the team jersey, which shows histograms for players belonging to different teams in the same game. For each detected faces, this context color histogram c is compared to a reference histograms r, using the χ^2 statistics. As a second verification step we perform eye detection directly using the intensity values. Pixels of the region of interest are first transformed into the *YCrCB* color space. Then, the eye map is obtained, combining two separate luminance and chrominance maps. Once the shapes present in the final map have been separated, roundness is checked to assess if they correspond to eye pupils value is greater than a threshold the shape is considered as possible eyes. After that, the position of the eye is considered and a region that has two eye-like regions in the appropriate positions is finally considered to be a face.

3.2 Detection and Recognition of Jersey's Numbers

Detection of numbers depicted on player's jerseys is achieved using the same approach as for faces. Official rules of most important soccer organization (like UEFA and FIFA) state that jerseys must be decorated with such numbers on their front, and that size of the numbers must be within a certain range. Moreover, numbers are in the range from 1 to 22, and remains assigned to each player for the entire tournament. We train a different detector for each number from 1 to 22. We found that this approach is far more reliable that having classifiers for digits 0-9, because two digits numbers are not always well separated, and so they tend to cause missed detections. Moreover, detecting each digit separately would force us to impose constraints on spatial arrangement of detected digits which are not easy to verify in the cases where numbers are not perfectly horizontal.

Each detector acts as a dichotomizer, allowing us to directly recognize which is the particular number that has been detected. Each classifier has been trained with 50 positive and 100 negative examples, the latter being randomly selected from images, while the former have been manually cropped. Other positive examples have been generated with graphic programs or obtained by small rotations of some selected images. Templates for numbers are such that bounding box side is about 30 pixels wide.

3.3 Superimposed Text Detection and Recognition

To locate text captions containing player's name and other useful information, we exploited typical production rules of sports videos. These are basically the fact that to enhance readability of characters, producers use luminance contrast (luminance is not spatially sub-sampled in the TV standards) and captions with names of athletes occupy a horizontal box. The algorithm for superimposed text detection we have developed is based on spatio-temporal analysis of image corners and has been described in detail in [4]. An image location is defined as a corner if the intensity gradient in a patch around is distributed along two preferred directions (non-isotropic condition). Therefore, in correspondence with corners the gradient auto–correlation matrix has large and distinct eigenvalues. Corners are detected from:

$$\mathbf{A} = \begin{pmatrix} \langle I_x^2 \rangle & \langle I_x I_y \rangle \\ \langle I_x I_y \rangle & \langle I_y^2 \rangle \end{pmatrix}$$

$$c(x, y) = \det\mathbf{A} - k\,\mathrm{tr}^2\mathbf{A} \text{ with } k = 0.04$$

if $c(x, y)$ is above a predefined threshold, where subscripts denote partial differentiation with respect to the coordinate axis, and brackets indicate Gaussian smoothing. The first term of the equation has a significant value only if both eigenvalues are different from zero, while the second term inhibits false corners along the borders of the image.

Following the text localization several steps for text recognition are performed. They involve binarization, temporal integration and image enhancement.

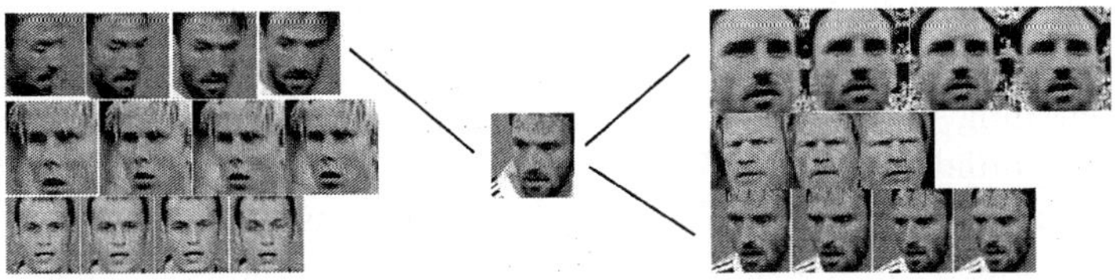

Fig. 4. Left - examples labeled by means of text or number. Right - an unlabeled example to be assigned to one of the labels. Lines represent possible correct pairings.

In our experiments, we have used a freely available OCR software [9]. The tool provides a good separation between different words, while making some mistakes in character recognition. In order to recognize player's names, we deal with this problem using an approximate string matching algorithm to perform query on a database of players' names.

3.4 Face Matching

To assign every non-identified face to one of the player classes we exploit the fact that players are a fixed and somewhat limited population. More in detail, we considered each annotated example as an individual, avoiding to merge clusters relative to the same player.

An example of this situation is given in Fig.4, where the unlabeled face in the center must be assigned to one of the labeled faces, which are (a subset of) faces annotated by means of number or text caption. The faces on the first row of the left side, and of the first and third row of the right side represent the same player. Considering each row as a distinct individual, we built a compact representation based on local facial features. This has the effects of increasing inter-class distances in our classification task, but at the cost of having an increased number of classes. Hence, for the unlabeled example there are three possible correct pairings. In practice, to label an unknown face, we require to find a face of the same player with a similar pose and expression.

To cope with the large variation of poses and expressions we followed a part-based approach to recognition, similarly to [15], using the SIFT descriptors [12]. We experimented with several part–based representation schemes, and obtained the most satisfying results using three SIFT descriptor centered on the two eyes (20×20 pixel, with the face size normalized to be 80 pixels wide), and on the midpoint of the eyes (15×30 pixels). This choice is motivated by the facts that a) these are the most robust facial features to detect and track troughout the shots and b) the lower part of the face is often characterized by appearance changes due to variation in expression, that exceed those due to identity changes. The basic SIFT descriptor has been modified to avoid to include in the descriptor non-face part of the image. In particular, we rely on skin–maps to adaptively compute the weights of the components of the SIFT descriptor. For each pixel of the patch, its weight in the descriptor is cut to zero as the pixel falls off the region defined by the skin–map.

The matching process begins by obtain a single face track for each of the frontal faces found in a shot. A face track is a set of consecutive faces of the same player in the same shot. The detected face is used as a starting point to initialize the track. First, a skin-tone model is built for the face. This is done by collecting an histogram in the C_bC_r space of the bounding box, and then using the dominant color as a skin tone. Then, eyes are tracked throughout the shot, using a simple correlation based tracker that uses eyes-centroids as measure. To avoid false track, the eye search is performed within a limited region (10 pixels) centered on the last observation, and completely included in the region delimited by the skin map. As the tracker looses the eye-tracks, the face track is closed and a compact representation of the whole track is produced.

Similarity between face tracks is computed using the minimum distance between the two sets. If U is a face track corresponding to a non–labeled player, and L is a labeled face track, their distance is computed as follows:

$$d(U, L) = \min_{i,j} \|U_i - L_j\|,$$

where U_i and L_j are two 384–length vector, and their distance is measured using the l_1 norm. A single track may be labeled with several labels. A threshold has been set such that no more than three labels are assigned to the same player. In the worst case, correction of multiple annotations must be done manually with little effort.

4 Highlights Detection Results

Experiments have been carried out with videos of soccer games provided by BBC Sports Library and recorded off-air from other broadcasters. Videos recorded at full PAL resolution and 25 fps. The overall test set includes over 100 sequences with typical soccer highlights, of duration from 15 seconds to 1.5 minutes. The relative frequency of the different types of highlights reflects that of a typical soccer game. Tables 1 and 2 show precision, misclassification and miss rates for the principal soccer highlights. It can be noticed that, for most of the highlights, correct detection is close to 90%.

5 Player Identification Results

The player identification method of Sect.3 has been tested on the same material of the experiments on highlight detection. On average, the system selected about 6000 frames for each game, providing 4 minutes of close-up shots with name/face association. The average number of players identified is 12 for game, without repetition. Figure 5 shows key–frames taken from shots where the either a face and a number have been found, or a face and text have been found. Table 3 reports performance of the number, face and text detectors, averaged on the

Table 1. Precision and misclassification rates of soccer highlight automatic annotation

HIGHLIGHT DETECTED	CLIP EVENT					
	Forward launch	Shot on goal	Placed kick	Attack act.	Counter att.	No highlight
Forward launch	**89.75%**	1.67%	0.00%	0.0%	0.00%	8.58%
Shot on goal	1.52%	**93.90%**	0.00%	0.00%	0.00%	4.58%
Placed kick	0.00%	0.00%	**89.75%**	0.00%	0.00%	10.25%
Attack action	1.50%	1.10%	0.00%	**96.40%**	1.00%	0.00%
Counter attack	0.00%	0.00%	0.00%	8.33%	**83.34%**	8.33%

Table 2. Miss rates of soccer highlight automatic annotation

HIGHLIGHT MISSES				
Forward launch	Shot on goal	Placed kick	Attack action	Counter attack
5.12%	13.05%	7.05%	25.00%	20.10%

Fig. 5. Examples of key frames selected by the system from a Euro 2004 game. The face in the last frame was not detected, but the player was correctly labeled using its number.

duration of a game. Reported ground truth (column "present"), is referred to single player close–up shots, those that are of interest for desired annotation. Table 4 reports average results obtained running the system on the duration of a game. Not surprisingly, detection of face-caption shots is most reliable than detection of face-number shots. This is mainly due to misdetections of the face and number detectors, while the closed caption detector correctly detects nearly all the shots where a caption was present. Moreover, the number of close-up shots detected is fairly low if compared with the total number of close-up shots, where identification is not performed because neither jersey's number nor text caption was present. However, it must be noticed that player's close up occurring during the most interesting moments of the game (after a goal for instance) are usually detected by the system.

Table 3. Face, number and text detector performances

Detector	**Present**	**Detected**	**Correct**	**False**	**Missed**
Face	112	98	90	8	22
Numbers	36	24	20	16	4
Text	12	11	11	1	0

Table 4. Detailed results of the annotation of a single game

		Correct
Total number of close-up shots	112	
Face-number shots present	36	
Numbers of distinct players present	18	
Face-number shots detected	24	20
Face-caption shots present	12	
Face-caption shots detected	11	11
Number of annotated shots	31	27
Number of distinct players identified	13	10

Fig. 6. Face matching experiment. Left: ground truth data. 9 players annotated with their name, plus a "null" class, comprised of unlabeled players. Right: results based on face matching. Some examples were not labeled, since they were not found similar to any labeled example. Crosses indicate incorrect assignments.

5.1 Face Matching Results

To test the face matching scheme of Sec. 3.4, we picked 10 correctly identified faces from the various games present in our testbed, and 30 non–labeled face tracks, for which ground truth was manually obtained. Of these, 25 tracks had a matching face in the annotated set, while the other 5 were completely new to the system. Results are shown in Fig. 6. To keep the result more readable, we avoid the multiple labeling scheme described in Sec. 3.4, and we simply assign a face track to the closest face in the labeled dataset. Also, in this experiment the goal is to test the performance of the face matching module, hence we deliberately avoid to use context information, such as the color of the player's jersey, to rule out obvious false matches (e.g., assigning a player to the wrong team).

6 Conclusions and Future Work

We presented solutions to perform automatic annotation of soccer video for the principal highlights and active players by exploiting a limited set of visual cues and a-priori knowledge of the rules and development of the soccer play. Improvements in the performance of player identification might require more discriminative face representation schemes and new and more effective solutions for jersey number detection.

Acknowledgments

This work has been partially funded by the European VI FP, Network of Excellence DELOS (2004-06).

References

1. J. Assfalg; M. Bertini; C. Colombo; A. Del Bimbo, A. and W. Nunziati; "Semantic annotation of soccer videos: automatic highlights identification", *Computer Vision and Image Understanding*, Volume 92, November–December 2003.
2. G. Baldi, C. Colombo, and A. Del Bimbo. "A compact and retrieval-oriented video representation using mosaics." *Proc. 3rd ICVS*, Amsterdam, 1999.
3. Tamara L. Berg, Alexander C. Berg, Jaety Edwards, Michael Maire, Ryan White, Yee-Whye Teh, Erik Learned-Miller, D. A. Forsyth. "Names and Faces in the News", *in Proc. of CVPR*, 2004.
4. M. Bertini, A. Del Bimbo, and P. Pala. "Content-based indexing and retrieval of TV news", *Pattern Recognition Letters*, 22(5), 2001.
5. Datong Chen, Jean-Marc Odobez and Herv Bourlard. "Text detection and recognition in images and video frames", *Pattern Recognition*, Volume 37, March 2004.
6. Ekin, A.; Tekalp, A.M.; Mehrotra, R.; "Automatic soccer video analysis and summarization", *IEEE Transcations on Image Processing*, July 2003.
7. M. Everingham, and A. Zisserman. "Automated Person Identification in Video"., *Proc. of CIVR*, 2004.
8. Y. Freund and R. E. Schapire. "A decision-theoretic generalization of on-line learning and an application to boosting", In *Proc. of Eurocolt 95*, Springer-Verlag, 1995.

9. GOCR: Open Source Character Recognition. *http://jocr.sourceforge.net/screenshots.html*
10. R. Hartley and A. Zisserman. "Multiple View Geometry in Computer Vision." Cambridge University Press, 2000.
11. S.S. Intille and A.F. Bobick. "Recognizing planned, multi-person action." *Computer Vision and Image Understanding* (1077-3142) 81(3):414-445, 2001.
12. D. Lowe, "Distinctive image features from scale–invariant keypoints", *International Journal of Computer Vision*, 60, 2, 2004.
13. M.Mottaleb and G.Ravitz. "Detection of Plays and Breaks in Football Games Using Audiovisual Features and HMM." In *Proc. of Ninth Int'l Conf. on Distributed Multimedia Systems*, pp. 154-160, 2003.
14. Shin'ichi Satoh, Yuichi Nakamura, and Takeo Kanade, "Name-It: Naming and Detecting Faces in News Videos," *IEEE MultiMedia*, Vol. 6, No. 1, January-March, 1999.
15. J. Sivic, M. Everingham, and A. Zissermann, "Person spotting: video shot retrieval for face sets", *Proceedings of CIVR*, July 2005.
16. C.G.M. Snoek and M. Worring. "Multimodal video indexing: a review of the state-of-the-art", Multimedia, Tools and Applications, Volume 25, January 2005.
17. G. Sudhir, J.C.M. Lee and A.K. Jain, "Automatic Classification of Tennis Video for High-level Content-based Retrieval." *Proc. of CAIVD'98*, pp. 81-90, 1998.
18. P. Viola and M. Jones. *"Rapid object detection using a boosted cascade of simple features"*, In Proc. CVPR, pages 511-518, 2001.
19. Xinguo Yu , Changsheng Xu , Hon Wai Leong , Qi Tian , Qing Tang , Kong Wah Wan. "Trajectory-based ball detection and tracking with applications to semantic analysis of broadcast soccer video." In *Proc. of ACM Multimedia*, November 02-08, 2003.
20. Xinguo Yu, Dirk Farin. "Current and Emerging Topics in Sports Video processing". *Proc. of IEEE ICME*, 2005.
21. W. Zhou, A. Vellaikal, and C.C.J. Kuo, "Rule-based video classification system for basketball video indexing." *Proc. of ACM Multimedia 2000 workshop*, 2000.

Conformal Geometric Algebra for 3D Object Recognition and Visual Tracking Using Stereo and Omnidirectional Robot Vision

Eduardo Bayro-Corrochano, Julio Zamora-Esquivel, and Carlos López-Franco

Computer Science Department, GEOVIS Laboratory,
Centro de Investigación y de Estudios Avanzados,
CINVESTAV, Guadalajara, Jalisco 44550, Mexico
edb@gdl.cinvestav.mx
http://www.gdl.cinvestav.mx/~edb

Abstract. In this paper the authors use the framework of conformal geometric algebra for the treatment of robot vision tasks. In this mathematical system we calculated projective invariants using omnidirectional vision for object recognition. We show the power of the mathematical system for handling differential kinematics in visual guided tracking.

1 Introduction

This paper shows the power of conformal geometric algebra for different tasks of robot vision. In this framework we calculate projective invariants using omnidirectional vision. These invariants are utilized for object recognition. We also treat the problem of the control of a robot binocular system which is used for 3D visual tracking. For the control strategy we utilize a novel geometric formulation of the involved Jacobian for the differential kinematics.

The rest of this paper is organized as follows: We give a brief description of the geometric algebra and also of the conformal geometric algebra in section II. In section III we explain the projective invariants. In section IV we explain the projective invariants using omnidirectional vision. Section V is devoted to the differential kinematics and control of a pan-tilt unit. The experimental analysis is given in section VI and the conclusions are in section VI.

2 Geometric Algebra

In general, a geometric algebra G_n is a n-dimensional vector space V^n over the reals. We also denote with $G_{p,q,r}$ a geometric algebra over $V^{p,q,r}$ where p, q, r denote the signature p, q, r of the algebra. If $p \neq 0$ and $q = r = 0$ the metric is Euclidean G_n, if just $r = 0$ the metric is pseudoeuclidean $G_{p,q}$ and if non of them are zero the metric is degenerate. See [3,2] for a more detailled introduction to conformal geometric algebra.

M. Lazo and A. Sanfeliu (Eds.): CIARP 2005, LNCS 3773, pp. 1079–1090, 2005.

We will use the letter e to denote the vector basis e_i. In a geometric algebra $G_{p,q,r}$, the geometric product of two basis vectors is defined as

$$e_i e_j = \begin{cases} 1 & for\ i = j \in 1, ..., \mathtt{p} \\ -1 & for\ i = j \in \mathtt{p}+1, ..., \mathtt{p}+\mathtt{q} \\ 0 & for\ i = j \in \mathtt{p}+\mathtt{q}+1, ..., \mathtt{p}+\mathtt{q}+\mathtt{r} \\ e_i \wedge e_j & for\ i \neq j \end{cases} \tag{1}$$

2.1 Conformal Geometric Algebra

In the Euclidean space the composite of displacements is complicated because rotations are multiplicative but translations are additive. In order to make translations multiplicative too, we use the Conformal Geometric Algebra [3,2].

In the generalized homogeneous coordinates for points in the Euclidean space, we need that they be null vectors and also lie on the intersection of the null cone N^{n+1} (the set of all null vectors) with the hyperplane

$$P^{n+1}(e, e_0) = \{X \in R^{n+1,1} \mid e(X - e_0) = 0\}, \tag{2}$$

that is

$$N_e^n = \mathcal{N}^{n+1} \cap \mathcal{P}^{n+1}(e, e_0) = \{x \in \mathcal{R}^{n+1,1} | X^2 = 0.\ X \cdot e = -1\} \tag{3}$$

which is called the homogeneous model of $\mathcal{E}^n$, also called the horosphere (see Fig. 1) in hyperbolic geometry.

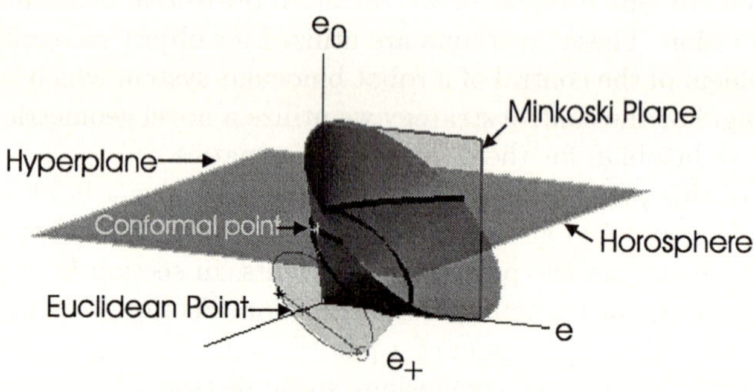

Fig. 1. Simplex at a_0 with tangent $a_1 \wedge a_2$

The points that satisfy the restrictions $X^2 = 0$ and $X \cdot e = -1$ are

$$X = \mathbf{x} + \frac{1}{2}\mathbf{x}^2 e + e_0 \tag{4}$$

where $\mathbf{x} \in \mathcal{R}^n$ and $X \in \mathcal{N}^n$. The origin is $e_0 = \frac{1}{2}(e_{n+1} - e_{n+2})$ and the point at infinity $e = e_{n+1} + e_{n+2}$.

Table 1. Entities in conformal geometric algebra

Entity	IPNS Representation	OPNS (Dual) Representation
Sphere	$S=\mathbf{p}+\frac{1}{2}(\mathbf{p}^2-\rho^2)e+e_0$	$S^*=A\wedge B\wedge C\wedge D$
Point	$X=\mathbf{x}+\frac{1}{2}\mathbf{x}^2e+e_0$	$X^*=S_1\wedge S_2\wedge S_3\wedge S_4$
Plane		$\Pi^*=A\wedge B\wedge C\wedge e$
Line		$L^*=A\wedge B\wedge e$
Circle	$Z=S_1\wedge S_2$	$Z^* = A\wedge B\wedge C$
Point Pair	$PP=S_1\wedge S_2\wedge S_3$	

Note that this is a bijective mapping. From now and in the rest of the paper the conformal points will be denoted by an italic uppercase letter (X), and the Euclidean points will be denoted by boldpoint at lowercase letters $\mathbf{x}$.

In table 1 we show the geometric entities of the conformal geometric algebra. Note that in the IPNS representation the point is a sphere with radius zero. In the dual representation the sphere is calculated using 4 points that lie on it.

Simplexes and Conformal Points. Evaluating the outer product of r linearly independent conformal points $a_0, a_1, \ldots, a_r$, where $r \leq n$ and n is the maximum grade of the algebra. The outer product of r conformal points is

$$a_0 \wedge a_1 \wedge \cdots \wedge a_r = \mathbf{A}_r + e_0\mathbf{A}_r^+ + \frac{1}{2}e\mathbf{A}_r^- - \frac{1}{2}E\mathbf{A}_r^\pm, \tag{5}$$

where

$$\begin{aligned}
\mathbf{A}_r &= \mathbf{a}_0 \wedge \mathbf{a}_1 \wedge \cdots \wedge \mathbf{a}_r,\\
\mathbf{A}_r^+ &= \sum_{i=0}^{r}(-1)^i\mathbf{a}_0 \wedge \cdots \wedge \breve{\mathbf{a}}_i \wedge \cdots \wedge \mathbf{a}_r = (\mathbf{a}_1 - \mathbf{a}_0)\wedge \cdots \wedge (\mathbf{a}_r - \mathbf{a}_0),\\
\mathbf{A}_r^- &= \sum_{i=0}^{r}(-1)^i\mathbf{a}_i^2\mathbf{a}_0 \wedge \cdots \wedge \breve{\mathbf{a}}_i \wedge \cdots \wedge \mathbf{a}_r,\\
\mathbf{A}_r^\pm &= \sum_{i=0}^{r}\sum_{j=i+1}^{r}(-1)^{i+j}(\mathbf{a}_i^2 - \mathbf{a}_j^2)\mathbf{a}_0 \wedge \cdots \wedge \breve{\mathbf{a}}_i \wedge \cdots \wedge \breve{\mathbf{a}}_j \wedge \cdots \wedge \mathbf{a}_r.
\end{aligned} \tag{6}$$

Note that A_r is the moment of the simplex with tangent (boundary) A_r^+. The outer product $a_0 \wedge a_1 \wedge \cdots \wedge a_r$ represents a sphere when $\mathbf{A}_r = 0$

$$a_0 \wedge a_1 \wedge \cdots \wedge a_r = -[e_0 - \frac{1}{2}e\mathbf{A}_r^-(\mathbf{A}_r^+)^{-1} + \frac{1}{2}\mathbf{A}_r^\pm(\mathbf{A}_r^+)^{-1}]E\mathbf{A}_r^+ \tag{7}$$

where the center and radius of the sphere

$$c = \frac{1}{2}\mathbf{A}_r^\pm(\mathbf{A}^+)^{-1}, \;\; \rho^2 = c^2 + \mathbf{A}_r^-(\mathbf{A}^+)^{-1}. \tag{8}$$

3D Rigid Motion. In conformal geometric algebra we can perform rotations by means of an entity called rotor which is defined by

$$R = exp\left(\frac{\theta}{2}\mathbf{l}\right), \tag{9}$$

where $\mathbf{l}$ is the bivector representing the dual of the rotation axis. To rotate an entity, we simply multiply it by the rotor R from the left and the reverse of the rotor $\tilde{R}$ from the right,

$$Y = RX\tilde{R}\,. \tag{10}$$

If we want to translate an entity we use a translator which is defined as

$$T = \left(1 + \frac{et}{2}\right) = exp\left(\frac{\mathbf{e}\mathbf{t}}{2}\right). \tag{11}$$

With this representation the translator can be applied multiplicatively to an entity similarly to the rotor, by multiplying the entity from the left by the translator and from the right with the reverse of the translator,

$$Y = TX\tilde{T}\,. \tag{12}$$

Finally, the rigid motion can be expressed using a *motor* which is the combination of a rotor and a translator

$$M = TR\,,, \tag{13}$$

thus the rigid body motion of an entity is described with

$$Y = MX\tilde{M}\,. \tag{14}$$

Also a motor can be defined using the exponential representation with a line representing its axis

$$M = exp\left(\frac{-\theta}{2}I_C L^*\right), \tag{15}$$

note that the line must be normalized to one.

3 Invariants

An invariant is a property that remains unchanged under certain class of transformation. Within the context of vision, we are interested in determining the invariants of an object under perspective projection. The cross-ratio of four collinear points is a well known 1D-invariant under projective transformations but it can be extended to 2D, so we can use it for image invariants. In the 2D case we need five points in the 3D case we need six points. In the 3D space these invariants can be interpreted as the cross-ratio of tetrahedral volumes.

Now, for the 2D case we need five points, an example of a 2D invariant is

$$Inv_2 = \frac{(\mathbf{X}_5 \wedge \mathbf{X}_4 \wedge \mathbf{X}_3) I_{p2}^{-1} (\mathbf{X}_5 \wedge \mathbf{X}_2 \wedge \mathbf{X}_1) I_{p2}^{-1}}{(\mathbf{X}_5 \wedge \mathbf{X}_1 \wedge \mathbf{X}_3) I_{p2}^{-1} (\mathbf{X}_5 \wedge \mathbf{X}_2 \wedge \mathbf{X}_4) I_{p2}^{-1}} , \tag{16}$$

where $I_{p2} = e_1 \wedge e_2 \wedge e_-$ denotes the pseudoscalar of the 2D projective space.

If we use conformal points the outer product of three points leads to a circle, so with four circles we can compute the 2D invariants. Also note that we use the A_r (6) part of the circle (the moment of the simplex) to calculate the invariant.

$$C_1 = X_5 \wedge X_4 \wedge X_3,\ C_2 = X_5 \wedge X_2 \wedge X_1, \tag{17}$$

$$C_3 = X_5 \wedge X_1 \wedge X_3,\ C_4 = X_5 \wedge X_2 \wedge X_4. \tag{18}$$

Let $A_{r,k}$ denote the A_r part of the k-circle C_k where $k = 1 \ldots 4$. Then the invariant using the moment A_r of the simplex is

$$Inv_2 = \frac{A_{r,1} I_E^{-1}\ A_{r,2} I_E^{-1}}{A_{r,3}^{+} I_E^{-1}\ A_{r,4}^{+} I_E^{-1}} . \tag{19}$$

4 Invariants and Omnidirectional Vision

The projective invariants do not hold in the catadioptric image, but they do in the image sphere. Therefore we must take some points in the catadioptric image and project them to the sphere. Once we do this we can proceed to calculate the invariants using four circles.

First we will show briefly that projective invariants in the plane are equivalent to projective invariants in the S^2 sphere (image sphere), see Fig. 2. According our previous work [1] we define the point F (in this case it will be equal to e_0), then the unit sphere is

$$S = e_0 - \frac{1}{2} e . \tag{20}$$

Now, let $x_1, x_2, ... x_5$ be points in the Euclidean space with conformal representation

$$X_i = \mathbf{x}_i + \frac{1}{2}\mathbf{x}_i^2 e + e_0, \ \ for\ i = 1 \ldots 5. \tag{21}$$

Then we project the points in the space to the sphere and that give us the projected points say $U_1, U_2, \ldots U_5$.

In the other hand, the image plane Π_I (in order to compare the invariants) is defined as

$$\Pi_I = e_2 + e . \tag{22}$$

We project first the points to the plane and then we intersect the plane with each line

$$Q_i = L_i^* \cdot \Pi_I \ for\ i = 1 \ldots 5. \tag{23}$$

The point Q_i is a *flatpoint* which is the outer product of a conformal point with the null vector e (the point at infinity). To obtain the conformal point from the *flatpoint* we can use

$$V_i = \frac{Q_i \wedge e_0}{(-Q_i \cdot E)E} + \frac{1}{2}\left(\frac{Q_i \wedge e_0}{(-Q_i \cdot E)E}\right)^2 e + e_0 \,. \tag{24}$$

Using (18) we calculate the two sets of four circles, one for the points U_i and one for V_i. With each set of circles we calculate the two invariants using (19), after comparing this two invariants we will see that them are the same. Therefore, we now know that if we project the points in the catadioptric image to the sphere we have again the projective invariants.

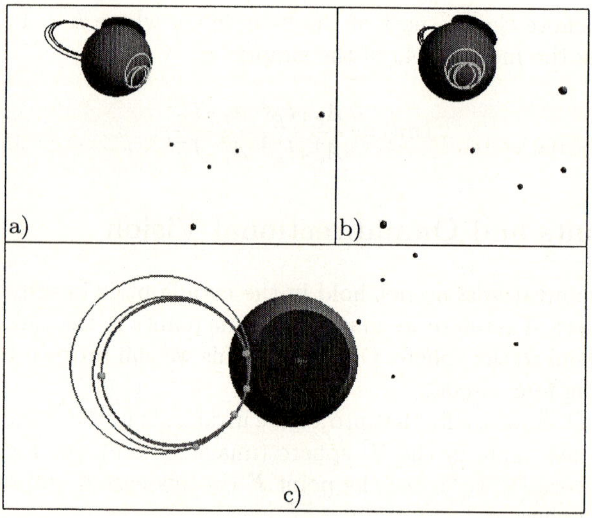

Fig. 2. Different views of points in the space projected to the (image) sphere and to the (image) plane used to compare the calculated invariants. a) Global view of points projected to the sphere and to the plane, b) Points projected in the sphere with the circles formed to calculate the invariants and c) Points projected in the plane with its circles formed to calculate the invariants.

We have seen a brief introduction to several topics necessaries to understand the experimental results. In the next section we will see an application of the given theory.

5 Differential Kinematic Control for a Pan-Tilt Unit

We will show an example using our formulation of the Jacobian. This is the control of a pan-tilt unit.

5.1 System

We can implement velocity control for a pan-tilt unit (PTU Fig. 3.a) easily assuming three degree of freedom (we call it virtual component), the PTU has similar kinematic behavior as a robot of three D.O.F.

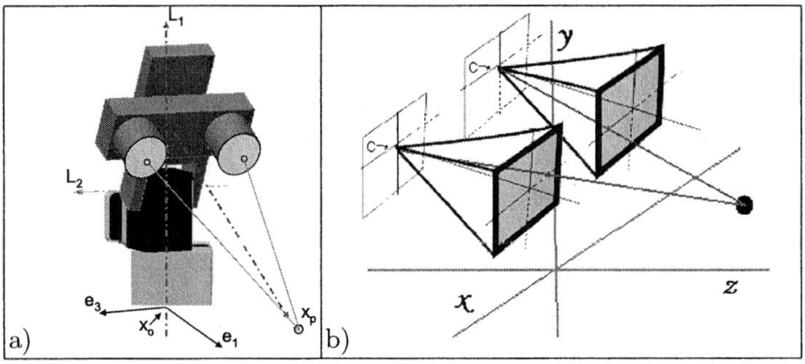

Fig. 3. a) Binocular stereo system fastened on a pan tilt unit. b) Abstraction of the stereo system.

In order to carry out a velocity control, we need first to compute the direct kinematics, this is very easy to do, because we know the axis lines:

$$L_1 = -e_{31},\ L_2 = e_{12} + d_1 e_1 e_\infty,\ L_3 = e_1 e_\infty. \tag{25}$$

Since $M_i = e^{-\frac{1}{2}q_i L_i}$ and $\widetilde{M_i} = e^{\frac{1}{2}q_i L_i}$, we can compute the position of end effector as:

$$x_p(q) = x'_p = M_1 M_2 M_3 x_p \widetilde{M_3}\widetilde{M_2}\widetilde{M_1}, \tag{26}$$

The estate variable representation of the system is as follows

$$\begin{cases} \dot{x}'_p = x' \cdot \left(L'_1\ L'_2\ L'_3\right) \begin{pmatrix} u_1 \\ u_2 \\ u_3 \end{pmatrix} \\ y = x'_p \end{cases} \tag{27}$$

where the position of end effector at home position x_p is the conformal mapping of $x_{p_e} = d_3 e_1 + (d_1 + d_2)e_2$, the line L'_i is the current position of L_i and u_i is the velocity of the i-junction of the system. As L_3 is an axis at infinity M_3 is a translator, that is, the virtual component is a prismatic junction.

5.2 Linearization Via Feedback

Now the following state feedback control law is chosen in order to get a new linear an controllable system.

$$\begin{pmatrix} u_1 \\ u_2 \\ u_3 \end{pmatrix} = \left(x'_p \cdot L'_1\ x'_p \cdot L'_2\ x'_p \cdot L'_3\right)^{-1} \begin{pmatrix} v_1 \\ v_2 \\ v_3 \end{pmatrix} \tag{28}$$

Where $V = (v_1, v_2, v_3)^T$ is the new input to the linear system, then we rewrite the equations of the system

$$\begin{cases} \dot{x}'_p = V \\ y = x'_p \end{cases} \tag{29}$$

5.3 Asymptotic Output Tracking

The problem of follow a constant reference x_t is solved computing the error between end effector position x'_p and the target position x_t as $e_r = (x'_p \wedge x_t) \cdot e_\infty$, the control law is then given by.

$$V = -ke \tag{30}$$

This error is small if the control system is doing it's job, it is mapped to an error in the joint space using the inverse Jacobian.

$$U = J^{-1}V \tag{31}$$

Computing the Jacobian $J = x'_p \cdot (L'_1 \; L'_2 \; L'_3)$

$$j_1 = x'_p \cdot (L_1),\; j_2 = x'_p \cdot (M_1 L_2 \widetilde{M}_1),\; j_3 = x'_p \cdot (M_1 M_2 L_3 \widetilde{M}_2 \widetilde{M}_1) \tag{32}$$

Once that we have the Jacobian is easy to compute the dq_i using Crammer's rule.

$$\begin{pmatrix} u_1 \\ u_2 \\ u_3 \end{pmatrix} = (j_1 \wedge j_2 \wedge j_3)^{-1} \cdot \begin{pmatrix} V \wedge j_2 \wedge j_3 \\ j_1 \wedge V \wedge j_3 \\ j_1 \wedge j_2 \wedge V \end{pmatrix} \tag{33}$$

This is possible because $j_1 \wedge j_2 \wedge j_3 = det(J) I_e$. Finally we have dq_i which will tend to reduce these errors. Due to the fact that the Jacobian has singularities then we should use the pseudo inverse of Jacobian.

5.4 Pseudo-Inverse of Jacobian

To avoid singularities we compute the pseudo inverse of Jacobian matrix $J = [j_1 \; j_2]$. Using the pseudo-inverse of Moore-Penrose

$$J^+ = (J^T J)^{-1} J^T \tag{34}$$

Now evaluating J in (34)

$$J^+ = \frac{1}{det(J^T J)} \begin{pmatrix} (j_2 \cdot j_2) j_1 - (j_2 \cdot j_1) j_2 \\ (j_1 \cdot j_1) j_2 - (j_2 \cdot j_1) j_1 \end{pmatrix} \tag{35}$$

And Using Clifford algebra we could simplify further this equation

$$det(J^T J) = (j_1 \cdot j_1)(j_2 \cdot j_2) - (j_1 \cdot j_2)^2 = (|j_1||j_2|)^2 - (|j_1||j_2|)^2 cos^2(\theta), \quad (36)$$

$$= (|j_1||j_2|)^2 sin^2(\theta) = |j_1 \wedge j_2|^2 \quad (37)$$

calling θ the angle between vectors. By the way each row of J^+ could be simplify as follows: $(j_2 \cdot j_2)j_1 - (j_2 \cdot j_1)j_2 = j_2 \cdot (j_2 \wedge j_1)$ and $(j_1 \cdot j_1)j_2 - (j_2 \cdot j_1)j_1 = j_1 \cdot (j_1 \wedge j_2)$.

Now the equation (34) can be rewritten as

$$J^+ = \frac{1}{|j_1 \wedge j_2|^2} \begin{pmatrix} j_2 \cdot (j_2 \wedge j_1) \\ j_1 \cdot (j_1 \wedge j_2) \end{pmatrix} = \begin{pmatrix} j_2 \cdot (j_2 \wedge j_1)^{-1} \\ j_1 \cdot (j_1 \wedge j_2)^{-1} \end{pmatrix} \quad (38)$$

Using this equation we can compute the input as $U = J^+ V$ that is equal to

$$U = (j_1 \wedge j_2)^{-1} \cdot \begin{pmatrix} V \wedge j_2 \\ j_1 \wedge V \end{pmatrix} \quad (39)$$

5.5 Visual Tracking

The target point is calculate using two calibrated cameras (see Figure 3.b), on each camera we estimate the center of mass of the object in movement in order to do a retroprojection and estimate the 3D point. to compute the mass center first we subtract the current image I_c to an image in memory I_a, the image in memory is the average of the last N images, this help us to eliminate the background.

$$I_k(t) = I_c(t) - I_a(t-1) * N, \;\; I_a(t) = (I_a(t-1) * N + I_c)/(N+1) \quad (40)$$

After that the moment of x and y is computed and they are divided by the mass (pixels in movement) that is, the intensity difference between the current image and the image on memory give us the mass center.

$$x_o = \frac{\int_0^n \int_0^m I_k y dx dy}{\int_0^n \int_0^m I_k dx dy}, \quad y_o = \frac{\int_0^n \int_0^m I_k x dx dy}{\int_0^n \int_0^m I_k dx dy} \quad (41)$$

When the camera moves the background changes and its necessary to reset N to 0 to restart the process of track.

6 Experimental Results

In this section we present two experiments: the first illustrates the use of the theory of invariants and omnidirectional vision for object recognition and the second the control of a binocular head for tracking.

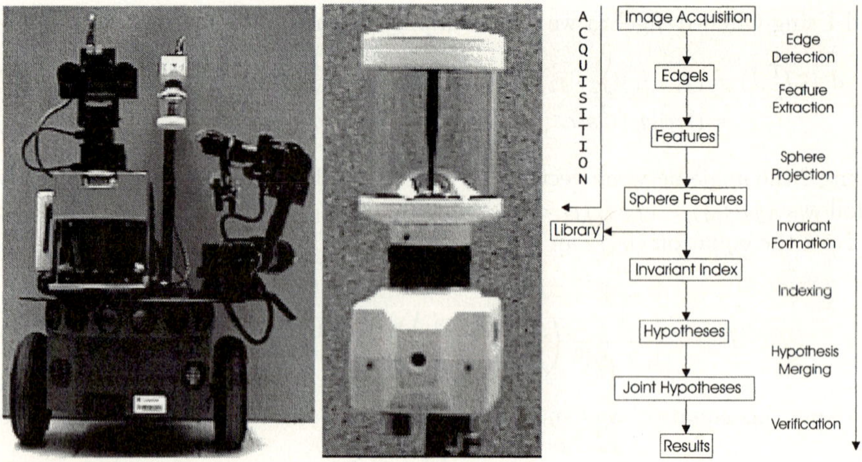

Fig. 4. a) Mobile robot. b) Omnidirectional vision system. c) Recognition procedure.

6.1 Object Recognition

The omnidirectional image has the advantage of a bigger field of view, see Fig. 4.a-b. This capability allows to see all the objects around the robot without moving it. In contrast to the stereo system, which does not see all the objects or in some cases none of them (see Fig. 5).

Before we use the omnidirectional system we must calibrate it with this we mean find the mirror center, focal length, skew and aspect ratio. The objective of the experiment is that the robot should recognize an object from different objects lying on three tables located around the robot. The recognition process consists of various steps that are show in Fig. 4.c .

To recognize an object we first take features from the catadioptric image, then these features are projected onto the unit sphere. With this features in the sphere we calculate the circles formed with them (see Eq. 18). Finally, the invariants are calculated with Eq. 19 which are equivalent to the projective invariants. These invariants are compared with the previously acquired invariants in the library to identify the object. The key points of an object are selected by hand. If they are accurate enough, our procedure can recognize the objects correctly. In general this kind of invariants are a bit sensitive to noise, due to the illumination changes and computations. In order to diminish the effect of noise in the data, we can compute several invariants related with the object, so that the accuracy of the recognition is increased. Utilizing an automatic corner detector the procedure of object recognition using our method can be carried out in real time.

Once that the object is recognized we rotate the robot until the object is in front of the stereo system. Since the object is now visible to the stereo camera, we can use an inverse kinematic approach to grasp the object. In our case we chose for the approach of [4] which is very interesting. Such approach models the

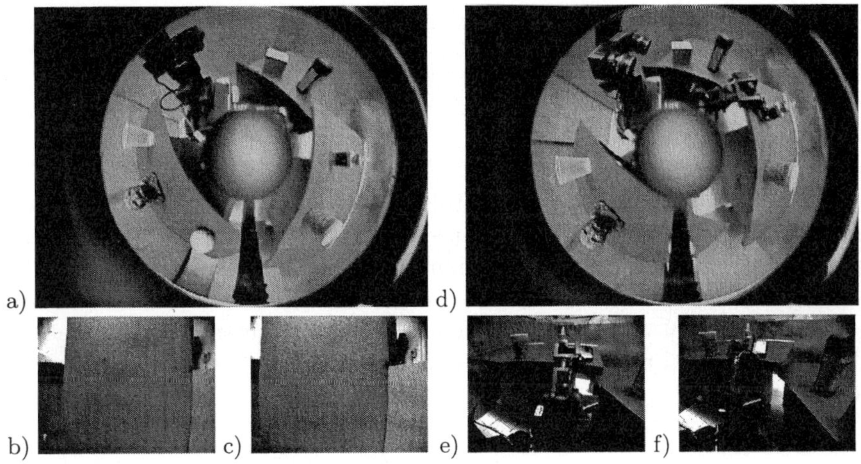

Fig. 5. Initial state of the experiment: a) Omnidirectional view, b-c) Left and right images of the stereo system (out of target). Robot grasps an object: d) Omnidirectional view, e-f) Left and right images of the stereo system (loocking at the target).

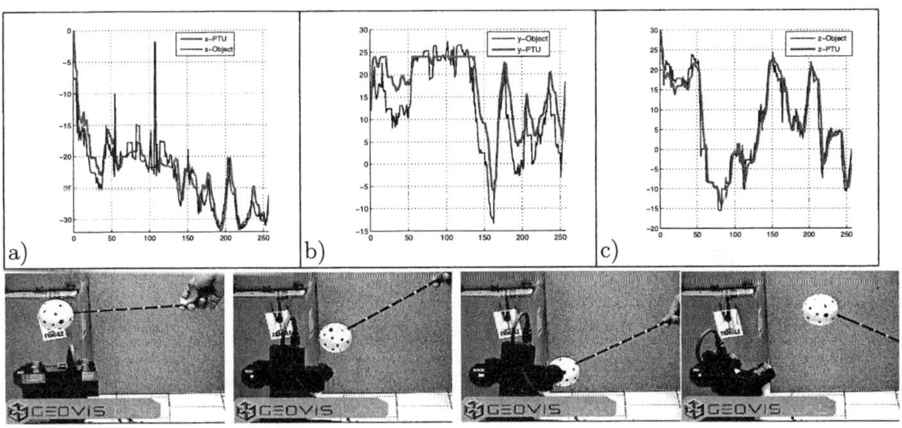

Fig. 6. (Upper row) Velocity components: a) x; b) y; c) z, (the rough curves are of the 3D object motion). (Lower row) Some views of a tracking sequence.

joints of the robot arm using spheres, circles, lines and planes which are entities very easy to handle in conformal geometric algebra. In Figures 5.d-f we show the robot grasping an object.

6.2 Visually Controlled Tracking

In Figure 6 we can appreciate the smooth trajectory of the tracking. The rough behavior of the 3D object motion is compensated by a PD controller using our geometric Jacobian approach. Note that 3D motion of the pan-tilt unit is not disturbed by the big peaks of the 3D object motion.

7 Conclusions

In this article we have chosen the coordinate-free system of conformal geometric algebra for the design of algorithms useful for robot perception and action. In this framework we calculate the invariants of circles in the sphere and used them to recognize objects with the advantage of the bigger field of view offered by the omnidirectional vision system. We also showed an interesting application of 3D tracking using a new formulation of a geometric Jacobian for the differential kinematics.

Acknowledgment

We are thankful to CONACYT Proyecto 49 Fondos de Salud for supporting this work.

References

1. Bayro-Corrochano E. and Lpez-Franco C. [2004]. Omnidirectional vision: unified model using conformal geometry. In Proc. of the 8th European Conf. on Computer Vision, ECCV2004, Prage, Czech Republic, Part I, pp. 536-548.
2. Bayro-Corrochano E. [2005]. Robot perception and action using conformal geometric algebra. In the *Hanbook of Geometric Computing. Applications in Patter Recognition, Computer Vision, Neuralcomputing and Robotics*, Eduardo Bayro-Corrochano (ed.), Chap. 14, Springer Verlag, Heidelberg, pp 405-457.
3. H. Li, D. Hestenes and A. Rockwood. [2001] Generalized homogeneous coordinates for computational geometry. In Geometric Computing with Clifford Algebra, G. Sommer (Ed.), Springer-Verlag, pp. 27-59.
4. Zamora-Esquivel J. and Bayro-Corrochano E. [2005] Static and differential geometry of robot devices using conformal computational geometry. Submitted elsewhere.

Author Index

Lecture Notes in Computer Science

For information about Vols. 1–3690

please contact your bookseller or Springer

Vol. 3807: M. Dean, Y. Guo, W. Jun, R. Kaschek, S. Krishnaswamy, Z. Pan, Q.Z. Sheng (Eds.), Web Information Systems – WISE 2005 Workshops. XV, 275 pages. 2005.

Vol. 3806: M. Kitsuregawa, E.J. Neuhold, A.H. H. Ngu, J.-Y. Chung, Q.Z. Sheng (Eds.), Web Information Systems – WISE 2005. XXI, 771 pages. 2005.

Vol. 3791: A. Adi, S. Stoutenburg, S. Tabet (Eds.), Rules and Rule Markup Languages for the Semantic Web. X, 225 pages. 2005.

Vol. 3789: A. Gelbukh, Á. de Albornoz, H. Terashima-Marín (Eds.), MICAI 2005: Advances in Artificial Intelligence. XXVI, 1198 pages. 2005. (Subseries LNAI).

Vol. 3785: K.-K. Lau, R. Banach (Eds.), Formal Methods and Software Engineering. XIV, 496 pages. 2005.

Vol. 3784: J. Tao, T. Tan, R.W. Picard (Eds.), Affective Computing and Intelligent Interaction. XIX, 1008 pages. 2005.

Vol. 3781: S.Z. Li, Z. Sun, T. Tan, S. Pankanti, G. Chollet, D. Zhang (Eds.), Advances in Biometric Person Authentication. XI, 250 pages. 2005.

Vol. 3780: K. Yi (Ed.), Programming Languages and Systems. XI, 435 pages. 2005.

Vol. 3779: H. Jin, D. Reed, W. Jiang (Eds.), Network and Parallel Computing. XV, 513 pages. 2005.

Vol. 3777: O.B. Lupanov, O.M. Kasim-Zade, A.V. Chaskin, K. Steinhöfel (Eds.), Stochastic Algorithms: Foundations and Applications. VIII, 239 pages. 2005.

Vol. 3775: J. Schönwälder, J. Serrat (Eds.), Ambient Networks. XIII, 281 pages. 2005.

Vol. 3773: A.Sanfeliu, M.Lazo Cortés (Eds.), Progress in Pattern Recognition, Image Analysis and Applications. XX, 1094 pages. 2005.

Vol. 3772: M. Consens, G. Navarro (Eds.), String Processing and Information Retrieval. XIV, 406 pages. 2005.

Vol. 3770: J. Akoka, S.W. Liddle, I.-Y. Song, M. Bertolotto, I. Comyn-Wattiau, W.-J. van den Heuvel, M. Kolp, J.C. Trujillo, C. Kop, H.C. Mayr (Eds.), Perspectives in Conceptual Modeling. XXII, 476 pages. 2005.

Vol. 3768: Y.-S. Ho, H.J. Kim (Eds.), Advances in Mulitmedia Information Processing - PCM 2005, Part II. XXVIII, 1088 pages. 2005.

Vol. 3767: Y.-S. Ho, H.J. Kim (Eds.), Advances in Mulitmedia Information Processing - PCM 2005, Part I. XXVIII, 1022 pages. 2005.

Vol. 3766: N. Sebe, M.S. Lew, T.S. Huang (Eds.), Computer Vision in Human-Computer Interaction. X, 231 pages. 2005.

Vol. 3765: Y. Liu, T. Jiang, C. Zhang (Eds.), Computer Vision for Biomedical Image Applications. X, 563 pages. 2005.

Vol. 3764: S. Tixeuil, T. Herman (Eds.), Self-Stabilizing Systems. VIII, 229 pages. 2005.

Vol. 3762: R. Meersman, Z. Tari, P. Herrero (Eds.), On the Move to Meaningful Internet Systems 2005: OTM Workshops. XXXI, 1228 pages. 2005.

Vol. 3761: R. Meersman, Z. Tari (Eds.), On the Move to Meaningful Internet Systems 2005: CoopIS, DOA, and ODBASE, Part II. XXVII, 653 pages. 2005.

Vol. 3760: R. Meersman, Z. Tari (Eds.), On the Move to Meaningful Internet Systems 2005: CoopIS, DOA, and ODBASE, Part I. XXVII, 921 pages. 2005.

Vol. 3759: G. Chen, Y. Pan, M. Guo, J. Lu (Eds.), Parallel and Distributed Processing and Applications - ISPA 2005 Workshops. XIII, 669 pages. 2005.

Vol. 3758: Y. Pan, D. Chen, M. Guo, J. Cao, J. Dongarra (Eds.), Parallel and Distributed Processing and Applications. XXIII, 1162 pages. 2005.

Vol. 3756: J. Cao, W. Nejdl, M. Xu (Eds.), Advanced Parallel Processing Technologies. XIV, 526 pages. 2005.

Vol. 3754: J. Dalmau Royo, G. Hasegawa (Eds.), Management of Multimedia Networks and Services. XII, 384 pages. 2005.

Vol. 3753: O.F. Olsen, L. Florack, A. Kuijper (Eds.), Deep Structure, Singularities, and Computer Vision. X, 259 pages. 2005.

Vol. 3752: N. Paragios, O. Faugeras, T. Chan, C. Schnörr (Eds.), Variational, Geometric, and Level Set Methods in Computer Vision. XI, 369 pages. 2005.

Vol. 3751: T. Magedanz, E.R. M. Madeira, P. Dini (Eds.), Operations and Management in IP-Based Networks. X, 213 pages. 2005.

Vol. 3750: J.S. Duncan, G. Gerig (Eds.), Medical Image Computing and Computer-Assisted Intervention – MICCAI 2005, Part II. XL, 1018 pages. 2005.

Vol. 3749: J.S. Duncan, G. Gerig (Eds.), Medical Image Computing and Computer-Assisted Intervention – MICCAI 2005, Part I. XXXIX, 942 pages. 2005.

Vol. 3747: C.A. Maziero, J.G. Silva, A.M.S. Andrade, F.M.d. Assis Silva (Eds.), Dependable Computing. XV, 267 pages. 2005.

Vol. 3746: P. Bozanis, E.N. Houstis (Eds.), Advances in Informatics. XIX, 879 pages. 2005.

Vol. 3745: J.L. Oliveira, V. Maojo, F. Martin-Sanchez, A.S. Pereira (Eds.), Biological and Medical Data Analysis. XII, 422 pages. 2005. (Subseries LNBI).

Vol. 3744: T. Magedanz, A. Karmouch, S. Pierre, I. Venieris (Eds.), Mobility Aware Technologies and Applications. XIV, 418 pages. 2005.

Vol. 3740: T. Srikanthan, J. Xue, C.-H. Chang (Eds.), Advances in Computer Systems Architecture. XVII, 833 pages. 2005.

Vol. 3739: W. Fan, Z.-h. Wu, J. Yang (Eds.), Advances in Web-Age Information Management. XXIV, 930 pages. 2005.

Vol. 3738: V.R. Syrotiuk, E. Chávez (Eds.), Ad-Hoc, Mobile, and Wireless Networks. XI, 360 pages. 2005.

Vol. 3735: A. Hoffmann, H. Motoda, T. Scheffer (Eds.), Discovery Science. XVI, 400 pages. 2005. (Subseries LNAI).

Vol. 3734: S. Jain, H.U. Simon, E. Tomita (Eds.), Algorithmic Learning Theory. XII, 490 pages. 2005. (Subseries LNAI).

Vol. 3733: P. Yolum, T. Güngör, F. Gürgen, C. Özturan (Eds.), Computer and Information Sciences - ISCIS 2005. XXI, 973 pages. 2005.

Vol. 3731: F. Wang (Ed.), Formal Techniques for Networked and Distributed Systems - FORTE 2005. XII, 558 pages. 2005.

Vol. 3729: Y. Gil, E. Motta, V. R. Benjamins, M.A. Musen (Eds.), The Semantic Web – ISWC 2005. XXIII, 1073 pages. 2005.

Vol. 3728: V. Paliouras, J. Vounckx, D. Verkest (Eds.), Integrated Circuit and System Design. XV, 753 pages. 2005.

Vol. 3726: L.T. Yang, O.F. Rana, B. Di Martino, J. Dongarra (Eds.), High Performance Computing and Communications. XXVI, 1116 pages. 2005.

Vol. 3725: D. Borrione, W. Paul (Eds.), Correct Hardware Design and Verification Methods. XII, 412 pages. 2005.

Vol. 3724: P. Fraigniaud (Ed.), Distributed Computing. XIV, 520 pages. 2005.

Vol. 3723: W. Zhao, S. Gong, X. Tang (Eds.), Analysis and Modelling of Faces and Gestures. XI, 4234 pages. 2005.

Vol. 3722: D. Van Hung, M. Wirsing (Eds.), Theoretical Aspects of Computing – ICTAC 2005. XIV, 614 pages. 2005.

Vol. 3721: A. Jorge, L. Torgo, P.B. Brazdil, R. Camacho, J. Gama (Eds.), Knowledge Discovery in Databases: PKDD 2005. XXIII, 719 pages. 2005. (Subseries LNAI).

Vol. 3720: J. Gama, R. Camacho, P.B. Brazdil, A. Jorge, L. Torgo (Eds.), Machine Learning: ECML 2005. XXIII, 769 pages. 2005. (Subseries LNAI).

Vol. 3719: M. Hobbs, A.M. Goscinski, W. Zhou (Eds.), Distributed and Parallel Computing. XI, 448 pages. 2005.

Vol. 3718: V.G. Ganzha, E.W. Mayr, E.V. Vorozhtsov (Eds.), Computer Algebra in Scientific Computing. XII, 502 pages. 2005.

Vol. 3717: B. Gramlich (Ed.), Frontiers of Combining Systems. X, 321 pages. 2005. (Subseries LNAI).

Vol. 3716: L. Delcambre, C. Kop, H.C. Mayr, J. Mylopoulos, Ó. Pastor (Eds.), Conceptual Modeling – ER 2005. XVI, 498 pages. 2005.

Vol. 3715: E. Dawson, S. Vaudenay (Eds.), Progress in Cryptology – Mycrypt 2005. XI, 329 pages. 2005.

Vol. 3714: H. Obbink, K. Pohl (Eds.), Software Product Lines. XIII, 235 pages. 2005.

Vol. 3713: L.C. Briand, C. Williams (Eds.), Model Driven Engineering Languages and Systems. XV, 722 pages. 2005.

Vol. 3712: R. Reussner, J. Mayer, J.A. Stafford, S. Overhage, S. Becker, P.J. Schroeder (Eds.), Quality of Software Architectures and Software Quality. XIII, 289 pages. 2005.

Vol. 3711: F. Kishino, Y. Kitamura, H. Kato, N. Nagata (Eds.), Entertainment Computing - ICEC 2005. XXIV, 540 pages. 2005.

Vol. 3710: M. Barni, I. Cox, T. Kalker, H.J. Kim (Eds.), Digital Watermarking. XII, 485 pages. 2005.

Vol. 3709: P. van Beek (Ed.), Principles and Practice of Constraint Programming - CP 2005. XX, 887 pages. 2005.

Vol. 3708: J. Blanc-Talon, W. Philips, D.C. Popescu, P. Scheunders (Eds.), Advanced Concepts for Intelligent Vision Systems. XXII, 725 pages. 2005.

Vol. 3707: D.A. Peled, Y.-K. Tsay (Eds.), Automated Technology for Verification and Analysis. XII, 506 pages. 2005.

Vol. 3706: H. Fuks, S. Lukosch, A.C. Salgado (Eds.), Groupware: Design, Implementation, and Use. XII, 378 pages. 2005.

Vol. 3704: M. De Gregorio, V. Di Maio, M. Frucci, C. Musio (Eds.), Brain, Vision, and Artificial Intelligence. XV, 556 pages. 2005.

Vol. 3703: F. Fages, S. Soliman (Eds.), Principles and Practice of Semantic Web Reasoning. VIII, 163 pages. 2005.

Vol. 3702: B. Beckert (Ed.), Automated Reasoning with Analytic Tableaux and Related Methods. XIII, 343 pages. 2005. (Subseries LNAI).

Vol. 3701: M. Coppo, E. Lodi, G. M. Pinna (Eds.), Theoretical Computer Science. XI, 411 pages. 2005.

Vol. 3700: J.F. Peters, A. Skowron (Eds.), Transactions on Rough Sets IV. X, 375 pages. 2005.

Vol. 3699: C.S. Calude, M.J. Dinneen, G. Păun, M. J. Pérez-Jiménez, G. Rozenberg (Eds.), Unconventional Computation. XI, 267 pages. 2005.

Vol. 3698: U. Furbach (Ed.), KI 2005: Advances in Artificial Intelligence. XIII, 409 pages. 2005. (Subseries LNAI).

Vol. 3697: W. Duch, J. Kacprzyk, E. Oja, S. Zadrożny (Eds.), Artificial Neural Networks: Formal Models and Their Applications – ICANN 2005, Part II. XXXII, 1045 pages. 2005.

Vol. 3696: W. Duch, J. Kacprzyk, E. Oja, S. Zadrożny (Eds.), Artificial Neural Networks: Biological Inspirations – ICANN 2005, Part I. XXXI, 703 pages. 2005.

Vol. 3695: M.R. Berthold, R.C. Glen, K. Diederichs, O. Kohlbacher, I. Fischer (Eds.), Computational Life Sciences. XI, 277 pages. 2005. (Subseries LNBI).

Vol. 3694: M. Malek, E. Nett, N. Suri (Eds.), Service Availability. VIII, 213 pages. 2005.

Vol. 3693: A.G. Cohn, D.M. Mark (Eds.), Spatial Information Theory. XII, 493 pages. 2005.

Vol. 3692: R. Casadio, G. Myers (Eds.), Algorithms in Bioinformatics. X, 436 pages. 2005. (Subseries LNBI).

Vol. 3691: A. Gagalowicz, W. Philips (Eds.), Computer Analysis of Images and Patterns. XIX, 865 pages. 2005.